Kerry Gavin
Illustrator
Page 570

Louise Fili
Graphic Designer
Page 196

Tom Kienberger
Graphic Designer
Page 114

1991
Artist's Market

Where & How to Sell
Your Artwork

Edited by
Lauri Miller

Cincinnati, Ohio

Acknowledgements

The editor wishes to thank Roseann Shaughnessy, Laurie Henry and Robin Gee for their assistance in preparing the 1991 edition of Artist's Market.

Managing Editor, Market Books Department: Constance J. Achabal

International Standard Serial Number 0161-0546
International Standard Book Number 0-89879-426-9

Contents

The Markets

Services & Opportunities

From the Editor

While there are some who say the art market is glutted because of the state of the economy and the high number of art-school graduates each year, from the *Artist's Market* vantage point it appears there is as healthy a demand for both fine and freelance commercial art as ever.

There are over 1,000 new markets in this edition (200 in galleries alone) and two new sections: Performing Arts and Record Companies. The markets in these two new sections, due to their creative natures, tend to allow the freelance artist greater artistic freedom than most industries. Athough they often work on limited budgets and pay little (or not at all), a record album cover or poster offers a large showcase for one's work, while a program guide read by thousands offers high visibility.

Even though high-technology will continue to influence the commercial art field, a recent study by the National Art Materials Trade Association (NAMTA) found there was little decrease in the amount of traditional art products computer-equipped companies are purchasing, which is the same message that art buyers conveyed on their returned *Artist's Market* questionnaires this year. There is a greater need for artists able to create computer design and graphics, yet the need for hand-done illustration and design is just as strong as it was last year.

The fax machine is another technology which continues to have a large impact on the lives of artists. It has opened the national market to artists living anywhere. New York-based Clare Wood, a Close-up on page 80, bemoans the fact that life is so expensive there, and the rates she must charge reflect this. Recently, she says, she bid on a project which was given to a Midwest artist "whose rates were so low, they were almost like student rates," making it difficult for the budget-tightened ad agency to pass up.

Another reason for optimism is the fact that designers, illustrators and gallery directors feel that the general population seems increasingly appreciative of good artwork. A few gallery directors mention the clientele is more knowledgeable and more interested in the work of emerging and regional artists. Designer Joel Fuller in *HOW* says, "This is a very exciting time for design in America right now. I get the sense of design becoming much more important to the average consumer and companies being much more aware of what the effects of design are."

In addition to the listings, this year's *Artist's Market* offers you visually and editorially interesting articles on how successful illustrators and designers self-promote and how art directors in advertising, art/design and the greeting card, magazine and newspaper industries feel about their fields; what they foresee in its future; and what they look for in freelance artwork. Following the "Business of Art" section, there is an article on copyright, which explains two recent developments in the federal copyright law and why they will have an impact on freelance artists. The introduction to each market section provides helpful information on the trends, art requirements and payment terms unique to each industry. From this year's Close-ups you will learn how these talented people got their start, things they have learned along the way and what advice they have to offer on the nuts and bolts of the business.

Oftentimes it is during moments of enthusiasm that we buy a book such as *Artist's Market*, to help us get on the path we so desire to be on. We read for awhile, note helpful suggestions and then place it on a shelf along with other books that are gathering dust. I hope you keep this edition off the shelf, read it and use it time after time to establish strong markets for your work.

Lauri Miller

How to Use Your Artist's Market

Markets in this book are organized according to their professional category, such as book publishers or magazines. However, you have probably found that your talents apply to many categories. For example, if you're a painter who also illustrates, you will find opportunities (for your fine art) not only in the gallery and art publisher sections, but also (for your illustration) in the magazine, book publishing and greeting card sections. Cartoonists look to advertising agencies, businesses, associations, greeting card companies, magazines, newspapers and syndicates. Because the companies' needs are so diverse, you will find opportunities for your work in almost every section, no matter what your specialty is.

Reading the market listings

Listings include information on whom to contact, what type of work is needed, how artists are used, payment method and amount. For an explanation of all the information given in the listings, match the numbered phrases in the sample listing with the corresponding numbers in the copy that follows.

(1)*CAREW DESIGN,, 200 Gate 5 Rd., Sausalito CA 94965. (415)331-8222. **(2)** President: Jim Carew. **(3)** Estab. 1975. **(4)** Specializes in corporate identity, direct mail and package design.
Needs: (5) Works with 15 freelance illustrators and 2-4 freelancer designers/year. Prefers local artists only. **(6)** Works on assignment only. Uses artists for brochure and catalog design and illustration, mechanicals, retouching, airbrushing, direct mail design, lettering, logos and ad illustration.
First Contact & Terms: (7) Send query letter with brochure, resume and tearsheets. **(8)** Samples are filed. Samples not filed are returned only if requested by artist. **(9)** Reports back only if interested. **(10)** Call to schedule an appointment to show a portfolio, **(11)** which should include roughs and original/final art. **(12)**Pays for production by the hour, $18-30. Pays for illustration by the project, $100-1,000. **(13)** Considers complexity of project, client's budget, skill and experience of artist, how work will be used, turnaround time and rights purchased when establishing payment. **(14)** Buys all rights.
Tips: (15) "The best way for an illustrator and a designer to get an assignment is to show a portfolio."

(1) New listings. An asterisk (*) precedes new listings.

(2) Contact information. Names of contact persons are given in most listings. If not, address your work to the art director or person most appropriate for that field.

(3) Established dates. Dates indicating when the market was established are given in this area of the listings. The risk is sometimes greater when dealing with new companies. So far as we know, all are reputable but some are unable to compete with larger, older companies. Many do survive, however, and become very successful.

(4) Company description. Company descriptions and/or client lists are provided to help you slant your work toward that specific business.

(5) Percentage of freelance work. The number or percentage of jobs assigned to freelance artists or the number of artists a market uses gives you an idea of the size of the market.

(6) Work on assignment. Many firms work on assignment only. Do not expect them to buy the art you send as samples. When your style fills a current need, they will contact you. This section also tells you what type of artwork the company needs.

(7) Submission requirements. Submit materials specified by the listing. If a market instructs you to query, please query. Do not send samples unless that is what they want you to do.

(8) Samples. Many art directors who want samples keep them on file for future reference. If you want your samples returned, include a self-addressed, stamped envelope (SASE) in your mailing package. Include an International Reply Coupon (IRC) if you are mailing to a foreign market.

(9) Reporting times. Reporting times vary, and some—such as this listing—will only contact you if interested in your work.

(10) Portfolio presentation. Markets want you to either mail portfolio materials or present them in person. Note whether to call or write for an appointment to show your portfolio.

(11) Portfolio contents. The type of samples you include in your portfolio reflect your understanding of the market; inappropriate samples signify a lack of market research.

(12) Payment terms.

(13) Payment factors. Markets often negotiate payment terms. Therefore, they list the factors they consider when establishing payment.

(14) Rights purchased. Note what rights the market purchases. If several types of rights are listed, it usually means the firm will negotiate. But not always. Be certain you and the art buyer understand exactly what rights you are selling. This design studio buys all rights.

(15) Advice. Read the tips at the end of many listings. They give you personalized advice or a view of general market information.

Submission Information

The Artist's Market *welcomes new listings. If you are a user of freelance design and illustration or if you are a gallery director seeking new artists to represent and would like to be considered for a listing in the next edition, contact the editor by March 1, 1990.*

The Artist's Market *also welcomes you to submit artwork for possible inclusion in the next edition. The policy for submission is as follows:*

(1) artwork must be submitted by a freelance artist or a market who uses freelance work;

(2) the artwork must have been published by one of the markets listed in the book.

If you have material to submit which fits these guidelines, send it to: Editor, Artist's Market, *1507 Dana Ave., Cincinnati, OH 45207.*

A Taste of Self-Promotion

In an ideal world an illustrator or designer would spend the whole of her waking day creating, while the business side of the job would magically take care of itself. But in this imperfect world, unless the artist lets the art buyer know who he is, what he can do, how well he can do it and why the art buyer needs his work—on a continuous basis—no one else will. This can be done by advertising in a creative directory, having one's portfolio reviewed and doing self-promotional mailings. For most there is a need for all three.

As Rose DeNeve, the author of *PROMO 1: The Ultimate in Graphic Designer's and Illustrator's Self-Promotion* writes in her introduction: "Sometimes a promotion's success is self-evident—the phone starts ringing as soon as it hits the street. But more often, the effect of self-promotion is difficult to quantify and likely builds over time." It means, she says, "that effective promotion will be created within a strategem—that is, through *thinking*—as a definite statement within a larger marketing effort; as a series of mailers, each touting another area of the artist's expertise; as a memorable holiday greeting; or as a clever moving announcement. An effective promotion can be as simple as an elegant poster or as complicated as a graphic identity system and comprehensive marketing plan."

To be effective self-promotion she says: a designer or illustrator trying to break into the market needs to produce more—and more dynamic—pieces than those artists more established. The pieces should be appropriate in terms of both the audience and the message; the unique point of view and style of the artist should be exhibited; they should carry an entertainment value, be they funny, clever or visually stunning; and they should be useful, telling a prospective client why as well as how to hire you.

The examples which follow will give you a taste of today's most impressive self-promotion, and hopefully inspire you to create unique promotions of your own.

The following illustrations and copy are pages excerpted from **PROMO 1: The Ultimate in Graphic Designer's and Illustrator's Self-Promotion** *by Rose DeNeve. reprinted with permission from North Light Books.*

▲ Sabin's moving announcement

A LIGHT TOUCH

Tracy Sabin
Illustration & Design
San Diego, California

When designer/illustrator
Tracy Sabin moved quarters,
he needed two things—an
attractive moving
announcement and new
stationery. Sabin saw these as
opportunities to put his light
and graceful illustration style
into the hands of current and
prospective clients. Produced
for a total cost of eighteen
hundred dollars for
composites and printing of
one thousand copies of each
piece, Sabin's new stationery
has brought many positive
comments—and the moving
announcement has brought
him all of his·mail.

▲ *Tracy Sabin's stationery package*

SIMPLE PLEASURES

Gina Federico
Graphic Design
New Canaan, Connecticut

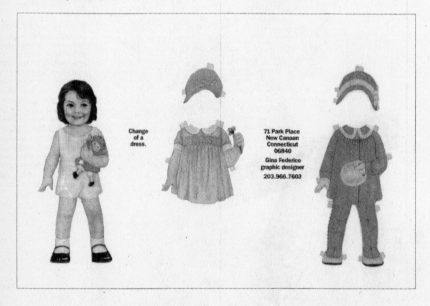

Change
of a
dress.

71 Park Place
New Canaan
Connecticut
06840

Gina Federico
graphic designer

203.966.7603

▲ *"Change of a dress" notice brought requests for samples of it from around the United States. Printing was done gratis*

Promotion for Gina Federico's graphic design studio stems from her own personal exuberance about life. "When something good or exciting happens," she says, "I like to let people know about it." Such a happy occasion can be a move to a new office, a change of studio affiliation, or simply the start of a new year. In any case, Federico's mailer-celebration is apt to be a simple execution, with a visual pun or other twist to make it memorable. Because she works alone, Federico strives to keep costs down, too, letting the concept, rather than its production, create the impression. "It's not marketing *per se*," she explains. "That's more or less a by-product." Still, Federico's low profile has earned her some plums—her work has been shown in the national design press and her business volume has grown steadily to where she's been able to establish her own independent design office.

▲ Three-dimensional mailer for Arlen Schumer and
Sherri Wolfgang's Dynamic Duo Studio

COMIC POWER

*The Dynamic Duo Studio
New York, New York*

Comic artists Arlen Schumer
and Sherri Wolfgang, who bill
themselves as the Dynamic
Duo, believe that the
potential of comic art in
advertising and editorial
illustration has barely been
tapped, and they want to
change that. A major
component of their strategy is
the promotion and
advertising they do for their
own comic art studio.
Because comic art is read and
loved by just about everyone,
these efforts have brought no
little attention to themselves
and their work. Of one ad,
which appeared in a major
illustration showcase,
Schumer says, "Before this ad
ran, we were doing 90
percent comp art and
storyboards. After it
appeared, the response and
jobs it engendered inverted
that ratio to 90 percent
finished illustration and 10
percent production art. Even
at a cost of seventy-five
hundred dollars, the ad paid
for itself many times over."

LETTER PERFECT

Paul Shaw/
Letter Design
New York, New York

By leaving out the flash and dazzle, Paul Shaw's simply designed promotions focus the recipient's attention on the artist's not inconsiderable skills in calligraphy. At the core of the scheme is an "Alphabet" series, a yearly effort that costs three to five hundred dollars each time and keeps the artist's name—and talents—before the eyes of current and potential clients. (Some of the alphabets have been framed and hung on client's walls.) The alphabets are augmented by occasional other pieces—a postcard showing hand-lettered typefaces, for example, or a moving announcement. As simple as they are, these mailers have been more than modestly successful—one, produced for the cost of mailing alone, garnered several letter-design jobs; another brought Shaw continuing work with a Soho gallery as a full-service designer.

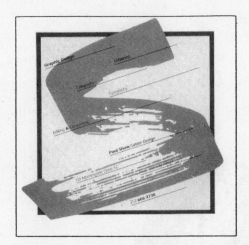

▲ *Logo mailer spurred requests for design input as well as lettering*

▲ *A more ambitious project, Letterforms serves as a calligraphy textbook as well as a style reference for clients. Copies are also sold through independent booksellers*

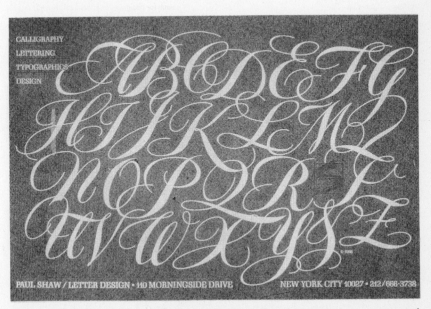

▲ Shaw's "Alphabet" mailer

▲ Postcard worked with Spencerian alphabet to increase commissions for
handdrawn letterforms—most notably for the movie and television industries

PICTURE THIS

Andrea Eberbach
Indianapolis, Indiana

In years past, illustrator Andrea Eberbach garnered most of her commissions via a series of color-printed illustrations, tucked in an envelope and sent to prospective clients. In 1989, however, Eberbach changed her tack by collecting the illustrations and creating a more comprehensive pamphlet. The new format both shows off her illustration style and gives Eberbach space to include a brief text describing her relationship to her work. While the earlier efforts were successful, Eberbach says the pamphlet has brought unprecedented numbers of inquiries, as well as better-paying and more interesting assignments. The reason? Perhaps because the words have given her pictures a context, helping clients understand Eberbach's artistic motivation.

Series of individual, color-printed illustration postcards, measuring 5¹/₂ x 8¹/₂

Front and back of Eberbach's most recent promotional pamphlet, measuring 9¹/₄ x 5¹/₄

CHANGING COURSES

*Sabina Fascione Alcorn
Cambridge, New York*

Sabina Fascione Alcorn once made her living as a textile designer, but the flat, stylized designs of that craft left her unfulfilled. Her real satisfaction came from the paintings she did for herself—watercolors, made from observation, in the style of the eighteenth-century French botanical illustrators. She longed to make these soul-felt works her source of income, but how to make the switch? Following the lead of her husband (artist Stephen Alcorn) and father-in-law (designer John Alcorn), she made a deal with fine photography printer Morgan Press: her illustrations in return for some poster/promotion pieces. The flower poster was particularly successful, and in an unexpected way: framed and hung in a major upstate New York nursery, the calendar was seen by a woman already writing a book on celebrated American gardens. She tracked Sabina down, and the illustrator soon signed a contract with Clarkson Potter to illustrate the book.

Sabina Fascione Alcorn's illustrated calendars for fine printer Morgan Press announced new color printing equipment. They brought the printer orders, the illustrator a major assignment, and both individual-copy sales.

A Roundtable of Art Directors

Art directors have a love for both art (they are oftentimes artists themselves) and the interactive and collaborative process. They are experts in their fields, cognizant of exactly what their companies' or clients' needs are. Sometimes they begin with a vision, either in the form of image or concept, and then look for the designer's or illustrator's style which matches it. Other times they see an artist's work on a promotional piece and say, "hey, that's great," file it and think of that style and concept when the right assignment comes along. Art directors often feel that one of the most rewarding parts of their job is encouraging and nurturing fresh and innovative work from freelance artists. How does one become the freelance artist whom the art director thinks of? This roundtable of art directors in advertising; design; book, magazine and newspaper publishing; and greeting cards is intended to give you a better idea of who and what an art director is and what he or she is looking for in a freelance artist.

Stavros Cosmopulos, "after 180 interviews and 179 rejections in a row," got a job with a small ad agency in Detroit. In 1960, he became an art director at Batten, Barton, Durstine & Osborne (BBD&O) in Boston, where he learned how big agencies work on big accounts like Pepsi Cola and Dodge Automobiles. Currently, he is chairman of the board and creative director at the agency of Cosmopulos, Crowley & Daly.

Rick Tharp is art director/designer at Tharp Did It, a five-person design firm in Los Gatos, California, which focuses on corporate, retail and visual identity and packaging design. His clients include BRIO Toys of Sweden, The Seagram Classics Wine Co. and Sebastiani Vineyards.

Steve Snider is art director at Little, Brown & Company. His design background is in advertising as well as publishing. He has been involved in book cover design for over 20 years.

Melinda Gordon was a freelance illustrator for many years. As the art director of Recycled Paper Products, Inc., she feels this background has helped her understand the pressures and frustrations of the illustrators and designers she works with.

David Loewy has worked at CMP Publications for five years and is presently art director of *VARBusiness* (Value Added Reseller), a computer business publication.

John Schmitz has a music, fine arts and literature background. He is art director of *The San Francisco Bay Guardian*, a news, art and entertainment weekly.

Describe the philosophy which guides you as an art director.

Cosmopulos: My philosophy is "keep it simple." I believe the world does not have any time to read ads, leave alone any of mine. My first rule of advertising is the ad or mailer must first attract attention to itself. Once you have their attention you have to pique their interest instantly (the second rule), say or show something in your ad that tells them "this is for you," otherwise they will move on to other things that attract their attention.

Tharp: My philosophy about design is much the same as that about life in general. It is simply to do the best I can do and enjoy it as much as possible. In the business of design, one must never lose sight of the fact that the client's problem dictates the solution. *That* comes first. If a freelancer can have fun doing it, keeping the problem in mind, what more could one ask for?

Snider: I do not think you can judge a book by its cover, but you should most certainly get a sense of the subject and tone of the book.

Gordon: Our company is unique in that we don't give assignments as such. We review unsolicited submissions each week, looking for new looks and ideas (or old ones with a great new twist). My function is to spot good cards and then offer encouragement and suggestions to the artists.

Loewy: I believe a successful illustration should not merely depict the exact title of the story, but should entice the reader by going deeper, provoking thought, emotion and mood. My philosophy is that the art and word should work together to convey an overall message, not by repeating each other, but by evoking differing thoughts. The end product should be an illustration that is not a literal translation, but a conceptual interpretation of the subject matter.

Schmitz: My philosophy is that art direction is "visual journalism." It is essential to work with editors and writers to tell a complete story. I also see art direction as demanding that one be both psychologist and sociologist—getting diverse, strong personalities to coexist and co-create. It is also a refined art—creating beauty simply in a specific medium.

How has your field been affected by socioeconomic factors and trends? What changes did you witness in the 80s and what do you foresee happening in the 90s?

Cosmopulos: The changes that have occurred in the 80s, as far as the print medium is concerned, have been as dramatic as any decade since I've been involved in the business. The methods of reproduction—scanning machines, better printing presses, better paper, more sophisticated typesetting, computers—they've all added a magical quality to the advertising and graphics arts industry. In the 90s I foresee more of the same—amazing technical breakthroughs and innovations that will challenge and inspire artists, photographers and art directors to heights never before imagined.

Tharp: We don't use computers for design in our office. The trend is in that direction, however. The particular projects will dictate when a computer is appropriate. I see too many students whose portfolios are focused on computer aided design, with concept taking a "back seat." When computers are no longer an issue, concept and traditional methods will become more valuable assets for the freelancer.

Snider: The poor economy in other fields, such as high-technology, has driven many collateral designers as well as advertising art directors, record album designers and magazine people into freelance design. The arena of good freelance people has increased tremendously.

Gordon: The card market has become well saturated in all areas. There seems to be a trend toward emotional cards—statements about just how much the sender cares about the card recipient and their relationship. The biggest changes I see are about ecology and conservation. Recycled Paper Products will continue to be the industry leader in these areas.

Loewy: During the 80s, the artist successfully refined the application of new tools, such as the computer, with a combination of collage and photo illustration. I believe that more computer artists will emerge in the 90s; but in spite of its rapid growth, I do not see computer graphics replacing the more conventional and traditional tools.

Schmitz: In the 80s there was the introduction of cultural diversity and positive and negative responses to technological advances. In the 90s there will be an acceptance and utilization of these forces. Also, design as communication will be more widely utilized and paid for, allowing for more work at the higher end of the quality scale.

How do you believe these changes affect the freelance artist?

Cosmopulos: Some artists will use the new machines as tools along with their unbridled imaginations to generate unparalleled styles, techniques and dimensions of art. Other artists who are more traditional won't have a need for them. The new machines will permit better, faster and higher fidelity reproduction. No one can ignore the advancing technologies—those that do will fall by the wayside.

Tharp: I don't think this is affecting the freelance illustrator, but the freelance designer is going to need access to all the computer peripherals that a larger studio would have in order to be efficient.

Snider: Freelancing has become much more competitive. Cost and speed are almost as important as talent.

Gordon: There are opportunities for artists whose work could not have been used before. We like to get both art and writing from the same person, which allows the artist tremendous freedom. At the same time, we must be much more selective than we were in the past, so the competition at the entry level is pretty fierce.

Loewy: The recent instability of the economy in general, and particularly in the publishing industry, has had a profound effect on the purchase of illustrative art for publications. The loss of advertising revenue and the reduced budgets of art departments have directly led to the cutting of expenditures on illustrative art. Sometimes to save money, publications will use stock art or reprints to cut costs. Although this may be beneficial to established artists, it does not promote new talent.

Schmitz: The amateur and half-interested will find less work as people's graphic design senses become sophisticated enough for many jobs to be done without professional help. More freelance artists will be in the area of consultation. More work *will* open up for serious illustrators and photographers.

What types of projects do you assign to freelancers?

Cosmopulos: All types of illustration assignments—from humor to realistic—using media ranging from crow quill to watercolors, acrylics to markers. We very rarely give out any graphic design or logo projects.

Tharp: Photography, illustration and calligraphy projects go to freelancers. All computer generated projects go to freelancers as well.

Snider: Book jackets: illustration, typography or total design.

Gordon: We do not assign projects. We look at everyday card submissions each week and at seasonals (12-18 months before any given season).

Loewy: I usually assign covers, spreads, full page and spots.

Schmitz: News and feature illustration, photography, promotional design and cartooning. All assignments are local (San Francisco Bay area) for time/deadline and "local support" reasons.

How do you find freelance artists? Do you use creative directories, referrals, samples which you have filed, reps . . .?

Cosmopulos: We use all the sources available to find the artist with the technique we want. We look in creative directories, samples we have filed and call artists' representatives.

Tharp: There is no particular resource we use for referencing freelancers. We assign from work we see via annuals, magazines and other print media, directories, reps and samples sent in or left behind.

Snider: I use all the reference materials I can, including reps.

Gordon: We are looking for greeting card and postcard artists, though we also consider submissions for post-it notes, note pads and mugs. We are listed in the *Artist's Market*, the *Writer's* Market and I attend the National Stationery Show each year in May, specifically to look at portfolios.

Loewy: I seek out illustrators through showcase books and my own files of mailed-in samples. I usually hesitate using artists' reps because it has been my experience that reps often turn down exciting editorial work without consulting the illustrator, based solely on whether the budget was large enough to be profitable for both of them.

Schmitz: Almost all of the new artists are solicited from mailed promo pieces.

What do you feel is the most effective self-promotion for a freelance artist? What do you find bothersome?

Cosmopulos: Most artists' self-promotion efforts are awful. They have a naive perspective of how their self-promotion is received at an art buyer's desk. I wrote an article titled: "How to Hook an Art Buyer" in the May 1990 issue of *The Artist's Magazine* covering this subject in detail. It would behoove anyone to get a copy.

Tharp: The best mode of self-promotion for beginning freelancers is to do a lot of high visibility pro-bono work, get as many samples as one can and send them to prospective art directors, designers and publications. If the freelancer is good and willing to go after the work, there are a lot of worthy projects out there with little or no budget. I find phone calls from freelancers bothersome. Don't call me, I'll call you, when the assignment's right.

Snider: Good printed samples are the best. Xeroxes are not very helpful. While it is nice to see slides, they are very bothersome for quick file reference.

Gordon: We prefer to have artists send a SASE requesting artist guidelines. Clever, lengthy letters will not influence us—the submissions must speak for themselves. Unfortunately, we are really much too busy to meet with artists, so people who insist on interviews are distressing, as are people who think that quantity necessarily equals quality.

Loewy: I believe the best way to get recognized as an illustrator is by promoting oneself with printed samples or by buying a page from a showcase book. I would strongly advise following up mailed-in samples with a phone call. If the art director does not have any work at the present time, ask if he would like to be kept up to date with more samples. If so, the artist's work will speak for itself. Hopefully, he/she will call you if he wants you.

Schmitz: I find mailed promo pieces, preferably accompanied by a resume/letter effective. "Creative" directories generally feature work by artists who can't get work because of stiff, archaic styles. Personal, *written* contact is essential. Phone calls are not accepted and inarticulate writers are inarticulate artists!

What do you seek in a freelancer — as an artist and as a person?

Cosmopulos: I look for certain styles of art that I can incorporate into the advertising that I am doing. Sometimes it's specific and other times I might be inspired by a style or piece of art that I see in a portfolio. As a person, he or she should be business-like and able to understand and communicate with me. There is nothing more discouraging than a project coming back when the artist didn't follow the instructions that I thought we had agreed upon (even when they were written down).

Tharp: The qualities we look for in artists are honesty, wit, enthusiasm and dedication to their "craft." Some artists are better at the board than they are in front of people. Those freelancers should either get a rep, or get into forensic medicine or embalming.

Snider: I look for someone who can think and express their interpretation visually, with a unique style. I like people who are honest and articulate. Needless to say, they must be capable of meeting deadlines and willing to make changes when there are valid reasons for doing so.

Gordon: Our ideal artist is very creative, professional, able to meet tight deadlines, self-motivated. I am always straightforward with the artists and expect the same from them. If there is a problem, I need to hear about it right away so we can fix it. Virtually all of our artists are really nice people — it's not a qualification, but it sure helps. We truly care about them, their happiness and success, and we work very closely with them.

Loewy: In my opinion, a freelance artist must, above all, be able to keep to schedule, have a good attitude, and have the talent to expand an art concept to its limits.

Schmitz: I look for freelance artists with an interest in the world around them, with intellect and a sense of responsibility, also consideration. They should be aware that my life as an art director is not dedicated to promoting the artist.

What do you look for in a portfolio?

Cosmopulos: Sometimes I need an artist whose portfolio contains work with a wide variety of styles and techniques; other times I'm looking for a specialist who works in a certain medium or technique. Artists should only show work they can handle easily within a given deadline. Showing too many things sometimes gets boring and might take up too much of the art buyer's time. Roughly 15 to 20 samples of your work is about right.

Tharp: When reviewing portfolios, we look for consistency within each style presented. We need to see a lot of work in a particular medium. This assures us the artist is proficient enough to guarantee the results that we may contract for. Too large a variety of work makes for a "forgettable" portfolio.

Snider: I look for ideas, style and expression.

Gordon: We want to see submissions that are geared to our product. The funniest joke in the world or the most beautiful painting may not be a card that works for us. Because we don't give assignments, tearsheets are not useful, and we are not set up to view slides.

Loewy: Ideally, an artist's portfolio should exploit to the fullest the artist's style, talent, innovation and creativity. It should not show Xerox copies of any work.

Schmitz: To put it simply, good artists get hired. The response from these artists is good and they win awards. Illustration and photography are not that subjective. You should include anything you are proud of and review all printed material available, especially that of your potential client, to determine the quality and appropriateness of your work.

What business skills would you like freelance artists to have?

Cosmopulos: Everyday business skills. Artists have a reputation of not being business-like. They should use reps. Agreeing on the price and getting the scope and dimension of the project right the first time may not make the illustration any better, but it goes a long way toward getting that next job. When I request a quote for a job, I expect it to include everything. I hate charges like research, photography, transportation, phone calls, shipping, etc., after the fact. I don't mind paying for those things, but they should be included in the original quote.

Tharp: On the subject of usage rights, I feel an artist, and that includes myself as a designer, should be fairly compensated for work provided. Many artists and their reps who demand additional, and sometimes unwarranted, compensation are attempting to "cash in" on the success of their work, but would not consider taking responsibility for the failure . . . if it happens. I do not advocate "responsibility for failure," but rather a fair practice of keeping things simple.

Snider: I look for just all-around professionalism.

Gordon: Basic business skills are fine. I expect new artists to keep their phone calls brief, pleasant and to the point. Everyone in the art department is patient, warm and dedicated to helping our artists, so I don't like to see those qualities abused.

Loewy: I think it is important for freelance artists to understand copyright laws for the mutual benefit of themselves and the publication. They should also be capable of reading over freelance purchase orders carefully before signing on a job.

Schmitz: A freelancer with good business conduct was the artist who didn't know if the first piece he did was good enough and so he did another. Both were excellent and on time. He was able to discuss the issues well with me and the editors and he took an interest. An example of poor business conduct is an artist that got work, did a good job, but had no confidence, even when he was praised by all. No follow-up was made; there was no interest in the work. How can I continue to work on that basis?

How does an illustrator/designer get started in your field?

Cosmopulos: With a lot of tenacity, perseverance, hard work, talent and self confidence.

The following pieces were submitted by the roundtable art directors as examples of successful freelance artwork. They explain why they work well and what the process was.

Stavros Cosmopulos (Cosmopulos, Crowley & Daly,

In 1860, when Willie Park, Sr. won the first British Open, Allendale had been a loss control champion for 25 years.

Reprinted with permission of Cosmopulos, Crowley & Daly

This is an illustration we commissioned freelance artist John Thompson to do for us for our client, Allendale Insurance Company. We chose the realistic style of Thompson because we wanted to show stability and dignity.

Rick Tharp (Tharp Did It):

The swan illustration for Sebastiani Vineyards' Eye of the Swan wine label was done for us by Michael Bull of San Francisco. Initially for a promotional poster, the client and consumer response was so positive that we were asked to redesign the entire package line. It reflects the character and style of this blush wine. A sketch was supplied on a cocktail napkin; Michael provided a rough within one week and a finished pen-and-ink illustration in three weeks.

Reprinted with permission of Tharp Did It

Reprinted with permission of Little, Brown & Company

Steve Snider (Little, Brown & Company):

The art by Paul Davis clearly said I Get on the Bus was an off-beat novel about an African American. It suggested the hallucinatory and erotic feel of the book. It was the result of discussion between Paul and me, [his establishing] the right communication before he began, and his subsequent interpretation.

Melinda Gordon (Recycled Paper Products):

The card was done by Kevin Pope. Kevin is a very funny artist with a unique point of view. He is always a pleasure to work with: prolific, well-focused and easy going. The art is playful and clever; the message is a groaner pun, yet says "Happy Birthday" very directly.

David Loewy (VARBusiness):

Many thought this cover, done by Mark Fredrikson in acrylic and airbrush, was the year's best cover. A thumbnail sketch was supplied, but he was told to adapt it to his style. I assigned it to him because he can take a concept to its limits. He has tight sketches and is flexible with ideas. This is a successful piece because it tells the story and reminds us of an experience we've all had (stepping into something messy); it also brings out humor and a surrealistic mood. Fredrikson was paid $2,000.

John Schmitz (San Francisco Bay Guardian):

This acrylic illustration was done by Ad McCauley for $50. My instructions were to read the story, so this artist got free rein. If artists can handle this, it's nice. I discovered him from a promo piece he mailed. I liked his style and the humor in his work. He was easy to work with, made the deadline and was good at interpreting the story. This illustration earned him an award of excellence from the Society of Newspaper Design.

Those that give up and get discouraged don't deserve to succeed.

Tharp: A freelance illustrator/designer gets started by doing pro-bono work, building a good portfolio, showing it to *everyone*, and getting (and keeping) good clients.

Snider: Create samples and show original works.

Gordon: I'm not up on other companies' procedures, but ours are simple: send a SASE for artists' guidelines; do some great cards; send them to us.

Loewy: The best way for an unpublished artist to get started in editorial illustration is to print or photograph samples of his/her best work and send the copies to magazine art directors in hope of a response.

Snider: Some schooling helps, whether formal or self-taught. Much reading and perusal of available design, work and self-promotion help. You must start with the obvious. If you can't design/illustrate a good business card, resume, etc., how can I hire you? 90 percent of designers' resumes are really bad.

What would you like freelance artists to know about your job and what your side of a project entails?

Cosmopulos: It is my responsibility to come up with the concept for the advertisement and translate that into verbal and visual images. When it comes to the illustration in the ad, sometimes I'm flexible in the way it should be done, sometimes I'm not; but even then, I'm always open to suggestions. The decision—for good or for bad—of what to accept and what to change is mine (our clients of course have the ultimate decision). If the illustrator can't work under these conditions, they shouldn't take the job.

Snider: A freelancer's project is just one of over a hundred that may be in progress, so do not bother me with something less than the very best product, and do not show me what you think I'll like. If I've asked you to work on a cover, it is for *your* style. Show me what *you* think is the best solution.

Gordon: All our artists are freelancers and we are here as a support system for them. The department is very small, but responsible for all art—from the time it comes in as a submission until the time it goes out for scanning. Consequently, we are always busy and most appreciative of artists who are professional.

Loewy: I believe the success of a conceptual illustration hinges on the combination of the proper art direction and the careful choice of artist to execute the director's concept. At CMP, concepts for illustrative pieces are conceived by a collaborative art and editorial effort. As art director, I then choose the artist based on his/her style, experience, craftsmanship and reputation. I translate our art concept to the illustrator either verbally or by thumbnail sketch. I commission 20-25 illustrations per monthly issue.

Schmitz: Time—there is never enough for an art director. That's why phone calls and casual portfolio reviews are so difficult. It's not because we hate you. That's why a kind, friendly human gets results.

The Business of Art

As a fine or freelance graphic artist, you have many jobs. You're not only expected to be a creative artist, but you're also your own secretary, salesperson, lawyer and accountant. Whether you're a painter, illustrator, graphic designer or cartoonist, you must constantly deal with the business of art. While some artists consider the business side a "necessary evil," every freelancer realizes the benefits good business practices provide. By selling your work in the most effective manner, you build your professional image while fulfilling your creative potential. Good business practices pave a smoother path for your journey to creative success.

This section provides general guidelines to securing and building your business through self-promotion, submitting your work and professional business practices. A special feature on copyright highlights two recent changes in copyright law and the importance of registering your work.

Who needs self-promotion?

Getting noticed is the most important step in establishing yourself. Your artwork needs to be noticed by the right people. The best way to do this is to plan an effective self-promotion campaign.

Loosely defined, self-promotion is the art of grabbing attention. It is an ongoing process of building name recognition and reputation. By promoting yourself, you let potential clients know who you are, what you do, how well you do it and why hiring you is a smart and profitable decision.

How do you do it? The name of the game is making the right contacts. At first, the best place to start is right in your own backyard. Local contacts are mainly established through word of mouth and referrals. Your friends, relatives and neighbors all have contacts; many might own a business. Volunteer to illustrate posters for local fundraising events. Join organizations, both art-related and community ones, to get acquainted with fellow artists and local business people. Begin to network with local artists, who will let you know which art directors are open to new talent. The more people who know you are available, the better your chances are of getting an assignment.

The next step—making contacts

After you complete a few assignments, the next step in establishing yourself as a professional artist is to develop a list of contacts, both within and out of your local area. Reading the listings in *Artist's Market* will help you determine where you want to sell your work. You can compile a mailing list of names, addresses, phone numbers and contact people of your best prospects. Note if the company wants to be contacted through the mail, by phone or through an agent and also what materials the art director likes to review. Also comb resource directories, trade publications and annuals such as *American Illustration, The Creative Black Book, Print's Regional Design Annual* or *Communication Art's Illustration Annual* for additional names and addresses.

Make a master list of your leads. Many artists keep index cards for each potential client. On each card you can note the client's specialty, the name of the art buyer, the firm's address and phone number. Then there is room to note your observations about the client—what type of style is used, a special feature spread or advertisement the company has done that you admire, or if the client has a certain slant to its work. The few extra minutes you spend in compiling these cards will pay off, because you will be able to send the right materials to potential clients.

You'll either make contact through the mail or by phone. Whether you call or write, be pleasant, clear, succinct and try to sound confident. Explain who you are, what your discipline is, and why your style is significant. If you have had many assignments, tell the art director where he may have seen your work and list some of your clients. The best way to use the telephone is in conjunction with an introductory letter mailed a week ahead of the call; then use the call itself to determine interest. Keep in mind that art directors and art buyers are very busy people; oftentimes they find phone calls annoying and may only be able to give you 15 seconds of their time. Make sure you know the name of the art buyer and the correct spelling of the name. Follow up your call by mailing samples of your work.

Your sample package

Your initial contact through the mail will be your sample package. The main purpose of this package is to provide a concise overview of your talents. Since you know your budget, you know how ambitious you can be with your package. No matter what the size, make it visually exciting. A small coordinated brochure and resume present a much better image than a sizable yet unimaginative package.

The contents of your promotional package can vary, but the basic components include: a cover letter, business card, samples and a self-addressed, stamped envelope (SASE). Optional materials are a self-addresssed, stamped reply card (with check-off responses to prompt action) and a client list if you have significant past experience.

The cover letter serves as an important first impression and personalizes your presentation—you're talking directly to someone about your best qualifications. A well-written, well-proofed cover letter on letterhead can make a positive statement about your ability to communicate, your intelligence and your business sophistication. Personally addressed letters will get through to art directors where telephone calls and other mailings cannot. Your cover letter should never be longer than one page, should be typed on your letterhead and should concisely state who you are, what you do, what services you can provide and what follow-up (if any) you plan to make. Indicate whether samples are to be returned or filed; if they are to be returned, be sure your SASE contains sufficient postage. If they are to be filed and you have not included a reply card, your SASE may be a #10 business-size envelope for a letter response.

A resume lists your arts-related experience, education and achievements. It spotlights your best features and your most outstanding qualifications. When designing your own, keep in mind that a resume is a list of items that pertain only to your career as an artist; it is not a lengthy autobiography.

Your resume should contain the following points:
- *Your professional name, address and phone number.*
- *Education and scholarships.* List only post-high school degrees if they're art-related and also nondegree studies such as art seminars, workshops and lectures.
- *Exhibitions.* Exhibitions pertain more to a painter, but an illustrator can list them as evidence of stature and appeal. Give the year of the exhibition, the name of the gallery and its location. Also note whether it is a one-person or group show. If you have several shows, it is wise to separate exhibitions under subheadings such as "Solo Shows" and "Group Shows." Also include invitational and juried shows. List these in reverse chronological order, listing the most recent and working backwards.
- *Competitions and awards.* You will need three or more awards and competitions to warrant a special category. Otherwise, list them under exhibitions.

You can also include commissions, special projects, professional affiliations, collections, notices and reviews (the publication, date and page number should be noted).

If you have just graduated from art school, emphasize the quality of your education (a note about prominent professors may help) over the lack of professional experience. Established artists emphasize prestigious accounts and awards, with their educational background as a last note. In other words, state your strongest evidence in the beginning, then back it up with additional strengths.

A brochure is your most versatile self-promotional piece. It can be a multi-fold printed piece, a one-page flyer or a multi-purpose booklet. Used as a solo piece, it can take the place of a resume by outlining background information as well as presenting examples of your work. Accompanying your promotional package, it can provide an overview of your talents, while more focused samples show your approach to specific markets. Since its basic purpose is as a piece art directors can file, the brochure should never be larger than 8½ × 11. When designing a brochure, keep in mind that it should contain at least one example of your work and complete contact information (name, address with zip code, and telephone number with area code). If the piece is to be mailed, keep one folded side blank so you can address and stamp it. Check standard mailing dimensions at the post office so that you won't incur extra postal charges.

A business card can be a calling card, an addendum to your package or a leave-behind after an interview. It should list your name, phone number and address plus a mention of your specialty. Use simple, clear type and standard dimensions (2 × 3½).

Samples are your visual candy; they are visual statements that best convey your style and technique. Select only the most appropriate and only the best; many art directors claim they judge you by the worst piece they see. Gear your samples to the specific needs of the market you're approaching.

Refer to the article, "A Taste of Self-Promotion" for effective examples of how top illustrators and designers promote themselves.

Types of samples

Art directors most commonly request to see transparencies, photographs, photostats, photocopies and tearsheets. Black-and-white work lends itself to photocopies and photostats (produced by a photographic process utilizing paper negatives). Color work is best depicted by either photographs or transparencies. (A transparency is a positive image on a translucent film base; a slide is a 35mm transparency in a mount.) Transparencies reproduce a greater range of tones than any other method of printing and can be made in varying sizes (2¼ × 2¼, 4 × 5 and 8 × 10). Tearsheets, which are examples of published work, bolster your professional image and give an art director a notion of how your work appears in print. They should be laminated to prevent tearing and folding. If you don't have any published work, give yourself an assignment. For example, if you want to break into package design, redesign a spaghetti sauce label or beer can. Never send original work.

Label everything. With photographs, photostats and photocopies, use the back to stamp your name, address and phone number (a pre-printed label hurries this process); use arrows to indicate which way is up; note the size of the original; and, if submitting several, mark each "1 of 5 photographs" or "2 of 5 photostats." These numbers may also refer to a separate information sheet which gives details of how the illustration or design was used. If you send one, add "See info sheet" under the number.

Slides are labelled in similar fashion. On the "front" (image is correct when held up to a light), list your name, size of original work, medium, number, and arrows indicating the top. If your slides are accompanied by an info sheet, indicate reference to it on the slides. Your full name, address and phone number may be printed on the reverse side.

How to present a portfolio

It is important that you follow-up with a phone call and request an appointment to show your portfolio to the art director, either through the mail or in person. If the art director suggests you drop off your portfolio, remember that a drop-off is not a turn-down and at many places this is automatic policy. It also may make it easier for you to meet with the art director the next time. If the art director says she is not interested, keep your chin up and call the next one on your list. If she has agreed, now is the chance to display the creative and professional artist you are.

The overall appearance of the portfolio affects your professional presentation. A neat, organized three-ring binder is going to create a better impression than a bulky, time-worn leather case. The most popular portfolios are simulated leather with puncture-proof sides that allow the use of loose samples. The size of the portfolio should be dictated by the size of your work. Avoid the large "student" variety because it is too bulky to spread across an art director's desk. The most popular sizes are between 11 × 14 and 18 × 24.

No matter what format you choose for the case, you must follow a few basic principles in presenting its contents. You are showing your portfolio to this art director because, based on the research you have done, you have determined that your work is appropriate for this market. The pieces in your portfolio should be germane to the company. If you're showing your portfolio to an ad agency art buyer, you're not going to bring a lot of greeting card samples. An art director will look for consistency of a particular style or technique. He wants to be sure that your work is solid and will continue to be so. Choose only your best work. Quality is better than quantity.

Select 10 or 12 examples of your best work and bring along 10 extra samples in case the client wants to see more of a particular type of work that you're not showing in your portfolio, interior illustration, for example.

Plan to spend anywhere from 10 to 30 minutes presenting your work. Try to be self-confident and remember that, for the most part, the less said, the better. Usually the art director just wants to see your work and may become irritated if subject to a life story. Allow her to flip the pages while you give a one-line description of each piece. If she has questions about one — the client, the purpose of the assignment, the result, etc., then that's your chance to talk.

If you were called in to talk about a specific job, this is the time to find out about its scope, budget and schedule, along with showing your portfolio. If you are introducing your work to a client for future assignments, make sure you leave behind samples (labelled with your name, address and telephone number) and your business card.

Since the drop-off policy is prevalent, have at least two or three portfolios at hand. One can be left when necessary, another can be used on personal calls, while the third can be sent to out-of-town prospects. Mini-portfolios are handy for simultaneous submissions. Let it be known that you will retrieve your portfolio either the next morning or the following evening. Most businesses are honorable; you don't have to worry about your case being stolen. However, things do get lost; make sure you've included only duplicates, which can be insured at a reasonable cost. Remember to tag each portfolio with your name and address so you can easily identify it.

For more specific information on portfolio presentations, read the "A Roundtable of Art Directors," at the front of the book.

Packaging your work

Your primary goal in packaging is to have your samples, portfolio or assigned work arrive undamaged. Before packaging original work, make sure you have a copy (photostat, photocopy, photograph, slide or transparency) in your file at home. If changes are necessary on an assigned job, you can then see on your copy what the art director is discussing over the phone. Most importantly, if your work is lost, you can make a duplicate.

Flat work can be packaged between heavy cardboard or Styrofoam. Cut the material slightly larger than the piece of flatwork and tape it closed. It is wise to include your business card or a piece of paper with your name and address on it on the outside of this packaging material in case the outer wrapper becomes separated from the inner packing. The work at least can then be returned to you.

The outer wrapping, depending on package size and quality of inner wrapping, may be a manila envelope, a foam-padded envelope, a "bubble" package (one with plastic "bubbles" lining the inside), or brown wrapping paper. Use reinforced tape for closures. Make sure one side is clearly addressed.

Check the various types of envelopes and packaging materials available at your local art supply, photography or stationery stores. If you're going to be doing a lot of mailing, buy in bulk quantities. The price is always lower.

Packing original works such as paintings takes several layers of protective coverings. The outer layer protects the work from physical damage, while the inner layer provides a cushion. The outer package must be sturdy, yet easy to open and repack. If you are mailing a flat work that is unframed, consider rolling it into a cardboard tube that can be found at appliance and furniture stores. A cardboard container is adequate for small pieces, but larger works should be protected with a strong outer surface, such as laminated cardboard, masonite or light plywood. Mounted, matted or framed pieces are irregularly shaped and require extra cushioning material such as Styrofoam. When packaging a framed work, wrap it in polyfoam or heavy cloth, cushion the outer container with spacers (any cushioning material that prevents a work from moving), then pack the artwork carefully inside so that it will not move when shipped.

Mailing

The U.S. Post Office mail classifications with which you will be most concerned are First Class and Fourth Class, more commonly called parcel post. First Class mail is the type used every day for letters, etc. If the piece you are mailing is not the usual letter size, make sure to mark it First Class. Fourth Class is used for packages weighing 1 to 70 pounds and not more than 108 inches in length and girth combined.

The greatest disadvantage to using these classes of mail is that you cannot be guaranteed when the package/letter will arrive. If time is of the essence, consider the special services offered by the post office such as Priority Mail, Express Mail Next Day Service and Special Delivery.

Today there is a growing number of airfreight services which make overnight delivery common. Check to see which ones are available in your area, but some of the more familiar names are Emery, Purolator and Federal Express. These firms offer varying rates according to weight of the package and urgency.

Certified mail includes a mailing receipt and provides a record of delivery at the addressee's post office. This type of mail is handled like ordinary mail, but you can request a return receipt on certain types of mail as your proof of delivery.

Cost is determined by weight, size and destination of the package and automatically includes insurance up to $100. You can purchase additional insurance.

UPS does have wrapping restrictions. Packages must be in heavy corrugated cardboard, with no string or paper on the outside, and be sealed with reinforced tape. UPS cannot guarantee how long it will take a package to arrive at its destination, but will track lost packages. It also offers Two-Day Blue Label Air Service to any destination in the U.S., and Next Day Service in specific zip code zones.

Greyhound Bus Lines and some commercial airlines also offer same-day or overnight package delivery. Check locally for rates and restrictions.

Finding the right price

Negotiation is the art of reaching a mutual agreement so that both parties feel satisfied with the outcome. When a client describes a project to you, you are hearing the client's needs and wants. She will never know *your* needs unless you speak up.

Each job will present you with a new and different pricing situation. Experience is often the best teacher, but even in the beginning, there are a few rules to follow. First, convey a positive attitude and listen carefully. Try to put yourself in your client's place so you can "hear" what he is really saying. When you speak, do it slowly and distinctly so the art buyer will slow down and listen to you.

So that you will be in a position to quote a price that is fair to both you and the client, you need to develop an hourly rate. This is especially important if you are a newcomer who can only estimate what your time is worth. After you establish an hourly rate and have completed many jobs, you will be able to quote a fee by knowing how long it usually takes to complete a similar assignment.

To arrive at an hourly rate, you need to know the annual salary of a person on staff who is doing similar work, such as a graphic designer on staff at an advertising agency. Take the annual salary, divide it by 52 (the number of weeks in a year) to get the weekly rate of pay. Then, divide the result by 40 (the number of hours in a work week) to arrive at the hourly rate for this type of job. Finally, add the extra expenses incurred in your overhead (rent, electricity, heat, supplies, etc.) by multiplying the result by 2.5. Check with other freelance artists to see if this figure is competitive and realistic. Remember that your prices should cover all costs and provide some profit.

Contracts

In simplest terms, a contract is an agreement between two or more persons containing an offer, acceptance and consideration. Contracts may be written, oral or tacit, but to protect yourself from misunderstandings and faulty memories, make it a practice to have a written contract signed and dated by you and the party you are dealing with.

The items you want specified in your contract will vary according to the assignment and the complexity of the project; but some basic points are: your fee (the basic fee, possibly a kill fee, payment schedule, advances, expense compensation, etc.); what service you are providing for the fee; deadlines; how changes will be handled; and return of original art.

Read carefully any contract or purchase order you are asked to sign. If the terms are complex, or if you do not understand them, seek professional advice before signing. If it is a preprinted or "standard" contract, look for terms which may not be agreeable to you. Because of a 1989 Supreme Court decision, "work for hire" is not as ominous as it once was—when it meant losing all rights to the work created. Now a freelance artist working at someone else's direction will still own rights to the work unless the type of work fits into the law's enumerated categories and she agrees in writing to transfer those rights.

Further information on contracts is available in *Business and Legal Forms for Illustrators*, *Business and Legal Forms for Graphic Designers* and *Legal Guide for the Visual Artist*, all by Tad Crawford; *The Artist's Friendly Legal Guide*; *Graphic Artists Guild Handbook Pricing and Ethical Guidelines*; and *Contracts for Artists* by William Gignilliat.

Recordkeeping

If you haven't kept good business records, all your talent and art skills will mean nothing when it comes time to give an account of your business profitability to the IRS. Recordkeeping is usually considered a drudgery by artists, yet it is an essential part of your business. A freelancer is an independent businessperson and, like any other entreprenuer, must be accountable for financial statements.

You don't have to be an accountant to understand basic recordkeeping principles. Two accounting terms that you'll need to know are the accounting period and the accounting method. Your accounting period determines the time frame you'll use to report income and claim deductions. Most likely you'll elect a calendar year accounting period, beginning January 1 and ending December 31. An accounting period other than a calendar year is known as a fiscal year.

Once you've selected your accounting period, you'll need to determine which accounting method best suits your business. Your accounting method will determine what income and expenses will be reported during a particular accounting period.

There are two basic accounting methods, the cash method and the accrual method. The cash method, which is used by most individuals, records income when it is received, or when a gallery or agent receives it for you. Similarly, expenses are recorded when you pay them. Expenses paid in advance can only be deducted in the year in which they occur. This method typically uses cash receipts and disbursement journals, which record payment when received and monthly paid expenses.

The accrual method is a little more involved. In this method, you report income at the time you earn it instead of when you receive it. Also, you deduct expenses at the time you incur them rather than when you pay them. If you use this method, which lists projects as they are invoiced or expenses as they are incurred, you will probably keep accounts receivable and accounts payable journals. The accrual method is best for artists with huge inventories.

You are free to choose any accounting method you wish. However, once you've made that decision, you may only change your accounting method with the approval of the IRS. In order to request a change of accounting method, you must file Form 3115, Application for Change in Accounting Method, with the Commissioner of the Internal Revenue Service in Washington, D.C. not more than six months after the beginning of the year in which you wish to make a change.

The next step to good recordkeeping is to decide which records to keep. A good rule is to keep any receipt related to your business. It's important to hold on to cancelled checks, sales slips, invoices, cash receipts, cash register tapes, bank statements, bills and receipts for goods and services you have bought. Ask for a receipt with every purchase. If you're entertaining a client at a business dinner, ask the waiter or cashier for a receipt. Keep a record of the date, place, cost, business relationship and the purpose of the meeting. Don't forget to record driving expenses. Keep your business and personal records separate. Also, if you're a painter and an illustrator, keep separate records for each pursuit.

Here are a few tips for setting up an effective recordkeeping system. The first thing you should do is to divide your income and expense records into separate headings. Then you should divide each into various subheadings. A handy method is to label your records with the same categories listed on Schedule C of the 1040 tax form. That way you'll be able to transfer figures from your books to the tax form without much hassle. Always make an effort to keep your files in chronological order.

There are various bookkeeping systems at your disposal. A single-entry bookkeeping system records expenses as they are incurred; you add them up at the end of the year. This can be recorded in a journal or diary. A double-entry system is more complicated, involving ledgers and journals in which every item is entered twice—once as a debit and once as a credit so the books are always in balance.

Taxes

Knowing what income you must report and what deductions you can claim are the two most important factors in computing your taxes. To know these factors, you must first determine whether you are a professional or a hobbyist. You must prove you are a professional in order to claim business-related deductions which reduce the amount of taxable income you have to report.

Some of the factors which set you apart as a professional are: conducting your activity in a business-like manner (such as keeping accurate records, keeping a business checking account); your expertise and training; the time you devote to your work and whether you have no other substantial source of income; and your history of income or losses. In the past a professional had to show two out of three years of profit. Now, under the Tax Reform

Act of 1986, you must show a profit for three years out of five to attain a professional status.

What is deductible?

As a professional who owns an unincorporated business, you must report business expenses and income on Schedule C of Form 1040, Profit (or Loss) from Business or Profession. The following costs of doing business are deductible on Schedule C:

• Advertising expenses. This includes the costs of direct mailings; ads placed or aired on television, radio or in the Yellow Pages; the cost of printing business cards and show invitations.

• Capital expenditures. A capital expenditure is the purchase of a "permanent" fixture such as a computer. If you spend less than $10,000 on one item which you use for your business, you may deduct the cost on your Schedule C. If you use the item only to a certain extent for your business, you can deduct that percentage of the item's cost on Schedule C.

• Car and truck expenses. There are two methods of handling this deduction. The IRS allows you to claim 24¢ per mile travelled in business-related trips, up to 15,000 miles, then 11¢ per mile after that. Or you can take a percentage of all auto-related expenses. No matter which method you elect, keep a travel log which notes the date, distance travelled and the reason for the trip. This information is vital if you are audited.

• Courses and seminars. Courses such as framing and slide photography workshops are deductible because they are related to your profession.

• Depreciation. The costs of business-related items priced over $10,000 can be "capitalized." By capitalizing an item, you deduct a percentage of the cost of the item each year for a certain number of years. The IRS determines the life of the item and the percentages allowed each year.

• Dues and publications. This includes membership fees and subscriptions to art-related magazines and newsletters.

• Freight. This deduction applies only to shipping commissioned works to clients or shipping entries to juried shows.

• Home office. If you use a portion of your home as your studio, you may deduct certain expenses. Refer to the subhead "Home office deduction" in this article for further details.

• Insurance. You can deduct insurance on artwork and your studio.

• Legal and professional expenses. These are deductible if applied to your business.

• Studio rental. This deduction is staightforward, unlike the home office deduction.

• Taxes. Taxes on real and personal property used in your business, and payroll or FICA taxes for your employees are deductible. Federal, state and local business taxes are claimed on Schedule A.

• Travel, meals and entertainment. Only 80% of expenses incurred in entertaining clients is deductible.

• Miscellaneous expenses. This includes framing, entry fees and postage, or any expense directly related to running your business.

Estimated tax is the method you use to pay tax on income which is not subject to withholding. You will generally make estimated tax payments if you expect to owe more than $500 at year's end and if the total amount of income tax that will be withheld during the year will be less than 90% of the tax shown on the previous year's return. In order to calculate your estimated tax, you must estimate your adjusted gross income, taxable income, taxes and credits for the year. Form 1040ES provides a worksheet which will help you estimate how much you will have to pay. Estimated tax payments are made in four equal installments due on April 15, June 15, September 15 and January 15. For more information, refer to IRS Publication 505, Tax Withholding and Estimated Tax.

The self-employment tax is a social security tax for individuals who are self-employed and therefore cannot have social security tax withheld from their paychecks. In order to be liable for self-employment tax, you must have a net self-employment income of $400 or more. Your net income is the difference between your self-employment income and your allowable business deductions. You will compute the amount of self-employment tax you owe on Schedule SE, Computation of Social Security Self-Employment Tax. Beginning in 1990, there is a deduction for self-employment tax. The deduction is calculated by multiplying by 7% the smaller of: your net income from self employment or $54,256 minus your wages subject to social security tax.

Depending on the level of your business and tax expertise, you may want to have a professional tax advisor to consult with or to complete your tax form. Most IRS offices have walk-in centers open year-round and offer over 90 free IRS publications containing tax information to help in preparation of your return. The booklet that comes with your tax return forms contains names and addresses of Forms Distribution Centers by region where you can write for further information. The U.S. Small Business Administration offers seminars on taxes, and arts organizations hold many workshops covering business management, often including detailed tax information. Inquire at your arts council, local arts organization or university to see if a workshop is scheduled.

You will be asked to provide your Social Security number or your Employer Identification number (if you are a business) to the person/firm for whom you are doing a freelance project. This information is now necessary in order to make payments.

Home office deduction

A home office deduction allows you to claim a business portion of the expenses incurred for the upkeep and running of your entire home. You may deduct business expenses that apply to a part of your home only if that part is used exclusively on a regular basis as your principal place of business at which you meet or deal with clients, or a separate structure used in your trade or business that is not attached to your residence. Your office must be a space devoted only to your artwork and its business activity.

You may have another business which generates more income than you derive from the sale of your art. For instance, you may have a fulltime job where you have an office at another location. You can still take your home office deduction as long as it's your principal place of business for your secondary source of income.

When a studio is part of the principal residence, deductions are possible on an appropriate portion of mortgage interest, property taxes, rent, repair and utility bills and depreciation.

There are two ways to determine what percentage of your home is used for business purposes. If the rooms in the house are approximately the same size, divide the number of rooms used as your office into the total number of rooms in your house. If your rooms differ in size, divide the square footage of your business area into the total square footage of your house.

Your total office deduction for the business use of your home cannot exceed the gross income that you derive from its business use. In other words, you cannot take a net business loss resulting from a home office deduction.

Because the IRS keeps close tabs on the home office deduction, you should keep a log of business activities taking place in your home office. Record the dates and times the office was used, what was discussed, and all sales and business transacted.

Consult a tax advisor to be certain you meet all of the requirements before attempting to take this deduction, since its requirements and interpretations frequently change.

Sales tax

Check regarding your state's regulations on sales tax. Some states claim that "creativity" is a service rendered and cannot be taxed, while others view it as a product you are selling and therefore taxable. Be certain you understand the sales tax laws to avoid being held liable for uncollected money at tax time. Write to your state auditor for sales tax information.

If you work on consignment with a shop or gallery, you are not responsible for collecting sales tax since it is the shop or gallery which is making the sale to the consumer. If you sell wholesale, you need not collect sales tax for the same reason. However, you must exchange resale numbers so both parties can show the numbers on their invoices.

In most states, if you are selling to a customer outside of your sales tax area, you do not have to collect sales tax. However, check to see if this holds true for your state.

Insurance

As a self-employed artist—whether you are working out of your home or a separate studio and not covered by any benefits package—there are two areas of coverage which you need to consider: personal insurance, which includes life, health and disability; and coverage for your business.

Life insurance can be viewed either on a short- or long-term basis. If you want to cover the needs of a specific duration, such as a home mortgage or a bank loan, seek term insurance at the lowest possible rates. Permanent life insurance is a long-term means of accumulating capital; the money which accumulates may be withdrawn, borrowed against or used to pay the premiums on the policy as you grow older.

For health insurance, many freelancers feel it is better to be covered for big problems (such as lengthy hospital stays or long-term nursing care) than for routine medical expenses. You may want to accept a higher total annual deductible—say $2,500 as opposed to $100—in exchange for reducing your premium drastically. Basic coverage protects you for a specified time that pays for most in-hospital costs. Major medical coverage picks up where the basic package stops. Major medical plans cover long-term, catastrophic illnesses; the deductible is usually $1,000 to $1,500 a year.

Disability insurance pays a monthly fee if you are unable to work. This form of protection is normally based on your earnings and your occupation; hazardous jobs require greater protection.

Whether your business is located at home or in an outside office, you should have a small business plan which provides coverage against loss due to fire, theft and liability for the contents of the studio. The more costly your equipment, the greater your coverage should be.

In case an illness prevents you from working, overhead expense protection covers expenses such as rent, electricity, telephone bills and employee salaries. It is available to businesses located outside the home. This short-term plan enables you to resume work after an illness without extra financial pressures.

If there is a condition that needs insuring, there is a policy for it. Compare the policies offered by several companies by sending away for brochures and interviewing agents. Many artists prefer to join a professional organization, such as the American Institute of Graphic Artists or the Graphic Artists Guild, which offers insurance benefits. Coverage under a group plan is significantly less expensive and may offer more comprehensive coverage than individual policies.

The Business of Copyright

by Alvalyn Lundgren-Ellis

Imagine yourself commissioned to design a humorous logo to be used on a T-shirt. You create the logo and receive payment for the specified usage. Some time later, you discover the T-shirt manufacturer has also used your design on hats, jackets and sweatshirts. You received a sum of money representing the use of your design on a T-shirt only, but the manufacturer has made a profit from the use of your design on other items which you, the creator of the design, have not been compensated for.

This situation is a common occurrence in the graphic arts field. Although common, it can be avoided if the artist knows about United States copyright law and how to use it in negotiating the sale of rights to his artwork. Wise use of copyright can mean the difference between making a living from your creative endeavors or not. It can bring additional income from your work, form equitable contracts between artists and art buyers, and establish a better atmosphere in which to create original artwork by having confidence that your work will not be copied for someone else's profit.

Making a living as an artist means more than having the talent and desire to do so. Both fine and graphic arts professionals need to think of themselves as business people and make knowledgeable business decisions to protect their livelihood and their artwork. Knowledge of copyright should be as basic to your art education as color mixing or fundamentals of drawing. Without this knowledge, you risk shortchanging yourself every time you sell the use of your work.

The artist's rights

As the creator of your artwork, you have certain inherent rights over your work and the ability to control how it is used. You have the exclusive right to reproduce, sell or distribute your work, create derivative works, and display your work publicly. This is the essence of copyright.

Copyright protection exists automatically from the moment a work is created in tangible form. You do not need to register your work to claim copyright for it. To be copyrightable, a work must be both original and creative. It can be graphic, pictorial or sculptural in nature, as long as it is totally your own and not derived from another source, and it must be a physical expression of an idea. It can be a single work or a series of related images. Examples of single works include logo designs, illustrations, fine art prints, oil paintings, transparencies, photos, surface design, globes, charts and diagrams. Copyrightable series include films, videos, filmstrips, motion pictures, slide shows and computer software programs.

Copyright protection cannot be claimed for any idea not fixed in tangible form, short

Alvalyn Lundgren-Ellis is an illustrator and graphic designer. She is a design and illustration educator and department chair for the Visual Arts department at Learning Tree University in Chatsworth, California. She was previously president of the Visual Artists' Association, a business-of-design support group, and is currently the legislative director.

phrases, utilitarian objects, typeface designs and calligraphic alphabets. However, any artistic motif or graphic which adorns a utilitarian object is copyrightable. For example, a logo and label design on a shampoo bottle are copyrightable, but the bottle itself is not. Your artistic style cannot by copyrighted, but the work you create in your particular style can be copyrighted.

Copyright exists separately from the original artwork and can be sold or transferred separately. You can sell an original illustration and retain all rights to it, or you can sell the rights and keep the original. You can also subdivide your copyright, transferring individual or groups of rights altogether or separately, at different times and to different entities. It is conceivable that you would sell a first reproduction right of an illustration to a greeting card company and a second right for the same illustration to a calendar publisher a month later. You can limit the duration of the copyright transfer and the geographic location as well. For instance, you can license your illustration to a greeting card company for a period of three years, to be distributed only within the continental United States. After that specified three-year period, all rights would revert back to you.

You exercise your copyright simply by placing copyright notice on your artwork. An example of proper copyright notice is: © 1991 Joe Artist. Whether you register your copyright or not, you should always place your copyright notice on all your work. Incorporating the copyright notice into the signature you use to sign your work is a good idea, as you will always automatically use it. Placing this notice signifies to the general public that you alone control the work, and it will deter potential infringement situations. You are making a public statement that the work and the rights to it belong to you and cannot be used by anyone else for profit or nonprofit unless you permit it through the sale or transfer of your copyright.

Copyright registration

If you distribute your work publicly in any manner (publish it), you will need to register your copyright over the work with the Copyright Office. Not only does registration reinforce your ownership of your work, but it provides you with recourse if someone does use your work without your permission. You can bring suit for infringement and are entitled to receive not only actual damages, but attorney's fees and statutory damages as well. Registering your copyright is simple and inexpensive. It requires completion of an application form, a ten dollar filing fee, and a "deposit" of copies of the work for which copyright is claimed. If the work has not been published, you need only to submit one photograph or other reproduction of the work. If the work has been published, you must supply two tearsheets or actual samples of the published work as deposits.

Once registered, copyright protection lasts for your lifetime plus 50 years. If a copyrighted work is a joint work created by two or more people, protection lasts for the lifetime of the last surviving author plus 50 years. If a work was created anonymously or pseudononymously (under an assumed name), protection lasts 75 years after the date of first publication or 100 years from the date of creation, whichever is shorter. Your copyright can be renewed by your heirs, who can enjoy any on-going profits from your work. You can transfer your copyright to your heirs in your will.

You may transfer part or all of your copyright through sale, gift, donation, or as a service in trade. However you transfer it, you must transfer it in writing, in a contract, or some other form of written documentation. In contrast, you can sell or transfer title to your original artwork through a verbal agreement only, although it is always wise to keep a written record of all transactions.

On March 1, 1989, the United States joined an international copyright treaty known as the Berne Convention for the Protection of Literary and Artistic Works. This extends automatic copyright protection of works by U.S. creators into the 79 Berne Convention member nations, and makes it easier to track, prevent and prosecute infringement of U.S. creative work abroad.

Infringement

Infringement (in the U.S. or abroad) occurs when someone copies a work owned by someone else or exercises an exclusive right over the work without authorization. A basic test for infringement is when a casual observer of both the original work and the copy can determine that one was derived directly from the other. If you base your artwork on research materials such as photographs clipped from magazines or other artwork, you must keep in mind that you might be borrowing from a copyrighted image and therefore infringing on somone else's copyrighted work. You need to alter your artwork enough so that the casual observer cannot notice a resemblance. Research materials should only be used as inspiration or resources and never copied exactly. Many artists have innocently borrowed from another artist's or photographer's work and have been guilty of infringement for doing so.

On occasion, your work might be reproduced without your permission but for purposes which will not harm your work or damage your artistic integrity. This kind of situation comes under the category of "fair use." Reproduction for the purposes of criticism, comment, education, research and reporting all come under the heading of fair use. An example of legitimate fair use is when a magazine, in reporting on the work of a particular artist, reproduces the work of the artist to illustrate the article. Or if you send out a press release about an exhibition of your original artwork and a newspaper picks up the story and, without your permission, reproduces your work to illustrate the coverage of the exhibition.

Work for hire

There are legitimate situations in which you create artwork but have no right to it or can't even claim it as your own. If you are a salaried employee of a company and you create artwork as a normal part of your employment, you cannot claim copyright for the work. Your employer is both creator and owner of the copyright and the original artwork and has the exclusive legal authority to exercise control over it. As an employee, you are part of the company. However, any work you do during personal time is your own, and you are able to claim copyright protection for it.

Sometimes, as a freelance artist, you will be asked by a commissioning party to sign a work-for-hire contract. In work for hire you assign all rights to your work, the ownership of the original art, and the right to claim authorship of your work over to the commissioning party. If you sign a work-for-hire agreement, you will, in essence, become an employee of the commissioning party for the duration of the job, but only in terms of your rights to your work. You work as an employee but receive no employee benefits. You cannot claim authorship of your work, nor can you technically include it in your portfolio. Work-for-hire agreements tend to give greater financial benefit to the commissioning party, leaving the real creator of the commissioned work out in the cold in terms of income and reputation. Work-for-hire agreements tend to be negotiated for fees lower than the actual value of the work being created. Current copyright law requires that work-for-hire agreements must be made in writing.

If you are confronted with "sign-it-or-lose-it" work-for-hire agreements, the best thing to do is to try to negotiate for something comparable, such as an all rights or a buyout contract, in which you transfer all rights to your work along with the ownership of the original artwork. In doing so, you can claim authorship of your work, use the work in your promotion and portfolio, and receive a more equitable fee for creating the work in the first place. If you cannot claim authorship of your work, no one will know you created the work, and no one will contact you to create a similar work for them. Your livelihood, which is based solely on the reputation and integrity of your work, could be jeopardized.

In June, 1989, the United States Supreme Court handed down a landmark decision on work for hire. The case involved a sculptor who was commissioned by a nonprofit organization to create a sculpture based on an idea conceived by the founder of the organization. The sculptor was reimbursed only for expenses, per his verbal agreement with the organization.

A dispute later arose between the organization and the sculptor as to who owned the sculpture. The Supreme Court decided the sculptor was the owner, under the copyright law, and that he was not an employee of the organization, nor was he creating a work for hire for the organization. How had the Supreme Court come to that decision? Remember, the sculptor had only a verbal agreement with the organization. Therefore, the commission could not have been a work for hire, nor was there any transfer of copyright. Also, ideas are not copyrightable; only the physical expression of one is.

Negotiating copyright

Now that you have a basic foundation in copyright, how do you use it when selling your work? The more extensively your work is to be used, the more you should require in payment. If you are selling the original art as well, you should require an extra fee for that. Always find out how your client intends to use your artwork, both in the near and distant future, and whether they want the original. Find out for how long they intend to use it and where.

International exposure of your work should command a higher fee, as the widespread use of your work will mean a greater profit base for your client. The more your work will benefit the client, the more the client should benefit you. Let's say you are commissioned by a book publisher to paint a cover illustration for a trade novel. The publisher intends to print only 50,000 copies of the novel, and you negotiate your fee on that basis. In your contract, you transfer a first North American reproduction right for use as a hardcover book jacket and reserve all other rights. The novel makes the best seller list for ten weeks in a row, and the publisher now wants to print another 25,000 hardcover copies and also print 50,000 in paperback, using your illustration again for each situation. Since you have reserved all other rights to your illustration, the publisher now needs to come back to you and negotiate fees for the additional two uses described above. If the publisher goes ahead and reproduces your illustration a second time without your authorization, he will be infinging your copyright. This may seem like a lot of work for the publisher, but you need to keep in mind that it was your illustration which helped make the book such a hit in the first place.

Always try to consider potential as well as actual uses for your work. If your client wants to negotiate a buyout with you, you should ask a fee much higher than if you are selling one right. Base your negotiations on the idea of receiving value for value, equal pay for equal benefit. That way, you will never shortchange yourself.

The future

Laws change, and, as copyright law in the United States underwent some revisions to accommodate the Berne Treaty requirements, it will change again. Professional artists will need to stay current with the laws or else risk making grievous errors. When you have questions, contact the Copyright Office or an attorney who deals with copyright law.

Additional information on copyright can be obtained by contacting the Copyright Office, Library of Congress, Washington DC 20559. To order copyright literature and forms, call (202)707-9100. To speak with an information specialist, call (202)479-0700.

Important note on the markets

● *Listings are based on editorial questionnaires and interviews. They are not advertisements (markets do not pay for their listings), nor are listings endorsed by the* Artist's Market *editor.*

● *Listings are verified prior to the publication of this book. If a listing has not changed from last year, then the art director has told us that his needs have not changed — and the previous information still accurately reflects what he buys.*

● *Remember, information in the listings is as current as possible, but art directors come and go; companies and publications move; and art needs fluctuate between the publication of this directory and when you use it.*

● *When looking for a specific market, check the index. A market might not be listed for one of these reasons: 1) It doesn't solicit freelance material, 2) It has gone out of business, 3) It requests not to be listed, 4) It did not respond to our questionnaire, 5) It doesn't pay for art (we have, however, included some nonpaying listings because we feel the final printed artwork could be valuable to the artist's portfolio), 6) We have received complaints about it and it hasn't answered our inquiries satisfactorily.*

● Artist's Market *reserves the right to exclude any listing that does not meet its requirements.*

Key to Symbols and Abbreviations

* New listing
ASAP As soon as possible
b&w Black and white
IRC International Reply Coupon
P-O-P Point-of-purchase display
SASE Self-addressed, stamped envelope
SAE Self-addressed envelope

The Markets

Advertising, Audiovisual & Public Relations Firms

The head of an ad agency once said, "I start worrying about losing an account the minute I get it. The minute I sign the contract, I'm one step closer to losing it." If the state of an agency's account has always been anxiety provoking, it must be close to breakdown inducing today.

The advertising business is in a slump and clients are watching their pennies. Ad spending last year barely kept up with inflation. More companies are demanding that agencies accept fixed-fee payments instead of percentage commissions. Mergers, among both clients and agencies, have led to belt-tightening—cost cutting and layoffs.

This has resulted in the creation of more inhouse advertising and media buying staff and a greater need for freelancers. Instead of dealing with account executives or other agency go-betweens, smaller businesses are increasingly turning to specialty shops that provide a few services, such as copywriting or illustration and design. Clients feel they receive more attention and eliminate extra expenses such as agency commissions.

With large agencies producing cautious and conservative design, smaller firms are making their mark, often producing bolder and more innovative campaigns. More and more smaller firms are hiring artists to design and illustrate print ads, brochures, posters, catalogs and direct-mail packages. Small companies often direct the finest illustration projects because they are more apt to accept new styles and are less dependent upon industry trends. Freelance artists tend to bring freshness and objectivity to a campaign which is difficult to obtain from agency employees. Illustrators who are in demand tend to have a unique style which evokes a strong emotional response, such as the work of Close-up Clare Wood.

This year, due to the popularity of the Simpsons, Teenage Mutant Ninja Turtles and Dick Tracy, cartoon characters are selling everything from insurance to frozen pizza. Another recognizable fad is the current movement away from hard-sell tactics to advertising that relies upon patterns of association such as visual cues and, in television, unusual sounds to sell a product. Hence, one watches a whole commercial with no idea of what is being "pushed," until the final moment when the product is shown.

Of course, these advertising trends should not dictate your style, but their popularity does open the market to artists specializing in these fields. Moreover, there were many art directors, who on the *Artist's Market* questionnaires, said they are looking for computer-literate artists.

Before submitting samples, make sure you understand what the agency does, what freelancers are used for, whether local artists are preferred, and the submission procedure required. Don't call if an art director prefers the first inquiry to be via a letter. While some art directors like to see conceptual work (roughs and comprehensives), others want to examine only finished pieces. There are art directors who want to see a variety of work; others expect the freelancer to have done a bit of market research and tailored samples and/or portfolio to their particular needs. Find out what each prefers. As with any query, always have duplicates of everything you send so the agency is free to keep material on file. Also, every submitted piece should be accompanied by a brief description of the project and the instructions you were given to complete it. Many art directors also like to be told what rate the artist charged and how long it took to do. The listings in this section will give you a bird's eye view of this market and the requirements of each firm.

Payment is either by the hour or by the project. The amount depends upon a variety of factors—the media involved (magazine, local newspaper, etc.), the size of the ad, and the company's budget, to name a few factors. Buyouts, one-time use, limited use and arrangements for final ownership of finished art are negotiated with the agency. If research and travel are required, make sure you know upfront who covers the expense.

Public relations firms

Many companies utilize public relations firms to handle publicity and maintain a favorable image for the firm. Freelancers in this area complete a variety of tasks, from logo design to brochure illustration. Remember to send plenty of samples when submitting to these firms. Give the company a clear view of the scope of your work, because assignments in this market cover a very broad spectrum. Payment depends on your experience, the project and the company involved.

Audiovisual firms

These firms produce instructional motion pictures, filmstrips, special effects, test commercials and corporate slide presentations for employee training and advertising. Computer graphics and electronic design are gaining in importance as audiovisual vehicles, and there are a growing number of video houses being established as animation specialists. Closely associated with this trend is television art. Many networks and local television stations hire freelancers to design slide shows, news maps, promotional materials and "bumpers" that are squeezed between commercials.

For the names and addresses of additional audiovisual firms, public relations contacts and advertising agencies, check the following sources: the *Standard Directory of Advertising Agencies*, the *Audio Video Market Place*, *O'Dwyer's Directory of Public Relations Firms*, the *Ad Week Agency Directory*, and the *Madison Avenue Handbook*. Weekly publications such as *Advertising Age* and *Adweek*, and the daily *The New York Times* business section are helpful for keeping up-to-date on industry news and trends.

Alabama

J.H. LEWIS ADVERTISING AGENCY INC., Box 6829, Mobile AL 36660. (205)476-2507. Senior Vice President/ Creative Director: Larry D. Norris. Ad agency. Clients: retail, manufacturers, health care and direct mail. Buys 15 illustrations/year.
Needs: Works with illustrators and designers. Uses artists for mechanicals and layout for ads, annual reports, billboards, catalogs, letterheads, packaging, P-O-P displays, posters, TV and trademarks.
First Contact & Terms: Prefers southern artists. Query. SASE. Reports in 5 days. No originals returned to artist at job's completion. Pays for design by the hour, $30-60. Pays for illustration by the project, $750-1,500. Pays promised fee for unused assigned work.

SPOTTSWOOD VIDEO/FILM STUDIO, 2520 Old Shell Rd., Mobile AL 36607. (205)478-9387. Contact: Manning W. Spottswood. Estab. 1976. AV/film/TV producer. Clients: industry, education, government and advertising. Produces mainly public relations and industrial films and tapes.

Needs: Assigns 5-15 freelance jobs/year. Artists "must live close by and have experience." Uses approximately 1 freelance illustrator/month. Works on assignment only. Uses freelance artists mainly for brochures. Also uses freelance artists for illustrations, maps, charts, decorations, set design, etc.

First Contact & Terms: Send resume or arrange interview by mail. Reports only if interested. Pays for illustration and design by the hour, $35 minimum; by the project, $150 minimum. Considers complexity of project, client's budget, skill and experience of artist, geographic scope of finished project, turnaround time, rights purchased and quality of work when establishing payment.

Tips: "We are very small and go from project to project—most of them very small."

Arizona

*CHARLES DUFF ADVERTISING, 301 W. Osborn Rd., Phoenix AZ 85013. (602)285-1660. Creative Director: Trish Spencer. Estab. 1948. Ad agency. Full-service multimedia firm. Specializes in agri-marketing promotional materials—literature, audio, video, trade literature. Product specialty animal health. Current clients include: Farnam, Veterinary Products Inc, Bee-Smart Products, Scentry, Inc.

Needs: Approached by 20 freelance artists/month. Works with 1 freelance illustrator/month. Prefers artists with experience in animal illustration: equine primarily and pets. Uses freelance artists mainly for the unusual, beauty and illustration. Also uses freelance artists for brochure, catalog and print ad illustration; retouching; billboards and posters. 35% of work is with print ads.

First Contact & Terms Send query letter with brochure photocopies, SASE, resume, photographs, tearsheets, slides and transparencies. Samples are filed or are returned by SASE only if requested by artist. Reports back within 2 weeks. Reviews portfolios "only by our request." Pays for illustration by the project, $300-600. Buys one-time rights.

FILMS FOR CHRIST ASSOCIATION, 2628 W. Birchwood Circle, Mesa AZ 85202. Contact: Paul S. Taylor. Motion picture producer and book publisher. Audience: educational, religious. Produces motion pictures, videos and books.

Needs: Works with 1-5 illustrators/year. Works on assignment only. Uses artists for books, catalogs and motion pictures. Also uses artists for storyboards, animation, slide illustration and ads. Generally prefers a tight, realistic style, plus some technical illustration.

First Contact & Terms: Query with resume and samples (photocopies, slides, tearsheets or snapshots). Prefers slides as samples. Samples returned by SASE. Reports in 1 month. Provide brochure/flyer, resume and tearsheets to be kept on file for future assignments. No originals returned to artist at job's completion. Considers complexity of project and skill and experience of artist when establishing payment.

PAUL S. KARR PRODUCTIONS, 2949 W. Indian School Rd., Box 11711, Phoenix AZ 85017. (602)266-4198. Contact: Paul Karr. Utah Division: 1024 N. 250 East, Box 1254, Orem UT 84057. (801)226-8209. Contact: Michael Karr. Film and video producer. Clients: industry, business, education, TV and cable.

Needs: Occasionally works with freelance filmmakers in motion picture and video projects. Works on assignment only.

First Contact & Terms: Advise of experience, abilities, and funding for project.

Tips: "If you know about motion pictures and video or are serious about breaking into the field, there are three avenues: 1) have relatives in the business; 2) be at the right place at the right time; or, 3) take upon yourself the marketing of your idea, or develop a film or video idea for a sponsor who will finance the project. Go to a film or video production company, such as ours, and tell them you have a client and the money. They will be delighted to work with you on making the production. Work, and approve the various phases as it is being made. Have your name listed as the producer on the credits. With the knowledge and track record you have gained you will be able to present yourself and your abilities to others in the film and video business and to sponsors."

 The asterisk before a listing indicates that the listing is new in this edition. New markets are often the most receptive to freelance submissions.

NORDENSSON LYNN & ASSOCIATES, 378 N. Main Ave., Tucson AZ 85701. Senior Art Director: Kathryn Polk. Estab. 1963. Ad agency/PR firm. "We are a multi-media, full-service firm strong in print." Specializes in health care, development (Real Estate), and financial. Current clients include: Intergroup of Arizona, Tobin Homes, Arizona Commerce Bank and El Dorado Hospital.
Needs: Works with 1 freelance illustrator/month. "We work with local artists (preferably with experience) and artists reps." Uses freelancers mainly for mechanicals and illustrations. Also uses freelance artists for print ad illustration, mechanicals, retouching and lettering. 80% of work is with print ads.
First Contact & Terms: Send query letter with resume, tearsheets, photocopies, slides and SASE. Samples are filed. Samples not filed are returned by SASE only if requested by artist. Reports back to the artist only if interested. Write to schedule an appointment to show a portfolio, include color and b&w samples, or mail original/final art, tearsheets, final reproduction/product, slides. Pays for design by the project, $200-500. Pays for illustration by the project, $75-2,500. Considers complexity of project, client's budget, turnaround time, skill and experience of artist, how work will be used and rights purchased when establishing payment. Rights purchased vary according to project.
Tips: "Get your foot in the door with an initial project, maybe at a lower-priced introductory offer and second project at regular fee."

Arkansas

MANGAN RAINS GINNAVEN HOLCOMB, 911 Savers Federal Bldg., Little Rock AR 72201. Contact: Steve Mangan. Ad agency. Clients: recreation, financial, consumer, industrial, real estate.
Needs: Works with 5 freelance designers and 5 freelance illustrators/month. Assigns 50 freelance jobs and buys 50 freelance illustrations/year. Uses freelance artists for consumer magazines, stationery design, direct mail, brochures/flyers, trade magazines and newspapers. Also uses freelance artists for illustrations for print materials.
First Contact & Terms: Query with brochure, flyer and business card to be kept on file. Include SASE. Reports in 2 weeks. Call or write to schedule an appointment to show a portfolio, which should include final reproduction/product. Pays for design by the hour, $42 minimum; all fees negotiated.

California

*AC&R, ADVERTISING, INC., 2010 Main St., Irvine CA 92713. (714)261-1770. FAX: (714)261-7515. Creative Group Secretary: Denise Pooler. Estab. 1960. Ad agency. Full-service, multimedia firm. Specializes in print, electronic media, outdoor design and collateral. Project specialties are consumer, automotive and retail. Current clients include: KAO Corp., Aaron Bros. Art Marts and PacTel Cellular.
Needs: Approached by 12 freelance artists/month. Works with 2 freelance illustrators and 1 freelance designer/month. Works mostly with artist reps and prefers artists with experience. Works on assignment only. Uses freelance artists mainly for work that can't be done in house. Also uses freelance artists for brochure, catalog, print, ad and slide illustration; storyboards; animatics; animation; retouching; TV/film graphics; lettering and logos. 80% of work is with print ads.
First Contact & Terms: Send query letter with samples that do not need to be returned. Samples are filed and are not returned. Reports back to the artist only if interested. Call or mail appropriate materials: the best examples of the artist's work. Pays for design by the hour, $18-35; by the day, $250-500. Pays for illustration by the hour, by the project or by the day. Buys all rights.

*AD VENTURES GROUP, INC., Suite 220, 3100 Lake Center Dr., Santa Ana CA 92704. Executive Vice President: Cathie Underwood. Estab. 1977. Ad agency. Full-service multimedia firm. Specializes in print ads, collateral, direct mail, P-O-P displays, TV and radio broadcast advertising. Product specialties are "mainly consumer products and services."
Needs: Approached by 5 freelance artists/month. Works with 1 freelance illustrator and 2 freelance designers/month. Prefers local artists only with experience in direct mail, fashion, consumer products and services and retail. Works on assignment only. Uses freelance artists for "everything." Also uses freelance artists for brochure, catalog and print ad design and illustration, storyboards, slide illustration, mechanicals, billboards, posters, TV/film graphics, lettering, logos and direct mail design. 50% of work is with print ads.
First Contact & Terms: Send query letter with brochure, photocopies, SASE, resume, photographs, tearsheets, photostats, slides, transparencies or other samples. "Some showing of their work and experience and their fees." Samples are filed or are returned by SASE only if requested by artists. Reports back to the artist only if interested. Write to schedule an appointment to show a portfolio. Mail appropriate materials. Portfolio should include: thumbnails, roughs, original, final art, b&w and color tearsheets, "a good representation of their abilities." Pays for design and illustration by the project. Buys all rights.

*ANKLAM FEITZ GROUP, 146 N. San Fernando Blvd., Burbank CA 91502. (818)842-5163. Creative Director: Barry Anklam. Full-service advertising and design agency providing ads, brochures, P-O-P displays, posters and menus. Clients: high-tech, electronic, photographic accessory companies and restaurants.

Needs: Works with 8 freelance artists/year. Assigns 15-20 jobs/year. Uses freelance artists mainly for brochure, newspaper and magazine ad illustration; mechanicals; retouching; direct mail packages; lettering and charts/graphs.

First Contact & Terms: Contact through artist's agent or send query letter with brochure showing art style. Samples are filed. Reports back only if interested. To show a portfolio, mail color and b&w tearsheets and photographs. Pays for design by the hour, $15-20. Pays for illustration by the project. Considers complexity of project, client's budget and turnaround time when establishing payment. Rights purchased vary according to project.

ALEON BENNETT & ASSOC., Suite 212, 13455 Ventura Blvd., Van Nuys CA 91423. President: Aleon Bennett. PR firm.

Needs: Works with 2 freelance artists/year. Works on assignment only. Uses freelance artists mainly for work on press releases and advertisements.

First Contact & Terms: Send query letter. Samples are not filed and are not returned. Does not report back.

RALPH BING ADVERTISING CO., 16109 Selva Dr., San Diego CA 92128. (619)487-7444. President: Ralph S. Bing. Ad agency. Product specialties are industrial (metals, steel warehousing, mechanical devices, glass, packaging, stamping tags and labels), political, automotive, food and entertainment.

Needs: Local artists only. Works on assignment only. Uses artists for consumer and trade magazines, brochures, layouts, keylines, illustrations and finished art for newspapers, magazines, direct mail and TV. Prefers pen & ink.

First Contact & Terms: "Call first; arrange an appointment if there is an existing need; bring easy-to-present portfolio. Provide portfolio of photocopies and tearsheets, and client reference as evidence of quality and/or versatility." Reports only if interested. No original work returned to artist at job's completion. Pays by the hour, $5-50 average; by the project, $10 minimum. Considers complexity of project and client's budget when establishing payment.

Tips: "Prefer to see samples of finished work; do not want to see classroom work."

*BOSUSTOW VIDEO, 3000 Olympic Blvd., Santa Monica CA 90404. (213)315-4888. Contact: Tee Bosustow. Video production firm. Clients: broadcast series, feature films, commercials, corporate, media promotion and home video.

Needs: Works with varying number of freelance artists depending on projects. Majority of work on in-house computer graphics system. Works on assignment only. Uses freelance artists mainly for titles, maps, graphs and other information illustration.

First Contact & Terms: Hires per job. Send brochure showing art style and resume only to be kept on file. Do not send samples; required only for interview. Reports only if interested. Pays by the project, $50-500. Considers complexity of project, skill and experience of artist, client's budget and turnaround time when establishing payment. Usually buys all rights; varies according to project.

COAKLEY HEAGERTY, 1155 N.First St., San Jose CA 95112-4925. (408)275-9400. Creative Directors: Susann Rivera and J. D. Keser. Art Director: Bob Peterson. Full-service ad agency. Clients: consumer, high-tech, banking/financial, insurance, automotive, real estate, public service. Client list provided upon request.

Needs: Works with 100 freelance artists/year. Assigns 500 freelance jobs/year. Works on assignment only. Uses freelance artists for illustration, retouching, animation, lettering, logos and charts/graphs.

First Contact & Terms: Send query letter with brochure showing art style or resume, slides and photographs. Samples are filed. Samples not filed are returned by SASE. Does not report back. Call to schedule an appointment to show a portfolio. Pays for illustration by the project, $600-5,000. Considers complexity of project, client's budget, skill and experience of artist and rights purchased when establishing payment. Rights purchased vary according to project.

*COPY GROUP ADVERTISING, Box 315, Encino CA 91316. Contact: Len Miller. Clients: resorts, travel spots, vacation areas and direct mail companies.

Needs: Uses freelance artists mainly for cartooning, illustration, spot drawing and humorous sketching. "Artists with experience in book publishing, advertising and greeting cards would probably have the skills we're looking for." Prefers pen & ink.

First Contact & Terms: Send a small sampling of material for review. Prefers photocopies as samples; *do not send original work*. Reports within 10 days. Pays by the project, $25-150.

DIMON CREATIVE COMMUNICATION SERVICES, Box 6489, Burbank CA 91510. (818)845-3748. Art Director: Bobbie Polizzi. Ad agency/printing firm. Serves clients in industry, finance, computers, electronics, health care and pharmaceutical.

First Contact & Terms: Send query letter with tearsheets, original art, photocopies and SASE. Provide brochure, flyer, business card, resume and tearsheets to be kept on file for future assignments. Portfolio should include comps; does not want to see newspaper ads. Pays for design by the hour, $20-50. Pays for illustration by the project, $75 minimum. Considers complexity of project, turnaround time, client's budget and skill and experience of artist when establishing payment.

*DJC & ASSOCIATES, Suite 202, 2021 N St., Sacramento CA 95814. (916)421-6310. Owner: Donna Cicogni. Ad agency. Assigns 120 jobs/year.
Needs: Works with 1 illustrator/month. Local artists only. Works on assignment only. Uses artists for consumer and trade magazines, stationery design, direct mail, TV, brochures/flyers and newspapers.
First Contact & Terms: Call to schedule an appointment to show a portfolio which should include original/ final art, final reproduction/product, etc. No originals returned to artist at job's completion. Negotiates pay.
Tips: "Have a variety of work to show: fashion, design, graphic etc."

*DOLPHIN MULTI-MEDIA PRODUCTIONS, INC., 1137 D San Antonio Rd., Palo Alto CA 94303. (415)962-8310. FAX: (415)962-8651. Operations Manager: Pam Johnson. Estab. 1972. AV firm. Full-service multimedia firm. Computer graphics, slides. Specializes in industrial multi-image, speaker support and collaterals. Product specialties are high-tech and biomedical industries, etc. Current clients include: Apple, New Zealand Government, Landor, ACS, J. Walter Thompson, Hills Bros., Levi's, Blue Shield, IBM, Oral B and Pac Bell.
Needs: Prefers artists with experience in computer graphics—Dicomed, Macintosh. Uses freelance artists mainly for computer slide production. Also uses freelance artists for storyboards, slide illustration and animation. 2% of work is with print ads.
First Contact & Terms: Send query letter with resume and slides. Samples are filed. Reports back to the artist only if interested. Mail appropriate materials: 35mm transparencies. Buys all rights.

DUDKOWSKI-LYNCH ASSOCIATES, INC., 150 Shoreline Highway Bldg. E, Mill Valley CA 94941. (415)332-5825. Vice President: Marijane Lynch. "We are a video facility providing Quantel Paintbox images to agencies, producers, corporations and institutions."
Needs: Works with 5 artists/year. "We need airbrush talent, motion graphics, cartoons, and general painting (any medium)." Prefers artists with strong art background and skill, and experience in video or film; best if artist has Quantel Paintbox experience. Uses artists for P-O-P displays, animation, films, video, logos and charts/graphs.
First Contact & Terms: Send resume. Samples are filed. Samples not filed are returned only if requested by artist. Reports back within 1 month. Call to schedule an appointment to show a portfolio, which should include color and b&w final reproduction/product, photographs and video tape. Pays for design by the hour, $15-40 or by the project. Pays for illustration by the image. Considers complexity of project, client's budget, turnaround time and skill and experience of artist when establishing payment. Rights purchased vary according to project.
Tips: "Send resume, follow up call in two weeks. Have samples of work."

*EVANS, OGILVIE & PARTNERS INC., Suite 370, 201 Lomas Santa Fe, Solana Beach CA 92075. (619)755-1577. FAX: (619)755-3293. Vice President Creative Director: David Evans. Estab. 1988. Ad agency. Full-service, multimedia firm. Specializes in marketing communications from strategies and planning through implementation in any media. Product specialties are real estate, identities, medical and high-tech. Current clients include: IDM Corp., Eastlake Development Co., Redlands Community Hospital.
Needs: Approached by 3-4 freelance artists/month. Works with 1-2 freelance illustrators and 3-4 freelance designers/month. Works only with artist reps/illustrators. Prefers local artists only with experience in listening, concepts, print and collaterals. Uses freelance artists mainly for comps, design, production and copy. Also uses freelance artists for brochure and print ad design and illustration, storyboards, mechanicals, retouching, billboards, posters, TV/film graphics, lettering and logos. 40% of work is with print ads.
First Contact & Terms: Send query letter with brochure, photocopies, resume and photographs. Samples are filed. Reports back to the artist only if interested. Write to schedule an appointment to show a portfolio or call. Portfolio should include: roughs, photostats, tearsheets, transparencies and actual produced pieces. Pays for design by the hour, $30-75; by the project, $150-10,000. Pays for illustration by the project, $75-3,500. Buys first rights, reprint rights or rights purchased vary according to project.

EXPANDING IMAGES, Suite 126, 18 Technology, Irvine CA 92718. (714)727-3203. President: Robert Denison. AV firm. Clients: mixed.
Needs: Works with 6 freelance artists/year. Uses freelance artists for graphics, photography, illustration and design.
First Contact & Terms: Works on assignment only. Send samples to be kept on file. Prefers tearsheets as samples. Samples not filed are returned by SASE only if requested. Reports only if interested. Pays by the project. Considers client's budget and skill and experience of artist when establishing payment. Buys all rights.

*HAYES • ROTHWELL, Suite 270, 4699 Old Ironsides Dr., Santa Clara CA 95054. (408)988-3545. FAX: (408)988-3545. Senior Art Director: Daniel Tiburcio. Estab. 1983. Ad agency. Full-service, multimedia firm. Specializes in ads and collateral. Product specialty is high technology. Current clients include: Abekas Video Systems, Cadence and Linear Technology.
Needs: Approached by 5 freelance artists/month. Works with 2-3 freelance illustrators and 2 freelance designers/month. Prefers local artists only. Uses freelance artists mainly for the overload work. Also uses freelance artists for brochure illustration, print ad illustration, mechanicals and lettering. 50% of work is with print ads.
First Contact & Terms: Send query with photocopies and photographs. Samples are filed. Reports back to the artist only if interested or does not report back, in which case the artist should try again! Mail appropriate materials: thumbnails, tearsheets and photographs. Payment for design and illustration is determined by budget. Rights purchased vary according to project.

DEKE HOULGATE ENTERPRISES, Box 7000-371, Redondo Beach CA 90277. (213)540-5001. Owner: Deke Houlgate. "Our main specialty is publicity; sports promotion; automotive industry provides most of our clientele. We do very little brochure or sales promotion work." Clients: sports and event promotion companies, automotive and specialty products. Client list provided with a SASE.
Needs: Works with 2 freelance artists/year. Assigns 6-12 jobs/year. Uses artists for design, illustration, magazines, retouching and press releases.
First Contact & Terms: Send query letter with brochure. Samples are sometimes filed or are returned by SASE. Reports back within 2 weeks. Write to schedule an appointment to show a portfolio. Pays artist's own rate. "I don't negotiate. Either budget covers artist's rate, or we can't use." Considers client's budget when establishing payment. Rights purchased vary according to project.

HUBBERT-KOVACH MARKETING COMMUNICATIONS, 3198-M Airport Loop, Costa Mesa CA 92626. Senior Art Director: Chris Klopp. Ad agency. Clients: real estate and miscellaneous (all product, service).
Needs: Works with 10-20 freelance artists/year. Local artists primarily (southern California). Uses freelance artists mainly for line art/paste-up, b&w and 4-color advertising collateral illustration and layout comps. Especially seeks professionalism (marker skills); efficiency (clean); and deadline awareness (fast turnaround).
First Contact & Terms: Send query letter with resume and samples to be kept on file. Accepts any kind of copy that is readable as samples. Samples not filed are returned by SASE. Reports back only if interested. Write for appointment to show portfolio. Pays by the hour, $15-50 average. Pays in 30 days. Considers complexity of the project, client's budget and turnaround time when establishing payment. Rights purchased vary according to project.

*DAVID JACKSON PRODUCTIONS (DJP, INC.), 1020 N. Cole St., Hollywood CA 90038. (213)465-3810. FAX: (213)465-1096. President: David Jackson. Estab. 1985. AV firm. Full-service, multimedia firm. Specializes in feature films, television shows, interactive video and records. Current clients include Gendarme and Executive One.
Needs: Approached by 2-3 freelance artists/month. Works with 2-3 freelance illustrators and 2 freelance designers/month. Prefers artists with experience in line drawing and airbrush. Works on assignment only. Uses freelance artists mainly for promo work and jacket art. Also uses freelance artists for brochure design and illustration, storyboards, animation, mechanicals, posters and TV/film graphics. 5% of work is with print ads.
First Contact & Terms: Send query letter with resume, SASE and tearsheets. Samples not filed and are returned by SASE. Reports back within 15-30 days. Mail appropriate materials: roughs, original, final art and tearsheets. Pays for design and illustration by the project. Payment is negotiable. Buys all rights.

LONGENDYKE/LOREQUE INC., Suite 10, 3100 W. Warner St., Santa Ana CA 92704. (714)641-9209. Lead Artist: David Longendyke and Tracy Skinner. "We are a slide graphic firm specializing in multi-image and videographic animation and special effects." Clients: AV producers, ad agencies.
Needs: Works with 4-5 freelance artists/year. Prefers local artists with knowledge of camera-ready art for AV. Uses artists for animation, logos, charts/graphs and camera-ready art for multi-image.
First Contact & Terms: Send resume and slides. Samples are filed. Samples not filed are returned only if requested by artist. Reports back only if interested. Write to schedule an appointment to show a portfolio, which should include original/final art and slides. Pays for design by the hour, $10-20. Considers complexity of project, turnaround time and skill and experience of artist when establishing payment.
Tips: "Artist must have knowledge of typesetting, multi-image screen formats and extensive use of Amberlith, and understand AV animation."

*EDWARD LOZZI & ASSOCIATES, Suite 101, 9348 Civic Center Dr., Beverly Hills CA 90210. FAX: (818)995-3376. Office Manager: Brian Cowan. Estab. 1979. PR firm. Full-service, multimedia firm. Specializes in magazine ads and documentaries. Product specialties are medical, entertainment, books and architectural.

Needs: Approached by 3-5 freelance artists/month. Works with 2-6 freelance illustrators and 2-6 designers/month. Prefers artists with experience in airbrush, pen and ink, washes and line drawing. Also uses freelance artists for brochure design and illustration, print ad design and illustration, storyboards, animation, billboards, posters and logos. 40% of work is with print ads.

First Contact & Terms: Send query letter with brochure, photocopies, SASE, resume, photographs and tearsheets. Samples are filed or are returned by SASE only if requested by artist. Reports back to the artist only if interested. Mail appropriate materials. Pays for design by the hour, $200 minimum; by the project, $500-1,000; by the day, $500 minimum. Pays for illustration by the hour, $150 minimum; by the project, $500-5,000; by the day, $500 minimum. Buys all rights.

*LUTAT, BATTEY & ASSOC., INC., 1475 S. Bascom Ave., Campbell CA 95008. (408)559-3030. Creative Director: Bruce Battey. Estab. 1976. Ad agency. Specializes in print advertising, both consumer and trade; also collaterals. Product specialties are computers and food.

Needs: Approached by 6-10 freelance artists/month. Works with 3 freelance illustrators and 5 freelance designers/month. Prefers artists with experience in high technology, food and fashion. Works on assignment only. Uses freelance artists mainly for all clients. Also uses freelance artists for brochure, catalog and print ad design and illustration, storyboards, slide illustration, mechanicals, retouching, billboards, posters, lettering, logos and desktop publishing. 60% of work is with print ads.

First Contact & Terms: Send query letter with brochure, resume, photographs and tearsheets. Samples are filed or are returned by SASE only if requested by artist. Reports back within days, only if interested. Write to schedule an appointment to show a portfolio. Mail appropriate materials: thumbnails, roughs, original, final art, b&w and color tearsheets, photographs and transparencies. Pays for design and illustration by the project. Rights purchased vary according to project.

LEE MAGID MANAGEMENT AND PRODUCTIONS, Box 532, Malibu CA 90265. (213)463-5998. President: Lee Magid. Estab. 1963. AV and PR firm. "We produce music specials and recordings."

Needs: Works with 4 freelance illustrators/month. Works on assignment only. Uses freelancers mainly for "anything print." Also uses artists for brochure, catalog and print ad design, storyboards, posters, TV/film graphics and logos. 50% of work is with print ads.

First Contact & Terms: Send query letter with brochure, photostats and SASE. Samples are filed or are returned by SASE only if requested by artist. Reports back to the artist only if interested. To show a portfolio, mail photostats; include color and b&w samples. Pays for design and illustration by the project. Considers how work will be used when establishing payment. Buys all rights or reprint rights.

Tips: "Send your work in, but keep originals. Send clear copy of work."

ON-Q PRODUCTIONS, INC., 618 E. Gutierrez St., Santa Barbara CA 93103. President: Vincent Quaranta. AV firm. "We are producers of multi-projector slide presentations. We produce computer-generated slides for business presentations." Clients: banks, ad agencies, R&D firms and hospitals.

Needs: Works with 10 freelance artists/year. Assigns 50 jobs/year. Uses freelance artists mainly for slide presentations. Also uses artists for illustration, retouching, animation and lettering.

First Contact & Terms: Send query letter with brochure or resume and slides. Samples are filed or are returned by SASE. Reports back only if interested. Write to schedule an appointment to show a portfolio, which should include original/final art and slides. Pays for design by the hour, $30 minimum, or by the project, $100 minimum. Pays for illustration by the hour, $25 minimum or by the project, $75 minimum. Considers complexity of project, client's budget, turnaround time and skill and experience of artist when establishing payment.

Tips: "Artist must be *experienced* in computer graphics and on the board. The most common mistake freelancers make are "poor presentation of a portfolio (small pieces fall out, scratches on cover acetate) and they do not know how to price out a job. Know the rates you're going to charge and how quickly you can deliver a job."

ORLIE, HILL & CUNDALL, INC., 20 Liberty Ship Way, Sausalito CA 94965. (415)332-3625. Contact: Alan Cundall. Ad agency.

Needs: Works with freelance artists when art department is overloaded. Uses freelance artists mainly for work on consumer magazines, stationery design, direct mail, brochures/flyers, trade magazines and newspapers. Also uses artists for layout, paste-up and type spec.

First Contact & Terms: Send query letter and resume to be kept on file for future assignments. No originals returned to artist at job's completion. Pays for design by the hour, $35 minimum, or by the project, fee determined in advance. Considers budget and complexity of project when establishing payment.

Tips: "We're an ad agency with expertise in direct marketing. What I want to see is brilliant selling ideas, magnificently interpreted into ads and other forms of communication."

*PALKO ADVERTISING, INC., Suite 207, 2075 Palos Verdes Dr. N., Lomita CA 90717. (213)530-6800. Contact: Judy Kolosvary. Ad agency. Clients: business-to-business, retail and high-tech.
Needs: Uses artists for layout, illustration, paste-up, mechanicals, copywriting and accurate inking. Produces ads, brochures and collateral material.
First Contact & Terms: Prefers local artists. Send query letter with brochure, resume, business card, "where you saw our address" and samples to be kept on file. Write for appointment to show portfolio. Accepts tearsheets, photographs, photocopies, printed material or slides as samples. Samples not filed returned only if requested. Reports back only if interested. Pays for design by the hour, $15-30. Pays for illustration by the hour, $15-30, or by the project, $50-1,500. Negotiates rights purchased.

*REID ADVERTISING AND PUBLIC RELATIONS, 3185-H Airway Ave., Costa Mesa CA 92626. (714)979-7990. FAX: (714)979-1510. President: John Reid. Ad agency and PR firm. Full-service, multimedia firm. Specializes in b&w newspaper and 4-color magazine ads, brochures and collaterals. Product specialty is new homes. Current clients include: Centex Homes and Taylor Woodrow Homes.
Needs: Approached by 2-3 freelance artists/month. Works with 1 freelance illustrator and 1-2 freelance designers/month. Prefers local artist with experience in real estate advertising. Works on assignment only. Uses freelance artists mainly for design and production. Also uses freelance artists for brochure design, print ad design, mechanicals, retouching, billboards, posters and logos. 50% of work is with print ads.
First Contact & Terms: Send query letter with brochure and photocopies. Samples are filed or returned by SASE only if requested by artist. Reports back to the artist only if interested. Mail appropriate materials: roughs and b&w and color photostats. Pays for design by the hour, $15-25 or by the project. Pays for illustration by the project, $250-750. Buys all rights.

RICHARD SIEDLECKI DIRECT MARKETING, Suite C-170, 2674 E. Main St., Ventura CA 93003-2899. (805)658-7000. Direct Marketing Consultant: Richard Siedlecki. Consulting agency. Clients: industrial, publishers, associations, air freight, consumer mail order firms and financial institutions. Client list provided for SASE.
Needs: Assigns 15 freelance jobs/year. Works with 2 freelance designers/month. Works on assignment only. Uses artists for consumer and trade magazines, direct mail packages, brochures, catalogs and newspapers.
First Contact & Terms: Artists should be "experienced in direct response marketing." Send query letter with brochure, resume and business card to be kept on file. Reports only if interested. Pays by the hour, $25 minimum; by the project, $250 minimum. Considers complexity of project and client's budget when establishing payment. "All work automatically becomes the property of our client."
Tips: Artists "must understand (and be able to apply) direct mail/direct response marketing methods to all projects: space ads, direct mail, brochures, catalogs."

*VIDEO RESOURCES, Box 18642, Irvine CA 92713. (714)261-7266. Producer: Brad Hagen. AV firm. Clients: automotive, banks, restaurants, computer, transportation and energy.
Needs: Works with 8 freelance artists/year. Southern California artists only with minimum 5 years of experience. Works on assignment only. Uses artists for graphics, package comps, animation, etc.
First Contact & Terms: Send query letter with brochure showing art style or resume, business card, photostats and tearsheets to be kept on file. Samples not filed are returned by SASE. Considers complexity of the project and client's budget when establishing payment. Buys all rights.

DANA WHITE PRODUCTIONS, INC., 2623 29th St., Santa Monica CA 90405. (213)450-9101. Owner/Producer: Dana C. White. AV firm. "We are a full-service audiovisual production company, providing multi-image and slide-tape, video and audio presentations for training, marketing, awards, historical, and public relations uses. We have complete inhouse production resources, including slidemaking, soundtrack production, photography, and A/V multi-image programming." Clients: "We serve major industry, such as GTE, Occidental Petroleum; medical, such as Oral Health Services, Whittier Hospital, Florida Hospital; schools, such as University of Southern California, Pepperdine University, and Clairbourne School; and public service efforts, such as fund-raising."
Needs: Works with 4-6 freelance artists/year. Assigns 12-20 freelance jobs/year. Prefers artists local to greater LA, "with timely turnaround, ability to keep elements in accurate registration, neatness, design quality, imagination and price." Uses artists for design, illustration, retouching, animation, lettering and charts/graphs.
First Contact & Terms: Send query letter with brochure or tearsheets, Photostats, photocopies, slides and photographs. Samples are filed or are returned only if requested. Reports back within 14 days only if interested. Call or write to schedule an appointment to show a portfolio. Payment negotiable by job.

Los Angeles

*THE ADVERTISING CONSORTIUM, 1219 S. La Brea, Los Angeles CA 90019. (213)937-5064. Contact: Jacci Abreu. Estab. 1985. Ad agency. Full-service, multimedia firm. Specializes in print, collaterals, direct mail, outdoor, broadcast.

Needs: Approached by 5 freelance artists/month. Works with 2 freelance illustrators and 4 freelance designers/month. Prefers local artists only. Works on assignment only. Uses freelance artists and·art directors for everything (nobody on staff). Also uses freelance artists for brochure, catalog and print ad design and illustration, mechanicals and logos. 80% of work is with print ads.
First Contact & Terms: Send query letter with brochure, resume, anything that does not have to be returned. Samples are filed. Write to schedule an appointment to show a portfolio. Portfolio should include: original/final art, b&w and color photostats, tearsheets, photographs, slides and transparencies. Pays for design by the project, based on budget and scope of work. Pays for illustration by the project, based on budget and scope of work.

*ANCHOR DIRECT MARKETING, Suite 100, 7926 Cowan Ave., Los Angeles CA 90045. (213)216-7855. FAX: (213)215-1655. President: Robert Singer. Estab. 1986. Ad agency. Specializes in direct response.
Needs: Number of freelance artists that approach each month varies. Prefers local artists and artists with experience in direct response and illustration. Works on assignment only. Uses freelance artists mainly for layout.
First Contact & Terms: Call to schedule an appointment to show a portfolio. Portfolio should include "direct response work."

*DELLA FEMINA, MCNAMEE WCRS, 5900 Wilshire Blvd., Los Angeles CA 90036. (213)937-8540. FAX: (213)937-7977. Art Buyer: Georgia Nelson. Ad agency. Full-service, multimedia firm. Specializes in magazine ads, collaterals, newspapers and TV. Product specialties are automotive and fast food. Current clients include: Carl's Jr., Isuzu, KSwiss, Magic Mountain, Jiffy Lube and CAL Fed Bank.
Needs: Approached by 10 freelance artists/month. Works with 6 freelance illustrators and a few freelance designers/year. Prefers artists with experience in advertising. Works on assignment only. Uses freelance artists mainly for storyboards/comps. Also uses freelance artists for print ad illustration, storyboards, animatics, animation, mechanicals, retouching, billboards, posters and TV/film graphics. 50% of work is with print ads.
First Contact & Terms: Send query letter with photocopies, resume, photographs, tearsheets, photostats and transparencies. Samples are filed. Reports back within 5 days. Call to schedule an appointment to show a portfolio or mail appropriate materials. Portfolio should include: thumbnails, roughs, b&w and color photostats, tearsheets, photographs and transparencies. Pays for illustration by the hour and by the day. Negotiates rights purchased.

GARIN AGENCY, Suite 614, 6253 Hollywood Blvd., Los Angeles CA 90028. (213)465-6249. Manager: P. Bogart. Ad agency/PR firm. Clients: real estate, banks.
Needs: Works with 1-2 freelance artists/year. Local artists only. Works on assignment only. Uses artists for "creative work and TV commercials."
First Contact & Terms: Send query letter with photostats or tearsheets to be kept on file for one year. Samples not filed are not returned. Does not report back. Negotiates pay; by the hour. Considers client's budget and turnaround time when establishing payment. Buys all rights.
Tips: "Don't be too pushy and don't overprice yourself."

*GUMPERTZ/BENTLEY/FRIED, 5900 Wilshire Blvd., Los Angeles CA 90036. (213)931-6301. Creative Director: John Johnson. Ad agency. Clients: stockbrokers, banks, food companies and visitors' bureaus.
Needs: Works with 3-4 illustrators and photographers/month. Uses freelance artists mainly for illustration. Negotiates pay.
First Contact & Needs: Call to arrange interview to show portfolio.

THE HALSTED ORGANIZATION, 4727 Wilshire Blvd., Los Angeles CA 90010. (213)937-4000. Contact: Production Manager. Ad agency, PR and marketing firm. Clients: manufacturers, medical/dental and sporting goods companies and general consumers. Client list provided upon request.
Needs: Works with 15-20 freelance artists/year. Prefers local artists with own studios. Uses artists for design, illustration, brochures, mechanicals, retouching, posters, direct mail packages, press releases, lettering and logos. Looks for "clean work, type spec ability is rewarded, photo retouch is great,"
First Contact & Terms: Send query letter with brochure showing art style or resume and tearsheets, photostats, photocopies, slides and photographs. Samples not filed are returned only if requested. Reports back within 10 days. Call to schedule an appointment to show a portfolio, which should include b&w roughs, original/final art and tearsheets. Pays for design by the hour, $12.50 up; by the project, $120-no limit; by the day, $100-no limit. Pays for illustration by the hour, $15-40; by the project, $100-no limit; by the day, $90-no limit. Considers complexity of project, turnaround time, client's budget, and rights purchased when establishing payment. Buys one-time rights or reprint rights; rights vary according to project.

HDM , 4751 Wilshire Blvd., Los Angeles CA 90010. (213)930-5000. Creative Director: Lee Kovel. "We are a general service ad agency." Clients: hotels, ATVs, motorcycle, food, pen and lighter manufacturers. Client list provided upon request.

Needs: Works with 200 freelance artists/year. Assigns 200 freelance jobs/year. Works on assignment only. Uses freelance artists for design, illustration, brochures, catalogs, P-O-P displays, mechanicals, retouching, billboards, posters, direct mail packages, lettering, logos, charts/graphs and advertisements.

First Contact & Terms: Send query letter with brochure showing art style or resume, tearsheets, photostats, photocopies, slides and photographs. Samples are filed. Does not report back. Write to schedule an appointment to show a portfolio, which should include color photostats, photographs, slides and video disks. Pays for design by the day, $300-600. Pays for illustration by the hour, $50-65; by the day, $300-400. Considers complexity of project, client's budget, turnaround time, skill and experience of artist, how work will be used and rights purchased when establishing payment. Negotiates rights purchased; rights purchased vary according to project.

NATIONAL ADVERTISING AND MARKETING ENTERPRISES, (N.A.M.E.), 7323 N. Figueroa, Los Angeles CA 90041. Contact: J. A. Gatlin.

Needs: Works on assignment only. Uses artists for graphic design, letterheads and direct mail brochures.

First Contact & Terms: Send query letter with tearsheets, photostats and photographs. Samples not returned. Sometimes buys previously published work. Reports in 4 weeks. To show a portfolio, mail appropriate materials. Pays by the hour, $15-40.

Tips: "Submit repros of art, not originals."

*RUBIN POSTAER & ASSOCIATES, (formerly Needham, Harper Worldwide, Inc.), Suite 900, 11601 Wilshire Blvd., Los Angeles CA 90025. (213)208-5000. Manager, Art Services: Annie Ross. Ad agency. Serves clients in automobile and heavy equipment industries and savings and loans.

Needs: Works with about 2 freelance illustrators/month. Uses freelancers for all media.

First Contact & Terms: Contact manager of art services for appointment to show portfolio. Selection based on portfolio review. Negotiates payment.

Tips: Wants to see variety of techniques.

San Francisco

*ANDERSON/ROTHSTEIN, INC., 139 Townsend, San Francisco CA 94107. (415)495-6420. FAX: (415)495-0319. Senior Art Director: Dean Narahara. Estab. 1980. Ad agency. Full-service, multimedia firm. Specializes in magazine ads and collaterals. Product specialty is food service.

Needs: Approached by 30 freelance artists/month. Works with 5 freelance illustrators and 9 freelance designers/month. Also uses freelance artists for brochure, catalog and print ad design and illustration, storyboards, mechanicals, retouching, TV/film graphics, lettering and logos. 70% of work is with print ads.

First Contact & Terms: Send query letter with brochure, photocopies, resume and photographs. Samples are filed. Reports back to the artist only if interested. Call to schedule an appointment to show a portfolio. Portfolio should include: roughs, original/final art, b&w and color photostats, photographs and transparencies. Buys all rights or rights purchased vary according to project.

ARNOLD & ASSOCIATES PRODUCTIONS, 2159 Powell St., San Francisco CA 94133. (415)989-3490. President: John Arnold. AV and video firm. Clients: general.

Needs: Works with 30 freelance artists/year. Prefers local artists (in San Francisco and Los Angeles), award-winning and experienced. "We're an established, national firm." Works on assignment only. Uses artists for multimedia, slide show and staging production.

First Contact & Terms: Send query letter with brochure, tearsheets, slides and photographs to be kept on file. Call to schedule an appointment to show a portfolio, which should include final reproduction/product and color photographs. Pays for design by the hour, $15-50; by the project $500-3,500. Pays for illustration by the project, $500-4,000. Considers complexity of the project, client's budget and skill and experience of artist when establishing payment.

BASS/FRANCIS PRODUCTIONS, 737 Beach St., San Francisco CA 94109. (415)441-4555. Production Manager: Jim Vastola. "A multi-media, full-service organization providing corporate communications to a wide range of clients."

Needs: Works with 10 freelance artists/year. Assigns 35 freelance jobs/year. Prefers solid experience in multi-image production. Works on assignment only. Uses freelance artists for mechanicals, lettering, logos, charts/graphs and multi-image designs. Prefers loose or impressionistic style.

First Contact & Terms: Send resume and slides. Samples are filed and are not returned. Reports back within 1 month only if interested. To show a portfolio, mail slides. Pays for design by the project, $100-1,000; by the day, $200-350. Pays for the illustration by the hour, $18-25; by the project, $100-250. Considers turnaround time, skill and experience of artist and how work will be used when establishing payment. Rights purchased vary according to project.

Tips: "Send resume, slides, rates. Highlight multi-media experience. Show slide graphics also."

CHARTMASTERS, 201 Filbert St., San Francisco CA 94133. (415)421-6591. Art Manager: Michael Viapiana. AV firm.
Needs: Works with 5-6 freelance artists/year. "Artists must sign W-2 form and work on premises as temporary employee." Uses artists for design, illustration, mechanicals, animation and charts/graphs. Experience in 35mm slide production, presentation and multi-image shows essential.
First Contact & Terms: Send resume and slides. Samples not filed are returned. Reports back only if interested. Call or write to schedule an appointment to show a portfolio. Pays for design by the hour. Considers complexity of project and skill and experience of artist when establishing payment. Rights purchased vary according to project.

*EXCELVISION, P.O. Box 14607, San Francisco CA 94114. (415)777-3226 ext. 388. Production Manager: Martin Dade. Estab. 1970. AV firm. Full-service, multimedia firm. Specializes in 3-D computer animation— "Extremely high-end product."
Needs: Approached by 4 freelance artists/month. Works with 3 freelance illustrators and 5 freelance designers/month. Prefers local artists only with experience in 3-D computer animation. Works on assignment only. Uses freelance artists mainly for 3-D computer animation. Also uses freelance artists for animation and TV/film graphics. 10% of work is with print ads.
First Contact & Terms: Send query letter with resume, photostats and slides. Samples are filed or are returned by SASE only if requested by artist. Reports back to the artist only if interested. Write to schedule an appointment to show a portfolio. Portfolio should include color slides and tranparencies. Pay for design "negotiable by job." Pay for illustration "negotiable by job."

*MEDIA SERVICES CORP., 10 Aladdin Terrace, San Francisco CA 94133. (415)928-3033. FAX: (415)441-1859. President: Gloria Peterson. Estab. 1974. Ad agency. Specializes in publishing and package design. Product specialties are publishing and consumer. Current clients include: City Life, Eatacup.
Needs: Approached by 3 freelance artists/month. Works with 1-2 freelance illustrators and 2 freelance designers/month. Prefers artists with experience in package design with CAD. Works on assignment only. Uses freelance artists mainly for support. Also uses freelance artists for mechanicals, retouching and lettering. 5% of work is with print ads.
First Contact & Terms: Send query letter with brochure, SASE, resume, photographs or slides and tearsheets or transparencies. Samples are filed or are returned by SASE only if requested by artist. Reports back to the artist only if interested. Mail appropriate materials: original/final art, tearsheets or 5×7 transparencies. Pay for design varies. Pay for illustration varies. Rights purchased vary according to project.

PURDOM PUBLIC RELATIONS, 395 Oyster Point, S. San Francisco, CA 94080. (415)588-5700. FAX: (415)588-1643. President: Paul Purdom. Estab. 1962. PR Firm. Full-service, multimedia firm. Product specialties are high-tech and business-to-business. Current clients include Sun Microsystems and Varian Associates.
Needs: Works with 1-2 freelance artists/month and 1-2 freelance designers/month. Works on assignment only. Prefers local artists for work on brochure and catalog design, slide illustration, mechanicals and TV/film graphics.
First Contact & Terms: Samples are not filed and are returned. Call to schedule an appointment to show a portfolio, which should include completed projects. Pays for design by the project and buys all rights.

HAL RINEY & PARTNERS, INC., 735 Battery, San Francisco, CA 94111. (415)981-0950. Contact: Jerry Andelin. Ad agency. Serves clients in beverages, breweries, computers, confections, insurance, restaurants, winery and assorted packaged goods.
Needs: Works with 5-6 freelance illustrators/month. Uses freelancers in all media.
First Contact & Terms: Call one of the art directors for appointment to show portfolio. Selection based on portfolio review. Negotiates payment based on client's budget, amount of creativity required from artist and where work will appear.
Tips: Wants to see a comprehensive rundown in portfolio on what a person does best—"what he's selling"—and enough variety to illustrate freelancer's individual style(s).

EDGAR S. SPIZEL ADVERTISING INC., 1782 Pacific Ave., San Francisco CA 94109. (415)474-5735. President: Edgar S. Spizel. AV producer. Clients: "Consumer-oriented from department stores to symphony orchestras, supermarkets, financial institutions, radio, TV stations, political organizations, hotels, real estate firms, developers and mass transit, such as BART." Works a great deal with major sports stars and TV personalities.
Needs: Uses artists for posters, ad illustrations, brochures and mechanicals.
First Contact & Terms: Send query letter with tearsheets. Provide material to be kept on file for future assignments. No originals returned at job's completion.

UNDERCOVER GRAPHICS, Suite 1-C, 20 San Antonio Pl., San Francisco CA 94133. (415)788-6589. Creative Director: Helen Schaefer. AV producer. Clients: musical groups, producers, record companies and book publishers.

Needs: Works with 2-3 freelance illustrators and 2-3 freelance designers/month. Uses artists for billboards, P-O-P displays, corporate identity, multimedia kits, direct mail, TV, brochures/flyers, album covers and books.

First Contact & Terms: Send query letter with brochure or resume, tearsheets, slides, photographs and/or photocopies. Samples returned by SASE. Provide brochures, tearsheets, slides business card and/or resume to be kept on file for future assignments. Reports in 4 weeks only if interested. To show a portfolio, mail roughs, original/final art, tearsheets and photographs. Originals returned to artist at job's completion. Pays $250-5,000, comprehensive layout and production; $10-25/hour, creative services; $25-500, illustration. Considers complexity of project, client's budget, skill and experience of artist and rights purchased when establishing payment. Pays original fee as agreed for unused assigned illustrations.

Tips: Artists interested in working with us should "be creative and persistent. Be different. Set yourself apart from other artists by work that's noticeably outstanding. Don't be content with mediocrity or just 'getting by' or even the 'standards of the profession.' Be *avant-garde.*"

Colorado

BROYLES ALLEBAUGH & DAVIS, INC., 31 Denver Technological Center, 8231 E. Prentice Ave., Englewood CO 80111. (303)770-2000. Executive Art Director: Kent Eggleston. Ad agency. Clients: industrial, high-tech, financial, travel and consumer clients; client list provided upon request.

Needs: Works with 12 freelance illustrators/year; occasionally uses freelance designers. Works on assignment only. Uses freelance artists for consumer and trade magazines, direct mail, P-O-P displays, brochures, catalogs, posters, newspapers, TV and AV presentations.

First Contact & Terms: Send business card, brochure/flyer, samples and tearsheets to be kept on file. Samples returned by SASE if requested. Reports only if interested. Arrange interview to show portfolio or contact through artist's agent. Prefers slides or printed pieces as samples. Negotiates payment according to project. Considers complexity of project, client's budget, skill and experience of artist, geographic scope of finished project, turnaround time and rights purchased when establishing payment.

*CINE DESIGN FILMS, Box 6495, Denver CO 80206. (303)777-4222. Producer/Director: Jon Husband. AV firm. Clients: automotive companies, banks, restaurants, etc.

Needs: Works with 3-7 freelance artists/year. Uses artists for layout, titles, animation and still photography. Clear concept ideas that relate to the client in question are important.

First Contact & Terms: Works on assignment only. Send query letter to be kept on file. Reports only if interested. Write for appointment to show portfolio. Pays by the hour, $20-50 average; by the project, $300-1,000 average; by the day, $75-100 average. Considers complexity of project, client's budget and rights purchased when establishing payment. Rights purchased vary according to project.

Connecticut

*THE BERNI COMPANY, Marketing Design Consultants, 666 Steamboat Rd., Greenwich CT 06830. (203)661-4747. Contact: Mark Eckstein. Clients: manufacturers and retailers of consumer package goods. Buys 50 illustrations/year. Write or call for interview; local professionals only.

Needs: Uses artists for illustration, layout, lettering, paste-up, retouching and type spec for annual reports, catalogs, letterheads, P-O-P displays, packaging, design, production and trademarks. Pays $15-50. Pays promised fee for unused assigned work.

BRADFORD ADVERTISING & PUBLIC RELATIONS, INC., 140 Ferry Rd., Old Saybrook CT 06475. (203)388-1282. FAX: (203)388-5298. Art Director: Lizann Michaud. Creative Director: Wil Bradford. Ad and PR agency. Clients: automotive, industry, bank and sporting goods.

Needs: Works with approximately 10 freelance artists/year. Prefers local artists. Works on assignment only. Uses freelance artists for design, illustration, brochures, catalogs, P-O-P displays, mechanicals, billboards, posters, direct mail packages, press releases, logos and advertisements.

First Contact & Terms: Send brochure. Samples are filed or are returned only if requested. Does not report back. Call to schedule an appointment to show a portfolio, which should include thumbnails, roughs, original/final art, tearsheets and slides. Pays for design by the hour, $25-100; by the project, $250-1,500; by the day, $250-500. Pays for illustration by the hour, $50-300; by the project, $100-1,000; by the day, $250-1,500. Considers complexity of project, client's budget, turnaround time, skill and experience of artist, how work will be used and rights purchased. Negotiates rights purchased; rights purchased vary according to project.

Tips: "When contacting our firm, please send samples of work."

*DONAHUE, INC., 227 Lawrence St., Hartford CT 06106. (203)527-1400. FAX: (203)247-9247. Senior Art Director: Kurt Whitmore. Estab. 1979. Ad agency. Full-service, multimedia firm. Specializes in collateral, trade ads. Product specialties are computer, tool and interior design firms.

Needs: Approached by 4-5 freelance artists/month. Works with 1-2 freelance illustrators and 3-4 freelance designers/month. Prefers artists with experience in reproduction, tight comps and mechanicals. Uses freelance artists mainly for "in-house." Also uses freelance artists for brochure design, catalog design and illustration, print ad design, mechanicals, posters, lettering and logos. 40% of work is for print ads.
First Contact & Terms: Send query letter with resume and tearsheets. Samples are filed. Reports back to the artist only if interested. Portfolio should include thumbnails, roughs, original/final art and tearsheets. Pays for design by the hour, $15-25. Pays for illustration by the project, $200-2,000. Rights purchased vary according to project.

ERIC HOLCH/ADVERTISING, 49 Gerrish Lane, New Canaan CT 06840. President: Eric Holch. Clients: companies who advertise in trade magazines.
Needs: Works with 10 freelance artists/year. Works on assignment only. Uses freelance artists mainly for advertisement and brochure illustration. Prefers food, candy, packages and seascapes as themes for advertising illustrations for brochures, ads, etc. Pays $100-3,000 average.
First Contact & Terms: Send query letter with brochure showing art style or samples to be kept on file. Write to schedule an appointment to show a portfolio, which should include roughs, photocopies and original/final art. Pays for design by the hour, $25-50. Pays for illustration by the project, $100-3,000. Buys one-time rights, all rights or negotiates rights purchased depending on project. Considers skill and experience of artist and client's preferences when establishing payment.

JACOBY/STORM PRODUCTIONS INC., 22 Crescent Rd., Westport CT 06880. (203)227-2220. President: Doris Storm. AV/TV/film producer. Clients: schools, corporations and publishers. Produces filmstrips, motion pictures, slide sets, sound-slide sets and videotapes.
Needs: Assigns 6-8 jobs/year. Uses artists for lettering, illustrations for filmstrips and designing slide show graphics.
First Contact & Terms: Prefers local artists with filmstrip and graphics experience. Query with resume and arrange interview. Include SASE. Reports in 2 weeks. Usually buys all rights. Pays $20-30/frame, lettering; $50-100/frame, illustrations. Pays on acceptance.

LISTENING LIBRARY, INC., 1 Park Ave., Old Greenwich CT 06870. (203)637-3616. Associate Editor: Suzanne Keenan. Produces educational AV productions.
Needs: Periodically requires illustrators for front covers for 3-4 catalogs/year. Uses artists for catalog and advertising design, advertising illustration, catalog and advertising layout and direct mail packages.
First Contact & Terms: Local (New York City, Westchester County, Fairfield County, etc.) artists only. Works on assignment only. Send resume and nonreturnable samples to be kept on file for possible future assignments. Samples not returned. Original work not returned to artist after job's completion. "Payment is determined by the size of the job and skill and experience of artist." Buys all rights.

*****REALLY GOOD COPY CO.**, 76 Whiting Ln., W. Hartford CT 06119. (203)233-6128. (203)233-7289. President: Donna Donovan. Estab. 1982. Ad agency. Full-service, multimedia firm. Specializes in print ads, collateral, direct mail and catalogs. Product specialties are consumer, financial and entertainment products. Current clients include: Levi Strauss & Co., Speidel, CIGNA, Dow Brands, YMCA, NASA and U.S. Postal Service.
Needs: Approached by 3-4 freelance artists/month. Works with 1 freelance illustrator and 1-2 freelance designers/month. Prefers local artists with experience in Macintosh design and production. Works on assignment only. Uses freelance artists for all projects. There are no on-staff artists. 50% of work is with print ads.
First Contact & Terms: Send query letter with description of background and experience. Samples are filed or are returned by SASE only if requested. Reports back to the artist if interested. Write to schedule an appointment to show a portfolio. Portfolio should include roughs and original/final art. Pays for design by the hour, $25-90. Pays for illustration by the project, $50-600.
Tips: "The most common mistake freelancers make is showing only finished pieces. I want to see roughs and comps, too, to feel confident about exposing my client to the designer and vice versa. Write first with some background to save your time and mine. I screen out 90% of artists before the interview."

Delaware

ALOYSIUS, BUTLER, & CLARK, Bancroft Mills, 30 Hill Rd., Wilmington DE 19806. (302)655-1552. Contact: John Hawkins. Ad agency. Clients: banks, industry, restaurants, real estate, hotels, businesses, transit systems, government offices.
Needs: Assigns "many" freelance jobs/year. Works with 3-4 freelance illustrators and 3-4 freelance designers/month. Uses artists for trade magazines, billboards, direct mail packages, brochures, newspapers, stationery, signage and posters.
First Contact & Terms: Local artists only "within reason (Philadelphia, Baltimore)." Send query letter with resume, business card and slides, photos, photostats, photocopies to be kept on file all except work that is "not worthy of consideration." Samples not kept on file returned only if requested. Reports only if interested.

Works on assignment only. Call for appointment to show portfolio. Pays by the project. Considers complexity of project, client's budget, and skill and experience of artist when establishing payment. Buys all rights.

CUSTOM CRAFT STUDIO, 310 Edgewood St., Bridgeville DE 19933. Audiovisual producer.
Needs: Works with 1 illustrator and 1 designer/month. Works with freelance artists on an assignment basis only. Uses freelance artists mainly for work on filmstrips, slide sets, trade magazine and newspapers. Also uses artists for print finishing, color negative retouching and airbrush work. Prefers pen & ink, airbrush, watercolor and calligraphy.
First Contact & Terms: Send query letter with slides or photographs, brochure/flyer, resume, samples and tearsheets to be kept on file. Samples returned by SASE. Reports in 2 weeks. No originals returned to artist at job's completion. Pays for design and illustration by the project, $25-100.

*LYONS, INC., 715 Orange St., Wilmington DE 19801. (302)654-6146. Vice President: P. Coleman DuPont. Advertising and graphic design/AV & video. Clients: consumer, corporate and industry.
Needs: Works on assignment only. Uses freelance artists mainly for art direction, graphic design, illustration, photography, storyboard art and multi-image design. Uses artists for advertising, collateral materials, publications, multimedia presentations and displays.
First Contact & Terms: Send resume. Prefers nonreturnable samples, slides or copies to be kept on file for future assignments. Samples returned by SASE. Pays by the hour or by assignment, $6-20/hour average. Complexity of assignment, overall budget and skill/experience of artist considered when establishing rate.

*PHOTO/ART, INC., Box 1742, Wilmington DE 19899. (302)658-7301. FAX: (302)658-7308. Art Director: Karen Kaler. Estab. 1935. Ad agency and AV firm. Does graphic design, computer-generated slides and photography. Specializes in collateral, brochures, booklets and slides. Product specialty is industry.
Needs: Number of freelance illustrators works with each month varies. Number of freelance designers works with each month varies. Prefers artists with experience in illustration. Works on assignment only. Uses freelance artists mainly for illustration and overload. Also uses freelance artists for brochure and print ad design and illustration, catalog illustration and lettering. 15% of work is with print ads.
First Contact & Terms: Send query letter with brochure, resume and photocopies. "Whatever works best for the artist." Samples are filed or are returned. Reports back to the artist only if interested. Write to schedule an appointment to show a portfolio. Portfolio should include roughs, original/final art and b&w and color samples. Pays for design and illustration by the project. Payment is negotiable. Rights purchased vary according to project.

SHIPLEY ASSOCIATES INC., 1300 Pennsylvania Ave., Wilmington DE 19806. (302)652-3051. Creative Director: Jack Parry. Ad/PR firm. Serves clients in harness racing, industrial and corporate accounts, insurance, real estate and entertainment.
Needs: Works with 2 freelance illustrators and 1 freelance designer/month. Assigns 9 freelance jobs/year. Works with freelance artists on assignment only. Uses artists for annual report illustration, mechanicals, brochure and sign design.
First Contact & Terms: Query with previously published work. Prefers layouts (magazine & newspaper), mechanicals, line drawings and finished pieces as samples. Samples not returned. Reports within 2 weeks. Provide resume, samples and tearsheets to be kept on file for possible future assignments. No originals returned at job's completion. Pays for design by the hour, $8 minimum. Negotiates payment.
Tips: Looks for "versatility and technique, individual style, good production skills."

District of Columbia

DE LA CROIX PRODUCTIONS INTERNATIONAL INC., P.O. Box 9751 NW, Washington DC 20016. (301)-990-1426. Executive Producer: Maximilien De Lafayette. Produces shows, plays, music and various artistic projects; recruits, trains, promotes and manages artists, actors, actresses, choreographers, designers, dancers, singers and stage directors as well as freelance painters and illustrators.
Needs: Works with 110 freelance artists/year. Uses artists for advertising, brochure, catalog and magazine/newspaper design, illustration and layout; AV presentations; exhibits; displays; signage; posters and design for plays and artistic productions.
First Contact & Terms: Send resume, at least 2 letters of reference and samples to be kept on file; write for appointment to show portfolio. Prefers photostats as samples. Reports within 2 weeks. Works on assignment only. Pays by the project. Considers skill and experience of artist when establishing payment.
Tips: Looks for "originality, new style, creativity, ability to meet work schedule, precision and flexibility when considering freelance artists."

ROBERT N. PYLE & ASSOCIATES, 3222 N. St. NW, Washington DC 20007. (202)333-8190. Account Executive: Nick Pyle. Estab. 1970. PR firm. "We provide everything—advertising, sales, public image, lobby work, media work, marketing, association management and press work. Specializes in food, metals, banks. Current clients include Welch's Independent Bakers Association and Elchem metals.

Needs: Works with various numbers of freelance illustrators and freelance designers/month. Uses freelancers mainly for special projects. Also uses artists for brochure, catalog and print ad design and illustration, storyboards, slide illustration, animatics, animation, mechanicals, retouching, billboards, posters, TV/film graphics, lettering and logos.

First Contact & Terms: Send query letter with brochure and resume. Samples are filed or are returned. Reports back to the artist only if interested. To show a portfolio, mail appropriate materials. Pays for design and illustration by the hour, $60 minimum; by the project, $60 minimum; by the day. Considers complexity of project, client's budget and how work will be used when establishing payment. Rights purchased vary according to project.

Tips: "We do everything by project as needs arise. We pay well and would like to know more contacts to call when needed."

Florida

COVALT ADVERTISING AGENCY, 12907 N.E. 7th Ave., North Miami FL 33161. (305)891-1543. Creative Director: Fernando Vasquez. Ad agency. Clients: automotive, cosmetic, financial, industrial, banks, restaurants and consumer products.

Needs: Prefers local artists; very seldom uses out-of-town artists. Artists must have minimum of 5 years of experience; accepts less experience only if artist is extremely talented. Works on assignment only. Uses artists for illustration (all kinds and styles), photography, mechanicals, copywriting, retouching (important), rendering and lettering.

First Contact & Terms: Send query letter with brochure, resume, business card, tearsheets, photostats and photocopies to be kept on file. Samples are filed and are not returned. Reports only if interested. Call for appointment to show portfolio, which should include photostats, photographs, slides, original final art or tearsheets. Pays for design by the hour, $35 minimum; by the project, $150 minimum. Pays for illustration by the project, $200 minimum. Considers complexity of project, client's budget, skill and experience of artist, and turnaround time when establishing payment. Buys all rights or reprint rights.

Tips: "If at first you don't succeed, keep in touch. Eventually something will come up due to our diversity of accounts. If I have the person, I might design something with his particular skill in mind."

PRUITT HUMPHRESS POWERS & MUNROE ADVERTISING AGENCY, INC., 516 N. Adams St., Tallahassee FL 32301. (904)222-1212. Production Manager: Beverly Smedeker. Ad agency. Clients: business-to-business, consumer. Media used includes billboards, consumer and trade magazines, direct mail, newspapers, P-O-P displays, radio and TV.

Needs: Uses artists for direct mail, brochures/flyers, trade magazines and newspapers. "Freelancers used in every aspect of business and given as much freedom as their skill warrants."

First Contact & Terms: Send resume. Provide materials to be kept on file for future assignments. Negotiates payment based on client's budget and amount of creativity required from artist. Pays set fee/job.

Tips: In portfolio, "submit examples of past agency work in clean, orderly, businesslike fashion including written explanations of each work. Ten illustrations or less."

*SANCHEZ & LEVITAN, INC., 1800 SW 27th Ave., Miami FL 33145. (305)442-1586. FAX: (305)442-2598. Art Director: Enrique Duprat. Ad agency and PR firm. Full-service, multimedia firm. Specializes in TV, radio and magazine ads, etc. Product specialty is consumer. Current clients include: Florida Lottery, NCNB National Bank, UpJohn Co.

Needs: Approached by 1 freelance artist/month. Prefers local artists only. Works on assignment only. Also uses freelance artists for print ad design, storyboards, slide illustration, mechanicals, TV/film graphics and logos. 35% of work is for print ads.

First Contact & Terms: Send query letter with brochure and resume. Samples are not filed and are returned by SASE only if requested by artist. Reports back to the artist only if interested. Write to schedule an appointment to show a portfolio.

*WEST & COMPANY MARKETING & ADVERTISING, Suite 2050, 100 S. Ashley Dr., Tampa FL 33602. (813)224-9378. Senior Art Director: Tim Ward. Ad agency. "We are a full-service, multimedia firm with in-house art and media departments." Product specialty is food and beverages.

Needs: Works with 3 freelance illustrators and 1 freelance designer/month. Prefers artists with experience in food design. Works on assignment only. Uses freelance artists mainly for newspaper and magazine design. Also uses freelance artists for print ad design and illustration, storyboards, mechanicals, retouching, billboards, posters and lettering. 70% of work is with print ads.

First Contact & Terms: Send query letter with resume. Samples are not filed and are returned. Reports back within 2 weeks. Write to schedule an appointment to show a portfolio. Portfolio should include original/final art, final production/product, color and b&w samples. Pays by the project. Rights purchased vary.

Tips: "We are looking for talent."

Georgia

CINEVISION CORPORATION, 1771 Tullie Cir., N.E., Atlanta GA 30329. (404)321-6333. President: Steve Newton. Estab. 1972. AV firm providing sales service and rental of professional 16mm/35mm/70mm/vistavision motion picture equipment and screening of motion pictures on location and in screening room facility in Atlanta. Current clients include AT&T, Bell South, Paramount Pictures, Columbia Pictures, Universal Pictures, MGM/UA, Warner Bros. and Disney Company.
Needs: Works on assignment only. Uses freelancers mainly for brochure design. 2% of work is with print ads.
First Contact & Terms: Send query letter with brochure. Samples are filed. Reports back within 10 days. To show a portfolio, mail tearsheets. Pays for design and illustration by the project. Considers client's budget when establishing payment.
Tips: "Have experience."

FILMAMERICA, INC., Suite 209, 3177 Peachtree Rd. NE, Atlanta GA 30305. (404)261-3718. President: Avrum M. Fine. AV firm. Clients: corporate and ad agencies.
Needs: Works with 2 freelance artists/year. Works on assignment only. Uses freelance artists for film campaigns. Especially important are illustration and layout skills.
First Contact & Terms: Send query letter with resume and photographs or tearsheets to be kept on file. Samples not filed are returned only if requested. Reports back only if interested. Write for appointment to show portfolio. Pays for design by the project, $1,000-2,000. Pays for illustration by the project, $1,500-2,500. Considers complexity of the project and rights purchased when establishing payment. Rights purchased vary according to project.
Tips: "Be very patient!"

PAUL FRENCH AND PARTNERS, INC., 503 Gabbettville Rd., LaGrange GA 30240. (404)882-5581. Contact: Ms. Gene Ballard. AV firm. Client list provided upon request.
Needs: Works with 3 freelance artists/year. Works on assignment only. Uses artists for illustration.
First Contact & Terms: Send query letter with resume and slides to be kept on file. Samples not filed are returned by SASE. Reports back only if interested. To show a portfolio, mail appropriate materials. Pays for design and illustration by the hour, $25-100 average. Considers client's budget when establishing payment. Buys all rights.
Tips: "Be organized."

GARRETT COMMUNICATIONS, Box 53, Atlanta GA 30301. (404)755-2513. President: Ruby Grant Garrett. Estab. 1979. Production and placement firm for print media. Clients: banks, organizations, products-service consumer. Client list provided for SASE.
Needs: Assigns 24 freelance jobs/year. Works with 2-3 freelance illustrators and 2 freelance designers/year. Experienced, talented artists only. Works on assignment only. Uses freelance artists for billboards, brochures, signage and posters. 100% of work is with print ads. Prefers loose or realistic style and technical illustration occasionally. Especially needs "help-wanted illustrations that don't look like clip art."
First Contact & Terms: Send query letter with resume and samples to be kept on file. Samples returned by SASE if not kept on file. Reports within 10 days. Write to schedule an appointment to show a portfolio which should include roughs and tearsheets. Pays for design by the hour, $15-35; by the project, $75-1,500. Pays for illustration by the project, $35-2,000. Considers client's budget, skill and experience of artist and turnaround time when establishing payment. Negotiates rights purchased.
Tips: Send "6-12 items that show scope of skills. My best advice to freelancers for an introduction into our company is to send a resume and three samples or copies of work for our files. Do not send samples or copies of fine art or paintings."

THE GORDON GROUP, INC., Suite 106, 3305 Breckinridge Blvd., Duluth GA 30136. (404)381-6662. President: M.J. Gordon. Ad agency/AV and PR firm; "full-service marketing communication programs." Clients: business-to-business, industry, service, non-retail, non-foods.
Needs: Assigns 20-30 freelance jobs/year. Uses freelance artists for trade magazines, direct mail packages, brochures, catalogs, filmstrips, stationery, signage, P-O-P displays, AV presentations and posters. Artists should make contact "any way they can." Works on assignment only. Pays by the hour, $20 minimum. Pay "depends on the job and the budget. We pay hourly or on a project basis." Considers complexity of project, client's budget, skill and experience of artist, turnaround time and rights purchased when establishing payment. Buys all rights, material not copyrighted.
Tips: "Don't spend a lot of money on materials. Turn us on with a creative letter instead."

*GROUP ATLANTA, (formerly The Broom Agency Inc.), Box 29335, Atlanta GA 30359. (404)442-1100. Creative Director: Ralph Broom. Full-service advertising agency. Clients: real estate, banks, health care, radio stations, government agencies, child care centers, car dealers.
Needs: Works with 20 freelance artists/year. Assigns 400 freelance jobs/year. Works on assignment only. Uses artists for design, illustration, mechanicals, retouching, animation, posters, direct mail packages, lettering, logos and charts/graphs.
First Contact & Terms: Send query letter with brochure or tearsheets, photostats, photocopies, slides and photographs. Samples are filed or are returned only if requested. To show a portfolio, mail thumbnails, roughs, photostats, tearsheets and color photographs. Pays for design and illustration by the project, $50 minimum. Considers complexity of project, client's budget and turnaround time when establishing payment.
Tips: "Send photocopied samples with cost charged on each."

KAUFMANN ASSOCIATES, 1626 Frederica Rd., St. Simons Island GA 31522. (912)638-8678. Creative Director: Harry J. Kaufmann. Ad agency. Clients: resort, food processor and bank.
Needs: Assigns "very few" freelance jobs/year. Works on assignment only. Works with 1 freelance illustrator/month. Uses artists for brochures.
First Contact & Terms: Send samples to be kept on file. Reports only if interested. Pays for design and illustration by the hour, $25-35; by the project, $100-800. Considers complexity of project, client's budget, and skill and experience of artist when establishing payment. Buys all rights.
Tips: "Organize credentials and samples for a brief but useful review."

LEWIS BROADCASTING CORP., Box 13646, Savannah GA 31406. Executive Vice President: Mr. Pierce. TV producer.
Needs: Uses freelance artists for direct mail brochures, billboards, posters, public service TV spots and motion picture work. Perfers pen & ink, charcoal/pencil, colored pencil, watercolor, acrylics, oils, pastels, markers, calligraphy and computer illustration. Works on assignment only.
First Contact & Terms: Send query letter with resume and printed photocopied samples. Reports in 2 weeks. Provide business card and resume to be kept on file. Originals returned to artist at job's completion. Pay "depends on job."
Tips: "Be willing to flesh out others' ideas."

*MCCANN-ERICKSON, 615 Peachtree St. N.E., Atlanta GA 30365. (404)881-3100. FAX: (404)881-3100. Associate Creative Director: David Farmer. Ad agency. Full-service, multimedia firm. Specializes in television and radio broadcast, all forms of print media, collateral and research. Product specialty is consumer. Current clients include: Georgia-Pacific, Coca-Cola USA, Six Flags, American Express Vacations and The *Atlanta Journal & Constitution.*
Needs: Approached by 25 freelance artists/month. Works with 10 freelance illustrators and 2 freelance designers/month. Works on assignment only. Uses freelance artists mainly for illustration, storyboards and comps. Also uses freelance artists for brochure design and illustration, print ad illustration, storyboards, slide illustration, animatics, animation, retouching, TV/film graphics, lettering and logos. 50% of work is print ads.
First Contact & Terms: Send query letter with brochure, photocopies, resume, photographs, tearsheets and transparencies. Samples are filed. Reports back to the artist only if interested. Call to schedule an appointment to show a portfolio. Portfolio should include "anything you feel is important to represent yourself." Pays for design by the hour, $25-75. Pays for illustration by the project, $250 minimum. Buys all rights or negotiates rights purchased.

PRINGLE DIXON PRINGLE, Suite 1500, Marquis One Tower, 245 Peachtree Center Ave., Atlanta GA 30303. (404)688-6720. Creative Director: Steve Pharr. Ad agency. Clients: fashion, financial, fast food and industrial firms; client list provided upon request.
Needs: Works with 2 freelance illustrators/month. Local artists only. Works on assignment basis only. Uses freelance artists for billboards, consumer and trade magazines, direct mail, P-O-P displays, brochures, catalogs, posters, signage, newspapers and AV presentations.
First Contact & Terms: Arrange interview to show portfolio. Payment varies according to job and freelancer.

*SAWYER RILEY COMPTON INC., Suite 800, 1100 Abernathy Rd., Atlanta GA 30328. (404)393-9849. FAX: (404)393-9953. Associate Creative Director/Art: Nick Driver. Ad agency, AV and PR firm. Specializes in ads, collaterals and scripts. Product specialty is business-to-business exclusively. Current clients include: Hitachi, Gates Energy Products, Komatsu, Baker, Elanco.
Needs: Approached by 2-3 freelance artists/month. Works with 1 freelance illustrator and 2 freelance designers/month. Works on assignment only. Also uses freelance artists for brochure, catalog and print ad design and illustration, storyboards, slide illustration, animatics, animation, mechanicals, retouching, posters, lettering and logos. 70% of work is for print ads.
First Contact & Terms: Send query letter with brochure, photographs, tearsheets, photostats and slides.

Samples are filed. Reports back to the artist only if interested. Does not report back; artist should "follow-up call." Call to schedule an appointment to show a portfolio. Portfolio should include original/final art and photographs. Pays for design by the hour, $35-80. Pays for illustration by the project. Buys all rights.

J. WALTER THOMPSON COMPANY, One Atlanta Plaza, 950 East Paces Ferry Rd., Atlanta GA 30326. (404)365-7300. Executive Art Director: Bill Tomassi. Executive Creative Director: Mike Lollis. Ad agency. Clients: mainly financial, industrial and consumer. This office does creative work for Atlanta and the southeastern U.S.
Needs: Works with freelance illustrators. Works on assignment only. Uses freelance artists for billboards, consumer magazines, trade magazines and newspapers.
First Contact & Terms: Send slides, original work, stats. Samples returned by SASE. Reports only if interested. No originals returned at job's completion. Call for appointment to show portfolio. Pays by the hour, $20-65 average; by the project, $100-6,000 average; by the day, $150-3,500 average. Considers complexity of project, client's budget, skill and experience of artist and rights purchased when establishing payment.
Tips: Wants to see samples of work done for different clients. Likes to see work done in different mediums. Likes variety and versatility. Artists interested in working here should "be *professional* and do top grade work." Deals with artists reps only.

TUCKER WAYNE/LUCKIE & COMPANY, (formerly Tucker Wayne & Co.), Suite 2700, 230 Peachtree St. NW, Atlanta GA 30303. (404)521-7600. Creative Department Business Manager: Rita Morris. Ad agency. Serves a variety of clients including packaged product, food, utility, transportation and agriculture/pesticide manufacturing.
Needs: A total of 8 art directors occasionally work with freelance illustrators. Uses freelancers for consumer and trade magazines, newspapers and TV.
First Contact & Terms: Call creative secretary for appointment. Selection based on portfolio review. Negotiates payment based on budget, where work will appear, travel expenses, etc.

Hawaii

*MILICI VALENTI GABRIEL DDB NEEDHAM WORLDWIDE, Amfac Bldg., 700 Bishop St., Honolulu HI 96813. (808)536-0881. Contact: Creative Director. Ad agency. Serves clients in food, finance, utilities, entertainment, chemicals and personal care products.
Needs: Works with 3-4 freelance illustrators/month. Artists must be familiar with advertising demands; used to working long distance through the mail; and be familiar with Hawaii. Uses freelance artists mainly for illustration, retouching and lettering for newspapers, multimedia kits, magazines, radio, TV and direct mail.
First Contact & Terms: Provide brochure, flyer and tearsheets to be kept on file for future assignments. No originals returned to artist at job's completion. Pays $200-2,000.

PACIFIC PRODUCTIONS, Box 2881, Honolulu HI 96802. (808)531-1560. Contact: Production Manager. AV producer. Serves clients in industry, government and education. Produces almost all types of AV materials.
Needs: Assigns 2 freelance jobs/year. Works with 3 freelance illustrators, 2 freelance animators and 2 freelance designers/year. Uses freelance artists for all types of projects.
First Contact & Terms: Artists located in Hawaii only. Send query letter and samples (photostats or slides preferred). Samples returned. Provide resume to be kept on file for possible future assignments. Works on assignment only. Reports in 2 weeks. Pays by the project. Payment varies with each client's budget. No originals returned to artist following publication. Negotiates rights purchased.

Idaho

I/D/E/A INC., One I/D/E/A Way, Caldwell ID 83605. (208)459-6357. Creative Director: Ben Shuey. Ad agency. Clients: direct mail.
Needs: Assigns 12-15 freelance jobs/year. Uses freelance artists for direct mail packages, brochures, airbrush and photographs.
First Contact & Terms: Call before sending query letter with brochure, resume and samples to be kept on file. Write for artists' guidelines. Prefers the "most convenient samples for the artist." Samples not kept on file are returned only if requested. Reports only if interested. Works on assignment only. Pays by the project, amount varies. Considers complexity of project, client's budget, and skill and experience of artist when establishing payment. Rights purchased vary with project.
Tips: "Most work goes into catalogs or brochures."

Illinois

*ANDREN & ASSOCIATES, INC., 6400 Keating Ave., Lincolnwood IL 60646. (312)267-8500. Contact: Kenneth E. Andren. Clients: beauty product and tool manufacturers, clothing retailers, laboratories, banks,

Michael Furuya was commissioned by Milici Valenti Gabriel to do this mixed media illustration for the GTE Hawaiian Telephone 1989 directory covers. He was provided with the theme "Children, Hawaii's Future," and was given eight weeks for the assignment. The senior administrator for GTE Hawaiian Telephone says, "Michael had a good understanding of what we were going for, in addition to a fresh style; he was a pleasure to work with and very dependable." The response, she says, "has been universally positive."

camera and paper product companies. Clients include Alberto Culver, Barton Brand, Nalco Chemical, Encyclopedia Britannica, Firestone, Reflector Hardware, Rust-O-Leum, Avon Products and National Safety Council. Client list available upon request.
Needs: Approached by 50 freelance artists/year. Works with 6 or more freelance illustrators and 6 or more freelance designers/year. Local artists only. Uses artists for catalogs, direct mail brochures, flyers, packages, P-O-P displays and print media advertising.
First Contact & Terms: Query with samples or arrange interview. Include SASE. Reports in 1-2 weeks. Pays $15 minimum/hour for animation, design, illustration, layout, lettering, mechanicals, paste-up, retouching and type spec.
Tips: "Send in resume prior to calling to schedule appointment to show portfolio."

ARBEN DESIGN, INC., 600 W. Roosevelt Rd., West Chicago IL 60185. (708)231-5077. President: David Elders. Estab. 1977. AV firm. "We are designers and manufacturers of studio sets (modular) for film and video industry. We also create related graphics, logos, signage and models." Current clients include Sears & Roebuck, WPTD-TV-Dayton and the National Safety Council.
Needs: Works with 2 freelance illustrators/month. Prefers local artists only with experience in marker renderings/perspective drawings. Uses freelancers mainly for studio set illustration. Also uses artists for catalog and print ad design and illustration, TV/film graphics and logos.
First Contact & Terms: Send query letter with resume and SASE. Samples are filed. Reports back to the artist only if interested. Write to schedule an appointment to show a portfolio, which should include original, final art; include color samples. Pays for design and illustration by the project, $50 minimum. Considers complexity of project and how work will be used when establishing payment. Buys all rights.

THE BEST COMPANY, 109 N. Main St., Rockford IL 61101. (815)965-3800. Vice President: Richard (Ric) Blencoe. Ad agency producing radio/TV commercials, brochures, newspaper and magazine ads, logo and corporate identity programs. Clients: mainly consumer accounts. Client list provided upon request.
Needs: Works with 10-20 freelance artists/year. Uses freelance artists mainly for design, illustration, brochures, consumer magazines, retouching, billboards, lettering and logos.
First Contact & Terms: Send query letter with brochure or resume, tearsheets, photostats and slides. Samples are filed or are returned only if requested. Reports back within 2 weeks only if requested. Call or write to schedule an appointment to show a portfolio or mail roughs, original/final art and tearsheets. Pays for

design by the hour, $20-45; by the project, $50 minimum. Pays for illustration by the hour, $50 minimum; by the project, $300 minimum. Considers complexity of project, client's budget and skill and experience of artist when establishing payment. Buys all rights; negotiates rights purchased.
Tips: "Do some research on agency and our needs to present portfolio in accordance. Will not see walk-ins."

BRACKER COMMUNICATIONS, 330 W. Frontage Rd., Northfield IL 60093. (708)441-5534. President: Richard W. Bracker. Ad agency/PR/publishing firm. Clients: construction, financial, acoustical, contractors, equipment manufacturers, trade associations, household fixtures, pest control products.
Needs: Works with 4-6 freelance artists/year. "Use only artists based in the Chicago area for the most part. We look for ability and have used recent graduates." Works on assignment only. Uses freelance artists for graphic design/key line. Especially important are type specing, design/layout and photo handling.
First Contact & Terms: Phone or send resume to be kept on file. Reviews any type of sample. Reports within 2 weeks. Write for appointment to show portfolio. Negotiates and/or accepts quotations on specific projects. Considers complexity of project, skill and experience of artist and turnaround time when establishing payment. Buys all rights.
Tips: "Don't make assumptions about anything."

BRAGAW PUBLIC RELATIONS SERVICES, 800 E. Northwest Hwy., Palatine IL 60067. (312)934-5580. Principal: Richard S. Bragaw. PR firm. Clients: professional service firms, associations and industry.
Needs: Assigns 12 freelance jobs/year. Local artists only. Works on assignment only. Works with 1 freelance illustrator and 1 freelance designer/month. Uses artists for direct mail packages, brochures, signage, AV presentations and press releases.
First Contact & Terms: Send query letter with brochure to be kept on file. Reports only if interested. Write to schedule an appointment. Pays by the hour, $25-75 average. Considers complexity of project, skill and experience of artist and turnaround time when establishing payment. Buys all rights.
Tips: "We do not spend much time with portfolios."

CAIN AND COMPANY (ROCKFORD), 2222 E. State St., Rockford IL 61108. (815)399-2482. Senior Art Director: Randall E. Klein. Ad agency/PR firm. Clients: financial, industrial, retail and service.
Needs: Assigns 6 freelance jobs/year. Uses freelance artists for consumer and trade magazines, billboards, direct mail packages, brochures, catalogs, newspapers, filmstrips, movies, stationery, signage, P-O-P displays, AV presentations, posters and press releases "to some degree."
First Contact & Terms: Send query letter with brochure, resume, business card, samples and tearsheets to be kept on file. Call or write for appointment to show portfolio. Send samples that show best one medium in which work is produced. Samples are not filed and are not returned. Reports only if interested. Works on assignment only. "Rates depend on talent and speed; could be anywhere from $5 to $30 an hour." Considers skill and experience of artist and turnaround time when establishing payment. Buys all rights.
Tips: "Have a good presentation, not just graphics."

JOHN CROWE ADVERTISING AGENCY, 1104 S. 2nd St., Springfield IL 62704. (217)528-1076. Owner: Bryan J. Crowe. Ad/art agency. Clients: industries, manufacturers, retailers, banks, publishers, insurance firms, packaging firms, state agencies, aviation and law enforcement agencies.
Needs: Buys 3,000 illustrations/year. Works with 4 freelance illustrators and 3 freelance designers/month. Works on assignment only. Uses artists for color separation, animation, lettering, paste-up and type spec for work with consumer magazines, stationery design, direct mail, slide sets, brochures/flyers, trade magazines and newspapers. Especially needs layout, camera-ready art and photo retouching. Prefers pen & ink, airbrush, watercolor and marker.
First Contact & Terms: "Send a letter to us regarding available work at agency. Tell us about yourself. We will reply if work is needed and request samples of work." Prefers tearsheets, original art, photocopies, brochure, business card and resume to be kept on file. Samples not filed returned by SASE. Reports in 2 weeks. Pays for design by the project, $5-50; pays for illustration by the project, $10-100. No originals returned to artist at job's completion. No payment for unused assigned illustrations.
Tips: "Current works are best. Show your strengths and do away with poor pieces that aren't your stonghold. A portfolio should not be messy and cluttered."

DATA COMMAND, INC., (formerly Imperial International Learning Corp.), Box 548, Kankakee IL 60901. (815)933-7735. President: Aggie Posthumus. AV producer. Serves clients in education, filmstrips, illustrated workbooks, microcomputer software.
Needs: Assigns multiple jobs/year. Works with variety of designers/year. Works on assignment only. Uses artists for original line art, color illustrations and graphic design, computer graphics.
First Contact & Terms: Send query letter and tearsheets to be kept on file. Samples returned only if requested. Reports back only if interested. Method and amount of payment are negotiated with the individual artist. No originals returned to artist following publication. Considers skill and experience of artist when establishing payment. Buys all rights.

DYNAMIC GRAPHICS, 6000 N. Forest Park Dr., Peoria IL 61614. Art Director: Frank Antal. Graphics firm for general graphic art user.

Needs: Works with 50 freelance artists/year. Works on assignment only. Uses artists for illustrations. Needs artists with "originality, creativity, professionalism."

First Contact & Terms: Send query letter with portfolio showing art style or tearsheets and photocopies. Samples not filed are returned. Reports back within 1 month. To show a portfolio, mail appropriate materials, which should include final reproduction/product or photostats. Pays by the project; "we pay highly competitive rates but prefer not to specify." Considers complexity of project, skill and experience of artist and rights purchased when establishing payment. Buys all rights.

Tips: "Submit styles that are the illustrator's strongest and can be used successfully, consistently."

ELVING JOHNSON ADVERTISING INC., 7804 W. College Dr., Palos Heights IL 60463. (708)361-2850. Art/Creative Director: Michael McNicholas. Ad agency. Serves clients in industrial machinery, construction materials, material handling, finance, etc.

Needs: Works with 2 freelance illustrators/month. Local artists only. Uses freelance artists for direct mail, brochures/flyers, trade magazines and newspapers. Also uses freelance artists for layout, illustration, technical art, paste-up and retouching. "We need technical illustration." Prefers pen & ink, airbrush, watercolor and markers.

First Contact & Terms: Call for interview. Pays for design and illustration by the project, $100 minimum.

Tips: "We find most artists through references and portfolio reviews."

LINEAR CYCLE PRODUCTIONS, Box 2827, Carbondale IL 62902-2827. (618)687-3515. Producer: Rich Brown. Estab. 1980. AV firm. "We are an agency specializing in audiovisual sales and marketing programs and also into teleproduction for CATV." Current clients include Katz, incorporated and McDave and Associates.

Needs: Works with 7-15 freelance illustrators and designers/year. Prefers artists with experience in teleproductions (broadcast/CATV/non-broadcast). Works on assignment only. Uses freelance artists for storyboards, animation, TV/film graphics, lettering and logos. 10% of work is with print ads.

First Contact & Terms: Send query letter with resume, photocopies, photographs, slides, transparencies, video demo reel and SASE. Samples are filed or are returned by SASE only if requested by artist. Reports back to the artist only if interested. To show a portfolio, mail audio/videotapes, photographs and slides; include color and b&w samples. Pays for design and illustration by the project $100 minimum. Considers skill and experience of artist, how work will be used and rights purchased when establishing payment. Negotiates rights purchased.

Tips: "We see a lot of sloppy work and samples, portfolios in fields not requested or wanted, poor photos, photocopies, graphics etc. Make sure that the materials are in a presentable situation."

*WALTER P. LUEDKE & ASSOCIATES, INC., Suite 1A, 4223 E. State St., Rockford IL 61108. (815)398-4207. FAX: (815)398-4239. President: W. P. Luedke. Estab. 1959. Ad agency. Full-service multimedia firm. Specializes in magazine ads, brochures, catalogs and consultation. Product specialty is industry.

Needs: Approached by 2 freelance artists/month. Works with 2 freelance illustrators and 2 freelance designers/month. Prefers artists with experience in technical layout, artwork, exp. views. Works on assignment only. Uses freelance artists mainly for artwork, layout, keyline. Also uses freelance artists for brochure, catalog and print ad design and illustration, storyboards, slide illustration, animatics, animation, mechanicals, retouching, billboards, posters, TV/film graphics, lettering and logos. 30% of work is with print ads.

First Contact & Terms: Send query letter with resume, photographs, tearsheets, photostats and slides. Samples are filed and are not returned. Reports back to the artist only if interested. Call to schedule an appointment to show a portfolio. Portfolio should include thumbnails, roughs, original/final art, b&w and color photostats, tearsheets, photographs, slides or "whatever." Pays for design by the hour, by the project or by the day (negotiable). Pays for illustration by the hour, by the project or by the day (negotiable). Buys all rights.

ARTHUR MERIWETHER, INC., 1529 Brook Dr., Downers Grove IL 60515. (312)495-0600. Production Coordinator: Lori Ouska. AV firm, design studio and communications service. Clients: industrial corporations (electronics, chemical, etc.) plus consumer clients.

Needs: Works with 10-20 freelance artists/year. Artists should have minimum 2 years of experience. Prefers local artists. Uses artists for keyline/paste-up, illustration and design. Especially important are knowledge of audiovisual and print production techniques.

First Contact & Terms: Send query letter with resume, business card, slides and tearsheets. Samples returned by SASE. Reports only if interested. Pays for design by the hour, $15-50. Pays for illustration by the project, $50-1,000. Rights purchased vary according to project; usually buys all rights.

Tips: Artists "should submit only their best work—don't try to show everything. Keep presentation brief. Know what type of work the client wants to see."

SWEET ADVERTISING AGENCY, 111 E. Hitt St., Mt. Morris IL 61054. (815)734-6520. Partner: Virginia A. Grek. Estab. 1933. Ad agency providing complete marketing services: print media, ad development and design, brochures and marketing support materials.
Needs: Prefers artist with experience in commercial graphics. Works on assignment only. Uses freelance artist for brochure and print ad illustration, retouching and lettering. 80% of work is with print ads. Also buys stock photos.
First Contact & Terms: Send query letter with brochure and tearsheets. Samples are filed or are returned. Reports back within 7 days. To show a portfolio, mail b&w and color tearsheets and final reproduction/product. Payment varies. Considers client's budget when establishing payment. Buys all rights.
Tips: "Get in on the ground floor and produce as many different styles as possible. Learn to follow instructions and build a good portfolio."

Chicago

AUDITIONS BY SOUNDMASTERS, Box 8135, Chicago IL 60680. (312)224-5612. Executive Vice President: R.C. Hillsman. Produces radio/TV programs, commercials, jingles and records.
Needs: Buys 125-300 designs/year. Uses freelance artists for animation, catalog covers/illustrations, layout, paste-up, multimedia kits and record album design.
First Contact & Terms: Mail 8x10 art. Include SASE. Reports in 3 weeks. Pays $500 minimum, animation; $100-350, record jackets; $50-225, layout; $35-165, paste-up. Material copyrighted.

E. H. BROWN ADVERTISING AGENCY, INC., 20 N. Wacker, Chicago IL 60606. (312)372-9494. Art Director: Arnold G. Pirsoul. Estab. 1920. Ad agency. Clients: insurance, schools, banks, corporations, electronics, high-tech, etc.
Needs: Works with 10 freelance illustrators and 6 freelance designers/year. Works on assignment only. Mainly uses freelancers for creative concept, also uses artists for design, illustration, newspapers, retouching, lettering, charts/graphs and advertisements. 40-50% of work is with print ads.
First Contact & Terms: Send photostats, photocopies and photographs. Samples are filed and are not returned. Reports back only if interested. Call or write to schedule an appointment to show a portfolio, which should include color and b&w roughs and tearsheets. Pays for design by the hour, $35-50. Pays for illustration by the project, $400-2,000. Considers complexity of project, client's budget, turnaround time, skill and experience of artist, how work will be used and rights purchased. Negotiates rights purchased; rights purchased vary according to project.
Tips: "Be precise and efficient about the job to be done. Avoid delays and be on time when the job is contracted. Stick with the estimate. Call us and we will make time to see samples. Show us a range of recent illustrations. Keep your portfolio updated, not heavy. Do not send cartoons or children's book illustrations."

*CLEARVUE, INC., 6465 N. Avondale, Chicago IL 60631. (312)775-9433. Contact: Curriculum Product Development. AV firm.
Needs: Works with 10-12 freelance artists/year. Works on assignment only. Uses freelance artists mainly for art for filmstrip programs.
First Contact & Terms: Send query letter to be kept on file. Prefers to review art boards or samples of actual filmstrips. Reports back within 10 days. Write for appointment to show portfolio. Pays $30-50 per frame—average program is 35-50 frames and in the case of video 10 to 20 minutes. Considers complexity of the project and budget when establishing payment. Buys all rights.
Tips: "Have some knowledge of educational filmstrip and video production requirements."

DARBY GRAPHICS, 4015 N. Rockwell, Chicago IL 60618. (312)583-5090. Creative Director: Tony Christian. Estab. 1930. In-house art department in full-service printing company providing audiovisual, design production services. Specializes in benefits, associations publications and hospitals. Current clients include Sears, McDonalds, Hewitt & Assoc., Bank Administration Institute, CECO and The Wyatt Comany.

The asterisk before a listing indicates that the listing is new in this edition. New markets are often the most receptive to freelance submissions.

Needs: Works with 2 freelance illustrators/year and 2 freelance designers/month. Prefers local artist with experience in keyline/production. Uses freelancers mainly for keylining, illustrating and computer/graphic design. Also uses freelance artists for brochure design and illustration, slide illustration, mechanicals and retouching. 10% of work is with print ads.

First Contact & Terms: Send query letter with resume, photocopies and slides. Samples are filed or are returned by SASE only if requested by artist. Reports back to the artist only if interested. Write to schedule an appointment to show a portfolio, which should include roughs and original/final art; include color and b&w samples. Pays for design by the hour, $15-25. Pays for illustration by the project, $100-1,000. Considers skill and experience of artist when establishing payment. Rights purchased vary according to project.

Tips: "Call us a week after writing to schedule an appointment. We do not want to see photocopies, 'fine art' samples from school or too much in a portfolio. Have a variety of the same thing or style. Like to see projects through all the various stages: conception, implementation, layout, paste-up and finished product."

FINANCIAL SHARES CORPORATION, 62 W. Huron, Chicago IL 60610. (312)943-8116. Contact: President. Training and PR firm. Helps financial institutions achieve profitable results through high-quality customized consulting services. Our services include: market research, strategic marketing planning, product design and pricing, public and investor relations and sales training. We also develop and implement sales incentive and measurement programs. Clients: financial institutions, law firms, technology firms and professional associations.

Needs: Works with 6 freelance artists/year. Assigns 50 jobs/year. Prefers local artists only. Uses freelance artists mainly for design of brochures, newspapers, logos, charts/graphs and advertisements.

First Contact & Terms: Send query letter with brochure. Reports back within 2 weeks. Write to schedule an appointment to show a portfolio, which should include original/final art, photostats and final reproduction/ product. Pays for design by the hour or project. Pays for illustrations by the project. Considers client's budget, turnaround time and skill and experience of artist when establishing payment. Rights purchased vary according to project.

Tips: "We need artists who know about the finance/banking field."

IMAGINE THAT!, Suite 4908, 405 N. Wabash Ave., Chicago IL 60611. (312)670-0234. President: John Beele. Ad agency. Clients: broadcast, insurance, University of Illinois sports program, pharmaceuticals, retail furniture stores, real estate and professional rodeo.

Needs: Assigns 25-50 freelance jobs and buys 15 freelance illustrations/year. Uses artists for layout, illustration, mechanicals and photography.

First Contact & Terms: Arrange interview to show portfolio with Sheila Dunbar. Pay is negotiable.

McCANN HEALTHCARE ADVERTISING, 625 N. Michigan Ave., Chicago IL 60611. (312)266-9200. Creative Director: Priscilla Kozel. Ad agency. Clients: pharmaceutical and health care companies.

Needs: Work load varies. Works on assignment only. Uses freelance artists mainly for layout and comps. Also uses freelancers for medical trade magazines, journal ads, brochures/flyers and direct mail to physicians. Especially needs sources for tight marker renderings and comp layouts.

First Contact & Terms: Send query letter with resume and samples. Call for appointment to show portfolio, which should include roughs, original/final art, final reproduction/product color and photostats and photographs. Reports within 2 weeks. A common mistake freelancers make in presenting portfolios is "not presenting work specific to need expressed. Too general, hodgepodge." Pays by the hour, $10-50. Negotiates payment based on client's budget, where work will appear, complexity of project, skill and experience of artist and turnaround time.

Tips: "Rendering with markers very important." Prefers to see original work rather than reproductions, but will review past work used by other ad agencies. Needs good medical illustrators but is looking for the best person—one who can accomplish executions other than anatomical. Artists should send resume or letter for files. When showing samples or portfolio "show how you got from A to Z. Show intermediate stages; it shows the thinking process."

MARKETING SUPPORT INC., 303 E. Wacker Dr., Chicago IL 60601. (312)565-0044. Executive Art Director: Robert Becker. Clients: plumbing, heating/cooling equipment, chemicals, hardware, ski equipment, home appliances, crafts and window coverings.

Needs: Assigns 300 freelance jobs/year. Works with 2-3 freelance illustrators/month. Local artists only. Works on assignment only. Uses freelance artists for filmstrips, slide sets, brochures/flyers and trade magazines. Also uses freelance artists for layout, illustration, lettering, type spec, paste-up and retouching for trade magazines and direct mail.

First Contact & Terms: Arrange interview to show portfolio. Samples returned by SASE. Reports back only if interested. Provide business card to be kept on file for future assignments. No originals returned to artist at job's completion. Pays by the hour, $15 minimum. Considers complexity of project, client's budget and skill and experience of artist when establishing payment.

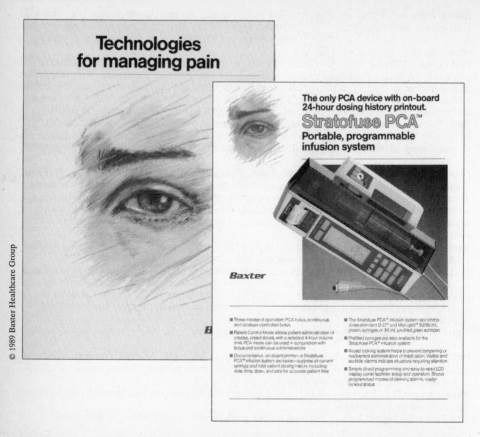

Technologies for managing pain

The only PCA device with on-board 24-hour dosing history printout.

Stratofuse PCA™
Portable, programmable infusion system

Baxter

Illustrator Gary Krejca's ability to meet deadlines and his attention to detail matches the need of McCann Healthcare Advertising. Krejca believes the piece is successful because "it's attention-getting. A difficult subject (i.e., discomfort in pain management) is shown, without being unpleasant."

NORTHWEST TELEPRODUCTIONS, 142 E. Ontario, Chicago IL 60611. (312)337-6000. General Manager: Mr. Carmen V. Trombetta. Senior Producer: Debbie Heagy. Estab. 1990. Videotape/film teleproducer. Clients: 40% are major Chicago advertising and PR firms and educational/industrial enterprises and 40% are corporate enterprises, and 20% are broadcast enterprises. Produces multimedia kits, slide sets, videotapes and films.
Needs: Works with 2-3 illustrators/month. Works on assignment only. Assigns 100 jobs/year. Uses artists for videotape teleproduction, television copy art, storyboard animation and computer animation.
First Contact & Terms: Query with resume, business card and slides which may be kept on file. Samples not kept on file are returned by SASE. Reports in 2-3 weeks. Original art returned to artist at job's completion. Pays by the project, $200 minimum.
Tips: "Artists must be familiar with film and videotape. We need more videotape and computer graphics artists. Show some examples of computer graphics."

Indiana

ASHER AGENCY, 511 W. Wayne, Fort Wayne IN 46802. (219)424-3373. Sr. Art Director: Mark Manuszak. Estab. 1974. Ad agency and PR firm. Clients: automotive firms, convention centers, financial/investment firms, area economic development agencies, health care providers and fast food companies.
Needs: Works with 10 freelance artists/year. Assigns 50 freelance jobs/year. Prefers area artists. Works on assignment only. Uses freelance artists mainly for illustration also for design, brochures, catalogs, consumer and trade magazines, retouching, billboards, posters, direct mail packages, logos and advertisements.

First Contact & Terms: Send query letter with brochure showing art style or tearsheets and photocopies. Samples are filed or are returned by SASE. Reports back only if interested. Write to schedule an appointment to show a portfolio, which should include roughs, original/final art, tearsheets and final reproduction/product. Pays for design by the hour, $20 minimum. Pays for illustration by the hour. Considers complexity of project, client's budget, turnaround time and skill and experience of artist when establishing payments. Buys all rights.

BLOOMHORST STORY O'HARA INC., 200 S. Meridian, Indianapolis IN 46225. (317)639-4436. Art Director: Ken Bloomhorst. Full-service Ad agency. Clients: retail.
Needs: Works with 30 artists/year. Uses freelance artists mainly for brochure, catalog, newspaper and magazine ad illustration; P-O-P displays; mechanicals; retouching; animation; films; lettering and charts/graphs.
First Contact & Terms: Send query letter with brochure showing art style or tearsheets, photocopies and slides. Samples are filed or are returned only if requested by artist. Does not report back. Call to schedule an appointment to show a portfolio, which should include color and b&w roughs, photostats, tearsheets, photographs and slides. Pays for illustration by the project, $100-10,000+. Considers complexity of project, client's budget, turnaround time, how work will be used and rights purchased. Rights purchased vary according to project.
Tips: "Please do not leave your phone number asking us to call you back to set up an interview."

C.R.E. INC., 400 Victoria Centre, 22 E. Washington St., Indianapolis IN 46204. (317)-631-0260. Creative Director: Mark Gause. Ad agency. Clients: primarily business-to-business.
Needs: Works with 15 freelance artists/year. Works on assignment only. Uses freelance artists for line art, color illustrations and airbrushing.
First Contact & Terms: Send query letter with resume, and photocopies to be kept on file. Samples not filed are returned. Reports back only if interested. Call or write to schedule an appointment to show a portfolio, or mail original/final art, final reproduction/product and tearsheets. Pays by the project, $100 minimum. Considers complexity of the project, client's budget, skill and experience of artist and rights purchased when establishing payment. Buys all rights.
Tips: "Show samples of good creative talent."

CALDWELL VAN RIPER, INC. ADVERTISING-PUBLIC RELATIONS, 1314 N. Meridian St., Indianapolis IN 46202. (317)632-6501. Secretary: Lori Morozowski. Ad agency/PR firm. Clients are a "good mix of" consumer (banks, furniture, food, etc.) and industrial (chemicals, real estate, insurance, heavy industry)."
Needs: Assigns 100-200 freelance jobs/year. Works with 10-15 freelance illustrators/month. Works on assignment only. Uses freelance artists for consumer and magazine ads, billboards, direct mail packages, brochures, catalogs, newspaper ads, P-O-P displays, storyboards, AV presentations and posters.
First Contact & Terms: Send query letter with brochure, samples and tearsheets to be kept on file. Call for appointment to show portfolio. Accepts any available samples. Samples not filed are returned by SASE only if requested. Reports only if interested. Pay is negotiated. Considers complexity of project, client's budget, skill and experience of artist and rights purchased when establishing payment. Buys all rights.
Tips: "Send 5 samples of best work (copies acceptable) followed by a phone call."

*GRAY, MILLER & MITSCH, Suite 305, 8910 Purdue Rd., Indianapolis IN 46268. (317)875-0580. FAX: (317)872-6023. Estab. 1985. Ad agency. Full-service, multimedia firm. Specializes in magazine ads and collaterals. Product specialty is business-to-business. Current clients include: E-A-R, Mallory, Business Furniture Corp.
Needs: Approached by 1 freelance artist/month. Prefers artists with experience. Uses freelance artists mainly for design assistance. Also uses freelance artists for brochure, catalog and print ad design and illustration, storyboards, slide illustration, animatics, animation, retouching, billboards, posters, TV/film graphics, lettering and logos. 45% of work is for print ads.
First Contact & Terms: Send query letter with brochure, resume, photocopies, photographs and tearsheets. Samples are filed or are returned. Reports back to the artist only if interested. Mail appropriate materials: thumbnails, roughs, original/final art, b&w and color photostats, tearsheets, photographs, slides and 4×5 transparencies. Pays for design by the hour, $25-40; by the project, $25-40; by the day $25-40. Pays for illustration by the project, $150-5,000. Buys one-time rights or rights purchased vary according to project.

BJ THOMPSON ASSOCIATES, INC., 201 S. Main St., Mishawaka IN 46544. (219)255-5000. Art Director: Tim Elliott. Estab. 1979. "We are a full-service advertising/public relations firm, with much of our work in print-media and collateral." Specializes in RV's, agriculture and home improvement. Current clients include: Jayco, Inc., Reese Products, Leer, Inc., Ziggity Systems and Champion Motor Coach.
Needs: Works with 6 freelance illustrators and 2 freelance designers/month. Prefers artists with experience in mechanical illustration and airbrush. Works on assignment only. Uses freelancers mainly for all print material. Uses freelance artists for brochure and print ad design and illustration, storyboards, slide illustration, retouching, billboards and posters. 70% of work is with print ads.

First Contact & Terms: Send query letter with resume and slides. Samples are not filed and are returned only if requested by artist. Reports back to the artist only if interested. Write to schedule an appointment to show portfolio, which should include color and b&w photostats, tearsheets, final reproduction/product and slides. Pays for design by the project, $25/hour minimum. Pays for illustration by the project, $50/hour minimum. Considers complexity of project, client's budget, turnaround time and skill and experience of artist when establishing payment. Buys all rights.

Iowa

*ADMARK ADVERTISING, 109 1st St. S.E., P.O. Box 779, Mason City IA 50401. (515)424-0191. Art Director: Jackie Loterbour. Estab. 1978. Ad agency. Full-service, multimedia firm. Product specialty is business-to-business. Current clients are mostly local.
Needs: Prefers local artists only. Works on assignment only. Uses freelance artists mainly for illustration and technical design. Also uses freelance artists for retouching. 50% of work is with print ads.
First Contact & Terms: Send query letter with brochure, photocopies, photostats and samples that do not need to be returned. Samples are filed and are not returned. Reports back to the artist only if interested. Mail appropriate materials: photostats, tearsheets and photographs. Pays for design and illustration by the project. Negotiates rights purchased and rights purchased vary according to project.

Kansas

*BRYANT, LAHEY & BARNES, INC., 5300 Foxridge Dr., Mission KS 66202. (913)262-7075. Art Director: Terry Pritchett. Ad agency. Clients: agriculture and veterinary firms.
Needs: Local artists only. Uses artists for illustration and production, including keyline and paste-up; consumer and trade magazines and brochures/flyers.
First Contact & Terms: Query by phone. Send business card and resume to be kept on file for future assignments. Negotiates pay. No originals returned to artist at job's completion.

MARKETAIDE, INC., Box 500, Salina KS 67402-0500. (913)825-7161. Production Manager: Eric Lamer. Full-service Ad/marketing/direct mail firm. Clients: financial, agricultural machinery, industrial, some educational, and fast food.
Needs: Prefers artists within one-state distance and possessing professional expertise. Works on assignment only. Uses freelance artists for illustrations, retouching, signage.
First Contact & Terms: Send query letter with resume, business card and samples to be kept on file. Accepts any kind of accurate representation as samples, depending upon medium. Samples not kept on file are returned only if requested. Reports only if interested. Write for appointment to show portfolio. Pays by the hour, $15-75 average; "since projects vary in size we are forced to estimate according to each job's parameters." Considers complexity of project, skill and experience of artist, how work will be used, turnaround time and rights purchased when establishing payment.
Tips: Artists interested in working here "should be highly-polished in technical ability, have a good eye for design and be able to meet all deadline commitments."

MARSHFILM ENTERPRISES, INC., Box 8082, Shawnee Mission KS 66208. (816)523-1059. President: Joan K. Marsh. Estab. 1969. AV firm. Clients: schools.
Needs: Works with 1-2 freelance artists/year. Works on assignment only. Uses freelance artists mainly for illustrating filmstrips. Artists must have experience and imagination.
First Contact & Terms: Send query letter, pay scale, resume and slides or actual illustrations to be kept on file "if it is potentially the type of art we would use." Samples not filed are returned. Reports within 1 month. Write for appointment to show portfolio. Pays for illustration by the project. Considers client's budget when establishing payment. Buys all rights.

Kentucky

SHEEHY, KNOPF, & SHAVER INC. ADVERTISING, Suite 107, 101 Bullitt Lane, Louisville KY 40222. (502)436-1314. Creative Director: Tom Koka. Estab. 1957. Ad agency. Clients: investment, entertainment, health care, interior design and industrial companies.
Needs: Works with 20 freelance illustrators and 50 freelance designers/year. Works on assignment only. Mainly uses freelancers for design and mechanicals. Also uses artists for illustration, retouching, animation and lettering. 60% of work is with print ads.
First Contact & Terms: Send query letter with brochure showing art style or resume and samples. Samples not filed are returned only if requested. Reports only if interested. Call or write to schedule an appointment to show a portfolio, which should include original/final art, final reproduction/product, color tearsheets, photostats and photographs. Pays for design by the hour, $20-40. Pays for illustration by the project, $200-

3,500. Rights purchased vary according to project. "We like to hear from students."

Tips: "Be concise. Make appointments before calling on anyone. Leave samples for reference of style and information on where to be reached including phone number. Call occasionally with updates."

WHAS TELEVISION: CBS 11, 520 W. Chestnut, Louisville KY 40201. (502)582-7840. Broadcast Design Director: Kim Trusty. Estab. 1950. Ad agency. "We are an in-house broadcast design firm for CBS Television, providing print, on-air and outdoor graphics as they relate to the station's needs."

Needs: Works with 3-6 illustrators and designers/year. Prefers artists with experience in illustration, photography, advertising print, or AVA/Quantel Paintbox graphics. Also, experience with ESS, Chyron Super Scribe, Macintosh and Vidifont helpful. "Prefer to work with reps, but will work with artists directly." Works on assignment only. Uses freelance artists for brochure and print ad illustration, storyboards, animation, retouching, billboards, TV/film graphics and logos. 30% of work is with print ads. "Bulk of work is computer graphics."

First Contact & Terms: Send query letter with tearsheets and transparencies. Samples are filed or are returned only if requested by artist. Reports back to the artist only if interested. Write to schedule an appointment to show a portfolio, or mail roughs, original, final art, tearsheets, final reproduction/product; include color and b&w samples. "Do not show photocopies, thumbnails or job performance appraisals." Pays for design by the hour, $15-40. Pays for illustration by the project, $200-6,000. Considers complexity of project, client's budget, turnaround time, skill and experience of artist, how work will be used and rights purchased when establishing payment. Negotiates rights purchased; rights purchased vary according to project.

Tips: "Mail a letter/resume with samples—be it a leave-behind card or tearsheets, but never mail merely a resume for a creative job. Creative self promo ideas get attention and stand out amidst stacks of resumes sent. Also keep in mind, you are creative—your resume must reflect your taste and talent. If I get a computer printout or a drab resume, I tend to believe this person's work will be similar and disqualify them."

Louisiana

CUNNINGHAM, SLY WADSACK INC., Box 4503, Shreveport LA 71134-0503. (318)861-6660. Creative Director: Harold J. Sly. Ad agency. Clients: industrial/financial.

Needs: Works with 6-10 freelance artists/year. Works on assignment only. Uses artists for layout/design, illustration, photo retouching, mechanical art and airbrushing. Especially looks for mechanical skills.

First Contact & Terms: Send query letter with brochure, resume, business card and samples to be kept on file. Samples not filed are returned only by request. Reports back only if interested. Pays by the hour, $20-50 average. Considers complexity of the project, client's budget and turnaround time when establishing payment. Rights purchased vary according to project.

DUKE UNLIMITED, INC., Suite 1709, 1 Galleria Blvd., Metairie LA 70002. (504)836-5150. President: Lana Duke. Estab. 1975. Ad agency. Clients: industrial, investment, medical, restaurants, entertainment, fashion and tourism.

Needs: Assigns 50 freelance jobs/year. Works with 6 freelance illustrators and 3 freelance designers/year. Works on assignment. Uses freelance artwork mainly for ads and brochures. Uses artists for consumer and trade magazines, billboards, direct mail packages, brochures, catalogs, newspapers, filmstrips, movies, stationery, signage, P-O-P displays, AV presentations, posters and press releases. 70% of work is with print ads.

First Contact & Terms: Send query letter with brochure, business card, photostats and tearsheets to be kept on file. Samples returned only if requested. Reports only if interested. Pays by the project, $100-2,500 average. The artist must provide a firm quotation in writing. Considers complexity of project, client's budget, skill and experience of artist, turnaround time and rights purchased when establishing payment. Buys all rights.

Tips: "In a portfolio, show line art, four-color illustration, airbrush and cartoons. Do not include fashion and furniture illustrations. Generally, artists include too many pieces, including mediocre or poor pieces with their best work. This takes up too much time."

*THE MABYN KEAN AGENCY, 8550 United Plaza Blvd., Baton Rouge LA 70809. (504)925-8278. FAX: (504)922-4422. President: Mabyn Shingleton. Estab. 1977. Ad agency. Full-service, multimedia firm. Specializes in brochures and collaterals. Current clients include: United Companies and Wright & Percy Insurance.

Needs: Approached by 3 freelance artists/month. Works with 3 freelance illustrators and 2 freelance designers/month. Prefers local artists only. Works on assignment only. Uses freelance artists mainly for design and mechanicals. Also uses freelance artists for brochure, catalog and print ad design and illustration, storyboards, animation, mechanicals, retouching, billboards, posters, TV/film graphics and logos. 25% of work is with print ads.

First Contact & Terms: Send query letter with brochure, resume, photographs, tearsheets and slides. Samples are filed or are returned. Reports back to the artist only if interested. Write to schedule an appointment to show a portfolio. Portfolio should include thumbnails, roughs and b&w and color photographs. Pays for design and illustration by the project. Rights purchased vary according to project, but usually all rights.

*SACKETT EXECUTIVE CONSULTANTS, 8600 Pontchartrain Blvd., New Orleans LA 70124. (504)282-2568. FAX: (504)282-0311. Art Director: Mrs. Shawn Nguyen. Estab. 1980. Ad agency and PR firm. Full-service, multimedia firm. Specializes in magazine/newspaper ads, direct mail, audiovisual TV/radio/film productions and political campaigns. Product specialties are retail and political. Current clients include: Canupo, Sound Trek and ABC Insurance.

Needs: Approached by 10 freelance artists/month. Works with 2 freelance illustrators and 1 freelance designer/month. Prefers artists with experience in food illustrations, architectural renderings and technical illustrations. Works on assignment only. Uses freelance artists mainly for illustration and presentation (or crash jobs). Also uses freelance artists for brochure, catalog and print ad design and illustration, animatics, animation, mechanicals, retouching, billboards, posters, TV/film graphics, lettering and logos. 40% of work is for print ads.

First Contact & Terms: Send query letter with brochure, photocopies, resume, tearsheets and photostats. Samples are filed. Samples are not returned. Reports back within 1 week. Call to schedule an appointment to show a portfolio. Portfolio should include original/final art, b&w and color photostats. Pays for design by the hour, $10-50; by the project, $100 minimum; and by the day, $80-400. Pays for illustration by the project, $500-3,000. Buys first rights and all rights.

Maryland

SAMUEL R. BLATE ASSOCIATES, 10331 Watkins Mill Dr., Gaithersburg MD 20879-2935. (301)840-2248. President: Samuel R. Blate. AV and editorial services firm. Clients: business/professional, U.S. government, some private.

Needs: Works with 5 freelance artists/year. Only works with artists in the Washington-Baltimore-Richmond metro area. Works on assignment only. Uses artists for cartoons (especially for certain types of audiovisual presentations), illustrations (graphs, etc.) for 35mm slides, pamphlet and book design. Especially important are "technical and aesthetic excellence and ability to meet deadlines."

First Contact & Terms: Send query letter with resume and tearsheets, photostats, photocopies, slides and photographs to be kept on file. "No original art, please, and SASE for return." Call or write for appointment to show portfolio, which should include final reproduction/product and color and b&w photographs. Samples are returned only by SASE. Reports only if interested. Pays by the hour, $20-40. "Payment varies as a function of experience, skills needed, size of project, and anticipated competition, if any." Also considers complexity of the project, client's budget, turnaround time and rights purchased when establishing payment. Rights purchased vary according to project, "but we prefer to purchase first rights only. This is sometimes not possible due to client demand, in which case we attempt to negotiate a financial adjustment for the artist."

Tips: "The demand for technically oriented artwork has increased. At the same time, some clients who have used artists have been satisfied with computer-generated art."

*CROSBY COMMUNICATIONS, 647 Ridgely Ave., Annapolis MD 21401. (301)266-1474. FAX: (301)266-1425. Art Director: Margy McArdle. Estab. 1970's. Ad agency. Specializes in collateral. Current clients include: Derand Wealth Advisors and AA Medical Center.

Needs: Approached by 1-2 freelance artists/month. Works with 1 freelance illustrator and 1 freelance designer/month. Prefers artists with experience in production and illustration. Works on assignment only. Uses freelance artists mainly for illustration and production. Also uses freelance artists for slide illustration, mechanicals, retouching, lettering and photography. 10% of work is with print ads.

First Contact & Terms: Send query letter with resume and tearsheets. Samples are filed. Reports back to the artist only if interested. Call to schedule an appointment to show portfolio. Portfolio should include originals/final art, tearsheets and slides. Pays for design by the hour, $20-30 or by the project. Pays for illustration by the project based on estimate given. Rights purchased vary according to project.

Tips: "Make sure presentation is clean and work is good. Don't waste art director's time with less than professional work. Leave samples of printed work."

IMAGE DYNAMICS, INC., Suite 1400, 1101 N. Calvert St., Baltimore MD 21202. (301)539-7730. Creative Director: Ann Lesche. Ad agency/PR firm. Clients: wide mix, specializing in restaurants and hotels, associations, colleges, hospitals and land developers.

Needs: Local artists only. Uses artists for illustration, design and paste-up; frequently buys humorous and cartoon-style illustrations. Prefers various styles in b&w and full-color.

First Contact & Terms: Call to arrange interview to show portfolio; "please do not drop in. Bring lots of b&w and color samples; have printed or produced work to show." Samples are returned. Reports only if interested. Provide business card and samples to be kept on file for possible future assignments. Pays by the project, $100-1,500, depending on project and budget. Considers complexity of project, client's budget, skill and experience of artist and turnaround time when establishing payment.

SHECTER & LEVIN ADVERTISING/PUBLIC RELATIONS, 2205 N. Charles St., Baltimore MD 21218. (301)889-4464. Production Executive: Virginia Lindler. Ad agency/PR firm. Serves clients in real estate, finance, professional associations, social agencies, retailing, apartments and manufacturing.

Needs: Works with 3-4 illustrators/month. Uses designers for billboards, consumer magazines, stationery design, direct mail, television, brochures/flyers, trade magazines and newspapers. Also uses artists for layouts and mechanicals for brochures, newspaper and magazine ads.
First Contact & Terms: Write for an interview to show portfolio. No originals returned to artist at job's completion. Negotiates pay.

MARC SMITH CO., Box 5005, Severna Park MD 21146. (301)647-2606. Art/Creative Director: Marc Smith. Ad agency. Clients: consumer and industrial products, sales services and PR firms.
Needs: Works with 3 illustrators/month. Local artists only. Uses freelance artists for layout, illustration, lettering, technical art, type spec, paste-up and retouching. Also uses freelance artists for illustration and design of direct mail, slide sets, brochures/flyers, trade magazines and newspapers; design for film strips, stationery, multimedia kits. Occasionally buys humorous and cartoon-style illustrations.
First Contact & Terms: Send query letter with brochure showing art style or tearsheets, photostats, photocopies, slides or photographs. Keeps file on artists; does not return original artwork to artist after completion of assignment. Call or write to schedule an appointment to show a portfolio, which should include color thumbnails, roughs, original/final art, final reproduction/product and tearsheets. Pays by the hour, $25-150, or negotiated.
Tips: "More sophisticated techniques and equipment are being used in art and design. Our use of freelance material has intensified. Project honesty, clarity and patience."

VAN SANT, DUGDALE & COMPANY, INC., The World Trade Center, Baltimore MD 21202. (301)539-5400. Executive Creative Director: Stan Paulus. Creative Director: Richard Smith. Ad agency. Clients: consumer, corporate, associations, financial, and industrial.
Needs: Number of freelance artists used varies. Works on assignment basis only. Uses freelance artists for consumer and trade magazines, brochures, catalogs, newspapers and AV presentations.
First Contact & Terms: Negotiates payment according to client's budget, amount of creativity required, where work will appear and freelancer's previous experience.

Massachusetts

CORNERSTONE ASSOCIATES, 123 Second Ave., Waltham MA 02154. (617)890-3773. Production managaer: Phil Sheesley or Art Director: Donna Ingemanson. Estab. 1978. "We are an audiovisual company specializing in meetings, multi-media, shows and speaker support slide presentations." Current clients include Reebok, DEC, Prime, and other local clients.
Needs: Works with 2 freelance designers/month. Prefers local artists only with experience in slide mechanicals and design. Also uses artists for storyboards and slide illustration.
First Contact & Terms: Send query letter with resume, slides and SASE. Samples are filed or are returned by SASE. Reports back to the artist only if interested. Call or write to schedule an appointment to show a portfolio, or mail original final art, final reproduction/product, photographs and slides. Considers complexity of project, client's budget, turnaround time, skill and experience of artist and how work will be used when establishing payment. Rights purchased vary according to project.
Tips: "Have a strong design sense; show you can execute extremely clean mechanicals; have a portfolio that shows these skills."

COSMOPULOS, CROWLEY & DALY, INC., 250 Boylston St., Boston MA 02116. (617)266-5500. Chairman of the Board/Creative Director: Stavros Cosmopulos. Associate Creative Director: Rich Kerstein. Advertising and marketing agency. Clients: banks, restaurants, industry, package goods, food and electronics.
Needs: Works with 6 freelance illustrators and 1 freelance animator/month. Works on assignment only. Uses artists for work on billboards, P-O-P displays, filmstrips, consumer magazines, stationery design, multimedia kits, direct mail, television, slide sets, brochures/flyers, trade magazines and newspapers.
First Contact & Terms: Send business card, photostats or slides. Samples not filed are returned by SASE. Reports only if interested. Make an appointment to show portfolio. No originals returned to artist at job's completion. Pays for design by the project, $250 minimum. Pays for illustration by the project, $100 minimum. Considers complexity of project, client's budget, geographic scope of finished project, turnaround time and rights purchased when establishing payment.
Tips: "Give a simple presentation of the range of work you can do including printed samples of actual jobs — but not a lot of samples. I look for specific techniques that an artist may have to individualize the art."

FLAGLER ADVERTISING/GRAPHIC DESIGN, Box 1317, Brookline MA 02146. (617)566-6971. President/Creative Director: Sheri Flagler. Specializes in corporate identity, brochure design, fashion and technical illustration. Clients: cable television, finance, real estate, fashion and direct mail agencies.

Needs: Works with 10-20 freelance artists/year. Works on assignment only. Uses artists for illustration, mechanicals, retouching, airbrushing, charts/graphs and lettering.
First Contact & Terms: Send resume, business card, brochures, photocopies or tearsheets to be kept on file. Call or write for appointment to show portfolio. Samples not filed are not returned. Reports back only if interested. Pays for design by the project, $150-1,500 average; for illustration by the project, $150-1,200 average. Considers complexity of project, client's budget and turnaround time when establishing payment.
Tips: "Send a range and variety of style showing clean, crisp and professional work."

*HARPER & COMPANY, INC., 274 Great Rd., Acton MA 01720. (508)263-5331. FAX: (508)635-9558. Creative Partner: Deb Harper. Estab. 1985. Ad agency. Full-service, multimedia firm. Specializes in magazine ads, collaterals, corporate identity and desk-top publishing. Product specialties high-tech and consumer.
Needs: Approached by 2-4 freelance artists/month. Works with 1 freelance illustrator and 2 freelance designers/month. Prefers artists with experience in high technology. Works on assignment only. Uses freelance artists mainly for overflow of design and most production. Also uses freelance artists for brochure design, catalog design and illustration, mechanicals, retouching and logos. 25% of work is with print ads.
First Contact & Terms: Send query letter with photocopies, resume and references. Samples are filed. Reports back within 2 weeks, only if interested. Mail appropriate materials: thumbnails, roughs, original/final art and color photostats. Pays by the project, $50-1,500. Pays for illustration by the project, $25-1,000. Buys all rights.

HELIOTROPE STUDIOS LTD., 21 Erie St., Cambridge MA 02139. (617)868-0171. Production Coordinator: Suzanne Sobert. Estab. 1984. AV firm. "We are a full-service, sophisticated facility for film and video production and post-production." Current projects include NBC-TV "Unsolved Mysteries" TV series; TWA/The Travel Channel; "Nova"-WGBH-TV, BBC-TV and corporate video projects.
Needs: Works with 6 freelance illustrators and 6 freelance designers/month. Works on assignment only. Uses freelancers mainly for set design and animation. Also uses artists for brochure design and storyboards.
First Contact & Terms: Send query letter with brochure. Samples are filed. Reports back to the artist only if interested. To show a portfolio, mail appropriate materials. Pays for design and illustration by the day, $100-400. Considers client's budget and turnaround time when establishing payment. Rights purchased vary according to project.
Tips: "Have excellent referrals and a solid demo tape of work."

*THE PHILIPSON AGENCY, Suite B201, 241 Perkins St., Boston MA 02130. (617)566-3334. FAX: (617)566-3363. President and Creative Director: Joe Philipson. Marketing design firm. Specializes in packaging, collaterals, P.O.P., corporate image, sales presentations, direct mail, business-to-business and high-tech.
Needs: Approached by 3-4 freelance artists/month. Works with 1 freelance illustrator and 3 freelance designers/month. Prefers artists with experience in design, illustration, comps and production. Works on assignment only. Uses freelance artists mainly for overflow and special jobs. Also uses freelance artists for packaging, brochure, catalog and print ad design and illustration, mechanicals, retouching, posters, lettering and logos. 65% of work is with print ads.
First Contact & Terms: Send query letter with brochure, photocopies, SASE, resume, photographs, tearsheets, photostats, slides and transparencies. Samples are filed or are returned by SASE. Reports back to the artist only if interested. Mail appropriate materials: roughs, original/final art, photostats, tearsheets, photographs and slides. Pays for design by the hour, $15-50; pays for illustration by the hour. Buys all rights.

*RAPP COLLINS MARCOA, (formerly Marcoa Dr Group Inc.), 40 Broad St., Boston MA 02109-4359. Creative Director: Dom Cimei. Direct marketing ad agency. Clients: industry, financial and publishing firms, utilities, healthcare and software firms.
Needs: Number of freelance artists used varies. Usually works with local freelancers. Works on assignment basis only. Uses freelance artists for direct mail, collateral and print.
First Contact & Terms: Arrange interview to show portfolio. "Write, then call." Payment varies according to job.
Tips: "Marginal samples lessen the impact of good stuff."

TR PRODUCTIONS, 1031 Commonwealth Ave., Boston MA 02215. (617)783-0200. Production Manager: Tom Cramer. AV firm. Clients: industry and high-tech.
Needs: Works with 5-10 freelance artists/year. Assigns 20-50 jobs/year. Prefers local artists. Works on assignment generally. Uses artists for slide graphics, layout, mechanical, computer graphics, charts/graphs, advertisements and 2-color and 4-color collateral design. Especially important is clean, accurate board work.
First Contact & Terms: For slide work, artist must have experience in design and mechanicals for slides/multi-image. Send query letter with brochure showing art style, resume and slides to be kept on file. Samples not filed are not returned. Reports only if interested. Call to schedule an appointment to show a portfolio. Pays by the hour, $10-25 average. Considers complexity of project, client's budget, skill and experience of

artist and turnaround time when establishing payment. Buys all audiovisual rights.

Michigan

*WILLIAM R. BIGGS/GILMORE ASSOCIATES, 200 E. Michigan Ave., Kalamazoo MI 49007. (616)349-7711. FAX: (616)349-3051. Creative Department Coordinator: Launa Rogers. Estab. 1973. Ad agency. Full-service, multimedia firm. Specializes in magazine and newspaper ads and collateral. Product specialties are consumer, business-to-business and healthcare.
Needs: Approached by 10 freelance artists/month. Works with 1-3 freelance illustrators and designers/month. Works both with artist reps and directly with artist and prefers artists with experience with client needs. Works on assignment only. Uses freelance artists mainly for completion of projects needing specialties. Also uses freelance artists for brochure, catalog and print ad design and illustration, storyboards, slide illustration, animatics, animation, mechanicals, retouching, billboards, posters, TV/film graphics, lettering and logos.
First Contact & Terms: Send query letter with brochure, photocopies and resume. Samples are filed. Reports back to artists only if interested. Call to schedule an appointment to show a portfolio. Portfolio should include all samples the artist considers appropriate. Pays for design and illustration by the hour and by the project. Rights purchased vary according to project.

BLAVIN, HARTZ & MOLNER, INC., Suite 153, 23077 Greenfield Rd., Southfield, MI 48075. (313)557-8011. President: Monroe "Bob" Molner. Clients: Variety of industries.
Needs: Buys 100-150 illustrations/year. Works on assignment only. Uses artists for print ads, TV storyboards, layouts and fashion and furniture illustrations.
First Contact & Terms: Query. SASE. Reports in 1 week. Pays $10-50, fashion or furniture illustration; $20-30/hour, layout. Pays original fee as agreed for unused assigned illustrations. No originals returned to artist at job's completion.

LEO J. BRENNAN, INC. Marketing Communications, (formerly Leo J. Brennan Advertising), 2359 Livernois, Troy MI 48083-1692. (313)362-3131. Financial and Administrative Director: Virginia Janusis. Estab. 1969. Ad agency, PR and marketing firm. Clients: mainly industry, automotive, banks and C.P.A.s.
Needs: Works with 10 freelance artists/year. Artist must be well experienced. Uses artists for design, illustration, brochures, catalogs, retouching, lettering, keylining and typesetting. 50% of work is with print ads.
First Contact & Terms: Send query letter with resume and samples. Samples not filed are returned only if requested. Reports only if interested. Call to schedule an appointment to show a portfolio, which should include thumbnails, roughs, original/final art, final reproduction/product, color and b&w tearsheets, photostats and photographs. Pay for design and illustration varies. Considers complexity of project, client's budget, skill and experience of artist and turnaround time when establishing payment. Buys all rights.

CREATIVE HOUSE ADVERTISING INC., Suite 301, 30777 Northwestern Hwy., Farmington Hills MI 48018. (313)737-7077. Executive Vice President/Creative Director: Robert G. Washburn. Estab. 1964. Advertising/marketing/promotion graphics/display/art firm. Clients: residential and commercial construction, land development, consumer, retail, finance and manufacturing. Assigns 20-30 jobs and buys 10-20 illustrations/year.
Needs: Works with 6 freelance illustrators and 4 freelance designers/year. Local artists generally. Uses freelance artists for work on filmstrips, consumer magazines, multimedia kits, direct mail, television, slide sets, brochures/flyers, trade magazines and newspapers. Uses freelance artists mainly for illustration, design and comp layouts of ads, brochures, catalogs, annual reports and displays. 50-60% of work is with print ads.
First Contact & Terms: Query with resume, business card and brochure/flyer to be kept on file. Samples returned by SASE. Reports in 2 weeks. No originals returned to artist at job's completion. Arrange interview to show portfolio, which should include originals, reproduced and published pieces. Pays for design by the project, $250-5,000. Pays for illustration by the project, $200-20,000. Considers complexity of project, client's budget and rights purchased when establishing payment. Reproduction rights are purchased as a buy-out.
Tips: "Flexibility is a necessity, do not send too much of the same style or technique. Send letter of introduction, samples and information then follow up with a call to make an appointment."

KLOCK ADVERTISING, INC., 701 E. 8 Mile Rd., Hazel Park MI 48030. (313)545-5415. Chairman of the Board: Jack Klock. Multimedia, full-service Ad agency. Clients: automotive, financial, health care, private schools, media and travel club.
Needs: Works with 5 freelance artists/year. Assigns 25 job/year. Prefers local artists. Works on assignment only. Uses artists for brochure, catalog and newspaper ad design and illustration; direct mail packages; magazine ad design and illustration; P-O-P displays; mechanicals; retouching and posters.
First Contact & Terms: Send brochure, tearsheets, photostats, photocopies and photographs. Samples are filed or are returned only if requested by artist. Reports back within 1 month only if interested. Call or write to schedule an appointment to show a portfolio or mail thumbnails, roughs, photostats, tearsheets and final reproduction/product. Pays for design and illustration by the project, $100-1,000. Considers complexity of project and client's budget when establishing payment. Buys all rights.

Tips: The most common mistake freelancers make in presenting samples or portfolios is "submitting materials that do not apply to our projects. Find out our needs first. We have a mix of straightforward industrial work plus more creative work for some clients."

LIGHT PRODUCTIONS, 1915 Webster, Birmingham MI 48009. (313)642-3502. Producer: Terry Luke. Estab. 1980. "We are an audiovisual service co. doing photography, video, print, and multi-image projects and public relations marketing." Current clients include CBS, Westinghouse, Capital Records, Dale Carnegie, Rockwell International and Bridgeport Machine.
Needs: Works with 2 freelance illustrators and 2 freelance designers/month. Prefers local artists only. Uses freelancers mainly for brochure design and storyboards. Also uses freelance artists for brochure design and illustration, catalog and print ad design, slide illustration, animation, mechanicals, retouching, posters, TV/film graphics, lettering and logos. 50% of work is with print ads.
First Contact & Terms: Send query letter with brochure, resume, photostats, photocopies, photographs, slides, transparencies and SASE. Samples are filed or are returned only if requested by artist. Reports back to the artist only if interested. Call or write to schedule an appointment to show a portfolio, which should include roughs, original/final art, photostats, final reproduction/product, photographs, slides, include color and b&w samples. Pays for design by the hour, $5-60; by the project, $20 minimum; by the day, $35-150. Pays for illustration by the project, $30 minimum. Considers complexity of project, client's budget, turnaround time, skill and experience of artist and rights purchased when establishing payment. Negotiates rights purchased; rights purchased vary according to project.
Tips: "The most common mistake freelancers make is having too much work and some is of lower quality. It is best to inquire first and bring samples oriented toward what we do."

LOVIO-GEORGE INC., 681 Forest, Detroit MI 48201. (313)832-2210. Creative Director: Martha Pompa. Estab. 1979. PR firm. "Marketing communications firm with full service capabilities, specializing in brochure development, logos, collateral/stationery packages." Specializes in real estate and retail. Current clients include: Robertson Brothers, Elkin Travel and Detroit Economic Growth Corp.
Needs: Works with 1 freelance illustrator and 2 freelance designers/month. Prefers local artists only. Works on assignment only. Uses freelancers mainly for brochure design. Also uses freelance artist for brochure illustration, print ad design and illustration, billboards, posters, logos and sales promotion mats. 25% of work is with print ads.
First Contact & Terms: Send query letter. Samples are not filed and are returned by SASE only if requested by artist. Reports back within 1 week. Call to schedule an appointment to show a portfolio, which should include roughs, original/final art, photostats, tearsheets; include color and b&w samples. Pays for design by the project, $75 minimum. Pays for illustration by the project, $50 minimum. Considers complexity of project, client's budget, turnaround time and skill and experience of artist when establishing payment.
Tips: "Make phone calls and get in to see the person face to face."

PHOTO COMMUNICATION SERVICES, INC., 6410 Knapp N.E., Ada MI 49301. (616)676-1499. Contact: M.L. Jackson. Estab. 1970. AV firm. Full-service, multimedia firm. Product specialties are corporate and industrial products. Current clients include: General Electric and Zondervan Publishing.
Needs: Approached by 2-3 freelance artists/month. Works with 1 freelance illustrator/month. Works on assignment only. Uses freelance artists mainly for animated illustration. Also uses freelance artists for brochure, catalog and print ad design and illustration, storyboards, slide illustration, animation, retouching, lettering and logos. 30% of work is with print ads.
First Contact & Term: Send query with brochure, SASE and tearsheets. Samples are filed or returned by SASE only if requested by artist. Reports back only if interested. Mail appropriate materials: tearsheets and transparencies. Pays for design and illustration by the hour $25 minimum, by the project $25 minimum and by the day $200 minimum. Rights purchased vary according to project.

THOMPSON ADVERTISING PRODUCTIONS, INC., 31690 W. 12 Mile Rd., Farmington Hills MI 48018. (313)553-4566. Vice President: Clay Thompson. Ad agency. Clients: automotive, marine and industrial.
Needs: Works with artists on illustration, layout, retouching, and creative concept. Artist should have a "strong sense of design communication."
First Contact & Terms: Send resume and samples. Samples not filed are returned only if requested. Call or write to schedule an appointment to show a portfolio, which should include thumbnails, roughs and original/final art. Pays for design and illustration by the hour, $10-25. Considers complexity of project, client's budget, and skill and experience of artist. Rights purchased vary according to project.
Tips: Artist should "be prepared to show samples of layout work and demonstrated skills and be prepared to quote a price. Portfolio should include original layouts and artwork. Do not show examples without a concept support."

J. WALTER THOMPSON USA, 600 Renaissance Center, Detroit MI 48243. (313)568-3800. Assistant Art Administrator: Maryann Inson. Ad agency. Clients: automotive, consumer, industry, media and retail-related accounts.

Needs: Deals primarily with established artists' representatives and art/design studios.

First Contact & Terms: Contact only through artist's agent. Assignments awarded on lowest bid. Call to schedule an appointment to show a portfolio, which should include thumbnails, roughs, original/final art, final reproduction/product, color tearsheets, photostats and photographs. Pays for design and illustration by the project.

Tips: Agency deals with proven illustrators from an "approved vendor's list." New vendors are considered for list periodically. "Portfolio should be comprehensive but not too large. Organization of the portfolio is as important as the sample. Mainly, consult professional rep."

Minnesota

*ALPINE MARKETING COMMUNICATIONS LTD., 3300 Edinborough Way, Minneapolis MN 55435. (612)832-8242. Vice President/General Manager: Jane Louseth. Estab. 1973. Ad agency. Full-service, multi-media firm. Specializes in sales support material and business-to-business advertising. Product specialties are real estate, finance and manufacturing.

Needs: Approached by 35 freelance artists/month. Works with 5 freelance illustrators and 6 freelance designers/month. Prefers artists with experience in food illustration and real estate renderings. Works on assignment only. Uses freelance artists for special projects. Also uses freelance artists for brochure design, print ad design and illustration, mechanicals, retouching and logos. 45% of work is with print ads.

First Contact & Terms: Send query letter with brochure, resume, tearsheets and slides. Samples are filed. Reports back only if interested. Mail appropriate materials: roughs, color photostats, photographs and transparencies. Pays for design by the project, $200-10,000. Buys all rights.

BADIYAN PRODUCTIONS INC., 720 W. 94 St., Minneapolis MN 55420. (612)888-5507. President: Fred Badiyan. AV firm. Client list provided upon request.

Needs: Works with 50 freelance artists/year. Works on assignment only. Uses freelance artists for design, brochures, mechanicals, press releases and motion pictures.

First Contact & Terms: Send query letter with brochure or resume, tearsheets, photocopies and slides. Samples are filed or are returned. Write to schedule an appointment to show a portfolio or mail appropriate materials. Pays for design and illustration by the hour or by the project.

Tips: "Send a letter and sample of work."

BUTWIN & ASSOCIATES ADVERTISING, INC., 8700 Westmoreland Lane, Minneapolis MN 55426. (612)546-0203. President: Ron Butwin. Estab. 1977. Ad agency. "We are a full-line ad agency working with both consumer and industrial accounts on advertising, marketing, public relations and meeting planning." Clients: banks, restaurants, clothing stores, food brokerage firms, corporations, full range of retail and service organizations, etc.

Needs: Works with 30-40 freelance illustrators and 20-30 freelance designers/year. Prefers local artists when possible. Uses artists for design, illustration, brochures, catalogs, newspapers, consumer and trade magazines, P-O-P displays, retouching, animation, direct mail packages, motion pictures and lettering. 60% of work is with print ads. Prefers pen & ink, airbrush, watercolor, marker, calligraphy and computer illustration.

First Contact & Terms: Send brochure or resume, tearsheets, photostats, photocopies, slides and photographs. Samples are filed or are returned only if SASE is enclosed. Reports back only if interested. Call to schedule an appointment to show a portfolio. Pays for design and illustration by the project; $25-1,500. Considers client's budget, skill and experience of artist and how work will be used when establishing payment. Buys all rights.

Tips: "Portfolios should include layouts and finished project." A problem is that "samples sent are often too weak to arouse enough interest."

FABER SHERVEY ADVERTISING, 160 W. 79th St., Minneapolis MN 55420. (612)881-5111. Creative Director: Paul D. Shervey. Ad agency. Clients: business-to-business, industry and farm.

Needs: Works with 25 freelance artists/year. Prefers local artists. Uses artists for retouching, line art, keyline and illustration.

First Contact & Terms: Send brochure and business card. Do *not* send samples. Does not report back. Call or write for appointment to show portfolio. Pays by the hour, $20-80 average. Considers complexity of project when establishing payment. Buys all rights.

EDWIN NEUGER & ASSOCIATES, 1221 Nicollet Mall, Minneapolis MN 55403. (612)333-6621. President: Ed Neuger. Estab. 1959. "We are a full-service public relations firm which specializes in financial relations for companies of all sizes." Clients: general. Client list provided upon request.

Needs: Works with 10 freelance artists/year. Assigns 25 jobs/year. Prefers local artists because "most assignments are not extremely large or time is a factor." Uses freelance artists mainly for annual reports. Also uses artists for design, illustration, brochures and catalogs.

First Contact & Terms: Samples are filed and are not returned. Does not report back. Call or write to schedule an appointment to show a portfolio. Pays by the project, such as on annual reports. Considers complexity of project, client's budget and skill and experience of artist. Buys all rights.

PIERCE THOMPSON & ASSOCIATES, INC., 6356 Smithtown Bay Rd., Excelsior MN 55331 (612)474-5502. President: Robert P. Thompson. Vice President: Kim Benike. Estab. 1955. PR firm. Full-service, multimedia firm. Specializes in newspaper and collaterals. Product specialties are telecommunications, insurance, construction, office products, etc.
Needs: Approached by 2 freelance artists/month. Works with 1 freelance illustrator and 1 freelance designer/year. Prefers local artists only. Works on assignment only. Uses freelancers mainly for layout. Also uses freelance artists for brochure, catalog and print ad design and illustration, retouching and logos. 10% of work is with print ads.
First Contact & Terms: Send query letter with brochure, photocopies, resume and photographs. Samples are filed. Reports back to the artists only if interested. Mail appropriate materials, not to be returned. Portfolio should include thumbnails, b&w and color tearsheets. Pays for design by the hour and by the project. Pays for illustration by the project. Buys all rights.
Tips: The most effective way for a freelancer to get started in public relations is "to show quality work, be an on-time performer and be a member of the team!"

RENNER BURNS ADVERTISING, INC., Suite 400, 7600 Parklawn Ave., Edina MN 55435. (612)831-7725. Art Director: Jeff Vlaming. Estab. 1977. Full service ad agency providing finished materials to client (publications, radio or TV stations). Specializes in public utilities. Current clients include Dairyland, Federal Land Co., Waldor Pump Sedgwick Heating & Air Conditioning and American Linen.
Needs: Works with 3 freelance illustrators/month. Prefers local artists. Works on assignment only. Uses freelancers mainly for illustration and photography. Also uses freelance artists for brochure, catalog and print ad illustration, animation, mechanicals, retouching, TV/film graphics, lettering and logos. 40% of work is with print ads.
First Contact & Terms: Send query letter with brochure and photographs. Samples are filed or are returned only if requested by artist. Reports back to the artist only if interested. Call to schedule an appointment to show a portfolio, which should include original, final art, final reproduction/product, photographs, slides; include color and b&w samples. Pays for illustration by the project, $100-2,000. Considers complexity of project, client's budget and turnaround time when establishing payment. Buys all rights.
Tips: "Have a good track record and fair prices (rates). Show needed style or talent in portfolio or mailed pieces."

Missouri

BRYAN/DONALD, INC. ADVERTISING, Suite 2712, 2345 Grand, Kansas City MO 64108. (816)471-4866. President: Don Funk. Multimedia, full-service Ad agency. Clients: food, fashion, pharmaceutical and real estate companies.
Needs: Works with 4 freelance artists/year. Assigns 35 jobs/year. Works on assignment only. Uses artists for design, illustration, brochures, catalogs, books, newspapers, consumer and trade magazines, P-O-P display, mechanicals, retouching, animation, billboards, posters, direct mail packages, lettering, logos, charts/graphs and advertisement.
First Contact & Terms: Send samples showing your style. Samples are not filed and are not returned. Reports back only if interested. Call to schedule an appointment to show a portfolio. Considers complexity of project and skill and experience of artist when establishing payment. Buys all rights.

*PARKER GROUP, INC., 6900 Delmar, St. Louis MO 63130. (314)737-4000. FAX: (314)727-3034. Director of Graphic Services: Mary Tuttle. Estab. 1979. Ad agency. Full-service, multimedia firm. Specializes in magazines, trade publication and newspaper ads. Product specialties are healthcare, consumer and business. Current clients include: Blue Cross and Blue Shield of Missouri.
Needs: Approached by 10 freelance artists/month. Works with 2 freelance illustrators and designers/month. Works with artist reps. Works on assignment only. Uses freelance artists mainly for illustration and some comp work. Also uses freelance artists for brochure and print ad design and illustration, catalog illustration, storyboards, slide illustration, mechanicals, retouching, billboards, posters, TV/film graphics, lettering and logos. 75% of work is with print ads.
First Contact & Terms: Contact only through artist rep or send query letter with photocopies, resume, tearsheets or photostats. Samples are filed and are not returned. Reports back only if interested. Write to schedule an appointment to show a portfolio or mail appropriate material: thumbnails, roughs, original/final art and b&w and color samples of "whatever is available." Pays for design by the hour, $25 minimum; by the project, $150 minimum; by the day, $400 minimum. Pays for illustration by the project, $150 minimum. Rights purchased vary according to project.

PREMIER FILM VIDEO & RECORDING, 3033 Locust St., St. Louis MO 63103. (314)531-3555. Secretary/Treasurer: Grace Dalzell. AV/film/animation/TV producer. Serves clients in business, religion, education and advertising. Produces videotape, motion 35mm, 16mm and Super 8mm, strip films, cassette dupes, 8-tracks and TV and radio spots.
Needs: Assigns 50-60 freelance jobs/year. Works with 8-10 freelance illustrators, "a few" freelance designers/month. Works on assignment only. Uses artists for strip film and slide presentations, TV commercials and motion picture productions.
First Contact & Terms: Send resume to be kept on file. "We do not accept samples; we review them during interviews only." Reporting time varies with available work. Pays by the project; method and amount of payment are negotiated with the individual artist. Pay varies with each client's budget. No originals returned to artist following publication; "copies supplied when possible." Buys all rights, but sometimes negotiates.
Tips: "In developing a brochure, begin by simply stating work capability and area of work most capable of producing, i.e., animation, cartoons, production, direction or editing—whatever you want to do for a living. Be specific."

Nebraska

MILLER FRIENDT LUDEMANN INC., 300 Corporate Center, 1235 K St., Lincoln NE 68508. (402)435-1234. Art Director: Dave Christiansen. Ad agency/PR firm. Clients: bank, industry, restaurant, tourist and retail.
Needs: Works on assignment only. Uses artists for consumer and trade magazines, billboards, direct mail packages, brochures, newspapers, stationery, signage, P-O-P displays, AV presentations, posters, press releases, trade show displays and TV graphics. "Freelancing is based on heavy workloads. Most freelancing is paste-up but secondary is illustrator for designed element."
First Contact & Terms: Send query letter with resume and slides to be kept on file. Samples not filed are returned by SASE. Reports back within 10 days. Write for appointment to show portfolio, "if regional/national; call if local." Portfolio should include thumbnails, roughs, original/final art, final reproduction/product, color tearsheets and photostats. Pays by the project, $100-1,500 average. Considers complexity of project, client's budget, skill and experience of artist, turnaround time and rights purchased when establishing payment. Buys all rights.
Tips: "Be prompt, have work done on time and be able to price your project work accurately. Make quality first."

J. GREG SMITH, Suite 102, Burlington Place, 1004 Farnam St., Omaha NE 68102. (402)444-1600. Art Director: Jane Yowell. Estab. 1974. Ad agency. Clients: financial, banking, associations, agricultural, travel and tourism.
Needs: Works with 3 illustrators and 1 designer/year. Works on assignment only. Mainly uses freelancers for mailers, brochures and projects also uses freelance artists for consumer and trade magazines, catalogs and AV presentations.
First Contact & Terms: Send query letter with brochure showing art style or photocopies. Reports only if interested. To show a portfolio, mail original/final art, final reproduction/product, color and b&w. Pays for design and illustration by the project, $500-5,000. Buys first, reprint or all rights.
Tips: Current trends include a certain "flexibility." Agencies are now able "to use any style or method that best fits the job."

Nevada

*DOYLE-MCKENNA & ASSOCIATES, 1175 Harvard Way, Reno NV 89502. (702)323-2181. FAX: (702)329-5899. Art Director: Brian Crane. Estab. 1955. Ad agency. Specializes in newspaper ads, brochures and collaterals. Product specialties are casinos and public utilities.
Needs: Approached by 1-5 freelance artists/month. Works with 2-3 freelance illustrators and 1-2 freelance designers/month. Works on assignment only. Mainly uses freelance talent for illustration, TV production, animation and paste-up. Also uses freelance artists for brochure, print ad and slide illustration, storyboards, animatics, mechanicals, retouching, TV/film graphics, lettering and logos. 70% of work is with print ads.
First Contact & Terms: Send query letter with brochure, photocopies, SASE, resume, photographs, tearsheets, photostats, slides and transparencies. Samples are filed or are returned by SASE only if requested by artist. Reports back within 5 days. Call or write to schedule an appointment to show a portfolio. Portfolio should include roughs, b&w and color photostats, tearsheets, photographs and slides. Pays for design by the hour, $50-100. Pays for illustration by the project, $50-2,000. Negotiates rights purchased.
Tips: "We see a lot of unprofessional presentations."

*STUDIOS KAMINSKI PHOTOGRAPHY LTD., 1040 Matley Lane, Reno NV 89502. (702)786-2615. President: T.J. Kaminski. AV/TV/film producer. Clients: education, industry and corporate. Produces filmstrips, motion pictures, multimedia kits, overhead transparencies, slide sets, sound-slide sets and videotapes.

Needs: Works with about 3 illustrators/year. Uses freelance artists mainly as illustrators to paint portraits from photos once in a while. Also uses freelance artists for slide illustration and retouching, catalog design and ad illustration.

First Contact & Terms: Arrange interview to show portfolio. Samples returned by SASE. Reports within 1 week. Works on assignment only. Provide brochure/flyer, resume or tearsheet to be kept on file for possible future assignments. Pays $30-60/hour; $200-500/day.

Tips: Have good samples and be qualified.

New Jersey

SOL ABRAMS ASSOCIATES INC., 331 Webster Dr., New Milford NJ 07646. (201)262-4111. President: Sol Abrams. PR firm. Clients: real estate, food, fashion, beauty, entertainment, government, retailing, sports, nonprofit organizations, etc. Media used include billboards, consumer and trade magazines, direct mail, newspapers, P-O-P displays, radio and TV.

Needs: Assigns approximately 6 freelance jobs/year. "For practical purposes, we prefer using artists in New Jersey-New York area." Works on assignment only. Uses artists for consumer magazines, billboards, brochures, catalogs, newspapers, stationery, signage, AV presentation and press releases.

First Contact & Terms: Send query letter with photographs and photostats, which may be kept on file. Samples not kept on file are returned by SASE. Reports only if interested. Pay varies according to client and job. Considers client's budget and skill and experience of artist when establishing payment. Buys all rights.

Tips: "As one who started his career as an artist before deciding to become a public relations consultant, I empathize with young artists. If material interests me and I cannot use it, I might develop leads or refer it to people and firms which may use it. Artists should be honest and sincere. Dedication and integrity are as important as talent."

DAVID H. BLOCK ADVERTISING, INC., 33 S. Fullerton Ave., Montclair NJ 07042 (201)744-6900. Executive Art Director and Vice President: Karen Deluca. Estab. 1939. Clients: finance, industry, consumer, real estate and bio-medical. Buys 100-200 illustrations/year.

Needs: Works with over 12 freelance illustrators and over 15 freelance designers/year. Prefers to work with "artists with at least 3-5 years experience in paste-up and 'on premises' work for mechanicals and design." Uses artists for illustration, layout, lettering, type spec, mechanicals and retouching for ads, annual reports, billboards, catalogs, letterheads, brochures and trademarks.

First Contact & Terms: Arrange interview. Include SASE. Reports in 2 weeks. Pays for design by the hour, $15-50. Pays for illustration by the project, $150-5,000.

Tips: "Please send some kind of sample of work. If mechanical artist, line art printed sample. If layout artist, composition of some type and photographs or illustrations. Mail samples first then follow with a phone call."

COOPER COMMUNICATIONS & PRODUCTIONS, INC., 18 S. Orange Ave., South Orange NJ 07079. (201)763-6148. President: Dan Cooper. Production Manager: Doris Burrell. Full-service ad agency with print, video and multi-image capabilities. Clients: all except retail—specializes in technology communications. Client list provided upon request.

Needs: Works with 4-5 freelance artists/year. Assigns 25 freelance jobs/year. Prefers local artists. Works on assignment only. Uses artists for design, illustration, brochures, catalogs, newspapers, P-O-P displays, mechanicals, animation, posters, direct mail packages, press releases, logos, charts/graphs and advertisements.

First Contact & Terms: Send query letter with brochure or resume. Samples are filed or are returned only if requested by artists. Reports back only if interested. Call or write to schedule an appointment to show a portfolio. Likes to see work samples and price list. Pays for design and illustration by the hour, $15-20 minimum. Considers complexity of project and turnaround time when establishing payment. Rights purchased vary according to project.

CREATIVE ASSOCIATES, 626 Bloomfield Ave., Verona NJ 07044. (201)857-3444. Producer: Harrison Feather. Estab. 1970. AV firm. "We are a multimedia production facility providing photography, video post-production, slide shows, computer graphics, desktop publishing, scriptwriting services for sales meetings, trade shows, speaker support and entertainment." Clients: high-tech, pharmaceutical, computer, R&D labs, engineering and marine. Client list provided with SASE.

Needs: Works with 5 freelance artists/year. Assigns 10 freelance jobs/year. Works on assignment only. Uses artists for design, illustration, motion pictures and charts/graphs.

First Contact & Terms: Send query letter with brochure or resume and slides. Samples are filed or are returned by SASE. Call to schedule an appointment to show a portfolio, which should include original/final art, slides and video cassette. Pays for design (computer generated art) by the project, $500 minimum. Pays for illustration by the project, $300 minimum. Considers complexity of project, client's budget, skill and experience of artist and how work will be used when establishing payment. Rights purchased vary according to project.

CREATIVE PRODUCTIONS, INC., 200 Main St., Orange NJ 07050. (201)676-4422. Partner: Gus J. Nichols. Estab. 1955. AV firm. Clients: pharmaceutical firms, manufacturers, chemical and financial firms.

Needs: Works with 30 freelance artists/year. Artists must be within 1 hour travel time to studio with 1 year of experience. Uses freelancers mainly for computer-generated slides and video graphics. Also uses artists for computer-generated charts and graphs. Especially important is "accuracy, neat work and the ability to take direction."

First Contact & Terms: Send resume to be kept on file. Call for appointment to show portfolio. Reports back only if interested. Pays by the hour, $15-25 average. Considers skill and experience of artist when establishing payment.

Tips: Artists "must have computer training/experience with business graphics and be able to create illustrations on computers."

DIEGNAN & ASSOCIATES, Box 298, Oldwick NJ 08858. (201)832-7951. President: Norman Diegnan. Estab. 1977. PR firm. Clients: commercial.

Needs: Works with 25 freelance illustrators/year. Assigns 25 freelance jobs/year. Works on assignment only. Uses artists for catalogs and AV presentations. 50% of work is with print ads.

First Contact & Terms: Send brochure and resume to be kept on file. Write for appointment to show portfolio; may also send portfolio. Reports only if interested. Pays artist's rate. Considers client's budget when establishing payment. Buys all rights.

IMAGE INNOVATIONS, INC., The Professional Center at Somerset, Suite 201, 29 Clyde Rd., Somerset, NJ 08873. (201)873-0700. President/Owner: Mark A. Else. Estab. 1974. AV firm providing marketing support and human resources programs (multi-image, print and video). Specializes in health care, pharmaceuticals, and computer software. Current clients include Warner-Lambert, Johnson & Johnson and Merck & Co.

Needs: Works with 2 freelance illustrators/year and 1 freelance designer/month. Prefers local artists only with experience in AV graphics. Works on assignment only. Uses freelancers mainly for brochure design. Also uses artists for storyboards, slide illustration, mechanicals, TV/film graphics and logos.

First Contact & Terms: Send query letter with photocopies. Samples are filed or are not returned. Does not report back. Call or write to schedule an appointment to show a portfolio, which should include thumbnails and final reproduction/product; include b&w samples. Pays for design and illustration by the project, $500-5,000. Considers complexity of project, client's budget, turnaround time and how work will be used when establishing payment. Buys all rights.

Tips: "Knock on doors with professionally assembled portfolio."

INSIGHT ASSOCIATES, Bldg. E, 373 Rt. 46 W., Fairfield NJ 07006. (201)575-5521. President: Raymond E. Valente. AV firm. Estab. 1979. "Full-service business communicators; multimedia, videotape, print materials, sales meetings ... all of the above from concept to completion." Clients: organizations in need of any audiovisual, audio and/or print." Client list provided upon request.

Needs: Works with 50-100 freelance artists/year. Assigns 50 freelance jobs/year. Works on assignment only. Uses artists for design, illustration, brochures, catalogs, P-O-P displays, mechanicals, retouching, animation, direct mail packages, press releases, lettering, logos, charts/graphs and advertisements. 40% of work is with print ads.

First Contact & Terms: Send query letter with brochure or resume. Samples are filed or filed are returned by SASE. Reports back within 3 weeks only if interested. Write to schedule an appointment to show a portfolio or mail brochure or resume. Pays by the project, amount varies. Considers complexity of project, client's budget, turnaround time and how work will be used when establishing payment. Rights vary according to project.

Tips: "Become acquainted with audiovisual needs, such as video graphics, slide-to-video transfer, etc." Common mistakes in showing a portfolio include "showing photocopies, not being organized and using a hard sell."

JANUARY PRODUCTIONS, INC., 210 6th Ave., Hawthorne NJ 07507. (201)423-4666. Art Director: Karen Neulinger. Estab. 1973. AV producer. Serves clients in education. Produces videos, sound filmstrips and read-along books and cassettes.

Needs: Assigns 1-5 jobs/year. Works with 1-5 freelance illustrators/year. "While not a requirement, an artist living in the same geographic area is a plus." Works on assignment only, "although if someone had a project already put together, we would consider it." Uses freelancers mainly for illustrating children's books. Also uses artists for artwork for filmstrips, sketches for books and layout work.

First Contact & Terms: Send query letter with resume, tearsheets, photocopies and photographs. To show a portfolio, call to schedule an appointment. Portfolio should include original/final art, color and tearsheets. Pays for design and illustration by the project. No originals returned following publication. Buys all rights.

Tips: "Include children-oriented drawings in your portfolio."

J. M. KESSLINGER & ASSOCIATES, 37 Saybrook Place, Newark NJ 07102. (201)623-0007. President: Joe Dietz. Advertising agency. Serves business-to-business clients.
Needs: Uses 1-2 freelance illustrators/month for illustration, mechanicals, direct mail, brochures, flyers, trade magazines and newspapers. Prefers local artists. Works on assignment only.
First Contact & Terms: Phone for appointment. Prefers photostats, tearsheets, slides as samples. Samples returned by SASE only if requested. Reports only if interested. Does not return original artwork to artist unless contracted otherwise. Negotiates pay. Pays by the hour, $15-50 average. Pay range depends on the type of freelance work, i.e. mechanicals vs. creative. Considers complexity of project, client's budget, skill and experience of artist and rights purchased when establishing payment.

OPTASONICS PRODUCTIONS, 186 8th St., Creskill NJ 07626. (201)871-4192. President: Jim Brown. Specializes in graphics, typesetting, multi-image, audio for AV, displays, and exhibits. Clients: industry and theatre.
Needs: Works with varied number of freelance artists/year. Prefers local artists. Works on assignment only. Uses artists for advertising, brochure and catalog design and illustration; and graphics for multi-image slide shows.
First Contact & Terms: Send query letter with brochure/flyer, business card or resume which will be kept on file. Negotiates payment.

RESULTS, INC., 30 Park Ave., Rutherford NJ 07070. (201)933-1222. Creative Director: D. Green. Estab.1954. Ad agency. Full-service agency specializing in print, collateral, graphic arts and image campaigns. Specializes in real estate and computer software. Current clients include Hartz Mountain, Alfred Sanzari and SKF.
Needs: Works with 3 freelance illustrators and 3 freelance designers/month. Uses freelancers mainly for (brochure) design. Also uses artists for brochure illustration, print ad design, storyboards and logos. 70% of work is with print ads.
First Contact & Terms: Send query letter with photocopies, photographs and slides. Samples are filed or are returned. Reports back to the artist only if interested. To show a portfolio mail tearsheets and final reproduction/product; include color and b&w samples. Consider complexity of project, client's budget and skill and experience of artist when establishing payment. Rights purchased vary accoring to project.

*STARBUCK CREATIVE SERVICES, 26 Steven Tr., West Orange NJ 07052. Senior Vice President: B. Siegel. Ad agency. Clients: health care. Client list provided for SASE.
Needs: Works with 2-5 freelance artists/year. Mainly use freelance talent for medical and pharmaceutical advertising, illustration and photography. Also uses artists for special projects and back-up.
First Contact & Terms: Send query letter with brochure, resume, business card and photostats, photographs, slides or tearsheets to be kept on file. Samples not filed are returned by SASE only if requested. Reports within 3 weeks. Write for appointment to show portfolio. Pays for design and illustration by the project. Considers complexity of the project, client's budget, skill and experience of artist, geographic scope for the finished product, turnaround time and rights purchased when establishing payment. Rights purchased vary according to project.

TAA INC., 65 Horse Hill Rd., Cedar Knolls NJ 07927. (201)267-2670. Production Manager: Lenear Carter. In-house ad agency. Clients: pharmaceutical marketing.
Needs: Assigns 3 freelance jobs/year. Works with 1 freelance illustrator/month. Works on assignment only. Uses artists for work on direct mail packages, brochures and posters.
First Contact & Terms: Send query letter with brochure to be kept on file. Samples not kept on file are returned only if requested. Reports only if interested. Write to schedule an appointment to show a portfolio. Pays for design by the hour, $25 minimum or by the project, $400 minimum. Pays for illustration by the project, negotiated. Considers "my own judgment on what job is worth before the work is done" when establishing payment. "If unforeseen complications arise, artist must tell me."
Tips: "Artists should know something about the company before they come in."

*TECHNICAL ART FOR INDUSTRY, 147 Williamson Ave., Bloomfield NJ 07003. (201)748-4334. Executive Manager/Sales: Douglas Quinn. Estab. 1985. Ad agency. Full-service, multimedia firm. Specializes in business-to-business. Product specialties are health care, heavy industry electronics, aerospace and defense.
Needs: Approached by 10 freelance artists/month. Works with 5-6 freelance illustrators and 2-3 freelance designers/month. Prefers artists with experience in airbrush/retouching, exployed view architectural, tech writers/Japanese translations and German translation. Uses freelance artists for mechanicals/art/copy. Also uses freelance artists for brochure, catalog, print ad and slide illustration, mechanicals and retouching. 85% of work is with print ads.
First Contact & Terms: Send query letter with photocopies, resume and photographs. Samples are filed and are not returned. Does not report back. Call to schedule an appointment to show a portfolio. Portfolio should include original/final art. "Sketches are as important to us as final art." Pays for design by the hour, $10-30; by the project, $100-2,000. Pays for illustration by the hour, $10-30; by the project, $50-2,000. Buys all rights.

Tips: "Don't send too many samples, 10-12 should do it. And work should be clear and portfolios should be a size easy to handle. Always do your very best no matter what the budget is. Always submit sketches or comps which best exhibit your talents. Whether interviewing or delivering your job, always keep in mind: Presentation Presentation Presentation."

TPS VIDEO SERVICES, Box 1233, Edison NJ 08818. (201)287-3626. Contact: R.S. Burks. Video production firm. Clients: industrial, broadcast.
Needs: Works with 50 freelance artists/year. Assigns 200 freelance jobs/year. Works on assignment only. Uses freelance artists for brochure design, P-O-P displays, mechanicals, retouching, animation, posters, lettering, logos and charts/graphs.
First Contact & Terms: Send query letter with resume and any type of sample. "Must have SASE included for return." Samples are filed. Reports back within 1 week only if interested. Write to schedule an appointment to show a portfolio.

*VAMCOM ADVERTISING, 202 Johnson Rd., Morris Plains NJ 07950. (201)539-1388. FAX: (201)539-2570. Executive Art Director: Dennis Simmons. Ad agency and PR firm. Full-service, multimedia firm. Specializes in magazine ads and collaterals. Product specialties are technical, medical and financial. Current clients include: AT&T, Employees Federal Credit Union, National Tourism Organization of Malta and Panasonic Industrial Company.
Needs: Approached by 2-3 freelance artists/month. Works with 1 freelance illustrator and 1 freelance designer/month. Works on assignment only. Uses freelance artists mainly for design. Also uses freelance artists for brochure and print ad design and illustration, mechanicals and retouching.
First Contract & Terms: Send query letter with photocopies and tearsheets. Samples are filed. Reports back to the artist only if interested. Call to schedule an appointment to show a portfolio. Portfolio should include thumbnails, roughs and original/final art. Pays for design by the hour, $15-25. Pays for illustration by the project. Rights purchased vary according to project.

New York

ACKERMAN ADVERTISING COMMUNICATIONS INC., 31 Glen Head Rd., Glen Head NY 11545. (516)759-3000. Creative Director: Skip Ackerman. Art Director: Fred Appel. Estab. 1973. Serves clients in food, finance and tourism.
Needs: Works with 12 freelance illustrators and 10 freelance designers/year. Local artists only. Uses artists for layout, paste-up, illustration and retouching for newspapers, TV, magazines, transit signage, billboards, collateral, direct mail and P-O-P displays. 85% of work is with print ads.
First Contact & Terms: Arrange interview. No originals returned. Pays by the project.

*WALTER F. CAMERON ADVERTISING INC., 50 Jericho Tpk., Jericho NY 11753. (516)333-2500. FAX: (516)333-2524. Art Director: Steven Levine. Estab. 1960. Ad agency. Full-service, multimedia firm. Specializes in magazine ads, collaterals and documentaries. Current clients include: G. Fried Carpet and Harrows Rolls.
Needs: Approached by 10-20 freelance artists/month. Works with 2 freelance illustrators and 2-4 freelance designers/month. Prefers local artists only with experience in automotive and retail. Uses freelance artists mainly for mechanicals/design comps for presentation. Also uses freelance artists for brochure, catalog and print ad design and illustration, storyboards, animatics, mechanicals, retouching, posters and logos. 90% of work is with print ads.
First Contact & Terms: Send query letter with brochure, photocopies, SASE, resume, photographs, tearsheets, photostats and slides. Samples are filed or are returned by SASE only if requested by artist. Reports back to the artist only if interested. Call, write to schedule an appointment to show a portfolio or mail appropriate materials: thumbnails, roughs, original/final art, b&w and color comps. Pays for design by the hour, $15-25; by the day, $100-150. Pays for illustration by the project, $100-3,000. Buys all rights.

*CHANNEL ONE PRODUCTIONS, INC., 82-03 Utopia Pkwy., Jamaica Estates NY 11432. (718)380-2525. President: Burton M. Putterman. AV firm. "We are a multimedia, film and video production company for broadcast, image enhancement and P-O-P displays." Clients: multi-national corporations, recreational industry and PBS.
Needs: Works with 25 freelance artists/year. Assigns 100 jobs/year. Prefers local artists. Works on assignment only. Uses freelance artists mainly for work on brochures, catalogs, P-O-P displays, animation, direct mail packages, motion pictures, logos and advertisements.
First Contact & Terms: Send query letter with resume, slides and photographs. Samples are not filed and are returned by SASE. Reports back within 2 weeks only if interested. Call to schedule an appointment to show a portfolio, which should include original/final art, final reproduction/product, slides, video disks and videotape. Pays for design by the project, $400 minimum. Considers complexity of project and client's budget when establishing payment. Rights purchased vary according to project.

*FASTFORWARD COMMUNICATIONS INC., 30 Virginia Rd., N. White Plains NY 10603. (914)684-0555. FAX: (914)684-0563. Vice President: J. Martorano. Estab. 1986. Ad agency and PR firm. Specialties are high technology and entertainment. Current clients include Six Flags, Nynex and AT&T.
Needs: Approached by 6 freelance artists/month. Works with 1 freelance illustrator and 1-2 freelance designers/month. Works on assignment only. Uses freelance artists mainly for Macintosh work. Also uses freelance artists for brochure and catalog design and illustration and TV/film graphics. 90% of work is with printed materials.
First Contact & Terms: Send query letter with samples, rates and resume. Samples are filed or returned by SASE. Reports back to the artist only if interested. Mail appropriate materials: thumbnails and roughs and b&w or color tearsheets. Pays for design and illustration by the project. Buys all rights or rights purchased vary according to project.

HERB GROSS & COMPANY, 84 Edgerton St., Rochester NY 14607. (716)244-3711. Producer/Director: Jim Hughes. Ad agency. "We are an ad agency/production company specializing in consumer and retail advertising. We are highly experienced in film, TV, radio and music production." Clients: retail chains, sporting goods, optical, automotive of any kind, office supplies and bedding.
Needs: Works with approximately 6 freelance artists/year; assigns 35 freelance jobs/year. Prefers experienced, flexible artists. Uses artists for brochure, catalog, newspaper and magazine ad illustration, mechanicals, billboards, direct mail packages and lettering.
First Contact & Terms: Send query letter with resume and tearsheets. Samples are filed and are not returned. Reports back only if interested. To show a portfolio, mail final reproduction/product, color and b&w photostats, tearsheets and photographs. Pays for design and illustration by the hour, $25 minimum; or by the project. Considers complexity of project, client's budget, turnaround time, skill and experience of artist and rights purchased when establishing payment. Buys all rights.

*ROBERT HABER ASSOCIATES, 40 Catlin Ave., Staten Island NY 10304. (718)780-3191. Director: Robert Haber. Estab. 1980. AV firm. Full-service, multimedia firm. Specializes in exhibition design for museums and industry. Current clients include: Staten Island Children's Museum and Newark Museum.
Needs: Approached by 3-4 freelance artists/month. Works with 1 freelance illustrator and 2 freelance designers/month. Works on assignment only. Also uses freelance artists for brochure and catalog design and illustration, print ad design, slide illustration, mechanicals and posters. 25% of work is with print ads.
First Contact & Terms: Send query letter with brochure, SASE, resume and slides. Samples are filed. Reports back within 2 weeks. Write to schedule an appointment to show a portfolio. Portfolio should include thumbnails, roughs, b&w and color slides. Pays for design by the project, $500-2,000. Pays for illustration by the project, $500-3,000. Rights purchased vary according to project.
Tips: "It is important that initial inquiry be via letter. The company will acknowledge all letter replies within 2 weeks."

HUMAN RELATIONS MEDIA, 175 Tompkins Ave., Pleasantville NY 10570. (914)769-7496. Editor-in-Chief: Michael Hardy. AV firm. Clients: junior and senior high schools, colleges, hospitals, personnel departments of business organizations.
Needs: Works with 5 freelance artists/year. Prefers local artists. Uses artists for illustration for videotape. "It is helpful if artists have skills pertaining to science-related topics." Computer graphics preferred for video, science illustration for artwork.
First Contact & Terms: Send query letter with resume and samples to be kept on file. Samples not filed are returned by SASE. Reports back only if interested. Call for appointment to show portfolio, which should include videotape, slides or tearsheets. Pays for illustration by the project, $65-1,500. Considers complexity of the project, number of illustrations in project, client's budget, skill and experience of artist and turnaround time when establishing payment. Rights purchased vary according to project.
Tips: "It is important that samples are seen before face-to-face interviews. We look for a strong, simple graphic style since the image may be on screen only 10 seconds. We require the ability to research and illustrate scientific subjects accurately."

McANDREW ADVERTISING, 2125 St. Raymond Ave., Bronx NY 10462. (212)892-8660. Art/Creative Director: Robert McAndrew. Estab. 1961. Ad agency. Clients: industrial and technical firms. Assigns 200 jobs and buys 120 illustrations/year.
Needs: Works with 5 freelance illustrators and 2 freelance designers/year. Uses mostly local artists. Uses freelance artists mainly for stationery design, direct mail, brochures/flyers and trade magazines. Prefers realistic, precise style. Prefers pen & ink, airbrush and occasionally markers. 50% of work is with print ads.
First Contact & Terms: Query with photocopies, business card and brochure/flyer to be kept on file. Samples not returned. Reports in 1 month. No originals returned to artist at job's completion. Call or write to schedule an appointment to show a portfolio, which should include roughs and final reproduction/product. Pays for illustration and design by the project, $35-300. Considers complexity of project, client's budget and skill and experience of artist when establishing payment.

Tips: Artist needs an "understanding of a product and the importance of selling it."

McCUE ADVERTISING & PUBLIC RELATIONS INC., 91 Riverside Dr., Binghamton NY 13905. Contact: Donna McCue. Ad/PR firm. Clients: retailers, nonprofit and industry.
Needs: Artists with at least 2 professional assignments only. Uses freelance artists mainly for work on direct mail, television, brochures or flyers, trade magazines, newspapers, mechanicals and logo design.
First Contact & Terms: Send a query letter with resume, brochure, flyer, business card and tearsheets to be kept on file. No originals returned at job's completion. Negotiates payment.

MESSER & SUSSLIN & OTHERS, INC., 264 N. Middletown Rd., Pearl River NY 10965. (914)735-3030. Senior Art Directors: Tony Vela, and Dan Susslin. Estab. 1973. Ad agency, "heavy in print." Current clients include Volvo, Western Union and English Leather.
Needs: Works with 2 freelance illustrators/month. Prefers local artist only with experience in illustration. Also uses artists for brochure, print ad and slide illustration; animatics; animation; retouching and lettering. 50% of work is with print ads.
First Contact & Terms: Send query letter with brochure and tear sheets. Samples are filed and are not returned. Reports back to the artist only if interested. Call to schedule an appointment to show a portfolio, which should include tearsheets, final reproduction/product; include color and b&w samples. Pays for illustration by the project, $200-5,000. Considers complexity of project, client's budget, skill and experience of artist and how work will be used when establishing payment. Rights purchased vary according to project.
Tips: "Have a good portfolio and a cooperative attitude."

THE NOTEWORTHY CO., 100 Church St., Amsterdam NY 12010. (518)842-2660. Contact: Carol Constantino. Advertising specialty manufacturer. Clients: advertising specialty jobbers with clients in health fields, real estate, banks, chain stores, state parks and community service groups. Buys 25 illustrations/year.
Needs: Uses artists for catalogs, packaging, litterbags, coloring books and pamphlets.
First Contact & Terms: Query with samples and SASE. Reports in 2 weeks. Provide resume and brochures to be kept on file for future assignments. No originals returned to artist at job's completion. Pays $200 minimum, litterbag design.

RICHARD-LEWIS CORP., Box 598, Scarsdale NY 10583. President: R. Byer. Product specialists are: machinery, tools, publishing, office supplies, chemicals, detergent, film and printing supplies.
Needs: Local artists only. Uses artists for illustration, retouching and some ad layout and mechanicals. Prefers airbrush and marker.
First Contact & Terms: Query with resume or arrange interview to show portfolio. Include SASE. Reports in 2-3 weeks. Pays by the hour; negotiates pay.

RONAN, HOWARD, ASSOCIATES, INC., 11 Buena Vista Ave., Spring Valley NY 10977-3040. (914)356-6668. Director: Howard Ronan. Ad/PR firm. Clients: video production products, lighting products, electronic components, book and video publishers and slide and filmstrip lab services.
Needs: Works with 2-3 freelance artists/year. Uses freelance artists mainly for mechanicals, retouching, charts/graphs and AV presentations.
First Contact & Terms: Send query letter. "Samples and/or other material will not be returned. Please do not send unordered material with a demand for return. It is an unwarranted burden on our shipping department." SASE. Reports immediately. Pays $25 minimum for illustrations, layout, lettering, paste-up, retouching and mechanicals for newspapers, magazines, catalogs and P-O-P displays. Pays promised fee for unused assigned illustrations.

*MICHAEL W. SCHOEN CO., 455 Central Ave., Scarsdale NY 10583. (914)472-4740. FAX: (914)472-4741. Owner: M. Schoen. Ad agency. Full-service, multimedia firm. Specializes in magazine ads and collaterals. Product specialty is industrial.
Needs: Prefers local artists only with experience in airbrush product illustration and ad agency experience. Works on assignment only. Also uses freelance artists for brochure, catalog and print ad design and illustration, mechanicals and retouching.
First Contact & Terms: Send query letter with resume. Samples are not filed and are returned by SASE only if requested by artist. Reports back to the artist only if interested. Call to schedule an appointment to show a portfolio. Pays for design and illustration by the project. Buys all rights.

*TOBOL GROUP, INC., 33 Great Neck Rd., Great Neck NY 11021. (516)466-0414. FAX: (516)466-0776. Estab. 1981. Ad agency. Product specialties are "50/50 business/consumer." Curent clients include: Weight Watchers, Republic Electronics, Mainco, Summit Mfg., Doxon, Inc. and Computer Breakthroughs.
Needs: Approached by 2 freelance artists/month. Works with 1 freelance illustrator and 1 freelance designer/ month. Works on assignment only. Also uses freelance artists for brochure, catalog and print ad design and illustration, mechanicals, retouching, billboards, posters, TV/film graphics, lettering and logos. 35% of work is with print ads.

First Contact & Terms: Send query letter with SASE and tearsheets. Samples are filed or are returned by SASE. Reports back within 1 month. Call to schedule an appointment to show a portfolio. Mail appropriate materials: thumbnails, roughs, original/final art, b&w and color tearsheets and transparencies. Pays for design by the hour, $25 minimum; by the project, $100-800. Pays for illustration by the project, $300-1,500. Negotiates rights purchased.

WALLACK & WALLACK ADVERTISING, INC., 33 Great Neck Rd., Great Neck NY 11021. (516)487-3974. Art Director: John Napolitano. Estab. 1982. Ad agency. "We specialize in promotion programs, image through printed materials." Clients: fashion eyewear, entertainment, health and fitness and industrial.
Needs: Works with 6 illustrators/year. Prefers artist with experience in product illustration. Uses artists for mechanicals; brochure, catalog and print ad illustration. Mechanical and print production skills are important. 50% of work is with print ads.
First Contact & Terms: Send query letter with tearsheets and photocopies to be kept on file. Samples returned only if requested. Reports only if interested. To show a portfolio, mail b&w and color roughs, tearsheets and final reproduction/product. Pays for design by the project, $150-1,500. Pays for illustration by the project, $150-5,000. Considers complexity of the project, client's budget, skill and experience of artist, turnaround time, geographic scope for the finished product, and rights purchased when establishing payment. Rights purchased vary according to project.
Tips: "Promote what you're proficient at. Allow potential clients the time to know you and your work (6 to 10 mailings). Follow-ups should be courteous and business like. If you're good, there's work for you. Neatness counts; if your handwriting is bad, type. Show work you're proud of, not work you think will impress."

WOLF MANSFIELD BOLLING ADVERTISING, INC., 506 Delaware Ave., Buffalo NY 14202. (716)854-2762. Executive Art Director: Tod Martin. Ad/PR firm, marketing communications. Serves clients in a variety of industries.
Needs: Assigns a minimum of 3 freelance jobs; buys 25 illustrations/year. Uses artists for illustrations, mechanicals, layout and retouching.
First Contact & Terms: Local artists primarily. Works on assignment only. Query with resume and arrange interview to show portfolio. Especially looks for "neatness and creativity of presentation." Include SASE. Reports in 3 weeks. Provide business card, brochure/flyer or resume to be kept on file for possible future assignments. Pays $12-50/hour.

New York City

*A.V. MEDIA CRAFTSMAN, INC., Room 600, 110 E. 23rd St., New York NY 10010. (212)228-6644. President: Carolyn Clark. Estab. 1967. AV firm. Full-service, multimedia firm. Specializes in slide shows, training videos and related brochures (educational). Product specialties are consumer and fashion forecasts. Current clients include: J.C. Penney Co., DuPont, Mountain Publishers and John Wiley & Co.
Needs: Approached by 20 or more freelance artists/month. Works with 2 freelance illustrators and 2 freelance designers/year. Prefers local artists only with experience in mechanicals for both slides or 4-color separations, (Mac Plus-Pagemaker). Works on assignment only. Uses freelance artists for mechanicals—traditional and Mac Pagemaker. Also uses freelance artists for brochure illustration, catalog design and mechanicals.
First Contact & Terms: Send resume, a few photocopied samples of your work and list of clients. Samples are filed or are not returned. Reports back to the artist only if interested. Pays for design by the hour, $10-15 (mechanicals); $18-20 per hour for Pagemaker. Pays for illustration by the project. Rights purchased vary according to project.

ADELANTE ADVERTISING INC., 386 Park Ave. S, New York NY 10016. (212)696-0855. President/Art Director: Sy Davis. Estab. 1973. Ad agency. Clients: national consumer. Client list available.
Needs: Works with 50 freelance illustrators and 5 freelance designers/year. Seeks experienced professionals. Sometimes works on assignment only. Uses artists for a variety of jobs. 40% of work is with print ads.
First Contact & Terms: Send query letter, brochure, resume and samples to be kept on file. Prefers photographs, slides or tearsheets as samples. Samples not filed are not returned. Reports only if interested. Call for appointment to show portfolio. Pays by the project, $150-5,000. Considers complexity of the project, client's budget, skill and experience of artist, geographic scope for the finished product and turnaround time when establishing payment. Rights purchased vary according to project.
Tips: "Be unique in style."

ANITA HELEN BROOKS ASSOCIATES, PUBLIC RELATIONS, 155 E. 55th St., New York NY 10022. (212)755-4498. President: Anita Helen Brooks. PR firm. Clients: fashion, "society," travel, restaurant, political and diplomatic and publishing. Special events, health and health campaigns.

Needs: Number of freelance jobs assigned/year varies. Works on assignment only. Uses artists for consumer magazines, newspapers and press releases. "We're currently using more abstract designs."
First Contact & Terms: Call for appointment to show portfolio. Reports only if interested. Payment determined by client's needs. Considers client's budget and skill and experience of artist when establishing payment.
Tips: Artists interested in working with us must provide "rate schedule, partial list of clients and media outlets. We look for graphic appeal when reviewing samples."

CANON & SHEA ASSOCIATES, INC., Suite 1500, 224 W. 35th St., New York NY 10001. (212)564-8822. Art Director: Jackie Elswaby. Estab. 1978. Ad/PR/marketing firm. Clients: business-to-business and financial services.
Needs: Assigns 20-40 freelance jobs and buys 50-60 freelance illustrations/year. Works with 20-30 freelance illustrators and 2-3 freelance designers/year. Mostly local artists. Mainly uses freelancers for mechanicals and illustrations. 85% of work is with print ads.
First Contact & Terms: Send query letter with brochure showing art style or resume and tearsheets. To show a portfolio, mail original/final art or write to schedule an appointment. Pays by the hour: $25-35, animation, annual reports, catalogs, trade and consumer magazines; $25-50, packaging; $50-250, corporate identification/graphics; $10-28, layout, lettering and paste-up.
Tips: "Artists should have business-to-business materials as samples and should understand the marketplace. Do not include fashion or liquor ads. Common mistakes in showing a portfolio include showing the wrong materials, not following up and lacking understanding of the audience."

THE CHRISTOPHERS, 12 E. 48th St., New York NY 10017. (212)759-4050. Editor: Joseph R. Thomas. Estab. 1945. Multimedia public service organization engaging in various publishing and TV ventures.
Needs: Works with 3 freelance artists/year. Prefers local artists with experience in nonprofit field. Works on assignment only. Uses freelance artwork mainly for pamphlets and books. Also uses freelance artists for brochure design and illustration and direct mail packages.
First Contact & Terms: Send query letter with brochure showing art style. Samples are filed or are returned by SASE. Reports back within 1 week. Pays for design and illustration by the project, $150 minimum. Buys all rights.

EFFECTIVE COMMUNICATION ARTS, INC., 221 W. 57th St., New York NY 10019. (212)333-5656. Vice President: W. J. Comcowich. Estab. 1965. AV firm. Produces films, videotapes and interactive videodiscs on science, medicine and technology. Specialize in pharmaceuticals, medical devices and electronics. Current clients include Pfizer, Inc., ICI Pharma, AT&T and Burroughs Wellcome.
Needs: Works with 2 freelance illustrators and 4 freelance designers/month. Prefers artist with experience in science and medicine. Works on assignment only. Uses freelancers mainly for animation. Also uses artists for brochure design, storyboards, slide illustration, mechanicals and TV/film graphics.
First Contact & Terms: Send query letter with resume, photographs and videotape. Samples are filed or are returned only if requested by artist. Reports back to the artist only if interested. Write to schedule an appointment to show a portfolio, which should include original/final art and videotape. Pays for design by the project; by the day, $200-350. Pays for illustration by the project, $150-750. Considers complexity of project, client's budget and skill and experience of artist when establishing payment. Buys all rights.
Tips: "Show good work; have good references."

*ELCON COMMUNICATIONS, 38 W. 38th St., New York NY 10018. (212)768-0073. FAX: (212)768-0079. Creative Director: Neil. Estab. 1988. Ad agency. Full-service, multimedia firm.
Needs: Approached by 5-10 freelance artists/month. Works with 2-5 freelance illustrators and 2-5 freelance designers/month. Prefers local artists only. Works on assignment only. 35% of work is with print ads.
First Contact & Terms: Send query letter with photocopies and samples. Samples are filed and are not returned. Reports back to the artist only if interested. Call or write to schedule an appointment to show a portfolio. Portfolio should include original/final art and tearsheets. Buys all rights or rights purchased vary according to project.

ERICKSEN/BASLOE ADVERTISING, LTD., 12 W. 37th St., New York NY 10018. Director of Creative Services: Catherine M. Reiss. Full-service Ad agency providing all promotional materials and commercial services for clients. Clients: entertainment, home video, TV, TV syndication, movies, etc.
Needs: Works with 50 freelance artists/year. Assigns 50 jobs/year. Works on assignment only. Uses freelance artists mainly for illustration, advertising, video packaging, brochures, catalogs, trade magazines, P-O-P displays, mechanicals, posters, lettering and logos. "Must be able to render celebrity likenesses." Prefers oils and colored pencil.
First Contact & Terms: Contact through artist's agent or send query letter with brochure or tearsheets and slides. Samples are filed and are not returned unless requested; unsolicited samples are not returned. Reports back within 1 week if interested or when artist needed for a particular project. Does not report back to all

Close-up

Clare Wood
Illustrator

When asked to describe one of her exhilarating experiences as a freelance illustrator, Clare Wood speaks of an event fairly early in her career. Five years ago, when she was doing editorial illustration for publications such as *McCall's, Redbook, Parents* and *The New York Times*, the art director from a major national magazine called at 11:30 one night when she was in bed with the flu. He was desperate for an illustrator to do four head and shoulder black-and-white portraits of royal family members by the next morning. "I thought it was a joke at first," she says. She explained that she was ill but would call a couple of her colleagues to see if they were available. When he said the fee would be $2,000, "it was an extraordinary rush; it was hysterical to think of earning this mind-boggling amount overnight. So I said 'okay,' and hung up. My hand didn't leave the phone; I just waited a few minutes and said no one else was available, but I was."

That art director had been in a bind and while this situation is unusual for editorial, it is, according to Wood, typical of advertising where the days are more hectic and longer. "During a massive advertising project I may be working seven days a week for weeks. I've had art directors calling me at 10 o'clock at night, on the weekends. You've got to be always available for them."

Her first major advertising assignment, a couple of years ago, was a full-color 15-piece project for Sharp Electronics. The art director had seen her ad in the *Adweek Portfolio*, called her a couple of days before Christmas and needed the assignment done by New Year's. "I needed the money and wanted to break into advertising. I was willing to sacrifice, really kill myself and work hard.

"If art directors find that you're pleasant to work with and willing to make changes, even at the last minute even if they're a little unreasonable, they're going to want to work with you, because they know if they're in a pinch they can depend on you. They want to make sure you're reliable and come through with a product they're happy with because their jobs depend on it."

Other characteristics of advertising she mentions are that the artist is unable to conceptualize because the client has usually already been sold a particular image. And that agencies are often looking for simplified, somewhat bland pictures of "perfect, beautiful people and perfect, beautiful things." Also she says one must satisfy "the account executive, the writer, many others from the agency, plus the committee from the client." As a result, "you end up doing a lot more at the rough stage. Then there are a lot more redos and changes, even on the finals." She says this leads to "a lot more time and a lot more work" and the "artwork by the end product often becomes not what I would have initially considered my creation."

Of course there are certain advantages to working in this industry. Because of the good budgets that ad agencies have to work with, she says she "can do the job the way it deserves to be done." She can hire models and photographers so she has optimal references from which to draw and an assistant to help her with such things as packaging. She has heard that due to the state of the economy and the high expense of photography, more art directors are now turning to illustrators.

When she was just starting, she says, "I couldn't figure it out, why my phone wasn't ringing. I didn't advertise, didn't understand how important that is. It was desperation finally—and other illustrators persuaded me that it was necessary."

She took out an ad in the *Graphic Artists Guild Directory of Illustration* and the *Adweek Portfolio* and now advertises in *RSVP*, which she says has been "fabulous for her." These directories not only expose her work to art directors who regularly consult them, but also leave her with 1,000-2,000 tearsheets to use as samples. She also buys mailing lists which are updated every three months "because art directors in advertising move around so much." She does not use computer printout labels which she thinks are bound to go unnoticed because they look like junk mail, but rather takes great care in having each envelope hand addressed. "I try to make it look personal."

Her way is time consuming and the cost of about $2,500 for each ad as well as the stamps she uses for her mailings is "a chunk of change," but well worth it she believes. From her last mailing of 400, she says she only got one phone call which lead to one job—"but it was a $12,000 job, so I was very happy, thrilled." While she has been too busy to send out mailings this often, she thinks it really ought to be done 2-3 times a year.

When speaking of portfolios, she passes on the advice she received from one of her illustration instructors: "Only put into your portfolio what you really love to do and then find the market that's good for it. She says it is also best to have a few samples of top quality rather than a lot of mediocre ones. "When I started out, I had only six pieces, but I felt they were really my best—none of them had been printed yet, but they really knocked people out because I had put a lot of myself into them. I had them photographed by a top quality place, which took some money that I didn't have at the time. But I just bit the bullet and did it because presentation is very important."

She says when an art director requests to see her portfolio, she follows up with a phone call the day after sending it to ask if there is anything else the art director would like to see. She says one could easily miss the job if, for example, the art director is looking for a flower sample and the flower greeting card is not in the portfolio.

Clare Wood

This ad of Wood's appears in the Graphic Artists Guild's Directory of Illustration. Smucker's was not a client, rather this illustration was a self-assignment for a portfolio piece. "Generally speaking," Wood says, "art directors call and say, 'I saw your [creative directory] ad piece and it really stood out. We wanted something realistic but with a difference.' " The illustration of "people seems to be my forte," she says, "and also creating a warm, emotional mood."

Another important piece of advice is: "One thing I've learned from being burned a lot—that a contract at the very beginning of the job is very important to protect yourself. Before I was smart enough, my contract didn't have a lot in it. My mistake was that I used to feel embarrassed to bring all these things up at the beginning. I wanted to have a nice relationship with the art director. I didn't want to bring up all these unpleasant subjects like kill fees and extra money for extra work. I learned to my chagrin that it was more painful in the middle of the job, if the job got cancelled for whatever reason, to have to fight for your 50 percent kill fee. It would be much less unpleasant to actually say it and get it over with in the beginning by having it in the contract." She recommends that the artist also request to get paid half of the fee in advance to cover expenses or perhaps a third up front, a third at the rough stage.

She has done a certain amount of philosophizing about the inherent tendency of people to take advantage of one another and what else she can do besides having a contract to guard against this. She has pondered whether she has trouble with the business side because women in general have a more difficult time than men discussing money, and has learned the importance of consulting with established and experienced illustrators and the Graphic Artists Guild when she is having difficulties with a particular assignment or art director. She heightens her business acumen by reading the business section of *The New York Times* and has come to accept that pleasing the client is the most important aspect of her job. While the most fulfilling remains those times when she feels "a rush, a surge of physical and emotional adrenalin, well-being and happiness" when she is doing the actual artwork.

—Lauri Miller

---

unsolicited samples. Call or write to schedule an appointment to show a portfolio; "only on request should a portfolio be sent." Pays for illustration by the project, $1,500-6,500. Considers complexity of project, client's budget, turnaround time, skill and experience of artist, how work will be used and rights purchased when establishing payment. Buys all rights and retains ownership of original.
Tips: "I need to see accurate likenesses in your portfolio." Has a portfolio-drop off policy.

FLAX/DE KRIG ADVERTISING, 9 E. 40th St., 10th floor, New York NY 10016. (212)683-3434. Art Director: Linda Ely. Estab. 1962. Clients: women's fashions, men's wear and fabrics. Assigns 100 freelance jobs and buys around 20 freelance illustrations/year.
Needs: Works with 3-5 freelance illustrators and 5-10 freelance designers/year. Uses artists for mechanicals, illustration, technical art, retouching and lettering for newspapers, magazines, fashion illustration, P-O-P displays, some cartooning and direct mail. 90% of work is with print ads.
First Contact & Terms: Local artists only. Arrange interview to show portfolio. Reports in 1 week. Pays for design by the project, $25 minimum; pays for illustration by the project, $100 minimum.
Tips: "I would like to see the artists ability, more loose comps and less school projects in a portfolio. Follow up with phone calls."

GETO & DE MILLY, INC., 130 E. 40th St., New York NY 10016. (212)686-4551. Senior Account Executive: Stuart Fischer. PR firm specializing in public relations, governmental affairs, political consulting. Clients: real estate developers and builders, nonprofit organizations and public officials.
Needs: Works with 15 freelance artists/year. Assigns 15 freelance jobs/year. Prefers local artists. Uses freelance artists for design, illustration, brochures, mechanicals, direct mail packages, lettering, charts/graphs and advertisements.
First Contact & Terms: Send query letter. Samples are not filed and are returned by SASE if requested. Reports back only if interested. Write to schedule an appointment to show a portfolio. Pays for design and illustration by the project, $250 minimum. Considers complexity of project, client's budget, turnaround time, skill and experience of artist, how work will be used and rights purchased. Rights purchased vary according to project.

GREY ADVERTISING INC., 777 3rd Ave., New York NY 10017. V.P. Art Buying Manager: Patti Harris. **Needs:** Works on assignment only. **First Contact & Terms:** Call for an appointment to show a portfolio, which should include original/final art. Pays by the project. Considers client's budget and rights purchased when establishing payment. **Tips:** "Most of our advertising is done with photography. We use illustrations on a very limited basis. Treat the work with respect and handle yourself in a businesslike fashion."

HERMAN & ASSOCIATES INC., 488 Madison Ave., New York NY 10022. (212)935-2832. CEO: Paula Herman. Estab. 1966. Serves clients in insurance, electronics/computers, travel and tourism. **Needs:** Works with 6-10 freelance illustrators/year. Works with 4 freelance designers/year. Prefers local artists who have worked on at least 2-3 professional assignments previously. Works on assignment only. Uses artists for mechanicals, illustration and retouching for newspapers and magazines. 55% of work is with print ads. **First Contact & Terms:** Send brochure showing art style and whatever best represents artist's work as samples. Samples returned by SASE. Reporting time "depends on clients." Reports back whether to expect possible future assignments. Write to schedule an appointment to show a portfolio. Pays for design by the hour, $25-35; by the project, $250 minimum; by the day, $400-500. Pays for illustration by the project, $300-2,000. **Tips:** "The illustrator should be an 'idea' contributor as well. Add to the concept or see another possiblity. Freelancers need to provide 'leave behinds,' reminders of their work. We are using more illustration, especially in the high-tech, electronics and travel-related areas (architecture, buildings, etc.) Send samples that show your versatility."

*HILL AND KNOWLTON, INC., 420 Lexington Ave., New York NY 10017. (212)697-5600. Corporate Design Group: Jim Stanton or Lorenzo Ottaviani. Estab. 1 yr.. PR firm. Full-service, multimedia firm. Specializes in annual reports, collaterals, corporate identity, advertisements. **Needs:** Works with 4-20 freelance illustrators and 2 freelance designers/month. Works on assignment only. Also uses freelance artists for storyboards, slide illustration, animatics, mechanicals, retouching and lettering. 10% of work is with print ads. **First Contact & Terms:** Send query letter with promo and samples. Samples are filed. Does not report back, in which case the artist should "keep in touch by mail – do not call." Call and drop-off only for a portfolio review. Portfolio should include dupe photographs. Pays for illustration by the project, $100-12,000. Negotiates rights purchased.

JIM JOHNSTON ADVERTISING INC., 49 W. 27th, 10th floor, New York NY 10001. (212)779-1257. Art/Creative Director: Doug Johnston. Serves clients in publishing, corporate and business-to-business. **Needs:** Works with 3-4 freelance illustrators/month. Uses artists for consumer magazines, trade magazines and newspapers. **First Contact & Terms:** Query with previously published work or samples and SASE, or arrange interview. Reports in 2 weeks. Provide tearsheets to be kept on file for possible future assignments. Payment by job: $250-6,500, annual reports; $250-2,000, billboards; $125-2,500, consumer magazines; $150-5,000, packaging; $250-1,000, P-O-P displays; $150-1,500, posters; $125-600, trade magazines; $100-1,000, letterheads; $200-1,500, trademarks; $300-2,500, newspapers. Payment by hour: $20 minimum, catalogs; $5-20, paste-up. Pays 25% of promised fee for unused assigned illustrations.

CHRISTOPHER LARDAS ADVERTISING, Box 1440, Radio City Station, New York NY 10101. (212)688-5199. President: Christopher Lardas. Estab. 1960. Ad agency. Clients: producers of paper products, safety equipment, chocolate-confectionery, real estate and writing instruments/art materials. **Needs:** Works with 3 freelance illustrators and 3 freelance designers/year. Local artists only; must have heavy experience. Works on assignment only. Uses artists for illustration, layout and mechanicals. 75% of work is with print ads. **First Contact & Terms:** Send query letter with brochure showing art style or photocopies to be kept on file. Looks for "realistic product illustrations." Samples not filed are returned only if requested. Reports back only if interested. Write for appointment to show portfolio, which should include roughs, original/final art or color and b&w tearsheets. Pays by the hour. Considers client's budget when establishing payment. Buys all rights. **Tips:** "Artists generally don't follow-up via mail! After artists make initial phone contact, we request a mail follow-up: e.g. photocopies of samples and business card for future reference. Few comply. Send examples of art you enjoy most."

MCCAFFERY & RATNER, INC., 370 Lexington Ave., New York NY 10017. (212)661-8940. Senior Art Director: John Bloch. Estab. 1983. Ad agency specializing in advertising and collateral material. Current clients include Bulova, Port Authority of New York and New Jersey, National Geographic Magazine, Windows on the World and NY Chevrolet Dealers.

Needs: Works with 6 freelance illustrators/year. Works on assignment only. Also uses artists for brochure and print ad illustration, mechanicals, retouching, billboards, posters, lettering and logos. 80% of work is with print ads.

First Contact & Terms: Send query letter with brochure, tearsheets, photostats, photocopies and photographs. Reports back to the artist only if interested. To show a portfolio, mail appropriate materials or drop off. Portfolio should include original/final art, tearsheets and photographs; include color and b&w samples. Pays for illustration by the project, $75-5,000. Considers complexity of project, client's budget, skill and experience of artist, how work will be used and rights purchased when establishing payment. Rights purchased vary according to project.

Tips: "Send mailers and drop off portfolio."

*MARINA MAHER COMMUNICATIONS, 645 Madison Ave., New York NY 10022. (212)759-7543. FAX: (212)355-6318. General Manager: Dale Kuron. Estab. 1983. AV and PR firm. Full-service multimedia firm. Specializes in mailers, A/V, brochures and collaterals. Product specialties are beauty, fashion and lifestyles. Current clients include: Procter & Gamble, Pierre Cardin and Nina Ricci. Prefers local artists only. Also uses freelance artists for brochure and catalog design and illustration, storyboards, slide illustration, mechanicals, retouching, posters, lettering, logos and letterheads.

First Contact & Terms: Send query letter with brochure, photocopies, resume, tearsheets and photostats. Samples are filed. Reports back to the artist only if interested. Call to schedule an appointment to show a portfolio. Portfolio should include "whatever specialty is." Rights purchased vary according to project.

MARTIN/ARNOLD COLOR SYSTEMS, 150 5th Ave., New York NY 10011. (212)675-7270. President: Martin Block. Vice President Marketing: A.D. Gewirtz. AV producer. Clients: industry, education, government and advertising. Produces slides, filmstrips and Vu Graphs, large blow-ups in color and b&w.

Needs: Assigns 20 jobs/year. Works with 2 freelance illustrators and 2 freelance designers/month. Works on assignment only. Uses freelance artists mainly for presentations and display.

First Contact & Terms: Send query letter with resume to be kept on file. Call or write to schedule an appointment to show a portfolio, which should include original/final art and photographs. Pays for design by the project; pays for illustration by the hour, $50 minimum. Original artwork returned to artist after publication. Negotiates rights purchased.

Tips: Artist should have "knowledge of computer graphics."

MARX MYLES GRAPHICS INC., 440 Park Ave. South, New York NY 10016. (212)683-2015. Vice President Sales: Sheldon H. Marx. Estab. 1981. Ad agency/design studio specializing in sales promotion, production and typography.

Needs: Uses freelance artists mainly for paste up ads, brochures, books and magazines. Prefers local artist only with experience in mechanicals, illustration and art design.

First Contact & Terms: Send query letter with samples. Samples are filed. Reports back within 1 week. Portfolio should include any appropriate samples. Pays for design by the hour, $10-20. Considers client's budget and skill and experience of artist when establishing payment.

MEDIA DESIGNS, 100 Park Ave., New York NY 10017. (212)818-8913. President/Creative Director: Scott Randall. Estab. 1983. Ad agency and AV firm. "We are a full-service firm providing sales materials, public image presentation, specializing in print and video production." Specializes in broadcast, media and travel.

Needs: Prefers local artists only with experience in design, production and advertising. Uses freelancers mainly for ads and collateral design. Also uses artists for brochure design, print ad design and illustration, storyboards, mechanicals and logos. 50% of work is with print ads.

First Contact & Terms: Send query letter. Samples are filed or are returned only if requested by artist. Reports back to the artist only if interested. Call or write to schedule an appointment to show a portfolio, which should include tearsheets and final reproduction/product. Pays for design by the hour, $20-25. Pays for illustration by the project, $250-750. Considers complexity of project, client's budget and skill and experience of artist when establishing payment. Rights purchased vary according to project.

 The asterisk before a listing indicates that the listing is new in this edition. New markets are often the most receptive to freelance submissions.

RUTH MORRISON ASSOCIATES, INC., 19 W. 44 St., New York NY 10036. (212)302-8886. Administrator: Maggie Minarich. Estab. 1972. PR firm. "Other assignments include logo/letterhead design, trade ads, invitations and product labels." Specializes in food, wine, home funishings, travel, hotel/restaurant, education, non-profit. Current clients include Fortnum & Mason, New Zealand Lamb Company, Liberty Imports Inc. and Christian Appalachian Project.
Needs: Prefers local artists only with experience in advertising and publishing. Uses freelancers mainly for brochure design, P-O-P materials and direct mail. Also uses artists for catalog and print ad design, mechanicals, posters, lettering and logos. 5% of work is with print ads.
First Contact & Terms: Send query letter with photocopies. Samples "of intent" are filed. Samples not filed are returned only if requested by artist. Does not report back. Write to schedule an appointment to show a portfolio, which should include original/final art. Considers complexity of project, client's budget, turnaround time, skill and experience of artist and how work will be used when establishing payment. Rights purchased vary according to project.

*MUIR CORNELIUS MOORE, INC., 79 Fifth Ave., New York NY 10003. (212)463-0686. Art Buyer: Sue Moseson. Estab. 1976. Specializes in business-to-business advertising, sales promotion, corporate identity, displays, direct mail and exhibits. Clients: financial, high-tech and consumer products.
Needs: Works with 25-50 freelance artists/year. Works on assignment only. Uses artists for design, illustration, mechanicals and lettering; brochures, catalogs, books, P-O-P displays, posters, direct mail packages, charts/graphs, AV materials, logos, exhibits and advertisements. 35% of work is with print ads.
First Contact & Terms: Send query letter with tearsheets and photographs to be kept on file. Prefers samples that do not have to be returned, but will return unfiled material by SASE. Reports only if interested. To show a portfolio, mail final reproduction/product and b&w tearsheets, photographs or call to schedule an appointment. Pays by the project. Considers complexity of project, client's budget, skill and experience of artist, how the work will be used, turnaround time and rights purchased when establishing payment.
Tips: "One of the more common mistakes freelancers make is a sloppy, poorly thought out presentation, containing no resume or client list."

NEWMARK'S ADVERTISING AGENCY INC., 253 W. 26th St., New York NY 10001. Art/Creative Director: Al Wasserman. Art/ad agency. Clients: manufacturing, industry, banking, leisure activity, consumer, real estate and construction firms.
Needs: Works with 1 freelance designer/every 5 months. Uses artists for illustration or cartoon and photo retouching, billboards, P-O-P display, consumer magazines, slide sets, brochures/flyers and trade magazines. Also uses artists for figure illustration, cartoons, technical art, paste-up, retouching and 3-D model building.
First Contact & Terms: Provide stat samples to be kept on file for future assignments. No originals returned to artist at job's completion. "Send repros first." Pays $8-15/hour, paste-up and $75-3,000 or more/job.

NOSTRADAMUS ADVERTISING, Suite 1128-A, 250 W. 57th St., New York NY 10107. Creative Director: B.N. Sher. Specializes in annual reports, corporate identity, publications, signage, flyers, posters, advertising and logos. Clients: ad agencies, book publishers, nonprofit organizations and politicians.
Needs: Works with 5 freelance artists/year. Uses artists for advertising design, illustration and layout; brochure design, mechanicals, posters, direct mail packages, charts/graphs, logos, catalogs, books and magazines.
First Contact & Terms: Send query letter with brochure, resume, business card, samples and tearsheets to be kept on file. Do *not* send slides as samples; will accept "anything else that doesn't have to be returned." Samples not kept on file are not returned. Reports only if interested. Call for appointment to show portfolio. Pays for design, mechanicals and illustration by the hour, $15-25 average. Considers skill and experience of artist when establishing payment.

*PHOENIX FILMS, INC., 468 Park Ave. S., New York NY 10016. (212)684-5910. President: Heinz Gelles. Vice President: Barbara Bryant. Clients: libraries, museums, religious institutions, U.S. government, schools, universities, film societies and businesses. Produces and distributes educational films.
Needs: Assigns 20-30 jobs/year. Local artists only. Uses artists for motion picture catalog sheets, direct mail brochures, posters and study guides.
First Contact & Terms: Query with samples (tearsheets and photocopies). Send SASE. Send recent samples of artwork and rates to Richard Sabol, Promotion Department. No telephone calls please. Reports in 3 weeks. Buys all rights. Keeps all original art "but will loan to artist for use as a sample." Pays for design and illustration by the hour or project. Rates negotiable. Free catalog upon written request.

PUBLIC RELATIONS ANALYSTS INC., 210 E. 47 St., New York NY 10017. (212)838-6330. Chairman: Eileen Milling. Multimedia PR consultants. Clients: technical products, education and health care. Client list provided upon request with an SASE.

Needs: Works with a few freelance artists/year. Works on assignment only. Uses freelance artists for design, mechanicals, retouching, lettering and logos.

First Contact & Terms: Send query letter with brochure or resume and tearsheets. Samples are filed. "Will contact artists only if there is a need for a specific assignment or the possibility of a job." Payment is negotiated. Considers complexity of project, client's budget, turnaround time and how work will be used when establishing payment. Rights purchased vary according to project.

Tips: "Determine if there is an immediate need for services; follow up; honor time/date of appointment; keep references current."

RICHARD H. ROFFMAN ASSOCIATES, Suite 6A, 697 West End Ave., New York NY 10025. (212)749-3647. President: Richard R. Roffman. PR firm. Clients: restaurants, art galleries, boutiques, hotels and cabarets, nonprofit organizations, publishers and all professional and business fields.

Needs: Assigns 24 freelance jobs/year. Works with 2 freelance illustrators and 2 freelance designers/month. Uses artists for consumer and trade magazines, brochures, newspapers, stationery, posters and press releases.

First Contact & Terms: Send query letter, SASE (for response) and resume to be kept on file; call or write for appointment to show portfolio. Do not mail samples. Prefers photographs and photostats as samples. Reports only if interested. Pays by the hour, $10-25 average; by the project, $75-250 average; by the day, $150-250 average. Considers complexity of project, client's budget and skill and experience of artist when establishing payment. Buys first rights or one-time rights. Returns material only if SASE enclosed.

Tips: "Realize that affirmative answers cannot always be immediate—do have patience. If you desire an answer in writing please enclose SASE for the reply, thank you."

*PETER ROGERS ASSOCIATES, 355 Lexington Ave., New York NY 10017. (212)599-0055. FAX: (212)682-4309. Art Directors: Laura Mandile, Tracy McFarlane and Deanne Paul. Ad agency. Full-service, multimedia firm. Specializes in magazine ads, TV commercials. Product specialties are beauty, fashion, jewelry and "any other high-end merchandise."

Needs: Approached by 20 freelance artists/month. Works with 1 freelance illustrator and 2 freelance designers/mechanical artists/month. Prefers artists with experience. Uses freelance artists for illustration, storyboards, animatics, retouching, graphics and lettering. 80% of work is with print ads.

First Contact & Terms: Send query letter with any relevant materials, mechanicals, stylists, fashion and still photographs and promo cards. Samples are filed. Call to schedule an appointment to show a portfolio or drop-off and pick-up next day. Pays for design/mechanicals by the hour, $18-30 minimum; or by the project. Pays for illustration by the hour, $25-50 or by the project. Negotiates rights purchased.

Tips: "Avoid unprofessional/sloppy presentations and 'pushiness.' Send samples or drop off book prior to calling. Prefer being contacted by reputable reps/agencies."

PETER ROTHHOLZ ASSOCIATES INC., 380 Lexington Ave., New York NY 10017. (212)687-6565. President: Peter Rothholz. PR firm. Clients: government (tourism and industrial development), publishing, pharmaceuticals (health and beauty products) and business services.

Needs: Works with 2 freelance illustrators and 2 freelance designers/month. Works on assignment only.

First Contact & Terms: Call for appointment to show portfolio, which should include resume or brochure/flyer to be kept on file. Samples returned by SASE. Reports in 2 weeks. Assignments made based on freelancer's experience, cost, style and whether he/she is local. No originals returned to artist at job's completion. Negotiates payment based on client's budget.

JASPER SAMUEL ADVERTISING, 406 W. 31st St., New York NY 10001. (212)239-9544. Art Director: Joseph Samuel. Ad agency. Clients: health centers, travel agencies, hair salons, etc.

Needs: Works with 5-10 freelance artists/year. Works on assignment only. Uses artists for advertising, brochure and catalog design, illustration and layout; product design and illustration on product.

First Contact & Terms: Send query letter with brochure, resume, business card, photographs and tearsheets to be kept on file. Samples not filed are returned. Reports within 1 month. Call or write for appointment to show portfolio. Pays by the project. Considers complexity of project and skill and experience of the artist when establishing payment.

SPACE PRODUCTIONS, 451 West End Ave., New York NY 10024. (212)986-0857. Contact: Producer. "We work in mass communications, using all types of AV materials, film, animation and TV, but the emphasis is on TV." Serves clients in advertising, industry, government and cultural and educational institutions. Produces commercials, information and entertainment programs, sales/marketing, P-O-P display and other types of properties.

Needs: Assigns 20-25 jobs/year. Uses a "dozen or more" illustrators, animators and designers/year. "No geographical restrictions, but artist-applicants should note that we are located in New York City." Uses artists for art direction, graphics, illustration, design/print and TV.

First Contact & Terms: Send resume and samples (copies, any type; subjects that suggest the individual style of an artist's work). Samples not filed are returned by SASE. Provide resume, samples, brochure/flyer, business card or tearsheets—"a small representative sampling"—to be kept on file for possible future assignments. Reports in 2 months. Pays $10-50/hour. Method and amount of payment are negotiated with the individual artist or agent. Payment depends on assignment and varies with each client's budget. Original artwork sometimes returned to artist following publication. Rights purchased vary, "depending on assignment and client."

V. STEFANELLI & ASSOCIATES, Suite 15, 409 E. 84th St., New York NY 10028. (212)439-1557. Producer: Vincent Stefanelli. Estab. 1986. Film/video producer of commercials, tapes, documentaries, fashion and music videos. Clients: advertising agencies, corporations, educators, retail, etc. Client list provided with SASE.
Needs: Works with 5 freelance artists/year. Assigns 50 jobs/year. Works on assignment only. Uses artists for design, illustration, consumer and trade magazines, P-O-P displays, mechanicals, animation, direct-mail packages, press releases, motion pictures, charts/graphs and advertisements.
First Contact & Terms: Send brochure. Samples are filed. Reports back within 3 weeks. Call to schedule an appointment to show a portfolio, which should include photographs. Pays for design and illustration by the hour, $30-75. Considers complexity of project, client's budget, turnaround time and skill and experience of artist when establishing payment. Rights purchased vary according to project.
Tips: "We are always looking for innovative styles and ideas!"

TALCO PRODUCTIONS, 279 E. 44th St., New York NY 10017. (212)697-4015. President: Alan Lawrence. TV/film producer. Clients: nonprofit organizations, industry, associations and PR firms. Produces motion pictures, videotapes and some filmstrips and sound-slide sets.
Needs: Assigns 4-10 jobs/year. Prefers local artists with professional experience.
First Contact & Terms: Send query letter with resume. SASE. Reports only if interested. Portfolio should include roughs, final reproduction/product, color, photostats and photographs. Pay varies according to assignment; on production. On some jobs, originals returned to artist after completion. Buys all rights. Considers complexity of project, client's budget and rights purchased when establishing payment.
Tips: "Do not send anything but a resume!"

*THE TARRAGANO COMPANY, Suite 303E, 200 Park Ave., New York NY 10166. (212)972-1250. President: Morris Tarragano. Ad agency and PR firm. Clients: manufacturers of products and services of all types. Media used include consumer and trade magazines, direct mail, newspapers, radio and TV.
First Contact & Terms: Write for an appointment to show portfolio and/or send resume. Selection based on review of portfolio and references. Negotiates payment based on amount of creativity required from artist and previous experience/reputation.

VAN VECHTEN & ASSOCIATES PUBLIC RELATIONS, 48 E. 64th St., New York NY 10021. (212)644-8880. President: Jay Van Vechten. PR firm. Clients: medical, consumer products, industry. Client list provided for SASE.
Needs: Assigns 20+ freelance jobs/year. Works with 2 freelance illustrators and 2 freelance designers/month. Works on assignment only. Uses artists for consumer and trade magazines, brochures, newspapers, stationery, signage, AV presentations and press releases.
First Contact & Terms: Send query letter with brochure, resume, business card, photographs or photostats. Samples not filed are returned by SASE. Reports back only if interested. Write for appointment to show a portfolio. Pays by the hour, $10-25 average. Considers client's budget when establishing payment. Buys all rights.

PETER VANE ADVERTISING, 401 Park Avenue South, New York NY 10016. (212)679-8260. Executive Vice President/Creative: Penny Vane. Estab. 1978. Ad agency. "We are an advertising agency specializing in direct marketing, providing marketing consultation, creative, production and media services to a wide range of consumer and business-to-business clients." Specializes in publishing, clubs and continuities, financial and trade. Current clients include Grolier, Highlights for Children, Medical Business Services, Scholastic, Time-Life and Playboy.
Needs: Prefers artists with experience in direct marketing. Works on assignment only. Uses freelancers mainly for direct mail, space ads and inserts. Also uses artists for brochure and print ad design and illustration, mechanicals and logos. 20% of work is with print ads.
First Contact & Terms: Send query letter with resume and photocopies. Samples are filed "if worthy of future reference" or are returned by SASE. Reports back to the artist only if interested. To show a portfolio, mail roughs, photostats and tearsheets. "Portfolios should show, whenever possible, both original concept (comp) and finished execution (printed piece)." Pays for design by the hour, $25-50. Considers complexity of project, client's budget, turnaround time, skill and experience of artist and how work will be used when establishing payment. Rights purchased vary according to project.

Tips: The most effective way for a freelancer to get started in advertising is to have "referrals, initiative and samples demonstrating transferable skills."

MORTON DENNIS WAX & ASSOCIATES INC., Suite 1210, 1560 Broadway, New York NY 10036. (212)302-5360. FAX: (212)302-5364. President: Morton Wax. Estab. 1956. PR firm. Clients: entertainment, communication arts and corporate.
Needs: Works with 10 freelance designers/year. Artists must have references and minimum 3 years of experience. Works on assignment only. Uses artists for trade magazine ads, brochures and other relevant artwork. 100% of work is with print ads.
First Contact & Terms: Send query letter with resume, photostats or tearsheets to be kept on file. Samples not filed are returned by SASE. Reports only if interested. Write for appointment to show portfolio. "We select and use freelancers on a per project basis, based on specific requirements of clients. Each project is unique." Considers complexity of project, client's budget, turnaround time and rights purchased when establishing payment. Rights vary according to project.

North Carolina

HEGE, MIDDLETON & NEAL, INC., Box 9437, Greensboro NC 27408. (919)373-0810. President: J.A. Middleton, Jr. Ad agency.
Needs: Assigns 200 freelance jobs/year. Works with 5 freelance illustrators and 5 freelance designers/month. Works on assignment only. Uses artists for consumer and trade magazines, billboards, direct mail packages, brochures, catalogs, newspapers, stationery, signage, P-O-P displays and posters.
First Contact & Terms: Send query letter with brochure, resume, business card, photographs and tearsheets to be kept on file. Samples returned by SASE if requested. Reports only if interested. Write for appointment to show portfolio. Pays by the project, $20-6,000. Considers complexity of project, client's budget, skill and experience of artist, geographic scope of finished project, turnaround time and rights purchased when establishing payment. Buys all rights.

IMAGE ASSOCIATES INC., 4314 Bland Rd., Raleigh NC 27609. (919)876-6400. President: David Churchill. Estab. 1984. AV firm. "Visual communications firm specializing in computer graphics and AV, multi-image, print and photographic applications."
Needs: Works with 1 freelance illustrator and 2 freelance designers/month. Prefers artists with experience in high-tech orientations and computer-graphics. Works on assignment only. Uses freelancers mainly for brochure design and illustration. Also uses freelance artists for print ad design and illustration, slide illustration, animation and retouching. 25% of work is with print ads.
First Contact & Terms: Send query letter with brochure, resume and tearsheets. Samples are filed or are returned by SASE only if requested by artist. Reports back to the artist only if interested. To show a portfolio, mail roughs, original/final art, tearsheets, final reproduction/product and slides. Pays for design and illustration by the hour, $35-75. Consider complexity of project, client's budget and how work will be used when establishing payment. Rights purchased vary according to project.

LEWIS ADVERTISING, INC., 1050 Country Club Ln., Rocky Mount NC 27804. (919)443-5131. Senior Art Director: Scott Brandt. Ad agency. Clients: fast food, communications, convenience stores, financial. Client list provided upon request with SASE.
Needs: Works with 20-25 freelance artists/year. Works on assignment only. Uses artists for illustration and part-time paste-up. Especially looks for "consistently excellent results, on time and on budget."
First Contact & Terms: Send query letter with resume, business card and samples to be kept on file. Call for appointment to show portfolio. Artists should show examples of previous work, price range requirements and previous employers. Samples not filed returned by SASE only if requested. Reports only if interested. Pays by project. Considers complexity of the project, client's budget, turnaround time and ability of artist when establishing payment. Buys all rights.

MORPHIS & FRIENDS, INC., Drawer 5096, 230 Oakwood Dr., Winston-Salem NC 27103. (919)723-2901. Director: Linda Anderson. Art Director: Laura Griffin. Ad agency. Clients: banks, restaurants, clothing, cable, industry and furniture.
Needs: Assigns 20-30 freelance jobs/year. Works on assignment only. Works with approximately 2 freelance illustrators/month. Uses freelance artists for consumer and trade magazines, billboards, direct mail packages, brochures and newspapers.
First Contact & Terms: Send query letter with photocopies to be kept on file. Samples not filed are returned only if requested. Reports only if interested. Call to schedule an appointment to show a portfolio, which should include roughs and final reproduction/product. Pays by the hour, $20 minimum. "Negotiate on job basis." Considers complexity of project, client's budget, skill and experience of artist, geographic scope of finished project, turnaround time and rights purchased when establishing payment. Buys all rights.
Tips: "Send a letter of introduction with a few samples to be followed up by phone call."

THOMPSON AGENCY, Suite M, 1415 South Church St., 112 S. Tyron St., Charlotte NC 28203. (704)333-8821. Contact: Joe Thompson. Ad agency. Clients: banks, resorts and soft drink, utility companies and insurance agencies.
Needs: Assigns approximately 50 freelance jobs/year. Works with 3 freelance illustrators/month. Works on assignment only. Uses freelance artists for consumer and trade magazines, billboards, direct mail packages, brochures, newspapers, signage, P-O-P displays and posters.
First Contact & Terms: Send query letter with brochure showing art style or photocopies to be kept on file. Samples returned by SASE if requested. To show portfolio, mail appropriate materials or write to schedule an appointment; portfolio should include final reproduction/product. Reports only if interested. Pays for design by the project, $500-7,500; pays for illustration by the project, $350-3,000. Considers complexity of project, client's budget, skill and experience of artist, turnaround time and rights purchased when establishing payment. Buys all rights.
Tips: "In general, we see a bolder use of ideas and techniques. We try to screen all work before appointment. Work must be professional and very creative.

*WILLIAMS/SPARLING ADVERTISING, 320 S. Elm St., Greensboro NC 27401. (919)273-9654. FAX: (919)273-1333. Contact: Scott Williams. Estab. 1987. Ad agency. Full-service, multimedia firm. Specializes in print, radio, TV production, collateral, media, special events coordination, promotion and sports/marketing. Product specialty is consumer package goods and corporate identity. Current clients include: Bank of North Carolina and United Arts Council.
Needs: Approached by 10 freelance artists/month. Works with 2 freelance illustrators and 4-6 freelance designers/month. Prefers specialists and artists with experience in all areas and wants top grade work. Uses freelance arts for brochure and print ad design and illustration, storyboards, slide illustration, animatics, animation, posters, TV/film graphics, lettering and logos. 15% of work is with print ads.
First Contact & Terms: Send query letter with brochure, photocopies, SASE and tearsheets. Samples are filed or returned by SASE. Reports back within 30 days. Mail appropriate materials: roughs and b&w and color photostats, tearsheets and transparencies. Pays for design by the hour $20-75; by the project $200-6,000, by the day, $150-400. Pays for illustration by the hour $40-100. Rights purchased vary according to project.

Ohio

BRIGHT LIGHT PRODUCTIONS, INC., Suite 810, 602 Main St., Cincinnati OH 45202. (513)721-2574. President: Linda Spalazzi. Estab. 1976. Audiovisual firm. "We are a full-service film/video communications firm producing TV commercials and corporate communications."
Needs: Works on assignment only. Uses freelancers mainly for art/design. Also uses artists for brochure and print ad design, storyboards, slide illustration, animatics, animation, TV/film graphics and logos.
First Contact & Terms: Send query letter with brochure and resume. Samples not filed are returned only if requested by artist. Write to schedule an appointment to show a portfolio, which should include roughs and photographs. Pays for design and illustration by the project. Considers complexity of project, client's budget, turnaround time, skill and experience of artist, how work will be used and rights purchased when establishing payment. Negotiates rights purchased.
Tips: "Don't give up!"

*BUTLER LEARNING SYSTEMS, 1325 W. Dorothy Lane, Dayton OH 45409. (513)298-7462. President: Don Butler. Produces training programs.
Needs: Works with 2 freelance artists/year. Local artists only. Uses freelance artists mainly for design, illustrations, catalogs and books.
First Contact & Terms: Contact by phone. Samples not filed are returned only if requested. Reports back within 7 days. Call to schedule an appointment to show portfolio, which should include thumbnails, roughs and original/final art. Payment varies. Considers complexity of project and client's budget when establishing payment. Buys all rights.

*EMERGENCY TRAINING DIVISION OF EDUCATIONAL DIRECTION, INC., Bldg. 200, 150 N. Miller Rd., Akron OH 44313. (216)836-0600. FAX: (216)836-4227. Sr. Vice President and Treasurer: Greg Spaid. Estab. 1967. AV firm. Specializes in textbooks, audiovisual slides and video training aids. Product specialty is emergency medical services. "We sell this to hospital, ambulance firms, fire departments, colleges, etc."
Needs: Approached by very few freelance artists/month. Works with 1 freelance illustrator and 1 freelance designer/month. Prefers local artists only. Works on assignment only. Uses freelance artists mainly for catalogs, ads, artwork illustrations, word slides, etc. Also uses freelance artists for brochure, catalog and print ad design and illustration, slide illustration, mechanicals and billboards. 2% of work is with print ads.
First Contact & Terms: Send query letter with brochure and resume. Samples are not filed and are returned. Reports back within 1 month. Call to schedule an appointment to show a portfolio. Pays for design by the hour. Pays for illustration by the project. Buys all rights.

FREEDMAN ADVERTISING, 814 Plum, Cincinnati OH 45202. (513)241-3900. Senior Art Director: Edward Fong. Estab. 1959. Ad agency. Full-service, multimedia firm. Product specialty consumer.
Needs: Approached by 6 freelance artists/month. Works with 2 freelance illustrators/month. Works only with artist reps. Prefers artists with experience in illustration. Works on assignment only. Also uses freelance artists for brochure design and illustration, storyboards, slide illustration, animatics, animation, mechanicals and retouching. 80% of work is with print ads.
First Contact & Terms: Send query letter with brochure and resume. Samples are filed and are not returned. Reports back within 1 week. Call to schedule an appointment to show a portfolio. Portfolio should include: thumbnails, roughs, original/final art and b&w transparencies. Pays for design by the hour, $15-20; by the project. Pays for illustration by the project $300-10,000. Buys all rights.

*HAYES PUBLISHING CO. INC., 6304 Hamilton Ave., Cincinnati OH 45224. (513)681-7559. Office Manager: Marge Lammers. AV producer/book publisher. Produces educational books, brochures and audiovisuals on human sexuality and abortion. Free catalog.
First Contact & Terms: Send slides and photographs. Samples returned by SASE. Reports in 2 weeks. Provide business card to be kept on file for possible future assignments. Pays by job.

IMAGEMATRIX, 2 Garfield Pl., Cincinnati OH 45202. (513)381-1380. President: Peter Schwartz. Total communications for business.
Needs: Works with 25 freelance artists/year. Local artists only; must have portfolio of work. Uses freelance artists for paste-up, mechanicals, airbrushing, storyboards, photography, lab work, illustration for AV; buys cartoons 4-5 times/year. Especially important is AV knowledge, computer graphics for video and slides and animation understanding.
First Contact & Terms: Works on assignment only. Artwork buy-out. Send business card and slides to be kept on file. Samples not filed are returned by SASE. Reports within 2 months. Write for appointment to show portfolio. Pays for design by the hour, $8-35; by the project, $90 minimum. Pays for illustration by the hour, $8-15; by the project, $150 minimum. Considers complexity of the project, client's budget, skill and experience of artist and turnaround time when establishing payment. Buys all rights.
Tips: "Specialize your portfolio; show an understanding of working for a 35mm final product. We are using more design for video graphics and computer graphics."

GEORGE C. INNES & ASSOCIATES, Box 1343, 110 Middle Ave., Elyria OH 44036. (216)323-4526. President: George C. Innes. Ad/art agency. Clients: industry and consumer.
Needs: Assigns 25-50 jobs/year. Works with 3-4 freelance illustrators/month. Works on assignment only. Uses freelance illustrators mainly for filmstrips, stationery design, technical illustrations, airbrush, multimedia kits, direct mail, slide sets, brochures/flyers, trade magazines, newspapers and books. Also uses freelance artists for layout and design for reports, catalogs, print ads, direct mail/publicity, brochures, displays, employee handbooks, exhibits, products, technical charts/illustrations, trademarks, logos and company publications. Prefers pen & ink, airbrush, watercolor, acrylics, oils, collage, markers and computer illustration.
First Contact & Terms: Send query letter with brochure showing art style or tearsheets, photostats, photocopies, slides and photographs. Samples not filed are not returned. Reports in 2 weeks. To show a portfolio, a freelance artist should mail appropriate materials. No originals returned to artist at job's completion. Pays for design and illustration by the hour, $5-30.

INSTANT REPLAY, 1349 E. McMillan, Cincinnati OH 45206. (514)861-7065. Contact: Director of Graphics. Estab. 1977. AV firm. "We are a full service film production/video production and video post production house with our own sound stage. We also do traditional with animation, paintbox animation with a Harry, and 3-D computer animation for broadcast groups, corporate entities and ad agencies. We do many corporate identity pieces as well as network afiliate packages, plus car dealership spots and general regional and national advertising for TV market." Current clients include Procter and Gamble, Merrell-Dow, Whirlpool, G.E. (Jernegine division), NBC, CBS, ABC, and FOX affiliates.
Needs: Works with 1 freelance designer/month. Prefers artists with experience in video production. Works on assignment only. Uses freelancers mainly for production. Also uses freelance artists for storyboards, animatics, animation and TV/film graphics. .01% of work is with print ads.
First Contact & Terms: Send query letter with resume, photocopies, slides and videotape. "Interesting samples are filed." Samples not filed are returned only if requested by artist. Reports back to the artist only if interested. Call to schedule an appointment to show a portfolio, which should include slides. Pays by the hour, $25-50; by the project and by the day (negotiated by number of days.) Pays for production by the day, $75-300. Considers complexity of project, client's budget and turnaround time when establishing payment. Buys all rights.

KRAEMER GROUP, 360 Gest St., Cincinnati OH 45203. (513)651-5858. Production Coordinators: Terri Miller. Estab. 1968. AV firm. "We are a full-service film and video production company. Services include scripting, casting, sets, directorial, multi-image shows, and shooting through post production of a project." Current clients include ad agencies, P&G and NCR.

Needs: Works with 2 freelance designers/month. Prefers artists with experience in film and video production. Uses freelancers mainly for production responsibilities (grips; sets, props, lighting, makeup, stylists, graphic designers). Also uses freelance artists for storyboards, animation, TV/film graphics, lettering and logos.
First Contact & Terms: Send query letter with brochure and resume. Samples are filed or are returned only if requested by artist. Reports back within 3-4 weeks. Write to schedule an appointment to show a portfolio, which should include photographs. Pays for design by the day, $175 minimum. Pays for illustration by the project. Considers complexity of project, client's budget, turnaround time, skill and experience of artist and rights purchased when establishing payment. Rights purchased vary according to project.
Tips: "Be willing to start out at entry level to establish one's self; then develop good credentials including reputation, examples of work and references."

LIGGETT-STASHOWER, 1228 Euclid Ave., Cleveland OH 44115. (216)348-8500. Executive Art Director: Larry Pillot. Full-service Ad agency. Clients: consumer/business/direct mail.
Needs: Works with 20 freelance illustrators/year. Local artists primarily. Works on assignment only. Uses freelance artists for work on billboards, consumer and trade magazines, direct mail, P-O-P displays, brochures, catalogs, posters, signage, newspapers and AV presentations.
First Contact & Terms: Query with resume of credits and samples. Payment is by the project; negotiates according to client's budget, amount of creativity required, where work will appear and freelancer's previous experience. Pays for design and illustration by the project, $200-2,000.

LOHRE & ASSOCIATES, 1420 E. McMillan St., Cincinnati OH 45206. (513)961-1174. Art Director: Charles R. Lohre. Ad agency. Clients: industrial firms.
Needs: Works with 2 illustrators/month. Local artists only. Works on assignment only. Uses freelance artists for trade magazines, direct mail, P-O-P displays, brochures and catalogs.
First Contact & Terms: Send query letter with resume and samples. Call or write to schedule an appointment to show portfolio, which should include final reproduction/product. Especially looks for "excellent line control and realistic people or products." Pays for design by the hour, $12 minimum; pays for illustration by the hour, $6 minimum.
Tips: Looks for artists who can draw well and have experience in working with metal fabrication.

CHARLES MAYER STUDIOS INC., 168 E. Market St., Akron OH 44308. (216)535-6121. President: C.W. Mayer, Jr. AV producer since 1934. Clients: mostly industrial. Produces film and manufactures visual aids for trade show exhibits.
Needs: Works with 1-2 freelance illustrators/month. Uses illustrators for catalogs, filmstrips, brochures and slides. Also uses artists for brochures/layout, photo retouching and cartooning for charts/visuals. In addition, has a large gallery and accepts paintings, watercolors, etc. on a consignment basis, 33%-40% commissions.
First Contact & Terms: Send slides, photographs, photostats or b&w line drawings or arrange interview to show portfolio. Samples not kept on file are returned. Reports in 1 week. Provide resume and a sample or tearsheet to be kept on file for future assignments. Originals returned to artist at job's completion. Negotiates pay.

MENDERSON & MAIER, INC., 2260 Park Ave., Cincinnati OH 45206. (513)221-2980. Art Director: Barb Phillips. Estab. 1954. Full-service Ad agency in all aspects of media. Specializes in business-to-business.
Needs: Works with 1 freelance illustrator/month. Prefers local artist only. Uses freelancers mainly for illustrations and production. Also uses freelance artist for brochure, catalog and print ad design and illustration, slide illustration, mechanicals, retouching and logos. 70% of work is with print ads.
First Contact & Terms: Contact only through artist rep; send resume and photocopies. Samples are filed and are not returned. Reports back within 6 days. To show a portfolio, mail photostats, tearsheets, final reproduction/product and photographs; include color and b&w samples. Pays for design by the hour, $10 minimum; by the project. Pays for illustration by the project. Considers complexity of project and client's budget when establishing payment. Buys all rights.
Tips: The most effective way for a freelancer to get started in advertising is "by any means which builds a sample portfolio."

ART MERIMS COMMUNICATIONS, 750 Prospect Ave., Cleveland OH 44115. (216)664-1113. President: Arthur M. Merims. Ad agency/PR firm. Clients: industry.
Needs: Assigns 10 freelance jobs/year. Prefers local artists. Works on assignment only. Works with 1-2 freelance illustrators and 1-2 freelance designers/month. Uses freelance artists mainly for work on trade magazines, brochures, catalogs, signage and AV presentations.
First Contact & Terms: Send query letter with samples to be kept on file. Call or write for appointment to show portfolio, which should include "copies of any kind" as samples. Pays by the hour, $20-50 or by the project. Considers complexity of project, client's budget and skill and experience of artist when establishing payment.
Tips: When reviewing samples, looks for "creativity and reasonableness of cost."

TELEPRODUCTIONS, State Rt. 59, Kent OH 44242. (216)672-2184. Creative Director: Gordon J. Murray. Estab. 1962. "Teleproductions is a university-based PBS television production facility that originates and supports programming for two television stations, a campus cable-network, and also functions as an academic support unit providing instructional television services."
Needs: Works with 2-3 freelance illustrators and 2-3 freelance designers/year. Prefers artists with experience in television, "but not required." works on assignment only. Uses freelancers mainly for brochure and set design and corollary materials. Also uses freelance artists for catalog and print ad design and illustration, storyboards, slide illustration, animation, mechanicals, posters, TV/film graphics, lettering and logos.
First Contact & Terms: Send query letter with resume and photocopies. Samples are filed. Reports back to the artist only if interested. "We will contact artist about portfolio review." Portfolio should include color and b&w samples, roughs, original/final art, tearsheets, final reproduction/product, photographs, slides. Pays for design and illustration by the project, $25-$350. Considers complexity of project, client's budget, turn-around time, how work will be used and rights purchased when establishing payment. Rights purchased vary according to project.
Tips: "Because of our afilliation with a university with an excellent design program, competition is keen but not exclusive. The diversity of our production often requires the skills of graphic designers, set designers, illustrators, sculptors, cartoonists, paste-up artists and production assistants. We are in the process of building a file of dependable, talented freelancers for future projects."

TRIAD, (Terry Robie Industrial Advertising, Inc.), 124 N. Ontario St., Toledo OH 43624. (419)241-5110. Vice President/Creative Director: Janice Robie. Ad agency/graphics/promotions. Clients: industrial, consumer, medical.
Needs: Assigns 30 freelance jobs/year. Works with 1-2 freelance illustrators/month and 2-3 freelance designers/month. Works on assignment only. Uses freelance artists for consumer and trade magazines, brochures, catalogs, newspapers, filmstrips, stationery, signage, P-O-P displays, AV presentations, posters and illustrations (technical and/or creative).
First Contact & Terms: Send query letter with resume and slides, photographs, photostats or printed samples to be kept on file. Samples returned by SASE if not kept on file. Reports only if interested. To show a portfolio, mail appropriate materials or write to schedule an appointment; portfolio should include roughs, original/final art, final reproduction/product and tearsheets. Pays by the hour, $10-60; by the project, $25-2,500. Considers client's budget, and skill and experience of artist when establishing payment. Negotiates rights purchased.
Tips: "We are interested in knowing your specialty."

Oregon

ADFILIATION ADVERTISING & DESIGN, 323 W. 13th Ave., Eugene OR 97401. President/Creative Director: Gary Schubert. Estab. 1976. Ad agency. "We provide full-service advertising to a wide variety of regional and national accounts. Our specialty is print media, serving predominantly industrial and business-to-business advertisers." Clients: forest products, heavy equipment, software and sporting equipment.
Needs: Works with approximately 4 freelance illustrators and 2 freelance designers/year. Assigns 20-24 jobs/year. Works on assignment only. Uses freelancers mainly for specialty styles. Also uses artists for brochure and magazine ad illustration, retouching, animation, films and lettering. 80% of work is with print ads.
First Contact & Terms: Send query letter, brochure, resume, slides and photographs. Samples are filed or are returned by SASE only if requested. Reports back only if interested. Write to schedule an appointment to show a portfolio. Pays for design by the hour, $25-40. Pays for illustrations by the hour, $25-40; by the project, $400-800. Considers complexity of project, client's budget, turnaround time and skill and experience of artist when establishing payment. Buys first rights, one-time rights, or all rights; rights purchased vary according to project.
Tips: "We're busy. So follow up with reminders of your specialty, utilizing current samples of your work and convenience of dealing with you. We are looking at more electronic illustration lately. Find out what the agency does most often and produce a relative example for indication that you are up for doing the real thing! Follow-up after initial interview of samples. Do not send fine art abstract subjects."

CREATIVE COMPANY, INC., 3276 Commercial St., SE, Salem OR 97302. (503)363-4433. President/Owner: Jennifer Larsen Morrow. Specializes in corporate identity, packaging and P-O-P displays. Clients: local consumer-oriented clients specializing in food products, professionals and trade accounts on a regional and national level.
Needs: Works with 3-4 freelance artists/year. Prefers local artists. Works on assignment only. Uses artists for design, illustration, retouching, airbrushing, posters and lettering. "Clean, fresh designs!"
First Contact & Terms: Send query letter with brochure, resume, business card, photocopies and tearsheets to be kept on file. Samples returned only if requested. Reports only if interested. Call for appointment to show portfolio. "We require a portfolio review. Years of experience not important if portfolio is good. We prefer one-on-one review to discuss individual projects/time/approach." Pays for design and illustration by

the hour, $20-50 average. Considers complexity of project and skill and experience of artist when establishing payment.

Tips: Common mistakes freelancers make in presenting samples or portfolios are: "1) poor presentation, samples not mounted or organized, 2) not knowing how long it took them to do a job to provide a budget figure, 3) not demonstrating an understanding of the printing process and how their work will translate into a printed copy, 4) just dropping in without an appointment, 5) not following up periodically to update information or a resume that might be on file."

Pennsylvania

AMERICAN ADVERTISING SERVICE, 121 Chestnut, Philadelphia PA 19106. Creative Director: Joseph Ball. Ad agency.
Needs: Uses freelance artists for advertising, billboards, package, graphic and cover design, commercials, exhibits and art renderings.
First Contact & Terms: Prefers personal contact, but mailed art or photocopies OK. Not responsible for art after submission.

TED BARKUS CO. INC., 1512 Spruce St., Philadelphia PA 19102. President/Creative Director: Allen E. Barkus. Ad agency/PR firm. Serves clients in finance, retailing, industrial products, consumer products, appliance manufacturers, fashion, food, publishing, travel destinations, and interior design.
Needs: Works with 2 freelance illustrators and 1 freelance designer/month. Local and New York artists with experience working with similar firms only. Works on assignment only. Uses freelance artists mainly for design of billboards, P-O-P displays, consumer and trade magazines, stationery, multimedia kits, direct mail, TV, slide sets and newspapers. Also uses freelance artists for illustration of brochures/flyers.
First Contact & Terms: Send business card, slides, photographs and b&w line drawings to be kept on file. Samples returned by SASE. Reports in 2 weeks. No original work returned after job completed. Pays by the project or by the hour, $10-25 average. Considers complexity of project and skill and experience of artist when establishing payment.

SHIMER VON CANTZ, The Bourse Building, Independence Mall East, Philadelphia PA 19106. (215)627-3535. Associate Creative Director: Zsuzsa Johnson. Estab. 1968. Ad agency and PR firm. "We are a marketing, advertising and public relations company providing complete programs to bring our clients to consumer and trade markets." Specializes in computers, computer aftermarket, real estate developers, industrial and medical. Current clients include Okidata Printers, Kokes (Union Valley) Developers, Goodall Rubber Products, and Fitzgerald Mercy Hospital.
Needs: Works with 1 freelance illustrator and 1 freelance designer/month. Works on assignment only. Uses freelancers mainly for illustration and mechanicals. Also uses freelance artists for brochure, catalog, print ad and slide illustration, storyboards, animatics, mechanicals, retouching, lettering and logos. 85% of work is with print ads.
First Contact & Terms: Send query letter with brochure, resume, tearsheets, photostats, photocopies, photographs, slides or transparencies and include SASE. Samples are filed. Samples not filed are returned by SASE only if requested by artist. Reports back to the artist only if interested. Call or write to schedule an appointment to show a portfolio; include color and b&w samples, or mail original, final art, final reproduction/product, photographs, slides. Pays for design by the hour, $15-25; by the project, $50 minimum; by the day, $150-300. Pays for illustration by the hour, $15-25; by the project, $50 minimum. Considers complexity of project, client's budget, turnaround time, skill and experience of artist, how work will be used and rights purchased when establishing payment. Rights purchased vary according to project.
Tips: "Show great work and be believable that it is yours. Be on time and professional. Do a *first* project at a reduced rate and be on time, on budget and great."

***COOK ASSOCIATES, INC.**, 900 Matsonford Rd., West Conshohocken PA 19428. (215)834-1111. FAX: (215)834-1213. Art Director: Robert Nowak. Ad agency. Specializes in sales promotional collaterals, dealer loader brochures and company brochures. Product specialties are health and beauty aids and pharmaceuticals. Current clients include: Smith Kline Beecham, Church & Dwight, Lehn & Fink and Glenbrook Labs.
Needs: Approached by 3-5 freelance artists/month. Works with 2 freelance illustrators and 2 freelance designers/month. Prefers local artists with experience in concept through production. No people just out of school; must have at least 5 years experience. Uses freelance artists mainly for layout and design. Also uses freelance artists for brochure and print ad design and illustration, mechanicals, retouching, posters and printed sales brochures. 99% of work is with print material.
First Contact & Terms: Send query letter with photocopies, resume non-returnables. Samples are filed or are returned by SASE only if requested by artist. Reports back to the artist only if interested. Portfolio should include thumbnails, roughs, original/final art and b&w and color tearsheets. Pays for design by the hour, $10-20. Pays for illustration by the project. Buys all rights.

EDUCATIONAL COMMUNICATIONS INC., 761 Fifth Ave., King of Prussia PA 19406. Creative Director: Joseph Eagle. Estab. 1969. AV firm. "ECI specializes in training programs for corporate clients. We work in all media but predominately in slides and video." Clients: automotive, pharmaceutical. Current clients include Dow, Merck, Subaru of America and Mack Trucks.

Needs: Works with 3-4 freelance artists/year. Prefers local artists with experience in A/V , slide art and computer graphics. Uses freelance artists for storyboards, slide illustration, animation and mechanicals. 2% of work is with print ads. Works on assignment only. Especially important are cartoon or technical illustration skills.

First Contact & Terms: Send query letter with resume, tearsheets, photostats, photocopies and slides to be kept on file. Samples are not returned. Does not report back. Write to schedule an appointment to show a portfolio, which should include b&w and color of original/final art, final reproduction/product, roughs, tearsheets and slides. Pays by the day, $100 minimum. Considers complexity of the project, and skill and experience of artist when establishing payment. Buys all rights.

Tips: "Work submitted must be clean, professional, and corporate in nature. Speed, ability to follow directions, and ability to think creatively are important. Ability to meet deadlines essential."

*HARDMAN EASTMAN STUDIOS, INC., 1400 E. Carson St., Pittsburgh PA 15203. (412)481-4450. General Manager: Barbara Jost. AV and video production firm. Clients: business and industry.

Needs: Works with 1-2 freelance artists/year. Local artists only. Works on assignment only. Uses artists for design, illustration, mechanicals and charts/graphs. Artists should have the "experience to design art for 35mm slide and TV crop format, also the ability to communicate with clients and translate input into what is required for end use."

First Contact & Terms: Send query letter with resume. Samples not filed are not returned. Reports only if interested. Write to schedule an appointment to show a portfolio, which should include roughs, original/final art, and color photographs. Payment varies. Considers complexity of project, client's budget, skill and experience of artist and turnaround time when establishing payment. Buys all rights.

Tips: "Do not call. Send letter and resume!"

JERRYEND COMMUNICATIONS, INC., Rt. #2, Box 356H, Birdsboro PA 19508. (215)689-9118. Vice President: Gerard E. End, Jr. Estab. 1980. Ad/PR firm. Clients: industry, credit unions, technical services, professional societies and automotive aftermarket.

Needs: Works with 5-10 freelance illustrators and 6-12 freelance designers/year. Works "primarily with local artists for time, convenience and accessibility." Works on assignment only. Mainly uses freelance artists for design and layout of ads and newsletters. 20-25% of work is with print ads.

First Contact & Terms: Send query letter with brochure showing art style to be kept on file. Samples not filed returned by SASE. Reports within 2 weeks. Call to schedule an appointment to show a portfolio, which should include roughs, final reproduction/product and tearsheets. Pays for design and illustration by the hour, $25-50 average. Considers complexity of project, client's budget, turnaround time and rights purchased when establishing payment. Buys all rights.

Tips: "Clients are interested in changing graphics and appearances. Call to determine our types of clients and needs. Must be willing to do on-the-spot sketches. If we have nothing for you at the time you call we will suggest other agencies who might have a need."

KINGSWOOD ADVERTISING, INC., 33 Cricket Tr, Ardmore PA 19003. Senior Vice President/Creative Director: John F. Tucker, Jr. Serves clients in consumer, industrial and scientific products and services.

Needs: Works with 3 freelance illustrators, 3 freelance designers/year. Prefers local artists. Works on assignment only. Uses artists mainly for illustration and occasional comps from roughs. Also uses artists for technical art, retouching, trade magazines, direct mail and collateral, P-O-P displays, stationery design and newspapers.

First Contact & Terms: Provide business card, brochure/flyer and samples to be kept on file. Prefers roughs through final as samples. Samples returned by SASE. No originals returned to artist at job's completion. Call to schedule an appointment to show a portfolio. Pays for design by the project, $100-500. Pays for illustration by the project, $200-1,000.

Tips: "Learn a little about our clients' products and their current ad and literature style, and possibly suggest an improvement here and there. Also know where your work appeared and what market it adderssed."

KRUSE CORPORATE IMAGE, INC., Morgantown Rd RD1, Box 61-B, Reading PA 19601. Owner/President: Dan Kruse. Creative Vice President: Joe Reighn. Estab. 1987. AV firm. "We provide multi-image/video production and related print materials for corporate image, product introduction and sales meetings." Clients: manufacturers, financial, medical, chemical, service.

Needs: Works with 2-4 freelance illustrators and 3-6 freelance designers/year. Assigns 10-15 jobs/year. Prefers local or regional artists. Works on assignment only. Uses freelance artists for design, animation and AV programming. Prefers pen & ink, watercolor, markers, and airbrush.

First Contact & Terms: Send query letter with resume. Samples are filed or are returned if requested. Reports back only if interested. Write to schedule an appointment to show a portfolio, which should include tearsheets and slides. Pays for design by the hour, $10-40. Pays for illustration by the hour, $20-50, or by the project. Considers complexity of project, client's budget and turnaround time when establishing payment. Rights purchased vary according to project.

Tips: "I look to see what style(s) artists handle best and how creative their solutions have been while still matching the requirements of the project. They sometimes fail to present materials as solutions to certain communication objectives—as all our projects are. I like to see examples of rough concept sketches through to final design."

LETVEN/DICCICCO ADVERTISING INC., 455 Business Center Dr., Horsham PA 19044. (215)957-0300. Executive Art Director: Ross Winters. Estab. 1967. Full-service, multimedia, business-to-business ad agency. "High Creative." Specializes in food and business-to-business. Current clients include Hatfield Meats, Primavera, Hallowell and Caulk Dental Supplies.

Needs: Works with 10 freelance illustrators and 25 freelance designers/month. Uses freelance artists mainly for paste-up and mechanicals, illustration, photography and copywriting. Also uses artists for brochure design and illustration, print ad illustration, slide illustration, animatics, animation, retouching, TV/film grapics, lettering and logos. 60% of work is with print ads.

First Contact & Terms: Send query letter with brochure, resume, tearsheets, photostats, photocopies, photographs, slides and SASE. Samples are filed or are returned by SASE only if requested by artist. Reports back to the artist only if interested. Write to schedule an appointment to show a portfolio, which should include roughs, original/final art, tearsheets, final reproduction/product, photographs, slides; include color and b&w samples. Pays for design by the hour, $15-50. Pays for illustration by the project. Considers client's budget, turnaround time, skill and experience of artist and rights purchased when establishing payment. Rights purchased vary according to project.

Tips: "Not everything they've had printed is worth showing—good ideas and good executions are worth more than mediocre work that got printed. Check on agency's client roster in the Red Book—that should tell you what style or look they'll be interested in."

THE NEIMAN GROUP, Harrisburg Transportation Center, Heath and Chesnut St., Harrisburgh PA 17101. Art Director: Craig Hunter. Estab. 1978. Full-service ad agency specializing in print collatoral and ad campaigns. Product categories include healthcare, banks, retail, and industry.

Needs: Works with 4 freelance illustrators and 2 freelance designers/month. Prefers local artists with experience in comping and roughs. Works on assignment only. Uses freelancers mainly for illustrations and comps. Also uses freelance artists for brochure design, mechanicals, retouching, lettering and logos. 50% of work is with print ads.

First Contact & Terms: Send query letter with resume, tearsheets, photostats and photographs. Samples are filed. Reports back to the artist only if interested. Write to schedule an appointment to show a portfolio, which should include color and b&w samples, thumbnails, roughs, original/final art, photographs. Pays for design by the hour, $10-35; by the project. Pays for illustration by the hour, $15-40. Buys all rights.

Tips: The most effective way for a freelancer to get started in advertising is to "keep at it, do good work."

NEW YORK COMMUNICATIONS, INC., 207 S. State Rd., Upper Darby PA 19082. Contact: Mike Davis. Estab. 1974. Motion picture/TV/marketing consulting firm. Clients: radio & TV stations and newspapers.

Needs: Uses freelance artists for storyboards. Works with 6 freelance illustrators and 3 freelance designers/ year. 5% of work is with print ads.

First Contact & Terms: Query with resume. Works on assignment only. Provide resume, sample storyboards, business card, to be kept on file for future assignments. Samples not kept on file returned by SASE. No originals returned to artist at job's completion. Pays for design by the project, $100-1,200. Pays for illustration by the project, $10-500. Considers skill and experience of artist and turnaround time when establishing payment.

Tips: Looks for "the ability to capture people's faces, detail and perspective. Include storyboards in your portfolio or you won't be considered. Don't include page design examples or portraits. Send three samples, plus a query letter and resume."

PERCEPTIVE MARKETERS AGENCY LTD., 1100 E. Hector St., Conshohocken PA 19428. (215)825-8710. Creative Director: Bill Middleton. Estab. 1972. Ad agency. Clients: retail furniture, contract furniture, commuter airline, lighting distribution company; several nonprofit organizations for the arts, a publishing firm, air freight company, trade painting products company, etc.

Needs: Works with 10-20 freelance artists/year. Uses mostly local talent. In order of priority, uses freelance artists for mechanicals, photography, illustration, comps/layout, photo retouching and design/art direction. Concepts, ability to follow instructions/layouts and precision/accuracy are important. 50% of work is with print ads.

First Contact & Terms: Send resume and photostats, photographs and tearsheets to be kept on file. Accepts as samples—"whatever best represents artist's work—but preferably not slides." Samples not filed are returned by SASE only. Reports only if interested. Call for appointment to show portfolio. Pays for design by the hour, $10-25. Pays for illustration by the project, $50-2,500. Considers complexity of the project, client's budget and turnaround time when establishing payment. Buys all rights.

Tips: "Freelance artists should approach us with unique, creative and professional work. And it's especially helpful to follow-up interviews with new samples of work, (i.e., to send a month later a 'reminder' card or sample of current work to keep on file.)"

*SHAPSON GERO & SOMMERS, INC., 260 S. Broad St., Philadelphia PA 19102. (215)545-4300. FAX: (215)546-8510. Senior Art Director: Ruth Banks. Estab. 1946. Ad agency. Full-service, multimedia firm. Specializes in media advertising and collateral, marketing communications, and PR support. Product specialties are business-to-business, consumer and trade. Current clients include City of Philadelphia, Department of Revenue/Water Revenue Department and Valley Forge Medical Center and Hospital.

Needs: Approached by 20-25 freelance artists/month. Works with 8-10 freelance illustrators/month; 2-3 freelance designers/month. Prefers artists with **experience** in advertising and corporate projects. Works on assignment only. Uses freelance graphic artists mainly for illustration of ads and brochures. Also uses freelance artists for brochure, catalog and print ad illustration, storyboards, slide illustration, mechanicals, retouching, billboards, posters, TV/film graphics, lettering, logos and photography. 50% of work is with print ads.

First Contact & Terms: Send query letter with brochure, photocopies, SASE, resume and non-returnable samples. Samples are filed or are returned by SASE *only*. Reports back to the artist only if interested. Write to schedule an appointment to show a portfolio or mail appropriate materials. Portfolio should include thumbnails, roughs, original/final art and b&w and color photostats or tearsheets. Pays for design by the hour or by the project. Pays for illustration by the project. Payment depends on the project. Rights purchased vary according to project.

THE SLIDEING BOARD, INC. a Division of SBI, International, 322 Blvd. of the Allies, Pittsburgh PA 15222. (412)261-6006. General Manager: Rob Dillon. "Audiovisual and multi-image production firm for sales, marketing, training and capabilities presentations." Clients: consumer, industry, finance and business-to-business.

Needs: Works with 10-15 graphic artists/year. Would like to work with freelance computer graphic artists. (*Not* desk-top publishing.) Assigns 30-50 jobs/year. Prefers local artists only. Uses artists for design, storyboards, mechanicals, lettering, charts/graphs and some illustration and animation.

First Contact & Terms: Call to schedule an appointment to show a portfolio and some slides. Pays for design and illustration by the hour, $5-20 or by the project, depending on complexity, client's budget, turnaround time and skill and experience of artist. Buys all rights.

Tips: Artists must "have knowledge of how to produce art for photography."

E.J. STEWART, INC., 525 Mildred Ave., Primos PA 19018. (215)626-6500. General Manager: Dave Bowers. TV producer. Clients: industry, education, government, interactive video and advertising. Produces videotape programs and commercials.

Needs: Assigns 50+ jobs/year. Works with 2 freelance illustrators and 2 freelance designers/month. Philadelphia area artists only. Works on assignment only. Uses freelance artists for set design and storyboards.

First Contact & Terms: Send resume, brochure/flyer and business card to be kept on file. Reports in 3 weeks. Method and amount of payment are negotiated with the individual artist. No originals returned to artists following publication. Buys all rights.

Tips: "There is more interest in computer generated animation in our field. 10% of work is cartoon-style illustrations."

Tennessee

*CARDEN & CHERRY, INC., 1220 McGavock St., Nashville TN 37203. (615)255-6694. FAX: (615)255-9302. Vice President Creative Services: Jud Phillips. Estab. 1953. Ad agency. Full-service, multimedia firm. Specializes in all aspects of print and broadcast. Product specialties are consumer and trade.

Needs: Approached by 10 freelance artists/month. Works with 2 freelance illustrators/month. Uses freelance artists mainly for illustration, retouching and mechanicals. Also uses freelance artists for print ad illustration, mechanicals, retouching and lettering. 40% of work is with print ads.

First Contact & Terms: Send query letter with SASE and anything returnable by SASE. Samples are filed or are returned by SASE. Reports back to the artist only if interested. Call to schedule an appointment to show a portfolio. Portfolio should include "anything, rough or finished." Pays for design by the hour, by the project. Pays for illustration by the project, (negotiable). Negotiates rights purchased.

CASCOM INTERNATIONAL, 707 18th Ave. S., Nashville TN 37203. (615)329-4112. President: Dennis Kostyk. Estab. 1977. AV firm specializing in graphic and cell animation, special effects. "80% produced on 35mm film, 20% on various computer animation systems." Current clients include 150 TV stations and 65 foreign distributors (TV networks and producers).

Needs: Works with 2 freelance illustrators and 2 freelance designers/month. Prefers artist with experience in film graphics. Works on assignment only. Uses freelancers mainly for print and graphic cell design and layout. Also uses freelance artists for brochure, catalog and print ad design and illustration, storyboards, animation, mechanicals and TV/film graphics. 5% of work is with print ads.

First Contact & Terms: Send query letter with brochure, resume, photographs, slides and transparencies. Samples are filed. Samples not filed are returned only if requested by artist. Reports back within 4 weeks or only if interested. To show a portfolio mail "anything that shows ability." Negotiates payment. Considers complexity of project, turnaround time and skill and experience of artist when establishing payment. Buys all rights.

Tips: The most effective way for a freelancer to get started in audiovisual is to have "good work, good experience, good attitude and good ideas."

*GOOD ADVERTISING, 5050 Poplar Ave., Memphis TN 38157. (901)761-0741. (901)682-2568. Associate Creative Director: Holland Henton. Estab. 1982. Ad agency. Full-service, multimedia firm. Specializes in print ads, collaterals and TV. Product specialties are consumer and business-to-business. Current clients include: Federal Express, Baptist Hospital and Big Star Supermarkets.

Needs: Approached by 2 freelance artists/month. Works with 2 freelance illustrators and 2 freelance designers/month. Prefers artists with experience in high-quality illustration. Also uses freelance artists for brochure and catalog design and illustration, retouching, lettering and logos. 30% of work is with print ads.

First Contact & Terms: Send query letter with brochure, tearsheets and transparencies. Samples are filed or are not returned. Reports back within 5 days. Mail appropriate materials: original/final art and color photographs. Pays for design by the hour, $25 minimum. Pays for illustration by the project. Buys all rights.

LETTER GRAPHICS, 180 Racine, Memphis TN 38111. (901)458-4584. Creative Director: Michael Somers. Creative support services for clients and agencies: art, design, logos, type, printing, illustration.

Needs: Works with 20 freelance artists/year. Prefers experienced professionals. Works on assignment only. Uses freelance artists for brochure, catalog, newspaper and magazine ad design and illustration, direct mail packages, P-O-P displays, mechanicals, retouching, animation, billboards, posters, films, lettering and logos.

First Contact & Terms: Send query letter with photocopies, slides or photographs. Samples are filed. Samples not filed are not returned. Reports back only if interested. Call or write to schedule an appointment to show a portfolio, which should include photocopies or photos of color. "Quotes based on work required." Considers client's budget, skill and experience of artist and rights purchased when establishing payment. Rights purchased vary according to project.

Tips: "Show me what you can do—I'll call when I have something that fits your talent."

THOMPSON & COMPANY, 65 Union Ave., Memphis TN 38103. Associate Creative Director: Trace Hallowell. Estab. 1981. Full-service ad agency specializing in beauty, financial and automotive. Current clients include Lustrasilk, First Tennessee Bank, United Southern Bank, Rotary Lift, Seabrook Wallcoverings and Teledyne.

Needs: Works with various number of freelance illustrators and designers/month. Works on assignment only. Uses freelancers mainly for ads. Also uses freelance artists for brochure design and illustration, print ad and slide illustration, storyboards, animatics, animation, mechanicals, retouching, billboards, posters, TV/film graphics, lettering and logos. 80% of work is with print ads.

First Contact & Terms: Send query letter with samples. Samples are filed or are returned only if requested by artist. Reports back to the artist only if interested. Write to schedule an appointment to show a portfolio, which should include "whatever is appropriate." Considers complexity of project, client's budget, turnaround time, skill and experience of artist, how work will be used and rights purchased when establishing payment. "Always a fair price." Rights purchased vary according to project.

Texas

ALAMO AD CENTER INC., 217 Arden Grove, San Antonio TX 78215. (512)225-6294. Art Director: Daniel Rocha. Ad agency/PR firm. Serves clients in medical supplies, animal breeding, food, retailing (especially jewelry), real estate and manufacturing.

Needs: Works with 6 freelance illustrators and 4 freelance designers/month. Local artists only. Works on assignment only. Uses freelance artists for work in consumer and trade magazines, brochures/flyers, album covers, architectural renderings and "overflow work."

First Contact & Terms: Send brochure, flyer, business card, resume and tearsheets to be kept on file. SASE. Reports within 4 weeks if interested. Arrange interview to show portfolio, which should include tearsheets. No originals returned at job's completion. Pay is negotiable. Considers skill and experience of artist when establishing payment.

*AUSTIN/TYLER, Suite 104, 3335 Keller Springs Rd., Carrollton TX 75006. (214)931-8617. Creative Director: Flay Mohle. Estab. 1989. Ad agency. Full-service, multimedia firm. Specializes in magazine ads, collaterals, packaging and broadcast. Product specialties are cosmetics, automotive and food/beverage. Current clients include: Berryman Products Inc., Gena Laboratories Inc., The First Intermark and Transmark International.
Needs: Approached by 1-3 freelance artists/month. Works with 0-1 freelance illustrator and 0-1 freelance designer/month. "Accomplished, professional talent with sound business practices. No preference as to areas of experience." Works on assignment only. Uses freelance artists for overflow design and production; short deadline illustration. Also uses freelance artists for brochure, print ad design, print ad illustration, storyboards, slide illustration, animation, mechanicals, retouching, billboards, TV/film graphics and logos. 85% of work is with print ads.
First Contact & Terms: Send query letter with brochure, resume, photostats and slides. Samples are filed and are not returned. Reports back within 2-3 weeks. Call to schedule an appointment to show a portfolio. Portfolio should include roughs, original/final art and b&w and color tearsheets, photographs and 4×5 transparencies. Pays for design by the project $350-3,500. Pays for illustration by the project, $175-6,000. Negotiates rights purchased or rights purchased vary according to project.

BERNETA COMMUNICATIONS, INC., 701 Park Pl., Amarillo TX 79101. (806)376-7237. Project Manager: Jeanette Moeller. Ad agency and AV firm. "We are a full-service communications and production firm." Clients: banks, automotive firms, museums, various businesses, hotels, motels, jewelry stores and politicians. Client list provided upon request.
Needs: Works with 12 freelance artists/year. Assigns 1,000 freelance jobs/year. Works on assignment only. Uses freelance artists for design, illustration, brochures, catalogs, animation, posters, direct mail packages, lettering, logos, charts/graphs and advertisements.
First Contact & Terms: Send query letter with brochure. Samples are filed. Samples not filed are returned only if requested. Reports back only if interested. To show a portfolio, mail color and b&w thumbnails, roughs, original/final art, photostats, tearsheets, final reproduction/product, photographs, slides and video disks. Pays for design by the project, $100-1,500. Pays for illustration by the project, $100-1,900. Considers complexity of project, client's budget, turnaround time, skill and experience of artist, how work will be used and rights purchased when establishing payment. Rights purchased vary according to project.
Tips: "Be organized. Be able to present yourself in a professional manner."

BOZELL JACOBS KENYON & ECKHARDT, Box 619200, Dallas-Ft. Worth Airport TX 75261-9200. (214)556-1100. Creative Directors: Glen Ashley, Neil Scanlan, Artie McGibbens. Ad agency. Clients: all types.
Needs: Works with 4-5 freelance illustrators/month. Works on assignment only. Uses freelancers for billboards, newspapers, P-O-P displays, TV and trade magazines.
First Contact & Terms: Call for appointment to show portfolio. Reports within 3 weeks. Provide business card, brochure/flyer, resume and samples to be kept on file for possible future assignments. Samples not kept on file are returned. Payment is negotiated.
Tips: Wants to see a wide variety including past work used by ad agencies and tear sheets of published art.

DYKEMAN ASSOCIATES INC., 4115 Rawlins, Dallas TX 75219. (214)528-2991. Contact: Alice Dykeman or Laurie Winters. PR/marketing firm. Clients: business, industry, sports, environmental, energy, health. Assigns 150 jobs/year.
Needs: Works with 5 freelance illustrators/designers per month. "We prefer artists who can both design and illustrate." Local freelance artists only. Uses freelance artists for design of brochures, exhibits, corporate identification, signs, posters, ads, title slides, slide artwork and all design and finished artwork for graphics and printed materials. Prefers tight, realistic style. Prefers pen & ink, charcoal/pencil, colored pencil and computer illustration.
First Contact & Terms: Arrange interview to show portfolio. Provide business card and brochures. No originals returned to artist at job's completion. Pays by the project, $250-3,000 average; "artist makes an estimate; we approve or negotiate." Considers complexity of project, creative compatibility, client's budget, skill and experience of artist and turnaround time when establishing payment.
Tips: "Be enthusiastic. Present an organized portfolio with a variety of work. Portfolio should reflect all that an artist can do. Don't include examples when you did a small part of the creative work. Have a price structure but be willing to negotiate per project." Finds most artists through portfolio reviews.

*EMERY ADVERTISING, 1519 Montana, El Paso TX 79902. (915)532-3636. Art Director: Henry Martinez. Ad agency. Clients: automotive firms, banks and restaurants.
Needs: Works with 5-6 freelance artists/year. Uses freelance artists mainly for design, illustration and production.
First Contact & Terms: Works on assignment only. Send query letter with resume and samples to be kept on file; call for appointment to show portfolio. Prefers tearsheets as samples. Samples not filed returned by SASE. Reports back. Payment for design and illustration is by the project, $250-2,500. Considers complexity of project, client's budget and turnaround time when establishing payment. Rights purchased vary according to project.
Tips: Especially looks for "consistency and dependability."

GOODMAN & ASSOCIATES, 3633 West 7th., Fort Worth TX 76107. (817)735-9333. Production Manager: Cindy Schafer. Ad agency. Clients: financial, fashion, industrial, manufacturing and straight PR accounts.
Needs: Works with 3-6 freelance illustrators/month. Uses freelance artists for billboards, consumer and trade magazines, direct mail, P-O-P displays, brochures, catalogs, posters, signage and AV presentations.
First Contact & Terms: Local artists only. Arrange interview to show portfolio. Works on assignment basis only. Payment is by the project, by the hour or by the day; negotiates according to client's budget.

HEPWORTH ADVERTISING COMPANY, 3403 McKinney Ave., Dallas TX 75204. (214)526-7785. Manager: S.W. Hepworth. Full-service Ad agency. Clients: finance, consumer and industry.
Needs: Works with 3-4 freelance artists/year. Uses artists for brochure and newspaper ad design, direct mail packages, magazine ad illustration, mechanicals, billboards and logos.
First Contact & Terms: Send a query letter with tearsheets. Samples are not filed and are returned only if requested by artist. Does not report back. Portfolio should include roughs. Pays for design and illustration by the project. Considers client's budget when establishing payment. Buys all rights.
Tips: Looks for variety in samples or portfolio.

KNOX PUBLIC RELATIONS, Suite A, Guthrie Creek Park, 708 Glencrest, Longview TX 75601. (214)758-6439. President: Donna Mayo Knox. Estab. 1974. PR firm. Clients: civic, social organizations, private schools and businesses.
Needs: Works with 1-3 freelance illustrators/year. Works on assignment only. Uses freelance artists mainly for work on brochures. Also uses freelance artists for billboards, stationery design, multimedia kits, direct mail and flyers. 35% of work is with print ads.
First Contact & Terms: Send query letter with brochure showing art style or resume and samples. Samples returned by SASE. Reports in 3 weeks. Call or write to schedule an appointment to show a portfolio. Originals returned to artist at job's completion. Pays for illustration by the hour, $40.
Tips: "Please query first. We like variety, but don't send too many samples of styles of design. We are not interested in past pay rates."

McCANN-ERICKSON WORLDWIDE, Suite 1900, 1360 Post Oak Blvd., Houston TX 77056. (713)965-0303. Senior Vice President/Creative Director: Jesse Caesar. Ad agency. Clients: all types including consumer, industrial, gasoline, transportation/air, entertainment, computers and high-tech.
Needs: Works with about 20 freelance illustrators/month. Uses freelancers in all media.
First Contact & Terms: Call for appointment to show portfolio. Selection based on portfolio review. Negotiates payment based on client's budget and where work will appear.
Tips: Wants to see full range of work including past work used by other ad agencies and tearsheets of published art in portfolio.

McNEE PHOTO COMMUNICATIONS INC., 9261 Kirby, Houston TX 77006. (713)796-2633. President: Jim McNee. AV/film producer. Serves clients in industry and advertising. Produces slide presentations, videotapes, brochures and films. Also a brokerage for stock photographs.
Needs: Assigns 20 freelance jobs/year. Works with 4 freelance illustrators/month. Prefers local artists with previous work experience. Uses freelance artists for brochures, annual reports and artwork for slides, film and tape.
First Contact & Terms: "Will review samples by appointment only." Provide resume, brochure/flyer and business card to be kept on file for possible future assignments. Works on assignment only. Reports within 1 month. Method of payment is negotiated with the individual artist. Pays by the hour, $30-60 average. Considers client's budget when establishing payment. No originals returned after publication. Buys all rights, but will negotiate.

MARTINEZ/SIBONEY, INC., #1070, 3500 Maple Ave., Dallas TX 75219-3901. (214)521-6060. Senior Art Director: Al Schmidt; Creative Coordinator: Debbie Diaz. Estab. 1985. Ad agency. "We are a full-service Hispanic advertising and marketing agency." Specializes in package goods, transportation and fast food.

Current clients: Frito-Lay, Dallas Area Rapid Transit, McIhenny Tabasco Sauce, Volkswagen of America, Whataburger and Southwestern Bell.

Needs: Works with freelance illustrators and freelance designers. Works only with artist reps. Uses freelance artists for brochure design and illustration, print ad illustration, storyboards, animatics, retouching and logos. 40% of work is with print ads.

First Contact & Terms: Send query letter with photocopies, photographs, slides, transparencies and SASE. Samples are filed or are returned by SASE only if requested by artist. Reports back within 1 week. Call to schedule an appointment to show a portfolio, which should include thumbnails, roughs, original/final art and final reproduction/product. Pays by the project, $500-5,000. Considers complexity of project, client's budget, turnaround time, skill and experience of artist, how work will be used and rights purchased when establishing payment. Buys all rights.

Tips: "Have a good track record. Must have referrals. Don't show everything you've produced since finishing art school."

TAYLOR BROWN, SMITH & PERRAULT INC., Suite 264, 4544 Post Oak Place, Houston TX 77027. (713)877-1220. Senior Vice President/Creative Director: Larry Reinschmiedt. Estab. 1983. Ad agency specializing in TV, radio, print and collateral. Specializes in automotive, oil and gas and utilities company. Current clients include Conoco, Houston Lighting and Power, Hi-lo automotive Parts, Westin Hotels and Chevron.

Needs: Works with 4 freelance illustrators/month. Prefers artists with experience in photography, illustration. Uses freelance artists for brochure and print ad illustration, storyboards, animatics, mechanicals, and retouching. 40% of work is with print ads.

First Contact & Terms: Send query letter with photocopies. Samples are filed. Samples not filed are not returned. Does not report back. Call or write to schedule an appointment to show a portfolio, which should include color and b&w samples, tearsheets, photographs and slides. Pays for design and illustration by the project. Considers complexity of project, client's budget and how work will be used when establishing payment. Negotiates rights purchased. The most effective way for a freelancer to get started in advertising is to "call on agencies, show portfolio, send samples and keep in touch."

*EVANS WYATT ADVERTISING, 5151 Flynn Pkwy., Corpus Christi TX 78411. (512)854-1661. Creative Director: E. Wyatt. Estab. 1975. Ad agency. Full-service, multimedia firm. Specializes in general and industrial advertising.

Needs: Approached by 2-4 freelance artists/month. Works with 2-3 freelance illustrators and 6-7 freelance designers/month. Works on assignment only. Uses freelance artists mainly for advertising art. Also uses freelance artists for brochure, catalog and print ad design and illustration, storyboards, retouching, billboards, posters, TV/film graphics, lettering, logos and industrial/technical art. 60% of work is with print ads.

First Contact & Terms: Send a query letter with brochure, photocopies, SASE, resume and photographs. Samples are filed and/or are returned by SASE only if requested by artist. Reports back within 10 days. Call to schedule an appointment to show a portfolio. Mail appropriate materials: thumbnails, roughs and b&w and color photostats, tearsheets and photographs. Pays by the hour, by the project, by the day and by arrangement. Buys all rights.

Utah

*ALAN FRANK & ASSOCIATES INC., 1524 S. 11th E., Salt Lake City UT 84105. (801)486-7455. Art Director: Kazuo Shiotani. Serves clients in travel, fast food chains and retailing. Mail art with SASE. Reports within 2 weeks.

Needs: Illustrations, animation and retouching for annual reports, billboards, ads, letterheads, TV and packaging. Minimum payment: $500, animation; $100, illustrations; $200, brochure layout.

*SOTER ASSOCIATES, INC., 209 N. 400 West, Provo UT 84601. (801)375-6200. FAX: (801)375-6280. President: N. Gregory Soter. Estab. 1970. Ad agency. Full service, multimedia firm. Specializes in collateral and magazine advertising. Product specialties are computer, banking and health care. Current clients include: Dynix, Deseret Bank, Roberts-Slade, City of Orem, Provo, etc.

Needs: Approached by 2 freelance artists/month. Works with 1 freelance illustrator and 3 freelance designers/month. Works on assignment only. Uses freelance artists for brochure design and illustration, print ad design and illustration, mechanicals, retouching, billboards and logos. 65% of work is with print ads.

First Contact & Terms: Send query letter with resume, photostats, photocopies, tearsheets or "whatever is your preference." Samples are filed. Reports back to the artist only if interested. Write to schedule an appointment to show a portfolio, which should include original/final art and b&w and color photographs. Payment for design and illustration negotiated. Rights purchased vary according to project.

Vermont

*MEDIA FORUM INTERNATIONAL, LTD., RFD 1, Box 107, W. Danville VT 05873. (802)592-3444. Managing Director: Desi K. Bognar. Estab. 1969. AV firm. Specializes in publishing and film/TV consulting. Product specialties are "broadcast/film; ethnic, biography. Own publications and products, mostly; overseas work."
Needs: Approached by several freelance artists/year. "We seek out talent and have our files." Works on assignment only. Uses freelance artists mainly for illustrations. "First contact and terms and payment are dependent on the type of project at the time—book, brochure, film or video."

© 1989 Carlton Communications

Lately, Some People Are Losing Sleep Over The Stability Of Their Bank.

Artist Charles Arnold of Richmond, Virginia rendered this advertisement in pen and ink for Carlton Communications, Inc. Creative director Daniel T. Chamberlain wanted an illustration that would "promote the stability of the Savings Bank." He says the piece is successful because it conveys the idea that the customer is "treated in a professional and friendly manner and knows that his money is truly safe."

Virginia

CARLTON COMMUNICATIONS, INC., 300 W. Franklin St., Richmond VA 23220. (804)780-1701. Creative Director: Dan Chamberlain. Estab. 1975. Full-service Ad and PR agencies specializing in economic development, hotels, health care, travel, real estate and insurance.
Needs: Works with 2 freelance illustrators and 1 freelance designer/month. Uses freelancers mainly for ads, brochures, direct mail, posters, photography and illustration. Also uses freelance artists for brochure, catalog and print ad design and illustration, storyboards, slide illustration, animatics, animation, mechanicals, retouching, billboards, posters, TV/film graphics, lettering and logos. 50% of work is with print ads.
First Contact & Terms: Send query letter with brochure, resume, tearsheets and photocopies. Samples are filed and are not returned. Reports back to the artist only if interested. Call or write to schedule an appointment to show a portfolio, which should include original/final art. Pays for design by the project, $100 minimum. Pays for illustration by the project, $50 minimum. Consider complexity of project and client's budget when establishing payment.
Tips: "The most common mistakes freelancers make in presenting a portfolio is that there is too much work, causing the book to have an unfocused look. Have perseverance and enthusiasm to excel, no matter how small the project."

DEADY ADVERTISING, 17 E. Cary St., Richmond VA 23219. (804)643-4011. President: Jim Deady. Specializes in industrial and financial, displays and publications. Clients: tobacco, zinc die castings and savings and loans.

Needs: Works with 10-12 freelance artists/year. Local or regional artists only with minimum of 2 years experience with an agency. Works on assignment only. Uses freelance artists for design, illustration, mechanicals, retouching and airbrushing; brochures, magazine and newspaper advertisements, radio and television commercials.

First Contact & Terms: Send query letter with resume to be kept on file; also send samples. Other samples are returned. Reports back only if interested. Call or write for appointment to show portfolio, which should include photostats. Pays for design by the hour, $35-75 average, or by the project, $250-2,500 average; for illustration by the project, $275-1,500 average. Considers client's budget, skill and experience of artist and turnaround time when establishing payment.

Tips: "Be on time with all projects."

*BERNARD HODES ADVERTISING, Suite 700, 1600 Wilson Blvd., Arlington VA 22209. (703)528-6253. FAX: (703)528-6308. Art Director: Glenn Kimmell. Estab. 1970. Ad agency. Full-service, multimedia firm. Specializes in recruitment advertising on a national level. Current clients include: Martin Marietta, Unysis, USF&G, Computer Sciences Corp. (CSC), Marriott Suites and Hechingers.

Needs: Approached by 20 freelance artists/month. Works with 15 freelance illustrators and 5 freelance designers/month. Prefers artists with experience in airbrush illustration, graphic design and high-tech corporate identity. Works on assignment only. Uses freelance artists for illustration and mechanical key. Also uses freelance artists for brochure and print ad design and illustration, mechanicals, retouching and posters. 90% of work is with print ads.

First Contact & Terms: Send query letter with brochure, photocopies, resume and tearsheets. Samples are filed. Reports back within 5 days only if interested. Write to schedule an appointment to show a portfolio. Portfolio should include thumbnails, roughs, original/final art and b&w and color photostats, tearsheets and 5×7 trancparencies. Pays for design by the hour, $12-25. Pays for illustration by the project $200-5,000. Buys all rights.

PAYNE ROSS & ASSOCIATES ADVERTISING, INC., 206 E. Jefferson St., Charlottesville VA 22901. (804)977-7607. Art Director: Bill LeSeuer. Ad agency. Clients: resorts, service industries, manufacturing and banks.

Needs: Works with 12-20 freelance artists/year. Uses freelance artists mainly for photography, illustration and copywriting; occasionally for paste-up.

First Contact & Terms: Send query letter with brochure showing art style or resume and tearsheets, photostats, slides, photographs and other printed pieces. Reports back only if interested. To show portfolio, mail appropriate materials, which should include original/final art, final reproduction/product, photostats and photographs. Pays for design by the hour, $15-40; pays for illustration by the project, $200-2,000. Pay varies according to "experience, type of work, etc." Considers skill and experience of artist and turnaround time when establishing payment. Rights purchased vary according to project.

Tips: "There is increasing popularity in use of illustration for brochure and print advertising. Also there is more acceptance of this by client, particularly photography and illustration together. We find more integration between copy and design in conceptual stage. Therefore designer, illustrator, photographer must be flexible."

SIDDALL, MATUS AND COUGHTER, Ross Bldg., 801 E. Main St., Richmond VA 23219. Art Directors: Jessica Welton, Dan Scarlotto, Ray Fesenmaier, Ed Paxton, Linda Held. Ad agency/PR firm. Clients: travel agencies, computer. land development, bank, chemical, retail industries.

Needs: Assigns 50 freelance jobs/year. Works on assignment only. Works with 4 freelance illustrators/month. Uses freelance artists for consumer and trade magazines, billboards, direct mail packages, brochures, newspapers and posters.

First Contact & Terms: Send query letter with samples and tearsheets to be kept on file. Call or write for appointment to show portfolio, which should include printed samples to be kept on file. Samples returned only if requested. Reports only if interested. Pays for design by the hour, $30-60. Pays for illustration by the project, up to $15,000. Considers complexity of project, client's budget, skill and experience of artist, geographic scope of finished project, turnaround time and rights purchased when establishing payment. Buys all rights.

Washington

*ELGIN SYFERD, 601, 1008 Western Ave., Seattle WA 98104. (206)442-9900. FAX: (206)223-6309. Art Director: Kevin Nolan. Estab. 1981. Ad agency. Full-service, multimedia firm. Specializes in magazine ads, collaterals, documentaries etc. Product specialty is consumers.

Needs: Approached by 20+ freelance artists/month. Works with 1+ freelance illustrator/month. Prefers local artists only. Works on assignment only. Uses freelance artists mainly for collaterals. Also uses freelance artists for brochure illustration, storyboards, retouching and logos.

First Contact & Terms: Send query letter with tearsheets. Samples are filed. Reports back within 3 weeks. Mail appropriate materials: color photostats, tearsheets and 4×5 transparencies. Pays for design by the project. Pays for illustration by the project. Negotiates rights purchased.

*FINE ADVERTISING, #929, 1904 Third Ave., Seattle WA 98101. (206)343-5929. FAX: (206)343-7911. Creative Director: Bruce Stigler. Estab. 1979. Ad agency. Creative shop. Specializes in radio, TV and print (newspaper, outdoor, magazine). Product specialties are travel, restaurant and real estate. Current clients include: Chalon International, Shuttle Express and Kidder Matthew.
Needs: Approached by 3-5 freelance artists/month. Works with 2-3 freelance illustrators and 1-2 freelance designers/month. Prefers local artists only. Prefers artists with experience in desktop publishing and agency experience. Uses freelance artists for logo design and collateral. Also uses freelance artists for brochure and catalog design and illustration, logos and production. 70% of work is with print ads.
First Contact & Terms: Send query letter with photocopies and resume. Samples are filed. Reports back to the artist only if interested. Write to schedule an appointment to show a portfolio. Portfolio should include b&w and color roughs and original/final art. Pays for design and illustration by the project, $100 minimum. Negotiates rights purchased.

West Virginia

GUTMAN ADVERTISING AGENCY, 500 Klos Tower, Wheeling WV 26003-2801. (304)233-4700. President: D. Milton Gutman. Ad agency. Clients: finance, resort, media, industrial supplies (tools, pipes) and furniture.
Needs: Works with 3-4 freelance illustrators/month. Local artists only except for infrequent and special needs. Uses artists for billboards, stationery design, TV, brochures/flyers, trade magazines and newspapers. Also uses artists for retouching work.
First Contact & Terms: Send materials to be kept on file for possible future assignments. Call for an appointment to show a portfolio. No originals returned at job's completion. Negotiates payment.

Wisconsin

ARTFORM COMMUNICATIONS, 205 W. Highland Ave., Milwaukee WI 53203. (414)224-9600. Contact: Art Director. AV producer. Clients: business, corporate, multi-image and videotapes. Assigns 100 freelance jobs/ year.
Needs: Works with 10 freelance illustrators/year. Uses freelance artists for stylized illustrations, human figures and animation. Works with production artists familar with producing film work, cutting rubylith, etc. for Marron Carrel special effects camera.
First Contact & Terms: Query with resume and samples (slides). Include SASE. Reports in 3 weeks. Provide resume and brochures/flyers to be kept on file for possible future assignments. No originals returned to artist at job's completion. Pays for design by the hour, $10-20.50. Pays for illustration by the hour, $10-30.50.
Tips: "Most of our artwork is now computer generated and that limits our use of freelancers." Looking for "work that relates directly to multi-image, logo design , hand lettering and computer graphics experience. We do not want to see mangy, poorly organized portfolios."

*THE BRADY COMPANY, N80-W12878 Kond Du Lac Ave., Box 878, Menomonee Falls WI 53051-0878. (414)255-0100. FAX: (414)255-3388. Creative Director: Mark Fossen. Estab. 1948. Ad agency. Full-service, multimedia firm. Specializes in high-tech medical. Current clients include: heavy industry.
Needs: Approached by 7 freelance artists/month. Works with 3 freelance illustrators and 1 freelance designer/month. Prefers local artists only with experience in business-to-business. Works on assignment only. Uses freelance artists mainly for overflow. Also uses freelance artists for brochure, catalog and print ad illustration, storyboards, slide illustration, animation, mechanicals, retouching, billboards, TV/film graphics and lettering. 20% of work is with print ads.
First Contact & Terms: Send query letter with brochure, photocopies, resume, photographs and tearsheets. Samples are filed and are returned by SASE only if requested by artist. Reports back to the artist only if interested. Mail appropriate materials: thumbnails, roughs, original/final art, tearsheets and photographs. Pays for design by the hour, $25-75; by the project, $5-5,000. Pays for illustration by the project $60-6,000. Buys all rights.

ROLING, RAV & DAVIS, 60 N. Williams St., Williams Bay WI 53191. Contact: Art Director. Estab. 1972. Full-service ad agency. "Lots of fashion accounts." Current clients include Hartmarx, Motorola, and Bike Athletic.
Needs: Works with 3 freelance illustrators and 1 freelance designer/month. Works on assignment only. Uses freelancers mainly for keyline and illustration. Also uses freelance artists for print ad illustration, storyboards and mechanicals. 20% of work is with print ads.

First Contact & Terms: Send query letter with resume and any samples. Samples are filed. Reports back to the artist only if interested. Write to schedule an appointment to show a portfolio. Payment negotiated. Considers complexity of project, client's budget and turnaround time when establishing payment.
Tips: "Be professional and work hard!"

Canada

PULLIN PRODUCTIONS, LTD., 822 Fifth Ave. SW, Calgary, Alberta T2P 0N3 Canada. Creative Director: Art Feinstough. AV firm.
Needs: Works with 4 freelance artists/year. Works on assignment only. Uses freelance artists for design, illustrations, brochures, P-O-P displays, animation, motion pictures, lettering and charts/graphs.
First Contact & Terms: Send query letter with resume and samples. Samples not filed are not returned. Reports only if interested. To show a portfolio, mail appropriate materials. Pays for design by the hour, $10-50. Considers complexity of project, client's budget, skill and experience of artist, how work will be used and turnaround time when establishing payment. Buys all rights.

WARNE MARKETING & COMMUNICATIONS, Suite 810, 111 Avenue Rd., Toronto, Ontario M5R 3M1 Canada. (416)927-0881. Creative Associate: Alyson S. Hayes.
Needs: Works with 8 freelance artists/year. Works on assignment only. Uses artists for design, illustrations, brochures, catalogs, P-O-P displays, mechanicals, retouching, billboards, posters, direct mail packages, logos, charts/graphs and advertisements. Artists should have "creative concept thinking." Prefers charcoal/pencil, colored pencil and markers.
First Contact & Terms: Send query letter with resume and photocopies. Samples not filed are not returned. Reports only if interested. Write to schedule an appointment to show a portfolio, which should include roughs and final reproduction/product. Pays for design by the project, $100 minimum. Pays for illustration by the project, $150 minimum. Considers complexity of project, client's budget, and skill and experience of artist when establishing payment. Buys all rights.
Tips: Artist should "send samples (photocopies) and wait for assignment. There is an increasing need for technical illustration."

Other Advertising, Audiovisual and Public Relations Firms

Each year we contact all firms currently listed in *Artist's Market* requesting they give us updated information for our next edition. We also mail listing questionnaires to new and established firms which have not been included in past editions. The following advertising, audiovisual and public relations firms either did not respond to our request to update their listings for 1991 (if they indicated a reason, it is noted in parentheses after their name), or they are firms which did not return our questionnaire for a new listing (designated by the words "declined listing" after their names).

Ad Methods Advertising, Inc.
ADI Advertising/Public Relations
Advertising Incorporated
Alimed, Inc.
Alpestrine Productions, Inc.
Anderson & Lembke (declined listing)
Animation Arts Associates Inc.
Avrett, Free and Ginsberg, Inc.
N.W. Ayer, Inc.
Babbit & Reiman Advertising (declined listing)
Banning Co. (requested to be deleted)
Barkin, Herman, Solochek & Paulsen, Inc.
Bayer Bess Vanderwarker (declined listing)
Big Time Picture Co., Inc. (requested to be deleted)
Borders, Perrin & Norrander (declined listing)
Brogan Kabot Advertising Consultancy, Inc.
Broyles Garamella Fitzgerald and Czysz (out of business)
Leo Burnett USA (declined listing)
Cabscott Broadcast Productions, Inc. (moved; no forwarding address)
Campbell and Wagman (declined listing)
Campbell-Mithun-Esty (declined listing)
Carter Advertising Inc. (moved; no forwarding address)
Champion Advertising Agency (asked not to be listed this year)
Chiat/Day/Mojo (declined listing)
Clarke Goward Fitts Matteson (declined listing)
Claypoole, Burk & Hummel
Colle & McVoy Advertising Agency, Inc. (out of business)
Frank J. Corbett, Inc.
Crawleys Animation Inc. (moved; no forwarding address)
Creative Resources Inc.
D'Arcy Masius Benton &

Bowles (declined listing)
DDB Needham Chicago (declined listing)
DDB Needham/Retail (declined listing)
Earle Palmer Brown (declined listing)
Educational Filmstrips & Video
Alan G. Eisen Co. Inc. (moved; no forwarding address)
Ellis, Diaz/Bozell (declined listing)
Entelek (moved; no forwarding address)
Evans/Kraft (declined listing)
Event Technical Support
Paul Fagan (no longer uses artwork)
Richard Falk Associates
Foote, Cone & Belding (declined listing)
Garfield-Linn & Company
Howard Gladstone & Associates (asked to be deleted)
Marc Glazer and Company, Inc.
Graham Hayward & Associates
Hanna-Barbera Productions Inc.
Homer & Durham Advertising, Ltd.
Houston Advertising (declined listing)
Hutcheson Schutze (declined listing)
Imagematrix Dallas
Imageworks Inc.
Informedia
Interface Video Systems, Inc.
January & Associates
Jocom International (no longer uses freelance artwork)
Ketchum Advertising (declined listing)
Knape & Knape (declined listing)
Koch/Marschall Productions, Inc. (no longer uses freelance artwork)
Lane Marketing Group, Inc. (moved; no forwarding address)
Lauren International Ltd.
Lerner Scott Corp. (moved; no forwarding address)

Long, Haymes & Carr (declined listing)
Lord & Bentley Persuasive Marketing
M.D.K. Allied (out of business)
McCann-Erickson, Los Angeles (declined listing)
Media Design Group
Moroch & Associates (declined listing)
Eric Mower & Associates
Mullen Advertising (declined listing)
Nelson/Ralston/Robb Communications (overstocked)
Ogilvy & Mather (declined listing)
O'Neil Griffin & Associates (declined listing)
Puskar Gibbon Chapin (declined listing)
The Russ Reid Co.
Rosenfield-Lane, Inc. (no longer uses freelance artwork)
Scott Lancaster Mills Atha (declined listing)
Society for Visual Education, Inc.
Sosa & Associates (declined listing)
The Tarragano Company
Telemation Productions, Inc.
J. Walter Thompson/West (declined listing)
Thompson-Marince (declined listing)
Tracey-Locke
Travis-Walz and Associates, Inc.
Troll Associates
Vickers & Benson/FKQ Inc. (out of business)
David Vine Associates
Vomack and Laban Advertising (moved; no forwarding address)
Wieden & Kennedy (declined listing)
Winterkorn Lillis Inc.
Wren Marketing Communications Co.
Young & Rubicam (declined listing)
ZM Squared

Designers give visual expression to information through the use of written and printed images. Uniting words and images, designers must also convey the client's message. Designer April Greiman in a recent *HOW* article says, "The design profession is a servant to and/or translator of culture."

The variety of freelance opportunities that art/design studios offer matches the diversity of projects studios handle. Studios provide all forms of visual communication for various businesses—corporate identity, product/brand identity, publication design, direct marketing materials, catalogs, annual reports, brochures, exhibits, direct mail pieces and so on.

Art studios are called upon mainly for illustration; your city's airbrush specialists probably call their business an art studio. Design studios offer not only a variety of design specialties but also illustration, layout, mechanicals and retouching.

Studios range in size, scope and purpose. There are one-person studios that generally turn to freelance help when the workload becomes too heavy. Then there are large operations with account executives who turn to outside help for either a fresh approach or for basic mechanical skills such as paste-up.

One design firm might specialize in a particular field, such as display design. Another studio's specialty is its ability to solve problems for a variety of clients. Some studios specialize in the type of product they design, such as annual reports or packaging. Other studios define themselves by their method of working, such as desktop publishing or other computer technologies.

Many designers feel the future is bright for their profession. Designer Joel Fuller says, "The mergers and acquisitions [because] of all the ad agency buyouts have destroyed advertising in a lot of ways. And I think that is good for the design firms, because they are doing more and more of that work."

Another sign of the times is the move to computers and desktop publishing for preparing design. Computers provide a new style of illustration, new ways of adding color to line art, and new control over the color separation process. Designers with computer skills are greatly in demand.

Despite fax machines, many studios still prefer to work with local artists because of the need to meet tight deadlines and to make last-minute changes. Consult your Yellow Pages and Business-to-Business directory to locate studios; follow up by researching the *Design Firm Directory* (names and addresses are noted, but there is no marketing information) for the studio's specialty.

Study the listings in this section to find out what type of work they do, who the art buyers are, what they have done in the past, who their clients are, and the size of the studios. Use your skills as a visual communicator to contact studios. Learn as much about prospects as you can before contacting them. Then send samples that match the prospect's needs along with a cover letter asking for a portfolio review. If a studio shows interest, find out what type of work might be available for you, then select appropriate pieces to show in your portfolio.

When showing a portfolio to a studio, bear in mind that what you are basically selling is yourself and what you can do for that studio. First, get to know the art buyer by asking about his current projects. When asked what you do, give an answer that is broadly specific. Rather than saying, "I'm a designer," say, "I specialize in corporate identity." Then mention that you have designed logos and identity systems for companies that are in the same league as your prospect.

Design your portfolio as carefully as you would design another client's project. Present your work in a neat, organized fashion. Show that you know how to pinpoint a client's needs by focusing on the needs of your current prospect. If you are showing your work to a studio that specializes in collateral material, present brochures instead of product designs. Identify what your involvement was in each project, such as designing the logo or lettering the piece. Since many art directors like to see how you conceptualize projects, save space at the end of your presentation to show a complete project from thumbnails to the final product.

Since studios usually bill clients by the hour or by the project, freelancers are similarly paid. Variables in pricing are use of color, turnaround time, rights purchased, complexity of the project and your reputation. When you are first discussing a project, ask whether or not you will retain a copyright and receive credit; some projects call for the company or client to retain all rights.

The most comprehensive directory of design firms is the *Design Firm Directory*. Other sources are *Adweek's Portfolio of Graphic Design*, the *Creative Black Book* and the *L.A. Workbook*. Consider joining a professional design organization, which puts you in touch with a network of designers both in your area and nationally: The Graphic Artists Guild, American Institute of Graphic Arts (AIGA), Society of Publication Designers, American Center for Design, Society of Illustrators and your local art director club. Also, membership in a business organization such as the International Association of Business Communicators provides contacts with businesses which might need your services. Magazines focused on design are *Print, HOW, Step-by-Step Graphics, Communication Arts, Metropolis, Folio, Upper & Lower Case* and *Graphis*.

A.T. ASSOCIATES, 63 Old Rutherford Ave., Charlestown MA 02129. (617)242-6004. Partners: Daniel N. Kovacevic and Annette Tecce. Specializes in industrial and graphic design, model making, corporate identity, signage, display and packaging. Clients: design firms, corporate clients, small businesses and ad agencies.
Needs: Works with 10-25 freelance artists/year. Prefers local artists, some experience necessary. Uses artists for model making, mechanicals, logos, brochures, P-O-P display, charts/graphs and design.
First Contact & Terms: Send resume and nonreturnable samples. Samples are filed. Reports back within 30 days only if interested. Call or write to schedule an appointment to show a portfolio, which should include thumbnails, roughs, original/final art and final reproduction/product and b&w and color tearsheets, photostats and photographs.Pays for design and illustration by the hour, $10-25; by the day, $48-200. Considers complexity of project, client's budget, skill and experience of artist, turnaround time and rights purchased when establishing payment. Rights purchased vary according to project.

AARON, SAUTER, GAINES & ASSOCIATES/DIRECT MARKETING, Suite 230, 320 E. McDowell Rd., Phoenix AZ 85004. (602)265-1933. President: Cameron G. Sauter. Specializes in brand identity, direct marketing, direct response ads, catalogs and P-O-P display for retail stores; banks; and industrial, mail order and service companies.
Needs: Works with 5-10 freelance artists/year. Uses artists for advertising, brochure and catalog design and illustration, mechanicals, retouching and direct mail packages.
First Contact & Terms: Seeks artists with professionalism, speed and experience only. Works on assignment basis. Send query letter with brochure, resume and business card to be kept on file. Prefers original work, photos or slides as samples. Samples returned by SASE if not kept on file. Reports back only if interested. Pays for design by the hour, $15-50 average; by the project, $100-1,000 average; by the day, $50-100 average. Pays for illustration by the hour, $25-75 average; by the project, $100-2,000 average; by the day, $100-150 average. Considers complexity of project, client's budget, skill and experience of artist and turnaround time when establishing payment. "All art is purchased with full rights and no limitations."

*LEONARD ALBRECHT ASSOCIATES, 15040 Golden W. Circle, Westminster CA 92683. (714)898-0553. Owner: Leonard Albrecht. Specializes in industrial design.
Needs: Works with 2-3 freelance artists/year. Uses artists for design, illustration, mechanicals and model making.
First Contact & Terms: Send query letter with brochure showing art style or resume. Reports within 10 days. Write to schedule an appointment to show a portfolio. Considers skill and experience of artist when establishing payment.

ANCO/BOSTON, 48 Eliot St., South Natick MA 01760. (508)650-1148. Graphic Director: Fran Jarvis. Art agency. Clients: educational publishers, commercial and industrial companies. Current clients include Merrill Publishers; Houghton-Mifflin Co., and Warren, Gorham & Lemont.
Needs: Approached by over 12 freelance artists/year. Works with approximately 6 freelance illustrators and 1-2 freelance designers/year. Local artists only. Uses artists for books, charts, graphs, technical art and paste-up. Most of the artwork required is one-color line art.
First Contact & Terms: Send query letter with resume and photocopies. All art becomes the property of Anco/Boston. To show portfolio, mail appropriate materials or call to schedule an appointment; send examples of work with resume. Pays for design by the project, $25 minimum; pays for illustration by the project, $10 minimum.
Tips: "We are interested only in b&w line art. Our work is for educational materials and is frequently of a technical nature."

*TODD R. ANDERSON STUDIO, 345 Canal St., Chicago, IL 60606. (312)876-1818. Owner: Todd Anderson. Estab. 1975. Specializes in brand identity, corporate identity; display, package and P-O-P design and signage. Clients: corporations. Current clients include Sears and Desoto. Client list not available.
Needs: Approached by 20 freelance artists/year. Works with 2 freelance illustrators and 2 freelance designers/year. Prefers local artists only. Works on assignment only. Uses illustrators mainly for packaging. Uses designers mainly for packaging and P-O-P. Also uses artists for brochure illustration, lettering, logos, P-O-P design and P-O-P illustration.
First Contact & Terms: Send query letter with resume. Samples are filed. Reports back to the artist only if interested. Call to schedule an appointment to show a portfolio, which should include b&w and color thumbnails, roughs and original/final art. Pays for design and illustration by the project, by bid. Rights purchased vary according to project.

*ANDREN & ASSOCIATES INC., 6400 N. Keating Ave., Lincolnwood IL 60646. (312)267-8500. Contact: Kenneth E. Andren. Clients: beauty product and tool manufacturers, clothing retailers, laboratories, banks, camera and paper products. Current clients include Alberto Culver, Barton Brand, Nalco Chemical, Encyclopedia Britannica, Firestone, Reflector Hardware, Rust-O-Leum, Avon Products, National Safety Council.
Needs: Assigns 6-7 jobs/month. Local artists only. Uses artists for catalogs, direct mail brochures, flyers, packages, P-O-P displays and print media advertising.
First Contact & Terms: Query with samples or arrange interview. Include SASE. Reports in 1-2 weeks. Pays $15 minimum/hour for animation, design, illustrations, layout, lettering, mechanicals, paste-up, retouching and type spec.

ANTISDEL IMAGE GROUP, INC., 3242 De La Cruz Blvd., Santa Clara CA 95054. (408)988-1010. President: G.C. Antisdel. Estab. 1970. Specializes in annual reports, corporate identity, displays, interior design, packaging, publications, signage and photo illustration. Clients: high technology 80%, energy 10%, and banking 10%. Current clients include IBM. Client list not available.
Needs: Approached by 40 freelance artists/year. Works with 15 freelance illustrators and 5 freelance designers/year. Works on assignment only. Uses artists for illustration, mechanicals, retouching, airbrushing, direct mail packages, model making, charts/graphs, AV materials and lettering.
First Contact & Terms: Send query letter with resume, business card and tearsheets to be kept on file. Reports back only if interested. Call or write to schedule an appointment to show a portfolio, which should include color, tearsheets, photographs and b&w. Pays for design by the hour, $8-50 or by the project $50-18,000. Pays for illustration by the project, $50-10,000. Considers complexity of project, client's budget, skill and experience of artist, how work will be used, turnaround time and rights purchased when establishing payment.
Tips: "Don't send crummy photocopies. Use styles which apply to hi-tech clients."

*ARK ANDRÉ RICHARDSON KING-ARCHITECTURAL GRAPHIC DESIGNERS, 220 South State St., Chicago IL 60604. (312)922-7757. FAX: (312)922-4093. President: André R. King. Estab. 1981. Specializes in corporate identity and signage. Clients: corporations, architects, developers and leasing management. Client list available upon request.

The asterisk before a listing indicates that the listing is new in this edition. New markets are often the most receptive to freelance submissions.

Needs: Approached by more than 12 freelance artists/year. Works with a few illustrators and designers/year. Uses illustrators mainly for architectural spot drawings. Uses designers mainly for architectural renderings. Also uses artists for brochure design and airbrushing.
First Contact & Terms: Send query letter with brochure and resume. Samples are filed or are returned. Reports back to the artist only if interested. Call to schedule an appointment to show a portfolio. Portfolio should include thumbnails, roughs and b&w photographs. Pays for design by the hour and by the project. Pays for illustration by the hour and by the project. Buys all rights.

THE ART WORKS, 4409 Maple Ave., Dallas TX 75219. (214)521-2121. Creative Director: Fred Henley. Estab. 1978. Specializes in illustration, annual reports, brand identity, corporate identity, packaging, publications and signage. Current clients include Southland, Bennetts Printing Co., Boy Scouts and Interstate Batteries. Client list available upon request.
Needs: Approached by 80 freelance artists/year. Works with 30-50 freelance illustrators and 30-50 freelance designers/year. Uses artists for illustration, advertising, brochure, catalog and book design, advertising, brochure and catalog layout; P-O-P displays, mechanicals, retouching, posters, direct mail packages, lettering and logos. "We are currently looking for freelance illustrators and designers to join our group and work in our studio."
First Contact and Terms: Send brochure, business card, slides and original work to be kept on file. Samples returned by SASE only if requested by artist. Reports within 7 days. Call or write for appointment to show portfolio. Pays for design by the hour, $35; by the project, $1,000; by the day, $150. Pays for illustration by the hour, $65; by the project, up to $5000; by the day, $200. Considers complexity of project, client's budget, skill and experience of artist and turnaround time when establishing payment.
Tips: Common mistakes freelancers make in presenting samples or portfolios are "repetition and showing school work." Advises artists to "send printed samples."

AXION DESIGN INC., 1638 Sherbrooke St. W., Montreal, Quebec H3H 1C9 Canada. (514)935-5409. President: J. Morin. Estab. 1983. Specializes in brand and corporate identity. Clients: Bell Canada, Petro Canada, Royal Bank and Air Canada.
Needs: Approached by 25 freelance artists/year. Works with 4 freelance illustrators and 5 freelance designers/year. Uses artists for brochure design, mechanicals, lettering and logos.
First Contact and Terms: Send resume. Reports back within 14 days. Write to schedule an appointment to show a portfolio. Considers complexity of project and skill and experience of artist when establishing payment. Buys all rights.
Tips: The most common mistakes freelancers make in presenting samples or portfolios is, "They do not understand the communication objectives that their work is meant to meet."

BARNSTORM DESIGN/CREATIVE, Suite 201, 2527 W. Colorado Ave., Colorado Springs CO 80904. (719)630-7200. Owner: Douglas D. Blough. Estab. 1975. Specializes in corporate identity, brochure design, multiimage slide presentations and publications. Clients: ad agencies, high-tech corporations and restaurants.
Needs: Works with 2-4 freelance artists/year. Works with local, experienced (clean, fast and accurate) artists on assignment. Uses freelancers mainly for paste-up, illustration and layout. Also uses artists for design, mechanicals, retouching, AV materials and calligraphy.
First Contact & Terms: Send query letter with resume and samples to be kept on file. Prefers "good originals or reproductions, professionally presented in any form" as samples. Samples not filed are returned by SASE. Reports only if interested. Call or write for appointment to show portfolio. Pays for design by the hour, $10 minimum. Pays for illustration by the project, $50 minimum, b&w; $200, color. Considers client's budget, skill and experience of artist, and turnaround time when establishing payment.
Tips: "Portfolios should reflect an awareness of these trends. We try to handle as much inhouse as we can, but we recognize our own limitations (particularly in illustration). Do not include too many samples in your portfolio."

*BATTERY GRAPHICS, 35 King St., Burlington VT 05401. (802)862-4449. Estab. 1979. Specializes in annual reports, corporate identity and collateral. Clients: area businesses, corporations, nonprofits and museums.
Needs: Approached by 20 freelance artists/year. Works with 3 freelance illustrators/year. Prefers local artists only. Works on assignment only. Uses designers mainly for brochure design and illustration, catalog design and retouching.
First Contact & Terms: Send query letter with resume, tearsheets and photocopies. Samples are filed. Reports back only if interested. If does not report back, the artist should call for follow up. To show a portfolio, call or mail "the best representation of your work." Rights purchased vary according to project.

*BCD INK, LTD. CREATIVITY DESIGN SERVICES, 108 E. 16th St., New York NY 10003. (212)420-1222. President: Emma Crawford. Specializes in package, publication and direct mail design. Clients: manufacturers, institutions and corporations. Current clients include Lancome Pratt Institute and Luggage and Leather Goods Manufacturers of America. Client list available upon request.

Needs: Approached by 40-50 freelance artists/year. Works with 5-10 freelance illustrators and 10-20 freelance designers/year. Prefers local artists with design skills and experience in mechanicals and computers (Mac Quark/Adobe Illustrator). Works on assignment only. Uses illustrators mainly for advertising packaging. Also uses artists for brochure design and illustration, catalog design and illustration, mechanicals, lettering, logos, ad design/poster illustration and design and direct mail design.

First Contact & Terms: Send query letter with tearsheets, resume, SASE and photocopies. Samples are filed, or are not returned, or are returned by SASE if requested by artist. Reports back to the artist only if interested. Call to schedule an appointment to show a portfolio. Portfolio should include thumbnails, roughs, original/final art, tearsheets, mechanicals and paste-up. Pays for design by the hour, $10-18. Pays for illustration by the project. Rights purchased vary according to project.

MAY BENDER DESIGN ASSOCIATES, 7 Deer Park Dr., Princeton Corp. Plaza, Monmouth NJ 08856. (201)329-8388. President: May Bender. Specializes in corporate identity, displays, packaging, product design and signage. Clients: manufacturers of consumer products. Current clients include R-J Reynolds, Bausch and Lomb.

Needs: Approached by 6-12 freelance artists each year. Works with 5-10 freelance illustrators and 3-5 designers/year. Uses artists for illustrations, mechanicals, retouching, design, comprehensives, airbrushing and lettering.

First Contact & Terms: Send brochure. Samples are filed. Samples not filed are returned only if requested. Call or write to schedule an appointment to show a portfolio, which should include original/final art. Pays for design by the hour, $35 and up, or by the project. Pays for mechanicals by the hour, $25. Considers complexity of project, client's budget and turnaround time when establishing payment. Rights purchased vary.

Tips: "MBDA specializes in packaging, industrial (product) design and corporate identity. I'm not interested in cute illustrations or such. I prefer strong, contemporary design and the like."

*SUZANNE BENNETT AND ASSOCIATES, 875 Avenue of the Americas, New York NY 10001. (212)564-8050. Contact: Suzanne Bennett. Specializes in direct mail, publications and book design. Clients: PR firms, magazine and book publishers and nonprofit organizations.

Needs: Works with 15 freelance artists/year. Uses artists for mechanicals, retouching, airbrushing and charts/graphs.

First Contact & Terms: Samples not filed are not returned. Does not report back. Write to schedule an appointment to show a portfolio. Considers client's budget, skill and experience of artist, how work will be used and turnaround time when establishing payment. Rights purchased vary according to project.

BARRY DAVID BERGER & ASSOCIATES, INC., 9 East 19th St., New York NY 10003. (212)477-4100. Contact: Amy Patten. Specializes in brand and corporate identity, P-O-P displays, product and interior design, exhibits and shows, corporate capability brochures, advertising graphics, packaging, publications and signage. Clients: product manufacturers and marketing organizations.

Needs: Works with 10 freelance artists/year. Uses artists for advertising illustration, mechanicals, retouching, direct mail package design, model making, charts/graphs, photography, AV presentations and lettering.

First Contact & Terms: Send query letter, then call for appointment. Works on assignment only. Prefers "whatever is necessary to demonstrate competence" as samples. Samples returned if not kept on file. Reports immediately. Provide brochure/flyer, resume, business card, tearsheets and samples to be kept on file for possible future assignments. Pays by the project for design and illustration.

J.H. BERMAN AND ASSOCIATES, Suite 550, 1201 Connecticut Ave., Washington DC 20036. (202)775-0892. Office Manager: Sara Greenbaum. Estab. 1974. Specializes in annual reports, corporate identity and signage. Clients: real estate developers, architects, high-technology corporations and financial-oriented firms (banks, investment firms, etc.).

Needs: Works with 10-15 (6 consistently) freelance artists/year. Mainly uses artists for architectural rendering and mechanical/production. Also uses artists for design, illustration, brochures, magazines, books, P-O-P displays, retouching, airbrushing, posters, model making, AV materials, lettering and advertisements.

First Contact & Terms: "Artists should be highly professional, with at least 5 years of experience. Highest quality work required. Restricted to local artists for mechanicals only." Send query letter with brochure, resume, business card and samples to be kept on file. Call or write for appointment to show portfolio or contact through agent. "Samples should be as compact as possible; slides not suggested." Samples not kept on file returned by SASE. Reports only if interested. Pays for design by the hour, $20-50. Pays for illustration by the project, $200 minimum. Considers complexity of project, skill and experience of artist, how work will be used, turnaround time and rights purchased when establishing payment.

Tips: Artists should have a "totally professional approach." The best way for illustrators or designers to break into our field is a "phone call followed by a strong portfolio presentation" which should include "original completed pieces."

*BINGENHEIMER DESIGN COMMUNICATIONS INC., 126 E. Center College St., Yellow Springs OH 45387. (513)767-2521. President: Bob Bingenheimer. Estab. 1979. Specializes in annual reports, brand identity, coporate identity, display, direct mail, package and publication design; signage and advertising. Clients: corporations, associations and the government. Current clients include NCR, Standard Register. Client list available upon request.

Needs: Approached by 2-10 freelance artists/year. Works with 2-5 freelance illustrators and 1-2 freelance designers/year. Prefers artists with experience in publications. Works on assignment only. Uses illustrators mainly for publications and editorial. Uses designers mainly for collateral. Also uses artists for retouching, airbrushing and ad illustration.

First Contact & Terms: Send query letter with SASE and slides. Samples are filed. Reports back only if interested. To show a portfolio, mail slides. Pays for design by the hour, $30-40. Rights purchased vary according to project.

BOB BOEBERITZ DESIGN, 247 Charlotte St., Asheville NC 28801. (704)258-0316. Owner: Bob Boeberitz. Estab. 1984. Specializes in graphic design. Clients: galleries, retail outlets, restaurants, textile manufacturers, record companies, publishers, universities, hotels and medical service suppliers. Current clients include Beacon Manufacturing Co., High Windy Audio, Whitford Press, Holbrook Farm and The Market Place. Client list not available.

Needs: Approached by several freelance artists/year. Works with 3-4 freelance illustrators and 1-2 freelance designers/year. Uses artists primarily for illustration, comps and mechanicals. Prefers pen & ink, airbrush and acrylic.

First Contact & Terms: Send query letter with brochure, resume, photostats, photocopies, photographs, business card, slides and tearsheets to be kept on file. "Anything too large to fit in file" is discarded. Reports only if interested. To show a portfolio, write to schedule an appointment or mail color and b&w original/final art, final reproduction/product. Pays for illustration by the hour $25 minimum or by the project, $50 minimum. Considers complexity of project, client's budget, skill and experience of artist and turnaround time when establishing payment. Buys all rights.

Tips: "Show sketches. Sketches help indicate how the person thinks. The most common mistakes freelance make in presenting samples or portfolio is in not showing how the concept was developed, what your role was in it. I always see the final solution, but never what went into it. In illustration, show both the art and how it was used." Portfolio should focus on what you do best. Portfolios should be neat, clean and flattering to your work. Show only the most memorable work, what you do best. Always have other stuff, but don't show everything. Be brief. Don't just toss a portfolio on my desk; guide me through it. A 'leave-behind' is helpful along with a distinctive looking resume."

BOELTS BROS. DESIGN, INC., 14 E. 2nd St., Tucson AZ 85705-7752. (602)792-1026. FAX: (602)792-9720. President: Eric Boelts. Estab. 1986. Specializes in annual reports, brand identity, corporate identity, display design, direct mail design, package design, publication design and signage. Client list available upon request.

Needs: Approached by 100 freelance artists/year. Works with 10 freelance illustrators and 5-10 freelance designers/year. Works on assignment only. Uses designers and illustrators for brochure, poster, catalog, P-O-P and ad illustration, mechanicals, retouching, airbrushing, charts/graphs and audiovisual materials.

First Contact & Terms: Send query letter with brochure, tearsheets and resume. Samples are filed. Reports back only if interested. Call to schedule an appointment to show portfolio. Portfolio should include roughs, original/final art, slides and transparencies. Pays for design by the hour and by the project. Pays for illustration by the project. Negotiates rights purchased.

Tips: When presenting samples or portfolios, artists "sometimes mistake quantity for quality. Keep it short and show your best work."

THE BOOKMAKERS, INCORPORATED, 298 E. South St., Wilkes-Barre PA 18702. (717)823-9183. President: John Beck. Specializes in publications and technical illustrations. Clients: mostly book publishers. Clients include Simon and Schuster, South-Western and Hunter College. Client list available upon request.

Needs: Works with 5-10 freelance illustrators/year. Uses artists for illustrations, brochures, catalogs, retouching, airbrushing, posters and charts/graphs.

First Contact & Terms: Send query letter with resume, tearsheets, photostats, photocopies, slides and photographs. Samples not filed are returned by SASE. Reports only if interested. Write to schedule an appointment to show a portfolio, which should include b&w thumbnails, roughs, original/final art, final reproduction/product, tearsheets and photostats. Pays for illustration by the project, $20-2,400. Considers complexity of project, client's budget, skill and experience of artist, how work will be used and turnaround time when establishing payment. Buys all rights.

Tips: "We are especially interested in versatility. Don't send too much. Send one good flyer or five illustrations of what you do best."

BOOKMAKERS LTD., 25 Sylvan Rd. South, Westport CT 06880. (203)226-4293. President: Gayle Crump. Specializes in publications and related sales promotion and advertising. Clients: trade and educational publishers. Client list not available.

Needs: Approached by 100 freelance artists/year. Works with 20-30 freelance illustrators and 2 freelance designers/year. "We are agents and designers. We represent artists for juvenile through adult markets."
First Contact & Terms: Send query letter with samples showing style (tearsheets, photostats, printed pieces or slides). Samples not filed are returned. Reports within 2 weeks. Considers skill and experience of artist when establishing payment.
Tips: The most comon mistake freelancers make in presenting samples or portfolios is "too much variety—not enough focus. Be clear about what you are looking for and what you can do in relation to the real markets available."

*BRAINCHILD DESIGNS, INC., 108E 16th St., New York NY 10003. (212)420-1222. President: Manny Goettel. Estab. 1978. Specializes in package and publication design. Clients: toys companies. Clients include Buddy L Corp. Like Like, Darda, Hinkle and JPI. Client list available upon request.
Needs: Approached by 100 freelance artists/year. Works with 1-2 freelance illustrators and 10-15 freelance designers/year. Prefers local artists with experience in mechanicals and packaging. Works on assignment only. Uses illustrators mainly for packaging. Uses designers mainly for packaging and mechanicals. Also uses artists for mechanicals, catalog, ad and direct mail design.
First Contact & Terms: Send query letter with tearsheets, resume and SASE. Samples are filed and are not returned. Reports back to the artist only if interested. Call to schedule an appointment to show a portfolio. Portfolio should include thumbnails, roughs, original/final art, photostats and tearsheets. Pays for design by the hour, $10-18. Pays for illustration by the project. Negotiates rights purchased.

*THE BRUBAKER GROUP, 10560 Dolcedo Way, Los Angeles CA 90077. (213)472-4766. Estab. 1968. Specializes in brand identity, display, interior and package design and technical illustration. Clients: aircraft and automobile manufacturers, toy and electronic companies and theme parks. Current clients include Disney, Mattel, Mazda, Exxon, Lear Jet Corp. and CBS. Client list available upon request.
Needs: Approached by 2-10 freelance artists/year. Works with 2-10 freelance illustrators and designers/year. Prefers artists with experience in product, model construction and consumer product design. Works on assignment only. Uses illustrators mainly for theme park environments and product design. Uses designers mainly for product, environmental and auto design. Also uses artists for brochure design and illustration, poster illustration and design, model making, charts/graphs and audiovisual materials.
First Contact & Terms: Send query letter with tearsheets, photostats, photographs and photocopies. Samples are filed. Samples not filed are not returned. Reports back to the artist only if interested. To show a portfolio, mail b&w photostats and photographs. Pays for design by the hour, $12-60, and by the project. Pays for illustration by the project. Buys all rights.

BUTLER, (formerly Butler Kosh Brooks), 940 N. Highland Ave., Los Angeles CA 90038. (213)469-8128. Vice President/Account Supervisor: Michael Masterson. Estab. 1987. Specializes in corporate identity, displays, direct mail, fashion, packaging and publications. Clients: film companies, fashion, medical and home video distributors.
Needs: Works with 12 freelance artists/year. Works on assignment only. Uses artists for design, brochures, catalogs, books, P-O-P, mechanicals, retouching, posters, model making, direct mail, lettering and logos.
First Contact & Terms: Send query letter with brochure or resume. Samples are filed. Samples not filed are returned by SASE. Reports back within 1 week only if interested. Pays for design and illustration by the hour, $15. Considers complexity of project, client's budget, skill and experience of artist, how work will be used, turnaround time and rights purchased when establishing payment. Rights purchased vary according to project.

*BYRNE DESIGN, 133 W. 19th St., New York NY 10011. (212)807-6671. FAX: (212)633-6194. Creative Director: Pierre Vilmenay. Estab. 1976. Specializes in annual reports and corporate identity. Clients: financial consultants and corporations. Current clients include Paine Webber; Alliance Capital and Peat Marwick. Client list available upon request.
Needs: Approached by 10 freelance artists/year. Works with 3-4 freelance illustrators and designers/year. Uses freelance illustrators and designers mainly for promotional brochures. Also uses artists for brochure design and illustration, mechanicals, lettering, logos and charts/graphs.
First Contact & Terms: Send query letter with brochure and resume. Samples are filed. Reports back only if interested or need arises. To show a portfolio, mail thumbnails, roughs and tearsheets. Pays for design by the hour, $25-50. Pays for illustration by the project. Rights purchased vary according to project.

*CARBONE SMOLAN ASSOCIATES, 170 Fifth Ave., New York NY 10010. (212)807-0011. FAX: (212)807-0870. Senior Designer: Beth Bangor. Estab. 1980. Specializes in corporate identity; display, package, publication and book design; signage and marketing communications. Clients: architects, financial services firms, museums, publishers, corporations and hoteliers. Clients include American Express, Smith Barney, The Rafael Group, Tiffany's, Deloitte & Touche, Merrill Lynch and The Pierpont Morgan Library. Client list available upon request.

Needs: Approached by hundreds of freelance artists/eyar. Works with more than 10 freelance illustrators and up to 10 designers/year. "Must follow drop-off policy—portfolios accepted on Wednesday mornings only 8:30-9:00 a.m. Only three accepted (per week)." Uses illustrators for book design and brochures. Uses designers mainly for "All of our work—from architectural signage to graphic design." Also uses artists for brochure design and illustration, catalog and book design and mechanicals.
First Contact & Terms: Send query letter with resume. Samples are filed or are returned by SASE if requested by artist. Reports back within 1-2 weeks. Write to schedule an appointment to show a portfolio. Portfolio should include tearsheets, photographs, slides and transparencies. Pays for design by the hour, $15-25. Pays for illustration by the project, $350-2,000. Buys one-time rights.

CAREW DESIGN, 200 Gate 5 Rd., Sausalito CA 94965. (415)331-8222. President: Jim Carew. Estab. 1975. Specializes in corporate identity, direct mail and package design.
Needs: Works with 15 freelance illustrators and 2-4 freelance designers/year. Prefers local artists only. Works on assignment only. Uses artists for brochure and catalog design and illustration, mechanicals, retouching, airbrushing, direct mail design, lettering, logos and ad illustration.
First Contact and Terms: Send query letter with brochure, resume and tear sheets. Samples are filed. Samples not filed are returned only if requested by artist. Reports back only if interested. Call to schedule an appointment to show a portfolio, which should include roughs and original/final art. Pays for production by the hour, $18-30. Pays for illustration by the project, $100-1,000+. Considers complexity of project, client's budget, skill and experience of artist, how work will be used, turnaround time and rights purchased when establishing payment. Buys all rights.
Tips: "The best way for an illustrator and a designer to get an assignment is to "show a portfolio.""

CAS ASSOCIATES, Box 4462, Diamond Bar CA 91765. Editor/President: Carl Schoner. Estab. 1988. Specializes in corporate identity, display, direct mail and publication design, signage and cartoons. Clients: small- to medium-size businesses in retail, wholesale and service-related industries. Does ad layout and design for real estate and mortgage companies, graphic design for sport clothing wholesalers.
Needs: Works with 10-20 freelance illustrators and designers/year. Prefers local artists, "but will consider all talent" with experience in graphic design. Prefers humorous cartoons and "clean" logos. Uses illustrators mainly for ad illustration. Uses designers mainly for logos and ad layout. Also uses artists for brochure, P-O-P and poster illustration and design, direct mail design, charts/graphs, lettering, logos, advertisement design and illustration. Especially needs "good cartoonists capable of producing characters for corporate advertising campaigns."
First Contact and Terms: Send photocopies. Samples are filed or are returned if accompanied by a SASE. Reports back within weeks only if interested. Write to schedule an appointment to show a portfolio, which should include roughs, original/final art and final reproduction/product. Pays by the project, $15 minimum. Considers complexity of project, turnaround time and rights purchased when establishing payment. Negotiates rights purchased.
Tips: "For cartoonists and logo designers, the key to assignments is highly imaginative, original artwork coupled with clean lines and only as much detail as is necessary. Original simplicity is the key. We prefer to work with professional graphic artists for logo designs, but we are very open to working with new talent for humorous illustrations and marketing materials."

*CATHEY ASSOCIATES, INC., Suite M-29, 8585 Stemmons, Dallas TX 75247. (214)638-0731. FAX: (214)637-6023. President: Gordon Cathey. Estab. 1975. Specializes in annual reports; brand identity; corporate identity; display, direct mail, package and publication design; and signage. Clients: corporations. Current clients include Frito-Lay, Inc., General Electric Plastics Division, Miller Brewing Company and the University of Texas at Dallas. Client list available upon request.
Needs: Approached by 20-30 freelance artists/year. Works with 4-6 freelance illustrators and 1-2 designers/year. Specifications vary with project demands. Works on assignment only. Uses illustrators mainly for brochures. Uses designers mainly for mechanicals. Also uses artists for lettering, P-O-P design and illustration, poster and ad illustration.
First Contact & Terms: Send query letter with brochure, tearsheets, photographs, photostats, slides and transparencies. Samples are filed. Reports back only if interested. To show a portfolio, call to schedule an appointment, or mail original/final art, photostats, tearsheets, photographs and transparencies (4×5 or larger). Payment is for design and illustration entirely dependent on project requirement. Rights purchased vary according to project.

*WALLACE CHURCH ASSOCIATES, INC., 330 East 48th St., New York NY 10017. (212)755-2903. FAX: (212)355-6872. Studio Manager: Susan Wiley. Specializes in corporate identity and package design. Clients: Fortune 500 food companies, personal and home producer companies and pharmaceutical corporations. Current clients include Kraft, Pillsbury, Gillette and Bristol-Myers. Client list available upon request.

Close-up

Tom Kienberger
Graphic Designer

When Tom Kienberger recently moved his design studio from Hollywood to Long Beach, he created a black-and-white moving announcement with a refined look. Below the graceful type of "From There to Here" appears an etched-like abstraction of an architectural relic. This announcement conveys the image he has of himself as a designer, the type of design he wants to do and the sort of client he wants to have. "I want to do very elegant work," he says. "I just want to do good, responsible design."

This designer, who does corporate identity, collateral, posters, packaging and advertisements (everything from the initial analysis and conceptualization to overseeing production) for such clients as the Museum of Contemporary Art in Los Angeles, CADAM INC., PAC TEL Properties and Westgroup Partners, speaks very calmly and confidently about his design work now, yet he clearly remembers how he felt when just starting out.

"I learned everything the hard way. Coming out of school, you don't know the printing process; you don't know what's available to you, how to get your suppliers and network together, how you do business, who you do business with. The first couple of months were actually frantic—it's like, who does my camera work, who should I use for my typesetting? A million decisions with no experience."

His first assignment was a $1,500 corporate identity and application project for a post-production house in Hollywood. "I was very green at the time. It's amazing how I would approach the job differently now. I didn't really have a formula for how to deal with a client and my own process at the same time. I think back on that and I think, those poor people."

Kienberger received his BFA from the Kansas City Art Institute and then did a year of graduate work at the Rhode Island School of Design. During this training, he picked up the philosophy which now guides him as a designer. "I was taught that the design solution comes out of understanding the problem and objectives. Once you understand what the client is trying to say, you can help illustrate that in a graphic way. I have clients who say, 'We don't have the copy written yet, but do a layout and we'll plug in the copy later.' That's completely wrong. The only way to design is to know what your client wants to say. The more you understand the problem, the better your solution will be."

He says he usually works very closely with the public relations or marketing department and asks many questions. "If you ask the right kinds of questions in the first meeting, you come away from the meeting with a direction. Objectives are not big complicated things. They should be few in number, articulate and realistic."

While Kienberger advises designers to go to art school—which for him was "powerful and energizing," he does not recommend going into business on one's own when just starting out, and suggests working for a studio first.

When he first started out, he did a lot of work for arts institutions because they offered opportunity, and he found the environments very creative and stimulating. He also did as much as he could. "I let everyone know what I was looking for. I mean I've done everything from shopping bags to etching on crystal to palm trees; but it was work and one thing led to another."

Kienberger is very professional about his work. He says he is up at 7 o'clock and in his studio when the phone starts ringing at 9 o'clock. "I don't consider myself as freelance," he says. "I mean I operate a business. I have a responsibility to my client; people rely on me and I have to follow through and be there. If I'm not, there's someone right around the corner who can do what I do and possibly do it better."

While many graphic designers believe self-promotion is very important, he has always let his work speak for itself and relies on referrals for the majority of his work. "In the beginning, I made hundreds of cold calls and never got a client that way. There have been a couple of times when there's been no work coming in and I have absolutely panicked and said, 'I've got to do some self-promotion and fast!' I have a capabilities brochure on myself that's been in the works for 1½ years and thankfully, I've been too busy to complete it." At one point he thought of advertising in a creative directory, but dismissed the idea after the few designers he called said they weren't getting any work out of them.

Another aspect to his success seems to be that he researches his client's market. He says that because many of his clients are in real estate, he subscribes to many of the real estate journals and periodicals of the Southwest. "It's a big plus if I can bring up an article that's pertinent to the subject at hand from one of the journals. Then my client knows I'm on top of things. I feel it's my job to know my client's field of business, to know the competition, the market and take that into account when I design for them."

Kienberger thinks the West Coast is now the leader in many fields of design. He says the market has gotten larger in California due to the Pacific Rim proximity, attracting designers from everywhere. He has two clients based in Japan now and believes that will spread into other contacts. "The Japanese are so sensitive to design. They really like graphics. Coming from their culture, they see it as energetic; they sense and feel the 'California spirit.'"

— Lauri Miller

Kienberger, who loves architecture, did this leasing brochure for PAC TEL Properties' Pacific Mutual Building. The brochure for the Museum of Contemporary Art is a reflection of how he also loves the arts.

Needs: Approached by 15-20 freelance artists/year. Works with 10-12 freelance illustrators and designers/year. Prefers artists with experience in food and personal care rendering. Works on assignment only. Uses illustrators mainly for package art. Uses designers mainly for graphics, package design and mechanicals. Also uses artists for mechanicals, retouching, airbrushing, lettering, logos and model making.

First Contact & Terms: Send query letter with portfolio. Samples are filed. Reports back only if interested. Portfolio should include "everything." Pays for design by the hour, $15-25, and by the project. Pays for illustration by the project, $500 minimum. Buys all rights.

*JANN CHURCH PARTNERS ADVERTISING & GRAPHIC DESIGN, INC., Suite 160, 110 Newport Center Dr., Newport Beach CA 92660. (714)640-6224. FAX: (714)760-5056. President: Jann Church. Estab. 1970. Specializes in annual reports; brand identity; corporate identity; display, interior, direct mail, package and publication design; and signage. Clients: real estate developers, medical/high technology corporations, private and public companies, etc. Current clients include The Nichols Institute, TCW Realty Advisors and the Environmental Systems Research Institute. Client list available upon request.

Needs: Approached by 100 freelance artists/year. Works with 3 freelance illustrators and 5 freelance designers/year. Works on assignment only. Uses designers and illustrators for all work.

First Contact & Terms: Send query letter with resume, photographs and photocopies. Samples are filed. Reports back only if interested. Mail appropriate materials. Portfolio should be "as complete as possible." Rights purchased vary according to project.

*CLIFF AND ASSOCIATES, 715 Fremont Ave., South Pasadena CA 91030. (818)799-5906. FAX: (818)799-9809. Owner: Greg Cliff. Estab. 1984. Specializes in annual reports, corporate identity, direct mail and publication design and signage. Clients: Fortune 500 coporations and performing arts companies. Current clients include Arco, Mattel, Yamaha, Times Mirror, Century 21, Avery, Quotron, Union Oil, Northrup and Southern California Edison.

Needs: Approached by 20 freelance artists/year. Works with 15 freelance illustrators and 20 designers/year. Prefers local artists and art center graduates. Uses illustrators and designers mainly for brochures. Also uses artists for mechanicals; lettering; logos; catalog, book and magazine design, P-O-P and poster design and illustration; and model making.

First Contact & Terms: Send query letter with resume and sample of work. Samples are filed. Does not report back. Call to schedule an appointment to show a portfolio. Portfolio should include thumbnails and b&w photostats and printed samples. Pays for design by the hour, $18-25. Pays for illustration by the project. Buys one-time rights.

Tips: "Make your resume and samples look like a client presentation."

*CN/DESIGN, 205 W. Milton Ave., Rahway NJ 07065. (201)382-1066. FAX: (201)382-8559. Vice President/Creative Director: Bradley B. Manier. Specializes in print advertising, collateral annual reports, corporate identity and direct mail design. Clients: corporations. Client list not available.

Needs: Approached by 25 freelance artists/year. Works with 2 freelance illustrators and 5 freelance designers/year. Uses illustrators mainly for advertising and posters. Uses designers mainly for collaterals. Also uses artists for brochure design, mechanicals, retouching, airbrushing, logos, poster and ad illustration, model making and charts/graphs.

First Contact & Terms: Send query letter with brochure, tearsheets, photostats and resume. Samples are filed. Reports back only if interested. Write to schedule an appointment to show a portfolio. Portfolio should include thumbnails, roughs, original/final art and tearsheets. Pays for design by the hour, $15-50. Pays for illustration by the project, $150-2,000. Rights purchased vary according to project.

WOODY COLEMAN PRESENTS, INC., 490 Rockside Rd., Cleveland OH 44131. (216)661-4222. President: Woody Coleman. Artist's agent. Clients: ad agencies, PR firms and direct corporations.

Needs: Works with 25 freelance artists/year. Artists must have three years of experience. Especially needs photorealistic with figure and product. Uses artists for illustrations.

First Contact & Terms: Send query letter with brochure showing art style or tearsheets, slides and 4x5 transparencies. Samples not filed are returned by SASE. Reports only if interested. To show a portfolio, mail color and 4x5 transparencies. Pays for illustration by the project, $400-10,000. Considers complexity of project, client's budget, skill and experience of artist, how work will be used, turnaround time and rights purchased when establishing payment.

Tips: Artist should send "8 of their 10 best samples within their area of expertise."

COMMERCIAL ARTS, LTD./MARKET DIRECT INC., 301 S. Elmont Dr., Apache Junction AZ 85220-4722. (602)878-3301. President: Lanie Bethka. Specializes in corporate identity, direct mail and publications. Clients: real estate companies, banks, software houses, light manufacturers, engineering firms, colleges, insurance groups and medical groups.

Needs: Works with 1-5 freelance artists/year. Prefers local artists. Works on assignment only. Uses artists for illustrations, retouching, charts/graphs, AV materials and lettering. Prefers tight, realistic style or technical illustrations; pen & ink, airbrush, acrylics, markers, computer illustration and mixed media.

First Contact & Terms: Send query letter with brochure or resume, tearsheets, photostats, photocopies, slides and photographs. Samples are filed or are returned only if requested. Write to schedule an appointment to show a portfolio, which should include thumbnails, roughs, orignal/final art, final reproduction/product, tearsheets, photostats, photographs, b&w and color. Pays for design by the project, $50-5,000 or more. Pays for illustration by the project, $35-1,000. Considers complexity of project, client's budget, skill and experience of artist, how work will be used and turnaround time when establishing payment. Buys all rights.

Tips: Finds most artists through portfolio reviews and samples.

CORPORATE GRAPHICS INC., 17th Floor, 655 Third Ave., New York NY 10017. (212)599-1820. Chairman/Art Director: Bennett Robinson. President: Michael Watras. Specializes in annual reports, corporate identity, brochures and other forms of corporate literature. Clients: various and international. Current clients include Bayer USA, Bell Atlantic and Cellular Communications.

Needs: Work with many freelance artists/year. Works on assignment only. Uses artists for illustration, mechanicals, charts, graphs. Portraiture and annual report illustration is also needed for products, maps, situations, etc.

First Contact & Terms: Send resume and tearsheets. Samples are filed or are returned only if requested by artist. Reports back only if interested. Portfolio drop offs: Mondays and Wednesdays, April 15-November 15 only. To show a portfolio, mail b&w and color tearsheets, photostats, photographs. Pays mechanical artists by the hour, $15-20. Considers complexity of a project, client's budget, skill and experience, how work is to be used and turnaround time when establishing payment.

Tips: "We want top notch quality and sophistication of style. Mechanical artists need to know stat camera and color-key skills. Show variety and range. Send mail pieces each 3-6 month as a way of staying in touch. Be persistent—but not by calling on the phone."

COUSINS DESIGN, 599 Broadway, New York NY 10012. (212)431-8222. Vice President: Morison Cousins. Specializes in packaging and product design. Clients: manufacturing companies.

Needs: Works with 10-12 freelance artists/year. Prefers local artists. Works on assignment only. Uses artists for design, illustration, mechanicals, retouching, airbrushing, model making, lettering and logos. Prefers airbrush, colored pencil and marker as media.

First Contact & Terms: Send query letter with brochure or resume, tearsheets and photocopies. Samples are filed and are returned only if requested. Reports back within 2 weeks only if interested. Write to schedule an appointment to show a portfolio, which should include roughs, final reproduction/product and photostats. Pays for design by the hour, $20-40. Pays for illustration by the hour, $20 minimum or a fee. Considers skill and experience of artist when establishing payment. Buys all rights.

CRAYON DESIGN & COMMUNICATION, 415 Le Moyne, PH2 Montreal Quebec H2Y 1Y5 Canada. (514)842-5938. Art Directors: Sol Lang or Mary Bogdan. Estab. 1980. Specializes in annual reports, brand identity, corporate identity, display, direct mail, package and publication design and signage.

Needs: Prefers local artists only with experience in concept and layout, "especially knowledge of type." Prefers latest trends. Also uses artists for brochure and catalog design and illustration, book magazine and newspaper design, P-O-P design and illustration, mechanicals, poster illustration and design, direct mail design, charts/graphs, logos, advertisement design and illustration.

First Contact and Terms: Send query letter with brochure, resume, tearsheets, slides, photographs and transparencies. Samples are filed or are returned by SASE only if requested by artist. Reports back only if interested. To show a portfolio, mail final reproduction/product, b&w and color tearsheets, photographs and transparencies. Pays by the hour, $11-25 (Canadian). Considers skill and experience of artist when establishing payment.

Tips: "Keep sending updated info and samples as career progresses. A phone call of inquiry would clarify if no assignments have been issued."

CREATIVE WORKS, Suite 300, 631 US Highway 1, North Palm Beach FL 33408. (407)863-4900. Graphics Dept. Head (Mechanicals): David Wright. Product and Interior Design Department Head: Robert Jahn. Specializes in corporate identity, collateral, signage, product and sales offices. Clients: ad agencies, PR firms, real estate developers, manufacturers and inventors. Client list not available.

Needs: Approached by 50 freelance artists/year. Works with 12 freelance illustrators and 50 freelance designers/year. Uses local (work inhouse), experienced artists. Uses artists for design, illustration, mechanicals, airbrushing, model making and drafting. Especially needs drafting/mechanical people.

First Contact & Terms: Send query letter with resume to be kept on file. Samples not kept on file are returned by SASE only if requested. Reports within 1 week. Write to schedule an appointment to show a portfolio, which should include original/final art and photographs. Pays by the project for drafting and mechanicals. Considers complexity of project, client's budget, skill and experience of artist and turnaround time when establishing payment.

Tips: Don't make the mistake of "showing samples which don't accurately represent your capabilities. Send distinctive graphic or artistic resume that is memorable and request an appointment."

JO CULBERTSON DESIGN, INC., 222 Milwaukee St., Denver CO 80206. (303)355-8818. President: Jo Culbertson. Estab. 1976. Specializes in annual reports, corporate identity, direct mail, publication and marketing design and signage. Clients: insurance companies and telecommunications companies, textbook publishers, healthcare providers and professional corporations. Current projects include product literature, food products packaging, annual reports, capabilities brochures and book design. Current clients include Great-West Life Assurance Co., Love Publishing Co., University of Colorado Health Services Center. Client list available upon request.

Needs: Works with 4 freelance illustrators and 2-3 freelance designers/year. Prefers local artists only. Works on assignment only. Uses illustrators mainly for book covers, presentation graphics and general illustration. Uses designers mainly for various print projects. Also uses artists for brochure design and illustration, catalog and P-O-P illustration, mechanicals, lettering and ad illustration.

First Contact and Terms: Send query letter with brochure, resume and samples. Samples are filed or are returned only if requested by artist. Reports back only if interested. Call to schedule an appointment to show a portfolio, which should include roughs, original/final art, final reproduction/product and b&w and color tearsheets and photostats. Pays by the hour, $12-20; or by the project. Considers complexity of project, client's budget, skill and experience of artist, how work will be used, turnaround time and rights purchased when establishing payment. Rights purchased vary according to project.

Tips: Common mistakes freelancers make in presenting samples are "not checking back periodically and not having an original approach—too much like others. Have persistance, develop personal, individualistic style(s)."

CULTURE & DESIGN STUDIO, 401 Fifth Ave., New York, NY 10016. (212)685-2838. Art Director: David Bruner. Estab. 1974. Specializes in direct mail and publication design. Clients include American Leadership Conference, CAUSA International and CG&S Advertising. Client list available upon request.

Needs: Approached by 8 freelance artists/year. Works with 5 freelance illustrators and 7 freelance designers/year. Prefers local artists only. "Mac literacy helps for designers." Works on assignment only. Uses illustrators mainly for magazine articles. Uses designers mainly for conference programs. Also uses artists for brochure, book, poster, direct mail and magazine design; mechanicals; AV material; logos; advertisement design and illustration.

Tips: Common mistakes freelancers make in presenting samples or portfolios are "repetition (slides of flat art already presented) and presenting everything they ever did, not discriminating and choosing a hierachy of their work. Keep it simple."

CWI INC., 255 Glenville Rd., Greenwich CT 06831. (203)531-0300. Contact: Geoffrey Chaite. Design studio. Specializes in packaging, annual reports, brand identity, corporate identity, P-O-P and collateral material, displays, exhibits and shows. Clients: manufacturers of packaged goods, foods, tools, drugs and tobacco, publishing, banks and sports. Client list not available.

Needs: Works with 5-8 freelance illustrators and 4 freelance designers/year. Minimum 8-10 years of experience. Uses artists for P-O-P displays, stationery design, multimedia kits, direct mail, slide sets, brochures/flyers, trade magazines, newspapers, layout, technical art, type spec, paste-up, retouching and lettering. Especially needs photography, illustration and paste-up.

First Contact & Terms: Send flyers, business card, tearsheets, b&w line drawings, roughs, previously published work, comps and mechanicals to be kept on file for future assignments. May return originals to artist at job's completion. Payment is negotiated.

Tips: "Original comps and art should be shown as much as printed units. Show how you created units in steps, i.e. show roughs, comps, pencils, mechanicals, etc."

*JOSEPH B. DEL VALLE, Suite 1011, 41 Union Square West, New York NY 10003. Director: Joseph B. Del Valle. Specializes in annual reports, publications, book design and illustration. Clients: major publishers and museums.

Needs: Works with approximately 6 freelance artists/year. Artists must have experience and be able to work on a job-to-job basis. Uses artists for design and mechanicals.

First Contact & Terms: Send query letter with resume. Reports only if interested. Call or write to schedule an appointment to show a portfolio, which should include final reproduction/product. Pays for design by the hour, $15-25. Considers client's budget and turnaround time when establishing payment.

DE NADOR & ASSOCIATES, 14 Yellow Ferry Harbor, Sausalito CA 94965. (415)332-4098. FAX: (415)332-7431. Coordinating Manager: Margaux. Estab. 1977. Specializes in annual reports, brand identity, corporate identity and publication design. Clients: ad agencies and corporations. Current clients include Brittania

Sportswear Ltd., HBR Hotels, Colliers International. Client list available upon request.

Needs: Approached by 60 freelance artists/year. Works with 2-5 freelance illustrators and 5-10 designers/year. Prefers local artists and artists with experience in technical fields. Works on assignment only. Also uses designers and illustrators for brochure design and illustration, mechanicals, ad design and illustration, P-O-P and mail design.

First Contact & Terms: Send query letter with resume, photographs and photocopies. Samples are filed. Reports back only if interested. To show a portfolio, call or mail thumbnails, roughs, photostats, tearsheets, photographs and transparencies. Pays for design by the hour, $10-35. Pays for illustration by the hour, $15-100. Buys all rights or varying according to project.

*DENTON DESIGN ASSOCIATES, 491 Arbor St., Pasadena CA 91105. (818)792-7141. President: Margi Denton. Estab. 1975. Specializes in annual reports, corporate identity and publication design. Clients: corporate and non-profit markets. Client list not available.

Needs: Approached by 20 freelance artists/year. Works with 5-10 freelance illustrators and 1-2 freelance designers/year. "Need illustrators from anywhere in the U.S." Works with illustrators on assignment only. Uses illustrators for publications, annual reports and brochures.

First Contact & Terms: Send query letter with tearsheets. Samples are filed and are not returned unless requested. Reports back only if interested. Pays for design and illustration by the project. Buys one-time rights; or rights purchased vary according to project.

DESIGN & PRODUCTION INCORPORATED, 7110 Rainwater Pl., Lorton VA 22079. (703)550-8640. Executive Vice President: Jay F. Barnwell, Jr. Specializes in display, interior design, signage and exhibition design. Clients: ad agencies, PR firms, architectural firms, institutions and major corporations. Current clients include Marriott, MCA, Disney and Honeywell. Client list not available.

Needs: Approached by 12-18 freelance artists/year. Works with 6-8 freelance illustrators and 8-12 freelance designers/year. Uses artists for brochures, catalogs, mechanicals, model making and exhibits.

First Contact & Terms: Prefers local artists who are established professionals. Works on assignment only. Send query letter with brochure, resume and samples to be kept on file; call for appointment to show portfolio. Prefers slides or tearsheets as samples. Samples not filed are returned by SASE. Reports within 2 weeks. Pays for design by the hour, $25-50 average; by the project, $1,000-15,000 average. Pays for illustration by the hour, $15-40 average; by the project, $1,000-3,000 average. Considers complexity of project, client's budget, and skill and experience of artist when establishing payment.

Tips: "Only experienced freelancers need apply. Develop a style, a definite, recognizable trait that can be associated to you exclusively."

DESIGN CONSULTANT INCORPORATED, 4907, 505 N. Lake Shore Dr., Chicago IL 60611. (312)642-4670. President: Frederic A Robertson. Estab. 1961. Specializes in brand and corporate identity, direct mail, package and publications design and signage. Clients: commercial, industrial and marketing. Current projects include naming, design identification and packaging for a new product.

Needs: Works with 3-4 freelance illustrators/year. Works with 10-20 freelance designers/year. Prefers local artists only with experience in technical and products illustration. Works on assignment only. Prefers clean line and color. Uses illustrators mainly for technical and product illustrations. Uses designers mainly for layout, development, comprehensive and art. Also uses artists for brochure and catalog design and illustration, P-O-P design and illustration, mechanicals, model making, charts/graphs, lettering, logos and poster, book, direct mail and ad design.

First Contact and Terms: Send query letter with brochure, resume and photocopies. Samples are filed. Reports back only if interested. To show a portfolio, mail roughs, original/final art, final reproduction/product and photostats and photocopies. Pays by the project, $200-1,500. Considers complexity of project, skill and experience of artist, how work will be used, turnaround time and rights purchased when establishing payment. Rights purchased vary according to project.

Tips: "Send resume and photocopies of range of work. State general cost of such work. We will file in reference and contact is needed. Range of hourly rate charged is also helpful."

DESIGN ELEMENTS, INC., #702, 201 W. Short, Lexington KY 40508. (606)252-4468. President: C. Conde. Estab. 1979. Specializes in corporate identity, package and publication design. "Work directly with end user (commercial accounts)." Client list not available.

Needs: Approached by 6-8 freelance artists/year. Works with 2-3 freelance illustrators and 2-3 freelance designers/year. Works on assignment only. Uses artists for brochure and P-O-P design and illustration, mechanicals, airbrushing, poster design, lettering and logos.

First Contact and Terms: Send query letter with brochure, resume, tearsheets and slides. Samples are filed or are returned only if requested by artist. Reports back only if interested. Call or write to schedule an appointment to show a portfolio. Pays by the hour, $15 minimum. Considers complexity of project, client's budget and skill and experience of artist when establishing payment. Buys all rights.

Tips: "Freelancers need to be more selective about portfolio samples—show items actually done by person presenting, or explain why not. Send resume and samples of work first."

*THE DESIGN OFFICE OF STEVE NEUMANN & FRIENDS, Suite 103, 3000 Richmond Ave., Houston TX 77098. (713)629-7501. FAX: (713)520-1171. Associate: Cynthia J. Whitney. Specializes in corporate identity and signage. Clients: hospitals, .
Needs: Works with 1 freelance designer/year. Artists must be local with computer experience. "We are 100% computerized." Uses artists for production and design. Also uses freelance designers for brochure design, lettering, logos and model making. Prefers pen & ink, colored pencil and calligraphy. Especially needs full-time and/or part-time production person.
First Contact & Terms: Send query letter with resume, references, business card and nonreturnable slides to be kept on file. Call for follow up after 15 days—ask for Cynthia Whitney. Pays for design by the hour, $8-12, based on job contract. Considers complexity of project, client's budget, skill and experience of artist, and how work will be used when establishing payment. Rights purchased vary according to project.

DESIGNWORKS, INC., Davis Square, 48 Grove St., Somerville, MA 02144. (617)628-8600. Design Director: Jennie R. Bush. Provides design for publishing industry. Specializes in educational publications. Clients: book publishers. Current clients include DC Heath, Anne R. Dow Assoc., Harvard University, Butterworth Publishing, and Zoland Books. Client list available upon request.
Needs: Approached by 20 freelance artists/year. Works with 6 freelance illustrators and 10 freelance designers/year. Prefers artists with three years of experience; local for design or paste-up. Works on assignment only. Uses artists for book illustration, charts/graphs, brochure and book design and mechanicals. Prefers styles "appropriate for educational materials." Prefers pen & ink, airbrush and colored pencil.
First Contact & Terms: Send query letter with brochure showing art style or resume, tearsheets or photocopies. Samples are filed or returned by SASE if requested. Reports back only if interested. To show a portfolio, mail thumbnails, roughs, original/final art, b&w tearsheets or photostats or call to schedule an appointment. Pays for design by the hour, $18-25. Pays for illustration by the project, $300-5,000. Considers complexity of project, client's budget when establishing payment.
Tips: "Make a neat presentation."

ANTHONY DI MARCO, 2948 Grand Route St. John, New Orleans LA 70119. (504)948-3128. Creative Director: Anthony Di Marco. Estab. 1972. Specializes in brand identity, publications, illustration sculpture, and costume design. Clients: numerous New Orleans Mardi Gras clubs, various churches, printers/agencies. Client list available upon request.
Needs: Approached by 20 or more freelance artists/year. Works with 2-4 freelance illustrators and 2-4 freelance designers/year. Seeks "local artists with ambition. Artists should have substantial portfolios and an understanding of business requirements." Mainly uses artists for fill-in and finish. Also uses artists for design, illustration, mechanicals, retouching, airbrushing, posters, model making, charts/graphs. Prefers highly polished, finished art; pen & ink, airbrush, charcoal/pencil, colored pencil, watercolor, acrylic, oil, pastel, collage and marker.
First Contact & Terms: Send query letter with resume, business card and slides and tearsheets to be kept on file. Samples not kept on file are returned by SASE. Reports back within 1 week if interested. Call or write for appointment to show portfolio. Pays for illustration by the project, $100 minimum. Considers complexity of project, skill and experience of artist, turnaround time and rights purchased when establishing payment.
Tips: "Keep professionalism in mind at all times. Artists should put forth their best effort. Apologizing for imperfect work is a common mistake freelancers make when presenting a portfolio. Include prices for completed works (avoid overpricing). The best way to introduce yourself to us is to call or write for a personal appearance."

DIAMOND ART STUDIO LTD., 11 E. 36th St., New York NY 10016. (212)685-6622. Creative Directors: Gary and Douglas Diamond. Vice President: Douglas Ensign. Art studio. Clients: agencies, corporations, manufacturers and publishers. Assigns 800 jobs/year.
Needs: Employs 10 illustrators/month. Uses artists for comprehensive illustrations, cartoons, charts, graphs, layout, lettering, logo design, paste-up, retouching, technical art and type spec. Prefers pen & ink, airbrush, colored pencil, watercolor, acrylic, pastel and marker.
First Contact & Terms: Send resume and tearsheets to be kept on file. SASE. Write for interview to show a portfolio. Pays for design by the hour. Pays for illustration by the hour and by project. Considers complexity of project, client's budget, skill and experience of artist, and turnaround time when establishing payment.
Tips: "Leave behind something memorable and well thought out."

DONATO & BERKLEY INC., 386 Park Ave. S, New York NY 10016. (212)532-3884. FAX (212)532-3921. Contact: Sy Berkley or Steve Sherman. Estab. 1956. Advertising art studio. Specializes in direct mail response advertising, annual reports, brand identity, corporate identity and publications. Clients: ad agencies, PR firms, direct response advertisers and publishers.

Needs: Works with 1-2 freelance illustrators and 1-2 freelance designers/month. Local experienced artists only. Uses freelance artwork mainly for video wraps and promotion. Also uses artists for consumer magazines, direct mail, brochures/flyers, newspapers, layout, technical art, type spec, paste-up, lettering and retouching. Especially needs illustration, retouching and mechanical paste-up. Prefers pen & ink, airbrush, watercolor and oil as media.

First Contact & Terms: Call for interview. Send brochure showing art style, flyers, business card, resume and tearsheets to be kept on file. No originals returned to artist at job's completion. Call to schedule an appointment to show a portfolio, which should include thumbnails, roughs, original/final art and final reproduction/product. Pays for design by the hour,$25-50 or by the project, $75-1,500. Pays for illustration by the project, $75-1,500. Considers complexity of project and client's budget when establishing payment.

Tips: "We foresee a need for direct response art directors and the mushrooming of computer graphics. Clients are much more careful as to price and quality of work. Include 8x10 chromes and original samples in a portfolio. Don't show school samples."

*EHN GRAPHICS, INC., 244 E. 46th St., New York NY 10017. (212)661-5947. President: Jack Ehn. Specializes in annual reports, book design, corporate identity, direct mail, publications and signage. Current clients include MacMillan and McGraw Hill. Client list available upon request.

Needs: Approached by 20 freelance artists/year. Works with 10-12 freelance artists/year. Uses artists for illustration, books, mechanicals, retouching and direct mail packages.

First Contact & Terms: Send query letter with samples. Samples not filed are returned only if requested. Reports only if interested. Call or write to schedule an appointment to show a portfolio, which should include original/final art and final reproduction/product. Considers complexity of project, client's budget, and skill and experience of artist when establishing payment.

RAY ENGLE & ASSOCIATES, 626 S. Kenmore, Los Angeles CA 90005. (213)381-5001. President: Ray Engle. Estab. 1963. Specializes in annual reports, corporate identity, displays, interior design, direct mail, packaging, publications and signage. Clients: ad agencies, PR firms, direct clients. Current clients include IBM, KCET and Hughes. Client list available upon request.

Needs: Approached by 200 freelance artists/year. Works with 4 freelance illustrators and 5 freelance designers/year. Prefers local artists; top quality only. Mainly uses artists for illustration. Also uses freelance artists for brochure and catalog design and illustration, book and magazine design, P-O-P display, mechanicals, retouching, airbrushing, posters, model making, charts/graphs, lettering and logos. Prefers pen & ink, airbrush, colored pencil, marker and calligraphy.

First Contact & Terms: Send query letter with brochure showing art style or resume and tearsheets, photostats, photocopies, slides or photographs. Samples are filed or are returned if accompanied by a SASE. Reports back only if interested. Call to schedule an appointment to show a portfolio. Mail b&w and color thumbnails, roughs, original/final art, final reproduction/product, tearsheets, photostats, photographs. Pays for design by the hour, $25-50; by the project, $100 minimum; by the day, $250 minimum. Pays for illustration by the project, $75 minimum. Considers complexity of project, client's budget, how work will be used, turn-around time and rights purchased when establishing payment. Rights purchased vary according to project.

Tips: "Think of how you can be of service to us—not how we can be of service to you. Send promotional piece, then follow up with a phone call. Be succinct, businesslike. Respect my time."

ERIKSON/DILLON ART SERVICES, 31 Meadow Rd., Kings Park NY 11754-3812. (516)544-9191. Art Director: Toniann Dillon. Specializes in publications and technical illustration. Clients: book publishers. Current clients include Lab Aids, Inc., and Global Book Co. Client list not available.

Needs: Approached by 25 freelance artists/year. Works with 8-10 freelance artists/year and 2 freelance designers/year. Local artists only. Uses artists for advertising illustration, book design and illustration, mechanicals, retouching and charts/graphs.

First Contact & Terms: Send query letter with resume and photocopies to be kept on file. Samples not kept on file are not returned. Does not report back. Call to schedule an appointment to show a portfolio, which should include final reproduction/product. Pays for design by the hour, $4.50-20; by the project, $50-1,000; by the day, $40-100. Pays for illustration by the hour, $4.50-$9; by the project, $25-$100; by the day, $40-80. Considers complexity of project and client's budget when establishing payment.

Tips: "Presentation should be at a size that can be accessed in a filing system. Leave copies of samples as reminder. Send updated samples. Call first—show only work relative to my needs."

FALCO & FALCO INCORPORATED, Williamsburg Commons, 6G Aver Court, East Brunswick NJ 08816. (201)390-0099. Art Director: Marie Falco. Specializes in annual reports, corporate identity and direct mail. Current clients include Shearson Lehman Hutton, Thomas Publishing Co., Surnoff Center and Prudential. Client list available upon request.

Needs: Approached by 25 freelance artists/year. Works with 10 freelance illustrators/year. Prefers local artists only with experience in corporate communications. Works on assignment only. Uses artists for brochure, catalog and P-O-P illustration; mechanicals; retouching and airbrushing.

First Contact and Terms: Send query letter with brochure, resume, tearsheets, photostats, photocopies, slides, photographs and transparencies; "any of these are fine." Samples are filed or are returned only if requested by artist. Reports back within 10 days. Call or write to schedule an appointment to show a portfolio, which should include roughs, original/final art, final reproduction/product, b&w and color tearsheets and photographs. Payment depends on project. Considers complexity of project, client's budget and how work will be used when establishing payment. Rights purchased vary according to project.
Tips: "Concentrate on your specialty. Don't make a sloppy presentation."

FINN STUDIO LIMITED, 154 E. 64th St., New York NY 10021. (212)838-1212. Creative Director: Finn. Estab. 1970. Clients: theatres, boutiques, magazines, fashion and ad agencies.
Needs: Uses artists for T-shirt designs, illustrations, calligraphy; creative concepts in art for fashion and promotional T-shirts.
First Contact & Terms: Mail slides. SASE. Reports within 4 weeks. Pays $50-500; sometimes also offers royalty.
Tips: "Too often artists bring in the wrong media of art for the product."

FITZPATRICK DESIGN GROUP, Suite 203, 2109 Broadway, New York NY 10023. (212)580-5842. Vice President: Robert Herbert. Retail planning and design firm. Current clients include Bloomingdale's, Jordan Marsh, Neiman Marcus, British Home Stores, Century 21, Dayton Hudson, Host/Marriott, Jenss. Client list available upon request (for potential clients only).
Needs: Approached by 10-20 freelance artists/year. Works with 2 freelance illustrators and 1 freelance designer/year. Prefers experienced freelancers with references. Works on assignment only. Uses freelance artists for interior design and renderings and design consulting.
First Contact & Terms: Send query letter with brochure showing art style or resume. Samples are filed. Samples not filed are returned by a SASE only if requested. "We usually ask the artist to call after we have had time to review the material." Write to schedule an appointment to show a portfolio, which should include photographs and whatever materials the artist thinks are pertinent. Negotiates payment. Considers complexity of project, skill and experience of artist, turnaround time and client's budget when establishing payment.
Tips: "While it is good to have an overall view of your work, you should also include specifics that relate to what we need done. For example, we primarily specialize in retail stores; we want to see examples of your experience in that area. Never call 'out of the blue.' Never show up without an appointment, and ask if there are specifics that you need to bring with you."

HANS FLINK DESIGN INC., 7-11 S. Broadway, White Plains NY 10601. (914)328-0888. President: Hans D. Flink. Specializes in brand identity, corporate identity, packaging and signage. Clients: corporate and packaged product companies.
Needs: Works with 10-20 freelance artists/year. Uses artists for design, illustration, P-O-P displays, mechanicals, retouching, airbrushing, model making, lettering, logos and package-related services.
First Contact & Terms: Send query letter with brochure and resume to be kept on file. Reports back only if interested. Call or write for appointment to show portfolio. Pays for design by the hour, $10-35 average; by the project, $500-3,000 average; by the day, $100-250 average. Pays for illustration by the project, $250-2,000 average. Considers complexity of project, client's budget, skill and experience of artist and how work will be used when establishing payment.

FREELANCE EXPRESS, INC., 111 E. 85th St., New York NY 10028. (212)427-0331. Multi-service company. Estab. 1988.
Needs: Uses artists for cartoons, charts, graphs, illustration, layout, lettering, logo design and mechanicals.
First Contact & Terms: Mail resume and photocopied samples that need not be returned. "Say you saw the listing in *Artist's Market*." Provide materials to be kept on file for future assignments. No originals returned to artist at job's completion.

*FREELANCE PROFESSIONALS OF CHICAGO, INC., Suite 660, 53 W. Jackson, Chicago IL 60604. (312)427-5077. FAX: (312)427-8501. Freelance Coordinator: Marc Stopeck. Specializes in annual reports, direct mail design and publication design, technical illustration and promotional materials. Clients: ad agencies, publishing companies, nonprofits and corporations. Client list not available.
Needs: Approached by 100 freelance artists/year. Works with 30 freelance illustrators and 20 designers/year. Prefers artists with experience in editorial illustration and designers with DTP experience. Uses illustrators mainly for editorial. Uses designers mainly for ads, brochures and newsletters. Also uses artists for catalog design, mechanicals, book design, magazine design and illustration, poster design and illustration, charts/graphs.
First Contact & Terms: Send query letter with resume and tearsheets. Samples are filed. Reports back within 1 month. Mail appropriate materials, roughs and tearsheets. Pays for design by the hour. Pays for illustration by the project. Rights purchased vary according to project.

FREEMAN DESIGN GROUP, 415 Farms Rd., Greenwich CT 06831. (203)968-0026. President: Bill Freeman. Estab. 1972. Specializes in annual reports, corporate identity, package and publication design and signage. Clients: corporations. Current projects include annual reports and company magazines. Client list available upon request.

Needs: Approached by 35 freelance artists/year. Works with 5 freelance illustrators and 5 freelance designers/year. Prefers artists with experience in production. Works on assignment only. Uses illustrators for mechanicals, retouching and charts/graphs.

First Contact & Terms: Send query letter with brochure showing art style, resume and tearsheets. Samples are filed or are returned if accompanied by SASE. "Does not report back." Call to schedule an appointment to show a portfolio or mail original/final art and tearsheets. Pays for design by the hour, $15-25; by the project, $150-3,000. Considers complexity of projects, client's budget, skill and experience of artist, how work will be used and rights purchased when establishing payment.

Tips: "Send us a sample of a promotional piece."

HELENA FROST ASSOCIATES, LTD., 117 E. 24th St., New York NY 10010. (212)475-6642. President: Helena R. Frost. Estab. 1986. Specializes in packaging, publications and textbooks "at all levels in all disciplines." Clients: publishers.

Needs: Works with over 100 freelance artists/year. Works on assignment only. Prefers realistic style. Uses artists for book design, mechanicals and charts/graphs.

First Contact & Terms: Send query letter with brochure. Samples are filed or are returned only if requested by artist. Does not report back. Write to schedule an appointment to show a portfolio, which should include roughs, final reproduction/product and tearsheets. Pays for design and illustration by the project. Considers client's budget, turnaround time and rights purchased when establishing payment. Buys one-time rights.

***FUNK & ASSOCIATES GRAPHIC COMMUNICATIONS**, 1234 Pearl St., Eugene OR 97401. (503)485-1932. President/Creative Director: David Funk. Estab. 1980. Specializes in annual reports, corporate identity, direct mail, package and publication design and signage. Clients: corporations, primarily industrial and high tech. Current clients include Spectra Physics, Department of Agriculture City of Eugene, Whittier Wood Producers. Client list available upon request.

Needs: Approached by 50-100 freelance artists/year. Works with 8-12 freelance illustrators and 10 freelance designers/year. "We have a wide variety of clients with diverse needs." Uses illustrators mainly for conceptual and technical illustration. Uses designers mainly for overflow projects and specialized skills. Also uses artists for brochure design, brochure illustration, mechanicals, lettering, P-O-P design, poster and ad illustration.

First Contact & Terms: Send query letter with resume and photocopies. Samples are filed. Reports back only if interested. Write to schedule an appointment to show portfolio. Portfolio should include thumbnails, roughs, original/final art and transparencies. Pays for design by the hour, $15-45, by the project, $200-5,000. Pays for illustration by the hour, $15 minimum. "Payment is usually done by bid." Negotiates rights purchased, and rights purchased vary according to project.

STEVE GALIT ASSOCIATES, INC., 5105 Monroe Rd., Charlotte NC 28205. (704)537-4071. President: Stephen L. Galit. Specializes in annual reports, corporate identity, direct mail, publications and technical illustrations. Clients: ad agencies and corporations.

Needs: Works with 15 freelance artists/year. Looks for "expertise, talent and capability." Uses freelance artists for brochure and catalog illustration, retouching, airbrushing, model making, charts/graphs and lettering.

First Contact & Terms: Send query letter with brochure showing art style or tearsheets, photostats, photocopies, slides or photographs. Samples are filed or are returned if accompanied by a SASE. Reports back only if interested. Call or write to schedule an appointment to show a portfolio. Negotiates payment. Considers client's budget, skill and experience of artist and how work will be used. Rights purchased vary according to project.

GILLIAN/CRAIG ASSOCIATES, INC., Suite 301, 165 8th St., San Francisco CA 94103. (415)558-8988. President: Gillian Smith. Estab. 1984. Specializes in annual reports, corporate identity, package and publication design and signage.

Needs: Works with 3-4 freelance illustrators/year. Prefers artists with experience in Macintosh computer design. Works on assignment only. Uses illustrators mainly for annual reports, sometimes brochures or collateral. Uses designers mainly for production, "but almost never".

First Contact and Terms: Send query letter with brochure, resume and tearsheets. Samples are filed or are returned if accompanied by a SASE. Reports back only if interested. To show a portfolio, mail appropriate materials or drop off portfolio. Pays by the project, $100-3,500, "depending on nature of project and amount of work." Rights purchased vary according to project.

GOLDSMITH YAMASAKI SPECHT INC, Suite 510, 900 N. Franklin, Chicago IL 60610. (312)266-8404. Industrial design consultancy. President: Paul B. Specht. Specializes in corporate identity, packaging, product design and graphics. Clients: industrial firms, institutions, service organizations, ad agencies, government agencies, etc.

Needs: Works with 6-10 freelance artists/year. "We generally use local artists, simply for convenience." Works on assignment only. Uses artists for design (especially graphics), illustration, retouching, model making, lettering and production art. Prefers collage and marker.

First Contact & Terms: Send query letter with resume and samples to be kept on file. Samples not kept on file are returned only if requested. Reports only if interested. Call or write to schedule an appointment to show a portfolio, which should include roughs and final reproduction/product. Pays for design by the hour, $20 minimum. Pays for illustration by the project; payment depends on project. Considers complexity of project, client's budget, skill and experience of artist, how work will be used, turnaround time and rights purchased when establishing payment.

Tips: "If we receive many inquiries, obviously our time commitment may necessarily be short. Please understand. We use very little outside help, but it is increasing (mostly graphic design and production art)."

ALAN GORELICK DESIGN, INC., Marketing Communications, 8 High St., Morristown NJ 07960-6807. President/Creative Director: Alan Gorelick. Estab. 1974. Specializes in corporate identity, displays, direct mail, signage, technical illustration and company and product literature. Clients: health care and pharmaceutical corporations, industry, manufacturers. Client list not available.

Needs: Approached by 150 freelance artists/year. Works with 10 freelance illustrators and 20 freelance designers/year. Works with "seasoned professional or extremely talented entry-level" artists only. Uses artists for design, illustration, brochures, mechanicals, retouching, airbrushing, posters, direct mail packages, charts/graphs, logos and advertisements.

First Contact & Terms: Send query letter with brochure, resume, business card, photostats, slides, photocopies and tearsheets to be kept on file. Samples not filed are returned by SASE only if requested. Reports only if interested. Write for appointment to show portfolio, which should include color and b&w thumbnails, roughs, original/final art, final reproduction/product, tearsheets, photostats and photographs. Pays for design by the hour, $20-50. Pays for illustration by the hour, $15-50; by the project, $250-5,000. Considers complexity of project, client's budget, and skill and experience of artist when establishing payment.

Tips: Requires "straight talk, professional work ethic and commitment to assignment." Looking for "neat work, neat appearance, and a broad selection from rough to finish. 'Current' printed pieces."

*TOM GRABOSKI ASSOCIATES, INC., Suite 11, 3315 Rice St., Coconut Grove FL 33133. (305)445-2522. FAX: (305)445-5885. President: Tom Graboski. Estab. 1980. Specializes in exterior/interior signage, environmental graphics, corporate identity, publication design and print graphics. Clients: corporations, museums, a few ad agencies. Current clients include Universal Studios, Florida, Royal Caribbean Cruise Line and The Equity Group.

Needs: Approached by 50-80 freelance artists/year. Works with approximately 4-8 freelance designers/mechanical artists/draftspersons/year. Prefers artists with a background in signage and knowledge of architecture. Freelance artists used in conjunction with signage projects and occasionally miscellaneous print graphics.

First Contact & Terms: Send query letter with resume. "We will contact designer/artist to arrange appointment for portfolio review. Portfolio should be representative of artist's work and skills; presentation should be in a standard portfolio format." Pays by the hour. Rights purchased vary per project.

*GRAFICA DESIGN SERVICE, 7529 Remmet Ave., Canoga Park CA 91303. (818)712-0071. FAX: (818)348-7582. Designer: Larry Girardi. Estab. 1974. Specializes in corporate identity, package and publication design, signage and technical illustration. Clients: ad agencies, corporations, government, medium size businesses. Current clients include West Oaks Advertising, C.R. Laurence, Windsor Publications. Client list available upon request.

Needs: Approached by 25-50 freelance artists/year. Works with 5-10 freelance illustrators and designers/year. Prefers local artists and artists with experience in airbrush and Apple Macintosh computer graphics. Works on assignment only. Uses illustrators mainly for technical illustration and airbrush illustration. Uses designers mainly for design-layout/thumbnails and comps. Also uses artists for brochure design and illustration, catalog design, mechanicals, retouching, airbrushing, lettering, logos, ad design, catalog illustration, P-O-P illustration, charts/graphs, ad illustration and Mac-computer production.

First Contact & Terms: Send query letter with brochure, resume, SASE, tearsheets, photographs, photocopies, photostats and slides. Samples are filed or are returned by SASE if requested. Reports back only if interested. To show a portfolio, mail thumbnails, roughs, b&w and color photostats, tearsheets, photographs, slides and transparencies. Pays for design by the hour, $15-50; by the project, $100-5,000. Pays for illustration by the hour and by the project. "The payment is based on the complexity of the project, the budget and the experience of the artist." Rights purchased vary according to project.

*GRAHAM DESIGN, Suite 210, 1825 K St. NW, Washington DC 20007. (202)833-9657. FAX: (202)466-8500. Senior Art Director: Stephanie McConnell. Estab. 1947. Specializes in annual reports, corporate identity, publication design and signage. Clients: corporations, associations and the government. Current clients include Heritage Foundation and Palmer National Bank. Client list available upon request.
Needs: Approached by "too many" freelance artists/year. Works with 12 freelance illustrators and 12 freelance designers/year. Prefers local artists only. Works on assignment only. Also uses artists for brochure design and illustration, mechanicals, airbrushing and logos.
First Contact & Terms: Send query letter with brochure and resume. Samples are filed. Does not report back, in which case the artist should call. Call or write to schedule an appointment to show a portfolio, which should include b&w and color thumbnails, photostats, slides, roughs, tearsheets, transparencies, original/final art and photographs. Pays for design and illustration by the hour, $30 minimum. Negotiates rights purchased.

*GRAPHIC ART RESOURCE ASSOCIATES, 257 West 10th St., New York NY 10014-2508. (212)929-0017. FAX: (212)929-0017. Owner: Robert Lassen. Estab. 1980. Specializes in annual reports, corporate identity, direct mail design, publication design, signage, print advertising and marketing communications. Clients: corporations and institutions. Current clients include United Mineral and Chemical Corp., Columbia University and Comvest Corp. Client list not available.
Needs: Approached by 24 freelance artists/year. Works with 1 freelance illustrator/year. Prefers "style, professionalism, flexibility and ability to follow instructions." Works on assignment only. Uses illustrators mainly "to provide effects I can't get with photos, including computer graphics." Uses designers mainly "to offer alternatives to my own designs." Also uses artists for retouching, airbrushing, lettering, model making, charts/graphs, ad illustration and computer graphics.
First Contact & Terms: Send query letter with brochure, tearsheets, resume, photographs, slides and transparencies. Some samples are filed; samples not filed are not returned. Does not report back, in which case artist should wait until he or she is called. Call to schedule an appointment to show portfolio. Portfolio should include whatever he/she thinks is appropriate. Pays by the project, $150. Pays for illustration by the project, $150. Rights purchased vary according to project.
Tips: Finds that "many young designers make designs for design's sake and lack awareness of design as a tool. Don't show me fashion. Don't show me proportional distortion except as humor. Don't show me bad typography."

*GRAPHIC DATA, 804 Tourmaline St., San Diego CA 92109. (619)274-4511. President: Carl Gerle. Estab. 1971. Specializes in publication design. Clients: industrial and publishing companies. Current clients include IEEE. Client list available upon request.
Needs: Approached by 20 freelance artists/year. Works with 2 freelance illustrators and 4 freelance designers/year. Prefers local artists and designers with interest in using computer design systems. Works on assignment only. Uses illustrators mainly for architectural, landscape and technical drawing. Uses designers mainly for architectural and publication design. Also uses artists for mechanicals, retouching, airbrushing, book design, poster illustration and design, model making and computer design.
First Contact & Terms: Send query letter with brochure, resume and photostats. Samples are filed. Reports back to the artist only if interested. Write to schedule an appointment to show a portfolio. Portfolio should include whatever the artist thinks is appropriate. Rights purchased vary according to project.

GRAPHIC DESIGN CONCEPTS, Suite 2, 4123 Wade St., Los Angeles CA 90066. President: C. Weinstein. Estab. 1980. Specializes in annual reports; corporate identity; displays; direct mail; package, publication and industrial design. "Our clients include public and private corporations, government agencies, international trading companies, ad agencies and PR firms." Current projects include new product development for electronic, hardware, cosmetic, toy and novelty companies.
Needs: Works with 15 freelance illustrators and 25 freelance designers/year. "Looking for highly creative idea people, all levels of experience." All styles considered. Uses illustrators mainly for commercial illustration. Uses designers mainly for product and graphic design. Also uses artists for brochure and catalog design and illustration; book, magazine, and newspaper design; P-O-P design and illustration; mechanicals; retouching; airbrushing; poster illustration and design; model making; direct mail design; charts/graphs; lettering; logos; advertisement design and illustration.
First Contact and Terms: Send query letter with brochure, resume, tearsheets, photostats, photocopies, slides, photographs and transparencies. Samples are filed or are returned if accompanied by SASE. Reports back within 10 days with SASE. Portfolio should include thumbnails, roughs, original/final art, final reproduction/product, tearsheets, transparencies and references from employers. Pays for design and illustration by the hour, $15 minimum. Considers complexity of project, client's budget, skill and experience of artist, how work will be used, turnaround time and rights purchased when establishing payment.
Tips: "Send a resume if available. Send samples of recent work or *high quality* copies. Everything sent to us should have a professional look. After all, it is the first impression we will have of you. Selling artwork is a business. Conduct yourself in a businesslike manner."

*GRAPHIC DESIGN INC., 23844 Sherwood, Center Line MI 48015. (313)758-0480. General Manager: Norah Heppard.
Needs: Works on assignment only. Uses artists for brochure design; catalog design, illustration and layout; direct mail packages; advertising design and illustration; and posters.
First Contact & Terms: Send query letter with resume and photocopies. Samples are filed or are returned only if requested. Reports back within 1 week. Write to schedule an appointment to show a portfolio or mail thumbnails, roughs, original/final art, final reproduction/product and color and b&w tearsheets, photostats and photographs. Pays by the project, $50-2,000. Considers complexity of project, available budget, turn-around time and rights purchased when establishing payment. Buys all rights.
Tips: Artists must have the "ability to make deadlines and keep promises."

GRAPHICUS CORPORATION, 2025 Maryland Ave., Baltimore MD 21218. (301)727-5553. Art Director: Charles Piccirilli. Estab. 1974. Specializes in design and advertising; also annual reports, advertising campaigns, direct mail, brand identity and corporate identity, displays, packaging, publications and signage. Clients: recreational sport industries, fleet leasing companies, technical product manufacturers, commercial packaging corporations, direct mail advertising firms, realty companies, banks, publishers and software companies.
Needs: Works with 2-3 freelance artists/year. Works on assignment only. Mainly uses freelancers for mechanicals and illustration. Also uses artists for advertising, brochure, catalog and poster illustration, retouching and AV presentations. Especially needs high-quality illustration.
First Contact & Terms: Send query letter with resume, photocopies and photographs; prefers originals as samples. Samples returned by SASE. Reports on whether to expect possible future assignments. To show a portfolio, mail roughs and original/final art or call to schedule an appointment. Pays for design and illustration by the hour, $20-45. Considers complexity of project, client's budget, and skill and experience of artist when establishing payment. Buys one-time or reprint rights; rights purchased vary according to project.
Tips: "Portfolios should include work from previous assignments. The most common mistake freelancers make is not being professional with their presentations. Send a cover letter with photocopies of work."

GROUP FOUR DESIGN, 147 Simsbury Rd., Avon CT 06001-0717. (203)678-1570. Principal: Frank von Holzhausen. Specializes in corporate communications, product design and packaging design. Clients: corporations dealing in consumer and office products.
Needs: Works with 5-10 freelance artists/year. Artists must have at least two years of experience. Uses artists for illustration, mechanicals, airbrushing and model making.
First Contact & Terms: Send query letter with resume and slides. Samples not filed are returned. Reports only if interested. To show a portfolio, mail roughs and original/final art. Pays mechanical artists by the hour, $12-20; pays for design by the hour, $30 and up. Considers client's budget, and skill and pertinent experience of artist when establishing payment.
Tips: "We look for creativity in all artists seeking employment and expect to see that in their resume and portfolio."

*HAMMOND DESIGN ASSOCIATES, INC., 206 W. Main, Lexington KY 40507. (606)259-3639. FAX: (606)259-3697. Vice-President: Kelly Johns. Estab. 1986. Specializes in annual reports; brand identity and corporate identity; display, direct mail, package and publication design and signage. Clients: corporations, universities and colleges. Client list not available.
Needs: Approached by 20-24 freelance artists/year. Works with 7 freelance illustrators/year. Works on assignment only. Uses illustrators mainly for brochures and ad illustration. Also uses illustrators for airbrushing, lettering, P-O-P and poster illustration and charts/graphs.
First Contact & Terms: Send query letter with brochure or resume. Samples are filed or returned by SASE if requested by artist. Reports back only if interested. To show a portfolio, mail thumbnails, roughs, photostats and tearsheets. Pays for design and illustration by the hour, $10-65, by the project, $100-1,000, by the day, $85-250. Buys all rights.

*THOMAS HILLMAN DESIGN, 193 Middle St., Portland ME 04101. (207)773-3727. Design Director: Thomas Hillman. Estab. 1984. Specializes in annual reports, corporate identity, direct mail design, package design and publication design. Clients: businesses and corporations.
Needs: Approached by 30-50 freelance artists/year. Works with 6-12 freelance illustrators/year. Prefers local artists and artists with experience in illustration. Works on assignment only. Uses illustrators mainly for collateral. Also uses illustrators for brochure, catalog and poster design.
First Contact & Terms: Send query letter with tearsheets and photocopies. Samples are filed. Samples not filed are returned by SASE if requested by artist. Reports back only if interested. To show a portfolio, call or mail tearsheets and copies. Pays for illustration by the project, $75-1,500. Buys all rights, or rights purchased vary according to project.

DAVID HIRSCH DESIGN GROUP, INC., Suite 622, 205 W. Wacker Dr., Chicago IL 60606. (312)329-1500. President: David Hirsch. Specializes in annual reports, corporate identity, publications and promotional literature. Clients: PR, real estate, financial and industrial firms.
Needs: Works with over 30 freelance artists/year. Uses artists for design, illustrations, brochures, retouching, airbrushing, AV materials, lettering, logos and photography.
First Contact & Terms: Send query letter with promotional materials showing art style or samples. Samples not filed are returned by SASE. Reports only if interested. Call to schedule an appointment to show a portfolio, which should include roughs, final reproduction/product, tearsheets and photographs. Considers complexity of project, client's budget and how work will be used when establishing payment.
Tips: "We're always looking for talent at fair prices."

*MEL HOLZSAGER/ASSOCIATES, INC., 275 Seventh Ave., New York NY 10001. (212)741-7373. President/Art Director: Mel Holzsager. Specializes in corporate identity, packaging and general graphic design. Clients: publishers and manufacturers.
Needs: Works with occasional freelance artists according to the work load. Prefers local artists. Uses artists for advertising and brochure illustration, mechanicals and retouching.
First Contact & Terms: Send brochure showing art style to be kept on file. Samples returned only if requested. Call or write to schedule an appointment to show a portfolio, which should include thumbnails, roughs and original/final art. Negotiates payment.
Tips: A mistake artists make is "trying to be too versatile. Specialization would be an advantage."

HUSTON AND COMPANY, Box 1034, Burlington VT 05402-1034. (802)864-5928. Principal: B. Huston. Specializes in interior design, packaging, publications and signage. Clients: manufacturers, communication departments, museums and corporations.
Needs: Works with 24 freelance artists/year. Works on assignment only. Uses artists for design, illustration, books, mechanicals and model making.
First Contact & Terms: Send query letter with resume. Samples not filed are returned only if requested. Reports only if interested. Call to show a portfolio, which should include thumbnails, roughs and photographs. Pays for design by the hour, $9-15. Pays for illustration by the hour, $25. Considers complexity of project, client's budget, skill and experience of artist, and turnaround time when establishing payment.

ELLIOT HUTKIN INC., 2253 Linnington Ave., Los Angeles CA 90064. (213)475-3224. Art Director: Elliot Hutkin. Estab. 1982. Specializes in publication design. Clients: corporations and publishers. Current projects: corporate magazine and travel magazine, miscellaneous corporate publications.
Needs: Works with 10 freelance illustrators and 1 freelance designer/year. Works on assignment only. Uses illustrators mainly for editorial illustration. Also uses artists for retouching, airbrushing, charts/graphs, lettering and logos.
First Contact and Terms: Send query letter with tearsheets, photocopies and photographs. Samples are filed or are returned if accompanied by a SASE. Reports back only if interested. Call to schedule an appointment to show a portfolio, which should include roughs, final reproduction/product, b&w and color tearsheets, photographs. Pays by the project, $75-2,500.
Tips: "Send samples of work (include *all* styles and black and white). Advertise in *LA Workbook*. Have local (LA) rep."

IDENTITY CENTER, Suite Q, 1340 Remington Rd, Schaumburg IL 60173. President: Wayne Kosterman. Specializes in brand identity, corporate identity, print communications and signage. Clients: corporations, hospitals and banks.
Needs: Works with 6-10 freelance artists/year. Prefers 3-5 years of experience minimum. Uses artists for illustration, mechanicals, retouching and lettering.
First Contact & Terms: Send resume and photocopies. Samples are filed or are returned. Reports back within 1 week. To show a portfolio, mail original/final art, photostats and photographs. Pays for design by the hour, $15-20. Pays for illustration by the hour, $10-25. Considers client's budget, skill and experience of artist and how work will be used when establishing payment. Buys one-time rights; rights purchased vary according to project.
Tips: "Not interested in amateurs or 'part-timers.'"

*IMAGE INK STUDIO, INC., 12708 Northup Way, Bellevue WA 98005. (206)885-7696. Creative Director: Dennis Richter. Specializes in annual reports, corporate identity and packaging for manufacturers. Current clients include Olympic Stain, Weyerhaeuser Paper Company, Attachmate. Client list available upon request.
Needs: Approached by 20 freelance artists/year. Works with 5 freelance illustrators and 15 freelance designers/year. Uses freelance artists for brochure and catalog illustration, mechanicals, retouching and airbrushing. Prefers pen & ink and airbrush.

First Contact & Terms: Send query letter with brochure showing art style or tearsheets. Samples are filed. Reports back only if interested. Call or write to schedule an appointment to show a portfolio, which should include tearsheets. Pays for illustration by the project, $50 minimum. Considers complexity of project, client's budget, skill and experience of artist and how work will be used when establishing payment. Buys one-time rights or all rights.

IMPRESSIONS, ABA INDUSTRIES, INC., 200 Powerhouse Rd., Roslyn Heights NY 11577-2198. Director Creative Services: Frand DeMarco. Estab. 1973. Specializes in brand identity, corporate identity, direct mail, sales promotion and marketing. Clients: NatWest Bank, Thompson Medical, Glenbrook Labs, Home Shopping Network.
Needs: Approached by 25-30 freelance artists/year. Works with 4-6 freelance illustrators and 8-10 freelance designers/year. Prefers artists with experience in all media, especially marker renderings. Uses illustrators mainly for technical illustration, spot work and comps. Uses designers mainly for large multi-element and specialty projects. Also uses artists for brochure design and illustration; catalog, book, P-O-P design and illustration; mechanicals; retouching; airbrushing; poster, direct mail and ad design; model making, lettering and logos. Especially needs mechanical artists with experience; comp artists (all media); and designers/art directors (promotion or corporate).
First Contact and Terms: Send query letter with resume, tearsheets, slides, photographs and transparencies. Samples are filed or are returned only if requested by artist. Reports back within 2 weeks. To show a portfolio, mail b&w and color thumbnails, roughs, original/final art, final/reproduction/product, tear sheet, photographs and transparencies. Pays for mechanical artists by the hour, $18-25/30. Pays for comp artists by the hour, $20-50. "Designers based on per project rate." Considers complexity of project, client's budget and skill and experience of artist when establishing payment. Rights purchased vary according to project.
Tips: "Show work in a portfolio that exhibits your ability to manage multi-element projects. We are very detail-oriented, so work must be clean and organized. Designers and mechanical artists should show sensitivity to type, i.e. letter spacing. Work must be contemporary but not trendy."

INDIANA DESIGN CONSORTIUM, INC., 416 Main St., Box 180, Lafayette IN 47902. (317)423-5469. Senior Art Director: Ellen Sprunger. Specializes in corporate identity, display, direct mail, publication, technical illustration and collateral. Clients: agricultural, health care, financial and business-to-business.
Needs: Approached by 5-10 freelance artists/year. Works with 5+ freelance illustrators and 3+ freelance designers/year. Prefers Midwest artists. Uses artists for brochure, catalog, ad, poster and P-O-P illustration; mechanicals; retouching; airbrushing; model making and lettering.
First Contact & Terms: Send resume, tearsheets and photocopies. Samples are filed or are returned by SASE. Reports back only if interested. Call or write to schedule an appointment to show a portfolio, which should include color tearsheets, final reproduction/product and photographs. Pays for design and illustration by the project. Considers complexity of project, client's budget, skill and experience of artist and turnaround time when establishing payment. Negotiates rights purchased.

INNO, 1850 Alma St., Atlanta GA 30381. (404)351-2042. Design Director: Lionel Gillespie. Estab. 1980. Specializes in product design. Clients: medical, consumer and industrial products. Client list not available.
Needs: Approached by 25-50 freelance artists/year. Works with 10+ freelance illustrators and 2-3 freelance designers/year. Prefers local artists only with experience in mechanicals. Works on assignment only. Uses designers mainly for presentation work in markers and wet media. Also uses artists for P-O-P design, model making and product design.
First Contact and Terms: Send query letter with resume and slides. Samples are not filed and are returned if accompanied by SASE. Reports back within 5 days. To show a portfolio, mail thumbnails, roughs and original/final art. Pays by the hour, $5-60; or by the project. Considers complexity of project, client's budget, skill and experience of artist and turnaround time when establishing payment. Buys all rights.
Tips: The most common mistake freelancers make in presenting samples or portfolios is "sloppy photography – poor grammar, poor verbal presentation." Looks for "quality and variety."

INNOVATIVE DESIGN & GRAPHICS, Suite 214, 1234 Sherman Ave., Evanston IL 60202-1343. (312)475-7772. Contact: Tim Sonder and Maret Thorpe. Clients: magazine publishers, corporate communication departments, associations.
Needs: Works with 3-15 freelance artists/year. Local artists only. Uses artists for illustration and airbrushing.
First Contact & Terms: To show a portfolio, send query letter with brochure showing art style or resume, tearsheets, photostats, slides and photographs. Reports only if interested. Pays for illustration by the project, $100-700 average. Considers complexity of project, client's budget and turnaround time when establishing payment.
Tips: "Interested in meeting new illustrators, but have a tight schedule. Looking for people who can grasp complex ideas and turn them into high-quality illustrations. Ability to draw people well is a must. Do not call for an appointment to show your portfolio. Send non-returnable tearsheets or self-promos, and we will call you when we have an appropriate project for you."

*PETER JAMES DESIGN STUDIO, 7520 NW 5th St., Plantation FL 33317. (305)587-2842. FAX: (305)587-2866. Creative Director: Jim Spangler. Estab. 1980. Specializes in business-to-business advertising, brand graphics, direct mail advertising identity and corporate name. Clients: manufacturers, corporations and industrial and hospitality companies. Client list available upon request.
Needs: Approached by dozens of freelance artists/year. Works with 6 freelance illustrators and designers/year. Prefers local artists and artists with experience in corporate design with 7 years experience minimum. Also uses artists for illustration, mechanicals, retouching, airbrushing, lettering and logo design.
First Contact & Terms: Send query letter with samples, tearsheets, photocopies and resume. Samples are filed or are returned by SASE if requested by artist. Reports back only if interested. Write to schedule an appointment to show a portfolio or mail tearsheets, comps and print samples. Pays for design by the hour, $15-25. Pays for illustration by the project only. Rights purchased vary according to project.

JMH CORPORATION, 921 E. 66th St., Indianapolis IN 46220. (317)255-3400. President: J. Michael Hayes. Specializes in corporate identity, packaging and publications. Clients: publishers, consumer product manufacturers, corporations and institutions.
Needs: Works with 10 freelance artists/year. Prefers experienced, talented and responsible artists only. Works on assignment only. Uses artists for advertising, brochure and catalog design and illustration; P-O-P displays; mechanicals; retouching; charts/graphs and lettering.
First Contact & Terms: Send query letter with brochure/flyer, resume and slides. Samples returned by SASE, "but we prefer to keep them." Reporting time "depends entirely on our needs." Write for appointment. Pay is by the project for design and illustration. Pays $500-2,000/project average; also negotiates. Considers complexity of project, client's budget, skill and experience of artist, how work will be used, turnaround time and rights purchased when establishing payment.
Tips: "Prepare an outstanding mailing piece and 'leave-behind' that allows work to remain on file."

JOHNSON DESIGN GROUP, INC., Suite 410, 200 Little Falls St., Falls Church VA 22046. (703)533-0550. Art Director: Leonard A. Johnson. Specializes in publications. Clients: corporations, associations and PR firms. Client list not available.
Needs: Approached by 15 freelance artists/year. Works with 15 freelance illustrators and 5 freelance designers/year. Works on assignment only. Uses artists for brochure and book illustration, mechanicals, retouching and lettering. Especially needs line illustration and a realistic handling of human figure in real-life situations.
First Contact & Terms: Send query letter with brochure/flyer and samples (photocopies OK) to be kept on file. Samples are not returned. Negotiates payment by the project.
Tips: The most common mistakes freelancers make in presenting samples or portfolios are "poor quality or subject matter not relevant." Artists should "have a printed 'leave behind' sheet or Xerox samples that can be left in the art director's files."

*BRENT A. JONES DESIGN, 328 Hayes St., San Francisco CA 94102. (415)626-8337. Principal: Brent Jones. Estab. 1983. Specializes in corporate identity and advertising design. Clients: corporations, museums, book publishers, retail establishments. Current clients include Harper & Row, Laventhol & Horwath and the California Academy of Sciences. Client list availble upon request.
Needs: Approached by 1-3 freelance artists/year. Works with 2 freelance illustrators and 1 freelance designer/year. Prefers local artists only. Works on assignment only. Uses illustrators mainly for renderings. Uses designers mainly for production. Also uses artists for brochure design and illustration, mechanicals, catalog illustration, charts/graphs and ad design and illustration.
First Contact & Terms: Send query letter with brochure and tearsheets. Samples are filed and are not returned. Reports back within 2 weeks only if interested. Write to schedule an appointment to show a portfolio, which should include slides, tearsheets and transparencies. Pays for design by the hour, $15-25. Rights purchased vary according to project.

*FREDERICK JUNGCLAUS, DESIGNER/ILLUSTRATOR, 145 E. 14th St., Indianapolis IN 46202. (317)636-4891. Owner: Fred Jungclaus. Specializes in annual reports, corporate identity, display, architectural rendering and 3-D photo props. Clients: ad agencies and architects. Current clients include Indianapolis Motor Speedway, Kahn's Meats, Gibraltar Corp. Client list not available.

The asterisk before a listing indicates that the listing is new in this edition. New markets are often the most receptive to freelance submissions.

Needs: Approached by 3-5 freelance artists/year. Works with 3-5 freelance illustrators and 2 freelance designers/year. Works on assignment only. Uses artists for retouching and airbrushing. Seeks artists capable of illustrating Indy-type race cars or antique cars.

First Contact & Terms: Send samples to be kept on file. Prefers prints or tearsheets as samples. Samples not filed are not returned. Call for appointment to show portfolio. Pays by the project. Considers skill and experience of artist and turnaround time when establishing payment.

AL KAHN GROUP, INC., 221 W. 82nd St., New York NY 10024. (212)580-3517. Vice President Marketing: Michele Strub. Estab. 1976. Specializes in ERC (Emotional Response Communications), graphic design, brochures, videos/films, and promotional material. Clients: colleges, universities, nonprofit organizations, medical and high tech. Current clients include Colorado Tech, Intertec, Synmex and Wilson College. Client list not available.

Needs: Approached by 90 freelance artists/year. Works with 15 freelance illustrators and 20 freelance designers/year. Prefers artists with experience in type, layout, grids, mechanicals, comps and creative visual thinking. Works on assignment only. Uses artists for rough comps, presentations, mechanicals, layout and general studio assistance. Also uses artists for model making, charts/graphs, logos, and advertisement, brochure and direct mail design.

First Contact & Terms: Send brochure/flyer or resume, slides, b&w photos and color washes. Samples returned only if requested. To show a portfolio, call to schedule an appointment. Portfolio should include thumbnails, roughs, final reproduction/product and b&w and color tearsheets, photostats, photographs and transparencies. Pays for design and illustration by the project, $500-2,500. Considers complexity of project and client's budget when establishing payment. Buys one-time rights.

Tips: "Call, send samples and arrange an interview. Creative thinking and a positive attitude are a plus." The most common mistake freelancers make in presenting samples or portfolios is "work does not match up to the samples they show."

KASOM DESIGN, 751 Bryant St., San Francisco CA 94107. (415)421-8282. Owner: Wayne Kasom. Estab. 1972. Specializes in product design (industrial design). Clients: manufacturers. Current projects include work for a bookbinding machine, computer data storage unit, cat scanning machine.

Needs: Works with 2-5 freelance designers/year. Uses designers for brochure design, mechanicals, model making and logos.

First Contact and Terms: Send resume. Samples are not filed and are returned if accompanied by a SASE. Reports back only if interested. Call to schedule an appointment to show a portfolio which should include roughs, original/final art and final reproduction/product. Pays by the hour, $12-30. Considers complexity of project, client's budget, skill and experience of artist and turnaround time when establishing payment. Buys all rights.

Tips: "Keep checking often."

*****KEITHLEY & ASSOCIATES, INC.**, 39 W. 14th St., New York NY 11001. (212)807-8388. Art Director: Monisha Sheth. Specializes in publications. Primary clients: publishing (book and promotion departments); secondary clients: small advertising agencies.

Needs: Works with 3-6 freelance artists/year. "Except for artists doing mechanicals and some design work, all work must be done in our studio. We prefer experienced artists (2 years minimum)." Uses artists for desktop publishing design, brochures, catalogs, books (design and dummy), mechanicals, retouching and charts/graphs.

First Contact & Terms: Call for appointment to show portfolio. Do not send samples. Reports only if interested. Pays for design by the hour, $18-25 average. Pays for mechanicals by the hour, $14-20 average. Considers client's budget, and skill and experience of artist when establishing payment.

LARRY KERBS STUDIOS INC., 419 Park Ave. S., New York NY 10016. (212)686-9420. Contact: Larry Kerbs or Jim Lincoln. Specializes in sales promotion design, some ad work and placement, annual reports, corporate identity, publications and technical illustration. Clients: industrial, chemical and insurance companies and PR firms.

Needs: Works with 3 freelance illustrators and 1 freelance designer/month. New York, New Jersey and Connecticut artists only. Uses artists for direct mail, layout, illustration, slide sets, technical art, paste-up and retouching for annual reports, trade magazines, product brochures and direct mail. Especially needs freelance comps through mechanicals; type specification.

First Contact & Terms: Mail samples or call for interview. Prefers b&w line drawings, roughs, previously published work as samples. Provide brochures, business card and resume to be kept on file for future assignments. No originals returned to artist at job's completion. Pays by the hour, $18-20, paste-up; $20-24, comprehensive layout; $22-28, design; negotiates payment by the project for illustration.

Tips: "Improve hand lettering for comps; strengthen typographic knowledge and application."

*DON KLOTZ ASSOCIATES, 298 Millstone Rd., Wilton CT 06897. (203)762-9111. FAX: (203)762-9763. President: Don Klotz. Estab. 1965. Specializes in corporate identity and package design. Clients: corporations and small businesses. Client list available upon request.

Needs: Approached by 23 freelance artists/year. Works with 2 freelance illustrators/year. Prefers artists with experience in packaging and food illustration. Uses illustrators mainly for packaging and trade ads. Also uses artists for brochure design and illustration, mechanicals, airbrushing, book design and model making.

First Contact & Terms: Send query letter with tearsheets and resume. Samples are filed or are returned. Reports back only if interested. Call to schedule an appointment to show portfolio. Portfolio should include thumbnails, b&w roughs and tearsheets. Pays for design and illustration by the hour. Rights purchased vary according to project.

LORNA LACCONE DESIGN, Suite 6E, 123 E. 54th St., New York NY 10022. (212)688-4583. President: Lorna Laccone. Estab. 1975. Specializes in general graphic design of brochures, logos and promotionals for communications firms and major retailers.

Needs: Works with 20 freelance artists/year. Prefers reliable local freelancers to work on premises or off. Uses freelance artists for brochure design, mechanicals and airbrushing. Especially needs neat, clean, fast mechanicals, comps/layouts.

First Contact & Terms: Send query letter with samples. Samples are not filed but returned if accompanied by a SASE. Reports back within 7-10 days. To show a portfolio, mail roughs, original/final art and tearsheets. "Published pieces are always nice to see, plus crisp comps." Pays for design by the hour, $25 minimum; by the project, $100 minimum. Pays for illustration by the hour, $25. minimum; by the project, $100 minimum. Considers complexity of project, project's budget and turnaround time when establishing payment.

Tips: "Would like to see crisp, clean comps, design work and fashion illustration. Do not send unprofessional looking portfolios with pieces out of order or in poor condition."

LEBOWITZ/GOULD/DESIGN, INC., 7 W. 22nd St., New York NY 10010. (212)645-0550. Associate: Cyndy Travis. Specializes in corporate identity, packaging, signage and product design. Clients: corporations, developers, architects, city and state agencies. Client list not available.

Needs: Approached by 12-15 freelance artists/year. Works with 2-3 freelance freelance illustrators/year. Works on assignment only. Uses freelance artists for mechanicals and drafting for architectural graphics.

First Contact & Terms: Send query letter with resume and slides. Samples are filed or are returned only if requested by artist. Call or write to schedule an appointment to show a portfolio, which should include roughs, final reproduction/product, photostats, photographs and reduced working drawings (where appropriate). Pays for mechanicals and drafting by the hour, $12 minimum. Considers client's budget and turnaround time when establishing payment. Buys all rights.

Tips: "Remember we do not always have free time to interview everyone that calls us—we look for people when we need them. We call you so make your resumes and samples available."

LEE GRAPHICS DESIGN, 395 19th St. NE, Salem OR 97301. (503)364-0907. Owner/Art Director: Lee Ericksen. Estab. 1980. Specializes in advertising, promotions, capabilities folders, brand identity, corporate identity, displays, direct mail, packaging, publications, signage and illustrations. "We are a full-service graphics studio." Clients: individuals, ad agencies and PR firms. Client list not available.

Needs: Works with approximately 3-4 freelance illustrators and 3-4 freelance designers/year. Artist must have "talent, creativity, basic design ability and computer intellect." Uses artist for design, illustration, brochures, catalogs, books, magazines, newspapers, P-O-P displays, mechanicals, airbrushing, posters, direct mail packages, charts/graphs, AV materials, lettering, logos, advertisements and anything that appears in print form. Prefers pen & ink, charcoal/pencil, colored pencil, collage and marker.

First Contact & Terms: Send query letter with resume. Call to schedule an appointment to show a portfolio, which should include thumbnails, roughs, color and b&w original/final art, final reproduction/product, tearsheets, photostats and photographs. Pays for design and illustration by the hour, $10-25. "Usually get estimate by artist." Considers complexity of project, client's budget, skill and experience of artist, how work will be used, turnaround time and rights purchased when establishing payment.

Tips: "Always show respect for your artwork with presentation; follow directions. Be versatile in all areas of graphics. The computer is becoming more important as an art skill. I now work with a Mac SE with Word 3.01, Page Maker, and Freehand. It would be a great advantage for a new artist to have at least a general background in this area. However, *computers are not designers; they are design tools.*"

LEKASMILLER, 3210 Old Tunnel Rd., Lafayette CA 94549. (415)934-3971. Production Manager: Audrey. Estab. 1979. Specializes in annual reports, corporate identity, direct mail and brochure design. Clients: corporate and retail. Current clients include: Civic Bank of Commerce, Tosco Refining Co., Voicepro and Ortho consumer products.

Needs: Approached by 75 freelance artists/year. Works with 1-3 freelance illustrators/year. Works with 5-10 freelance designers/year. Prefers local artists only with experience in design and production. Works on assignment only. Uses artists for brochure design and illustration, mechanicals, direct mail design, logos, ad design and illustration.

First Contact and Terms: Send resume and photocopies. Samples are filed or are returned if accompanied by a SASE. Reports back only if interested. To show a portfolio, mail thumbnails, roughs, final reproduction/product, tearsheets and transparencies. Pays by the hour, $8-12. Consider skill and experience of artist when establishing payment. Negotiates rights purchased.
Tips: "Mail resume and samples – then follow-up with a phone call."

LEO ART STUDIO, Suite 610, 320 Fifth Ave., New York NY 10001. (212)736-8785. Art Director: Robert Schein. Specializes in textile design for home furnishings. Clients: wallpaper manufacturers/stylists, glassware companies, furniture and upholstery manufacturers. Current clients include Waverly, Burlington House, Blumenthal Printworks, Columbus Coated, Eisenhart Wallcoverings and Town and Country. Client list available upon request.
Needs: Approached by 35-50 freelance artists/year. Works with 1-2 freelance illustrators and 10-15 freelance designers/year. Prefers artists trained in textile field, not fine arts. Must have a portfolio of original art designs. Should be able to be in NYC on a fairly regular basis. Works both on assignment and speculation. Prefers realistic and traditional styles. Uses artists for design, airbrushing, coloring and repeats. "We are always looking to add full-time artists to our inhouse staff (currently at 7). We will also look at any freelance portfolio to add to our variety of hands."
First Contact & Terms: Send query letter with resume. Do not send slides. "We prefer to see portfolio in person. Contact via a phone is OK – we can set up appointments within a day or two notice." Samples are not filed and are returned. Reports back within 5 days. Call or write to schedule an appointment to show a portfolio, which should include original/final art. Pays for design by the project, $400-800. "Payment is generally two-thirds of what design sells for – slightly less if reference material art material, or studio space is requested." Considers complexity of project, skill and experience of artist and how work will be used when establishing payment. Buys all rights.
Tips: "Do not call if you are not a textile artist. Artists must be able to put design in repeat, do color combinations and be able to draw well on large variety of subjects – florals, Americana, graphics, etc. We will look at student work and advise if it is correct field. We do not do fashion or clothing design."

LEONE DESIGN GROUP INC., 7 Woodland Ave., Larchmont NY 10538. President: Lucian J. Leone. Specializes in corporate identity, publications, signage and exhibition design. Clients: museums, corporations, government agencies. Client list not available.
Needs: Approached by 30 freelance artists/year. Works with 10-15 freelance designers/year. Uses artists for exhibition design, brochures, catalogs, mechanicals, model making, charts/graphs and AV materials.
First Contact & Terms: Send query letter with resume, samples and photographs. Samples are filed unless otherwise stated. Samples not filed are returned only if requested. Reports back within 2 weeks. Write to schedule an appointment to show a portfolio, which should include thumbnails, b&w and color original/final art, final reproduction/product and photographs. Pays for design by the hour or project. Considers client's budget and skill and experience of artist when establishing payment.

*THE LEPREVOST CORPORATION, Suite 6, 29350 Pacific Coast Hwy., Malibu CA 90265. (213)457-3742. President: John LePrevost. Specializes in corporate identity, record covers, television and film design. Current clients include Public Broadcasting Service (PBS), Fox Television and Greenpeace.
Needs: Approached by 30 freelance artists/year. Works with 10 freelance designers/year. Prefers "talented and professional" artists only. Works on assignment only. Uses artists for animation and film design and illustration; lettering and logo design. Animation and design becoming more sophisticated.
First Contact & Terms: Call for appointment. Samples not returned. Provide information to be kept on file for possible future assignments; reports back. Payment by the project for both design and illustration. Considers complexity of project, client's budget, skill and experience of artist, how work will be used, turnaround time and rights purchased when establishing payment.

*WES LERDON ASSOCIATES, INDUSTRIAL DESIGN, Box 21204, 2403 Abington Rd., Columbus OH 43221-0204. (614)486-8188. Senior Designer: Mark Schultz. Estab. 1976. Specializes in corporate identity, technical illustration and product design. Clients: manufacturers of electronic, computer and medical products. Current clients include Westinghouse, AEG, Harris and Gould. Client list not available.
Needs: Approached by 6-8 freelance artists/year. Works with 2 freelance illustrators and designers/year. Prefers artists with experience in product illustration. Uses illustrators mainly for products. Uses designers mainly for products and corporate identity. Also uses artists for mechanicals, logos, model making and product development.
First Contact & Terms: Send query letter with resume and photocopies. Samples and filed or returned. Reports back in 2 weeks. If does not report back, call as a follow-up. Call to schedule an appointment to show portfolio, which should include thumbnails, roughs, original/final art and b&w samples. Pays for design and illustration by the hour, $13-35. Rights purchased vary according to project.
Tips: The most common mistake freelancers make in presenting their work is "too much reliance on slides and not enough original art (slides look better than originals)."

*LUCY LESIAK DESIGN, 445 East Illinois St., Chicago IL 60611. (312)836-7850. FAX: (312)836-7851. President: Lucy Lesiak. Estab. 1982. Specializes in corporate identity, publication design, book design and collateral. Clients: corporations, professional associations, non-profits. Current clients include Hamilton Investments, Scott Foresman and Co., Richard D. Irwin, Inc., and the College of American Pathologists. Client list available upon request.

Needs: Approached by 25-30 freelance artists/year. Works with 4-6 freelance illustrators and 2-3 designers/year. Works on assignment only. Uses illustrators mainly for educational text books. Uses designers mainly for book design. Also uses freelance artists for brochure design, mechanicals, retouching, airbrushing, lettering, poster illustration and charts/graphs.

First Contact & Terms: Send query letter with brochure, tearsheets, photographs, photocopies and slides. Samples are filed. Reports back only if interested. Call to schedule an appointment to show portfolio, which should include original/final art, slides and tearsheets. Pays for design by the hour, $15-35. Pays for illustration by usage and size of illustration, $25-1,200. Rights purchased vary according to project.

LESLEY-HILLE, INC., 32 E. 21st St., New York NY 10010. (212)677-7570. President: Valrie Lesley. Specializes in annual reports, corporate identity, publications, advertising and sales promotion. Clients: nonprofit organizations, hotels, restaurants, investment, oil and real estate, financial and fashion firms.

Needs: Works with "many" freelance artists/year. "Experienced and competent" artists. Uses artists for illustration, mechanicals, airbrushing, model making, charts/graphs, AV materials and lettering.

First Contact & Terms: Send query letter with resume, business card and samples to be kept on file. Accepts "whatever best shows work capability" as samples. Samples not filed are returned by SASE. Reports only if interested. Call or write for appointment to show portfolio. Pay varies according to project. Considers complexity of project, client's budget, skill and experience of artist and turnaround time when establishing payment.

Tips: Designers and artists must "be *able to do* what they say they can and agree to do . . . professionally and on time!"

*LORENC DESIGN, INC., Suite 460, 3475 Lenox Rd., Atlanta GA 30326. (404)266-2711. President: Mr. Jan Lorenc. Specializes in corporate identity, display, packaging, publication, architectural signage design and industrial design. Clients: developers, product manufacturers, architects and institutions. Current clients include Gerald D. Hines Interests, MCI, City of Raleigh NC, City of Birmingham AL, HOH Associates. Client list available upon request.

Needs: Approached by 25 freelance artists/year. Works with 5 freelance illustrators and 10 freelance designers/year. Local senior designers only. Uses artists for design, illustration, brochures, catalogs, books, P-O-P displays, mechanicals, retouching, airbrushing, posters, direct mail packages, model making, charts/graphs, AV materials, lettering and logos. Especially needs architectural signage designers.

First Contact & Terms: Send brochure, resume and samples to be kept on file. Prefers slides as samples. Samples not kept on file are returned. Call or write for appointment to show portfolio, which should include thumbnails, roughs, original/final art, final reproduction/product and color photostats and photographs. Pays for design by the hour, $10-25; by the project, $100-3,000. Considers complexity of project, client's budget, and skill and experience of artist when establishing payment.

Tips: The most common mistake freelancers make in presenting samples or portfolios is "apologizing for problems in portfolios, problems with clients." Looks for "attention to detail."

*LUBELL BRODSKY INC., 270 Madison Ave., New York NY 10016. (212)684-2600. Art Director: Ed Brodsky and Ruth Lubell. Specializes in corporate identity, direct mail, promotion and packaging. Clients: ad agencies and corporations.

Needs: Works with 10 freelance artists/year. Works on assignment only. Uses artists for illustration, mechanicals, retouching, airbrushing, charts/graphs, AV materials and lettering.

First Contact & Terms: Send business card and tearsheets to be kept on file. Reports back only if interested. Considers complexity of project, client's budget, skill and experience of artist and turnaround time when establishing payment.

JACK LUCEY/ART & DESIGN, 84 Crestwood Dr., San Rafael CA 94901. (415)453-3172. Contact: Jack Lucey. Estab. 1960. Art agency. Specializes in annual reports, brand identity, corporate identity, publications, signage, technical illustration and illustrations/cover designs. Clients: businesses, agencies and freelancers. Current clients include U.S. Air Force, TWA Airlines, California Museum of Art & Industry, Lee Books, High Noon Books. Client list available upon request.

Needs: Approached by 12 freelance artists/year. Works with 2 freelance illustrators and designers/year. Uses mostly local artists. Uses artists for illustration and lettering for newspaper work. Especially needs agricultural painting and corporation illustrations. Prefers oil, watercolor and pen & ink. Uses freelancers mainly for type and airbrush.

First Contact & Terms: Query. Prefers photostats and published work as samples. Provide brochures, business card and resume to be kept on file for future assignments. No originals returned to artist at job's completion. Pays for design and illustration by the hour, $50 minimum.

Tips: "We would like to see an upgrade of portfolios." Some common mistakes freelancers make is "a limited variety of subject matter and often the use of only one medium used by artist; also limitation, of black & white and no color or color and no black & white. I would like to see more comps and preliminary layouts and roughs along with the finished or camera-ready art work. (Some true idea of time involved to do roughs and complete finished art.) Roughs show thought process involved."

*SUDI MCCOLLUM DESIGN, 3244 Cornwall Dr., Glendale CA 91206. (818)243-1345. FAX: (818)956-3347. Contact: Sudi McCollum. Specializes in corporate identity and publication design. Clients: corporations and small businesses. Current clients include Huntley Research Institute and AEOS. Client list not available.

Needs: Approached by a few graphic artists/year. Works with a couple of freelance illustrators and a couple of freelance designers/year. Works on assignment only. Uses designers mainly for assistance in production. Also uses artists for retouching, airbrushing, catalog illustration and charts/graphs.

First Contact & Terms: Send query letter with "whatever you have that's convenient." Samples are filed. Reports back to the artist only if interested. Write to schedule an appointment to show a portfolio. Portfolio should include tearsheets and original/final art. For payment artist does estimate per project. "I am a small design studio. I do most all design and illustration myself. I don't normally use outside help."

MCDANIEL ASSOCIATES, 724 Pine St., San Francisco CA 94108. Art Director: Jan Stageberg. Estab. 1978. Specializes in corporate identity, direct mail, package and publication design. Clients: Financial institutions, high-tech, toys, food and home products. Current projects include collateral design, brand identity, direct mail campaigns, package design, product support materials, logo and logotype design.

Needs: Approached by 50-75 freelance artists/year. Works with 3-4 freelance illustrators/year. Works with 20 freelance designers/year. Prefers local artists only. Works on assignment only. Prefers promotional and corporate, trendy b&w conservative styles. Uses illustrators mainly for spot illustrations, package design, airbrush and line art. Uses designers mainly for packaging and collateral design. Also uses artists for brochure design, mechanicals, airbrushing, poster design, model making, direct mail design, charts/graphs, lettering and logos.

First Contact and Terms: Send resume, tearsheets, photostats, photocopies and photographs. Samples are filed or are returned only if requested by artist. Reports back only if interested. Write to schedule an appointment to show a portfolio or mail appropriate materials. Pays for design by the hour, $15-25. Pays for illustration by the project. Considers complexity of project, client's budget and skill and experience of artist when establishing payment. Rights purchased vary according to project.

Tips: "Be responsible to see the job through. Have excellent craftsmanship. Show attention to detail. Be serviceable. Let us know your role in producing the art—show sketches and marker comps if possible."

ROB MacINTOSH COMMUNICATIONS, INC., 93 Massachusetts Ave., Boston MA 02115. President: Rob MacIntosh. Specializes in annual reports, advertising design and collateral. Clients: manufacturers, graphic arts industry, nonprofit/public service agencies.

Needs: Works with 12 freelance artists/year. Portfolio and work experience required. Uses artists for advertising and brochure design, illustration and layout, mechanicals, retouching and charts/graphs. Occasionally uses humorous and cartoon-style illustrations.

First Contact & Terms: Send samples to be kept on file. Irregular sizes or abundant material will not be filed. "Never send original work unless it's a printed sample. A simple, compact presentation is best. Often Photostats are adequate." Reports only if interested and "generally only when we require more information and/or services." Pays for design by the day, $100 minimum. Pays for illustration by the project, $100 minimum. Considers complexity of project, client's budget, skill and experience of artist and turnaround time when establishing payment.

*MACMILLAN CREATIVE SERVICES GROUP, Suite 203, 212 W. Superior, Chicago IL 60640. (312)944-5115. Art Director: Jeffen Shaw. Estab. 1987. Specializes in creative directories and trade publications. "We publish creative directories with our clients being the advertiser in our publications and the firms that use our publications." Client list not available.

Needs: Approached by 30 freelance artists/year. Works with 20 freelance illustrators and 2-5 freelance designers/year. Works on assignment only. Uses illustrators mainly for editorial and promotional work. Uses designers mainly for promotional work. Also uses artists for lettering, model making and charts/graphs.

First Contact & Terms: Send query letter with brochure, SASE, tearsheets, photographs, photocopies, slides and transparencies. Samples are filed or are returned by SASE if requested by artist. Reports back to the artist only if interested. Call or write to schedule an appointment to show portfolio. Portfolio should include original/final art and b&w or color tearsheets, photographs, slides and transparencies. Trades ad space for design or illustration or when budgeted pays by the project based on use. Rights purchased vary according to project.

*TED MADER & ASSOCIATES, Suite 416, 911 Western, Seattle WA 98104. Creative Head: Ted Mader. Specializes in corporate identity, brand identity, displays, direct mail, fashion, packaging, publications and signage. Uses freelance artists for mechanicals, retouching, airbrushing, model making, charts/graphs, AV materials and lettering. Client list available upon request.
First Contact & Terms: Send resume and samples. Samples are filed. Write to schedule an appointment to show a portfolio. Considers skill and experience of artist when establishing payment. Rights purchased vary according to project.

AARON MARCUS AND ASSOCIATES, 1196 Euclid Ave., Berkeley CA 94708-1640. (415)527-6224. Principal: Aaron Marcus. A consulting, training, and product development firm that researches, plans and develops the visual design of user interfaces and electronic publishing documents, including information displays for computer graphics systems. Clients: corporations, manufacturers, government, utilities.
Needs: Works with 5-10 freelance artists/year. Prefers Macintosh experience; usually local designers with 3 years information-oriented graphic design experience. Uses artists for brochure and catalog design and illustration; book, magazine and newspaper design; P-O-P displays (especially on computer screens); mechanicals; charts/graphs/diagrams; AV materials; logos and screen design. Especially needs info-oriented graphic designers with Macintosh experience, symbol designers and chart, diagram designers.
First Contact & Terms: Send query letter with resume and photocopies. Samples are filed. Samples not filed are not returned. Reports back within 1 month. Call or write to schedule an appointment to show a portfolio, or mail original/final art, final reproduction/product, b&w and color tearsheets, photostats, photographs or photocopies. Pays for design and illustration by the hour, $5-25. Considers complexity of project, client's budget, skill and experience of artist, how work will be used, turnaround time and rights purchased when establishing payment.
Tips: "We don't need general graphic artists. We're a specialized studio doing pioneering work in computer graphics design and need people who have serious motivation and/or experience in our project areas."

MARKET DIRECT, INC., 5929 Rockhill Rd., Kansas City MO 64110-3115. (816)523-0482. President: Lanie Bethka. Estab. 1979. Specializes in brand identity, corporate identity and display, direct mail and package design. Clients: food and transportation companies. Current clients include May Co., Famous Corned Beef Co. and Apple Courier, Inc.
Needs: Approached by 50-100 freelance artists/year. Works with 5 or 6 freelance illustrators and designers/year. Prefers local artists and artists with experience in product illustration, cartooning and direct mail. Works on assignment only. Uses illustrators mainly for product illustrations. Designers mainly for direct mail, display and package design. Also uses brochure design and illustration, catalog design and illustration, airbrushing, P-O-P design and illustration, direct mail design and ad illustration.
First Contact & Terms: Send query letter with brochure, tearsheets, photostats, resume, photographs, slides, photocopies and transparencies. Samples are filed or are returned. Does not report back, in which case the artist should call. "We contact when the project fits the artist's style or talent." Portfolio should include all that is appropriate. Pays for design by the hour, $55-100; by the project, $100-2,000. Pays for illustration by the hour, $45-100; by the project, $45-2,000. Rights purchased vary according to project.

STEVE MEEK INC., 2215 S. Ford, Chicago IL 60616. President: Steve Meek. Estab. 1986. Specializes in corporate identity. Clients: Fortune 500 corporations, small businesses and art studios. Current clients include: USG, Canteen, Arthur Anderson, GBC and Pathway Financial. Client list not available.
Needs: Approached by 25 freelance artists/year. Works with 6 freelance illustrators/year. Works on assignment only. Prefers rough, loose style. Uses illustrators mainly for brochures and posters. Also uses artists for airbrushing and ad illustration.
First Contact and Terms: Send query letter with tearsheets and photocopies. Samples are filed or are not returned. Reports back within 1 month. Write to schedule an appointment to show portfolio, which should include final reproduction/product. Pays by the project, $250-2,500. Considers client's budget, skill and experience of artist and how work will be used when establishing payment. Buys one-time rights.
Tips: "Lighten up and be enthusiastic."

DONYA MELANSON ASSOCIATES, 437 Main St., Boston MA 02129. Contact: Donya Melanson. Art agency. Clients: industries, associations, publishers, financial and government. Current clients include Hygienetics, Inc., Alliance to Save Energy and American Public Health Association. Client list available upon request.
Needs: Approached by 30 freelance artists/year. Works with 4-5 freelance illustrators/year. Most work is handled by staff, but may occasionally use illustrators and designers. Local artists only. Uses artists for stationery design, direct mail, brochures/flyers, annual reports, charts/graphs and book illustration.
First Contact & Terms: Query with brochure, resume, photostats and photocopies. Reports in 1-2 months. Provide materials (no originals) to be kept on file for future assignments. Originals returned to artist after use only when specified in advance. To show a portfolio, call or write to schedule an appointment or mail thumbnails, roughs, original/final art, final reproduction/product and color and b&w tearsheets, photostats and photographs. Pays $10-25/hour, cartoons, design, illustration, lettering, retouching, technical art and logo

design. Pays $10-20/hour, mechanicals. Considers complexity of project, client's budget, skill and experience of artist and how work will be used when establishing payment.

Tips: "Be sure your work reflects concept development."

*BOB MILLER & ASSOCIATES, Suite 100-B, 2012 H Street, Sacramento CA 95814. (916)448-3878. FAX: (916)448-2605. President: Bob Miller. Estab. 1978. Specializes in annual reports; corporate identity; signage; direct mail, package, publication and advertising design. Clients: food processor manufacturers, ad agencies, small manufacturers, museums and retailers. Current clients include Farmers' Rice Cooperative, Blue Diamond Growers, Crystal Cream & Butter Co. and Mason Paint Co. Client list available upon request.

Needs: Approached by 40-50 freelance artists/year. Works with 1-2 freelance illustrators and designers/year. Prefers artists with experience in design and production. Works on assignment only. Uses illustrators mainly for "styles of illustration that can't be done by our studio." Uses designers mainly for "overflow work or a unique style." Also uses artists for brochure design and illustration; catalog, ad, book, magazine, newspaper, P-O-P and direct mail design; mechanicals; retouching; airbrushing; lettering; illustration, poster design and illustration; model making and charts/graphs.

First Contact & Terms: Send query letter with resume. Samples are filed or are not returned. Does not report back, in which case the artist should "follow up with a phone call." Call to schedule an appointment to show a portfolio. Portfolio should include "anything that will give creditability to portfolio." Pays for design by the hour, $12-15, by the day, $84-105. Pays for illustration by the project, $100-2,000. Rights purchased vary according to project.

MILLER+SCHWARTZ, 3359 Coy Dr., Sherman Oaks CA 91423. (818)907-1493. Creative Director: David Schwartz. Specializes in real estate collateral. Clients: commercial real estate companies.

Needs: Works with 20 freelance artists/year. Works on assignment only. Uses artists for illustration, mechanicals, retouching, airbrushing and lettering.

First Contact & Terms: Send resume. Samples are filed and are not returned. Reports back only if interested. Call to schedule an appointment to show a portfolio, which should include roughs and printed pieces. Pays for mechanicals by the hour, $15-20. Pays for illustration by the project. Considers complexity of project, client's budget, how work will be used, turnaround time and rights purchased when establishing payment. Rights purchased vary according to project.

MIRANDA DESIGNS INC., 745 President St., Brooklyn NY 11215. (718)857-9839. President: Mike Miranda. Estab. 1970. Specializes in annual reports, solving marketing problems, corporate identity, direct mail, fashion, packaging, publications and signage. Clients: agencies, PR firms, corporate and retail companies. Current clients include N.Y.C.B.O.E. Client list not available.

Needs: Approached by 30 freelance artists/year. Mainly uses freelancers for mechanicals, illustration and design. Works with 20 freelance illustrators and 5 freelance designers/year. Works with all levels from juniors to seniors in all areas of specialization. Works on assignment only. Uses freelance artists for brochure design and catalog design and illustration, magazine and newspaper design, mechanicals, model making, direct mail packages, charts/graphs and design of advertisements.

First Contact & Terms: Send query letter with resume and photocopies. Samples are filed. Samples not filed are not returned. Does not report back. Call to schedule an appointment to show a portfolio, which should include thumbnails, roughs, original/final art and final reproduction/product. Pays for design and illustration by the hour, $10 minimum,"for juniors to whatever the market demands and budget permits." Considers complexity of project, client's budget and skill and experience of artist when establishing payment. Rights purchased vary according to project.

Tips: "Be professional, but not standoffish. Show a variety of subject material and media."

MITCHELL STUDIOS DESIGN CONSULTANTS, 1111 Fordham Ln., Woodmere NY 11598. (516)374-5620. Principal: Steven E. Mitchell. Estab. 1922. Specializes in brand identity, corporate identity, display, direct mail and packaging. Clients: major corporations.

Needs: Works with 20-25 freelance artists/year. "Most work is done in our studio." Uses artists for design, illustration, mechanicals, retouching, airbrushing, model making, lettering and logos.

First Contact & Terms: Send query letter with brochure, resume, business card, photostats, photographs and slides to be kept on file. Reports only if interested. Call or write for appointment to show portfolio, which should include roughs, original/final art, final reproduction/product and color photostats and photographs. Pays for design by the hour, $25 minimum; by the project, $150 minimum. Pays for illustration by the project, $250 minimum. Considers complexity of project, client's budget, skill and experience of artist, how work will be used, turnaround time and rights purchased when establishing payment.

Tips: "Call first. Show actual samples, not only printed samples. Don't show student work."

MIZEREK ADVERTISING, 48 E. 43rd St., New York NY 10017. (212)986-5702. President: Leonard Mizerek. Estab. 1975. Specializes in catalogs, jewelry, fashion and technical illustration. Clients: corporations—various product and service-oriented clientele. Current clients include: Spain and Time Life.

Needs: Approached by 20-30 freelance artists/year. Works with 10 freelance designers/year. Experienced artists only. Works on assignment only. Uses artists for design, illustration, brochures, retouching, airbrushing and logos.

First Contact & Terms: Send query letter with tearsheets and photostats. Reports only if interested. Call to schedule drop off or an appointment to show a portfolio, which should include original/final art and tearsheets. Pays by the project, $500-2,500. Considers client's budget and turnaround time when establishing payment.

Tips: "Contact by mail; don't press for interview. Let the work speak for itself. Show commercial product work, not only magazine editorial."

*MOODY GRAPHICS, 143 Second St., San Francisco CA 94105. (415)495-5186. President: Carol Moody. Specializes in annual reports, corporate identity, direct mail, publications and technical illustration. Clients: hotels, banks, small companies—corporate and retail.

Needs: Works with 0-2 freelance illustrators/year. Works with 1-2 freelance designers/year. "Artists work in my studio. They should have mechanical experience and good mechanical abilities; stat camera experience helpful." Works on assignment only. Uses artists for design, illustration, brochures, catalogs, mechanicals, retouching, airbrushing, direct mail packages, charts/graphs, lettering, logos and advertisements.

First Contact & Terms: Call or write for appointment to show portfolio. Samples not kept on file returned by SASE. Reports only if interested. Pays for design, mechanical assembly by the hour, $15-25 average. Pays for illustration, technical drawing by the hour, $15-25 average. Considers skill and experience of artist when establishing payment.

Tips: "Show paste-ups as well as printed samples." The most common mistake freelancers make is showing "too much of the same type of work. They should show 1-3 of best and weed out the rest—like 3 best letterhead designs, 3 best brochures, etc."

MOSSMAN ASSOCIATES, Suite 5, 1388 NW 2 Ave., Boca Raton FL 33432. Account Supervisor: Stanley Mossman. Specializes in corporate identity, direct mail, publications, health care institution brochures, book jacket and book design. Clients: publishers, manufacturers, hospitals, agencies, nonprofit institutions, etc.

Needs: Works with 3-5 freelance artists/year. Interested in "local artists with strong portfolio, a few years of experience, neat work and understanding of mechanicals." Uses artists for design, mechanicals, charts/graphs and photography.

First Contact & Terms: Send query letter with resume, business card and samples to be kept on file. Prefers copies, tearsheets and mock-ups as samples. Reports back within 5 days. Call or write for appointment to show portfolio. Considers complexity of project and skill and experience of artist when establishing payment.

Tips: Especially looks for creative samples or clean and organized portfolio. A mistake artists make is "not knowing their own limitations, not being honest about their skills."

*SID NAVRATILART, 1305 Clark Bldg., Pittsburgh PA 15222. (412)471-4322. Contact: Sid Navratil. Specializes in annual reports, corporate identity, desk-top publishing, direct mail, publication, signage, technical illustration and 3-dimensional designs. Clients: ad agencies and corporations. Current clients include PPG Industries, Pittsburgh National Bank, Ketchums Communications. Client list not available.

Needs: Approached by 10 freelance artists/year. Works with 5 freelance illustrators/year. Experienced artists only with a minimum of 5 years of experience; "I prefer artist to work on my premises at least during revision work, if that is possible." Works on assignment only. Uses artists for design, illustration, brochures, mechanicals, retouching, airbrushing, charts/graphs, lettering, logos and advertisements.

First Contact & Terms: Send resume, photocopies and business card to be kept on file. Material not filed is returned only if requested. Reports within 10 days. Write for appointment to show portfolio. Pays for design and illustration by the hour, $20-30 average. Considers complexity of project, client's budget and skill and experience of artist when establishing payment.

Tips: "In illustration, we prefer the daring, innovative approach. The subject is usually industrial in nature, done for corporations such as PPG, USS, Alcoa and Rockwell. 1) Telephone first; 2) Send resume; 3) Follow up with second call and make appointment. Do not send expensive photos and brochures. A brief resume with few Xerox copies of work is sufficient."

LOUIS NELSON ASSOCIATES INC., 80 University Pl., New York NY 10003. (212)620-9191. Contact: Louis Nelson. Estab. 1980. Specializes in environmental design, brand identity, corporate identity, display, interior design, packaging, publications, signage, product design, exhibitions and marketing. Clients: corporations, associations and governments; Port Authority, California Museum of Service & Industry and the Hill Group. Client list available upon request.

Needs: Approached by 25-30 freelance artists/year. Works with 3-5 freelance illustrators and 10 freelance designers/year. Works on assignment only. Uses freelance artwork mainly for specialty graphics and three-dimensional design. Uses artists for design, illustration, mechanicals, model making and charts/graphs.

First Contact & Terms: Considers "quality, point-of-view for project and flexibility." Send query letter with brochure showing art style or tearsheets, slides and photographs. Samples are returned only if requested. Reports within 2 weeks. Write to schedule an appointment to show a portfolio, which should include roughs, color final reproduction/product and photographs. Pays for design by the hour, $8-35 average; by the project, $60-5,000 average. Pays for illustration by the project, $100-500 average. Considers complexity of project, client's budget, skill and experience of artist and rights purchased when establishing payment.

Tips: "I want to see how the person responded to the specific design problem and to see documentation of the process—the stages of development. The artist must be versatile and able to communicate a wide range of ideas. Mostly, I want to see the artist's integrity reflected in his/her work."

NICHOLS GRAPHIC DESIGN, 80 8th Ave., New York NY 10011. President: Mary Ann Nichols. Estab. 1978. Specializes in corporate identity, direct mail and publications. Clients: ad agencies, PR firms, publishers, children's fashion manufacturers, industrial manufacturers and mailing houses. Current clients include Journal of Democracy, Koplik, Yarborough Time, Westcon and In-Store Advertising. Client list not available.

Needs: Approached by 10-15 freelance artists/eyar. Works with 3-4 freelance artists/year. Prefers local artists. Works on assignment only. Uses freelance artists for brochure and catalog illustration, mechanicals, retouching, airbrushing, direct mail packages, charts/graphs and lettering. "Currently doing computer graphics. Freelancers with a computer/design background would be essential."

First Contact & Terms: Send query letter, resume and "samples you can spare." Samples are filed and are not returned. Reports back only if interested. Portfolio should include thumbnails, roughs, original/final art (if available) and final reproduction/product. Pays for design by the hour, $15-18. Pays for illustration by the project. Considers complexity of project, client's budget, skill and experience of artist and how work will be used when establishing payment. Rights purchased vary according to project.

Tips: "Organization is essential" when presenting a portfolio. Often portfolios are "sloppy, too many things to look at—(generally time is limited). Send resume and printed pieces that need not be returned."

TOM NICHOLSON ASSOCIATES, INC., 535 Fifth Ave., 24th Fl., New York NY 10017. (212)490-9262. Principal: Tom Nicholson. Estab. 1987. Specializes in design of interactive computer programs. Clients: corporations, museums, government agencies. Current clients include Citibank and IBM. Client list available upon request.

Needs: Approached by "very few" freelance artists/year. Works with 6-10 freelance illustrators and 6 freelance designers/year. Prefers local artists. Uses illustrators mainly for computer illustration and animation. Uses designers mainly for computer screen design and concept development. Also uses artist for mechanicals, charts/graphs and AV materials. Especially needs designers with interest (not necessarily experience) in computer screen design plus a strong interest in information design.

First Contact and Terms: Send query letter with resume; include tearsheets and slides if possible. Samples are filed or are returned. Reports back within 1 week. Write to schedule an appointment to show a portfolio, which should include thumbnails, original/final art and tearsheets. Considers complexity of project, client's budget and skill and experience of artist when establishing payment. Buys one-time or all rights; rights purchased vary according to project.

*NORWOOD OLIVER DESIGN ASSOCIATES, 501 American Legionway, Point Pleasant Beach NJ 08742. (201)295-1200. Vice President: Madan P. Vazirani A.I.A. Interior design firm. Clients: department stores, malls, restaurants, hotels, and other commercial and retail clients. Current clients include Bergdorf Goodman, Bonwit Teller, Hess's and Reynolds. Client list not available.

Needs: Approached by 5 freelance artists/year. Works with 5 freelance illustrators and 2 freelance designers/year. Prefers renderers that have 5-10 years experience and within driving distance. Works on assignment only. Uses renderers for interior design and renderings, architectural renderings, design consulting, model making and wall hangings. Especially needs perspective renderings of interiors.

First Contact & Terms: Send resume and photocopies. Samples are filed or are not returned. Write to schedule an appointment to show a portfolio, which should include color photostats and photographs. Pays per rendering, $300-500. Considers client's budget, skill and experience of artist, and "whether piece is b&w, color or airbrush" when establishing payment. Buys first rights.

NOTOVITZ DESIGN ASSOCIATES, INC., (formerly Notovitz & Perrault Design, Inc.), 47 E. 19 St., New York NY 10003. (212)677-9700. President: Joseph Notovitz. Specializes in corporate design (annual reports, literature, publications), corporate identity and signage. Clients: finance and industry.

Needs: Works with 10 freelance artists/year. Uses artists for brochure, poster, direct mail and booklet illustration; mechanicals; charts/graphs and logo design.

First Contact & Terms: Send resume, slides, printed pieces and tearsheets to be kept on file. Samples not filed are returned by SASE. Reports in 1 week. Call for appointment to show portfolio, which should include roughs, original/final art and final reproduction/product. Pays for design by the hour, $15-50; by the project, $200-1,500. Pays for illustration by the project, $100-5,000; also negotiates.

Tips: "Send pieces which reflect our firm's style and needs. They should do a bit of research in the firm they are contacting. If we never produce book covers, book cover art does not interest us."

*TIMOTHY OAKLEY DESIGNS, 3921 Kaualio Pl., Honolulu HI 96816. (808)732-8706. Owner/Senior Art Director: Tim Oakley. Estab. 1980. Specializes in brand identity, corporate identity, direct mail and package design and airbrushing. Clients: agencies, record companies. Current clients include Sheraton Hotels and Capital Records. Client list available upon request.
Needs: Approached by 10-20 freelance artists/year. Works with 2-5 freelance illustrators and designers/year. Works only with artist reps and prefers local artists only. Works on assignment only. Uses illustrators mainly for national products. Uses designers mainly for local material. Also uses designers and illustrators for brochure design and illustration, lettering, logos, model making, charts/graphs, audiovisual materials and ad illustration.
First Contact & Terms: Call first; then send query letter with brochure, resume, photographs and slides. Samples sometimes filed. Samples not filed are returned by SASE if requested by artist. Reports back only if interested. Write to schedule an appoinment to show a portfolio. Portfolio should include thumbnails, photostats, slides, tearsheets and transparencies (2×4 or 4×5). Pays for design by the hour, \$35-50; by the project, \$250-2,500. Pays for illustration by the hour, \$40-100. Buys all rights.

OPTISONICS PRODUCTIONS, 186 8th St., Creskill NJ 07626. (201)871-4192. President: Jim Brown. Specializes in graphics, typesetting, multi-image, audio for AV, displays, exhibits and print media. Clients: industry and theatre.
Needs: Works with varied number of freelance artists/year. Prefers local artists. Works on assignment only. Uses artists for advertising, brochures, catalogs and for graphics for multi-image slide show.
First Contact & Terms: Send query letter with brochure/flyer, business card or resume which will be kept on file. Negotiates payment.

PANOGRAPHICS, Rt. 1, Box 139, Windfall Rd., Utica NY 13502. (315)797-9194. Owner: Lawrence Stepanowicz. Estab. 1980. Specializes in direct mail and publications. Clients: ad agencies and businesses.
Needs: Works with 10-15 freelance artists/year. Prefers local artists. Works on assignment only. Uses artists for brochure design and illustration; catalog, book and magazine design; mechanicals; direct mail packages; logos; cartoons and caricatures.
First Contact and Terms: Send query letter with brochure, tearsheets, photostats, photocopies, slides and photographs. Samples are filed or are returned if accompanied by SASE. Reports back only if interested. Call or write to schedule an appointment to show a portfolio, or mail original/final art. Pays for design and illustration by the hour, \$10-25; by the project, \$35 minumum. Considers complexity of project, client's budget, skill and experience of artist and how work will be used when establishing payment. Buys all rights.
Tips: "Let us know who and where you are, especially if in central New York State."

PAPAGALOS AND ASSOCIATES, 313 E. Thomas, Phoenix AZ 85012. (602)279-2933. Creative Director: Nicholas Papagalos. Specializes in advertising, brochures, annual reports, corporate identity, displays, packaging, publications and signage. Clients: major regional, consumer and business-to-business.
Needs: Works with 10-20 freelance artists/year. Works on assignment only. Uses artists for illustration, retouching, airbrushing, model making, charts/graphs, AV materials and lettering.
First Contact & Terms: Send query letter with brochure or resume and samples. Samples are filed or are returned only if requested. Reports back within 5 days. Call or write to schedule an appointment to show a portfolio, which should include thumbnails, roughs, final reproduction/product, photostats and photographs. Pays for design and illustration by the project, \$100 minimum. Considers complexity of project, client's budget, skill and experience of artist, how work will be used, turnaround time and rights purchased when establishing payment. Rights purchased vary according to project.
Tips: In presenting samples or portfolios, "two or three samples of the same type/style are enough."

PERSECHINI & COMPANY, #303, 1575 Westwood Blvd., Los Angeles CA 90024. (213)478-5522. Contact: Shannon Heiman. Estab. 1979. Specializes in annual reports, corporate identity, display, packaging, publications and signage. Clients: healthcare, real estate, hospitality, institutional ad agencies, PR firms and internal communications departments. Current clients include National Medical Enterprises, UCLA and Mannin Sclvage & Lee. Client list not available.
Needs: Approached by 50-100 freelance artists/year. Works with 5-6 freelance illustrators and 1 freelance designer/year. Works on assignment basis only. Uses artists mainly for design and illustration; also for mechanicals, retouching, airbrushing and lettering. Occasionally uses humorous and cartoon-style illustrations.
First Contact & Terms: Send query letter with brochure, business card and photostats and photocopies to be kept on file. Samples not kept on file are returned by SASE. Reports back only if interested. Pays for design by the hour, \$15-25 average. Pays for illustration by the project, \$150-5,000 average. Considers complexity of project, client's budget, skill and experience of artist, how work will be used, turnaround time and rights purchased when establishing payment.

Tips: "Most of our accounts need a sophisticated look for their ads, brochures, etc. Occasionally we have a call for humor. Do a lot of mailings of current or new work so we can update files and are always reminded."

PETRO GRAPHIC DESIGN ASSOCIATES, 315 Falmouth Dr., Rocky River OH 44116. (216)356-0429. Principal/Graphic Designer: Nancy Petro. Estab. 1976. Specializes in corporate identity, direct mail and collateral design, design for print communications and ads. "We work directly for clients, predominantly in two areas: (1) builders/developers (including shopping malls) and (2) lawncare industry ad. Client list not available.
Needs: Approached by 20-25 freelance artists/year. Works with 6-8 freelance illustrators/year and 3-5 freelance designers/year. Works on assignment only. Uses illustrators mainly for ads and brochures. Uses designers mainly for back-up when overloaded. Also uses artists for mechanicals, retouching, airbrushing, lettering, ad illustration and fashion illustration.
First Contact and Terms: Send query letter with brochure, resume, tearsheets, photostats and photocopies. Samples are filed. Samples not filed are returned if accompanied by a SASE. Reports back only if interested. Call or write to schedule an appointment to show a portfolio, or mail b&w and color final reproduction/ product, tearsheets, photostats and photographs. Pays by the hour, $20-65; by the project, $50-5,000 ("depends on scope of project")." Considers complexity of project, client's budget, skill and experience of artist, how work will be used, turnaround time and rights purchased when establishing payment. Negotiates rights purchased; rights purchased vary according to project. "Show an identifiable, unique product that is of high quality."
Tips: "Don't show weak work. Show work that is of high quality and can be matched (in quality) if you are hired for a job. Please send samples or copies of your work. Your work is your best salesman. Any designer can evaluate the work and know if it fills a need—without undue demands on the designer's time."

PLATINUM DESIGN, INC., 14 W. 23rd St., 2nd Floor, New York NY 10010. Art Director: Melissa Norton. Estab. 1985. Specializes in annual reports, corporate identity, direct mail packages and publication design. Clients include *Business Week*, *Fortune*, *Seventeen* and Warner. Current projects include corporate logos, letterhead designs and special ad sections.
Needs: Works with 15 freelance illustrators/year. Works with 5 freelance designers/year. Prefers artists with experience in editorial and computer graphics for charts. Works on assignment only. Uses designers mainly for editorial design or type retouching. Also uses illustrators and designers for magazine design, mechanicals, retouching, airbrushing, charts/graphs and lettering.
First Contact and Terms: Send query letter with brochure, resume and samples. Samples are filed or are returned if accompanied by a SASE. Reports back only if requested. To show a portfolio, mail appropriate materials. Pays by the hour, $10-20; by the project, $75-3,000+. Considers client's budget, how work will be used and rights purchased when establishing payment. Rights purchased vary according to project.
Tips: "Send note and sample material for files. Do not call."

© 1989 Fortune Magazine

Platinum Design, Inc. of New York does much publication design. This special advertising section featuring the advantages of various information systems was done for Fortune magazine. Art director Melissa Norton is looking for freelance artists with experience in editorial and computer graphics.

PORRAS & LAWLOR ASSOCIATES, 15 Lucille Ave., Salem NH 03079. (603)893-3626. Art Director: Victoria Porras. Estab. 1980. Specializes in corporate identity, direct mail and publications. Clients: banks, high-tech industry and colleges. Client list available on request.
Needs: Approached by 25 freelance artists/year. Works with 3 freelance illustrators and 2 freelance designers/ year. Prefers artists living in New England with two years of experience. Uses freelance artists for brochure illustration, mechanicals, airbrushing, AV materials and lettering.
First Contact & Terms: Send query letter with brochure showing art style or samples. Samples are filed. Reports back only if interested. Call or write to schedule an appointment to show a portfolio, which should include thumbnails, original/final art, final reproduction/product or photographs (whatever is applicable to artist). Pays for design by the hour, $15-25. Pays for illustration by the project, $120-3,000. Considers complexity of project, client's budget, skill and experience of artist, turnaround time and rights purchased when establishing payment. Negotiates rights purchased; rights purchased vary according to project.
Tips: "In your portfolio include examples of corporate identity and publications. Don't talk about bad things that happened while you were doing the work."

PRESENCE, 5533 Sebastopol Rd., Sebastopol CA 95472. (707)829-8797. Principal: Valerie Randall. Estab. 1978. Specializes in direct mail, package and 3-D promotional design. Clients: major corporations, ad agencies and PR firms. Current clients include: Lori Strauss, Speigel, Inc., Cost Plus and International Greetings. Client list not available.
Needs: Works with 1 freelance illustrator/year. Works with 2 freelance designers/year. Prefers artists with experience in print production. Works on assignment only. Uses artists for P-O-P design, mechanicals, model making and direct mail design. Especially needs paper structure; designers who understand packaging.
First Contact and Terms: Send query letter with resume, tearsheets, photostats, photocopies and photographs. Samples are filed or are returned if accompanied by a SASE. Reports back within 1 month. Call or write to schedule an appointment to show a portfolio, which should include roughs, original/final art, final reproduction/product and color tearsheets, photostats and photographs. Pays by the hour, $10-30. Considers complexity of project, client's budget, skill and experience of artist, how work will be used, turnaround time and rights purchased when establishing payment. Rights purchased vary according to project.
Tips: "Send query letter with resume; (we check how letter is laid out, spelling and punctuation to give us a clue about work habits.) Also send samples in any form; will return if SASE provided. We will respond within one month regardless. Call or write to schedule an appointment. We devote one day per month specifically for portfolio reviews."

PRODUCT SYSTEMS INTERNATIONAL INC., 40 N. Cherry St., Lancaster PA 17602. (717)291-9042. Director, Client Development: Nancy B. Rogers. Estab. 1987. Specializes in graphic design, product design/development, package design/packaging, merchandising.
Needs: Works with 20 freelance artists/year. Artists should be within driving distance; "prefer freelancers to work inhouse." Works on assignment only. Uses artists for illustration, brochures, catalogs, mechanicals, model making, charts/graphs, lettering, logos, advertisement and market research. Prefers airbrush, charcoal/ pencil and marker.
First Contact & Terms: Send query letter with brochure, resume and business card to be kept on file; slides to be returned. Samples not kept on file are returned. Reports within 30 days. To show a portfolio, write to schedule an appointment and mail thumbnails, roughs, final reproduction/product and photographs. Pays for design by the hour, $10-30; pays for illustration by the hour, $10-$30. Considers complexity of project, and skill and experience of artist when establishing payment.

PRODUCTION INK, 2826 Northeast 19th Dr., Gainesville FL 32609. (904)377-8973. Contact: Terry VanNortwick. Estab. 1979. Specializes in publications, marketing and advertising.
Needs: Works with 6-10 freelance artists/year. Works on assignment only. Uses artists for brochure illustration, airbrushing and lettering.
First Contact & Terms: Send resume, samples, tearsheets, photostats, photocopies, slides and photography. Samples are filed or are returned if accompanied by SASE. Reports back only if interested. Call or write to schedule an appointment to show a portfolio, which should include original/final art. Pays for illustration by the project, $100 minimum. Considers complexity of project, client's budget, skill and experience of artist,

The asterisk before a listing indicates that the listing is new in this edition. New markets are often the most receptive to freelance submissions.

how work will be used, turnaround time, and rights purchased when establishing payment. Buys reprint rights; rights purchased vary according to project.

Tips: "Send slide samples for our files. Check with us regularly."

PUBLISHING SERVICES, 812 S. Mitchell, Bloomington IN 47401. (812)334-8914. Creative Director: Kristin Herzog. "We design and produce several education publications."

Needs: Works with 10 freelance illustrators/year. Buys 20 freelance illustrations/year. Uses artists mainly for b&w, inside articles.

First Contact & Terms: Send samples, tearsheets and photocopies. Pays by the project $100-200.

Tips: "Make sure name, address and phone are on all samples. Samples get separated and passed around. Calling is not usually a good idea."

THE PUSHPIN GROUP, 215 Park Ave. S., New York NY 10003. (212)674-8080. President: Seymour Chwast; Partner: Phyllis Rich Flood. Specializes in annual reports, brand identity, corporate identity, packaging, publications and signage. Clients: individuals, ad agencies, corporations, PR firms, etc.

Needs: Works with 5-6 freelance artists/year. Generally prefers designers to illustrators. Uses artists for design, illustrations, brochures, books, magazines, mechanicals, retouching, airbrushing, charts/graphs and lettering.

First Contact & Terms: Send query letter with resume, tearsheets, photostats and photocopies. Samples not filed are returned only if requested. Reports only if interested. Call or write to schedule an appointment to show a portfolio, which should include roughs, original/final art, final reproduction/product, color and b&w tearsheets, photostats, photographs and b&w. Pays for design by the hour, $15-20. Considers complexity of project, client's budget, skill and experience of artist, and turnaround time when establishing payment.

*QUADRANT COMMUNICATIONS CO., INC., Suite 1602, 595 Madison Ave., New York NY 10022. (212)421-0544. FAX: (212)421-0483. President: Robert Eichinger. Estab. 1973. Specializes in annual reports, corporate identity, direct mail design, publication design and technical illustration. Clients: corporations. Current clients include AT&T, Citibank, NYNEX and Polo/Ralph Lauren. Client list available upon request.

Needs: Approached by 50 freelance artists/year. Works with 12 freelance illustrators and 6 freelance designers/year. Prefers artists with experience in publication production. Works on assignment only. Uses illustrators and designers mainly for publications, trade show collateral and direct mail design. Also uses artists for brochure design and illustration, catalog design, mechanicals, retouching, magazine design, and charts/graphs.

First Contact & Terms: Send query letter with resume. Samples are filed. Reports back only if interested. Call to schedule an appointment to show a portfolio. Portfolio should include tearsheets and photographs. Pays by the hour or by the project, "The payment depends on the nature of the project, the client's budget and the current market rate." Rights purchased vary according to project.

*QUALLY & COMPANY INC., Suite 2502, 30 E. Huron, Chicago IL 60611. (312)944-0237. Creative Director: Robert Qually. Specializes in advertising, graphic design and new product development. Clients: major corporations.

Needs: Works with 20-25 freelance artists/year. "Artists must be good and have the right attitude." Works on assignment only. Uses artists for design, illustration, mechanicals, retouching and lettering.

First Contact & Terms: Send query letter with brochure, resume, business card and samples to be kept on file. Samples not kept on file are returned by SASE. Reports back within several days. Call or write for appointment to show portfolio. Considers complexity of project, client's budget, skill and experience of artist, how work will be used, turnaround time and rights purchased when establishing payment.

Tips: Looking for talent, point of view, style, craftsmanship, depth and innovation in portfolio or samples. Sees "too many look-alikes, very little innovation."

THE QUARASAN GROUP, INC., Suite 300, 630 Dundee Rd., Northbrook IL 60062. (708)291-0700. President: Randi S. Brill. Project Managers: Kendall Clark, Kathy Kasper, Jean Lograsso and Jay Skilton. Specializes in books. Clients: book publishers. Client list not available.

Needs: Approached by 300 freelance artists/year. Works with 140-175 freelance illustrators and 3-5 designers/year. Artists with publishing experience only. Uses artists for illustration, books, mechanicals, charts/graphs, lettering and production. Also uses extensive desktop artwork and computer graphics.

First Contact & Terms: Send query letter with brochure or resume and samples addressed to ASD to be circulated and to be kept on file. Prefers "anything that we can retain for our files; photostats, photocopies, tearsheets or dupe slides that do not have to be returned" as samples. Reports only if interested. Pays for production by the hour, $12-20 average; for illustration by the piece/project, $25-1,000 average. Considers complexity of project, client's budget, how work will be used and turnaround time when establishing payment. "For illustration, size and complexity are the key factors."

Tips: Common mistakes freelancers make are "not identifying work clearly and not submitting samples that can be kept. Follow our procedure as explained by the receptionist; have patience; it really is the best way to showcase your talents with Quarasan."

MIKE QUON DESIGN OFFICE, INC., 568 Broadway, New York NY 10012. (212)226-6024. President: Mike Quon. Specializes in corporate identity, display, direct mail, packaging, publications and technical illustrations. Clients: corporations and ad agencies (e.g. American Express, HBO, IBM, Clairol and AT&T). Client list available upon request.
Needs: Approached by 25-30 graphic artists each year. Works with 5-6 freelance illustrators and 4-5 freelance designers/year. Prefers good/great people "local doesn't matter." Works on assignment only. Prefers graphic style. Uses artists for design, brochures, P-O-P displays, mechanicals, model making, charts/graphs and lettering. Prefers pen & ink. Especially needs precision inking people.
First Contact & Terms: Send query letter with resume, tearsheets and photocopies. Samples are filed or are returned if accompanied by a SASE. Reports back only if interested. Write to schedule an appointment to show a portfolio or mail thumbnails, roughs and tearsheets. Pays for design by the hour, $12-20. Pays for illustration by the project, $50-500 and up. Considers complexity of project, client's budget, skill and experience of artist, turnaround time and rights purchased when establishing payment. Buys one-time rights; rights purchased vary according to project.

*R.H.GRAPHICS, INC., 23 E. 22nd St., New York NY 10010. (212)505-5070. President: Roy Horton. Vice President: Irving J. Mittleman. Specialized in brand identity, corporate identity, display, direct mail and packaging. Current clients include Revlon, Clairol, Wallace Lab, World Gold. Client list not available.
Needs: Approached by 25 freelance artists/year. Works with 1-3 freelance illustrators/year. Artists must have ten years of experience. Especially needs mechanicals and ruling. Uses artists for P-O-P displays, mechanicals, retouching, airbrushing and lettering.
First Contract & Terms: Send query letter with brochure showing art style or resume and tearsheets. Reports only if interested. Write to show a portfolio, which should include roughs and original/final art. Pays for design by the hour, $18-25. Pays for illustration by the project, $50-250. Considers client's budget, and skill and experience of artist when establishing payment.
Tips: Wants to see "actual art and variety."

*JOHN RACILA ASSOCIATES, 340 W. Butterfield Rd., Elmhurst IL 60126. (312)279-0614. Creative Director: John Neher. Specializes in brand identity, corporate identity, display, interior design, packaging, publication and signage. Clients: manufacturers of consumer goods.
Needs: Prefers local artists to work on premises, minimum three years of experience or consumer product experience. Works on assignment only. Uses artists for design, illustration, mechanicals, retouching, airbrushing, model making, AV material, lettering and advertisement.
First Contact & Terms: Send query letter with brochure. Samples are filed or are returned only if requested. Reports back only if interested. Call to schedule an appointment to show a portfolio, which should include roughs, original/final art, final reproduction/product and color tearsheets. Pays for design by the hour, $8 minimum. Pays for illustration by the project, $50 minimum. Considers complexity of project, client's budget, skill and experience of artist and turnaround time when establishing payment. Buys all rights.

READ INK, Suite 19, 2000 Vallejo St., San Francisco CA 94123. Art Director: Elizabeth Read. Estab. 1987. Specializes in publications and advertising. Clients: publishers, art agencies and corporations.
Needs: Works with 12 freelance illustrators and 7 freelance designers/year. Prefers to see samples before contacting. Works on assignment only. Uses artists for brochure and book design and collateral. Setting up freelance sample file of creative talent to draw upon.
First Contact and Terms: Send brochure or resume, tearsheets, photostats, photocopies, slides and/or photographs. Samples are filed or are returned if accompanied by a SASE. Reports back within 3 weeks. To show a portfolio, mail final reproduction/product, b&w and color tearsheets, photostats and photographs. Pays for design and illustration by the project. Considers complexity of project, client's budget, skill and experience of artist, how work will be used, turnaround time and rights purchased when establishing payment. Rights purchased vary according to project.
Tips: "Too often artists don't show their best work in their portfolio. It's important to weed out your portfolio and show only your best work."

RITTER & RITTER, INC., 45 W. 10th St., New York NY 10011. (212)505-0241. Art Director: Valerie Ritter. Estab. 1968. Specializes in annual reports, corporate identity, book covers, brochures, catalogs and promotion for publishers, corporations, nonprofit organizations and hospitals. Client list available upon request.
Needs: Approached by 50 artists/year. Works with 2 freelance illustrators and designers/year according to firm's needs. Does not always work on assignment only; "sometimes we need a freelance on a day-to-day basis." Uses freelance artwork mainly for catalogs and brochures. Uses fine artists for advertising illustration

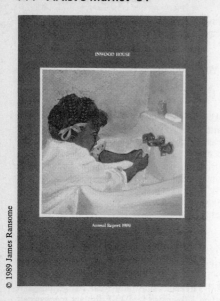

These are two examples of freelance artwork commissioned by Ritter & Ritter, Inc. of New York City. Jersey City, New Jersey artist James Ransome was assigned this annual report illustration for Inwood House. According to Art director Valerie Ritter, "James met deadlines and had an extremely specific image he wanted to convey. His style was suited to the client's and our art directional images." It was done in oil paint; Ransome sold one-time rights to the piece. Les Kantwrek designed this wood-cut and charcoal cover for Newsweek's Education Division. Ritter wanted "a strong image of a fraying rope. L. Kantwrek's style was appropriate to my vision."

and covers, and graphic designers for brochure design, mechanicals, charts and graphs. Prefers "elegant, understated, sensitive design without self-conscious trendiness."

First Contact & Terms: Prefers experienced artists, although "talented 'self-starters' with design expertise/education are also considered." Send query letter with brochure, resume and samples to be kept on file. "Follow up within a week of the query letter about the possibility of arranging an appointment for a portfolio review." Prefers printed pieces as samples. Samples not filed are returned by SASE. Pays for mechanicals by the hour, $14-20. Pays for design by the project, $100-1,000 average; or by the day, $90-150 average. Pays for illustration by the project, $50-500 average. Considers complexity of the project, client's budget, skill and experience of the artist and turnaround time when establishing payment.

Tips: "Don't try to be something for everyone. Most illustrators (with rare exceptions) are not designers and should not think of showing amateurish design attempts. Also be respectful of art directors' time. Know what you'd like to say in advance, rehearse beforehand and have timely dates ready to set up an appointment. There's no need to diminish the impact of a few good pieces by including less successful ones" in an attempt "to make a portfolio look more substantial."

DEBORAH RODNEY CREATIVE SERVICES, Suite 205, 1640 5th St., San Monte CA 90401. (213)394-0590. Contact: Deborah Rodney. Estab. 1975. Specializes in advertising design and collateral. Clients: ad agencies and direct clients. Current projects include Caesar's Tahoe direct mail and ads and posters for a children's store (Westside Kids).

Needs: Works with 3-5 freelance illustrators/year. Prefers local artists. Uses illustrators mainly for finished art and lettering. Uses designers mainly for logo design. Also uses artists for mechanicals, charts/graphs, advertisement design and illustration. Especially needs "people who do good marker comps and inking."

First Contact and Terms: Send query letter with brochure, resume, tearsheets and photocopies. Call to schedule an appointment to show a portfolio, or mail final reproduction/product and tearsheets or "whatever best shows work." Pays by the hour, $15-20; by the job $100-1,500. Considers complexity of project, client's budget, how work will be used, turnaround time and rights purchased when establishing payment. Negotiates rights purchased.

*ARNOLD SAKS ASSOCIATES, 350 E. 81st St., New York NY 10028. (212)861-4300. FAX: (212)535-2590. Vice President, Production: Anita Fiorillo. Estab. 1967. Specializes in annual reports and corporate communications. Clients: corporations. Current clients include Goldman Sachs, Bristol-Myers Squibb, Philip Morris, Peat Marwick, NYNEX and ALCOA. Client list available upon request.

Needs: Approached by 10 freelance artists/year. Works with 1 or 2 freelance mechanical artists and 1 freelance designer/year. "Mechanical artists; accuracy and speed are important. Also a willingness to work late nights and some weekends." Uses illustrators occasionaly for annual reports. Uses designers mainly for in-season annual reports. Also uses artists for brochure design and illustration, mechanicals and charts/graphics.

First Contact & Terms: Send query letter with brochure and resume. Samples are filed. Reports back to the artist only if interested. Write to schedule an appointment to show a portfolio. Portfolio should include finished pieces. Payment depends on experience and terms and varies depending upon scope and complication. Rights purchased vary according to project.

JACK SCHECTERSON ASSOCIATES INC., 53/16 251 Place, Little Neck NY 11362. (718)225-3536. Contact: Jack Schecterson. Estab. 1967. Art/ad agency. Specializes in packaging, product design, annual reports, brand identity, corporate identity, and P-O-P displays. Clients: manufacturers of consumer/industrial products.

Needs: Uses local artists. Works on assignment only. Uses artists for annual reports, catalogs, direct mail brochures, exhibits, flyers, packaging, industrial design, slide sets, album covers, corporate design, graphics, trademark, logotype design, sales promotion, audiovisuals, P-O-P displays and print media advertising. Especially needs package and product designers.

First Contact & Terms: Send query letter with brochure showing art style or resume and tear sheets, or write for appointment. Samples returned by SASE. Reports "as soon as possible." Pays by the project for design and illustration; negotiates payment. Reproduction rights purchased.

Tips: "Portfolio samples should be printed pieces backed up with magic marker roughs."

SCHROEDER BURCHETT DESIGN CONCEPTS, 40 Park Ave., New York NY 10016. Designer & Owner: Carla Schroeder Burchett. Estab. 1972. Specializes in packaging, drafting and marketing. Clients: manufacturers.

Needs: Works on assignment only. Uses artists for design, mechanicals, lettering and logos.

First Contact & Terms: Send resume; "if interested, will contact artist or craftsperson and will negotiate." Write for appointment to show portfolio, which should include thumbnails, final reproduction/product and photographs. Considers skill and experience of artist when establishing payment.

Tips: "Creativity depends on each individual. "Artists should have a sense of purpose and dependability."

DEBORAH SHAPIRO DESIGNS, 150 Bentley Ave., Jersey City NJ 07304. (201)432-5198. Owner: Deborah Shapiro. Estab. 1981. Specializes in annual reports, brand identity, corporate identity, direct mail, packaging and publications. Clients: corporations and manufacturers.

Needs: Works with 10 freelance artists/year. Works on assignment only. Uses artists for illustration, retouching and airbrushing and photography.

First Contact & Terms: Send query letter with brochure or resume, tearsheets, photostats and photocopies. Samples are filed and are not returned. Reports back only if interested. To show a portfolio, mail original/final art, final reproduction/product, tearsheets and photographs. Pays for illustration by the project, $200-2,000. Considers complexity of project, client's budget, skill and experience of artist, how work will be used, turnaround time and rights purchased when establishing payment. Buys one-time rights.

Tips: "We do not want to see student works. Do not send too many samples. Send assignment oriented pieces."

*SHAREFF DESIGNS, 81 Irving Place, New York NY 10003. (212)475-3963. Designer: Ira Shareff. Specializes in brand identity, corporate identity, displays, packaging, publications, signage, technical illustration, hand lettering, financial graphics and murals. Clients: publishers, ad agencies and independent clients. Current clients include: Spice Market, Inc., Creative Concepts, Inc. and Sarerino, Inc. Client list available upon request.

Needs: Approached by 20 freelance artists/year. Works with 4 freelance designers/year. Uses artists for illustration, catalogs, mechanicals, retouching, airbrushing, model making, charts/graphs and AV materials.

First Contact & Terms: Artists must have 3 years' experience in the required areas. Works on assignment only. Send resume and samples. Prefers photocopies or tearsheets as samples. Samples are returned only if requested. Considers complexity of project, client's budget and turnaround time when establishing payment.

Tips: The most common mistakes freelancers make in presenting samples are "poor verbal presentations and poorly presented work (not in any order, no consistency of style, format, etc.)."

ROGER SHERMAN PARTNERS, INC., Suite 300, 13530 Michigan Ave., Dearborn MI 48126. (313)582-8844. Contact: Bonnie Bobich. Interior design and contract purchasing firms providing architectural and interior design for commercial restaurants, stores, hotels and shopping centers and complete furnishing purchasing. Clients: commercial firms.

Needs: Artists with past work experience only, able to provide photos of work and references. Works on assignment only. Uses artists for architectural renderings, furnishings, landscape and graphic design, model making and signage; also for special decor items as focal points for commercial installations, such as paintings, wood carvings, etc.

First Contact & Terms: Send query letter with brochure/flyer or resume and samples to be kept on file. Prefers slides and examples of original work as samples. Samples not returned. Reporting time depends on scope of project. Call or write for appointment. Negotiates payment; varies according to client's budget.

*SMALLKAPS ASSOCIATION, INC., 21 Beacon Dr., Port Washington NY 11050. (516)767-5168. FAX: (516)944-5618. President: Marla Kaplan. Estab. 1976. Specializes in brand and corporate identity, direct mail and publication design, signage and technical illustration. Clients: ad agencies, publishers, small and large corporations. Current clients include McGraw-Hill, American Cancer Society and Oxbridge Communications, Inc.

Needs: Approached by 20 freelance artists/year. Works with 3 freelance illustrators and 5 freelance designers/year. Prefers local artists with experience in mechanicals and comps. Works on assignment only. Also uses artists for brochure design and illustration; catalog, ad, P-O-P and direct mail design; retouching; airbrushing; lettering; logos; P-O-P and direct mail design; charts/graphs and audiovisual materials.

First Contact & Terms: Send query letter with resume, SASE, tearsheets and photocopies. Samples are filed or are returned by SASE if requested by artist. Reports back to the artist only if interested. Call to schedule an appointment to show a portfolio. Portfolio should include thumbnails, roughs, original/final art and photostats. Pays for design by the hour, $10-20; by the day, $80-150. Pays for illustration by the project, $100-1,000. Negotiates rights purchased.

SMITH & DRESS, 432 W. Main St., Huntington NY 11743. (516)427-9333. Contact: A. Dress. Specializes in annual reports, corporate identity, display, direct mail, packaging, publications and signage. Clients: corporations.

Needs: Works with 3-4 freelance artists/year. Local artists only. Works on assignment only. Uses artists for illustration, retouching, airbrushing and lettering.

First Contact & Terms: Send query letter with brochure showing art style or tearsheets to be kept on file (except for works larger than 8½x11). Pays for illustration by the project. Considers client's budget and turnaround time when establishing payment.

SMITH DESIGN ASSSOCIATES, 205 Thomas St., Box 558, Glen Ridge NJ 07028. (201)429-2177. Freelance Artist: Lucille Simonetti, 14 Edgemere Rd., Livingston NJ 07039. Clients: food processors, cosmetics firms, various industries, corporations, life insurance, office consultant. Current clients: Popsicle, Good Humor, Inter-Continental Hotels, Sony and Schering Plough. Client list available upon request.

Needs: Approached by over 100 freelance artists/year. Works with 10-20 freelance illustrators and 2-3 freelance designers/year. Requires quality and dependability. Uses freelance artists for advertising and brochure design, illustration and layout; interior design, P-O-P and design consulting.

First Contact & Terms: Send query letter with brochure showing art style or resume, tearsheets and photostats. Samples are filed or are returned only if requested by artist. Reports back within 1 week. Call to schedule an appointment to show a portfolio, which should include color roughs, original/final art and final reproduction. Pays for design by the hour, $15-30. Pays for illustration by the hour, $25 minimum. Considers complexity of project and client's budget when establishing payment. Buys all rights. Also buys rights for use of existing non-commissioned art.

Tips: "Know who you're presenting to, the type of work we do and the quality we expect."

*HARRY SPRUYT DESIGN, Box 555, Block Island RI 02807. Principal: Harry Spruyt. Specializes in environmental product design consulting and invention. Clients: product manufacturers, design firms, consultants, ad agencies and individuals. Current clients include Scott Paper Co. Client list available upon request.

Needs: Works with various number of freelance artists/year. Works on assignment only. Uses artists/designers for accurate perspective drawings of products (concepts), design and material research and model making.

First Contact & Terms: Portfolio should include thumbnails, roughs, original/final art, final reproduction/product and color photographs of models. "I want to see samples closest to my current needs such as sketches showing the process leading up to these examples, models and time estimates. I do not want to see photos of sketches. Pays for design and illustration by the hour, $20 and up; by the project, $200 and up; by the day, $120 and up. Considers "usable work, competence in following guidelines and meeting mutually agreeable delivery dates" when establishing payment.

Tips: "We integrate what's shown by freelancer with what's heard and seen at an interview in an efficient use of time."

*MICHAEL STANARD, INC., 996 Main St., Evanston IL 60202. (708)869-9820. FAX: (708)869-9826. Executive Designer: Lisa Fingerhut. Estab. 1978. Specializes in annual reports; brand and corporate identity; display, package and publication design; and signage. Clients: corporations and associations. Current clients

Popsicle® Twister® is a new twist on an old favorite. We've taken all natural orange or cherry flavors and swirled them around an all natural lemon flavored center. It adds up to an exciting icy flavor that will zap kids' mouths with great Popsicle® taste!

© 1990 Smith Design Associates

Artists Erich Buechel of Bloomfield, New Jersey and Lucille Simonetti of Livingston, New Jersey collaborated on this piece for Smith Design Associates. Following a tight layout and sample styles, they completed the project in two weeks. According to president James C. Smith, the artists were chosen for their "specific talent for airbrush, and/or bright colors. In addition, they demonstrated commitment to instructions, deadlines, etc."

include Kraft, General Foods, City of Evanston, Big Ten Conference and TNT North America. Client list available upon request.

Needs: Approached by numerous freelance artists/year. Works with 5-10 freelance illustrators and 1-2 freelance designers/year. Works on assignment only. Uses illustrators for a variety of work.

First Contact & Terms: Send query letter with resume. Samples are not filed and are returned by SASE if requested by artist. Reports back to the artist only if interested. To show a portfolio, mail appropriate materials. Pays by the project. Negotiates rights purchased.

*STRATEGIC DESIGN GROUP, 823 E. Main St., Richmond VA 23219. (804)648-9000. FAX: (804)783-1865. Director of Graphics: Craig Caldwell. Estab. 1980. Specializes in corporate identity and signage. Clients: healthcare-related companies. Current clients include University of Virginia Medical Center; St. Agnes Hospital, Baltimore; Children's Hospital of the King's Daughters, Norfolk, VA. Client list available upon request.

Needs: Approached by 6-10 freelance artists/year. Works with 1-2 freelance illustrators and 3-4 designers/year. Prefers local artists and artists with experience in environmental graphics. Uses designers mainly for production. Also uses freelance designers for mechanicals, logos, model making, charts/graphs and audiovisual material.

First Contact & Terms: Send query letter with resume and photocopies. Samples are filed. Reports back only if interested. Call or write to schedule an appointment to show portfolio, which should include thumbnails, original/final art and b&w and color photostats. Pays for design by the hour, $10-15. Buys all rights.

GORDON STROMBERG DESIGN, 5423 N. Artesian St., Chicago IL 60625-2201. (312)275-9449. Estab. 1974. Specializes in annual reports;, corporate identity; interior, direct mail, publication and book design; and signage. Clients: professional offices, large nonprofit groups, organizations, companies and service groups, publishers. Client list not available.

Needs: Approached by 40-50 freelance artists/year. Works with 3-4 freelance illustrators. "We have not worked with freelance designers recently." Prefers local artists with "flexibility in style, doing high quality work." Works on assignment only. Uses illustrators for newsletters, folders and books. Also uses artists for brochure, poster, ad and medical illustration; mechanicals, retouching, lettering, and charts/graphs.

First Contact & Terms: Send query letter with items I needn't return: "brochure, resume, tearsheets, photographs, photocopies, photostats, slides and transparencies," preferably of things related to a printed project. Samples are filed or are returned by SASE if requested by artist. Reports back within a few days only if interested and SASE sent. To show a portfolio, mail appropriate materials "and request appointment if local." Portfolio should include thumbnails, roughs, original/final art, b&w and color photostats, tearsheets, photographs, slides and transparencies. Pays for design and illustration by the project or by the day. "I work payment out after I see the work." Rights purchased vary according to project and client needs.

STUDIO GRAPHICS, 7337 Douglas St., Omaha NE 68114. (402)397-0390. Owner: Leslie Hanson. Specializes in corporate identity, displays, direct mail, packaging, publications and signage. Clients: agencies, corporations, direct with print advertisers, marketing organizations and restaurant chains.
Needs: Works with 2 freelance artists/year. Works on assignment only. Uses artists for illustration, retouching, airbrushing and AV materials.
First Contact & Terms: Send query letter with resume and samples "as available." Samples are filed or are returned by SASE only if requested. Reports back only if interested. Write to schedule an appointment to show a portfolio, which should include "samples as available." Pays for design and illustration by the project, $100 minimum. Considers complexity of project and client's budget when establishing payment. Negotiates rights purchased; rights purchased vary according to project.

TESSING DESIGN, INC., 3822 N. Seeley Ave., Chicago IL 60618. (312)525-7704. Principals: Arvid V. Tessing and Louise S. Tessing. Estab. 1975. Specializes in corporate identity, marketing promotions and publications. Clients: publishers, educational institutions and nonprofit groups.
Needs: Works with 8-12 freelance artists/year. Works on assignment only. Uses freelancers mainly for publications. Also uses artists for design, illustrations, books, magazines, mechanicals, retouching, airbrushing, charts/graphs and lettering.
First Contact & Terms: Send query letter with brochure. Samples are filed. Samples not filed are not returned. Reports back only if interested. Call to schedule an appointment to show a portfolio, which should include original/final art, final reproduction/product and photographs. Pays for design by the hour, $35-50. Pays for illustration by the project, $75 minimum. Considers complexity of project, client's budget, skill and experience of artist, how work will be used, turnaround time and rights purchased when establishing payment. Rights purchased vary according to project.
Tips: "We prefer to see original work or slides as samples. Work sent should always relate to the need expressed. Our advice for artists to break into the field is as always; call prospective clients, show works and follow-up."

THARP DID IT, Suite 21, 50 University Ave., Los Gatos CA 95030. (408)354-6726. Art Director/Designer: Rick Tharp. Estab. 1975. Specializes in brand identity, corporate identity, display, packaging and signage. Clients: direct. Current clients include BRIO Scanditoy (Sweden), Sebastiani Vineyards and Harmony Foods. Client list not available.
Needs: Approached by 250-350 artists/year. Works with 5-10 freelance illustrators and 1 freelance designer/year. Prefers local artists/designers with experience. Works on assignment only. Uses artists for illustrations.
First Contact & Terms: Send query letter with brochure, resume or printed promotional material. Samples are filed. Samples not filed are returned by SASE. Reports back within 2 years only if interested. To show a portfolio, mail appropriate materials. Pays for illustration by the project, $50-10,000. Considers client's budget and how work will be used when establishing payment. Rights purchased vary according to project.
Tips: "In order for a portfolio to be memorable, it should focus on a limited number of styles and techniques. This applies to illustrators. Designers should have a wide variety of very good work. We do not see portfolios unless we initiate the review, after reviewing samples."

TOKYO DESIGN CENTER, Suite 928, 548 S. Spring St., Los Angeles CA 90013. (213)680-1294. Creative Art Director: Joe Hayakawa. Estab. 1979. Specializes in corporate identity, advertising, catalogs and packaging. Clients: fashion, cosmetic, architectural and industrial firms.
Needs: Works with 4 freelance artists/year. Uses artists for brochures, catalogs, books, P-O-P displays, mechanicals, airbrushing, charts/graphs and advertisements.
First Contact & Terms: Samples are filed and are not returned. Send samples to be kept on file. Samples not kept on file are not returned. Reports only if interested. Pays for design and illustration by the project, $250-3,000. Considers client's budget when establishing payment.
Tips: "Show printed samples, not transparencies. Send a promotional piece and information."

*TOLLNER DESIGN GROUP, 1475 S. Bascom Ave., Campbell CA 95008. (408)371-8100. FAX: (408)371-4294. President: Lisa Tollner. Estab. 1980. Specializes in corporate identity, direct mail design, package design and collateral. Clients: ad agencies and corporations. Current clients include Cisco Systems, Valid Logi and Valley Fair Shopping Center. Client list available upon request.
Needs: Approached by 50 freelance artists/year. Works with 15 freelance illustrators/year. Prefers local artists only. Works on assignment only. Also uses freelance illustrators for brochure, catalog, P-O-P, poster and ad illustration; retouching; airbrushing; lettering; model making; charts/graphs and audiovisual materials.
First Contact & Terms: Send query letter with tearsheets, photographs, photocopies, photostats, slides and transparencies. Samples are filed. Reports back only if interested. Call or write to schedule an appointment to show portfolio. Portfolio should include tearsheets, photographs, slides and transparencies. Pays for illustration by the project, $150-2,500. Rights purchased vary according to project.

*TOTAL DESIGNERS, Box 888, Huffman TX 77336. (713)324-4249. President: Ed Lorts. Specializes in corporate identity, display, signage, technical illustration and exhibit and interior design. Current clients include Hines Interests, Trammel Crow, Central Park Associates. Client list available upon request.
Needs: Approached by 3 or 4 freelance artists/year. Works with 1 or 2 freelance illustrators and designers/year. Works on assignment only. Uses artists for brochure and catalog illustration, P-O-P displays, mechanicals and logos. Especially needs entry-level artist.
First Contact & Terms: Send query letter with brochure, resume and samples. Samples are filed or are returned. Reports back only if interested. Call or write to schedule an appointment to show portfolio, which should include thumbnails, roughs and original/final art. Pays for design by the project, $100 minimum. Pays for illustration by the project, $250. Considers complexity of project, skill and experience of artist, turnaround time and rights purchased when establishing payment. Buys all rights; rights purchased vary according to project.
Tips: "Bring turnkey projects, thumbnails and roughs through to finished. Don't show old material."

*CHIP TRAVERS GRAPHIC DESIGN, 2360 E. Broadway, Tucson AZ 85719. (602)792-1018. FAX: (602)884-9825. Specializes in annual reports; corporate identity; display, direct mail and publication design; signage and promotional graphics. Clients: hotels, corporations, hospitals, direct clientele. Current clients include McCollough, Larson Co. and Magma Copper. Client list available upon request.
Needs: Approached by 50 freelance artists/year. Works with 5-7 freelance illustrators and 10-15 designers/year. Prefers local artists and qualified professionals. Works on assignment only. Uses illustrators mainly for annual reports and posters and covers. Uses designers mainly for ads, publications and logos. Also uses artists for brochure/illustration; mechanicals; retouching; airbrushing; catalog, P-O-P and poster illustration; model making; ad illustration and audiovisual materials.
First Contact & Terms: Send query letter with brochure and resume. Samples are returned. Reports back only if interested. Write to schedule an appointment to show a portfolio. Portfolio should include b&w tearsheets, slides and transparencies (35mm/4×5). Pays for design and illustration by the project. Rights purchased vary according to project.

TRIBOTTI DESIGNS, 15234 Morrison St., Sherman Oaks CA 91403. (818)784-6101. Contact: Robert Tribotti. Estab. 1970. Specializes in graphic design, annual reports, corporate identity, packaging, publications and signage. Clients: PR firms, ad agencies and corporations.
Needs: Works with 2-3 freelance artists/year. Prefers local artists only. Works on assignment only. Mainly uses freelancers for brochure illustration. Also uses artists for catalogs, mechanicals, retouching, airbrushing, charts/graphs, lettering and advertisement. Prefers marker, pen & ink, airbrush, pencil, colored pencil and computer illustration.
First Contact & Terms: Send query letter with brochure. Reports back only if interested. Call to schedule an appointment to show a portfolio, which should include thumbnails, roughs, original/final art, final reproduction/product and b&w and color tearsheets, photostats and photographs. Pays for design and illustration by the project, $75-1,500. Considers complexity of project, client's budget, skill and experience of artist, how work will be used and rights purchased when establishing payment. Buys one-time rights; negotiates rights purchased. Rights purchased vary according to project.
Tips: "We will consider experienced artists only. Must be able to meet deadline. Send printed samples and follow up with a phone call."

*THE T-SHIRT GALLERY LTD., 154 E. 64th St., New York NY 10021. (212)838-1212. Vice President: Flora Azaria. Specializes in t-shirts. Current clients include *Seventeen Magazine* and Peter Max Studio. Client list not available.
Needs: Approached by 10 freelance artists/year. Works with 8 freelance illustrators and 9 freelance designers/year. Uses artists for design and illustrations.
First Contact & Terms: Send query letter with resume and samples. Samples not filed are returned only if requested. Reports within weeks. To show a portfolio, mail appropriate materials. Pays for design by the project, $50-500. Pays for illustrations by the project, $50-500. Considers how work will be used when establishing payment.

UNIT 1, INC., 1556 Williams St., Denver CO 80218. (303)320-1116. President: Chuck Danford. Estab. 1969. Specializes in annual reports, brand identity, corporate identity, direct mail, packaging, publications and signage. Current clients include Saunders Construction Inc., Hazen Research, Analytical Surveys, Inc. and Western Mobile Inc. Client list not available.
Needs: Approached by 25 freelance artists/year. Works with 1 or 2 freelance illustrators and 5-10 freelance designers/year. Uses freelancers mainly for design and production. Also uses artists for design, brochures, catalogs, P-O-P displays, mechanicals, posters, direct mail packages, charts/graphs, logos and advertisements.
First Contact & Terms: Send resume and samples to be kept on file. Samples not kept on file are returned. Reports only if interested. Call or write for appointment to show portfolio. Pays for design and production by the project. Considers skill and experience of artist when establishing payment.

Tips: "Show printed pieces whenever possible; don't include fine art. Explain samples, outlining problem and solution. If you are new to the business develop printed pieces as quickly as possible to illustrate practical experience."

UNIVERSAL EXHIBITS, 9517 E. Rush St., South El Monte CA 91733. (213)686-0562. President: M.A. Bell. Estab. 1946. Specializes in display and interior design. Clients: ad agencies, companies and museums. Current clients include Litton Industries, Yamaha, Hasbro and Lockheed. Client list not available.
Needs: Approached by 5-7 freelance artists/year. Works with 2 freelance illustrators and 6 freelance designers/year. Prefers local artists, up to 40 miles, with sketching abilities. Works on assignment only. Uses artists for design and model making.
First Contact & Terms: Send resume and slides to be kept on file; reviews original art. Samples not kept on file are returned only if requested. Reports back within 5 days. Call for appointment to show portfolio. Pays for design by the hour, $22-35 average. Considers client's budget and turnaround time when establishing payment.
Tips: "Think trade shows and museums."

WARHAFTIG ASSOCIATES, INC., 48 W. 25th St., New York NY 10010. Production Coordinator: Chik Fung. Estab. 1982. Specializes in collateral, advertising, sales promotion for Fortune 500 companies.
Needs: Works with 20-30 freelance artists/year. Prefers very experienced artists. Uses freelance artwork mainly for mechanicals and illustration. Also uses freelance artists for brochure design and illustration, magazine design, retouching, charts/graphs, AV materials, lettering, logos and design of advertisements.
First Contact & Terms: Send query letter with resume and tearsheets. Samples not filed are returned if accompanied by a SASE. Does not report back. Write to schedule an appointment to show a portfolio, which should provide an adequate representation of style, concepts, work. Pays for design by the hour, $20-40. Pays for illustration by the project. Considers complexity of project, client's budget, skill and experience of artist, how work will be used, turnaround time and rights purchased when establishing payment. Rights purchased vary according to project.
Tips: "Do not show that *one* piece that is not consistent in quality with the rest of your portfolio. Don't thow your work into a portfolio with a zipper that doesn't work. Send material for us to keep on file."

*SUSAN B. WENZEL ELEMENTS, Box 331, 4521 Campus Dr., Irvine CA 92715. Owner: Susan Wenzel. Design studio providing advertising and design for small companies.
Needs: Works with 4 or more freelance artists/year. Uses artists for advertising and brochure design, illustration and layout; catalog and fashion illustration; calligraphy; paste-up; mechanicals; posters; direct mail and annual reports. Prefers "avant-garde '90s!"
First Contact & Terms: Send query letter with brochure or resume, tearsheets, photostats, photocopies and photographs. Samples not filed are returned only if requested. Reports back within 60 days. Write to schedule an appointment to show a portfolio, which should include thumbnails, roughs, final reproduction/product, tearsheets and photostats. Pays for design by the hour, $35-75. Pays for illustration by the hour, $35-100; by the project, $250-500. Considers complexity of project, client's budget, skill and experience of artist, how work will be used, turnaround time and rights purchased when establishing payment.
Tips: "Soft sell and know time is your best friend."

*WEYMOUTH DESIGN, INC., 332 Congress St., Boston MA 02210-1217. (617)542-2647. FAX: (617)451-6233. Office Manager: Judith Hildebrandt. Estab. 1973. Specializes in annual reports and corporate collateral. Clients: corporations and small businesses. Client list not available.
Needs: Approached by "tons" of freelance artists/year. Works with 10 freelance illustrators and 5 freelance designers/year. Prefers artists with experience in corporate annual report illustration. Works on assignment only. Uses illustrators mainly for annual reports. Uses designers mainly for mechanicals. Also uses illustrators for brochure and poster illustration.
First Contact & Terms: Send query letter with resume or illustration samples. Samples are filed. Samples not filed are returned by SASE if requested by artist. Reports back within 5 days. For illustration and photography does not report back, in which case the artist should call for a portfolio review in April-June only. Pays for design by the hour, $18-35. Pays for illustration by the project; "artists usually set their own fee to which we do or don't agree." Rights purchased vary according to project.

*WHITEFLEET DESIGN INC., 440 E. 56th St., New York NY 10022. (212)319-4444. Contact: Design Production. Specializes in annual reports, brand and corporate identity, display, exhibits and shows, packaging, publications, signage and slide shows. Clients: large computer and engineering corporations, retail stores, hospitals, banks, architects and industry.
Needs: Works with 8 freelance artists/year. Uses artists for brochure and catalog layout, mechanicals, retouching, model making, charts/graphs, AV presentations, lettering and logo design. Especially needs good artists for mechanicals for brochures and other print. Prefers Swiss graphic style.

First Contact & Terms: Send brochure/flyer and resume; submit portfolio for review. Prefers actual printed samples or color slides. Samples returned by SASE. Reports within 1 week. Provide brochure/flyer, resume and tearsheets to be kept on file for possible future assignments. Pays $10-15/hour for mechanicals; pays by the project for illustration.

WISNER ASSOCIATES, Advertising, Marketing & Design, 2237 N.E. Wasco, Portland OR 97232. (503)228-6234. Creative Director: Linda Wisner. Estab. 1979. Specializes in brand identity, corporate identity, direct mail, packaging and publications. Clients: small businesses, manufacturers, restaurants, service businesses and book publishers. Client list not available.
Needs: Approached by 20-30 freelance artists/year. Works with 7-10 freelance artists/year. Prefers experienced artists and "fast clean work." Works on assignment only. Uses artists for illustration, books, mechanicals, airbrushing and lettering.
First Contact & Terms: Send query letter with resume, photostats, photocopies, slides and photographs to be kept on file. Prefers "examples of completed pieces, which show the abilities of the artist to his/her fullest." Samples not kept on file are returned by SASE only if requested. Reports only if interested. To show a portfolio, call to schedule an appointment or mail thumbnails, roughs, original/final art and final reproduction/product. Pays for illustration by the hour, $15-30 average. Pays for paste-up/production by the hour, $10-25. Considers complexity of project, client's budget, skill and experience of artist, how work will be used and turnaround time when establishing payment.
Tips: "Bring a complete portfolio with up-to-date pieces."

*MICHAEL WOLK DESIGN ASSOCIATES, 4265 Braganza St., Coconut Grove FL 33133. (305)667-3031. President: Michael Wolk. Estab. 1985. Specializes in corporate identity, display and interior design and signage. Clients: Corporate and private. Client list available upon request.
Needs: Approached by 10 freelance artists/year. Works with 5 freelance illustrators and 5 freelance designers/year. Prefers local artists only. Works on assignment only. Uses illustrators mainly for brochures. Uses designers mainly for interiors and graphics. Also uses artists for brochure design and illustration, mechanicals, logos and catalog illustration.
First Contact & Terms: Send query letter with slides. Samples not filed and are returned by SASE. Reports back to the artist only if interested. Mail appropriate materials: slides. Rights purchased vary according to project.

BENEDICT NORBERT WONG MARKETING DESIGN, 55 Osgood Pl., San Francisco CA 94133. (415)781-7590. President/Creative Director: Ben Wong. Specializes in direct mail and marketing design. Clients: financial services companies (banks, savings and loans, insurance companies, stock brokerage houses) and direct mail marketing firms (ad agencies, major corporations).
Needs: Works with 15 freelance artists/year. Uses artists for design, illustration, brochures, catalogs, mechanicals, retouching, posters, direct mail packages, charts/graphs, lettering, logos and advertisements. Especially needs "experienced designers in area of direct mail."
First Contact & Terms: Send query letter with resume, business card and samples to be kept on file. Prefers tearsheets as samples. Reports back if interested. Call for appointment to show portfolio. "Payment depends on experience and portfolio." Considers complexity of project, client's budget, skill and experience of artist, how work will be used, turnaround time and rights purchased when establishing payment.
Tips: "Please show imaginative problem-solving skills which can be applied to clients in direct marketing."

*YAMAGUMA & ASSOCIATES, Suite 230, 1570 The Alameda, San Jose CA 95126. (408)279-0500. FAX: (408)293-7819. Production Manager: Gaye Sakakuchi. Estab. 1980. Specializes in corporate identity; display, direct mail and publication design; signage and marketing. Clients: high technology, government and business-to-business. Current clients include the Port of San Francisco. Client list available upon request.
Needs: Approached by more than 100 freelance artists/year. Works with 3-4 freelance illustrators and 4-6 designers/year. Works on assignment only. Uses illustrators mainly for 4-color, airbrush and technical work. Uses designers mainly for logos, layout and production. Also uses brochure design and illustration, catalog design, mechanicals, retouching, lettering, logos, ad design, catalog illustration, book design, magazine design, newspaper design, P-O-P design and illustration, poster illustration and design, model making, direct mail design, charts/graphs, audiovisual materials and ad illustration.
First Contact & Terms: Send query letter with brochure, tearsheets, photostats, resume, photographs, slides, photocopies and transparencies. Samples are filed. Reports back only if interested. To show a portfolio, mail thumbnails, roughs, original/final art, b&w and color photostats, tearsheets, photographs, slides and transparencies. Pays for illustration and design by the project. Rights purchased vary according to project.

Other Art/Design Studios

Each year we contact all firms currently listed in *Artist's Market* requesting they give us updated information for our next edition. We also mail listing questionnaires to new and established firms who have not been included in past editions. The following art/design studios either did not respond to our request to update their listings for 1991 (if they indicated a reason, it is noted in parentheses after their name), or they are studios which did not return our questionnaire for a new listing (designated by the words "declined listing" after their names).

Ad Systems Inc. (moved; no forwarding address)
Primo Angeli Inc. (declined listing)
The Art Directors (declined listing)
Basic/Bedell Advertising Selling Improvement Corp.
Bass/Yager & Associates (declined listing)
Lawrence Bender & Associates (declined listing)
Tom Bowler Design (asked to be deleted)
Michael Brock Design (declined listing)
Carré Noir Inc. (asked to be deleted)
The Chestnut House Group Inc.
Communication Design (declined listing)
Crosby Associates (declined listing)
Cross Associates (declined listing)
Curry Design (declined listing)
D.F.I. Inc.
Design North (asked to be deleted)
Diagram Design (declined listing)
The Duffy Group (declined listing)
Rod Dyer Group (declined listing)
Marsha Drebelbis Studio

Edges (asked to be deleted)
Editing, Design & Production (out of business)
The Flack Studio (no longer does commercial work)
Stephanie Furniss Design
Gailen Associates, Inc. (asked to be deleted)
Milton Glaser (declined listing)
Eric Gluckman Communications, Inc.
Graphic Group
The Graphic Suite (asked to be deleted)
April Greiman, Inc. (declined listing)
Paige Hardy & Associates
Mark Heideman Graphic Design
Hillman/Design Focus
Grant Hoekstra Graphics, Inc.
Hornall Anderson Design Works (declined listing)
The Hoyt Group, Inc.
The Ink Tank (declined listing)
David Kageyama Designer (asked to be deleted)
Kelly & Co., Graphic Design, Inc.
KNT Plusmark Inc.
Krames Communications
Krudo Design Atelier, Ltd.
F. Patrick La Salle Design/Graphics
Legal Arts
M & Co. (declined listing)
McGuire Willis & Associates

Manhattan Design (declined listing)
MG Design Associates Inc.
Mirenburg & Company (asked to be deleted)
Clement Mok Designs (declined listing)
Barbara Moses Design
Muller & Company
Multimedia Group
Office of Michael Manwaring (declined listing)
Precision Graphics
Roy Ritola, Inc.
Philip Ross Associates Ltd. (asked to be deleted)
John Ryan & Company
Schafer Associates Visual Communications Group
Schema (asked to be deleted)
Serigraphics Etc.
Sherin & Matejka, Inc.
Sibley/Peteet Design (declined listing)
Stepan Design
Thomas & Means Associates, Inc.
Vanderbyl Design (declined listing)
Vignelli Associates (declined listing)
Westgroup Communication, Inc. (asked to be deleted)
Zender & Associates (asked to be deleted)

Art publishing offers artists the opportunity to gain widespread exposure for their work, as well as the chance to earn repeat income from the sale of one image. Depending on the type of print or reproduction published, you can reach buyers of every income, geographic location and background.

Although the terms are sometimes used interchangeably, the difference between prints and reproductions lies in the way they are produced. Prints, also called original graphics or handpulled prints, are copies of original works produced by hand or through nonmechanical means. These may be lithographs, serigraphs, linocuts, engravings, woodcuts or etchings.

The nature of the printmaking process limits the number of prints that can be produced at one time. The quantity is limited to the number of impressions possible before the plate or other printing surface wears out, but quantities are often limited to 250 or 500, a number set by the publisher to add value. Because quantity is limited, prints usually command a higher price than most reproductions.

Reproductions are copies produced on an offset press or by photomechanical means and quantities are limited only by the market. Unlimited reproductions are often called posters. Years ago posters were used primarily for advertising, but today they're considered affordable art suitable for framing and display. The poster industry experienced a leap in sales in the mid-1980s and the market remains steady.

While some artists choose to publish their own work, this requires a knowledge of printing processes and marketing savvy, as well as the financial means. Art publishers produce prints or reproductions for the artist.

Some art publishers will produce the print or reproduction and leave the marketing to the artist or to a separate distributor. Many are publisher/distributors, handling production, distribution and sales. And some publisher/distributors market work published by the artist or another publisher, as well as their own publications.

Galleries, art dealers, printers and other businesses may be art publishers. Many poster publishers sell to wholesale outlets—frame shops, chain poster stores, manufacturers and retail outlets. Publishers of limited edition prints look for works with fine art appeal to sell to high-end interior designers, corporate collectors and galleries. Sales of limited edition prints are growing. Many new buyers of prints are those that purchased posters in the past and are choosing to upgrade their collection.

Art publishing is market-driven. Artists interested in working with a publisher should keep an eye out for trends. Study the market by visiting poster shops, frame stores and galleries. Art, architecture, decorating and interior design publications are helpful resources. Check copies of trade publications such as *Decor* and *Art Business News* and consumer magazines such as *Architectural Digest*, *Interior Design* and *Metropolitan Home* for features on interior design trends and new ideas in the market.

Other helpful sources include the Pantone Color Institute and the Color Marketing Group. These organizations publish an annual list of popular colors. If possible, attend some trade shows so you can meet designers and publishers. Art Expo and Art Buyers Caravan are large national shows and *Decor* magazine sponsors a series of eight regional trade fairs.

Once you've selected a publisher, send a query letter with a brief bio or list of galleries which have represented your work. Tearsheets can be helpful because they show publishers your work is reproducible. Most publishers ask for slides. Be sure to label slides individually and include an SASE for their return. Indicate position, size and media of the original on each slide, as well as your name and contact information. For artists looking for distribution only, you can send slides, but at some point you will be asked to send the actual reproductions.

A few publishers offer flat fees, but most offer royalty agreements. Royalties for posters are based on the wholesale price and range from about 2.5 to 5 percent. For prints, royalties are based on the retail price and can range from 5 to 20 percent. A number of factors determine price, including the artist's experience and reputation, the quality of the reproduction, printing costs, sales potential and the amount of promotion needed. Keep in mind that publishers will often hold back royalties on a specific number of prints to pay for printing and promotion costs. Make sure you clearly understand the arrangement.

Before you sign a contract with a publisher, check if it indicates exactly how much and what type of promotion you will receive. Find out what rights you are selling. Try to retain the right to reproduce your work in another form, while selling the publisher the right to publish your work in a certain type of print and for a limited amount of time. Other items to look for in your contract include a description of the work, size and type of reproduction, payment, insurance terms, a guarantee or credit line and copyright notice. Always retain ownership of your original work.

Some artists worry about control of the final product. A good publisher will give you approval over the final print and most will arrange for you to see a press proof. The more you learn about what can and cannot be done in certain printing processes, the better. Try to arrange to talk to a printer. Different processes, papers and inks can result in different effects. It is often very difficult to match original colors exactly. Knowing what to expect beforehand can help eliminate headaches for the printer and the publisher, as well as for yourself.

*AARON ASHLEY, INC., Suite 1905, 230 5th Ave., New York NY 10001. (212)532-9227. Contact: Philip D. Ginsburg or Budd Wiesenburg. Produces unlimited edition fine quality 4-color offset and hand-colored reproductions for distributors, manufacturers, jobbers, museums, schools and galleries. Current clients include major U.S. and overseas distributors, the National Gallery and the Metropolitan Museum of Art. Approached by 100+ artists/year. Publishes more than 25 new artists/year. Pays royalties or fee. Offers advance. Negotiates rights purchased. Requires exclusive representation for unlimited editions. Provides written contract. Query, arrange interview or submit slides or photos. Include SASE. "Do not send originals." Reports immediately.
Acceptable Work: Seeking artwork with decorative appeal for designer market. Considers oil paintings and watercolor. Prefers realistic or representational works. Artists represented include Jacqueline Penney and M.H. Hurlimann Armstrong. Editions created by working from an existing painting.

ADVANCE GRAPHICS, 982 Howe Rd., Martinez CA 94553. Photo editor: Steve Henderson. Art publisher handling unlimited edition offset reproductions. Current clients include Sears, Penney's, Macy's and Union Bank. Approached by 100 artists/year. Publishes the work of 50 and distributes the work of 10 emerging artists/year. Publishes and distributes the work of 1-2 mid-career artists/year. Publishes and distributes the work of 1-2 established artists/year. Pays $200-400. "Successful published artists can advance to royalty arrangement. Artists keep originals." Send query letter with photographs, slides and SASE.
Acceptable Work: Seeking artwork with creative artistic expression, fashionableness and decorative appeal. Considers oil, acrylic, watercolor, airbrush and mixed media. Prefers "trendy, inspirational and decorative art." Western art and pictures of dogs needed. Artists represented include Sue Dawe, Ron Kimball, A.

 The asterisk before a listing indicates that the listing is new in this edition. New markets are often the most receptive to freelance submissions.

Sutherland and B. Garcia. Editions created by collaborating with the artist and by working from an existing painting.

AEROPRINT, (AKA SPOFFORD HOUSE), South Shore Rd., Box 154, Spofford NH 03462. (603)363-4713. Owner: R. Westervelt. Estab. 1972. Art publisher/distributor handling limited editions (maximum 250 prints) of offset reproductions and unlimited editions for galleries and collectors. Clients: aviation art collectors. Seeking artwork with creative artistic expression. Publishes/distributes the work of 17 artists/year. Publishes the work of 1 emerging artist/year. Publishes and distributes the work of 12 mid-career artists/year. Publishes and distributes the work of 4 established artists/year. Payment method is negotiated. Offers an advance. Negotiates rights purchased. Does not require exclusive representation. Provides a written contract and shipping from firm. To show a portfolio, mail appropriate materials which should include color or b&w thumbnails, roughs, original/final art, photostats, tearsheets, slides, transparencies or final reproduction/product.
Acceptable Work: Considers pen & ink, oil, acrylic, pastel, watercolor, tempera or mixed media. Prefers "aviation subject matter only." Artists represented include Dietz, Corning, Kotula, Willis, Ryan, Deneen and Cohen.
Tips: A common mistake artists make when presenting their work is "incomplete or undeveloped talent, prematurely presented for publishing or introduction to project."

*AESTHETIC IMPRESSIONS, 12455 Branford, Arleta CA 91331. (818)897-2259. Manager: David Garcia. Estab. 1980. Art publisher. Publishes and distributes posters and foil prints. Clients: small and large distributors. Current clients include: Western Graphics and Prints Plus.
Needs: Seeking art for the commercial market. Considers lithographs and foil prints. Prefers animal, fantasy themes and landscapes. Artists represented include Kirk Reynart and Carol Hoss. Editions created by collaborating with the artist and by working from an existing painting. Approached by few artists/year. Publishes and distributes the work of 2 established artists/year.
First Contact & Terms: Send query letter with brochure showing art style. Samples are filed. Reports back within 1 week. Call or write to schedule an appointment to show a portfolio. Portfolio should include slides, transparencies and photographs. Payment method is negotiated. Offers an advance. Negotiates rights purchased. Provides a written contract.
Tips: "Prints should deal with animals or landscapes."

ALL SALES CO., INC., 3219 N. Cherry St., Hammond LA 70401. (504)542-8530. President: Tim Curry. Estab. 1973. Art publisher and distributor. Publishes and distributes unlimited and limited editions.
Needs: Seeking artwork with decorative appeal for the designer market. Considers oil, watercolor, acrylic, pastel and mixed media. Editions created by collaborating with the artist and by working from an existing painting. Approached by many artists/year. Number of emerging artists published each year varies. Publishes the work of 5-10 emerging artists/year. Publishes the work of 5 and distributes the work of 30+ established artists/year.
First Contact & Terms: Send query letter with resume and slides. Samples are filed or returned by SASE. Reports back only if interested. Mail appropriate materials: tearsheets and slides. Payment method is negotiated. Offers an advance when appropriate. Buys reprint rights or negotiates rights purchased. Provides in-transit insurance.
Tips: "Artists approaching us must have commercial quality. Our specialties are wildlife, golf and country themes."

AMERICAN ARTS & GRAPHICS, INC., 10315 47th Ave. W., Everett WA 98204-3436. Licensing Coordinator: Shelley Pedersen. Estab. 1948. Publishes posters for a teenage market; minimum 5,000 run. Approached by 100 artists/year. Publishes the work of 40 emerging, mid-career and established artists/year. Distributes the work of 60 emerging, mid-career and established artists/year. "Our main market is family variety stores, record and tape stores, and discount drug stores." Current clients include: Walmart, K-Mart, Fred Meyer, Longs, Osco and Payless. Artist's guidelines available. Send query letter with tearsheets, photostats, photocopies, slides and photographs; then submit sketch or photo of art. Include SASE. Reports in 2 weeks. Usually pays royalties of 10¢ per poster sold and an advance of $500-1,000 against future royalties.
Acceptable Work: Seeking artwork with decorative appeal (popular trends). Prefers 7x11" sketches; full-size posters are 23x35". Prefers airbrush, then acrylic and oil. Artists represented include Gail Gastfield, Robert Prokop, Robert Contreras and Gwen Connelly. Editions created by working from an existing painting.
Tips: "Research popular poster trends; request a copy of our guidelines."

*AMERICAN MASTERS FOUNDATION, 10688 Haddington, Houston TX 77043. (713)932-6847. FAX: (713)932-7861. Executive Assistant: Allison Ince. Estab. 1971. Art publisher. Publishes handpulled originals, unlimited and limited editions.

Needs: Seeking artwork with creative artistic expression, fashionableness and decorative appeal for the serious collector, commercial market and designer market. Considers oil, watercolor, acrylic, mixed media, gouache and tempera. Prefers traditional, realist, floral, Victorian, impressionistic styles and landscapes. Artists represented include P. Crowe, L. Dyke, C. Frace, L. Gordon, C.J. Frazier and Pearson. Editions created by collaborating with the artist and by working from an existing painting. Approached by 50-75 artists/year. Publishes the work of 1 artist/year. Publishes the work of 6 mid-career artists/year. Publishes the work of 2 established artists/year.

First Contact & Terms: Send query letter with brochure showing art style or resume, slides and photographs. Samples are not filed and are returned. Reports back within 2 months. Mail appropriate materials: original/final art and photographs. Payment method is negotiated. Offers an advance when appropriate. Buys all rights. Requires exclusive representation of artist. Provides in-transit insurance and shipping from firm.

*AMERICAN QUILTING ART, Box S-3283, Carmel CA 93921. (408)659-0608. Sales Manager: Erica Summerfield. Art publisher of offset reproductions, unlimited editions and handpulled originals. Publishes/distributes the work of 1 emerging, 1 mid-career and 1 established artist/year. "We want more." Payment method is negotiated. Offers an advance when appropriate. Buys all rights. Prefers exclusive representation of the artist. Provides in-transit insurance, insurance while work is at firm and shipping from firm. Send query letter with brochure showing art style or "any available material." Samples are filed or or are returned by SASE. Reports back within 2 weeks. Write to schedule an appointment to show a portfolio.

Acceptable Work: Seeking artwork with decorative appeal. Considers watercolor, pen & ink line drawings, oil, acrylic, pastel, tempera and mixed media. Artists represented include Mary Rutherford.

ANGEL GIFTS INC., 1900 W. Stone, Fairfield IA 52556. (515)472-5481. Art Director: Susan Stainback. Estab. 1981. Art publisher/distributor handling limited editions (maximum 250 prints), unlimited editions (minimum 250 prints) and posters for print galleries and department stores. Publishes/distributes the work of 6 artists/year. Payment method is negotiated. Offers an advance when appropriate. Negotiates rights purchased. Does not require exclusive representation. Provides insurance while work is at firm. Send query letter with brochure showing art style and transparencies (size 4x5 35mm 2¼"). Samples not filed are returned by SASE. Reports back to the artist regarding his query/submission within 3 weeks.

Acceptable Work: Considers oil, acrylic, watercolor and tempera. Prefers contemporary, original themes, photorealistic works, and art deco portraits. Prefers individual works of art and pairs. Maximum size of acceptable work 28" × 22".

Tips: "Send examples, name, address and phone number with request for guidelines and SASE."

HERBERT ARNOT, INC., 250 W. 57th St., New York NY 10107. (212)245-8287. President: Peter Arnot. Vice President: Vicki Arnot. Art distributor of original oil paintings. Clients: galleries. Approached by "hundreds of artists/year." Distributes work for 250 artists/year. Pays flat fee, $100-1,000 average. Provides promotion and shipping to and from distributor. Send query letter with brochure, resume, business card, slides, photographs or original work to be kept on file. Samples are filed or are returned by SASE. Reports within 1 month. Call or write for appointment to show portfolio.

Acceptable Work: Seeking artwork with creative artistic expression, decorative appeal for the serious collector and designer market. Considers oil and acrylic paintings. Has wide range of themes and styles—"mostly traditional/impressionistic, not modern."

Tips: "Professional quality, please."

ART EDITIONS, INC., 352 W. Paxton Ave., Salt Lake City UT 84101. (801)466-6088. Contact: Ruby Reece. Art printer for limited and unlimited editions, offset reproductions, posters and advertising materials. Clients: artists, distributors, galleries, publishers and representatives. Provides insurance while work is at firm. Send photographs, slides, transparencies (size 4x5 – 8x10") and/or originals. "Contact offices for specific pricing information. Free information packet available upon request." Samples are filed. Samples not filed are returned by SASE. Reports back within 2 weeks.

ART IMAGE INC., 1577 Barry Ave., Los Angeles CA 90025. (213)826-9000. President: Allan Fierstein. Publishes and produces unlimited and limited editions that are pencil signed and numbered by the artist. Also distributes etchings, serigraphs, lithographs and watercolor paintings. "Other work we publish and distribute includes handmade paper, cast paper, paper weavings and paper construction." All work sold to galleries, frame shops, framed picture manufacturers, interior decorators and auctioneers. Approached by 36 artists/year. Publishes and distributes the work of 4 emerging artists/year. Publishes and distributes the work of 2 mid-career artists/year. Publishes and distributes the work of 6 established artist/year. Negotiates payment. Requires exclusive representation. Provides shipping and a written contract. Send query letter with brochure showing art style, tearsheets, slides, photographs and SASE. Reports within 1 week. To show a portfolio, mail appropriate materials or write to schedule an appointment; portfolio should include photographs.

Acceptable Work: Seeking artwork with decorative appeal for the designer market. "All subject matter and all media in pairs or series of companion pieces." Artists represented include Robert White, Peter Wong and Sue Ellen Cooper. Editions created by collaborating with the artist.

Tips: "We are publishing and distributing more and more subject matter from offset limited editions to monoprints, etchings, serigraphs, lithographs and original watercolor paintings."

*ART IN MOTION, 1612 Ingleton, Burnaby, BC V5C 5R9 Canada. (604)299-8787. FAX: (604)299-5975. President: Garry Peters. Art publisher and distributor. Publishes and distributes limited editions, offset reproductions and posters. Clients: galleries, distributors world wide and picture frame manufacturers.
Needs: Seeking artwork with creative artistic expression, fashionableness, decorative appeal and art for the serious collector, commercial and designer market. Considers oil, watercolor, acrylic, and mixed media. Prefers decorative to wildlife. Artists represented include Joyce Kamihura and Lue Raffin. Editions created by collaborating with the artist and by working from an existing painting. Approached by 75 artists/year. Publishes the work of 3-5 emerging, mid-career and established artists/year. Distributes the work of 2-3 emerging and established artists/year.
First Contact & Terms: Send query letter with brochure showing art style or resume and tearsheets, slides, photostats, photography and transparencies. Samples are filed or are returned by SASE if requested by artist. Reports back within 2 weeks only if interested. If does not report back the artist should call. To show a portfolio, call or mail appropriate materials: photostats, slides, tearsheets, transparencies and photographs. Pays royalties of 15%. Payment method is negotiated. "It has to work for both parties. We have artists making $200 a month and some that make $8,000 a month or more." Offers an advance when appropriate. Negotiates rights purchased. Requires exclusive representation of artist. Provides in-transit insurance, insurance while work is at firm, promotion, shipping to and from firm and a written contract.
Tips: "We are looking for a few good artists, make sure you know your goals, and hopefully we can help you accomplish them, along with ours."

ART RESOURCES INTERNATIONAL, LTD., 98 Commerce Rd., Stamford CT 06902-4506. (203)967-4545, FAX: (203)967-4545. Vice President: Robin E. Bonnist. Estab. 1980. Art publisher. Publishes unlimited edition offset lithographs. Does not distribute previously published work. Clients: galleries, department stores, distributors, framers throughout the world. Approached by hundreds of artists/year. Publishes the work of 10-20 emerging, 5-10 mid-career and 5-10 established artists each year. Also uses artists for advertising layout and brochure illustration. Pays by royalty (3-10%), or flat fee of $250-1,000. Offers advance in some cases. Requires exclusive representation for prints/posters during period of contract. Provides in-transit insurance, insurance while work is at publisher, shipping to and from firm, promotion and a written contract. Artist owns original work. Send query letter with brochure, tearsheets, slides and photographs to be kept on file or returned only if requested and SASE is included; prefers to see slides or transparencies initially as samples, then reviews originals. Samples not kept on file returned only by SASE. Reports within 1 month. Appointments arranged only after work has been sent with SASE.
Acceptable Work: Considers oil and acrylic paintings, pastel, watercolor, mixed media and photography. Prefers pairs or series, triptychs, diptychs. Editions created by collaborating with the artist and by working from an existing painting.
Tips: "Please submit decorative, fine quality artwork. We prefer to work with artists who are creative, professional and open to art direction. Write to the company, including a short bio-date and slides of the work they would like us to publish."

ART SPECTRUM, division of Mitch Morse Gallery, Inc., 334 E. 59th St., New York NY 10022. (212)593-1812. President: Mitch Morse. Art dealer and distributor. Distributes limited editions (maximum of 300 prints) and handpulled originals — all 'multi-original' editions of lithographs, etchings, collographs, serigraphs. Serves galleries, frame shops, hotels, interior designers, architects and corporate art specifiers. Distributes the works of 15-20 artists/year. Negotiates payment method. Offers advance. Negotiates rights purchased. Provides promotion and shipping. Artist owns original art. Send query letter with resume, slides and photographs to be kept on file. Call or write for appointment to show portfolio, which should include original/final art and photographs. Samples not kept on file are returned. Reports within 1 week.
Acceptable Work: Considers original fine art prints only. Offers "subjects primarily suitable for corporate offices. Not too literal; not too avant-garde." Prefers series; unframed (framed unacceptable); 30x40"maximum.
Tips: "Do not stop by without appointment. Do not come to an appointment with slides only — examples of actual work must be seen. No interest in reproductive (photo-mechanical) prints — originals only. Submit work that is "an improved version of an existing 'look' or something completely innovative." Actively seeking additional artists who do original paintings on paper. Trends show that the "current demand for contemporary has not yet peaked in many parts of the country. The leading indicators in the New York City design market point to a strong resurgence of Old English."

ARTHURIAN ART GALLERY, 5962 N. Elston, Chicago IL 60646. Owner: Art Sahagian. Estab. 1985. Art distributor/gallery handling limited editions, handpulled originals, bronze, watercolor, oil and pastel. Current clients include Gerald Ford, Nancy Reagan, John Budnik and Dave Powers.

Needs: Seeking artwork with creative artistic expression, fashionableness and decorative appeal for the serious and commercial collector. Artists represented include Robert Barnum, Nancy Fortunato, Art Sahagian and Christiana. Editions created by collaborating with the artist. Approached by 25-35 artists/year. Publishes the work of 3-5 and distributes the work of 45-50 emerging artists/year. Publishes the work of 3-6 and distributes the work of 10-20 mid-career artists/year. Publishes the work of 3-6 and distributes the work of 15-25 established artists/year.

First Contact & Terms: Pays flat fee, $100-1,000 average. Rights purchased vary. Provides insurance while work is at firm, promotion and a written contract. Send query letter with brochure showing art style or resume, photocopies, slides and prices. Samples not filed returned by SASE. Reports within 30 days. To show a portfolio, mail appropriate materials or write to schedule an appointment. Portfolio should include original/final art, final reproduction/product and color photographs. Considers complexity of project, client's budget, and skill and experience of artist when establishing payment.

Tips: "Make your work show good craftsmanship, appeal to the public and provide enough quantity for distribution."

This piece by artist Wayne Stuart Shilson entitled "Tea Time at the Moana" was commissioned by Arthur's International of Honolulu, Hawaii. President Marvin C. Arthur believes the painting "demonstrates both the high qualities of this master and the pointillism technique. It is restful to look at, creative in style and historical in nature."

ARTHUR'S INTERNATIONAL, Box 10599, Honolulu HI 96816. President: Marvin C. Arthur. Estab. 1959. Art distributor handling original oil paintings primarily. Distributes limited and unlimited edition prints. Approached by many artists/year. Clients: galleries, collectors, etc. "We pay a flat fee to purchase the original. Payment made within 5 days. We pay 30% of our net profit made on reproductions. The reproduction royalty is paid after we are paid." Artists may be handled on an exclusive or non-exclusive basis. Send brochure, slides or photographs to be kept on file; no originals unless requested. Artist biographies appreciated. Samples not filed returned by SASE. Reports back normally within 1 week.

Acceptable Work: Seeking artwork with creative artistic expression for the serious collector. Considers all types of original artwork. Artists represented include Wayne Takazono, Wayne Stuart Shilson and Paul J. Lopez. Editions created by collaborating with the artist or by working from an existing painting. Purchases have been made in pen & ink, charcoal, pencil, tempera, watercolor, acrylic, oil, gouache and pastel. "All paintings should be photographic in texture or have an eye appeal of the subject matter that is not a modern art puzzle."

Tips: "We like artwork that is realistic. Send photos and/or slides, background info and SASE. Do not send any original paintings unless we have requested it. Having a track record is nice, but it is not a requirement. Being known or unknown is not the important thing; being talented and being able to show it to our taste is what is important."

*ARTIQUE UNLIMITED ASSOCIATION, INC., 1710 S. Jefferson, Box 3085, Cookeville TN 38502. (615)526-3491. FAX: (615)528-8904. Contact: Yvette Crouch. Estab. 1985. Art publisher and distributor. Publishes and distributes limited and unlimited editions. Clients: art galleries, gift shops, furniture stores and department stores.

Needs: Seeking artwork with creative artistic expression, decorative appeal and art for the designer market. Considers oil, watercolor and acrylic. Artists represented include Debbie Kingston, D. Morgan, Mary Bertrand and Lena Liu. Editions created by collaborating with the artist or by working from an existing painting. Publishes the work of 27 and distributes the work of 22 emerging artists/year.

First Contact & Terms: Send query letter with slides or photographs. Samples are not filed and are returned by SASE only. Reports back within 4-8 weeks. Mail appropriate materials. Pays royalties. Does not offer an advance. "Our contract for artists is for a number of years for all printing rights." Requires exclusive representation rights. Provides promotion, shipping from firm and a written contract.

*ARTISTS' ENTERPRIZES, Box 1274, Kaneohe HI 96744. (808)239-8933. FAX: (808)239-9186. Creative Director: Larry LeDoux. Estab. 1978. Distributor, advertising and public relations firm for artists and galleries. "We are publishing and marketing consultants" Distributes handpulled originals, posters, limited editions and offset reproductions. Clients: artists and art galleries. Current clients include N. Jonas Englund and Shipstore Galleries.

Needs: Seeking artwork with creative artistic expression, fasionableness, decorative appeal and art for the serious collector, commercial and designer market. Considers oil, watercolor, acrylic, pastel, pen and ink and mixed media. Artists represented include David Friedman and Vie Kersting. Editions created by collaborating with the artist and by working from an existing painting. Approached by 15-20 artists/year. Distributes the work of 2-4 emerging artists, 4-6 mid-career artists and 2-4 established artists/year.

First Contact & Terms: Send query letter with brochure showing art style and resume with tearsheets, slides and photographs. Samples are filed or are returned by SASE. Reports back within 90 days if interested. Pays on consignment basis: Firm receives 10% commission. "Artist receives monies from all sales less sales expenses, including telephone, shipping, sales commission (10%) and firm fee (10%)." Artist retains all rights. Provides promotion, a written contract, consulting, marketing, sales, PR and advertising.

Tips: "We specialize in helping artists become better known and in helping them fund a promotional campaign through sales. If you are ready to invest in yourself, we can help you as we have helped the Makk family, Robert Lyn Nelson and Andrea Smith."

ARTISTS' MARKETING SERVICE, 160 Dresser Ave., Prince Frederick MD 20678. President: Jim Chidester. Estab. 1987. Distributor of limited and unlimited editions, offset reproductions and posters. Clients: galleries, frame shops and gift shops. Current clients include John Shaw, Paula Fitzpatrick and John Morrow. Approached by 200-250 artists/year. Publishes the work of 1 and distributes the work of 10-15 emerging artists/year. Distributes the work of 20-30 mid-career and 3-5 established artists/year. Pays on consignment basis (50% commission). Offers an advance when appropriate. Purchases one-time rights. Does not require exclusive representation of artist. Provides shipping to and from firm. Send query letter with brochure, tearsheets and photographs. Samples are filed or returned by SASE only if requested by artist. Reports back within weeks. To show a portfolio, mail tearsheets and slides.

Acceptable Work: Seeking artwork with decorative appeal and art for the commercial collector and designer market. Prefers traditional themes: landscapes, seascapes, nautical, floral, wildlife, Americana, impressionistic and country themes.

Tips: "We are only interested in seeing work from self-published artists who are interested in distribution of their prints. We are presently *not* reviewing originals for publication."

*ARTISTWORKS WHOLESALE INC., 32 S. Lansdowne Ave., Lansdowne PA 19050. (215)626-7770. Art Coordinator: Helen Casale. Estab. 1981. Art publisher. Publishes and distributes posters and cards. Clients: galleries, decorators and distributors worldwide.

Needs: Seeking artwork with creative artistic expression, fashionableness and decorative appeal for the commercial and designer markets. Considers oil, watercolor, acrylic, pastel, mixed media and photography. Prefers contemporary and popular themes, realistic and abstract. Editions created by collaborating with artist and by working from an existing painting. Approached by 100 artists/year. Publishes and distributes the work of 1-2 emerging artists, 3-4 mid-career artists and 10-15 established artists/year.

First Contact & Terms: Send query letter with brochure showing art style or resume, slides, photographs and transparencies. Samples are not filed and are returned by SASE. Reports back within 1 month. Write to schedule an appointment to show a portfolio or mail appropriate materials: original/final art, photographs and slides. Payment method is negotiated. Offers advance when appropriate. Negotiates rights purchased. Requires exclusive representation of artist. Provides in-transit insurance, insurance while work is at firm, promotion, shipping to and from firm and a written contract.

Tips: "Artistworks is always looking for high quality well-executed work from artists working in a variety of media."

*ATLANTIC ARTS, INC., Suite 405, 410 Severn Ave., Annapolis MD 21403. (301)263-2554. FAX: (301)263-1367. Manager: Cynthia Shinn. Estab. 1982. Art publisher/distributor. Publishes and distributes handpulled originals, limited editions and monotypes. Clients: galleries, art consultants and corporations.

Needs: Seeking artwork with creative expression, fashionableness and decorative appeal, for the commercial and designer market. Considers oil, watercolor, acrylic, pastel, mixed media and works on paper. Prefers contemporary themes and styles. Editions created by collaborating with the artist and by working from an existing painting. Approached by 20-30 artists/year.

First Contact & Terms: Send query letter with brochure showing art style and resume with tearsheets, photostats, slides, photographs and transparencies. Reports back only if interested. Call or write to schedule an appointment to show a portfolio. Portfolio should include original/final art. Payment method is negotiated. Offers an advance when appropriate. Negotiates rights purchased. Sometimes requires exclusive representation of artist.

*TAMORA BANE GALLERY, 8025 Melrose Ave., Los Angeles CA 90046. (213)205-0555. FAX: (213)205-0794. Vice President: Tamara Bane. Estab. 1987. Art publisher and gallery. Publishes handpulled originals.

Needs: Seeking art for the serious collector. Considers oil, acrylic, pastel and mixed media. Prefers representational styles. Artists represented include Mel Ramos and Eyvind Earle. Editions created by collaborating with the artist and by working from an existing painting. Approached by more than 100 artists/year. Distributes the work of 2 emerging artists/year. Publishes the work of 1 and distributes the work of 4 mid-career artists/year. Publishes and distributes the work of 4 established artists/year.

First Contact & Terms: Send query letter with brochure or resume and tearsheets, photostats, photocopies, slides, photographs and transparencies. Samples are not filed and are returned. Reports back only if interested. Mail appropriate materials: tearsheets, slides and transparencies. Pays on consignment basis: firm receives 50% commission or payment method is negotiated. Offers an advance when appropriate. Sometimes requires exclusive representation of artist. Provides in-transit insurance, insurance while work is at firm, promotion, shipping to and from firm and a written contract.

Tips: "Please be original. We prefer somewhat established artists."

*BENTLEY HOUSE LIMITED, Box 5551, Walnut Creek, CA 94596. (415)935-3186. FAX: (415)935-0213. Administrative Assistant: Terri Sher. Estab. 1986. Art publisher. Publishes limited and unlimited editions, offset reproductions, posters and canvas transfers. Clients: framers, galleries, distributors in North America and Europe, and framed picture manufacturers.

Needs: Seeking artwork with decorative appeal for the residential, commercial and designer markets. Considers oil, watercolor, acrylic and mixed media. Prefers traditional styles, realism and impressionism. Artists represented include R. Zolan, C. Valente, A. Gethen, J. Akers and P. Jeannoit. Editions created by collaborating with the artist or by working from an existing painting. Approached by 200 artists/year. Publishes the work of 2 emerging artists, 8 mid-career artists and 18 established artists/year.

First Contact & Terms: Send query letter with brochure showing art style or resume, tearsheets, slides and photographs. Samples are not filed and are returned by SASE if requested by artist. Reports back within 3 months. "We will call artist if we are interested." Pays royalties of 10%; payment method is negotiated or payment is royalty plus free prints. Does not offer an advance. Buys all reproduction rights. Usually requires exclusive representation of artist. Provides promotion, a written contract, insurance while work is at firm and shipping from firm.

Tips: "Bentley House Limited sells high quality products which can be found in finer retailers worldwide. Our product is too expensive for mass merchandisers like K-Mart. As a result, we look for high quality images produced by experienced artists."

BERNARD PICTURE CO., Hope Street Editions, Box 4744, Stamford CT 06907. (203)357-7600. Art Coordinator: Susan Murphy. Estab. 1951. Art publisher/distributor. Produces unlimited editions using 4-6-color lithography for galleries, picture framers, and manufacturers worldwide. Publishes 60 artists/year. Buys all rights. "Artwork is ultimately published in series of four related images, but individual pieces will be considered." Send slides or photographs and SASE; "a follow-up call is helpful. Will contact if interested."

Acceptable Work: Preferred subjects include country, Southwestern, tropical/Hawaiian, florals, still lifes, panoramic landscapes, animals and whimsical scenes; others are welcome. Will consider any medium, the most popular being oil, acrylic, watercolor, pen & ink, mixed media and photography.

BIG, (Division of the Press Chapeau), Govans Station, Box 4591, Baltimore City MD 21212-4591. (301)433-5379. Director: Philip Callahan. Estab. 1976. Distributor/catalog specifier of original tapestries, sculptures, crafts and paintings to architects, interior designers, facility planners and corporate curators, throughout US. Current clients include: Arco Inc., Cuhza Architects, State of NC, Iowa Better Business Bureau. Presentations are done through BIG BOX (slide catalog) and individual presentations to clients. Approached by 50-150 artists/year. Publishes the work of 20 and distributes the work of 100 emerging artists/year. Publishes the work of 10 and distributes the work of 20 mid-career artists/year. Publishes the work of 6 and distributes the work of 15 established artists/year. Pays $500-30,000. Payment method is negotiated (artist sets net pricing).

Offers an advance. Does not require exclusive representation. Provides in-transit insurance, insurance while work is at firm, promotion, shipping to firm, and a written contract. "All participating artists are included in unique slide catalog, distributed to A+D community throughout US. 100 artists per edition. Only highest quality considered." Send query letter with slides. Samples are filed or are returned by SASE. Reports back within 5 days. Call to schedule an appointment to show a portfolio which should include slides.

Acceptable Work: Seeking art for the serious and commercial collector, and the designer market. "What corporate America hangs in its board rooms, highest quality traditional, landscapes, contemporary abstracts; but don't hesitate with unique statements, folk art or regional themes. In other words, we'll consider all catagories as long as the craftsmanship is there." Prefers individual works of art. Artists represented include Snyder, Toyko and Estrin. Editions created by collaborating with the artist.

Tips: "Use judgement in NET pricing. Remember that in most cases your work is being resold. Don't put yourself out of the marketplace. Selling a quantity of pieces at fair realistic prices is usually more profitable than trying to make a 'killing' on each work. Negotiate pricing with your agents and representatives so as to create a win-win business arrangement."

C.R. FINE ARTS LTD., 249 A St., Studio 35, Boston MA 02210. (617)654-2960. President: Carol Robinson. Estab. 1982. Art publisher/distributor/gallery handling originals, limited editions and posters. Clients: corporate collectors, art consultants and galleries. Publishes 6 artists/year; represents work of 300 artists/year. Payment method is negotiated. Negotiates rights purchased. Provides promotion, gallery exposure, representation in an extensive slide library, and a written contract for publishing projects. Send query letter with resume, transparencies and slides. Samples not filed returned by SASE only. Reports within 1 month. Call to schedule an appointment to show a portfolio, which should include slides and transparencies.

Acceptable Work: Considers pastel, watercolor and oil paintings. Prefers contemporary, abstract works, landscapes, sculpture, 3-Ds, tapestry and traditional images.

Tips: We are interested in representing innovative and emerging artists who not only wish to be published, but also those who have a body of originals that are available.

*CALIFORNIA FINE ART PUBLISHING CO., 4621 W. Washington Blvd., Los Angeles CA 90016. (213)930-2410. FAX: (213)930-2417. President: Ron Golbus. Estab. 1974. Art publisher and distributor. Publishes and/or distributes handpulled originals, limited and unlimited editions and offset reproductions. Clients: contract interior designers and galleries. Current clients include Hyatt, Hilton and Sheraton.

Needs: Seeking artwork with creative artistic expression, fashionableness and decorative appeal for the commercial and designer market. Considers oil, watercolor, acrylic, pastel, pen & ink and mixed media. Prefers all types of themes and styles. Artists represented include Haskeel and Calero. Editions created by collaborating with the artist and by working from an existing painting. Publishes the work of 5-10 emerging artists/year.

First Contact & Terms: Send query letter with brochure showing art style or resume and tearsheets, photostats, photocopies, slides, photographs and transparencies. Samples are filed or are returned. Reports back within 30 days. To show a portfolio call or mail appropriate materials. Portfolio should include thumbnails, roughs and b&w and color tearsheets, photographs and transparencies. Pays flat fee, royalties, on consignment basis or payment method is negotiated. Offers an advance when appropriate. Buys first rights, all rights or negotiates rights purchased. Requires exclusive representation of artist.

Tips: "We are looking for artists willing to develop 'current market trends.' We are looking for fresh art, new looks and a workable relationship."

*CARIBBEAN ARTS, INC., 985 Westchester Pl., Los Angeles CA 90019. (213)732-4601. Director: Bernard Hoyes. Art publisher/distributor of limited and unlimited editons, offset reproductions and handpulled originals. Clients: galleries, stores, bookstores, corporations, art dealers and collectors. Current clients include: Things Graphic and Fine Art, Vargas and Associates. Works with 2-3 artists/year. Pays $50-1,200 flat fee; 15% royalties or on consignment. Payment method is negotiated. Offers an advance. Purchases first rights or negotiates rights purchased. Provides in-transit insurance, insurance while work is at firm, promotion, shipping from firm and a written contract. Send query letter with brochure or resume and slides. Samples are filed. Samples not filed are returned only if requested. Reports back within 10 days. Call or write to schedule an appointment to show a portfolio, which should include original/final art.

Acceptable Work: Seeks art for the serious collector. Considers oil paintings, pastel and watercolor. Prefers original themes and primitivism. Prefers individual works of art. Maximum size 30x40". Editions created by working from an existing painting.

Tips: "Do a lot of original work."

CASTLE ARTS, Box 587A, Altamont NY 12009. (518)861-6979. President: Edward A. Breitenbach. Estab. 1983. Distributor handling limited editions, posters, etchings, original oils and sketches for galleries, subdistributors and gift shops. Distributes the work of one artist/year. Pays flat fee. Does not require exclusive representation. Provides promotion. "We are only handling one artist at this time. Will consider others in the future."

Acceptable Work: Fantasy, novelty, surrealism only. Represents T.E. Breitenbach. Editions created by collaborating with the artist.

*CAVANAUGH EDITIONS, 400 Main St., Half Moon Bay, CA 94019. (415)726-7110. Marketing Director: Cheryl Shriver. Estab. 1989. Art publisher. Publishes and/or distrubites limited editions. Clients: galleries.
Needs: Seeking artwork with decorative appeal for the commercial and designer market. Prefers primitive styles; will consider realistic. Artists represented include Joanne Case and Woody Jackson. Editions created by collaborating with the artist and by working from an existing painting. Approached by 150 artists/year. Publishes and distributes the work of 2 established artists/year.
First Contact & Terms: Send query letter with brochure showing art style or resume. Samples are filed. Reports back only if interested. Write to schedule an appointment to show a portfolio, which should include original/final art, photographs, slides or transparencies. Payment method is negotiated. Does not offer an advance. Negotiates rights purchased. Provides insurance while work is at firm and a written contract.

*CHILD GRAPHICS PRESS, Box 7771, Hilton Head Island SC 29938. (800)543-4880. Contact: Bea Harmon. Estab. 1988. Art publisher and distributor. Publishes and distributes posters. Clients: framers, galleries, schools and libraries.
Needs: Seeking artwork with creative expression and decorative appeal for the designer market. Considers oil, watercolor and acrylic. Prefers art related to children's literature. Artists represented include Etienne Delessert, John Howe and Roberto Innocenti. Editions are usually created by working from an existing painting. Approached by more than 50 artists/year. Publishes the work of 1 and distributes the work of 2 emerging artists/year. Publishes the work of 4 and distributes the work of 8+ mid-career artists/year. Publishes the work of 4 and distributes the work of 15+ established artists/year.
First Contact & Terms: Send query letter with brochure showing art style or resume with tearsheets, photostats, photocopies and photographs. Samples are not filed and are returned by SASE. Reports back within 3 months. Write to schedule an appointment to show a portfolio. Portfolio should include thumbnails, original/final art, photostats, tearsheets and photographs. Payment method is negotiated. Offers advance when appropriate. Negotiates rights purchased. Provides promotion and a written contract.
Tips: "We are looking for artwork related to well-known children's literature, contemporary with upbeat colors and vivid imagery."

COLONIAL ART CO., THE, 1336 NW 1st St., Oklahoma City OK 73106. (405)232-5233. Estab. 1919. Distributor of offset reproductions for galleries. Publishes/distributes the work of "thousands" of artists/year. Payment method is negotiated. Offers an advance when appropriate. Does not require exclusive representation of the artist. Send sample prints. Samples not filed are returned only if requested by artist. Reports back only if interested. To show a portfolio mail appropriate materials.

*GREG COPELAND INC., 10-14 Courtland St., Paterson NJ 07503. (201)279-6166. FAX: (201)279-6235. Creative Director: Philip Hopkins. Estab. 1969. Art publisher, distributor and gallery. Clients: wholesale, retail and designers.
Needs: Seeking artwork with creative artistic expression and decorative appeal for the designer market. "We are very well known for contemporary themes and styles but are expanding into traditional ones." Editions created by collaborating with the artist and by working from an existing painting. Approached by 20-30 artists/year. Distributes the work of 3-6 emerging artists, 2-4 mid-career artists and 2 established artists/year.
First Contact & Terms: Send query letter with brochure showing art style or resume and tearsheets, slides and photographs. Samples filed or returned by SASE if requested by artist. Reports back only if interested. Write to schedule an appointment to show a portfolio. Pays flat fee. Does not offer an advance. Negotiates rights purchased. Provides promotion.

*CREGO EDITIONS, 3960 Dewey Ave., Rochester NY 14616. (716)621-8803. Owner: Paul Crego Jr. Distributor. Publishes and distributes limited editions and originals.
Needs: Seeking artwork with decorative appeal for the serious collector, the commercial and designer markets. Considers oil, watercolor, acrylic, pen & ink and mixed media. Artists represented include David Kibuuka. Editions created by collaborating with the artist. Approached by 25 artists/year. Publishes and distributes the work of 1 emerging artist, 1 mid-career artist and 1 established artist/year.
First Contract & Terms: Send query letter with brochure showing art style or resume and photocopies and photographs. Samples are filed or returned by SASE if requested by artist. Reports back only if interested. Mail appropriate materials: original/final art, photographs and slides. Pays flat fee, royalties or payment method is negotiated. Buys first-rights, all rights or negotiates rights purchased. Requires exclusive representation. Provides in-transit insurance, insurance while work is at firm, promotion, shipping to and from firm and a written contract.

CROSS GALLERY, INC., 180 N. Center, Suite 1, Box 4181, Jackson WY 83001. (307)733-2200. Director: Mary Schmidt. Estab. 1982. Art publisher, distributor and gallery. Publishes/distributes limited editions, offset reproductions and handpulled originals; also sells original works. Clients: galleries, retail customers and corporate businesses. "We are just getting started and are developing galleries in other areas of the US for distributing work." Approached by 100 artists/year. Payment method is negotiated. Offers an advance when appropriate. Requires exclusive area representation of the artist. Provides insurance while work is at firm and shipping from firm. Send query letter with resume, tearsheets, photostats, photographs, slides and transparencies. Samples are filed. Samples not filed are returned by SASE. Reports back within "a reasonable amount of time." Call to schedule an appointment to show a portfolio or mail color photostats, tearsheets, slides and transparencies.

Acceptable Work: Seeking artwork with creative artistic expression for the serious collector. Artists represented include Penni Cross and other lesser known artists. Editions created by collaborating with the artist and by working from an existing painting. Considers pen & ink line drawings, oil and acrylic paintings, pastel, watercolor, tempera, and mixed media. Prefers Western Americana with an emphasis on realism as well as contemporary art.

Tips: "We look for originality. Presentation is very important."

CUPPS OF CHICAGO, INC., 831-837 Oakton St., Elk Grove IL 60007. (312)593-5655. President: Dolores Cupp. Estab. 1964. Distributor of original oil paintings for galleries, frame shops, designers and home shows. Approached by 75-100 artists/year. Distributes the work of "many" emerging, mid-career and established artists/year. Pays flat fee; or royalties of 10%. Offers an advance when appropriate. Negotiates rights purchased. Provides promotion and a written contract. Send query letter with brochure showing art style or resume and photographs. Samples are filed. Samples not filed are returned only if requested. Reports back only if interested. Call or write to schedule an appointment to show a portfolio, which should include original/ final art.

Acceptable Work: Seeking artwork with creative artistic expression, fashionableness and decorative appeal for the serious collector, commercial collector and designer market. Artists represented include Carlos Cavidad and Sonia Gil Torres. Editions created by collaborating with the artist and by working from an existing painting. Considers oil and acrylic paintings. Considers "almost any style—only criterion is that it must be well done." Prefers individual works of art.

Tips: "Work must look professional. Please send actual artwork or photos—don't like slides."

DANMAR PRODUCTIONS, INC., 7387 Ashcroft, Houston TX 77081. (713)774-3343. Vice President: Marlene Goldfine. Estab. 1985. Art publisher of limited and unlimited editions, handpulled originals for galleries, designers and contract framers. Publishes work of 10-15 artists/year. Pays 10% royalties. Payment method is negotiated. Negotiates rights purchased. Requires exclusive representation. Provides insurance while work is at firm, promotion, shipping from firm and a written contract. Send query letter with brochure or tearsheets, photographs, slides and transparencies. Samples not filed are returned by SASE. Reports back within 10 days. To show a portfolio, mail original/final art and color tearsheets, slides and final reproduction/product.

Acceptable Work: Considers oil, acrylic, pastel, watercolor and mixed media. Prefers textured and dimensional fine art.

Tips: "We are looking to work with talented people who maintain a professional attitude. Originality is important and color is critical in our industry. We welcome all new talent and offer a quick, honest appraisal. Abstracts and florals seem to be more popular this year."

*DEVON EDITIONS, 770 Tamalpais Blvd., Corte Madera CA 94925. (415)924-9102. Art Director: Dallas Saunders. Estab. 1989. Art publisher. Publishes and/or distributes posters. Clients: retail stores of all types, decorators, designers, etc.

Needs: Seeking artwork with decorative appeal for the serious collector, commercial and designer markets. Considers oil, watercolor, acrylic, pastel and photography (b&w only). Prefers traditional painting of all styles and b&w photography. Artists represented include Howard Behrens, Max Hayslette, Marco Sassone, Aaron Chang, Arthur Elgort, and artists from the Philadelphia Museum of Art and The Fleischer Museum. Editions created by collaborating with artist and by working from an existing painting. Approached by hundreds of artists/year. Publishes and distributes the work of 2-3 emerging artists/year. Publishes and distributes the work of 5-7 mid-career artists/year. Publishes the work of 10-15 and distributes the work of over 100 established artists/year.

First Contact & Terms: Send query letter with brochure showing art style or resume and tearsheets, slides, photographs and transparencies. Samples are not filed and are returned by SASE if requested by artist. Reports back within 3 weeks. Mail appropriate materials: original/final art and b&w tearsheets, photographs, slides and transparencies. Payment discussed upon decision to publish only. Requires exclusive representation of artist. Provides in-transit insurance, insurance while work is at firm, promotion, shipping from firm and a written contract. There services are upon acceptance only.

Tips: "Keep portfolio small and show only your best examples in quality 35mm slides for first submission, $4 \times 5''$ transparencies also acceptable."

DODO GRAPHICS, INC., Box 585, 145 Cornelia St., Plattsburgh NY 12901. (518)561-7294. FAX (518)561-6720. Manager: Frank How. Art publisher of offset reproductions, posters and etchings for galleries and frame shops. Publishes the work of 5 artists/year. Payment method is negotiated. Offers an advance when appropriate. Buys all rights. Requires exclusive representation of the artist. Provides a written contract. Send query letter with brochure showing art style or photographs and slides. Samples are filed. Samples not filed are returned by SASE. Reports back within 3 months. Write to schedule an appointment to show a portfolio, which should include original/final art and slides.

Acceptable Work: Considers pastel, watercolor, tempera, mixed media and airbrush. Prefers contemporary themes and styles. Prefers individual works of art, 16x20″ maximum.

Tips: "Do not send any originals unless agreed upon by publisher."

*EDELMAN FINE ARTS, LTD., Suite 1503, 1140 Broadway, New York NY 10001. (212)683-4266. Vice President: H. Heather Edelman. Art distributor of original oil paintings. "We now handle watercolors, lithographs, serigraphs and 'work on paper' as well as original oil paintings." Clients: over 900 galleries worldwide. Approached by 75 artists/year. Distributes the work of 25 emerging, 35 mid-career and 75 established artists/year. Pays $50-1,000 flat fee or works on consignment basis (20% commission). Buys all rights. Provides in-transit insurance, insurance while work is at firm, promotion, shipping from firm and written contract. Send query letter with brochure, resume, tearsheets, photographs and "a sample of work on paper or canvas" to be kept on file. Call or write for appointment to show portfolio or mail original/final art and photographs. Reports as soon as possible.

Acceptable Work: Seeking artwork with creative artistic expression and decorative appeal for the serious collector and designer market. Considers oil and acrylic paintings, watercolor and mixed media. Especially likes Old World and impressionist themes or styles. Artists represented include Rembrandt, Chagall, Miro and Picasso.

Tips: Portfolio should include originals and only best work.

EMPORIUM ENTERPRISES, INC., 235 Preston Royal Shopping Center, Dallas TX 75230. (214)357-7772. FAX: (214)357-7770. President/CEO: Fernando Piqué. Estab. 1983. Art publisher/distributor/gallery/frame shop. Publishes/distributes limited editions, offset reproductions and posters. Clients: galleries, frame shops, department stores and gift shops. Publishes/distributes the work of 1-3 artists/year. Payment method is negotiated. Offers an advance when appropriate. Negotiates rights purchased. Requires exclusive representation of the artist. Provides a written contract. Send query letter with brochure. Samples are filed with registration of $5. Reports back only if interested. Call or write to schedule an appointment to show a portfolio or mail appropriate materials.

Acceptable Work: Seeking artwork with creative artistic expression. Considers oil, acrylic, pastel, watercolor and mixed media. Prefers individual works of art and unframed series. Editions created by collaborating with the artist.

Tips: "Be patient. We can't represent everyone."

*ESSENCE ART, 929-8 Lincoln Ave., Holbrook NY 11741. (516)589-9420. President: Mr. Jan Persson. Estab. 1989. Art publisher and distributor. Publishes and distributes posters, limited editions and offset reproductions. "All are African-American images." Clients: galleries and framers.

Needs: Seeking artwork with creative artistic expression and decorative appeal for the commercial market. Considers all media. Prefers African-American themes and styles. Artists represented include Dane Tilghman, Cal Massey, Synthia Saint-James. Editions created by collaborating with artist and by working from an existing painting. Approached by 20 artists/year. Publishes the work of 3 and distributes the work of 10 emerging artists/year. Publishes the work of 1 and distributes the work of 20 mid-career artists/year. Publishes the work of 2 and distributes the work of 20 established artists/year.

First Contact & Terms: Send query letter with slides, photographs and transparencies. Samples are filed or are returned by SASE if requested by artist. Reports back within 2 months. To show a portfolio, mail photographs and transparencies. Pays royalties of 10% and payment method is negotiated. Does not offer an advance. Buys reprint rights. Provides insurance while work is at firm, promotion, shipping from firm and a written contract.

Tips: "We are looking for artwork with good messages."

ATELIER ETTINGER INCORPORATED, 155 Avenue of the Americas, New York NY 10013. (212)807-7607. FAX (212)691-3508. President: Eleanor Ettinger. Estab. 1975. Flatbed limited edition lithographic studio. "All plates are hand drawn, and proofing is completed on our Charles Brand hand presses. The edition is printed on one of our 12-ton, Voirin presses, classic flatbed lithographic presses hand built in France over 100 years ago. Atelier Ettinger is available for contract printing for individual artists, galleries and publishers." Approached by 50-100 artists/year. Publishes the work of 1 emerging artist/year. Publishes and distributes the work of 3 mid-career artists/year. Publishes and distributes the work of 4 established artists/year. Provides insurance while work is on premises. For printing estimate, send good slides or transparencies, finished paper size, and edition size required.

Acceptable Work: Seeking artwork with creative artistic exprssion, fashionableness and decorative appeal for the serious collector, commercial collector and designer market. Artists represented include Malcolm Lepke, Mel Odom, George Staurinos, Norman Rockwell and Alice Neel. Editions created by collaborating with the artist and by working from an existing painting.

Tips: "The work must be unique and non-derivative. We look for artists who can create 35-50 medium to large scale works per year and who are not already represented in the five art field."

ELEANOR ETTINGER INCORPORATED, 155 Avenue of the Americas, New York NY 10013. (212)807-7607. FAX (212)691-3508. President: Eleanor Ettinger. Estab. 1975. Established art publisher of limited edition lithographs, limited edition sculpture, unique works (oil, watercolor, drawings, etc.). Currently distributes the work of 21 artists. "All lithographs are printed on one of our Voirin presses, flat bed lithographic presses hand built in France over 100 years ago." Send query letter with visuals (slides, photographs, etc.), a brief biography, resume (including a list of exhibitions and collections) and SASE for return of the materials. Reports within 14 days.
Acceptable Work: Prefers American realism. Considers oil, watercolor, acrylic, pastel, mixed media, pen & ink and pencil drawings. Payment method is negotiated.
Tips: "Our focus for publication is towards the School of American Realism. Properly label each visual."

*F A ASSOCIATES, Box 691, Cotati CA 94931. (707)664-9003. Business Owner: Linda Fogh. Estab. 1986. Art publisher and distributor. Publishes and distributes handpulled originals, limited editions and offset reproductions. Clients: private collectors, designers and corporate collectors.
Needs: Seeking artwork with creative artistic expression for the serious collector and designer market. Considers all subjects, all media representational. Artists represented include K. Mallary, J. Rideout, L. Brullo, and A. Grendahl-Kuhn. Editions created by collaborating with the artist and by working from an existing painting.
First Contact & Terms: Send query letter with resume and slides, photographs and print samples if available. Samples are filed or are returned by SASE if requested by artist. Reports back within 2 weeks. To show portfolio, mail appropriate materials: photographs, slides and original work if requested. Payment method is negotiated. Does not offer an advance. Negotiates rights purchased. Provides in-transit insurance, shipping from firm and a written contract.
Tips: "Include complete information about each image: size, medium, price, year completed, SASE; without the foregoing no response is made."

*FINE ART LTD., 6135F Northbelt Dr., Norcross GA 30071. (404)446-6400 or (800)922-2781. FAX: (404)416-0904. Director: Mr. Emile Valhuerdi. Estab. 1983. Distributor of oil paintings. Clients: designers.
Needs: Seeking artwork with decorative appeal for the designer market. Considers oil only. Prefers traditional and impressionist styles. Artists represented include Candi, Jackson and Torrens. Approached by over 100 artists/year. Distributes the work of 400-500 mostly unknown artists/year.
First Contact & Terms: Send query letter with brochure showing art style or resume and photographs. Samples are not filed and are returned by SASE. Reports back within 2 weeks. Call to schedule an appointment to show a portfolio which should include original/final art and photographs. Pays flat fee $500, royalties of 100% or payment method is negotiated. Does not offer an advance. Buys all rights. Provides in-transit insurance, insurance while work is at firm and shipping from firm.
Tips: "Send photos."

*RUSSELL A. FINK GALLERY, Box 250, 9843 Gunston Rd., Lorton VA 22199. (703)550-9699. Contact: Russell A. Fink. Art publisher/dealer. Publishes offset reproductions using five-color offset lithography for galleries, individuals and framers. Publishes and distributes the works of 1 emerging artist and 1 mid-career artist/year. Publishes the work of 2 and distributes the work of 3 established artists/year. Pays 10% royalties to artist or negotiates payment method. Negotiates rights purchased. Provides insurance while work is at publisher and promotion and shipping from publisher. Negotiates ownership of original art. Send query letter with slides or photographs to be kept on file. Call or write for appointment to show portfolio. Samples returned if not kept on file.
Acceptable Work: Seeking artwork with creative artistic expression for the serious collector. Considers oil, acrylic and watercolor. Prefers wildlife and sporting themes. Prefers individual works of art; framed. "Submit photos or slides of at least near-professional quality. Include size, price, media and other pertinent data regarding the artwork. Also send personal resume and be courteous enough to include SASE for return of any material sent to me." Artists represented include Manfred Schatz, Ken Carlson, John Loren Head, Robert Abbett and Rod Crossman. Editions created by working from an existing painting.
Tips: "Looks for composition, style and technique in samples. Also how the artist views his own art. Mistakes artists make are arrogance, overpricing, explaining their art and underrating the role of the dealer."

FOXMAN'S OIL PAINTINGS LTD., 1712 S. Wolf Rd., Wheeling IL 60090. (312)679-3804. Secretary/Treasurer: Harold Lederman. Art distributor of limited and unlimited editions, oil paintings and watercolors for galleries, party plans and national chains. Publishes the work of 4 and distributes work of 115 artists/year. Payment method is negotiated. Negotiates rights purchased. Requires exclusive representation. Provides promotion, shipping from firm and a written contract. Send query letter with resume, tearsheets, photographs and slides.

Samples are not filed and are returned. Reports back within 2 weeks. Call to schedule an appointment to show a portfolio, which should include original/final art.

Acceptable Work: Considers oil paintings, pastel, airbrush, watercolor, acrylic and collage. Prefers simple themes: children, barns, countrysides; black art and other contemporary themes and styles. Prefers individual works of art. Maximum size 48×60".

*FRAME HOUSE GALLERY, 10688 Haddington, Houston TX 77043. (713)465-4332. FAX: (713)932-7861. Executive Assistant: Allison Ince. Estab. over 25 years ago. Art publisher. Publishes handpulled originals, unlimited and limited editions.

Needs: Seeking artwork with creative artistic expression, fashionableness and decorative appeal for the serious collector, commercial and designer markets. Considers oil, watercolor, acrylic, mixed media, gouache, tempera. Prefers traditionalism, realism, florals, landscapes, Victorian styles and impressionism. Artists represented include Alan M. Hunt, Lynn Kaatz, James Crow, Christa Kieffer and Jim Harrison. Editions created by collaborating with the artist and by working from an existing painting. Approached by 25-50 artists/year. Publishes the work of 1 emerging artist, 3 mid-career artists and 2 established artists/year.

First Contact & Terms: Send query letter with brochure showing art style or resume and slides and/or photographs. Samples are not filed and are returned. Reports back within 2 months. To show a portfolio, mail original/final art and photographs. Payment method is negotiated. Offers an advance when appropriate. Buys all rights. Provides in-transit insurance and shipping from firm.

FRONT LINE GRAPHICS, INC., 9808 Waples St., San Diego CA 92121. (619)552-0944. Creative Director: Todd Haile. Estab. 1981. Publisher/distributor of posters, prints and limited editions for galleries, decorators, and poster distributors worldwide. Publishes the work of 12-18 freelance artists/year. Publishes/distributes the work of 24 artists/year. Approached by 50 artists/year. Publishes the work of 20 emerging artists/year. Payment method is negotiated. Requires exclusive representation of the artist. Provides promotion and a written contract. Send query letter with slides. Samples not filed are returned only if requested by artist. Reports back within 1 month. Call to schedule an appointment to show a portfolio, which should include original/final art and slides.

Acceptable Work: Seeking artwork with fashionableness and decorative appeal for the commercial collector and designer market. Considers oil, acrylic, pastel, watercolor and mixed media. Prefers conetmporary interpretations of landscapes, seascapes, florals and abstracts. Prefers pairs. Minimum size 22×30". Artists represented include Keith Mallett, Neil Loeb and Dale Terbush. Editions created by collaborating with the artist.

Tips: "Front Line Graphics is looking for artists who are flexible and willing to work with us to develop art that meets the specific needs of the print and poster marketplace. Front Line Graphics' standing as a major publisher in the art publishing industry is related to the fresh new art and artists we actively seek out on an on-going basis."

GALAXY OF GRAPHICS, LTD., 460 W. 34th St., New York NY 10001. (212)947-8989. President: Reid A. Fader. Estab. 1983. Art publisher. Publishes and distributes unlimited editions. Clients: galleries, distributors, and picture frame manufacturers.

Needs: Seeking artwork with creative artistic expression, fashionableness and decorative appeal for the commerical market. Artists represented include Hal Larsen, Glenna Kurz and Alain Moulis. Editions created by collaborating with the artist and by working from an existing painting. Considers any media. "Any currently popular and generally accepted themes." Approached by several hundred artists/year. Publishes and distributes the work of 6-12 emerging artists, 6-12 mid-career artists, and 25 established artists/year.

First Contact & Terms: Send query letter with resume, tearsheets, slides, photographs, and transparencies. Samples are not filed and are returned by SASE. Reports back within 1-2 weeks. Call to schedule an appointment to show a portfolio. Pays royalties of 10%. Offers an advance. Buys all rights. Provides in-transit insurance, insurance while work is at firm and a written contract.

*GALLERIE VENDOME, INC., Candlebrook Village, 777 Federal Rd., Box 558, Brookfield CT 06804. (203)775-1363. FAX: (203)775-3666. President: Marc Andre Chiffert. Estab. 1984. Art publisher, distributor and gallery. Publishes and distributes handpulled originals, limited editions, oils and sculpture. Clients: corporate and "yuppie."

Needs: Seeking artwork with creative artistic expression for the serious collector. Considers oil, acrylic and mixed media. Prefers no specific themes or styles. Artists represented include Laporte, Gantner, Gaveau and Schenck. Editions created by collaborating with artist. Approached by 15-20 artists/year. Publishes the work of 2 emerging artists and 2 mid-career artists/year. Distributes the work of 3-4 emerging and 2-3 mid-career artists/year.

First Contact & Terms: Send query letter with brochure showing art style, tearsheets and slides. Samples are filed or are returned by SASE if requested by artist. Reports back within 2 months. Mail appropriate materials: photographs and slides. Payment method is negotiated. Offers an advance when appropriate. Buys all rights. Provides in-transit insurance, insurance while work is at firm, promotion, shipping to and from firm and a written contract.

Tips: "Be considerate and professional" when approaching Gallerie Vendome. "We are presently seeking artists on the theme of buildings and construction."

GALLERY PUBLISHERS, 137 Orange Ave., Coronado CA 92118. (619)435-1808. FAX: (619)435-8272. Contact: Julie Harper or Jim. Estab. 1986. Art publisher of limited editions. Clients: wholesale to the trade with emphasis on national distribution. Approached by 50-100 artists/year. Publishes and distributes the work of 3-5 emerging, 3-5 mid-career, and 3-5 established artists/year. Payment is negotiated. Offers an advance when appropriate. Negotiates rights purchased. Provides promotion and a written contract. Send query letter. Samples are filed. Samples not filed are returned. Reports back within 45 days. To show a portfolio, mail tearsheets, slides transparencies and photos.
Acceptable Work: Considers all painted or drawn media, i.e. oil, acrylic, watercolor, pastel, charcoal, pencil, etc. Artists represented include Luis Preciado, Ken Tarlton and Patricia Vetter.
Tips: "We prefer to keep them on file for possible future use."

GALLERY REVEL, 96 Spring St., New York NY 10012. (212)925-0600. Assistant Director: Shelley O'Connor. Gallery handling oil and bronze sculpture. Distributes the work of 15 artists/year. Pays flat fee of $200 average or consigns work; payment is negotiated. Send query letter with brochure showing art style or resume and slides. Samples not filed are returned. Reports back within 15 days. Call to schedule an appointment to show a portfolio, which should include original/final art and slides.
Acceptable Work: Considers oil and acrylic paintings, all on canvas. Prefers impressionistic landscapes, realism and bronze sculpture.
Tips: "I am not interested in figurative and depressive work."

***GANGO EDITIONS,** Suite 520, 135 S.W. Ash, Portland OR 97204. (800)852-3662. (503)223-0925. Administrative Assistant: Elaine Graves. Estab. 1982. Art publisher. Publishes posters. Clients: poster galleries, art galleries and major distributors. Current clients include Bruce McGraw Graphics, Editions Ltd. West, Tunkel Art Source and many overseas distributors.
Needs: Seeking artwork with creative artistic expression and decorative appeal for the commercial and designer markets. Considers, oil, watercolor, acrylic, pastel and mixed media. Prefers landscapes and abstract styles. Artists represented include Carol Grigg, Sidonie Caron and Carolyn Dewey. Editions created by working from an existing painting. Approached by more than 100 artists/year. Publishes the work of more than 10 and distributes the work of more than 50 emerging artists/year. Publishes the work of 3 and distributes the work of more than 200 established artists/year.
First Contact & Terms: Send query letter with slides and photographs. Samples are filed "if we see potential" or are returned by SASE. Reports back within 2 weeks. Write to schedule an appointment to show a portfolio or mail appropriate materials. Portfolio should include slides and photographs. Pays royalties or payment method is negotiated. Offers advance when appropriate. Negotiates rights purchased. Requires exclusive representation of artist. Provides insurance while work is at firm, promotion and a written contract.
Tips: "We are interested in fresh ideas for the poster market rather than reworked old ideas. We are always actively seeking new artists. Artists need to be aware of current fashion colors."

LEN GARON FINE ARTS, 1742 Valley Greene Rd., Paoli PA 19301. (215)296-3481. Director/Owner: Len Garon. Estab. 1976. Art publisher/distributor handling limited and unlimited editions of offset reproductions, posters and handpulled originals. Clients: galleries, frame shops, corporate art consultants and interior designers. Approached by 64-70 artists/year. Publishes the work of 2 and distributes the work of 10 emerging artists/year. Publishes the work of 5 and distributes the work of 15 mid-career artists/year. Publishes the work of 8 and distributes the work of 15 established artists/year. Payment method is negotiated. Offers an advance when appropriate. Does not require exclusive representation of the artist. Provides promotion and a written contract. Send query letter with brochure, tearsheets and photographs. Samples are filed and are not returned. Reports back within 2 weeks. To show a portfolio mail tearsheets and transparencies.
Acceptable Work: Seeking artwork with creative artistic expression and decorative appeal for the serious collector and the designer market. Considers oil, acrylic, pastel, watercolor and mixed media. Prefers impressionist, original themes. Prefers unframed series. Maximum size of acceptable work: 24×36". Artists represented include Len Garon, Judy Antonelli, Des Toscano, Kim Johnson and Barbara Hails. Editions created by collaborating with the artist and by working from an existing painting.
Tips: "Be patient in developing a new market for your work. Success is a marathon—not a sprint. Keep a positive attitude and go for your goal."

GENESIS FINE ARTS, 853 SW 174th St., Seattle WA 98166. (206)248-3848. Marketing Director: Ron Lowrie. Art publisher/distributor/wholesale gallery handling limited editions (maximum 250 prints), handpulled originals and posters for wholesale trade, designers and galleries. Publishes/distributes the work of 7 artists/year. Payment method is negotiated (primarily flat fee per image/print). Offers an advance when appropriate. Negotiates rights purchased. Requires exclusive representation, except locally. Provides promotion and a written contract. Send query letter with brochure showing art style and slides. Samples not filed are returned.

Reports back to the artists regarding his query/submission within 1 month. Call or write to schedule an appointment or mail appropriate materials to show a portfolio, which should include slides and transparencies.

Acceptable Work: Considers pastel, watercolor, mixed media and monoprints. Prefers individual works of art. Maximum size 38 × 50".

*GENRE LTD. INC. – ART PUBLISHERS, 620 S. Glenoaks Blvd., Burbank CA 91502. (818)843-7200. President: Mrs. Akiko Morrison. Art publisher of limited editions, offset reproductions, unlimited editions, posters and licensed characters. Clients: catalog/direct mail, corporate, department stores, galleries, chains, high-end. Approached by 30 artists/year. Publishes the work of 2 and distributes the work of 1 emerging artist/year. Distributes the work of 1 mid-career artist/year. Publishes and distributes the work of 3 established artists/year; 8 freelance artists/year. Pays flat fee, $250-2,000; royalties of 10% for posters; or on consignment basis. Payment method is negotiated. Offers an advance when appropriate. Buys reprint rights negotiates rights purchased. Provides a written contract. Send query letter with brochure showing art style or slides and SASE. Samples are filed or are returned only if requested. Reports back within 2 weeks. Call to schedule an appointment to show a portfolio or mail slides. "SASE a must."

Acceptable Work: Seeking artwork with decorative appeal for the designer market. Considers children's art, traditional art subjects, original cartoon images, pen & ink line drawings, oil and acrylic paintings and mixed media. "We can create titles." Prefers unframed series.

*GERARD GALLERY, 400 Main St., Half Moon Bay, CA 94019. (415)726-0203. Manager: Laura Guluzzy. Estab. 1990. Gallery. Features original art and private collectors and limited editions. Clients: tourists.

Needs: Seeking artwork with decorative appeal for the serious collector and commercial market. Considers oil, acrylic, pen & ink and mixed media. Prefers landscapes and seascapes. Artists represented include Georgia Crittenden Bemis, Woody Jackson, Joan Colleen Baker, Joanne Case and John Herendeen. Editions created by working from an existing painting. Approached by 150 artists/year.

First Contact & Terms: Send query letter with brochure showing art style or resume, tearsheets, slides or photographs. Samples are filed. Reports back only if interested. Write to schedule an appointment to show a portfolio, which should include original/final art, photographs, slides or transparencies. Payment method is negotiated. Does not offer an advance. Provides insurance while work is at firm and a written contract.

*GESTATION PERIOD, Box 8280, 1946 N. 4th St., Columbus OH 43201. (614)294-4659. Owner: Bob Richman. Estab. 1971. Distributor. Distributes unlimited editions and posters. Clients: art galleries, framers and bookstores.

Needs: Seeking artwork with creative artistic expression.

First Contact & Terms: Send query letter with resume, tearsheets and published samples. Samples are filed or returned by SASE. Reports back within 2 months. Negotiates rights purchased. Provides promotion.

Tips: "We are currently seeking published prints for distribution."

*GIRARD/STEPHENS FINE ART DEALERS, 4002 28th Ave., Temple Hills MD 20748. (301)423-7563. Creative Director: Yvette Bailey. Estab. 1987. Publishes and distributes handpulled originals and limited editions. Clients: galleries, decorators and framers.

Needs: Seeking artwork with creative artistic expression for the serious collector. Considers oil, watercolor, acrylic and mixed media. Prefers contemporary themes and styles. Artists represented include Jeff Donaldson, Neil Harpe and Stephen Watson. Editions created by working from an existing painting. Approached by 10-12 artists/year. Publishes and distributes the work of 4 emerging artists/year. Distributes the work of 2 mid-career artists and 1 established artist/year.

First Contact & Terms: Send query letter with resume and slides. Samples not filed are returned by SASE. Reports back within 30 days. To show portfolio, mail appropriate materials: slides. Pays 10% royalty. Offers advance when appropriate. Buys one-time rights. Provides insurance while work is at firm, shipping from firm and a written contract.

Tips: "We look for artists that demonstrate technical ability as well as an aesthetic or social philosophy."

*THE GOLF SHOP COLLECTION, Box 14609, Cincinnati OH 45250. (513)241-7789. FAX: (513)241-7975. President: J.A. Olman. Estab. 1970. Art publisher and distributor. Clients: picture framers, art galleries and golf pros.

Needs: Seeking artwork with decorative appeal for the commercial market. Considers oil, watercolor and acrylic. Prefers scenes of golf and people. Artists represented include Kuchno, Crofut, Cost and Moss. Editions created by collaborating with the artist and by working from an existing painting.

First Contact & Terms: Send query letter with resume and photographs. Samples are not filed and are returned by SASE. Reports back within 3 weeks. Write to schedule an appointment to show a portfolio. Portfolio should include: original/final art and photographs. Pays flat fee, $250; or on consignment basis: firm receives 35% commission. Does not offer advance. Buys all rights. Provides insurance while work is at firm and a written contract.

*GRAPHICOR, 433 E. Maple St., Miamisburg OH 45342. Art Coordinator: Judy James. Estab. 1978. Printer and distributor of fine art reproductions. Distributes limited editions and offset reproductions.
Needs: Seeking artwork with decorative appeal. Considers oil, watercolor, acrylic, pastel and pen & ink. Seeking all themes and styles. "We need variety." Artists represented include Pat Whipp. Editions created by working from an existing painting. Approached by 200 artists/year. Distributes the work of 100-200 emerging artists, 10-50 mid-career artists, and 5-10 established artists.
First Contact & Terms: Send query letter with slides and limited edition prints. Samples are not filed and are returned. Reports back within 1 month. Call to schedule an appointment to show a portfolio or mail appropriate materials. Pays on consignment basis: firm receives 50% commission. Does not offer an advance. Provides insurance while work is at firm and a written contract.
Tips: "Be patient. It takes 6-12 months to begin marketing new work."

GRAPHIQUE DE FRANCE, 46 Waltham St., Boston MA 02118. (617)482-5066. Contact: Ellen Conklin. Estab. 1979. Art publisher and distributor handling offset reproductions, posters and silkscreens. Clients: galleries and foreign distributors. Publishes/distributes the work of 30-40 aritists/year. Pays royalties of 10%. Buys reprint rights or "rights to image in poster form." Provides promotion and written contract. Send slides and transparencies. Samples are filed or returned by SASE. Reports back within 4 weeks. To show a portfolio, mail origial/final art, color and b&w slides and transparencies.
Acceptable Work: Considers oil, pastel and watercolor. "Our catalog is representative of a variety of styles. Preference depends on the work itself." Prefers individual works of art. Maximum size $44 \times 60''$.
Tips: "Put your name on the sample (i.e. slide or transparency, etc.) and address. Include SASE for return. Samples must be seen by GDF before I can schedule a meeting with the artist/agent."

GRAPHIQUE DU JOUR, INC., 2231 Faulkner Rd., Atlanta GA 30324. President: Daniel Deljou. Estab. 1980. Art publisher/distributor handling limited editions (maximum 250 prints), handpulled originals and monoprints/monotypes for designers and architects. Approached by over 100 artists/year. Publishes the work of 10-15 and distributes the work of 10 emerging artists/year. Publishes and distributes the work of 15 mid-career artists/year. Publishes the work of 20 established artists/year. Pays flat fee, $200-800; royalties of 10-15%; also sells on consignment basis; 40-50% commission; payment method is negotiated. Offers an advance when appropriate. Negotiates rights purchased. Requires exclusive representation. Provides promotion, a written contract and shipping from firm. Send query leter with photographs, slides and transparencies. Samples not filed are returned only if requested by artist. Reports back to the artist regarding his query/submission only if interested. To show a portfolio, mail original/final art.
Acceptable Work: Seeking artwork with creative artistic expression and decorative appeal for the serious collector, commercial collector and designer market. Considers oil, acrylic, pastel, watercolor and mixed media. Prefers contemporary themes. Prefers individual works of art pairs, or unframed series. Maximum size $30 \times 40''$ image of published pieces. Artists represented include Kamy, Lee White, Donna Pinter, Ken Weaver, Michaela Sutillo and Alan Parker. Editions created by collaborating with the artist and by working from an existing painting.
Tips: "We would like to add a line of traditional art with a contemporary flair. Be original. Don't follow the trend, but hope to start one."

*GREGORY EDITIONS, 21220 Erwin, Woodland Hills CA 91367. (818)713-1999. FAX: (818)713-0250. President: Mark Eaker. Estab. 1988. Art publisher and distributor. Publishes and distributes handpulled originals and limited editions.
Needs: Seeking artwork with creative artistic expression. Considers oil and acrylic. Artists represented include Stan Solomon and Ting Sculpture. Editions created by working from an existing painting.
First Contact & Terms: Send query letter with brochure showing art style. Call to schedule an appointment to show a portfolio, which should include photographs and transparencies. Requires exclusive representation of artist. Provides in-transit insurance, insurance while work is at firm, promotion, shipping from firm and a written contract.

*GUILDHALL, INC., 2535 Weisenberger, Fort Worth TX 76107. (817)332-6733; 1-800-356-6733. President: John M. Thompson III. Art publisher/distributor of limited and unlimited editions, offset reproductions and handpulled originals for galleries, decorators, offices and department stores. Also provides direct mail sales to retail customers. Current clients include over 500 galleries nationwide. Pays $250-2,500 flat fee; 10-20% royalties; 33% commission on consignment; or payment method is negotiated. Negotiates rights purchased. Requires exclusive representation for contract artists. Provides insurance while work is at firm, promotion, shipping from firm and a written contract. Send query letter with resume, tearsheets, photographs, slides and 4×5 transparencies. Samples are not filed and are returned only if requested. Reports back within 2 weeks. Call or write to schedule an appointment to show a portfolio, or mail thumbnails, color and b&w tearsheets, slides and 4x5 transparencies.

Acceptable Work: Seeking artwork with creative artistic expression for the serious collector, commercial collector and designer market. Considers pen & ink, oil, acrylic, watercolor, and bronze and stone sculptures. Prefers historical Native American, Western, abstract, equine, wildlife, landscapes and religious themes. Prefers individual works of art. Artist represented include Chuck DeHaan, Tom Deveo and Wayne Baize. Editions created by collaborating with the artist and by working from an existing painting. Approached by 150 artists/year. Publishes the work of 5 and distributes the work of 15 emerging artists/year. Publishes the work of 5 and distributes the work of 12 mid-career artists/year. Publishes the work of 10 and distributes the work of 15 established artists/year.

Tips: "Assure us that you have earned the title of artist."

*HADLEY HOUSE PUBLISHING, 14200 23rd Ave. N., Plymouth MN 55447. (612)559-9213. FAX: (612)559-7692. Vice President-Publishing: Joyce A. Olson. Estab. 1974. Art publisher, distributor and gallery. Publishes and distributes handpulled originals, limited and unlimited editions and offset reproductions. Clients: wholesale and retail.

Needs: Seeking artwork with creative artistic expression and decorative appeal for the serious collector. Considers oil, watercolor, acrylic, pastel and mixed media. Prefers wildlife, Western landscapes and Americana themes and styles. Artists represented include Olaf Wieghorst, Kenneth Riley, Terry Redllin, Clark Hulings, Bryan Moon and Ozz Franca. Editions created by collaborating with artist and by working from an existing painting. Approached by 200-300 artists/year. Publishes the work of 3-4 and distributes the work of 1 emering artist/year. Publishes the work of 15 and distributes the work of 2 mid-career artists/year. Publishes the work of 8 established artists/year.

First Contact & Terms: Send query letter with brochure showing art style or resume and tearsheets, slides, photographs and transparencies. Samples are filed or are returned. Reports back within 4-6 weeks. Call to schedule an appointment to show a portfolio, which should include b&w slides, original/final art and transparencies. Pays royalties. Buys one-time rights or reprint rights. Requires exclusive representation of artist. Provides insurance while work is at firm, promotion, shipping from firm, a written contract and advertising through dealer showcase.

*WILLIAM HAVU FINE ART, 2565 Blake St., Denver CO 80205. (303)297-1625. Owner: Bill Havu. Estab. 1983. Art publisher and distributor. Publishes and distributes handpulled originals. Clients: corporation consultants. Current clients include Victor Huff & Associates (V.H.A.), Viacom Productions and Associates III.

Needs: Seeking artwork with creative artistic expression. Considers monotypes. Prefers abstract styles and landscapes. Artists represented include David Grojean, Tony Ortega, Sam Scott and Roy Wilce. Editions created by collaborating with artist. Approached by 15 artists/year. Publishes the work of 1 and distributes the work of 4 emerging artists/year. Publishes the work of 10 and distributes the work of 25 mid-career artists/year. Publishes the work of 10 and distributes the work of 15 established artists/year.

First Contact & Terms: Send query letter with resume, tearsheets, slides and photographs. Samples are not filed and are returned by SASE if requested by artist. Reports back within 1 week. Write to schedule an appointment to show a portfolio. Portfolio should include tearsheets, photographs and slides. Pays on consignment basis: firm receives 50% commission. "When publishing monotypes, the artist and firm split the net profit 50/50." Does not offer advance. Provides insurance while work is at firm and shipping from firm.

Tips: "We advise that work be of high quality regardless of the subject. It should be well crafted."

ICART VENDOR GRAPHICS, 8568 Pico Blvd., Los Angeles CA 90035. (213)653-3190. Director: Sandy Verin. Estab. 1972. Art publisher/distributor/gallery. Produces limited and unlimited editions of offset reproductions and handpulled original prints for galleries, decorators, corporations, collectors. Publishes the work of 3-5 artists/year. Distributes the work of 30-40 artists/year. Pays flat fee, $250-1,000; royalties (5-10%) or negotiates payment method. Offers advance. Buys all rights. Usually requires exclusive representation of the artist. Provides insurance while work is at publisher. Negotiates ownership of original art. Send brochure, photographs, not slides. Samples returned by SASE. Reports back within 1 month.

Acceptable Work: Considers oil, acrylic, watercolor and mixed media, also serigraphy and lithography. Prefers unusual appealing subjects. Likes airbrush. Prefers Art Deco period styles. Prefers individual works of art, pairs, series; 30x40" maximum.

Tips: "Be original with your own ideas. Present clean, neat presentations in original or photographic form (no slides). No abstracts please. Important colors this year include earth tones, greens and blues. Popular styles include impressionism and landscapes."

IMAGE CONSCIOUS, 147 Tenth St., San Francisco CA 94103. (415)626-1555. Creative Director: Joan Folkmann. Estab. 1980. Art publisher/distributor of offset and poster reproductions. Clients: poster galleries, frame shops, department stores, design consultants, interior designers and gift stores. Current clients include Z Gallerie, Deck the Walls and Decor Corporation. Approached by hundreds of artists/year. Publishes the work of 1 and distributes the work of 50 emerging artists/year. Publishes the work of 1 and distributes the work of 200 mid-career artists/year. Publishes the work of 2 and distributes the work of 700 established artists/

year. Payment method is negotiated. Negotiates rights purchased. Provides promotion, shipping from firm and a written contract. Send query letter with brochure, resume, tearsheets, photographs, slides and/or transparencies. Samples are filed or are returned by SASE. Reports back within 1 month.

Acceptable Work: Seeking artwork with creative artistic expression and decorative appeal for the designer market. Considers oil, acrylic, pastel, watercolor, tempera, mixed media and photography. Prefers individual works of art, pairs or unframed series. Artists represented include Mary Silverwood, Aleah Koury, Doug Keith, Jim Tanaka, Gary Braasch and Lawrence Goldsmith. Editions created by collaborating with the artist and by working from an existing painting.

Tips: "Research what type of product is currently in poster shops. Note colors, sizes and subject matter trends."

*IMCON, Box 365, West Milford NJ 07480. (201)728-2909. FAX: (201)728-5444. President: Fred Dankert. Estab. 1986. Fine art printer. Prints handpulled originals and limited editions. Clients: galleries and distributors.

Needs: Seeking artwork with creative artistic expression for the serious collector. Considers oil, watercolor, acrylic, pastel and pen and ink. Editions created by collaborating with the artist and by working from an existing painting. Approached by 50-100 artists/year. Publishes and distributes the work of 4 mid-career artists/year. Publishes and distributes the work of 2 established artists/year.

First Contact & Terms: Send query letter with resume, photographs and transparencies. Samples are filed or are returned by SASE if requested by artist. Reports in 1 month. Call or mail appropriate materials: transparencies, original/final art and photographs. Payment method is negotiated. Does not offer an advance. Buys all rights. Provides insurance while work is at firm and in some cases promotion.

Tips: "Artists should be willing to work with us to produce original prints either directly or from their existing work. We do *not* reproduce; we create new images. Artists should have market experience."

ARTHUR A. KAPLAN CO. INC., 460 W. 34th St., New York NY 10001. (212)947-8989. President: Reid Fader. Estab. 1956. Art publisher of unlimited editions and offset reproduction prints. Clients: galleries, department stores and picture frame manufacturers. Approached by 350 artists/year. Publishes and distributes the work of 12-25 emerging and 12-25 mid-career and established artists/year. Publishes and distributes the work of 25-50 established artists/year. Pays a royalty of 5-10%. Offers advance. Buys all rights. Requires exclusive representation. Provides insurance while work is at firm, promotion, shipping from firm and a written contract. Send resume, tearsheets, slides, photographs and original art to be kept on file. Material not filed is returned. Reports within 2-3 weeks. To show a portfolio, mail appropriate materials or call to schedule an appointment. Portfolio should include original/final art, final reproduction/product, color tearsheets and photographs.

Acceptable Work: Seeking artwork with decorative appeal. Considers oil, acrylic, pastel, watercolor, mixed media, photography. Artists represented include Lena Liu, Justin Coopersmith and Gloria Eriksen. Editions created by collaborating with artist and by working from an existing painting.

Tips: "We cater to a mass market and require fine quality art with decorative and appealing subject matter. Don't be afraid to submit work—we'll consider anything and everything."

*MARTIN LAWRENCE LIMITED EDITIONS, 16250 Stagg St., Van Nuys CA 91406. (818)988-0630. Art publisher. Publishes limited edition graphics, fine art posters and originals by internationally known, up-and-coming and new artists. Publishes and distributes the work of 4 emerging artists/year.

First Contact & Terms: Contact by mail only. Send good quality slides or photographs, pertinent biographical information and SASE. Exclusive representation required.

Acceptable Work: Seeking artwork with decorative appeal for the serious and commercial collector. Prefers oil, acrylic, watercolor, serigraphs, lithographs, etchings and sculpture. Artists represented include Pergoca, Yamagata, King, Rios, Warhol, Scharf, Haring and Cutrone. Editions created by collaborating with the artist and by working from an existing painting.

LESLI ART, INC., Box 6693, Woodland Hills CA 91365. (818)999-9228. President: Stan Shevrin. Estab. 1965. Artist agent handling paintings for art galleries and the trade. Works with 20 artists/year. Payment method is negotiated. Offers an advance. Provides national distribution, promotion and written contract. Send query letter with photographs and slides. Samples not filed are returned by SASE. Reports back within 1 month. To show a portfolio, mail slides and color photographs.

Acceptable Work: Considers oil paintings and acrylic paintings. Prefers realism and impressionism—figures costumed, narrative content, landscapes, still lifes and florals. Maximum size 36×48".

Tips: "Considers only those artists who are serious about their work begin exhibited in important galleries throughout the United States and Europe."

LESLIE LEVY PUBLISHING, Suite D, 7342 E. Thomas, Scottsdale AZ 85251. (602)945-8491. Director: Gary Massey. Materials to be sent to: Leslie Levy Gallery, 7141 E. Main St., Scottsdale AZ 85251. (602)947-0937. Estab. 1976. Art publisher and distributor of limited editions, offset reproductions, unlimited editions, posters

Close-up

Paul Liptak
Director of Acquisitions
Bruce McGaw Graphics, Inc.

If you're interested in having your work published, you have picked a good time according to Paul Liptak, director of acquisitions for Bruce McGaw Graphics. The market for fine art prints and posters experienced a sales boom about five years ago and continues to be a strong market, he says — and this means more opportunities for both new and experienced artists.

More good news is that the market is not dominated by any one or two styles, subjects or artists. "We're looking at everything and anything and we're definitely interested in seeing the work of new artists," Liptak says. One of the largest publishers and distributors of fine art reproductions, Bruce McGaw Graphics will publish 150 to 160 pieces this year and will distribute three times as many from other publishers.

Liptak started in the sales department, but took over acquisitions about five years ago when the company became more involved in publishing. In his search for new artists, he visits shows, art fairs, museums, galleries, libraries and even restaurants displaying art. Although he actively solicits work from artists he's worked with before, Liptak finds work from many new artists in the 1,500 to 1,600 unsolicited submissions he receives each year.

To stay on top of trends, he reads magazines and books and listens carefully to clients and customers — owners and buyers for frame shops and poster stores, interior designers and corporate art collectors. Bruce McGaw Graphics maintains a showroom, but most of their products are sold through their catalog. Top customers receive additional supplements and samples of new prints. The company also advertises in trade magazines and at trade shows, including the large New York and Los Angeles Art Expos.

"Corporate sales have shown a very strong increase," Liptak says. Although it's hard to pinpoint any one style or media that appeals to the corporate client, "they tend to buy images that fit in with the corporate atmosphere and colors that coordinate with their office space."

Liptak will look at just about every type of image, but says he especially needs more work featuring sports, and more abstract images. The market seems saturated with black-and-white photography and Monet-type impressionistic works at this time, but he is quick to say he wouldn't hesitate to publish a strong image in either of these areas.

To get a feel for the market, Liptak advises artists to visit poster stores and frame shops. The posters most prominently displayed are usually best sellers. It pays to be aware of trends, but, he says, "I'm more interested in seeing what I don't already have. Artists should resist being too influenced by publishers' catalogs."

To submit to Bruce McGaw Graphics, artists should send 20 to 30 slides. If interested, Liptak will show them to his colleagues on staff first. Then he will have a number of "mini designs" worked up to see how the images translate to the poster format. He will also show them to customers to gauge their response. "It's an extensive research and review process. It can take up to three months. But we want to be as sure as we can — for ourselves, our customers and the artist."

The initial print run is usually 3,000 units. Artists are paid on a royalty basis, but the company keeps royalties from the first 500 or 600 prints sold to cover production costs, Liptak explains.

Once accepted, the inhouse design staff will add border treatments, select the typeface and determine border colors to fit the image. Sometimes special treatments such as foil stamping or embossing are added. Artists or their representatives are consulted on the design and final approval is left to the artist.

The print and poster market has changed dramatically in the last 20 years, says Liptak. Better paper, ink and production methods continue to improve the overall quality. In recent years there seems to be more focus on the relationship between the image and the design and more attention is paid to borders and other design elements, he says.

Design, color and medium contribute to the attractiveness of the print or poster, but, cautions Liptak, the image still sells the piece. Not all images make good posters. Some are better suited to gift items, stationery, cards or only as originals. It takes research and experience to learn what makes a good poster or print image, he says.

His advice to artists is simple—once you have an image or images you feel will work well as reproductions, send them out. Take advantage of a market hungry for new images and open to new artists.

—Robin Gee

Ty Wilson's "The Date," Liptak says, "captures the elegance of romance. To create a dramatic effect on his simplistic line drawings, we incorporated foil stamping." Yuriko Takata's "Vase Du Fleur" is an example, he says, of one of Takata's many styles. He says, "Yuriko has been a part of our roster of artists for over nine years—the longest of any artist." Reprinted with permission of the artists

and miniature prints and calendars. Approached by hundreds of artists/year. Publishes the work of 5-8 emerging, 15 mid-career and 10 established artists/year. Pays 2½% of retail each for posters "which are sold quarterly." Insists on reprint rights. Requires exclusive publishing of the artist for the type of print/poster being published. Send query letter with resume, tearsheets, photographs, slides or transparencies—"highest quality of any of the above items." Slides, etc. are returned by SASE. "Portfolio will not be seen unless interest is generated by the materials sent in advance."

Acceptable Work: Seeking artwork with creative artistic expression, fashionableness and decorative appeal for the serious collector, commercial collector and designer market. Current clients include: Steve Hanks, Doug West and Stephen Morath. Editions created by collaborating with the artist and by working from an existing painting. Considers oil, acrylic, pastel, watercolor, tempera, mixed media and photographs.

Tips: "First, don't call us before sending materials. After we review your materials, we will contact you if we are interested. We are known in the industry for our high quality prints and excellent skilled artists. We intend to remain the same. If you feel the representation and/or publication of your art would uphold our reputation, we welcome your submission of materials. We are looking for art unlike what we and other publishers are publishing."

LOLA LTD./LT'EE, 1028 Hill St., Greensboro NC 27408. (919)275-8005. Owner: Lola Jackson. Art publisher and distributor of limited editions, offset reproductions, unlimited editions and handpulled originals. Clients: art galleries, architects, picture frame shops, interior designers, major furniture and department stores and industry. Approached by 100 artists/year. Publishes the work of 5 emerging and 5 mid-career artists/year. Distributes the work of 40 emerging and 40 mid-career artists/year. Publishes and distributes the work of 5 established artists/year. Payment method is negotiated. "Our standard commission is 50% less 30-50% off retail." Offers an advance when appropriate. Provides insurance while work is at firm, shipping to firm and a written contract. Send query letter with brochure showing art style or resume, tearsheets, photostats, photographs, photocopies or transparencies. "Actual sample is best." Samples are filed or are returned only if requested. Reports back within 2 weeks. To show a portfolio, mail original/final art or final reproduction/product.

Acceptable Work: Seeking artwork with creative artistic expression and decorative appeal for the commercial collector and designer market. "Handpulled graphics are our main area"; also considers oil, acrylic, pastel, watercolor, tempera or mixed media. Prefers unframed series, 30x40" maximum. Artists represented include Tupper, Whittle and Morga-Reagan. Editions created by collaborating with the artist.

Tips: "Send a cover letter, with an actual sample and the price the artist needs. Example: Retail, less 50, less 50. We do not pay for samples. We have sales reps throughout U.S. to sell for you. We are presently looking for more reps."

LONDON CONTEMPORARY ART, 729 Pinecrest, Prospect Heights IL 60070. (708)459-3990. Assistant Marketing Director: Kim Bayer. Estab. 1977. Art publisher and distributor. Publishes and distributes handpulled originals and limited editions. Clients: corporate/residential designers, consultants and retail galleries.

Needs: Seeking artwork with creative artistic expression, fashionableness and decorative appeal for the designer market. Considers oil, watercolor, acrylic, pastel and mixed media. Prefers abstract and impressionistic styles and Midwest and Mediterranean landscapes. Artists represented include Dodsworth, Penny and Tarkai. Editions created by collaborating with artist and by working from an existing painting. Approached by 50-75 artists/year. Publishes and distributes the work of 2 emerging artists/year. Publishes and distributes the work of 40 mid-career artists/year. Publishes and distributes the work of 5 established artists/year.

First Contact & Terms: Send query letter with resume, slides and photographs. Samples are filed. Does not report back, "in which case the artist should contact us." Mail appropriate materials: color slides. Payment method is negotiated. Offers advance when appropriate. Negotiates rights purchased. Requires exclusive representation of artist. Provides insurance while work is at firm, promotion, shipping from firm and a written contract.

Tips: "Send visuals and a bio first, then follow-up with a call."

BRUCE MCGAW GRAPHICS, INC., 230 Fifth Ave., New York NY 10001. (212)679-7823. Acquisitions: Paul Liptak. Send query letter with brochure showing art style or resume, tearsheets, photostats, photocopies, slides and photographs. Samples not filed are returned by SASE. Reports within weeks. To show a portfolio, mail color tearsheets and photographs. Considers skill and experience of artist, saleability of artwork, client's preferences and rights purchased when establishing contract.

MARCO DISTRIBUTORS, 1412 S. Laredo, Aurora CO 80017. (303)752-4819. President: Mark Woodmansee. Art publisher and distributor of limited editions, handpulled originals, oil washes and oil on canvas. Clients: corporations, galleries and interior designers. Publishes the work of 2 artists/year. Distributes the work of 10 artists/year. Pays flat fee or royalty of 20%; or negotiates payment method. Buys all rights, reprint rights or negotiates rights purchased. Requires exclusive representation. Provides promotion, shipping to and from firm and a written contract. Send brochure and samples to be kept on file. Prefers photographs, tearsheets or original work as samples. Samples not filed are not returned. Reports back to artist. Call or write for appointment to show portfolio or contact through artist's agent.

Acceptable work: Considers oil and acrylic paintings, pastel, watercolor, mixed media, serigraphs, stone lithographs, plate lithographs and woodcuts. Especially likes landscapes, unique figures and impressionist styles.

Tips: "Send photos of your work; follow with a call."

*MARI HUBÉ, 132 E. 82nd St., New York NY 10028. (212)772-2525. FAX: (212)517-9376. President: Marilyn Goldberg. Estab. 1988. Art publisher and distributor. Publishes and distributes handpulled originals, unlimited editions, posters, limited editions, sculpture and tapestry for museum giftshops, boutiques and galleries throughout the US and the world.

Need: Seeking artwork with fashionableness and decorative appeal for the serious collector, commercial and designer markets, especially artwork with decorative appeal for the designer market. Considers acrylic and mixed media. Prefers contemporary styles and themes. Artists represented include Picasso, Tsuruta and Wilkinson. Editions created by collaborating with the artist. Approached by 100 artists/year. Publishes the work of 1 emerging, 1 mid-career and 1 established artist/year. The number of artists distributes the work of each year varies.

First Contact & Terms: Send query letter with brochure showing art style or resume, tearsheets, slides, photographs and transparencies. Samples are filed or are returned. Reports in 1 month. To show portfolio, mail photographs, slides and transparencies. Payment method is negotiated. Offers an advance when appropriate. Negotiates rights purchased. Provides insurance while work is at firm and shipping from firm.

Tips: "Decorative-type art in pastel colors is very popular now. Also, bright colors on white."

MARIGOLD ENTERPRISES, LTD., 132 E. 82nd St., New York NY 10028. (212)772-2525. President: Marilyn Goldberg. Art publisher/distributor/gallery handling limited editions, posters, tapestry and sculpture for galleries, museums and gift boutiques. Current clients include the Guggenheim Museum and Metropolitan Museum of Art. Approached by 100 artists/year. Publishes the work of 1 emerging, mid-career and established artist/year. Distributes the work of 3 emerging, mid-career and established artists/year. Payment method is negotiated. Offers advance when appropriate. Negotiates rights purchased. Exclusive representation is not required. Provides insurance while work is at firm, shipping to firm and a written contract. Send query letter with resume, slides and transparencies. Samples are filed or returned. Reports within 2 weeks. Call or write to schedule an appointment to show a portfolio or mail slides and transparencies.

Acceptable Work: Seeking artwork with decorative appeal for the designer market. Considers oil, acrylic, pastel, watercolor and mixed media. Prefers individual works of art, unframed series. Artists represented include Pablo Picasso, Ichiro Isonita. Editions created by collaborating with the artist.

Tips: "Decorative-type art in pastel, light, airy pleasant feel is very popular."

*THE MARKS COLLECTION, 239 Cherokee St., NE, Marietta GA 30060. (404)425-7982. President: Jim Marks. Estab. 1981. Art publisher. Publishes unlimited and limited editions. Clients: persons interested in the Civil War; Christian and secular.

Needs: Seeking art for the serious collector. Considers oil, acrylic and mixed media. Prefers Christian, nature and Civil War themes. Artists represented include Michael Gnatek and William Maugham. Editions created by collaborating with the artist. Publishes and distributes the work of 2 established artists/year.

First Contact & Terms: Send query letter with brochure showing art style and slides and photographs. Samples are filed. Reports back only if interested. If does not report back, phone for discussion. Payment depends upon the use and distribution: royalties or flat fee. Offers an advance when appropriate. Provides a written contract.

Tips: "Phone first to give an overview of your style, subject matter, etc."

DAVID MARSHALL, Box 24635, St. Louis MO 63141. (314)997-3003. President: Marshall Gross. Estab. 1972. Art distributor/gallery handling original acrylic paintings, serigraphs, paper construction, cast paper and sculpture. Clients: designer showrooms, architects, designers, galleries, furniture stores and department stores. Approached by 10-15 artists/year. Distributes the work of 2-4 emerging artists, 4-6 mid-career artists and 4-6 established artists/year. Distribution items pay flat fee of $15-50 each if artists will reproduce. Payment method can be negotiated. Send query letter with brochure showing art style or photographs. Samples are not filed and are returned only if requested by artist. Reports within 7 days. Call to schedule an appointment to show a portfolio, which should include roughs, slides and color photos.

Acceptable Work: Seeking fashionableness and decorative appeal for the serious collector, commercial collector and designer market. Considers pastel, watercolor and cast paper. Prefers contemporary, impressionist and primitive/original themes and styles. Prefers individual works of art and unframed series; 36×40″ maximum. Artists represented include Christine, Mills and Ro. Editions created by collaborating with the artist.

Tips: "Glass and mirror designs are given special consideration. Cannot use limited editions or traditional styles. Send samples. We represent all types of shows from professional to street fairs. Current color trend in the Home Furnishings Industry are a must. Artist must be willing to reproduce his or her own work for the duration of our catalog—2-3 years."

*MASTER ART PRESS, INC., Box 8, Getzville NY 14068. (800)777-2044. FAX: (716)691-9548. Contact: Wendy Werner. Art publisher and distributor. Publishes and distributes offset reproductions. Clients: galleries, frameshops and distributors.
Needs: Seeking artwork with creative expression for the serious collector. Considers oil, watercolor and acrylic. Prefers realistic but imaginative themes and styles. Artists represented include Luke Buck, Bill Burkett, Darrell Davis and Margaret M. Martin. Editions created by working from an existing painting. Publishes and distributes the work of 8 established artists/year.
First Contact & Terms: Send query letter with resume, tearsheets, slides and photographs. Samples are not filed and are returned by SASE if requested by artist. Reports back within 3 weeks. Call to schedule an appointment to show a portfolio. Portfolio should include original/final art, photographs and slides. Pays royalty. Requires exclusive representation of artist. Provides in-transit insurance, insurance while work is at firm, promotion, shipping from firm and a written contract.

*THE MEISNER GALLERY, 115 Schmitt Blvd., Farmingdale NY 11735. (516)249-0680. FAX: (516)249-0697. Gallery Director: Mitch Meisner. Estab. 1970. Art publisher and gallery. Publishes and distributes limited editions and sculpture. Clients: retail galleries worldwide.
Needs: Seeking art for the serious collector and commercial market. Considers sculpture to be cast in bronze or acrylic. Prefers figurative styles. Artists represented include Michael Wilkinson, Isidore Margulies and Dante Liberi. Approached by more than 100 artists/year. Publishes the work of 3 and distributes the work of 5 emerging artists/year. Publishes the work of 3 and distributes the work of 10 mid-career artists/year. Publishes the work of 6-10 and distributes the work of 30+ established artists/year.
First Contact & Terms: Send query with resume, tearsheets and photographs. Samples are filed. Reports back within 1 month. Call to schedule an appointment to show a portfolio. Portfolio should include b&w and color tearsheets, photographs, slides and transparencies. Payment method is negotiated. Offers advance when appropriate. Negotiates rights purchased. Requires exclusive representation of artist. Provides insurance while work is at firm, promotion and a written contract.
Tips: "We specialize in figurative sculpture but we are open to new and interesting ideas. At this time pieces 12-20″ high are the best size."

*METROPOLITAN EDITIONS, LTD., Suite 333, 9903 Santa Monica Blvd., Beverly Hills CA 90212. (213)446-6000. Executive Director: Kurt Justin McKay. Estab. 1988. Art publisher and distributor. Publishes/distributes handpulled originals, posters, limited editions and books. Clients: U.S. galleries.
Needs: Seeking art for the serious collector, commercial and designer markets. Considers all media. Prefers realism, figuratives, fantasy. Artists represented are Gil Borivel, Dakota and Salazar. Editions created by collaborating with the artist and by working from an existing painting. Approached by 100 artists/year.
First Contact & Terms: Send query letter with resume and "any samples." Samples are not filed "if rejected" and are returned by SASE only. Reports back only if interested. To show a portfolio, mail appropriate samples. Payment method is negotiated. Negotiates rights purchased. Requires exclusive representation of artist. Provides in-transit insurance, insurance while work is at firm, promotion, shipping from firm and a written contract.
Tips: "Only the good die young."

MONTMARTRE ART COMPANY, INC., 24 S. Front St., Bergenfield NJ 07621. (201)387-7313 or (800)525-5278. President: Ann B. Sullivan. Estab. 1959. Wholesale art dealer to trade. Clients: galleries, decorators, designers and art consultants. Distributes the work of 25 freelance artists/year. Payment method is negotiated. Offers an advance when appropriate. Requires exclusive representation. Provides insurance while work is at firm and shipping from firm. Send query letter with brochure showing art style or any of the following: resume, tearsheets, photostats, photographs, photocopies, slides and transparencies. Samples not filed are returned by SASE. Reports back within 7-10 days. Call to schedule an appointment to show a portfolio which should include original/final art, slides and transparencies.
Acceptable Work: Considers oil, acrylic, watercolor and mixed media. Prefers contemporary, traditional themes etc. Prefers unframed series.
Tips: "Montmartre buys original artwork, (ie: oil, acrylic etc.) distributes and promotes the work to galleries, designers etc., nationally and internationally. We will work with artists to help make certain works more saleable to our client market. We also help artists get their work published in the print and poster market."

MITCH MORSE GALLERY INC., 334 E. 59th St., New York NY 10022. (212)593-1812. President: Mitch Morse. Art distributor. Produces limited edition handpulled originals for framers, galleries, interior designers, architects, hotels and better furniture stores. Distributes the work of 15-20 artists/year. Negotiates payment. Offers advance. Provides promotion and shipping. Send query letter with resume, slides, photographs and SASE. Reports back within 1 week.

Acceptable Work: Prefers the unframed realistic, impressionistic and romantic paintings, lithographs, serigraphs and etchings; individual works; 4x6' maximum.

Tips: "There is continued emphasis on color as a major ingredient in the selection of art and greater interest in more traditional subject matter. Actively seeking additional artists who do original paintings on paper."

RIE MUNOZ LTD., 210 Ferry Way, Juneau AK 99801. Estab. 1979. Art publisher/distributor/gallery handling limited and unlimited editions of offset reproductions and handpulled originals, plus art cards, cloisonne pins and books. Clients: gift shops, book stores, galleries, frame and museum shops. Approached by 5-10 artists/year. Publishes and distributes the work of 3 established artists/year. Pays royalties of 10-20%; or on consignment basis (40% commission). Offers an advance when appropriate. Buys one-time rights. Provides insurance while work is at firm, promotions and a written contract. Send resume, tearsheets, slides and transparencies. Samples are not filed and are returned. To show a portfolio, mail original/final art.

Acceptable Work: Seeking artwork with creative artistic expression and decorative appeal for the serious collector and commercial collector. Considers pen & ink line drawings, oil, acrylic, watercolor and mixed media. Prefers Alaskan or Canadian artists only. Artists represented include Rie Muñoz, John Fehringer and Jo Ann George. Editions created by working from an existing painting.

Tips: "We do not want to see 'non'-Alaskan themes. Our most popular themes include fishing, eskimos and wildlife. We also focus on art depicting lifestyles in the villages. If you are in town, make an appointment to show a portfolio."

THE NATURE COMPANY, 750 Hearst Ave., Berkeley CA 94710. (415)644-1337. Product Development Director: Lon Murphy. Art publisher/distributor of unlimited editions. Publishes work of 8-14 artists/year. Pays $250-800 flat fee or royalties; wholesale commission. Negotiates rights purchased. Provides in-transit insurance, insurance while work is at firm, promotion, shipping and from firm and a written contract. Send query letter with brochure showing art style or tearsheets, photostats, photographs, slides and transparencies. Samples are filed or are returned only if requested. Reports within 2 months. To show a portfolio, mail roughs, color and b&w photostats, tearsheets, slides and transparencies.

Acceptable Work: Will receive all media. Considers pen & ink line drawings, oil, acrylic, pastel, watercolor, tempera and mixed media. "Must be natural history subjects (i.e, plants, animals, landscapes). Avoid domesticated plants, animals, and people-made objects."

NEW DECO, INC., Suite 3, 6401 E. Rogers Circle, Boca Raton FL 33487. (407)241-3901 or (800)543-3326. President: Brad Morris. Estab. 1984. Art publisher/distributor. Produces limited editions using lithography and silkscreen for galleries, also publishes/distributes unlimited editions. Publishes several artists/year. Needs new designs for reproduction. Pays flat fee. Offers advance. Negotiates rights purchased. Provides promotion, shipping and a written contract. Negotiates ownership of original art. Send brochure, resume and tearsheets, photostats or photographs to be kept on file. Samples not kept on file are returned. Reports only if interested. Call or write for appointment to show portfolio, which should include tearsheets.

Tips: "We find most of our artists from *Artists's Market*, advertising, trade shows and referrals."

NEW YORK GRAPHIC SOCIETY, Box 1469, Greenwich CT 06836. (203)661-2400. President: Larry Tolchin. Art publisher/distributor of offset reproductions, limited editions, posters and handpulled originals. Clients: galleries, frame shops, museums and foreign trade. Publishes and distributes the work of 10 emerging artists/year. Pays flat fee or royalty. Offers advance. Buys all print reproduction rights. Provides in-transit insurance from firm to artist, insurance while work is at firm, promotion, shipping from firm and a written contract; provides insurance for art if requested. Send query letter with slides or photographs. Write for artist's guidelines. All submissions returned to artists by SASE after review. Reports within 2 months.

Acceptable Work: Considers oil, acrylic, pastel, watercolor, mixed media and colored pencil drawings. Distributes posters only. Publishes/distributes serigraphs, stone lithographs, plate lithographs and woodcuts.

Tips: "We publish a broad variety of styles and themes. However, we do not publish experimental, hardedge, sexually explicit or suggestive material. Work that is by definition fine art and easy to live with, that which would be considered decorative, is what we are always actively looking for."

*GEORGE NOCK STUDIOS, Box 2848, Reston VA 22090. (703)471-4113. Director: George Nock. Art publisher. Publishes and distributes handpulled originals, unlimited editions, posters, limited editions and original bronze sculpture. Clients: multi-national corporations and private collectors. Current clients include Elke Sommers, Joe Namath, Howard Cosell, Jim Vance and Guy Coheleach.

Needs: Seeking artwork with creative artistic expression for the serious collector. Considers pen & ink and bronze sculpture. Prefers realistic and abstract styles. Artists represented include George Nock and Verdell. Editions created by collaborating with the artist. Approached by 6-10 artists/year. Publishes and distributes the work of 1 emerging, 1 mid-career and 1 established artist/year.

First Contact & Terms: Send query letter with brochure showing art style. Samples are not filed and are returned by SASE if requested by artist. Reports back within 1 week. Portfolio should include photographs and slides. Payment method is negotiated. Buys all rights. Provides promotion.

NORTH BEACH FINE ARTS, INC., 2565 Blackburn St., Clearwater FL 33575. President: James Cournoyer. Art publisher and distributor handling limited edition graphics and posters. Clients: galleries, architects, interior designers and art consultants. Pay negotiable. Negotiates rights purchased. Provides insurance when work is at firm, promotion, written contract and markets expressly-select original handmade editions of a small number of contemporary artists. Send query letter with brochure, resume, tearsheets, photostats, photocopies, slides and photographs to be kept on file. Accepts any sample showing reasonable reproduction. Samples returned by SASE only if requested. Reports back within 2 months. To show a portfolio, mail original/final art, color and b&w tearsheets, photostats and photographs.

Acceptable Work: Considers pen & ink line drawings, mixed media serigraphs, stone lithographs, plate lithographs, woodcuts and linocuts. Especially likes contemporary, unusual and original themes or styles. Looking for artists doing own original graphics, high quality prints to distribute.

Tips: Wants "original prints and posters by serious, experienced, career-oriented artists with a well-developed and thought-out style."

*PACIFIC EDGE PUBLISHING, INC., 206 N. Coast Hwy., Laguna Beach CA 92651. (714)497-5630. President: Paul C. Jillson Estab. 1988. Art publisher. Publishes handpulled originals. Clients: fine art galleries.

Needs: Seeking art for the serious collector and commercial market. Considers oil. Prefers representational to semi-abstract styles. Artists represented include Maria Bertran. Editions created by working from an existing painting. Approached by 20 artists/year. Publishes the work of 1 emerging and 1 mid-career artist/year.

First Contact & Terms: Send query letter with brochure showing art style or resume and tearsheets and photographs. Samples not filed are returned by SASE if requested by artist. Reports back within 10 days. Call to schedule an appointment to show a portfolio. Portfolio should include photographs. Pays royalties. Negotiates rights purchased. Requires exclusive representation of artist. Provides in-transit insurance, insurance while work is at firm, promotion, shipping from firm and a written contract.

PETERSEN PRINTS, 6725 Sunset Blvd., Los Angeles CA 90028. Director: Donna Lasky. Produces limited editions (maximum 950 prints) using offset lithography for galleries, department stores and sporting merchandisers. Publishes the work of 15-25 artists/year. Buys all rights. Requires exclusive representation of the artist. Provides in-transit insurance, insurance while work is at publisher, promotion, shipping from publisher and a written contract. Artist owns original art. Send query letter with brochure, resume, slides or photographs to be kept on file. Samples not kept on file are returned by SASE. Reports back within 3 weeks. Write for appointment to show portfolio.

Acceptable Work: Considers oil, acrylic, gouache, mixed media and watercolor. Prefers paintings of wildlife and outdoor subjects; individual works of art.

Tips: "We do not want to see newspaper clippings in a portfolio. However, there should be a complete biography."

PORTRAITS OF NATURE, Box 217, Youngwood PA 15697. (412)925-9508. Director: Candace E. Crimboli. Estab. 1975. Art publisher handling limited editions for galleries. Publishes/distributes the work of 7 artists/year. Payment method is negotiated. Buys reprint rights. Does not require exclusive representation of the artist. Provides promotion and contract while work is at firm. Send query letter with resume and slides – at least 20 – of most recent work. Samples not filed are returned by SASE only. Reports back within 2 months. Write to schedule an appointment to show a portfolio which should include original/final art.

Acceptable Work: Considers oil, acrylic, pastel, watercolor, tempera and mixed media. Prefers contemporary, floral and outdoor themes. Prefers individual works of art.

POSNER GALLERY, 207 N. Milwaukee St., Milwaukee WI 53202. (414)273-3097. President: Judith L. Posner. Estab. 1964. Art publisher/distributor/gallery. Produces limited and unlimited editions of offset reproductions and original serigraphs and lithographs. Approached by 100 artists/year. Publishes and distributes the work of 1 emerging artist, 2-5 mid-career artists and 3-5 established artists/year. Current clients include: Megan Graphics, Edition Limited and Mitchell Beja. Pays royalty, or on consignment (50% commission). Buys all rights. Requires exclusive representation of artist. Provides promotion and shipping from firm. Send resume, photographs and slides. Samples are returned by SASE only if requested. Reports within 10 days.

Acceptable Work: Seeking creative artistic expression, fashionableness and decorative appeal, for the serious collector, commercial collector and designer market. Considers all media. Prefers individual works of art. Specializes in contemporary themes. Artists represented include Crane and Peticus. Editions created by collaborating with the artist and by working from an existing painting.

Tips: "Must be contemporary. No surrealist, space themes or strange subject matter."

POSTERS INTERNATIONAL, 1200 Castlefield Ave., Toronto Ontario M6B-1G2. (416)789-7156. Vice President: Esther Cohen. Estab. 1976. Art publisher/distributor/gallery handling limited editions (maximum 250 prints), handpulled originals and posters for galleries, restaurants, hotels, designers, and retailers. Approached by 100 artists/year. Publishes the work of 5 emerging, 5 mid-career and 6 established artists/year. Distributes the work of 15 emerging, 15 mid-career and 12 established artists/year. Payment method is negotiated. Offers an advance when appropriate. Negotiates rights purchased. Does not require exclusive representation. Provides in-transit insurance, insurance while work is at firm, promotion, shipping from firm and a written contract. Send query letter with brochure showing art style and tearsheets, photographs, slides and transparencies. Samples are sometimes filed. Samples not filed are returned only if requested by artist. Reports back to the artist regarding his query/submission within 3 weeks only if interested. To show a portfolio call or mail color and b&w slides and transparencies. "Outside of the shipments should indicate samples have no commercial value. Value at $1."

Acceptable Work: Seeking artwork with creative artistic expression, fashionableness and decorative appeal for the serious collector, commercial collector and designer market. Considers pen & ink, oil, acrylic, pastel, watercolor, tempera and mixed media. Prefers commercial, contemporary, original and trendy themes. Prefers individual works of art, pairs and unframed series.

Tips: "Any art that can have mass appeal, we would consider publishing any originals or limited editions. Should also have commerical appeal."

THE PRESS CHAPEAU, Govans Station, Box 4591, Baltimore City MD 21212-4591. (301)433-5379. Director: Philip Callahan. Estab. 1976. Publishes original prints only, "in our own atelier or from printmaker." Clients: architects, interior designers, corporations, institutions and galleries. Also sells to US government through GSA schedule. Current clients include Arco, Inc., state of NC and the Iowa Better Business Bureau. Publishes the work of 36 and distributes the work of 135 artists/year. Pays flat fee $100-2,000. Payment method is negotiated. Offers advance. Purchases 51% of edition or right of first refusal. Does not require exclusive representation. Provides insurance, promotion, shipping to and from firm and a written contract. Contact only through artist's agent. Send query letter with slides. Samples are filed. Samples not filed are returned by SASE. Reports back within 5 days. Write to schedule an appointment to show a portfolio which should include slides.

Acceptable Work: Considers original handpulled, etchings, lithographs, woodcuts and serigraphs. Prefers professional, highest museum quality work in any style or theme. Suites of prints are also viewed with enthusiasm. Prefers unframed series.

Tips: "Our clients are interested in investment quality original handpulled prints. Your resume is not as important as the quality and craftsmanship of your work."

*PRESTIGE ART GALLERIES, INC., 3909 W. Howard St., Skokie IL 60076. (708)679-2555. President: Louis Schutz. Estab. 1960. Art gallery. Publishes and distributes paintings and mixed media artwork.

Needs: Seeking art for the serious collector. Considers oil. Prefers realism and French impressionism. Artists represented are Erte, Simbari, Agam and King. Editions created by collaborating with the artist and by working from an existing painting. Approached by 100 artists/year. Publishes and distributes the work of 2 emerging artists, 4 mid-career artists and the work of 5 established artists/year.

First Contact & Terms: Send query letter with resume and tearsheets, photostats, photocopies, slides, photographs and transparencies. Samples are not filed and are returned by SASE. Reports back within two weeks. To show portfolio, mail appropriate materials. Payment method is negotiated. Offers an advance. Buys all rights. Provides insurance while work is at firm, promotion, shipping from firm and a written contract.

Tips: "Be professional."

*PRIMROSE PRESS, Box 302, New Hope PA 18938. (215)862-5518. President: George Knight. Art publisher. Publishes limited edition reproductions for galleries. Clients: galleries, framers, designers, cost consultants, distributors, manufacturers and catalogs. Approached by 300 artists/year. Publishes the work of 2-4 and distributes the work of 1-2 emerging artists/year. Publishes the work of 3-5 and distributes the work of 2-3 mid-career artists/year. Publishes the work of 4-6 and distributes the work of 3-5 established artists/year. Pays royalties to artist of 10-20%. Buys one-time rights. Provides in-transit insurance, insurance while work is at publisher, shipping from publisher and a written contract. Artist owns original art. Send query letter with tearsheets and slides to be kept on file. Prefers slides as samples. Samples returned by SASE if not kept on file. Reports within 10 days.

Acceptable Work: Seeks art for the serious collector, commercial collector and the designer market. Considers pen & ink line drawings, oil and acrylic paintings, watercolor and mixed media. Publishes representational themes. Prefers individual works of art; 40×30" maximum. Editions created by working from an existing painting.

*QUANTUM MECHANICS, Suite B, 14140 Live Oak, Baldwin Park CA 91706. (818)962-6526. FAX: (818)960-7648. Sales Manager: Gene Ashe. Estab. 1986. Art publisher. Publishes and produces PC computer-generated based graphics package. Clients: ad agencies and distributors.

© 1987 Primrose Press

President George Knight of New Hope, Pennsylvania-based Primrose Press owns all rights to this piece by artist Peter Keating. Created in steel pen and colored inks, the painting conveys "rural elegance," as the title suggests. Keating, who has been published by Primrose Press for 10 years, "takes deadlines seriously and is very professional in his approach to print projects," says Knight. He was paid on a royalty basis.

Needs: Seeking artwork with creative expression for the commercial market. Considers mixed media. Themes and styles are "whatever the client requests." Editions created by collaborating with the artist.

First Contact & Terms: Send query letter with resume and "disk with graphic files." Samples are filed. Reports back within 4 weeks. To show a portfolio, mail "graphic files of work." Pay, rights purchased and services are negotiable. Offers advance when appropriate. Requires exclusive representation.

Tips: "We believe that this marketing idea is so unique that any and all approaches are considered. We only encourage artists who would welcome editing suggestions to their work to make submissions."

*R J DESIGN, INC., Box 5359, Plymouth MI 48170. (313)454-0666. President: Robert Rudzik. Estab. 1984. Art publisher and distributor. Publishes and distributes posters. Clients: frame shops and distributors. Current clients include Image Conscious, Modern Art Editions and the Decor Corp.

Needs: Seeking artwork with decorative appeal. Considers any media. "Prefers popular themes that are unique and entertaining." Artists represented include R. Rudzik. Editions created by collaborating with the artist. Approached by 10 artists/year. Publishes and distributes the work of 1 emerging artist/year.

First Contact & Terms: Send query letter with brochure showing art style. Samples are filed. Reports back only if interested. To show a portfolio, mail color transparencies and photographs. Payment is negotiated. Does not offer an advance. Negotiates rights purchased. Provides insurance while work is at firm, shipping from firm and a written contract.

Tips: "We are looking for artists who are interested in developing images for the poster market."

*H.W. RINEHART FINE ARTS, INC., 245 W. 75th St., New York NY 10023. (212)362-3281. FAX: (212)721-4431. President: Harriet Rinehart. Estab. 1982. Art publisher. Publishes posters. Clients: galleries, distributors and hotel designers worldwide.

Needs: Seeking artwork with fashionableness and decorative appeal for the designer market. Considers oil, watercolor, acrylic, pastel, soft colors and gentle artwork. "Nothing is automatically precluded. It depends on the quality." Prefers landscapes, scenery and still lifes (no nudes). Artists represented include Thomas McKnight and Elizabeth Horowitz. Editions created by collaborating with the artist or by working from an existing painting. Approached by 25-30 artists/year. Publishes the work of 1 mid-career and 1 established artist/year. "I publish work when it looks right only. No set number per year is required."

First Contact & Terms: Send query letter with brochure showing art style or resume, slides, photographs and transparencies. Samples not filed are returned by SASE if requested by artist. Reports back within 2 weeks. Call to schedule an appointment to show a portfolio. Portfolio should include "whatever best shows your work." Pays flat fee, $1,000-2,500; royalties, 10%; or payment method is negotiated. "Payment depends on the artist's needs. I have at least 5 different agreements with different artists." Offers an advance when appropriate. Buys reprint rights. Requires exclusive representation of artist. Provides insurance while work is at firm, promotion, shipping from firm and a written contract.

Tips: "Ask for a catalog in advance to see if your work fits the publisher you are considering. Don't simply send slides to everyone."

*SALEM GRAPHICS, INC., Box 15134, Winston-Salem NC 27103. (919)727-0659. Contact: Robert C. Baker. Estab. 1981. Art publisher and distributor. Publishes and distributes unlimited editions, limited editions and offset reproductions. Clients: art galleries and frame shops.
Needs: Seeking artwork with creative artistic expression, fashionableness and decorative appeal for the serious collector, commercial and designer markets. Considers oil, watercolor, acrylic and pastel. Artists represented include R.B. Dance, Vivien Weller and Mildred Kratz. Editions created by collaborating with the artist and by working from an existing painting. Approached by 50-100 artists/year. "We publish and/or distribute the work of approximately 15 artists, mostly established."
First Contact & Terms: Send query letter with tearsheets, slides, samples of existing prints and transparencies. Samples are not filed. Reports back ASAP. To show a portfolio, mail color tearsheets, photographs, slides and transparencies. Requires exclusive representation of artist. Provides insurance while work is at firm.

SCAFA-TORNABENE ART PUBLISHING CO. INC., 100 Snake Hill Rd., West Nyack NY 10994. (914)358-7600. Director of Art and Design: Rosemary Maschak. Produces unlimited edition offset reproductions for framers, commercial art trade and manufacturers worldwide. Approached by 15-200 artists/year. Publishes and distributes the work of 50 emerging and 50 mid-career artists/year. "We work constantly with our established artists." Pays $200-350 flat fee for each accepted piece. Published artists (successful ones) can advance to royalty arrangements with advance against 5-10% royalty. Buys only reproduction rights (written contract). Artist maintains ownership of original art. Requires exclusive publication rights to all accepted work. Send query letter first with slides or photos and SASE and then arrange interview. Reports in about 2 weeks.
Acceptable Work: Seeking artwork with decorative appeal for the commercial collector and designer market. Considers unframed decorative paintings, watercolor, posters, photos and drawings; usually pairs and series. Prefers trendy, inspirational and decorative art. Prefers airbrush, watercolor, acrylic, oil, gouache, collage and mixed media. Artists represented include Carlos Rios, Andres' Orpinas and Anni Muller. Editions created by collaborating with the artist and by working from an existing painting.
Tips: Always looking for something new and different. "Study the market first. See and learn from what stores and galleries display and sell. For trends we follow the furniture market as well as bath, kitchen and all household accessories. Send slides or photos of your work, and give me a call approximately two weeks from contact and please be patient. I answer all inquiries personally."

TED SCHWARTZ FINE ARTS, Box 3033, Colorado Springs CO 80934. (719)578-5910. Owner: Ted Schwartz. Estab. 1980. Art publisher/distributor handling handpulled originals for galleries, frame stores and designers. Approached by 10-20 artists/year. Publishes and distributes the work of 2-5 emerging and 5-10 mid-career artists/year. Payment method is negotiated. "We purchase art outright on per piece basis. Range paid $10-100." Negotiates rights purchased. Does not require exclusive representation. Send query letter with brochure showing art style and tearsheets, photographs and slides. Samples are not filed and are returned only if requested by artist. Reports back to the artist regarding his query/submission within 2 weeks. Write to schedule an appointment to show a portfolio which should include original/final art.
Acceptable Work: Seeking art for the serious collector, commercial collector and designer market. Works with original printmakers only. "We are interested in *high quality* contemporary and representational imagery. Most interested in mezzotints, etchings and collographs." Prefers individual works of art: 30×40″. Artists represented include Bill Wheeler, Jack Willis and Tony Saladino. Editions created by collaborating with the artist.
Tips: "Send photos (slides, etc.) showing quality of work with biography, pricing requirements, etc. No offset lithographs. Popular subjects include landscapes, contemporary abstract, seascapes, etc."

SGL, Suite A, 190 Shepard Ave., Wheeling IL 60090. (708)215-2911. Vice President: Mr. Rami Ron. Estab. 1984. Art publisher/distributor handling art for qualified art galleries. Approached by 50 artists/year. Publishes/distributes the work of unlimited artists/year. Payment method is negotiated. Negotiates rights purchased. Requires exclusive representation. Provides a written contract. Send query letter with resume, tearsheets, photographs, slides and all possible materials defining work. Samples are not filed and are returned. Reports back to the artist regarding his query/submission within 1 month. To show a portfolio, mail color tearsheets and slides.
Acceptable Work: Seeking artwork with creative artistic expression for the serious collector. We are open to all media. Prefers original themes. Prefers individual works of art. Maximum size no limit. Artists represented include Frederik Hart, Frank Gallo and Felix de Weldon. Editions created by collaborating with artists.
Tips: "We look for new, exciting ideas. We find most artists through personal recommendations, trade shows and magazines."

*SOMERSET HOUSE PUBLISHING CORP., 10688 Haddington, Houston TX 77043. Contact: New Art Department. Clients: 5,000 retail art galleries. Approached by 50-100 artists/year. Publishes 1 emerging, 5 mid-career and 1 established artist/year. Payment method is negotiated. Send query letter with slides. Samples are filed or returned. Reports within months. To show a portfolio, mail slides and photographs. Considers saleability of artwork when establishing payment. Buys first rights.

Acceptable Work: Seeking artwork with creative artistic expression, fashionableness and decorative appeal for the serious collector, commercial collector and designer market. Artists represented include G. Harvey, Tim Cox, Dennis Schmidt, Paula Vaughan, Barbara Mock and Vivian Hollan Swain. Editions created by collaborating with the artist and by working from an existing painting. Special interests: nautical/seascapes and wildlife themes.

Tips: "Submit a good variety of slides or photos not already in print."

SOUTHEASTERN WILDLIFE EXPOSITION, Box 20159, Charleston SC 29413-0159. (803)723-1748. Estab. 1983. Art publisher, distributor and gallery handling limited editions, unlimited editions, handpulled originals and posters for galleries and representatives. Royalties and payment is negotiated. Offers an advance when appropriate. Negotiates rights purchased. Provides in-transit insurance, insurance while work is at firm, promotion and a written contract. Send query letter with resume and slides. Samples are filed or are returned only if requested. Reports only if interested. To show a portfolio, mail tearsheets and slides.

Acceptable Work: Considers pen & ink line drawings, oil, acrylic, pastel, watercolor and mixed media. Also considers carvings and sculpture. Prefers wildlife and individual works of art. Artists represented include Larry Martin, Rick Kelley and Art LaMay. Editions created by collaborating with the artist.

Tips: "Portfolio should include six slides of work, biography, names of shows exhibited in and number of limited editions published."

*SUGARBUSH PRINTS, 4616 Draper Ave., Montreal, Quebec H4A 2P4 Canada. (514)482-8351. Contact: Norma Shadley. Art publisher and distributor. Publishes and distributes limited editions.

Needs: Seeking artwork with creative artistic expression and art for the commercial market. Considers oil, watercolor, acrylic, pastel and mixed media. Artists represented include Paul Rupert. Editions created by collaborating with artist.

First Contact & Terms: Contact through artist agent or send query letter with brochure showing art style or resume and tearsheets, slides, photographs and transparencies. Samples are not filed and are returned. Call to schedule an appointment to show a portfolio or mail appropriate materials: color tearsheets, slides and transparencies. Pays royalties. Offers an advance when appropriate. Buys all rights. Requires exclusive representation of artist.

SUMMERFIELD EDITIONS, 2019 E. 3300 S., Salt Lake City UT 84109. (801)484-0700. Owner: Majid Omana. Estab. 1986. Art publisher, distributor and gallery handling offset reproductions, limited editions, posters and art cards for galleries, department stores, card stores and gift shops. Current clients: Kimball Art Center and Image Conscious. Approached by 100 artists/year. Publishes and distributes the work of 4 emerging and 4 mid-career artists/year. Pays royalties of 10% plus signing fee. Offers an advance when appropriate. Negotiates rights purchased; prefers to buy all rights. Provides a written contract. Send query letter with brochure showing art style or resume, tearsheets, photostats, photocopies, slides and transparencies. Samples are filed. Samples not filed are returned only if requested. Reports back within 3 months if interested. Call or write to schedule an appointment to show a portfolio, or mail tearsheets, slides and transparencies.

Acceptable Work: Seeking artwork with decorative appeal for the serious collector, commercial collector and designer market. Considers pastel, watercolor and mixed media. Prefers Americana, country, Southwest and contemporary themes. Prefers individual works of art. Artists represented include Karen Christensen and Ann Argyle. Editions created by working from an existing painting.

Tips: "Color photos or slides and/or finished art are preferred. We also like to see a resume. We do not want to see uncompleted, sloppy work."

TEE-MARK LTD., Box 2206, Charlotte NC 28247. (704)588-4038. Vice-President: Harvey Plummer. Estab. 1982. Art publisher/distributor handling limited editions (maximum 950 prints) of offset reproductions and handpulled originals for galleries and golf pro shops. Current clients include: USGA, PGA/World Golf Hall of Fame, TPC, *Gold Magazine*. Approached by 10 artists/year. Distributes the work of 2 emerging artists and 1 mid-career artist/year. Publishes the work of 1 and distributes the work of 5 established artists/year. Pays flat fee; $100-1,000, royalties of 10% or on consignment basis: firm receives 35% commission. Payment method is negotiated. Purchases all rights. Requires exclusive representation. Provides in-transit insurance, insurance while work is at firm, promotion, shipping to and from firm and a written contract. Send query letter with brochure showing art style and tearsheets, photographs, photocopies and transparencies. Samples are filed. Reports back to artist regarding his query/submission within 1 month. Call or write to schedule an appointment to show a portfolio which should include original/final art, tearsheets, slides, transparencies and final reproduction/product.

Acceptable Work: Seeking artwork with creative artistic expression and decorative appeal for the serious collector. Considers oil, acrylic, watercolor and mixed media. Tee-Mark specializes in golf artwork. Prefers individual works of art and pairs. Maximum size 40×50″. Artists represented include Ken Reed and Marci Role. Editions created by collaborating with the artist.

TELE GRAPHICS, 607 E. Walnut St., Pasadena CA 91101. President: Ron Rybak. Art publisher/distributor handling limited editions, offset reproductions, unlimited editions and handpulled originals. Clients: galleries, picture framers, interior designers and regional distributors. Approached by 30-40 artists/year. Publishes the work of 1-4 emerging artists/year. Negotiates payment method. Offers advance. Negotiates rights purchased. Requires exclusive representation. Provide promotions, shipping from firm and a written contract. Send query letter with resume and samples. Samples not filed returned only if requested. Reports within 30 days. Call or write to schedule an appointment to show a portfolio, which should include original/final art. Pays for design by the project. Considers skill and experience of artist, and rights purchased when establishing payment.
Acceptable Work: Seeking artwork with decorative appeal for the serious collector. Artists represented include Joy Broe, Sherrie Russell and John Running. Editions created by collaborating with the artist and by working from an existing painting.
Tips: "Be prepared to show as many varied examples of work as possible. Show transparencies or slides plus photographs to show a particular style. We are not interested in seeing only 1 or 2 pieces."

*TERRITORIAL ENTERPRISE, INC., Suite 14, 868 Tahoe Blvd., Incline Village NV 89451. (702)832-7400. FAX: (702)333-9406. Art Director: David Delacroix. Estab. 1858. Art publisher and distributor of various paper products and limited editions. Clients: galleries and frame shops. Current clients include Art Attack and other Lake Tahoe galleries.
Needs: Seeking artwork with creative artistic expression. Considers pen & ink. Prefers unique, different fantasy and romantic themes and styles. Artists represented include Muzzio, Ben Intendi and S. Croce. Editions created by working from an existing painting. Approached by 10 artists/year. Publishes the work of 1-3 emerging artists/year. Publishes and distributes the work of 5 mid-career and 1 established artist/year.
First Contact & Terms: Send query letter with brochure showing art style. Samples are filed. Reports back within 2 weeks. Pays flat fee. Offers advance when appropriate. Buys all rights. Provides shipping from firm.
Tips: "We are only interested in the unique and unusual. We are looking for quality illustration only, no abstract."

VALLEY COTTAGE GRAPHICS, Box 564, Valley Cottage NY 10989. (914)358-7605 or 358-7606; or (800)431-2902. Distributors: Rosemary Maschak or Ms. Sheila Berkowitz. Publishes "top of the line" unlimited edition posters and prints. Clients: galleries and custom frame shops nationwide. Buys reproduction rights (exclusively) and/or negotiates exclusive distribution rights to "special, innovative, existing fine art publications." Query first; submit slides, photographs of unpublished originals, or samples of published pieces available for exclusive distribution. Reports within 2-3 weeks.
Acceptable Work: Prefers large, contemporary pieces; 18x24″, 22x28″, 24x36″.

*VARGAS & ASSOCIATES ART PUBLISHING, Back Bay Annex, Box 1410, Boston MA 02117. (617)482-7680. FAX: (617)482-2257. Publisher: Elba Vargas. Estab. 1988. Art publisher and distributor. Publishes and distributes serigraphs, limited and open edition offset reproductions. Clients: galleries, frame shops, museums and decorators with worldwide distribution.
Needs: Seeking artwork with creative artistic expression, for the serious collector and commercial market. Considers oil, watercolor, acrylic, pastel pen & ink and mixed media. Prefers ethnic themes. Artists represented include Paul Goodnight, William Tolliver, Arlene Case, James Ransome and Ray Beasley. Approached by over 100 artists/year. Publishes/distributes the work of about 30 artists.
First Contact & Terms: Send query letter with resume, slides and/or photographs. Samples are filed or are returned by SASE if requested by artist. Reports back only if interested. To show portfolio, mail photographs. Payment method is negotiated. Offers an advance. Requires exclusive representation of the artist.

VOYAGEUR ART, 2828 Anthony Ln. S, Minneapolis MN 55418. President: Lowell Thompson. Estab. 1980. Art publisher of limited editions, posters, unlimited editions and original lithographs for galleries, frame shops, poster shops, retail catalog companies and corporations. Approached by 200 artists/year. Publishes and distributes the work of 1-2 emerging artists/year. Publishes the work of 8-10 and distributes the work of 2 mid-career artists/year. Publishes the work of 15 and distributes the work of 2 established artists/year. Payment method is negotiated. Prefers exclusive representation of artist. Provides in-transit insurance, insurance while work is at firm, promotion and a written contract. Send query letter with brochure or resume, tearsheets, photographs, slides or transparencies and SASE. Samples are filed or returned only if requested. Reports back within 2 months. Artists represented include Arnold Alamiz, Linda Roberts and Daniel Smith. Editions created by collaborating with the artist and by working from an existing painting.

© 1989 Paul Goodnight

"Paul Goodnight is our biggest seller," says Elba Vargas of Vargas & Associates of Boston. In this print "Listen to the Hipbones," it is unclear whether these women are African-Americans, Sengaleses, Haitians or Brazilians. As the director of the Museum of the National Center of Afro-American Art says, "It is the root of their gestures that gives the picture its sense of kindred expression."

Acceptable Work: Considers oil and acrylic paintings, pastel, watercolor, tempera, and mixed media. Prefers traditional works with original themes, primitivism and photorealistic works. "Will consider all submissions."

JAMES D. WERLINE STUDIO, 4938 Beechwood Rd., Cincinnati OH 45244. (513)831-5004. Partner: Dee A. Werline. Estab. 1978. Art publisher handling limited editions of offset reproductions for galleries and museums. Approached by 8-10 artists/year. Publishes the work of 2 established artists/year. Pays royalties of 10% (wholesale). Buys reprint rights. Requires exclusive representation. Provides insurance, shipping from firm and a written contract. Send query letter with brochure, resume, tearsheets and slides. Samples are filed or returned only if requested by artist. Reports back within 3-4 weeks. Call to schedule an appointment to show a portfolio, or mail original/final art, color tearsheets, slides and final reproduction/product.
Acceptable Work: Seeking artwork with creative artistic expression for the serious collector. Considers oil, acrylic, pastel, watercolor and tempera. Prefers original themes and individual works of art. Artists represented include Debbie Hook, James D. Werline and Don Paul Kirk.

EDWARD WESTON EDITIONS, 19355 Business Center Dr., Northridge CA 91324. (818)885-1044. Vice President/Secretary: Ann Weston. Art publisher, distributor and gallery handling limited and unlimited editions, offset reproductions and handpulled originals. Approached by hundreds of artists/year. Publishes and distributes the works of 1-2 emerging artists and as many established artists/year as possible. Pays flat fee; royalty of 10% of lowest selling price; or negotiates payment method. Sometimes offers advance. Buys first rights, all rights, reprint rights or negotiates rights purchased. Requires exclusive representation. Provides promotion and written contract. Send brochure and samples to be kept on file. Prefers original work as samples. Samples not filed returned by SASE. "Publisher is not responsible for returning art samples." Reports within 2 months. Write for appointment to show portfolio.

Acceptable Work: Seeking artwork with decorative appeal for the serious collector, commercial collector and designer market. Considers all media. Especially likes "new, different, unusual techniques and style." Artists represented include Elke Sommer, Stevel Leal, Charles Bragg and P. Noyer. Editions created by collaberating with the artist and by working from an existing painting.

WINDY CREEK INC., 1855 S. 350 E, Bluffton IN 46714. (219)824-5666. President: Bob Hayden. Art publisher and distributor of limited editions, unlimited editions and posters for galleries, mail order and gift shops. Publishes/distributes the work of 3 artists/year. Payment method is negotiated. Offers an advance when appropriate. Negotiates rights purchased. Provides promotion. Send query letter with brochure showing art style or photocopies. Samples are filed or are returned only if requested. Reports back within weeks. Write to schedule an appointment to show a portfolio.
Acceptable Work: Considers pen & ink line drawings, oil, acrylic and watercolor. Prefers wildlife art. Prefers individual works of art and unframed series.

ZOLA FINE ART, 8163 Melrose Ave., Los Angeles CA 90046. (213)655-6060. President: Lisa Zola. Estab. 1986. Art publisher/distributor/gallery. Distributes original artwork in variety of media. Clients: banks, corporations, hotels; also distributes to art consultants. Current clients include: Southern California Gas Company, Bateman Eichler, Hill Richards and Kenneth Leventhal & Company. Approached by 100 artists/year. Distributes the work of 20-30 emerging, 20-30 mid-career and 20-30 established artists/year. Payment method is negotiated. Provides insurance while work is at firm, promotion, return shipping and a written contract. Send query letter with brochure, resume, tearsheets, photographs, slides or transparencies. Samples are returned. Reports back within 1 month. To show a portfolio mail slides, transparencies, bio, price list and SASE.
Acceptable Work: Seeking art for the serious collector and designer market. Considers mixed media, gouache, oil acrylic, pastel, watercolor, drawings, sculpture, ceramic and original prints. Prefers contemporary styles and landscapes. Prefers individual works of art and unframed series. Artists represented include Gerald Brommer, Linda Vista and Nick Capaci. Editions created by collaborating with the artist.
Tips: "I don't want actual artwork sent initially. Portfolios should include several examples of work, detail photos, any press clippings, bios and price list." Preferred subjects are landscapes, architectural and non-objective. Label slides and photographs with size name and medium. Include a price list reference."

Other Art Publishers and Distributors

Each year we contact all firms currently listed in *Artist's Market* requesting they give us updated information for our next edition. We also mail listing questionnaires to new and established firms which have not been included in past editions. The following art publishers and distributors either did not respond to our request to update their listings for 1991 (if they indicated a reason, it is noted in parenthese after their name), or they are firms which did not return our questionnaire for a new listing (designated by the words "declined listing" after their names).

Keith Alexander Editions
Art Access, Inc.
Art Beats (asked to be deleted)
The Art Group
Art Selections; New England Graphic Images
Art Source (asked to be deleted)
Atlantic Gallery Publications
Robert Bane Editions (declined listing)
Become A Poster (out of business)
Mitchell Beja (declined listing)
Canadian Art Prints Inc.
Michelle Carter & Associates
Joan Cawley Gallery (declined listing)
The Chasen Portfolio
Cirrus Editions
Class Publications, Inc.
Collectors Editions (declined listing)
Colonia Art Publications

Creativ Haus Incorporated
Del Bello Gallery
Fidelity Arts of California, Inc. (declined listing)
Fine Art Resources, Inc. (asked to be deleted)
The 5 G Collection Art Plus & Collectors Art Plus
Foxfire Div., TOB, Inc.
Gallery in a Vineyard
Gallerie Vendome Inc. (declined listing)
Geme Art Inc.
Graphic Originals Inc., (moved; no forwarding address)
Haddad's Fine Arts Inc.
Har-El Printers and Publishers
Impact
Island Art Publishers
Janus Lithographs
Kane Graphics (declined listing)
Lakar Publishing
Lynns Prints (asked to be deleted)

Mirage Editions (declined listing)
Mixed-Media, Ltd.
Morosstudio Originals, Inc. (declined listing)
National Art Source & Services Corp. (out of business)
Oaksprings Impressions
Panache Editions Ltd.
Rave Collections
Segal Fine Art (declined listing)
Shadowlight Impressions
Springdale Graphics
Stanton Arts
Sterling Portfolio, Inc.
John Szoke Graphics Inc.
Touchstone Publishers (declined listing)
The Winn Art Group (declined listing)
Diane Wolf Gallery (moved; no forwarding address)

Book Publishers

Once run by people who considered books something more than moneymakers, book publishing has grown into an international megabusiness. The major publishing houses are currently in the hands of a few. Time and Warner merged, so that now Little, Brown & Company has two parents; Robert Murdock owns Harper & Row, which recently merged with William Collins; Robert Maxwell owns Macmillan, Inc., which includes Charles Scribner & Son and Atheneum; and S.I. Newhouse owns Random House, which includes Alfred A. Knopf, Crown Publishers, Vintage Books, Pantheon Books, and over a dozen other imprints. The industry is reeling from this unprecedented number of changes in ownership and leadership, extraordinarily high advances to authors, and a huge number of returns from bookstores. There will probably be more staff reduction and production cost-cutting, which, on the bright side, lead to more freelance opportunities.

Art directors at publishing houses call on freelance artists to design and illustrate book covers and interiors, as well as catalogs and direct mail pieces. Book design utilizes artists skilled in typography, type specification and layout. The designer may initiate the ideas for text illustration or the suggestion may come from the art director during initial planning stages.

Most assignments for freelance work are for jackets/covers. The cover must represent the contents of the book and attract the consumer. While the cover establishes the relative importance of the author, title and subtitle, it must also identify its market—a romance novel requires a different cover than a scholarly title.

Covers for trade titles (larger format books almost exclusively sold in bookstores) have adopted a looser style of illustration rather than the traditional realistic approach. Many houses are publishing paperback originals, often in series form, skipping the hardcover editions completely. Thus, their covers must convey the book's uniqueness while tying it to a series. The nicely designed trade paperback is the format currently favored for contemporary fiction. Often tagged "quality" paperbacks, their covers show inventive typography and matte-paper jackets. Louise Fili was one of the creators of this look. Read her Close-up in this section to see what she believes a book cover should be.

Mass-market titles (books sold on newsstands as well as in bookstores) especially rely on their covers to catch the consumer's eye. They often employ bright colors and usually focus on one or two of the book's characters or a symbol that summarizes the story.

It seems that children's books are the most dynamic area of the market. According to the Association of American Publishers, store sales of juvenile hardcover books grew 19.1 percent last year, compared to a 1.8 percent growth in adult hardcover sales. The number of children age 12 and under is expected to rise to 50 million by 1995, from 46 million now. Time/Warner is starting a book club for children and Doubleday may do the same. According to an article in *Publishers Weekly*, as the competition for children's books heightens, art directors are becoming more daring and experimental in creating a new look. They are moving away from ultra-realism and expressing a need for fresh work, more sophisticated graphics, and an emphasis on mood and character.

For those appalled at the prospect of publishing conglomerates offering as much diversity of style and opinion as the three major networks, there is hope in the small presses, which continue to grow as a force in the publishing field. There are now between 14,000 to 20,000 small publishers. In independent bookstores, books produced by small alternative publishers stand on shelves next to those of major houses. Small presses feature literature, New Age, regional, instructional, travel and computer books. With an emphasis on quality, small press books generally use conceptual illustrations that border on fine art.

Publishers large and small have turned to computer technologies to streamline production. Computers are also being used for book design, page makeup and for actual artwork. Lisa Torri, of Brooks/Cole Publishing Company in California, says, "There is an extremely strong trend in college textbook publishing toward the use of computers as both an illustration and design tool. We utilize the computer in every aspect of our design department."

Artwork is generally geared to the specific theme of a book. Therefore, art directors call upon a variety of styles to fill their diverse needs. Have your samples on file with as many publishers as possible, so you will be represented when the need arises for your type of work. Write and request a catalog of a publisher's titles to get an idea of the type of books it produces and go to bookstores to get an overview of what is being done.

Art directors generally prefer to receive five to ten samples (never originals) along with a concise cover letter stating what you have to offer. If you are called for a portfolio review, show your best work in the area the art director shows a need. Also include a few pieces that show other specialties in case the art director might also have other interests.

Payment varies according to the project. Fees depend upon the expected sales of the book, the format (hardcover or paperback), the complexity of the project, deadlines and rights purchased. Additional factors involve reuse of the artwork in promotional materials and reprints. Make sure you review all aspects of the assignment with the art buyer.

In this section's listings, we have included the types and approximate number of books published to give you a better understanding of the scope of the house you are considering. We have also broken the listings into subheads to give you as many specifics as possible on the three main job opportunity areas in book publishing—book design, jackets/covers and text illustration.

For further information on this market, refer to *Writer's Market, Novel and Short Story Writer's Market, Children's Writer's and Illustrator's Market, Literary Market Place, Books in Print,* and *International Directory of Little Magazines and Small Presses.* The trade magazine *Publishers Weekly* provides weekly updates on the industry.

*ABARIS BOOKS, 42 Memorial Plaza, Pleasantville NY 10570. (914)747-9298. FAX: (914)747-4166. Managing Editor: Elizabeth A. Pratt. Estab. 1973. Book publisher. Publishes hardcover originals and paperback reprints. Types of books include scholarly art and art history books. Specializes in prints and drawings. Publishes 6-8 titles/year. Recent titles include *The Royal Horse and Rider* and several volumes of *The Illustrated Bartsch.* 25% require freelance design. Book catalog free on request.
Needs: Approached by 25-30 freelance designers/year. Works with 2-3 freelance designers/year. Prefers designers with experience in art books and museum catalogs. "We are looking for very specialized experience in this area. It is a prerequisite not just a preference." Also uses freelance artists for jacket/cover, book, direct mail and catalog design. Works on assignment only.
First Contact & Terms: Send query letter with resume and appropriate samples, slides and photos. Samples are filed. Reports back within 2 months only if interested. Write to schedule an appointment to show a portfolio. Portfolio should include photostats, original/final art and photographs.
Book Design: Assigns 2-3 freelance design jobs/year. Pays by the project.
Jackets/Covers: Assigns 2-3 freelance design jobs/year. Pays by the project.
Tips: Look of design used is "straightforward, clean, simple, elegant (*not* advertising/high-level marketing style). Subdued/understated. Have appropriate experience and recommendations; professional and complete portfolio. Contact by letter first."

 The asterisk before a listing indicates that the listing is new in this edition. New markets are often the most receptive to freelance submissions.

ACADIA PUBLISHING CO., Box 170, Bar Harbor ME 04609. (207)288-9025. President: Frank J. Matter. Independent book producer/packager. Estab. 1981. Publishes hardcover originals, trade paperback originals, hardcover reprints and trade paperback reprints. Publishes nonfiction and fiction. Types of books include biography, cookbooks, instructional, juvenile, reference, history, guides, romance, historical, mainstream/contemporary and literary. Specializes in New England subjects. Publishes 8-10 titles/year. 33% require freelance illustration. Recent titles include *The Eloquent Edge*, *The Lost Tales Of Horatio Alger* and *My Dear Sarah Anne*. Book catalog free for SASE with 1 first-class stamp.

First Contact & Terms: Approached by 100 freelance artists/year. Works with 3 freelance illustrators and 3 freelance designers/year. Works with freelance artists for jacket/cover illustration and design and text illustration. Works on assignment only. Send query letter with resume, tearsheets and SASE. Samples are filed or returned by SASE if requested. Reports back about queries/submissions within 1 month. Call or write to schedule appointment to show portfolio which should include slides, SASE, original/final art, tearsheets, final reproduction/product and slides. Considers complexity of project, skill and experience of artist, project's budget and rights purchased when establishing payment.

Jackets/Covers: Assigns 3 freelance design and 3 freelance illustration jobs/year. Pays by the project; rate negotiated.

Text Illustration: Assigns 3 freelance jobs/year. Pays by the project, $100 minimum.

Tips: "We do not want to see portfolios without querying first and do not send original artwork without inquiring first. Include SASE. New trends include more 4-color art, simplicity, better harmony of text and illustration through research and inspiration of artists and more computer generated art. Book design is leaning toward larger margins and more white space, simple and modern."

A.D. BOOK CO., 6th Floor, 10 E. 39th St., New York NY 10157-0002. (212)889-6500. Art Director: Doris Gordon. Publishes hardcover and paperback originals on advertising design and photography. Publishes 12-15 titles/year; 4-5 require freelance designers; 1-2 require freelance illustrators.

First Contact & Terms: Send query letter which can be kept on file and arrange to show portfolio (4-10 tearsheets). Samples returned by SASE. Buys first rights. Originals returned to artist at job's completion. Free catalog. Advertising design must be contemporary.

Book Design: Pays $100 minimum.

Jackets/Covers: Pays $100 minimum.

AIRMONT PUBLISHING CO., INC., 401 Lafayette St., New York NY 10003. (212)598-0222. Vice President/Publisher: Barbara J. Brett. "Airmont Books are all reprints of classics. We are not buying any cover art, but at any time in the future when we may need art, we will consider artists we have worked with on our Avalon Books, published by our Thomas Bouregy Company. See that listing."

ALLYN AND BACON INC., College Division, 160 Gould St., Needham MA 02194. (617)455-1200. Cover Administrator: Linda Knowles Dickinson. Publishes hardcover and paperback textbooks. Publishes over 120 titles/year; 50% require freelance cover designs. Recent titles include *Personal Selling*, *Marketing*, *College Physics* and *Understanding Families*.

First Contact & Terms: Approached by 20-30 freelance artists/year. Needs artists/designers experienced in preparing art and mechanicals for print production. Designers must be strong in book cover design and contemporary type treatment.

Jackets/Covers: Assigns 85 freelance design jobs/year; assigns 2-3 freelance illustration jobs/year. Pays for design by the project, $300-550. Pays for illustration by the project, $150-500. Prefers sophisticated, abstract style. Prefers pen & ink, airbrush, charcoal/pencil, watercolor, acrylic, oil, collage and calligraphy. "Always looking for good calligraphers."

Tips: "Keep stylistically and technically up to date. Learn *not* to over-design: read instructions, and ask questions. Introductory letter must state experience and include at least photocopies of your work. We prefer designers/artists based in the Boston area. Let me thumb through your portfolio at my own rate. Don't give me a pony show over every piece. Don't pester me. If I like what I see, and you can stay on budget, you'll probably get an assignment. Being pushy closes the door."

AMERICAN ATHEIST PRESS, 7215 Cameron Rd., Austin TX 78752. (512)458-1244. Editor: R. Murray-O'Hair. Estab. 1963. "The American Atheist Press, a nonprofit, nonpolitical, educational publisher, specializes in the publication of atheist and freethought paperbacks and reprints, as well as criticism of religion. It also publishes a monthly magazine, the *American Atheist*." Publishes 8 titles/year; 40% require freelance illustration. Recent titles include *Women, Food, and Sex in History*.

First Contact & Terms: Works with 60 freelance artists/year. Send query letter with brochure showing art style; "anything showing style is fine." Samples are filed. Reports back within 3 months on submissions only if interested. Does not report back on queries. Originals returned to artist at job's completion if artist requests. Call or write to schedule an appointment to show a portfolio, which should include roughs, original/final art, photostats, tearsheets or final reproduction/product. Considers complexity of project, skill and experience of artist and project's budget when establishing payment. Negotiates rights purchased.

Book Design: Assigns 3 freelance illustration jobs/year. Pays by the project, $25-500.
Jackets/Covers: Assigns 3-6 freelance design and 3-6 freelance illustration jobs/year. Pays by the project, $100-250.
Text Illustration: Assigns 3 freelance jobs/year. Pays by the project, $25-500.
Tips: "If the artist has a minimum price for his work, he should include that with his basic information; it saves time later on. Often a 'cause' press cannot meet an artist's monetary expectations."

APPLEZABA PRESS, Box 4134, Long Beach CA 90804. (213)591-0015. Publisher: D.H. Lloyd. Estab. 1977. Specializes in poetry and fiction paperbacks. Publishes 2-4 titles/year. 40% require freelance illustration. Recent titles include *Gridlock: Anthology of Poetry about Southern California*.
First Contact & Terms: Approached by 20 freelance artists/year. Works with 4 freelance illustrators and 1 freelance designer/year. Mainly uses art for covers. Works on assignment only. Send query letter with brochure, tearsheets and photographs to be kept on file. Samples not filed are returned by SASE. Reports only if interested. Originals returned to artist at job's completion. Portfolio should include 8-10 samples, such as slides or photocopies of b&w work. Considers project's budget and rights purchased when establishing payment. Rights purchased vary according to project.
Jackets/Covers: Assigns 1 freelance design job/year. Prefers pen & ink and collage. Pays by the project, $30-100.
Tips: "Usually use cover art that depicts the book title and contents. Usually b&w and one color." The most common mistake illustrators and designers make in presenting their work is "sending samples of art that is inconsistent with our needs, i.e., we receive many fantasy illustration samples and we don't publish fantasy."

APRIL PUBLICATIONS, INC., Box 1000, Staten Island NY 10314. Art Director: Verna Hart. Specializes in paperback nonfiction. Publishes 25 titles/year.
First Contact & Terms: Works with 10 freelance artists/year. Works on assignment only. Send query letter with samples to be kept on file. Prefers photostats as samples. Samples not filed are returned by SASE. Reports only if interested. Considers project's budget and rights purchased when establishing payment. Buys all rights.

ARCsoft PUBLISHERS, Box 132, Woodsboro MD 21798. (301)845-8856. President: A.R. Curtis. Specializes in original paperbacks, especially in space science, computers and miscellaneous high-tech subjects. Publishes 12 titles/year.
First Contact & Terms: Works with 5 freelance artists/year. Works on assignment only. Send query letter with brochure, resume and non-returnable samples. Samples not filed are not returned. Reports back within 3 months only if interested. Original work not returned after job's completion. Considers complexity of project, skill and experience of artist, project's budget and turnaround time when establishing payment. Buys all rights.
Book Design: Assigns 5 freelance illustration jobs/year. Pays by the project.
Jackets/Covers: Assigns 1 freelance design and 5 freelance illustration jobs/year. Pays by the project.
Text Illustration: Assigns 5 freelance jobs/year. Pays by the project.
Tips: "Artists should not send in material they want back. All materials received become the property of ARCsoft Publishers."

ART DIRECTION BOOK CO., 6th Floor, 10 E. 39th St., New York NY 10157-0002. (212)889-6500. Art Director: Doris Gordon. Specializes in hardcover and paperback books on advertising art and design. Publishes 15 titles/year; 50% require freelance design.
First Contact & Terms: Works with 5 freelance artists/year. Professional artists only. Call for appointment. Drop off portfolio. Samples returned by SASE. Originals returned to artist at job's completion. Buys one-time rights.
Book Design: Assigns 10 freelance jobs/year. Uses artists for layout and mechanicals. Pays by the job, $100 minimum.
Jackets/Covers: Assigns 10 freelance design jobs/year. Pays by the job, $100 minimum.

ARTIST'S MARKET, Writer's Digest Books, 1507 Dana Ave., Cincinnati OH 45207. Contact: Lauri Miller. Annual hardcover directory of freelance markets for graphic and fine artists. Send b&w samples—photographs, photostats or good quality photocopies of artwork. "Since *Artist's Market* is published only once a year, submissions are kept on file for the next upcoming edition until selections are made. Material is then returned by SASE." Buys one-time rights.
Needs: Buys 50-60 illustrations/year. "I need examples of art that have been sold to one of the listings in *Artist's Market*. Thumb through the book to see the type of art I'm seeking. The art must have been freelanced; it cannot have been done as staff work. Include the name of the listing that purchased the work, what the art was used for, and the payment you received." Pays $25 to holder of reproduction rights and free copy of *Artist's Market* when published.

ARTS END BOOKS, Box 162, Newton MA 02168. (617)965-2478. Editor and Publisher: Marshall Brooks. Specializes in hardcover and paperback originals and reprints of contemporary literature. Publishes 2 titles/year. Recent titles include *Rattlesnake Logic*, by Leonard Cirino.
First Contact & Terms: Approached by 60 freelance artists/year. Please query. Photocopies are OK.
Book Design: Pays by the project.
Jackets/Covers: Pays by the project.
Text Illustration: Prefers pen & ink work. Pays by the project.
Tips: "We have more of a fine arts emphasis than not. Mainstream commercial artwork is not suited to the work that we do. Originality is essential. The artwork used is a cross between Pierre Bonnard, Rockwell Kent and Vanessa Bell."

ASHLEY BOOKS INC., 4600 W. Commercial Blvd., Tamarac FL 33319. (305)731-2221. President: Billie Young. Estab. 1971. Publishes hardcover originals; controversial, medical and timely fiction and nonfiction. Publishes 50 titles/year; 40% require freelance design or illustration. Recent titles include *Vinnie and the Malpractice Epidemic*. Mainly uses artists for book subjects, also uses artists for promotional aids.
First Contact & Terms: Prefers artists experienced with book publishing or record album jacket experience. Do not send material that needs to be returned. Arrange interview to show portfolio. Buys first rights. Negotiates payment. Free catalog for SASE with 45¢ postage.
Book Design: Assigns 35 jobs/year. Uses artists for layout and paste-up.
Jackets/Covers: Assigns 35 jobs/year. "Cover should catch the eye. A cover should be such that it will sell books and give an idea at a glance what the book is about. A cover should be eye catching so that it draws one to read further."
Tips: "As a result of an upsurge in consumer interest in cooking, more cookbooks will be produced generating more illustrations and more artwork."

*ASIAN HUMANITIES PRESS, Box 3523, Fremont CA 94539. (415)659-8272. FAX: (415)659-8272. Publisher: M.K. Jain. Estab. 1976. Book publisher. Publishes hardcover originals, trade paperback originals and reprints and textbooks. Types of books include reference and literary fiction books on religion and philosophy. Specializes in Asian literature, religions, languages and philosophies. Publishes 10 titles/year. Recent titles include *The Wind and The Waves: Four Modern Korean Poets*. 80% require freelance illustration; 100% require freelance design. Book catalog free by request.
Needs: Approached by 10 freelance artists/year. Works with 2 freelance illustrators and designers/year. Buys 8 freelance illustrations/year. Prefers artists with experience in scholarly and literary works relating to Asia. Uses freelance artists mainly for cover/jacket design. Also uses freelance artists for jacket/cover illustration and catalog design.
First Contact & Terms: Send query letter with brochure, resume, tearhseets and photostats. Samples are filed. Reports back to the artist only if interested. To show a portfolio, mail photostats and tearsheets. Rights purchased vary according to project. Originals are not returned at job's completion.
Jackets/Covers: Assigns 10 freelance design and 8 freelance illustration jobs/year. Prefers "camera ready mechanicals with all type in place."
Tips: "The best way for a freelance graphic artist to get an assignment is to have a great portfolio and relevant referrals. Familiarity with Asian art is helpful, though not mandatory."

*THE ASSOCIATED PUBLISHERS, INC., 1407 14th St. NW, Washington DC 20005-3704. (202)265-1441. Managing Director: W. Leanna Miles. Estab. 1920. Book publisher. Publishes textbooks. Types of books include history and "all materials pertaining to the Black experience." Publishes about 2 titles/year. Recent titles include *The Role of the Black Church* and *The Father of Black History*. 25% require freelance illustration; 50% require freelance design. Book catalog available for $2.
Needs: Approached by 3-5 freelance artists/year. Works with 2 freelance illustrators and designers/year. Prefers artists with experience in the Black experience. Uses freelance artists mainly for annual study kits. Also uses freelance artists for jacket/cover and text illustration; book, direct mail and catalog design. Works on assignment only.
First Contact & Terms: Send query letter with brochure and resume. Samples are filed. Reports back to the artist only if interested. Negotiates rights purchased.
Book Design: Assigns 2-5 freelance design and illustration jobs/year. Pays by the project, $200-1,500.
Jackets/Covers: Assigns 2-5 freelance design and illustration jobs/year. Pays by the project, $200-1,500.
Text Illustration: Assigns 2-5 freelance design and illustration jobs/year. Pays by the project, $200-1,500. Prefers a mixture of media and style.

*AUGSBURG PUBLISHING HOUSE, Box 1209, 426 S. 5th St., Minneapolis MN 55440. (612)330-3300. Contact: Photo-Editor/Designers. Publishes paperback Protestant/Lutheran books (45 titles/year), religious education materials, audiovisual resources, periodicals. Recent titles include *The Church's Bible*, *Witness Sunday School Curriculum* and *Wail No More*? Also uses artists for catalog cover design; advertising circulars; advertising layout, design and illustration. Negotiates pay, b&w and color.

First Contact & Terms: "Majority, but not all, of the artists are local." Works on assignment only. Call, write, or send slides or photocopies. Reports in 5-8 weeks. Samples not filed are returned by SASE. Reports back on future assignment possibilities. Provide brochure, flyer, tearsheet, good photocopies and 35mm transparencies; if artist is willing to have samples retained, they are kept on file. Buys all rights on a work-for-hire basis. May require designers to supply overlays on color work.
Book Design: Assigns 45 jobs/year. Uses designers primarily for cover design, occasionally inside illustration, sample chapter openers. Pays $600-1,000, cover design.
Text Illustration: Negotiates pay for 1-, 2-, and 4-color.
Tips: The most common mistake illustrators and designers make in presenting their work is "lack of knowledge of company product and the contemporary Christian market."

AVON BOOKS, Art Department, 105 Madison Ave., New York NY 10016. (212)481-5663. Publisher: Carolyn Reidy. Art Director: Tom Egner. Publishes paperback originals and reprints—mass market, trade and juvenile. Estab. 1942. Publishes 300 titles/year; 85% require freelance illustrators.
First Contact & Terms: Works with 60 freelance artists/year. Works on assignment only. Send resume and samples to be filed or drop off portfolio. Accepts any type sample. Samples returned only by request. Reports within 1 month. Works on assignment only. Original work returned to the artist after job's completion. Considers complexity of the project, skill and experience of the artist and project's budget when establishing payment.
Book Design: Assigns 20 freelance jobs/year. Uses artists for all aspects. Payment varies.
Jackets/Covers: Assigns 150 freelance design and 150 freelance illustration jobs/year.
Tips: "Portfolio should include a sample for our files; a cover letter or resume is a plus. Also include a response card. I do not want to see illustrations for very young children's books, editorial or fashion illustration."

BAEN BOOKS, 260 Fifth Ave., New York NY 10001. (212)532-4111. Publisher: Jim Baen. Editor: Toni Weisskopf. Estab. 1983. Publishes science fiction and fantasy. Publishes 84-96 titles/year. 75% require freelance illustration; 80% require freelance design. Recent titles include *Sassinak* and *Warhorse*. Book catalog free for request.
First Contact & Terms: Approached by 1,000 freelance artists/year. Works with 10 freelance illustrators and 4 freelance designers/year. Buys 64 freelance illustrations/year. Send query letter with slides, transparencies (color only) and SASE. Samples are filed. "Happy with artists we are currently using, so not presently reviewing portfolios." Reports back within 1 month. Originals returned to artist at job's completion. Considers complexity of project, skill and experience of artist, project's budget, turnaround time and rights purchased when establishing payment. Buys exclusive North American rights.
Jackets/Covers: Assigns 64 freelance design and 64 freelance illustration jobs/year. Pays by the project, $200 minimum, design; $1,000 minimum, illustration.
Tips: The best way for a freelance illustrator to get an assignment is to show a "good portfolio, high quality samples within science fiction, romantic realism genre. Do not send black-and-white illustrations."

BANDANNA BOOKS, 319 Anacapa St., Santa Barbara CA 93101. Publisher: Sasha Newborn. Estab. 1981. Publishes textbooks, trade paperback originals and reprints. Publishes nonfiction and fiction. Types of books include language, philosophy, classics and poetry. Specializes in classics and humanism. Publishes 4 titles/year. 50% require freelance illustration. Recent titles include *Sappho*, *Ghalib's Ghazals* and *Areopagitica*. Book catalog not available.
First Contact & Terms: Approached by 10 freelance artists/year. Buys 10 freelance illustrations/year. Works with illlustrators mainly for woodblock silhouette art. Also works with artists for cover and text illustration. Send query letter with SASE and photographs. Samples are not filed and are returned by SASE only if requested. Reports back about queries/submissions within 6 weeks only if interested. Originals not returned to artist at job's completion. To show a portfolio mail thumbnails and photographs. Considers project's budget when establishing payment.
Book Design: Pays by the project, $50-200.
Jackets/Covers: Prefers b&w scratchboard or woodblock, medallion bust or silhouettes, miniatures, engraving and coin-minting. Pays by the project, $50-200.
Tips: "I need pieces that work very small."

BASCOM COMMUNICATIONS CO., 399 E. 72nd St., New York NY 10021. President: Betsy Ryan. Estab. 1983. Specializes in juvenile and adult hardcover and paperback originals. Publishes 10 titles/year; 50% require freelance illustration. Recent titles include *The Doctor's Guide to Headache Relief* and *Hampstead High* (series).
First Contact & Terms: Approached by 150 freelance artists/year. Works with 3 freelance artists/year. Works on assignment only. Send query letter with brochure showing art style. Samples are filed and are not returned. Does not report back. Originals returned to artist at job's completion. Write to schedule an appointment to show a portfolio, which should include original/final art, tearsheets and final reproduction/product. Considers

complexity of project, project's budget and turnaround time when establishing payment.

Book Design: Assigns 5 freelance design and 5 freelance illustration jobs/year. Pays by the hour, $15 minimum.

Jackets/Covers: Assigns 5 freelance design and 5 freelance illustration jobs/year. Pays by the project.

Text Illustration: Assigns 5 freelance jobs/year. Pays by the project.

*BEHRMAN HOUSE, INC., 235 Watchung Ave., West Orange NJ 07052. (201)669-0447. FAX: (201)669-9769. Projects Editor: Adam Siegel. Estab. 1921. Book publisher. Publishes textbooks. Types of books include pre-school, juvenile, young adult, history (all of Jewish subject matter) and Jewish texts and textbooks. Specializes in Jewish books for children and adults. Publishes 7 titles/year. Recent titles include *A Child's Bible, My Jewish World* and *How Do I Decide?* 70% require freelance illustration; 80% require freelance design. Book catalog free by request.

Needs: Approached by 10 freelance artists/year. Works with 4 freelance illustrators and 6 freelance designers/year. Buys 5 freelance illustrations/year. Prefers artists with experience in illustrating for children; "helpful if Jewish background." Uses freelance artists mainly for children's textbooks. Also uses freelance artists for jacket/cover illustration and design, book design and text illustration. Works on assignment only.

First Contact & Terms: Send query letter with brochure, resume, photocopies and photostats. Samples are filed. Reports in 1 month. To show a portfolio, call or mail b&w photostats and original/final art. Rights purchased vary according to project. Originals are returned at the job's completion.

Book Design: Assigns 5 freelance design and 3 freelance illustration jobs/year. Pays by the project.

Jackets/Covers: Assigns 6 freelance design and 4 freelance illustration jobs/year. Pays by the project.

Text Illustration: Assigns 6 freelance design and 4 freelance illustration jobs/year. Pays by the project.

Tips: "Send us a sample of work, and if style and quality of work is appropriate for one of our projects, we will contact artist."

*THE BENJAMIN/CUMMINGS PUBLISHING CO., 390 Bridge Pkwy., Redwood City CA 94065. Contact: Production Manager. Specializes in college textbooks in biology, chemistry, computer science, mathematics, nursing and allied health. Publishes 40 titles/year; 90% require freelance design and illustration.

First Contact & Terms: Approached by 100 freelance artists/year. Works with 25-75 freelance artists/year. Specializes in 1, 2, and 4-color illustrations-technical, biological and medical. "Heavily illustrated books tying art and text together in market-appropriate and innovative approaches. Our biologic texts require trained bio/med illustrators. Proximity to Bay Area is a plus, but not essential." Works on assignment only. Original artwork not returned to artist at job's completion. Send query letter with resume and samples. Samples returned only if requested. Pays by piece, $20-150 average.

Book Design: Assigns 30 jobs/year. "From manuscript, designer prepares specs and layouts for review. After approval, final specs and layouts are required. On our books, which are dummied, very often the designer is contracted as dummier at a separate per page fee." Pays $3-6.50/page, dummy.

Jackets/Covers: Assigns 40 jobs/year. Pays by the job, $500-2,000.

*ROBERT BENTLEY PUBLISHERS, 1000 Massachusetts Ave., Cambridge MA 02138. (617)547-4170. Publisher: Michael Bentley. Book publisher. Publishes hardcover originals and reprints and trade paperback originals. Publishes reference books. Specializes in automotive technology and automotive how-to. Publishes 15-20 titles/year. Recent titles include *Bosch Fuel Injection and Engine Management Including High Performance Tuning.* 50% require freelance illustration; 80% require freelance design. Book catalog free for SASE with 45¢ stamp.

Needs: Works with 3-5 freelance illustrators and 10-15 freelance designers/year. Buys 100+ freelance illustrations/year. Perfers artists with "technical illustration background, although a down to earth/user friendly style is welcome." Also uses freelance artists for jacket/cover illustration and design, book design, text illustration, direct mail design and catalog design. Works on assignment only.

First Contact & Terms: Send query letter with resume, SASE, tearsheets and photocopies. Samples are filed. Reports in 3-5 weeks. To show a portfolio, mail thumbnails, roughs and b&w tearsheets and photographs. Buys all rights. Originals are not returned at the job's completion.

Book Design: Assigns 10-15 freelance design and 3-5 freelance illustration jobs/year. Pays by the project.

Jackets/Covers: Pays by the project. Media and style preferred depends on marketing requirements.

Text Illustration: Prefers ink on mylar or adobe postscript files.

Tips: "Send us photocopies of your line artwork and resume."

BETTERWAY PUBLICATIONS, INC., Box 219, Crozet VA 22932. (804)823-5661. President and Production Manager: Jackie Hostage. Estab. 1980. Publishes hardcover and trade paperback originals. Publishes nonfiction, instruction, reference, self-help and genealogy. Specializes in home building and remodeling, small business and finance. Publishes 22-24 titles/year. 40% require freelance illustration; 100% freelance design. Book catalog free by request.

First Contact & Terms: Works with 5-6 freelance illustrators and 2-3 freelance designers/year. Buys 80-100 freelance illustrations/year. Works with illustrators mainly for interior line art. Also works with artists for jacket/cover illustration and design, book and catalog design. Works on assignment only. Send query letter with resume, photocopies, SASE and photographs. Samples are filed or are returned by SASE. Reports back only if interested. Originals returned to artist at job's completion. To show a portfolio, mail final reproduction/product. Considers complexity of project, skill and experience of artist and turnaround time when establishing payment. Buys all rights.
Book Design: Assigns 15-20 freelance design and 12-15 freelance illustration jobs/year. Pays by the hour, $10-35; by the project, $350-2,500.
Jackets/Covers: Assigns 20-24 freelance design and 10-12 freelance illustration jobs/year. Prefers contemporary, high-tech themes. "Computer generated for some titles." Pays by the hour, $10-50; by the project, $250-2,000.
Text Illustration: Assigns 10-12 freelance jobs/year. Prefers line art. Pays by the hour, $10 minimum; by the project, $250 minimum.
Tips: "Send good samples appropriate to our current needs. Show reliability of turnaround time and willingness to work on a royalty basis for larger projects."

*BLUE BIRD PUBLISHING, Suite 306, 1713 E. Broadway, Tempe AZ 85282. (602)968-4088. Owner/Publisher: Cheryl Gorder. Estab. 1985. Book publisher. Publishes trade paperback originals. Types of books include young adult, reference and general adult nonfiction. Specializes in parenting and home education. Publishes 6 titles/year. Recent titles include: *Dr. Christman's Learn-to-Read Book* and *The Sixth Sense—Practical Tips for Everyday Safety*. 50% require freelance illustration; 25% require freelance design. Book catalog free for SASE with 1 first-class stamp.
Needs: Approached by 3 freelance artists/year. Works with 3 freelance illustrators and 1 freelance designer/year. Buys 20-35 freelance illustrations/year. Prefers local artists only. Uses freelance artists mainly for illustration. Also uses freelance artists for jacket/cover illustration and design, text illustration and catalog design. Works on assignment only.
First Contact & Terms: Send query letter with brochure and photocopies. Samples are filed. Reports in 6 weeks. To show a portfolio, mail b&w samples and color tearsheets. Rights purchased vary according to project. Originals are not returned at the job's completion.
Book Design: Assigns 3 freelance illustration jobs/year. Pays by project, $20-250.
Jackets/Covers: Assigns 1 freelance design and 1 freelance illustration job/year. Pays by the project, $50-200. Prefers "a modern and geometric style and black-and-white, but will consider alternatives."
Text Illustration: Assigns 3 freelance illustration jobs/year. Pays by the project, $20-250. Prefers line art.

BLUE DOLPHIN PUBLISHING, INC., 13386 N. Bloomfield Rd., Nevada City CA 95959. (916)265-6923. President: Paul M. Clemens. Estab. 1985. Publishes hardcover and trade paperback originals. Publishes biography, cookbooks, humor and self-help. Specializes in comparative spiritual traditions, lay psychology and health. Publishes 8 titles/year. 10% require freelance illustration; 10% freelance design. Book catalog 65¢ with first-class stamp.
First Contact & Terms: Works with 2 freelance illustrators and designers/year. Works with illustrators mainly for book covers. Also works with freelance artists for jacket/cover design and text illustration. Works on assignment only. Send query letter with tearsheets. Samples are filed or are returned by SASE only if requested. Reports back about queries/submissions within 4-8 weeks. Originals returned to artist at job's completion. To show a portfolio, mail original/final art and final reproduction/product. Considers project's budget when establishing payment. Negotiates rights purchased.
Book Design: Assigns 1-2 freelance design and 1-2 freelance illustration jobs/year. Pays by the hour, $6-12; by the project, $100-500.
Jackets/Covers: Assigns 1-2 freelance design and 1-2 freelance illustration jobs/year. Pays by the hour, $6-12; by the project, $100-500.
Tips: "Send query letter with brief sample of style of work."

BLUE LANTERN STUDIO/Green Tiger Press, Box 62009, San Diego CA 92162. Art Director: Sandra Darling. Estab. 1970. Specializes in original gift and children's books with "imaginative and unusual themes and illustrations." Publishes 10-15 titles/year. 70% require freelance illustration. Recent titles include *Carl Goes Shopping, Robert and the Balloon Machine* and *The Flying White Hot Dog*.
First Contact & Terms: Approached by 300 freelance artists/year. Works with 7-10 freelance artists/year. Works on assignment only. Send query letter with samples to be kept on file "if interested." Write for artists' guidelines. Prefers slides and photographs as samples. "Never send originals." Samples not filed are returned by SASE. Reports back to the artist within 3 months. Originals returned at job's completion. Considers project's budget and rights purchased when establishing payment. Rights purchased vary according to project.

Text Illustration: Assigns 7-10 freelance jobs/year. Payment is usually on a royalty basis.
Tips: "We are looking for artists who have a subtle style and imagination. We look for art containing a romantic, visionary or imaginative quality. We also welcome nostalgia and the 'world of child' themes. We do not publish science fiction or cartoons. Artists should have a good variety of samples including human figures, especially children." The most common mistake freelancers make is to "present work too amateur to be considered."

BOOK DESIGN, Box 193, Moose WY 83012. Art Director: Robin Graham. Specializes in hardcover and paperback originals of nonfiction, natural history. Publishes over 3 titles/year.
First Contact & Terms: Works with 16 freelance artists/year. Works on assignment only. Send query letter with "examples of past work and one piece of original artwork which can be returned." Samples not filed are returned by SASE if requested. Reports back within 20 days. Originals not returned to artist at job's completion. Write to schedule an appointment to show a portfolio. Considers complexity of project, skill and experience of artist, project's budget and turnaround time when establishing payment. Negotiates rights purchased.
Book Design: Assigns 6 freelance design jobs/year. Pays by the project, $50-3,500.
Jackets/Covers: Assigns 2 freelance design and 4 freelance illustration jobs/year. Pays by the project, $50-3,500.
Text Illustration: Assigns 26 freelance jobs/year. Prefers technical pen illustration, maps (using airbrush, overlays etc.), watercolor illustration for children's books, calligraphy and lettering for titles and headings. Pays by the hour, $5-20; by the project, $50-3,500.
Tips: "We are looking for top-notch quality only."

THOMAS BOUREGY & CO., INC. (AVALON BOOKS), 401 Lafayette St., New York NY 10003. (212)598-0222. Vice President/Publisher: Barbara J. Brett. Estab. 1950. Book publisher. Publishes hardcover originals. Types of books include adventure, romance and Westerns. Publishes 60 titles/year. Recent titles include *Warriors of the Andes* (adventure), *Dangerous Odyssey* (mystery romance), *Justice at Blackwater* (Western) and *The Promise of Summer* (romance). 100% require freelance illustration. Book catalog not available. Works with 6 freelance illustrators and 1 freelance designer/year. Buys 60 freelance illustrations/year. Prefers local artists and artists with experience in dust jackets. Uses freelance artists mainly for dust jackets. Also uses freelance artists for jacket/cover illustration. Works on assignment only.
First Contact & Terms: Send brochure. Samples are filed "if they fit our needs." Samples not filed are returned by SASE if requested. Reports back if interested. Call to schedule an appointment to show a portfolio, which should include tearsheets. Buys all rights. Originals are not returned at job's completion.
Jackets/Covers: Assigns 60 freelance illustration jobs/year. Pays by the project, $250. Prefers oil or acrylic.

*BOWLING GREEN UNIVERSITY POPULAR PRESS, Bowling Green University, Bowling Green OH 43403. (419)372-2981. Managing Editor: Pat Browne. Publishes hardcover and paperback originals on popular culture, folklore, women's studies, science fiction criticism, detective fiction criticism, music and drama. Publishes 15-20 titles and 8 journals/year.
First Contact & Terms: Send previously published work and SASE. Reports in 2 weeks. Buys all rights. Free catalog.
Jackets/Covers: Assigns 20 jobs/year. Pays $50 minimum, color washes, opaque watercolors, gray opaques, b&w line drawings and washes.

BRIARCLIFF PRESS, 11 Wimbledon Court, Jericho NY 11753. (516)681-1505. Editorial/Art Director: Trudy Settel. Estab. 1981. Publishes hardcover and paperback cookbook, decorating, baby care, gardening, sewing, crafts and driving originals and reprints. Publishes 18 titles/year; 50% require freelance design and illustration. Uses artists for color separations, lettering and mechanicals. Assigns 25 jobs/year; pays $5-10/hour. Also assigns 5 advertising jobs/year for catalogs and direct mail brochures; pays $5-10/hour.
First Contact & Terms: Works with 3-5 freelance illustrators and 5-7 freelance designers/year. Send query letter and SASE; no samples until requested. Artists should have worked on a professional basis with other firms of this type. Reports in 3 weeks. Buys all rights. No advance. Pays promised fee for unused assigned work.
Book Design: Assigns 25/year. Pays $6 minimum/hour, layout and type spec.
Jackets/Covers: Buys 24/year. Pays $100-300, b&w; $250-500, color.
Text Illustration: Uses artists for text illustrations and cartoons. Buys 250/year. Pays $10-30, b&w; $25-50, color.
Tips: "Do not send originals,"

BROADMAN PRESS, 127 9th Ave. N., Nashville TN 37234. (615)251-2630. Art Director: Jack Jewell. Estab. 1891. Religious publishing house. 20% of titles require freelance illustration. Recent titles include *I Love Life* and *How to Succeed in College*. Book catalog free on request.

First Contact & Terms: Works with 15 freelance illustrators and 10 freelance designers/year. Artist must be experienced, professional illustrator. Works on assignment only. Send query letter with brochure and samples to be kept on file. Call or write for appointment to show portfolio. Send slides, tearsheets, photostats or photocopies; "samples *cannot* be returned." Reports only if interested. Pays for illustration by the project, $250-1,500. Negotiates rights purchased.

Needs: Works with 25 freelance artists/year. Uses artists for illustration. "We publish for all ages in traditional and contemporary styles, thus our needs are quite varied."

Tips: "We actively search for 'realist' illustrators who can work in a style that looks contemporary." Looks for "the ability to illustrate scenes with multiple figures, to accurately illustrate people of all ages, including young children and babies, and to illustrate detailed scenes described in text. Common mistakes freelancers make is that work is not high enough in quality, or art is obviously copied from clipped photos of celebrities."

BROOKS/COLE PUBLISHING COMPANY, 511 Forest Lodge Rd., Pacific Grove CA 93950. (408)373-0728. Art Director: Vernon T. Boes. Art Coordinator: Lisa Torri. Estab. 1967. Specializes in hardcover and paperback college textbooks on mathematics, psychology, chemistry, political science, computers, statistics and counseling. Publishes 100 titles/year. 85% require freelance illustration.

First Contact & Terms: Works with 24 freelance illustrators and 25 freelance designers/year. Works with illustrators for technical line art and covers. Works with designers for cover and book design and text illustration. Works on assignment only. Send query letter with brochure, resume, tearsheets, photostats, photographs and SASE. Samples are filed or are returned by SASE. Reports back only if interested. Write to schedule an appointment to show a portfolio, which should include roughs, photostats, tearsheets, final reproduction/product, photographs, slides and transparencies. Considers complexity of project, skill and experience of artist, project's budget and turnaround time. Negotiates rights purchased.

Book Design: Assigns 20 freelance design and many freelance illustration jobs/year. Pays by the project, $250-1,000.

Jackets/Covers: Assigns 20 freelance design and many freelance illustration jobs/year. Pays by the project, $250-900.

Text Illustration: Assigns 85 freelance jobs/year. Prefers ink/Macintosh. Pays by the project, $50 minimum.

Tips: "Provide excellent package in mailing of samples and cost estimates. Follow up with phone call. Don't be pushy. Be polite, professional and patient. We do not want to see redundant sample material or material that you were only partially responsible for. Research our company's needs and products."

WILLIAM C. BROWN PUBLISHERS, 2460 Kerper Blvd., Dubuque IA 52001. (319)588-1451. Vice President and Director, Production and Design: Beverly A. Kolz. Visual/Design Manager: Faye M. Schilling. Estab. 1944. Publishes hardbound and paperback college textbooks. Publishes 200 titles/year; 10% require freelance design; 50% require freelance illustration. Also uses artists for advertising. Pays $35-350, b&w and color promotional artwork.

First Contact & Terms: Works with 15-20 freelance illustrators and 5-10 freelance designers/year. Works with artists mainly for illustrations. Works on assignment only. Send query letter with resume, brochure, tearsheets or 8½x11" photocopies or finished 11x14" or smaller (transparencies if larger) art samples or call for interview. Reports in 4 weeks. Samples returned by SASE if requested. Reports back on future assignment possibilities. Buys all rights. Pays half contract for unused assigned work.

Book Design: Assigns 50-70 freelance design jobs/year; assigns 75-100 freelance illustration jobs/year. Uses artists for all phases of process. Pays by the project, $400 minimum; varies widely according to complexity. Pays by the hour, mechanicals.

Jackets/Covers: Assigns 70-80 freelance design jobs and 20-30 freelance illustration jobs/year. Pays $100-350 average and negotiates pay for special projects.

Text Illustrations: Assigns 75-100 freelance jobs/year. Considers b&w and color work. Prefers mostly continuous tone, some line drawings; ink preferred for b&w. Pays $25-300.

Tips: "In the field, there is more use of color. There is need for sophisticated color skills—the artist must be knowlegeable about the way color reproduces in the printing process. The designer and illustrator must be prepared to contribute to content as well as style. Tighter production schedules demand an awareness of overall schedules. *Must* be dependable. Prefer black-and-white and color 35 mm slides over photocopies. Send cover letter with emphasis on good portfolio samples. Do not send samples that are not a true representation of your work quality."

*ARISTIDE D. CARATZAS, PUBLISHER, Box 210, 30 Church St., New Rochelle NY 10802. (914)632-8487. Managing Editor: John Emerich. Publishes books about archaeology, art history, natural history and classics for specialists in the above fields in universities, museums, libraries and interested amateurs. Accepts previously published material. Send letter with brochure showing artwork. Samples not filed are returned by SASE. Reports only if interested. To show a portfolio, mail appropriate materials or call or write to schedule an appointment. Buys all rights or negotiates rights purchased.

Close-up

Louise Fili
Graphic Designer

"I had always been interested in books ever since I was a child," says Louise Fili, former art director of Pantheon Books. "I thought I would grow up to be a writer and every week I would start writing a novel, but I realized the only reason I did that was to have an excuse to design the jacket. I would design a jacket, write about two pages, and then I would stop. It never occurred to me that you could grow up and make a living doing jackets."

By the middle of her senior year at Skidmore College, Louise Fili did know she wanted to be a graphic designer and in December of that year, followed her instinct and went to New York City. There she interned at the Museum of Modern Art and enrolled in the School of Visual Arts for her final semester.

Shortly after, she started doing freelance work on special project picture books for Alfred A. Knopf of Random House. "Type had been my major interest in school and I did like working in publishing where you don't really have a client. In other areas of design the client always seems to have the last word, even though the client doesn't always have the best taste. In publishing, although there are always disagreements, you're all part of the same family and are ostensibly working together." She worked at Knopf until those special projects ran out.

She then went to work for Herb Lubalin, where she was hired to handle the PBS account and work on editorial and packaging design. "That was a big thrill for me. He was the god of typography." And then there were the book jackets, which allowed her complete independence. "I found that when you work in a design studio like that of Herb Lubalin, clients come to the studio because they want every comp that comes out of that studio to come out of Herb Lubalin's pen. Whereas with the book jackets, I would work directly with the art director from the publisher and Herb often never saw the work that I was doing."

In 1978 she began her 11-year career as the art director at Pantheon. Then, she says "book jackets were a totally different entity. There was a certain type of book jacket that everyone expected. They were very, very dull. I tried to see what I could do that had never been done before. I used artists who didn't normally do book covers and especially tried to open things up in the areas of type—the use of it, the size of it, the colors. One of the first things I did was to use matte laminations and matte paper stock on paperback books, which up until that time had hardly ever been done, and now that's routine."

She says it was always a challenge to create a design that was not commercial in the marketing sense. "Usually the only way to slip it by the marketing department was to do it on a book that nobody cared about." She says this is what happened with *The Lover*; its cover has won numerous awards and the manager of B. Dalton was quoted as saying she credits the success of the book to the jacket. "What it took me a long time to prove, which I think I eventually did, was that something could be just as arresting or more arresting if it is quietly beautiful then if it has to scream out at you and compete with a million other screaming jackets."

For freelancers just starting out she advises, "Go to the bookstores and look at everything that was done 10 years ago, 30 years ago and especially what is being done now and why. When I was first interested in books, I looked at everything and made myself aware of who was doing the best job and who I wanted to be. It does take time to come around to understanding the book jacket medium."

She thinks carefully done promotional mailings are very important, pieces which show the work well and are targeted to the right people. "At Random House we used to get mail twice a day and it would take me a half an hour each time to just go through it. Of course I got faster and more ruthless as time went on. If it was just addressed to the art director, I would throw it out because if they didn't go through the trouble to fine out who the art director is and this was just a mass mailing, it was probably a piece of junk."

As far as portfolios go, "I think all you need are 10 really good samples. If you need more than 10, there's something probably wrong with the first 10. They should be geared to whoever you're showing them to. If it's book jackets, then show them great book jackets or something that could relate to book jackets like album or magazine covers."

It seems that part of why Louise Fili has been so successful is that she has a true love for books. She always reads the manuscripts before beginning to design the cover, believing there is a responsibility to remain true to the material. "What's exciting about it," she says, "is that you start with an unedited manuscript and very often not even a real title and then as an art director or designer, one has the power to shape it in a way that will attract a reader. The jacket is the first thing that's going to influence someone to take it seriously."

— *Lauri Miller*

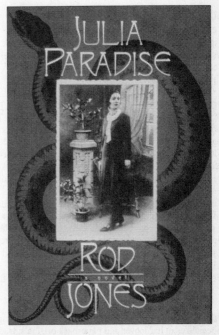

Designed by Fili, these two book covers convey her belief that "when you read a book, you become intimate with it and the jacket for the course of a week or more. It can be insulting if by the time you finish it, you see that the cover was inappropriate or that the person in the illustration really wouldn't have looked like that."

Reprinted with permission of the artist

*CAROLINA WREN PRESS, Box 277, Carrboro NC 27510. (919)560-2738. Art Director: Martha Lange. Estab. 1973. Book publisher. Publishes trade paperback originals. Types of books include contemporary fiction, experimental fiction, pre-school and juvenile. Specializes in books for children in a multi-racial and non-sexist manner, and women's and black literature. Publishes 3 titles/year. Recent titles include *Boy Toy* and *Love, or a Reasonable Facsimile*. 50% require freelance illustration. Book catalog free by request.
Needs: Approached by 20 freelance artists/year. Works with 3 freelance illustrators/year. Buys 20 freelance illustrations/year. Prefers artists with experience in children's literature. Also uses freelance artists for jacket/cover and text illustration. Works on assignment only.
First Contact & Terms: Send query letter with resume, tearsheets, photocopies and illustrations; should include children and adults—no cartoons. Samples are filed or are returned by SASE if requested by artist. "No submissions should be made until requested for specific projects." To show a portfolio, mail b&w and color tearsheets. Rights purchased vary according to project. Originals are returned to the artist at the job's completion.
Jacket/Covers: Assigns 3 freelance illustration jobs/year. Pays by the project, $50-150.
Text Illustration: Assigns 3 freelance illustration jobs/year. Payment is 5% of print run-in books.
Tips: "Understand the world of children in the 1990s. Draw sufficiently realistically so racial types are accurately represented and the expressions can be interpreted. Our books have a classical, modern and restrained look."

CHARLESBRIDGE PUBLISHING, (formerly Mastery Education), 85 Main St., Watertown MA 02172. Managing Editor: Elena Wright. Estab. 1980. Specializes in paperback originals of teacher-directed instruction books. "We have 400 titles this year. 90 were new, K-8th grade materials. We have a new trade book division for science/nature books." Recent titles include *The Yucky Reptile Book* and *Going Lobstering*.
First Contact & Terms: Works with 4 freelance illustrators/year. Artists should have experience in educational textbooks or children's tradebooks. Works on assignment only. Send resume, tearsheets and photocopies. Samples not filed are returned by SASE. Reports only if interested. No originals returned to artist at job's completion. Considers complexity of project and project's budget when establishing payment. Buys all rights.
Book Design: Works with 12 freelance designers/year. Pays by the project.
Text Illustration: Assigns few jobs/year. Pays by the project.
Tips: "Look at what is good in children's trade book art and show how you can transplant that excitement into elementary textbooks. School books require realistic line art of children at exact proportions for each year of age. No cartoon-style exaggerated features. We need real-looking kids, of all races, depicted to show their dignity and intelligence. Local talent wanted."

*CHATHAM PRESS, INC., Box A, Old Greenwich CT 06870. (203)531-7807. FAX: (203)622-6688. Contact: R. Salvaggio. Estab. 1971. Book publisher. Publishes hardcover originals and reprints, and trade paperback originals and reprints. Types of books include travel, cookbooks and photography. Specializes in photography, the ocean, beach, coastline and other New England topics. Publishes 6 titles/year. 25% require freelance illustration; 25% require freelance design. Book catalog free for SASE with $1.50 first-class stamps.
Needs: Approached by 40 freelance artists/year. Works with 3 freelance illustrators and 3 freelance designers/year. Uses freelance artists for jacket/cover illustration and design, book design and text illustration. Works on assignment only.
First Contact & Terms: Send query letter with resume, SASE and appropriate samples. Samples are not filed and are returned by SASE if requested by artist. Reports back to the artist only if interested. To show a portfolio, mail appropriate materials. Buys first rights, one-time rights, reprint rights or all rights. Originals are returned at the job's completion. Pays by the project, $100.
Jackets/Covers: Assigns 3 freelance design jobs and 3 freelance illustration jobs/year. Pays by the project, $100.
Text Illustration: Assigns 3 freelance design and 3 freelance illustration jobs/year. Pays by project, $100.

*CHICAGO REVIEW PRESS, 814 N. Franklin, Chicago IL 60610. (312)337-0747. Editor: Linda Matthews. Specializes in hardcover and paperback originals; trade nonfiction: how-to, travel, cookery, popular science, Midwest regional. Publishes 12 titles/year; 2% require freelance illustration and all require cover jacket design. Recent titles include *The Art of Construction, Chicago Tribune Cookbook, Chicago with Kids* and *Our Sisters' London, Feminist Walking Tours*.
First Contact & Terms: Approached by 50 freelance artists/year. Works with 5 freelance artists/year. Send query letter with resume and tearsheets or phone. Samples are filed or are returned by SASE. Reports back only if interested. Originals not returned to artist at job's completion "unless there are special circumstances." Call to show a portfolio, which should include tearsheets, final reproduction/product and slides. Considers project's budget when establishing payment. Buys one-time rights.

Book Design: Assigns 2 freelance design jobs/year. Pays by the project, $35-400.
Jackets/Covers: Assigns 10 freelance design and 5 freelance illustration jobs/year. Pays by project, $400.
Tips: "Design and illustration we use is sophisticated, above average, innovative and unusual."

THE CHILD'S WORLD, INC., Box 989, Elgin IL 60121. Editor: Janet McDonnell. Book publisher. Estab. 1968. Publishes nonfiction and fiction. Types of books include juvenile and childrens'. Publishes 50 titles/year; 100% require freelance illustration. Recent titles include The *Dinosaur Series*, The *Discovery World Series* and The *Play With Series*.
First Contact & Terms: Approached by 200-300 freelance artists/year. Works with 15 freelance illustrators/year. Works with illustrators mainly for text illustration of children's books and catalog covers. Also works with freelance artists for cover illustration. Works on assignment only. Send query letter with tearsheets, resume and SASE. Samples are filed or are returned by SASE only if requested. No originals returned to artist at job's completion. Considers complexity of project and skill and experience of artist when establishing payment. Buys all rights.
Text Illustration: Assigns 20-50 freelance jobs/year. Payment varies.
Tips: "Study our market and send appropriate samples (slides are not helpful). Send color samples of work for young children. New trends are leaning toward more sophisticated yet simple design for even the young child." Often sees "samples which show a style much too 'old' looking for our audience; or the subject matter is inappropriate."

*CHRISTIAN BOARD OF PUBLICATION, Box 179, St. Louis MO 63166. Director of Product Development, Design and Promotion: Guin Stemmler. Publishes several paperbacks annually. Recent titles include *Worldly Spirituality*, *Inner Peace* and *Story Weaving*. Also publishes magazines, curriculum, catalogs and advertising pieces. Uses artists for design and illustration of curriculum, books, direct mail brochures and displays.
First Contact & Terms: Approached by 50 freelance artists/year. Send query letter with resume, SASE, brochure or copies of work to be kept on file. Reports in 6-8 weeks. Buys all rights. Originals not returned to artist at job's completion. Works on assignment only. Samples returned by SASE.
Jackets/Covers: Assigns a few jobs/year. Pays $300 minimum, 2-color; $350, 4-color.
Text Illustration: Assigns many jobs/year. Pays $50 minimum, 2-color; $60 minimum, 4-color.
Tips: The most common mistake illustrators and designers make in presenting their work is bringing "wrong samples such as fashion or industrial art; we do age-level religious and educational materials. Do clean, accurate work on time. Know the religious field (willing to do research), but in modern approach."

*CLEIS PRESS, Box 14684, San Francisco CA 94114. (415)864-3385. FAX: (415)864-3385. Production Coordinator: Frédérique Delacoste. Estab. 1980. Publishes trade paperback originals. Types of books include contemporary and experimental fiction. Publishes 6 titles/year. Recent titles include *COSMOPOLIS, Urban Fiction by Women*. 50% require freelance illustration; 100% require freelance design. Book catalog available for SASE and 2 first-class stamps. Approached by 2-3 freelance artists/year. Prefers local artists only. Uses freelance artists for jacket cover illustration and design.
First Contact & Terms: Send query letter with photographs. Samples are filed and are not returned. To show a portfolio, mail appropriate materials. Originals returned at the job's completion.
Book Design: Assigns 5 freelance design jobs/year. Pays by the project, $375 minimum.
Jackets/Covers: Assigns 8 freelance design and 8 freelance illustration jobs/year. Pays by the project, $375 minimum.

CLIFFS NOTES INC., Box 80728, Lincoln NE 68501. Contact: Michele Spence. Publishes educational and trade (Centennial Press) books. Recent titles include *Bluff Your Way in Gourmet Cooking* (Centennial Press), *Cliffs Enhanced ACT Preparation Guide* (Cliff Notes).
First Contact & Terms: Approached by 30 freelance artists/year. Uses artists for educational posters. Works on assignment only. Samples returned by SASE. Reports back on future assignment possibilities. Send brochure, flyer and/or resume. No originals returned to artist at job's completion. Buys all rights. Artist supplies overlays for color art.
Jackets/Covers: Uses artists for covers and jackets.
Text Illustration: Uses technical illustrators for mathematics, science, miscellaneous.

COMPUTER TECHNOLOGY RESOURCE GUIDE, Box 294, Rhododendron OR 97049. (503)622-4798. Editor: Michael P. Jones. Estab. 1986. Book about computers and computer accessories, services, books "and anything else related to computers" for beginners to advanced users of computers plus those involved with providing technical assistance to users. Circ. 2,500. Accepts previously published material. Original artwork returned to the artist after publication. Sample copy: $8. Art guidelines for SASE with 1 first class stamp.
Cartoons: Buys 1-3 cartoons/issue from freelancers. Prefers single-panel, double-panel and multi-panel with and without gagline; b&w line drawings, b&w washes and color washes. Send query letter with samples of style, roughs and finished cartoons. Samples are filed or are returned by SASE. Reports back within 2 months. Write for appointment to show a portfolio. Buys one-time rights. Pays in copies.

Illustrations: Buys 10 illustrations/issue from freelancers. "We want to see computers being used and featured in artwork." Send query letter with brochure or resume, tearsheets, photostats, photocopies, slides and photographs. Samples not filed are returned by SASE. Reports back within 2 months. To show a portfolio, mail thumbnails, roughs, original/final art, final reproduction/product, color and b&w tearsheets, photostats and photographs. Buys one-time rights. Pays in copies on publication.

Tips: "I am looking for good quality black-and-white sketches. Give me a good sample of what you can draw, even if you haven't done much in the way of computers. Send me whatever you have, and I'll be able to get a good idea from the samples. Your portfolio should include sketches on any subject. Give us enough to get a good grasp on what you can do."

*CONARI PRESS, 713 Euclid Ave., Berkeley CA 94708. (415)527-9915. FAX (415)527-9915. Please call first. Editor: Mary Jane Ryan. Estab. 1987. Book publisher. Publishes hardcover and trade paperback originals. Types of books include self-help, cookbooks and general non-fiction guides, etc. Publishes 5 titles/year. "Next year it will be as many as 10." Recent titles include *Civil War on Consumer Rights* and *Working with the Ones You Love*. 25% require freelance illustration. Book catalog free for SASE with 1 first class stamp.

Needs: Approached by 5 freelance artists/year. Uses freelance artists for jacket/cover illustration and design. Works on assignment only.

First Contact & Terms: Send query letter with resume and tearsheets. Samples are filed. Reports back to the artist only if interested. To show a portfolio, mail tearsheets. Rights purchased vary according to project. Originals are returned at job's completion.

Jackets/Covers: Assigns 3-5 freelance design jobs/year. Pays by the project, $500-800.

Text Illustration: Assigns 1-3 freelance jobs/year. Pays by the project, $200-600.

Tips: "To get an assignment with me you should have dynamic designs and reasonable prices."

CONTEMPORARY BOOKS, 180 N. Michigan, Chicago IL 60601. (312)782-9181. Art Director: Georgene Sainati. Book publisher. Publishes hardcover originals and trade paperback originals. Publishes nonfiction and fiction. Types of books include biography, cookbooks, instructional, humor, reference, self-help, romance, historical and mainstream/contemporary. Publishes 140 titles/year. 5% require freelance illustration. Recent titles include *Black Tie Only* (novel), *Arnold* (biography of Arnold Schwarzenegger), and *Greatest Sports Excuses* (humor). Book catalog not available.

First Contact & Terms: Approached by 150 freelance artists/year. Works with 10 freelance illustrators/year. Buys 7-10 freelance illustrations/year. Works with illustrators mainly for covers. Also works with freelance artists for jacket/cover illustration and text illustration. Works on assignment only. Send query letter with brochure and resume. Samples are filed or are not returned. Does not report back. Originals sometimes returned to artist at job's completion when requested. To show a portfolio, mail tearsheets and final reproduction/product. Considers complexity of project, skill and experience of artist and project's budget when establishing payment. Buys reprint rights.

Jackets/Covers: Assigns 7 freelance illustration jobs/year. Pays by the project, $600-1,200.

Text Illustration: Assigns 3 freelance jobs/year. Prefers stipple or line and wash. Pays by the hour, $15-25.

Tips: "Several samples of the same technique aren't really necessary unless they treat vastly different subjects. Plese send samples first, then follow up with a call."

*COUNCIL FOR INDIAN EDUCATION, 517 Rimrock Rd., Billings MT 59102. (406)252-7451. Editor: Hap Gilliland. Estab. 1970. Book publisher. Publishes trade paperback originals. Types of books include contemporary fiction, historical fiction, instruction, adventure, biography, pre-school, juvenile, young adult and history. Specializes in Native American life and culture. Recent titles include *Sacajawea: a Native American Heroine* and *Vision of the Spokane Prophet*. 80% require freelance illustration. Book catalog free for SASE with 1 first class stamp.

Needs: Approached by 5 freelance artists/year. Works with 1-3 freelance illustrators/year. Buys 40-100 freelance illustrations/year. Uses freelance artists mainly for illustrating children's books. Works on assignment only.

First Contact & Terms: Send query letter with SASE and photocopies. Samples are filed. Reports back within 2 months. To show a portfolio, mail b&w photostats. Buys one-time rights. Originals are returned at the job's completion.

Book Design: Assigns 4 freelance illustration jobs/year. "We are a small nonprofit organization publishing on a very small budget to aid Indian education. Contact us only if you are interested in illustration for $5 per picture."

Jacket/Covers: Assigns 4 freelance illustration jobs/year. Prefers b&w pen & ink only.

Text Illustration: Assigns 4 freelance illustration jobs/year. Prefers realistic pen & ink.

Tips: Look of design used is "realistic/Native American style."

COWLEY PUBLICATIONS, 980 Memorial Dr., Cambridge MA 02138. (617)876-3507. Marketing Director: Jeff McArn. Book publisher. Estab. 1980. Publishes trade paperback originals; nonfiction. Types of books include religion. Specializes in contemporary theology, spirituality and books of interest to clergy.

First Contact & Terms: Works with 2 freelance designers/year for jacket/cover design. Works on assignment only. Send query letter with resume and samples. Samples are filed or are returned by SASE only if requested. Reports back about queries/submissions within 1 month. Originals not returned to artist at job's completion. To show a portfolio, mail final reproduction/product. Considers project's budget when establishing payment.
Jackets/Covers: Assigns 2 freelance design jobs/year. Pays by the project, $200-400.

*CPI, 145 E. 49th St., New York NY 10017. (212)753-3800. Contact: Tatiana Sayig. Publishes hardcover originals, workbooks and textbooks for ages 4-14. Publishes 40 titles/year; 100% require freelance illustration. Recent titles include *Wonders of Science.*
First Contact & Terms: Approached by 500 freelance artists/year. Uses artists for instructional software, workbooks, textbooks and scientific illustration. Works on assignment only. Send query letter with flyer, tearsheets, photocopies and SASE. Reports back only for future assignment possibilities. Originals are not returned to artist at job's completion. Buys all rights. Free artist's guidelines.
Text Illustration: Assigns 100 freelance jobs/year. "Submit samples of b&w line and color action subjects. In general, realistic and representational art is required." Pays by the project, $35-200, opaque watercolor or any strong color medium except fluorescents.
Tips: "Don't send fine-artsy work, and send a good sampling of work. Most important is b&w work."

*CRAFTSMAN BOOK CO., 6058 Corte del Cedro, Carlsbad CA 92009. (619)438-7828. Marketing Manager: Bill Grote. Estab. 1957. Book publisher. Publishes paperback reference books. Types of books include self-help. Specializes in construction. Publishes 4 titles/year. Recent titles include *Contractor's Guide to the Building Code.* 10% require freelance illustration. Book catalog free by request.
Needs: Approached by 10 freelance artists/year. Works with 1 freelance illustrator/year. Buys 1-5 freelance illustrations/year. Prefers artists with experience in illustration. Uses freelance artists mainly for line drawings or full-color cover illustrations. Also uses freelance artists for jacket/cover design and direct mail and catalog design.
First Contact & Terms: Send query letter with brochure, resume and tearsheets. Samples are filed. Reports back within 3 days only if interested; if does not report back, the artist should call. To show a portfolio, mail original/final art. Rights purchased vary according to project. Originals returned at the job's completion.
Book Design: Assigns 6 freelance design and 3 freelance illustration jobs/year. Pays by the project.
Jackets/Covers: Pays by the project, $100-360.
Text Illustration: Assigns 2 freelance design jobs/year. Pays by the hour, $10-15. Prefers computer generated art from scanned photos.

CROSSROAD/CONTINUUM, 370 Lexington Ave., New York NY 10017. Production Manager: Ilene Levy. Book publisher. Estab. 1980. Publishes hardcover originals, trade paperback originals, hardcover reprints and trade paperback reprints. Publishes nonfiction. Types of books include biography, reference and religious. Specializes in religion/literary. Publishes 100 titles/year. 5% require freelance illustration; 75% require freelance design. Recent titles include *Beyond the Mirror*, by Nouwan; *Continuum Counseling Series* and *Sex, Race and God*, by Thistlethwaite.
First Contact & Terms: Approached by 20 freelance artists/year. Works with 1 freelance illustrator and 25 freelance designers/year. Buys 5 freelance illustrations/year. Works with illustrators mainly for occasional cover or inside needs. Also works with artists for book design and jacket/cover design. Works on assignment only. Send query letter with brochure, resume and tearsheets. Samples are filed or are returned by SASE only if requested. Reports back about queries/submissions only if interested. Originals returned to artist at job's completion. Write to schedule an appointment to show a portfolio, which should include original art, tearsheets and final reproduction/product. Considers complexity of project and project's budget when establishing payment. Buys all rights.
Book Design: Assigns 15 freelance design and 1-2 freelance illustration jobs/year. Pays by the project, $250-300.
Jackets/Covers: Assigns 80 freelance design jobs/year. Prefers all types of styles with minimal photo research involved. Pays by the project, $400-600.
Text Illustration: Assigns 1-2 freelance jobs/year. Pays by the project; rate varies.
Tips: "Send information that can be kept on hand and follow up with a phone call shortly afterwards. I look at portfolios and if an acceptable price is reached and they are in the area, I will give artists a chance."

*CROSSWAY BOOKS, A Division of Good News Publishers (formerly Good News Publishers/Crossway Books), 1300 Crescent St., Wheaton IL 60187. Contact: Art Guye. Nonprofit Christian book publisher. Publishes hardcover and trade paperback originals and reprints. Type of books include fiction (contemporary, mainstream, historical, science fiction, fantasy, adventure, mystery), biography, juvenile, young adult, reference, history, self-help, humor, and books on issues relevant to contemporary Christians. Specializes in Christian fiction. Publishes 30-35 titles/year. 65% require freelance illustration; 35% require freelance design. Recent titles include *Piercing the Darkness, Heart of Stone, In the Midst of Wolves* and *The Francis A. Schaeffer Trilogy.* Book catalog free for (9 × 12) SASE with adequate postage.

First Contact & Terms: Approached by 150-200 freelance artists/year. Works with 15 freelance illustrators and 10 freelance designers/year. Assigns 20 freelance illustration and 30 freelance design projects per year. Uses artists mainly for book cover illustration/design. Also uses artists for advertising, brochure design, related promotional materials, layout, and production. Send query letter with 5-10 nonreturnable samples or quality color photocopies of printed or original art for files. "Please do not send materials that need to be returned." Samples not filed are returned by SASE. Reports back only if interested. Buys "all book and promotional rights." Returns originals to artist. Considers complexity of project, proficiency of artist and projects budget when establishing payment.

Jackets/Covers: Assigns 26 freelance illustration and 14 freelance design jobs/year. Prefers realistic and semi-realistic color illustration in all media. Looks for ability to consistently render the same children or people in various poses and situations (as in series books). Pays by the project, $200-2,000.

Tips: "We are looking for Christian artists who are committed to spreading the Gospel through quality literature. Since we are a nonprofit organization, we may not always be able to afford an artist's 'going rate.' Quality and the ability to meet deadlines are critical. A plus would be a designer who could handle all aspects of a job from illustration to final keyline/mechanical. If an artist is interested in production work (type spec and keylining) please include your hourly rate and a list of references that may be contacted. Also looking for designers who can do imaginative typographic design treatments and exciting calligraphic approaches for covers."

CROWN PUBLISHERS, INC., 201 E. 50th St., New York NY 10022. Design Director: Ken Sansone. Art Director: Jim Davis. Specializes in fiction, nonfiction and illustrated nonfiction. Publishes 250 titles/year. Recent titles include *An Inconvenient Woman*, by Dominick Dunne; *The Plains of Passage*, by Jean M. Auel and *London Fields*, by Martin Amis.

First Contact & Terms: Approached by several hundred freelance artists/year. Works with 50 artists/year. Prefers local artists. Works on assignment only. Send query letter with brochure showing art style. Reports only if interested. Original work returned at job's completion. Considers complexity of project, skill and experience of artist, project's budget, turnaround time and rights purchased when establishing payment. Rights purchased vary according to project.

Book Design: Assigns 20-30 freelance design and very few freelance illustration jobs/year. Pays by the project.

Jackets/Covers: Assigns 100 freelance design and/or illustration jobs/year. Pays by the project.

Text Illustration: Assigns very few jobs/year.

Tips: "No single style, we use different styles depending on nature of the book and its perceived market. Become familiar with the types of books we publish. For example, don't send juvenile or sci-fi."

CUSTOM COMIC SERVICES, Box 726, Glenside PA 19038. Art Director: Scott Deschaine. Estab. 1985. Specializes in educational comic books for promotion and advertising for use by business, education, and government. "Our main product is full-color comic books, 16-32 pages long." Prefers pen & ink, airbrush and watercolor. Publishes 12 titles/year. Recent titles include *McGruff's Surprise Party*, *The Guiding Hand* and *Let's Talk About It*.

First Contact & Terms: Approached by 150 freelance artists/year. Works with 24 freelance artists/year. "We are looking for artists who can produce finished artwork for educational comic books from layouts provided by the publisher. They should be able to produce consistently high-quality illustrations for mutually agreeable deadlines, with no exceptions." Works on assignment only. Send query letter with business card and nonreturnable samples to be kept on file. Samples should be of finished comic book pages; prefers photostats. Reports within 6 weeks; must include SASE for reply. Considers complexity of project and skill and experience of artist when establishing payment. Buys all rights.

Text Illustration: Assigns 18 freelance jobs/year. "Finished artwork will be black-and-white, clean, and uncluttered. Artists can have styles ranging from the highly cartoony to the highly realistic." Pays $100-250/page of art.

Tips: A common mistake freelance artists make is "not sending appropriate material—comic book artwork."

DAW BOOKS, INC., 375 Hudson St., New York NY 10014. (212)366-2096. Art Director: Betsy Wollheim. Estab. 1971. Publishes hardcover originals and reprints and mass market paperback originals and reprints. Publishes science fiction, fantasy and horror. Publishes 72 titles/year. 50% require freelance illustration. Recent titles include *Stone of Farewell*, by Tad Williams and *The Heirs of Hammerfell*, by Marion Zimmer Bradley. Book catalog free request.

First Contact & Terms: Works with approximately 10 freelance illustrators/year. Buys over 36 freelance illustrations/year. Works with illustrators for covers. Works on assignment basis only. Send query letter with brochure, resume, tearsheets, slides, transparencies and SASE. Samples are filed or are returned by SASE only if requested. Reports back about queries/submissions within 2-3 days. Originals returned to artist at job's completion. Call to schedule an appointment to show a portfolio which should include original/final art, final reproduction/product and transparencies. Considers complexity of project, skill and experience of artist and project's budget when establishing payment. Buys first rights and reprint rights.

Jacket Covers: Assigns over 36 freelance illustration jobs/year. Payment is negotiable.

Tips: We have a drop-off policy for portfolios. We accept them on Tuesdays, Wednesdays and Thursdays and report back within a day or so. Portfolios should contain science fiction, fantasy, and horror color illustrations *only*. We do not want to see anything else."

DELMAR PUBLISHERS INC., Box 15-015, 2 Computer Dr. W., Albany NY 12212. Contact: Art Manager. Estab. 1946. Specializes in original hardcovers and paperback textbooks—science, computer, health, mathematics, professions and trades. Publishes 70 titles/year. Recent titles include *Manufacturing Technology* and *Communications Technology*.

First Contact & Terms: Approached by 200 freelance artists/year. Works with 40 freelance artists/year. Prefers text illustrators and designers, paste-up artists, technical/medical illustrators and computer graphic/ AUTOCAD artists. Works on assignment only. Send query letter with brochure, resume, tearsheets, photostats, photocopies, slides or photographs. Samples not indicated to be returned will be filed for one year. Any material needed back must return via certified mail. Not responsible for loss of unsolicited material. Reports back only if interested. Original work not returned after job's completion. Considers complexity of project, project's budget and turnaround time when establishing payment. Buys all rights.

Book Design: Assigns 15 freelance design jobs/year. Pays by the project, $100-600.

Jacket/Covers: Assigns 60 freelance design jobs/year. Pays by the project, $250-500.

Text Illustration: Assigns up to 15 freelance jobs/year. Prefers ink on mylar or vellum—simplified styles. Two-color application is most common form. Four-color art is needed less frequently but still a requirement. Charts, graphs, technical illustration and general pictorials are common. Pays by the project.

Tips: "Quote prices for samples shown. Quality and meeting deadlines most important. Experience with publishing a benefit." Look of design and illusration used is "basic, clean, conservative, straightforward textbook technical art."

*DEVONSHIRE PUBLISHING CO., Box 85, Elgin IL 60121. (708)624-1953. Vice President: Don Reynolds. Estab. 1985. Book publisher. Publishes trade paperback originals. Types of books include contemporary, mainstream, historical, science fiction, instruction, mystery, history and humor. Specializes in fiction. Publishes 2-3 titles/year. Recent titles include *The Making of Bernie Trumble*. 100% require freelance illustration and design. Book catalog free for SASE with 1 first-class stamp.

Needs: Approached by 5 freelance artists/year. Works with 1 freelance designer/year. Buys 2-3 freelance illustrations/year. Uses freelance artists mainly for cover design. Also uses freelance artists for jacket/cover illustration and design, and catalog design. Works on assignment only.

First Contact & Terms: Send query letter with SASE and photocopies. Samples are not filed and are returned by SASE. Reports back within 1 month. To show a portfolio, mail roughs and photostats. Buys one-time rights. Originals are not returned at the job's completion.

Book Design: Assigns 2-3 freelance design and 2-3 freelance illustration jobs/year. Pays by the project, $300-1,500.

Jackets/Covers: Assigns 2-3 freelance design and 2-3 freelance illustration jobs/year. Pays by the project, $300-1,500.

Tips: "Be specific when applying—what is it how much?"

*DIAL BOOKS FOR YOUNG READERS, 375 Hudson St., New York NY 10014. Editor: Toby Sherry. Specializes in juvenile and young adult hardcovers. Publishes 40 titles/year. 40% require freelance illustration. Recent titles include *The Talking Eggs*, by Robert Sansoucie.

First Contact & Terms: Approached by 400 freelance artists/year. Works with 20 freelance artists/year. Prefers artists with some book experience. Works on assignment only. Send query letter with brochure, tearsheets, photostats, slides and photographs. Samples are filed and are not returned. Reports back only if interested. Originals returned at job's completion. Call to schedule an appointment to show a portfolio, which should include original/final art and tearsheets. Considers complexity of project, skill and experience of artist and project's budget when establishing payment. Rights purchased vary."

Book Design: Assigns 20 freelance design and 30 freelance illustration jobs/year.

Jackets/Covers: Assigns 2 freelance design and 8 freelance illustration jobs/year.

DILLON PRESS, 242 Portland Ave. S, Minneapolis MN 55415. (612)333-2691. Publisher: Uva Dillon. Specializes in hardcovers of juvenile nonfiction (Gemstone Books) and fiction for school library and trade markets. Publishes 40 titles/year.

First Contact & Terms: Works with 5 freelance artists/year. Works on assignment only. Send query letter with resume and samples to be kept on file. Call or write for appointment to show portfolio. Prefers slides and tearsheets as samples. Samples not filed are returned by SASE. Reports back within 6 weeks. Originals not returned to artist. Considers complexity of the project, skill and experience of artist and project's budget when establishing payment. Rights purchased vary according to project.

Book Design: Assigns 10 freelance jobs/year. Pays by the hour or by the project, negotiated so as competitive with other publishers in area.

Jackets/Covers: Assigns 10 freelance design and 10 freelance illustration jobs/year. Pays by the hour or by the project, negotiated so as competitive with other publishers in area.

Text Illustration: Assigns 10 freelance jobs/year. Seeks a variety of media and styles. Pays by the hour or by the project, negotiated so as competitive with other publishers in area.

*DRAMA BOOK PUBLISHERS, 260 Fifth Ave., New York NY 10001. (212)725-5377. Estab. 1967. Book publisher. Publishes hardcover originals and reprints, trade paperback reprints and textbooks. Types of books include costume, theater and performing arts. Publishes 8 titles/year. 10% require freelance illustration; 25% require freelance design.

Needs: Works with 2-3 freelance designers/year. Prefers local artists only. Uses freelance artists mainly for jackets/covers. Also uses freelance artists for book, direct mail and catalog design and text illustration. Works on assignment only.

First Contact & Terms: Send query letter with brochure and tearsheets. Samples are filed. Reports back to the artist only if interested. To show a portfolio, mail appropriate materials. Rights purchased vary according to project. Originals are not returned at the job's completion.

Book Design: Pays by the project.

Jackets/Covers: Pays by the project.

*EASTVIEW EDITIONS, INC., Box 783, Westfield NJ 07091. (201)820-9636. Manager: Mr. N. Glenn. Specializes in hardcover and paperback books on "all the arts" — fine arts, architecture, design, music, dance, antiques, hobbies, nature and history. Publishes 12 titles/year. Uses artists for book design, jacket/cover design and text illustration. Also "looking for people who want cooperative publication."

First Contact & Terms: Send outline and description of work; "no samples that must be returned, only 'second generation' illustrations." Pays in royalties, fees.

*ENTELEK, Ward-Whidden House/The Hill, Box 1303, Portsmouth NH 03802. Editorial Director: Albert E. Hickey. Publishes paperback education originals, specializing in computer books and software. Recent titles include *Sail Training For High Risk Youth*.

First Contact & Terms: Approached by 25 freelance artists/year. Query with samples. Prefers previously published work as samples. Include SASE. Reports in 1 week. Free catalog. Works on assignment only. Provide brochure, flyer and tearsheets to be kept on file for possible future assignments. Pays $300, catalogs and direct mail brochures.

Needs: Works with 1 freelance artist and 1 freelance designer for advertising/year. Especially needs cover and brochure designs.

*M. EVANS AND COMPANY, INC., 216 E. 49th St., New York NY 10016. (212)688-2810. Managing Editor: Joseph Mills. Estab. 1956. Book publisher. Publishes hardcover and trade paperback originals. Types of books include contemporary fiction, biography, young adult, history, self-help, cookbooks, westerns and romances. Specializes in westerns, romance and general nonfiction. Publishes 40 titles/year. Recent titles include *Paris 2005*, *Born in Blood* and *Italian Vegetarian Cooking*. 50% require freelance illustration. 50% require freelance design.

Needs: Approached by 25 freelance artists/year. Works with 20 freelance illustrators and designers/year. Buys 20 freelance illustrations/year. Prefers local artists only. Uses freelance artists for jacket/cover illustration and design and book design. Works on assignment only.

First Contact & Terms: Send query letter with brochure and resume. Samples are filed. Reports back to the artist only if interested. Call to schedule an appointment to show a portfolio which should include original/final art and photographs. Rights purchased vary according to project. Originals are not returned at the job's completion.

Book Design: Assigns 20 freelance design and 20 freelance illustration jobs/year. Pays by the project, $375-425.

Jackets/Covers: Assigns 20 freelance design jobs/year. Pays by the project $900-1,500. Media and style preferred depend on subject. "We rarely use text illustrations."

Tips: "We decide what to use based on the artist's portfolio."

*EXPOSITION PHOENIX PRESS, 6721 NW 16th Terrace, Fort Lauderdale FL 33073. (305)975-9603. President: Dr. Panchula. Estab. 1939. Book publisher (subsidy and investment publishing). Publishes hardcover originals and reprints, mass market paperback originals and textbooks. Types of books include contemporary, historical and science fiction, instruction, adventure, mystery, biography, pre-school, juvenile, history, self-helf, travel, humor, cookbooks and religion. Specializes in self-help. Publishes approx. 100 titles/year. Recent titles include *Humanimals*, *Fred Said* and *Side Tracked*. 20% require freelance illustration; 5% require freelance design. Book catalog free for SASE with 1 first-class stamp.

Needs: Approached by 30+ artists/year. Works with 4-5 freelance illustrators/year. Buys 12+ freelance illustrations/year. Prefers artist with experience in many different styles. Uses freelance artists mainly for dust jackets and children's books. Works on assignment only.
First Contact & Terms: Send query letter with brochure and SASE. Samples are filed or are returned by SASE if requested by artist. Reports in 1 month. To show a portfolio, mail roughs. Rights purchased vary according to project. Originals returned at the job's completion by request only.
Book Design: Pays by the project.
Jackets/Covers: Assigns 20 freelance design jobs and 20 freelance illustration jobs/year. Pays by the project, $75-200.
Text Illustration: Pays by the project, $75-200.

*FACTS ON FILE, 460 Park Ave. S., New York NY 10016. (212)683-2244. FAX: (212)683-3633. Art Director: Jo Stein. Estab. 1940. Book and news digest publisher. Publishes hardcover originals and trade paperback reprints. Types of books include instruction, biography, young adult, reference, history, self-help, travel and humor. Specializes in general reference. Publishes 200 titles/year. Recent titles include *Guinness Book of Records* and *Encyclopedia of Evolution*. 10% require freelance illustration; 50% require freelance design. Book catalog free by request.
Needs: Approached by 100 freelance artists/year. Works with 10 freelance illustrators and 50 freelance designers/year. Buys 10 feelance illustrations. Use freelance artists mainly for jacket and direct mail design. Also use freelance artists for book direct mail design, text illustration and paste-up. Works on assignment only.
First Contact & Terms: Send query letter with SASE, tearsheets and photocopies. Samples are filed. Reports back only if interested. Call to show a portfolio, which should include thumbnails, roughs and color tearsheets, photographs and comps. Rights purchased vary according to project. Originals returned at the job's completion.
Book Design: Assigns 10 freelance design and 10 freelance illustration jobs/year. Pays by the project, $500-750.
Jackets/Covers: Assigns 50 freelance design and 10 freelance illustration jobs/year. Pays by the project $500-750. Media and style preferred vary per project.
Text Illustration: Assigns 10 freelance design and 10 freelance illustration jobs/year. Payment is "per piece, negotiated."

*FAIRCHILD PUBLICATIONS BOOKS & VISUALS, 7 E. 12th St., New York NY 10003. (212)887-1884. FAX: (212)887-1865. Production Manager: Juanita Brown. Estab. 1966. Book publisher. Publishes hardcover originals and reprints and textbooks. Types of books include instruction, reference, history and fashion. Specializes in fashion, textiles and merchandising. Publishes 5-10 titles/year. 85% require freelance illustration; 100% require freelance design. Book catalog free by request.
Needs: Works with varied number of freelance illustrators and 4-5 freelance designers/year. Number of freelance illustrations bought varies. Prefers local artists only, with experience in fashion illustration. Uses freelance artists mainly for text and cover design. Also uses freelance artists for jacket/cover illustration and book design.
First Contact & Terms: Send query letter with brochure, photographs and photostats. Samples are filed. Reports back to the artist only if interested. Call to schedule an appointment to show a portfolio, which should include b&w and color tearsheets, slides and photographs. Buys all rights. Originals are not returned at job's completion.
Book Design: Assigns 5-10 freelance design and 2-3 freelance illustration jobs/year. Pays by the project based on budget requirements; negotiated.
Jackets/Covers: Assigns 5-10 freelance design and 1-2 freelance illustration jobs/year. Pays by the project. Media preferred depends on job halftones, whether it is something from inside text or an illustration.
Text Illustration: Assigns 1-2 freelance design jobs/year.
Tips: "Be punctual; bring portfolio and ask questions about the project. Talk a little about yourself."

*FALCON PRESS PUBLISHING CO., INC., 318 N. Last Chance Gulch, Helena MT 59601. (406)442-6597. FAX: (406)443-0751. Editorial Director: Chris Cauble. Estab. 1978. Book publisher. Publishes hardcover originals and reprints, trade paperback originals and reprints, and mass market paperback originals and reprints. Types of books include historical fiction, instruction, adventure, pre-school, juvenile, young adult, travel, humor and cookbooks. Specializes in recreational guidebooks, high-quality, four-color photo books. Publishes 40 titles/year. Recent titles include *Scenic Byways*, *Nature Conservancy Calendar* and *New Mexico On My Mind*. Book catalog free by request.
Needs: Approached by 6 freelance artists/year. Works with 4 freelance illustrators/year. Buys 40 freelance illustrations/year. Prefers artists with experience in illustrating children's books. Uses freelance artists mainly for illustrating children's books. Also uses freelance artists for jacket/cover illustration and design, book design and text illustration. Works on assignment only.

First Contact & Terms: Send query letter with resume, tearsheets, photographs, photocopies and photostats. "Samples should be in the form of one of these options." Samples are not filed and are returned by SASE if requested by artist. Reports back to the artist only if interested. To show a portfolio, mail thumbnails, roughs, original/final art and b&w photostats, slides, dummies, tearsheets, transparencies and photographs. Buys all rights. Originals are returned at the job's completion.

Book Design: Assigns 3 freelance illustration jobs/year. "We have inhouse artists."

Jackets/Covers: Assigns 3-4 freelance illustration jobs/year. Pays by the project, $250-650. No preferred media or style; "although to-date, most covers have been watercolors."

Text Illustration: Assigns 3 freelance design and 3 freelance illustrations/year. Pays by the project, $500-1,500. No preferred media or style.

Tips: "Be acquainted with our children's series of books, *Highlights in American History* and *Interpreting the Great Outdoors*; and have a good portfolio."

*FANTAGRAPHICS BOOKS, INC., 7563 Lake City Way., Seattle WA 98115. (206)524-1967. FAX: (206)524-1967. Publisher: Gary Groth. Estab. 1976. Book publisher. Publishes hardcover originals and reprints and trade paperback originals and reprints. Types of books include contemporary, experimental, mainstream, historical science fiction, young adult and humor. "All our books are comic books or graphic stories." Specializes in fictional comics. Publishes 100 titles/year. Recent titles include *Love and Rockets*, *The Comic Journal*, *Amazing Heroes*, *Hate Magazine* and *Usagi Yojimbo*. 15% require freelance illustration. Book catalog free by request.

Needs: Approached by 500 freelance artists/year. Works with 15 freelance illustrators/year. Must be interested in and willing to do comics. Uses freelance artists mainly for comic book interiors and covers.

First Contact & Terms: Send query letter with resume, SASE, photocopies and finished comics work. Samples are not filed and are returned by SASE. Reports back to the artist only if interested. Call or write to schedule an appointment to show a portfolio, which should include original/final art and b&w samples. Buys one-time rights or negotiates rights purchased. Originals are returned at the job's completion.

Book Design: Payment for book design, jackets/covers and text illustration is on a royalty basis.

Tips: "We want to see completed comics stories. We don't make assignments, but instead look for interesting material to publish that is pre-existing. We want cartoonists who have an individual style, who create stories that are personal expressions."

FARRAR, STRAUS & GIROUX, INC., 19 Union Square West, New York NY 10003. (212)741-6900. Art & Production Director: Dorris Janowitz. Book publisher. Estab. 1946. Publishes hardcover and trade paperback originals and trade paperback reprints. Publishes nonfiction and fiction. Types of books include biography, cookbooks, juvenile, self-help, historical and mainstream/contemporary. Publishes 120 titles/year. 40% require freelance illustration; 40% freelance design.

First Contact & Terms: Works with 12 freelance designers/year. Works with freelance artists for jacket/cover and book design. Send brochure, tear sheets and photostats. Samples are filed and are not returned. Reports back only if interested. Originals returned to artist at job's completion. Call to write to schedule an appointment to show a portfolio, which should include photostats and final reproduction/product. Considers complexity of project and project's budget when establishing payment. Buys one-time rights.

Book Design: Assigns 40 freelance design jobs/year. Pays by the project, $300-450.

Jackets/Covers: Assigns 40 freelance design jobs/year. Pays by the project, $750-1,500.

Tips: The best way for a freelance illustrator to get an assignment is "to have a great portfolio and referrals."

FELL PUBLISHERS, 2131 Hollywood Blvd., Hollywood FL 33020. (305)925-5242. President: Donald L. Lessne. Specializes in hardcovers, paperbacks and magazines—mostly trade books. Publishes 20 titles/year.

First Contact & Terms: Works with 5 freelance artists/year. Prefers local artists only. Works on assignment only. Send brochure showing art style or photocopies. Samples not filed are returned only if requested. Reports back within 30 days. No originals returned to artist at job's completion "unless specifically requested that they need them back." Considers rights purchased when establishing payment. Rights purchased vary according to project.

Book Design: Assigns 20 freelance design and 20 freelance illustration jobs/year. Pays by the project, $400-1,000.

Jackets/Covers: Assigns 20 freelance design and a variable amount of freelance illustration jobs/year. Pays by the project, $400-1,000.

Tips: "We are looking for fresh approaches to creative art in the trade area. We are looking for contemporary artists; we are looking for self-starters that do market research to deliver the best product."

*FIVE STAR PUBLICATIONS, Box 3142, Scottsdale AZ 85271-3142. (602)941-0770. Publisher: Linda F. Radke. Estab. 1985. Book publisher. Publishes trade paperback originals. Types of books include juvenile, reference and self-help. Specializes in child care and children's books. Publishes 4 titles/year. Recent titles include *Shakespeare for Children: The Story of Romeo and Juliet and Nannies, Maids & More: The Complete*

Guide for Hiring Household Help. 25% require freelance illustration; 100% require freelance design. Book catalog free for SASE with 2 first-class stamps.

Needs: Works with 2 freelance illustrators and 1 freelance designer/year. Bought 60 freelance illustrations last year. Prefers artists with experience. Uses freelance artists mainly for book illustration, brochures, cover design. Also uses freelance artists for jacket/cover illustration and text illustration and direct mail design. Works on assignment only.

First Contact & Terms: Send query letter with brochure and resume. Samples are filed. Reports back to the artist only if interested. Rights purchased very according to project.

Book Design: Pays by the project.

Jackets/Covers: Assigns 4 freelance design and 2 freelance illustration jobs/year. Pays by the project. Media and style preferred depend on the assignment.

Text Illustration: Assigns 2 freelance design and 2 freelance illustration jobs/year. Pays by the project. Payment is negotiable. Prefers realism.

Tips: "If artist is to be considered, we require the willingness to do one sample drawing as related to the assignment."

THE FREE PRESS, A DIVISION OF MACMILLAN, PUB. CO., 866 Third Ave., New York NY 10022. Manufacturing Director: W.P. Weiss. Specializes in hardcover and paperback originals, concentrating on professional and tradebooks in the social sciences. Publishes 70 titles/year. Recent titles include *A Force for Change*, *Social Marketing*, *Our Country* and *Apprenticeship for Adulthood*.

First Contact & Terms: Approached by dozens of freelance artists/year. Works with 10 artists/year. Prefers artists with book publishing experience. Works on assignment only. Send query letter with brochure showing art style or resume and nonreturnable samples. Samples not filed are returned by SASE. Reports only if interested. Original work returned after job's completion. Considers complexity of project, skill and experience of artist, project's budget, turnaround time and rights purchased when establishing payment. Buys all rights.

Book Design: Assigns 70 freelance design jobs/year. Pays by the project.

Jackets/Covers: Assigns 70 freelance design jobs/year. Pays by the project.

Text Illustration: Assigns 35 freelance jobs/year. "It is largely drafting work, not illustration." Pays by the project.

Tips: "Have book industry experience!"

FRIENDSHIP PRESS PUBLISHING CO., 475 Riverside Dr., New York NY 10115. (212)870-2280. Art Director: E. Paul Lansdale (Room 552). Specializes in hardcover and paperback originals, reprints and textbooks; "adult and children's books on social issues from an ecumenical perspective." Publishes over 10 titles/year; many require freelance illustration. Recent titles include *Born of the Sun*, *Mythmakers — Gospel, Culture and the Media* and *The Electronic Lifeline*.

First Contact & Terms: Approached by over 12 freelance artists/year. Works with over 10 freelance artists/year. Works on assignment only. Send brochure showing art style or resume, tearsheets, photostats, slides, photographs and "even black & white photocopies. Send nonreturnable samples." Samples are filed or are not returned. Reports back only if interested. Originals returned to artist at job's completion. To show a portfolio, call or write to schedule an appointment; or mail thumbnails, roughs, original/final art, photostats, tearsheets, final reproduction/product, photographs, slides, transparencies or dummies. Considers skill and experience of artist, project's budget and rights purchased when establishing payment.

Jackets/Covers: Assigns 10 freelance design and over 5 freelance illustration jobs/year. Pays by the project, $300-500.

Text Illustration: Assigns over 8 freelance jobs/year. Pays by the project, $30-70, b&w.

FUNKY PUNKY AND CHIC, Box 601, Cooper Station, New York NY 10276. (212)533-1772. Creative Director: R. Eugene Watlington. Specializes in paperback originals on poetry, celebrity photos and topics dealing with New Wave, high fashion. Publishes 4 titles/year; 50% require freelance design; 75% require freelance illustration.

First Contact & Terms: Works with 20 freelance artists/year. Send query letter with business card, photographs and slides. Samples not kept on file are returned by SASE. Reports only if interested. Write for appointment to show a portfolio. Originals not returned to artist at job's completion. Considers complexity of project and project's budget when establishing payment. Buys all rights.

Book Design: Assigns 1 freelance job/year. Pays by the project, $100-300 average.

Jackets/Covers: Assigns 3 freelance illustration jobs/year. Pays by the project, $50-75 average.

Text Illustration: Assigns 2 freelance jobs/year. Pays by the project, $50-75 average.

GESSLER PUBLISHING CO. INC., 55 W. 13th St., New York NY 10011. (212)627-0099. Marketing Director: Paula Dunn. Estab. 1932. Publishes trade hardcover and paperback originals and reprints and textbooks. Publishes cookbooks, instruction and reference. Specializes in French, Spanish and German titles. Book catalog free by request.

First Contact & Terms: Works with illustrators mainly for cover art on catalog. Also works with artists on jacket/cover, direct mail and catalog design. Works on assignment only. Send query letter. Samples are not filed and are not returned. Reports back only if interested. Originals occasionally returned to artist at job's completion. Call to schedule an appointment to show a portfolio, which should include original/final art, tearsheets and final reproduction/product. Considers project's budget when establishing payment. Negotiates rights purchased.

*C.R. GIBSON, 32 Knight St., Norwalk CT 06856. (203)847-4543. Creative Services Coordinator: Marilyn Schoenleber. Publishes 100 titles/year. 95% require freelance illustration.
First Contact & Terms: Works with approximately 70 freelance artists/year. Works on assignment—"most of the time." Send tearsheets, photostats, slides, photographs, sketches and published work. Samples are filed or are returned by SASE. Reports back within 1 month only if interested. Call to schedule an appointment to show a portfolio or mail tearsheets, slides and published samples. Considers complexity of project, project's budget and rights purchased when establishing payment. Negotiates rights purchased.
Book Design: Assigns at least 65 freelance design jobs/year. Pay by the project, $1,200 minimum.
Jackets/Covers: Assigns 20 freelance design jobs/year. Pays by the project, $500 minimum.
Text Illustration: Assigns 20 freelance jobs/year. Pays by the hour, $15 minimum; by the project, $1500 minimum.
Tips: "Submit by mail a cross-section of your work—slides, printed samples, finished art no larger than a mailing envelope. Enclose SASE in the envelope."

*GLENCOE/MCGRAW-HILL, a Macmillan/McGraw-Hill Company, 809 W. Detweiller, Peoria IL 61615. (309)691-4454. Vice President of Art/Design/Production: Donna M. Faull. Specializes in secondary educational materials (hardcover, paperback, filmstrips, software), especially in inudstrial and computer technology, home economics and family living, social studies, career education, etc. Publishes over 100 titles/year.
First Contact & Terms: Works with over 30 freelance artists/year. Works on assignment only. Send query letter with brochure, resume and "any type of samples." Samples not filed are returned if requested. Reports back in weeks. Original work not returned after job's completion; work-for-hire basis with rights to publisher. Considers complexity of the project, skill and experience of the artist, project's budget, turnaround time and rights purchased when establishing payment. Buys all rights.
Book Design: Assigns over 30 freelance design and over 30 freelance illustration jobs/year. Pays by the hour, $10-40; pays by the project, $300-3,000 and upward (very technical art, lots of volume).
Jackets/Covers: Assigns over 50 freelance design jobs/year. Pays by the project, $200, 1-color; 4,000, complete cover/interiors for textbooks.
Text Illustration: Assigns over 50 freelance jobs/year. Pays by the hour, $10-40.
Tips: "Try not to call and never drop in without an appointment."

GLOBE BOOK COMPANY, 190 Sylvan Ave., 2nd Fl., Englewood Cliffs NJ 07632. (201)592-2640. Art Director: Gianella Garrett. Specializes in high school level textbooks, social studies, language arts, science and health. Publishes 80 titles/year; 50% require freelance illustration.
First Contact & Terms: Works with 40 freelance artists/year. Works on assignment only. Send query letter with brochure showing art style or tearsheets, photostats or any printed samples. Samples are filed and are not returned. Reports back only if interested. Originals returned to artist at job's completion. Call to schedule an appointment to show a portfolio, or mail original/final art, tearsheets and photographs. Considers complexity of project, project's budget and turnaround time when establishing payment. Buys one-time rights.
Book Design: Assigns several freelance design jobs/year. Pays by the project.
Jackets/Covers: Assigns several freelance design jobs/year. Pays by the project.
Text Illustration: Assigns several freelance jobs/year. Does not want juvenile illustration. Pays by the project.
Tips: "Looking for individuals who can produce four-color, one-color or preseparated work and four-color maps. We need technical and medical illustrators. Also, need freelance dummying and book and cover designers."

GLOBE PEQUOT PRESS, 138 West Main St., Box Q, Chester CT 06412. (203)526-9571. Production manager: Kevin Lynch. Estab. 1947. Publishes hardcover and trade paperback originals and reprints. Publishes biography, cookbooks, instruction, self-help, history and travel. Specializes in regional subjects: New England, Northwest, Southeast bed and board country inn guides. Publishes 70 titles/year. 40% require freelance illustration; 1% require freelance design. Book catalog free for SASE with 1 first-class stamp.
First Contact & Terms: Works with 10 freelance illustrators and 2 freelance designers/year. Buys 500 freelance illustrations/year. Works with illustrators mainly for b&w pen and ink. Also works with artists for jacket/cover illustration text illustration and direct mail design. Works on assignment only. Send query letter with brochure, resume and photostats. Samples are filed and are not returned. Reports back within 2 weeks only if interested. Originals not returned to artist at job's completion. Call or write to schedule an appointment to show a protfolio which should include roughs, original/final art, photostats, tearsheets and dummies.

Considers complexity of project, project's budget and turnaround time when establishing payment. Buys all rights.

Book Design: Assigns 1 freelance design and 28 freelance illustration jobs/year. Pays by the hour, $10-25; by the project.

Jackets/Covers: Assigns 25 freelance design and 5 freelance illustration jobs/year. Prefers realistic style. Pays by the project, $150-500.

Text Illustration: Assigns 28 freelance jobs/year. Prefers b&w pen and ink line drawings. Pays by the project, $150-5,000.

Tips: "Design and illustration we use is classic/friendly but not corny."

GOOSE LANE EDITIONS LTD., 248 Brunswick St., Fredericton N.B. Canada E3B 1G9. (506)454-8319. Art Director: Julie Scriver. Book publisher. Estab. 1958. Publishes hardcover originals and trade paperback originals. Publishes poetry, fiction and nonfiction. Types of books include biography, cookbooks, fiction, reference and history. Publishes 10-15 titles/year. 10% require freelance illustration; 5% require freelance design. Recent titles include *No Hay Fever & A Railway, Summers in St. Andrews* and *The Collected Letters of Sir Charles G.D. Roberts.* Book catalog free for SASE with Candian first-class stamp.

First Contact & Terms: Approached by 3 freelance artists/year. Works with 5-6 freelance illustrators and 2-3 freelance designers/year. Works with illustrators mainly for cover illustration. Also works with artists for text illustration. Works on assignment only. Send query letter with resume, slides, transparencies and SASE. Samples are filed or are returned by SASE. Reports back about queries/submissions within 1 month. Originals returned to artist at job's completion. Call or write to schedule an apointment to show a portfolio which should include roughs, original/final art, final reproduction/product and slides. Considers complexity of project, skill and experience of artist and project's budget when establishing payment. Negotiates rights purchased.

Jackets/Covers: Assigns 5-6 freelance illustration jobs/year. Prefers to work with artists in the region. Prefers painting—dependent on nature of book. Pays by the project, $200-600.

Text Illustration: Assigns 1-2 freelance jobs/year. Prefers line drawing. Pays by the project, $100-600.

*GRAPEVINE PUBLICATIONS, INC., Box 118, Corvallis OR 97339-0118. (503)754-0583. Managing Editor: Chris Coffin. Estab. 1983. Book publisher. Publishes trade paperback originals and textbooks. Types of books include instruction and self-help. Specializes in instruction in computers, technology, math and science. Publishes 60 titles/year. Recent titles include *Lotus Be Brief, an Easy Course in Using the HP-48SX.* 90% require freelance illustration; 10% require freelance design. Book catalog free by request.

Needs: Approached by 10-20 freelance artists/year. Works with 3-5 freelance illustrators and 0-1 freelance designers/year. Buys 200-400 freelance illustrations/year. Uses freelance artists mainly for color cover illustration and pen & ink illustration in text.

First Contact & Terms: Send query letter with brochure, resume, SASE and photographs. Samples are filed or are returned by SASE if requested by artist. Reports back within 1 month. To show a portfolio, mail appropriate materials: b&w and color photographs. Buys all rights. Originals are not returned at the job's completion.

Book Design: Assigns 1-2 freelance design and 10-20 freelance illustration jobs/year. Pays by the project, $200-1,000.

Jackets/Covers: Assigns 10-15 freelance illustration jobs/year. Pays by the project, $500-1,000. Prefers pastel, watercolor or acrylic; original illustrations.

Text Illustration: Assigns 10-20 freelance illustration jobs/year. Pays by the project, $500-5,000. Prefers pen & ink; characters sketched and developed throughout text.

GREAT COMMISSION PUBLICATIONS, 7401 Old York Rd., Philadelphia PA 19126. (215)635-6515. Art Director: John Tolsma. Publishes paperback originals educational and promotional materials for two Presbyterian denominations.

First Contact & Terms: Works with 6 freelance artists/year. Seeks experienced illustrators, usually local artists, but some may be from out-of-state. Works on assignment only. Send query letter with brochure, resume, business card and tearsheets to be kept on file. Material not filed is returned only if requested. Reports only if interested. No originals returned at job's completion. Considers complexity of project, skill and experience of artist and the project's budget when establishing payment. Buys all rights.

Text Illustration: Assigns 100-150 jobs per year. Prefers stylized illustration, primarily figure work with some Biblical art; 1-, 2- and 4-color art. Pays by the project, $1,000 maximum. Assigns from 1-13 projects at one time.

GUERNICA, Box 633, Station N.D.G., Montreal, Quebec H4A 3R1 Canada. (514)256-5599. President: Antonio D'Alfonso. Book publisher. Estab. 1978. Specializes in hardcover and paperback originals. Publishes fiction and nonfiction. Types of books include historical, mainstream/contemporary, biography and reference. Publishes 8-10 titles/year. Recent titles include *Conscience and Coercion,* by Antonio Gualtieri; *Arrangiarsi* and *The Italian Immigration Experience in Canada.*

First Contact & Terms: Approached by 12 freelance artists/year. Works with illustrators mainly for covers. Also works with freelance aritsts for book design. Works on assignment only. Send query letter with tear-sheets. Samples not filed are returned by Canadian SASE. Reports back within 1 month. To show a portfolio mail appropriate materials which should include tearsheets. Considers project's budget when establbishing payment. Buys one-time rights and reprint rights.
Book Design: Pays by the project, $100-300.
Jackets/Covers: Pays by the project, $100-300.
Text Illustration: Pays by the project, $100-300.
Tips: "We try to be singular in our design. Our books are now all 4½ × 7½ and we use artwork as graphics. Just send samples, with address stamped on the back of your work."

HARCOURT BRACE JOVANOVICH, INC., 1250 Sixth Ave., San Diego CA 92101. (619)699-6568. Art Director, Children's Books: Michael Farmer. Trade Books: Vaughn Andrews. Specializes in hardcover and paperback originals and reprints. Publishes "general books of all subjects (not including text, school or institutional books)." Publishes 250 titles/year. 100% require freelance illustration. Recent titles include *In the Beginning*, *Swan Lake* and *Tales From Margaritaville*.
First Contact & Terms: Approached by 500 freelance artists/year. Works with 200 freelance artists/year, "experienced artists from all over the world." Works on assignment only. Send query letter with brochure, tearsheets and photostats. Samples are filed or are returned by SASE. Reports back within 8 weeks. Originals returned to artist at job's completion. To show a portfolio, mail photostats, tearsheets, final reproduction/product, photographs and photocopy of book dummy if it's a children's book. Considers complexity of project, skill and experience of artist and project's budget when establishing payment. Buys all rights.
Book Design: Assigns 50 freelance design and 50 freelance illustration jobs/year. Pays by the project, $300-600.
Jackets/Covers: Assigns 250 freelance design and 200 freelance illustration jobs/year. Pays by the project, $750-$1,400.
Text Illustration: Assigns 50 freelance jobs/year. Prefers that all work be rendered on flexible paper. Pays by the project, amount varies.
Tips: "Send samples along with a cover letter and background experience. Look at our books before you consider us, to see if your artwork is somewhat appropriate to our style."

*HARRISON HOUSE PUBLISHING, 1029 N. Utica, Tulsa OK 74110. (918)582-2126. Art Supervisor: Doug Belew. Estab. 1975. Publishes hardcover and trade paperback originals and mass market paperback originals. Publishes nonfiction and fiction: cookbooks, instruction, juvenile, reference, self-help, Christian and romance (Christian). Specializes in Christian teaching books. Publishes 24 titles/year. 10% require freelance illustration; 50% require freelance design. Recent titles include *The Unique Woman*, *More than Conquerors*, and *Grief*.
First Contact & Terms: Approached by 60 freelance artists/year. Works with 1 freelance illustrator and 3 freelance designers/year. ("Would like to use more.") Works with illustrators mainly for jacket/cover, book and text illustration. Works on assignment only. Send query letter with brochure, tearsheets, slides and transparencies. Samples are filed. Call to schedule an appointment to show a portfolio, or mail appropriate materials. Considers complexity of project, skill and experience of artist, project's budget, turnaround time and rights purchased when establishing payment.
Jackets/Covers: Pays by the project, $300-500.
Text Illustration: Pays by the project, $300-1,200.
Tips: "We're looking for freelance artists portraying a positive look—contemporary, fresh, clean. We desire a New York look on a Tulsa budget. Will give consistent work if good."

*HARVEST HOUSE PUBLISHERS, 1075 Arrowsmith, Eugene OR 97402. (503)343-0123. Production Manager: Fred Renich. Specializes in hardcovers and paperbacks of adult fiction and nonfiction, children's books and youth material. Publishes 55 titles/year.
First Contact & Terms: Works with 5 freelance artists/year. Works on assignment only. Send query letter with brochure or resume, tearsheets and photographs. Samples are filed. Reports back only if interested. Originals sometimes returned to artist at job's completion. Call or write to schedule an appointment to show a portfolio or mail tearsheets and final reproduction/product. Considers complexity of project, skill and experience of artist, project's budget and turnaround time when establishing payment. Buys all rights.
Jackets/Covers: Assigns 50 freelance design and 10 freelance illustration jobs/year.
Text Illustration: Assigns 5 freelance jobs/year. Pays approximately $125/page.
Needs: Uses artists for inside illustrations and cover design. "Must be relevant to textbook subject and grade level." Occasionally uses freelance book designers. "Recent major el/hi series have used thousands of 4-color cartoon-type illustrations, as well as realistic scientific paintings, and a variety of 'story' pictures for reading books; also black line work for workbooks and duplicating masters." Payment is usually by project, and varies greatly, "but is competitive with other textbook publishers."

HEMKUNT PRESS, A-78 Naraina Indl. Area Ph.I, New Delhi 110028 India. Phone: 505079. Director: Mr. G.P. Singh. Specializes in educational text books, illustrated general books for children and also books for adults. Subjects include religion and history. Publishes 30-50 titles/year.
First Contact & Terms: Works with 7-8 freelance artists/year. Works on assignment only. Send query letter with resume and samples to be kept on file. Prefers photographs and tearsheets as samples. Samples not filed are not returned. Reports only if interested. Originals not returned to artist. Considers complexity of project, skill and experience of artist and project's budget when establishing payment. Buys all rights.
Book Design: Assigns 40-50 titles/year. Payment varies.
Jackets/Covers: Assigns 30-40 freelance design jobs/year. Payment varies.
Text Illustration: Assigns 30-40 jobs/year. Pays by the project, $50-600.

T. EMMETT HENDERSON, PUBLISHER, 130 W. Main St., Middletown NY 10940. (914)343-1038. Contact: T. Emmett Henderson. Publishes hardcover and paperback local history, American Indian, archaeology and genealogy originals and reprints. Publishes 2-3 titles/year; 100% require freelance design; 100% require freelance illustration.
First Contact & Terms: Send query letter. No work returned. Reports in 4 weeks. Buys book rights. Originals returned to artist at job's completion. Works on assignment only. Send resume to be kept on file for future assignments. Check for most recent titles in bookstores. Artist supplies overlays for cover artwork. No advance. No pay for unused assigned work. Assigns 5 advertising jobs/year; pays $10 minimum.
Book Design: Assigns 2-4 jobs/year. Uses artists for cover art work, some text illustration. Prefers representational style.
Jackets/Covers: Assigns 2-4 jobs/year. Uses representational art. Pays $20 minimum, b&w line drawings and color-separated work.
Text Illustrations: Pays $10 minimum, b&w. Buys 5-15 cartoons/year. Uses cartoons as chapter headings. Pays $5-12 minimum, b&w.

HERALD PRESS, 616 Walnut Ave., Scottdale PA 15683. (412)887-8500, ext. 244. Art Director: James M. Butti. Specializes in hardcover and paperback originals and reprints of inspirational, historical, juvenile, theological, biographical, fiction and nonfiction books. Publishes 24 titles/year. Recent titles include: *The Deserter*, *Changing Lenses*, *Edge of Dawn*, and *Who Is My Neighbor*. Estab. 1908. 60% require freelance illustration. Catalog available.
First Contact & Terms: Approached by 75-100 freelance artists each year. Works with 12 illustrators/year. Prefers oil, pen & ink, colored pencil, watercolor, and acrylic. Works on assignment only. Send query letter with brochure or resume, tearsheets, photostats, slides and photographs. Samples are not filed and are returned by SASE. Reports back within 2 weeks. Originals not returned to artist at job's completion "except in special arrangements." To show a portfolio, mail original/final art, photostats, tearsheets, final reproduction/product, photographs and slides. "Portfolio should include approximate time different jobs or illustrations had taken." Considers complexity of project, skill and experience of artist and project's budget when establishing payment. Buys all rights.
Jackets/Covers: Assigns 8 freelance design and 8 freelance illustration jobs/year. Pays by the project, $150 minimum.
Text Illustration: Assigns 6 freelance jobs/year. Pays by the project, $300-600 (complete project).
Tips: "Design we use is colorful/realistic/religious. When sending samples, show a wide range of styles and subject matter—otherwise you limit yourself."

*HOLIDAY HOUSE, 40 E. 49th St., New York NY 10017. (212)688-0085. Vice President Design and Production: David Rogers. Specializes in hardcover children's books. Publishes 45 titles/year; 30% require freelance illustration. Recent titles include: *Little Grunt & the Big Egg* and *Jason & the Golden Fleece*.
First Contact & Terms: Approached by 75-125 freelance artists/year. Works with 10-15 freelance artists/year. Prefers art suitable for children and young adults. Works on assignment only. Samples are filed or are returned by SASE. Reports back only if interested. Originals returned to artist at job's completion. Call to schedule an appointment to show a portfolio, which should include "whatever the artist likes to do and think's he does well." Considers complexity of project, skill and experience of artist and project's budget when establishing payment. Buys one-time rights.
Book Design: Pays by the hour, $15-20.
Jackets/Covers: Assigns 10-15 freelance illustration jobs/year. Prefers watercolor, then acrylic and charcoal/pencil. Pays by the project, $900.
Text Illustrations: Assigns 5-10 jobs/year. Pays royalty.
Tips: "Show samples of everything you do well and like to do." A common mistake is "not following size specifications."

HOMESTEAD PUBLISHING, Box 193, Moose WY 83012. Art Director: Carl Schreier. Estab. 1980. Specializes in hardcover and paperback originals of nonfiction, natural history, Western art and general Western regional literature. Publishes over 6 titles/year. 75% require freelance illustration. Book catalog free for SASE with 4 first class stamps.

First Contact & Terms: Works with 50 freelance illustrators and 20 freelance designers/year. Works on assignment only. Prefers pen & ink, airbrush, charcoal/pencil and watercolor. Send query letter with samples to be kept on file or write for appointment to show portfolio. Prefers to receive as samples "examples of past work, if available (such as published books or illustrations used in magazines, etc.). For color work, slides are suitable; for b&w technical pen, photostats. And one piece of original artwork which can be returned." Samples not filed are returned by SASE only if requested. Reports within 10 days. No original work returned after job's completion. Considers complexity of project, skill and experience of artist, project's budget and turnaround time when establishing payment. Rights purchased vary according to project.

Book Design: Assigns 6 freelance jobs/year. Pays by the project, $50-3,500 average.

Jackets/Covers: Assigns 2 freelance design and 4 freelance illustration jobs/year. Pays by the project, $50-3,500 average.

Text Illustration: Assigns 26 freelance jobs/year. Prefers technical pen illustration, maps (using airbrush, overlays, etc.), watercolor illustrations for children's books, calligraphy and lettering for titles and headings. Pays by the hour, $5-20 average; by the project, $50-3,500 average.

Tips: "We are using more graphic, contemporary designs. We are looking for the best quality, well-written publications that are available."

HUMANICS LIMITED, Box 7447, Atlanta GA 30309. (404)874-2176. FAX: (404)874-1976. Acquisitions Editor: Katherine Buttler. Estab. 1976. Book publisher. Publishes hardcover and trade paperback originals and educational activity books. Types of books include instruction, pre-school, juvenile, self-help and New Age. Specializes in self-help, psychology, educational resource, nutrition, peace and environment. Publishes 12 titles/year. Recent titles include *Make the Circle Bigger: We Need Each Other; Tao of Sailing; Cambio, Chameleon* and *Home At Last*. 10% require freelance illustration and design. Book catalog free for SASE with 2 first class stamps.

Needs: Approached by 24-30 freelance artists/year. Works with 3 freelance illustrators and 2 freelance designers/year. Buys 60 freelance illustrations/year. Uses freelance artists for text illustration. Works on assignment only.

First Contact & Terms: Send query letter with resume, SASE, photocopies and slides. Samples are filed or are returned by SASE if requested by artist. Reports back to the artist only if interested. Call to schedule an appointment to show a portfolio or mail appropriate materials. Rights purchased vary according to project. Originals are not returned at the job's completion.

Book Design: Assigns 2 freelance design and 3-5 freelance illustration jobs/year. Pays by the project, $150 minimum, pays royalties.

Jackets/Covers: Assigns 4 freelance illustration jobs/year. Pays by the project, $150 minimum, pays royalties.

Text Illustration: Assigns 2 freelance design and 3 freelance illustration jobs/year.

Tips: "Send examples of your work, preferably related to our subject matter. Follow up with a call. Make appointment for portfolio review if possible."

*CARL HUNGNESS PUBLISHING, Box 24308, Speedway IN 46224. (317)244-4792. Editorial Director: Carl Hungness. Publishes hardcover automotive originals. Publishes 2-4 titles/year.

First Contact & Terms: Send query letter with samples and SASE. Reports in 2 weeks. Offers $100 advance. Buys one-time or all rights. No pay for unused assigned work. Free catalog.

HUNTER HOUSE PUBLISHERS, Box 847, Claremont CA 91711. Production Manager: Paul J. Frindt. Specializes in hardcover and paperback originals on adult and young adult nonfiction, areas of health and psychology. Publishes 6-11 titles/year.

First Contact & Terms: Works with 2-3 freelance artists/year. Prefers local artists. Works on assignment only. Send query letter with resume, slides and photographs. Samples are filed or are returned by SASE. Reports back within weeks. Originals not returned to artist at job's completion. Write to schedule an appointment to show a portfolio, which should include thumbnails, roughs, original/final art, photographs, slides, transparencies and dummies. Considers complexity of project, skill of artist, project's budget, turnaround time and rights purchased when establishing payment. Buys all rights.

Book Design: Assigns 2-3 freelance design and 2-4 freelance illustration jobs/year. Pays by the hour, $7.50-15; by the project, $250-750.

Jackets/Covers: Assigns 3-6 freelance design and 4-8 freelance illustration jobs/year. Pays by the hour, $10-25; by the project, $250-750.

Text Illustration: Assigns 1-3 freelance jobs/year. Pays by the hour, $10-18; by the project, $150-450.

Tips: "We work closely with freelancers and prefer designers/illustrators/artists who are open to suggestion, feedback, and creative direction. Much of the time may be spent consulting; we don't appreciate impatient or excessively defensive responses. In book design we are conservative, in cover and illustration rather conceptual and somewhat understated but interested in originality."

*HURTIG PUBLISHERS LTD., Suite 1302, Oxford Tower, 10235-101 St., Edmonton, Alberta, T5J 3G1 Canada. (403)426-2359. Contact: Editorial Dept. Specializes in hardcover and paperback originals of nonfiction, primarily on Canadian-oriented topics. Publisher of The Canadian Encyclopedia. Recent titles include *The*

Junior Encyclopedia of Canada and *Masterpieces of Canadian Art from the National Gallery of Canada*.
First Contact & Terms: Approached by about 25 freelance artists/year. Artists must have "considerable experience and be based in Canada." Send query letter to be kept on file; "almost all work is specially commissioned from current sources." Reports within 3 months. Considers complexity of project, skill and experience of artist, project's budget, turnaround time and rights purchased when establishing payment. Rights purchased vary according to project.
Tips: Books contain "mostly historical photographs or reproductions of fine art. Don't try to contact us by phone. Send samples that we can keep on file but remember that we use almost *no* freelance graphic artists."

Illustrator Carol Heyer of Thousand Oaks, California rendered this Prismacolor colored-pencil piece for Ideals Publishing Corporation. She says editor Pat Pringy was looking for "soft colors, detailed pieces and a contrast between the 'peaches and cream' appearance of Beauty and the darker, more intense figure of Beast." She learned of Ideals from Artist's Market and now is working on another project for them, the sequel Excalibur.

IDEALS PUBLISHING CORP., Nelson Place at Elm Hill Pike, Nashville TN 37214. (615)885-8270. Children's Book Editor: Peggy Schaefer. Specializes in original children's books.
First Contact & Terms: Works with 10-12 freelance artists/year. Works on assignment only. Send query letter with brochure showing art style, tearsheets, photostats, slides and photographs. Samples are filed or are returned by SASE only if requested. Does not report back. Originals not returned to artist at job's completion. To show a portfolio, mail appropriate materials. Considers skill and experience of artist and project's budget when establishing payment.

IGNATIUS PRESS, Catholic Publisher, 2515 McAllister St., San Francisco CA 94118. Production Editor: Carolyn Lemon. Art Editor: Roxanne Lum. Estab. 1978. Catholic theology and devotional books for lay people, priests and religious readers.
First Contact & Terms: Works on assignment only. Will send art guidelines "if we are interested in the artist's work." Accepts previously published material. Send brochure showing art style or resume and photocopies. Samples not filed are not returned. Reports only if interested. To show a portfolio, mail appropriate materials; "we will contact you if interested." Pays on acceptance.

Jackets/Covers: Buys cover art from freelance artists. Prefers Christian symbols/calligraphy and religious illustrations of Jesus, saints, etc. (used on cover or in text). "Simplicity, clarity, and elegance are the rule. We like calligraphy, occasionally incorporated with Christian symbols. We also do covers with type and photography." Prefers pen & ink, charcoal/pencil. "Since we are a nonprofit Catholic press, we cannot always afford paying the going rate for freelance art, so we are always appreciative when artists can give us a break on prices and work *ad maiorem Dei gloriam.*"
Tips: "I do not want to see any schmaltzy religious art."

*INSTRUCTIONAL FAIR, Box 1650, Grand Rapids MI 49501. Production Manager: Jackie Servis. Publisher of educational material, elementary level, all curriculum areas. These are supplemental materials. Clients: elementary school teachers.
First Contact & Terms: Works with several freelance artists/year. Works on assignment only. Send query letter with photostats. Samples are filed or are returned only if requested by artists. Reports back within 1-2 months, only if interested. Write to schedule an appointment to show a portfolio, or mail original/final art and final reproduction/product. Pays by the project, amount negotiated. Considers client's budget and how work will be used when establishing payment. Buys all rights.

INTERNATIONAL MARINE PUBLISHING CO. Seven Seas Press, Box 220, Camden ME 04843. (207)236-4837. Production Director: Molly Mulhern. Imprint of TAB Books. Estab. 1969. Specializes in hardcovers and paperbacks on marine (nautical) topics. Publishes 25 titles/year. 50% require freelance illustration. Book catalog free for request.
First Contact & Terms: Works with 20 freelance illustrators and 20 freelance designers/year. Works with freelance illustrators mainly for interior illustration. Prefers local artists. Works on assignment only. Send resume and tearsheets. Samples are filed. Reports back within 4 weeks. Originals are not returned to artist at job's completion. To show a portfolio, mail original/final art and tearsheets. Considers project's budget when establishing payment. Buys one-time rights.
Book Design: Assigns 20 freelance design and 20 freelance illustration jobs/year. Pays by the project, $150-550; by the hour, $12-30.
Jackets/Covers: Assigns 20 freelance design and 3 freelance illustration jobs/year. Pays by the project, $100-300; by the hour, $12-30.
Text Illustration: Assigns 20 freelance jobs/year. Prefers technical drawings. Pays by the hour, $12-30; by the project, $30-80 per piece.
Tips: Do your research! See if your work fits with what we publish! "Write with a resume and sample; then follow with a call; then come by to visit."

KALEIDOSCOPIX, INC., Children's Book Division, Box 389, Franklin MA 02038-0389. (508)528-6211. Editor: J.A. Kruza. "Kaleidoscopix, Inc. has two divisions: book publishing and audio cassette publishing. The products of both are marketed to an upscale audience like tourists through seacoast gift stores. Titles include historical and nautical material relevant to the area, tourism guides, and children's books for ages 3-7. Our books feature stories which present a problem that is solved by the hero through his/her own effort."
First Contact & Terms: "We are reviewing manuscripts and/or illustrations. And we are contracting with effective communicators with either in-depth knowledge, or storytelling or singing ability."
Text Illustration: Send a summary letter with slides, photographs, photostats and photocopies. Samples are filed or are returned by SASE. Reports back within 15-45 days. Call to schedule an appointment to show a portfolio, which should include original/final art, final reproduction/product and photographs. Buys all rights. Pays $25 and up, b&w; $50 and up, color, inside; on publication. Pays by the project, $300-2,000.
Tips: "Photocopies of representative style and technique show what your skills are. Sometimes an IBM full color photocopy or slide shows your sense for color. Send them."

*KITCHEN SINK PRESS, No. 2 Swamp Rd., Princeton WI 54968. (414)295-6922. FAX: (414)295-6878. Editor-in-Chief: David Schreiner. Estab. 1969. Book and comic book publisher. Publishes hardcover originals and reprints and trade paperback originals and reprints. Types of books include science fiction, adventure, fantasy, mystery, humor, graphic novels and comic books. Publishes 24 books and 48 comic books. Recent titles include Al Capp's *Li'l Abner*, Will Eisner's *A Life Force* and Mark Schultz's *Cadillacs & Dinosaurs*. 20%

The asterisk before a listing indicates that the listing is new in this edition. New markets are often the most receptive to freelance submissions.

require freelance illustration; 10% require freelance design. Book catalog free by request.

First Contact & Terms: Approached by more than 100 freelance artists/year. Works with 10-20 freelance illustrators and 2-3 freelance designers/year. Buys 300 freelance illustrations/year. Prefers artists with experience in comics. Uses freelance artists mainly for covers, contributions to anthologies and new series. Also uses freelance artists for jacket/cover illustration, comic book covers and text illustration. Works on assignment only although "sometimes a submission is accepted as is." Send query letter with tearsheets, SASE and photocopies. Samples are filed or are returned by SASE. Reports back within 3-4 weeks. Mail appropriate materials only. "We do not encourage portfolio viewing because of our remote location." Rights purchased vary according to project. Originals are returned at the job's completion.

Book Design: Assigns 2-3 freelance design and many freelance illustration jobs/year. Pays by the project, $600-1,000.

Jackets/Covers: Assigns 6-8 freelance design jobs/year. Pays by the project, $200-400. Prefers line art with color overlays.

Tips: "Dazzle us with your samples."

LEISURE BOOKS, a division of Dorchester Publishing Co., Inc., Suite 1008, 276 5th Ave., New York NY 10001. (212)725-8811. Managing Editor: Carolyn Pittes. Estab. 1972. Specializes in paperback, originals and reprints, especially mass market category fiction—historical romance, western, adventure, horror. Publishes 144 titles/year. 90% require freelance illustration.

First Contact & Terms: Buys from 24 freelance artists/year. "We work with freelance art directors; editorial department views all art initially and refers artists to art directors. We need highly realistic, paperback illustration; oil or acrylic. No graphics, fine art, representational art or photography." Works on assignment only. Send samples by mail—no samples will be returned without SASE. Reports only if samples are appropriate or if SASE is enclosed. Call for appointment to drop off portfolio. Original work returned after job's completion. Considers complexity of project and project's budget when establishing payment. Usually buys first rights, but rights purchased vary according to project.

Jackets/Covers: Pays by the project.

Tips: "Talented new artists are welcome. Be familiar with the kind of artwork we use on our covers. If it's not your style, don't waste your time and ours."

LIBRARIES UNLIMITED, Box 3988 Englewood CO 80155-3988. (303)770-1220. Marketing Director: Shirley Lambert. Estab. 1964. Specializes in hardcover and paperback original reference books concerning library science and school media for librarians, educators and researchers. Publishes 45 titles/year. 2% require freelance illustration. Book catalog free by request.

First Contact & Terms: Works with 4-5 freelance artists/year. Works on assignment only. Send query letter with resume and photocopies. Samples not filed are returned only if requested. Reports within 2 weeks. No originals returned to artist at job's completion. Considers complexity of project, skill and experience of artist, and project's budget when establishing payment. Buys all rights.

Book Design: Assigns 2-4 freelance illustration jobs/year. Pays by the project, $100 minimum.

Jackets/Covers: Assigns 45 freelance design jobs/year. Pays by the project, $250 minimum.

Tips: "We look for the ability to draw or illustrate without overly-loud cartoon techniques. We need the ability to use two-color effectively, with screens and screen builds. We ignore anything sent to us that is in four-color. We also need a good feel for typefaces, and we prefer experience with books."

LITTLE, BROWN AND COMPANY, 34 Beacon St., Boston MA 02106. (617)227-0730. Art Director: Steve Snider. Specializes in trade hardcover and paperback originals and reprints. Publishes 300 titles/year. 50% require freelance illustration.

First Contact & Terms: Works with approximately 50 freelance artists/year. Works on assignment only. Send query letter with brochure, resume, tear sheets, Photostats and photographs. Samples are filed. Samples not filed are returned only if requested by artist. Reports back only if interested. Originals returned to artist at job's completion. Call to schedule an appointment to show a portfolio, which should include original/final art, tear sheets, final reproduction/product and photographs. Considers complexity of project, project's budget and turnaround time when establishing payment.

Jackets/Covers: Assigns freelance design and illustration jobs/year. Pays by the project, $700 minimum.

*LLEWELLYN PUBLICATIONS, Box 64383, St. Paul MN 55164. Art Director: Terry Buske. Estab. 1901. Book publisher. Imprint of Llewellyn. Publishes hardcover originals, trade paperback originals and reprints, mass market originals and reprints and calendars. Types of books include reference, self-help, metaphysical, occult, mythology, health, women's spirituality and New Age. Specializes in New Age and magic. Publishes 60 titles/year. Recent titles include *Teutonic Magic, Dream Lover, Gypsy Love Magick, Book of Goddesses* and *Wicca*. 60% require freelance illustration. Book catalog free by request.

First Contact & Terms: Approached by 200 freelance artists/year. Works with 15 freelance illustrators/year. Buys 150 freelance illustrations/year. Prefers artists with experience in book covers, New Age material and realism. Uses freelance artists mainly for book covers and interiors. Works on assignment only. Send query

When art director of Little, Brown & Company Steve Snider assigned this book cover illustration to Ken Maryanski, who he has known for several years, he gave him the manuscript to read, specifying that he wanted something lighthearted, humorous, erotic— a little bawdy. Snider says this is a successful piece because it evokes the tongue-in-cheek, slightly sexy tone of the book.

© 1989 Little, Brown & Company

letter with brochure, SASE, tearsheets, photographs and photocopies. Samples are filed or are returned by SASE. Reports back within 1 month, only with SASE. To show a portfolio, mail b&w and color tearsheets, photographs and slides. Negotiates rights purchased.

Jackets/Covers: Assigns 40 freelance illustration jobs/year. Pays by the illustration, $150-600. Media and style preferred "are usually realistic, well-researched, airbrush, acrylic, oil, colored pencil. Artist should know our subjects."

Text Illustration: Assigns 15 freelance illustration jobs/year. Pays by the project, $30-100. Media and style preferred "are pencil, pen & ink, usually very realistic; there are usually people in the illustrations."

Tips: "Know what we publish and send similar samples. I need artists who are aware of occult themes, knowledgable in the areas of metaphysics, divination, alternative religions, women's spirituality, and who are professional and able to present very refined and polished finished pieces. Knowledge of history, mythology and ancient civilization are a big plus."

LODESTAR BOOKS, imprint of E.P. Dutton, 315 Hudson St., New York NY 10014. (212)366-2626. Senior Editor: Rosemary Brosnan. Publishes young adult fiction (12-16 years) and nonfiction hardcovers, fiction and nonfiction for ages 9-11 and 10-14, nonfiction and fiction picture books. Publishes 25-30 titles/year.

First Contact & Terms: Send query letter with samples or drop off portfolio. Especially looks for "knowledge of book requirements, previous jackets, good color, strong design and ability to draw people and action" when reviewing samples. Prefers to buy all rights.

Jackets/Covers: Assigns approximately 10-12 jackets/year to freelancers. Pays $700 minimum, color.

Tips: In young adult fiction, there is a trend toward "covers that are more realistic with the focus on one or two characters. In nonfiction, strong, simple graphic design, often utilizing a photograph. Three-color jackets are popular for nonfiction; occasionally full-color is used."

*LOOMPANICS UNLIMITED, Box 1197, Port Townsend WA 98368. Editorial Director: Steve O'Keefe. Estab. 1975. Book publisher. Publishes trade paperback originals. Types of books include instruction, reference and self-help. Specializes in crime, police science, fake I.D. and underground economy. Publishes 25 titles/year. Recent titles include *Techniques of Burglar Alarm Bypassing* and *How to Disappear.* 50% require freelance illustration; 10% require freelance design. Book catalog available for $3.

First Contact & Terms: Approached by 6 freelance artists/year. Works with 4-5 freelance illustrators and 1-2 freelance designers/year. Buys 250 freelance illustrations/year. Prefers artists with "good line drawing skills." Uses freelance artists mainly for how-to illustrations and diagrams. Also uses freelance artists for cover illustration and design and text illustration. Works on assignment only. Send query letter with photocopies. Samples are filed. Reports back within 3 weeks. To show a portfolio, mail b&w and color tearsheets. Buys all rights. Originals are not returned at the job's completion.

Jackets/Covers: Assigns 10 freelance illustration jobs/year. Pays by the project, $150-300. Media and style preferred varies.
Text Illustration: Assigns 12 freelance illustration jobs/year. Pays per drawing, $20. Prefers "strong line drawings, diagrams and technical illustrations."
Tips: "Send photocopies of good line drawings. Our pay rate is low, but payment is reliable."

*LUCENT BOOKS, Box 289011, San Diego CA 92128-9011. (619)485-7424. Managing Editor: Bonnie Szumski. Estab. 1988. Book publisher. Publishes nonfiction for libraries and classrooms. Specializes in biography, preschool, juvenile and young adult. Specializes in controversial issues and disasters. Publishes 30 titles/year. Recent titles include *Pompeii: World Disasters*, *The Black Death* and *The Armenian Earthquake*. 30% require freelance illustration. Book catalog free for SASE.
First Contact & Terms: Approached by 15-20 freelance artists/year. Buys 100-150 freelance illustrations/year. Prefers artists with experience in "young adult books with a realistic style in pen & in or pencil, able to draw creatively, not from photographs." Uses freelance aritsts mainly for *The World Disaster Series* and technical drawings for the Encyclopedia series. Also uses freelance artists for jacket/cover and text illustration. Works on assignment only. Send query letter with resume, tearsheets and photocopies. Samples are filed. Reports back to the artist only if interested. To show a portfolio, mail appropriate materials. Buys all rights. Originals are not returned at the job's completion.
Book Design: Pays by the project.
Jackets/Covers: Pays by the project.
Text Illustration: Assigns 8-10 freelance illustration jobs/year. Pays by the project. Prefers pencil and pen & ink.
Tips: "We have a very specific style in mind and can usually tell immediately from samples whether or not the artist's style suits our needs."

*MADISON BOOKS, 4720 Boston Wy., Lanham MD 20706. (301)459-5308. FAX: (301)459-2118. Design Director: Gisele Byrd. Estab. 1984. Book publisher. Publishes hardcover and trade paperback originals. Types of books include biography, history, and books about popular culture and current events. Specializes in biography, history and popular culture. Publishes 16 titles/year. Recent titles include *Hattie: The Life of Hattie McDaniel* and *The Hunt for "Tokyo Rose"*. 40% require freelance illustration; 100% require freelance design. Book catalog free by request.
First Contact & Terms: Approached by 20 freelance artists/year. Works with 4 freelance illustrators and 12 freelance designers/year. Buys 2 freelance illustrations/year. Prefers artists with experience in book jacket design. Uses freelance artists mainly for book jackets. Also uses freelance artists for book and catalog design. Works on assignment only. Send query letter with tearsheets, photocopies and photostats. Samples are filed or are returned by SASE if requested by artist. Reports back to the artist only if interested. Call to schedule an appointment to show a portfolio which should include roughs, original/final art, tearsheets, photographs, slides and dummies. Buys all rights.
Book Design: Assigns 2 freelance design and 2 freelance illustration jobs/year. Pays by the project, $1,000-2,000.
Jackets/Covers: Assigns 16 freelance design and 2 freelance illustration jobs/year. Pays by the project, $600-1,000. Prefers typographic design, photography and line art.
Tips: "We are looking for an ability to produce trade-quality designs within a limited budget. Books have large type, clean lines, covers that 'breathe'. Common mistakes are portfolios which do not include any cover designs, when I'm trying to hire experienced cover designers. If you have not designed jackets for a publishing house, but want to break into that area have at least 5 'fake' titles designed to show ability."

METAMORPHOUS PRESS INC., 3249 NW 29th Ave., Box 10616, Portland OR 97210. (503)228-4972. Publisher: David Balding. Estab. 1982. Specializes in hardcover and paperback originals, general trade books, mostly nonfiction and self-help. "We are a general book publisher for a general audience in North America." Publishes at least 5 titles/year. 10% require freelance illustration. Recent titles include *Challenge of Excellence*, *Beliefs* and *Self-Rescue*.
First Contact & Terms: Approached by 200 freelance artists/year. Works with 2 freelance designers and 2 freelance illustrators/year. "We're interested in what an artist can do for us—not experience with others." Works on assignment only. Send query letter with brochure, business card, photostats, photographs, and tearsheets to be kept on file. Samples are not returned. Reports within a few days usually. Considers complexity of project and project's budget when establishing payment. Rights purchased vary according to project.
Book Design: Rarely assigns freelance jobs. "We negotiate payment on an individual basis according to project."
Jackets/Covers: Will possibly assign 1-2 jobs in both freelance design and freelance illustration this year. Payment would vary as to project and budget.
Text Illustration: Assigns 1-2 freelance jobs/year. Payment varies as to project and budget.

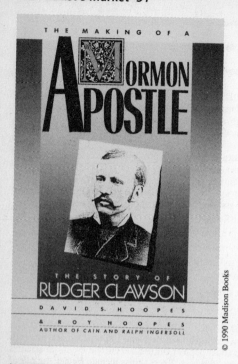

THE MAKING OF A
Mormon Apostle
THE STORY OF
RUDGER CLAWSON
DAVID S. HOOPES
& ROY HOOPES
AUTHOR OF CAIN AND RALPH INGERSOLL

© 1990 Madison Books

Design director of Madison Books, Gisele Byrd, told Washington D.C.-based artist Ann Masters that she wanted to "produce an eye-catching, trade-oriented jacket design, using the provided photographs in some way. Byrd assigned the piece to Masters because of her "ability to design using photographs in a non-traditional way, as well as her typographic skills." She says it is successful because it "captures the essence of the book's contents." Masters sold all rights to this design.

*MILKWEED EDITIONS, Suite 505, Hennepin, Minneapolis MN 55403. (612)332-3192. Art Director: R.W. Scholes. Estab. 1979. Book publisher. Publishes trade paperback originals. Types of books include contemporary and historical fiction, poetry, essays, visual and collaborations. Specializes in contemporary subjects. Publishes 8-10 titles/year. Recent titles include *Coming Home Crazy* and *An Alphabet of China Essay*. 70% require freelance illustration; 10% require freelance design. Book catalog free for SASE with 65¢ first-class stamps.

First Contact & Terms: Approached by 20 freelance artists/year. Works with 4 freelance illustrators/year.Buys 100 freelance illustrations/year. Prefers artists with experience in books illustration. Uses freelance artists mainly for fiction and poetry jacket/cover illustration and text illustration. Works on assignment only. Send query letter with resume, SASE and tearsheets. Samples are filed or are returned by SASE if requested by artist. Reports back within 3-6 weeks. Call to schedule an appointment to show a portfolio, which should include best possible samples. Rights purchased vary according to project. Originals returned at the job's completion.

Book Design: Assigns 80 freelance illustration jobs/year. Pays by the project, $25 minimum.

Jackets/Covers: Assigns 3 freelance illustration jobs/year. Pays by the project, $50 minimum. "Prefer a range of different media—according to the needs of each book."

Text Illustration: Assigns 20 freelance illustration jobs/year. Pays by the project, $25 minimum. Prefers various mediums and styles.

Tips: "Show ability and interest—call back."

*MINNE HA! HA!, Box 14009, Minneapolis MN 55414. Editor/Publisher: Lance Anger. Specializes in paperback originals on political humor, cartoons and cartooning. Also publishes bimonthly humor magazine with 20,000+ circulation. Publishes 1 title/every other year. Recent title includes *Buy This Too*, by Pete Wagner.

First Contact & Terms: Approached by 20-25 freelance artists/year. Works with 3-10 freelance artists/year. "Fine artists encouraged to showcase here." Send query letter with brochure, resume, business card, samples and tearsheets to be kept on file. Samples not kept on file are not returned. Reports only if interested. Write for appointment to show a portfolio. Originals returned to artist at job's completion. Considers project's budget and cooperative profit-sharing when establishing payment. Buys one-time rights.

Book Design: Assigns 1-3 freelance jobs/year. Pay is negotiable.

Jackets/Covers: Assigns 1-3 freelance design jobs/year.

Text Illustration: Assigns 1-3 freelance jobs/year.

Tips: "We are using more art integrated with words/text." Looking for "new wavey, artsy fartsy, funny funny funny work. Do not send originals! Sending resumes is not necessary either. Send a selection of photocopied line art; the funnier the better."

*MODERN PUBLISHING, 155 E. 55th St., New York NY 10022. (212)826-0850. Art Director: Paul Matarazzo. Specializes in hardcovers, paperbacks and coloring books. Publishes approximately 100 titles/year. Recent titles include *Reader Teady* and *New Kids on the Block.*

First Contact & Terms: Approached by 10-30 freelance artists/year. Works with 15 freelance artists/year. Works on assignment only. Send query letter with resume and samples. Samples not filed are returned only if requested. Reports only if interested. Original work not returned at job's completion. Considers turnaround time and rights purchased when establishing payment. Buys all rights.

Jackets/Covers: Pays by the project, $100-200 average, cover, "usually 4 books per series."

Text Illustration: Pays by the project, $15-20 average, page (line art), "48-382 pages per book, always 4 books in series."

Tips: "Do not show samples which don't reflect the techniques and styles we use. Reference our books and book stores to know our product line better."

WILLIAM MORROW & CO. INC., (Lothrop, Lee, Shepard Books), 105 Madison Ave., New York NY 10016. (212)889-3050. Art Director: Cindy Simon. Specializes in hardcover originals and reprint children's books. Publishes 70 titles/year. 100% require freelance illustration. Book catalog free for SASE with 3 first-class stamps.

First Contact & Terms: Works with 30 freelance artists/year. Uses artists mainly for picture books and jackets. Works on assignment only. Send query letter with resume and samples, "followed by call." Samples are filed. Reports back within 3-4 weeks. Originals returned to artist at job's completion. Portfolio should include original/final art and dummies. Considers complexity of project and project's budget when establishing payment. Negotiates rights purchased.

Book Design: "Most design is done on staff." Assigns 1 or 2 freelance design jobs/year. Pays by the project.

Jackets/Covers: Assigns 1 or 2 freelance design jobs/year. Pays by the project.

Text illustration: Assigns 70 freelance jobs/year. Pays by the project.

Tips: "Be familiar with our publications."

*MOSAIC PRESS MINIATURE BOOKS, 358 Oliver Rd., Cincinnati OH 45215. (513)761-5977. Publisher: Miriam Irwin. Estab. 1977. Book publisher. Publishes hardcover originals. Types of books include miniature books. Publishes 4 titles/year. Recent titles include *Trees of Minnesota* and *Victorian Christmas.* 100% require freelance illustration. Book catalog free for SASE with 45¢ first-class stamps. "Ask for artists' guide."

First Contact & Terms: Approached by 12 freelance artists/year. Works with 2 freelance illustrators/year. Prefers local artists, but not necessarily. Uses freelance artists mainly for pen & ink drawings. Also uses freelance artists for text illustration. Works on assignment only. Send query letter which includes phone number with SASE and photocopies of pen & ink illustrations under 6". Samples are not filed and are returned by SASE if requested by artist. Reports back within 2 weeks, if SASE enclosed. Call to schedule an appointment to show portfolio which should include pen & ink only. Buys one-time rights. Originals are sometimes returned at the job's completion.

Book Design: Pays by the project.

Jackets/Covers: Assigns 5 freelance illustration jobs/year. Pays by the project, ($50, 1 copy of the book and 40% discount on all Mosaic Press books). Prefers b&w pen & ink under 6". "They must reduce well."

Text Illustration: Assigns 10 freelance illustration jobs/year. Pays by the project. $40, 5 copies of the book and 40% discount on all Mosaic Press books). Prefers b&w pen and ink under 6" tall.

*MOUNTAIN LION, INC., Box 257, Route 206, Rocky Hill NJ 08553. (609)924-8369. Managing Editor: Martha Wickenden. Produces hardcover and paperback originals for publishers on sports, health, how-to, fitness and large format pictorials. Publishes 10-12 titles/year; 30% require freelance illustration. Recent titles include *Rotisserie & Fantasy* and *Baseball League Guide, 1990.*

First Contact & Terms: Works with 4-5 freelance artists/year. Prefers artists who have some experience with publishing. Works on assignment only. Send query letter with resume, tearsheets, photostats, duplicate slides and photographs or other samples. Samples are filed or are returned only if requested. Reports back within 1 week. Originals not returned to artist at job's completion. To show a portfolio, mail thumbnails, photostats, tearsheets, final reproduction/product, duplicate photographs and slides. Considers complexity of project, skill and experience of artist, project's budget, turnaround time and rights purchased when establishing payment. Negotiates rights purchased.

Book Design: Assigns 10-12 freelance design jobs/year. Pays $300-500, depending on complexity.

Jackets/Covers: Assigns 10-12 freelance design jobs/year. Pays fixed fee, $200-400, depending on complexity.

Text Illustration: Assigns 4-5 freelance jobs/year. Pays by the job, per specs.

Tips: Looking for "humorous, technical or diagrammatic illustration and design which is heavy with text, stats and highly illustrated with photographs (170-200 for 160 pg. book). Work with us, we'll work with you. Show a 'can-do' attitude."

*JOHN MUIR PUBLICATIONS, Box 613, Santa Fe NM 87504. (505)982-4078. President: Steven Cary. Publishes trade paperback nonfiction. "We specialize in travel books, auto repair manuals, children's books, environmental and parenting books and are always actively looking for new illustrations in these fields." Prefers pen & ink, colored pencil, acrylic and calligraphy. Publishes 36 titles/year.
First Contact & Terms: Works with 10-12 freelance artists/year. Prefers local artists. Send query letter with resume and samples to be kept on file. Write for appointment to show portfolio. Accepts any type of sample "as long as it's professionally presented." Samples not filed are returned by SASE. Originals not returned at job's completion. Considers complexity of project, skill and experience of artist, project's budget, turnaround time and rights purchased when establishing payment. Buys all rights.
Jackets/Covers: Assigns 25-30 freelance design and freelance illustration jobs/year, mostly 4-color. Pays by the project, $250 minimum.
Text Illustration: Assigns 20 freelance jobs/year. Usually prefers pen & ink. Negotiates payment.

NATURAL SCIENCE PUBLICATIONS, INC., 2406 NW 47th Terrace, Gainesville FL 32606. (904)371-9858. Editor: Ross Arnett. Book publisher. Estab. 1947. Publishes hardcover originals, trade paperback originals and textbooks. Publishes reference and technical books. Specializes in natural science. Publishes 12-14 titles/year. 5% require freelance illustration and freelance design. Recent titles include *Florida Butterflies*, *Endangered Animals of Thailand* and *Biography of the West Indies*. Book catalog free for request.
First Contact & Terms: Approached by 20-25 freelance artists/year. Works with 1 freelance illustrator/year. Works with 1 freelance designer/year. Buys 50-100 freelance illustrations/year. Uses freelance artists for jacket/cover illustration and design, book design and text illustration. Works on assignment only. Send query letter with brochure, resume and SASE. Samples are filed. Reports back within 10 days. Originals returned to artist at job's completion. To show a portfolio, mail appropriate materials. Considers complexity of project, skill and experience of artist, project's budget and rights purchased when establishing payment. Buys one-time rights.
Tips "Illustrators must work with authors."

NBM PUBLISHING CO., 35-53 70th St., Jackson Heights NY 11372. (718)458-3199. Publisher: Terry Nantier. Publishes graphic novels including *The Silent Invasion* and *Vic & Blood* for an audience of 18-24 year olds. Genres: adventure, fantasy, mystery, science fiction, horror and social parodies. Themes: science fiction, fantasy, mystery and social commentary. Circ. 5-10,000. Original artwork returned after publication.
Book Design: Approached by 60-70 freelance artists/year. Works with 6 freelance designers/year. Uses freelance artists for lettering, paste-up, layout design and coloring. Prefers pen & ink, watercolor and oil for graphic novels submissions. Send query letter with resume and samples. Samples are filed or are returned by SASE. Reports back within 2 weeks. To show a portfolio, mail photocopies of original pencil or ink art. Pays by the project, $200 minimum.
Tips: "We are interested in submissions for graphic novels. We do not need illustrations or covers only!"

THE NEW ENGLAND PRESS, Box 575, Shelburne VT 05482. (802) 863-2520. Contact: Managing Editor. Specializes in paperback originals on regional New England subjects, nature. Publishes 12 titles/year; 60% require freelance illustration. Recent titles include *Yankee Wisdom: New England Proverbs*, *Star in the Shed Window* and *Poetry of James Hayford*.
First Contact & Terms: Approached by 20+ freelance artists/year. Works with 6-8 freelance artists/year. Northern New England artists only. Send query letter with brochure showing art style or resume. Samples are filed. Reports back only if interested. Originals not usually returned to artist at job's completion, but negotiable. To show a portfolio, mail "anything that shows talent." Considers complexity of project, skill and experience of artist, project's budget and turnaround time when establishing payment. Negotiates rights purchased.
Book Design: Assigns 8-10 freelance design and 6-8 freelance illustration jobs/year. Payment varies.
Jackets/Covers: Assigns 4-5 freelance illustration jobs/year. Payment varies.
Text Illustration: Assigns 6-8 freelance jobs/year. Payment varies.
Tips The most common mistake illustrators and designers make in presenting their work is "they never write a query letter—they just send stuff." Design and illustrations used are "more folksy than impressionistic, etc."

NEW READERS PRESS, 1320 Jamesville Ave., Syracuse NY 13210. Art Director: Steve Rhodes. Estab. 1960. Publishes trade paperback originals and textbooks. Publishes nonfiction and fiction: instructional, educational history, romance, historical, mainstream/contemporary. Specializes in reading and writing for young adult and adult new readers. Publishes 20-30 titles/year. 20% require freelance illustration; 0-5% freelance design. Book catalog free for request.
First Contact & Terms: Works with 5-10 freelance illustrators and 3-5 freelance designers/year. Buys 50-100 freelance illustrations/year. Works with illustrators mainly for spots and technical illustration. Also uses artists for jacket/cover and text illustration. Works on assignment only. Send query letter with tearsheets, photostats and SASE. Samples are filed or are returned by SASE only if requested. Reports back only if

interested. Call or write to schedule an appointment to show a portfolio, which should include roughs, original/final art, photographs and transprencies (2¼″ or 4×5). Considers complexity of project, project's budget and turnaround time when establishing payment. Buys one-time rights; negotiates rights purchased.

Book Design: Assigns 3-5 freelance design and 10-15 freelance illustration jobs/year. Pays by the hour, $10-50.

Jackets/Covers: Assigns 3-5 freelance design and 5-10 freelance illustration jobs/year. Prefers contemporary themes. Pays by the hour, $10-50; by the project, $100-500.

Text Illustration: Assigns 10-20 freelance jobs/year. Prefers b&w pen, pencil, watercolor, wash, etc. "Often illustrations include figures of people with a variety of ethnic and cultural backgrounds." Pays by the hour, $10-25; by the project, $10-150.

Tips: Looks for "flexibility in style or medium. We appreciate clean and fresh artwork from artists with little experience to "seasoned pros." Send photocopies of artwork. We especially like to work with artists in central New York area due to easier communication and faster turnaround."

NEW SOCIETY PUBLISHERS, 4527 Springfield Ave., Philadelphia PA 19143. (215)382-6543. Marketing: Marie Bloom. Estab. 1981. Specializes in books and other resources on nonviolent social change. Publishes 12-16 titles and 2 calendars/year. Recent titles include *Reimaging America: The Arts of Social Change, Who's Calling the Shots?* and *Turtle Talk.* Book catalog free on request.

First Contact & Terms: Approached by 3-5 freelance artists/year. Works with several freelance artists/year. Works with artists for cover designs on assignment only. Send query letter with samples to be kept on file. Prefers photostats and photographs. Samples not filed are returned only by SASE. Reports only if interested. Original work sometimes returned to the artist. Considers complexity of the project, project's budget and rights purchased when establishing payment. Negotiates rights purchased.

Covers: Assigns 4-6 freelance design jobs/year. Pays by the project, $50 for 3 sketches. If one is accepted then $200 for completed mechanicals. Additional must be negotiated – for complex jobs.

Text Illustration: Assigns 1-2 jobs/year. Prefers pen & ink line drawings. Pays by the hour, $5-10 or negotiated by the project.

Tips: "Portfolios should include black-and-white as well as color samples, two of each medium, also roughs and final design. Send the range of work, not just slick pieces." The look of design and illustration used is "contemporary and plain."

*NEW WORLD LIBRARY, 58 Paul Dr., San Rafael CA 94903. (415)472-2100. Editor: Katherine Dieter. Book publisher. Types of books include instruction and self-help. Specializes in psychology, philosophy and self-improvement. Publishes 4 titles/year. 25% require freelance illustration; 100% require freelance design. Book catalog frce for request.

First Contact & Terms: Works with freelance artists for jacket/cover illustration and design, book and catalog design and text illustration. Works on assignment only. Send query letter with brochure, resume, tearsheets and SASE. Samples are filed or are returned by SASE only if requested. Reports back only if interested. Originals are not returned at job's completion unless requested. Write to schedule an appointment to show a portfolio, which should include original/final art, tearsheets and final reporduction/product. Negotiates rights purchased.

Book Design: Assigns 6 freelance design and 1 freelance illustration jobs/year. Pays by the project, $350 and up.

Jackets/Covers: Assigns 6 freelance design and 1 freelance illustration jobs/year. Pays by the project, $400.

Text Illustration: Assigns 1 freelance job/year. Pays by the hour, $15.

NEWBURY HOUSE PUBLISHERS, 10 E. 53 St., New York NY 10022. (212)207-7373. Production Coordinator: Cynthia Funkhouser. Specializes in textbooks emphasizing English as a second language. Publishes 25 titles/year; 50% require freelance illustration. Recent titles include *Noteworthy: Listening and Notetaking Skills* and *Issues for Today: An Effective Reading Skills Text.*

First Contact & Terms: Works with 12 freelance artists/year. Works on assignment only. Send query letter with resume and photocopies. Samples are filed and are not returned. Reports back only if interested. Originals not returned at job's completion. Write to schedule an appointment to show a portfolio, which should include roughs, original/final art and final reproduction/product. Considers skill and experience of artists and project's budget when establishing payment. Buys all rights.

Book Design: Assigns 12 freelance design jobs/year. Pays by the project, $200 and up.

Text Illustration: Assigns 12 freelance jobs/year. Prefers line art and ink drawings. Pays per illustration or per project, $20 and up.

Tips: "Designers should have experience in el-hi and/or college book design with samples available to show. Artists should be able to show photocopies of published tearsheets. We use both cartoons and serious illustrations. We seek artists who are able to portray a broad range of ethnic identities in their drawings." A common mistake is that "the look of the illustrations is frequently too juvenile for our books; these books are for adults."

NORTHWOODS PRESS, Box 88, Thomaston ME 04861. Editor: Robert Olmsted. Part of the Conservatory of American Letters. Estab. 1972. Specializes in hardcover and paperback originals of poetry. Publishes approximately 12 titles/year. 10% require freelance illustration. Recent titles include *Dan River Anthology, 1990*; *Looking for the Worm* and *Bound*. Book catalog free for SASE.
First Contact & Terms: Approached by 40-50 freelance artists/year. Works with 3-4 freelance illustrators and 3-4 freelance designers/year. Send query letter to be kept on file. Reports within 10 days. Originals returned to artist at job's completion. Considers complexity of project, skill and experience of artist, project's budget, turnaround time and rights purchased when establishing payment. Buys one-time rights and occasionally all rights.
Jackets/Covers: Assigns 4-5 freelance design jobs and 4-5 freelance illustration jobs/year. "The author provides the artwork and payment."
Tips: Portfolio should include "art suitable for book covers—contemporary, usually realistic."

OCTAMERON PRESS, 4805A Eisenhower Ave., Alexandria VA 22304. Editorial Director: Karen Stokstod. Estab. 1976. Specializes in paperbacks—college financial and college admission guides. Publishes 10-15 titles/year. Recent titles include *College Match* and *Financial Aid Financer*.
First Contact & Terms: Approached by 25 freelance artists/year. Works with 1-2 freelance artists/year. Local artists only. Works on assignment only. Send query letter with brochure showing art style or resume and photocopies. Samples not filed are returned. Reports within 1 week. Original work returned at job's completion. Considers complexity of project and project's budget when establishing payment. Rights purchased vary according to project.
Jackets/Covers: Works with 15 freelance designers and illustators/year. Pays by the project, $200-400.
Text Illustration: Works with variable number of freelance artists/year. Prefers line drawings to photographs. Pays by the project, $35-75.

ODDO PUBLISHING, INC., Box 68, Fayetteville GA 30214. (404)461-7627. Vice President: Charles W. Oddo. Estab. 1964. Specializes in hardcovers of juvenile fiction. Publishes 6-10 titles/year; 100% require freelance illustration. Recent titles include *Bobby Bear at the Circus* and *Bobby Bear's Magic Show*. Prefers cartoon and/or realistic work, airbrush, watercolor, acrylic and oil. Book catalog free for SASE with $1.25 first class stamps.
First Contact & Terms: Approached by over 300 freelance artists/year. Works with 3 freelance artists/year. Send query letter with brochure, resume, business card, or tearsheets to be kept on file. Accepts "whatever is best for artist to present" as samples. Samples not kept on file are returned by SASE only if requested. Reports back only if interested. Works on assignment only. Write for appointment to show portfolio. No originals returned to artist at job's completion. Buys all rights.
Book Design: Assigns 3 freelance jobs/year. Pays for illustration and design combined by the project, $250 minimum.
Text Illustration: Assigns 3 freelance jobs/year. Artwork purchased includes science fiction/fantasy.
Tips: Portfolio should include "human form to show that artist can illustrate accurately. Chances are if an artist can illustrate people that look real, his or her talents are highly refined. We also look for quality cartoon-illustrating ability. We expect to see various styles to indicate the artist's versatility. Our artwork relates the feeling of the story as if text was not present."

ONCE UPON A PLANET, INC., 65-42 Fresh Meadow Lane, Fresh Meadows NY 11365. Art Director: Alis Jordan. Estab. 1978. Publishes humorous, novelty 32-page-books for the gift and stationery market. Recent titles include *Over 40 Quiz Book* and *Golfer's Prayer Book*. Uses artists for text illustration only.
First Contact & Terms: Approached by 200 freelance artists/year. Send samples showing art style. Works on assignment only. If originals are sent, SASE must be enclosed for return. Reports in 2-4 weeks. Prefers to buy all rights, but will negotiate. Payment is negotiated on an assignment basis.
Text Illustration: Assigns 5-10 freelance jobs/year. Uses b&w line drawings and washes.
Tips: "Samples should include a very small selection of b&w illustrations with or without washes similar to those found in the *New Yorker* magazine. We are not interested in fine art, animals, calligraphy, 'cute' children's books, etc."

ORCHARD BOOKS, 387 Park Ave. S., New York NY 10016. (212)686-7070. Publisher: Norma Jean Sawicki. Book publisher. Division of Franklin Watts. Estab. 1987. Publishes hardcover childrens books only. Specializes in picture books and novels for children and young adults. Also publishes nonfiction for young children. Publishes 50 titles/year. 100% require freelance illustration; 50% freelance design. Book catalog free for SASE with 2 first-class stamps.
First Contact & Terms: Works with 50+ freelance illustrators/year. Works on assignment only. Send query letter with brochure, tearsheets slides and transparencies. Samples are filed or are returned by SASE only if requested. Reports back about queries/submissions only if interested. Originals returned to artist at job's completion. Call or write to schedule an appointment or mail appropriate materials to show a portfolio, which should include thumbnails, tearsheets, final reproduction/product, slides and dummies or whatever

artist prefers. Considers complexity of project, skill and experience of artist and project's budget when establishing payment. Buys all rights.

Book Design: Assigns 50 freelance design jobs/year. Pays by the project, $650 minimum.

Jackets/Covers: Assigns 25 freelance deisgn jobs/year. Pays by the project, $650 minimum.

Text Illustration: Assigns 50 freelance jobs/year. Pays by the project, minimum $2,000 advance against royalty.

Tips: Send a "great portfolio."

OTTENHEIMER PUBLISHERS, INC., 300 Reisterstown Rd., Baltimore MD 21208. (301)484-2100. Art Director: Diane Parameros Shea. Estab. 1890. Specializes in mass market-oriented hardcover and paperback originals and reprints—encyclopedias, dictionaries, self-help, cookbooks, children's and novelty. Publishes 200 titles/year. 80% require freelance illustration. Recent titles include *A Taste of America Cookbook, Down the Yellow Brick Road: The Making of the Wizard of Oz, The Norman Rockwell Illustrated Cookbook, It's Raining Cats and Dogs* and *Discovering Dinosaurs.*

First Contact & Terms: Approached by 3-8 freelance artists/year. Works with 5-10 freelance illustrators and 2-5 freelance designers/year. Prefers professional graphic designers and illustrators. Works on assignment only. Send query letter with resume, slides, photostats, photographs, photocopies or tearsheets to be kept on file. Samples not filed are returned by SASE. Reports back only if interested. Call or write for appointment to show portfolio. "I do not want to see unfinished work, sketches, or fine art such as student figure drawings." Original work not returned at job's completion. Considers complexity of project, project's budget and turn-around time when establishing payment. Buys all rights.

Book Design: Assigns 20-40 freelance design jobs/year and 25 illustration jobs/year. Pays by the project, $50-2,000 average.

Jackets/Covers: Assigns over 25 freelance design and over 25 freelance illustration jobs/year. Pays by the project, $100-1,000 average, depending upon project, time spent and any changes.

Text Illustration: Assigns over 30 jobs/year. Prefers water-based color media and b&w line work. Prefers graphic approaches as well as very illustrative. "We cater more to juvenile market." Pays by the project, $25-2,000 average.

Tips: Prefers "art geared towards children, clean work that will reproduce well. I also look for the artist's ability to render children/people well, which is a problem for some. We use art that is realistic, stylized and whimsical but not cartoony. We cater to mass market but are trying to get a tradebook look into our products more and more. The more samples, the better. Don't even expect to get any work if you only work in b&w. We haven't the need; be very, very patient—I have people on file for years before I may need them for a job. A sure control of one's media should also be present. Very few freelancers are able to present a nice resume. I like it when people have taken the time and effort to record their art history."

OXFORD UNIVERSITY PRESS, English Language Teaching (ESL), 200 Madison Ave., 9th Fl, New York NY 10016. Art Buyer: Paula Radding. Estab. 1584. Specializes in textbooks emphasizing English language teaching. Also produces wall charts, picture cards, etc. Recent titles include *East West 3, On Course 2, New Oxford Picture Dictionary English/Navajo.*

First Contact & Terms: Approached by about 300 freelance artists/year. Works with 75 freelance artists/year. Uses artists mainly for editorial illustration. Works on assignment only. Send query letter with brochure, resume, tearsheets, photostats, slides or photographs. Samples are filed. Reports back only if interested. Originals returned to artist at job's completion. To show a portfolio, mail original/final art, photostats, tearsheets, final reproduction/product, slides and transparencies. Considers complexity of project, skill and experience of artist and project's budget when establishing payment. Artist retains copyright.

Text Illustration: Assigns 75-100 freelance jobs/year. Uses "black line, half-tone and 4-color work in styles ranging from cartoon to realistic. Our greatest need is for natural, contemporary figures from all ethnic groups, in action and interaction." Pays by the project, $100-2,500.

Tips: "Please wait for us to call you. You may send new samples to update your file at any time. Do not send wildlife/botanical samples and political cartoons, both of which we never use. Show us people in your illustration samples."

PADRE PRODUCTIONS, Box 840, Arroyo Grande CA 93421-0840. Contact: Lachlan MacDonald. Estab. 1974. Book publisher and independent book producer/packager. Imprints include Bear Flag Books, The Country-woman's Press, Helm Publishing, International Resources, the Press of MacDonald & Reinecke and Channel X. Publishes hardcover originals and trade paperback originals, nonfiction and fiction. Types of books include biography, cookbooks, humor, juvenile, reference, self-help, history, travel and science fiction. Specializes in California history, nature and travel. Publishes 10-12 titles/year. 50% require freelance illustration; 5% require freelance design. Book catalog free for SASE with 3 first-class stamps.

First Contact & Terms: Buys 100 freelance illustrations/year. Works with artists for jacket/cover illustration and text illustration. Works on assignment only. Send query letter with brochure, resume, slide duplicates, photographs and photostats. Samples are filed or are returned by SASE only if requested. Reports back about queries/submissions only if interested. Originals returned to artist at job's completion. Considers project's budget and rights purchased when establishing payment. Negotiates rights purchased.

Jackets/Covers: Pays by the project, $50-200.

Text Illustration: Pays by the project, $50-1,000.

Tips: "Send query letter with SASE, slides or printed samples of art (no originals) and outline of a book idea. Include sample chapter or captions you intend to provide. We prefer artist with complete book ideas. However, we keep a file of samples so we can contact an artist whose style suits manuscripts going into production. We are always looking for exceptional line art to illustrate short fiction."

 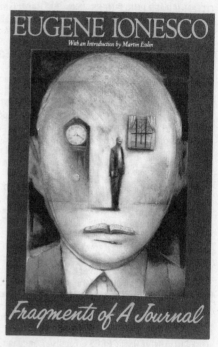

These covers for Paragon House were designed by artists David Lui and David Shannon of New York City. Art director Susan Newman says Lui was selected to do the cover for Metaphysics *because he has an understanding of philosophy and New Age material and is able "to find all the right images for the ideas that flow through the book and unify them into one." Newman says Shannon was the appropriate artist for the cover illustration of* Eugene Ionesco: Fragments of a Journal *because "he is a very heavy conceptual artist and Ionesco is a very heavy conceptual writer." She says both artists are very professional and take a lot of time in the beginning to conceptualize. Shannon, she says, presented her with six possibilities, and "every one of them was incredible." Both artists received approximately $1,500 each for selling one-time rights to their work.* © 1990 Paragon House

PARAGON HOUSE, 90 Fifth Ave., New York NY 10011. (212)620-2820. Art Director: Susan Newman. Estab. 1982. Publishes trade hardcover originals, reprints and textbooks. Publishes biography, history, New Age, humor, reference, self-help, technical, collected poems and collected letters. Specializes in biography and history. Publishes over 100 titles/year. 25-30% require freelance illustration; 60% require freelance design. Recent titles include *The Gentleman in the Parlour*, *A Touch of Genius* and *The Great Good Place*.

First Contact & Terms: Approached by 50-100 freelance artists/year. Works with 25 + freelance illustrators and 20 + freelance designers/year. Buys 25 + freelance illustrations/year. Works with illustrators mainly for jacket illustration and design. Works on assignment only. Send query letter with resume, tearsheets, slides, transparencies, photographs, photostats brochure or color photocopies. Samples are filed. Reports back only if interested. Originals returned to artist at job's completion. Call or write to schedule an appointment to show a portfolio which should include original/final art, photostats, tearsheets, final reproduction/product, photographs or transparencies. Buys first or one-time rights.

Book Design: Assigns 40% freelance design and 10-15% freelance illustration jobs/year. Pays by the project, $300-500.
Jacket/Covers: Assigns 40% freelance design and 25% freelance illustration jobs/year. Pays by the project, $800-1,500.
Text Illustration: Assigns very few freelance jobs/year. Pays by the project, $300 minimum.
Tips: "Keep sending material; I love to see new work. When you are looking to get an appointment with an art director, try to make sure they are assigning work for a list; if they are not working on a list, they might forget you."

*PEACHPIT PRESS, INC., 1085 Keith Ave., Berkeley CA 94708. (415)527-8555. FAX: (415)524-9775. Production Coordinator: Naomi Gardner. Estab. 1987. Book publisher. Types of books include instruction and computer. Specializes in desktop publishing. Publishes 5-8 titles/year. Recent titles include *Canned Art: Clip Art for the Macintosh* and *Learning PostScript: A Visual Approach*. 100% require freelance design. Book catalog free by request.
Needs: Approached by 2-3 artists/year. Works with 4 freelance designers/year. Prefers local artists with experience in computer book cover design. Uses freelance artists mainly for covers, flyers and brochures. Also uses freelance artists for direct mail and catalog design. Works on assignment only.
First Contact & Terms: Send query letter with resume, photographs and photostats. Samples are filed. Reports back to the artist only if interested. Call to schedule an appointment to show a portfolio which should include original/final art and color samples. Buys all rights. Originals are not returned at job's completion.
Book Design: Payment is negotiable.
Jackets/Covers: Assigns 5-8 freelance design jobs/year. Payment is negotiable.

PEANUT BUTTER PUBLISHING, 200 2nd Ave. W., Seattle WA 98119. (206)281-5965. Contact: Editor. Estab. 1972. Specializes in paperback regional and speciality cookbooks for people who like to dine in restaurants and try the recipes at home. Publishes 30 titles/year. 100% require freelance illustration. Recent titles include *Soap's On, Cooking Russian in America* and *The Low-Cholesterol Cookbook*. Book catalog free for SASE with 1 first class stamp.
First Contact & Terms: Approached by 70 freelance artists/year. Works on assignment only. Send brochure showing art style or tearsheets, photostats and photocopies. Samples not filed are returned only if requested. Reports only if interested. To show a portfolio, mail appropriate materials. Pays for design by the project, $400 minimum. Pays for illustration by the project, $100 minimum. Negotiates rights purchased.
Tips: Books contain pen & ink and 4-color photos."Don't act as if you know more about the work than we do. Do exactly what is assigned to you."

PELICAN PUBLISHING CO., Box 189, 1101 Monroe St., Gretna LA 70053. (504)368-1175. Production Manager: Dana Bilbray. Publishes hardcover and paperback originals and reprints. Publishes 40-50 titles/year. Types of books include travel guides, cookbooks and childrens' books.
First Contact & Terms: Approached by over 200 freelance artists/year. Works on assignment only. Send query letter, 3-4 samples and SASE. Samples are not returned. Reports back on future assignment possibilities. Originals are not returned at job's completion. Buys all rights.
Book Design: Assigns variable number of freelance jobs/year. Payment varies.
Jackets/Covers: Assigns variable number of freelance jobs/year. Payment varies.
Text Illustration: Assigns variable number of freelance jobs/year. Payment varies.
Tips: "Let me know if you've ever worked in the book illustrating industry. Show color, children's oriented work and comment on understanding of book design."

*PHAROS BOOKS/UNITED MEDIA, 200 Park Ave. 6E, New York NY 10166. (212)692-3700. FAX: (212)692-3758. Art Director: Bea Jackson. Book publisher. Imprint of World Almanac, Pharos Books and Topper Books. Publishes hardcover originals and reprints, trade paperback originals and reprints and mass market paperback originals and reprints. Types of books include instruction, biography, juvenile, young adult, reference, history, self-help, travel and humor. Specializes in nonfiction trade. Publishes 50 titles/year. Recent titles include *World Almanac Book of Facts, The Kinsey Institute New Report on Sex* and *Miss Manners Guide for the Turn of the Milleneum*. 20% require freelance illustration; 45% require freelance design. Book catalog free by request.
Needs: Approached by 50 artists/year. Works with 10 freelance illustrators and 15 freelance designers/year. Buys 20 freelance illustrations/year. Uses freelance artists mainly for cover design, illustration, maps, etc. Also uses freelance artists for mechanicals, dummies jacket/cover and illustration, book and catalog design and text illustration. Works on assignment only.
First Contact & Terms: Send query letter with brochure, resume, tearsheets and photographs. Samples are filed. Does not report back, in which case the artist should wait to be called (or follow up after 4 weeks). To show a portfolio, mail thumbnails, roughs, original/final art, tearsheets, dummies and printed samples. Originals are returned at job's completion.

Book Design: Assigns 10 freelance design and 20 freelance illustration jobs/year. Pays by the project, $300-650.

Jackets/Covers: Assigns 20 freelance design and 10 freelance illustration jobs/year. Pays by the project, $500-1,200. "We look for a solid contemporary trade look that's not too trendy."

Text Illustration: Assigns 8 freelance design and 8 freelance illustration jobs/year. Pays by the project, $150-2,000. Prefers styles appropriate for juveniles and nonfiction trade.

Tips: "Show that you can produce good work, quickly and within budget. I do not re-hire a freelancer when revisions, price negotiations and keeping schedules are a significant problem."

PICTURE BOOK STUDIO, 10 Central St., Saxonville MA 01701. Publisher: Robert Saunders. Produces children's picture books. Publishes 25 books/year with 10-12 illustrations in each. Recent titles include *The Baby Who Would Not Come Down*, *Magical Hands* and *Jeremy Quacks*. "Request a catalog."

First Contact & Terms: Approached by 250 freelance artists/year. Prefers artwork that is "fresh and original, with childlike spontaneity and warmth." Prefers watercolor, then pen & ink, colored pencil, pastel and collage. Send query letter with slides. Samples not filed are returned by SASE. Reports back within 1 month. "We must always see slides first. Do not call." Originals returned to artist at job's completion. Buys worldwide book rights.

Tips: "A common mistake made by many illustrators who submit artwork is to show that they can work in a variety of styles. Mr. Saunders looks especially for uniqueness, not flexibility. I want to see work which the illustrator likes to do most." Look of design and illustration is "lyrical, expressionistic with a contemporary flavor."

PLAYERS PRESS, Box 1132, Studio City CA 91604. Associate Editor: Marjorie Clapper. Specializes in children's books.

First Contact & Terms: Buys up to 30 illustrations/year from freelancers. Works on assignment only. Send query letter with brochure showing art style or resume and samples. Samples not filed are returned by SASE. Reports back only if interested. To show a portfolio, mail thumbnails, original/final art, final reproduction/product, tearsheets, photographs and as much information as possible. Buys all rights. Payment varies.

*PLYMOUTH MUSIC CO., INC., 170 NE 33rd St., Ft. Lauderdale FL 33334. (305)563-1844. General Manager: Bernard Fisher. Specializes in paperbacks dealing with all types of music. Publishes 60-75 titles/year; 100% require freelance design, 100% require freelance illustrations.

First Contact & Terms: Works with 10 freelance artists/year. Artists "must be within our area." Works on assignment only. Send brochure, resume and samples to be kept on file. Samples not kept on file are returned. Reports back within 1 week. Call for appointment to show a portfolio. Originals not returned to artist at job's completion. Considers complexity of project when establishing payment. Buys all rights.

Jackets/Covers: Assigns 5 freelance design and 5 freelance illustration jobs/year. Pays by the project.

POCKET BOOKS, 1230 6th Ave., New York NY 10020. (212)698-7000. FAX: (212)698-7337. Vice President/Executive Art Director: Barbara Buck. Estab. 1939. Book publisher. Imprint of Simon and Schuster. Publishes hardcover originals and reprints, trade paperback originals and reprints and mass market paperback originals and reprints. Types of books include contemporary, experimental, mainstream, historical, science fiction, instruction, adventure, mystery, biography, juvenile, young adult, reference, history, self-help, travel, humor and cookbooks. Publishes more than 700 titles/year. 60% require freelance illustration; 50% require freelance design.

Needs: Approached by 100+ freelance artists/year. Works with 100-150 freelance illustrators and 20-30 freelance designers/year. "The work speaks for itself—I don't care where the artist lives." Uses freelance artists mainly for fiction jacket/cover illustration and design. Works on assignment only.

First Contact & Terms: Send query letter with tearsheets, transparencies or color Photocopies. Do not call! Samples are filed and are not returned. "We are not *responsible*." Reports back to the artist only if interested. For a portfolio review do not call. "Drop off any day but Friday—at your own risk." Portfolio should include tearsheets and transparencies (at least 4×5). Rights purchased vary according to project. Originals returned at the job's completion. Payment is negotiable, by the project.

Jackets/Covers: Assigns hundreds of freelance design and illustration jobs/year. Payment is negotiable by the project. "I use all styles."

Tips: "Keep me current on your work by dropping off portfolios and leaving new tearsheets behind for my files. Label all tearsheets."

*POLKA ● DOT PRESS, (formerly Java Publishing Co.), Box 25203, Colorado Springs CO 80936. (719)548-1844. Publisher: Bruce Fife. Estab. 1985. Book publisher. Publishes hardcover and trade paperback originals. Types of books include instruction and humor. Specializes in humor, recreation and performing arts. Publishes 3-8 titles/year. Recent titles include *Strutter's Complete Guide to Clown Makeup*. 80% require freelance illustration and design. Book catalog free for SASE with 2 first class stamps.

Needs: Uses freelance artists mainly for cover design and text illustration. Works on assignment only.
First Contact & Terms: Send query letter with brochure and photocopies. Samples are filed. Reports back to the artist only if interested. To show a portfolio, mail appropriate materials.
Book Design: Pays by the project.
Jackets/Covers: Assigns 6 freelance design jobs/year.
Text Illustration: Assigns 6 freelance illustration jobs/year. Pays by the project.

PRAEGER PUBLISHERS, 1 Madison Ave., New York NY 10010. (212)685-6710. Art Director: Carole A. Russo. Publishes textbooks and hardcover and trade paperback originals. Publishes 200 titles/year. Recent titles include *Public Relations Writing, Communication Tomorrow* and *Propaganda/A Pluralistic Perspective*.
First Contact & Terms: Approached by 200-250 freelance artists/year. Works with 7 freelance designers/year, mainly for jacket/cover design. Works on assignment only. Send query letter with tearsheets. Samples are filed and are not returned. Reports back only if interested. Originals not returned at job's completion. Call or write to show a portfolio, which should include original/final art and final reproduction/product. Considers project's budget when establishing payment.
Jackets/Covers: Assigns 35 freelance design jobs/year. Prefers "scholarly" looking design. Pays by the project, $200-500.
Tips: "Want to see type designs mainly; never use illustrations or photographs." Show me what would apply to Praeger, not everything you've ever published. Also, proofread any literature you mail out; especially to a book publisher!

THE PRAIRIE PUBLISHING COMPANY, Box 2997, Winnipeg MB R3C 4B5 Canada. (204)885-6496. Publisher: Ralph E. Watkins. Specializes in paperback juvenile fiction and local history. Publishes 3 titles/year. Recent titles include *The Tale of Johathan Thimblemouse, Humour is the Best Sauce* and *The Homeplace*.
First Contact & Terms: Approached by 5 freelance artists/year. Works with 3-4 freelance artists/year. Works on assignment only. Send query letter with resume and tearsheets. Samples are filed or are returned. Reports back within weeks. Originals not returned at job's completion. To show a portfolio, mail roughs. Considers skill and experience of artist and project's budget when establishing payment. Negotiates rights purchased.
Book Design: Pays by the project, $100-150.
Jackets/Covers: Pays by the project, $100-150.
Text Illustration: Prefers line drawings. Pays by the project, $100-150.
Tips: "The work should not appear too complete. What I look for is open-ended art."

*BYRON PREISS VISUAL PUBLICATIONS, INC., 24 W. 25th St., New York NY 10010. (212)645-9870. Art Director: Steve Brenniulmeyer. Specializes in hardcover and paperback science fiction, fantasy, animal and nature, young adult and children's. Publishes 100 titles/year; 85% require freelance illustration. Recent titles include *The Dungeon, First Contact* and the *Camelot World Series*.
First Contact & Terms: Approached by over 4 freelance artists/week. Works with 50 freelance artists/year. Prefers pen & ink, airbrush, charcoal/pencil, colored pencil, watercolor, acrylic, oil, pastel and computer illustration. Works on assignment only. Send query letter with brochure showing art style or tearsheets, photostats, photographs or "color reproductions of any color art." Samples are filed or are returned by SASE only if requested. Reports back only if interested. Originals returned to artist at job's completion. Call or write to schedule an appointment to show a portfolio, which should include the "best samples possible." Considers complexity of project, skill and experience of artist, project's budget, turnaround time and rights purchased when establishing payment. Negotiates rights purchased.
Book Design: Assigns 10 freelance design and 50 freelance illustration jobs/year. Pay varies per project.
Jackets/Covers: Assigns approximately 20 freelance design and 50 freelance illustration jobs/year. Pay varies per project.
Text Illustration: Assigns 50 freelance jobs/year. Pay varies per project.
Tips: "Please consider subject matter of our books when showing artwork. We use bright colors for children's illustrations. Send one or two color photocopies of best work for our files."

*THE PRESS OF MACDONALD & REINECKE, Box 840, Arroyo Grande CA 93421-0840. (805)473-1947. Editor: Lachlan MacDonald. Estab. 1974. Book publisher. Publishes hardcover originals and trade paperback originals and reprints. Types of books include fiction, biography, juvenile, young adult, poetry and drama. Publishes 2-4 titles/year. Recent titles include *Avigation* and *Voices from the Well*. 15% require freelance illustration. Book catalog free for SASE with 1 first class stamp.
Needs: Approached by 100 freelance artists/year. Works with 2-3 freelance illustrators/year. Buys 50 freelance illustrations/year. Prefers artists with experience in line art. Uses freelance artists mainly for full page text illustration.
First Contact & Terms: Send query letter with brochure, resume, SASE, tearsheets and photocopies. Samples are filed. Reports back to the artist only if interested. To show a portfolio, mail appropriate materials. Portfolio should include printed samples. Do not send originals. Buys one-time rights or negotiates rights purchsed. Originals are not returned at the job's completion.

Book Design: Pays by the project, $25-600.
Jackets/Covers: Assigns 2-3 freelance design jobs/year. Pays by the project, $25-100.
Text Illustration: Assigns 2-3 freelance illustration jobs/year. Pays by the project, $25-500. Prefers line drawings with precise detail.

*PRUETT PUBLISHING COMPANY, 2928 Pearl St., Boulder CO 80301. Project Editor: Jim Pruett. Specializes in hardcover and paperback originals on Western history, outdoor themes, Americana and railroads. Publishes 20 titles/year. Recent titles include *Taming Mighty Alaska*, *Seasonal* and *Ghosts on the Range*. Also uses freelancers for brochure, catalog and advertising design. Assigns 20-25 projects/year. Pays by the project.
First Contact & Terms: Approached by 15-20 freelance artists/year. Works with 4-5 freelance artists/year. Prefers local artists. Works on assignment only. Send query letter with samples showing art style. Samples not filed are returned only if requested with SASE. Considers complexity of project, skill and experience of artist, project's budget and turnaround time when establishing payment. Rights purchased vary according to project.
Book Design: Assigns 20 freelance design and 0-1 freelance illustration jobs/year. Pays by the project, $150-400.
Jackets/Covers: Assigns 20 freelance design and 5-10 freelance illustration jobs/year. Pays by the project, $200-550.
Text Illustration: Assigns 0-1 freelance jobs/year. Pays by the project, $200-500.
Tips: Looking for "historic illustrations and photographs. Photography is a big part of our design. Do not send cartoons and children's illustrations. It is rare we work with artists from other states as we have a lot of talent here, unless they have a particular style like historic illustration that is hard to find locally."

PULSE-FINGER PRESS, Box 488, Yellow Springs OH 45387. Contact: Orion Roche or Raphaello Farnese. Publishes hardbound and paperback fiction, poetry and drama. Publishes 5-10 titles/year. Also uses artists for advertising design and illustration. Pays $25 minimum for direct mail promos.
First Contact & Terms: Send query letter. "We can't use unsolicited material. "Inquiries without SASE will not be acknowledged." Prefers local artists. Works on assignment only. Reports in 6 weeks. Samples returned by SASE; reports back on future assignment possibilities. Send resume to be kept on file for future assignments. Artist supplies overlays for all color artwork. Originals returned to artist at job's completion. Buys first serial and reprint rights.
Jackets/Covers: "Must be suitable to the book involved; artist must familiarize himself with text. We tend to use modernist/abstract designs. Try to keep it simple, emphasizing the thematic material of the book." Pays $25-100, b&w jackets, on acceptance.

G.P. PUTNAM'S SONS, (Philomel Books), 200 Madison Ave., New York NY 10016. (212)951-8700. Art Director, Children's Books: Nanette Stevenson. Publishes hardcover and paperback juvenile books. Publishes 100 titles/year.
First Contact & Terms: "We take drop-offs on Tuesday mornings. Please call in advance with the date you want to drop off your portfolio." Originals returned to artist at job's completion. Works on assignment only. Samples returned by SASE. Provide flyer, tearsheet, brochure and photocopy or stat to be kept on file for possible future assignments. Free catalog.
Jackets/Covers: "Uses full-color paintings, tight style."
Text Illustration: "Uses a wide cross section of styles for story and picture books."

RAINTREE PUBLISHERS, 310 W. Wisconsin Ave., Milwaukee WI 53203. (414)273-0873. Art Director: Suzanne Beck. Specializes in educational material for children. Publishes 40 titles/year; 90% require freelance illustrators.
First Contact & Terms: Works with 12 freelance artists/year. Send slides, tearsheets or photocopies or submit portfolio for review. Do not call in person. Provide samples to be kept on file for possible future assignments. Samples not kept on file are returned by SASE. Reports in 2-4 weeks. Works on assignment only. Originals sometimes returned to artist at job's completion. Buys all rights.
Jackets/Covers: Assigns 12 illustration jobs/year. Payment varies depending on job and artist's experience.
Text Illustration: Assigns 12 jobs/year. Payment varies depending on job and artist's experience.

*RANDOM HOUSE, INC., (Juvenile), 225 Park Ave., New York NY 10003. (212)254-1600. Art Director: Cathy Goldsmith. Specializes in hardcover and paperback originals and reprints. Publishes 150 titles/year. 100% require freelance illustration.
First Contact & Terms: Works with 100-150 freelance artists/year. Works on assignment only. Send query letter with resume, tearsheets and photostats; no originals. Samples are filed or are returned. "No appointment necessary for portfolios. Come in on Wednesdays only, before noon." Considers complexity of project, skill and experience of artist, project's budget, turnaround time and rights purchased when establishing payment. Negotiates rights purchased.

Book Design: Assigns 5 freelance design and 150 freelance illustration jobs/year. Pays by the project.
Text Illustration: Assigns 150 freelance jobs/year. Pays by the project.

READ'N RUN BOOKS, Box 294, Rhododendron OR 97049. (503)622-4798. Publisher: Michael P. Jones. Estab. 1985. Specializes in fiction, history, environment, wildlife for children through adults. "Varies depending upon subject matter. Books for people who do not have time to read lengthy books." Publishes 2-6 titles/year. Accepts previously published material. Original artwork returned to the artist after publication. Sample copy: $6. Art guidelines for SASE with 1 first-class stamp.
First Contact & Terms: Buys 30 illustrations/year from freelancers. Prefers pen & ink, airbrush, charcoal/pencil, markers, calligraphy and computer illustration. Send query letter with brochure or resume, tear sheets, Photostats, photocopies, slides and photographs. Samples not filed are returned by SASE. Reports back within 1-2 months, "depending on workload." To show a portfolio, mail thumbnails, roughs, original/final art, final reproduction/product, color and b&w tearsheets, photostats and photographs. Buys one-time rights. Pays in copies, on publication.
Tips: "We publish books on wildlife, history and nature. We will be publishing short-length cookbooks." In portfolios, "I want to see a lot of illustrations showing a variety of styles. There is little that I actually don't want to see. We have a tremendous need for illustrations on the Oregon Trail (i.e., oxen-drawn covered wagons, pioneers, mountain men, fur trappers, etc.) and illustrations depicting the traditional way of life of Plains Indians and those of the North Pacific Coast and Columbia River with emphasis on mythology and legends."

RESOURCE PUBLICATIONS INC., Suite 290, 160 E. Virginia, San Jose CA 95112. Art Director: Terri All. Estab. 1973. Publishes paperback originals related to celebration and the arts. Publishes 12 titles/year. Book catalog free for SASE with 2 first-class stamps.
First Contact & Terms: Uses artists for design and production. Assigns 20 design jobs/year. Pays $15-25/hour; catalogs, direct mail brochures, letterhead and magazines. Send query letter with samples and SASE. Reports in 6-8 weeks. Assigns 12-16 production jobs/year. Pays $6-15/hour, paste-up. No advance. Buys all rights. Free catalog.
Book Design: Assigns 1-4/year. Pays $15-25/hour, layout and type spec.
Jackets/Covers: Buys 1-4/year. Pays $45-125, b&w; $50-250, color.

*ROSS BOOKS, Box 4340, Berkeley CA 94704. (415)841-2474. Managing Editor: Elizabeth Yerkes. Estab. 1977. Book publisher. Publishes trade paperback originals, textbooks and hardcover reprints. Types of books include instruction, young adult, reference, self-help, cookbooks, adult science, holography and computer books. Specializes in holography and computers. Publishes 7 titles/year. Recent titles include *Holography Marketplace 2nd Edition* and *Language Flashcard*. 40% require freelance illustration; 40% require freelance design. Book catalog free for SASE with 2 first-class stamps.
Needs: Approached by 100-300 freelance artists/year. Works with 2-4 freelance illustrators and 12 freelance designers/year. Number of freelance illustrations purchased each year varies. Prefers artists with experience incomputer generated diagrams and illustration. Also uses freelance artists for jacket/cover illustration, book design, text illustration and direct mail design. Works on assignment only.
First Contact & Terms: Send query letter with resume and photocopies. Samples are filed. Reports back to the artist only if interested and SASE enclosed. Rights purchased vary according to subject. Originals returned at the job's completion.
Book Design: Assigns 2-4 freelance design and 2-4 freelance illustration jobs/year. Pays by the project, $500 maximum.
Text Illustration: Assigns 2-4 freelance design and 2-4 freelance illustration jobs/year. Pays by the project, $500 maximum.
Tips: "Computer illustration ability should be demonstrated."

SANTILLANA PUBLISHING CO. INC., 6 Industrial Pkwy., Northvale NJ 07647. (201)767-6961. 901 W. Walnut St., Compton CA 90220. (808)245-8584. President: Sam Laredo. Production Manager: Al Green. Specializes in hardcover and paperback juvenile and teen textbooks and workbooks. Publishes 35 titles/year.
First Contact & Terms: Works with 8-10 freelance artists/year. Prefers pen & ink, airbrush, colored pencil, watercolor, acrylic and computer illustration. Works on assignment only. Send query letter with brochure, tearsheets or "anything we don't have to return" to be kept on file. Call or write for appointment to show portfolio. Samples not filed are returned by SASE. Reports back only if interested. No originals returned to artist at job's completion. Considers skill and experience of artist, project's budget and rights purchased when establishing payment. Negotiates rights purchased.
Text Illustration: All jobs assigned to freelancers. Pays by the project, $200-5,000 average.
Tips: Looks for "lots of details, strong lines, good color."

SCARBORUGH HOUSE, a division of Book Crafters, (formerly Stein and Day), Box 459, Chelsea MI 48118. (313)475-1210. Contact: Art Department. Publishes hardcover, paperback, original and reprint mass market fiction and nonfiction. Publishes 100 titles/year; 10% require freelance design, 20% freelance cover illustrations.

First Contact & Terms: Prefers local artists with experience in publishing, but young unpublished artists are welcome to submit. Send query letter with brochure showing art style or resume and nonre-turnable samples. Especially looks for clean, smooth art, good color design and layout; also a variety of technical skills. Include SASE. Works on assignment only. Reports back on future assignment possibilities. Portfolios accepted at Westchester office for review. Artist provides overlays for color covers. Buys all rights. 15% kill fee. Pays on publication. Free catalog.

Jackets/Covers: Assigns 15 freelance design and 25 freelance illustration jobs/year. Pays by the project, $500-1,200 average; mass market cover illustration, $700-1,500 average.

Text Illustration: Assigns 3-5 freelance jobs/year. Pays by the project, $150-500 average. "We use very little text illustration but on occasion we require maps or b&w line drawings."

Tips: "Our covers are very diversified. All styles and designs are considered. A book can make it or break it by its cover. Simple design executed properly is the best design. Artist is selected for the best style that matches my layout and concept."

SCHANES PRODUCTS & SERVICES, (formerly Blackthorne Publishing, Inc., 786 Blackthorne Ave., El Cajon CA 92020. (619)698-8183. FAX: (619)588-4678. Art Director: Steven J. Schanes. Specializes in paperback originals and reprints, comic books, signed prints and trade books. Publishes 200 titles/year.

First Contact & Terms: Approached by 50 freelance artists/year. Works with 50 freelance artists/year. "We look for professional standards in the artists we work with." Send query letter with brochure, resume, and samples to be kept on file; originals will be returned. Prefers slides and photostats as samples. Samples not filed are returned. Reports within 3 weeks. Originals returned to artist after job's completion. Considers complexity of the project, skill and experience of artist, project's budget and turnaround time when establishing payment. Rights purchased vary according to project.

Book Design: Assigns 50 freelance jobs/year. Pays by the project, depending on the job, from $50 for a spot illustration to $15,000 for a complete comic book series.

Jackets/Covers: Assigns 15 freelance design and 30 freelance illustration jobs/year. Pays by the hour, $5-40 average; by the project, $50-10,000 average.

Text Illustration: Assigns 15 jobs/year. Prefers pen & ink. Pays by the hour, $5-40 average; by the project, $50-10,000 average.

Tips: Looking for illustration which is "accurate, based on knowledge of human anatomy. Study basic drawing."

*SCHIFFER PUBLISHING, LTD., 1469 Morstien Rd., West Chester PA 19380. (215)696-1001. President: P. Schiffer. Specializes in books for collectors and artists. Recent titles include *Quintiles and Tredeciles*, *Horary Astrology* and *Planets in Synastry*.

First Contact & Terms: Approached by over 24 freelance artists/year. Works on assignment only. Send query letter with resume and tearsheets, photostats, photocopies, slides and photographs. Samples not filed are returned by SASE. Reports only if interested. Negotiates rights purchased.

Tips: "Send large, clear examples."

SCHOLASTIC INC., 730 Broadway, New York NY 10003. Art Director: David Tommasino. Specializes in hardcover and paperback originals and reprints of young adult, biography, classics, historical romance and contemporary teen romance. Publishes 250 titles/year; 80% require freelance illustration. Recent titles include *The Baby-sitters Club*, *Friends 4-ever* and *Dear Diary*.

First Contact & Terms: Approached by 100 freelance artists/year. Works with 75 freelance artists/year. Prefers local artists with experience. Uses freelance artwork mainly for young adult/romance, historical, classical and biographies. Send query letter with brochure showing art style or tearsheets. Samples are filed or are returned only if requested. Reports back within 2 weeks only if interested. Originals returned to artist at job's completion. Considers complexity of project and skill and experience of artist when establishing payment. Buys first rights.

Jackets/Covers: Assigns 200 freelance illustration jobs/year. Pays by the project, $1,500-3,500.

Tips: "In your portfolio, show tearsheets or proofs only of printed covers. I want to see oil, acrylic tightly rendered; illustrators should research the publisher. Go into a bookstore and look at the books. Gear what you send according to what you see is being used."

*SCHOLIUM INTERNATIONAL INC., 99 Seaview Blvd., Port Washington NY 11050. (516)484-3290. President: A. L. Candido. Publishes scientific and technical books.

First Contact & Terms: Send photocopies or transparencies. Uses artists for jacket design, direct mail brochures and advertising layouts/art.

*SCIENCE TECH PUBLISHERS, 701 Ridge St., Madison WI 53705. (608)238-8664. Managing Editor: Katherine M. Brock. Specializes in hardcover science and technical books, also production services for other publishers. Publishes 5-6 titles/year; 90% require freelance illustration. Recent titles include *Biology of Microorganisms* (production of entire book), published by Prentice-Hall.

First Contact & Terms: Approached by 20 freelance artists/year. Works with 3-6 freelance artists/year. Needs artists skilled in technical art. Works on assignment only. Send query letter with brochure showing art style or resume. Samples are filed or are returned only if requested. Reports back within 3 weeks. Originals not returned to artist at job's completion. Call to schedule an appointment to show a portfolio, which should include "a good selection" of work. Considers complexity of project, skill and experience of artist and project's budget when establishing payment. Buys all rights. Finds most artists through references, word-of-mouth, portfolio reviews and samples received through the mail.

Text Illustration: Assigns 3-6 freelance jobs/year. Prefers scientific illustration—graphs, line art, bar graphs, diagrams pen & ink, airbrush, collage and computer illustration with overlays. Pays by the hour, $8-45.

Tips: "Provide a good selection of work and especially final printed pieces in which the work was used." Follow up on a phone call by sending your *resume* for us to have in hand and file for future reference.

*SCOJTIA PUBLISHING CO., 6457 Wilcox Station, Los Angeles CA 90038. Managing Editor: Patrique Quintahlen. Estab. 1986. Book publisher. Imprint of Jordan Enterprises Publishing Co. Publishes hardcover and trade paperback originals. Types of books include contemporary, experimental, mainstream, historical, science fiction, instruction, adventure, fantasy, biography, pre-school, juvenile, young adult, reference, history, self-help, travel, humor and cookbooks. Specializes in contemporary, experimental and historical fiction; pre-school; juvenile; young adult; self-help; biography; history and reference. Publishes 2-5 titles/year. Recent titles include *Roommates, College Sublets, Living in the Dorm* and *The Boy Who Opened Doors*. 80% require freelance illustration; 50% require freelance design. Book catalog not available.

Needs: Approached by 50 freelance artists/year. Works with 5 freelance illustrators and 2 freelance designers/year. Buys 24 freelance illustrations/year. Uses freelance artists mainly for text illustration and book covers. Also uses freelance artists for book design and direct mail design. Works on assignment only.

First Contact & Terms: Send query letter with resume, SASE, tearsheets, photographs, photocopies and photostats. Samples are filed. Reports back with 4 months. To show a portfolio, mail roughs, original/final art and b&w and color photostats, dummies, tearsheets and photographs. Rights purchased vary according to project. Originals are not returned at job's completion unless requested.

Book Design: Assigns 2 freelance design and 2 freelance illustration jobs/year. Pays by the hour, $10-20; by the project, $50-1,500.

Jackets/Covers: Assigns 2 freelance design and 2 frelance illustration jobs/year. Pays by the hour, $5-15; by the project, $50-500. Prefers "painting styles with a Monet, Degas look and color."

Text Illustration: Assigns 2 freelance design and 5 freelance illustration jobs/year. Pays by the hour, $5-15; by the project, $50-500. Prefers line drawings.

Tips: "An artist with a diversity of styles, reflecting an understanding of the natural abstract, curious, forever discovering desire and motivation of children and adults is most likely to get an assignment with Scojtia. Color, unique characters (animals), realistic drawings that are comfortable with topics of fantasy are the pictures we look for."

SILVER BURDETT & GINN, 250 James St., Morristown NJ 07960. (201)285-8103. Director Art & Design: Doug Bates. Book publisher. Estab. 1890. Publishes textbooks and nonfiction. Types of books include instruction, technical and history. Specializes in math, science, social studies, English, music and religion. Publishes approx. 75 titles/year. 100% require freelance illustration; 20% require freelance design. Recent titles include *Mathematics: Exploring Your World, Science Horizons, World of Language* and *People in Time and Place*. Book catalog not available.

First Contact & Terms: Approached by 40 freelance artists/year. Works with 100 freelance illustrators and 10 freelance designers/year. Buys 1,000 freelance illustrations/year. Works with illustrators mainly for illustration of pupils' text. Also works with artists for jacket/cover illustration and design, book design and text illustration. Works on assignment only. Send query letter with resume and tearsheets. Samples are filed or are returned by SASE only if requested. Reports back about queries/submissions only if interested. Originals returned to artist at job's completion. Call to schedule an appointment to show a portfolio, which should include thumbnails, roughs, original/final art, tearsheets and final reproduction/product. Considers complexity of project and skill and experience of artist when establishing payment. Negotiates rights purchased.

Book Design: Assigns approx. 10 freelance design jobs/year. Pays by the project.
Text Illustration: Assigns 1,000 freelance illustrations jobs/year. Pays by the project, $75-1,200.
Tips: The look of design and illustration used is "contemporary, but warm and friendly, inviting; lively, but functional. "Show portfolio—preferably work appropriate to text book and educational publishing."

SIMON AND SCHUSTER BOOKS FOR YOUNG READERS, 1230 Ave. of the Americas, New York NY 10020. Contact: Art Director. Specializes in hardcover and paperback juvenile trade books, for ages 3-12. Publishes 50 hardcover and 20 paperbacks/year.
First Contact & Terms: Assigns 50 freelance jobs/year "but only to artists we have previously met and selected. We pay an advance or flat fee."

SINGER MEDIA CORP., 3164 Tyler Ave., Anaheim CA 92801. (714)527-5650. FAX: (214)527-0268. Contact: John J. Kearns. Licenses paperback originals and reprints; mass market, Western, romance, sophisticated romance, mystery, science fiction, nonfiction and biographies. Licenses 200 titles/year through affiliates; 95% require freelance designers for book covers. Also buys 3,000 cartoons/year to be internationally syndicated to newspaper and magazine publishers—also used for topical books.
First Contact & Terms: Approached by 100+ freelance artists/year. Send query letter with photocopies and tearsheets to be kept on file. Do not send original work. Material not filed is returned by SASE. Reports in 2 weeks. Pays 50% of syndication fee received; books, 15% USA, 20% foreign. Buys first and reprint rights. Originals returned to artist at job's completion. Artist's guidelines $1.
Book Design: Assigns "many" jobs/year. Uses artists for reprints for world market. Prefers clean, clear, uncluttered style.
Jackets/Covers: Popular styles: Western, romance, mystery, science fiction/fantasy, war and gothic. "We are only interested in color transparencies for paperbacks." Duplicates only. Offers advance.
Tips: "Study the market. Study first the best seller list, the current magazines, the current paperbacks and then come up with something better if possible or something new. We now utilize old sales for reprint." Looking for "new ideas, imagination, uniqueness. Every artist is in daily competition with the best artists in the field. A search for excellence helps. We get hundreds of medical cartoons, hundreds of sex cartoons. We are overloaded with cartoons showing inept office girls but seldom get cartoons on credit cards, senior management, aerobics, fitness, romance. We have plenty on divorce, but few on nice romance and love. We would like more positive and less negative humor. Can always use good travel cartoons around the world. Merged with Media Trans Asia which publishes 32 magazines in Hong Kong, Thailand and India, including inflight magazines for Asian and Mid Eastern Airlines." Also looking for "jacket covers for paperbacks. Young people, sexy but decent."

*****SOURCEBOOKS, INC.**, Box 372, Naperville IL 60566. (708)961-2161. Publisher: Dominique Raccah. Publishes hardcover and trade paperback originals. Types of books include reference, business and finance; nonfiction only. "We have 2 divisions—sourcebooks trade: business/finance general trade and financial sourcebooks: banking/finance/accounting professional books." Recent titles include *Outsmarting the Competition: Practical Approaches to Finding and Using Competitive Information.* 100% require freelance illustration; 100% require freelance design.
Needs: Approached by few freelance artists/year. Works with 3-4 freelance illustrators and 2-3 freelance designers/year. Buys 10-15 freelance illustrations/year. Prefers artists with experience in cover design. Uses freelance artists mainly for cover and book design. Also uses freelance artists for jacket/cover and text illustration, direct mail and catalog design. Works on assignment only.
First Contact & Terms: Send query letter with brochure, resume, tearsheets, photographs and photocopies. Samples are filed and are not returned. Reports back to the artist only if interested. To show a portfolio, mail "whatever best represents the artist's work for our files." Buys all rights. Originals are not returned at job's completion.
Book Design: Assigns 10 freelance design and few freelance illustration jobs/year. Pays by the project.
Jackets/Covers: Assigns 10 freelance design jobs/year. Pays by the project, $400-1,500.
Text Illustration: "Text illustration is rarely done separately."
Tips: "We're currently looking to expand our roster of cover designers. An artist should be very familiar with book cover design to work with us. Strong, dynamic covers are of paramount importance in selling books. To get an assignment, show us some terrific work."

SOUTHERN HISTORICAL PRESS, INC., 275 W. Broad St., Greenville SC 29601. (803)859-2346 or 233-2346. President: The Rev. Silas Emmett Lucas, Jr. Specializes in hardcover and paperback originals and reprints on genealogy and history. Publishes 40 titles/year.
First Contact & Terms: Works with 1 freelance artist/year. Works on assignment only. Send query letter and samples to be kept on file. Call or write for appointment to show portfolio. Prefers tearsheets or photographs as samples. Samples not filed are returned by SASE if requested. Reports back only if interested. Original work not returned after job's completion. Considers complexity of project, skill

and experience of artist, project's budget and turnaround time when establishing payment. Buys all rights.

Needs: Assigns 5 freelance book design, cover design and illustration and text illustration jobs/year.

*SPINSTERS/AUNT LUTE, Box 410687, San Francisco CA 94141. (415)558-9655. Production Manager: Debra DeBondt. Estab. 1978. Book publisher. Publishes hardcover and trade paperback originals and trade paperback reprints. Types of books include contemporary, experimental, historical, science fiction, fantasy, mystery, biography/"mythography", young adult and self-help. Specializes in lesbian/feminist. Publishes 5-10 titles/year. Recent titles include *The Journey, Why Can't Sharon Kowalski Come Home?* 100% require freelance illustration. Book catalog free by request.

Needs: Approached by 30 freelance artists/year. Works with 6 freelance illustrators/year. Buys 5-10 freelance illustrations/year. Prefers artists with experience in lesbian and/or feminist publishing. Uses freelance artists mainly for covers/jackets. Works on assignment only.

First Contact & Terms: Send query letter with resume, tearsheets, photographs, photocopies slides and transparencies upon request. Samples are filed. Reports back to the artist only if interested. To show a portfolio, mail original/final art and color slides, tearsheets, transparencies and photographs. Rights purchased vary according to project. Originals returned at job's completion.

Jackets/Covers: Assigns 5-10 freelance illustration jobs/year. Pays by the project, $200-350. Prefers watercolor or pastel.

STAR PUBLISHING, Box 68, Belmont CA 94002. Managing Editor: Stuart Hoffman. Specializes in original paperbacks and textbooks on science, art, business. Publishes 12 titles/year. 33% require freelance illustration.

First Contact & Terms: Works with 7-8 artists/year. Send query letter with resume, tearsheets and photocopies. Samples not filed are returned only by SASE. Reports back only if interested. Original work not returned after job's completion. Rights purchased vary according to project.

Book Design: Assigns 12 freelance design and 20 freelance illustration jobs/year. Pays by the project.

Jackets/Covers: Assigns 5 freelance design jobs/year. Pays by the project.

Text Illustration: Assigns 6 freelance jobs/year.

STEMMER HOUSE PUBLISHERS, INC., 2627 Caves Rd., Owings Mills MD 21117. (301)363-3690. President: Barbara Holdridge. Specializes in hardcover and paperback fiction, nonfiction, art books, juvenile and design resource originals. Publishes 10 titles/year; 50% require freelance design, 75% require freelance illustration.

First Contact & Terms: Approached by over 50 freelance artists/year. Works with 10 freelance artists/year. Works on assignment only. Send brochure/flyer, tearsheets, photocopies or color slides to be kept on file; submission must include SASE. Do not send original work. Material not filed is returned by SASE. Call or write for appointment to show portfolio. Reports in 6 weeks. Works on assignment only. Originals returned to artist at job's completion on request. Negotiates rights purchased.

Book Design: Assigns 1 freelance design and 2 freelance illustration jobs/year. Pays by the project, negotiated.

Jackets/Covers: Assigns 2 freelance design jobs/year. Prefers paintings. Pays by the project, $300 minimum.

Text Illustration: Assigns 8 jobs/year. Prefers full-color artwork for text illustrations. Pays by the project on a royalty basis.

Tips: Looks for "draftmanship, flexibility, realism, understanding of the printing process." A common mistake freelancers make in presenting samples or portfolios is "presenting original work only without printed samples and not sending an SASE for material to be returned." Books are "rich in design quality and color, stylized while retaining realism; not airbrushed. 1) Review our books. 2) Propose a strong picture-book manuscript with your illustrations."

STONE WALL PRESS INC., 1241 30th St. NW, Washington DC 20007. Publisher: Henry Wheelwright. Publishes paperback and hardcover originals; environmental, backpacking, fishing, outdoor themes. Publishes 1-2 titles/year; 10% require freelance illustration. Recent titles include *Adventures in Conservation, Basic Trout Fishing* and *Where Rivers Run.*

First Contact & Terms: Approached by 20 freelance artists/year. Prefers artists who are accessible. Works on assignment only. Send query letter with brochure showing art style. Samples returned by SASE. Reports back only if interested. Buys one-time rights. Originals returned to artist at job's completion.

Book Design: Assigns 1 freelance job/year. Uses artists for composition, layout, jacket design. Prefers realistic style—color or b&w. Artist supplies overlays for cover artwork. Pays cash upon accepted art.

Text Illustration: Buys b&w line drawings.

Tips: Looking for "clean, basic, brief, concise, expendable samples."

SUPPORT SOURCE, 420 Rutgers Ave., Swarthmore PA 19081. Publisher: Jane Heald. Specializes in paperback originals on "caregiving to the elderly and spiritual life education." Publishes 1 title/year.
First Contact & Terms: Approached by 5 freelance artists/year. Send brochure showing art style. Samples are filed or are returned by SASE. Originals returned to artist at job's completion. To show a portfolio, mail final reproduction/product, photostats and tearsheets. Considers complexity of project and project's budget when establishing payment. Negotiates rights purchased.
Text Illustration: Prefers line drawings. Pays by the project, $20 each.
Tips: "Build our file of samples so that we will have a selection of styles to choose from when planning each book. Elaborate color work not appropriate for us. Show us b&w only."

*SWAMP PRESS, 323 Pelham Rd., Amherst MA 01002. President: Ed Rayher. Specializes in hardcover and paperback originals of literary first editions. Publishes 2 titles/year.
First Contact & Terms: Works with 3 freelance artists/year. Send query letter with brochure or photostats. Samples are filed or are returned by SASE. Reports back within 2 months. Originals are returned to artist at job's completion. To show a portfolio, mail photostats, tearsheets and slides. Considers complexity of project and project's budget when establishing payment. Buys one-time rights.
Book Design: Assigns 3 freelance illustration jobs/year. Pays in copies of the book—$50 maximum.
Jackets/Covers: Assigns 3 freelance illustration jobs/year. Pays in copies—$25 maximum.
Text Illustration: Assigns 3 freelance jobs/year. Pays in copies—$50 maximum.
Tips: "Send four or five photocopies or slides. Woodcuts, engravings, linocuts are wonderful, especially if we can use your blocks."

*TECHNICAL ANALYSIS, INC., 3517 SW Alaska St., Seattle WA 98126-2730. (206)938-0570. Art Director: Christine Morrison. Estab. 1982. Magazine, books and software producer. Publishes trade paperback reprints and magazines. Types of books include instruction, reference, self-help and financial. Specializes in stocks, options, futures and mutual funds. Publishes 3 titles/year. 100% require freelance illustration; 10% require freelance design. Book catalog not available.
Needs: Approached by 100 freelance artists/year. Works with 40 freelance illustrators and 5 freelance designers/year. Buys 100 freelance illustrations/year. Uses freelance artists for magazine article illustration. Also uses freelance artists for text illustration and direct mail design. Works on assignment only.
First Contact & Terms: Send query letter with brochure, resume, SASE, tearsheets, photographs, photocopies, photostats, slides and transparencies. Samples are filed. Reports back within 6-8 weeks. Write to schedule an appointment to show a portfolio or mail tearsheets. Buys first rights or reprint rights. Most originals are returned to artist at job's completion.
Book Design: Assigns 5 freelance design and 100 freelance illustration jobs/year. Pays by the project, $30-230.
Jackets/Covers: Assigns 1 freelance design and 15 freelance illustration jobs/year. Pays by the project $30-230.
Text Illustration: Assigns 5 freelance design and 100 freelance illustration jobs/year. Pays by the project, $30-230.

TOR BOOKS, 49 W. 24th St., New York NY 10018. Editor: Patrick N. Hayden. Specializes in hardcover and paperback originals and reprints: espionage, thrillers, horror, mysteries and science fiction. Publishes 180 titles/year; heavy on science fiction.
First Contact & Terms: All covers are freelance. Works on assignment only. Send query letter with color photographs, slides or tearsheets to be kept on file "unless unsuitable"; call for appointment to show portfolio. Samples not filed are returned by SASE. Reports back only if interested. Original work returned after job's completion. Considers skill and experience of artist, and project's budget when establishing payment. "We buy the right to use art on all editions of book it is commissioned for and in promotion of book."
Jackets/Covers: Assigns 180 freelance illustration jobs/year. Pays by the project, $500 minimum.

TRAVEL KEYS BOOKS, Box 160691, Sacramento CA 95816. (916)452-5200. Publisher: Peter B. Manston. Specializes in paperback originals on travel, antiques and home security. Publishes 3-7 titles/year; 100% require freelance illustration. Recent titles include *Manston's Europe '90*, (annual) and *Manston's Italy*.
First Contact & Terms: Works with 4 freelance artists/year. "We contract only on a work-for-hire basis. All books include between 15 and 60 illustrations, usually pen & ink drawings." Works on assignment only. Send query letter with brochure showing art style or tearsheets and photostats. Some samples are filed and retained, but samples not filed are returned. Reports back within 2 months. Originals not returned to artist at job's completion. Considers skill of artist and project's budget when establishing payment. Buys all rights or unlimited rights to reproduction.

Text Illustration: Assigns 4 freelance jobs/year. Prefers representational pen & ink for most projects. Pays by the hour, $20; by the project, $1,450 maximum.

Tips: "Please query first, request catalog with SASE (3 first-class stamps)." The most common mistakes freelancers make in presenting their work are "failure to include a sample or photocopy of a sample of their work, and failure to include SASE."

TROLL ASSOCIATES, Book Division, 100 Corporate Dr., Mahwah NJ 07430. Vice President: Marian Frances. Specializes in hardcovers and paperbacks for juveniles 3-15 year olds. Publishes over 100 titles/year; 30% require freelance design and illustrations.

First Contact & Terms: Works with 30 freelance artists/year. Prefers artists with 2-3 years of experience. Send query letter with brochure/flyer or resume and tearsheets or photostats. Samples usually returned by SASE only if requested. Reports in 1 month. Works on assignment only. Originals usually not returned to artist at job's completion. Write to schedule an appointment to show a portfolio, or mail original/final art, photostats and tearsheets. Considers complexity of project, skill and experience of artist, project's budget and rights purchased when establishing payment. Buys all rights or negotiates rights purchased.

THE TRUMPET CLUB/DELL PUBLISHING COMPANY, 666 5th Ave., New York NY 10103. Art Director: Ann Hofmann. Estab. 1985. Mail-order school book club specializing in paperbacks and related promotional material. Publishes juvenile fiction and nonfiction. Recent titles include *Camp Funny Ha Ha*, *100 Amazing Americans* and *Poisonous Creatures*.

First Contact & Terms: Works with 25 freelance artists/year. Prefers local mechanical people only. Prefers local illustrators, but out-of-towners okay. Send query letter, resume or tearsheets. Samples are filed and are not returned. Reports back only if interested. "We only report if we are interested or you can call for an appointment to show your portfolio. We prefer illustrators with children's book experience, but we will consider others, too." Originals returned after job's completion. Call or write to schedule an appointment to show a portfolio, which should include photostats, final reproduction/product, slides or transparencies. Considers complexity of project and project's budget when establishing payment.

Tips: "We are looking for freelance mechanical people, designers and illustrators. Designers and mechanical people may work on or off premises, depending on the complexity of the project. Designers must be able to carry a job through to production. We are now looking for MacIntosh designers and typesetters familiar with Pagemaker, Quark, and Freehand."

TYNDALE HOUSE PUBLISHERS, INC., 351 Executive Dr., Wheaton IL 60189. (708)668-8300. Creative Director: William Paetzold. Specializes in hardcover and paperback originals on "Christian beliefs and their effect on everyday life with a Middle-American look." Publishes 80-100 titles/year; 25% require freelance illustration. Recent titles include *The Quotable Lewis*, *Grace Livingston Hill*, *McGee & Me!* and *Video and Books for Kids*.

First Contact & Terms: Approached by 40-50 freelance artists/year. Works with 15-20 freelance artists/year. Send query letter, tearsheets and/or slides. Samples are filed or are returned by SASE. Reports back only if interested. Negotiates whether originals returned to artist at job's completion. To arrange to show a portfolio, mail tearsheets, slides and SASE. Considers complexity of project, skill and experience of artist, project's budget and rights purchased. Negotiates rights purchased.

Jackets/Covers: Assigns 20 freelance illustration jobs/year. Prefers progressive but friendly style. Pays by the project, $400 and up.

Text Illustrations: Assigns 20 freelance jobs/year. Prefers progressive but friendly style. Pays by the project, $100 and up.

Tips: "Only show your best work. We are looking for illustrators who can tell a story with their work and who can draw the human figure in action when appropriate." A common mistake is "neglecting to make follow-up calls. 1) Be able to leave filable sample(s). 2) Be available; by friendly phone reminders, sending occasional samples. 3) Schedule yourself wisely, rather than missing a deadline."

*UAHC PRESS, 838 5th Ave., New York NY 10021. (212)249-0100. Director of Publications: Stuart L. Benick. Produces books, filmstrips and magazines for Jewish school children and adult education. Recent titles include *What Happens After I Die? Jewish Views of Life After Death* and *The Mystery of Being Jewish*. Free catalog.

First Contact & Terms: Approached by 20 freelance artists/year. Send samples or write for interview. SASE. Reports within 3 weeks. Pays for design by the project, $150 minimum. Pays for illustration by the project, $50 minimum.

Needs: Buys book covers and illustration.

Tips: Seeking "clean and catchy" design and illustration.

*THE UNICORN PUBLISHING HOUSE, INC., 120 American Rd., Morris Plains NJ 07950. (201)292-6852. Art Director: Heidi K.L. Corso. Specializes in original and reprint hardcovers, especially juvenile and adult classics. Publishes 14 titles/year for ages 4-adult. Recent titles include *The Owl and The Pussycat, The Elf and the Doormouse, Alice in Wonderland* and *Hans Christian Andersen*.
First Contact & Terms: Approached by 750 freelance artists/year. Works with 12 freelance artists/year. Send query letter with brochure, resume, tearsheets and photocopies. Samples are not returned. Original work returned after job's completion. Considers complexity of project, skill and experience of artist and project's budget when establishing payment. Negotiates rights purchased.
Book Design: Assigns 12 freelance illustration jobs/year. Pays by the project, $300 minimum.
Text Illustration: Assigns 12 freelance jobs/year. "No preference in medium—art must be detailed and realistic." Pays by the project, "depends on the number of pieces being illustrated."
Tips: "In a portfolio, we're looking for realism in a color and b&w medium. We want to see how they do people, animals, architecture, natural settings, fantasy creatures; in short, we want to see the range that artists are capable of. We do not want to see original artwork. Usually the biggest problem we have is receiving a group of images which doesn't show us a true range of capacity."

UNIVELT INC., Box 28130, San Diego CA 92128. (619)746-4005. Manager: H. Jacobs. Publishes hardcover and paperback originals on astronautics and related fields; occasionally publishes veterinary first-aid manuals. Publishes 10 titles/year; all have illustrations.
First Contact & Terms: Prefers local artists. Send query letter with resume, business card and/or flyer to be kept on file. Samples not filed are returned by SASE. Reports in 4 weeks on unsolicited submissions. Buys one-time rights. Originals returned to artist at job's completion. Free catalog.
Jackets/Covers: Assigns 10 freelance jobs/year. Uses artists for covers, title sheets, dividers, occasionally a few illustrations. Pays $50-100 for front cover illustration or frontispiece.
Tips: "Illustrations have to be space-related. We obtain most of our illustrations from authors and from NASA."

THE UNIVERSITY OF ALABAMA PRESS, Box 870380, Tuscaloosa AL 35487-0380. (205)348-5180. Production Manager: A.F. Jacobs. Specializes in hardcover and paperback originals and reprints of academic titles. Publishes 40 titles/year; 33% require freelance design.
First Contact & Terms: Works with 4-6 freelance artists/year. Requires book design experience, preferably with university press work. Works on assignment only. Send query letter with resume, tearsheets and slides. Samples not filed are returned only if requested. Reports back within a few days. Originals not returned to artist at job's completion. To show a portfolio, mail tearsheets, final reproduction/product and slides. Considers project's budget when establishing payment. Buys all rights.
Book Design: Assigns 10-15 freelance design jobs/year. Pays by the project, $250 minimum.
Jackets/Covers: Assigns 10-15 freelance design jobs/year. Pays by the project, $250 minimum.

*THE UNIVERSITY OF CALGARY PRESS, 2500 University Drive NW, Calgary AB T2N 1N4 Canada. (403)220-7578. FAX: (403)282-6837. Production Coordinator: Sandy Baker. Estab. 1981. Book publisher. Publishes hardcover originals and reprints, trade paperback originals and reprints and textbooks. Types of books include biography, reference, history and scholarly. Publishes 12-14 titles/year. Recent titles include *Sitar Music in Calcutta* and *Alexander Cameron Rutherford: A Gentleman of Strathcona*. Book catalog free by request.
Needs: Approached by 1-2 freelance artists/year. Prefers artists with experience in scholarly book design. Uses freelance artists mainly for covers.Works on assignment only.
First Contact & Terms: Send query letter with resume and photostats. Samples are filed. Reports back within 2-3 weeks. Write to schedule an appointment to show a portfolio, which should include thumbnails, photostats and photographs. Rights purchased vary according to project. Originals returned at job's completion.
Jackets/Covers: Assigns 12 freelance design jobs/year. Pays by the project, $150-300.

*UNIVERSITY OF IOWA PRESS, University of Iowa, Iowa City IA 52242. Director: Paul Zimmer. Publishes scholarly works, short fiction series, some trade books. Publishes 30 titles/year; 20 require freelance scholarly book design, 2 require freelance illustration or photography.
First Contact & Terms: Query with 2-3 samples; originals not required. Works on assignment only. Samples returned by SASE. Check for most recent titles in bookstores. Free catalog.
Book Design: Assigns 20 freelance jobs/year. Pays $350 to draw specifications and prepare layouts. Pays $350 minimum, book design; $350, jacket.

UNIVERSITY OF NEBRASKA PRESS, 901 N. 17th St., Lincoln NE 68588-0520. (402)472-3581. Designer: Richard Eckersley. Specializes in hardcover and paperback originals, reprints and textbooks on English and American literature, criticism and literature in translation, economics, political science, music, the American West, the American Indian, food production and distribution, agriculture, natural history, modern history of Western Europe, Latin American studies and Bison paperback reprints (ficton, memoirs, biography, etc.). Recent titles include *Billy the Kid, Dr. Jeckyll & Mr. Hyde* and *Yosemite-The Embattled Wilderness.*

First Contact & Terms: Approached by 40 freelance artists/year. Works with 6 freelance artists/year. "Work judged solely on merit and appropriateness." Works on assignment only. Send query letter with brochure showing art style or resume, tearsheets, photostats, slides and photographs. Samples are filed or are returned by SASE. Reports back within 2 weeks. Originals returned to artist at job's completion. Call or write to schedule an appointment to show a portfolio, or mail photostats, tearsheets, final reproduction/product, photographs, slides and transparencies. Considers complexity of project, skill and experience of artist and project's budget. Negotiates rights purchased. Finds most artists through references/word-of-mouth, portfolio review and samples received through the mail.

Book Design: Assigns 8 freelance design and 1 freelance illustration jobs/year. Pays by the project, $300-850.

Jackets/Covers: Assigns 12 freelance design jobs/year. Prefers pen & ink, airbrush, charcoal/pencil, watercolor, acrylic, oil, pastel and collage. "Both line and four-color process. Subjects very varied in main list; styles range from minimalist abstractions to naturalistic. Paperbacks mostly 19th century Western subjects. We also require calligraphy on occasion." Pays by the project, $250-600.

Text Illustration: Assigns 2 freelance jobs/year. Prefers mostly line subjects (pen, woodcut, scratchboard, etc.) Pays by the project, $250-1,000.

Tips: "Illustrators should be conversant with graphic reproduction. Book designers are required to supply accurate tissues and detailed type specifications." A common mistake freelancers make is "not examining our list to see the sort of work we are likely to commission. Search out our books in the store in order to select the most relevant samples to send us."

UNIVERSITY OF PENNSYLVANIA PRESS, 418 Service Dr., Philadelphia PA 19104. Director: Thomas M. Rotell. Design & Production Manager: Carl E. Gross. Publishes scholarly books and texts, hardcover and paperback originals and reprints. Publishes 60-70 titles/year. Recent titles include *Virginia Piedmont Blues, Writing about Eakins, The Voice of My Beloved* and *Emperor of Culture.*

First Contact & Terms: Approached by 30 freelance artists/year. Uses artists for advertising layout; catalog illustration; direct mail, book and cover design. Assigns 30-40 advertising jobs/year. Prefers pen & ink, airbrush, acrylic and calligraphy. Minimum payment, $400, catalogs or direct mail brochures. Assigns 60-70 production jobs/year. Pays $9/hour minimum, mechanicals and paste-ups. Arrange interview; local artists only. Include SASE. Buys all rights. No advance. Negotiates payment for unused assigned work. Free catalog.

Book Design: Assigns 60-70 jobs/year. Uses artists for layout, type spec; all design shipped out-of-house. Pays $350-375/job, text layout; $375/job, type spec.

Jackets/Covers: Assigns 35-40 jobs/year. Pays for design by the job, $350-375 average; $300-350, b&w line drawings and washes, gray opaques and color-separated work.

Text Illustration: Pays $10-15/hour, maps, charts.

Tips: Production of books has doubled. Artists should have some experience in book and jacket design. Looking for "elegant, clean design and fine line illustration." Common mistakes designers make are "poorly rendered comp layouts, text typeface sizes too large for column width, insufficient leading between lines of type."

URBAN & SCHWARZENBERG, INC., (Medical Publishers), 7 E. Redwood St., Baltimore MD 21202. Editor-in-Chief: Charles W. Mitchell. Book publisher. Estab. 1976. Publishes hardcover originals, trade paperback originals and textbooks. Publishes nonfiction. Types of books include instruction, reference and clinical medicine. Specializes in clinical medicine, texts for students and reference. Publishes 12 titles/year. 10% require freelance illustration. Recent titles include *Orthopaedic Injuries in the Elderly* and *Art and Science of Bedside Diagnosis.* Book catalog free for request.

First Contact & Terms: Approached by 8 freelance artists/year. Works with 3 freelance medical illustrators/year. Send query letter with brochure, resume, slides, transparencies, SASE and photostats. Samples are filed or are returned by SASE only if requested. Reports back about queries/submissions within 2 weeks. Originals not returned to artist at job's completion. Write to schedule an appointment and mail appropriate materials to show a portfolio, which should include original/final art, photostats, final reproduction/product and slides. Considers complexity of project, skill and experience of artist, project's budget and turnaround time when establishing payment. Buys all rights.

Tips: Uses many half-tone and line illustrations. A common mistake freelanceers make is "sending the wrong kind of work for samples, i.e., not sending detailed line drawings when bidding on a surgery text. Allow me to keep samples of your work."

VALLEY OF THE SUN PUBLISHING, subsidiary of Sutphen Corp., Box 38, Malibu CA 90265. Art Director: Julie Mitchell. Book publisher. Also publishes audio, video and music cassettes. Estab. 1972. Publishes trade and mass market paperback originals. Subjects include self-help, metaphysical and New Age titles. Publishes 100 titles/year. 50% require freelance illustration. Recent titles include the self-help audio and New age music audio tapes *Increasing Self-Discipline, Stress Control, Inner Vistas* and *Soulmate Suite.*

First Contact & Terms: Approached by 20 freelance artists/year. Buys 50 freelance illustrations/year. Works with illustrators mainly for audio and video package cover art. Also works with artists for jacket/cover illustration. Works on assignment only. Send query letter with slides, transparencies, self-promotion materials and SASE. Samples are filed or are returned by SASE. Reports back only if interested. Originals returned to artists at job's completion. Write to schedule an appointment to show a portfolio, which should include original/final art, tearsheets, photographs, slides and transparencies. Considers project's budget when establishing payment. Buys first rights.

Jackets/Covers: Assigns 30-40 freelance illustration jobs/year. Pays by the project, $100 minimum.

Text Illustration: Assigns 10-20 freelance jobs/year. Pays by the project, $100 minimum.

Tips: "We use surrealistic or fantasy illustration, can be realistic or abstract. I look for eye-catching color. Send black-and-white prints or 35mm or 2¼ × 2¼ transparencies that can be kept on file. Artist can also send self-promotion materials that can be kept on file."

VICTORY PRESS, 543 Lighthouse Ave., Monterey CA 93940-1422. Contact: Eileen Hu. Estab. 1988. Publishes trade paperback originals and children's fiction. Recent titles include *Adventures of Monkey King* and *Chan Mi Gong: Chinese Meditation for Health.*

First Contact & Terms: Approached by 10 freelance artists/year. Send resume and photocopies. Samples not filed are returned by SASE. Buys all rights.

Text Illustration: Pays by the project, minimum $100; pen & ink sketches, $10-20 illustration.

Jackets/Covers: Color, minimum $100.

Tips: "If possible, include copies of published work."

*J. WESTON WALCH, PUBLISHER, Box 658, Portland ME 04104-0658. (207)772-2846. Managing Editor: Richard Kimball. Specializes in supplemental secondary school materials including books, poster sets, filmstrips and computer software. Publishes 120 titles/year.

First Contact & Terms: Works with 20 freelance artists/year. Works on assignment only. Send query letter with resume and samples to be kept on file unless the artist requests return. Write for artists' guidelines. Prefers photostats as samples. Samples not filed are returned only by request. Reports within 6 weeks. Original work not returned to the artist after job's completion. Considers project's budget when establishing payment. Rights purchased vary according to project.

Jackets/Covers: Assigns 20 freelance design and illustration jobs/year. Pays by the hour, $12-20 by the project, $100 minimum.

Text Illustration: Assigns 10 freelance jobs/year. Prefers b&w pen & ink. Pays by the hour, $12-20 by the project, $100 minimum.

WARNER BOOKS INC., 666 Fifth Ave., New York NY 10103. (212)484-3151. Vice President and Creative Director: Jackie Meyer. Publishes mass market paperbacks, adult trade hardcovers and children's books. Publishes 400 titles/year; 20% require freelance design, 80% require freelance illustration. Recent titles include *The Gold Coast, The Fortune* and *Red Phoenix*. Works with countless freelance artists/year. Buys hundreds of designs and illustrations from freelance artists/year.

First Contact & Terms: Approached by 250 freelance artists/year. Works on assignment only. Send brochure or tearsheets and photocopies. Samples are filed or are returned by SASE. Reports back only if interested. To show a portfolio, mail appropriate materials. Originals returned to artist at job's completion (artist must pick up). Pays $650 and up/design; $1,000 and up/illustration. Negotiates rights purchased. Check for most recent titles in bookstores.

Jackets/Covers: Uses realistic jacket illustrations. Payment subject to negotiation.

Tips: Industry trends include "more graphics and stylized art. Looks for "photorealistic style with imaginative and original design and use of eyecatching color variations." Artists shouldn't "talk too much. Good design and art should speak for themselves."

*WEBB RESEARCH GROUP, Box 314, Medford OR 97501. (503)664-4442. Owner: Bert Webber. Estab. 1979. Book publisher. Publishes hardcover and trade paperback originals. Types of books include biography, reference, history and travel. Specializes in the history and development of the Pacific Northwest and the Oregon Trail. Recent titles include *Rajneeshpuram: Who Were Its People*, a book on American & Japanese relocation in World War II and *Oregon Trail Diaries of Jane Gould*. 5% require freelance illustration. Book catalog free for SASE with 2 first class stamps.

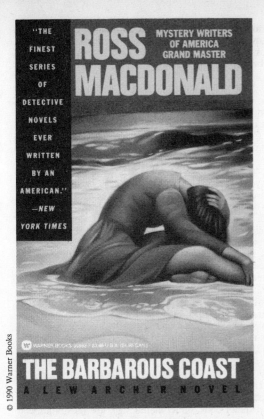

"THE FINEST SERIES OF DETECTIVE NOVELS EVER WRITTEN BY AN AMERICAN." —NEW YORK TIMES

ROSS MACDONALD

MYSTERY WRITERS OF AMERICA GRAND MASTER

THE BARBAROUS COAST
A LEW ARCHER NOVEL

© 1990 Warner Books

This pastel book-cover illustration by Gary Kelly "creates the right mood for a mystery," according to Warner Books creative director Jackie Meyer. The Cedar Falls, Iowa artist was given a copy of the book so he could come up with an image for the cover and completed the assignment in three months. Meyer assigned the project to him because he "comes up with great creative solutions and likes to read books and problem solve. His work is stylized and contemporary. He also is a pleasure to work with." He sold first rights to the artwork and all rights to the design.

Needs: Approached by more than 10 freelance artists/year. Uses freelance artists for localizing travel maps and doing sketches of Oregon Trail scenes. Also uses freelance artists for jacket/cover and text illustration. Works on assignment only.

First Contact & Terms: Send query letter with SASE and Xerox samples of Oregon Trail subjects. Samples are not filed and are returned by SASE if requested by artist. Reports back to the artist only if interested and a SASE is received. Portfolios are not reviewed. Rights purchased vary according to project. Originals are often returned to the artist at the job's completion.

Jackets/Covers: Assigns over 15 freelance design jobs/year.

Text Illustration: Assigns 6 freelance illustration jobs/year. Payment for book design, jackets/covers and text illustration negotiated based on specific assignment.

Tips: "Know our subjects and send a couple samples. Please send SASE if return or comments wanted. We find the work of those who *know the Oregon trail* to be the best."

SAMUEL WEISER INC., Box 612, York Beach ME 03910. (207)363-4393. Vice President: B. Lundsted. Specializes in hardcover and paperback originals, reprints and trade publications on metaphysics/oriental philosophy/esoterica. Recent titles include *Tibetan Buddhist Medicine & Psychiatry*, by Terry Clifford, Ph.D.; *Aspects and Personality*, by Dr. Karen Hamaker-Zondag; and *Astrology for Lovers*, by Dr. Liz Greene. Publishes 20 titles/year.

First Contact & Terms: Approached by 15 or so freelance artists/year. Works with 4 freelance artists/year. Send query letter with resume, slides, book covers and jackets. Samples are filed or are returned by SASE only if requested by artist. Reports back within 1 month only if interested. Originals returned to artist at job's completion. To show a portfolio, mail tearsheets and slides. Considers complexity of project, skill and experience of artist, project's budget, turnaround time and rights purchased when establishing payment. Buys one-time non-exclusive rights. Finds most artists through references/word-of-mouth, portfolio reviews and samples received through the mail.

Jackets/Covers: Assigns 20 freelance design jobs/year. Prefers airbrush, watercolor, acrylic and oil. Pays by the project, $200-600.

Tips: "We're interested in artists with professional experience with cover mechanicals—from inception of design to researching/creating image to type design, color-separated mechanicals to logo in place. It helps if we can see the work. We like printed color shots, or slides, or even photos of the work so we can see basically what we are getting. We return this if the artist requests that we do, but we really like to keep what we think we might be able to use down the road a bit. For example, we have one photo that we just now are using, but I saw it over three years ago for the first time and had nothing to use it on. Don't send us drawings of witches, goblins and demons, for that is not what our field is about. You should know something about us before you send materials. Send SASE for catalog."

*WESTERN PRODUCER PRAIRIE BOOKS, Box 2500, Saskatoon SK S7K 2C4 Canada. (306)665-3548. FAX: (306)653-1255. Editorial Director: Jane McHughen. Estab. 1951. Book publisher. Publishes hardcover originals and trade paperback originals and and reprints. Types of books include mainstream fiction, biography, young adult, history and humor. Specializes in natural history. Publishes 22 titles/year. Recent titles include *A Question of Courage*, by Irene Morck and *Barefoot on the Prairie*, by Ferne Nelson. 25% require freelance illustration; 100% require freelance design. Book catalog free for SASE.
Needs: Approached by 10 freelance artists/year. Works with 6 freelance illustrators and 2 freelance designers/year. Buys 20 freelance illustrations/year. Prefers local artists only with experience in book cover art. Uses freelance artists mainly for cover illustrations. Also uses freelance artists for jacket/cover and book design and text illustration. Works on assignment only.
First Contact & Terms: Send query letter with resume and slides. Samples are filed. Reports back to the artist only if interested. To show a portfolio, mail appropriate materials. Rights purchased vary according to project. Originals are returned at job's completion.
Book Design: Assigns 3 freelance design and 3 freelance illustration jobs/year. Pays by the project.
Jackets: Assigns 22 freelance design and 6 freelance illustration jobs/year. Pays by the project.
Text Illustration: Assigns 6 freelance design and 6 freelance illustration jobs/year. Pays by the project.

*WESTPORT PUBLISHERS, INC., 4050 Pennsylvania, Kansas City MO 64111. (816)756-1490. FAX: (816)756-0159. Managing Editor: Terry Faulkner. Estab. 1983. Book publisher. Publishes hardcover and trade paperback originals. Types of books include instruction, biography, juvenile, reference, history, self-help, travel, cookbook, psychology-related and parenting. Publishes 24-30 titles/year. Recent titles include *Little People*, *Making of Two Dakotas*, *Celebrate! Parties for Kids* and *Colorful Kansas City*. 70% require freelance illustration; 80% require freelance design. Book catalog available with SASE.
Needs: Approached by 3-5 freelance artists/year. Works with 3-5 freelance illustrators and 3-5 freelance designers/year. Buys 25-50 freelance illustrations/year. Uses freelance artists mainly for covers, juvenile/self-help titles. Also uses freelance artists for book, direct mail design, text illustration and catalog design. Works on assignment only.
First Contact & Terms: Send query letter with brochure, resume, SASE, tearsheets and photocopies. Samples are filed. Reports back within 3 weeks. To show a portfolio, mail thumbnails, b&w photostats, dummies, roughs and tearsheets. Rights purchased vary according to project. Originals are returned at the job's completion.
Book Design: Assigns 5-10 freelance design and 5-10 freelance illustration jobs/year. Pays by the project, $100 and up.
Jackets/Covers: Assigns 24-30 freelance design and 24-30 freelance illustration jobs/year. Pays by the project.
Text Illustration: Assigns 15 freelance design and 3-5 freelance illustration jobs/year. Pays by the project, $150 and up.
Tips: "Get experience with books similar in subject area to our list."

ALBERT WHITMAN & COMPANY, 5747 W. Howard St., Niles IL 60648. Editor: Kathleen Tucker. Specializes in hardcover original juvenile fiction and nonfiction—many picture books for young children. Publishes 23 titles/year; 100% require freelance illustration.
First Contact & Terms: Works with 20 freelance artists/year. Prefers working with artists who have experience illustrating juvenile trade books. Works on assignment only. Send brochure/flyer or resume and "a few slides and photocopies of original art and tearsheets that we can keep in our files. Do *not* send original art through the mail." Samples not returned. Reports to an artist if "we have a project that seems right for him. We like to see evidence that an artist can show the same children in a variety of moods, poses and environments." Original work returned to artist at job's completion "if artist holds the copyright." Rights purchased vary.
Cover/Text Illustration: Cover assignment is usually part of illustration assignment. Assigns 18 freelance jobs/year. Prefers realistic and semi-realistic art. Pays by flat fee or royalties.
Tips: Especially looks for "an artist's ability to draw people, especially children and the ability to set an appropriate mood for the story."

WILSHIRE BOOK CO., 12015 Sherman Rd., North Hollywood CA 91605. (213)875-1711 or (818)983-1105. President: Melvin Powers. Publishes paperback reprints; psychology, self-help, inspirational and other types of nonfiction. Publishes 25 titles/year.

First Contact & Terms: Local artists only. Call if interested. Buys first, reprint or one-time rights. Negotiates pay. Free catalog.
Jackets/Covers: Assigns 25 jobs/year. Buys b&w line drawings.

WISCONSIN TALES & TRAILS, INC., Box 5650, Madison WI 53705. (608)231-2444. Publisher: Howard Mead. Estab. 1960. Publishes adult trade books. Specializes in hardcover and paperback originals and reprints. "Only those that relate in some way to Wisconsin." 3 categories: Wisconsiana, guides, nature/ environment. Publishes 1-2 titles/year. Recent titles include *Ah, Wisconsin*.
First Contact & Terms: Approached by 50 freelance artists/year. Works on assignment only. Send query letter and samples to be kept on file for future assignments. Samples returned by SASE "if requested." Reports back on future assignment possibilities. Buys one-time rights. Return of original artwork "depends on individual contract or agreement negotiated."
Book Design: Pays by the project, $300-1,000.
Jackets/Covers: Pays by the project, $200 minimum.
Text Illustration: Assigns 1-2 freelance jobs/year. Pays by the project, $300-1,000.
Tips: Also publishes bimonthly magazine, *Wisconsin Trails*. "We have been using freelance artwork regularly in our magazine, b&w and color. Send a variety of samples using both b&w and color. Don't send originals. Looking for elegant photographs."

*WOODALL PUBLISHING COMPANY, 28167 N. Keith Dr., Lake Forest IL 60045. (708)362-6700. Vice President of Operations: Deborah Spriggs. Specializes in paperback annuals on camping. Publishes 3 titles/year. Recent titles include *Woodall's Campground Directory*, *Tent Camping Guide*, *RV Buyer's Guide* and *Favorite Recipes from America's Campgrounds*.
First Contact & Terms: Approached by 6 freelance artists/year. Works with 4 freelance artists/year. Works on assignment only. Call for appointment to show portfolio. Reports within 4 weeks. No original work returned at job's completion. Considers complexity of project, skill and experience of artist and project's budget when establishing payment. Rights purchased vary according to project.
Book Design: Assigns 3-4 jobs/year. Pays by the project.
Jackets/Covers: Assigns 2 freelance design and illustration jobs/year. Pays by the project.
Text Illustration: Pays by the project.
Tips: Looking for "outdoors, fun and relaxing" themes and styles. "Find out about our products before presenting sampler."

WOODSONG GRAPHICS INC., Box 238, New Hope PA 18938. (215)794-8321. President: Ellen Bordner. Specializes in paperback originals covering a wide variety of subjects, "but no textbooks or technical material so far." Publishes 3-6 titles/year. Recent titles include *Dogs & You*, by Doris Phillips and *Snowflake Come Home*, by John Giegling.
First Contact & Terms: Approached by several hundred freelance artists/year. Works with 1-5 freelance artists/year depending on projects and schedules. Works on assignment only. Send query letter with brochure and samples to be kept on file. Any format is acceptable for samples, except originals. Samples not filed are returned by SASE. Reports only if interested. Originals returned to artist at job's completion. Considers complexity of assignment, skill and experience of artist, project's budget and turnaround time when establishing payment. Rights purchased vary according to project.
Book Design: Assigns 2-3 freelance jobs/year. Pays by the project, $400 minimum.
Jackets/Covers: Assigns 3-6 freelance illustration jobs/year. Pays by the project, $100 minimum.
Text Illustration: Assigns 2-3 freelance jobs/year. Medium and style vary according to job. Pays by the project, $250 minimum.
Tips: Looks for a "realistic style in illustration, generally with an upbeat 'mood.' A willingness to submit some samples specifically created for the project at hand would be tremendously helpful. Our needs are often quite specialized. Animal illustrations are a particular interest here."

WRITER'S DIGEST BOOKS/NORTH LIGHT, F&W Publishing, 1507 Dana Ave., Cincinnati OH 45207. Art Director: Carol Buchanan. Publishes 25-30 books annually for writers, artists, photographers, plus selected trade titles. Send non-returnable photocopies of printed work to be kept on file. Works on assignment only.
Text Illustration: Uses artists for text illustration and cartoons.
Tips: Uses artists for ad illustration and design, book jacket illustration and design and direct-mail design.

*WRITER'S PUBLISHING SERVICE CO., 1512 Western Ave., Box 1273, Seattle WA 98111. (206)284-9954. Publisher: William R. Griffin. Estab. 1976. Book publisher. Publishes hardcover originals and reprints, trade paperback originals and textbooks. Types of books include contemporary, experimental, historical, science fiction, instruction, adventure, fantasy, mystery, biography, pre-school, reference, history, self-help, humor and cookbooks. Specializes in "all subjects; a separate division does only cleaning and maintenance subjects." Publishes 25 titles/year. Recent titles include *Living Through Two World Wars*, by Lehman and *How to Sell and Price Contract Cleaning*, by Davis. 90% require freelance illustration; 50% require freelance design. Book catalog available for $3.

Needs: Approached by 250 freelance artists/year. Works with 50 freelance illustrators and 20 freelance designers/year. Buys over 300 freelance illustrations/year. Prefers artists with experience. Uses freelance artists mainly for illustration, design, covers. Also uses freelance artists for direct mail and catalog design. Works on assignment only.

First Contact & Terms: Send query letter with brochure, resume, tearsheets, photocopies and other samples of work. Samples are filed. Reports back to the artist only if interested. Call or write to schedule an appointment to show a portfolio, which should include roughs, dummies and other samples. Rights purchased vary according to project. Originals returned at job's completion.

Book Design: Assigns 30 freelance design and 20 freelance illustration jobs/year. Pays by the hour, $7-30; by the project, $3-1,500.

Jackets/Covers: Assigns 10 freelance design and 20 freelance illustration jobs/year. Pays by the hour; by the project.

Text Illustration: Assigns 10 freelance design and 20 freelance illustration jobs/year. Pays by the hour or by the project.

Tips: "We are always looking for cleaning and maintenance related art and graphics."

*WYRICK & COMPANY, 12 Exchange St., Charleston SC 29401. (803)722-0881. FAX: (803)722-6771. President: C.L. Wyrick, Jr.. Estab. 1986. Book publisher. Publishes hardcover and trade paperback originals and trade paperback reprints. Types of books include contemporary and mainstream fiction, biography, travel, humor, art and photography books. Publishes 6-8 titles/year. Recent titles include *Porgy, Toiling in Soil*. 75% require freelance illustration; 100% require freelance design.

Needs: Approached by 8-12 freelance artists/year. Works with 2-3 freelance illustrators and 2-3 freelance designers/year. Buys 8-20 freelance illustrations/year. Prefers local artists with experience in book design and illustration. Uses freelance artists mainly for book jackets and text illustration. Also uses freelance artists book and catalog design. Works on assignment only.

First Contact & Terms: Send query letter with resume, tearsheets, transparencies and SASE. Samples are filed or are returned by SASE. Reports back within 2-3 months. To show a portfolio, mail tearsheets, photographs, slides and transparencies. Buys one-time rights. Originals are returned at the job's completion.

Book Design: Assigns 6-8 freelance design and 1-3 freelance illustration jobs/year. Pays by the project.

Jackets/Covers: Assigns 6-8 freelance design and 2-4 freelance illustration jobs/year. Pays by the project.

Text Illustration: Assigns 2-3 freelance design and illustration jobs/year. Pays by the project.

Tips: "Send samples of work suitable for book illustrations or cover design—not ads or unrelated work."

YE GALLEON PRESS, Box 25, Fairfield WA 99012. (509)283-2422. Editorial Director: Glen Adams. Estab. 1937. Publishes rare Western history, Indian material, antiquarian shipwreck and old whaling accounts and town and area histories; hardcover and paperback originals and reprints. Publishes 20 titles/year; 10% require freelance illustrators. Book catalog free for SASE.

First Contact & Terms: Works with 2 freelance illustrators/year. Query with samples and SASE. No advance. Pays promised fee for unused assigned work. Buys book rights.

Text Illustration: Buys b&w line drawings, some pen & ink drawings of a historical nature; prefers drawings of groups with facial expressions and some drawings of sailing and whaling vessels. Pays for illustration by the project, $10-35.

Tips: " 'Wild' artwork is hardly suited to book illustration for my purposes. Many correspondents wish to sell oil paintings which at this time we do not buy them. It costs too much to print them for short edition work."

*ZOLAND BOOKS, INC., 38A Huron Ave., Cambridge MA 02138. (617)864-6252. Design Director: Lori Pease. Estab. 1987. Book publisher. Publishes hardcover originals and reprints and trade paperback originals and reprints. Types of books include contemporary and mainstream fiction, biography, juvenile, travel, poetry, fine art and photography. Specializes in literature. Publishes 6-10 titles/year. Recent titles include *The Earth Shines Secretly—A Book of Days*, by Marge Piercey, art by Nell Blaine; *The Collected Poems of Beatrice Hawley*, edited by Denise Levertov and *Marge Piercy*, art by Nell Blaine. 10% require freelance illustration; 100% require freelance design. Book catalog free by request.

Needs: Works with 2 freelance illustrators and 6 freelance designers/year. Buys 3 freelance illustrations/year. Uses freelance artists mainly for book and jacket design. Also uses freelance artists for jacket/cover illustration and catalog design. Works on assignment only.

First Contact & Terms: Send query letter with brochure, resume, tearsheets, photocopies and photo-stats. Samples are filed or are returned by SASE if requested by artist. Reports back to the artist only if interested. To show a portfolio, mail roughs and tearsheets. Rights purchased vary according to project. Originals returned at job's completion.

Book Design: Assigns 6-10 freelance design and 1-3 freelance illustration jobs/year. Pays by the project, $400.

Jacket/Covers: Assigns 6-10 freelance design and 1-3 freelance illustration jobs/year. Pays by the project, $500.

Tips: "Show work in as professional a manner as possible. We prefer classic design with a contemporary twist."

Other Book Publishers

Each year we contact all firms currently listed in *Artist's Market* requesting they give us updated information for our next edition. We also mail listing questionnaires to new and established firms which have not been included in past editions. The following book publishers either did not respond to our request to update their listings for 1991 (if they indicated a reason, it is noted in parentheses after their name), or they did not return our questionnaire for a new listing (designated by the words "declined listing" after their names).

Alyson Publications, Inc. (over-stocked)
Arbor House (declined listing)
Astara Inc.
The Athletic Press
Atlantic Monthly Press (declined listing)
AUM Publications
Avery Publishing Group (asked to be deleted)
Baker Book House (over-stocked)
Bantam Books (declined listing)
The Best Sellers
Blue Heron Press (asked to be deleted)
Camelot Books (declined listing)
Carnival Enterprises
Carol Communication (asked to be deleted)
Catholic Book Publishing Co.
Chronicle Books
David C. Cook Publishing Company
Creative Graphics International, Inc.
Data Command
Doubleday and Co. Inc.

Dutton Children's Books (declined listing)
Enslow Publishers
Faber & Faber, Inc., (declined listing)
The Franklin Library (over-stocked)
Golden West Books
Harlequin Books (asked to be deleted)
Harper & Row Publishers, Inc. (declined listing)
Heinle & Heinle Publishers, Inc. (overstocked)
Henry Holt & Co.
Houghton Mifflin Co., (declined listing)
Human Kinetics Publishers
Incentive Publications Inc.
Jalmar Press
Judson Press
Kar-Ben Copies, Inc.
B. Klein Publications Inc.
Lake View Press (asked to be deleted)
Living Flame Press
Longman Financial Services Institute, Inc.
MacMillan Publishing Co.
Milady Publishing Corp.

Moon Publications, Inc. (no longer uses freelance artwork)
Mott Media Inc., Publishers (needs have changed)
Thomas Nelson Publishers (asked to be deleted)
Nelson-Hall Publishers
W.W. Norton Co., Inc. (declined listing)
Oness Press
Charles Scribner's Sons (declined listing)
Scroll Press Inc.
Sierra Club Books
South End Press (needs have changed)
Surfside Publishing Inc.
Texas Monthly Press (asked to be deleted)
Thompson & Company, Inc.
Time-Life Books (declined listing)
Vitachart, Inc.
J. Weston Walch, Publisher
Walker & Company
Winston-Derek, Inc.
Women's Aglow Fellowship
Zaner-Bloser Educational Publishers

There are over 3.5 million businesses in this country, and that adds up to a goldmine of opportunities for freelance artists. Businesses—which range from local supermarkets to multi-million dollar corporations—need artists who can design and illustrate collateral materials, print ads, annual reports and point-of-purchase displays, to name only a few assignments.

Retail, service and merchandising businesses provide freelance opportunities both locally and nationally. Don't overlook potential clients in your own town. Consult this section and the *Yellow Pages* for businesses in your area. New businesses require artwork for letterheads, brochures and advertisements. Professionals such as doctors may need you to design informational brochures. The grocery store just down the block might need a new approach to its advertisements in the local paper. Keep your name on file by sending samples and a business card to businesses you think might need a graphic facelift or regular contributions. Once you have established a good reputation with one business, word of mouth and referrals will bring extra assignments.

Businesses require a variety of styles to match the diversity of their products and marketing strategies. Realistic work is generally needed for product renderings in catalogs and in print advertising. Collectible manufacturers look for a realistic but fine art approach to plate illustration. Fashion firms call for realism in their catalogs and ads but desire a freer hand for fashion editorial. Read this section's Close-up on Luis Peres of Polo/Ralph Lauren for insight on this industry. Familiarity with signage and design of point-of-purchase displays and exhibits increases your chances of working with exhibit, display and sign firms. Architectural, interior and landscape design firms are also included in this section; they usually require that freelancers have good draftsmanship, a knowledge of blueprints and building materials, plus a good sense of perspective.

Do your homework before contacting businesses. Research the company's specialty, its size and its products. Ask for an annual report, which not only documents the financial results of a company's fiscal year but frequently offers a candid perspective on its employees, facilities and marketing plans. Then send samples that match the company's needs.

Find the name of the art buyer during your initial call; then send a sample package. Make appointments in advance to show your portfolio and then select work that reflects the company's specialty. Always leave a reminder behind so that it can be filed for future reference.

Before accepting an assignment, make sure you understand what rights will be purchased. Businesses often buy all rights (called a "buy-out") to artwork because they reuse it. Negotiate your payment so that it reflects the buy-out.

Stay current with economic and business trends by reading the financial pages in newspapers and periodicals; this way you will know what type of businesses are thriving and which ones are in trouble. Attend trade shows to see the latest trends in your field and to make valuable contacts; trade magazines list the dates and locations of upcoming shows. To increase your knowledge of the exhibit, display and sign field, refer to the trade magazine *Visual Merchandising & Store Design*. Read *Women's Wear Daily*, as well as fashion magazines, for trends in the fashion industry. Collectible plate manufacturers are listed in this section of the book and more names and addresses are listed in *The Bradford Book of Collector's Plates* and in *Plate World*. For additional names and information regarding architecture and interior design firms, consult the directory *Profile* and the magazines *The AIA Journal*, *Architectural Digest* and *Interior Design*.

*ABBEY PRESS, Hill Dr., St. Meinrad IN 47577. Creative Director: Jo Anne Calucchia. Manufacturer/distributor/mail-order catalog providing Christian products, greeting cards, wall decor and sculpture. Clients: Christian bookstores, gift stores and retail catalog.

Needs: Approached by 50 freelance artists/year. Works with 20-50 freelance illustrators and 5 freelance designers/year. Buys 200-300 freelance designs and illustrations/year. Artist must have knowledge of art preparation for reproduction; prefers 3 years experience in greeting cards. Works on assignment only. Uses artists for 3-dimensional product design, illustration on product and model making. Prefers gouache or watercolor. "Quick turnaround time is required."

First Contact & Terms: Send query letter with resume, tearsheets, slides and photographs. Samples not filed are returned by SASE. Reports back within 1 month. Pays for design by the project, $75 minimum. Pays for illustration by the project, $200 minimum.

Tips: "Our products are of a religious and/or inspirational nature. We need full-color illustrations from experienced artists who know how to prepare art for reproduction. Familiarize yourself with current looks and trends in the Christian market."

ABEL LOVE, INC., 20 Lakeshore Dr., Newport News VA 23602. (804)877-2939. Buyer: Abraham Leiss. Estab. 1985. Distributor of gifts, hobby, art and craft supplies and drafting material. Clients: retail stores and college bookstores. Current clients include Hampton Hobby House and the NASA Visitors Center.

Needs: Approached by 100 freelance artists/year. Works with 10 freelance illustrators and 1 freelance designer/year. Uses freelance artists for catalog design, illustration and layout. Send query letter with slides, photographs and transparencies. Samples are filed. Reports back ASAP. Pays for design and illustration by the project. Rights purchased vary according to project.

*ABRACADABRA MAGIC SHOP, 125 Lincoln Blvd., Dept. AM90, Middlesex NJ 08846. (201)805-0200. President: Robert Bokor. Manufacturer/mail order specializing in fun products for men and boys, marketed via mail order.

Needs: Approached by 3-4 freelance artists/year. Works with 2 freelance illustrators and 2 freelance designers/year. Assigns 6 jobs to freelance artists/year. Uses freelance artists mainly for catalogs. Local artists only. Works on assignment only. Uses artists for advertising and catalog design, illustration and layout; packaging design and layout.

First Contact & Terms: Send query letter with resume and photocopies. Samples not filed are returned by SASE. Reports back within 1 month. To show a portfolio, mail appropriate materials. Pays for design by the project, $50-1,000; per illustration. Considers client's budget when establishing payment.

Tips: "We are currently looking for freelance cartoonists to illustrate products for catalogs."

*ACADIA CO., INC., 330 7th Ave., New York NY 10001. (212)695-3900. Design Director: Susan P. Cherson. Converter. "Our goods must reflect the national retail market (K-Mart/Walmart/Sears). Labels: "The Acadia Co., Inc."

Needs: Works with 15 freelance artists/year. Prefers local artists only with experience in repeats, an excellent color sense and a major understanding of home furnishings. Uses freelance artists mainly for creative repeats and colorings. Also uses freelance artists for textile and pattern design, paste-up and mechanicals (for pillow tickings only). No style preferred. Special needs are "someone with an exceptional color sense in home furnishings."

First Contact & Terms: Send query letter with brochure showing art style. Samples are filed or are returned by SASE if requested by artist. Reports back only if interested. Write to schedule an appointment to show a portfolio with enclosed phone number. Portfolio should include color thumbnails. Pays by the project, $75-800. Buys all rights.

Tips: The best way for illustrators or designers to introduce themselves to Acadia Co., Inc. is "first by recommendations and then by portfolio review."

 The asterisk before a listing indicates that the listing is new in this edition. New markets are often the most receptive to freelance submissions.

ACCENTS, INC., 3208 Factory Dr., Pomona CA 91768. Marketing Manager: Charles Fixa. Estab. 1960. Manufacturer of party paper such as napkins, plates and cups. Clients: grocery and party store trade.
Needs: Approached by 10 freelance artists/year. Works with 1-2 freelance artist/year. Assigns 1-2 jobs/year. Prefers local artists only with experience in party paper industry. Uses freelance artists mainly for design for napkins. Prefers contemporary design. Also uses freelance artists for advertising design, illustration and layout and other design.
First Contact and Terms: Send query letter with brochure and tearsheets. Samples are filed or are returned only if requested by artist. Reports back within 1 month. Call or write to schedule an appointment to show a portfolio, which should include original/final art and final reproduction/product. Pays for design and illustration by the project. Considers complexity of project and client's budget when establishing payment. Negotiates rights purchased.

*ADELE'S GROUP, Suite 91, 24436 Clipstone, Woodland Hills CA 91367. (213)276-5566. Contact: Shirley Margulis. Licensor and retailer of personalized gifts including acrylic and oak desk accessories, stained glass boxes, novelty clocks, personalized gift items from any medium. Sells to "high-quality-conscious" customers.
Needs: Approached by 10-15 freelance artists/year. Works with 100-150 freelance artists/year. Uses artists for product design, model making and lettering. "We always will consider any type of item that can be personalized in some way, shape or form." Prefers wood, acrylic, glass or a combination thereof.
First Contact & Terms: Send query letter with brochure or photocopies and photos to be kept on file. Samples not filed are returned by SASE. Reports back only if interested. Write for appointment to show a portfolio, which should include thumbnails, b&w photographs or actual samples. Pays for design by the hour, $10-15; by the project, $10-300. Considers rights purchased when establishing payment.
Tips: "Consider first that we only purchase items we or you can personalize. A beautiful picture can't be personalized." Common mistakes freelancers make in presenting samples or portfolios is to "talk too much and show sloppy samples. Also, they don't know how to cost out their item. We require a firm price and commitment."

*ADVANCE SPECTACLE CO., INC., 3710 Commercial Ave., Northbrook IL 60062. President: S.F. Levine. Mail-order business offering eyeglasses and products for senior citizens.
Needs: Works with 1 freelance artist/year. Assigns 20 freelance jobs/year. Prefers local artists. Works on assignment only. Uses artists for advertising, brochure and catalog design, illustration and layout.
First Contact & Terms: Send query letter with brochure. Samples are filed. Reports back only if interested. Write to schedule an appointment to show a portfolio. Pays for design and illustration by the project. Considers complexity of project and client's budget when establishing payment. Negotiates rights purchased.

AERO PRODUCTS RESEARCH INC., 11201 Hindry Ave., Los Angeles CA 90045. (213)641-7242. Director of Public Relations: J. Parr. Aviation training materials producer. Produces line of plastic credit and business cards and advertising specialty items.
Needs: Works with about 4 freelance illustrators and 2 freelance designers/month. Prefers local artists. Uses artists for brochures, catalogs, advertisements, graphs and illustrations.
First Contact & Terms: Send query letter with brochure/flyer and tearsheets to be kept on file. Originals not returned to artist at job's completion. Negotiates pay according to experience and project.

*AFRICAN FABRIC PRINTS/AFRICAN GARMENTS INC., Box 91, New York NY 10108. (212)447-5046. Contact: Vince Jordan.
Needs: Uses artists for fashion and textile design and ready-to-wear patterns.
First Contact & Terms: Mail tearsheets, original art or design ideas. Reports in 5-6 weeks. Pays $50 minimum.

AHPA ENTERPRISES, Box 506, Sheffield AL 35660. Marketing Manager: Allen Turner. Estab. 1976. Media products producer/marketer. Provides illustration, fiction, layout, video production, computer-printed material, etc. Specializes in adult male, special-interest material. Clients: limited-press publishers, authors, private investors, etc.
Needs: Approached by 20 freelance artists/year. Works with about 5 freelance artists/year. Assigns 40-50 jobs to freelance artists/year. Seeking illustrators for illustration of realistic original fiction or concepts. Wants only those artists "who are in a position to work with us on an intermittent but long-term basis." Prefers a tight, realistic style; pen & ink, airbrush, colored pencil and watercolor. Works on assignment only.
First Contact & Terms: Send query letter with resume and photocopies or tearsheets, photostats, photographs and new sketches to be kept on file. Samples not filed are returned by SASE only if requested. Reports back only if interested (within 3-7 days). Pays for illustration by the project, $40-500. Considers complexity of the project and number and type of illustrations ordered when establishing payment. Buys all rights.
Tips: "This is an excellent place for capable amateurs to 'turn pro' on a part-time, open-end basis. We are most inclined to respond to artists whose cover letters indicate a willingness to adapt to our particular market needs. We are not inclined to respond to an illustrator who seems to be 'over-selling' himself."

*ALBEE SIGN CO., 561 E. 3rd St., Mt. Vernon NY 10553. (914)668-0201. President: William Lieberman. Produces interior and exterior signs and graphics. Clients are banks and real estate companies.
Needs: Works with 6 freelance artists for sign design, 6 for display fixture design, 6 for P-O-P design and 6 for custom sign illustration. Local artists only. Works on assignment only.
First Contact & Terms: Query with samples (pictures of completed work). Previous experience with other firms preferred. Include SASE. Reports within 2-3 weeks. No samples returned. Reports back as assignment occurs. Provide resume, business card and pictures of work to be kept on file for future assignments. Pays by job.

ALLBILT/FASHION WORLD UNIFORM CORP., 38-09 43rd Ave., Long Island City NY 11101. (718)706-1414. Senior Designer: Teresa Bajandas. Manufacturer of custom designed uniforms for the hotel and travel industries. "We work with interior designers and architects in developing a uniform program consistent with the theme and image of each project be it hotel or airline." AllBilt and Fashion World labels.
Needs: Works with 4-8 freelance artists/year. Uses freelance artists for accessory design and fashion illustration. Prefers loose figure illustrations and realistic product rendering.
First Contact & Terms: Send query letter with brochure, tearsheets, photostats and photocopies. Samples not filed are returned only if requested by artist. Reports back only if interested. Write to schedule an appointment to show a portfolio, which should include original/final art. Pays for illustration by the project, $100-5,000. Considers complexity of project when establishing payment.

*ALVA MUSEUM REPLICAS, 220 Old Country Rd., Mineola NY 11501. (516)739-0085. Contact: Gregory Glasson. Manufacturer and distributor of sculpture replicas. Clients: museum shops, department stores, libraries and universities. For contract casting, mail color slides or photos stating size, medium, showing all views and SASE.

*AMERICAN ARTISTS, Division of Graphics Buying Service, Suite 7, 42 Sherwood Terrace, Lake Bluff IL 60044. (708)295-5355. Manufacturer of limited edition plates, figurines and lithographs. Specializes in horse and cat themes, but considers others. Clients: wholesalers and retailers.
Needs: Approached by 10 freelance artists/year. Works with 5 freelance illustrators and 2 freelance designers/year. Uses artists for plate and figurine design and illustration; brochure design, illustration and layout. Open to most art styles.
First Contact & Terms: Send query letter with resume and samples. Prefers transparencies or slides but will accept photos—color only. Samples not filed are returned only if requested or if unsuitable. Reports within 1 month. Call or write for appointment to show a portfolio. Payment varies and is negotiated. Rights purchased vary. Considers complexity of project, skill and experience of artist, how work will be used and rights purchased when establishing payment.

AMERICAN BOOKDEALERS EXCHANGE, Box 2525, La Mesa CA 92041. Editor: Al Galasso. Publisher of *Book Dealers World*, targeted to self-publishers, writers and mail order book dealers. Clients: self-publishers, writers, business opportunity seekers.
Needs: Works with 3 freelance artists/year. Prefers artists with at least a year's experience. Works on assignment only. Uses artists for advertising, brochure and catalog design and illustration.
First Contact & Terms: Send query letter with photostats to be kept on file. Samples not kept on file are returned only if requested. Reports only if interested. Pays by the project, $25-200 average. Considers complexity of project, skill and experience of artist, turnaround time and rights purchased when establishing payment.

*AMERICAN TRADITIONAL STENCILS, RD 281, Bow St., Northwood NH 03261. (603)942-8100. FAX: (603)942-8919. Owner: Judith Barker. Estab. 1970. Manufacturer of brass and laser cut stencils and 24 karat gold finish charms. Clients: retail craft, art and gift shops. Current clients include Williamsburg Museum, Henry Ford Museum and some Ben Franklin stores.
Needs: Approached by 1-2 freelance artists/year. Works with 1 freelance illustrator/year. Assigns 2 jobs to freelance artists/year. Prefers artists with experience in graphics. Works on assignment only. Uses freelance artists mainly for stencils. Prefers b&w camera-ready art. Also uses freelance artists for advertising illustration and product design. Send query letter with brochure showing art style and photocopies. Samples are filed or are returned. Reports back in 2 weeks. Call to schedule an appointment to show a portfolio, which should include roughs, original/final art and b&w tearsheets. Pays for design and illustration by the project. Payment is negotiated. Rights purchased vary according to project.

ARCHITECTURE BY SCHLOH, 213 Bean Ave., Los Gatos CA 95030. (408)354-4551. Estab. 1965. Architectural firm providing architectural services for high-end custom homes. Clients: residential.
Needs: Works with 3 freelance illustrators and 2 freelance designers/year. Uses artists mainly for technical drawings. Local artists preferred. Works on assignment only. Uses artists for advertising and brochure design, architectural renderings and model making.

First Contact & Terms: Send query letter with brochure and photocopies. Samples are filed. Reports back within 2 weeks. Write to schedule an appointment to show a portfolio, which should include photographs. Pays for illustration by the hour, $40-50; pays for design by the hour, $20-35. Considers complexity of project and client's budget when establishing payment. Buys first rights.

THE ASHTON-DRAKE GALLERIES, 9200 N. Maryland Ave., Niles IL 60648. (708)966-2770, Artist Relations: Scott Wolff. Product Development: Ed Bailey-Mershon. Estab. 1985. Direct response marketer of limited edition collectibles, such as porcelain dolls, figurines and other uniquely executed artwork sold in thematic continuity series. Clients: collectible consumers represent all age groups.
Needs: Approached by 200 freelance artists/year. Works with 250 freelance doll artists, sculptors, costume designers and illustrators/year. Works on assignment only. Uses artists for concept illustration, collectible design, prototype specifications and sample construction. Prior experience in giftware design, doll design, greeting card and book illustration a plus. Subject matter is children and mothers, animals and nostalgia scenes. Prefers "cute, realistic and naturalistic human features; animated poses."
First Contact & Terms: Send inquiry letter with resume, copies of samples to be kept on file, except for copyrighted slides, which are duplicated and returned. Prefers slides, photographs, tearsheets or photostats (in that order) as samples. Samples not filed are returned. Reports within 45 days. Pays for design by the project, $500-5,000. Pays for illustration by the project, $25-500. Concept illustrations are done "on spec" to $200 maximum. Contract for length of series on royalty basis with guaranteed advances. Considers complexity of the project, project's budget, skill and experience of the artist, and rights purchased when establishing payment.
Tips: "Do not send actual products." The most common mistake freelancers make in presenting samples or a portfolio is "sending actual products, ribbons and awards and too many articles on their work. Especially looking for doll artists who work in clay or sculptors and costume designers."

*BAGINDD PRINTS, 2171 Blount Rd., Pompano Beach FL 33069. (305)971-9000. FAX: (305)973-1000. Manager: Arnold S. Reimer. Estab. 1977. Manufacturer of handpainted and silk screened designer wallcovering and fabrics. Clients: interior designers.
Needs: Approached by 10-15 freelance artists/year. Works with 6 freelance designers/year. Prefers local artists with experience in textile design. Uses freelance artists mainly for wallcovering and fabrics. Also uses freelance artists for product design. Send slides and photographs. Samples are not filed and are returned. Reports back in 1 week. Call to schedule an appointment to show a portfolio, which should include original/final art and photographs. Buys first rights or all rights.

BAIMS, 408 Main, Pine Bluff AR 71601. (501)534-0121. Contact: David A. Shapiro. Estab. 1896. Retailer. Carries Haggar, Van Heusen and other labels.
Needs: Works with 2-3 freelance illustrators and designers/year. Assigns 25-100 jobs/year. Uses artists for ad illustration.
First Contact & Terms: Send a query letter with resume, business card and samples to be kept on file. Reports in 2 weeks. Call or write to arrange an appointment to show a portfolio. Pays $5-20/job.
Tips: "Send non-returnable samples of clothing illustrations. We do not want to see samples with emphasis on things other than our needs."

BANKERS LIFE & CASUALTY COMPANY, 1000 Sunset Ridge Rd., Northbrook IL 60062. (312)498-1500. Manager-Communications/Graphics: Charles S. Pusateri. Insurance firm.
Needs: Works with 3-5 freelance artists/year. Works on assignment only. Uses freelance artists mainly for sales materials. Also uses artists for advertising and brochure design, illustration and layout; posters and signage. Prefers pen & ink, airbrush, pencil, marker and calligraphy.
First Contact & Terms: Send query letter with resume and printed pieces to be kept on file. Samples returned only if requested. Reports within 2 weeks only if interested. Write to schedule an appointment to show a portfolio, which should include thumbnails, roughs and final reproduction/product. Pays for design by the project, $50-100. Pays for illustration by the project, $25-75. Considers complexity of project, skill and experience of artist and turnaround time when establishing payment. Rights purchased vary according to project.
Tips: "Follow rules but don't give up. Timing is essential. The best way for an artist to break into our field is by sending a letter followed by a phone call."

BASS PRO SHOPS, 1935 S. Campbell, Springfield MO 65898. Art Dept. Manager: Marla Leighton. Distributor. "We specialize in outdoor gear, fishing tackle, hunting, camping and boating for sportsmen."
Needs: Approached by 50-60 freelance artists/year. Works with 10-20 freelance illustrators and 20-30 freelance designers/year. Assigns 40-50 jobs to freelance artists/year. Works on assignment only. Uses freelance artists for advertising design and illustration, brochure design and illustration, product design, rendering of product, P-O-P display, display fixture design and signage.

First Contact & Terms: Send query letter with resume, tearsheets, photostats, slides and photographs. Samples are filed and are not returned. Reports back only if interested. Call to schedule an appointment to show a portfolio which should include thumbnails, roughs, final reproduction/product and tearsheets. Pays for design by the hour, $10 minimum. Pays for illustration by the hour, $20 minimum. Considers skill and experience of artist and rights purchased when establishing payment. Buys all rights.

BAXTER HODELL DONNELLY PRESTON, INC. ARCHITECTS, 3500 Red Bank Rd., Cincinnati OH 45227. Marketing Coordinator: Cynthia A. Jackson. Estab. 1939. "BHDP offers comprehensive services in programming, planning, architecture, interior design and product management. The company has earned a national reputation for quality and innovation—especially on large buildings with complex functional requirements. Our experience covers a broad range of projects, including office buildings, manufacturing, research and development facilities, schools and major department stores." Current clients include P&G, Merrill Dow and Mead Data Central.
Needs: Approached by 10 freelance artists/year. Works with approximately 3 freelance illustrators and copywriters and 2 graphic designers/year. Uses freelance artists for interior rendering, architectural rendering, model making and copywriting.
First Contact & Terms: Send query letter with brochure showing art style or resume and sample. Samples are filed or are returned only if requested by artist. Reports back within days. Write to schedule an appointment to show a portfolio or mail a sample. Considers complexity of project, skill and experience of artist, turnaround time, client's budget and rights purchased when establishing payment. Negotiates rights purchased.
Tips: "We have limited time for meetings. Prefer contact by mail, and it's best to include a sample of work. All contacts are kept in files for future resources. Budgets are a considered factor."

*BEROL USA, 105 Westpark Dr., Box 2248, Brentwood TN 37024-2248. (615)371-1199. Art Product Group Manager: Terry Butler. Manufactures writing instruments, drawing materials and art supplies (Prismacolor Art Pencils, Art Markers and Art Stix® artist crayons). Current clients include: Alvin Co, Koenig Charrette.
Needs: Approached by 200 freelance artists each year. Works with 5 freelance illustrators and 8 freelance designers each year. Assigns 25 jobs to freelance artists/year. Uses artists for illustration and layout for catalogs, ads, brochures, displays, packages. Artists must use Prismacolor and/or Verithin products only. Uses freelance artists mainly for illustration and finished art. Prefers traditional styles and media.
First Contact & Terms: Query with photographs and slides to be kept on file. Samples returned only by request. Reports within 2 weeks. Call or write to schedule an appointment to show a portfolio; portfolios not necessary. Pays by the project, $300 maximum. Rights purchased vary according to project.
Tips: "Hand-colored photographs (with Prismacolor® Art Pencils) becoming very popular."

*LYNWOOD BROWN AIA AND ASSOCIATES, INC., 1220 Prince St., Alexandria VA 22314. (703)836-5523. FAX: (703)548-7899. President: L. Brown. Architectural firm providing architecture and engineering. Clients: commercial, industrial, institutional and residential.
Needs: Works with 2-3 freelance artists/year. Uses artists for interior design, architectural rendering and model making.
First Contact & Terms: Works on assignment only. Send query letter with brochure; call for appointment to show portfolio. Prefers photos or prints as samples. Samples not filed are returned by SASE only if requested. Reports within 30 days. Pays for design by the hour, $9-20 average; for illustration by the hour, $8-18 average. Considers client's budget, skill and experience of artist and turnaround time when establishing payment.

*C.J. PRODUCTS, INC., 100 Christmas Pl., Weston WV 26452. (304)269-6111. FAX: (304)269-6115. Technical Director: Jay Hayes. Estab. 1978. Manufacturer of Christmas displays. Clients: national retail chains.
Needs: Approached by 30 freelance artists/year. Works with 6 freelance illustrators and 12 freelance designers/year. Assigns 12 jobs to freelance artists/year. Prefers artists with experience in display, signage, sculpture and photography. Uses freelance artists mainly for special projects. Also uses freelance artists for brochure design, illustration and layout; catalog design, illustration and layout; product rendering and design; model making and P-O-P displays.
First Contact & Terms: Send query letter with brochure showing art style, resume, tearsheets and photocopies. Samples are filed or returned by SASE only if requested by artist. Reports back only if interested. Write to schedule an appointment to show a portfolio or mail thumbnails, roughs, b&w and color photostats, tearsheets, photographs, slides and transparencies. Pays for design and illustration by the hour and by the project. Buys all rights.

CABELA'S, THE WORLD'S FOREMOST OUTFITTER, 812 13th Ave., Sidney NE 69160. Catalog Director: Jim Beardsley. Estab. 1960. Direct-mail firm specializing in quality fishing, hunting and outdoor gear.
Needs: Approached by 50-75 freelance artists/year. Works with 15 freelance artists and 6 freelance designers/year. Assigns 35-50 freelance jobs/year. Prefers artists with experience in wildlife and cutaway (4-color). Prefers acrylic. Uses freelance artists mainly for cover design. Also uses freelance artists for catalog illustration and rendering of product.

First Contact & Terms: Send query letter with brochure showing art style, tearsheets, slides and photographs. Samples are filed or are returned. Reports back within 1 week. To show a portfolio, mail roughs, original/final art and color and b&w photographs and slides. Pays for design by the project, $300-500. Pays for illustration by the project, $300-1,500. Considers complexity of project, turnaround time and rights purchased when establishing payment. Buys one-time and all rights.

CAN CREATIONS, INC., Box 8576, Pembroke Pines FL 33084. President: Judy Rappoport. Estab. 1984. Manufacturer of decorated plastic pails directed to juvenile market. Clients: balloon and floral designers, party planners and suppliers, department stores, popcorn and candy retailers.
Needs: Approached by 8-10 freelance artists/year. Works with 2-3 freelance designers/year. Assigns 5 freelance jobs/year. Prefers local artists only. Works on assignment only. Uses freelance artists mainly for "design work for plastic containers." Also uses artists for advertising design, illustration and layout; brochure design; posters; signage; magazine illustration and layout.
First Contact & Terms: Send query letter with tearsheets and photostats. Samples are not filed and are returned by SASE only if requested by artist. Reports back within 2 weeks. Call or write to schedule an appointment to show a portfolio, which should include roughs and b&w tearsheets and photostats. Pays for design by the project, $75 minimum. Pays for illustration by the project, $150 minimum. Considers client's budget and how work will be used when establishing payment. Negotiates rights purchased.
Tips: "We are looking for cute and very simple designs, not a lot of detail."

CANTERBURY DESIGNS, INC.. Box 4060, Martinez GA 30917-4060. (800)241-2732 or (404)860-1674. President: Angie A. Newton. Estab. 1977. Publisher and distributor of charted design books; counted cross stitch mainly. Clients: needlework specialty shops, wholesale distributors (craft and needlework), department stores and chain stores.
Needs: Works with 12-20 freelance artists/year. Uses artists mainly for counted cross-stitch design.
First Contact & Terms: Send query letter with samples to be returned. Prefers stitched needlework, paintings, photographs or charts as samples. Samples not filed are returned. Reports within 1 month. Call for appointment to show portfolio. Payment varies. "Some designs purchased outright, some are paid on a royalty basis." Considers complexity of project, salability, customer appeal and rights purchased when establishing payment.
Tips: "When sending your work for our review, be sure to photocopy it first. This protects you. Also, you have a copy from which to reconstruct your design should it be lost in mail. Also, send your work by certified mail. You have proof it was actually received by someone."

*CAP FERRAT JEANS, Suite 1103, 1411 Broadway, New York NY 10018. (212)869-1808. FAX: (212)869-3442. Senior Vice President: Jack Marine. Estab. 1960. Manufacturer and importer of women's jeans for ages 16-40. Label: Cap Ferrat.
Needs: Approached by 2 freelance artists/year. Works with 1-2 freelance artists/year. Prefers artists with experience in labeling designs, tops and bottoms. Uses freelance artists mainly for new concepts. Also uses freelance artists for advertising, product and fashion design and catalog illustration. No style preferred. Special needs are "development of shirt line to complement jean line—for export program." Send query letter with brochure showing art style. Samples are not filed and are returned by SASE if requested by artist. Reports back only if interested. Call to schedule an appointment to show a portfolio, which should include roughs. Pays for design and illustration by the project, $50-500. Rights purchased vary according to project.
Tips: Artists should "be sure they understand the denim market."

*VAL CARLSON, ARCHITECT, AIA, P.C., 159 Center St., Shelton CT 06484. (203)735-2677. President: Val Carlson. Architectural, interior, and landscape design; city planning and construction management firm. Clients: institutional, educational, ecclesiastical, residential, state, hospital and commercial.
Needs: Works with 2 freelance artists/year. Prefers artists with several years of experience. Works on assignment only. Uses freelance artists for architectural rendering, furnishings, art restoration and new art murals and paintings
First Contact & Terms: Send query letter with brochure showing art style or resume, photocopies and photographs. Samples are filed and are not returned. To show a portfolio, mail original/final art, final reproduction and photographs. Pays for design by the project, $1,000-20,000. Pays for illustration by the project, $200-1,000. Considers complexity of project, skill and experience of artist and turnaround time. Buys all rights.
Tips: "Submit brochures, work references and typical quotes." Needs freelance artists for "restoration of ecclesiastical artwork, murals, stations of the cross, etc."

*HUGH DAVID CARTER-ARCHITECT-AIA, Suite 4, 819½ Pacific Ave., Santa Cruz CA 95060. (408)458-1544. Architect: H.D. Carter. Architectural firm specializing in upper-end residential projects, both new and remodeled, some office and interiors.

Needs: Works with 2 freelance artists/year. Works on asignment only. Uses freelance artists for advertising design and illustration, interior rendering, landscape design, architectural rendering, charts, maps and model making.

First Contact & Terms: Send query letter with brochure, resume, tearsheets, photostats, photocopies, slides or photographs. Samples are filed or are returned by SASE. Reports back within 1 month. Call to schedule an appointment to show a portfolio, which should include thumbnails, roughs, original/final art and final reproduction. Pays for design by the hour, $15-50. Pays for illustration by the hour, $15-60; by the project, $150-600. Considers complexity of project, how work will be used and amount of work when establishing payment. Negotiates rights purchased.

Tips: "Come by with an appointment only."

*THOMAS PAUL CASTRONOVO, ARCHITECT, 1175 Main St., Akron OH 44310. Clients: residential and commercial. Mail slides or b&w photos. Reports in 10 days.

Needs: Uses artists for architectural and interior rendering, paintings, sculpture and model building. Pays by job.

*CERAMO STUDIO, 116-19 101 Ave., Richmond Hill NY 11419. (718)849-2323. Owner: Marvin Rosen. Estab. 1975. Manufacturer of porcelain gift items with kiln-fire design. Clients: gift shops and souvenir stores. Current clients include Marriott Host and Ogden Food.

Needs: Prefers design for porcelain products. Uses freelance artists for product design. Send query letter with brochure showing art style. Samples are filed or are returned by SASE only if requested by artist. Reports back to the artist only if interested. To show a portfolio, mail appropriate materials. Pays for design by the project.

CHICAGO COMPUTER AND LIGHT, INC., 5001 N. Lowell Ave., Chicago IL 60630-2610. (312)283-2749. President: Larry Feit. Estab. 1976. Manufacturer of gift items for upscale gift shops. Clients: gift stores and major public museums.

Needs: Works with 3 freelance artists/year. Assigns 6 jobs/year. Works on assignment only. Uses freelance artists mainly for catalog sheets, package design and letterhead. Also uses freelance artists for advertising, brochure and catalog design, illustration and layout; rendering of product; P-O-P displays; posters; model making and signage.

First Contact and Terms: Send query letter with brochure, resume, tearsheets, photostats and photographs. Samples are filed or are returned by SASE. Reports back within 1 week. Call or write to schedule an appointment to show a portfolio, which should include roughs, original/final art and color and b&w tearsheets, photostats and photographs. Pays for design and illustration by the hour, $10-60. Considers complexity of project and how work will be used when establishing payment. Buys all rights; negotiates rights purchased.

Tips: "Send samples, follow up with a call, then wait."

COMMUNICATIONS ELECTRONICS, Dept. AM, Box 1045, Ann Arbor MI 48106-1045. (313)973-8888. Editor: Ken Ascher. Estab. 1969. Manufacturer, distributor and ad agency (10 company divisions). Clients: electronics, computers.

Needs: Works with approximately 400 freelance illustrators and 100 freelance designers/year. Uses artists for advertising, brochure and catalog design, illustration and layout; product design; illustration on product; P-O-P displays; posters and renderings. Prefers pen & ink, airbrush, charcoal/pencil, watercolor, acrylic, marker and computer illustration.

First Contact & Terms: Send query letter with brochure, resume, business card, samples and tearsheets to be kept on file. Samples not filed are returned by SASE. Reports within 1 month. Call or write for appointment to show portfolio. Pays for design and illustration by the hour, $15-100; by the project, $10-15,000; by the day, $40-800. Considers complexity of project, skill and experience of artist, how work will be used, turnaround time and rights purchased when establishing payment.

*CREATIONS BY PHYLLIS CO., 30 N.E. 125th Place, Portland OR 97230. (503)254-3344. Owner: Phyllis Altman. Estab. 1975. Manufacturer of porcelain music boxes, dolls, carousels, etc. Clients: distributors. Current clients include Show Stoppers.

Needs: Works with 1 freelance illustrator and 1 freelance designer/year. Prefers local artists only with experience in china painting. Uses freelance artists mainly for piece work. Prefers traditional and Victorian. Also uses freelance artists for catalog design and illustration.

First Contact & Terms: Call to find out what needs are. Payment is negotiated. Rights purchased vary according to project.

JERRY CUMMINGS ASSOCIATES INC., Suite 301, 420 Boyd St., Los Angeles CA 90013. (213)621-2756. Contact: Jerry Cummings. Estab. 1970. Landscape architecture firm. Clients: commercial and residential.
Needs: Assigns 20-30 freelance renderings/year. Works on assignment only. Works with artists for landscape architectural rendering. Prefers loose yet realistic landscape illustration. Prefers marker, then pen & ink.
First Contact & Terms: Send query letter with brochure showing art style or resume and photographs. Reports within 2 weeks. Samples returned by SASE. Reports back on future possibilities. Call or write to schedule an appointment to show portfolio, which should include original/final art. Pays for design by the hour, $15-30. Pays for illustration by the hour, $25-35. Considers complexity of project, client's budget and skill and experience of artist when establishing payment.
Tips: "Include landscape renderings in your portfolio. Do not include portraits or abstract art designs."

*CUSTOM HOUSE OF NEEDLE ARTS, INC., Box 1128, Norwich VT 05055. (802)649-3261. FAX: (802)649-2216. Owner/President: Carolyn Purcell. Manufacturer of traditional crewel embroidery kits. Clients: needle-work shops and catalog shoppers.
Needs: Approached by 2-3 freelance artists/year. Works with a varying number of freelance designers/year. Uses artists for product design. "We hope the artist is a crewel stitcher and can produce sample model. We don't want to see inappropriate designs for traditional crewel embroidery."
First Contact & Terms: Send query letter with samples and any pertinent information to be kept on file. Prefers colored drawings or photos (if good closeup) as samples. Samples not filed are returned by SASE only if requested. Reports within 1 month. Pays royalty on kits sold.
Tips: "We emphasize *traditional* designs; for pictures, pillows, bellpulls, chair seats and clock faces."

CUSTOM STUDIOS INC., 1333 W. Devon Ave., Chicago IL 60660. (312)761-1150. President: Gary Wing. Estab. 1960. Custom T-shirt manufacturer. "We specialize in designing and screen printing custom T-shirts for schools, business promotions, fundraising and for our own line of stock."
Needs: Works with approximately 20 freelance illustrators and 20 freelance designers/year. Assigns 50 free-lance jobs/year. Especially needs b&w illustrations (some original and some from customer's sketch). Uses artists for direct mail and brochures/flyers, but mostly for custom and stock T-shirt designs.
First Contact & Terms: Send query letter with resume, photostats, photocopies or tearsheets; "do not send originals as we will not return them." Reports in 3-4 weeks. Call or write to schedule an appointment to show a portfolio or mail b&w tearsheets or photostats to be kept on file. Pays by the project, $10-60. Considers turnaround time and rights purchased when establishing payment. For designs submitted to be used as stock T-shirt designs, pays 5-10% royalty. Rights purchased vary according to project.
Tips: "Send 5-10 good copies of your best work. Do not get discouraged if your first designs sent are not accepted."

*DAMART, 3 Front St., Rollinsford NH 03869. Advertising Manager: Benjamin M. Giles. Estab. 1970. Manu-facturer, mail order, retailer and in-house advertising agency. "At Damart we sell world famous thermolac-tyl® underwear, socks, gloves, slippers and many accessories for women age 35 and men age 40 + ." Clients: mail order companies.
Needs: Works with 4-8 freelance artists/year. Assigns 40-60 jobs to freelance artists/year. Prefers artists with experience in direct-response advertising. Works on assignment only. Uses freelance artists for all work, including advertising, brochure and catalog design, illustration and layout; posters and signage.
First Contact & Terms: Send query letter with brochure showing art style or resume, tearsheets, photostats, slides and photographs. Samples are filed and are not returned. Reports back only if interested. Write to schedule a portfolio review. Portfolio should include thumbnails, roughs, original/final art, final reproduction/product. Pays for design and illustration by the project, $100 minimum. Buys all rights or negotiates rights purchased.

DAUPHIN ISLAND ART CENTER, 1406 Cadillac Ave., Box 699, Dauphin Island AL 36528. Owner: Nick Colquitt. Estab. 1984. Distributor and retailer for marine and/or nautical decorative art.
Needs: Approached by 12-14 freelance artists/year. Works with 8-10 freelance artists/year. Prefers local artists only with experience in marine and nautical themes; uses freelance artists mainly for retail items. Also uses artists for advertising, brochure and catalog illustration and wholesale and retail art.
First Contact & Terms: Send query letter with brochure and nautical samples. Samples not filed are returned only if requested by artist. Reports back within 3 weeks. To show a portfolio, mail original/final art and final reproduction/product. Pays for design by the project. Considers skill and experience of artist and "retailabil-ity" when establishing payment. Negotiates rights purchased.
Tips: "Send samples of marine/nautical decorative art suitable for retail."

*E & B MARINE INC., 201 Meadow Rd., Edison NJ 08818. (201)819-7400. FAX: (201)819-4771. Manager of Creative Services: Barbara Weinstein. Estab. 1947. Specialty retailer of boating equipment with more than 40 locations. Also direct-mail catalogue publisher of boating supplies and accessories.

Needs: Approached by more than 10 freelance artists/year. Works with more than 10 freelance illustrators and more than 50 freelance designers/year. Assigns more than 300 jobs to freelance artists/year. Prefers local artists only with experience in retail and/or catalog. Works on assignment only. Uses freelance artists mainly for paste-up, layout, design and illustration. Prefers line art, some 4-color illustration. Also uses freelance artists for advertising design, illustration and layout; brochure design and layout; catalog design, illustration and layout; signage; P-O-P displays.

First Contact & Terms: Send query letter with resume and tearsheets and photocopies. Samples are filed. Reports back to the artist only if interested. Write to schedule an appointment to show a portfolio, which should include roughs, original/final art and b&w and color tearsheets and photographs. Do not call. Pays for design by the hour, $10-25; by the project. Pays for illustration by the project, $25-1,000. Buys all rights.

*EMERSON RADIO CORPORATION, 1 Emerson Lane, North Bergen NJ 07047. Director of Advertising and Public Relations: Sharon Fenster; Advertising Assistant: Jill Robbins. Manufacturer.

Needs: Approached by over 100 freelance artists/year. Works with 2 freelance illustrators and 5 freelance designers/year. Prefers New York, New Jersey-area artists. Works on assignment only. Uses freelance artists mainly for brochures and catalogs. Also uses artists for advertising design, illustration and layout.

First Contact & Terms: Send query letter with brochure showing art style. Samples not filed are returned only if requested. Reports back only if interested. Write to schedule an appointment to show a portfolio, which should include final reproduction/product and color samples.

ENESCO CORPORATION, 1 Enesco Plaza, Elk Grove Village IL 60007. (708)593-3979. Contact: Creative Director of Licensed Design Development. Producer and importer of fine giftware and collectibles, such as ceramic, porcelain bisque and earthenware figurines, plates, hanging ornaments, bells, thimbles, musical ornaments, picture frames, magnets, decorative housewares, music boxes, dolls, tins, candles, plush, crystal and brass. Clients: gift stores, card shops and department stores.

Needs: Works with 326 freelance artists/year. Assigns 2,000 freelance jobs/year. Prefers artists with experience in gift product development. Uses freelance artists mainly for licensed product development. Also uses artists for product design and rendering and sculpture.

First Contact & Terms: Send query letter with brochure, resume, tearsheets, photostats and photographs. Samples are filed or are returned. Reports back within 2 weeks. Write to schedule an appointment to show a portfolio, or mail original/final art and photographs. "I work with 326 independent artists, and design studios on a *licensing basis*. We license their art/product designs under a royalty contract."

Tips: "Contact me by *mail only*. Send samples or portfolio's work for review. If your talent is a good match to Enesco's product development, I'll contact you to discuss licensing. Everything must be addressed to my attention and will be returned within two weeks."

*EPSILON DATA MANAGEMENT, INC., 50 Cambridge St., Burlington MA 01803. (617)273-0250. Creative Director, Design: Thomas Flynn. Full-service direct-response advertising and direct-mail company for commercial and nonprofit organizations. Clients: 250 diversified clients nationwide, nonprofit and commercial.

Needs: Works with 40 freelance artists/year. Uses artists for direct-mail packaging; advertising, brochure and catalog design, illustration and layout; and signage.

First Contact & Terms: Uses local artists generally with three years direct-response experience, plus "must work fast and accurately on very tight deadlines." Send query letter with brochure, resume, business card, samples and tearsheets to be kept on file. Considers photostats, slides, photographs or original work as samples. Samples not kept on file are not returned. Reports only if interested. Works on assignment only. Pays by the hour, $50-80 average; by the project, $150-3,000 average; by the day, $150-300 average. Considers complexity of project, skill and experience of artist and turnaround time when establishing payment.

Tips: "Be well experienced in direct-response advertising, and Macintosh II design experience with illustrator packages is a plus."

EVERYTHING METAL IMAGINABLE, INC. (E.M.I.), 401 E. Cypress, Visalia CA 93277. (209)732-8126. Executive Vice President: Dru McBride. Estab. 1967. Wholesale manufacturer. "We manufacturer lost wax bronze sculpture. We do centrifugal white metal casting; we do resin casting (cold cast bronze, alabaster walnut shell, clear resin etc.)." Clients: wholesalers, premium incentive consumers, retailers.

Needs: Approached by 5 freelance artists/year. Works with 5 freelance designers/year. Assigns 5-10 jobs to freelance artists/year. Prefers artists that understand centrifugal casting, bronze casting and the principles of mold making. Works on assignment only. Uses artists for figurine sculpture and model making. Prefers a tight, realistic style.

First Contact & Terms: Send query letter with brochure or resume, tearsheets, photostats, photocopies and slides. Samples not filed are returned only if requested. Reports back only if interested. Call to show a portfolio, which should include original/final art and photographs "or any samples." Pays for design by the project, $500-10,000. Considers complexity of project, client's budget, how work will be used, turnaround time and rights purchased. Buys all rights.

Tips: "Artists must be conscious of detail in their work, be able to work expediently and under time pressure. Must be able to accept criticism of work from client, and price of program must include completing work to satisfaction of customers."

*EXPRESSIVE DESIGNS, INC., 2343 W. Stirling Rd., Ft. Lauderdale FL 33312. (305)966-4666. FAX: (305)966-4668. Vice President: Mark Satchell. Estab. 1973. Manufacturer of plastic drinkware and fine collectible porcelain figurines. Current clients include Disney World, J.C. Penney Co. Department Stores and Federated Department Stores.
Needs: Approached by 3-4 freelance artists/year. Works with 1-2 freelance illustrators/year. Assigns 10-12 jobs to freelance artists/year. Works on assignment only. Uses freelance artists mainly for plastic drinkware and figurines. Prefers contemporary beach patterns. Also uses freelance artists for product design and model making. Send query letter with brochure showing art style. Samples are filed. Reports back in 2 weeks. Call to schedule and appointment to show a portfolio, which should include color samples and photographs. Pays for design by the project, $300-500. Pays for illustration by the project, payment negotiated. Rights purchased vary according to project.

*FABIL MFG. CORP, 95 Lorimer St., Brooklyn NY 11206. (212)757-6100. Vice President: Ron Reinisch. Manufacturer and importer of boys' and girls' outerwear and rainwear, boys' sportswear, swimwear and shirts. Label: Members Only.
Needs: Approached by 10 freelance artists/year. Works with 3 freelance illustrators and 4 freelance designers/year. Works with 3 freelance illustrators and 4 freelance designers/year. Local artists only, with experience in children's wear. Also uses artists for catalog design, illustration and layout and fashion design and illustration.
First Contact & Terms: Send query letter with samples. Samples are filed or are returned only if requested. Reports back within 3 weeks, only if interested. Write to schedule an appointment to show a portfolio or mail appropriate materials. Pays for illustration by the project, $50-75. Considers complexity of project, skill and experience of artist and client's budget when establishing payment. Buys all rights.

*FAME SHIRTMAKERS LTD., 350 Fifth Ave., New York NY 10118. (212)947-2815. FAX: (212)629-0091. Vice President: Arthur K. Fried. Estab. 1975. Manufacturer and importer of "young men's high fashion sport clothes," ages 18-35. Labels: Fame, Ziziano and Marc Daniels.
Needs: Approached by 2-3 freelance artists/year. Works with 1-2 freelance artists/year. Prefers artists with experience in men's fashion. Uses freelance artists mainly for fashion ideas and design. Prefers sketches. Special needs include new ideas.
First Contact & Terms: Send query letter with resume. Reports back within 2 weeks. Call to schedule an appointment to show a portfolio, which should include thumbnails and photographs. Pays for design and illustration by the project, $100. Negotiates rights purchased.
Tips: "Shop the market for my product and address my line compared to the market."

FISHMAN & TOBIN, 34 W. 33rd St., New York NY 10001. Director of Marketing: Lisbeth Kramer. Estab. 1914. Manufacturer of "suits and casual clothing for sizes 2-7, 8-20 and young men, all under one label, TFW, whose image is that of contemporary fashion, well made at very affordable prices."
Needs: Approached by 25 freelance artists/year. Works with a minimum of 5 freelance artists/year. Prefers local artists "with enough experience to have a fairly good portfolio. Recent students are fine if work is good, but prefer those experienced with *deadlines*." Uses freelance artists mainly for ads and direct-mail pieces, P-O-P displays, hangtags and labels.
First Contract & Terms: Send query letter with brochure, tearsheets, photostats, photocopies and slides. Samples are filed or are returned only if requested by artist. Reports back within days only if interested. Write to schedule an appointment to show a portfolio, which should include thumbnails, original/final art, final reproduction/product, tearsheets, photostats and photographs. Payment depends on project, experience and "volume of business we can offer." Considers complexity of project, skill and experience of artist, client's budget, how work will be used and turnaround time when establishing payment. Negotiates rights purchased.
Tips: "I seek professionalism as well as talent. I seek artists who are as excited about the particular project as I am. I seek artists looking for new challenges and exposure. I seek artists looking to build a steady clientele."

*FITZPATRICK DESIGN GROUP, INC., Suite 203, 2109 Broadway, New York NY 10023. (212)580-5842. FAX: (212)580-5849. Vice President: Robert Herbert. Retail planning and design firm.
Needs: Works with 10 freelance artists/year. Prefers experienced freelancers with references. Works on assignment only. Uses freeelance artists for drafting, renderings, graphics, colors and materials.
First Contact & Terms: Send query letter with brochure showing art style or resume. Samples are filed or are returned by a SASE only if requested. "We usually ask the artist to call after we have had time to review the material." Write to schedule an appointment to show a portfolio, which should include photographs and whatever materials the artist thinks are pertinent. Negotiates payment. Considers complexity of project, skill and experience of artist, turnaround time and client's budget when establishing payment.

Tips: "Never call 'out of the blue'. Never show up without an appointment." I seek new talent. One *does not* have to have fashion exposure. The retail industry has been greatly affected by buyouts and takeovers—creating less work, layoffs and a general slowdown in renovations and new projects."

FRANKLIN ELECTRIC, 400 Spring St., Bluffton IN 46714. Manager of Corporate Communications: Mel Haag. Manufacturer of submersible and fractional H.P. motors for original equipment manufacturers and distributors.
Needs: Works with 8 freelance artists/year. "Freelance artists must be proven." Works on assignment only. Uses artists for advertising and brochure design, illustration and layout; catalog design and layout and posters.
First Contact & Terms: Send query letter with brochure showing art style or resume, tearsheets, slides and photographs. Samples not filed are returned only if requested. Reports only if interested. Call to schedule an appointment to show a portfolio, which should include roughs, original/final art, final reproduction/product and color tearsheets. Pays for design and illustration by the hour, $30 minimum; payment is negotiated.
Tips: "I look for all styles and subjects. I am very interested in new techniques and styles."

FRELINE, INC., Box 889, Hagerstown MD 21740. Art Director: Mark Kretzer. Estab. early 1970s. Manufacturer and developer of library promotional aids—posters, mobiles, bookmarks, T-shirt transfers, reading motivators and other products to promote reading, library services and resources. Clients: school and public libraries and classroom teachers.
Needs: Approached by about 50 freelance artists/year. Works with 10-15 freelance illustrators/year. Works on assignment only. Uses freelance artists mainly for posters, bulletin boards, displays, mobiles and T-shirt designs. Also uses artists for graphic design and promotional materials. Prefers pen & ink, airbrush, colored pencil, watercolor, acrylic, pastel, collage and gouache. Most assignments for 4-color process.
First Contact & Terms: Experienced illustrators only. Send query letter with resume and tearsheets to be kept on file. Slides sent for review will be returned. Reports within 15 days. Pays by the project, $85-1,000. Considers complexity of project, skill and experience of artist, turnaround time and rights purchased when establishing payment.
Tips: "Portfolios with an emphasis on illustration suit our needs best. We prefer illustration with bright color, humor and fun. Do not send photocopies of sketches only. Submitting slides is an excellent way of presenting yourself. Our market caters to library usage and education, grade school level up to college."

G.A.I. INCORPORATED, Box 30309, Indianapolis IN 46230. (317)257-7100. President: William S. Gardiner. Licensing agents. "We represent artists to the collectibles and gifts industries. Collectibles include high-quality prints, collector's plates, figurines, bells, etc. There is no up-front fee for our services. We receive a commission from any payment the artist receives as a result of our efforts." Clients: Lenox, Enesco, The Bradford Exchange and The Hamilton Group.
Needs: Approached by 100+ freelance artists/year. Works with 5 freelance illustrators and 5 freelance designers/year. Works on assignment only. "We are not interested in landscapes, still lifes or modern art. A realistic—almost photographic—style seems to sell best to our clients. We are primarily looking for artwork featuring people or animals. Young animals and children usually sell best. Paintings must be well done and should have an emotional appeal to them."
First Contact & Terms: Send query letter with resume and color photographs; do *not* send original work. Samples not kept on file are returned by SASE. Reports in 1-3 months. Payment: "If we are successful in putting together a program for the artist with a manufacturer, the artist is usually paid a royalty on the sale of the product using his art. This varies from 4%-10%." Considers complexity of project, skill and experience of artist, how work will be used and rights purchased when establishing payment; "payment is negotiated individually for each project."
Tips: "We are looking for art with broad emotional appeal."

GARDEN STATE MARKETING SERVICES, INC., Box 343, Oakland NJ 07436. (201)337-3888. President: Jack Doherty. Estab. 1976. Service-related firm providing public relations and advertising services, mailing services and fulfillment. Clients: associations, publishers, manufacturers.
Needs: Approached by 15 freelance artists/year. Works with 4 freelance illustrators and 4 freelance designers/year. Assigns 10 jobs to freelance artists/year. Works on assignment only. Uses artists for advertising and brochure design, illustration and layout; display fixture design; P-O-P displays and posters.
First Contact & Terms: Send query letter with resume, business card and copies to be kept on file. Samples not kept on file are returned. Reports only if interested. To show a portfolio, mail thumbnails, original/final art, final reproduction/product, b&w and color tearsheets and photographs. Pays for design by the hour, $25 minimum. Considers complexity of project, skill and experience of artist and how work will be used when establishing payment.

DANIEL E. GELLES ASSOC., INC., Mohonk Rd., High Falls NY 12440. (914)687-7681. Vice President: Robert S. Gelles. Estab. 1956. Interior design firm which also designs and manufactures visual merchandise, display fixtures, etc. "We design custom fixturing for both manufacturers and stores (retailers). We do store floor

Emithsburg, Maryland artist Patricia Topper's ability to meet deadlines, and her openness to suggestions in creating this oil painting from a thumbnail sketch matched the needs of Freline, Inc., Hagerstown, Maryland. Art director Mark D. Kretzer says the piece is successful because "it has a very pleasant and happy message and conveys the promotion of reading."

layouts, plans, etc. We also maintain a stock fixturing line which requires updating consistently." Clients: both large and small, hard and soft goods manufacturers. Current clients include Sears, Roebuck & Co., Bloomingdales, Record World, Koret of California and Calvin Klein."

Needs: Works with 2-3 freelance illustrators/year. Prefers artists with some experience in the field of visual merchandising or P-O-P displays. Uses freelance artists mainly for full-color renderings of store layouts and fixtures. Also uses artists for interior design and rendering and concepts for display ideas, P-O-P displays, etc.

First Contact & Terms: Send resume and "any clear facsimile that would indicate artist's style and technique." Samples are filed. Call or write to schedule an appointment to show a portfolio, which should include thumbnails, roughs, original/final art, actual renderings (color) and original concepts. Pays for design by the project, $100-500; illustration by the project, $50-300. Considers complexity of project and skill and experience of artist when establishing payment. Negotiates rights purchased.

Tips: "Would like to see color drawings, obliques and freehand illustrations with at least one human figure; prefer anything that gets the concept across *clearly* without abstraction. Do not send scale models, slides or pencil drawings."

GELMART INDUSTRIES, INC., 180 Madison Ave., New York NY 10016. (212)889-7225. Vice President and Head of Design: Ed Adler. Manufacturer of high fashion socks, gloves, headwear, scarves and other knitted accessories. "We are prime manufacturers for many major brands and designer names." Current clients include "major stores."

Needs: Approached by 6 freelance artists/year. Works with 2 freelance designers/year. Uses freelance artists mainly for textile or package design. Also uses artists for fashion accessory design. Prefers pen & ink, colored pencil, watercolor, acrylic, collage and marker.

First Contact & Terms: Call for appointment to show a portfolio. Pays by the project.

Tips: "The best way for designers to introduce themselves is to "bring a few sketches of clothing accessories."

GIBBONS COLOR LABORATORY INC., 606 N. Almont Dr., Los Angeles CA 90069. (213)2762-3010. Vice President: Alfredo Arozamena. Estab. 1953. "We are a custom lab specializing in film processing, printing and all related matters." Specializes in architectural, portfolio model, interior and landscape representations.

Current clients include 20th Century Fox, Lucille Ball Productions and Kenny Rogers Productions.
Needs: Works with 25 freelance designers/month. Uses artists for print ad design and illustration, retouching and logos.
First Contact and Terms: Send query letter.
Tips: "A common mistake freelancers make in presenting a portfolio is a lack of good quality photographic prints or design in order to save money. Many of them do not realize that a good print or design, as expensive as it could be, can be the difference between getting a job or not."

GOES LITHOGRAPHING CO., 42 W. 61st St., Chicago IL 60621. Marketing Director: W.J. Goes. Manufacturer of all-year and holiday letterheads. Clients: printers and businesses.
Needs: Uses artists for letterheads.
First Contact & Terms: Send pencil sketches or thumbnail sketches. Samples are returned by SASE. Reports back only if interested. Portfolio should include thumbnail sketches. "No final work should be sent at this time." Considers how work will be used when establishing payment. Buys reprint rights.
Tips: "Listen to what we want and are looking for. Thumbnail work is the first step for use. Call for some of our samples."

GOLDBERGS' MARINE, 201 Meadow Rd., Edison NJ 08818. (201)819-7400. Manager Creative Services: Barbara Weinstein. Produces 18 mail-order catalogs of pleasure boating equipment and water-sport gear for the active family.
Needs: Approached by over 100 freelance artists/year. Works with 6-10 freelance illustrators and over 25 freelance designers/year. Artists must be "flexible with knowledge of 4-color printing, have a willingness to work with paste-up and printing staff, and exhibit the ability to follow up and take charge." Uses freelance artists mainly for catalog layout, design and illustration. Also uses artists for brochure design, illustration and layout; retail events and signage. "Seasonal freelance work is also available."
First Contact & Terms: Send query letter with brochure, business card, printed material and tearsheets to be kept on file. "Original work (mechanicals) may be required at portfolio showing." Reports only if interested. Call for appointment to show portfolio. Pays by the project. Considers complexity of project, how work will be used and turnaround time when establishing payment.
Tips: "Boating and/or retail experience is helpful and a willingness to do research is sometimes necessary. Long-term relationships usually exist with our company. We have plenty of work for the right people. With so many artists vying for work, you really must stand out of the crowd without being crazy. Approach it from a business standpoint."

*THE GRANDOE CORPORATION, 74 Bleeker St. Gloversville NY 12078. (518)725-8641. FAX: (518)725-9088. Designer/Advertising Manager: Doty Hall. Estab. 1890. Design studio, importer and manufacturer of accessories: ski, golf and dress gloves; knit sets and body-glove sportlines for men and women age 16-100. Label: grandoe.
Needs: Approached by 10 freelance artists/year. Works with 2-3 freelance artists/year. Prefers artists with experience in mock-up packaging, graphic art and package design. Uses freelance artists mainly for mock-ups, mechanicals and print-ready work. Also uses freelance artists for advertising, brochure, catalog, fashion, accessory and package design; P-O-P displays; paste-up; mechanicals and direct mail. Prefers "clean and graphic, as opposed to fine art" styles. Special needs are mechanicals, paste-up and package design.
First Contact & Terms: Send query letter with brochure showing art style or resume and photocopies. Samples are filed or are returned. Reports back if interested. Write to schedule and appointment to show a portfolio, which should include original/final art. Pays for design by the hour, $35-50. Pays for illustration by the hour, $25-30. Buys all rights.

GREAT AMERICAN AUDIO CORP., INC., 33 Portman Rd., New Rochelle NY 10801. President: Nina Joan Mattikow. Estab. 1976. Audio publishers: products range from old-time radio, self-help, humor, children's, books-on-tape, etc.
Needs: "We do not buy actual work. All artwork is commissioned by us." Works with 5 freelance illustrators/year. Mainly uses freelancers for package illustration. Also uses artists for product and P-O-P design, advertising illustration and layout. Prefers full-color inks or tempera for product illustration. "Art must be customized to suit us. We look for a particular style of work."
First Contact & Terms: Artists must be in New York metropolitan area. Send query letter with brochure and resume to be kept on file. Do not send samples. Write for appointment to show portfolio. Finished original art seen by appointment only. Reports only if interested. Works on assignment only. No originals returned to artist at job's completion. Pays for design by the project, $250-2,000 average. Pays for illustration by the project, $100-2,000. Buys all rights.

THE GREAT MIDWESTERN ICE CREAM COMPANY, Box 1717, 209 N. 16 St., Fairfield IA 52556. (515)472-7595. President: Jamie Vollmer. Manufacturer. "We manufacture an excellent ice cream which we feel is the new standard in the industry. We sell it through supermarkets, restaurants and our beautiful stores." Clients are grocery shoppers and ice cream lovers.

Needs: Works with 15+ freelance artists/year. Uses freelance artists for advertising, brochure and catalog design, illustration and layout; product design; illustration of the product; P-O-P displays; display fixture design; posters; model making; signage; and fashion clothing design for franchise employees and customers (T-shirts, etc.).

First Contact & Terms: Send query letter with resume and samples. Samples not filed are returned with SASE. Reports back only if interested. Call to schedule an appointment to show a portfolio. Pays for design by the project, $3,000; pays for illustration by the project, $1,000. Considers complexity of project, client's budget, skill and experience of artists, how work will be used and rights purchased when establishing payment.

Tips: "We are a highly creative company that prefers art on the cutting edge. We are looking for all types of art—from painting to cartoons—that uses ice cream as the theme."

GREEN & ASSOCIATES, Suite C-26, 115 S. Royal St., Alexandria VA 22314. (703)370-3078. Contact: James F. Green. Interior design firm providing residential and contract interior design and space planning plus custom furniture design. Clients: residential, corporate offices and retail design.

Needs: Number of freelance artists works with/year varies. Prefers local artists; "sometimes we require on-site inspections." Works on assignment only. Uses artists for interior design and interior and architectural rendering.

First Contact & Terms: Send query letter with brochure, resume and photostats or photographs, color preferred, to be kept on file. Reports only if interested. Pays for design and illustration by the project, $250 minimum. "Persons we work with must be able to make themselves available to our clients and staff. We will appreciate good art without regard to reputation of artist, etc." Considers complexity of project, client's budget and skill and experience of artist when establishing payment.

THE HAMILTON COLLECTION, Suite 1000, 9550 Regency Square Blvd., Jacksonville FL 32225. (904)723-6000. Director Product Development: Jean Montgomery; Senior Art and Production Director for commercial art/advertising: Linda Olsen. Direct-marketing firm for collectibles: limited edition art, plates, sculpture and general gifts. Clients: general public, specialized lists of collectible buyers and retail market.

Needs: Approached by 25-30 freelance artists/year. Works with 5 freelance artists in creative department and 15 in product development/year. Assigns 400-500 jobs to freelance artists/year. Only local artists with three years of experience for mechanical work. For illustration and product design, "no restrictions on locality, but must have *quality* work and flexibility regarding changes which are sometimes necessary. Also, a 'name' and notoriety help." Uses artists for advertising mechanicals, brochure illustration and mechanicals, and product design and illustration.

First Contact & Terms: Send query letter with samples to be kept on file, except for fine art, which is to be returned (must include a SASE or appropriate container with sufficient postage). Samples not kept on file are returned only if requested by artist. Reports within 2-4 weeks. Call or write for appointment to show portfolio. Pays for design by the hour, $10-50. Pays for illustration by the project, $50-5,000. Pays for mechanicals by the hour, $20 average. Considers complexity of project, skill and experience of artist, how work will be used and rights purchased when establishing payment.

Tips: Prefers conservative, old fashioned, realistic style. "Attitude and turnaround time important." In presenting portfolio, don't "point out mistakes, tell too much, tell not enough, belittle work or offer unsolicited opinions. Be prepared to offer sketches on speculation."

HAMPSHIRE PEWTER COMPANY, Box 1570, 9 Mill St., Wolfeboro NH 03894-1570. (603)569-4944. Vice President: J.H. Milligan. Estab. 1974. Manufacturer of handcast pewter tableware, accessories and Christmas ornaments. Clients: jewelry stores, department stores, executive gift buyers, tabletop and pewter speciality stores, churches, and private consumers.

Needs: Works with 3-4 freelance artists/year. "We prefer New-England based artists for convenience." Works on assignment only. Uses freelancers mainly for illustration and models. Also uses artists for brochure and catalog design, product design, illustration on product and model making.

First Contact & Terms: Send brochure and photographs. Samples are not filed and are returned only if requested. Reports back to the artist within weeks. Call to schedule an appointment to show a portfolio, or mail b&w roughs and photographs. Pays for design and illustration by the hour, $10 minimum. Considers complexity of project, client's budget and rights purchased. Buys all rights.

Tips: "Inform us of your capabilities. We commission work by the project. For artists who are seeking a manufacturing source, we will be happy to bid on manufacturing of designs, under private license to the artists, all of whose design rights are protected. If we commission a project, we intend to have exclusive rights to the designs by contract as defined in the Copyright Law and we intend to protect those rights."

HANSEN LIND MEYER, Suite 1100, 800 N. Magnolia, Orlando FL 32803. (407)422-7061. Director of Design: Charles W. Cole, Jr. Estab. 1963. Architectural/interior design firm providing complete architecture and engineering services. Clients: commercial, health care, justice and government. Current clients include University of Florida Clinics, Arlington County Sheriff's Department and Orange County Courts.

Needs: Approached by 6 freelance artists/year. Works with 10 freelance illustrators/year. Works on assignment only. Uses freelance artists mainly for architectural renderings. Also uses artists for interior and landscape renderings, maps and model making. Prefers watercolor, colored pencil, tempera and marker.
First Contact & Terms: Send query letter with resume and samples. Samples not filed are returned only if requested. Reports only if interested. To show a portfolio, mail thumbnails, final reproduction/product and color photographs. Pays for illustration by the project, $750-6,000. Considers complexity of project, client's budget, skill and experience of artist, and turnaround time when establishing payment.
Tips: The most common mistake freelancers make in presenting samples or portfolios is "poor quality reproductions and lack of coordinated professional images. Samples should be representative examples of architectural renderings completed for clients."

*HANSLEY INDUSTRIES, INC., 3 East 54th St., New York, NY 10022. (212)688-4040. Senior Designer: Debra Mattioli. Estab. 1950. Manufacturer of active sportswear/performance wear for boys 4-7 and 8-20 and men. Labels: private labels.
Needs: Approached by 6-10 freelance artists/year. Works with 4-5 freelance artists/year. Prefers artists with experience in boys'/men's swimwear, surfwear and skatewear. Uses freelance artists mainly for screen development and logos. Special needs are trendy looks for kids' sportswear. Send query letter with brochure showing art style or resume and "anything available." Samples are filed or are returned by SASE if requested by artist. Reports back only if interested. Call to schedule an appointment to show a portfolio, which should include original/final art and b&w and color photographs. Pays for design and illustration by the project. Buys all rights.

*HEP CAT, INC., 419 E. Iris Dr., Nashville TN 37204. (615)386-9705. Owner: Anna Grupke. Estab. 1986. Mail order company selling imprinted sportswear through direct mail; cat designs in particular.
Needs: Works with 5 freelance illustrators and designers/year. Assigns 10-20 jobs to freelance artists/year. Prefers artists with experience in T-shirt design and screen printing. Wants high quality realistic work on whimsical and humorous designs. Works on assignment only. Uses freelance artists mainly for designs imprinted on shirts. Prefers pen & ink, paintings and pastel. Send resume and tearsheets, photostats, photocopies, slides and photographs. "No original art." Samples are filed or are returned by SASE only if requested by artist. Reports back only if interested. To show a portfolio mail photostats, photographs and slides. Pays for design and illustration by the project, $200-300. Buys all rights.

*HERFF JONES, Box 6500, Providence RI 02940-6500. (401)331-1240. Art Director: Fred Spinney. Manufacturer of class ring jewelry; motivation/recognition/emblematic awards—service pins, medals, medallions and trophies. Clients: high-school and college-level students; a variety of companies/firms establishing recognition programs.
Needs: Works with 6 freelance artists/year. "Previous experience in this field helpful but not necessary. Must be strong in illustration work." Works on assignment only. Uses artists for product illustration.
First Contact & Terms: Send query letter with brochure, resume, business card, slides and photos to be kept on file; originals will be returned. Samples not kept on file returned by SASE. Reports only if interested. Write for appointment to show portfolio. Pays by the project, $25-100 average. Considers complexity of project, skill and experience of artist and turnaround time when establishing payment.
Tips: Artists approaching this firm "should be of a professional level. The artist should have a good versatile background in illustrating as well as having some mechanical drawing abilities, such as hand lettering."

IGPC, 460 W. 34th St., 10th Floor, New York NY 10001. (212)869-5588. Contact: Art Department. Agent to foreign governments; "we produce postage stamps and related items on behalf of 40 different foreign governments."
Needs: Approached by 50 freelance artists/year. Works with more than 75-100 freelance illustrators and designers/year. Assigns several hundred jobs to freelance artists/year. Artists must be within metropolitan NY or tri-state area. "No actual experience required except to have good, tight art skills (4-color) and excellent design skills." Works on assignment only. Uses artists for postage stamp art. Prefers tight, realistic style and technical illustration. Prefers airbrush, watercolor and acrylic.
First Contact & Terms: Send samples. Reports back within 5 weeks. Portfolio should contain "4-color illustrations of realistic, tight flora, fauna, technical subjects, autos or ships. Also include reduced samples of original artwork." Pays by the project. Considers government allowance per project when establishing payment.
Tips: "Artists considering working with IGPC must have excellent 4-color abilities (in general or specific topics, i.e., flora, fauna, transport, famous people, etc.); sufficient design skills to arrange for and position type; the ability to create artwork that will reduce to postage stamp size and still hold up to clarity and perfection. All of the work we require is realistic art. In some cases, we supply the basic layout and reference material; however, we appreciate an artist who knows where to find references and can present new and interesting concepts. Initial contact should be made by phone for appointment, (212)629-7979."

*THE IMAGE GROUP, 398 S. Grant Ave., Columbus OH 43215. (614)221-1016. Contact: Richard Henry Eiselt. Architecture/interior design firm. Clients: commercial.

Needs: Uses artists for restaurant design, architectural and full-color rendering, graphic and interior design, painting, sculpture, signage and wall art.

First Contact & Terms: Mail photos or transparencies. Pay varies according to client's budget and skill and experience of artist.

INDIANA KNITWEAR CORPORATION, Box 309, 230 E. Osage St., Greenfield IN 46140. (317)462-4413. Merchandise Manager: W. E. Garrison. Estab. 1930. Manufacturer of knit sportswear for young men and boys 8-18, 4-7 and 2-4. Label: Indy Knit.

Needs: Works with 6-8 freelance artists/year. Uses freelance artists mainly for screen print art.

First Contact & Terms: Send query letter with brochure showing art style. Samples not filed are returned only if requested by artist. Reports back within 1 week. Call to schedule an appointment to show a portfolio, which should include roughs, original/final art and final reproduction/product. Pays for design by the project. Pays for illustration by the project, $150-500. Considers complexity of project, skill and experience of artist and turnaround time when establishing payment. Negotiates rights purchased.

Tips: "All artwork we buy must be applicable for screen print on knits. The ideas must be timely."

INFO VIEW CORPORATION, INC., 124 Farmingdale Road, Wethersfield CT 06109. (203)721-0270. President: Larry Bell. Sells desktop publishing systems to corporations. Works with graphic artists to create visuals for newsletters, product-sell sheets, promotional materials and trade advertising.

Needs: Works on assignment only. Works with graphic artists in New York and Connecticut. Buys 40+ sketches/year. Looks for unique style. Prefers artists that have a feeling for current trends.

First Contact & Terms: Query with SASE. Reports in 2 weeks. Provide photocopy of recent work to be kept on file for future assignments. Pays by the project.

INTERNATIONAL RESEARCH & EVALUATION, 21098 Ire Control Ctr., Eagan MN 55121. (612)888-9635. Art Director: Ronald Owen. Estab. 1972. Private, nonpartisan, interdisciplinary research firm that collects, stores and disseminates information on-line, on demand to industry, labor and government on contract/subscription basis. "Conducts and produces a wide spectrum of creative exercises for client product introductions and marketing research probes."

Needs: Works with 50-65 freelance illustrators and 31-37 freelance designers/year. Works on assignment only. Uses artists for advertising, brochure and catalog design, illustration and layout; product design and P-O-P display.

First Contact & Terms: Artists should request "Capabilities Analysis" form from firm. Reports only if interested. Pays for design by the project, $125-10,000; pays for illustration by the project, $125-$5,000. Considers how work will be used when establishing payment.

INTIMATE FASHIONS INC., 15 E. 32 St., New York NY 10016. (212)686-1530. President: Ben Segan. Estab. 1964. Manufacturer of ladies' lingerie.

Needs: Local artists only. Uses artists for brochure design, illustration and layout and fashion illustration.

First Contact & Terms: Send brochure showing art style. Pays for design by the project. "We pay amount artist asks."

IT FIGURES STUDIO, 302 E. Ayre St., Newport DE 19804. Partners: Ray Daub or Mary Berg. Estab. 1979. Manufacturer/service-related firm. "IFS designs and creates animated (mechanical) figures, animated exhibits and attractions, museum figures (lifecast) and sets, stage sets and props for industrial videos and meetings, and puppet characters for film and video." Clients: department stores, museums, businesses, corporations and film/video producers. Current clients include DuPont Co., The Smithsonian, Lazarus Dept. Stores, Inc. and Dayton Hudson Corp.

Needs: Approached by 20 freelance artists/year. Works with 1-3 freelance illustrators and 1-3 freelance designers/year. Assigns 1-10 jobs to freelance artists/year. Prefers local artists only. Uses freelance artists mainly for sculpture, mold making, set building and conceptual art. Also uses artists for advertising design, illustration and layout; brochure and catalog design and layout; product design and rendering; model making and make-up.

First Contact and Terms: Send query letter with resume, slides and photographs. Samples are filed or are returned only if requested by artist. Reports back only if interested. Call or write to schedule an appointment to show a portfolio. Pays for design and illustration by the project, $100 minimum. Considers complexity of project, client's budget and skill and experience of artist when establishing payment. Buys all rights.

Tips: "After submitting a resume, artists should attempt to arrange for a meeting providing examples of their strengths and interests. Show overt enthusiasm with the follow-up after one submission of your resume/portfolio."

*J. JOSEPHSON, INC., 20 Horizon Blvd., S. Hackensack NJ 07606. Director of Marketing: Leslie Meisner. Manufacturer of wallcoverings. "We also provide them to the public in the form of sample books." Serves wallcovering and paint stores, interior designers and architects.

Needs: Approached by 12 freelance artists/year. Works with 2 freelance illustrators and 2 freelance designers/year. Uses freelance artists mainly for developing full collections of wallcovering and book cover designs. Also uses freelance artists for P-O-P displays and display fixture design.

First Contact & Terms: Send tearsheets. Samples are filed or are returned only if requested by artist. Reports back only if interested. Call to schedule an appointment to show a portfolio which should include original/final art and final reproduction/product. Pays for design by the project. Considers complexity of project, skill and experience of the artist and rights purchased when establishing payment. Negotiates rights purchased.

*JBACH DESIGNS, Box 7962, Atlanta GA 30357. Architectural/interior and landscape design/photography/graphics firm. Clients: residential, commercial. Specializes in greeting cards, displays, automobile racing promotion and photography, and package and P-O-P design.

Needs: Works with 10 freelance artists/year. Uses artists for advertising and brochure design, landscape and interior design, architectural and interior rendering, design consulting, furnishings and graphic design.

First Contact & Terms: Send query letter with brochure, resume and business card to be kept on file. Write for appointment to show portfolio; write for artists' guidelines. Reports within days. Pay varies according to assignment. Considers complexity of project, client's budget, skill and experience of artist, how work will be used, turnaround time and rights purchased when establishing payment.

Tips: "The direction for the 1990's for JBACH DESIGNS is more interaction between artist and client to achieve a higher design attitude. JBACH DESIGNS is being structured as a network of designers and artists."

JEWELITE SIGNS, LETTERS & DISPLAYS, INC., 154 Reade St., New York NY 10013. (212)966-0433. Vice President: Bobby Bank. Produces signs, letters, silk screening, murals, hand lettering, displays and graphics. Current clients include Transamerica, Duggal Labs, Steve Morn and MCI.

Needs: Approached by 15+ freelance artists/year. Works with 12 freelance artists/year. Assigns 20+ jobs to freelance artists/year. Works on assignment only. Uses artists for hand-lettering, walls, murals, signs, interior design, architectural renderings, design consulting and model making. Prefers airbrush, lettering and painting.

First Contact & Terms: Call or send query letter. Call to schedule an appointment to show a portfolio, which should include photographs. Pays for design and illustration by the project, $75 and up. Considers complexity of project and skill and experience of artist when establishing payment.

KELSEY NATIONAL CORP., 3030 S. Bundy, Los Angeles CA 90066. Director of Communications: Susan Stepan. Estab. 1963. Service-related firm providing small group health and life insurance products. Clients: small businesses of under 100 employees nationwide.

Needs: Works with 3-4 freelance artists/year. Assigns over 50 freelance jobs/year. Prefers local artists. Works on assignment only. Uses artists for advertising mailers; brochure design, illustration and layout; posters and signage.

First Contact & Terms: Send query letter. Samples are filed. Reports back only if interested. Call or write to schedule an appointment to show a portfolio, which should include original/final art, final reproduction/product and tearsheets. Pays for illustration by the project. "We ask for an estimate by job and have no specific hourly rate in mind." Considers client's budget, skill and experience of artist and turnaround time when establishing payment. Buys all rights.

Tips: "Exceptional creativity is not wanted by the company. We need someone to take much information and put it in clear, clean, readable materials. Show me examples of mailers and collaterals done for business-to-business clients in a moderate price range. Don't show consumer advertising or high-end jobs."

KOZAK AUTO DRYWASH, INC., 6 S. Lyon St., Box 910, Batavia NY 14020. (716)343-8111. President: Ed Harding. Manufacturer and direct marketer of automotive cleaning and polishing cloths and related auto care products distributed by direct mail and retail. Clients: stores with car-care lines, consumers and specialty groups.

Needs: Works with up to 2 freelance artists/year. Uses artists for advertising design and illustration, P-O-P display, packaging design and direct response advertising.

First Contact & Terms: Prefers artist located within a convenient meeting distance with experience in desired areas (P-O-P, packaging, direct response). Works on assignment only. Send query letter with brochure, resume and business card to be kept on file. Material not filed returned only if requested. Reports within 2 weeks. Pays by the project. Considers complexity of project, skill and experience of artist, and how work will be used when establishing payment.

KRISCH HOTELS, INC. KHI Advertising, Inc., Box 14100, Roanoke VA 24022. (703)342-4531. Director of Communications: Julie Becker. Estab. 1985. Service-related firm providing all advertising, in-room and P-O-P pieces for service, wholesale and retail businesses for tourists, meetings, conventions and food service (inhouse department). Clients: hotels/motels, restaurants/lounges, apartment complexes, wholesale businesses and printing firms.

Needs: Approached by 20-30 freelance artists/year. Works with 5-10 freelance illustrators and 2-4 freelance designers/year. Prefers local artists. Works on assignment only. Uses artists for advertising and brochure illustration; inroom pieces; direct mail; illustration product; P-O-P display; posters and signage. Prefers pen & ink, airbrush, charcoal/pencil and computer illustration.

First Contact & Terms: Send query letter with resume and photocopies. Samples not filed are not returned. Reports only if interested. Call or write to schedule an appointment to show a portfolio, which should include roughs, original/final art, tearsheets and photostats. Pays for design and illustration by the hour, $10 minimum; by the project, $25 minimum; by the day, $100 minimum. Considers complexity of project, client's budget, how work will be used, turnaround time, and rights purchased when establishing payment. Finds most artists through references/word-of-mouth.

Tips: "Increased competition in all markets leads to more sophisticated work attitudes on the part of our industry. Artists should know their own abilities and limitations and be able to interact with us to achieve best results. Send a letter of introduction with non-returnable samples (photocopies are okay). *Please* no original art."

KRON-TV, NBC, 1001 Van Ness Ave., San Francisco CA 94119. (415)441-4444. Design Manager: Steve Johnston. TV/film producer. Produces videotapes and still photos.

Needs: Works with 1-2 freelance artists/year for ad illustration, 1-2 for advertising design and 1-5 for product design. Local artists only. Uses artists for design and production of all types of print advertising, direct mail brochures, promotion and sales pieces. Especially needs computer graphic art.

First Contact & Terms: Query. Provide resume and business card to be kept on file for future assignments.

Tips: "We're looking for experienced designers with heavy production knowledge that would enable them to handle a job from design concept through printing."

KVCR—TV RADIO, 701 S. Mount Vernon Ave., San Bernardino CA 92410. (714)888-6511 or 825-3103. Station Manager: Lew Warren. Specializes in public and educational radio/TV.

Needs: Assigns 1-10 jobs/year. Uses artists for graphic/set design, set design painting and camera-ready cards.

First Contact & Terms: Query and mail photos or slides. Reports in 2 weeks. Samples returned by SASE. Pays $20-30, camera-ready cards.

LABUNSKI ASSOCIATES ARCHITECTS, Suite A3, 3301 S. Expressway 83, Harlingen TX 78550. (512)428-4334. President: R.A. Labunski. Architectural firm providing architecture, planning, construction, management, design, space planning, interiors, advertising. Clients: commercial, retail, residential, corporate, banks, hotel/motel/restaurant and schools.

Needs: Approached by 4-5 freelance artists/year. Works with 2-3 freelance illustrators and 2-3 freelance designers/year. Works on assignment only. Uses artists for ad design, illustration and layout; brochure design; interior and architectural rendering; design consulting; furnishings and model making. Prefers textured media.

First Contact & Terms: Desires "affordable, practical" artists with referrals/references. Send query letter with brochure, resume and business card to be kept on file; also send samples. Samples returned by SASE. Reports within 2 weeks. Call or write for appointment to show portfolio. Pays by the project. Considers complexity of project, client's budget, and skill and experience of artist when establishing payment.

LANE & ASSOCIATES, ARCHITECTS, 1318 N., "B," Box 3929, Fort Smith AR 72913. (501)782-4277. Owner: John E. Lane, AIA-ASID. Estab. 1979. Architectural and interior design firm providing architecture and interiors for remodeling and new construction; also art consultant. Clients: residential, religious, commercial, institutional and industrial.

Needs: Approached by 10-20 freelance artists/year. Works with 10-12 freelance artists/year. Works on assignment only. Uses artists occasionally for architectural rendering, charts, graphic design and advertising illustration; selects or commissions art pieces for clients: paintings, drawings, sculpture, photographs, macrame, tapestry (all mediums). Also arranges art exhibits for large local bank—"would like sources of talent for various media: painting, sculpture, photography, drawing, etc." Prefers pen & ink, watercolor, acrylic, oil, pastel and collage.

First Contact & Terms: Prefers to be able to meet in person with artist. Send query letter with brochure showing art style or resume and tearsheets or photographs for file and retention. Payment varies. Considers complexity of project, client's budget, skill and experience of artist, how work will be used, turnaround time, and rights purchased when establishing payment.

*EDWARD LAURENCE & CO. DIVISION OF WEBSTER WALLPAPER CO., INC., 2747 Webster Ave., Bronx NY 10458. (212)367-1910. FAX: (212)295-7265. President: E. Nerenberg. Estab. 1950. Manufacturer of silkscreened and hand-printed vinyl wallcovering and fabric. Cilents: wallcovering distributors and showrooms.

Needs: Works with 3-4 freelance illustrators and 2-3 freelance designers/year. Prefers local artists with experience in wallcovering design. Works on assignment only. Uses freelance artists mainly for wallcovering and fabric design. Prefers contemporary styles. Also uses freelance artists for advertising design, illustration and layout; catalog design, illustration and layout; signage; P-O-P displays and posters. Send resume and samples that best represent the artist's work. Samples are filed or are returned. Reports back only if interested. Call or write to schedule an appointment to show a portfolio or mail appropriate materials. Portfolio should include original/final art. Buys all rights.

*LEISURE AND RECREATION CONCEPTS INC., 2151 Fort Worth Ave., Dallas TX 75211. (214)942-4474. President: Michael Jenkins. Designs and builds amusement and theme parks.
Needs: Assigns 200 jobs/year. Uses artists for exhibits/displays, sketches of park building sections and bird's eye views of facilities.
First Contact & Terms: Query with samples or previously used work, or arrange interview. Include SASE. Reports in 1 week. Pay determined by job.

*THE LUCKMAN PARTNERSHIP, INC., 9220 Sunset Blvd., Los Angeles CA 90069. (213)274-7755. Assistant Director of Design: John Janulaw. Architectural firm. Clients: office buildings, hotels, educational facilities, sports facilities, theaters and entertainment centers. Current clients include California State College Los Angeles.
Needs: Approached by 8 freelance artists/year. Works with 3-4 freelance artists/year. Assigns 5 freelance jobs/year. Prefers local artists. Works on assignment only. Uses freelance artists for interior rendering, architectural rendering and model making. Prefers ad marker, airbrush and watercolor.
First Contact & Terms: Send query letter with resume, tearsheets and photocopies. Samples are filed or are returned only if requested by artist. Call to schedule an appointment to show a portfolio, which should include roughs and color photographs. Pays for illustration by the project, $500-20,000. Considers complexity of project, skill and experience of artist, turnaround time, and client's budget when establishing payment. Buys all rights.

MARATHON OIL COMPANY, 539 S. Main St., Findlay OH 45840. (419)422-2121. Graphics Supervisor: Fred J. Sessanna. Estab. 1887. Department specializes in brand and corporate identity, displays, direct mail package and publication design and signage. Clients: corporate customers.
Needs: Works with 4-5 freelance illustrators/year. Prefers local artists only. Works on assignment only. Uses illustrators mainly for publications. Also uses artists for brochure and P-O-P design and illustration, book design, mechanicals, retouching, airbrushing, poster illustration and design, model making, direct mail design, lettering, logos, advertisement design and illustration.
First Contact and Terms: Send query letter with resume and samples. Samples are filed or are returned only if requested by artist. Reports back only if interested. Call or write to schedule an appointment to show a portfolio, which should include roughs, original/final art, final reproduction/product, b&w and color photographs. Pays by the hour, $8-30; by the project. Considers complexity of project, client's budget and skill and experience of artist when establishing payment. Buys all rights.
Tips: "Have your name and samples in our file."

MARBURG WALLCOVERINGS, 1751 N. Central Park Ave., Chicago IL 60647. General Manager: Mike Vukosavich. Manufacturer and distributor which designs, styles and manufactures decorative wall coverings. Clients: wholesale distributors, contractors and architects. Current clients include Carousel Design, Winfield Design, F.G. Anderson, Sancar and Wallquest.
Needs: Approached by 2-4 freelance artists/year. Works with 2-3 freelance artists/year. Uses freelance artists mainly for pattern designs. Prefers bilingual English/German artists. Works on assignment only. Uses artists for product design.
First Contact & Terms: Send query letter with brochure or tearsheets. Samples are filed or are returned only if requested. Reports back only if interested. To show a portfolio, mail thumbnails and color tearsheets. Payment is negotiable. Considers client's budget, and skill and experience of artist when establishing payment. Buys first rights or reprint rights.

*ROBERT S. MARTIN & ASSOCIATES REGISTERED ARCHITECTS, (formerly Martin & Dethoff Registered Architects), 422 Franklin St., Reading PA 19602. Contact: Robert S. Martin. Architectural/interior design firm. Clients: commercial.
Needs: Works with 4 freelance artists/year. Works on assignment only. Uses artists for architectural rendering and furnishings.
First Contact & Terms: Send query letter with resume to be kept on file. Reports back only if interested. Pays for design by the hour, $25-50. Pays for illustration by the project, $500-1,000. Considers complexity and size of project when establishing payment.
Tips: Needs illustrators who are "fast and not expensive." Looks for "strong delineation and color."

*MARURI USA CORP., 7541 Woodman Place, Van Nuys CA 91405. Director/Sales and Marketing: Edward J. Purcell. Manufacturer of wholesale limited edition porcelain figurines and ceramic giftware. Clients: retailers.
Needs: Works with 3-5 freelance artists/year. Works on assignment only. Uses artists for figurine design and illustration; advertising, brochure and catalog design and illustration.
First Contact & Terms: Send query letter with brochure, resume, photographs and tearsheets to be kept on file. Samples not filed are returned only if requested. Reports only if interested. Write for appointment to show a portfolio. Pays for design by the project, $500 minimum. Pays for illustration by the project, $100 minimum.

MAYFAIR INDUSTRIES INC., Suite 5301, 350 Fifth Ave., New York NY 10018-0110. President: Robert Postal. Estab. 1935. Manufacturer of T-shirts, sweat shirts and sportswear. Prefers screen printed tops and bottoms (fun tops). Directed towards ages 2-30. Labels: B. J. Frog, Jane Colby Primo, Pilgrim and Rrribbit Rrribbit.
Needs: Works with 10 freelance artists/year. Uses artists for pattern design. Prefers cartoon style, young look.
First Contact & Terms: Send query letter with brochure showing art style. Samples not filed are returned only if requested. Reports only if interested. To show a portfolio, mail appropriate materials. Pays for illustration by the project, $100-2,500. Considers complexity of project when establishing payment.

*MEMBERS ONLY, A Division of Europe Craft Imports, 445 Fifth Ave., New York NY 10016, (212)686-5050. Director of Marketing: Kathy Coulter. Estab. 1980. Manufacturer and importer of men's apparel—sportswear and outerwear for a core group of 25-35 year olds. "Themes and styles vary from season to season." Label: Members Only. "We also do sub-labels for each season."
Needs: Works with 2-3 freelance artists/year. "Prefers someone who has graphic experience related to fashion who can handle project from creative to final camera ready art work."
First Contact & Terms: Send query letter with brochure showing art style or slides. Samples are filed or are returned only if requested by artist. Call to schedule an appointment to show a portfolio, which should include appropriate samples. Pays for design and illustration by the project. Buys all rights.

METROPOLITAN WATER DISTRICT OF SOUTHERN CALIFORNIA (MWD), Box 54153, 1111 Sunset Blvd., Los Angeles CA 90054. (213)250-6496. Graphic Arts Designer: Mario Chavez. Supplies water for southern California. "MWD imports water from the Colorado River and northern California through the state water project. It imports about half of all the water used by some 15 million consumers in urban southern California from Ventura to Riverside to San Diego counties. MWD wholesales water to 27 member public agencies which, along with about 130 subagencies, delivers it to homes, businesses and even a few farms in MWD's 5,200-square-mile service area."
Needs: Works with 4-6 freelance artists/year. "Color artwork for publication is separated on scanner, it should be flexible; final agreement (contract) is purchase order, based upon verbal agreement of artist accepting assignment. All artwork is vested in Metropolitan Water District unless agreed upon." Works on assignment only. Uses artists for brochure/publications design, illustration and layout.
First Contact & Terms: Send query letter with brochure showing art style. Samples not filed are returned by SASE. Reports only if interested. Call to schedule an appointment to show a portfolio, which should include b&w roughs, original/final art and tearsheets. Pays for design by the project, $100 minimum. Pays for illustration by the project, $50 minimum.
Tips: "Phone calls should be kept short and to a minimum. Public affairs of MWD is interested in skillful execution of conceptual artwork to illustrate articles for its publication program. Number of projects is limited."

J. MICHAELS INC., 182 Smith St., Brooklyn NY 11201. (718)852-6100. Advertising Manager: Ron Brown. Estab. 1886. Retailer of furniture and home furnishings for young married couples ages 20-45.
Needs: Works with 5 freelance illustrators/year. Uses artists mainly for mechanicals. Also uses freelance artists for ad illustration, P-O-P display, calligraphy, paste-up and posters. "We use a lot of line ink furniture illustrations." Prefers tight, realistic style, pen & ink, pencil, wash.
First Contact & Terms: Send query letter with brochure or nonreturnable samples, such as photocopies. Samples are filed and are not returned. Reports back only if interested. "Mail photocopies. If I want to see more, I will call." Pays for illustration by the project, $50 (for items like charts on TV). Considers complexity of project and skill and experience of artist when establishing payment. Buys all rights.
Tips: "We are a furniture retailer. Show me furniture illustrations that can print in newspapers."

MOSTAD & CHRISTENSEN, Box 1709, Oak Harbor WA 98277. Marketing Manager: Michele Hardenbergh. Estab. 1978. Service-related firm. "We sell marketing products (newsletters, brochures) to CPAs to promote their services to prospective clients." Clients: Certified Public Accountants and public accountants.

Needs: Works with 3 freelance artists/year. Assigns 3 freelance jobs/year. Works on assignment only. Uses freelance artists mainly for product design. Also uses freelance artists for brochure design, illustration and layout and catalog illustration.
First Contact & Terms: Send query letter with brochure showing art style, tearsheets and photographs. Samples are filed or are returned only if requested by artist. Reports back within 1 month. To show a portfolio, mail roughs, original/final art and photographs. Pays for design by the project, $2,000-5,000. Considers complexity of project when establishing payment. Buys all rights.
Tips: "We need artists who are creative, yet conservative. Our market is fairly conservative, very professional and businesslike. Artists who have worked on brochure design for professionals would be good candidates for our firm."

*MURPHY INTERNATIONAL SALES ORGANIZATION, 11444 Zelzah Ave., Granada Hills CA 91344. (818)363-1410. President: F.S. Murphy. Distributor and service-related firm providing retrofit, covering materials, new products and patents. Clients: building and home owners.
Needs: Works with 2 freelance artists/year. Uses artists for advertising, brochure and catalog design, and product illustration. Prefers loose, impressionistic style; calligraphy and computer illustration.
First Contact & Terms: Send samples to be kept on file. Write for art guidelines. Prefers photocopies as samples. Samples not filed are not returned. Reports back only if interested. Pays by the hour, $25 minimum. Considers how work will be used when establishing payment.
Tips: "Design should be realistic. Art is becoming more simple and less dramatic."

*MURRAY HILL PRESS, 56 Central Dr., Farmingdale NY 11735. (516)454-0800. President: Ralph Ceisler. Printer. Clients: commercial.
Needs: Approached by 3 freelance artists/year. Assigns 12 jobs/year; uses mostly local artists. Uses artists for catalogs, direct mail brochures, flyers and P-O-P display. "Need good catalog-brochure art. Must be creative. Artist preferably should be from Long Island for better access."
First Contact & Terms: Send query letter with tearsheets and SASE. Reports in 2 weeks. Call or write to schedule an appointment to show a portfolio, which should include thumbnails, roughs, original/final art and final reproduction/product. Pays for design and illustration by the project, $100 minimum. Pay depends strictly on job and is negotiable. Rights purchased vary according to project.
Tips: "Have samples showing rough through completion."

MVP CORP. INC., 88 Spence St., Bayshore NY 11706. (516)273-8020 or (800)367-7900. President: Harold Greenberg. Estab. 1975. Manufacturer of imprinted sportswear, T-shirts, jackets and sweatshirts, etc., for all ages.
Needs: Works with 3 freelance artists/year. Uses freelance artists mainly for special projects. Also uses artists for fashion illustration.
First Contact & Terms: Send resume. Samples are filed or are returned only if requested by artist. Reports back within 7 days only if interested. Write to schedule an appointment to show a portfolio, which should include roughs. Pays weekly, $500 and up. Considers skill and experience of artist when establishing payment.
Tips: "Looking for full time!"

*NATIONAL POTTERIES, 7800 Bayberry Rd., Jacksonville FL 32256-6893. (904)737-8500. FAX: (904)737-9526. Art Director: Barbara McDonald. Estab. 1940. Manufacturer and distributor of design giftware—decals, 3-dimensional, baby, novelty and seasonal. Clients: wholesale and retail.
Needs: Approached by 25 freelance artists/year. Works with 15 freelance illustrators and designers/year. Assigns 250 jobs to freelance artists/year. Prefers local artists with experience in mechanicals for sizing decals and design work in giftware. Works on assignment only. Uses freelance artists mainly for mechanicals and product design. Prefers pen & ink, pencil color separations for decal use; 3-dimensional illustration for product. "Background with a seasonal product such as greeting cards is helpful. 75% of our work is very traditional and seasonal. We're also looking for a higher-end product, an elegant sophistication." Also uses freelance artists for catalog design and layout, product rendering and mechanicals. Send resume, tearsheets, slides, photostats, photographs, photocopies and transparencies. Samples are filed or returned by SASE only if requested by artist. Reports back in 2 weeks. Portfolio should include samples which show a full range of illustration style. Pays for design by the project. Pays for illustration by the hour, $10-20; pays for mechanicals, $10-15. Buys all rights.

NETWORK IND./CLASS KID LTD., 350 Fifth Ave., New York NY 10118. Design Directors: Maggie Meltzer and Susan Trombetta. Estab. 1978. Importer of men's and boys' sportswear. Labels: Laguna, Pro-Keds, Evenkeel. Clients include Sears, JC Penney and Walmart.
Needs: Approached by 10-15 freelance artists/year. Works with 6-8 freelance illustrators and 2-4 freelance designers/year. Assigns "at least 1-2 jobs to freelance artists every week." Uses artists for fashion, textile and screen print design. Prefers marker, then pen & ink, colored pencil and computer illustration.

First Contact & Terms: Send query letter with resume and photocopies. Samples not filed are not returned. Reports back only if interested. To show a portfolio, mail color roughs (concepts) and original/final art. Pays for design by the hour, $10-20; by the project, $15-100. Pays for illustration by the hour, $90-150; by the project, $10-100. Considers complexity of project and skill and experience of artist when establishing payment.
Tips: "Show flat sketches of garments for illustration. Show cartoon art, textile designs or illustrations to show color sense and skill. Do not show photographs or rough fashion illustrations. If an artist is in the New York area, we can see them immediately. Occasional phone calls are good, because it keeps the artist in our mind. Most of our artists have been recommended by friends."

*NIEDERMEYER-AMERICA LTD., Box 4078, Portland OR 97208-4078. (503)222-6496. FAX: (503)222-6498. Sales: Jim Niedermeyer. Estab. 1980. Distributor of palm leaf hats, printed casual wear and straw hats for industrial and retail clients.
Needs: Works on assignment only. Uses freelance artists mainly for design and promotion. Also uses freelance artists for advertising design, illustration and layout; brochure design, illustration and layout; and catalog design, illustration and layout.
First Contact & Terms: Send query letter with brochure showing art style. Samples are not returned. Call to schedule an appointment to show a portfolio. Pays for design and illustration by the project. Rights purchased vary according to project.

*NOVEL TEE DESIGNS, 5439 Bayberry Dr., Norfolk VA 23502. Art Director: Vernell Peebles. Estab. 1985. Manufacturer and distributor of imprinted T-shirts, sweatshirts, aprons and nighshirts for retail shops and tourist-oriented, ski-resort, beach/surf, seasonal and cartoon/humorous designs. Clients: Gift shops, surf shops and department stores.
Needs: Approached by 50-100 freelance artists/year. Works with 4-6 freelance illustrators and 2-5 freelance designers/year. Assigns 50 jobs to freelance artists/year. Prefers artists with experience in silkscreen printing, art and design. Works on assignment only. Uses freelance artists mainly for T-shirts, sweatshirts, aprons and nightshirts and apparel graphic designs. "We are looking for designs that will appeal to women ages 18-40 and men ages 15-40; also interested in ethnic designs."
First Contact & Terms: Send query letter with brochure showing art style or resume, tearsheets and photostats. Samples are filed or are returned only if requested by artist. Reports back within 1 month only if interested. To show a portfolio, mail thumbnails, roughs, original/final art, final reproduction/product and tearsheets. Pays for design and illustration by the project, $25-100. Negotiates rights purchased.
Tips: "Artists should have past experience in silkscreening art. Understanding the type of line work needed for silkscreening and originality. We are looking for artists who can create humorous illustrations for a product line of T-shirts. Graphic designs are also welcomed. Have samples showing rough through completion."

*OBION-DENTON, 34 W. 33rd St., New York NY 10001. (212)563-6070. Art Director: Sandra Von Hagen. Estab. 1865. Manufacturer of children's sleepwear for 0-14 year olds. Labels: Dr. Denton, The Original Dr. Denton and OBION.
Needs: Approached by 50 freelance artists/year. Works with 25-30 freelance artists/year. Prefers artists with experience in screen print and heat transfer design and set-up. Uses freelance artists mainly for screen and transfer print design. Also uses freelance artists for catalog illustration, textile design, paste-up, mechanicals and storyboards. Prefers campy and contemporary styles.
First Contact & Terms: Send query letter with resume and photocopies. Samples are filed. Reports back only if interested. Call to schedule an appointment to show a portfolio, which should include original/final art and photostats. Pays for design by the project, $125-225. Buys all rights.
Tips: "Shop the market and show originality to compete with what is in the stores currently and going forward."

OSSIPOFF, SNYDER & ROWLAND (ARCHITECTS) INC., 1210 Ward Ave., Honolulu HI 96814. President: Sidney E. Snyder, Jr., AIA. Architecture/planning/interior design firm. Clients: commercial (offices), residential, institutional, religious and educational. Current clients include state of Hawaii.
Needs: Approached by 15 freelance artists/year. Works with 2-3 freelance artists/year. Artist should be in Hawaii for this contact. Works on assignment only. Uses artists for interior design, architectural rendering, furnishing, model making and fine art in building projects.
First Contact & Terms: Send query letter with brochure showing art style. Reports back. Write to schedule an appointment to show a portfolio. Payment determined by job.
Tips: "Interested in high quality."

*PATTERN PEOPLE, INC., 10 Floyd Rd., Derry NH 03038. (603)432-7180. Vice President: Michael S. Copeland. Estab. 1988. Design studio servicing various manufacturers. Designs wallcoverings and textiles with "classical elegance and exciting new color themes for all ages."

Needs: Approached by 5-8 freelance artists/year. Works with 10-15 freelance artists/year. Prefers artists with experience in various professional mediums. Uses freelance artists mainly for original finished artwork. Also uses freelance artists for textile and wallcovering design. "We use all styles but they must be professional." Special needs are "floral (both traditional and contemporary); textural (faux finishes, new woven looks, etc.) and geometric (mainly new wave contemporary)."
First Contact & Terms: Send query letter with photocopies, slides and photographs. Samples are filed. Reports back within 1 month. Write to schedule an appointment to show a portfolio, which should include original/final art and color samples. Pays for design by the project, $100-1,000. Buys all rights.
Tips: "The best way to break in is by attending the annual Surtex Design show in New York."

*PDT & COMPANY ARCHITECTS/PLANNERS, 8044 Montgomery Rd., Cincinnati OH 45236. (513)891-4605. Project Architect: Mark Browning. Clients: commercial, institutional and multi-family residential.
Needs: Approached by over 10 artists/year. Works with over 7 freelance illustrators and over 5 freelance designers/year. Uses artists for brochure layout, architectural and interior rendering and landscape design. Works on assignment only. Especially needs brick and stone sculptors and renderers. Prefers marker; gouache; mixed media; and stone, bronze and neon sculpture.
First Contact & Terms: Send query letter with brochure showing art style or resume and photographs. Samples are filed or are returned if requested by artist. Reports back in 3 weeks. Call or write to schedule an appointment to show a portfolio or mail photographs. All fees negotiable. Considers skill and experience of artist, client's budget and rights purchased when establishing payment. Negotiates rights purchased.

PEN NOTES, INC., 134 Westside Ave., Freeport NY 11520-5499. (516)868-1966/5753. President: Lorette Konezny. Produces children's learning books and calligraphy kits for children ages 3 and up, teenagers and adults.
Needs: Prefers New York artists with book or advertising experience. Works on assignment only. Also uses freelance artists for calligraphy, P-O-P display and mechanicals. Prefers pen & ink. Prefers realistic style with true perspective and color.
First Contact & Terms: Send query letter with brochure, photostats and photocopies. Samples are filed or are returned only if requested by artist. Call or write to schedule an appointment to show a portfolio or mail original/final art, final reproduction/product and color and b&w tearsheets and photostats. Original artwork is not returned after job's completion. Pays by the project, $100-6,000. Buys all rights.
Tips: "Work must be clean, neat and registered for reproduction. The style must be geared for children's toys. You must work on deadline schedule set by printing needs."

PENDLETON WOOLEN MILLS, 218 SW Jefferson, Portland OR 97201. (503)226-4801. Menswear Communications Manager: Patti McGrath; Womenswear Communications Manager: Pat McKevitt. Manufacturer of men's and women's sportswear, blankets and piece goods.
Needs: Approached by 10 freelance artists/year. Works with 3 freelance illustrators/year. Assigns job to 1 freelance artist/year. Seeks local artist for line art. Uses artists for advertising illustration. Prefers b&w and traditional styles.
First Contact & Terms: Send query letter with samples to be kept on file. Call for appointment to show portfolio. Reports back within 3 weeks. Considers complexity of project, available budget and how work will be used when establishing payment. Pays for illustration by the project, $40 minimum.

PICKARD, INC., 782 Corona Ave., Antioch IL 60002. (708)395-3800. FAX: (708)395-3827. Director of Marketing: Patti Kral. Estab. 1893. Manufacturer of fine china dinnerware, limited edition plates and collectibles. Clients: upscale stores, consumers and collectors. Current clients include Cartier, Tiffany & Co., Marshall Field's and Bradford Exchange.
Needs: Assigns 2-3 jobs to freelance artists/year. Uses freelance artists mainly for china patterns and plate art. Prefers designers for china pattern development with experience in home furnishings. Tabletop experience is a plus. Wants painters for plate art who can paint people and animals well. Prefers any medium with a fine art or photographic style. Works on assignment only. Send query letter with brochure showing art style or resume and color photographs, tearsheets, slides or transparencies. Samples are filed or are returned as requested. Reports back within 3 months. Negotiates fees, royalties and rights purchased.

PINEHURST TEXTILES INC., Box 1628, Asheboro NC 27204. (919)625-2153. Contact: Bonna R. Leonard. Estab. 1946. Manufactures ladies' lingerie, sleepwear and leisurewear; nylon tricot, 100% cotton, woven satin, woven polyester/cotton, brushed polyester and fleece; Pinehurst Lingerie label.
Needs: Approached by 5-10 freelance artists/year. Works with 1 freelance illustrator/year. Uses freelance work mainly for catalogs. Seasonal needs: spring and summer due September 1; fall and winter due March 1. Prefers pen & ink, watercolor and acrylic.
First Contact & Terms: Pays for illustration by the project, $75 minimum or by the hour, $25 minimum.
Tips: "Live in this area and do fashion illustration."

Close-up

Luis Pérez
Associate Art Director
Polo/Ralph Lauren Corporation

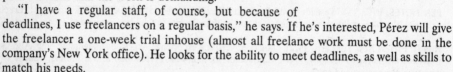

Freelance artists interested in working in the fashion industry must have lots of self discipline, says Luis Pérez, associate art director for the Polo/Ralph Lauren Corporation. Pérez handles all the company's menswear lines and is often working on several garments at once. The pace is hectic and the work is demanding.

"I have a regular staff, of course, but because of deadlines, I use freelancers on a regular basis," he says. If he's interested, Pérez will give the freelancer a one-week trial inhouse (almost all freelance work must be done in the company's New York office). He looks for the ability to meet deadlines, as well as skills to match his needs.

The ability to render garments realistically is essential, he says. "Final drawings must look exactly like the finished product." In fact Pérez moved up quickly in the company, from freelancer to associate art director, in part due to his ability to draw realistically. For the past several months he's been going through the company's huge collection of sketches to make sure they fit the firm's emphasis on realism.

A few years ago, he explains, fashion illustration often used a sweeping, minimal style—"one fast stroke and it was fine." He still sees work from freelancers with this type of style and many seem to lack basic drawing skills. "You need an almost classical training for this type of work," he says. "I look for freelancers who have excellent anatomy skills. Too few seem to be able to draw feet or hands well."

Since color is so important, freelancers also need to be able to mix colors and match them to the designers' specifications. Designers supply sketches of fabrics needed. Fabric sketches are handled in a different department and are sent out to freelance silk screeners and graphic designers.

Pérez works with about 12 freelance illustrators each year. Each season the art director and design staff plan the line, deciding the look they want, the number and type of garments. This may include everything from outerwear to socks.

Seasons are planned one year in advance. They are divided into four: "Fall," by far the largest season, followed by "Spring," "Cruise" and "Summer. The design staff meets regularly with Lauren, whose influence can be seen in all the firm's products from menswear to home fashions. Designer and president Ralph Lauren has final approval on all lines.

Freelancers draw from the firm's extensive library of sketches. "For example," says Pérez, "we must have 100 drawings of cardigan sweaters." The sketches give the illustrators the basic garment, and they follow the designers' instructions to draw the specific garment needed.

Freelance graphic designers are also needed in the menswear department. "We're developing new logos constantly and there's a demand for people who can provide us with camera-ready work."

To approach Pérez, send a query letter with a resume, tearsheets or photostats of your work. If he's interested, Pérez will then ask to see a portfolio. "I've been surprised to find many portfolios are not well presented," he says. "Work must be clean and artists should, at the very least, have a business card and samples they can leave as 'keepers.' Again it comes to discipline. I feel that if freelancers do not take time to prepare a professional portfolio, then they may not be able to discipline themselves to do the work here."

Pérez advises freelance artists to practice the basics and learn the matching and mixing of colors. "Try to expand on your skills. If you don't do hands well, don't try to fake it—practice them," he says. "And pay attention to details. It's those little details that can make a big difference."

—Robin Gee

This piece done by Pérez himself is an example of the realistic rendering which Polo/Ralph Lauren is looking for. From this illustration, one has as precise a sense of patterns and textures as one would from a black-and-white photograph. This example also attests to the importance of having excellent anatomical skills.

*PLYMOUTH MILLS, INC., 330 Tompkins Ave., Staten Island NY 10304. (718)447-6707. President: Alan Elenson. Manufacturer of imprinted sportswear: T-shirts, sweatshirts, fashionwear, caps, aprons and bags. Clients: mass merchandisers/retailers.

Needs: Approached by 25 freelance artists/year. Works with 8 freelance illustrators and 8 freelance designers/year. Assigns 100 jobs to freelance artists/year. Uses freelance artists mainly for screenprint designs. Also uses freelance artists for advertising and catalog design, illustration and layout and product design.

First Contact & Terms: Send brochure and resume. Reports back only if interested. Pays for design and illustration by the hour or by the project. Considers complexity of the project and how work will be used when establishing payment.

*POLO/RALPH LAUREN CORPORATION, 40 West 55 St., New York NY 10019. (212)603-2710. FAX: (212)977-5137. Associate Art Director: Luis F. Pérez. Coordinator: Bennetta Barrett. Design studio for fashion (men's wear). "The clothing has a very strong Americana feeling for young boys (4-7) to adult men." Labels: Polo and Ralph Lauren.

Needs: Approached by 80-over 100 freelance artists/year. Works with 12 freelance artists/year. Prefers local artists only with experience in realistic fashion illustration and marker—a must. Must work in house only. Uses freelance artists mainly for rendering flats of garments and male figures. Also uses freelance artists for accessory design and fashion illustration. Prefers realistic styles. "Artists with style required, with the ability for fast execution of assignments."

First Contact & Terms: Send query letter with resume and tearsheets and photostats. Samples are not filed and are returned by SASE if requested by artist. Reports back only if interested. To show a portfolio, mail b&w and color photostats and tearsheets. Pays for illustration by the hour, $10-20. Buys all rights.

Tips: "Please be sure the work you are showing is the type or style the firm or studio is looking for. Be completely prepared!"

THE POPCORN FACTORY, 13970 W. Laurel Dr., Lake Forest IL 60045. Marketing Director: Tom Downes. Estab. 1979. Manufacturer of cans of popcorn and other gift items, sold via catalog to mail order and over 50 buyers at Christmas, Valentine's, Easter, etc.

Needs: Works with 5-10 freelance artists/year. Assigns 50-100 freelance jobs/year. Prefers local artists only with experience in catalog work. Works on assignment only. Uses freelance artists mainly for cover illustration, flyers and ads. Also uses artists for advertising, brochure and catalog design and illustration.

First Contact & Terms: Send query letter with brochure. Samples are filed. Reports back within 1 month. Write to schedule an appointment to show a portfolio, or mail original/final art and photographs. Pays for design by the project, $500-$2,000. Pays for illustration by the project, $500-$1,500. Considers complexity of project, skill and experience of artist and turnaround time when establishing payment. Buys all rights.

Tips: "Send cartoons, classic illustration, Rockwell-style pencil/watercolor, a mix of photography/illustration. Show ads, flyers, inserts, letters and brochures from rough layout through final art."

POURETTE MFG. INC., 6910 Roosevelt Way NE, Seattle WA 98115. (206)525-4488. President: Don Olsen. Estab. 1952. Manufacturer and distributor specializing in candlemaking supplies and soap making supplies. Clients: anyone interested in selling candlemaking supplies or making candles.

*PRELUDE DESIGNS, 1 Hayes St., Elmsford NY 10523. (914)592-4300. Art Director: Madalyn Grano. Produces wallpaper, fabric and T-shirts.

Needs: Designs for the juvenile wallpaper/fabric market and both the adult and youth T-shirt markets. Occasionally hires artists for paste-up and color paint-up. Prefers artists experienced in tempera or gouache paints. Patterns submitted for wallcoverings or fabrics should be done to the following dimensions (or fractions thereof): 27W × 25¼L or 27L (6 colors maximum). Designs submitted for T-shirts should be done in the following dimensions: Youth 8W × 9L (or smaller); Adult 13W × 16L (or smaller). Also 6-color maximum and in any medium. Generally looking for fresh designs with an unusual "look." Prefers simple styles and themes dealing with current social trends.

First Contact & Terms: Send query letter with resume and samples of artwork. Include SASE if you wish samples returned. Portfolios may be shown by appointment only, and should include only those designs or patterns that apply to either juvenile wallcoverings/fabrics, or adult or youth T-shirts. Pays royalty of 3-5%. Original artwork returned at completion of project.

Tips: "Many artists don't follow-up with a phone call. In a busy art department, I can't always think to get back to people."

*PREMIER WALLCOVERINGS, Suite A, 2130 Hwy. 35, 121 Sea Girt NJ 08750. (201)974-1014. FAX: (201)974-1463. President: Anthony Cirillo. Estab. 1986. Manufacturer of wallcovering and fabric designs for all of the design home furnishings. Label: Schumacher.

Needs: Approached by more than 50 freelance artists/year. Works with more than 5 freelance illustrators and more than 20 freelance designers/year. Assigns over 100 freelance jobs/year. Prefers unique artists. Uses freelance artists for new and concept designs. Also uses freelance artists for product design. Send query letter with brochure showing art style or tearsheets and any previous work. Samples are filed or are returned. Reports back only if interested. Call or write to schedule an appointment to show a portfolio or mail roughs. Pays for design by the project; pays royalties. Rights purchased vary according to project.

*PRESTIGELINE, INC., 5 Inez Dr., Brentwood NY 11717. (516)273-3636. Director of Marketing: Stuart Goldstein. Manufacturer of lighting products.
Needs: Uses artists for advertising and catalog design, illustration and layout and product illustration. Prefers b&w line drawings. Produces seasonal material for Christmas, Mother's Day, Father's Day, Thanksgiving, Easter, back-to-school and graduations; submit work 3-4 months before season.
First Contact & Terms: Send resume, business card and photostats. Call for appointment to show a portfolio. Samples returned by SASE. Reports within 2 weeks. Buys all rights. Payment method is negotiable.
Tips: "There is an increased demand for b&w line art for newspaper advertisements."

PRISS PRINTS, INC., Suite 105, 3960 Broadway Blvd., Garland TX 75043. (800)543-4971; Texas: (214)278-5600. President: Toni Fischer Morath. Estab. 1972. Manufacturer. "We manufacture pressure sensitive wall decorations used primarily in children's rooms." Clients: retail stores selling wallcoverings and/or children's products. Current clients include: Target, Sears, J.C. Penney, Ames, Caldor and Kay-Bee.
Needs: Approached by 25 freelance artists/year. Works with 8 freelance illustrators and 2 freelance designers/year. Assigns 20 jobs to freelance artists/year. Uses freelancers mainly for product design. Also uses artists for advertising and brochure design, illustration and layout; illustration on product and signage.
First Contact & Terms: Send query letter with photostats. Samples are filed or are returned. Reports back only if requested; if not interested, all submissions returned. To show a portfolio, mail photostats. Pays for design and illustration by the project, $100 minimum. Considers complexity of project and interpretation of instructions when establishing payment. Buys all rights.
Tips: "Don't overwhelm me with long letters and too many samples. Don't send any originals unless requested. Send whimsical line art and illustrations."

*PULPDENT CORPORATION OF AMERICA, 80 Oakland St., Watertown MA 02172. (617)926-6666. Director of Product Information: Jane Hart Berk. Manufacturer/distributor of dental supplies including instruments, pharmaceuticals, X-ray supplies, sterilizers, needles, articulating paper, etc. Clients: dental-supply dealers and dentists.
Needs: Works with 3-5 freelance artists/year. Works with local artists only. Works on assignment only. Uses artists for advertising, brochure and catalog design, illustration and layout; photography and technical illustration.
First Contact & Terms: Send query letter with business card, photostats and tearsheets. Samples are filed. Reports within 6 weeks. Call or write for appointment to show a portfolio. Pays by the project, $40 minimum. Considers complexity of project and skill and experience of artist when establishing payment; "how much our product is worth determines to some extent the amount we are willing to invest in designing, etc."
Tips: "We prefer simple, not-too-trendy designs aimed at the dental professional."

*RAINBOW CREATIONS, INC., 216 Industrial Dr., Ridgeland MS 39157. (601)856-2158. President: Steve Thomas. Estab. 1973. Manufacturer of contract wallcovering: scenics, murals, borders and wallpaper prints. Clients: architects, interior designers and health-care institutions. Current clients include national distribution network.
Needs: Approached by 10 freelance artists/year. Works with 3 freelance illustrators and 2 freelance designers/year. Assigns 10 jobs to freelance artists/year. Prefers artists with experience in pattern design and silk screen. Works on assignment only. Uses freelance artists mainly as a source for new designs. Prefers silk screen and contemporary styles. Also uses freelance artists for product design. Send query letter with resume, photographs and photocopies. Reports back in 1 month. To show a portfolio, mail photostats, photographs and slides. Pays for design by the project, $100-700. Rights purchased vary according to project.

DARIAN RAITHEL & ASSOCIATES, 8623 Old Perry Hwy., Pittsburgh PA 15237. (412)367-4357. President: Darian Raithel. Estab. 1982. Architectural, interior design and landscape design firm providing total planning and design of retail stores, restaurants, offices and some residences. Current clients include Klay's Cafe, Derby's Deli, Coach Home Men's Stores and Merrill Lynch (now Prudential Preferred Realty).
Needs: Approached by 8-10 freelance artists/year. Works with 5-8 freelance artists/year. Uses freelance artists mainly for presentations. Also uses freelance artists for interior design and rendering, design consulting and furnishings. Especially needs drafting on a freelance basis.
First Contact & Terms: Send brochure showing art style or resume. Samples are filed or filed are returned. Reports back within 2 weeks. Call or write to schedule an appointment to show a portfolio, which should include color thumbnails, roughs and photographs. Pays for design by the hour, $6-12. Pays for illustration by the hour, $6-20. Considers skill and experience of artist when establishing payment. Buys one-time rights.
Tips: "Show freehand perspective illustrations, detail, specification drawings and plans in your portfolio. Don't oversell yourself. Organize your portfolio and make it neat."

RECO INTERNATIONAL CORPORATION, Collector's Division, Box 951, 138-150 Haven Ave., Port Washington NY 11050. (516)767-2400. Manufacturer/distributor of limited editions, collector's plates, lithographs and figurines. Clients: stores.
Needs: Works with 4 freelance artists/year. Uses artists for plate and figurine design and limited edition fine art prints. Prefers romantic and realistic styles.
First Contact & Terms: Send query letter and brochure to be filed. Write for appointment to show a portfolio. Reports within 3 weeks. Negotiates payment.

*RED CALLIOPE AND ASSOCIATES, INC., 13003 Figueroa St., Los Angeles CA 90061. (213)516-6100. FAX: (213)516-7170. Vice President of Design: Bonni Weisman. Estab. 1969. Manufacturer of infant clothing for newborns. Label: Red Calliope.
Needs: Approached by 8-15 freelance artists/year. Works with 7-10 freelance artists/year. Prefers artists with experience in infant and clothing design, juvenile textiles and illustration. Uses freelance artists mainly for complete design. Also uses freelance artists for product, textile and pattern design and displays. Style "must look 'baby.'"
First Contact & Terms: Send query letter with brochure showing art style or resume and photographs, photocopies or "anything appropriate." Samples are not filed and are returned. Reports back within 1 week. Call to schedule an appointment to show a portfolio, which should include appropriate materials. Pays for design by the project, $300-2,500. Pays for illustration by the project, $300-1,000. Rights purchased vary according to project.
Tips: "Prepare a portfolio after doing market research and then call."

RKT&B (ROTHZEID KAISERMAN THOMSON & BEE, P.C., ARCH & PLANNERS), 30 W. 22nd St., New York NY 10010. Partner: Carmi Bee. Architectural firm that designs buildings (new construction, restoration, rehab., medical facilities, retail, housing, offices).
Needs: Works with 3-10 freelance artists/year. Works on assignment only. Uses artists for brochure design and architectural rendering.
First Contact & Terms: Send query letter with brochure showing art style. Samples not filed are returned by SASE. Reports only if interested. To show a portfolio, mail appropriate materials. Payment varies. Considers complexity of project, client's budget, skill and experience of artist, how work will be used, turnaround time and rights purchased when establishing payment.

*ROCKY MOUNT UNDERGARMENT, 1536 Boone St., Rocky Mount NC 27801. (919)446-6161. FAX: (919)442-4412. Designer: Sharon Beary. Estab. 1959. Manufacturer of lingerie, undergarments and night-shirts (screen prints) for female children, young ladies and women. Labels: Blossoms, Hang Ten and Capezio.
Needs: Approached by many freelance artists/year. Works with 10-15 freelance artists/year. Prefers local artists (not exclusively) with experience in textile design and graphic art for screen prints. Uses freelance artists mainly for textile print and screen prints. Also uses freelance artists for advertising illustration, textile design and package design. Special needs are textile print design and screen print design.
First Contact & Terms: Send query letter with brochure showing art style or resume and tearsheets, photostats, photocopies and "whatever is available and effective." Samples are filed. Reports back only if interested. Write to schedule an appointment to show a portfolio, which should include original/final art, photostats and actual fabrics. Pays for design by the project. Payment "to be discussed."
Tips: "We are receptive to all inquiries to textile print design. Looking for fresh new ideas."

THE ROSENTHAL JUDAICA COLLECTION, by Rite Lite, 260 47th St., Brooklyn NY 11220. (718)439-6900. President: Alex Rosenthal. Estab. 1948. Manufacturer and distributor of a full range of Judaica ranging from mass-market commercial goods to exclusive numbered pieces. Clients: gift shops, museum shops and jewelry stores.
Needs: Approached by 10 freelance artists/year. Works with 4 freelance designers/year. Works on assignment only. Uses freelance artists mainly for new designs for Judaic giftware. Also uses artists for brochure and catalog design, illustration and layout and product design. Prefers ceramic and brass.
First Contact & Terms: Send query letter with brochure or resume, tearsheets and photographs. Samples are filed. Reports back only if interested. Call to schedule an appointment to show a portfolio, which should include original/final art and color tearsheets, photographs, and slides. Pays for design by the project, $500 minimum. Considers complexity of project, client's budget, skill and experience of artist and turnaround time when establishing payment. Buys all rights. "Works on a royalty basis."
Tips: Do not send originals.

RSVP MARKETING, Suite 5, 450 Plain St., Marshfield MA 02050. (617)837-2804. President: Edward C. Hicks. Direct marketing consultant services—catalogs, direct mail and telemarketing. Clients: primarily industry and distributors.

Needs: Works with 7-8 freelance artists/year. Desires "primarily local artists; must have direct marketing skills." Uses artists for advertising, copy brochure and catalog design, illustration and layout.
First Contact & Terms: Send query letter with resume and finished, printed work to be kept on file. Reports only if interested. Pays for design by the job, $400-5,000. Pays for illustration by the hour, $25-85. Considers skill and experience of artist when establishing payment.

*ST. ARGOS CO., INC., 11040 W. Hondo Pkwy., Temple City CA 91780. (818)448-8886. FAX: (818)579-9133. Manager: Roy Liang. Estab. 1987. Manufacturer of Christmas decorations, paper bags and postcards. Clients: gift shops.
Needs: Approached by 3 freelance artists/year. Works with 6 freelance illustrators and 4 freelance designers/year. Assigns 2 jobs to freelance artists/year. Prefers artists with experience in Christmas and product design. Uses freelance artists mainly for design. Prefers Victorian and classic styles. Also uses freelance artists for brochure illustration and posters. Send resume, slides and photographs. Samples are filed. Reports back in 1 month. Write to schedule an appointment to show portfolio, which should include color slides. Payment for design and illustration, percentage of volume sold. Buys all rights.

JANET SCHIRN INTERIORS, 401 N. Franklin St., Chicago IL 60610. President: Janet Schirn. Interior design firm providing contract and residential interior design. Clients: business, restaurant and mercantile (wholesale).
Needs: Uses artists for graphics and fine art.
First Contact & Terms: Send letter with resume and samples. Pays by the project. Considers client's budget and skill and experience of artist when establishing payment.
Tips: "Better quality work is necessary; there is greater client sophistication. Just show your work—no sales pitch."

SCHMID, 55 Pacella Park Dr., Randolph MA 02368. (617)961-3000. Art Director: Luis Lapitz. Estab. 1930. Manufacturer and distributor producing giftware such as music boxes, figurines and picture frames in earthenware and porcelain. Seasonal lines include: Christmas, Valentine's Day, Easter, etc. from a nostalgic to whimsical "look." Other themes include; Mother's Day, wedding, and baby. Clients: gift shops, department stores, jewelry stores and specialty shops.
Needs: Assigns 60-100 freelance jobs/year. Prefers artists with experience in giftware or greeting card design. Works on assignment only. Uses freelance artists mainly for product design. "We assign concept art and freelance artist is responsible for pencil roughs and color once pencil concept is approved."
First Contact & Terms: Send query letter with photocopies and other nonreturnable samples. Samples are filed or are returned by SASE only if requested by artist. Reports back within 1 month only if interested. Write to schedule an appointment to show a portfolio, should include roughs, original/final art, color and b&w tearsheets. Pays for design and illustration by the project. Considers complexity of project and how work will be used when establishing payment. Buys all rights.
Tips: "A 'greeting card style' is a plus. We are looking for illustrators who can portray figures and/or animals."

*SEA SIDE COTTAGE, 61 Bridle Path, Somers CT 06071. (203)749-0524. Owner: Phyllis Foltz. Estab. 1988. Manufacturer and distributor of floral design: dried and silk floral pieces and accessories. Clients: florist and gift shops/direct mail.
Needs: Works with 3 freelance illustrators/year. Prefers local artists, with experience in catalog work. Works on assignment only. Uses freelance artists mainly for catalog and advertising. Also uses freelance artists for brochure design, illustration and layout and magazine layout for *Florist (FTD)* and *Giftware News.*
First Contact & Terms: Send query letter with brochure showing art style. Samples are filed. Reports back only if interested. To show a portfolio, mail thumbnails, photostats, tearsheets and photographs. Pays for design and illustration by the project. Buys first rights.

*RICHARD SEIDEN INTERIORS, 238 N. Allen St., Albany NY 12206. (518)482-8600. President: Richard Seiden. Interior design firm. Provides residential and contract interior design. Clients: residential.
Needs: Works with 4 freelance artists/year for graphic design; 3, signage design; 2, model making; 3, murals; 4, wall hangings; 3, landscape design; 2, charts/graphs; and 2, stained glass. Works on assignment only.
First Contact & Terms: Send query letter with resume, tearsheets, photostats and SASE. Reports in 3 weeks. Provide materials to be kept on file for future assignments. Pays $150-1,800, original wall decor; also according to project. To show a portfolio, mail roughs. Pays for design by the hour, $25 minimum. Considers complexity of project, skill and experience of artist and client's budget when establishing payment.
Tips: Prefers to see photos rather than slides, if possible.

*SEM PARTNERS, INC., 100 E. Prince St., Drawer Q, Beckley WV 25802. (304)255-6181. Contact: J. Blair Frier, AIA, Principal. Architectural firm offering architectural planning, programming, construction administration and consulting. Clients: commercial, residential, education, state and federal, health care.

Needs: Uses artists for interior design, design consulting and model making.

First Contact & Terms: Works on assignment only. Send brochure and samples to be kept on file. Call for appointment to show portfolio. Samples not filed are returned only if requested. Reports within 1 month. Pays for design by the project. Considers complexity of the project and client's budget when establishing payment.

*SERIGRAPHIC PRODUCTIONS, INC., 3318 Pageland Hwy., Monroe NC 28110. (704)283-0886. President: Jeff Wood. Estab. 1989. Manufacturer and design studio that does high quality screenprinting on fashion apparel. "We tend to print high-end boutique apparel for all ages." Labels: Klondike Dry Goods, Drowning Creek Native Regalia.

Needs: Works with 5-10 freelance artists/year. Prefers artists with a working knowledge of screen printing artwork. Uses freelance artists mainly for new lines and custom designs. Also uses freelance artists for fashion design and illustration, package design and mechanicals. Prefers all types of printable artwork.

First Contact & Terms: Send query letter with brochure showing art style, slides and printed shirts, etc. Samples are filed or are returned only if requested by artist. Reports back within 5 days. Call to schedule an appointment to show a portfolio, which should include roughs, original/final art, final reproduction/product, color photographs and printed samples. Pays for design and illustration by the project, $25-500. Buys reprint rights or all rights. Payment is negotiable on new lines.

Tips: "We do mechanical screen printing separations. We are very interested in talented separation artists. Be professional! Our clients demand quality. We handle accounts such as HBO, DC Comics/Viacom, Atlantic Records, BME. These people know what they like."

SHERRY MFG. CO., INC., 3287 N.W. 65 St., Miami FL 33147. Art Director: Jeff Seldin. Estab. 1948. Manufacturer of silk-screen T-shirts with beach and mountain souvenir themes. Label: Sherry's Best. Current clients include Walt Disney Co., Club Med and Kennedy Space Center.

Needs: Approached by 50 freelance artists/year. Works with 10 freelance artists/year. Assigns 350 jobs to freelance artists/year. Prefers artists that know the T-shirt market and understand the technical aspects of T-shirt art. Prefers colorful graphics or highly stippled detail.

First Contact & Terms: Send query letter with brochure showing art style or resume, photostats and photocopies. Samples are not filed and are returned only if requested. Reports back within 2 weeks. Call or write to schedule an appointment to show a portfolio, which should include thumbnails, roughs, original/final art, final reproduction/product and color tearsheets, photostats and photographs. Pays for design and illustration by the project, $100-400 ($400 figure includes separations). Considers complexity of project, skill and experience of artist and volume of work given to artist when establishing payment. Buys all rights.

Tips: "Know the souvenir T-shirt market and have previous experience in T-shirt art preparation. Send sample copies of work with resume to my attention."

*SIEGEL DIAMOND ARCHITECTS, 10780 Santa Monica Blvd., Los Angeles CA 90025. (213)474-3244. Architecture firm providing planning and limited interior design services. Clients: commercial and residential. Buys 6 renderings/year.

Needs: Works with 3 freelance artists for architectural rendering; 3, graphic design; and 2, landscape design. Local artists only. Works on assignment only.

First Contact & Terms: Query with samples and arrange interview to show portfolio; no calls. Samples returned by SASE; reports back on future assignment possibilities. Work must be reproducible in b&w, i.e. line drawing with color added. Provide resume and business card to be kept on file for future assignments. Pays for design and illustration by the project.

TOM SNYDER PRODUCTIONS, INC., 90 Sherman St., Cambridge MA 02140. Art Director: Annette Donnelly. Developer of educational computer software for ages 5-adult; develops software, documentation, ancillary materials (music, art, books). Clients: schools, department stores, program stores.

Needs: Approached by over 30 freelance artists/year. Work with 2-3 freelance illustrators and 1 freelance designer/year. Uses artists for b&w and color work; brochure design, illustration and layout; product illustration; package design and computer graphics. Prefers pen & ink, charcoal/pencil, watercolor, oil, computer illustration and woodblock prints.

First Contact & Terms: Works on assignment only. Send query letter with resume and samples to be kept on file. Prefers photocopies as samples. Samples not filed are returned by SASE only if requested. Reports back only if interested. Pays by the hour, $15-25 average. Considers complexity of the project, skill and experience of the artist, how work will be used, and turnaround time when establishing payment.

Tips: "Let your work speak for itself. Just send photocopies and be patient. When an appropriate job comes up and your work is on file, we'll call you. A confident style and ability is important, but creativity is what I really look for in a portfolio."

SOPP AMERICA INC., One Chris Ct., Dayton NY 08810. Marketing Manager: Rick Novello. Estab. 1985. Manufacturer/distributor of ribbons, bows and giftwrap. Clients: card and gift shops, mass market and floral accounts.

Needs: Works with 3 freelance artists/year. Assigns 12 freelance jobs/year. Prefers artists with experience in P-O-P and advertising. Works on assignment basis only. Uses freelance artists mainly for advertising design, layout and P-O-P displays. Also uses freelance artists for advertising illustration, brochure design, illustration and layout and catalog design, illustration and layout.

First Contact & Terms: Send query letter with brochure showing art style. Samples are filed. Reports back only if interested. Call to schedule an appointment to show a portfolio which should include original/final art, final reproduction/product and tearsheets. Pays for design and illustration by the project. Considers client's budget when establishing payment. Buys all rights.

SPENCER GIFTS, INC., 1050 Black Horse Pike, Pleasantville NJ 08232. (609)645-5526. Art Director: James Stevenson. Estab. 1965. Retail gift chain located in approximately 500 malls in 43 states; gifts range from wall decorations to 14k gold jewelry.

Needs: Assigns 12-20 freelance jobs/year. Prefers artists with professional experience in advertising. Uses artists for package design and illustration, hard line art, fashion illustration, (airbrush).

First Contact & Terms: Query with nonreturnable samples, previously published work or arrange interview to show portfolio. With samples, enclose phone number where you can be reached during business hours. Pays for illustration by the project, $100-1,000. Will contact only upon job need.

Tips: "Send examples of airbrush art."

SPORTAILOR, INC., 6501 N.E. 2nd Ct., Miami FL 33138. (305)754-3255. FAX: (305)754-6559. Director of Marketing: Stan Rudman. Manufacturer and distributor of men's and boys' apparel (mostly sportswear) for toddlers-senior citizens. Labels: Sun Country Surfwear, Sun Country active wear, Weekender Sport.

Needs: Works with 3 freelance artists/year. Works on assignment only. Uses artists for advertising design, fashion design and illustration.

First Contact & Terms: Send query letter with brochure showing art style or samples and photocopies. Samples are filed or are returned only if requested. Reports back within 1 week. Call to schedule an appointment to show a portfolio, which should include color roughs and original/final art. "Show all the work you can do." Payment depends on the size of project; "it can be a $25 job or a $200 job." Considers client's budget when establishing payment.

Tips: "We are looking for an artist who can easily sketch from photographs for catalog work as well as a fashion designer who understands the surf market and knows how to come up with a boys' and young men's look."

*STAMP COLLECTORS SOCIETY OF AMERICA, Box 3, W. Redding CT 06896. Executive Vice President and Creative Director: Malcolm Decker. Philatelic marketing firm. Develops mail-order/direct response buyers of stamps using publications and mailing lists.

Needs: Approached by 12 freelance artists/year. Work with 2 freelance illustrators and 4 freelance designers/year. Prefers local (Westchester, New Haven, Fairfield County and New York City) designers; "experience requirement is determined by the job complexity." Works on assignment only. Use freelance artists mainly for spot illustrations. Also uses artists for advertising and brochure design, illustration and layout; product, album and editorial design; and "full-dress" direct-mail packages. Prefers ink and line drawings.

First Contact & Terms: Send query letter and resume; "if interested, we'll call you. Show your portfolio and leave-behind or send in samples or photocopies as requested." Pays by the hour, by the project or offers a retainer. Considers complexity of project, and skill and experience of the designer when establishing payment.

Tips: "Send a comprehensive, detailed resume listing all the clients served, noting those for whom the most work was done."

*PAUL STUART, Madison Ave at 45th St., New York NY 10017. (212)682-0320. P.R. Director/Ad Manager: Julie Oddy. Retailer and designer of updated traditional merchandise for 35-year-olds and older.

Needs: Approached by 10-20 freelance artists/year. Works with 2-3 freelance artists/year. Uses freelance artists mainly for direct mail and postcards. Also uses freelance artists for catalog illustration and layout.

First Contact & Terms: Send query letter with brochure showing art style. Samples are filed. Reports back only if interested. Call to schedule an appointment to show a portfolio, or mail appropriate materials. Payment depends on project. Buys all rights.

STUDIO 38 DESIGN CENTER, 38 William St., Amityville NY 11701. (516)789-4224. Vice President: Andrea Reda. Estab. 1972. Self-contained manufacturer of wallpaper for national clients.

Needs: Approached by 30 freelance artists/year. Works with about 10 freelance designers and 10 freelance illustrators/year. Uses artists for wallpaper. Assigns 80 jobs to freelance artists/year. Prefers pen & ink, airbrush, colored pencil, watercolor, pastel and marker.

First Contact & Terms: Portfolio should include color geometrics and florals; no figures. Pays for design by the project, $50-600.

Tips: "Call and make an appointment."

*ROBERT J. STURTCMAN—ARCHITECT, Drawer TT, Taos NM 87571. (505)758-4933. Owner: R. Sturtcman. Architectural/interior design firm. Clients: residential, schools and office/retail.
Needs: Uses artists for advertising and brochure design, interior and architectural rendering and model making.
First Contact & Terms: Send query letter with brochure showing art style. Samples not filed are returned by SASE. Reports back within 30 days. Write to schedule an appointment to show a portfolio. Pays for design by the hour, $15 minimum. Considers client's budget when establishing payment.

SUN HILL INDUSTRIES, INC., 48 Union St., Stamford CT 06906. Art Director and Product Development Manager: Nancy Mimoun. Estab. 1977. Manufacturer of Easter egg decorating kits, plastic home-office stationery items, health and beauty aids (organizers and novelties). Clients: discount chain and drug stores and mail-order catalog houses. Clients include K-Mart, Walmart, Walgreens, Caldor and Revco.
Needs: Approached by 10 freelance artists/year. Works with 2-3 freelance illustrators and 1-2 freelance designers/year. Assigns 5-6 freelance jobs/year. Works on assignment only. Uses artists for product and package design, rendering of product and model making. Prefers marker and acrylic.
First Contact & Terms: Send query letter with brochure and resume. Samples are filed or are returned only if requested by artist. Reports back only if interested. Pays for design by the hour, $25 minimum; by the project, $350 minimum. Pays for illustration by the hour, $25 minimum; by the project $350 minimum. Considers complexity of project and turnaround time when establishing payment. Buys all rights.
Tips: "Send all information; don't call; include package designs. Do not send mechanical work."

SUNDBERG, CARLSON AND ASSOCIATES, INC., 914 West Baraga Ave., Marquette MI 49855. (906)228-2333. Designer/Illustrator: Mike Lempinen. Estab. 1980. Architectural/interior design/engineering firm providing architectural , interior and graphic design and illustration; architectural renderings and model making.
Needs: "We are interested in seeing artwork for brochures, advertising, and architectural rendering services, and are especially interested in beginning a file on available art services; freelance, art houses, publication firms, etc." Works with 2-3 freelance illustrators and designers/year. Uses freelance artwork mainly for architectural rendering and promotional materials.
First Contact & Terms: Send query letter with brochure showing art style or resume, tearsheets, photostats and printed pieces. Samples not filed are not returned. Reports only if interested. To show a portfolio, mail appropriate materials. Pays by the hour, $6-15. Considers complexity of project, client's budget, and skill and experience of artist when establishing payment.
Tips: "Please do not send returnable pieces, slides or photos. We can not return unsolicited materials. The best way for freelancers to break in is to try to gain experience through part-time work and volunteering. For our firm, show a strong portfolio."

*SUTTON SHIRT CORP., 350 5th Ave., New York NY 10118. (212)239-4880. FAX: (212)629-0041. Merchandiser: Irene Mantia. Estab. 1969. Manufacturer of "stylish but moderately priced clothing."
Needs: Approached by 6 freelance artists/year. Works with 6 freelance artists/year. Prefers local artists only. Uses freelance artists mainly for fashion illustration. Also uses freelance artists for package design, paste-up and mechanicals. Prefers "attention to detail with flair."
First Contact & Terms: Send query letter with brochure showing art style. Samples are filed. Reports back only if interested. Call to schedule an appointment to show a portfolio, which should include thumbnails, roughs and original/final art. Pays for illustration by the project, $50.
Tips: "Call and set up a formal interview."

*SYLVOR CO., INC., 126 11th Ave., New York NY 10011. (212)929-2728. FAX: (212)691-2319. Owner: Bonnie Sylvor. Estab. 1929. Manufacturer of window displays for department stores and party planners. Clients: department stores, corporate parties and shops. Current clients include Saks Fifth Ave., Bloomingdales and Elizabeth Arden.
Needs: Approached by 20 freelance artists/year. Works with 5 freelance designers/year. Assigns 8 jobs to freelance artists/year. Prefers local artists only. Works on assignment only. Uses freelance artists mainly for overload and rush projects. Prefers poster style and flat painting that looks dimensional. Also uses freelance artists for product rendering and design, model making and signage.
First Contact & Terms: Send query letter with resume, slides, photographs, transparencies and other samples that do not need to be returned. Resumes are filed; samples are not filed. Does not report back, in which case the artist should call. Call to schedule an appointment to show a portfolio, which should include b&w photostats, slides and photographs. Pays for design by the project "or design piece. For work done on the premises, pays by the hour, $8 minimum." Buys all rights.

TALICOR, INC., 190 Arovista Circle, Brea CA 92621. (714)993-9800. President: Lew Herndon. Estab. 1971. Manufacturer and distributor of educational and entertainment games and toys. Clients: chain toy stores, department stores, specialty stores and Christian bookstores.

Needs: Works with 4-6 freelance illustrators and 4-6 freelance designers/year. Prefers local artists. Works on assignment only. Mainly uses artists for game design. Also uses artists for advertising, brochure and catalog design, illustration and layout; product design; illustration on product; P-O-P displays; posters and magazine design.
First Contact & Terms: Send query letter with brochure. Samples are not filed and are returned only if requested. Reports back only if interested. Call or write to schedule an appointment to show a portfolio. Pays for design and illustration by the project, $100-5,000. Negotiates rights purchased.

TEACH YOURSELF BY COMPUTER SOFTWARE, INC., Suite 1000, 349 W. Commercial St., East Rochester NY 14445. (716)381-5450. President: Lois B. Bennett. Estab. 1978. Publisher of educational software for microcomputers. Clients: schools, individuals, stores.
Needs: Approached by 10 freelance artists/year. Works with 2 freelance illustrators and 2 freelance designers/year. Local artists only. Works on assignment only. Uses artists for advertising, brochure and catalog design, illustration and layout; and illustration on product.
First Contact & Terms: Send query letter with brochure, resume, photostats, photographs, photocopies, slides or tearsheets to be kept on file. Samples not filed are returned by SASE. Reports back within 6 weeks. Write for appointment to show a portfolio, which should include roughs, photostats and photographs. Pays for design and illustration by the hour. Considers complexity of project, skill and experience of artist, how work will be used, turnaround time, and rights purchased when establishing payment. Buys all rights.
Tips: "I like to see a variety of work to see their dimensions. Let your work speak for itself—don't talk too much during a review."

THOG CORPORATION, Box 424, Tallmadge OH 44278. Sales Manager: Don Martin. Provides equipment for the graphic arts industry.
Needs: Approached by 6 freelance artists/year. Works with 2-3 freelance artists/year. Uses freelance artists for advertising, brochure and catalog design, illustration and layout; and product design.
First Contact & Terms: Send query letter. Samples are filed. Reports back only if interested. Write to schedule an appointment to show a portfolio, which should include roughs and photostats. Pays for design and illustration by the project, $25 minimum. Considers complexity of project, client's budget, and rights purchased when establishing payment. Buys all rights.
Tips: "We use a lot of custom line art."

TRIBORO QUILT MFG. CORP., 172 S. Broadway, White Plains NY 10605. (914)428-7551. Sales Manager: Alvin Kaplan. Produces infants' wear and bedding under the Triboro label; for chain and department stores.
Needs: Works with freelance artists for infants' and childrens' embroidery and fabric designs.
First Contact & Terms: Call for interview or provide resume, business card and brochure to be kept on file. Reports in 1 week. Samples returned by SASE; reports back on future assignment possibilities.

*PHILIP TUSA DESIGN INC., Box 14, Roosevelt Island Station, New York NY 10044. (212)753-2810. President: Philip M. Tusa. Specializes in interior design. Clients: commercial firms, corporations and residential customers.
Needs: Works on assignment only. Uses artists for illustration, model making, interior rendering and drafting.
First Contact & Terms: Send query letter with resume, tearsheets, photostats, photocopies, slides and photographs. Reports back only if interested. Call to schedule an appointment to show a portfolio, which should include thumbnails, roughs, original/final art, final reproduction/product and b&w and color tearsheets, photostats and photographs. Pays for illustration by the hour, $10 minimum; by the project, $100 minimum.
Tips: "The need for 'low overhead' prompts small companies to increase the use of freelance work. Keep in touch!"

UNIFORMS MANUFACTURING INC., Box 5336, W. Bloomfield MI 48033. (313)332-2700 or (800)222-1474. President: L.P. Tucker. Manufacturer of all types of wearing apparel—smocks, lab coats, shirts, trousers, coveralls, dresses, aprons, cotton gloves, polyester and knits; Uniform label. Catalog available on request.
Needs: Works with 3 freelance artists/year. Works on assignment only. Uses artists for advertising, brochure and catalog design; advertising illustration and direct mail promotions.
First Contact & Terms: Send brochure/flyer and slides as samples. Samples returned by SASE. Reports back as soon as possible. Negotiates payment.

*V.M. DESIGNS, INC., 217 S Front St., Burbank CA 91502. (818)840-9011. FAX: (818)840-8637. President: Dennis Buckley. Estab. 1980. Manufacturer of custom decoratives for retail stores. Current clients include major national and regional department and specialty stores.
Needs: Approached by 6-8 freelance artists/year. Works with 3 freelance illustrators and 2 freelance designers/year. Wants dependable quality work. Uses freelance artists mainly for product development. Also uses freelance artists for product rendering and design and model making. Send query letter with photographs

and photocopies. Samples are filed. Reports back in 1 month. Call to schedule an appointment to show a portfolio, which should include thumbnails, roughs and photographs. Pays for design and illustration by the project, a percentage of sale. Buys all rights.

VISUAL AID/VISAID MARKETING, Box 4502, Inglewood CA 90309. (213)473-0286. Manager: Lee Clapp. Estab. 1961. Distributes sales promotion aids, marketing consultant service, – involved in all phases. Clients: manufacturers, distributors, publishers and graphics firms (printing and promotion) in 23 SIC code areas.
Needs: Approached by 12-15 freelance artists/year. Works with 3-5 freelance artists/year. Assigns 4 jobs to freelance artists/year. Uses artists mainly for printing ads. Also uses artists for advertising, brochure and catalog design, illustration and layout; product design; illustration on product; P-O-P display; display fixture design and posters. Buys some cartoons and humorous and cartoon-style illustrations. Additional media: fiber optics, display/signage, design/fabrication.
First Contact & Terms: Works on assignment only. Send query letter with brochure, resume, business card, photostats, duplicate photographs, photocopies and tearsheets to be kept on file. Originals returned by SASE. Reports back within 2 weeks. Write for appointment to show a portfolio. Pays for design by the hour, $5-75. Pays for illustration by the project, $100-500. Considers complexity of project, skill and experience of artist and turnaround time when establishing payment.
Tips: "Do not say 'I can do anything.' We want to know best media you work in (pen & ink, line drawing, illustration, layout, etc.)."

*VISUAL CONCEPTS, 5410 Connecticut Ave., Washington DC 20015. (202)362-1521. Owner: John Jacobin. Estab. 1984. Service-related firm. Specializes in visual presentation, mostly for retail stores. Clients: retail and interior stores for residential and commercial spaces. Current clients include: Up Against the Wall and In Detail.
Needs: Approached by 5-10 freelance artists/year. Works with 3 freelance designers/year. Assigns 10-20 freelance artists/year. Prefers local artists with experience in visual merchandising and 3-D art. Works on assignment only. Uses freelance artists mainly for design and installation. Prefers contemporary or any classic styles. Also uses freelance artists for advertising design and layout, brochure and catalog illustration, signage and P-O-P displays.
First Contact & Terms: Contact through artist rep or send query letter with brochure showing art style or resume and samples. Samples are filed. Reports in 2 weeks. Call to schedule an appointment to show a portfolio, which should include thumbnails, roughs and color photographs or slides. Pays for design by the hour, $6.50-15 and up. Rights purchased vary according to project.

*VOGUE PATTERNS, 161 Sixth Ave., New York NY 10013. (212)620-2733. Associate Art Director: Christine Lipert. Manufacturer of clothing and knitting patterns with the Vogue labels.
Needs: Approached by 50 freelance artists/year. Works with 10-20 freelance illustrators and 1-5 freelance designers/year. Assigns 18 magazine illustration jobs and 100-150 catalog illustration jobs to freelance artists/year. "Artists must be proficient in fashion illustration." Uses freelance artists mainly for catalog illustration for *Vogue Patterns* catalog book, *Vogue Magazine* and *Vogue Knitting* magazine. "The nature of catalog illustration is specialized; every button, every piece of top-stitching has to be accurately represented. Editorial illustration should have a looser, editorial style. We are open to all media and styles."
First Contact & Terms: Send query letter with resume, tearsheets, slides and photographs. Samples not filed are returned by SASE. Reports back within one month. Call or write to schedule an appointment to show a portfolio, which should include original/final art, final reproduction/product, and color tearsheets. Pays by the project. Considers complexity of the project and turnaround time when establishing payment.
Tips: "Drop off comprehensive portfolio or send a current business card and sample. When a job becomes available, we will call illustrator to view portfolio again."

WRIGHT'S KNITWEAR CORP., 34 W. 33 St., New York NY 10001. (212)239-0808. Merchandise Manager: Robert Shields. Estab. 1850. Manufacturer and mill for print T-shirts, sweats and tanks for ages 4-7 and 8-18, young men's and juniors. Labels: Exit, Nowayout and Private Label.
Needs: Works with 12 freelance artists/year. Uses freelance artists mainly for screen print graphics.
First Contact & Terms: Send query letter with brochure, tearsheets, photostats and photocopies. Reports back within 4 weeks only if interested. Call to schedule an appointment to show a portfolio. Pays for design and illustration by the project. Considers complexity of project when establishing payment. Buys all rights.

YORK DISPLAY FINISHING CO., INC., 240 Kent Ave., Brooklyn NY 11211. (718)782-0710. President: Stanley Singer. Manufacturer and display firm providing P-O-P advertising displays in vacuum-formed plastic, corrugated cardboard and paper. Clients: display agencies, printers, artists, etc.

Needs: Works with 2 freelance artists/year. New York City metro area artists, thoroughly experienced in P-O-P design only. Uses artists for P-O-P design and model making.
First Contact & Terms: Send query letter with resume or business card to be kept on file. Reports in 3 weeks. Samples returned by SASE. Pays by the project, $100-1,500 average.

Other Businesses

The following businesses appeared in the 1990 edition of *Artist's Market* but are not in the 1991 edition. Those which did not respond to our request for an update of their listings may have done so for a variety of reasons—they may be out of business for example, or they may be overstocked with submissions. If they indicated a reason, it is noted in parentheses after the name.

Abbey Associates-Landscape Architects
All-State Legal Supply Co.
Ampaco Inc.
Art Stone Theatrical
Astro-Mechanical Dogs & Tricks
Automatic Mail Services, Inc.
Axion Design
Balloon Arts, Inc.
The Balloon Factory (asked to be deleted)
Barthelmess Inc. USA (asked to be deleted)
Bradmill U.S.A. Ltd.
Cenit Letters, Inc.
Childcraft Education Corp.
Christopher Enterprises
Clasyk Graphics & Design (asked to be deleted)
Cosrich, Inc. (asked to be deleted)
Crown Parian Ltd. (asked to be deleted)
Darien Raithel & Associates
Day Dream Publishing
Design Look, Inc.

Discoveries Inc.
Displayco (needs have changed)
Exhibit Builders Inc.
Fantasee Lighting
First Impressions (asked to be deleted)
General Motors Corp.
Giftco, Inc. (asked to be deleted)
Grandview Sportswear
Incolay Studios Inc.
King Kole International
KDI
Klingspor Abrasives, Inc.
Klitzner Ind., Inc.
Kraftbilt
Lillian Vernon Corp.
Loon Mountain Recreation Corp.
Meyer Scherer and Rockcastle, Ltd.
National Pen Corp (no longer uses freelance artwork)
P.O.P. Displays, Inc. (asked to be deleted)
Palmloom Co. (asked to be

deleted)
Perfect Pen and Stationery Co. Ltd.
Philadelphia T-Shirt Museum
Pickhardt & Siebert USA
Precision Graphic Services Inc. (asked to be deleted)
Quality Artworks, Inc.
S. Rosenthal & Co. Inc.
Royal Copenhagen Inc.
Royal Lace, Division of Mafcote Industries
The Social Secretary (asked to be deleted)
Sportsminded Inc.
Springboard Software, Inc.
Squeegee Printers
Transamerica Life Companies
Triboro Quilt Mfg. Corp.
Uarco, Inc.
UMSI Incorporated
Vermont T's
Vid America
Windsor Art Products, Inc.
Woodmere China Inc.

Galleries

The relationship between an artist and a gallery is mutually beneficial. A gallery provides space for you to exhibit your work to the public, and when it shows and sells your work, it allows you to devote more time to your art. Without artists, galleries wouldn't be in business. Ideally, the exhibition of your work should prove profitable to both you and the gallery.

If you have developed your own recognizable style and have established a reputation in your area through shows at a university or fairs, you may be ready to begin your search for a gallery. Although exhibiting in a far away city may seem more prestigious, you should begin your search close to home. After all, it is the area where you've developed your reputation and a gallery director may already be familiar with your work. It's also easier to keep an eye on sales and to replace works that have sold. Later, when you are more firmly established in your career, you can extend your range and work with galleries outside your area. You will find they are more willing to work with an artist who is a seasoned professional.

Finding the right gallery

One of your first considerations should be whether a gallery is right for you and your work. If this is your first approach to a gallery, you may find cooperative galleries more open to your work. An artist becomes a member of a cooperative by submitting an application with slides of finished work; the work is juried by a committee of cooperative members. If accepted, the artist may exhibit work in exchange for a fee and a commitment to spend time on such tasks as gallery sitting, housekeeping and maintenance. Some cooperatives take small commissions (20 to 30 percent); others do not charge a commission. When considering a cooperative gallery, decide if you can afford to take time away from your work to fulfill your obligation to the cooperative and whether you are comfortable knowing your work will not be sold by professional salespeople. Sales duties here will be handled by the cooperative members—your fellow artists. Another option is a nonprofit gallery. Read this section's Close-up on Connie Butler, curator of Artists Space, for information on this type of gallery.

There are a growing number of cafes, restaurants and bars, which display the work of local artists. Because these seem like good starting points for an artist desiring to have her work seen, a few such places have been included in the listings this year, such as the Rockridge Cafe in Oakland, California and the Virginia Inn in Seattle. Also, owners of office buildings are increasingly showing an interest in exhibiting artwork in their lobbies. One Manhattan property owner was quoted in *The New York Times* as saying, "Thousands of people come into the building everyday and I wanted them to be able to walk through the lobby and enjoy art. The tenants like it and take a great deal of interest in what's there and what's coming next." He said it was simply good business to demonstrate that a developer could take the time to do something that might please the public. Perhaps you know of such a cafe, restaurant or developer in your area.

In a retail gallery, your work is handled by a professional sales staff—*selling* the work is the gallery's major concern. Your work will either be bought outright or handled on consignment. The benefits to you include knowing your work is being marketed aggressively and being able to devote your full attention to the creative, not the selling side, of your art. In exchange for selling, promoting and publicizing your work, the gallery receives a commission of 40 to 60 percent. If your work sells for $2,500 and the gallery receives a 50 percent commission, you will both receive $1,250 for the sale.

Also, many museums sell work through their own shops, and they often "rent" work for a specified amount of time. You may also wish to consider establishing your own temporary gallery, if you enjoy selling and marketing your work. Some malls will arrange temporary leases of empty store space at a reduced price, but a new long-term tenant can displace you. If this sounds like an approach you would be interested in, check with a mall manager in your area. When considering any kind of gallery space for your work, avoid vanity or subsidy galleries where you pay not only for exhibition space, but for promotion as well.

After you have decided which type of gallery will best suit your needs, do some research to narrow your search to a few galleries in your area. Talk to other artists to see what information they have about galleries. Visit the galleries as though you were a customer and investigate the following aspects:

● How long has the gallery been in business? A newer gallery may be more open to artists, but not as stable financially as a more established gallery.

● Does the gallery feature emerging artists? Ask how many group shows the gallery presents annually – the more group shows, the more artists (including new artists) the gallery works with.

● What are the gallery's hours? A few hours of exhibition time on weekends won't get your work the attention it deserves. In tourist towns, the gallery may be open only during specific seasons.

● Does the gallery have a specialty? If the work featured is not anything like your work in style or subject matter, don't assume it's because no one has submitted similar work. The gallery probably limits the kinds of work it will consider.

● What is the gallery's price range? Do you think it's so high it will discourage the kinds of customers you see buying your work?

● How knowledgeable is the sales staff? If they can answer your questions about other artists' works, your work will probably receive the same kind of attention.

Approaching the gallery

After you select the galleries that interest you, call each gallery director (address him by name, not title) and ask for an appointment to show your work. Never bring a portfolio into a gallery without an appointment. If the gallery isn't reviewing new work, ask if you can send a brochure or sample to be kept on file. If you get an interview, plan your presentation to fit the particular gallery. Bring 15 to 20 professional transparencies or duplicate slides, your leave-behinds (a current brochure, resume, artist's statement and business card) and two or three originals. If you work in several media, show an original in each category, backed up by slides of other works in that media. Choose works appropriate to the gallery and don't drag along everything you have ever done. You will risk confusing and boring the gallery director, and you will have to transport all that work to and from the gallery.

Setting terms

A presentation does not guarantee a gallery will agree to handle your work. Don't be discouraged by a rejection – there are more galleries. Even more importantly, don't be so swept away by an acceptance that you have your work on display before you fully understand the obligations and responsibilities involved. You should know the answers to these questions before agreeing on representation:

● Will your work be sold on consignment? If so, what is the gallery's commission?

● How long will the agreement last? To a new artist, a lifetime deal might sound fantastic – but you will have second thoughts when your career begins to grow.

● What is the extent of the gallery's representation? Is it exclusive? If so, in what area—within 100 miles or in the entire state? Are works sold from your studio included in the agreement?

● Who pays for promotion, insurance and shipping? Generally, the gallery pays for promotional costs and inhouse insurance; shipping costs are often shared.

● Will the gallery provide names and addresses of people who buy your work so you can stay in touch with them? One sale could lead to another. The gallery owner may want to keep this information for himself. If so, ask that names of past buyers be provided; allow the names of prospective buyers to be kept confidential.

● Does the gallery set the retail price, or do you? Often, it's a compromise, but you should be consulted.

● How much publicity will the gallery provide? The more the gallery publicizes your work or show, the better your sales will be, and the more your reputation will grow. Be sure your show will be covered in press releases, and that you know how much display time your work will receive.

● Are statements of account provided on a regular basis? If not, how will you know if the gallery is selling your work, and how much it owes you?

● What happens if the gallery folds? You are guaranteed the return of your artwork under the Uniform Commercial Code, but make sure your agreement acknowledges this.

● Will you be able to remove your work during the run of your contract? You might want to enter some of your pieces in a juried show or need to take a piece down to photograph it. Be sure you clarify this point with the gallery director before you sign the contract.

When setting terms, be sure to bring along your own agreement in case the gallery doesn't provide a contract. (North Light Books' *The Artist's Friendly Legal Guide* includes contracts and agreements you can use.) Be sure you have a signed receipt before you leave any work. Before you make a commitment, clear up all the details. All verbal agreements should be confirmed in writing.

Broadening your scope

Because many galleries require they be the exclusive purveyor of an artist within a certain area, once you have had a local gallery show, you are ready to broaden your scope by querying other galleries, first within the same region, then farther away. To develop a sense of which galleries are right for you, look to the myriad of art publications which contain reviews and advertising (the pictures that accompany a gallery's ad can be very illuminating). A few such publications are *ARTnews, Art in America, The New Art Examiner* and regional publications such as *Artweek* (west coast), *Southwest Art, Artpaper* (based in Minneapolis) and *Art New England*. To find out more about what art magazines cover your area of interest, call the library in that city and if they don't know, they'll direct you to someone who does. The most complete list of galleries (though it lacks marketing information) is found in *Art in America's Guide to Galleries, Museums and Artists*. Other directories include *Art Now, U.S.A.'s National Art Museum and Gallery Guide, The Artist's Guide to Philadelphia Galleries*, and *Washington Art*.

The sample package you send to these galleries will contain the same types of material as before, but it should emphasize your successful shows and sales record. Be sure your slides are of high quality—the lighting should be even, with no glare; the piece should be centered; the colors should be accurate; and the forms should be perfect. So you have room to label them clearly and neatly, make sure they're set in plain mounts. Label each one with the title of the piece, its size, the medium, your name plus copyright symbol, the date, and an arrow indicating the top of the slide. Be sure you update your file to include your most recent work.

Also refer to "Getting a Gallery's Attention" in the September, October, and November

1988 issues of *The Artist's Magazine*. This information is not dated and is very helpful.

Alabama

FINE ARTS MUSEUM OF THE SOUTH, Box 8426, Mobile AL 36689. (205)343-2667. Assistant Director: David McCann. Clientele: tourists and general public. Sponsors 6 solo and 12 group shows/year. Average display time 6-8 weeks. Interested in emerging, mid-career and established artists. Overall price range: $100-5,000; most artwork sold at $100-500.
Media: Considers all media and all types of print.
Style: Exhibits all styles and genres. "We are a general fine arts museum seeking a variety of style, media and time periods." Looking for "historical significance."
Terms: Accepts work on consignment (20% commission). Retail price set by artist. Exclusive area representation not required. Gallery provides insurance, promotion, contract; shipping costs are shared. Prefers framed artwork.
Submissions: Send query letter with resume, brochure, business card, slides, photographs, bio and SASE. Write to schedule an appointment to show a portfolio, which should include slides, transparencies and photographs. Replies only if interested within 3 months. Files resumes and slides. All material is returned with SASE if not accepted or under consideration.
Tips: As trend sees "regional centers becoming more and more viable."

GADSDEN MUSEUM OF ARTS, 2829 W. Meighan Blvd., Gadsden AL 35904. (205)546-7365. Director: Sherrie Hamil. Museum. Estab. 1965. Clientele: students, adults, and tourists. Sponsors 5 solo and 6 group show/year. Average display time 4 weeks. Interested in emerging and established artists. Overall price range: $50-5,000.
Media: Considers all media. Most frequently exhibits watercolor, oil and photography.
Style: Exhibits impressionism, realism, primitivism, painterly abstraction and conceptualism. Considers all genres. Prefers landscapes, wildlife and portraits. "The Gadsden Museum of Arts displays its permanent collection of artwork (paintings, prints, sculptures and historical memorabilia) and exhibits monthly showings of art groups and individual artists works."
Terms: Accepts work on consignment (30% commission). Retail price set by gallery and artist. Gallery provides insurance, promotion and contract; artist pays for shipping. Prefers framed artwork.
Submissions: Send query letter with resume, slides, photographs and bio. Write to schedule an appointment to show a portfolio, which should include slides. Replies in 1 month. All material is returned if not accepted under consideration.

*DORIS WAINWRIGHT KENNEDY ART CENTER GALLERY, 900 Arkadelphia Rd., Birmingham AL 35254. (205)226-4928. Assistant Professor of Art: Steve Cole. College art gallery (Birmingham Southern College). Estab. 1965. Represents emerging and mid-career artists. Sponsors 8 shows/year. Average display time 3 weeks. Open September through May. Located in center of campus; 1484 sq ft.; 149 linear feet running wall space. 100% of space for special exhibitions. Clientele: 100% private collectors. Overall price range: $50-3,700; most artwork sold at $400-1,000.
Media: Considers original handpulled prints, woodcuts, wood engravings, linocuts, engravings, mezzotints, etchings, lithographs and serigraphs. Most frequently exhibits drawings, sculpture and paintings.
Style: Exhibits all styles. Genres include all genres.
Terms: "This gallery exists for the benefit of our students and the community. There is no commission on work(s) sold." Gallery provides insurance and promotion; artist pays for shipping. Prefers framed artwork.
Submissions: Send resume, slides and SASE. Replies in 1 month. Files resume.

Alaska

STONINGTON GALLERY, 415 F Street, in the Old City Hall, Anchorage AK 99501. (907)272-1489. Manager: Jane Purinton. Retail gallery. Estab. 1984. Clientele: 60% private collectors, 40% corporate clients. Represents 50 artists. Sponsors 9 solo and 15 group shows/year. Average display time 3 weeks. Interested in

The asterisk before a listing indicates that the listing is new in this edition. New markets are often the most receptive to freelance submissions.

emerging, mid-career and established artists. Overall price range: $100-5,000; most work sold at $500-1,000.

Media: Considers oil, acrylic, watercolor, pastel, mixed media, collage, works on paper, sculpture, ceramic, craft, fiber, glass and all original handpulled prints. Most frequently exhibited media: oil, mixed media and all types of craft.

Style: Exhibits all styles. "We do not want the Americana, Southwestern, Western and wild, but we have no pre-conceived notions as to what an artist should produce." Prefers landscapes, florals and figurative works. The Stonington Gallery specializes in original works by artists from Alaska and the Pacific Northwest. In addition, we are the only source of high-quality crafts in the state of Alaska. We continue to generate a high percentage of our sales from jewelry and ceramics, small wood boxes and bowls and paper/fiber pieces. Patrons tend to require that metal, clay and wood items be functional, but not so for paper/fiber or mixed media works."

Terms: Accepts work on consignment (40% commission). Retail price set by artist. Exclusive area representation required. Gallery provides insurance, promotion, contract and shipping costs from gallery. Prefers framed artwork.

Submissions: Send letter of introduction with resume, slides, bio and SASE. Write to schedule an appointment to show a portfolio, which should include slides. All material is returned if not accepted or under consideration.

Arizona

SUZANNE BROWN GALLERY, 7160 Main St., Scottsdale AZ 85251. (602)945-8475. Director: Ms. Lee Brotherton. Retail gallery and art consultancy. Estab. 1962. Located in downtown Scottsdale. "Recently opened a second gallery, specializing in contemporary American Art." Clientele: valley collectors, tourists, international visitors; 70% private collectors; 30% corporate clients. Represents 60 artists. Sponsors 3 solo and 2 group show/year. Average display time 4 weeks. Interested in emerging and established artists. Overall price range: $500-20,000; most work sold at $1,000-10,000.

Media: Considers oil, acrylic, watercolor, pastel, drawings, mixed media, collage, sculpture, ceramic, craft, fiber, glass, lithographs, monoprints and serigraphs. Most frequently exhibits oil, acrylic and watercolor.

Style: Exhibits realism, painterly abstration and post modern works; will consider all styles. Genres include landscapes, florals, Southwestern and Western (contemporary) themes. Prefers contemporary Western, Southwestern and contemporary realism. "Contemporary American Art, specializing in art of the New West. Suzanne Brown Gallery and Suzanne Brown Contemporary exhibit realistic and abstract paintings, drawings and sculpture by American artists. Some of these regionally and nationally acclaimed artists are Veloy Vigil, Ed Mell and Patrick Coffaro."

Terms: Accepts work on consignment. Retail price set by gallery and artist. Exclusive area representation required. Gallery provides insurance promotion, contract and shipping costs from gallery. Prefers framed artwork.

Submissions: Send query letter with resume, brochure, slides, photographs, bio and SASE. Replies in 2 weeks. All material is returned if not accepted or under consideration.

Tips: "We only accept slides (no appointments are made), resume and any other visuals that artists which to send. Please enclose SASE. Include a complete slide identification list, including availability of works and prices."

EL PRADO GALLERIES, INC., Tlaquepaque Village, Box 1849, Sedona AZ 86336. (602)282-7390. President: Don H. Pierson. Retail galleries. Estab. 1976. Represents 98 emerging, mid-career and established artists. Exhibited artists include Keith Lindberg, John Cogan. Sponsors 7 shows/year. Average display time 1 week. Open all year. One gallery located in Santa Fe, NM; 3 galleries are in Sedonas Tlaquepaque Village: 10,000 sq. ft. "Each gallery is different in lighting, grouping of art and variety. 95% private collectors, 5% corporate collectors. Accepts artists from all regions. Overall price range: $75-125,000.

Media: Considers oil, acrylic, watercolor, pastel, mixed media, collage, works on paper, sculpture, ceramic, craft, fiber and glass. Considers offset reproductions, woodcuts, engravings, lithographs, wood engravings, mezzotints, serigraphs, linocuts and etchings. Most frequently exhibits oil, acrylic and watercolor.

Style: Exhibits all styles and genres.. Prefers landscapes, Southwestern and Western. Does not want to see avant-garde.

Terms: Accepts work on consignment (45% commission). Retail price set by the gallery and the artist. Gallery provides insurance, promotion; gallery and artist pay for shipping. Prefers unframed work.

Submissions: Send query letter with photographs. Call or write to schedule an appointment to show a portfolio, which should include photographs. Replies in 3 weeks. Files material only if interested.

Tips: "The artist must show original work, not photocopies unless they show photos; must send SASE."

EL PRESIDIO GALLERY, 120 N. Main Ave., Tucson AZ 85701. (602)884-7379. Director: Henry Rentschler. Retail gallery. Estab. 1981. "Located in historic adobe building with 14' ceilings next to the Tucson Museum of Art." Clientele: locals and tourists, 70% private collectors 30% corporate clients. Represents 20 artists. Sponsors 3 solo and 4 group shows/year. Average display time 2 months. Accepts artists from mostly the West and Southwest. Interested in emerging and established artists. Overall price range: $500-20,000; most artwork sold at $1,000-5,000.

Media: Considers oil, acrylic, watercolor, mixed media, works on paper, sculpture, ceramic, glass, egg tempera and original handpulled prints. Most frequently exhibited media: oil, watercolor and acrylic.

Style: Exhibits impressionism, expressionism, realism, photorealism and painterly abstraction. Genres include landscapes, Southwestern, Western, wildlife and figurative work. Prefers realism, representational works and abstraction (mostly representational abstracts).

Terms: Accepts work on consignment (50% commission). Retail price set by gallery and artist. Exclusive area representation required. Gallery provides insurance, promotion and contract; artist pays for shipping. Prefers framed artwork.

Submissions: Send query letter with resume, brochure, slides, photographs, bio and SASE. Call or write to schedule an appointment to show a portfolio, which should include originals, slides, transparencies and photographs. Replies in 2 weeks.

Tips: "Have a professional attitude. Be willing to spend money on good frames."

ELEVEN EAST ASHLAND I.A.S., 11 E. Ashland, Phoenix AZ 85004. (602)271-0831. Director: David Cook. Estab. 1986. Located in an old farm house. Sponsors 13 solo and mixed group shows/year. Average display time 3 weeks. Interested in emerging, mid-career and established artists. Overall price range: $100-5,000; most artwork sold at $100-800.

Media: Considers all media. Most frequently exhibits photography, painting, mixed media and sculpture.

Style: Exhibits all styles, preferably contemporary. "This is a proposal exhibition space open to all artists excluding Western and Southwest styles (unless contemporary style); not traditional."

Terms: Accepts work on consignment (25% commission); rental fee for space; rental fee covers 1 month. Retail price set by artist. Exclusive area representation not required. Artist pays for shipping.

Submissions: Accepts proposal to schedule shows 6 months at a time. Send query letter with resume, brochure, business card, slides, photographs, bio and SASE. Call or write to schedule an appointment to show a portfolio, which should include slides and photographs. Replies only if interested within 1 month. Files all material. All material is returned if not accepted or under consideration. Deadline: end of November for shows 1/91-6/91.

*ETHERTON/STERN GALLERY, 135 S. 6th Ave., Tucson AZ 85701. (602)624-7370. FAX: (602)792-4569. Contact: Terry Etherton, Michael Stern or Sharon Alexandra.

Profile: Retail gallery and art consultancy. Estab. 1981. Located "downtown; 3,000 sq. ft.; in historic building—wood floors, 16' ceilings." Represents 50+ emerging, mid-career and established artists. Exhibited artists include Holly Roberts, Fritz Scholder, James G. Davis and Mark Klett. Sponsors 7 shows/year. Average display time 5 weeks. Open from September to June. 75% of space for special exhibitions; 10% of space for gallery artists. Clientele: 50% private collectors, 25% corporate collectors, 25% museums. Overall price range: $100-50,000; most work sold at $500-2,000.

Media: Considers oil, acrylic, drawing, mixed media, collage, sculpture, ceramic, all types of photography, original handpulled prints, woodcuts, wood engravings, linocuts, engravings, mezzotints, etchings and lithographs. Most frequently exhibits photography, painting and sculpture.

Style: Exhibits expressionism, neo-expressionism, primitivism, post modern works. Genres include landscapes, portraits and figurative work. Prefers expressionism, primitive/folk and post-modern.

Terms: Accepts work on consignment (50% commission). Buys outright for 50% of retail price (net 30 days). Retail price set by gallery and artist. Gallery provides insurance and promotion; shipping costs are shared. Prefers framed artwork.

Submissions: Only "cutting edge" contemporary—no decorator art. Send resume, brochure, slides, photographs, reviews, bio and SASE. Call or write to schedule an appointment to show a portfolio, which should include slides. Replies in 6 weeks only if interested. Files slides, resumes and reviews.

Tips: "Become familiar with the style of our gallery and with contemporary art scene in general."

*GALERIA MESA, 155 N. Center, Box 1466, Mesa AZ 85211-1466. (602)644-2242. Gallery Curator: Jeffory Morris. Owned and operated by the City of Mesa. Estab. 1981. Represents emerging, mid-career and established artists. "5-8 exhibits are national juried exhibitions. Artists vary with every exhibit. Other exhibits are rented or locally curated." Sponsors 9 shows/year. Average display time 1 month. Open September through July. Located downtown; 1,300 sq. ft., "wood floors, 14' ceilings and monitored security." 100% of space for special exhibitions. Clientele: "cross section of Phoenix metropolitan area." 95% private collectors, 5% corporate collectors. "Artists selected only through national juried exhibitions." Overall price range: $20-10,000; most artwork sold at $200-2,500.

" 'Reliquary for Childhood Dreams' is a contemporary piece that is very well-executed and makes reference to the artist's personal life," says Terry Etherton, director of Etherton/Stern Gallery in Tuscon, Arizona. Artist Randy Spalding created the polychromed wood and metal piece as part of a series in a three-person show.

Media: Considers all media. Considers original handpulled prints, woodcuts, engravings, lithographs, wood engravings, mezzotints, monotypes, serigraphs, linocuts and etchings. No media preference.
Style: Exhibits all styles. No genre preferred.
Terms: Artwork is not accepted on consignment. There is a 25% commission. Retail price set by the artist. Gallery provides promotion and pays for shipping costs from gallery if using UPS. Artist pays for shipping to the gallery and return if not using UPS. Requires framed artwork.
Submissions: Send a query letter with a request for a prospectus. "We do not offer a portfolio review. Artwork is selected through national juried exhibitions. Slide entry only." Replies in two months. Files artist statement and resume.
Tips: "Artists are encouraged to write or call for current exhibition prospectuses." Sees trend toward "greater conservatism."

*HUSBERG FINE ARTS GALLERY, Suite 1, 7133 E. Stetson Dr., Scottsdale AZ 85251. (602)947-7489. Owner: Allan Husberg. Retail gallery. Estab. 1969. Represents 46 artists; emerging, mid-career and established. Exhibited artists include Frank McCarthy and Arnold Friberg. Sponsors 4 shows/year. Average display time 3 months. Open all year. Located downtown; 4,000 sq. ft.; "relaxed comfortable atmosphere with rough-sawn pine walls." Clientele: collectors from all over U.S. 98% private collectors. "We represent artists exclusively for Arizona." Overall price range: $500-95,000; most artwork sold at $5,000.
Media: Considers oil, watercolor, pastel and sculpture. Most frequently exhibits oil, watercolor and sculpture.
Style: Exhibits impressionism, realism and photorealism. Genres include landscapes, florals, Americana, Southwestern, Western, wildlife and figurative work. Prefers Western, landscapes and figurative.
Terms: Accepts work on consignment (40% commission). Retail price set by the artist. Gallery provides varied services; shipping costs from gallery.
Submissions: Send query letter with slides, bio, brochure, photographs and SASE. Call to schedule an appointment to show a portfolio, which should include slides and photographs. Replies in 2 weeks. Files letters and bios.
Tips: "If visiting in person, have slides or photos, and an original or two if possible." Feels that "the art-buying public is more aware of "quality" than ever before. They are more frugal than in past years and more discriminating."

*SUE MALINSKI GALLERY, Suite 203, 16901 Village Dr. W., Surprise AZ 85374; and 6423 N. 51st Pl., Paradise Valley AZ 85253. (602)840-0412 and (602)583-0701. Owner: Sue Malinski. Retail and wholesale gallery. Estab. 1982. Represents 8 artists; mid-career and established. Interested in seeing the work of emerging artists. Exhibited artists include Paul Kuo and Margaretha. Sponsors 2 shows/year. Average display time 3 months. Open all year. Located in the mall (Surprise) and a home gallery (Paradise Valley); 1,600 sq. ft. (Surprise) and 1,800 sq. ft (Paradise Valley); "Southwest adobe walls." Clientele: "tourists and professionals." 60% private collectors, 2% corporate collectors. Overall price range: $50-4,500; most work sold at $150-350.

Media: Considers oil, acrylic, watercolor, pastel, works on paper, woodcuts, engravings, lithographs, posters and serigraph. Most frequently exhibits watercolor, pastel and works on paper.

Style: Exhibits conceptualism, impressionism and realism. Genres include landscapes, florals and Southwestern. Prefers Southwest, oriental and florals.

Terms: Accepts work on consignment (50% commission). Buys outright for 50% of retail price (net 30 days). Retail price set by the gallery and the artist. Gallery provides promotion. Artist pays for shipping or shipping costs are shared. Prefers framed artwork.

Submissions: Send query letter with brochure, business card, slides, photographs, reviews and bio. Call to schedule an appointment to show a portfolio, which should include photographs. Replies in 3-4 weeks. Files all material.

Tips: Artists should have "a few years of sales behind them, such as mall or area shows."

*MARY PEACHIN'S ART COMPANY, 3955 E. Speedway, Tucson AZ 85712. (602)881-1311. Retail gallery, wholesale gallery and art consultancy. Estab. 1979. Represents "hundreds" of emerging artists. Exhibited artists include Coffaro, Larry Fodor and Jack Eggman. Open all year. "Two galleries, one in midtown, one in Oro Valley; 3,500 sq. ft. 90% of space for gallery artists. Clientele: 50% private collectors, 50% corporate collectors. Overall price range: $25-2,000; most artwork sold at $100-900.

Media: Considers oil, acrylic, watercolor, pastel, mixed media, collage, works on paper, sculpture, ceramic, fiber, glass, engravings, etchings, lithographs, serigraphs, posters and offset reproductions. Most frequently exhibits monoprints, lithographs and reproductions.

Style: Exhibits painterly abstraction, impressionism, hard-edge geometric abstraction and all styles. Genres include landscapes, florals, Southwestern, Western, figurative work and all genres. Prefers landscapes, figurative work and abstraction.

Terms: Accepts work on consignment (50% commission). Buys outright for 50% of retail price (net 30 days). Retail price set by gallery and artist. Gallery provides insurance and promotion; artist pays for shipping. Prefers framed artwork.

Submissions: Send resume, slides, bio, photographs and SASE. Call to schedule an appointment to show portfolio, which should include photographs. Replies in 1 week; follow up with call. Files all material.

*JOANNE RAPP GALLERY/THE HAND AND THE SPIRIT, 4222 North Marshall Way, Scottsdale AZ 85251. (602)949-1262. Owner/Director: Joanne Rapp. Retail gallery. Represents 200 artists/year; emerging and established. Exhibited artists include Edward Moulthrop, Peter Shire, Johathon Bonner and Ann Keister. Sponsors 15 shows/year. Average display time 1 month. Open all year. Located downtown; 2,800 sq. ft.; "clean and contemporary." 80% of space for special exhibitions. Overall price range: $100-up.

Media: Considers mixed media, works on paper, fiber, glass, wood and metal. Most frequently exhibits wearable art, wood, fiber and clay.

Style: Exhibits contemporary craft.

Terms: Accepts work on consignment. Retail price set by the artist. Gallery provides promotion and contract. Shipping costs are shared.

Submissions: Jurying is July of each year. Send query letter with resume, slides, descriptive price list, bio and SASE. Write to schedule an appointment to show a portfolio, which should include originals, photographs, slides, clips and SASE. Replies in 1-2 months. Files bio, slides, clips, photographs and transparencies. "Director, gallery owner reviews work from slides; appointment requests should be done in writing with SASE."

SAVAGE GALLERIES, 7112 Main St., Scottsdale, AZ 85251. (602)945-7114. Director: Gwen Meisner. Retail gallery. Estab. 1960. Represents 30 artists; emerging, mid-career and established. Exhibited artists include Charles H. Pabst and George Burrows. Average display time 6 months. Open all year. Located downtown on "Gallery Row"; 2,500 sq. ft.; "large, open gallery with separate viewing room. Artist's works are all hung together." 100% of space for gallery artists. Clientele: "winter visitors, tourists, retired couples, successful young business people, upper middle income." 80% private collectors, 20% corporate clients. Overall price range: $350-35,000; most artwork sold at $1,000-5,000.

Media: Considers oil, acrylic, watercolor and sculpture. Most frequently exhibits oil, sculpture and water-color.

Style: Exhibits impressionism and realism. Genres include landscapes, Western and Southwestern. Prefers realism and impressionism.

Terms: Accepts work on consignment (50% commission). Retail price set by the gallery. Gallery provides insurance and promotion. Artist pays for shipping. Prefers framed artwork.

Submissions: Living American artists only. Send query letter with resume, slides, bio, brochure, photographs and SASE. Call to schedule an appointment to show a portfolio, which should include originals and photographs. Replies in 3-6 weeks. Files brochure and resume.

Tips: "Please send slides or photos along with a bio or brochure—if we have interest, an interview will then be scheduled."

UNION GALLERIES, UNIVERSITY OF ARIZONA, Box 10,000, Tucson AZ 85720. Arts Coordinator: Karin Erickson. Nonprofit gallery. Estab. 1982. Clientele: 100% private collectors. Represents 300 artists. Sponsors 3 solo and 10 group shows/year. Average display time is 3 weeks. Interested in emerging and established artists. Overall price range: $40-5,000; most artwork sold at $40-300.

Media: Considers oil, acrylic, watercolor, pastel, pen & ink, drawings, mixed media, collage, works on paper, sculpture, ceramic, crafts, fiber, glass, installations, photography, performance and prints. Most frequently exhibits photography, watercolors and clay. "I am interested in exhibiting more installation pieces."

Style: Exhibits hard-edge/geometric abstractions, color field, painterly abstraction, conceptualism, post-modern, surrealism, expressionism, neo-expressionism and realism. Genres include landscapes, figurative and nonobjective work. Prefers painterly abstraction, realism and post-modern works. "We do not cater to any specific style of artwork. We are interested in a well-rounded schedule of exhibitions of art, culture, history and information."

Terms: Accepts work on consignment (25% commission). Retail prices set by artist. Exclusive area representation not required. Gallery provides insurance, promotion and contract; artist pays for shipping.

Submissions: Send query letter and clippings. "Since we jury once a year, artists are notified *when* to send materials. Write to have name put on mailing list to announce annual slide review. Slides are reviewed in the spring. I do not want to have artwork submitted that cannot be exhibited. Not all artwork has to be framed, as long as it can be shown in a professional way. No work in progress."

Arkansas

*INDIAN PAINTBRUSH GALLERY, INC., Highway 412 W., Siloam Springs AR 72761. (501)524-6920. Owner: Nancy Van Poucke.

Profile: Retail gallery. Estab. 1979. Represents over 50 mid-career and established artists. Interested in seeing the work of emerging artists. Exhibited artists include Troy Anderson and Bert Seabourn. Sponsors 2-3 shows/year. Average display time 2 weeks. Open all year. Located on bypass; 1,800 sq. ft. 66% of space for special exhibitions. Clientele: Indian art lovers. 80% private collectors, 20% corporate collectors. Only artists of native American descent. Overall price range: $5-5,000; most work sold at $5-2,000.

Media: Considers oil, acrylic, watercolor, pastel, pen & ink, drawings, mixed media, works on paper, sculpture, ceramic, woodcuts, lithographs, etchings, posters, serigraphs and offset reproductions. Most frequently exhibits paintings, sculpture, knives, baskets, pottery.

Style: Exhibits Native American. Genres include Americana, Southwestern, Western.

Terms: Accepts work on consignment (60-70% commission). Buys outright for 50% of retail price. Retail price set by gallery. Gallery provides insurance and promotion; artist pays for shipping. Prefers unframed artwork.

Submissions: Only artists of Native American descent. Send personal information. Call to schedule an appointment to show portfolio, which should include "prints, etc." Replies in 2 weeks.

California

*ADAMS FINE ARTS GALLERY, 2724 Churn Creek Rd., Redding CA 96002. (916)221-6450. Owner/Director: Susanne Adams. Retail gallery. Estab. 1984. Represents 14 emerging and mid-career artists. Exhibited artists include Susan F. Greaves (featured in *American Artist Magazine*, August 1988) and Janet Turner. Sponsors 4 shows/year. Average display time 3 months. Open all year. Located in a new growth area, 2 blocks from the malls; 1,200 sq. ft.; "known for its quality—good reputation, regular art shows and newly remodeled interior." 50% of space for special exhibitions. Clientele: "Above average income." 70% private collectors, 30% corporate collectors. Overall price range: $100-2,000; most artwork sold at $300-700.

Media: Considers oil, acrylic, watercolor, pastel, mixed media, collage, works on paper, sculpture, craft and fiber. Considers original handpulled prints, woodcuts, engravings, lithographs, wood engravings, mezzotints, serigraphs, linocuts and etchings. Most frequently exhibits oil, watercolor and sculpture.

Style: Exhibits primitivism, painterly abstraction, imagism, impressionism, realism and photorealism. Genres include landscapes, Americana, Southwestern, Western and wildlife. Prefers wildlife, landscapes and Western. "I look for style, color, originality and composition." No "copy-cat styles, vulgarity, nudes that are offensive."

Terms: Artwork is accepted on consignment and there is a 40% commission or "the artist establishes the price they want (wholesale) and the gallery sets the retail price and retains the difference." Retail price set by the gallery. Gallery provides insurance, promotion and contract. Artist pays for shipping. Prefers framed artwork "but must be quality, professionally framed."

Submissions: Send query letter with resume, brochure, business card, slides or photographs and bio. Write to schedule an appointment. Portfolio should include originals and photographs. Replies in 2 weeks. Files "everything. We have extensive art files that are updated regularly and used frequently."

*ART ATELIER KAFKA, 6069 W. Sunset Blvd., Hollywood CA 90028. (213)464-3938. Consulting Curator: Kristian Von Ritzhoff. Retail gallery and rental gallery. Estab. 1985. Represents 1 emerging and established artist per show and large b&w photography. Exhibited artists include Hans Hostrich. Sponsors 6 shows/year. Average display time 2 months. Open all year. Located in Hollywood; 2,000 sq. ft.; "allows good coverage, nice reception, garden setting, skylights." 80% of space for special exhibitions; 80% for gallery artists. Clientele: movie stars and well-known artists. Overall price range: $1,000-2,100; most artwork sold at $1,400.

Media: Considers oil, acrylic, watercolor, pastel, sculpture, photography, original handpulled prints and lithographs.

Style: Exhibits post modern works, photorealism and hard-edge geometric abstraction. Prefers abstraction, photography and expressionism.

Terms: Accepts work on consignment (10% commission). Retail price set by the gallery and the artist. Gallery provides insurance, promotion and contract. Artist pays for shipping. Prefers unframed artwork.

Submissions: "Prefers eccentric but aesthetic oils and watercolors. For photographs prefer 4' × 4' sizes. Send query letter with slides and reviews. Call to schedule an appointment to show a portfolio, which should include slides and photographs. Replies in 3 weeks.

THE ART COLLECTOR, 4151 Taylor St., San Diego CA 92110. Curator: Jane Thompson. Retail gallery. Art consultancy. Estab. 1972. Open all year. Clientele: 25% private collectors, 75% corporate clients. Represents 550 artists. Sponsors 3 solo and 1 group shows/year. Average display time 1 month. Interested in emerging, mid-career and established artists. Overall price range: $200-100,000; most work sold at $700-10,000.

Media: Considers oil, acrylic, watercolor, pastel, mixed media, collage, works on paper, sculpture and ceramic. Most frequently exhibits handmade paper, mixed media and watercolor.

Style: Exhibits realism, photorealism, color field and painterly abstraction. Genres include landscapes, florals and Southwestern themes. Prefers abstraction, realism, ceramic and glass. "We have a large storage space and so we keep a lot of art for our clients. In the 18 years we have gone from a graphic gallery (2 employees) with individual clients to a more varied gallery with clients ranging from interior designers to private and corporate collectors."

Terms: Accepts work on consignment (50% commission). Retail price set by artist. Gallery provides insurance, promotion, contract and shipping costs from gallery.

Submissions: Send query letter, SASE and slides. Include sizes, cost (net or retail) and SASE. Write to schedule an appointment to show a portfolio, which should include originals, slides and transparencies, not larger than 4 × 5'. Replies in 3 weeks. Files slides.

*BARCLAY SIMPSON FINE ARTS, 3669 Mount Diablo Blvd., Lafayette CA 94549. (415)284-7048. Owner: Sharon Simpson. Retail gallery. Estab. 1981. Represents 12-15 emerging and mid-career artists/year. Exhibited artists include Joseph Way and Ron Pokrasso. Sponsors 10 shows/year. Average display time 4 weeks. Open all year. Located downtown; 2,500 sq. ft. upper gallery, 1,000 sq. ft. lower gallery. 80% of space for special exhibitions, 20% for gallery artists. Clientele: collectors and corporations. Overall price range: $100-25,000; most artwork sold at $4,500.

Media: Considers oil, acrylic, watercolor, pastel, drawing, mixed media, collage and sculpture, original handpulled prints, woodcuts, engravings, lithographs, mezzotints, linocuts and etchings. Most frequently exhibits painting, prints and sculpture.

Style: Exhibits expressionism, painterly abstraction, minimalism and color field. All genres considered. Prefers abstraction, expressionism and color field.

Terms: Accepts work on consignment (50% commission). "We work with the artist on pricing." Gallery provides promotion and contract (at times). Prefers unframed artwork.

Submissions: Send query letter with resume, slides, bio, SASE and reviews. Replies in 4-6 weeks.

Tips: "We are looking for excellent quality slides and artist's statement regarding work."

*BC SPACE GALLERY & PHOTOGRAPHIC ART SERVICES, 235 Forest Ave., Laguna Beach CA 92651. (714)497-1880. Director: Mark Chamberlain. Alternative space and art consultancy. Estab. 1973. Represents emerging and mid-career artists. Has current showings plus previous exhibitors on consultancy or referral

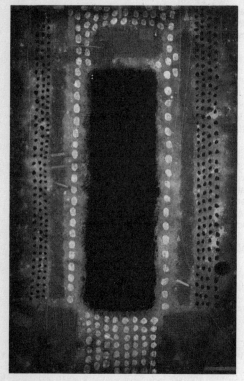

"Heironymous," a watercolor piece by Benicia, California artist Joseph Way, was handled on consignment by The Barclay Simpson Fine Arts Gallery, which has represented him for five years. The owners of Barclay Simpson were introduced to Way's work at a one-man show in the home of an early enthusiast of his work. Later, the owners contacted him and asked if he'd like to be represented by them. According to Way, The Barclay Simpson Gallery "is run by people who are tireless in their efforts to market the work of those they believe in."

© 1988 Joseph Way

basis. Sponsors 7 shows/year. Average display time 6 weeks. Open all year. Located near Main Street; 1,500 sq. ft.; "featuring contemporary photography, innovative and experimental work." Clientele: young, interested in contemporary art and photography. 80% private collectors, 20% corporate collectors. Overall price range: $200-3,000; most work sold at: $300-900.

Media: Considers mixed media, photography and anything photo derived. Considers original handpulled prints and any other type of prints. Most frequently exhibits photography, mixed media, sculptural work.

Style: Exhibits expressionism, surrealism, imagism, conceptualism, post modern works, impressionism, photorealism, sculptural; all styles and genres. Prefers innovative, bold and issue oriented work.

Terms: Artwork is accepted on consignment and there is a 40% commission. Retail price set by the artist. Gallery provides insurance and promotion and artist pays for shipping. Prefers unframed artwork.

Submissions: Send query letter with resume, slides, bio and SASE. Call or write to schedule an appointment to show a portfolio, which should include slides and "whatever is needed to typify work." Replies in 8 weeks. Files slides and bio.

Tips: "We prefer work with a social concern, not just random imagery. Please be patient with our response time."

*PHILL BERMAN GALLERY, 3820 S. Plaza Dr., Santa Ana CA 92704. (714)754-7485. Retail gallery. Estab. 1987. Represents 11 artists/year; emerging, mid-career and established. Exhibited artists include Marty Bell Dealer, Susanna Denton and Ruth Mayer. Sponsors 8 shows/year. Average display time 3-4 months. Open all year. Located "among 7 restaurants in a village in the heart of a major business area"; 609 sq. ft.; "we feature traditional art with warm, comfortable feelings shown in a comfortable setting." 20% of space for special exhibitions, 80% for gallery artists. Clientele: 95% private collectors, 5% corporate collectors.

Media: Considers oil, acrylic, watercolor, pastel, limited editions, offset reproductions, serigraphs and etchings. Most frequently exhibits canvas transfers, oil and watercolor.

Style: Exhibits impressionism and realism. Exhibits landscapes, wildlife and Southwestern.

Terms: Accepts work on consignment (50% commission). Retail price set by the artist. Gallery provides insurance and promotion. Artist pays for shipping. Prefers framed artwork.

Submissions: Not interested in abstract art or high detailed art. Call to schedule an appointment to show portfolio, which should include originals. "Bring in work after 9:30 Monday to Thursday. Pre-call for appointment after 6:30 Tuesday to Friday. Call Phill and request an appointment. I want an artist that I can see and speak with." Files all items received.

Tips: "If you have no plan to grow, don't stop in or call. I want to be part of your growth."

"The Tell," a 632 foot long sculpted photographic mural, was created by Mark Chamberlain, he says, "to solicit the involvement of the residents of Orange County in the future of this natural landscape." The work is "Phase VIII" of the Laguna Canyon Project, a ten-year photo-documentation of the Laguna Canyon Road, and is sponsored by BC Space Gallery of Los Angeles.

*BIOTA GALLERY, 8500 Melrose Ave., West Hollywood CA 90069. (213)289-0979. Director: Kathryn Bidart. Retail gallery. Estab. 1987. Represents emerging and mid-career artists. Exhibited artists include Lee Spear Webster and Peter Ritzer. Sponsors 9-10 shows/year. Average display time 5 weeks. Open all year. Located in West Hollywood — "prominent gallery area of Los Angeles; 1,200 sq. ft.; well located in an architecturally important building with 20 ft. ceilings. Opens onto beautiful atrium." 50% of space for special exhibitions. Clientele: "middle-to upper-income. Both first-time collectors and established collectors." 90% private collectors, 10% corporate collectors. Overall price range: $500-10,000; most work sold at $1,000-5,000.
Media: Considers oil, acrylic, watercolor, pastel, mixed media, sculpture, original handpulled prints, lithographs, etchings; photo-mechanically reproduced prints. Mostly exhibits oil, acrylic and watercolor.
Style: Exhibits expressionism, neo-expressionism, painterly abstraction, impressionism and realism. Genres include landscapes and florals.
Terms: Accepts work on consignment (50% commission). Retail price set by the gallery. Gallery provides insurance, promotion and contract. Artist pays for shipping. Prefers framed artwork.
Submissions: "Our focus is work inspired by nature, concern with environmental issues. We donate 10% of our annual profits to environmental organizations." Send query letter with resume, slides, bio, brochure, photographs, SASE, business card and reviews. Call to schedule an appointment to show a portfolio, which should include slides, photographs and transparencies. Replies in 5 weeks.

J.J. BROOKINGS GALLERY, Mail: Box 1237, San Jose CA 95108. (408)287-3311. Street address: 330 Commercial St. Director: Timothy Duran. Retail gallery. Estab. 1970. Clientele: 80% private collectors, 20% corporate clients. Represents 20 artists. Sponsors 4 solo and 2 group shows/year. Average display time 2 months. Interested in mid-career and established artists. Overall price range: $200-30,000; most artwork sold at $1,000-5,000.
Media: Considers all media except offset reproductions and posters. Most frequently exhibits photographs, paintings and prints.
Style: Exhibits all styles. Prefers abstraction and realism. "We pride ourselves in presenting a wide range of art not only in price, but in styles, size and recognition of the artist. Quality is the only consideration, though it is doubtful that we will show much politically oriented, social documentary or erotic work."
Terms: Accepts work on consignment (usually 50% commission). Retail price set by gallery and artist. Gallery provides insurance, promotion and contract. Prefers framed artwork.
Submissions: Send query letter with resume, brochure, business card, slides, photographs, bio and SASE. Write to schedule an appointment to show a portfolio, which should include slides, transparencies and photographs. Replies in 2-3 weeks. All material is returned if not accepted or under consideration.
Tips: "A professional, well thought-out presentation is a must."

*CANDY STICK GALLERY, 381 Main St., Box 55, Ferndale CA 95536. (707)786-4600. Fine Art Director: Deborah Wright or Gallery Director: Carol Lake. Retail and rental gallery. Estab. 1962. Represents 30 emerging, mid-career and established artists. Exhibited artists include Bill McWhorter and Jim McVicker. Sponsors 4 shows/year. Average display time 3 months. Open all year. Located downtown; 3,000 sq. ft.; "built in 1900, 20′ Victorian ceilings, white walls." 10% of space for special exhibitions; 70% for gallery artists; and 20% other. Clientele: tourists, locals, mostly upper middle income. 90% private collectors, 10% corporate collectors. Overall price range: $100-7,000; most artwork sold at $200-1,500.
Media: Considers oil, acrylic, drawings, sculpture, glass, watercolor, mixed media, ceramic, pastel, craft, original handpulled prints, wood engravings, etchings, lithographs and serigraphs. Most frequently exhibits oil, watercolor and mixed media.
Style: Exhibits photorealism, color field, painterly abstraction, impressionism, realism and "all styles will be considered." Genres include landscapes, Western, florals and wildlife. Prefers realism, impressionism and photorealism.
Terms: Artwork is accepted on consignment (40% commission). Retail price set by the gallery and the artist and gallery provides promotion. Artist pays for shipping. Prefers framed artwork. "We also have two print racks—one for fine originals, one for prints of unframed, matted work."
Submissions: Call to schedule an appointment to show a portfolio, which should include originals and photographs. Replies in 1 month. Files all material sent, if interested.
Tips: "Allow gallery to contact the artist. Be prepared to accept the decision of the director in a professional manner."

*CENTER FOR THE VISUAL ARTS, Suite 100, 1333 Broadway, Oakland CA 94612. (415)451-6300. President, Board of Directors: Jackque Warren. Nonprofit gallery. Clientele: gallery owners, consultants, collectors and general public. Interested in seeing the work of emerging, mid-career and established artists. Sponsors 6 solo and 6 group shows/year. Average display time is 6 weeks-2 months. "CVA is a nonprofit artists membership organization. We are not a commercial gallery."
Media: Considers oil, acrylic, watercolor, pastels, pen & ink, drawings, sculpture, ceramic, fiber, photography, craft, mixed media, collage and glass.
Style: Exhibits a wide variety of styles.
Terms: Nonprofit membership fee plus donation of time and referral. Retail price set by artist. Exclusive area representation not required. Gallery provides insurance, promotion and contract; artist pays for shipping.
Submissions: Send query letter.
Tips: Looks for artists with a "professional attitude and professional approach to work."

*CENTRAL CALIFORNIA ART LEAGUE, 1402 I St., Modesto CA 95354. (209)529-3369. Gallery Director: Milda Laukkanen. Cooperative, nonprofit sales and rental gallery. Estab. 1951. Represents 66 emerging, mid-career and established artists. Exhibited artists include Don Morell, Dolores Longbotham, Barbara Brown, Milda Laukkanen and Dale Laitinen. Sponsors 12 shows/year. Average rental and sales display time 3 months. Open all year. Located downtown; 2,500 sq. ft.; in "a historic building, a former county library, consisting of 2 large gallery rooms, entry, large hallway and two classrooms. (Auditorium shared with historical museum upstairs)." 10% of space for special exhibitions, 90% for gallery artists. Clientele: 75% private collectors, 25% corporate clients. Overall price range: $50-1,300; most artwork sold at $300-800.
Media: Considers oil, pen & ink, works on paper, fiber, acrylic, drawing, sculpture, watercolor, mixed media, ceramic, pastel, collage, photography and original handpulled prints. Most frequently exhibits watercolor, oil and acrylic.
Style: Exhibits impressionism, realism and all styles. All genres. Prefers realism, impressionism and photorealism.
Terms: Artwork is accepted on consignment (30% commission), a Co-op membership fee plus a donation of time (30% commission) and a rental fee for space, which covers 3 months. Retail price set by the artist. Gallery provides insurance. Prefers framed artwork.
Submissions: Call to schedule an appointment to show a portfolio, which should include 5 completed paintings, ready for judging one day a week. Replies in 1 week.

CLAUDIA CHAPLINE GALLERY, 3445 Shoreline Highway, Box 946, Stinson Beach CA 94970. (415)868-2308. Owner: Claudia Chapline. Retail gallery. Estab. 1987. Represents 12 emerging, mid-career and established artists. Exhibited artists include Whitson Cox, Harold Schwarm, Billy Rose, Gary Stephens and Gillian Hodge. Sponsors 12 shows/year. Average display time 5 weeks. Open all year. "Located on Highway One in a coastal resort village; 3,000 sq. ft. plus a sculpture garden; designed by Val Agnoli, architect. The gallery has four exhibition spaces with skylights and a sculpture garden at the foot of Mt. Tamalpais." 50% of space for special exhibitions. Prefers Northern California artists. Overall price range: $50-12,000; most artwork sold at $500-3,000.

Media: Considers oil, acrylic, watercolor, pastel, drawings, mixed media, collage, works on paper, sculpture, unique ceramics and craft, fiber, glass, photography, printmaking, original handpulled prints, woodcuts, engravings, lithographs, wood engravings, mezzotints, serigraphs, linocuts and etchings. Most frequently exhibits paintings, drawings/printmaking and sculpture.

Style: Exhibits painterly abstraction, post modern works and contemporary styles. Prefers contemporary and post modern.

Terms: Artwork is accepted on consignment and there is a 50% commission. Retail price set by the gallery. Gallery provides insurance and promotion and artist pays for shipping. Prefers framed artwork.

Submissions: Send query letter with resume, slides, SASE and reviews. Write to schedule an appointment to show a portfolio. Portfolio should include originals, slides, photographs and transparencies. Replies in 2 months if SASE is provided. Files slides and resumes if interested.

Tips: "Become familiar with the gallery and its approach. Include SASE."

*COCO BIEN OBJET D'ART, 1442-1444 So. Coast, Laguna Beach CA 92657. (714)494-3804. Owner: Colleen Baker-Huber. Retail gallery. Estab. 1986. Represents 50 artists; emerging, mid-career and established. Exhibited artists include Alvaro Rodriguez and Lucian Peytong. Average display time 6 months. Open all year. Located on main state highway at south side of town; 600 sq. ft.; "quaint villa' atmosphere and tourist area; black, grey, white decor shows paintings well." 100% of space for gallery artists. Clientele: "mostly tourists looking for local art." 80% private collectors. Overall price range: $75-5,000; most artwork sold at $500-700.

Media: Considers oil, acrylic, watercolor, pastel, mixed media, paper sculpture and original handpulled prints. Most frequently exhibits oil/acrylic paintings, watercolor and sculpture.

Style: Exhibits expressionism, painterly abstraction, impressionism and photorealism. Exhibits all genres. Prefers impressionism, painterly abstraction and photorealism.

Terms: Rental fee for space; covers 1-month or 6-months, agreement plus 15% commission. Retail price set by the gallery. Gallery provides promotion; pays for shipping costs from gallery or shipping costs are shared. Prefers framed artwork.

Submissions: Send query letter with slides, bio and SASE; "if interested, artist will be contacted for private interview and portfolio showing." Replies in 2 weeks. "Only info and slides on artists accepted."

COUTURIER GALLERY, 166 N. La Brea Ave., Los Angeles CA 90036. (213)933-5557. Gallery Director: Darrel Couturier. Retail gallery. Estab. 1985. Clientele: major museums, corporate and private; 70% private collectors, 30% corporate clients. Represents 24 artists. Sponsors 6 solo and 2 group shows/year. Average display time 5 weeks. Interested in emerging, mid-career and established artists. Overall price range: $500-250,000; most artwork sold at $200-25,000.

Media: Considers oil, watercolor, pastel, pen & ink, drawings, mixed media, sculpture, ceramic, egg tempera, woodcuts, wood engravings, linocuts, engravings, mezzotints, etchings, lithographs, pochoir and serigraphs. Most frequently exhibits ceramic, painting and sculpture.

Style: Exhibits contemporary painting, sculpture and ceramics. The focus of exhibitions is on political and social issues, though not exclusively. Figurative and non-figurative works considered—but only of a high degree of craft and technique.

Terms: Accepts work on consignment or buys outright. Retail price set by gallery and artist. Exclusive area representation required. Gallery provides insurance, promotion and contract; artist pays for shipping. Prefers framed artwork.

Submissions: Send query letter with resume, brochure, business card, slides, photographs, bio and SASE. Call or write to schedule an appointment to show a portfolio, which should include originals, slides, transparencies and photographs. Replies in 1 week. Files resume and photos. All material returned if not accepted or under consideration.

Tips: Sees trend toward "lots more art by people with little technical skill; hopefully, a new breed of artists trained to handle and incorporate today's technology in their work (e.g., computers, lasers, holograph, new metals and plastics)."

*DEPHENA'S FINE ART GALLERY, 2316 J St., Sacramento CA 95816. (916)441-3330. Director: Dephena Mathews. Retail and rental gallery and art consultancy. Estab. 1984. Represents 30 established artists. Interested in seeing the work of emerging artists. Exhibited artists include A. Wolff and Tasia. Sponsors 8 shows/year. Average display time 1 month. Open all year. Located in mid-town, 1,250 sq. ft. 50% for special exhibitions; 100% of space for gallery artists. Clientele: corporate and professional. Overall price range: $200-35,000; most artwork sold at $700-3,000.

Media: Considers oil, pen & ink, paper, acrylic, sculpture, glass, watercolor, mixed media, ceramic, pastel, original handpulled prints, linocuts, etchings, lithographs, serigraphs and posters.

Style: Exhibits expressionism, impressionism and realism. Genres include landscapes, florals, Americana, Southwestern, Western, wildlife, portraits and figurative work. Prefers Americana, impressionist, contemporary realism, figurative and decorative abstract.

Terms; Artwork is accepted on consignment (50% commission). Retail price is set by the artist. Gallery provides contract. Artist pays for shipping. Prefers framed artwork.
Submissions: Send query letter with resume, brochure, slides, photographs and bio. Write to schedule an appointment to show a portfolio, which should include originals, photographs, slides and transparencies. Replies only if interested within 1 month. Files resume, slides, brochures and photographs.
Tips: "Be cognizant of the Director's time."

THE OLGA DOLLAR GALLERY, 210 Post St., 2nd Floor, San Francisco CA 94108. (415)398-2297. Director: Olga Dollar. Retail gallery. Estab. 1976. Clientele: Corporations and collectors. Represents 25 artists. Sponsors 10 solo and 2 group shows/year. Average display time: 4 weeks. Interested in established artists. Overall price range: $500-30,000; most work sold at $500-5,000.
Media: Considers oil, acrylic, watercolor, pastel, pen & ink, drawings, mixed media, collage, works on paper, sculpture, engravings, mezzotints, etchings and lithographs. Most frequently exhibits acrylic, pastel, sculpture and works on paper.
Style: Exhibits realism, color field and painterly abstraction. Genres include landscapes, Americana, still life and figurative work. Prefers realism, abstraction and mixed media. "The gallery's new direction is toward expressive, abstract, on-the-edge contemporary American art. We exhibit well-known artists as well as selcted emerging artists (MFA in major schools)."
Terms: Accepts work on consignment (50% commission). Retail price set by gallery. Exclusive area representation required. Gallery provides insurance, promotion, contract, shipping costs from gallery. Prefers framed artwork.
Submissions: Send query letter with resume, slides and SASE. Replies in 1-2 months.
Tips: "Understand the direction of the gallery and follow the shows. Make a point to visit and view the work."

*DONLEE GALLERY OF FINE ART, 1316 Lincoln Ave., Calistoga CA 94515. (707)942-0585. Also has location at 2375 Alamo Pintado Ave., Los Olivos CA 93441, (805)686-1088. Owner: Ms. Lee Love. Retail gallery. Estab. 1985. Represents 28 artists. Interested in mid-career and established artists. Exhibited artists include Ralph Love and James Coleman. Sponsors 3 shows/year. Average display time 2 months. Open all year. Located downtown; 1,200 sq. ft.; "warm Southwest decor, somewhat rustic." 100% of space for gallery artists. Clientele: 100% private collectors. Overall price range: $500-15,000; most artwork sold at $1,000-3,500.
Media: Considers oil, acrylic, watercolor and sculpture. Most frequently exhibits oils, bronzes and alabaster.
Style: Exhibits impressionism and realism. Genres include landscapes, Southwestern, Western and wildlife. Prefers Southwest, landscapes and Western. No abstract art.
Terms: Accepts work on consignment (40% commission). Retail price set by the artist. Gallery provides insurance and promotion. Artist pays for shipping. Prefers framed artwork.
Submissions: Accepts only artists from Western states. Send query letter with resume, brochure, photographs, reviews and bio. Write to schedule an appointment to show a portfolio, which should include photographs. Replies only if interested within 2 weeks. Files "all info."
Tips: "Don't just drop in—make an appointment. No agents."

*FRANCINE ELLMAN GALLERY, 671 N. Lacienega Blvd., Los Angeles CA 90069. (213)652-7879. Director: Francine Ellman. Retail gallery. Estab. 1984. Represents 18 emerging, mid-career and established artists. Exhibited artists include Cindy Kane and Jacqueline Warren. Sponsors 6 shows/year. Average display time 1 month. Open all year, except Christmas week and part of August." Located on the Westside—gallery area; 1,500 sq. ft.; "former artists' loft, 15' ceiling, courtyard entrance and mezzanine." 75% of space for special exhibitions. 75% of space for gallery artists. 50% private collectors, 50% corporate. Overall price range: $300-300,000; most artwork sold at $5,000-20,000.
Media: Considers all media; original handpulled prints, woodcuts, engravings, lithographs, wood engravings, mezzotints, serigraphs, linocuts and etchings. Most frequently exhibits paintings, sculpture and works on paper.
Style: Exhibits expressionism, neo-expressionism, painterly abstraction, imagism, conceptualism, minimalism, color field, post modern works, impressionism, realism, photorealism and hard-edge geometric abstraction. Genres include landscapes, wildlife and figurative work. Prefers expressionism, abstraction and figurative work.
Terms: Artwork is accepted on consignment (50% commission). Retail price set by the gallery. Gallery provides insurance, promotion and contract. Gallery pays for shipping costs from gallery. Prefers framed artowrk.
Submissions: Send query letter with resume, slides, SASE, reviews and price info. Call after acceptance of slide portfolio. Portfolio should include originals. Replies in 1 month. Files slides, resume, price info and reviews.

*FRESNO ART MUSEUM, 2233 N. First St., Fresno CA 93703. (209)485-4810. Manager: Jerrie Peters. Nonprofit gallery. Estab. 1957. Clientele: general public and students; 100% sales to private collectors. Sponsors 13 solo and 12 group shows/year. Average display time is 2 months. Interested in emerging and established artists. Overall price range: $250-25,000; most artwork sold at $300-1,000.

Media: Considers all media.

Style: Considers all styles. "Our museum is a forum for new ideas yet attempts to plan exhibitions coinciding within the parameters of the permanent collection."

Terms: Accepts work on consignment (40% commission). Retail price set by gallery and artist. Exclusive area representation not required. Gallery provides insurance, promotion and contract; shipping costs are shared.

Submissions: Send query letter, resume, slides and SASE.All materials are filed.

*GALLERY AMERICANA, Box 6146, Carmel CA 93921. (408)624-5071. Director: Richard LaRue. Retail gallery. Estab. 1969. Represents 65 emerging, mid-career and established artists. Exhibited artists include Rosemary Miner and Ray Swanson. Sponsors 12 shows/year. Average display time 1 month. Open all year. Located downtown; 7,000 sq. ft.; "large amount of window display area." 15% of space for special exhibitions. Clientele: 90% private collectors, 10% corporate collectors. Overall price range: $1,000-60,000; most artwork sold at $4,000-6,000.

Media: Considers oil, acrylic and sculpture. Prefers oil and acrylic.

Style: Exhibits expressionism, impressionism and realism. Considers all genres.

Terms: Artwork is accepted on consignment (50% commission). Retail price set by the artist. Gallery provides insurance, promotion and contract. Artist pays for shipping. Prefers framed artwork.

Submissions: Send query letter with slides, bio, brochure and photographs. Call to schedule an appointment to show portfolio. Portfolio should include slides, photographs or transparencies. Replies in 1 week. Does not file submissions.

*GALLERY 57, 204 N. Harbor Blvd., Fullerton CA 92632. (714)870-9194. Director of Membership: D. Engel. Nonprofit and cooperative gallery. Estab. 1984. Represents 20-30 emerging artists. Exhibited artists include Carol Anne Fallis and Darrell Burdette. Sponsors 11 shows/year. Average display time 1 month. Open all year. Located downtown; 1,000 sq. ft., part of "gallery row" in historic downtown area. 100% of space for special exhibitions; 100% for gallery artists. Clientele: wide variety. Because nonprofit, artists handle sales outside gallery. Accepts only artists from southern California able to participate in cooperative activities.

Media: Considers, oil, acrylic, watercolor, pastel, drawings, mixed media, collage, works on paper, sculpture, installation, photography, neon and original handpulled prints. Most frequently exhibits mixed media, painting and sculpture.

Style: All styles. Prefers neo-expressionism, primitivism and post modern works.

Terms: There is a Co-op membership fee plus a donation of time. Retail price set by the artist. Gallery provides insurance and promotion. Artist pays for shipping. Prefers framed work.

Submissions: Send query letter with resume, or bio and slides. Call or write to schedule an appointment to show a portfolio, which should include slides and 1 or 2 originals. Replies in 2-4 weeks. Files nothing.

Tips: "Slides are reviewed by the membership on the basis of content, focus and professionalism. The gallery requires a commitment toward a supportive cooperative experience in terms of networking and support."

*GALLERY 912½, 912½ S. Broadway, Santa Maria CA 93454. (805)922-5005. Partner/Co-owner: Anne Whitten. Rental gallery. Estab. 1982. Represents 50 artists; emerging, mid-career and established. Has 50 members. Exhibited artists include Betsy Jones and Betty Biggs. Sponsors 6 shows/year. Average display time 4 weeks. Open all year. Located downtown; 700 sq. ft.; "we feature Central Coast artists and craftsmen." 10% of space for special exhibitions; 90% for gallery artists. Clientele: repeat. 100% private collectors. Overall price range: $10-800; most work sold at $125-250.

Media: Considers oil, acrylic, watercolor, pastel, sculpture, ceramic, craft, fiber, glass, photography, etchings and serigraphs. Most frequently exhibits pottery, watercolors and glass.

Style: Exhibits realist, traditional and all styles. Genres include landscapes, Western and florals. Prefers landscapes, florals and seascapes.

Terms: Rental fee for space; covers 1 month and 15% commission. Retail price set by artist. Gallery provides insurance, promotion and contract. Artist pays for shipping. Prefers framed artwork.

Submissions: Send query letter with resume, slides, bio and SASE. Call or write to schedule an appointment to show a portfolio, which should include originals and slides. Replies in 2 weeks. Files all material.

*GALLERY WEST, 107 S. Robertson Blvd., Los Angeles CA 90048. (213)271-1145. Director: Roberta Feuerstein. Retail gallery. Estab. 1971. Located near showrooms catering to interior design trade and several restaurants. Represents 25 artists. Sponsors 6 solo and 3 group shows/year. Average display time is 5 weeks. Interested in emerging and established artists. Overall price range: $500-25,000; most artwork sold at $3,500-6,500.

Media: Considers oil, acrylic, watercolor, pastel, mixed media, collage, works on paper, sculpture, ceramic, craft, fiber and limited edition original handpulled prints. Prefers paintings.

Style: Exhibits color field, painterly abstraction, photorealistic and realistic works. Prefers abstract expressionism, trompe l'oeil and realism.

Terms: Accepts work on consignment (50% commission). Retail price set by gallery and artist. Exclusive area representation required. Gallery provides insurance, promotion and contract; shipping costs are shared.

Submissions: Send query letter, resume, slides and SASE. Slides and biography are filed.

*GREENLEAF GALLERY, 14414 Oak St., Saratoga CA 95070. (408)867-3277. Owner: Janet Greenleaf. Director: Chris Douglas. Retail gallery and art consultancy. Estab. 1979. Represents 35 to 40 emerging and established artists. Exhibited artists include Gregory Deane, Yuriko Takata and Tomi Kobara. Sponsors 7 shows/year. Average display time 3 weeks on wall, 3 months in inventory. Open all year. Located downtown; 2,000 sq. ft.; "featuring a great variety of work in diverse styles and media. We have become a resource center for designers and architects, as we will search to find specific work for all clients." 50% of space for special exhibitions, 50% for gallery artists. Clientele: professionals, collectors and new collectors. 50% private collectors, 50% corporate clients. Prefers very talented emerging or professional fulltime artists—already established. Overall price range: $400-15,000; most artwork sold at $500-4,000.

Media: Considers oil, acrylic, watercolor, pastel, mixed media, collage, works on paper, sculpture, glass, original handpulled prints, lithographs, serigraphs, etchings and monoprints. Most frequently exhibits original oil and acrylic, watercolor and monoprints.

Style: Exhibits expressionism, neo-expressionism, painterly abstraction, minimalism, impressionism, realism or "whatever I think my clients want—it keeps changing." Genres include landscapes, florals, wildlife and figurative work. Prefers all styles of abstract, still lifes (impressionistic), landscapes and florals.

Terms: Artwork is accepted on consignment (50% commission). "The commission varies." Retail price is set by the artist. Gallery provides promotion and contract. Artist pays for shipping. Shipping costs are shared. Prefers framed or unframed work, "it depends on work."

Submissions: Send query letter with resume, slides, bio, photographs, SASE, business card, reviews and "any other information you wish—I do not want just slides, always photos as well." Call or write to schedule an appointment for a portfolio review, which should include originals. If does not reply, the artist should phone. Files "everything that is not returned. Usually throw out anything over 2 years old."

*HENLEY'S GALLERY ON THE SEA RANCH, 1000 Annapolis Rd., The Sea Ranch CA 95497. (707)785-2951. Owner: Marion H. Gates. Retail gallery. Estab. 1981. Represents more than 70 artists; emerging, mid-career and established. Exhibited artists include Miguel Dominguez and Duane Gordon. Sponsors 6 shows/year. Average display time 3-4 weeks. Open all year. Located in a commercial area of a second home community; 1,800 sq. ft.; "interesting architecture, incorporates 3 floors." 30% of space for special exhibitions; 65% for gallery artists. Clientele: "medium to upperscale." Overall price range: $200-21,000; most artwork sold at $1,500-3,000.

Media: Considers oil, acrylic, watercolor, pastel, pen & ink, drawings, mixed media, works on paper, sculpture, ceramic, crafts, glass, local photography, original handpulled prints and etchings. Most frequently exhibits watercolor, gouache and oil.

Style: Exhibits realism. Genres include landscapes and figurative work. Prefers landscapes and illustrations.

Terms: Accepts work on consignment (40-50% commission). Retail price set by the artist. Gallery provides insurance, promotion and contract. Artist pays for shipping. Prefers unframed artwork.

Submissions: Send query letter with resume, slides, bio, photographs and SASE. Call or write to schedule an appointment to show a portfolio, which should include originals and slides. Replies in 2 weeks. Files resume.

Tips: Does not want to see "non-loyalty to the gallery and its ongoing efforts." Looks for "a brighter contemporary look."

*HOLOS GALLERY, 1792 Haight St., San Francisco CA 94117. (415)221-4717. FAX: (415)221-4815. President: Gary Zellerbach. Retail and wholesale gallery. Estab. 1979. Represents 20 artists; emerging, mid-career and established. Interested in seeing the work of emerging artists. Exhibited artists include John Kaufman and Lon Moore. Sponsors 4 shows/year. Average display time 3 months. Open all year. Located in a neighborhood shopping area near Golden Gate Park; 600 sq. ft. 50% of space for special exhibitions; 50% for gallery artists. Clientele: 90% private collectors, 10% corporate collectors. Overall price range: $25-5,000; most artwork sold at $50-500.

Media: Considers holograms and holograms with mixed media. Exhibits "just holograms!"

Style: Exhibits surrealism, realism, photorealism and all styles. All genres. Prefers realist, abstract and conceptual styles.

Terms: Accepts work on consignment (50% commission) and bought outright for 50% of retail price (net 30-90 days). Retail price set by the gallery. Gallery provides insurance, promotion and shipping costs to and from gallery. Prefers framed artwork.

Submissions: Send query letter with resume, slides, SASE and reviews. Write to schedule an appointment to show a portfolio, which should include originals. Replies in 2-3 weeks. Files resume and slides.

INTERNATIONAL GALLERY, 643 G St., San Diego CA 92101. (619)235-8255. Director: Stephen Ross. Retail gallery. Estab. 1980. Clientele: 99% private collectors. Represents over 50 artists. Sponsors 6 solo and 6 group shows/year. Average display time is 2 months. Interested in emerging, mid-career and established artists. Overall price range: $15-10,000; most artwork sold at $25-500.
Media: Considers sculpture, ceramic, craft, fibers, glass and jewelry.
Style: "Gallery specializes in contemporary crafts (traditional and current) folk and primitive art as well as naif art."
Terms: Accepts work on consignment. Retail price is set by gallery and artist. Exclusive area representation not required. Gallery provides insurance, promotion and contract; shipping costs are shared.
Submissions: Send query letter, resume, slides and SASE. Call or write to schedule an appointment to show a portfolio, which should include slides and transparencies. Resumes, work description and sometimes slides are filed.
Tips: Sees trend toward "established artists having work made offshore in limited editions."

*KURLAND/SUMMERS GALLERY, 8742 A Melrose Ave., Los Angeles CA 90069. (213)659-7098. Director: Ruth T. Summers. Retail gallery. Estab. 1981. Represents 20-25 artists; mid-career and established. Interested in seeing the work of emerging artists. Exhibited artists include Christopher Lee and Colin Reid. Sponsors 8 shows/year. Average display time 5-6 weeks for a major exhibition; 1 month for other work. Open all year. Located 2 blocks east of Beverly Hills; 2,200 sq. ft.; "excellent lighting system, good architecture for showing work both in a home and a gallery setting." 50% of space for special exhibitions. Clientele: 85% private collectors, 15% corporate collectors. Overall price range: $600-60,000; most artwork sold at $2,500-6,500.
Media: Considers wood furniture/ceramic wall reliefs. Most frequently exhibits glass and works on paper by artists working in glass.
Style: Exhibits conceptualism, photorealism and hard-edge geometric abstraction. Prefers sculpture, geometric abstraction and photorealism.
Terms: Accepts work on consignment (50% commission). Retail price set by the artist. Gallery provides insurance, promotion and pays shipping costs from gallery. Artist pays for shipping costs to gallery. Prefers framed artwork.
Submissions: Send query letter with resume, slides, bio, brochure, photographs, SASE, business card, reviews and cover letter. Call or write to schedule an appointment to show a portfolio, which should include slides, photographs, transparencies, reviews, articles and photographs of installation. Replies in 2-3 weeks. Files bio, slides and cover letter.
Tips: "Be sure that your work is compatible with what we show, we specialize in contemporary non-functional glass, often incorporating non-glass elements." A developing trend seems to be that "more sophisticated artwork and work from Eastern Europe is coming into forefront."

*LIZARDI/HARP GALLERY, 290 West Colorado Blvd., Pasadena CA 91105. (818)792-8336. Director: Grady Harp and Armando Lizardi. Retail gallery and art consultancy. Estab. 1982. Clientele: 90% private collectors, 10% corporate clients. Represents 15 artists. Sponsors 10 solo and 2 group shows/year. Average display time is 4 weeks. Interested in emerging, mid-career and established artists. Overall price range: $400-20,000; most artwork sold at $2,000-8,000.
Media: Considers oil, acrylic, watercolor, pastel, pen & ink, drawings, mixed media, collage, sculpture, installation and original handpulled prints. Most frequently exhibits oil, pastel and sculpture.
Style: Exhibits surrealism, primitivism, impressionism, expressionism, neo-expressionism and realistic works. Genres include landscapes and figurative work. "Our gallery emphasizes quality of craftsmanship no matter the style or medium. Works musts show evidence of sophistication of technique. We mix established and emerging artists and are less interested in 'leading edge or fad' than quality."
Terms: Accepts work on consignment (50% commission). Retail price is set by gallery and artist. Exclusive area representation required. Gallery provides insurance, promotion and contract; artist pays for shipping.
Submissions: Send query letter, resume, brochure, slides, photographs and SASE. Write to schedule an appointment to show a portfolio, which should include slides and transparencies. A completed application is filed. Don't "bother us with constant phone calls inquiring about application."

LOS ANGELES MUNICIPAL ART GALLERY, Barnsdall Art Park, 4804 Hollywood Blvd., Los Angeles CA 90027. (213)485-4581. Edward Leffingwell, Director: Curator: Marie de Alcuaz. Nonprofit gallery. Estab. 1971. Sponsors 6 solo and 6 group shows/year. Average display time is 6 weeks. Accepts primarily Los Angeles artists. Interested in emerging and established artists.
Media: Considers oil, acrylic, watercolor, pastel, pen & ink, drawings, sculpture, ceramic, fibers, photography, craft, mixed media, performance art, collage, glass, installation, original handpulled prints and offset reproductions.

Style: Exhibits contemporary works. "The Los Angeles Municipal Art Gallery organizes and presents exhibitions which primarily illustrate the significant developments and achievements of living Southern California artists. The gallery strives to present works of the highest quality in a broad range of media and styles. We seek to provide a national and international forum for Los Angeles artists by participating in exchange and travelling shows. Our programs are to be significant for Southern California and are reflective of the unique spirit of this region and the grand wealth and diversity of the cultural activities in the visual arts in the city of Los Angeles."

Terms: Gallery provides insurance, promotion and contract.

Submissions: Send query letter, resume, brochure, slides and photographs. Write to schedule an appointment to show a portfolio. Slides and resumes are filed.

*MAYHEW WILDLIFE GALLERY, 400 Kasten St., Mendocino CA 95460. (707)937-0453. Owner: Meridith Carine. Retail gallery. Estab. 1980. Represents a broad scope of artists from Northern California: emerging, mid-career, and established. Exhibited artists include George Sumner and James D. Mayhew. Sponsors 2 major shows/year. Display time varies. Open all year. Located in the village of Mendocino, an art community with small shops; "modern interior quaint New England architecture in a coastal town." 30% of space for special exhibitions; 70% for gallery artists. Clientele: "locals and tourists who enjoy wildlife and are environmentally aware." 10% private collectors. Overall price range: $25-10,000; most work sold at $25-500.

Media: Considers oil, acrylic, watercolor, pastel, pen & ink, drawings, mixed media, works on paper, sculpture, glass, original handpulled prints, offset reproductions, woodcuts, wood engravings, linocuts, engravings, mezzotints, etchings, lithographs, posters and serigraphs. Most frequently exhibits bronze, watercolor and etchings.

Style: Exhibits impressionism (environmental), realism, photorealism and abstract sculpture. Genres include landscapes, florals and wildlife. Prefers wildlife, florals and landscapes.

Terms: Accepts work on consignment (60% commission). Retail price set by the artist. Gallery provides insurance and promotion; shipping costs are shared. Prefers framed artwork.

Submissions: Send query letter with resume, slides, bio, brochure and photographs. "We prefer being contacted for appointments first." Portfolio should include originals. Replies only if interested with 3 months. Files brochures or catalogs.

Tips: "Please contact us by phone to express your interest as a first step."

*MERRITT GALLERY, 1109 S. Mooney Blvd., Visalia CA 93277. (209)627-1109. Director: Luci Merritt. Retail gallery. Estab. 1983. Represents 25-30 mid-career and established artists. Exhibited artists include Melanie Taylon Kent. Sponsors 2-4 shows/year. Average display time 4 months. Open all year. Located in strip center, main thoroughfare; 700 sq. ft. 25% of space for special exhibitions.

Terms: Accepts work on consignment (40% commission). Retail price set by artist. Gallery provides insurance and promotion; artist pays for shipping. Prefers framed artwork.

Submissions: Send resume, bio and slides or photographs. Write to schedule an appointment to show portfolio, which should include photographs or slides and bio. Replies in 2 weeks. Files current artist's inventory.

Tips: "Do not bring originals unless requested; present professional portfolio and frame to professional standards." There seems to be "a move toward more limited edition prints and graphics, a more knowledgable clientele and the purchase of fewer second rate 'originals'. There is a continuing market for art as part of home or office decor."

MONTEREY PENINSULA MUSEUM OF ART, 559 Pacific St., Monterey CA 93940. (408) 372-5477. Director: Jo Farb Hernandez. Nonprofit museum. Estab. 1959. Features nine galleries. Sponsors approximately 32-35 exhibitions/year. Average display time is 4-12 weeks.

Media: Considers all media.

Style: Exhibits contemporary, abstract, impressionistic, figurative, landscape, primitive, non-representational, photorealistic, Western, realist, neo-expressionistic and post-pop works. "Our missions as an educational institution is to present a broad range of all types of works."

Terms: No sales. Museum provides insurance, promotion and contract; shipping costs are shared.

Submissions: Send query letter, resume, slides and SASE. Resume and cover letters are filed.

*NEWSPACE, LOS ANGELES, 5241 Melrose Ave., Los Angeles CA 90038. (213)469-9353. Director: Joni Gordon. Retail gallery. Estab. 1975. Represents 17 artists; emerging, mid-career and established. Exhibited artists include Martha Alf and Peter Zokosky. Sponsors 10 shows/year. Average display time 1 month. Closed during August. Located in Hollywood. Clientele: 80% private collectors, 20% corporate collectors. Overall price range: $600-20,000; most work sold at $1,500-10,000.

Media: Considers oil, acrylic, watercolor, pastel, pen & ink, drawings, mixed media, collage, works on paper, sculpture, ceramic, fiber, glass, installation, photography, original handpulled prints, woodcuts, etchings and lithographs. Most frequently exhibits oil on canvas, acrylic on canvas and mixed media.

Style: Exhibits expressionism, painterly abstraction, surrealism, minimalism, color field, realism, photorealism and hard-edge geometric abstraction. All genres.
Terms: Accepts work on consignment (40-50% commission). Retail price set by the gallery. Gallery provides insurance and promotion; shipping costs are shared. Prefers artwork unframed.
Submissions: Send query letter with resume, slides, bio and SASE. Write to schedule an appointment to show a portfolio, which should include photographs, slides and transparencies. Replies in 3 weeks.

*NORTH VALLEY ART LEAGUE GALLERY, 1126 Parkview Ave., Redding CA 96002. (916)243-1023. President: George Schilens. Nonprofit gallery. Estab. 1983. Represents 170 emerging, mid-career and established artists. Exhibited artists include Susan Greaves and George Nagel. Sponsors 17 shows/year. Average display time 1 month. Open all year. Located mid-town; 2,530 sq. ft.; 1930 vintage cottage. Clientele: mainly average income. 95% private collectors, 5% corporate clients. Overall price range: $50-1,500; most artwork sold at $150-200.
Media: Considers oil, acrylic, watercolor, pastel, pen & ink, drawings, mixed media, collage, works on paper, sculpture, ceramic, fiber, glass, photography, original handpulled prints, woodcuts, engravings, lithographs, pochoir, wood engravings, mezzotints, serigraphs, linocuts and etchings. Most frequently exhibits watercolor, oil and acrylic.
Style: Exhibits all styles and genres. Prefers landscapes, florals and Western.
Terms: Artwork is accepted on consignment (20% commission). Retail price is set by the artist. Gallery provides promotion. Artist pays for shipping. Prefers framed artwork.
Submissions: "All artists are encouraged. All members may show."
Tips: "We are a non-juried gallery except for special shows. We encourage all levels to participate in our general gallery exhibits."

*OFF THE WALL GALLERY, Suite 11, 2123 Main St., Huntington Beach CA 92648. (714)536-6488. "We also have a location at 4336 Katella Ave., Los Alamitos CA 90720." Estab. 1981. Represents 50 artists; mid-career and established. Interested in seeing the work of emerging artists. Exhibited artists include Robert Blue and Howard Behrens. Sponsors 2 shows/year. Average display time 3 weeks. Open all year. Located in outdoor mall; 1,000 sq. ft.; "creative matting and framing with original art hand-cut into mats." 30% of space for special exhibitions. Clientele: "mostly private—some corporate." 95% private collectors, 5% corporate clients. Overall price range: $10-9,000; most artwork sold at $200-1,000.
Media: Considers mixed media, collage, sculpture, ceramic and craft, original handpulled prints, offset reproductions, engravings, etchings, lithographs, pochoir, serigraphs and posters. Most frequently exhibits serigraphs, lithographs and posters.
Style: Exhibits expressionism, primitivism, conceptualism, impressionism, realism and photorealism. Genres include landscapes, florals, Americana, Southwestern and figurative work. Prefers impressionism, realism and primitivism.
Terms: Accepts work on consignment (50% commission). Buys outright for 50% of retail price (net 30 days). Retail price set by the artist. Gallery provides promotion; shipping costs from gallery, or artist pays for shipping. Prefers unframed artwork.
Submissions: Send query letter with brochure and photographs. Call to schedule an appointment to show a portfolio, which should include originals and photographs. Replies only if interested within 1 week. Files photographs, brochures and tearsheets.

*OLD CHURCH GALLERY, 990 Meadow Gate Rd., Box 608, Meadow Vista CA 95722. (916)878-1758. Gallery Directress: Donna Mae Halsted. Retail gallery; alternative space; art consultancy; frame shop; offers art classes/workshops/seminars; cultural center for literary, musical and children's entertainment. Estab. 1987. Represents 11 emerging, mid-career and established artists. Exhibited artists include Pamela Cushman and Margot Seymour Schulzke, P.S.A. Sponsors 6 1-or 2-person shows/year. Average display time 6 weeks. Open all year. Located down "town" in a small but rapidly growing village in the foothills of the Sierra Mountains; 1,600 sq. ft. "We are expanding to over 3,000 ft., to be finished in September 1990. In October of 1990 we are holding our first annual Mountains & Meadows Conservation Fine Arts Festival." 60% of space for special exhibitions. Clientele: 95% private collectors, 5% corporate clients. "We represent only local artists in all media. However, we do consider out of area artists for invitational shows, classes, workshops and seminars." Overall price range: $150-2,000; most work sold at $150-800.
Media: Considers most media and types of prints. Most frequently exhibits watercolor, pastel and oil.
Style: Exhibits painterly abstraction, impressionism, realism and photorealism. "Any style well planned and professionally executed is accepted when in good moral taste." Genres include landscapes, florals, Americana, Southwestern, Western, wildlife, portraits and figurative work. Prefers realism, impressionism and abstraction.
Terms: Artwork is accepted on consignment (40% commission). The gallery and the artist set the price together. Gallery provides insurance, promotion and contracts. "Works are usually hand delivered. In the case of our national open show the artist pays for shipping and insurance." Prefers framed artwork. "We ask the artist to use archival-quality framing."

Submissions: Send query letter with resume, bio, photographs, reviews, slides, SASE, business card, tearsheets, history of exhibitions and awards, collections in which your art appears, list of other galleries exhibiting your work, list of writings you have done in the art field and education in art. Call or write to schedule an appointment to show a portfolio, which should include originals, photographs, slides and transparencies. Replies in 3-6 weeks. Files resume and bio, 3-6 samples of the artist's work, news releases and significant articles about the artist and/or work.

ORLANDO GALLERY, 14553 Ventura Blvd., Sherman Oaks CA 91403. Co-Director: Robert Gino. Retail gallery. Estab. 1958. Represents 30 artists. Sponsors 22 solo shows/year. Average display time is 4 weeks. Accepts only Los Angeles artists. Interested in emerging, mid-career and established artists. Overall price range: up to $35,000; most artwork sold at $2,500.
Media: Considers oil, acrylic, watercolor, pastel, pen & ink, drawings, mixed media, collage, works on paper, sculpture, ceramic and photography. Most frequently exhibits oil, watercolor and acrylic.
Style: Exhibits painterly abstract, conceptual, primitive, impressionism, photo-realism, expressionism, neo-expressionism, realism and surrealism. Genres include landscapes, florals, Americana, figurative work and fantasy illustration. Prefers impressionism, surrealism and realism. Does not want to see decorative art.
Terms: Accepts work on consignment. Retail price is set by artist. Exclusive area representation required. Gallery provides insurance and promotion; artist pays for shipping.
Submissions: Send query letter, resume and slides. Portfolio should include slides and transparencies.

PALO ALTO CULTURAL CENTER, 1313 Newell Rd., Palo Alto CA 94303. (415)329-2366. Curator: Signe Mayfield. Nonprofit gallery. Estab. 1971. Exhibits the work of regional and nationally known artists in group and solo exhibitions. Interested in established or emerging, mid-career artists who have worked for at least 3 years in their medium. Overall price range: $150-10,000; most artwork sold at $200-3,000.
Media: Considers oil, acrylic, watercolor, pastel, pen & ink, drawings, sculpture, ceramic, fiber, photography, mixed media, collage, glass, installations, decorative art (i.e., furniture, hand-crafted textiles etc.) and original handpulled prints. "All works on paper must be suitably framed and behind plexiglass." Most frequently exhibits ceramics, painting, photography and fine arts and crafts.
Style: Our gallery specializes in contemporary and historic art.
Terms: Accepts work on consignment (10-30% commission). Retail price is set by gallery and artist. Exclusive area representation not required. Gallery provides insurance, promotion and contract; artist pays for shipping.
Submissions: Send query letter, resume, slides, business card and SASE.

*THE JOHN PENCE GALLERY, 750 Post St., San Francisco CA 94109. (415)441-1138. Proprietor/Director: John Pence. Retail gallery or art consultancy. Estab. 1975. Clientele: collectors, designers, businesses and tourists, 85% private collectors, 15% corporate clients. Represents 16 artists. Sponsors 7 solo and 2 group shows/year. Average display time 4 weeks. Interested in emerging, mid-career and established artists. Overall price range: $450-65,000; most artwork sold at $4,500-8,500.
Media: Primarily considers oil and pastel. Will occasionally consider watercolor and bronze.
Style: Exhibits painterly abstraction, impressionism, realism and academic realism. Genres include landscapes, florals, Americana, portraits, figurative work and still life. "We deal eclectically. Thus we may accept someone who is the best of a field or someone who could become that. We are *actively involved* with the artist, not merely reps." Looks for "consistency, interesting subjects, ability to do large works."
Terms: Accepts work on consignment (50% commission) or buys outright (33% markup). Retail price is set by gallery and artist. Exclusive area representation required. Gallery provides insurance and promotion.
Submissions: Send query letter, resume and slides. "No appointments. Send for application/instructions." Resumes are filed.

*RED RIVER GALLERY, 23564 Calabasas Rd., Calabasas CA 91302. (818)710-0027. Owner: John Sullivan. Retail gallery. Estab. 1988. Represents 18 emerging, mid-career and established artists. Exhibited Guy Rowbury and Buck Taylor. Sponsors 5 shows/year. Average display time 4 months. Open all year. Located in the suburbs; 750 sq. ft.; "across the street from the oldest house in the San Francisco Valley. We are in 'Old Town Calabasas' former stagecoach stop. 15% of space for special exhibitions, 85% for gallery artists. Clientele: 95% private collectors, 5% corporate clients. Overall price range: $150-4,000; most artwork sold at $250-800.
Media: Considers oil, acrylic, watercolor, pastel, pen & ink, drawings, mixed media, bronze sculpture, original handpulled prints, offset reproductions, engravings, lithographs, posters and serigraphs. Most frequently exhibits opaque watercolor, oil and mixed media.
Style: Exhibits expressionism and realism. Genres include Southwestern, Western and portraits. Prefers Western realism.
Terms: Artwork is accepted on consignment (40% commission) or buys outright (50% of the retail price; net 60 days). Retail price set by the gallery and artist. Gallery provides insurance, promotion, contract and shipping costs from gallery. Prefers framed artwork.

Submissions: Send query letter with slides, photographs and business card. Write to schedule an appointment to show a portfolio, which should include slides and photographs. Replies only if interested within 3 weeks. Files "art that appeals to me that I might want in the gallery later."
Tips: "Come in and look at the gallery. See what we have displayed, what our prices are and whether you would fit in or not. We run a very friendly gallery and consider our artists all good friends."

*ROCKRIDGE CAFÉ, 5492 College Ave., Oakland CA 94618. (415)653-6806. Manager: Brenda Kienan. Café gallery. Estab. 1983. Exhibits emerging artists. Membership varies. Exhibited artists include Jerry Doty, photographer and Sandy Diamond, calligraphy designer. Sponsors 20 shows/year. Average display time 5 weeks. Open all year. Located in a commercial/residential area; "we have space for 2 shows (group or one-person) per 5-week span of time. We do not 'represent' any artists; we have 2 large, airy dining rooms with natural light." Clientele: urban professional dining room clientele, 500-1,000 people daily. 100% private collectors. No sculpture. Overall price range: $50-1,000; most artwork sold at $100-300.
Media: Considers oil, acrylic, watercolor, pastel, pen & ink, drawings, mixed media, collage, works on paper, ceramic (flat), craft (flat), fiber, glass (flat), photography. "Will consider any 2-D media." Considers all types of prints. Most frequently exhibits photography, paintings of all types and mixed media.
Style: Exhibits all styles and genres. "We'll consider any genre or subject matter that would be appropriate to the dining room clientele, by which we mean that we cannot consider subject matter that would be very disturbing or offensive to someone who is eating."
Terms: Artwork is accepted on consignment (no commission). Artist sets retail price. Gallery provides basic promotion. Artist pays for shipping. Prefers framed artwork.
Submissions: Send query letter with resume, slides or photographs and SASE or call for information. Call to schedule an appointment to show a portfolio, which should include slides or photographs. Replies in 3 weeks. Files resumes.
Tips: "Samples should include work you would like to have shown, not a representative sampling. Show us 8-15 pieces."

*SAN FRANCISCO ART INSTITUTE, WALTER/McBEAN GALLERY, 800 Chestnut St., San Francisco CA 94133. (415)771-7020. Director: Jean-Edith Weiffenbach. Nonprofit gallery. Estab. 1968. Clientele: audience of general art community, artists, teachers and students. Exhibits work in 8 shows/year of between 2 and 8 artists/show. Interested in emerging and mid-career artists. Average display time is 5 weeks. "We exhibit work by artists of any nationality, creed and gender. We do not offer works for sale."
Media: Considers all media.
Style: Exhibits contemporary, abstract and figurative works. "We exhibit all media and styles, including performance, installation, painting, sculpture, video and photography."
Terms: Retail price is set by artist. Exclusive area representation not required. Gallery provides insurance, shipping, promotion and contract.
Submissions: Send query letter, resume and slides. Work is reviewed for general curatorial interest, although it is not generally selected for exhibition through submissions or a slide jurying process.
Tips: Sees trend toward "world art from culturally specific and diverse communities, plus the emergence of new technologies in art; art that has a social concern; art that does not function in the current art market and has no commodity value."

*THE SAN FRANCISCO MUSEUM OF MODERN ART RENTAL GALLERY, Building A, Fort Mason, San Francisco CA 94123. (415)441-4777. Director: Marian Parmenter. Nonprofit gallery and art consultancy. Estab. 1978. Amount of exhibition space 1,500 sq. ft. Clientele: Corporations and private collectors; 40% private collectors, 60% corporate clients. Represents 70% of our stable. Sponsors 3 solo or 2 group shows/year. "All work is stored, not really 'displayed' in racks except sculpture and the exhibiting artists." Interested in emerging, mid-career and established artists. Overall price range: $100-15,000; most artwork sold at $1,000-5,000.
Media: Considers oil, acrylic, watercolor, pastel, drawings, mixed media, collage, sculpture, installation, photography and original handpulled prints. Most frequently exhibited media: painting, sculpture and photography. Does not want to see fiber and clay.
Style: Exhibits hard-edge/geometric abstraction, painterly abstraction, minimalism, post-modern, pattern painting, surrealism, primitivism, photorealism, expressionism, neo-expressionism and realism. Genres include landscapes and figurative work. "Work chosen to be exhibited is chosen for quality, not style or theme."
Terms: Accepts work on consignment (40% commission). Retail price is set by gallery. Exclusive area representation not required. Gallery provides insurance, promotion and contract; artist pays for shipping.
Submissions: Send query letter, resume, slides and SASE.

*SHIPMANS PLACE GALLERY & GIFTS, 27075 Highland Ave., Highland CA 92346. (714)862-2711. Owner-Artist: Barbara Shipman. Retail gallery. Estab. 1974. Represents 15 established artists, "but it varies." Exhibited artists include Jeff Owens, Ben Avril and Barbara Shipman. Sponsors 2 shows/year, "but it varies." Average display time 2 months. Open all year. "Located on state highway 330 in Highland; 300 sq. ft., sometimes more; 1906 restored house." 100% of space for gallery artists. Clientele: 75% private collectors, 25% corporate collectors. Overall price range: $50-800; most work sold at $250-500. "I show more expensive work by appointment."

Media: Considers oil, acrylic, watercolor, pastel, pen & ink, drawings, mixed media, collage, works on paper, sculpture and ceramic. "I show very few prints." Most frequently exhibits watercolor, oil and acrylic.

Style: Exhibits expressionism, painterly abstraction, impressionism, realism and all styles. Genres include landscapes, florals, Americana, Southwestern, Western, wilfelife, portraits, figurative work and all genres. Prefers landscapes, florals and Southwestern.

Terms: Accepts work on consignment (30% commission). Retail price set by the artist. Provides promotion and contract; shipping costs are shared. Prefers framed artwork.

Submissions: Send query letter with reviews. Prefers in person. Call to schedule an appointment to show a portfolio, which should include originals and photographs. Replies only if interested within 2 weeks. Files artists' bios.

Tips: Bring 3 pieces of varied artwork to the gallery.

*SUNBIRD GALLERY, 243 Main St., Los Altos CA 94022. (415)941-1561. FAX: (415)941-9071. Director: Carolyn Duque. Retail gallery. Estab. 1983. Represents 20-25 artists; emerging, mid-career and established. Exhibited artists include Veloy Vigil and Frank Howell. Sponsors 5-6 shows/year. Open all year. Located in downtown Los Altos; 2,500 sq. ft.; "a very large open space, good for viewing a variety of work." 50% of space for special exhibitions; 100% for gallery artists. Clientele: 99% private collectors, 1% corporate collectors. Overall price range: $80-16,500; most work sold at $2,000-4,000.

Media: Considers oil, acrylic, watercolor, pastel, drawings, mixed media, collage, works on paper, sculpture, ceramic, original handpulled prints, woodcuts, engravings, etchings, lithographs and serigraphs. Most frequently exhibits oil, lithographs, acrylic and watercolor.

Style: Exhibits expressionism, primitivism, painterly abstraction, impressionism and realism. Genres include landscapes, florals and Southwestern. Prefers Southwestern, realism and expressionism.

Terms: Accepts work on consignment (40-50% commission). Retail price set by the gallery and the artist. Gallery provides insurance, promotion and contract; shipping cost from gallery. Prefers framed artwork.

Submissions: Send query letter with resume, slides, bio, brochure and SASE. Write to schedule an appointment to show a portfolio, which should include slides and photographs. Replies in 3 weeks. If does not reply, the artist should "call and request slides back in SASE." Files slides or photos and bios.

TOPAZ UNIVERSAL, 4632 W. Magnolia Blvd., Burbank CA 91505. (818)766-8660. Director: Diane Binder. Retail gallery. Estab. 1982. Located in the center of movie studio and metro media area. Clientele: 60% private collectors. Represents 8 artists. Sponsors 2 solo and 4 group shows/year. Average display time is 3 months. Interested in established artists. Overall price range: $2,000-100,000; most work sold at $6,000-25,000.

Media: Considers oil, acrylic, watercolor, pastel, pen & ink, drawings, sculpture, mixed media, performance and original handpulled prints.

Style: Exhibits contemporary, impressionistic, figurative and neo-expressionistic works. Specializes in contemporary, figurative and expressionistic works.

Terms: Accepts work on consignment (50% commission). Buys outright. Retail price is set by gallery and artist. Exclusive area representation not required. Gallery provides insurance, promotion and contract; shipping costs are shared.

Submissions: Send query letter with resume and brochure.

*VIEWPOINTS ART GALLERY, 315 State St., Los Altos CA 94303. (415)941-5789. Contact: Rob Mason. Cooperative gallery. Estab. 1973. Represents 15 mid-career and established artists. Is not interested in seeing the work of emerging artists. Exhibited artists include Helen Kunic and Carolyn Hofstetter. Sponsors 5 shows/year. Average display time 1 month. Open all year. Located downtown; 500 sq. ft. 15% of space for special exhibitions, 85% for gallery artists. Clientele: local residents; 95% private collectors, 5% corporate clients. Accepts only artists living close enough to spend time at the gallery. Overall price range: $35-1,000; most artwork sold at $350-450.

Media: Considers oil, acrylic, watercolor, pastel, pen & ink, drawings, mixed media, collage, sculpture, ceramic, fiber, woodcuts, etchings and serigraphs. Most frequently exhibits watercolor, oil, sculpture and pottery.

Style: Exhibits impressionism and realism. All genres. Prefers landscapes, florals and figurative work.

Terms: Artwork is accepted on consignment (35% commission). Co-op membership fee plus a donation of time (no commission). Retail price is set by the artist. Gallery provides promotion. Artist pays for shipping. Prefers framed artwork.

Submissions: Send query letter with resume, slides or photographs. Call to schedule an appointment to show a portfolio, which should include originals. Replies in 1 month. Files lists of perspective members and resumes and applications.

Tips: "Come in and look us over first. You should decide if your work is right for our gallery or vice versa before discussing application for membership."

*WESTERN VISIONS, 408 Broad St., Nevada City CA 95959. (916)265-6239. Owner: John Soga. Retail and wholesale gallery. Estab. 1983. Represents 20 emerging, mid-career and established artists. Exhibited artists include Bev Doolittle and Judy Larson. Sponsors 7 shows/year. Average display time 1 month. Open all year. Located in the New York Hotel; 800 sq. ft. 50% of space for special exhibits. Clientele: "upper middle class." 90% private collectors, 10% corporate collectors. Overall price range: $200-7,000; most artwork sold at $1,200.
Media: Considers acrylic, watercolor, pastel, pen & ink, mixed media, offset reproductions, lithographs, posters and serigraphs. Most frequently exhibits offset reproductions, serigraphs and lithographs.
Style: Exhibits imagism, impressionism and realism. Genres include landscapes, florals, Americana, Southwestern, Western and wildlife. Prefers Western, wildlife and camouflage.
Terms: Artwork is accepted on consignment (40% commission) or bought outright (50% of retail; net 30 days). Retail price is set by the gallery and artist. Gallery provides insurance, promotion and contract. Artist pays for shipping. Prefers unframed artwork.
Submissions: Send query letter with slides, bio, brochure and photographs. Call or write to schedule an appointment to show a portfolio, which should include slides and photographs. Replies only if interested within 1 week.
Tips: "We are looking for good artists who do Western and wildlife, especially camouflage art of any kind."

*WINDWALKER GALLERY, Suite E, 28601 Front St., Temecula CA 92390. (714)699-1039. Director: Gwen Anderson. Retail gallery. Estab. 1988. Represents 15 emerging, mid-career and established artists. Exhibited artists include Robert Freeman and Cat Corcilius. Sponsors 2 shows/year. Average display time 3 months. Open all year. Located in Old Town, 1,400 sq. ft., "located in 'Old West' type building. Interior architecture is Southwest with arches and movable display walls and art stands." 25% of space for special exhibitions. Clientele: 100% private collectors. Accepts only artists from New Mexico, Arizona, Colorado, Oklahoma and California. Prefers only Native American and Southwest styles. Original art only. Overall price range: $400-4,000; most artwork sold at $700-2,000.
Media: Considers oil, acrylic, watercolor, pastel, mixed media, sculpture, ceramic and fiber. Most frequently exhibits paintings, sculpture and ceramics.
Style: Exhibits painterly abstraction, conceptualism, impressionism and realism. Genres include landscapes, Southwestern, Western, portraits and figurative work. Most frequently exhibits Southwestern, landscapes and Western.
Terms: Artwork is accepted on consignment (50% commission). Retail price set by the gallery and the artist. Gallery provides insurance and promotion. Artist pays for shipping. Prefers framed artwork.
Submissions: Send query letter with resume, slides, bio, brochure, photographs and SASE. Portfolio should include originals. Replies in 3 weeks. Files "photos/slides of work that interests me and that I may want to display at a later date. All other is returned with SASE."
Tips: "Please visit the gallery to see what type of work is displayed. NEVER walk into the gallery with an armload of originals without an appointment."

*THE WING GALLERY, 13734 Riverside Dr., Sherman Oaks CA 91423. (818)981-9464. FAX: (818)981-ARTS. Director: Robin Wing. Retail gallery. Estab. 1974. Represents 100+ artists; emerging, mid-career, established. Exhibited artists include Doolittle and Wysocki. Sponsors 6 shows/year. Average display time 2 weeks-3 months. Open all year. Located in suburban-retail area; 3,500 sq. ft. 80% of space for special exhibitions. Clientele: 90% private collectors, 10% corporate collectors. Overall price range: $50-50,000; most work sold at $150-5,000.
Media: Considers oil, acrylic, watercolor, pen & ink, drawings, sculpture, ceramic, craft, glass, original handpulled prints, offset reproductions, engravings, lithographs, monoprints and serigraphs. Most frequently exhibits offset reproductions, watercolor and sculpture.
Style: Exhibits primitivism, impressionism, realism and photorealism. Genres include landscapes, Americana, Southwestern, Western, wildlife. Prefers wildlife, Western and landscapes/Americana.
Terms: Accepts work on consignment (40-50% commission). Retail price set by the gallery and the artist. Gallery provides insurance, promotion and contract; shipping costs rare shared. Prefers unframed artwork.
Submissions: Send query letter with resume, slides, bio, brochure, photographs, SASE, reviews and price list. Call or write to schedule an appointment to show a portfolio, which should include slides, photographs and transparencies. Replies in 1-2 months. Files current information and slides.

Colorado

BOULDER ARTS CENTER, 1750 13th St., Boulder CO 80302. (303)443-2122. BCVA Board of Directors: Exhibitions Committee. Nonprofit gallery. Estab. 1976. Exhibits the work of 60 individuals and 10 groups/year. Sponsors 4 solo and 8 group shows/year. Average display time is 6 weeks. "Emphasis is on Colorado artists." Interested in emerging and established artists. Overall price range: $200-17,000; most artwork sold at $850-2,500.

Media: Considers all media.

Style: Exhibits contemporary, abstract, figurative, non-representational, photo-realistic, realistic and neo-expressionistic works.

Terms: Accepts work by invitation only. Retail price is set by artist. Exclusive area representation not required. Gallery provides insurance, promotion and contract; artist pays for shipping.

Submissions: Send query letter, resume, slides and SASE. Press and promotional material, slides and BCVA history are filed.

*EMMANUEL GALLERY & AURARIA LIBRARY GALLERY, HEC PO Box 4615-S, Denver CO 80204. (303)556-8337. FAX: (303)556-3447. Director: Carol Keller. Nonprofit gallery and university gallery. Estab. 1976. Represents emerging, mid-career and established artists. Members are from 3 colleges. Sponsors 24 shows/year. Average display time 3-4 weeks. Open during semesters all year. Located on the downtown campus; about 1,000 sq. ft.; "the oldest standing church structure in Denver, a historical building built in 1876." 100% of space for special exhibitions. Clientele: private collectors or consultants. Wide price range.

Media: Considers all media and all types of prints. Most frequently exhibits painting, photography and sculpture.

Style: Exhibits neo-expressionism, conceptualism, minimalism, color field, post modern works, realism, photorealism and all styles. All genres.

Terms: It is a nonprofit gallery and there is a consignment during exhibit. A 25% commission donation is accepted. Retail price set by the artist. Gallery provides insurance and promotion. Shipping costs are negotiated.

Submissions: Send query letter with resume, slides, SASE and reviews. Call or write to schedule an appointment to show a portfolio, which should include slides and resume. Replies ASAP.

*EMPIRE ART GALLERY, 5 E. U.S. 40, Empire CO 80438. (303)569-2365. Owner: Dorothy Boyd. Retail gallery. Estab. 1976. Represents 25 artists; emerging, mid-career and established. Exhibited artists include Gregory Perillo and Jim Faulkner. Sponsors 4 shows/year. Average display time 6 months. Open all year. Located downtown; 1,200 sq. ft.; restored 1860 mining building. 20% of space for special exhibitions; 80% for gallery artists. Clientele: investors and art collectors. 95% private collectors, 5% corporate collectors. Overall price range: $50-13,000; most artwork sold at $500-1,000.

Media: Considers oil, acrylic, watercolor, pastel, pen & ink, drawings, mixed media, works on paper, sculpture, ceramic and craft, original handpulled prints, offset reproductions, engravings, lithographs, serigraphs and posters. Most frequently exhibits oil, pastel and watercolor.

Style: Exhibits expressionism, primitivism, impressionism, realism and photorealism. No abstract work. All genres. Prefers portraits, wildlife and landscapes.

Terms: Accepts work on consignment (40% commission). Retail price set the by artist. Gallery provides insurance, promotion and contract; shipping costs from gallery. Prefers framed artwork.

Submissions: Send query letter with resume and photographs. Call or write to schedule an appointment to show a portfolio, which should include originals and photographs. Replies in 2 months. Files resumes and photos.

Tips: "We prefer to see original work. We like work professionally presented."

*HAYDEN HAYS GALLERY, Broadmoor Hotel, Colorado Springs CO 80906. (719)577-5744. President: Terry Hays. Retail gallery. Estab. 1979. Represents 20 artists; emerging, mid-career and established. Exhibited artists include William Hook and Jacqueline Rochester. Sponsors 2-3 shows/year. Open all year. 1,400 sq. ft. 100% of space for gallery artists. Clientele: "all types and out-of-town visitors." 90% private collectors, 10% corporate collectors. Overall price range: $25-10,000; most artwork sold at $550-2,500.

Media: Considers oil, acrylic, watercolor, pastel, pen & ink, drawings, mixed media, collage, sculpture, engravings, mezzotints, etchings, lithographs and serigraphs. Most frequently exhibits oil, acrylic, and watercolor.

Style: Exhibits expressionism, primitivism, impressionism and realism. Genres include landscapes, florals, Southwestern and figurative work. Prefers figurative, landscapes and Southwestern.

Terms: Accepts work on consignment (60% commission). Retail price set by the artist. Gallery provides insurance and promotion; shipping costs are shared. Prefers framed artwork.

Submissions: Send query letter with slides and bio. Call to schedule an appointment to show a portfolio, which include slides. Replies only if interested within 1 month. Files "bio, 1-2 slides (to keep)."

INKFISH GALLERY, 949 Broadway, Denver CO 80203. (303)825-6727. Gallery Director: Paul Hughes. Retail gallery and art consultancy. Estab. 1975. Clientele: 60% local, 30% out of state, 10% tourist. 80% private collectors, 20% corporate clients. Represents 25 artists. Sponsors 6 solo and 6 group shows/year. Average display time 3 weeks. Interested in emerging, mid-career and established artists. Overall price range: $100-50,000; most artwork sold at $500-5,000.

Media: Considers oil, acrylic, watercolor, pastel, pen & ink, drawings, mixed media, collage, works on paper, sculpture, ceramic, glass, installations, woodcuts, wood engravings, linocuts, engravings, mezzotints, etchings and lithographs. Most frequently exhibits paintings, works on paper and sculpture.

Style: Exhibits neo-expressionism, surrealism, minimalism, primitivism, color field, painterly abstraction, conceptualism, post modern works and hard-edge geometric abstraction. Considers all genres. No "Cowboy and Indian" art. Prefers non-representational work. "Inkfish Gallery specializes in contemporary art with a focus on Colorado artists. We have been in business 15 years and are seeing a much better understanding and acceptance of contemporary art."

Terms: Accepts work on consignment (50% commission). Retail price set by gallery and artist. Exclusive area representation not required. Gallery provides insurance, promotion and shipping costs from gallery. Prefers framed artwork.

Submissions: Send query letter with resume, brochure, slides, photographs and bio. Call to schedule an appointment to show a portfolio, which should include originals, slides, transparencies and photographs. Replies in 2-3 weeks. Files bios and slides. All material is returned if not accepted or under consideration.

*MOYERS GALLERY AND FRAMING, 214½ N. Tejon St., Colorado Springs CO 80903. (719)633-2255. Retail gallery and custom framing facility. Estab. 1982. Represents 10-12 artists; emerging, mid-career and established. Exhibited artists include Lora Coley and Marilyn Kikman. Sponsors 2 shows/year. Average display time 1 month. Open all year. Located "downtown; 1,000 sq. ft.; unique frames and mouldings." 40% of space for special exhibitions. Clientele: businessmen and women. 80% private collectors. Overall price range: $2,000-2,500; most work sold at $400-500.

Media: Considers oil, acrylic, watercolor, pastel, pen & ink, drawings, collage, photography, etchings, lithographs, serigraphs and posters. Most frequently exhibits oil, watercolor and pastel.

Style: Exhibits expressionism, primitivism, impressionism and realism. Genres include landscapes, florals, Americana, Southwestern, wildlife and portraits. Prefers impressionism and realism.

Terms: Accepts work on consignment (40-60% commission). Buys outright for 50% of retail price (net 30 days). Retail price set by the gallery. Gallery provides promotion; shipping costs are shared. Prefers unframed artwork.

Submissions: Send query letter with slides, bio, photographs. Write to schedule an appointment to show a portfolio, which should include originals and photographs. Replies only if interested within 2 weeks. Files slides, letters and photographs.

*REISS GALLERY, 429 Acoma St., Denver CO 80204. (303)778-6924. Director: Rhoda Reiss. Retail gallery. Estab. 1978. Represents 160 artists; emerging, mid-career and established. Exhibited artists include Sica, Kevan Krasnoff and Jim Foster. Sponsors 3-4 shows/year. Average display time 6-8 weeks. Open all year. Located just 6 blocks south of downtown; 2,100 sq. ft.; "in an old Victorian house." 40% of space for special exhibitions. Clientele: "corporate and interior designers." 30% private collectors, 70% corporate collectors. Overall price range: $100-12,000; most artwork sold at $600-1,000.

Media: Considers oil, acrylic, watercolor, pastel, mixed media, collage, works on paper, sculpture, ceramic, fiber, glass, original handpulled prints, offset reproductions, woodcuts, engravings, lithographs, posters, wood engravings, mezzotints, serigraphs, linocuts and etchings. Most frequently exhibits oil, prints and handmade paper.

Style: Exhibits painterly abstraction, color field, impressionism and pattern painting. Genres include landscapes, florals, Southwestern and Western. Prefers abstract, landscape and Southwestern. Does not want to see "figurative work or traditional oil paintings."

Terms: Accepts work on consignment (50% commission). Retail price set by the artist. Gallery provides insurance and promotion; artist pays for shipping. Prefers unframed artwork.

Submissions: Send query letter with resume, slides, bio, brochure, photographs, SASE and reviews. Call to schedule an appointment to show a portfolio, which should include originals, photographs and slides. Replies in 2-4 weeks. Files bios, slides and photos.

Tips: Suggests "that artist send work in large scale. Small pieces do not work in corporate spaces. Contemporary work shows best in our gallery. I look at craftsmanship of work, composition and salability of subject matter."

TAOS CONNECTIONS OF DENVER, 162 Adams St., Denver CO 80206. (303)393-8267. Owner: Robert J. Covlin. Retail gallery. Estab. 1983. Clientele: 80% private collectors, 20% corporate clients. Represents 20 artists. Sponsors 6 solo shows/year. Average display time is 3 months. Accepts only regional artists (Southwest contemporary). Interested in emerging and established artists. Overall price range: $150-8,000; most artwork sold at $500-1,000.

Media: Considers oil, acrylic, watercolor, pastel, drawings, mixed media, sculpture and original handpulled prints. Most frequently exhibits oil, watercolor and mixed media.

Style: Exhibits impressionistic, expressionistic and realistic works. Genres exhibited include landscapes, architectural interpretations, florals and figurative work. "Taos Connections of Denver features Southwestern contemporary art for the art collector's home, office or gift-giving pleasures; including oil, watercolor and other media, metal and stone sculpture, hand-painted furniture, pottery and glassware. Art by respected regional and Southwestern artists."

Terms: Accepts work on consignment (40% commission). Retail price is set by gallery and artist. Exclusive area representation required. Gallery provides insurance and promotion; shipping costs are shared.

Submissions: Send query letter, resume and photographs. All received material is filed.

Tips: "We look for good, solid work with a Southwest feeling."

3RD AVE. GALLERY, (formerly Peter Heineman Fine Arts), 2424 E. 3rd Ave., Denver CO 80206. (303)321-6992. Owner: Diane Patterson. Retail gallery. Estab. 1987. Clientele: 98% private collectors; 2% corporate clients. Represents 4 artists. Sponsors 10 solo and 5 group shows/year. Average display time: 2 weeks. Interested in emerging and established artists. Overall price range: $0-3,000; most work sold at $400-700.

Media: Considers oil, acrylic, watercolor, pastel, pen & ink, drawings, mixed media, collage, works on paper, egg tempera, woodcuts, wood engravings, linocuts, engravings, mezzotints, etchings, lithographs, pochoir and serigraphs. Most frequently exhibits oil, watercolor and etchings/engravings.

Style: Exhibits all styles and all genres. "I have concentrated on collecting quality oil paintings, mostly by unknown artists, which can be sold at moderate price levels for average consumers. Usually a very large eclectic collection here defying any specific theme or concept."

Terms: Accepts work on consignment (40% commission). Retail price set by gallery and artist. Exclusive area representation not required. Gallery provides insurance, promotion, contract; artist pays for shipping. Prefers framed artwork.

Submissions: Send query letter with resume, brochure, slides, photographs, bio and SASE. Write to schedule an appointment to show a portfolio, which should include originals. Replies only if interested within 1 week.

Tips: "Keep your prices down to where people can afford them."

*TURNER ART GALLERY, 301 University Blvd., Denver CO 80206. (303)355-1828. Owner: Kent Lewis. Retail gallery. Estab. 1929. Represents 12 emerging, mid-career and established artists. Exhibited artists include Scott Switzer and Charles Fritz. Sponsors 6 shows/year. Open all year. Located in Cherry Creek North; 4,200 sq. ft. 50% of space for special exhibitions. Clientele: 90% private collectors. Overall price range: $1,000-10,000.

Media: Oil, acrylic, watercolor, pastel, sculpture and antique prints. Most frequently exhibits oil, watercolor and sculpture.

Style: Exhibits representational. All genres.

Terms: Retail price set by the gallery and the artist. Gallery provides insurance, promotion, contract and shipping costs from gallery.

Submissions: Call or send slides and bio. Replies in 1 week. Files work of accepted artists.

*THE WHITE HART GALLERY, 843 Lincoln, Steamboat Springs CO 80487. (303)879-1015. Owner: Cynthia Nelson. Retail gallery. Estab. 1986. Represents over 100 artists; emerging, mid-career and established. Exhibited artists include Veloy Vigil and Merrill Mahaffey. Sponsors 3 shows/year. Average display time 6 months. Open all year. Located downtown; 3,000 sq. ft. 20% of space for special exhibitions. Clientele: "resort clients and regulars." 80% private collectors, 20% corporate collectors. Overall price range: $100-10,000; most artwork sold at $250-1,500.

Media: Considers oil, acrylic, watercolor, pastel, pen & ink, drawings, mixed media, works on paper, sculpture, ceramic, fiber, glass, installation, original handpulled prints, woodcuts, wood engravings, linocuts, engravings, mezzotints, etchings, lithographs, serigraphs and posters. Most frequently exhibits paintings; sculpture (bronze, wood, metal); prints (contemporary graphics); interior design.

Style: Exhibits expressionism, painterly abstraction, impressionism and realism. Genres include Western and Southwestern. Prefers Southwestern, Western and contemporary.

Terms: Accepts work on consignment (40% commission). Buys outright for 50% of retail price (net 30 days). Retail price set by the artist. Gallery provides insurance (60% of price), promotion and contract; artist pays for shipping. Prefers framed artwork.

Submissions: Send query letter with resume, slides, bio and SASE. Write to schedule an appointment to show a portfolio, which should include originals or slides. Files slides and bios.

Tips: Looking for "great color, unique style. We're not selling as much wall art as sculpture and three dimensional."

Connecticut

MONA BERMAN FINE ARTS, 78 Lyon St., New Haven CT 06511. (203)562-4720. Director: Mona Berman. Private gallery and art consultancy. Estab. 1979. Clientele: 10% private collectors, 90% corporate clients. Represents 30 artists. Interested in emerging, mid-career and established artists. Overall price range: $400+; most artwork sold at $500-4,000.

Media: Considers oil, acrylic, watercolor, pastel, drawings, mixed media, collage, works on paper, sculpture, photography and limited edition original handpulled prints. Most frequently sells all except large sculpture.
Style: Exhibits variety of styles. Prefers "fine contemporary and ethnographic art."
Terms: Accepts work on consignment (50% commission). Retail price is set by gallery and artist. Exclusive area representation not required. Gallery provides insurance and promotion; artist pays for shipping.
Submissions: Send query letter, resume, brochure, labeled slides, price list and SASE. "Appointments only after preliminary slide review." Various material is filed.

*FISHER GALLERY AT THE FARMINGTON VALLEY ARTS CENTER, 25 Bunker Lane, Avon CT 06001. (203)678-1867. Director: Betty Friedman. Nonprofit gallery. Estab. 1974. Represents 200 emerging, mid-career and established artists. Sponsors 4 shows/year. Average display time 2 months. Open all year. Located in downtown Avon; 865 sq. ft.; "in 19th-century brownstone factory building once used for manufacture of safety fuses." 30% of space for special exhibitions. Clientele: 5% private collectors, 5% corporate collectors. Mostly contemporary craft. Overall price range: $100-2,000; most artwork sold at $150-350.
Media: Considers oil and acrylic (small), watercolor, pastel (small), pen & ink, drawings, mixed media, collage, works on paper, sculpture (small), ceramic, craft, fiber, glass, photography and functional crafts; all types of prints (small) except posters. Most frequently exhibits ceramics, jewelry and prints.
Style: Contemporary strictly. Prefers contemporary, abstract and functional. "No 'crafty' items."
Terms: Accepts work on consignment (40% commission). Retail price set by artist and sometimes the gallery. Gallery provides insurance, promotion and contract; artist pays for shipping to gallery. Prefers framed artwork.
Submissions: Mostly contemporary craft. Send resume, slides, bio, brochure, SASE and reviews. Write to schedule an appointment to show portfolio, which should include originals. Replies in 1 month. Files 3 slides, resume and letter.
Tips: "Write—do not call."

ARLENE MCDANIEL GALLERIES, 10 Phelps Lane, Simsbury CT 06070. (203)658-1231 or 658-9761. President: Arlene McDaniel. Retail gallery. Estab. 1972. Clientele: 50% private collectors; 50% corporate clients. Represents 20 artists. Sponsors 5 group shows/year. Interested in emerging and established artists. Overall price range: $2,500-5,000; most work sold at $500-10,000.
Media: Considers oil, acrylic, watercolor, pastel, pen & ink, drawings, mixed media, collage, sculpture, woodcuts, wood engravings, linocuts, engravings, mezzotints, etchings and lithographs. Prefers oil, watercolor and acrylic.
Style: Exhibits impressionism, realism, color field, painterly abstraction and post modern works. Genres include landscapes, florals and figurative work. Prefers landscapes and abstraction. "We don't feel that we are representing any specific "ism" in the art produced today, but rather intuitively seek individuals who are striving for a high level of quality in their form of expression. Thus, the mediums overlap the styles which overlap philosphies."
Terms: Accepts work on consignment (50% commission). Buys outright (50% retail price; 30 net days). Exclusive area representation required. Gallery provides insurance; shipping costs are shared. Prefers framed artwork.
Submissions: Send query letter with resume, brochure, slides, photographs and bio. Call or write to schedule an appointment to show a portfolio, which should include originals, slides, transparencies and photographs. Replies only if interested within 1 week. Files slides and bios.

SMALL SPACE GALLERY, Arts Council of Greater New Haven, 70 Audobon St., New Haven CT 06511. (203)772-2788. Director: Bill Storandt. Alternative space. Estab. 1985. Sponsors 10 solo shows/year. Average display time: 4-6 weeks. Prefers emerging area artists/Arts Council Members (Greater New Haven). Interested in emerging artists. Overall price range: $35-3,000.
Media: Considers oil, acrylic, watercolor, pastel, pen & ink, drawings, mixed media, collage, works on paper, egg tempera only if wall hangings, woodcuts, wood engravings, linocuts, engravings, mezzotints, etchings, lithographs, pochoir, serigraphs.
Style: Exhibits all styles and genres. "The Small Space Gallery was established to provide our artist members with an opportunity to show their work. Particularly those who were just starting their careers. We're not a traditional gallery, but an alternative art space.
Terms: AAS Council requests 10% donation on sale of each piece. Retail price set by artist. Exclusive area representation not required. Gallery provides insurance (up to $10,000) and promotion.
Submissions: Send query letter with resume, brochure, slides, photographs and bio. Call or write to schedule an appointment to show a portfolio, which should include originals, slides, transparencies and photographs. Replies only if interested. Files publicity, price lists and bio.

ARIE VAN HARWEGEN DEN BREEMS-fine art, 571 Riverside Ave., Wesport CT 06880. (203)222-0099. Director: Arie den Breems. Retail gallery. Estab. 1972. Clientele: 80% private collectors; 20% corporate clients. Represents 3 artists. Sponsors 3 solo shows/year. Average display time: 6 weeks. Interested in emerging and established artists. Overall price range: $1,000-45,000; most work sold at $4,000-7,000.

Media: Considers oil, acrylic, watercolor, pastel, pen & ink and drawings. Most frequently exhibits oil and works on paper.

Style: Exhibits impressionism, expressionism, neo-expressionism, neo-expressionism and realism. Genres include landscapes. "I deal with primarily nineteenth and early twentieth century art. I am interested in seeing the work of artists who paint with a sensitive approach to the landscape. The work should show personality."

*WILDLIFE GALLERY, 172 Bedford St., Stamford CT 06901. (203)324-6483. FAX: (203)324-6483. Director: Patrick R. Dugan. Retail gallery. Represents 72 artists; emerging, mid-career and established. Exhibited artists include R. Bateman and R.T. Peterson. Sponsors 4 shows/year. Average display time 3 months. Open all year. Located downtown; 1,200 sq. ft. 30% of space for special exhibitions, 25% for gallery artists. Clientele: 20% private collectors, 10% corporate collectors. Overall price range: $300-10,000; most artwork sold at $500-3,000.

Media: Considers oil, acrylic, watercolor, pastel, original handpulled prints, woodcuts, wood engravings, engravings, lithographs and serigraphs. Most frequently exhibits acrylic, oil and watercolor.

Style: Exhibits realism. Genres include landscapes, florals, Americana, Western and wildlife. Prefers realism. Does not want to see "impressionism, over-priced for the quality of the art."

Terms: Accepts work on consignment (50% commission). Retail price set by the gallery. Gallery provides promotion and contract; shipping costs are shared. Prefers unframed artwork.

Submissions: Send query letter with photographs, bio and SASE. Write to schedule an appointment to show a portfolio, which should include originals and photographs. Replies only if interested within 2 weeks. Files "all material, if qualified."

Tips: "Must be work done within last six months." Does not want "art that is old that artists have not been able to sell." Sees trend toward "more country scenes, back to 18th-century English art."

Delaware

DELAWARE CENTER FOR THE CONTEMPORARY ARTS, 103 E. 16th St., Wilmington DE 19801. (301)656-6466. Director: Izzy Mead. Nonprofit gallery. Estab. 1979. Clientele: Mostly middle- to upper-middle class locals; 100% private collectors. Represents 250 artists. Sponsors 9 solo/group shows/year. Average display time is 4 weeks. Interested in emerging and established artists. "Lean toward emerging artists." Overall price range: $50-4,000; most artwork sold at $500.

Media: Considers all media.

Style: Exhibits contemporary, abstracts, impressionism, figurative, landscape, non-representational, photorealism, realism and neo-expressionism. Prefers regional contemporary works.

Terms: Accepts work on consignment (35% commission). Retail price is set by gallery and artist. Exclusive area representation not required. Gallery provides insurance and promotion; shipping costs are shared.

Submissions: Send query letter, resume, slides and photographs. Write to schedule an appointment to show a portfolio. Slides are filed.

DIMENSIONS, INC., (formerly Dover Art League), 59 S. Governor Ave., Dover DE 19901. (302)674-9070. Director: Jean Francis. Private gallery. Estab. 1984. Clientele: 3% private collectors. Represents 45 artists but expanding. Sponsors 8 solo and 12-14 group shows/year. Average display time is 1-3 months. Overall price range: $45-1,500; most artwork sold at $100-300.

Media: Considers oil, acrylic, watercolor, pastel, pen & ink, drawings, sculpture, fiber, mixed media, collage, glass, installation and original handpulled prints.

Style: Exhibits landscapes, florals and realism. "Our gallery represents original art in a broad spectrum of both style and media, be it contemporary or not. Our second concept, or reason for existing, is that an organization such as ours in which many of the artists in the area meet and socialize at least once a month bridges the isolation gap many of us experience."

Terms: Accepts work on consignment (30% commission). Retail price is set by artist. Exclusive area representation not required. Gallery provides some promotion and a contract; shipping costs paid by artist.

Submissions: Send query letter, resume and slides. Call or write to schedule an appointment to show a portfolio. Resume, slides, brochure and card are filed.

UNIVERSITY GALLERY, UNIVERSITY OF DELAWARE, 301 Old College, Newark DE 19716. (302)451-1251. Director/Curator: Belena S. Chapp. Nonprofit university museum. Estab. 1978. Clientele: students, faculty, regional and national. Sponsors 1-2 solo and 1-2 group shows/year. Average display time is 6 weeks. Interested in emerging and established artists.

Media: Considers all media. Most frequently exhibits printmaking, painting and sculpture.

Style: Considers all styles. Genres include landscapes, Americana, portraits, figurative work and fantasy illustration. "As an educational institution, we make an effort to exhibit a broad range of contemporary and historical exhibitions and do not make a practice of focusing on one special area."

Submissions: Send query letter, resume, brochure, business card, slides, photographs and SASE. Write to schedule an appointment to show a portfolio, which should include originals, slides and transparencies. Resume and materials are filed. "Slides are filed if the artist allows us to keep them."

District of Columbia

AARON GALLERY, 1717 Connecticut Ave. NW, Washington DC 20009. (202)234-3311. Assistant Director: Annette Aaron. Retail gallery and art consultancy. Estab. 1970. Clientele: 60% private collectors, 40% corporate clients. Represents 18 artists; emerging, mid-career and established. Sponsors 12 solo and 16 group shows/year. Average display time is 2-4 weeks. Overall price range: $500 and up; most artwork sold at $2,000-10,000.
Media: Considers oil, acrylic, watercolor, pastel, pen & ink, drawings, mixed media, collage, sculpture, ceramic, glass installation, works on paper and original handpulled prints. Most frequently exhibits sculpture, acrylic on paper or canvas and original prints.
Style: Exhibits hard-edge/geometric abstraction, color field, post-modern, primitivism, expressionistic and neo-expressionistic works. Prefers post-expressionistic work. "Our gallery specializes in abstract expression in painting on canvas—fine colorist, luminescence and sculpture—intense in very contemporary themes."
Terms: Accepts work on consignment (40-50% commission). Retail price is set by gallery and artist. Exclusive area representation required. Gallery provides insurance, promotion and contract; shipping costs are shared.
Submissions: Send query letter, resume, brochure, business card, slaids, and SASE. Write to schedule an appointment to show a portfolio, which should include originals and photographs. Slides, resume and brochure are filed.

AMERICAN WEST GALLERY, 1630 Connecticut Ave. NW, Washington DC 20009. (202)265-1630. Contact: Owner. Retail gallery. Estab. 1985. Open year round. Clientele: local collectors and tourists. Represents 25-30 artists. Accepts only artists from the Western U.S. Interested in emerging and established artists. Overall price range: $100-52,000.
Media: Considers oil, acrylic, watercolor, pastel, pen & ink, drawings, mixed media, collage, works on paper, sculpture, ceramic, woodcuts, wood engravings, engravings, mezzotints, etchings, lithographs and serigraphs.
Style: Exhibits impressionism, expressionism, realism, photorealism, surrealism, minimalism and primitivism. Genres include landscapes, wildlife, portraits and figurative work also Americana, Southwestern and Western themes. "We want to bring East the best of what's happening in the West: paintings, sculpture and ceramics mostly. We are quite diverse in style and theme."
Terms: Accepts work on consignment (50% commission). Retail price set by gallery and artist. Exclusive area representation required. Artist pays for shipping.
Submissions: Send query letter with resume, slides, SASE, photographs and bio. To show a portfolio mail slides, transparencies and photographs. Label each with media, size, title and price." Replies in 2 months.
Tips: "Be concise. Don't be too pushy, defensive or sensitive."

ARTEMIS (formerly THE ART SOURCE, INC.), #205, 1120 20th St. NW, Washington DC 20036. (202)775-0916. Owner: Sandra Tropper. Retail and wholesale gallery and art consultancy. Estab. 1980 as The Art Source, Inc. Located downtown. Clientele: 40% private collectors, 60% corporate clients. Represents more than 100 artists, "so we do not sponsor specific shows." 50% of total space devoted to hanging the work of gallery artists. Interested in emerging and mid-career artists. Overall price range: $100-10,000; most artwork sold at $500-1,500.
Media: Considers oil, acrylic, watercolor, mixed media, collage, works on paper, sculpture, ceramic, craft, fiber, glass, installations, woodcuts, engravings, mezzotints, etchings, lithographs, pochoir, serigraphs and offset reproductions. Most frequently exhibits prints, contemporary canvases and paper/collage.
Style: Exhibits impressionism, expressionism, realism, minimalism, color field, painterly abstraction, conceptualism and imagism. Genres include landscapes, florals and figurative work. "My goal is to bring together clients (buyers) with artwork they appreciate and can afford. For this reason I am interested in working with many, many artists."
Terms: Accepts work on consignment (50% commission). Retail price set by dealer and artist. Exclusive area representation not required. Gallery provides insurance and contract; shipping costs are shared. Prefers unframed artwork.
Submissions: Send query letter with resume, slides, photographs and SASE. Write to schedule an appointment to show a portfolio, which should include originals, slides, transparencies and photographs. Replies only if interested within 1 month. Files slides, photos, resumes and promo material. All material is returned if not accepted or under consideration.
Tips: Notices trend toward "abstraction, as well as a longer term trend toward impressionism (unfortunately often second rate)"

ATLANTIC GALLERY, INC., 1055 Thomas Jefferson St. NW, Washington DC 20007. (202)337-2299. FAX: (202)944-5471. Director: Virginia Smith. Retail gallery. Estab. 1976. Clientele: 70% private collectors, 30% corporate clients. Represents 10 artists. Sponsors 5 solo shows/year. Average display time is 3 weeks. Interested in mid-career and established artists. Exhibited artists include John Stuart and Alan Maley. Overall price range: $100-20,000; most artwork sold at $600-800.
Media: Considers oil, watercolor and limited edition prints. Most frequently exhibits oils, watercolor and limited edition prints.
Style: Exhibits realism and impressionism. Prefers marine art, florals and landscapes.
Terms: Accepts work on consignment (40% commission). Retail price is set by gallery and artist. Exclusive area representation required. Gallery provides insurance, promotion and contract; artist pays for shipping.
Submissions: Send query letter, resume and slides. Portfolio should include originals and slides.

BIRD-IN-HAND BOOKSTORE & GALLERY, 323 Seventh St. SE, Washington DC 20003. (202)543-0744. Owner: Christopher Ackerman. Retail gallery. Estab. 1983. Clientele: mostly private collectors. Represents 60 artists. Sponsors 12 solo and 8 group shows/year. Average display time is 2 weeks. Interested in emerging artists. Overall price range: $60-650; most artwork sold at $200-300.
Media: Considers oil, watercolor, pastel, pen & ink, drawings, photography and original handpulled prints. Most frequently exhibits prints, watercolor and photography.
Style: Exhibits representational and abstract work. No "horror."
Terms: Accepts work on consignment (40% commission). Retail price is set by gallery and artist. Exclusive area representation not required. Gallery provides promotion and contract; shipping and insurance costs are shared.
Submissions: Send query letter, resume, slides and SASE. Write to schedule an appointment to show a portfolio. Resumes are filed.
Tips: "Write a letter to contact us. We will send information on how to present work."

FOXHALL GALLERY, 3301 New Mexico Ave. NW, Washington DC 20016. (202)966-7144. Director: Jerry Eisley. Retail gallery. Sponsors 6 solo and 6 group shows/year. Average display time is 3 months. Interested in emerging and established artists. Overall price range: $500-20,000; most artwork sold at $1,500-6,000.
Media: Considers oil, acrylic, watercolor, pastel, sculpture, mixed media, collage and original handpulled prints (small editions).
Style: Exhibits contemporary, abstract, impressionistic, figurative, photorealistic and realistic works and landscapes.
Terms: Accepts work on consignment (50% commission). Retail price is set by gallery and artist. Exclusive area representation required. Gallery provides insurance.
Submissions: Send resume, brochure, slides, photographs and SASE. Call or write to schedule an appointment to show a portfolio.

GATEHOUSE GALLERY, Mount Vernon College, 2100 Foxhall Rd. NW, Washington DC 20007. (202)331-3416 or 3448. Associate Professor and Gatehouse Gallery/Director: James Burford. Nonprofit gallery. Estab. 1978. Clientele: college students and professors. Sponsors 7 solo and 2-3 group shows/year. Average display time: 3 weeks. Interested in emerging and established artists.
Media: Considers all media. Most frequently exhibits photography, drawings, prints and paintings.
Style: Exhibits all styles and all genres. "The exhibitions are organized to the particular type of art classes being offered."
Terms: Accepts work on consignment (20% commission). Retail price set by artist. Exclusive area representation not required. Gallery provides promotion and contract; artist pays for shipping.
Submissions: Send query letter with resume, brochure, slides and photographs. Call or write to schedule an appointment to show a portfolio, which should include originals, slides and photographs. Replies in 1 month. Files resume. All material is returned if not accepted or under consideration.

GILPIN GALLERY, INC., 655 15th St. NW, Washington DC 20005. (202)393-2112. President: Maryanne Kowalesky. Retail gallery. Estab. 1982. Clientele: 80% private collectors, 20% corporate clients from Washington DC area. Represents 25 artists. Sponsors 4 solo shows/year. 90% of total space devoted to special exhibitions. Interested in emerging and established artists.
Media: Considers paintings, drawings, wearable prints and sculpture.
Style: Exhibits representational, impressionist, expressionist and abstract works.
Terms: Accepts work on consignment (50% commission). Buys outright (50% retail price). Retail price set by gallery and artist. Exclusive area representation not required. Gallery provides insurance, some promotion, contract and shipping from gallery. Prefers artwork framed.
Submissions: Send query letter with brochure and bio. Call or write to schedule an appointment to show a portfolio, which should include originals and photographs. Replies only if interested within 1 month. Files all material. All material is returned if not accepted or under consideration.
Tips: "Do not approach us on weekends or holidays. We prefer appointments."

*THE INTERNATIONAL SCULPTURE CENTER, 1050 Potomac St. NW, Washington DC 20007. (202)965-6066. FAX: (206)965-7318. Curator of Exhibitions: Sarah Tanguy. Nonprofit gallery. Represents emerging artists. Sponsors 4 shows/year. Average display time 3 months. Open all year. Located in Georgetown; "exhibition space is throughout office space; on three floors and in garden." 100% of space for special exhibitions. Clientele: architects, landscape architects, designers, art consultants and practicing artists. Overall price range: $300-5,000.
Media: Considers oil, acrylic, watercolor, pastel, pen & ink, drawings, mixed media, collage, works on paper, indoor (free-standing and pedestal) and outdoor sculpture, ceramic, craft, fiber, glass and photography. Most frequently exhibits sculpture, painting and photography.
Style: All styles. Prefers contemporary sculpture, conceptualism and contemporary figurative.
Terms: Retail price set by the artist. Gallery provides insurance. Artist provides transportation. Prefers framed artwork.
Submissions: Send query letter with resume, slides, bio and SASE. Write to schedule an appointment to show a portfolio, which should include slides and transparencies. Replies in 3 weeks to 2 months. "Files all artists that would be considered unless the artist requests immediate return. Slides also sent to Sculpture Source at artist's request."

*THE INTERNATIONAL SCULPTURE CENTER AT ARNOLD & PORTER, 1050 Potomac St. NW, Washington DC 20007. (202)965-6066. FAX: (202)965-7318. Curator of Exhibitions: Sarah Tanguy. Corporate art space. Estab. 1988. Represents emerging artists. Exhibited artists include John Ruppert and Jann Rosen-Queralt. Sponsors 8 shows/year. Average display time 6 weeks. Open all year. Located "in up-scale multi-use complex in central business district: space is situated off main lobby for the offices of senior partners at Washington's largest law firm, Arnold & Porter. Space is art nouveau in design, and very adaptable to various style and media." 100% of space for special exhibitions. Clientele: firm members, their clients, local galleries, museums and corporate curators. Accepts artists from Mid-Atlantic (Richmond, VA to northern MD). Space designed to show sculpture and related drawings. Overall price range: $300-10,000; most artwork sold at $800-2,500.
Media: Considers mixed media, collage, indoor (free-standing and pedestal) and outdoor sculpture, ceramic, craft and installation. Most frequently exhibits sculpture, working drawings and marquettes/models.
Style: Prefers contemporary sculpture using found objects, steel and wood; contemporary figurative; and conceptualistic sculpture.
Terms: Retail price set by the artist. Gallery provides insurance and promotion. Artist pays shipping.
Submissions: Send query letter with resume, slides, bio and SASE. Write to schedule an appointment to show a portfolio, which should include slides and transparencies (optional). Replies in 3 weeks to 2 months. Files "all artists that would be considered unless the artist requests immediate return. Slides also sent to Sculpture Source at artist's request."

*OSUNA GALLERY, 1919 Q St. NW, Washington DC 20009. (202)296-1963. FAX: (202)296-1965. Director: Andrew Cullinan. Retail gallery. Estab. 1969. Represents 20 emerging, mid-career and established artists. Exhibited artists include Carlos Alfonzo and Anne Truitt. Sponsors 10 shows/year. Average display time 1 month. Open all year. 1,500 sq. ft. 100% of space for gallery artists. Clientele: 80% private collectors, 20% corporate collectors. Overall price range: $1,000-20,000; most artwork sold at $5,000-8,000.
Media: Considers oil, acrylic, watercolor, pastel, pen & ink, drawings, mixed media, collage, works on paper and sculpture. Most frequently exhibits oil, acrylic, sculpture.
Style: Exhibits painterly abstraction, color field and realism.
Terms: Accepts work on consignment (50% commission). Gallery provides insurance and promotion; gallery pays for shipping costs from gallery. Prefers framed artwork.
Submissions: Send resume, slides, bio and SASE. Write to schedule an appointment to show a portfolio, which should include slides and transparencies. Replies in 3 weeks. Files slides and resume.

HOLLY ROSS GALLERY, 516 C St. NE, Washington DC 20002. (202)544-0400. Art Consultant: Sheryl Ameen. Retail gallery and art consultancy. Estab. 1981. Located in capitol hill. Clientele: 60% private collectors, 40% corporate clients. Represents 700 artists. Interested in emerging, mid-career and established artists. Overall price range: $75-10,000; most artwork sold at $900-3,500.
Media: Considers all media. Most frequently exhibits paintings, prints and sculpture.
Style: Exhibits impressionism, expressionism, realism, photorealism and painterly abstraction. Genres include landscapes, Americana, Southwestern, Western and figurative work. Prefers abstraction, photorealism and realism. "Our business is based in the service-oriented consulting field. Most of our sales are through our consultants. Working with a client to help them find that perfect piece is what our business is all about. We also do museum picture-quality framing and canvas/paper conservation work."
Terms: Accepts work on consignment (40% commission). Retail price set by artist. Exclusive area representation not required. Gallery provides insurance, contract and shipping costs from gallery negotiable.
Submissions: Send query letter with resume, slides and price information. Call or write to schedule an appointment to show a portfolio, which should include originals and slides. Replies in 2-4 weeks. Files bio, slides and some original work. All material is returned if not accepted or under consideration.

ANDREA RUGGIERI GALLERY, %2030 R St., Washington DC 20009. (202)265-6191. Owner: Andrea F. Ruggieri. Retail gallery. Estab. 1986. Clientele: 40% private collectors, 5% corporate clients. Represents 10 artists. Sponsors 8 solo and 2 group shows/year. Average display time is 1 month. Interested in emerging and established artists. Overall price range: $300-100,000.

Media: Considers oil, watercolor, pastel, pen & ink, drawings, mixed media, sculpture and prints.

Style: Exhibits representational works and abstraction. "We specialize in contemporary painting, works on paper and sculpture."

Terms: Accepts work on consignment (50% commission). Retail price is set by gallery and artist. Exclusive area representation required. Gallery provides all promotion and contract; artist pays for 50% of shipping.

Submissions: Send letter, resume, brochure, slides and SASE. "Slides of artists we are interested in are given consideration over a period of 1 month."

SCULPTURE PLACEMENT, LTD., Box 9709, Washington DC 20016. (202)362-9310. Curator: Paula A. Stoeke. Art management business. Estab. 1980. Clientele: 50% private collectors; 50% corporate clients. Sponsors 20 solo and 2 group shows/year. Average display time: 6 weeks. Considers only large outdoor sculpture. Interested in emerging and established artists. Overall price range: $60,000-180,000; most work sold at $80,000.

Media: Considers sculpture, especially bronze sculpture, cast metal and stone.

Style: Exhibits realistic and abstract sculpture. "We arrange exhibitions of travelling sculpture for corporate locations, museums, sculpture gardens and private estates. We are exclusive agents for the American realist, bronze sculptor J. Seward Johnson, Jr."

Submissions: Send query letter with slides, photographs and SASE. "Do not contact us by phone." Replies only if interested within 3 months.

Tips: "Simply send a couple of slides with letter. We keep slide bank. Please do not contact by phone." Wants to see "fine craftsmanship (no pedestal pieces, please)".

SPECTRUM GALLERY, 1132 29th St. NW, Washington DC 20007. (202)333-0954. Director: Anna G. Proctor. Retail/cooperative gallery. Estab. 1966. Open year round. Clientele: 85% private collectors, 15% corporate clients. Represents 29 artists. Sponsors 10 solo and 3 group shows/year. Average display time: 4 weeks. Accepts only artists from Washington area. Interested in established artists. Overall price range: $50-3,500; most artwork sold at $450-900.

Media: Considers oil, acrylic, watercolor, pastel, pen & ink, drawings, mixed media, collage, works on paper, sculpture, ceramic, fiber, woodcuts, mezzotints, etchings, lithographs and serigraphs. Most frequently exhibits acrylic, watercolor and oil.

Style: Exhibits impressionism, realism, minimalism, painterly abstraction, pattern painting and hard-edge geometric abstraction. Genres include landscapes, florals, Americana, portraits and figurative work. "Spectrum Gallery, one of the first cooperative galleries organized and operated in the Washington area, was established to offer local artists an alternative to the restrictive representation many galleries were then providing. Each artist at Spectrum is actively involved in the shaping of Gallery policy as well as the maintenance and operation of the Gallery. The traditional, the abstract, the representational and the experimental can all be found here. Shows are changed every four weeks and each artist is represented at all times. Presently there are 29 members of the Gallery."

Terms: Co-op membership fee plus donation of time; 35% commission. Retail price set by artist. Exclusive area representation not required. Gallery provides promotion and contract.

Submissions: Bring actual painting at jurying; application forms needed to apply.

Tips: "Artists must live in the Washington area because of the co-operative aspect of the gallery."

TAGGART & JORGENSEN GALLERY, 3241 P St. NW, Washington DC 20007. (202)298-7676. Gallery Manager: Lauren Rabb. Retail gallery. Estab. 1978. Located in Georgetown. Clientele: 80% private collectors, 10% corporate clients. Represents 2 living artists. Interested in seeing the work of emerging, mid-career and established artists. Sponsors 2 group shows/year. Average display time: 1 month. "Interested only in artists working in a traditional, 19th century-style." Overall price range: $1,000-1,000,000; most artwork sold at $20,000-500,000.

Media: Considers oil, watercolor, pastel, pen & ink and drawings.

Style: Exhibits impressionism and realism. Genres include landscapes, florals and figurative work. Prefers figurative work, landscapes and still lifes. "We specialize in 19th and early 20th century American and European paintings, with an emphasis on American Impressionism. We are interested only in contemporary artists who paint in a traditional style, using the traditional techniques. As we plan to handle very few contemporary artists, the quality must be superb. Please keep in mind that almost all of our inventory is period."

Terms: Buys outright (50% retail price; immediate payment). Retail price set by gallery and artist. Exclusive area representation required. Gallery provides insurance, promotion, contract and shipping costs to and from gallery. Prefers unframed artwork.

Submissions: "Please call first; unsolicited query letters are not preferred. Looks for technical competence. We do *not* want to see anything done in acrylic!"
Tips: "Collectors are more and more interested in seeing traditional subjects handled in classical ways. Works should demonstrate excellent draughtsmanship and quality."

TOUCHSTONE GALLERY, 2130 P St., Washington DC 20037. (202)223-6683. Director: Luba Dreyer. Cooperative gallery. Estab. 1977. Clientele: 80% private collectors, 20% corporate clients. Represents 35 artists. Sponsors 9 solo and 4 group shows/year. Average display time 3 weeks. Interested in emerging, mid-career and established artists. Overall price range: $200-5,000; most artwork sold at $600-2,000.
Media: Considers all media. Most frequently exhibits paintings, sculpture and prints.
Style: Exhibits all styles and all genres. "We show mostly contemporary art from the Washington DC area."
Terms: Co-op membership fee plus donation of time; 40% commission. Retail price set by artist. Exclusive area representation not required. Prefers framed artwork.
Submissions: Send query letter with SASE. Portfolio should include originals and slides. All material is returned if not accepted or under consideration. The most common mistake artists make in presenting their work is "showing work from each of many varied periods in their careers."

*WASHINGTON PROJECT FOR THE ARTS, 400 7th St. NW, Washington DC 20004. (202)347-4813. Contact: Program Review Committee. Alternative space. Estab. 1975. Interested in seeing the work of and representing emerging and mid-career artists. Has 1,200 members. Sponsors 12 shows/year. Average display time 8-10 weeks. Open all year. Located downtown, near the Mall, 7,500 sq. ft.; artist-designed bookstore, stairway, bathrooms, apartment and media facilities. 100% of space for special exhibitions. Clientele: young, 25-35, well-educated professionals. No sales.
Media: Considers all types, including video, performance and book art. Most frequently exhibits painting, sculpture, print and video media and photography.
Style: Contemporary.
Terms: Artists are paid an honorarium or commission for their work. Gallery provides insurance and promotion. Gallery pays for shipping costs to and from gallery. Prefers framed artwork.
Submissions: Send resume, slides, bio, brochure, photographs, SASE, business card and reviews; as much information as possible. Write to schedule an appointment to show a portfolio. Replies in 3 months. Will file all materials.
Tips: Looks for artists who have "the ability to ask difficult questions in their work, thereby stimulating discussion on the important issues of our times." Trends include "multi-culturalism in exhibitions; artists of various ethnic and religious backgrounds who explore community issues and address social and political issues."

Florida

*ALBERTSON-PETERSON GALLERY, 329 S. Park Ave., Winter Park FL 32789. (407)628-1258. FAX: (407)628-0596. Director: Judy Albertson. Retail gallery and art consultancy. Estab. 1984. Represents 15-20 artists; emerging, mid-career and established. Sponsors 4-6 shows/year. Average display time 3½ weeks. Open all year. Located downtown; 3,000 sq. ft.; "on a prominent street, a lot of glass, good exposure." 75% of space for special exhibitions, 75% for gallery artists. Clientele: 50% private collectors, 50% corporate collectors. Overall price range: $5,000-12,000; most work sold at $100-3,000.
Media: Considers oil, acrylic, watercolor, pastel, mixed media, collage, works on paper, sculpture, ceramic, craft, glass, photography, woodcuts, wood engravings, engravings, lithographs, etchings. Most frequently exhibits paintings, sculpture, glass and clay.
Style: Exhibits painterly abstraction, imagism, color field, pattern painting and all contemporary work.
Terms: Accepts work on consignment (50% commission). Retail price set by the gallery. Gallery provides insurance, promotion and contract; shipping costs are shared. "We want canvas-stretched works on paper not framed works."
Submissions: Send query letter with resume, slides, bio, photographs, SASE and reviews. Call or write to schedule an appointment to show a portfolio, which should include slides, bio, resume and statement. Replies in 1 month. "We always give some answer." Files bios and reviews.
Tips: "Know our gallery and the kind of work we like to exhibit—i.e. quality and contemporary feeling."

BACARDI ART GALLERY, 2100 Biscayne Blvd., Miami FL 33137. (305)573-8511. Director, Coordinator of the Advisory Committee: Juan Espinosa. Nonprofit gallery. Estab. 1963. Sponsors 4 solo and 6 group shows/year. Average display time 5 weeks. Interested in emerging and established artists.
Media: Considers all media.
Style: Considers all styles. "As a community service in the visual arts, we seek to bring important artists or collections to our community, as well as present notable examples of either from our own resources in South Florida."

Terms: "We do not charge fee, commission or buy works." Gallery provides insurance, promotion and contract.
Submissions: Send query letter with resume, slides and SASE. Resume and slides are filed "if given permission to retain them."
Tips: "Looks for quality and professional standards."

*CLAYTON GALLERIES, INC., 4105 S. MacDill Ave., Tampa FL 33611. (813)831-3753. Director: Cathleen Clayton. Retail Gallery. Estab. 1986. Represent 28 emerging and mid-career artists. Exhibited artists include Billie Hightower and Richard Protovin. Sponsors 7 shows/year. Average display time 5-6 weeks. Open all year. Located in the southside of Tampa 1 block from the bay; 1,400 sq. ft.; "post modern interior with glass bricked windows, movable walls, center tiled platform." 30% of space for special exhibitions. Clientele: 40% private collectors, 60% corporate collectors. Prefers Florida artists. Overall price range: $70-20,000; most artwork sold at $500-4,000.
Media: Considers most media and types of prints. Most frequently exhibits oil, acrylic and sculpture. Does not want to see photo-offset lithography or commercial art.
Style: Considers expressionism, neo-expressionism, primitivism, painterly abstraction, imagism, minimalism and post modern works. Genres include landscapes and figurative work. Prefers post modern, painterly abstraction and primitivism.
Terms: Accepts work on consignment (50% commission). Retail price set by gallery. Gallery provides insurance and promotion; artist pays for shipping. Prefers unframed artwork.
Submissions: Prefers Florida artists. Send resume, slides, bio, SASE and reviews. Write to schedule an appointment to show a portfolio, which should include photographs and slides. Replies in 1 month. Files slides and bio, if interested.
Tips: Looking for artist with "professional background i.e., B.A. or M.F.A. in art, awards, media coverage, reviews, collections, etc." Sees trend toward original regional art placement in corporate and private collections, more risks taken on content and unknown artists."

THE DE LAND MUSEUM OF ART INC., 449 E. New York Ave., De Land FL 32724. (904)734-4371. Executive Director: Harry Messersmith. Museum. Represents 700 emerging, mid-career, and established artists. Sponsors 6-8 shows/year. Open all year. Located "downtown; 2,000 sq. ft.; in a house that was constructed in 1900." Clientele: 95% private collectors, 5% corporate collectors. Overall price range: $100-5,000; most work sold at $300-1,200.
Media: Considers oil, acrylic, watercolor, pastel, works on paper, sculpture, ceramic, woodcuts, wood engravings, engravings and lithographs. Most frequently exhibits watercolor, sculpture, photographs and prints.
Style: Exhibits expressionism, surrealism, imagism, impressionism, realism and photorealism; all genres. Prefers landscapes, figurative and wildlife works.
Terms: Accepts work on consignment (30% commission), for exhibition period only. Retail price set by artist. Gallery provides insurance, promotion and contract; shipping costs are shared. Prefers framed artwork.
Submissions: Send resume, slides, bio, brohcure, SASE and reviews. Write to schedule an appointment to show a portfolio, which should include slides. Replies in 3 weeks. Files slides and resume.
Tips: "Artists should have a developed body of artwork and an exhibition history that reflects the artists development."

*EDISON COMMUNITY COLLEGE, GALLERY OF FINE ART, Box 6210, 8099 College Pky., Ft. Myers FL 33906. (813)489-9313. Curator: James H. Williams. Nonprofit gallery, college gallery. Estab. 1979. Has about 200 members. Sponsors 14-15 shows/year. Average display time 1 month. Open all year. Located on college campus; 4,500 sq. ft. 100% of space for special exhibitions. Clientele: general public. Most work sold at $50-1,000.
Media: Considers all fine art media; no offset lithographs except some signed posters. Most frequently exhibits painting, sculpture, ethnic and folk art.
Style: Exhibits all styles and genres "except wildlife and Americana."
Terms: Artists accepted for exhibition may sell art objects on view. Retail price set by artist. Gallery provides insurance and promotion; gallery pays for shipping costs "usually one way, sometimes both ways for major artists." Prefers framed artwork.
Submissions: Send resume and slides. Write to schedule an appointment to show a portfolio, which should include slides or transparencies. Replies in 3 months. Files resumes.
Tips: "Slides and resumes should reflect actual work and collections/exhibition record, with references."

*FLORIDA STATE UNIVERSITY GALLERY & MUSEUM, Copeland & W. Tennessee St., Tallahassee FL 32306-2037. (904)644-6836. Gallery Director: Allys Palladino-Craig. University gallery and museum. Estab. 1970. Represents over 100 artists; emerging, mid-career and established. Sponsors 12-22 shows/year. Average display time 3-4 weeks. Located on the university campus; 8,000 sq. ft. 100% of space for special exhibitions.

Media: Considers all media, including electronic imaging and performance art. Most frequently exhibits painting, sculpture and photography.

Style: Exhibits all styles "but portraiture, Western, wildlife nor florals has figured in an exhibition in recent memory." Prefers contemporary figurative and non-objective painting, sculpture, print making.

Terms: "Sales are almost unheard of; the gallery takes no commission." Retail price set by the artist. Gallery provides insurance and promotion; gallery pays for shipping costs to and from gallery for invited artists.

Submissions: Send query letter with resume, slides, bio, brochure, photographs, SASE and reviews. Write to schedule an appointment to show a portfolio, which should include slides. Replies in 1½-2 months.

Tips: "Almost no solo shows are granted; artists are encouraged to enter our competition—the FL National (annual deadline for two-slide entries is Halloween; show is in the spring; curators use national show to search for talent.)"

FOSTER HARMON GALLERIES OF AMERICAN ART, 1415 Main St., Sarasota FL 34236. (813)955-1002. Owner/Director: Foster Harmon. Retail gallery and art consultancy. Naples gallery estab. 1964, Sarasota galleries estab. 1980. Clientele: 95% private collectors, 5% corporate clients. Represents 75 artists. Sponsors about 16 solo and about 10 group shows/year. Average display time 3 weeks. Interested in emerging Florida artists and nationally established artists. Overall price range: $350-350,000; most artwork sold at $2,000-100,000.

Media: Considers oil, acrylic, watercolor, pastel, pen & ink, drawings, mixed media, collage, works on paper, sculpture, glass sculpture, egg tempera and original handpulled prints. Prefers paintings, sculpture and drawings.

Style: Exhibits impressionism, expressionism, neo-expressionism, realism, photorealism, surrealism, painterly abstraction and hard-edge geometric abstraction; considers all styles. Genres include landscapes, florals, Americana and figurative work. The purpose of the gallery is "to bring the works of nationally distinguished artists to Sarasota and to provide exhibitions for outstanding artists from throughout the state of Florida."

Terms: Accepts work on consignment (40-50% commission). Retail price set by artist. Exclusive area representation required. Gallery provides insurance and promotion; artist pays for shipping. Prefers framed artwork.

Submissions: Send query letter with resume, brochure, slides and SASE. Call or write to schedule an appointment to show a portfolio, which should include originals; "this is after previous step." Replies in weeks. All material is returned if not accepted or under consideration.

Tips: Artist "should already be represented in museums and other public collections."

GALERIE MARTIN, 417 Town Center Mall, Boca Raton FL 33431 (407)395-3050. Retail gallery. Estab. 1968. Clientele: 85% private collectors; 15% corporate clients. Represents 75 artists. Sponsors 4 solo and 8 group shows/year. Average display time: 3 weeks. Accepts only artists that are exclusively ours. Interested in emerging and established artists. Overall price range: $1,500-30,000; most work sold at $900-7,500.

Media: Considers oil, acrylic, watercolor, mixed media, sculpture, lithographs and serigraphs. Most frequently exhibits oil, acrylic and sculpture.

Style: Exhibits impressionism, expressionism, primitivism, painterly abstraction and pattern painting. Genres include landscapes, figurative work; considers all genres. Prefers impressionism, expressionism and abstraction. Looks for "new concepts of art that are pleasing to the eye."

Terms: Accepts work on consignment (50% commission). Buys outright (50% retail price; net 30 days). Retail price set by gallery and artist. Exclusive area representation required. Gallery provides insurance and promotion; shipping costs are shared.

Submissions: Send query letter with resume and slides. Call or write to schedule an appointment to show a porfolio, which should include originals. Replies only if interested within 2 weeks.

Tips: "Professionalism is a must."

***GALLERY CAMINO REAL,** Gallery Center: 608 Banyan Trail, Boca Raton FL 33431. (407)241-1606 or 1607. Associate Director: William Biety. Retail gallery. Estab. 1971. Represents 25 emerging, mid-career and established artists. Interested in seeing the work of emerging artists. Exhibited artists include Jules Olitski and Robert Lowe. Sponsors 10 shows/year. Average display time 3 weeks. Open all year. Located in central Boca Raton; 3,500 sq. ft.; "high-tech industrial spaces; a center with five galleries." 40% of space for special exhibitions. Clientele: collectors, designers, corporations. 60% private collectors. "We only review work submitted through the mail." Overall price range: $500-500,000; most artwork sold at $4,000-30,000.

Media: Considers oil, acrylic, watercolor, pastel, drawings, mixed media, collage, works on paper, sculpture, ceramic, fiber, original handpulled prints, woodcuts, wood engravings, linocuts, engravings, mezzotints, etchings, lithographs and serigraphs. Most frequently exhibits paintings, sculpture and clay.

Style: Exhibits expressionism, neo-expressionism, painterly abstraction, minimalism, color field and photorealism. Prefers painterly abstract, figurative and color field works.

Terms: Accepts work on consignment (50% commission). Retail price set by artist. Gallery provides insurance and promotion; shipping costs are shared. Prefers framed artwork.

Submissions: "We only review work submitted through the mail." Send resume, slides, bio and reviews. Write to schedule an appointment to show a portfolio, which should include slides and transparencies. Replies in 2 weeks. Files "only resumes of artists of interest."

Tips: "Include return postage-paid envelope for return of materials; be as familiar as possible with the gallery and the work exhibited there."

*CAROL GETZ GALLERY, 3390 Mary St. (Mayfair 2nd floor), Coconut Grove FL 33133. (305)448-3243. Director/Owner: Carol Getz. Retail gallery. Estab. 1987. Represents 12 mid-career and established artists. Interested in seeing the work of emerging artists. Exhibited artists include Michelle Spark, Judith Glantzman, Steve Miller, Marilyn Minter and Michael Mogavero. Sponsors 8 shows/year. Average display time 6 weeks. Open fall and spring. Located in center of Coconut Grove; 900 sq. ft.; "glass walls, so the work can be seen even when gallery is closed." 100% of space for special exhibitions. Clientele: all ages—mostly upper middle class. 85% private collectors, 15% corporate collectors. Overall price range: $400-15,000; most artwork sold at $4,000-6,000.

Media: Considers oil, acrylic, watercolor, pastel, pen & ink, drawings, mixed media, collage, works on paper, woodcuts, linocuts, engravings, mezzotints, etchings, lithographs, pochoir and serigraphs. Most frequently exhibits paintings, prints and drawings.

Style: Exhibits expressionism, neo-expressionism, primitivism, painterly abstraction, conceptualism, minimalism and realism. Prefers new image (combination of object and abstraction) and figurative abstraction.

Terms: Accepts work on consignment (40-50% commission). Retail price set by gallery and artist. Gallery provides insurance and promotion; gallery pays for shipping costs to and from gallery. Prefers unframed artwork.

Submissions: Accepts only artists from New York area (NJ, CT, etc.). Prefers only paintings, drawings and prints. "Artist must have shown before at reputable galleries and have a comprehensive resume." Send resume, slides and bio. Call to schedule an appointment to show a portfolio. Replies in 1 month.

Tips: "Send slides and resumes first with SASE."

GREENE GALLERY, 1090 Kane Concourse, Miami FL 33154. (305)865-6408. President: Barbara Greene. Retail gallery/art consultancy. Open fall, winter and spring. Clientele: 75% private collectors; 25% corporate clients. Sponsors 8-10 group shows/year. Average display time: 4 weeks. Interested in emerging and established artists.

Media: Considers oil, acrylic, watercolor, pastel, pen & ink, drawings, mixed media, collage, works on paper, sculpture, ceramic, woodcuts, wood engravings, linocuts, engravings, etchings, lithographs, pochoir and serigraphs. Most frequently exhibits paintings, prints and sculptures.

Style: Exhibits very little realism—but more, minimalism, color field, painterly abstraction, conceptualism, post modern works and hard-edge geometric abstraction. Genres include landscapes, florals and figurative work. Prefers abstraction, geometric and post modernism. "The gallery handles paintings and prints by leading and emerging artists. Geometric and abstact art is the gallery's main interest. The gallery is also interested in new image work of high quality."

Terms: Exclusive area representation required.

Submissions: Send query letter with resume, slides, SASE, photographs and bio. Call or write to schedule an appointment to show a portfolio, which should include originals, slides, transparencies and photographs. Replies in 1 weeks. Files slides, photo, bio and reviews.

*THE HANG-UP, INC., 3850 S. Osprey Ave., Sarasota FL 34239. (813)953-5757. President: F. Troncale. Retail gallery. Estab. 1971. Represents 25 emerging and established artists. Sponsor 6 shows/year. Average display time 1 month. Open all year. Located "south of town, but soon to relocate downtown;" 1,300 sq. ft. 50% of space for special exhibitions; 50% of space for gallery artists. Clientele: 75% private collectors, 25% corporate collectors. Overall price range: $1,000-5,000; most artwork sold at $500-1,000.

Media: Considers oil, acrylic, watercolor, mixed media, collage, works on paper, sculpture, original hand-pulled prints, lithographs, etchings, serigraphs, posters and offset reproductions. Most frequently exhibits paintings, graphics and sculpture.

Style: Exhibits expressionism, painterly abstraction, surrealism, impressionism, realism and hard-edge geometric abstraction. Genres include landscape and all genres. Prefers abstraction, impressionism and surrealism.

Terms: Accepts artwork on consignment (40% commission) or buys outright for 50% of the retail price (net 30 days). Retail price set by gallery. Gallery provides insurance, promotion and contract; shipping costs are shared. Prefers unframed work.

Submissions: Send resume, brochure, slides, bio and SASE. Write to schedule an appointment to show a portfolio which should include originals and photographs. Replies in 1 week.

IMAGE GALLERY, 500 N. Tamiami Trail, Sarasota FL 34236. (813)366-5097. Director: Ruth Katzman. Retail gallery. Estab. 1977. Clientele: specializes in fine crafts, jewelry and wearable art. Represents 50 artists; represents emerging and mid-career artists. Sponsors 4 solo and 3 group shows/year. Average display time is 1 month. Interested in emerging and established artists. Overall price range: $50-5,000; most artwork sold at $500-2,500.
Media: Considers sculpture, ceramic, fiber, craft, mixed media and glass.
Style: Exhibits contemporary works. Currently seeking "good work—exciting, new, innovative and creative."
Terms: Accepts work on consignment (50% commission) or buys outright (net 30 days). Retail price is set by gallery or artist. Exclusive area representation required. Gallery provides insurance and promotion; shipping costs are shared.
Submissions: Send query letter with resume, brochure, business card, slides, photographs and SASE if return is requested. Call or write to schedule an appointment to show a portfolio.

*IRVING GALLERIES, 332 Worth Ave., Palm Beach FL 33480. (407)659-6221. FAX: (407)659-0567. Director: Holden Luntz. Retail gallery. Estab. 1959. Represents 15 artists; established. Not interested in seeing the work of emerging artists. Exhibited artists include Botero and Frankenthaler. Closed for August. Located on main shopping street in town; 2,600 sq. ft. 100% of space for gallery artists. Clientele: "major 20th century collectors." 85% private collectors, 15% corporate collectors. Overall price range: $2,000 and up; most work sold at $20,000 and up.
Media: Considers oil, acrylic, watercolor, pastel, pen & ink, drawings, mixed media, works on paper and sculpture. Most frequently exhibits acrylic, oil, and bronze.
Style: Exhibits expressionism, painterly abstraction, color field, post modern works and realism. Genres include landscapes, florals and Americana.
Terms: Prefers framed artwork.
Submissions: Send query letter with resume, slides and bio. Call or write to schedule an appointment to show a portfolio, which should include slides and transparencies. Replies in 3 weeks.

*J. LAWRENCE GALLERY, 1010 E. New Haven Ave., Melbourne FL 32901. (407)728-7051. Director/Owner: Joseph L. Conneen. Retail gallery. Estab. 1980. Represents 180 mid-career and established artists. Interested in seeing work of emerging artists. Exhibited artists include Kiarly. Sponsors 10 shows/year. Average display time 3 weeks. Open all year. Located downtown; 4,000 sq. ft. 50% of space for special exhibitions. Clientele: 80% private collectors, 20% corporate collectors. Overall price range: $2,000-50,000; most work sold at $2,000-5,000.
Media: Considers oil, acrylic, watercolor, pastel, sculpture, ceramic, glass, original handpulled prints, mezzotints, lithographs and serigraphs. Most frequently exhibits oil, watercolor and silkscreen.
Style: Exhibits expressionism, painterly abstraction, impressionism, realism, photorealism and hard-edge geometric abstraction; all genres. Prefers realism, abstract and hard-edge works.
Terms: Accepts work on consignment (40% commission). Retail price set by gallery. Gallery provides insurance and promotion; artist pays for shipping.
Submissions: Prefers resumes from established artists. Send resume, slides and SASE. Write to schedule an appointment to show a portfolio, which should include originals and slides.

NAPLES ART GALLERY, 275 Broad Ave. S., Naples FL 33940. (813)262-4551. Owners: Warren C. Nelson and William R. Spink. Retail gallery. Estab. 1965. Clientele: 95% private collectors, 5% corporate clients. Represents 63 artists. Sponsors 13 solo and 20 group shows/year. Average display time is 3 weeks. Interested in emerging and established artists. Overall price range: $2,000-30,000; most artwork sold at $2,000-15,000.
Media: Considers oil, acrylic, watercolor, drawings, mixed media, collage, works on paper, sculpture and glass. Most frequently exhibits oils, acrylics and glass. Currently looking for glass and paintings.
Style: Exhibits primitivism, impressionism, photorealism, expressionism and realism. Genres include landscapes, florals, Americana, figurative work and fantasy. Most frequently exhibits realism, impressionism and abstract. Currently seeking abstract.
Terms: Accepts work on consignment. Retail price is set by artist. Exclusive area representation required. Gallery provides insurance, promotion and agreement; shipping costs are shared.
Submissions: Send query letter with resume and slides. Write to schedule an appointment to show a portfolio, which should include slides and transparencies.

NORTON GALLERY OF ART, 1451 S Olive Ave., West Palm Beach FL 33401. (407)832-5194. Director: Christina Orr-Cahall; Acting Curator of Collections: Brett I. Miller. Museum. Estab. 1940. Open year round. Closed Mondays. Clientele: 50% residents, 50% tourists. Sponsors 2 solo and 4 group shows/year. Average display time for a temporary exhibit 6 weeks. Interested in emerging and established artists.
Submissions: Send query letter with resume, slides, photographs and bio. Call or write to schedule an appointment to show a portfolio, which should include slides, transparencies and photographs. Replies in 2 weeks. Files slides and resumes.

*NUANCE GALLERIES, 720 S. Dale Mabry, Tampa FL 33609. (813)875-0511. Owner: Robert A. Rower. Retail gallery. Estab. 1981. Represents 50 artists; mid-career and established. Exhibited artists include Mary Alice Braukman and Alvar. Sponsors 3 shows/year. Open all year. 3,000 sq. ft.
Terms: Accepts work on consignment (50% commission). Retail price set by the gallery and the artist. Gallery provides insurance and contract; shipping costs are shared.
Submissions: Send query leter with slides and bio. Replies in 1-2 weeks.
Tips: "Be professional; set prices (retail) and stick with them."

PARK SHORE GALLERY, #302, 4330 Gulf Shore Blvd. N., Naples FL 33940. (813)434-0833. Artistic Director: Evan J. Obrentz. Retail gallery. Estab. 1984, renamed and relocated in 1987. Located in a collection of Venetian-styled waterfront shops and eateries with courtyards, walkways and original sculpture. Clientele: upscale tourists, winter residents and locals; 60% private collectors, 10% corporate clients. Represents 66 artists. Sponsors 6 solo and 7-8 group shows/year. Average display time for exhibitions 2½ weeks; for gallery artists 2-3 months. Interested in established artists. Overall price range: $300-35,000; most artwork sold at $2,000-12,000.
Media: Considers oil, acrylic, watercolor, mixed media, collage, sculpture, ceramic, glass, etchings, lithographs and serigraphs. Prefers paintings, bronze sculptures and fine prints.
Style: Exhibits impressionism, expressionism, neo-expressionism, realism, surrealism, painterly abstraction and post modern works. Genres include landscapes, florals, Southwestern and figurative work. Prefers impressionism, realism and figurative work. "Quality is our overall measure of acceptance; professionalism is desired."
Terms: Accepts work on consignment (50% commission). Retail price set by gallery and artist. Exclusive area representation required. Gallery provides insurance, promotion, contract and shipping costs from gallery. Prefers framed artwork.
Submissions: Send query letter with resume, brochure, slides, photographs, bio and SASE. Write to schedule an appointment to show a portfolio, which should include originals, slides, photographs and suggested retail price list. Replies only if interested within 4 weeks. Files resume, bio and brochures. All material is returned if not accepted or under consideration.

PENSACOLA MUSEUM OF ART, 407 S. Jefferson, Pensacola FL 32501. (904)432-6247. Director: Kevin J. O'Brien. Nonprofit gallery/museum. Estab. 1954. Open year round. Located in the historic district. Renovated 1906 old city jail. Clientele: 90% private collectors; 10% corporate clients. Sponsors 3 solo and 19 group shows/year. Average display time: 6-8 weeks. Interested in emerging and established artists. Overall price range: $200-20,000; most work sold at $500-3,000.
Media: Considers all media. Most frequently exhibits painting, sculpture, photography and new-tech (i.e. holography, video art, computer art etc.).
Style: Exhibits neo-expressionism, realism, photorealism, surrealism, minimalism, primitivism, color field, post modern works, imagism; all styles and genres.
Terms: Retail price set by gallery and artist. Exclusive area representation not required. Gallery provides insurance, promotion and shipping costs.
Submissions: Send query letter with resume, slides, SASE and video tape. Call or write to schedule an appointment to show a portfolio, which should include originals, slides, transparencies and video tape. Replies in 2 weeks. Files guides and resume.
Tips: "Grow a long mustache and act like Leroy Nieman."

*STEIN GALLERY, 3105 Bay to Bay Blvd., Tampa FL 33629. (813)831-9987. Director: Barbara Hill. Retail gallery. Estab. 1986. Represents 50 artists; mid-career. Interested in seeing the work of emerging artists. Exhibited artists include Eleanor Blair and Josette Urso. Sponsors 8 shows/year. Average display time 6-8 weeks. Open all year. Located south of downtown; 2,100 sq. ft; "excellent window exposure on a busy intersection, a spacious exhibition area." 80% of space for special exhibitions, 20% for gallery artists. Overall price range: $30-6,000; most work sold at $300-2,000.
Media: Considers oil, acrylic, watercolor, pastel, drawing, mixed media, works on paper, sculpture, ceramic, photography, original handpulled prints, lithographs and etchings. Most frequently exhibits mixed media, oil or acrylic and mixed media constructions.
Style: Exhibits expressionism, painterly abstraction, minimalism, post modern works, realism, photorealism, hard-edge geometric abstraction and all styles. Genres include landscapes, florals and figurative work. Prefers painterly abstraction, realism and expressionism.
Terms: Accepts work on consignment (50% commission). Retail price set by the gallery and the artist. Gallery provides insurance, promotion and contract; artist pays for shipping. Prefers framed artwork.
Submissions: Send query letter with resume, slides, bio, SASE and reviews. Call to schedule an appointment to show a portfolio, which should include photographs, slides and resume, reviews, invitations, catalogs or monograph. Replies in 1 month. Files work of accepted artists.

*THE SUWANNEE TRIANGLE G, Dock St., Box 341, Cedar Key FL 32625. (904)543-5744. Manager: Clair Teetor. Retail gallery. Estab. 1983. Represents 25 emerging and mid-career artists. Full-time exhibited artists include Connie Nelson and Kevin Hipe. Open all year. Located in the historic district; 400 sq. ft.; "directly on the Gulf of Mexico." 25% space for special exhibitions. 100% private collectors. Interested in seeing the work of emerging artists. Overall price range: $50-500; most artwork sold at $150-1,200.
Media: Considers oil, watercolor, pastel, ceramic, craft, jewelry, glass, offset reproductions, posters, serigraphs and etchings. Most frequently exhibits watercolor, oil and craft.
Style: Exhibits contemporary crafts and jewelry, painterly abstraction and imagism.
Terms: Artwork is bought outright for 50% of the retail price (net 30 days). Retail price set by the gallery. Gallery provides promotion and contract. Shipping costs are shared. Prefers framed artwork.
Submissions: Send query letter with resume, slides, bio, SASE and reviews. Call to schedule an appointment to show a portfolio. What portfolio should include is up to the discretion of artist. Replies only if interested within 3 weeks. Files material of future interest.
Tips: "Be prepared with well thought-out presentation. Do not monopolize time with frequent phone calls."

THE THOMAS CENTER GALLERY, 302 NE 6th Ave., Box 490, Gainesville FL 32602. (904)374-2197. Visual Arts Coordinator: Mallory McCane O'Connor. Nonprofit gallery. Estab. 1980. Clientele: "serves the community as a cultural center." Sponsors 3 solo and 8 group shows/year. Average display time is 1 month. "We concentrate on regional artists." Interested in emerging, mid-career and established artists.
Media: Considers all media.
Style: Considers all styles. "We have to be careful about anything that is too controversial or that deals with explicit sex or violence. This doesn't mean that the work must be bland and boring, however."
Terms: Accepts work on consignment (20% commission). Retail price is set by artist. Exclusive area representation not required. Gallery provides insurance, promotion and contract; shipping costs may be shared.
Submissions: Send query letter with resume, brochure, slides and SASE. Write to schedule an appointment to show a portfolio. Resume and 2 slides are filed.

UPHAM GALLERY, THE, 348 Corey Ave., St. Petersburg Beach FL 33706. (813)360-5432. Director: Carol Upham. 4 connected retail galleries, a workshop/classroom area, darkroom and studio. Also corporate art consultancy. Estab. 1985. Clientele: local residents and tourists; 60% private collectors, 40% corporate clients. Represents about 140 artists; emerging, mid-career and established. 6 group shows/year. Average display time is 6 weeks. Overall price range: $35-10,000; most artwork sold at $150-1,000.
Media: Considers all media except crafts and performance art. Most frequently exhibits mixed media, photography, acrylics, watercolors and sculpture.
Style: Exhibits hard-edge geometric abstraction, color field, painterly abstraction, conceptual, primitivism, impressionistic, photo-realistic, expressionistic, neo-expressionistic, realism and surrealism. Genres include landscapes, florals, Americana, portraits, figurative work and fantasy illustration. Most frequently exhibits photorealism, realism and Florida landscapes. "We are currently seeking artists on a national level to give workshops at the Upham Teaching Studio." No nudes or pornography.
Terms: Accepts work on consignment (40% commission). Retail price is set by artist. Gallery provides insurance, promotion and contract; artist pays for shipping.
Submissions: Send query letter with resume, brochure, up to 20 slides and SASE. Slides, resumes, brochures and articles are filed. Write to schedule an appointment to show a portfolio which should include originals, slides and photographs. Replies in 3 weeks. All material is returned if not accepted or under consideration.
Tips: "Please send a typed resume with slides. You are showing us that you are a professional, with well-established credits and are serious about your art."

VALENCIA COMMUNITY COLLEGE ART GALLERIES, 701 N. Econlockhatchee Trail, Orlando FL 32825. (305)299-5000. Gallery Curator: Judith Page. Nonprofit gallery. Estab. 1982. Clientele: 100% private collectors. Sponsors 1 solo and 5 group shows/year. Average display time is 6 weeks. Interested in emerging, mid-career and established artists.
Media: Considers all media. Most frequently exhibits sculpture, paintings and drawings.
Style: Considers all styles. Looks for "individuality, passion." Does not want to see commercial work.
Terms: Accepts work on consignment (no commission). Retail price is set by artist. Exclusive area representation not required. Gallery provides insurance, shipping costs, promotion and contract.
Submissions: Send query letter with resume, slides, photographs and SASE. Write to schedule an appointment to show a portfolio, which should include slides and transparencies. Resumes and other biographical material are filed.

*FRANCES WOLFSON ART GALLERY, 300 NE 2nd Ave., Miami FL 33132. (305)347-3278. Director of Galleries: Sheldon Lurie. Nonprofit gallery. Estab. 1976. Represents emerging, mid-career and established artists. Exhibited artists include James McGarrell and Arnold Roche Rabell. Sponsors 8 shows/year. Average display time 1 month. Open winter, fall and spring. Located downtown; 3,500 sq. ft. 100% of space for special exhibitions. Overall price range: $100-100,000.

Media: Consider oil, acrylic, watercolor, pastel, pen & ink, drawings, mixed media, works on paper, sculpture, ceramic, fiber, installation, photography, original handpulled prints, woodcuts, wood engravings, linocuts, engravings, mezzotints, etchings, lithographs, pochoir and serigraphs. Most frequently exhibits paintings, work on paper and sculpture.
Style: Exhibits all styles and genres.
Terms: Retail price set by the artist. Gallery provides insurance and promotion; gallery pays for shipping costs. Prefers framed artwork.
Submissions: Send query letter with resume, slides, bio and reviews. Write to schedule an appointment to show a portfolio, which should include slides. Replies in 2-3 weeks. Files correspondence and resume.

Georgia

ALIAS GALLERY, Suite F-2, 75 Bennett St., Atlanta GA 30309. President: Sarah A. Hatch. (404)352-3532. Retail gallery and custom/archival framing. Estab. 1985. Clientele: all great art appreciators—artist to upper middle class; 90% private collectors, 10% corporate clients. Represents artists. Sponsors 1 solo and 2 group shows/year. Average display time is 4-6 weeks. "My standards for quality work are very high." Interested in emerging, mid-career and established artists. Overall price range: $100-3,500; most artwork sold at $250-1,000.
Media: Considers oil, acrylic, watercolor, pastel, mixed media, installations, photography and unique handpulled prints. Most frequently exhibits paintings and pastels.
Style: Exhibits conceptual and expressionistic work. "The ideal work is the true vital expression of the artist and his or her ability to create a work which stands on its own merits. It has a 'life' of its own. Am always looking for a new idea, technique or style."
Terms: Central gallery space is booked with thematic shows. 30-40% commission. Retail price is set by artist. Gallery provides insurance, promotion and contract.
Submissions: Call or write for application and more information about upcoming shows. Send SASE.
Tips: "I lean toward bright color, but I have seen dark works with their own special kind of brightness. I do not want to see commercial or decorative art." Send SASE for current gallery prospectus.

*ARTIST ASSOCIATES, INC., 3261 Roswell Rd. NE, Atlanta GA 30305. (404)261-4960. Manager: C. Riley. Retail and cooperative gallery. Estab. 1961. Represents 30 mid-career artists. Has 30 members. Sponsors 6 shows/year. Average display time 1 month. Open all year. Located in Buckhead; 3,000 sq. ft.; "with nice wall space, in the oldest area of its kind in Atlanta." 25% of space for special exhibitions, 100% for gallery artists. Clientele: residents and designers. 50% private collectors, 50% corporate collectors. Overall price range: $200-3,000.
Media: Considers oil, acrylic, watercolor, pastel, pen & ink, drawings, mixed media, collage, ceramic, original handpulled prints, etchings and serigraphs.
Style: Exhibits expressionism, painterly abstraction, surrealism, conceptualism, minimalism, post modern works, impressionism, realism; all styles and genres.
Terms: Accepts work on consignment (40% commission). Retail price set by the artist. Gallery provides insurance, promotion and contract; artist pays for shipping. Prefers framed artwork.
Submissions: Send query letter with resume, slides and photographs. Write to schedule an appointment to show a portfolio, which should include originals and photographs. Replies in 1 month.
Tips: "Be prepared to leave 10-20 slides plus resume at least one month for the selection committee."

*THE ATLANTA COLLEGE OF ART GALLERY, 1280 Peachtree Street NE, Atlanta GA 30309. (404)898-1157. Director: Lisa Tuttle. Nonprofit gallery. Estab. 1984. Clientele: general public and art students. Sponsors 10 group shows/year. Average display time is 5 weeks. Interested in emerging, mid-career and established artists.
Media: Considers all media. Most frequently exhibits paintings, drawings, sculpture, prints, photography and installations.
Style: Considers all styles. "We primarily sponsor group exhibitions which are organized in a variety of ways: curated, juried, invitational, rentals, etc."
Terms: Accepts work on consignment (30% commission). Retail price is set by artist. Exclusive area representation not required. Gallery provides insurance, promotion and contract; shipping costs are shared.
Submissions: Send query letter with resume, slides and SASE. Write to schedule an appointment to show a portfolio, which should include slides.
Tips: "We are a nonprofit exhibition space and do *not* 'represent' artists per se."

FAY GOLD GALLERY, 247 Buckhead Ave., Atlanta GA 30305. (404)233-3843. Owner: Fay Gold. Retail gallery. Estab. 1980. Open year round. Clientele: 50% private collectors; 50% corporate clients. Represents 25 artists. Sponsors 18 solo and 4 group show/year. Average display time 4 weeks. Interested in emerging and established artists. Overall price range: $200-350,000; Most work sold at $2,000-20,000.

Media: Considers any media and all types of prints. Most frequently exhibits painting, photography, works on paper and sculpture.
Style: Exhibits all styles. Genres include landscapes, Americana and figurative work. Prefers abstracts, landscapes and figurative works. "We specialize in contemporary art of all mediums."
Terms: Accepts work on consignment (50% commission). Retail price set by gallery and artist. Exclusive area representation required. Gallery provides insurance and promotion.
Submissions: Send query letter with resume, slides and SASE. "We contact artists for a portfolio review if we are interested." Replies in 1 month. All material is returned if not accepted or under consideration.

*ANN JACOB GALLERY, 3500 Peachtree Rd. NE, Atlanta GA 30326. (404)262-3399. Director: Yvonne M. Jacob. Retail gallery and art consultancy. Estab. 1968. Represents 75 emerging, mid-career and established artists. Exhibited artists include Ben Smith and Mario Glushankoff. Sponsors 4 shows/year. "We always show our stable of artists even if there is a show at the same time." Open all year. Located in Buckhead; 2,200 sq. ft. 50% of space for special exhibitions. Clientele: 75% private collectors, 25% corporate collectors.
Media: Considers oil, acrylic, watercolor, drawing, mixed media, collage, works on paper, sculpture, ceramic, craft, fiber, glass, woodcuts, wood engravings, engravings, mezzotints, etchings, lithographs and serigraphs. Most frequently exhibits acrylic on canvas, bronze sculpture and art glass.
Style: Exhibits all styles and genres. Prefers painterly abstraction, expressionism and realism.
Terms: Accepts work on consignment (50% commission). Retail price set by gallery and artist. Gallery provides promotion and contract; gallery pays for shipping from gallery. Prefers framed artwork.
Submissions: Send resume, slides, bio, photographs and SASE. Call or write to schedule an appointment to show a portfolio, which should include slides, photographs and resume. Replies in 2 weeks.
Tips: "Please send information, including slides; then, if interested we will be in touch."

EVE MANNES GALLERY, Suite A, 116 Bennett St., Atlanta GA 30309. (404)351-6651. Retail gallery and art consultancy. Estab. 1980. Clientele: major corporate and private clients; 40% private collectors, 60% corporate clients. Represents 30-34 artists. Sponsors 4 solo and 6 group shows/year. Average display time is 4-6 weeks. Interested in emerging, mid-career and established artists. Overall price range: $500-20,000 plus larger commission prices; most artwork sold at $500-3,000.
Media: Considers oil, acrylic, watercolor, pastel, paper, sculpture, ceramic, fiber, glass, photography and mono prints. Most frequently exhibits pastel, oil or acrylic on canvas, sculpture (metal, wood), ceramic or glass. Currently looking for oil or acrylic on canvas.
Style: Exhibits hard-edge geometric abstraction, painterly abstraction, pattern painting, expressionism and realism. Genres include landscapes and figurative abstract. Most frequently exhibits color abstract, sculpture and landscapes. Currently seeking landscape realism. Seeks "challenging, vital work in both abstract and representational style. We welcome artists with strong, individual visions who explore personal and universal themes."
Terms: Accepts work on consignment (50% commission). Retail price is set by gallery or artist. Exclusive area representation required. Gallery provides insurance, promotion and contract; shipping costs are shared.
Submissions: Send query letter with resume, brochure and slides. Write to schedule an appointment to show a portfolio, which should include originals and slides. Slides, bio, postcards and catalogs are filed.
Tips: Looking for "consistency in artwork and images, confidence, friendliness, responsibility and commitment to gallery and self." Does not want to see "arrogant self-centered persons unwilling to work with gallery to help in sales." Current trend seems to be that "artists and galleries are having to work together more often in processing sales (possibly splitting discounts to established clientele)."

PEACHTREE GALLERY, LTD., 2277 Peachtree Rd. NE, Atlanta GA 30309. (404)355-0511. Manager: Gladys G. Lippincott. Retail gallery. Estab. 1983. Interested in established artists and posthumous works. Location: Buckhead area of Atlanta (in city limits) where there are other art and antiques specialists. Clientele: 80% private collectors, 20% corporate clients. Overall price range: $250-15,000; most artwork sold at $500-3,000.
Media: Considers oil, watercolor, pastel, pen & ink, drawings, mixed media, woodcuts, wood engravings, linocuts, engravings, mezzotints, etchings and lithographs. Most frequently exhibits oil, watercolor and lithographs.
Style: Exhibits impressionism, expressionism and realism. Prefers landscapes, florals, Americana, wildlife, figurative work and all genres. "Peachtree Gallery, Ltd., deals primarily in oil, watercolor and works on paper by listed American artists of the late 19th and early 20th centuries. The gallery's collection includes some English and French pieces. Scenes of the South and works by Southern artists are featured."
Terms: Accepts artwork on consignment or buys outright. Retail price set by gallery. Gallery provides promotion. Artist pays for shipping. Prefers framed artwork.
Submissions: Call to schedule an appointment to show a portfolio. Files bio, resume and brochure. Gallery does not handle contemporary artists. We are happy to see work by contemporary artists so that we can refer to it when we receive inquiries. We keep info on file.
Tips: "We see a growing interest in works by women artists and by both male and female artists of the WPA period and later."

*SWAN COACH HOUSE ART GALLERY, 3110 Slaton Dr., Atlanta GA 30305. (404)266-2636. Chairman: Becky Warner. Retail gallery. Estab. 1975. Represents mid-career and established artists. Interested in seeing the work of emerging artists. Exhibited artists include Linda Anderson and George Beattie. Sponsors 14 shows/year. Average display time 3½ weeks. Open all year. Located in Buckhead, north of downtown; 625 sq. ft.; "with a natural skylight, a beautiful architectural design." 100% of space for special exhibitions. 90% private collectors, 10% corporate collectors. Overall price range: $500-100,000; most work sold at $3-5,000.
Media: Considers oil, acrylic, watercolor, pastel, pen & ink, drawings, mixed media, collage, works on paper, sculpture, ceramic, glass, photography, original handpulled prints. "We rarely exhibit prints." Most frequently exhibits acrylic, oil and watercolor.
Style: Exhibits all styles and genres.
Terms: Accepts work on consignment (45% commission); there is a rental fee for space, covers 1 month. Retail price set by the artist. Gallery provides insurance and promotion; shipping costs are shared. Prefers framed artwork.
Submissions: Send query letter with resume, slides and SASE. Write to schedule an appointment to show a portfolio which should include slides. Replies in 3 months. Files resume.

Hawaii

HALE O KULA GOLDSMITH GALLERY, Box 416, Holualoa HI 96725. (808)324-1688. Owner: Sam Rosen. Retail gallery. Estab. 1981. Clientele: tourist and local trade; 100% private collectors. Interested in seeing the work of mid-career and established artists. Specializes in miniature art. Overall price range: $100-3,000; most artwork sold at $100-1,000.
Media: Considers sculpture, craft and mixed media.
Style: Exhibits contemporary, abstract, impressionism, floral, realism and neo-expressionism.
Terms: Accepts work on consignment (40% commission). Retail price is set by artist. Exclusive area representation not required. Gallery provides promotion and contract; shipping costs are shared.
Submissions: Send query letter with resume and slides. Write to schedule an appointment to show a portfolio.

INTERNATIONAL CONNOISSEURS, Box 1274, Kaneohe HI 96744. (808)239-8933. Owner: Larry LeDoux. Art consultancy. Estab. 1978. Clientele: 60% private collectors, 40% corporate clients. Represents 6 artists. Sponsors 2-4 solo shows/year. Interested in emerging, mid-career and established artists. Overall price range: $15-20,000; most artwork sold at $30-6,000.
Media: Considers oil, acrylic, watercolor, pastel, pen & ink, drawings, mixed media, collage, woodcuts, wood engravings, linocuts, engravings, mezzotints, etchings, lithographs and serigraphs. Most frequently exhibits oils and acrylics, reproductions and serigraphs.
Style: Exhibits realism, impressionism, expressionism and surrealism. Genres include landscapes and wildlife. Prefers surrealism and impressionism. "We are basically an artist's agency specializing in the marketing of artists through national media campaigns supported by mail-order sales, mailings and telemarketing. Our purpose is to create a national identity through exposure and retail sales, and generate continuing wholesale income through establishment of a network of galleries."
Terms: Accepts work on consignment. Retail price set by gallery and artist. Exclusive area representation not required.
Submissions: Send query letter with resume, brochure, slides, photographs, bio and SASE. Replies in 3 weeks. Files brochures. Most material is returned if not accepted or under consideration.
Tips: "We are looking for artists who want to invest in themselves whatever is necessary to create a national identity and following." Strong interest continues in impressionism and expressionism, not realistic treatment, but recognizable subjects.

QUEEN EMMA GALLERY, 1301 Punchbowl St., Honolulu HI 96813. (808)547-4397. Director: Masa Morioka Taira. Nonprofit gallery located in the main lobby of The Queen's Medical Center. Estab. 1977. Clientele: M.D.s, staff personnel, hospital visitors, community-at-large; 90% private collectors. Sponsors 8 solo and 4 group shows/year. Average display time is 3-3½ weeks. Interested in emerging, mid-career and established artists. Overall price range: $50-1,000; most artwork sold at $100-300.
Media: Considers all media.
Style: Exhibits contemporary, abstract, impressionism, figurative, primitive, non-representational, photorealism, realism neo-expressionism, landscapes and florals. Specializes in humanities-oriented interpretive, literary, cross-cultural and cross-disciplinary works. Interested in folk art, miniature works and ethnic works. "Our goal is to offer a variety of visual expressions by regional artists, including emergent and thesis shows by honors students and MFA candidates."

Terms: Accepts work on consignment (30% commission). Retail price is set by artist. Exclusive area representation not required. Gallery provides promotion and contract.
Submissions: Send query letter with resume, brochure, business card, slides, photographs and SASE. "Prefer brief proposal or statement or proposed body of works." Preference given to local artists.
Tips: "The best introduction to us is to submit your proposal with a dozen slides of works created with intent to show. Show professionalism, honesty, integrity, experimentation, new direction and readiness to show." Sees trend toward "global, environmental concerns, the use of non-traditional materials, expression and presentations and new technologies."

THE VILLAGE GALLERY, 120 Dickenson St., Lahaina HI 96761. (808)661-4402. Owner/Manager: Linda Shue. Retail gallery. Estab. 1970. Clientele: tourists, return visitors, those with a second home in Hawaii, 85% private collectors, 15% corporate clients. Represents 100 artists. Sponsors 10 solo and 4 group shows/year. Average display time varies. Interested in emerging and established artists. Overall price range: $10-10,000; most work sold at $800-3,000.
Media: Considers oil, acrylic, watercolor, pastel, pen & ink, drawings, mixed media, collage, works on paper, sculpture, ceramic, fiber and glass. Most frequently exhibits oil, watercolor and mixed media.
Style: Exhibits impressionism, realism, color field and painterly abstraction. Genres include landscapes, florals, figurative work; considers all genres. Prefers impressionism, painterly abstraction and realism.
Terms: Accepts work on consignment 50% commission. Retail price set by gallery and artist. Exclusive area representation required. Shipping costs are shared. Prefers artwork framed.
Submissions: Send query letter with resume, slides, and photographs. Write to schedule an appointment to show a portfolio, which should include originals, slides and photographs. Replies in 2 weeks. All material is returned if not accepted or under consideration.

Idaho

OCHI GALLERY, 1322 Main, Boise ID 83702. (208)342-1314. Owners: Denis or Roberta Ochi. Retail gallery and art consultancy. Estab. 1974. Sponsors 4 solo and 2 group shows/year. Average display time is 4-6 weeks. Interested in emerging and established artists. Overall price range: $500-100,000.
Media: Considers all media.
Style: Considers all styles. Most frequently exhibited styles: contemporary and realism. "We are always looking for good art regardless of style."
Terms: Accepts work on consignment. Retail price is set by gallery or artist. Exclusive area representation required.
Submissions: Send query letter with resume, slides and photographs. Write to schedule an appointment to show a portfolio, which should include originals, slides and transparencies. Slides, transparencies and "any pertinent information on artist's career" are filed.

Illinois

ARTEMISIA GALLERY, 700 N. Carpenter, Chicago IL 60622. (312)226-7323. President: Marlene Baues. Cooperative and nonprofit gallery/alternative space. Estab. 1973. 18 members. Sponsors 60 solo shows/year. Average display time 4 weeks. Interested in emerging and established artists. Overall price range: $150-10,000; most work sold at $600-2,500.
Media: Considers oil, acrylic, watercolor, pastel, pen & ink, drawings, mixed media, collage, works on paper, sculpture, ceramic, craft, fiber, glass, installation, photography, egg tempera, woodcuts, wood engravings, linocuts, engravings, mezzotints, etchings, lithographs, pochoir and serigraphs. Prefers paintings, sculpture and installation. "Artemisia is a cooperative art gallery run by artists. We try and promote women artists."
Terms: Co-op membership fee plus donation of time; rental fee for space; rental fee covers 1 month. Retail price set by artist. Exclusive area representation not required. Gallery provides insurance; artist pays for shipping.
Submissions: Send query letter with resume, slides and SASE. Write to schedule an appointment to show a portfolio, which should include slides. Replies in 6 weeks. All material is returned if not accepted or under consideration.
Tips: "Send clear, readable slides, labeled and marked 'top' or with red dot in lower left corner."

ARTPHASE I, INC., 1376 W. Grand Ave., Chicago IL 60622. (312)243-9800. Owner: Elizabeth Wangler. Art consultancy. Estab. 1986. Clientele: 50% private collectors; 50% corporate clients. Represents about 40 artists. Sponsors 11-12 group shows/year. Interested in emerging and established artists.
Media: Considers oil, acrylic, watercolor, pastel, drawings, mixed media, collage, works on paper, sculpture, ceramic, craft, fiber, egg tempera, woodcuts, wood engravings, linocuts, engravings, mezzotints, etchings and lithographs. Most frequently exhibits prints/drawings, paintings and 3-D ceramics, etc.

Style: Exhibits expressionism, neo-expressionism, realism, photorealism, minimalism, primitivism, color field, painterly abstraction, conceptualism and post modern works. Genres include landscapes and figurative work. Prefers painterly abstraction, neo-expressionism and expressionism. "Artphase I handles art in a variety of media. Our selections are based on our appreciation of the work rather than medium or price. We also maintain a slide registry in the gallery, which is actively presented to architects, designers and corporations."
Terms: Accepts work on consignment (50% commission). Gallery provides insurance, promotion and contract; shipping costs are shared.
Submissions: Send query letter with resume, brochure, slides, photographs, bio and SASE. Replies in 2-4 weeks. Files slides and resumes.

CAIN GALLERY, 1016 North Blvd., Oak Park IL 60301. (708)383-9393. Owner: Priscilla Cain. Retail gallery. Estab. 1973. Open all year. Clientele: 80% private collectors, 20% corporate clients. Represents 75 artists. Sponsors 3 solo shows/year. Average display time for a work 6 months. Interested in emerging and established artists. Overall price range: $100-6,000; most artwork sold at $300-600.
Media: Considers oil, acrylic, watercolor, mixed media, collage, sculpture, ceramic, woodcuts, engravings, mezzotints, etchings, lithographs and serigraphs. Most frequently exhibits acrylic, watercolor and serigraphs.
Style: Exhibits impressionism, realism, surrealism, painterly abstraction, imagism and all styles. Genres include landscapes, florals, figurative work and all genres. Prefers impressionism, abstraction and realism. "Our gallery is a showcase for living American artists—mostly from the Midwest, but we do not rule out artists from other parts of the country who attract our interest. We have a second gallery in Saugatuck, Michigan, which is open during the summer season. The Saugatuck gallery attracts buyers from all over the country."
Terms: Accepts artwork on consignment (45% commission). Retail price set by artist. Exclusive area representation required. Gallery provides insurance, promotion, contract and shipping costs from gallery. Prefers framed artwork.
Submissions: Send query letter with resume and slides. Call or write to schedule an appointment to show a portfolio, which should include originals and slides. Replies in 2 weeks.

CHIAROSCURO, 750 N. Orleans, Chicago IL 60610. (312)988-9253. Secretary: Ronna Isaacs or President: Peggy Wolf. Retail gallery. Estab. 1987. Located in Chicago's River North Gallery District. Clientele: 95% private collectors; 5% corporate clients. Represents over 200 artists. Sponsors 10 group shows/year. Average display time 1 month. Interested in emerging artists. Overall price range: $30-2,000; most work sold at $50-150.
Media: Considers oil, acrylic, watercolor, pastel, mixed media, works on paper, sculpture, ceramic, craft, furniture and glass. Most frequently exhibits paintings, craft and furniture.
Style: Exhibits expressionism, neo-expressionisms, realism, photorealism, surrealism, primitivism, color field, painterly abstaction, imagism, pattern painting and hard-edge geometric abstraction. Prefers figurative work. "We like to specialize in affordable art for the beginning collector."
Terms: Accepts work on consignment (50% commission). Retail price set by gallery and artist. Exclusive area representation required in River North Gallery District. Gallery provides insurance; shipping costs are shared.
Submissions: Send query letter with resume, slides, photographs, bio and SASE. Call or write to schedule an appointment to show a portfolio, which should include originals, slides and photographs. Replies in 3 weeks. Files resumes and slides. All material is returned if not accepted or under consideration.
Tips: "Include bio and price list with all slides."

CONTEMPORARY ART WORKSHOP, 542 W. Grant Pl., Chicago IL 60614. (312)472-4004. Administrative Director: Lynn Kearney. Nonprofit gallery. Estab. 1949. Clientele: art-conscious public, well informed on art; 75% private collectors, 25% corporate clients. Average display time is 3½ weeks "if it's a show, otherwise we can show the work for an indefinite period of time." Interested in emerging, mid-career and established artists. Overall price range: $300-5,000; most artwork sold at $1,500.
Media: Considers oil, acrylic, watercolor, mixed media, works on paper, sculpture, and original handpulled prints. Most frequently exhibits paintings, sculpture and works on paper.
Style: "Any good work" is considered.
Terms: Accepts work on consignment (⅓ commission). Retail price is set by gallery or artist. Exclusive area representation not required. Gallery provides insurance and promotion.
Submissions: Send query letter with resume, slides and SASE. Slides and resume are filed.
Tips: "Looks for a professional approach, fine art school degree (or higher), and high quality work in whatever medium. Artists a long distance from Chicago will probably not be considered." The most common mistake artists make in presenting their work is "showing too wide a range of their work—over too many past years."

CORPORATE ART SOURCE INC., 900 N. Franklin St., Chicago IL 60610. (312)751-1300. Owner: Kathleen Bernhardt. Retail gallery. Estab. 1975. Located in River North gallery area. Clientele: 10% private collectors; 90% corporate clients. Represents 200 artists. Sponsors 4 group shows/year. Average display time 4 weeks.

Interested in emerging and established artists. Overall price range: $200-100,000; most work sold at $500-5,000.

Media: Considers oil, acrylic, watercolor, pastel, pen & ink, drawings, mixed media, collage, works on paper, sculpture, ceramic, fiber, glass, egg tempera, woodcuts, wood engravings, linocuts, engravings, mezzotints, etchings, lithographs, pochoir and serigraphs. Most frequently exhibits works on paper, canvas and sculpture.
Style: Exhibits expressionism, realism, surrealism, color field, painterly abstraction and imagism. Considers all genres. Prefers realism, painterly abstraction and color field. "Corporate Art Source specializes in meeting the needs of architects, designers and our corporate clientele. Our staff of art consultants are experienced in working with blueprints and color boards and are able to recommend artwork for each particular space based on budget requirements, taste and environmental needs."
Terms: Accepts artwork on consignment (50% commission) or buys outright (40% retail price; net 30 days). Retail price set by gallery and artist. Gallery provides insurance and contract; artist pays for shipping.
Submissions: Send query letter with resume, slides and bio. Portfolio should include originals and slides. Replies in 2 weeks.

FREEPORT ART MUSEUM AND CULTURAL CENTER, 121 N. Harlem Ave., Freeport IL 61032. (815)235-9755. Contact: Director. Estab. 1975. Clientele: 30% tourists; 60% local; 10% students. Sponsors 2 solo and 10 group shows/year. Average display time 5 weeks. Interested in emerging and established artists.
Media: Considers oil, acrylic, watercolor, pastel, pen & ink, drawings, mixed media, collage, works on paper, sculpture, ceramic, craft, fiber, glass, installation, photography, egg tempera, original handpulled prints, woodcuts, wood engravings, linocuts, engravings, mezzotints, etchings, lithographs, pochoir and serigraphs.
Style: Exhibits all styles and genres. "We are a regional museum serving Northwest Illinois, Southern Wisconsin and Eastern Iowa. We have extensive permanent collections and 12-15 special exhibits per year representing the broadest possible range of regional and national artistic trends."
Terms: Gallery provides insurance and promotion. Shipping costs are shared. Prefers artwork framed.
Submissions: Send query letter with resume, slides, SASE, brochure, photographs and bio. Write to schedule an appointment to show a portfolio, which should include originals, slides and photographs. Replies in 1-2 months. Files resumes.
Tips: "Send information in December or January."

GALERIE AMERICANA, Suite 1907, 320 W. Illinois, Chicago IL 60610. (312)337-2670. Director: Derrick Beard. Retail and wholesale gallery/alternative space/art consultancy. Estab. 1985. Clientele: tourists, private collectors and walk-ins. 80% private collectors; 10% corporate clients. Represents 50 artists. Sponsors 3 solo and 3 group shows/year. Average display time 6 weeks. Accepts only artists from U.S., Carribbean and Latin America. Interested in established artists. Overall price range: $200-10,000; most work sold at $1,000-3,000.
Media: Considers oil, acrylic, watercolor, pastel, pen & ink, drawings, mixed media, collage, works on paper, sculpture, craft, photography, egg tempera, woodcuts, wood engravings, linocuts, engravings, etchings, lithographs, serigraphs, offset reproductions and posters. Most frequently exhibits oil, prints and drawings.
Styles: Exhibits all styles and genres. Prefers post-modernism, social realism and primitivism. "Our gallery is based on the belief that we should serve those minorities who have a social theme and/or a sensitivity to developments in society. We look for older artists who express a social statement and who were active during the '30s, '40s, '50s."
Terms: Accepts artwork on consignment (50% commission) or buys outright (35% retail price; net 60 days.) Retail price set by gallery and artist. Exclusive area representation required. Gallery provides insurance, promotion and contract; shipping costs are shared. Prefers framed artwork.
Submissions: Send query letter with resume, brochure, business card, slides, photographs, bio and SASE. Write to schedule an appointment to show a portfolio, which should include slides, transparencies and photographs. Replies in 4 weeks. Files resume, slides/photographs. All material is returned if not accepted or under consideration.
Tips: "Please write, do not call. By appointment only! Include *best* examples of work."

*GALESBURG CIVIC ART CENTER, 114 East Main St., Galesburg IL 61401. (309)342-7415. Director: Steve Fors. Nonprofit gallery. Estab. 1965. Represents 250 members; emerging artists. Exhibited artists include Celeste Rehm and Clare Smith. Sponsors 20 shows/year. Average display time 1 month. "We are closed the month of August." Located downtown; 1,400 sq. ft.; "We have 3 gallery spaces: 2 exhibition and 1 consignment gallery." 100% of space for gallery artists. Overall price range: $100-10,000; most artwork sold at $100-300.
Media: Considers oil, acrylic, watercolor, pastel, pen & ink, drawings, mixed media, collage, works on paper, sculpture, ceramic, craft, fiber, glass, installation, photography, original handpulled prints, woodcuts, wood engravings, linocuts, engravings, mezzotints, etchings, lithographs, pochoir and serigraphs. Most frequently exhibits paintings, prints and ceramic.
Style: Exhibits expressionism, neo-expressionism, painterly abstraction, minimalism, color field, post modern works, realism, hard-edge geometric abstraction and all styles. Genres include landscapes, florals and figurative work. Prefers neo-expressionism, realism and painterly abstraction.

Terms: Accepts work on consignment (30% commission). Retail price set by the artist. Gallery provides insurance and promotion; artist pays for shipping. Prefers framed artwork.
Submissions: Accepts only artists from Midwest. Send query letter with resume, slides and bio. Call to schedule an appointment to show a portfolio, which should include slides. Replies in 1 month.

*GALLERIA RENATA, 507 N. Wells St., Chicago IL 60610. (312)644-1607. Owner/Director: Renata Terzakis. Retail gallery. Estab. 1987. Represents 15 emerging and mid-career artists. Exhibited artists include Barry Gross and Charles Nivens. Sponsors 6-7 shows/year. Average display time 4-6 weeks. Open all year. Located in downtown, Chicago's River North; 2,500 sq. ft.; "ground floor loft space with 2 large street-level bay windows, 14' ceilings. Bi-level exhibition space main floor for special current exhibitions, lower level for constant representation of gallery artists." 66% of space for special exhibitions. Clientele: 85% private collectors, 15% corporate clients. Overall price range: $500-50,000; most artwork sold at: $1,000-10,000.
Media: Considers oil, acrylic, drawings, mixed media, collage, works on paper, sculpture, fiber, glass and installation. Most frequently exhibits oil, acrylic and sculpture.
Style: Exhibits expressionism, painterly abstraction, conceptualism, color field, realism and photorealism. Genres include landscapes, florals and figurative work. Prefers expressionism, realism and abstractionism.
Terms: Artwork is accepted on consignment (50% commission). Retail price set by the gallery and the artist. Gallery provides insurance and promotion. Artist pays for shipping. Prefers framed artwork.
Submissions: Send query letter with resume, slides, bio and SASE. Call or write to schedule an appointment to show a portfolio, which should include slides, photographs and transparencies. Replies in 1 month. Files material of interest for future reference.

GALLERY TEN, 514 E. State St., Rockford IL 61104. (815)964-1743. Contact: "any partner." Retail gallery. Estab. 1986. "We are a downtown gallery representing visual artists in all media." Clientele: 50% private collectors, 50% corporate clients. Represents 400 artists. Interested in emerging, mid-career and established artists. Average display time 6 weeks. Overall price range: $4-10,000; most artwork sold at $50-300.
Media: Considers all media.
Style: Exhibits fresh and contemporary styles and all genres. "Nine artist-partners organize continually rotating shows with themes such as figurative, holiday, the fine art of craft, architecture, fiber and handmade paper in the main gallery. We also have sales gallery for handcrafted and innovative objects and jewelry. All work must be for sale and ready to hang."
Terms: Retail price set by artists (40% commission). Exclusive area representation not required. Gallery provides promotion. Prefers framed artwork.
Submissions: Send query letter with slides, photographs and SASE. Replies in 2 weeks. All material is returned if not accepted or under consideration.
Tips: Looks for "creative viewpoint—professional presentation and craftsmanship."

GROVE ST. GALLERY, 919 Grove St., Evanston IL 60201. (708)866-7341. Gallery Director: Chris or George. Retail gallery. Estab. 1889. Clientele: 60% private collectors; 40% corporate clients. Represents 15 artists. Sponsors 6 solo and 5 group shows/year. Average display time 4 weeks. Interested in emerging and established artists. Overall price range: $500-25,000; most work sold at $2,500-10,000.
Media: Considers oil, acrylic, watercolor, pastel, glass and serigraphs. Most frequently exhibits oil.
Style: Exhibits impressionism. Genres include landscapes, florals, Southwestern and Western themes and figurative work. Prefers Mediterranean landscapes, florals and Southwestern/Western works.
Terms: Accepts artwork on consignment. Retail price set by artist. Exclusive area representation required. Gallery provides partial insurance and promotion; shipping costs are shared. Prefers artwork framed.
Submissions: Send query letter with resume, slides, brochure, photographs and bio. Call or write to schedule an appointment to show a portfolio, which should include originals, slides, transparencies and photographs. Replies in 3 weeks. Files photographs or slides. All material is returned if not accepted or under consideration.

*GWENDA JAY GALLERY, 2nd Floor, 301 W. Superior, Chicago IL 60610. (312)664-3406. Assistant Director: Emily Britton. Retail gallery. Estab. 1988. Represents 23 artists; mid-career artists mainly, but emerging and established, too. Exhibited artists include Paul Sierra and Eric Shultis. Sponsors 11 shows/year. Average

 The asterisk before a listing indicates that the listing is new in this edition. New markets are often the most receptive to freelance submissions.

display time 4 weeks. Open all year. Located in River North area; 2,200 sq. ft.; "we have a view of the Hancock building and are level with the El (elevated trains of Chicago)." 85% of space for 1-2 person exhibitions, 15% for gallery artists. Clientele: "all types—budding collectors to corporate art collections." Overall price range: $500-12,000; most artwork sold at $1,000-6,000.

Media: Considers oil, acrylic, mixed media and sculpture. "If there is an architectural theme, we may consider prints of limited editions only." Most frequently exhibits oil and egg tempera.

Style: Exhibits "eclectic styles and a personal vision." Genres include some landscapes and some figurative work. "We prefer eclectic styles. We are not looking for one style."

Terms: Accepts work on consignment (50% commission). Retail price set by the gallery. Gallery provides insurance, promotion and contract; shipping costs are shared.

Submissions: Send query letter with resume, slides, bio and SASE. Write to schedule an appointment. "We contact once slides have been reviewed." Portfolio should include originals, slides, photographs and transparencies. Replies in 2-4 weeks.

Tips: "Please send slides with resume and an SASE first. We will reply and schedule an appointment if we wish to see more. Please be familiar with the gallery's style." Looking for "consistent style and dedication to career. No original works until we've seen slides. There is no need to have work framed excessively. The work should stand well on its own, initially."

CARL HAMMER GALLERY, 200 W. Superior St., Chicago IL 60622. (312)266-8512. Director: Carl Hammer. Retail gallery. Estab. 1980. Open all year. Clientele: collectors, students, artists and visitors. Represents 20 artists. Sponsors 5 solo and 5 group shows/year. Average display time 4-5 weeks. Accepts only on aesthetic basis. Interested in emerging and established artists. Overall price range: $350-20,000; most artwork sold at $2,500-7,000.

Media: Considers oil, acrylic, watercolor, pastel, drawings, mixed media, collage, sculpture and fiber. Most frequently exhibits sculptures, paintings and mixed media.

Style: Exhibits works by self-taught and outsider artists, both historical and contemporary. "Works include paintings, drawings, textiles (Afro-American, Amish, American vintage and contemporary), eccentric furniture, architectural features, circus banners, assemblage and unique objects from American material culture. Work is accepted on aesthetic basis only, and is not based on inclusion in a certain category. Contemporary artists with academic backgrounds are exhibited as well (4-5 shows per year)."

Terms: Accepts artwork on consignment (commission varies) or buys outright (retail price varies). Retail price set by gallery. Exclusive area representation usually required. Gallery provides insurance, promotion and contract.

Submissions: Send query letter with slides, SASE and photographs. Replies in up to 2 months.

Tips: "Artists should be very familiar with the gallery focus and direction. We rarely choose work from submitted slides."

HYDE PARK ART CENTER, 1701 E. 53rd St., Chicago IL. (312)324-5520. Executive Director: Rhonda Silverstein. Nonprofit gallery. Estab. 1939. Clientele: general public. Sponsors 1 solo and 7 group shows/year. Average display time is 4-6 weeks. "Restricted to Illinois artists not currently affiliated with a retail gallery." Overall price range: $100-10,000.

Media: Considers all media.

Terms: Accepts work "for exhibition only." Retail price is set by artist. Exclusive area representation not required. Gallery provides insurance and contract.

Submissions: Send query letter with resume, slides and SASE.

ILLINOIS ARTISANS SHOP, State of Illinois Center, 100 W. Randolph St., Chicago IL 60601. (312)917-5321. Administrative Manager: Ellen Gantner. Retail gallery operated by the nonprofit Illinois State Museum Society. Estab. 1985. Clientele: tourists, conventioneers, business people, Chicagoans. Represents 400 artists. Interested in emerging, mid-career and established artists. Average display time is 6 months. "Accepts only juried artists living in Illinois." Overall price range: $10-4,000; most artwork sold at $250.

Media: Considers all media. "The finest examples in all mediums by Illinois artists."

Style: Considers all styles. "Seeks contemporary, traditional folk and ethnic arts from all regions of Illinois. 'Cute' crafts are not welcome in our shop."

Terms: Accepts work on consignment (50% commission), retail price is set by gallery and artist. Exclusive area representation not required. Gallery provides promotion and contract.

Submissions: Send resume and slides. Accepted works are selected by a jury. Resume and slides are filed. "The finest work can be rejected if slides are not good enough to assess."

*N.A.M.E., 700 N. Carpenter, Chicago IL 60622. (312)226-0671. Director: Irene Tsatsos. Nonprofit gallery. Estab. 1973. Represents emerging, mid-career and established artists. Has 75 members. Sponsors 8 shows/year. Average display time 5 weeks. Open all year. At River West; 2,000 sq. ft.

Media: Considers all media.

Style: Exhibits new work and new genres.

Terms: Retail price set by the artist. Gallery takes no commission. Gallery provides promotion; shipping costs are shared.

Submissions: "No portfolio reviews."

Tips: "There are 3 deadlines a year—1/15, 5/15, 9/15. Proposals are acknowledged immediately and decided upon within three months after review deadline."

*NAB GALLERY, 1433 Wolfram, Chicago IL 60657. (312)525-5418. Contact: Associate Director. Cooperative gallery, alternative space, nonprofit gallery. Estab. 1974. Represents emerging, mid-career and established artists. Has 6 members. Exhibited artists include Craig Anderson, John Kurtz and Marguerite Sandrock. Sponsors 4-6 shows/year. Average display time 5 weeks. Open fall, spring and winter. Located "downtown; NAB curates exhibits for spaces throughout Chicago." 90% of space for special exhibitions. Overall price range: $500-3,000.

Media: Considers all media. Most frequently exhibits paintings, drawings and prints.

Style: Exhibits all styles and genres.

Terms: There is a co-op membership fee plus a donation of time. There is a rental fee for space, which covers 1 month. Retail price set by the artist. Gallery provides promotion; artist pays for shipping.

Submissions: Send SASE and whatever best communicates artist's intent. Write to schedule an appointment to show a portfolio, which should include slides. Replies in 1 month with SASE. Files "completed exhibitions."

Tips: "Original work only. Since we are nonprofit, no emphasis on selling; rather, promotion. Always include SASE."

ISOBEL NEAL GALLERY, LTD., Suite 200, 200 Superior St., Chicago IL 60610. (312)944-1570. President: Isobel Neal. Retail gallery. Estab. 1986. Clientele: 90% private collectors, 10% corporate clients. Represents about 12 artists. Sponsors 2 solo and 5 group shows/year. Average display time 6 weeks. Features African-American artists. Interested in emerging, mid-career and established artists. Overall price range: $300-12,000; most artwork sold at $500-3,000.

Media: Considers oil, acrylic, watercolor, pastel, pen & ink, drawings, mixed media, collage, works on paper, sculpture, ceramic, fiber, photography, egg tempera, woodcuts, wood engravings, linocuts, engravings, mezzotints, etchings, lithographs and serigraphs. Most frequently exhibits oil, acrylic and sculpture.

Style: Exhibits impressionism, expressionism, realism, color field, painterly abstraction and hard-edge geometric abstraction; considers all styles. Genres include landscapes and figurative work. "The Isobel Neal gallery was founded to provide an opportunity for African-American artists to showcase their work and to enhance their visibility in the mainstream gallery system and in the community. The work ranges from figurative to abstract, sometimes with black imagery, but often not."

Terms: Accepts work on consignment (50% commission). Retail price set by gallery and artist. Exclusive area representation required. Gallery provides insurance, promotion and contract. "Under certain circumstances, the gallery will share shipping cost." Prefers framed artwork.

Submissions: Send query letter with resume, slides, bio and SASE. Call or write to schedule an appointment to show a portfolio. Replies in several months. Files slides, bio, resume and articles. All material is returned if not accepted or under consideration.

Tips: "Slides should be labeled properly and should be of good viewing quality." Common mistakes artists make in submitting work are "submitting photos instead of slides, not including a slide listing, not fully labeling slides, not cropping slides well, no SASE and submitting all of their work and not just their best. If at all possible, visit the gallery to see what we show."

NEVILLE-SARGENT GALLERY, 708 N. Wells and 311 W. Superior, Chicago IL 60610. (312)664-2787. Director: Kim Goldfarb. Retail gallery and art consultancy. Estab. 1974. Converted from industrial warehouse. Clientele: 50% private collectors; 50% corporate clients. Represents 30 artists. Sponsors 5 solo and 7 group shows/year. Average display time 3 weeks. Interested in emerging and established artists. Overall price range: $400-20,000; most work sold at $800-3,500.

Media: Considers oil, acrylic, watercolor, pastel, mixed media, collage, works on paper, sculpture and monotypes. Most frequently exhibits oil/acrylic canvases, steel/bronze sculptures and mixed media/handmade paper.

Style: Exhibits expressionism, neo-expressionism, realism, photorealism, primitivism and painterly abstraction. Genres include city scenes, landscapes and figurative work. Prefers painterly abstraction, realism and expressionism. "Neville-Sargent does not limit itself to a particular category of art. In an effort to satisfy our clients, who have a broad range of interests within the arts, we carry local and international artists, abstract and realist works in a variety of price ranges. Our philosophy is to embrace diversity and quality. The collection is eclectic. Though there is an increasing emphasis on sculpture, we are however open to significant work in the mediums stated above."

Terms: Accepts work on consignment (100% commission). Retail price set by gallery and artist. Exclusive area representation required. Gallery provides insurance, promotion and contract; shipping costs are shared.
Submissions: Send query letter with resume, slides and SASE. Call to schedule an appointment to show a portfolio, which should include originals. Replies in 1 month. Files "material that interests us." All material is returned if not accepted or under consideration.
Tips: "Quality of slides and presentation of slides is essential. Always enclose SASE."

*NIU ART MUSEUM, Northern Illinois University, DeKalb IL 60115. (815)753-1936. FAX: (815)753-0198. Museum Director: Lynda Martin. University museum. Estab. 1970. Represents emerging, mid-career and established artists. Exhibited artists include Miriam Schapiro and Faith Ringgold. Sponsors 20 shows/year. Average display time 6 weeks. Open all year. Located in DeKalb, Illinois and Chicago; space varies by gallery; "one is located in a renovated 1895 auditorium." 50% of space for special exhibitions.
Media: Considers all media and all types of prints.
Style: Exhibits all styles and all genres.
Terms: "All sales are referred to the artist." Retail price set by the artist. Gallery provides insurance and promotion; shipping costs to and from gallery are shared.
Submissions: Send query letter with resume and slides. Replies in 6 months. Files "maybes."

*NORTHERN ILLINOIS UNIVERSITY ART GALLERY IN CHICAGO, 212 W. Superior, Chicago IL 60610. (312)642-6010. Director: Peggy Doherty. Nonprofit university gallery. Estab. 1984. Represents emerging, mid-career and established artists. Sponsors 6 shows/year. Average display time 6-7 weeks. Open all year. Located in Chicago gallery area (near downtown); 1,656 sq. ft. 100% of space for special exhibitions. Overall price range: $100-50,000.
Media: Considers all media.
Style: Exhibits all styles and genres.
Terms: "No charge to artist and no commission." Retail price set by the artist. Gallery provides insurance and promotion; shipping costs are shared, depending on costs. Prefers framed artwork.
Submissions: Send query letter with resume, slides, SASE, reviews and statement. Call to schedule an appointment to show a portfolio. Replies in 3-4 weeks. Files resumes, bios, statements and paperwork.
Tips: "Always include SASE. Artists often expect too much: critiques of their work and immediate exhibitions. Work for exhibition is rarely selected at the first viewing."

© 1987 Margaret J. Miller

"Bloomin V," one of a series of fiber quilts designed by Margaret J. Miller, was exhibited in a show which traveled to Northern Illinois University Art Museum after it was in Sao Paulo, Brazil. The Woodinville, Washington artist says she wished to convey "three-dimensional design, unexpected color placement and a feeling of vastness, as though the piece occupies more space on the wall than it actually does."

NINA OWEN, LTD., 212 W. Superior St., Chicago IL 60610. (312)664-0474. Director: Audrey Owen. Gallery and art consultancy. Estab. 1985. Clientele: professionals—designers, architects, developers; 33% private collectors, 67% corporate clients. Represents 100 artists. Sponsors 3 solo and 3 group shows/year. Average display time is 2 months. Accepts sculptors only. Overall price range: $3,000-25,000. Most artwork sold at $4,500-5,000.

Media: Considers sculpture—metal, wood—mixed media, ceramic, fiber and glass. Most frequently exhibits steel, glass and wood sculptures. Currently looking for glass sculpture.
Style: Prefers "finely-executed abstract sculpture."
Terms: Accepts work on consignment. Retail price is set by gallery and artist. Exclusive area representation not required. Gallery provides insurance, promotion and contract; shipping costs are shared.
Submissions: Send query letter with resume, slides and SASE. Call or write to schedule an appointment to show a portfolio, which should include originals, slides or maquette (optional). Files slides and printed material of sculptors in our slide registry (approximately 50 artists not exhibited in gallery, but submitted for commissions).

THE PEORIA ART GUILD, 1838 N. Knoxville Ave., Peoria IL 61603. (309)685-7522. Director: Duffy Armstrong. Retail gallery for a nonprofit organization. Also has rental program. Estab. 1888. Clientele: 90% private collectors; 10% corporate clients. Represents 200 artists. Sponsors 6 solo and 2 group shows/year. Average display time 6 weeks. Interested in emerging mid-career and established artists. Overall price range: $25-2,000; most work sold at $125-500.
Media: Considers oil, acrylic, watercolor, pastel, mixed media, collage, works on paper, sculpture, ceramic, fiber, glass, photography, woodcuts, wood engravings, linocuts, engravings, mezzotints, etchings, lithographs and serigraphs. Most frequently exhibits acrylic/oil, watercolor and etchings/lithographs.
Style: Exhibits all styles. Genres include landscapes, florals and figurative work. Prefers landscapes, realism and painterly abstraction. "The Peoria Art Guild has a large and varied consignment gallery that supplies all the two-dimensional work to our extensive art rental program. Realistic watercolors, acrylics and oils work into this program easily with painterly abstractions and color field work always a possibility. The main gallery primarily exhibits newly emerging and established Midwestern artists with no restriction to style."
Terms: Accepts work on consignment (40% commission). Retail price set by artist. Gallery provides insurance, promotion and contract. Prefers artwork framed.
Submissions: Send query letter with resume, slides and SASE. Call to schedule an appointment to show a portfolio, which should include originals. Replies in 2 months. Files resume, slides and statement. All material is returned if not accepted or under consideration.

RANDOLPH STREET GALLERY, 756 N. Milwaukee, Chicago IL 60622. (312)666-7737. Contact: Exhibition Committee or Time Arts Committee. Nonprofit gallery. Estab. 1979. Sponsors 10 group shows/year. Average display time is 1 month. Interested in emerging, mid-career and established artists.
Media: Considers all media. Most frequently exhibits mixed media and performance.
Style: Exhibits hard-edge geometric abstraction, painterly abstraction, minimalism, conceptual, post-modern, feminist/political, primitivism, photorealism, expressionism and neo-expressionism. "We curate exhibitions which include work of diverse styles, concepts and issues, with an emphasis on works relating to social and critical concerns."
Terms: Accepts work on consignment (20% commission). Retail price is set by artist. Exclusive area representation not required. Gallery provides shipping costs, promotion, contract and honorarium.
Submissions: Send resume, brochure, slides, photographs and SASE. "Live events and exhibitions are curated by a committee which meets monthly." Resumes, slides and other supplementary material are filed.
Tips: Sees trend toward "a greater commitment to the community—art is no longer an 'ivory-tower' phenomenon."

REZAC GALLERY, 2nd Floor, 301 W. Superior, Chicago IL 60610. (312)751-0481. Owner/Director: Suzan Rezac. Retail gallery. Estab. 1988. Open all year. Features customized display cases in bleached oak, 5 huge windows facing south. Clientele: 100% private collectors. Represents 15 artists. Sponsors 3 solo and 3 group shows/year. Average display time 6 weeks. Prefers jewelry and sculpture. Interested in emerging and mid-career artists. Overall price range: $500-15,000; most artwork sold at $900-5,000.
Media: Considers sculpture, jewelry, glass, installation and photography. Most frequently exhibits goldsmithing, sculpture and installation.
Style: Exhibits minimalism, conceptualism, post modern works and hard-edge geometric abstraction. Prefers geometric abstraction, conceptualism and minimalism. "Rezac Gallery specializes in avant-garde decorative arts, with a prejudice towards metalsmithing and goldsmithing. Group exhibitions are always planned around a theme (i.e.: "Information as Ornament," "Gold"). The works are selected to fit the theme. This allows us to tie the decorative and fine arts, creating dialogue between the two fields. For one of the purposes of the gallery is to make the decorative arts as legitimate as their fine art counterparts."
Terms: Accepts work on consignment (50% commission). Retail price set by gallery and artist. Exclusive area representation required. Gallery provides insurance, promotion, contract and shipping costs from gallery.
Submissions: Send query letter with resume, brochure, slides, photographs and bio. Call or write to schedule an appointment to show a portfolio, which should include slides and transparencies. Replies in 3 weeks. File slides, 4×5″ and resumes.
Tips: "Make an appointment *after* you have sent slides. Looks for talent, integrity, professional approach and good craftsmanship. Don't show us over-designed or poorly made works."

ESTHER SAKS GALLERY, 311 W. Superior, Chicago IL 60610. (312)751-0911. Director: Esther Saks. Assistant Director: Jane Saks. Retail gallery. Estab. 1983. Clientele: 75% private collectors, 10% corporate clients. Represents 25 artists. Sponsors 9 solo and 3 group shows/year. Average display time 4 weeks. Interested in emerging and established artists. Overall price range: $250-14,000; most work sold at $1,000-4,000.
Media: Considers oil, acrylic, watercolor, drawings, mixed media, collage, works on paper, sculpture, ceramic, fiber, glass and original handpulled prints. Most frequently exhibits ceramic, works on paper and paintings.
Style: Exhibits neo-expressionism, surrealism and painterly abstraction. Genres include figurative work. "The Esther Saks Gallery offers contemporary artworks in a variety of media with a strong focus on ceramic sculpture. The gallery has a continuing commitment to work that affirms idea and image over technique and materials, while still revealing the hand and sensibility of the artist."
Terms: Accepts work on consignment (50% commission). Retail price set by gallery and artist. Exclusive area representation required. Gallery provides insurance, promotion, contract and shipping costs from gallery.
Submissions: Send query letter with resume, slides and SASE. Portfolio should include slides. "Include older pieces as well as new." Replies in 2 months. Follow your submissions with a phone call about a month after submitting."

SOUTHPORT GALLERY, 3755 N. Southport, Chicago IL 60613. (312)327-0372. Owner: Donna Wolfe. Retail gallery. Estab. 1988. Located near Wrigley Field and Music Box Theatre. Clientele: neighborhood people as well as the theatre crowd. Represents 3 artists. Sponsors 4 solo shows/year. Average display time 4 weeks. Accepts only artists from Chicago. Interested in emerging artists. Overall price range: $100-1,000; "we do exhibit and sell work for over $1,000."
Media: Considers oil, acrylic, watercolor, pen & ink, drawings, mixed media, collage, sculpture and photography. Most frequently exhibits watercolor, oil, pen & ink and etchings.
Style: Exhibits impressionism, realism, photorealism, surrealism, primitivism, color field, painterly abstraction and figurative work. Prefers realism, surrealism and photorealism. "Ideally, we seek emerging artists, offering them the opportunity to exhibit their work under standards that require it to be presented in a very professional manner. More established artists have found Southport gallery to be the perfect place to have an exhibit of their etchings, drawings or smaller works that fit within our price range."
Terms: Accepts work on consignment (50% commission). Retail price set by gallery and artist. Exclusive area representation not required. Gallery provides promotion and contract, opening reception and announcements. Prefers artwork framed.
Submissions: Send query letter with resume, slides, brochure, photographs, business card and bio. Call to schedule an appointment to show a portfolio, which should include originals, slides and photographs. Replies only if interested within 3 weeks. Files resume, bio and photos.
Tips: "Keep in mind our general price range and the fact that our gallery is small and therefore not suitable for exhibits of entirely large pieces (60×64). Qualities we look for include enthusiasm, professionalism and pride. Present a fair representation of your work and be secure about the way you present it."

*STATE OF ILLINOIS ART GALLERY, Suite 2-100, 100 W. Randolph, Chicago IL 60601. (312)814-5322. Administrator: Debora Duez Donato. Museum. Estab. 1985. Represents emerging, mid-career and established artists. Sponsors 6-7 shows/year. Average display time 7-8 weeks. Open all year. Located "in the Chicago loop; in the State of Illinois Center designed by Helmut Jahn." 100% of space for special exhibitions.
Media: All media considered.
Style: Exhibits all styles and genres.
Terms: "We exhibit work, do not handle sales." Gallery provides insurance and promotion; artist pays for shipping. Prefers framed artwork.
Submissions: Accepts only artists from Illinois. Send resume, slides, bio and SASE. Write to schedule an appointment to show a portfolio, which should include slides. Replies in 2 months.

UNIVERSITY OF ILLINOIS AT CHICAGO—CAMPUS PROGRAMS, 750 S. Halsted, M/C118, Chicago IL 60607. (312)413-5070. FAX: (312)413-5043. Director: Teri Gimpel. Nonprofit gallery. Estab. 1965. Represents emerging, mid-career and established artists. Exhibited artists include Ken Thurlbeck, Wallace Kirkland, Paula Henderson and Karl Kuehn. Sponsors 18 shows/year. Average display time 3 weeks. Open September-May. Located near downtown Chicago, Mongomery Ward Gallery: 1,131′; The Chicago Gallery: 2,906′; and The Art Lounge 720′. Clientele: University community, students, staff and faculty. Work must fit within university guidelines. Overall price range: $150-8,000.
Media: "We consider all media as long as it can fit through the door." Considers all types of prints.
Style: Exhibits all styles and all genres.
Terms: The gallery receives 20% of all sales. Retail price set by the artist. Gallery provides insurance and promotion. Artist pays for shipping. Prefers framed artwork.
Submissions: Send query letter with resume, slides, SASE and statement. Write to schedule an appointment to show a portfolio, which should include originals and slides. Replies in 4 months. Files none of material received.

Tips: "Work is chosen by committee which is why UIC has no style preference. We have three exhibition spaces: A Montgomery Ward gallery, the Chicago gallery and the Art Lounge."

RUTH VOLID GALLERY LTD., 225 W. Illinois St., Chicago IL 60610. (312)644-3180. Director: Karma Gardner. Retail gallery and art consultancy. Estab. 1970. Clientele: architects, designers, corporations, private collectors; 20% private collectors; 80% corporate clients. Represents 200 artists. Sponsors 2 solo and 8 group shows/year. Interested in emerging and established artists. Overall price range: $500-10,000.
Media: Considers oil, acrylic, watercolor, pastel, pen & ink, drawings, mixed media, works on paper, sculpture, ceramic, craft, fiber, glass, installation, photography, woodcuts, wood engravings, linocuts, engravings, mezzotints, etchings, lithographs, pochoir and serigraphs. Most frequently exhibits painting, sculpture and photography.
Style: Exhibits all styles.
Terms: Accepts work on consignment (50% commission). Retail price set by gallery and/or artist. Exclusive area representation required. Gallery provides insurance, promotion, contract; artist pays for shipping.
Submissions: Send query letter with resume, slides and SASE. Replies in 1 week. Files slides, articles and brochure. All material is returned if not accepted or under consideration.

ZAKS GALLERY, 620 N. Michigan Ave., Chicago IL 60611. (312)943-8440. Director: Sonia Zaks. Retail gallery. Represents 25 artists. Sponsors 10 solo and 1 group shows/year. Average display time is 1 month. Interested in emerging, mid-career and established artists. Overall price range: $350-15,000, "sculpture commissions higher prices."
Media: Considers oil, acrylic, watercolor, pastel, pen & ink, drawings, sculpture and mixed media.
Style: Specializes in contemporary paintings, works on paper and sculpture.
Terms: Accepts work on consignment. Retail price is set by gallery and artist. Exclusive area representation required. Gallery provides insurance and contract.
Submissions: Send query letter with resume and slides. Write to schedule an appointment to show a portfolio.
Tips: "A common mistake some artists make is presenting badly taken and unmarked slides. Artists may write to the gallery and enclose a resume and about one dozen slides."

Indiana

*ARTLINK, 1030 Broadway, Fort Wayne IN 46802. (219)424-7195. Artistic Director: Betty Fishman. Nonprofit gallery. Estab. 1979. Represents emerging and mid-career artists. Membership 400 (not all artists). Sponsors 8 shows/year. Average display time 5-6 weeks. Open all year. Located 5 blocks from central downtown; 1,600 sq. ft. 100% of space for special exhibitions. Clientele: "upper middle class." Overall price range: $100-500; most artwork sold at $100.
Media: Considers all media, including prints. Prefers work for annual print show and annual photo show, sculpture and painting.
Style: Exhibits expressionism, neo-expressionism, painterly abstraction, conceptualism, color field, post modern works, photorealism, hard-edge geometric abstraction, all styles and all genres. Prefers imagism, abstraction and realism.
Terms: Accepts work on consignment (30% commission). Retail price set by the artist. Gallery provides insurance, promotion and contract; shipping costs from gallery or shipping costs are shared. Prefers framed artwork.
Submissions: Send query letter with resume, slides and SASE. Reviewed by 14 member panel. Replies in 2 weeks. "Jurying takes place four times per year unless it is for a specific call for entry. A telephone call will give the artist an idea of the next jurying date."
Tips: Common mistakes artists make in presenting work are "bad slides and sending more than requested—large packages of painted material." Developing trends seem to be "higher prices, more 'crafts' in fine arts galleries, joint efforts by artists and gallery making higher demands on professionalism of the artist."

*ECHO PRESS, 1901 E. Tenth St., Bloomington IN 47403. (812)855-0476. Curator: Pegram Harrison. Retail gallery and contemporary print publishers. Estab. 1979. Represents 15 emerging, mid-career and established artists. Exhibited artists include Steven Sorman and Sam Gilliam. Average display time 2 months. Open all year. 1,000 sq. ft. 33% of space for special exhibitions. "We are a print workshop with gallery space: ⅔ workshop, ⅓ gallery." Clientele: 50% private collectors, 50% corporate collectors. Overall price range: $200-10,000; most work sold at $1,000-4,000.
Media: Considers lithographs, etchings, original handpulled prints, woodcuts, linocuts, engravings and etchings.
Style: Exhibits neo-expressionism, painterly abstraction and post modern works.
Terms: "We show our own publications." Retail price set by the gallery. Gallery provides insurance and promotion; shipping costs are shared.
Submissions: Send resume, slides, bio and reviews. Files bio, reproduction and review.

EDITIONS LIMITED GALLERY, 2727 E. 86th St., Indianapolis IN 46240. (317)253-7800. Director: Bridget Webster. Retail gallery. Represents emerging, mid-career and established artists. Sponsors 4 shows/year. Average display time 1 month. Open all year. Located "north side of Indianapolis; hardwood floors, track lighting, exposed ceiling, white walls." Clientele: 60% private collectors, 40% corporate collectors. Overall price range: $100-8,500; most artwork sold at $500-750.

Media: Considers oil, acrylic, watercolor, pastel, pen & ink, drawings, mixed media, collage, works on paper, sculpture, ceramic, craft, fiber, glass, photography, original handpulled prints, woodcuts, engravings, mezzotints, etchings, lithographs, pochoir and serigraphs. Most frequently exhibits mixed media, acrylic and pastel.

Style: Exhibits all styles and genres. Prefers abstract, landscapes and still lifes.

Terms: Accepts work on consignment (50% commission). Retail price set by the gallery. "I do discuss the prices with artist before I set a retail price." Gallery provides insurance, promotion and contract; shipping costs are shared. Prefers unframed artwork.

Submissions: Send query letter with slides and bio. Portfolio should include originals, slides, resume and bio. Replies in 1 month. Files bios, reviews, slides and photos.

Tips: Does not want to see "hobby art." Please send "a large enough body of work."

*WILLIAM ENGLE GALLERY, 415 Massachusetts Ave., Indianapolis IN 46204. (317)632-1391. President: William E. Engle. Retail gallery. Estab. 1981. Represents 50 mid-career and established artists; interested in seeing the work of emerging artists. Exhibited artists include Lilian Fendig and Hirokazu Yamaguchi. Sponsors 4-5 shows/year. Open all year. Located downtown in the gallery area, 1,100 sq. ft.; "high ceilings, long walls." 100% of space for special exhibitions. Clientele: 70% private collectors, 30% corporate clients. Overall price range: $100-10,000; most artwork sold at $400.

Media: Considers oil, acrylic, watercolor, pastel, pen & ink, drawings, mixed media, collage, works on paper, sculpture, ceramic, craft, fiber, glass, photography, original handpulled prints, woodcuts, lithographs, serigraphs, linocuts and etchings. Most frequently exhibits ceramic, painting and watercolor.

Style: Exhibits expressionism, painterly abstraction, conceptualism, post modern works, impressionism, realism and hard-edge geometric abstraction. All genres. Prefers figurative work, landscapes and Western.

Terms: Artwork is accepted on consignment (50% commission). Retail price set by the artist. Gallery provides promotion and contract. Gallery pays for shipping costs from gallery. Prefers framed artwork.

Submissions: Send query letter with resume, slides, bio, brochure, photographs, SASE, business card and reviews. Write to schedule an appointment to show a portfolio, which should include slides and photographs. Replies in 2 weeks.

Tips: "Be imaginative."

THE FORT WAYNE MUSEUM OF ART SALES AND RENTAL GALLERY, 311 E. Main St., Ft. Wayne IN 46802. (219)424-1461. Gallery Business Manager: Jean Fabish. Retail and rental gallery. Estab. 1983. Clientele: 90% private collectors, 10% corporate clients. Represents 175 artists. "We stress Indiana, Ohio, Illinois and Kentucky artists." Interested in emerging, mid-career and established artists. Overall price range: $75-4,500; most artwork sold at $250-650.

Media: Considers oil, acrylic, watercolor, pastel, pen & ink, sculpture, photography, mixed media, collage and original handpulled prints.

Style: "We try to show the best regional artists available. We jury by quality, not salability." Exhibits impressionism, expressionism, realism, photorealism and painterly abstraction. Genres include landscapes, florals, Americana, Southwestern, Western and wildlife. Prefers landscapes, abstractions and florals. "We do not do well with works that are predominantly figures or still life."

Terms: Accepts work on consignment (30% commission). Retail price is set by artist. Exclusive area representation not required. Gallery provides insurance, promotion and contract. Artist pays for shipping. Prefers framed artwork.

Submissions: Send query letter with resume, brochure, slides, photographs, bio and SASE. Write to schedule an appointment to show a portfolio which should include originals and slides. Replies in 2-4 weeks. Slides and resumes are filed.

Tips: Common mistakes artists make in presenting their work are "poor framing, some send very poor slides."

*GALLERY 614, 0350 C.R., N. Coronna IN 46730. (219)281-2752. Vice President: Mary Green. Retail gallery. Estab. 1973. Represents 4 artists; emerging and mid-career. Exhibited artists include R. Green and M. Viles. Sponsors 2 shows/year. Average display time 6 months. Open by appointment all year. Located in a rural area; 1,600 sq. ft.; "with track lighting, wooden and slate floors—plush." 50% of space for special exhibitions, 50% for gallery artists. Clientele: doctors, lawyers and businesspeople. 100% private collectors. Overall price range: $750-3,000; most artwork sold at $750-1,000.

Media: Considers oil, watercolor, pastel, photography, carbro and carbon printing. Most frequently exhibits carbro and carbon prints.
Style: Exhibits painterly abstraction and impressionism. Genres include landscapes, florals, portraits and figurative work. Prefers portraits, landscapes and still lifes.
Terms: Accepts work on consignment (30% commission). Retail price set by the gallery and the artist. Gallery provides insurance and promotion; shipping costs are shared. Prefers framed artwork.
Submissions: Send query letter with resume, slides and bio. Call to schedule an appointment to show a portfolio, which should include originals, photographs and slides. Replies only if interested within 2 weeks. Files all inquiries.

*PATRICK KING CONTEMPORARY ART, 427 Massachusetts Ave., Indianapolis IN 46204. (317)634-4101. Director: Patrick King. Retail gallery. Estab. 1981. Clientele: private, corporate and museum. Represents 30 artists. Interested in emerging and mid-career artists. Sponsors 4 solo and 5 group shows/year. Average display time is 5 weeks. "Gallery consigns works from exhibition to inventory for sales and presentations." Accepts only artists with 5-8 years of professional experience. Overall price range: $300 and up; most artwork sold at $600-3,500.
Media: Considers oil, acrylic, pastel, sculpture, ceramic, fiber, craft, mixed media and installation. Specializes in painting, sculpture and textile.
Style: Exhibits contemporary, abstract, figurative, non-representational, realist works and landscapes.
Terms: Accepts work on consignment (50% commission). Retail price is set by gallery. Exclusive area representation required. Gallery provides promotion; shipping costs are shared.
Submissions: Send query letter with resume, slides, photographs and SASE. Files "correspondence, resumes, slides and photographs of all artists accepted for representation. All other portfolios returned provided artist sends SASE with initial query."

MOREAU GALLERIES, Saint Mary's College, Notre Dame IN 46556. (219)284-4655. Directors: William Tourtillotte. Nonprofit gallery. Estab. 1968. Sponsors 6 solo and 2 group shows/year. Average display time is 1 month. Interested in emerging, mid-career and established artists. Overall price range: $100-10,000.
Media: Considers all media and original handpulled prints. Most frequently exhibits paintings, drawings, sculpture and ceramic.
Style: Exhibits hard-edge geometric abstraction, color field, painterly abstraction, minimalism, conceptualism, post-modernism, pattern painting, feminist/political works, photorealism, expressionism and neo-expressionism. Exhibits all genres. "We are an educational facility. We try to show a variety of styles and media from regional, national and international artists."
Terms: Retail price is set by artist. Exclusive area representation not required. Gallery provides insurance, shipping, promotion and contract.
Submissions: Send query letter, resume, slides and SASE. "Gallery board meets each November to screen proposals for following year." Slides, resumes and show flyer are filed.
Tips: "We look for stimulating, challenging work. The work must be quality in execution. We generally look for very contemporary work."

NEW HARMONY GALLERY OF CONTEMPORARY ART, 506 Main St., New Harmony IN 47631. (812)682-3156. Director: Connie Weinzapfel. Nonprofit gallery. Estab. 1975. Clientele: 80% private collectors, 20% corporate clients. Represents approximately 130 artists. Interested in emerging, mid-career and established artists. Sponsors 3 solo and 7 group shows/year. Average display time is 6 weeks. Accepts only Midwest artists. Overall price range: $50-5,000; most artwork sold at $100-500.
Media: Considers all media and original handpulled prints. Most frequently exhibits paintings (oil and acrylic), mixed media and sculpture.
Style: Considers all contemporary styles.
Terms: Accepts work on consignment (35% commission). Retail price is set by artist. Exclusive area representation not required. Gallery provides insurance, promotion and contract.
Submissions: Send query letter, resume, brochure, slides and SASE. Call to schedule an appointment to show a portfolio, which should include originals. Slides and resumes are filed or returned, and reviewed quarterly.
Tips: Does not want to see "sloppy slides, poor craftsmanship, non-punctuality and talking at length about work." A trend seems to be that there is "more focus on regional art," that it is no longer so "centralized in New York."

Iowa

*ART GUILD OF BURLINGTON, INC., Box 5, 7th and Washington, Burlington IA 52601. (319)754-8069. Director: Lois Rigdon. Nonprofit gallery and museum rental shop. Estab. 1978. Represents emerging, mid-career and established artists. Has over 400 members. Exhibited artists include Connie Bieber and Jim Spring. Sponsors 12 shows/year. Average display time 3 weeks. Open all year. Located in historic Heritage Hill area;

2,400 sq. ft. "c. 1876 German Methodist Church restored and adapted to use as gallery, gift shop and classrooms." 35% of space for special exhibitions. Clientele: 75% private collectors, 25% corporate collectors. Price range: $25-1,000; most artwork sold at $75-500.

Media: Considers oil, acrylic, watercolor, pastel, pen & ink, drawings, mixed media, collage, works on paper, sculpture, fiber, glass, photography, original handpulled prints, woodcuts, wood engravings, linocuts, engravings, mezzotints, etchings, lithographs and serigraphs. Most frequently exhibits watercolor, prints and pottery.

Style: Exhibits surrealism, realism, photorealism and all styles. Genres include landscapes, florals, Southwestern, wildlife, portraits and figurative work.

Terms: Work accepted on consignment (20% commission). Retail price set by artist. Gallery provides insurance and promotion; artist pays for shipping. Prefers framed artwork.

Submissions: Send resume, slides, bio, brochure, SASE and business card. Call or write to schedule an appointment to show a portfolio, which should include originals and slides. Replies in 1 month. Files resume and slides.

*BLANDEN MEMORIAL ART MUSEUM, 920 Third Ave. S., Fort Dodge IA 50501. (515)573-2316. Director: Margaret Carney Xie. Nonprofit municipal museum. Estab. 1930. Clientele: schoolchildren, senior citizens, tourists. 75% private collectors, 25% corporate clients. Sponsors 8 solo and 6 group shows/year. Average display time is 1 month. Interested in emerging, mid-career and established artists.

Media: Most frequently exhibits paintings, prints and ceramic works.

Style: Exhibits painterly abstraction. Genres include landscapes and florals.

Submissions: Send query letter with resume, brochure, slides and SASE. Write to schedule an appointment to show a portfolio, which should include originals and slides. Slides, resumes and brochures are filed.

Tips: Looking for artists with a "unique view, excellence in vision and creativity." Does not want to see "copycat artists."

BRUNNIER GALLERY AND MUSEUM, Iowa State University, 290 Scheman Bldg., Ames IA 50011. (515)294-3342. Museum Store Manager: Kathy Barth. Estab. 1989. Clientele: university, community, and conventioneers. "The store will not sponsor shows, only the museum." Average display time 2 months. Interested in emerging and mid-career artists.

Media: Considers works on paper, sculpture, ceramic, fiber, glass, enamel and porcelain. Most frequently exhibits glass, ceramic and porcelain.

Style: "The museum store will be used as an educational tool to expose our community to affordable decorative arts and artists as well as various art forms and techniques."

Terms: Accepts artwork on consignment (30% commission) or buys outright (50% retail price; net 30 days). Retail price set by gallery and artist. Exclusive area representation not required. Gallery provides insurance and promotion.

Submissions: Send query letter with resume, brochure, slides and photographs. Call or write to schedule an appointment to show a portfolio, which should include originals and slides.

Tips: "We have a small space and have to work with limited areas." Sees trend toward "more collecting; glass and unusual jewelry are popular."

*CORNERHOUSE GALLERY, 2753 First Ave. SE, Cedar Rapids IA 52402. (319)365-4348. Director: Janelle McClain. Retail gallery. Estab. 1976. Represents 75 emerging artists. Exhibited artists include John Preston and Stephen Metcalf. Sponsors 2 shows/year. Average display time 6 months. Open all year. 3,000 sq. ft.; "converted 1907 house with 3000 sq. ft. matching addition devoted to framing, gold leafing and gallery." 15% of space for special exhibitions. Clientele: "residential/commercial, growing collectors." 60% private collectors. Overall price range: $5-75,000; most artwork sold at $200-1,000.

Media: Considers oil, acrylic, watercolor, pastel, drawings, mixed media, collage, works on paper, sculpture, ceramic, fiber, glass, original handpulled prints, woodcuts, wood engravings, linocuts, engravings, mezzotints, etchings, lithographs and serigraphs. Most frequently exhibits oil, acrylic, original prints and ceramic works.

Style: Exhibits painterly abstraction, conceptualism, color field, post modern works and impressionism. Exhibits all genres. Prefers abstraction, impressionism and post modern.

Terms: Accepts work on consignment (40% commission). Retail price set by artist. Gallery provides insurance and promotion; gallery pays for shipping costs from gallery. Prefers unframed artwork.

Submissions: Send resume, brochure, photographs and bio. Write to schedule an appointment to show a portfolio, which should include originals and photographs. Replies in 1 month. Files bio and samples.

Tips: Do not "stop in unannounced."

PERCIVAL GALLERIES, INC., 520 Walnut, Valley National Bank Bldg., Des Moines IA 50309-4104. (515)243-4893. Director: Bonnie Percival. Retail gallery. Estab. 1969. Clientele: corporate, private and beginning collectors; 50% private collectors. Represents 20 artists. Sponsors 7 solo and 1 group shows/year. Average display time is 3 weeks. Interested in emerging and established artists. Most artwork sold at $500-1,000.

Media: Considers oil, acrylic, watercolor, pastel, pen & ink, sculpture, mixed media, collage, glass, installation, original handpulled prints and posters.

Style: Exhibits contemporary, abstract and realist. "Must meet our standards of high quality."

Terms: Accepts work on consignment. Retail price is set by gallery or artist. Exclusive area representation required. Gallery provides insurance and promotion.

Submissions: Send query letter with resume, brochure, slides, photographs, business card and SASE. Call or write to schedule an appointment to show a portfolio. Biographies and slides are filed.

*SIOUX CITY ART CENTER — THE SHOP, 513 Nebraska St., Sioux City IA 51101. (712)279-6272. FAX: (712)279-6309. Manager: Cynthia Urbanos. Gift gallery/rental gallery. Estab. 1938. Represents 75 artists; emerging and mid-career. Interested in seeing the work of emerging artists. Exhibited artists include Lance Hidy and Jack Wilkes. Sponsors 4 shows/year. Average display time 1 month. Located in downtown Sioux City; "gallery just off the front reception area; carpeted walls for easier installation; track lighting." 10% of space for special exhibitions. Clientele: 80% private collectors, 20% corporate collectors. Overall price range: $10-5,000; most work sold at $20-200.

Media: Considers oil, acrylic, watercolor, pastel, pen & ink, drawings, mixed media, works on paper, sculpture, ceramic, glass, photography, original handpulled prints, woodcuts, wood engravings, linocuts, engravings, mezzotints, etchings, lithographs, serigraphs and posters. Most frequently exhibits paintings, prints and ceramics.

Style: Exhibits all styles and genres. Prefers figurative, landscapes and non-figurative works.

Terms: Accepts work on consignment (35% commission). Retail price set by the gallery. Gallery provides insurance, promotion and contract; pays for shipping costs from gallery. Prefers framed artwork.

Submissions: Accepts only upper-Midwest artists. Send query letter with resume, slides, bio and SASE. Write to schedule an appointment to show a portfolio, which should include slides. Replies in 2 months. Files resumes.

Kansas

*ARTFRAMES . . . Bungalo Gallery, 912 Illinois St., Lawrence KS 66044. (913)842-1991. Partner/Gallery Director: Gary M. Smith. Retail gallery, cooperative gallery (private), alternative space, art consultancy of community-based fine arts and crafts. Estab. 1989. Represents 75 emerging, mid-career and established artists. Exhibited artists include Stan Herd, Christine Musgrave and Elizabeth "Grandma" Layton. Sponsors 4-8 shows/year. Average display time 5-8 weeks. Open all year. Located "near the historic downtown shopping center" and the KU (Kansas University) campus; 18,000 sq. ft.; (6,000 sq. ft. outdoor sculpture garden center), 3 floors in 65-year-old bungalow with wood floors, woodwork and multi-level spaces." 2,500 sq. ft of space for special exhibitions, 15,500 sq. ft. for gallery artists. Clientele: "community leaders, academic, business leaders." 65% private collectors, 20% corporate collectors. Overall price range: $65-21,000; most artwork sold at $65-950.

Media: Considers oil, acrylic, watercolor, pastel, pen & ink, drawings, mixed media, collage, sculpture, ceramic, craft (fine), fiber, glass, photography, original handpulled prints, etchings, lithographs and serigraphs. Most frequently exhibits watercolor, oil, acrylic and mixed media.

Style: Exhibits all styles and genres. Prefers landscapes, literal and abstract.

Terms: Accepts work on consignment (35% commission). Retail price set by gallery and artist. Gallery provides insurance, promotion and contract; gallery pays for shipping costs from gallery. Requires framed artwork.

Submissions: Send resume, bio, brochure, photographs, SASE, business card and reviews. No slides. Call to schedule an appointment to show a portfolio, which should include originals and photographs. Replies in 1 month. Files "full package."

Tips: "Come in person. It is necessary for proper consignment. Coffee is free."

*GALLERY ELLINGTON, 350 N. Rock Rd., Wichita KS 67206. (316)682-9051. FAX: (316)682-8384. Owner: Howard Ellington. Retail gallery. Estab. 1978. Represents 10 mid-career and established artists. Exhibited artists include Birger Sandzer and Todd Matson. Sponsors 1 show/year. Average display time 6 months. Open all year. Located on the East Side; 250 sq. ft. 100% of space for special exhibitions. Clientele: "upper class." 80% private collectors, 20% corporate collectors. Overall price range: $50-25,000; most artwork sold at $500.

Media: Considers oil, watercolor, woodcuts, engravings, etchings, lithographs and serigraphs. Most frequently exhibits oils, lithographs and block prints.

Style: Exhibits impressionism. Genres include landscapes and Southwestern. Prefers Southwestern and impressionism.

Terms: Accepts work on consignment (30 or 40% commission). Retail price set by artist; shipping costs are shared. Prefers framed artwork.

Submissions: Accepts only artists from Southwest/prairie printmakers. Send resume and photographs. Call to schedule an appointment to show a portfolio, which should include originals. Replies only if interested.

*GALLERY OF FINE ARTS TOPEKA PUBLIC LIBRARY, 1515 W. 10th, Topeka KS 66604. Gallery Director: Larry Peters. Nonprofit gallery and museum. Estab. 1973. Represents emerging, mid-career and established artists. Sponsors 8 shows/year. Average display time 1 month. Open all year. Located "1 mile west of downtown; 1,200 sq. ft., clean and attractive interior, security, professional installation and cases for small or fragile works." 100% of space for special exhibitions.

Media: Considers all media, woodcuts, woods engravings, mezzotints, etchings and lithographs. Most frequently exhibits 3D arts, paintings and drawings.

Style: Exhibits neo-expressionism, painterly abstraction, post modern works, realism and photorealism. Genres include landscapes, Southwestern and figurative work.

Terms: "If work is chosen for exhibition, there is no commission." Retail price set by artist. Gallery provides insurance; artist pays for shipping. Prefer framed artwork.

Submissions: Prefers only Nebraska, Kansas, Missouri, and Oklahoma artists—will accept others. "Size and weight are of importance: two people must easily handle all works." Send resume, slides and reviews. Call or write to schedule an appointment to show portfolio, which should include slides. Replies in 3 weeks. Files resume. "May be booked 1-2 years in advance."

Tips: "I want work to jump out and get my attention. (A good, quiet work may do this as well as a vibrant, exciting work)." Doesn't want to see "poor slides or photo prints, not enough work presented or no resume— Don't tell me more than I wish to know. I prefer a slide portfolio that I may view at my leisure without the artist being present. I see it becoming more competitive to get shows. Artists are going to really have to be into marketing to make a living."

WICHITA ART MUSEUM SALES/RENTAL GALLERY, 619 Stackman Dr., Wichita KS 67203. (316)268-4921. Chairperson: Barbara Rensner. Nonprofit retail and rental gallery. Estab. 1963. Clientele: tourists, residents of city, students; 99% private collectors, 1% corporate clients. Represents 119 artists. Sponsors 2 group shows/year. Average display time is 6 months. Accepts only artists from expanded regional areas. Interested in emerging and established artists. Overall price range: $5-1,800; most artwork sold at $5-500.

Media: Considers oil, acrylic, watercolor, pastel, mixed media, collage, works on paper, sculpture, ceramic, fiber, glass and original handpulled prints.

Style: Exhibits hard-edge/geometric abstraction, impressionism, photorealism, expressionism and realism. Genres include landscapes, florals, portraits and figurative work. Most frequently exhibits photorealism and impressionism.

Terms: Accepts work on consignment (30% commission).Retail price is set by artist. Exclusive area representation not required. Gallery provides insurance and contract.

Submissions: Send query letter with resume. Resumes and brochures are filed.

*THE WICHITA GALLERY OF FINE ART, Fourth Financial Center, 100 N. Broadway KS 67202. (316)267-0243. Co-owner: Robert M. Riegle. Retail gallery. Estab. 1977. Clientele: affluent business professionals; 80% private collectors, 20% corporate clients. Represents 25 emerging, mid-career and established artists. Sponsors 3 group shows/year. Average display time 6 months. Overall price range: $100-10,000; most artwork sold at $500-1,500.

Media: Considers oil, acrylic, watercolor, pastel, sculpture and original handpulled prints. Most frequently exhibits oil, watercolor and sculpture. Currently looking for watercolor.

Style: Exhibits impressionistic, expressionistic and realist styles. Genres include landscapes, florals and figurative work. Most frequently exhibited styles: impressionism, realism and expressionism. "Style is secondary to quality." Does not want to see "trite or faddish work."

Terms: Accepts work on consignment (40% commission). Retail price is set by gallery or artist. Exclusive area representation required. Gallery provides insurance, promotion and contract; shipping costs are shared.

Submissions: Send query letter with resume, brochure, slides, photographs and SASE. Call or write to schedule an appointment to show a portfolio, which should include originals. Letters are filed.

Tips: Seeking "full-time professional artists, producing consistently high quality art, adhering to ethical standards. Show prints rather than slides and have a good resume of education and background."

Kentucky

*CAPITAL GALLERY OF CONTEMPORARY ART, 314 Lewis St., Frankfort KY 40601. (502)223-2649. Co-owner: Cecelia Hromyak. Retail gallery. Estab. 1981. Represents 20 emerging, mid-career and established artists. Exhibited artists include Diane Tesler and Ellen Glasgow. Sponsors 8-10 shows/year. Average display time 4-6 weeks. Open all year. Located "downtown in a historic building." Clientele: private collectors—young professionals; 80% private collectors, 20% corporate collectors. Overall price range: $50-7,000; most artwork sold at $50-500.

Media: Considers oil, acrylic, watercolor, pastel, pen & ink, drawings, mixed media, collage, works on paper, sculpture, ceramic, craft, fiber, glass and original handpulled prints, woodcuts, wood engravings, linocuts, engravings, mezzotints, etchings, lithographs and serigraphs. Most frequently exhibits oil, watercolor and prints.

Style: Exhibits all styles. Prefers realism, impressionism, primitivism.
Terms: Accepts work on consignment (40% commission), or buys outright for 50% of retail price (net 60-90 days). Retail price set by artist. Gallery provides promotion; shipping costs are shared. Prefers framed artwork.
Submissions: Send resume, slides and bio. Write to schedule an appointment to show a portfolio, which should include originals and slides. Replies in 1 month. Files resumes and slides.
Tips: "Come look at the gallery first." Sees trend toward "more private collectors in middle income."

*GEORGETOWN COLLEGE GALLERY, Mulberry St., Georgetown College, Georgetown KY 40324. (502)863-8106. Chairman, Art Department: James McCormick. Nonprofit gallery. Estab. 1940. Clientele: area; faculty and students. Sponsors 4 or 5 solo and 1 or 2 group shows/year. Average display time is 3 weeks. Interested in emerging, mid-career and established artists. Overall price range: $100-800.
Media: Considers all media.
Style: Considers all styles.
Terms: Accepts work on consignment. Retail price is set by artist. Exclusive area representation not required. Gallery provides insurance and promotion; shipping costs are shared.
Submissions: Send query letter with resume and slides.
Tips: Sees trend toward "increasing conservativism."

*KENTUCKY ART & CRAFT GALLERY, 609 West Main St., Louisville KY 40202. (502)589-0102. Director of Marketing: Sue Rosen. Retail gallery operated by the private nonprofit Kentucky Art & Craft Foundation, Inc. Estab. 1984. Represents more than 400 emerging, mid-career and established artists. Exhibited artists include Arturo Sandoval and Sarah Frederick. Sponsors 12 shows/year. Open all year. Located downtown in the historic Main Street district; 3,000 sq. ft.; the gallery is "a Kentucky tourist attraction located in a 120-year-old cast iron building." 33% of space for special exhibitions. Clientele: tourists, the art-viewing public and schoolchildren. 10% private collectors, 5% corporate clients. Overall price range: $3-20,000; most artwork sold at $25-500.
Media: Considers mixed media, works on paper, sculpture, ceramic, craft, fiber and glass. Most frequently exhibits ceramics, fiber and wood.
Terms: Artwork is accepted on consignment (40% commission). Retail price set by the artist. Gallery provides insurance, promotion, contract and shipping costs from gallery.
Submissions: Contact gallery for jury application and guidelines first then send query letter with resume and 5 slides. Replies in 2-3 weeks. "If accepted, we file resume, slides, signed contract, promotional materials, PR about the artist and inventory pricing."
Tips: "The artist must live or work in a studio within the state of Kentucky."

LOUISVILLE VISUAL ART ASSOCIATION, 3005 Upper River Rd., Louisville KY 40207. (502)561-8635. Executive Director: John P. Begley. Nonprofit gallery. Estab. 1909. Clientele: general public. Sponsors 11 theme exhibits/year. "The Louisville Visual Art Association is Louisville's leading contemporary art center offering an active program of exhibitions, classes and special events. The organization was formed by the merger of two of the city's primary visual arts groups, the Water Tower Art Association and the Louisville Art Gallery. The gallery is housed at the historic landmark Water Tower." Average display time is 6 weeks. Interested in emerging and established artists.
Media: Considers all media.
Style: Considers all styles. "Looking for contemporary artwork—all media and crafts. Must have high aesthetic and technical qualities. Professional artists only."
Terms: Accepts work on consignment (30% commission). "Prices are printed on a price sheet and on labels." Retail price is set by artist. Exclusive area representation not required. Gallery provides insurance, shipping costs, promotion and contract.
Submissions: Send query letter with resume and slides. Resumes, slides if available, and other materials showing artists' work are filed.

*PADUCAH ART GUILD, INC., 200 Broadway, Paducah KY 42001. (502)442-2453. Executive Director: Dan Carver. Nonprofit gallery. Estab. 1957. Represents emerging, mid-career and established artists. Has 450 members. Sponsors 8 shows/year. Average display time 6-8 weeks. Open all year. Located downtown; 1,800 sq. ft.; "in historic building that was farmer's market." 90% of space for special exhibitions. Clientele: professionals and collectors. 90% private collectors. Overall price range: $200-8,000; most artwork sold at $200-1,000.
Media: Considers oil, acrylic, watercolor, pastel, pen & ink, drawings, mixed media, collage, works on paper, sculpture, ceramic, craft, fiber, glass, photography, original handpulled prints, woodcuts, wood engravings, linocuts, mezzotints, etchings, lithographs and serigraphs. Most frequently exhibits oil, acrylic and mixed media.

Style: Exhibits all styles. Genres include landscapes, florals, Americana and figurative work. Prefers realism, impressionism and abstraction.
Terms: Accepts work on consignment (25% commission). Retail price set by artist. Gallery provides insurance and promotion; shipping costs are shared. Prefers framed artwork.
Submissions: Send resume, slides, bio, SASE and reviews. Replies in 1 month.
Tips: "Do not call. Send submissions—see above. Must have large body of work."

PARK GALLERY, 3936 Chenoweth Square, Louisville KY 40207. (502)896-4029. Owners: Ellen Guthrie and Martha Juckett. Retail gallery. Estab. 1973. Clientele: 80% private collectors. Represents 20 artists. Sponsors 6 solo and 1 group shows/year. Average display time is 1 month. Interested in emerging and established artists. Overall price range: $100-3,000; most artwork sold at $300-1,000.
Media: Considers oil, acrylic, watercolor, pastel, sculpture, ceramic, fiber, craft, mixed media, glass, limited-edition original handpulled prints and handmade jewelry.
Style: Exhibits contemporary, landscape, floral and primitive works. Specializes in eclectic, affordable art.
Terms: Accepts work on consignment (40% commission) or buys outright (net 30 days). Retail price is set by gallery or artist. Gallery provides insurance, promotion and contract; shipping costs are shared.
Submissions: Send query letter with resume, brochure, slides and photographs. Call or write to schedule an appointment to show a portfolio. All materials are filed.
Tips: Looks for "quality and originality or uniqueness. No repetition, commercialism or mass-produced items."

Louisiana

*CASELL GALLERY, 818 Royal St., New Orleans LA 70116. (504)824-0671. Owner: Kim Casell. Retail gallery and art consultancy. Estab. 1969. Clientele: locals and tourists; 85% private collectors, 15% corporate clients. Represents 8-12 artists. Sponsors 4 group shows/year. Average display time is 3 months. Interested in emerging, mid-career and established artists. Overall price range: $65-1,500; most artwork sold at $65-350.
Media: Considers oil, acrylic, watercolor, pastel, pen & ink, drawings, photography, prints and graphics. Most frequently exhibits serigraph, lithograph and etching.
Style: Exhibits hard-edge geometric abstraction, impressionism, photorealism, expressionism, neo-expressionism and realism. Genres include landscapes and Americana. Most frequently exhibits city scenes, landscapes and realism. "We are looking for regional realism that tourists and locals feel comfortable with and wish to collect. We also like to have the latest fad that seems to have a short popular span and then fades. We will feature artists who have unique style and talent and will attract attention in the future. But mainly we like local scenes."
Terms: Accepts work on consignment (50% commission), or buys outright (net 30 days). Retail price is set by gallery or artist. Exclusive area representation not required. Gallery provides insurance and promotion.
Submissions: Send brochure and photographs. Write to schedule an appointment to show a portfolio, which should include photographs. Brochure and resumes are filed.

LE MIEUX GALLERIES, 332 Julia St., New Orleans LA 70130. (504)565-5354. President: Denise Berthiaume. Retail gallery and art consultancy. Estab. 1983. Clientele: 75% private collectors; 25% corporate clients. Represents 18 artists. Sponsors 4 solo and 5 group shows/year. Accepts only artists from the Southeast. Interested in established artists.
Media: Considers oil, acrylic, watercolor, pastel, drawings, mixed media, works on paper, sculpture, ceramic, glass and egg tempera. Most frequently exhibits oil, watercolor and drawing.
Style: Exhibits impressionism, neo-expressionism, realism and hard-edge geometric abstraction. Genres include landscapes, florals, wildlife and figurative work. Prefers landscapes, florals and paintings of birds.
Terms: Accepts work on consignment (50% commission). Retail price set by gallery and artist. Exclusive area representation required. Gallery provides insurance, promotion and contract; artist pays for shipping. Prefers artwork unframed.
Submissions: Send query letter with resume, slides and photographs. Write to schedule an appointment to show a portfolio, which should include slides and photographs. Replies in 3 months. All material is returned if not accepted or under consideration.
Tips: "Give me the time and space I need to view your work and make a decision; you cannot sell me on liking or accepting it; that I decide on my own."

STONER ARTS CENTER, 516 Stoner Ave., Shreveport LA 71101. (318)222-1780. Director: Linda T. Snider. Nonprofit gallery. Estab. 1972. Sponsors 7 solo or 2-person shows/year. Average display time is 6 weeks. Interested in emerging and established artists. Most artwork sold at $300-3,000 for large paintings; $100 or less for craft items in sales gallery.
Media: Considers oil, acrylic, watercolor, pen & ink, drawings, mixed media, collage, works on paper, sculpture, ceramic, fiber, glass, installation, photography and original handpulled prints. Most frequently exhibits oil, acrylic, mixed media and sculpture.

Style: Exhibits painterly abstraction, minimalism, conceptualism, surrealism, primitivism, impressionism and neo-expressionism. "The Stoner Arts Center is a contemporary gallery and exhibits varied styles and media. We do not exhibit realistic, sentimental work but will consider all media. We exhibit the works of reputable artists who have shown on a regional and national level, but we are always open to new and promising talent."

Terms: Accepts work on consignment (40% commission) in sales gallery. Retail price is set by artist. Exclusive area representation not required. Gallery provides insurance, promotion and contract.

Submissions: Send query letter with resume, slides and SASE.

Tips: "Visit the gallery first to see if your work would fit in. Then send slides, resume and statement; show a professional attitude. Artists often assume that they can schedule a show immediately."

Maryland

ARTISTS CIRCLE, LTD., 11544 Spring Ridge Rd., Potomac MD 20854. (301)921-0572. Gallery Manager: Cathy Caulk. Art consultancy. Estab. 1972. "No exhibitions. Gallery art shown by appointment to designers, architects and clients." Located in suburb. Clientele: 5% private collectors; 95% corporate clients. Represents 1,000 artists. Interested in emerging and established artists. Overall price range: $300-500,000; most work sold at $500-6,000.

Media: Considers oil, acrylic, watercolor, pastel, drawings, mixed media, collage, works on paper, sculpture, ceramic, fiber, glass, photography, egg tempera, woodcuts, wood engravings, engravings, mezzotints, etchings, lithographs, pochoir, serigraphs and offset reproductions.

Style: Exhibits impressionism, expressionism, neo-expressionism, realism, color field, painterly abstraction, post modern works, pattern painting and hard-edge geometric abstraction. Considers all styles. Genres include landscapes, Americana and subjects regional to Washington DC, Maryland or Virginia. Prefers abstracts and landscapes. "We are committed to placing the highest quality fine art in the corporate and business community. As the first art consultant in the Washington DC metropolitan area, we have a long standing professional relationship with the business and development community as well as the hundreds of artists throughout the country we represent. Because the corporate needs and market are so broad, we sell and show a wide range of media and styles. We often work closely with the developer and space planner when we are placing art. Unlike most art consultants, we maintain a 2,000 sq. foot gallery/office space, a large inventory of samples and existing pieces and have a full-time staff of 5 people."

Terms: Accepts work on consignment (50-40% commission) or buys outright (50% retail price; net 30 days). Retail price set by artist. "We reserve the right to advise an artists on prices if warranted." Gallery provides insurance and contract (if needed or for commissions); client pays shipping. Prefers artwork unframed.

Submissions: Send query letter with resume, brochure, slides and bio. Call to schedule an appointment to show a portfolio. Replies in 1-2 weeks. Files slides and artist info. All material is returned if not accepted or under consideration.

Tips: One trend is "the use, as well as acceptance, of professional art consultants as a viable source for corporate fine art, rather than galleries, also a greater use of signature sculpture by developers. It is interesting how many galleries now contact us in hopes of showing their artists to the corporate and business market. This did not happen in the past."

819 GALLERY, 819 S. Broadway, Fells Point, Baltimore MD 21231. (301)732-4488. Director: Stephen Salny. Retail gallery. Estab. 1986. Open February through December. Located on the waterfront in historic Fells Point. "Moving to expanded quarters next door at 817 S. Broadway by 1991. Will retain name of 819 Gallery." Clientele: locals, tourists from Washington DC, Philadelphia and Virginia, 100% private collectors. Represents 20 artists. Sponsors 6 solo shows/year. Average display time 6 weeks-2½ months. Interested in emerging artists. Overall price range: $500-2,500.

Media: Considers oil, acrylic, watercolor, mixed media, collage, works on paper, ceramic and glass. Most frequently exhibits original works on paper.

Style: Exhibits impressionism, painterly abstraction and hard-edge geometric abstraction. Genres include landscapes and florals. Prefers abstract expressionism, painterly abstraction and realism. "We show contemporary art of emerging artists, both regional and from other states and countries. I'm partial to works on paper. I also exhibit pottery on a continual basis, very selectively. An exhibit of ceramics is held from November-Christmas for the holiday season."

Terms: Accepts work on consignment (50% commission). Retail price set by artist. Exclusive area representation required. Gallery provides contract; artist pays for shipping. Prefers archival-quality framed artwork.

Submissions: Send query letter with resume, business card, slides, bio and SASE. Replies in 6 weeks. All material is returned if not accepted or under consideration.

Tips: "Looks for good organization in addition to reliability, professionalism and accuracy. Follow submission rules." Common mistakes artists make in presenting their work are that "they do not listen to the gallery requirements. They stop by unannounced, usually at a busy time for the gallery."

*THE GALLERY AT ST. MARY'S COLLEGE OF MARYLAND, St. Mary's City MD 20686. (301)862-0246. Director: Jonathan Ingersoll. Nonprofit gallery. Estab. 1971. Represents artists; emerging, mid-career and established. Sponsors 10 shows/year. Average display time 1 month. Open all year. Rural location; 1,600 sq. ft. 100% of space for special exhibitions.
Media: Considers "anything."
Style: Exhibits all styles and genres. No barns or fishing boats.
Terms: Gallery provides insurance and shipping costs. Prefers framed artwork, but will shrink wrap.
Submissions: Send letter, bio and examples.
Tips: "The best way for artists to be introduced to our gallery is to have someone respected in the art world introduce them. Otherwise a good letter with resume and good examples of the work."

GLEN ECHO GALLERY, 7300 MacArthur Blvd., Glen Echo MD 20812. (301)492-6266. Director: Britt Reeves. Nonprofit gallery. Estab. 1974. Located in suburban Washington DC in a round stone tower dating from 1891. Clientele: 100% private collectors. Represents 25 artists. Sponsors 6 solo and 6 group shows/year. Average display time: 4 weeks. Accepts only artists from local area, mainly work of artists-in-residence at Glen Echo Arts Park. Interested in emerging artists. Overall price range: $50-1,000; most work sold at $50-200.
Media: Considers oil, acrylic, watercolor, drawings, mixed media, sculpture, ceramic, craft, fiber, glass, photography, woodcuts, wood engravings, linocuts, engravings, mezzotints, etchings, lithographs, pochoir and serigraphs. Most frequently exhibits paintings, ceramic and mixed media.
Style: Exhibits impressionism, realism, surrealism, primitivism and painterly abstraction. Genres include landscapes, portraits and figurative work. Prefers surrealism, realism and abstraction.
Terms: Accepts work on consignment (20% commission). Retail price set by artist. Gallery provides insurance, promotion and contract. Prefers artwork framed.
Submissions: Send query letter with resume and slides; "late August exhibition review for following year." Call to schedule an appointment to show a portfolio. Replies in 1 month after panel reviews. All material is returned if not accepted or under consideration.

HOLTZMAN ART GALLERY, Towson State University, Towson MD 21204. (302)321-2808. Director: Christopher Bartlett. Nonprofit gallery. Estab. 1973. Clientele: students, Baltimore general public and private collectors. Sponsors 2 solo and 5 group shows/year. Average display time is 3 weeks. Interested in established artists. Overall price range: $50-10,000; most artwork sold at $100-1,000.
Media: Considers oil, acrylic, watercolor, pastel, pen & ink, drawings, mixed media, collage, works on paper, sculpture, ceramic, craft, fiber, glass, installation, photography, performance art, original handpulled prints and silkscreens. Most frequently exhibits paintings, watercolor and sculpture.
Style: Considers all styles and genres. "We exhibit a broad range of contemporary styles and media which also encompass diverse subject matter or themes as an educational resource to students and as displays of both traditional and avant-garde contemporary work."
Terms: Retail price is set by artist. Exclusive area representation not required. Gallery provides insurance, promotion and contract.
Submissions: Send query letter and resume. Resumes are filed. Slides are requested after initial contact.

MEREDITH GALLERY, 805 N. Charles St., Baltimore MD 21201. (301)837-3575. President: Judith Lippman. Retail gallery. Estab. 1977. Clientele: commercial and residential. Exhibits the work of 4-6 individuals and 5-7 groups/year. Sponsors 5 solo and 5 group shows/year. Average display time is 2 months. Interested in emerging and established artists. Overall price range: $200-5,000; most artwork sold under $2,000.
Media: Considers watercolor, ceramic, fiber, craft, glass, artist-designed furniture and original handpulled prints.
Style: Exhibits contemporary, abstract, figurative, realistic works and landscapes. Specializes in contemporary American crafts and artist-designed furniture.
Terms: Accepts work on consignment. Retail price is set by gallery and artist. Exclusive area representation required. Gallery provides insurance, promotion and contract; shipping costs are shared.
Submissions: Send query letter, resume, slides, SASE and price list. "Slides, resume and price list are filed if we are interested."
Tips: "Looks for excellent craftsmanship, innovative design and quality in your field."

PARTNERS GALLERY, LTD., 4724 Hamden Ln., Bethesda MD 20814. (301)657-2781. Contact: Susan Turner. Retail gallery. Estab. 1987. Clientele: 60% private collectors, 40% corporate clients. Represents approximately 30 artists. Sponsors 8-9 group shows/year. Average display time 4-7 weeks. "Must be good work and high quality." Interested in emerging and established artists. Overall price range: $1,500-9,000; most artwork sold at $2,500-3,000.

Media: Considers oil, acrylic, watercolor, pastel, pen & ink, drawings, mixed media, collage, works on paper, sculpture, ceramic, craft, fiber, glass and egg tempera, also considers wood engravings, linocuts, engravings, mezzotints, etchings, lithographs, pochoir and serigraphs. Most frequently exhibits oils, acrylics and fine ceramic craftwork.

Style: Exhibits expressionism, realism, photorealism, painterly abstraction and imagism. Genres include landscapes, Southwestern, portraits, figurative work and all genres. Prefers realism, figurative work and representationalism. "Partners Gallery Ltd. was founded upon and committed to the concept of partnership with the artist, the community and the collector."

Terms: Accepts artwork on consignment (50% commission). Retail price set by gallery and artist. Exclusive area representation sometimes required. Gallery provides insurance while in gallery, promotion and shipping costs from gallery. Prefers framed artwork.

Submissions: Send query letter with resume slides, SASE, brochure, photographs, business card and bio. Write to schedule an appointment to show a portfolio, which should include originals, slides and photographs. Replies in 1 month. Files only samples we are interested in.

TOWN CENTER GALLERY, INC., 250 Hungerford Dr., Rockville MD 20850. (301)424-7313. Manager: Connie Woolard. Cooperative gallery. Estab. 1972. Clientele: 90% private collectors; 10% corporate clients. Represents 22 artists. "Gallery offers space to non-members. Gallery members feature show hangs for 1 month, 12 times/year, if no special shows are scheduled." Interested in emerging, mid-career and established artists. Overall price range: $50-2,500; most artwork sold at $50-500.

Media: Considers oil, acrylic, watercolor, pastel, pen & ink, drawings, mixed media, collage, works on paper, sculpture, ceramic, egg tempera, woodcuts, wood engravings, linocuts, engravings, mezzotints, etchings, lithographs, serigraphs and offset reproductions. Most frequently exhibits watercolors or acrylics, oils and prints.

Style: Exhibits impressionism, expressionism and realism. Genres include landscapes, florals, Americana, wildlife and figurative work. Prefers landscapes, florals and still-lifes.

Terms: Co-op donation of time; 35% commission. Rental fee for space; rental fee for non-members covers 1 month. Retail price set by artist. Exclusive area representation not required. Prefers framed artwork.

Submissions: Send query letter with resume, business card, slides, bio and SASE. Call or write to schedule an appointment to show a portfolio, which should include originals, slides, transparencies and photographs. Replies in 3 weeks.

Tips: "A special show might be best consideration for anyone living outside the immediate area, as members are required to give working time, etc., since we are a co-operative gallery. Special non-member shows offered three times a year. The other months are group shows with one large wall for featuring a member each month or if a *special show* (non-member) has been requested, that space is used instead for 'special' (non-member) show." Sees trend toward "a real increased interest in original art; many beginning collectors."

Massachusetts

*ALPHA GALLERY, 121 Newbury St., Boston MA 02116. (617)536-4465. Directors: Joanna E. Fink and Alan Fink. Estab. 1967. Clientele: 70% private collectors, 25% corporate clients. Represents 15 artists. Sponsors 8-9 solo and 1-3 group shows/year. Average display time is 3½ weeks. Interested in emerging and established artists. Price range: $500-500,000; most artwork sold at $1,000-10,000.

Media: Considers oil, acrylic, watercolor, pastel, pen & ink, drawings, mixed media, sculpture and original handpulled prints. Most frequently exhibits oil on canvas, prints and works on paper.

Style: Exhibits painterly abstraction, expressionistic and realism. Genres include landscapes and figurative work. Most frequently exhibits figurative and new image works, expressionism. Prefers "strong, figurative, non-decorative oils, in which the paint itself is as important as what is portrayed."

Terms: Accepts work on consignment (50% commission). Retail price is set by gallery and artist. Exclusive area representation required. Gallery provides insurance, promotion mailing costs; shipping costs are shared.

Submissions: Send query letter with resume, slides and SASE.

CAPE MUSEUM OF FINE ARTS, 800 Main St., Rte. 6A, Dennis MA 02638. (508)385-4477. Director: Suzanne M. Packer. Museum. Estab. 1981, opened to public in 1985. Represents 75 artists. Sponsors 1 solo and 5 group shows/year. Average display time 6 weeks-2 months. Accepts only artists from region or associated with Cape Cod. Interested in emerging and established artists.

Media: "We accept all media." No offset reproductions or posters. Most frequently exhibits oil, sculpture, watercolor and prints.

Style: Exhibits all styles and all genres. "The CMFA provides a year-round schedule of art-related activities and programs for the Cape community: exhibitions, Cinema Club, lectures, bus trips and specially planned events for all ages. The permanent collection focuses on art created by Cape artists from the 1900 to the present date."

Submissions: Send query letter with resume and slides. Write to schedule an appointment to show a portfolio, which should include originals. All material is returned if not accepted or under consideration.

Tips: "We encourage artist to leave with the Museum their resume and slides so that we can file it in our archives." Wants to see works by "innovators, creators . . . leaders. Museum quality works. Artist should be organized. Present samples that best represent your abilities and accomplishments."

CLARK GALLERY, INC., Box 339, Lincoln Station, Lincoln MA 01773. (617)259-8303. Assistant Director: Pamela C. Cochrane. Retail gallery. Estab. 1976. Clientele: Boston and environs; 80% private collectors, 20% corporate clients. Represents 36 artists. Sponsors 18 solo and 2 group shows/year. Average display time is 4 weeks. Interested in emerging and established artists. Overall price range: $200-20,000; most artwork sold at $500-3,500.

Media: Considers oil, acrylic, watercolor, pastel, drawings, mixed media, collage, works on paper, sculpture, ceramic, glass and original handpulled prints.

Style: Exhibits painterly abstraction, expressionism, realism, figuration and personal narration. Genres include landscapes, portraits and figurative work. Prefers expressionism, realism and abstraction. "We concentrate on Boston area artists primarily. We are very eclectic in our selection."

Terms: Accepts work on consignment (50% commission). Retail price is set by gallery and artist. Exclusive area representation required. Gallery provides insurance, promotion and contract; artist pays for shipping.

Submissions: Send query letter, resume, slides and SASE. Letters and resumes are filed.

Tips: "Send a proper packet. Visit the gallery to see the type of work we show."

*FAUVE GALLERY, 18 Main St., Amherst MA 01002. (413)256-0321. Contact: Leonard Jazwiecki. Retail gallery, art consultancy and framer. Estab. 1974. Represents 12-15 artists; emerging, mid-career and established. Exhibited artists include John Grillo and Leonel Góngora. Sponsors 12 shows/year. Average display time 1 month. Open all year. Located on the commons—downtown; 1,200 sq. ft.; "natural wood pine floors, wide walls." 90% of space for special exhibitions. Clientele: corporate to walk-in. 50% private collectors, 50% corporate collectors. Overall price range: $100-5,000; most artwork sold at $100-1,200.

Media: Considers oil, acrylic, watercolor, pastel, pen & ink, drawings, mixed media, collage, works on paper, sculpture, ceramic, craft, fiber, glass, photography, original handpulled prints, woodcuts, wood engravings, engravings, mezzotints, etchings, lithographs, pochoir, serigraphs and posters. Most frequently exhibits oil, acrylic and mixed media.

Style: Exhibits expressionism, primitivism, painterly abstraction, impressionism, realism, photorealism and all genres.

Terms: Accepts work on consignment (40% commission). Regional exclusivity for 12 months. Retail price set by the gallery. Gallery provides insurance and contract; artist pays shipping. Prefers framed artwork. "But we will frame at 20% off materials."

Submissions: Prefers artists from all areas. Send query letter with resume, slides, bio, brochure, photographs, SASE and reviews. Write to schedule an appointment to show a portfolio, which should include originals, photographs, slides and transparencies. Replies in 6 weeks. Files all material.

Tips: "Only send the best work with good quality slides."

*THE GALLERY AT CORNERSTONE, 123 2nd Ave., Waltham MA 02154. (617)890-3773. FAX: (617)890-8049. Gallery Coordinator: Emily Blau. Estab. 1984. Represent emerging and mid-career artists. Sponsors 8 shows/year. Average display time 6 weeks. Open all year. 150 sq. ft. 100% of space for special exhibitions. Most work sold at $200-1,000.

Media: Considers photography.

Style: Exhibits all genres.

Terms: Retail price set by the artist. Gallery provides promotion; artist pays for shipping. Prefers framed artwork.

Submissions: Send query letter resume, slides and bio. Call and write to schedule an appointment to show a portfolio, which should include originals. Replies only if interested in 3 weeks. Files "everything that could be of future use."

*GALLERY EAST, THE ART INSTITUTE OF BOSTON, 700 Beacon St., Boston MA 02215. (617)262-1223. Exhibitions Directors: Janet Cavellero/Martin Mugar. Nonprofit gallery. Estab. 1911. Clientele: students and private individuals. Sponsors 1 solo and 6 group shows/year. Average display time 1 month. Interested in emerging and established artists.

Media: Considers oil, acrylic, watercolor, pastel, pen & ink, drawings, mixed media, collage, works on paper, sculpture, ceramic, installation, photography and original handpulled prints. Most frequently exhibits photography, oil/acrylic and graphic design.

Style: Exhibits landscapes, portraits and figurative work. "The AIB is *not* a commercial gallery. It is an educational nonprofit gallery."
Terms: Accepts work on consignment (33% commission). Retail price is set by gallery and artist. Gallery provides insurance, promotion and contract; shipping costs are shared.
Submissions: Send query letter, resume, brochure, slides and SASE. Portfolio should include slides and transparencies. Resumes are filed.

GALLERY ON THE GREEN, 1837 Mass Ave., Lexington MA 02173. (617)861-6044. Director: Partricia L. Heard. Retail gallery and art consultancy. Estab. 1980. Represents 30 artists. Sponsors 5 solo and 2 group shows/year. Average display time 6 weeks. Interested in mid-career and established artists.
Media: Considers oil, acrylic, watercolor, pastel, pen & ink, drawings, mixed media, collage, works on paper, sculpture, ceramic, fiber, glass, egg tempera and original handpulled prints. Most frequently exhibits oil, acrylic and watercolor.
Style: Exhibits impressionism, expressionism, realism, painterly abstraction and imagism. Genres include landscapes, florals, wildlife, portraits and figurative work. Prefers landscapes. "Carefully limited eclecticism."
Terms: Accepts work on consignment (50% commission). Retail price set by gallery and artist. Exclusive area representation required during exhibition. Gallery provides insurance, promotion, contract and shipping costs from gallery. Prefers framed artwork.
Submissions: Send query letter with resume, slides and SASE. Call to schedule an appointment to show a portfolio, which should include slides and transparencies. Replies in 3 weeks. Files slides and resumes. All material is returned if not accepted or under consideration.
Tips: "In corporate work there is a great need for large scale, realistic or semi-realistic work at reasonable prices." Sees trend toward "interest in fine crafts; work reflecting care for the environment."

*R. MICHELSON GALLERIES, 132 Main St., Northampton MA 01060 and 25 S. Pleasant St., Amherst MA 01002. (413)586-3964 and (413)253-2500. Owner: R. Michelson. Retail gallery. Estab. 1976. Represents 25 artists/year; emerging, mid-career and established. Exhibited artists include Barry Moser and Leonard Baskin. Sponsors 10 shows/year. Average display time 1 month. Open all year. Located downtown; the Northampton gallery has 1,500 sq. ft.; the Amherst gallery has 1,800 sq. ft. 50% of space for special exhibitions, 50% for gallery artists. Clientele: 85% private collectors, 15% corporate collectors. Overall price range: $50-25,000; most artwork sold at $300-5,000.
Media: Considers oil, acrylic, watercolor, pastel, pen & ink, drawings, works on paper, original handpulled prints, woodcuts, wood engravings, linocuts, engravings, mezzotints, lithographs, pochoir, serigraphs and posters. Most frequently exhibits works on paper and paintings.
Style: Exhibits expressionism, neo-expressionism, imagism, realism, photorealism and figurative works. All genres. Prefers realism, photorealism and expressionism.
Terms: Accepts work on consignment (50% commission) and buys outright. Retail price set by the gallery and the artist. Framed or unframed artwork accepted.
Submissions: Send query letter with resume, slides, bio, brochure, SASE and reviews. Replies in 1 month. Files slides.

*PATÉ POSTE'S SKYLIGHT GALLERY, 43 Charles St., Boston MA 02114. (617)720-2855. FAX: (617)723-7683. Art Director: Jeanne Antill. Alternative Space. Estab. 1986. Represents 16 mid-career artists. Interested in seeing the work of emerging artists. Exhibited artists include Ricky Leacock and Thomas Rebek. Sponsors 8 shows/year. Average display time 4 weeks. Open all year. Located downtown Boston/Beacon Hill; 800 sq. ft. 70% of space for special exhibitions. 60% private collectors, 40% corporate collectors. Overall price range: $500-2,500.
Media: Considers oil, acrylic, watercolor, pastel, mixed media, collage and photography. Most frequently exhibits oil, photography, and watercolor.
Style: Exhibits expressionism, painterly abstraction, impressionism and photorealism.
Terms: Retail price set by the gallery and the artist. Gallery provides insurance and promotion; artist pays for shipping. Prefers framed artwork.
Submissions: Accepts only artists from New England and NY. Send query letter with resume and SASE. Write to schedule an appointment to show a portfolio. Replies in 2 months.

*PUCKER SAFRAI GALLERY, INC., 171 Newbury St., Boston MA 02116. (617)267-9473. FAX: (617)424-9759. Director: Bernard Pucker. Retail gallery. Estab. 1967. Represents 30 artists; emerging, mid-career and established artists. Exhibited artists include Samuel Bak and Brother Thomas. Sponsors 8 shows/year. Average display time 4-5 weeks. Open all year. Located in the downtown retail district. 5% of space for special exhibitions, 95% for gallery artists. Clientele: private clients from Boston, all over the US and Canada. 90% private collectors, 10% corporate clients. Overall price range: $20-200,000; most artwork sold at $5,000-20,000.

Media: Considers oil, acrylic, watercolor, pastel, pen & ink, drawings, mixed media, sculpture, ceramic, photography, woodcuts, engravings, lithographs, wood engravings, mezzotints, serigraphs, linocuts and etchings. Most frequently exhibits paintings, prints and sculpture.
Style: Exhibits all styles. Genres include landscapes and figurative work.
Terms: Terms of representation vary by artist, usually it is consignment. Retail price set by the gallery. Gallery provides promotion. Artist pays shipping. Prefers unframed artwork.
Submissions: Send query letter with resume, slides, bio and SASE. Write to schedule an appointment to show a portfolio, which should include originals and slides. Replies in 3 weeks. Files resumes.

*SMITH COLLEGE MUSEUM OF ART, Elm St. at Bedford Terrace, Northampton MA 01063. (413)585-2770. FAX: (413)585-2075. Associate Curator of Painting and Sculpture: Linda Muehlig. Museum. Estab. 1879. Interested in seeing the work of emerging artists. Sponsors 8-10 shows/year. Average display time 2 months. Open all year. Located "on Smith College campus; 17,500 sq. ft.; exterior sculpture courtyard."
Media: Considers all media, including all types of prints except reproductions.
Style: Exhibits works of all periods and styles.
Terms: Acquisitions are made by purchase or gift. Gallery pays for shipping costs to and from gallery.
Submissions: Send query letter with whatever is available. Write to schedule an appointment to show a portfolio, which should include appropriate materials. Replies in about 1 month. Files letter, resume, photos and reviews.

SOUTH SHORE ART CENTER, 119 Ripley Rd., Cohasset MA 02025. (617)383-9548. Executive Director: Lanci Valentine. Nonprofit gallery. Estab. 1954. Represents 125 artists; emerging, mid-career and established. Exhibited artists include Virginia Avery and Berj Kailian. Sponsors 10 shows/year. Average display time 5-6 weeks. Open all year. Located in "Cohasset Village, convenient to municipal parking; 2,200 sq. ft.; 1987 facility, 32′ ceiling." 60% of space for special exhibitions, 40% for gallery artists. Clientele: 90% private collectors, 10% corporate clients. Overall price range: $100-5,000; most artwork sold at $300-700.
Media: Considers oil, acrylic, watercolor, pastel, pen & ink, drawings, mixed media, collage, works on paper, sculpture, ceramic, craft, fiber, glass, installation, photography, original handpulled prints, woodcuts, engravings, lithographs, wood engravings, mezzotints, serigraphs, linocuts and etchings. Most frequently exhibits paintings, sculpture and photography.
Style: Exhibits all styles and genres. Prefers landscapes and still lifes.
Terms: Accepts work on consignment (40% commission). Artists pay $40/year fee. Retail price set by the artist. Gallery provides promotion; artist pays for shipping.
Submissions: Submit original work, resume and slides; considers twice a year. Write to schedule an appointment to show a portfolio, which should include originals and slides. Replies in 1 week. Files slides and resume.

TENNYSON GALLERY, 237 Commercial St., Provincetown MA 02657. (508)487-2460. Owner: Linda Tennyson. Retail gallery. Estab. 1985. Clientele: 95% private collectors, 5% corporate clients. Represents 30-35 artists. Sponsors 7 group shows/year. Average display time 3 weeks. Interested in emerging and established artists. Overall price range: $250-6,000; most artwork sold at $350-950.
Media: Considers all media, including original handpulled prints. Considers woodcuts, wood engravings, linocuts, engravings, mezzotints, etchings, lithographs and serigraphs. Most frequently exhibits oil/acrylic, pastel, glass and sculpture.
Style: Exhibits impressionism, realism and painterly abstraction. Genres include landscapes, florals, wildlife, portraits and figurative work. Prefers impressionism, realism and painterly abstraction. Metamorphosis, our jewelry store, has been in business for 14 years, while Tennyson Gallery continues in its 5th year. We look for artists who strive for excellence in their work."
Terms: Accepts artwork on consignment (50% commission). Retail price set by artist. Exclusive area representation required. Artist pays for shipping. Prefers framed artwork.
Submissions: Send query letter with resume, slides, SASE, brochure, photographs and bio. Write to schedule an appointment to show a portfolio, which should include originals, slides, transparencies and photographs. Replies in 1 month. Files resumes, slides, photographs and transparencies.

TOWNE GALLERY, 28 Walker St., Lenox MA 01240. (413)637-0053. Owner: James Terry. Retail gallery. Estab. 1977. Clientele: 95% private collectors, 5% corporate clients. Represents 25 artists. Sponsors 1 solo and 2 group shows/year. Average display time 4 weeks. Interested in emerging and established artists. Overall price range: $100-3,500; most artwork sold at $350-650.
Media: Considers oil, acrylic, watercolor, pastel, mixed media, collage, paper, sculpture, ceramic, craft, fiber, glass, mezzotints, etchings, lithographs and serigraphs. Most frequently exhibits serigraphs, collagraphs and ceramics.
Style: Exhibits color field, painterly abstraction and landscapes. "The gallery specializes in contemporary abstracts for the most part. We also show large ceramics as an addition to the fine arts." No political statements.

Terms: Accepts work on consignment (60% commission). Retail price set by gallery and artist. Exclusive area representation required. Gallery provides insurance, promotion and contract; artist pays for shipping. Prefers framed artwork.

Submissions: Send query letter with resume, brochure, slides, photographs, bio and SASE. Write to schedule an appointment to show a portfolio, which should include originals, "after query letter is responded to." Replies only if interested within 6 months. Files bios and slides. All material is returned if not accepted or under consideration.

Tips: "Use professional slides. The current trend seems to be back to realism in the traditional media."

Michigan

ART TREE SALES GALLERY, 461 E. Mitchell, Petoskey MI 49770. (616)347-4337. Manager: Anne Thurston. Retail gallery of a nonprofit arts council. Estab. 1982. Clientele: heavy summer tourism; 99% private collectors, 1% corporate clients. Represents 108 artists. Sponsors annual "Great ARt" competition and exhibition in August. Best of Show may be published as a limited print and unlimited poster edition. Sponsors 2 week one person exhibits November through May, 1 week one person exhibits June through October. Prefers Michigan artists. Interested in emerging, mid-career and established artists. Overall price range: $6-2,000; most artwork sold at $20-300.

Media: Considers oil, acrylic, watercolor, pastel, mixed media, collage, works on paper, sculpture, ceramic, fiber, glass, original handpulled prints, offset reproductions and posters.

Style: Exhibits painterly abstraction, impressionism, photorealism, expressionism and realism. Genres include landscapes, florals, Americana and figurative work.

Terms: Accepts work on consignment (33⅓% commission). Retail price is set by gallery and artist. Exclusive area representation not required. All work is accepted by jury. Gallery provides insurance and promotion; artist pays for shipping.

Submissions: Send query letter, resume, brochure, photographs and SASE. Write to schedule an appointment to show a portfolio, which should include originals, slides and photos.

Tips: We especially concentrate on theme shows or single-medium shows, or small solo exhibitions. Our audience tends to be conservative, but we enjoy stretching that tendency from time to time. We exhibit the work of Michigan artists who show and sell on a consignment basis." Common mistakes artists make in presenting their work are not having it ready for presentation: not framed, matted, titled, ready for display and protected from public contact; slides or photos poorly taken."

JESSE BESSER MUSEUM, 491 Johnson St., Alpena MI 49707. (517)356-2202. Director: Dennis R. Bodem. Chief of Resources: Robert E. Haltiner. Nonprofit gallery. Estab. 1962. Clientele: 80% private collectors, 20% corporate clients. Sponsors 5 solo and 16 group shows/year. Average display time is 1 month. Prefers northern Michigan artists, but not limited. Interested in emerging and established artists. Overall price range: $10-2,000; most artwork sold at $50-150.

Media: Considers oil, acrylic, watercolor, pastel, pen & ink, drawings, mixed media, collage, works on paper, sculpture, ceramic, craft, fiber, glass, installations, photography, original handpulled prints and posters. Most frequently exhibits prints, watercolor and acrylic.

Style: Exhibits hard-edge geometric abstraction, color field, painterly abstraction, pattern painting, primitivism, impressionism, photorealism, expressionism, neo-expressionism, realism and surrealism. Genres include landscapes, florals, Americana, portraits, figurative work and fantasy illustration.

Terms: Accepts work on consignment (25% commission). Retail price is set by gallery and artist. Exclusive area representation not required. Gallery provides insurance, promotion and contract.

Submissions: Send query letter, resume, brochure, slides and photographs. Write to schedule an appointment to show a portfolio, which should include slides. Letter of inquiry and brochure are filed.

THE GALLERY SHOP/ANN ARBOR ART ASSOCIATION, 117 W. Liberty, Ann Arbor MI 48104. (313)994-8004. Gallery Shop Director: Tarb Jamison. Estab. 1978. Clientele: private collectors and corporations. Gallery Shop represents 200 artists, primarily regional. Overall price range: $2,000; most 2-dimensional work sold at $450; 3-dimensional work from $25-100. "Proceeds help support the Art Association's education programs and shows."

Media: Consider original work in virtually all two- and three- dimensional media, jewelry, original handpulled prints and etchings.

Style: "The gallery specializes in well-crafted and accessible artwork. Many different styles are represented."

Terms: Accepts work on consignment (33% commission for members). Retail price is set by artist. Exclusive area representation not required. Gallery provides contract; artist pays for shipping.

Submissions: Send query letter, resume, brochure, slides and SASE. Resume, cover letter, slides are filed for jury.

Tips: "We are particularly interested in new work in glass, ceramics, wood and metal at this time."

GALLERY YAKIR, 12944 Borgman Ave., Huntington Woods MI 48070. (313)548-4300. Director: Joanna Abramson. Retail gallery. Estab. 1985. Clientele: 95% private collectors, 5% corporate clients. Represents 26 artists. Sponsors 1 solo and 2 group shows/year. Average display time 6 weeks. Interested in mid-career artists. Overall price range: $100-15,000; most artwork sold at $300-3,500.
Media: Considers oil, watercolor, pastel, pen & ink, mixed media, collage, works on paper, sculpture, glass, woodcuts, wood engravings, linocuts, etchings, lithographs and posters. Most frequently exhibits sculpture, prints and watercolor.
Style: Exhibits abstract, impressionism, minimalism and painterly abstraction; considers all styles. Genres include landscapes, portraits and figurative work; considers all genres. Specializes in Israeli art.
Terms: Accepts work on consignment (40% commission). Retail price set by gallery and artist. Exclusive area representation required. Gallery provides insurance, promotion and contract; shipping costs are shared. Prefers framed artwork.
Submissions: Send query letter with resume, brochure, slides or photographs and bio. Call to schedule an appointment to show a portfolio, which should include slides or transparencies or photographs. Replies in 3 weeks. Files "everything I might be interested in." All material is returned if not accepted or under consideration.
Tips: "Send bio, photos/slides and any articles written about your work." Sees trend toward "tougher competition, softening prices."

LINDA HAYMAN GALLERY, 32500 Northwestern Hwy., Farmington Hills MI 48018. Owner: Linda Hayman. Retail gallery. Estab. 1979. Clientele: banks, doctor's offices, general offices. Represents emerging, mid-career and established artists.
Style: Prefers contemporary styles, original themes and photorealism.
Terms: Accepts work on consignment (50% commission).
Submissions: Send query letter with brochure, slides and photographs. Call or write to schedule an appointment to show a portfolio, which should include slides and photographs. Replies in 2 weeks.
Tips: Notices that "traditional is coming back, even in real contemporary rooms."

*KALAMAZOO INSTITUTE OF ARTS, 314 South Park St., Kalamazoo MI 49007. (616)349-7775. Curator: Helen Sheridan. Nonprofit gallery. Estab. 1924. Clientele: broad cross section of the general public and tourists; 90% private collectors, 2% corporate clients. Sponsors 12 solo and 20 group shows of 2 or more artists/year. Average display time is 4 weeks. Interested in emerging and established artists. Overall price range: $100-5,000; most artwork sold under $500.
Media: Considers oil, acrylic, watercolor, pastel, pen & ink, drawings, mixed media, collage, works on paper, sculpture, ceramic, craft, fiber, glass, installation, photography and original handpulled prints.
Style: Exhibits hard-edge geometric abstraction, color field, painterly abstraction, post modern, pattern painting, surrealism, photorealism, expressionism, neo-expressionism and realism. Genres include landscapes, portraits and figurative work.
Terms: Accepts work on consignment (30% commission in sales from gallery; museum shop shows only Michigan artists and takes 40% commission). Retail price is set by artist. Gallery provides insurance, promotion and contract; artist pays for shipping.
Submissions: Send query letter, resume, slides, reviews and catalogs. Call or write to schedule an appointment to show a portfolio, which should include originals and slides. Resume and supporting materials are filed. "Works are reviewed by an exhibition committee once a month."

ROBERT L. KIDD GALLERY, 107 Townsend St., Birmingham MI 48009. (313)642-3909. Associate Director: Sally Parsons. Retail gallery and ad consultancy. Estab. 1976. Clientele: 50% private collectors; 50% corporate clients. Represents approximately 125 artists. Sponsors 8 solo and 3 group shows/year. Average display time is 4 weeks. Interested in emerging and established artists. Overall price range: $200-18,000; most artwork sold at $800-5,000.
Media: Considers oil, acrylic, watercolor, pastel, mixed media, works on paper, sculpture, ceramic, fiber and glass. Most frequently exhibits acrylic, oil and sculpture.
Style: Exhibits color field, painterly abstraction, photorealism and realism. Genres include landscapes. "We specialize in original contemporary paintings, sculpture, fiber, glass, clay and handmade paper by Americans and Canadians."
Terms: Accepts work on consignment. Retail price is set by gallery and artist. Exclusive area representation required. Gallery provides insurance and promotion; shipping costs are shared.
Submissions: Send query letter, resume, slides and SASE.
Tips: Looks for "high quality technical expertise and a unique and personal conceptual concept. Understand the direction we pursue and contact us with appropriate work."

*KRESGE ART MUSEUM, Michigan State University, E. Lansing MI 48824. Director: Susan Bandes. Museum. Estab. 1959. Represents emerging, mid-career and established artists. Gallery is closed mid-August to mid-September. Located on the MSU campus; 4,000 sq. ft. 70% of space for special exhibitions. Clientele:

the local community. 100% private collectors. Overall price range: $200-20,000; most artwork sold at $200-5,000.

Media: Considers oil, acrylic, watercolor, pastel, pen & ink, drawings, mixed media, works on paper, sculpture, ceramic, glass, photography, original handpulled prints, woodcuts, wood engravings, linocuts, engravings, mezzotints, etchings, lithographs, pochoir, serigraphs and posters. Most frequently exhibits prints, paintings and photographs.

Style: Exhibits all styles and genres. Prefers contemporary styles.

Terms: 10-20% commission added to price. Retail price set by the artist. Gallery provides insurance; sometimes shipping costs and sometimes artist pays for shipping. Prefers framed artwork.

Submissions: Send query letter with resume, slides and bio. Write to schedule an appointment to show a portfolio, which should include slides and transparencies. Replies in 1 month. Files resume.

Tips: "We tend to do group shows of specific media rather than solo exhibits."

*MUSKEGON MUSEUM OF ART, 296 W. Webster, Muskegon MI 49440. (616)722-2600. FAX: (616)726-5567. Curator: Henry Matthews. Museum. Estab. 1912. Represents emerging, mid-career and established artists. Sponsors 22 shows/year. Average display time 6 weeks. Open all year. Located downtown; 13,000 sq. ft. "Through the process of selection we offer 6-10 one-artist shows a year, as well as opportunity to show in the "Regional" competition."

Media: Considers oil, acrylic, watercolor, pastel, pen & ink, drawings, mixed media, collage, works on paper, sculpture, ceramic, craft, fiber, glass, installation, photography, original handpulled prints, woodcuts, wood engravings, linocuts, engravings, mezzotints, etchings, lithographs, serigraphs and posters.

Style: Exhibits expressionism, neo-expressionism, primitivism, painterly abstraction, surrealism, imagism, conceptualism, minimalism, color field, post modern works, impressionism, realism, photorealism, pattern painting, hard-edge geometric abstraction; all styles and genres.

Terms: Accepts work on consignment (25% commission) "in our gift shop." Retail price set by the artist. Gallery provides insurance, promotion and contract. Prefers framed artwork.

Submissions: Most one-artist shows have a Michigan base. Send query letter with resume, slides, bio, SASE and reviews. Write to schedule an appointment to show a portfolio, which should include originals, photographs, slides, transparencies or any combination thereof. Replies in 1 month. Files "those that we feel might have the possibility of a show."

*JOYCE PETTER GALLERY, 134 Butler, Saugatuck MI 49453. (616)857-7861. Owner: Joyce Petter. Retail gallery. Estab. 1973. Represents 50 artists; emerging, mid-career and established. Exhibited artists include Harold Larsen and Fran Larsen. Sponsors 9 shows/year. Average display time 2 weeks. Open all year. Located downtown on a main street; 4,000 sq. ft.; "a restored Victorian in community known for art." 50% of space for special exhibitions, 50% for gallery artists. Clientele: 80% private collectors, 20% corporate collectors. Overall price range: $100-8,000; most artwork sold at $700-2,000.

Media: Considers oil, acrylic, watercolor, pastel, pen & ink, drawings, mixed media, collage, works on paper, sculpture, ceramic, craft, glass, original handpulled prints, woodcuts, wood engravings, linocuts, engravings, etchings, lithographs and serigraphs, "anything not mechanically reproduced." Most frequently exhibits oil, watercolor and pastel/acrylic.

Style: Exhibits painterly abstraction, surrealism, impressionism, realism, hard-edge geometric abstraction and all styles and genres. Prefers landscapes, abstracts, and "art of timeless quality."

Terms: Accepts work on consignment (50% commission). Retail price set by the artist. Gallery provides insurance, promotion and contract; shipping costs from gallery. Prefers framed artwork.

Submissions: Send query letter with resume and photographs. Call or write to schedule an appointment to show a portfolio, which should include originals and photographs. Replies in 1 month. Files only material of gallery artists.

Tips: "Art is judged on its timeless quality. We are not interested in the 'cutting edge.'"

RUBINER GALLERY, Suite 430A, 7001 Orchard Lake, West Bloomfield MI 48322. (313)626-3111. President: Allen Rubiner. Retail gallery. Estab. 1964. Clientele: 60% private collectors; 40% corporate clients. Represents 25 artists. Sponsors 5 solo and 3 group shows/year. Interested in emerging and established artists. Overall price range: $300-6,000; most artwork sold at $300-3,000.

Media: Considers oil, acrylic, watercolor, pastel, mixed media, collage, works on paper, sculpture and original handpulled prints.

Style: Exhibits painterly abstraction, impressionism and realism. Genres include landscapes, florals and figurative work. Prefers realism and abstraction.

Terms: Accepts work on consignment (50% commission). Retail price is set by gallery and artist. Exclusive area representation required. Gallery provides insurance and promotion; shipping costs are shared.

Submissions: Send query letter, slides and photographs. Call or write to schedule an appointment to show a portfolio, which should include originals. Resumes and slides are filed.

Minnesota

ARTBANQUE GALLERY, 300 First Ave. N., Minneapolis MN 55401. (612)342-9300. Director: Richard Halonen. Retail gallery and consultancy. Estab. 1982. Clientele: 60% private collectors, 40% corporate clients. Represents 15-20 artists. Sponsors 9 solo and 11 group shows/year. "The gallery's upper level features shows six weeks long and the lower level is for gallery artists." Average display time is 6 weeks. Interested in emerging and established artists. Overall price range: $500-5,000; most artwork sold at $1,000-3,000.
Media: Considers oil, acrylic, watercolor, pastel, pen & ink, drawings, mixed media, collage, works on paper, sculpture, ceramic, fiber, glass, installation, photography, original handpulled prints and monotype prints.
Style: Exhibits painterly abstraction, post-modern, primitivism, expressionism and neo-expressionism. Genres include landscapes and figurative work. "The exhibitions of gallery artists, which includes primarily painters, sculptors and photographers, feature current work with a seemingly 'cutting edge.'"
Terms: Accepts work on consignment (50% commission). Retail price is set by gallery and artist. Exclusive area representation required. Gallery provides insurance, promotion and contract; shipping costs are shared.
Submissions: Send query letter, resume, slides and SASE. Call or write to schedule an appointment to show a portfolio, which should include slides and transparencies. Resume, bio and slides are filed.

MCGALLERY, 400 1st Ave., Minneapolis MN 55401. (612)339-1480. Gallery Director: M.C. Anderson. Retail gallery. Estab. 1984. Clientele: collectors and art consultants; 60% private collectors, 40% corporate clients. Represents 30 artists. Sponsors 8 two-person shows/year. Average display time is 6 weeks. Interested in emerging, mid-career and established artists. Overall price range: $800-11,000; most artwork sold at $1,500.
Media: Considers oil, acrylic, pastel, drawings, mixed media, collage, works on paper, art glass, ceramic, photography and original handpulled monotypes. Most frequently exhibits works on paper, art glass, ceramic and sculpture.
Style: Exhibits painterly abstraction, post modern, expressionism and neo-expressionism. Prefers "artists that deal with art in a new perspective and approach art emotionally. They usually have an excellent color sense and mastery of skill."
Terms: Accepts work on consignment (50% commission). Retail price is set by artist. Exclusive area representation required. Gallery provides promotion and contract; artist pays for shipping.
Submissions: Send query letter, resume, slides and photographs. Call or write to schedule an appointment to show a portfolio, which should include originals, slides and/or transparencies.

J. MICHAEL GALLERIES, 3916 W. 50th St., Edina MN 55424. (612)920-6070. FAX: (612)920-4312. Sales Manager: Marlys Peterson. Retail gallery. Estab. 1978. Represents 400+ artists; established. Interested in seeing the work of emerging artists. Exhibited artists include Jiang and Lou Roman. Sponsors 4 shows/year. Average display time 6 months. Open all year. Located in Minneapolis suburban location; 4,000 sq. ft. 30% of space for special exhibitions. Clientele: 75% corporate, 15% residential, 10% designers; 20% private collectors, 80% corporate collectors. Overall price range: $100-5,000; most artwork sold at $500-1,000.
Media: Considers oil, acrylic, watercolor, pastel, mixed media, collage, works on paper, sculpture, ceramic, fiber, original handpulled prints, offset reproductions, woodcuts, linocuts, engravings, mezzotints, etchings, lithographs, serigraphs and posters. Most frequently exhibts watercolor, lithographs and etchings.
Style: Exhibits painterly abstraction, color field, impressionism and realism. All genres. Prefers landscapes, florals and Americana.
Terms: Accepts work on consignment (50% commission). Buys outright for 35-50% of retail price (net 30 days). Retail price set by the gallery and the artist. Gallery provides insurance, promotion and contract; shipping costs are shared. Prefer unframed artwork.
Submissions: Send query letter with resume, slides, bio, brochure and photographs—all nonreturnable. Call or write to schedule an appointment to show a portfolio, which should include originals and slides. Replies only if interested in 4 weeks. Files slides, photographs, bios and other visuals.

MINNESOTA MUSEUM OF ART, Landmark Center, 5th & Market, St. Paul MN 55102-1486. (612)292-4355. Curator of Exhibition: Katherine Van Tassell. Museum. Estab. 1927. Clientele: tourists. Sponsors 1-2 solo and 8-12 group shows/year. Average display time: 3 months. Accepts only artists from upper-Midwest. Interested in emerging artists.
Media: Considers all media but offset reproductions and posters. Most frequently exhibits paintings, prints, drawings and photographs.
Style: Exhibits all styles and genres. "Our museum specializes in American art primarily from 1850-1950. We are also committed to displaying the works of contemporary, emerging Midwestern artists. In addition we have a collection of non-western art and present exhibitions from this collection."
Terms: "We mostly show the work of artists in two month exhibitions for coverage only, no particular terms. We take 10% of commission if an artist should (which is rare) sell a work from our show." Retail price set

by artist. Gallery provides insurance, promotion, contract and shipping costs to and from gallery. Prefers artwork framed.

Submissions: Send query letter with resume, slides, bio and SASE. Write to schedule an appointment to show a portfolio. "We prefer not to schedule appointments until after we have seen slides and resume." Replies in 1 month. Files slides and resume.

Tips: "Our contemporary artists must be from Midwest region. It would help if they've seen our galleries and have some idea of our programs."

*NORMANDALE COLLEGE CENTER GALLERY, 9700 France Ave, So. Bloomington MN 55431. (612)830-9340. FAX: (612)896-4571. Director of Student Life: Gail Anderson Cywinski. College gallery. Estab. 1975. Represents 6 artists/year; emerging, mid-career and established. Sponsors 6 shows/year. Average display time 2 months. Open all year. Suburban location; 30 running feet of exhibition space. 100% of space for special exhibitions. Clientele: students, staff and community. Overall price range: $25-750; most artwork sold at $100-200.

Media: Considers oil, acrylic, watercolor, pastel, pen & ink, drawings, mixed media, collage, works on paper, sculpture, ceramic, craft, fiber, glass, photography, original handpulled prints, offset reproductions, woodcuts, wood engravings, linocuts, engravings, mezzotints, etchings, lithographs, pochoir, serigraphs and posters. Most frequently exhibits watercolor, photography and prints.

Style: Exhibits all styles and genres.

Terms: "We collect 10% as donation to our foundation." Retail price set by the artist. Gallery provides insurance, promotion and contract; artist pays for shipping. Prefers framed artwork.

Submissions: "Send query letter; we will send application and info." Portfolio should include slides. Replies in 2 months. Files "our application/resume."

THE RAVEN GALLERY, 3827 W. 50th St., Minneapolis MN 55410. (612)925-4474. Owner/Director: Jerry Riach. Retail gallery. Estab. 1973. Represents many artists; emerging, mid-career and established. Exhibited artists include Tsonakwa and Amy Cordova. Sponsors 9 shows/year. Average display time 5 weeks. Open all year. Located at the southwest corner of the city of Minneapolis; 1,400 sq. ft.; "the gallery is located in a unique shopping area of numerous privately owned specialty shops; its interior is divided into 2 bays, one of which is used for feature display while the other is used to display rotating stock." 33% of space for special exhibitions. Clientele: 95% private collectors, 5% corporate collectors. Overall price range: $50-10,000; most artwork sold at $500-1,500.

Media: Considers acrylic, watercolor, pastel, drawings, mixed media, sculpture, ceramic, craft, photography, original handpulled prints, woodcuts, lithographs, serigraphs and etchings. Most frequently exhibits original handpulled prints, sculpture and original painting.

Style: Exhibits art of native people of North America and Australia. Genres include landscapes, Southwestern, wildlife, portraits and figurative work. Prefers wildlife, figurative work and landscapes.

Terms: Accepts work on consignment (50% commission). Buys outright for 40% of retail price (net 30 days). Retail price set by the gallery and the artist. Gallery provides insurance and promotion; pays for shipping costs from gallery. Prefers unframed artwork.

Submissions: Accepts only tribal artists from North America and Australia. Send query letter with resume, slides, bio and photographs. Call or write to schedule an appointment to show a portfolio, which should include originals, photographs, slides and background information on the artist and the art. Replies in 1 month. Files biographical and cultural information.

*STEPPINGSTONE GALLERY, 45 Washington Ave., Hutchinson MN 55350. (612)587-4688. Owner/Manager: Linda. Retail gallery. Estab. 1983. Represents 6-8 artists; emerging and mid-career. Exhibited artists include T. Soucek, B. Hillman and B. Haas. Sponsors 2 shows/year. Average display time 1-2 months. Open all year. Located downtown; 1,000 sq. ft.; "remodeled building, brick walls." 95% private collectors, 5% corporate clients. Overall price range: $25-200; $25-100.

Media: Considers oil, acrylic, watercolor, pastel, pen & ink, mixed media, works on paper, ceramic, original handpulled prints, woodcuts, engravings, lithographs, etchings and offset reproductions. Most frequently exhibits watercolor and etchings.

Style: Exhibits all styles and genres. Prefers impressionism, realism and abstraction.

Terms: Accepts work on consignment (40% commission). Retail price set by the artist. Gallery provides promotion; artist pays for shipping. Prefers framed artwork.

Submissions: Send query letter with brochure, photographs and reviews. Write to schedule an appointment to show a portfolio, which should include originals and photographs. Replies only if interested within 1-2 weeks.

THE WOMEN'S ART REGISTRY OF MINNESOTA, 414 First Ave. N., Minneapolis MN 55401. (612)332-5672. Contact: Artists Panel. Nonprofit membership women's art gallery. Estab. 1976. Represents over 300 artists, emerging, mid-career and established. Has 1,500 members. Exhibited artists include Jantje Vischer and Phyllis Wiener. Sponsors 8 shows/year. Average display time 6 weeks. Open all year. Located downtown in the warehouse district; 2,500 sq. ft upstair balcony (47.1 × 18.10). 100% of space for special exhibitions (twice a year/specialty shows). Clientele: 50% private collectors, 50% corporate collectors. Overall price range: $150-5,000.

Media: Considers oil, acrylic, watercolor, pastel, pen & ink, drawings, mixed media, collage, works on paper, sculpture, ceramic, craft, fiber, glass, installation, photography, performance, readings and video. Most frequently exhibits painting, sculpture and photography.

Style: Exhibits all styles and genres.

Terms: Accepts work on consignment (30% commission). Rental fee space; covers 1 year. Retail price set by the artist. Gallery provides insurance, promotion and contract; artist pays for shipping. Prefers framed artwork.

Submissions: Send query letter with resume, slides and SASE. Call to schedule an appointment to show a portfolio, which should include slides. Replies in 4-6 weeks. Files "resume and slides selected for a future show."

Mississippi

MERIDIAN MUSEUM OF ART, 628 25th Ave., Box 5773, Meridian MS 39302. (601)693-1501. Director: John Marshall. Nonprofit gallery. Estab. 1970. Sponsors solo and group shows. Average display time is 4-6 weeks. Interested in emerging and established artists.

Media: Considers oil, acrylic, watercolor, pastel, pen & ink, drawings, mixed media, collage, works on paper, sculpture, ceramic, fiber, glass, installations, photography, performance and original handpulled prints. Most frequently exhibits painting, drawing, sculpture, oil, pencil and wood.

Style: Exhibits color field, painterly abstraction, post modern, neo-expressionism, realism and surrealism. Genres include landscapes, figurative work and fantasy illustration.

Terms: "We no longer accept works for sale at the Meridian Museum of Art." Exclusive area representation not required. Gallery provides insurance, promotion and contract; artist pays for shipping.

Submissions: Send query letter, resume, brochure, slides, photographs and SASE. Write to schedule an appointment to show a portfolio, which should include originals and slides. Biographical and object-related material are filed.

MISSISSIPPI MUSEUM OF ART, 201 E. Pascagoula St., Jackson MS 39201. (601)960-1515. Chief Curator: Elise Smith. Nonprofit museum. Estab. 1911. Clientele: all walks of life/diverse.

Media: Considers oil, acrylic, watercolor, pastel, pen & ink, drawings, mixed media, collage, works on paper, sculpture, ceramic, craft, fiber, glass, installation, photography, performance art and original handpulled prints. Most frequently exhibits paintings, watercolor and photography.

Style: Exhibits all styles and genres.

Submissions: Send query letter, resume, slides and SASE. Slides and resumes are filed.

Missouri

*BARUCCI'S ORIGINAL GALLERIES, 13496 Clayton Rd., St Louis MO 63131. (314)878-5090. President: Shirley Schwartz. Retail gallery and art consultancy. Estab. 1977. Clientele: affluent young area; 70% private collectors, 30% corporate clients. Represents 25 artists. Sponsors 3-4 solo and 1 group shows/year. Average display time is 2 months. Interested in emerging and established artists. Overall price range: $500-2,000.

Media: Considers oil, acrylic, watercolor, pastel, collage and works on paper. Most frequently exhibits watercolor, oil and acrylic.

Style: Exhibits painterly abstraction, primitivist and impressionistic works. Genres include landscapes and florals. Currently seeking impressionistic landscapes.

Terms: Accepts work on consignment (50% commission). Retail price is set by gallery or artist. Gallery provides a contract.

Submissions: Send query letter with resume, slides and SASE. Write to schedule an appointment to show a portfolio, which should include originals and slides. Slides, bios and brochures are filed.

BOODY FINE ARTS, INC., 1425 Hanley Industrial Court, St. Louis MO 63144. Retail gallery and art consultancy. "Gallery territory includes 15 Midwest/South Central states. Staff travels on a continual basis, to develop collections within the region." Estab. 1978. Clientele: 30% private collectors, 70% corporate clients. Represents 100 artists. Sponsors 6 group shows/year. Interested in mid-career and established artists. Overall price range: $500-200,000.

Media: Considers oil, acrylic, watercolor, pastel, drawings, mixed media, collage, sculpture, ceramic, fiber, glass, works on handmade paper, photography, neon and original handpulled prints.
Style: Exhibits color field, painterly abstraction, minimalism, impressionism and photorealism. Prefers non-objective, figurative work and landscapes.
Terms: Accepts work on consignment or buys outright. Retail price is set by gallery and artist. Exclusive area representation required. Gallery provides insurance, promotion and contract; shipping costs are shared.
Submissions: Send query letter, resume and slides. Write to schedule an appointment to show a portfolio, which should include originals, slides and transparencies. All material is filed.
Tips: "Organize your slides."

CHARLOTTE CROSBY KEMPER/KANSAS CITY ART INSTITUTE, 4415 Warwick, Kansas City MO 64111. (816)561-4852. Exhibitions Director: Sherry Cromwell-Lacy. Nonprofit gallery. Clientele: collectors, students, faculty, general public. Sponsors 8-10 shows/year. Average display time is 4-6 weeks. Interested in emerging and established artists.
Media: All types of artwork are considered.
Submissions: Send query letter.

LEEDY-VOULKOS GALLERY, 1919 Wyandotte, Kansas City MO 64108. (816)474-1919. Director: Sherry Leedy. Retail gallery. Estab. 1985. Clientele: 50% private collectors, 50% corporate clients. Represents 25-30 artists. Sponsors 6 two-person, 1 group and 2 solo shows/year. Average display time is 6 weeks. Interested in emerging, mid-career and established artists. Price range: $500-25,000; most artwork sold at $5,000.
Media: Considers oil, acrylic, watercolor, works on paper, mixed media, sculpture, ceramic, glass, installation, photography and original handpulled prints. Most frequently exhibits painting and clay sculpture.
Style: Exhibits abstraction, expressionism and realism. "I am interested in quality work in all media. While we exhibit work in all media our expertise in contemporary ceramics makes our gallery unique."
Terms: Accepts work on consignment (50% commission). Retail price is set by gallery and artist. Exclusive area representation required. Gallery provides insurance, promotion and contract; shipping costs are shared.
Submissions: Send query letter, resume, slides, prices and SASE. Call or write to schedule an appointment to show a portfolio, which should include originals, slides and transparencies. Bio, vita, slides, articles, etc. are filed.
Tips: "Have an idea of what our gallery represents and show professionalism. If the artist expects us to devote time to previewing their work, they should devote some time to exploring our gallery and have some idea of what we do. We have added a second location, 2012 Baltimore, where we have an additional 5,000 sq. ft. of exhibition space. Exhibitions run concurrently with the L-V Gallery."

MORTON J. MAY FOUNDATION GALLERY, Maryville College, 13550 Conway, St. Louis MO 63141. (314)576-9300. Director: Nancy N. Rice. Nonprofit gallery. Represents 6 artists/year; emerging, mid-career and established. Sponsors 10 shows/year. Average display time 1 month. Open all year. Located on college campus. 10% of space for special exhibitions. Clientele: college community. Overall price range: $100-4,000.
Media: Considers oil, acrylic, watercolor, pastel, pen & ink, drawings, mixed media, collage, works on paper, sculpture, ceramic, fiber, installation, photography, original handpulled prints, woodcuts, engravings, lithographs, wood engravings, mezzotints, linocuts and etchings. Most frequently exhibits oil, watercolor and prismacolor.
Style: Exhibits expressionism, primitivism, painterly abstraction, realism, photorealism and hard-edge geometric abstraction. Considers all genres.
Terms: Artist receives all proceeds from sales. Retail price set by the artist. Gallery provides insurance and promotion; artist pays for shipping. Prefers framed artwork.
Submissions: Prefers St. Louis area artists. Send query letter with resume, slides, bio, brochure and SASE. Call to schedule an appointment to show a portfolio, which should include slides, photographs and transparencies. Replies only if interested within 3 months.
Tips: "Make an appointment and bring examples of actual work." Does not want to see "hobbyists'/crafts fair art."

*PRO-ART, 5595 Pershing Ave., St. Louis MO 63112. (314)361-4442. Artistic Director: Michael Holohan. Retail gallery and art consultancy. Estab. 1985. Represents 25-30 artists; emerging and mid-career. Exhibited artists include Mark Pharis and Chris Gustin. Sponsors 10 shows/year. Average display time 1 month. Open all year. Located in St. Louis' Central West End; 2,000 sq. ft. Clientele: private collectors, corporate clients. Overall price range: $200-10,000; most artwork sold at $1,000.
Media: Considers drawing, sculpture and ceramic. Most frequently exhibits ceramic.
Style: Prefers ceramic vessels and sculpture.
Terms: Accepts work on consignment (50% commission). Gallery provides insurance, promotion and contract; shipping costs are shared.
Submissions: Prefers "mostly ceramics. Some drawings, but rarely." Send query letter with resume, slides, bio and SASE. Call to schedule an appointment to show a portfolio, which should include photographs. Replies in 2 months. Files resumes.

Tips: "Come visit or find out about the kind of work and artists we represent."

Montana

ART IN THE ATRIUM, 401 N. Broadway, Billings MT 59101. (406)657-1200. Director: Bernadine Fox. Nonprofit gallery. Estab. 1980. Clientele: broad scope. Exhibits the work of 13 individuals and 1 group/year. Average display time is 1 month. Accepts only regional artists. Overall price range: $100-1,500.
Media: Considers oil, acrylic, watercolor, pastel, pen & ink, drawings, fiber, photography, mixed media, original handpulled prints, offset reproductions and posters. Prefers watercolor, 35 × 40″ framed size, or less.
Style: Exhibits contemporary, abstract, Americana, impressionistic, figurative, landscape, floral, primitive, non-representational, photorealistic, Western, realistic, neo-expressionistic and post-pop styles. "Our gallery specializes in contemporary and Western art by living regional artists."
Terms: Accepts work on consignment. Retail price is set by gallery and artist. Exclusive area representation not required. Gallery provides promotion; artist pays for shipping.
Submissions: Send query letter, resume and slides. "All material is returned to the artist."

CUSTER COUNTY ART CENTER, Box 1284, Pumping Plant Rd., Miles City MT 59301. (406)232-0635. Executive Director: Susan McDaniel. Nonprofit gallery. Estab. 1977. Clientele: 90% private collectors, 10% corporate clients. Sponsors 8 group shows/year. Average display time is 6 weeks. Interested in emerging and established artists. Overall price range: $200-10,000; most artwork sold at $300-500.
Media: Considers oil, acrylic, watercolor, pastel, pen & ink, drawings, mixed media, collage, works on paper, sculpture, ceramics, fibers, glass, installations, photography and original handpulled prints. Most frequently exhibits paintings, sculpture and photography.
Style: Exhibits painterly abstraction, conceptualism, primitivism, impressionism, expressionism, neo-expressionism and realism. Genres include landscapes, Western, portraits and figurative work. "Our gallery is seeking artists working with traditional and non-traditional Western subjects in new, contemporary ways." Specializes in Western, contemporary and traditional painting and sculpture.
Terms: Accepts work on consignment (30% commission). Retail price is set by gallery and artist. Exclusive area representation not required. Gallery provides insurance, promotion and contract; shipping expenses are shared.
Submissions: Send query letter, resume, brochure, slides, photographs and SASE. Write to schedule an appointment to show a portfolio, which should include originals, "a statement of why the artist does what he/she does" and slides. Slides and resumes are filed.

*GALLERY 16, 608 Central, Great Falls MT 59404. (406)453-6103. Advertising Director: Judy Ericksen. Retail and cooperative gallery. Estab. 1969. Represents 100 artists; emerging, mid-career, established. Has 15 members. Exhibited artists include Val Knight and Kay Fiest. Sponsors 10 shows/year. Average display time 3 months. Open all year. Located downtown; 600 sq. ft.; "wide open space with good light, movable center section that can be altered easily to make a dramatic change in the interior space." 25% of space for exhibited artists. The balance for members and cosigners. Space devoted to showing the work of gallery artists varies. Clientele: "wide variety, due to the variety of shows; all ages, mainly leaning toward contemporary taste." 85% private collectors, 15% corporate collectors. Overall price range: $10-9,000; most artwork sold at $10-800.
Media: Considers oil, acrylic, watercolor, pastel, pen & ink, drawings, mixed media, collage, works on paper, sculpture, ceramic, fiber, glass, installation, photography, hand-made garments and jewelry, original handpulled prints, woodcuts, engravings, lithographs, wood engravings, serigraphs, linocuts and etchings. "We accept some commercially prepared prints if we also have originals by the artist." Most frequently exhibits ceramic, watercolor and jewelry.
Style: "We are open to almost any style if the quality is there. We lean toward contemporary material. There are many other opportunities for the display of Western art in this area."
Terms: Accepts work on consignment (35% commission). Retail price set by the artist. Gallery provides insurance, promotion and contract. Artist pays for shipping. Framed and unframed artwork accepted.
Submissions: Prefers contemporary work in all media. Send query letter with resume, slides, bio and SASE. Call to schedule an appointment to show a portfolio, which should include slides. Files materials of artists whose work is accepted.
Tips: "Montana is remote. Unless work can be easily shipped or artist can make delivery, it is best to check to see if shipping would be prohibitive."

*GLACIER GALLERY, 1498 Old Scenic Highway, 2 East, Kalispell MT 59901. (406)752-4742. Contact: Gallery. Retail gallery and art consultancy. Estab. 1969. Clientele: 95% private collectors, 5% corporate clients. Number of exhibitions vary each year. Average display time is 4 weeks. Interested in emerging, mid-career and established artists. Overall price range: $100-150,000; most artwork sold in excess of $10,000.

Media: Considers all media and original handpulled prints. Most frequently exhibits oil, bronze and etchings.
Style: Genres include landscapes, Americana and Western works and wildlife. Looking for "variety within the artists' works."
Terms: Accepts work on consignment (33-40% commission) or buys outright. Retail price is set by gallery and artist. Exclusive area representation not required. Gallery provides insurance ("to a limit"), promotion and contract; artist pays for shipping.
Submissions: Send query letter, resume, brochure, slides and photography. Write to schedule an appointment to show a portfolio. Various material is filed.
Tips: Feels the "contemporary art market is slow."

*HARRIETTE'S GALLERY OF ART, 510 1st Ave. No., Great Falls MT 59405. (406)761-0881. Owner: Harriette Stewart. Retail gallery. Estab. 1970. Represents 20 artists; emerging mid-career and established. Exhibited artists include King Kuka and Lorraine Kuehntopp. Sponsors 1 show/year. Average display time 6 months. Open all year. Located downtown; 1,000 sq. ft. 100% of space for special exhibitions. Clientele: 90% private collectors, 10% corporate collectors. Overall price range: $100-10,000; most artwork sold at $200-750.
Media: Considers oil, acrylic, watercolor, pastel, pen & ink, mixed media, sculpture, original handpulled prints, lithographs and etchings. Most frequently exhibits watercolor, oil and pastel.
Style: Exhibits expressionism. Genres include landscape, floral and Western.
Terms: Accepts work on consignment (33⅓% commission). Buys outright for 50% of retail price. Retail price set by the gallery and the artist. Gallery provides promotion; "buyer pays for shipping costs." Prefers framed artwork.
Submissions: Send query letter with resume, slides, brochure and photographs. Write to schedule an appointment to show a portfolio, which should include originals. Replies only if interested within 1 week.

HAYNES FINE ARTS GALLERY, MSU School of Art, Bozeman MT 59717. (406)994-2562. Director: John Anacker. Nonprofit gallery. Estab. 1974. Clientele: students and community. Sponsors 1 solo and 11 group shows/year. Average display time is 4 weeks. Interested in emerging and established artists.
Media: Considers all media and original handpulled prints. Most frequently exhibits painting, ceramic and sculpture.
Style: Exhibits abstraction, conceptualism, post-modernism, expressionism, neo-expressionism, realism and figurative work. Prefers contemporary work.
Terms: Accepts work on consignment (20% commission). Gallery provides insurance, promotion and contract; shipping costs are shared.
Submissions: Send query letter, resume and sample of work. Write to schedule an appointment to show a portfolio. Resumes are filed.
Tips: Looks for "contemporary ideas and creativity."

*HOLE IN THE WALL GALLERY, 123 E. Main St., Ennis MT 59729. (1-800)992-9981. FAX: (406)682-7440. Manager: Kathy Spositer. Retail gallery. Estab. 1978. Represents 60 artists emerging (in the future), mid-career and established. Exhibited artists include Gary Carter and Lee Stroncek. Sponsors 4 shows/year. Average display time 2 weeks. Open all year. Located downtown on Main Street; 2,000 sq. ft.; "using antiques for display." 25% of space for special exhibitions, 75% for gallery artists. Clientele: wealthy collectors. 75% private collectors, 25% corporate collectors. Overall price range: $100-30,000.
Media: Considers oil, acrylic, watercolor, pastel, pen & ink, mixed media, sculpture and lithographs. Most frequently exhibits oil, watercolor and bronze.
Style: Genres include landscapes, Western and wildlife. Prefers Western, wildlife and landscapes.
Terms: Accepts work on consignment (33⅓% commission). Retail price set by the artist. Gallery provides promotion. Gallery pays for shipping costs from gallery, artist pays for shipping to gallery. Prefers framed artwork.
Submissions: Send query letter with resume, slides, bio, brochure, photographs, SASE, business card and reviews. Call to schedule an appointment to show a portfolio, which should include originals, photographs, slides and transparencies. Replies in 2 weeks. Files resume, brochure and bio.
Tips: "Artists must do Western, wildlife work, be professional and established."

Nebraska

*GALLERY 72, 2709 Leavenworth, Omaha NE 68105. (402)345-3347. Director: Robert D. Rogers. Retail gallery and art consultancy. Estab. 1972. Clientele: individuals, museums and corporations. 75% private collectors, 25% corporate clients. Represents 10 artists. Sponsors 4 solo and 4 group shows/year. Average display time is 3 weeks. Interested in emerging, mid-career and established artists. Overall price range: $750 and up.
Media: Considers oil, acrylic, watercolor, pastel, pen & ink, drawings, mixed media, collage, sculpture, ceramic, installation, photography, original handpulled prints and posters. Most frequently exhibits paintings, prints and sculpture.

Style: Exhibits hard-edge geometric abstraction, color field, minimalism, impressionism and realism. Genres include landscapes and figurative work. Mostly exhibits color field/geometric, impressionism and realism.
Terms: Accepts work on consignment (commission varies), or buys outright. Retail price is set by gallery or artist. Gallery provides insurance and promotion; shipping costs are shared.
Submissions: Send query letter with resume, slides and photographs. Call to schedule an appointment to show a portfolio, which should include originals, slides and transparencies. Vitae and slides are filed.

© 1990 John Himmelfarb

John Himmelfarb's work, "Triangles," done in acrylic on canvas, was handled by Gallery 72 in Omaha, Nebraska, on consignment. The gallery contacted the Oak Park, Illinois artist after viewing his work in an exhibit. Himmelfarb says, "Gallery 72 has had a major impact on my career, making important connections and [resulting in] sales nationally."

*HAYMARKET ART GALLERY, 119 S. 9th St., Lincoln NE 68508. (402)475-1061. Director: Vonni Sparks. Retail gallery. Estab. 1968. Clientele: "We are seeing a growth in our membership and thus a change in clientele. *New* relationships are emerging rapidly and we are establishing bonds with younger clients regularly, as well as maintaining 'regular' clientele." Represents over 100 emerging, mid-career and established artists. Sponsors 6-8 solo and/or group shows/year. Overall price range: $4.50-2,000; most artwork sold at $300.
Media: Considers original artwork of all media and original handpulled prints.
Style: "Our ideal concept is to display at all times the widest possible variety of works produced by artists of this region, focusing on the emerging artist."
Terms: Accepts work on consignment (40% commission). Retail price is set by gallery and artist. Exclusive area representation not required. Gallery provides promotion and contract; artist pays for shipping.
Submissions: "Resume and slides are considered by Exhibition Committee. Phone calls welcome."

Nevada

THE BURK GAL'RY, 1229 Arizona St., Box 246, Boulder City NV 89005. (702)293-4514. Owner: Cindy Miller. Retail gallery. Estab. 1972. Open year round. "Gallery feartures old structure (1932), off-white walls, ceiling spots and moveable walls to accommodate a variety of art." Clientele: 98% private collectors; .02% corporate clients. Represents 30 artists. Sponsors 6 solo and 2 group shows/year. Average display time: 3 months. Accepts only artists from Southwestern U.S. Interested in emerging and established artists. Overall price range: $100-10,000; most work sold at $100-1,500.
Media: Considers oil, acrylic, watercolor, pastel, pen & ink, drawings, mixed media, collage, sculpture, ceramic, engravings, lithographs, etchings, serigraphs and offset reproducfions. Most frequently exhibits watercolor, oil and bronze.
Style: Exhibits realism, photorealism and primitivism. Genres include landscapes, Southwestern, Western, wildlife and portraits. Prefers Southwestern themes, wildlife and landscapes. "Our gallery specializes in watercolors dealing with the Southwest and contemporary themes."
Terms: Accepts work on consignment (40% commission). Retail price set by artist. Exclusive area representation required.
Submissions: Send query letter with resume, slides and SASE.

*MINOTAUR GALLERY, 3200 Las Vegas Blvd. S., Las Vegas NV 89109. (702)737-1400. President: R.C. Perry. Retail gallery and art consultancy. Estab. 1980. Clientele: 95% private collectors, 5% corporate clients. Represents 2,000 artists on a rotating basis. Sponsors 5 solo and 3 group shows/year. Interested in emerging and established artists. Overall price range: $1,000-100,000; most artwork sold at $2,000-10,000.

Media: Considers oil, acrylic, watercolor, pastel, pen & ink, drawings, mixed media, works on paper, sculpture, ceramic, craft, glass and original handpulled prints. Most frequently exhibits prints, paintings and sculpture.

Style: Exhibits painterly abstraction, impressionism, expressionism, realism and surrealism. Genres include landscapes, florals, Americana and Western styles, portraits, figurative work and fantasy illustration. "We are a department store of fine art covering a wide range of styles and taste levels."

Terms: Accepts work on consignment or buys outright. Retail price is set by gallery and artist. Exclusive area representation required. Gallery provides insurance, shipping, promotion and contract.

Submissions: Send query letter, resume, brochure, slides and photographs.

NEVADA MUSEUM OF ART, 549 Court St., Reno NV 89501. (702)329-3333. Contact: Director. Museum. Estab. 1931. Located downtown in business district. Sponsors 18 solo shows/year. Average display time: 4-6 weeks. Interested in emerging and established artists.

Style: "NMA is a nonprofit private art museum with two separate facilities: Hawkins House, 2,000+ square feet of gallery space for representation work of all media; E.L. Wiegand Museum, a new contemporary museum with 8,000+ square feet for all media and format. Museum curates individual and group exhibitions for emerging as well as established artists. Museum has active acqusition policy for West/Great Basin artists."

New Hampshire

*MCGOWAN FINE ART, INC., 10 Hills Ave., Concord NH 03301. (603)225-2515. Owner/Art Consultant: Mary McGowan. Gallery Director: Dorothy Glendinning. Retail gallery and art consultancy. Estab. 1980. Represents emerging, mid-career and established artists. Sponsors 4 shows/year. Average display time 1 month. Located just off Main Street. 75-100% of space for special exhibitions. Clientele: residential and corporate. Most work sold at $125-1,000.

Media: Considers oil, acrylic, watercolor, pastel, mixed media, collage, works on paper, sculpture, original handpulled prints, woodcuts, wood engravings, linocuts, engravings, mezzotints, etchings, lithographs and serigraphs. Most frequently exhibits limited edition prints, monoprints and oil/acrylic.

Style: Exhibits painterly abstraction and all styles. Genres include landscapes.

Terms: Accepts work on consignment (40% commission). Retail price set by the artist. Gallery provides insurance and promotion. Gallery pays for shipping costs from gallery, or artist pays for shipping. Prefers unframed artwork.

Submissions: Send query letter with resume, slides and bio. Replies in 1 month. Files "bio, reviews, slides if possible."

New Jersey

ARC-EN-CIEL, 64 Naughright Rd., Long Valley NJ 07853. (201)876-9671. Owner: Ruth Reed. Retail gallery and art consultancy. Estab. 1980. Clientele: 50% private collectors, 50% corporate clients. Represents many artists. Sponsors 3 group shows/year. Average display time is 6 weeks-3 months. Interested in emerging, mid-career and established artists. Overall price range: $50-8,000; most artwork sold at $250-1,500.

Media: Considers oil, acrylic, papier mache and sculpture. Most frequently exhibits acrylic, painted iron and oil.

Style: Exhibits surrealism, primitivism and impressionism. "I exhibit country-style paintings, naif art from around the world. The art can be on wood, iron or canvas. I also have some papier mache."

Terms: Accepts work on consignment or buys outright (50% markup). Retail price is set by gallery and artist. Exclusive area representation required. Gallery provides insurance; shipping costs are shared.

Submissions: Send query letter, resume, photographs, slides and SASE. Call or write to schedule an appointment to show a portfolio. Photographs are filed.

Tips: Looks for "originality and talent. No over-priced, over-sized *hokey*, commercial art."

*ART FORMS, 16 Monmouth St., Red Bank NJ 07701. (201)530-4330. Director: Charlotte T. Scherer. Art consultancy. Estab. 1984. Represents 12 artists; emerging. Exhibited artists include Paul Bennett Hirsch and Sica. Average display time 1 month. Open all year. Located in downtown area; 2,000 sq. ft.; "gallery has art

The asterisk before a listing indicates that the listing is new in this edition. New markets are often the most receptive to freelance submissions.

deco entranceway, tin ceiling, SoHo appeal." 50% of space for special exhibitions. Clientele: 60% private collectors, 40% corporate collectors. Overall price range: $500-30,000; most artwork sold at $2,500-7,000.
Media: Considers all media. Most frequently exhibits mixed media, oil, acrylic and ceramic.
Style: Exhibits neo-expressionism. Prefers neo-expressionism, op-art and minimalist works.
Terms: Accepts work on consignment (50% commission). Retail price set by the artist. Gallery provides insurance, promotion and contract, and pays shipping costs from gallery. Prefers unframed artwork.
Submissions: Send query letter with resume, slides and bio. Write to schedule an appointment to show a portfolio, which should include originals and slides. Replies in 3 weeks. Files resume and slides.
Tips: "Galleries are more willing to show emerging artists and are promoting individuals' work that they believe in, vs. showing solely the work of established artists and past trends."

BARRON ARTS CENTER, 582 Rahway Ave., Woodbridge NJ 07095. (201)634-0413. Director: Linda Samsel. Nonprofit gallery. Estab. 1977. Clientele: culturally minded individuals mainly from the central New Jersey region, 80% private collectors, 20% corporate clients. Represents 2 artists. Interested in mid-career and established artists. Sponsors several solo and group shows/year. Average display time is 1 month. Interested in emerging and established artists. Overall price range: $500-5,000.
Media: Considers oil, acrylic, watercolor, pastel, pen & ink, drawings, mixed media, collage, works on paper, sculpture, ceramic, craft, fiber, glass, installation, photography, performance and original handpulled prints. Most frequently exhibits acrylic, photography and mixed media.
Style: Exhibits painterly abstraction, impressionism, photorealism, realism and surrealism. Genres include landscapes and figurative work. Prefers painterly abstraction, photorealism and realism.
Terms: Accepts work on consignment. Retail price is set by artist. Exclusive area representation not required. Gallery provides insurance, promotion and contract; artists responsible for shipping.
Submissions: Send query letter, resume and slides. Call to schedule an appointment to show a portfolio. Resumes and slides are filed.
Tips: Most common mistakes artists make in presenting their work are "improper matting and framing and poor quality slides."

*MARY H. DANA WOMEN ARTISTS SERIES–DOUGLASS COLLEGE LIBRARY, Rutgers University, New Brunswick NJ 08903. (201)932-7739. FAX: (201)932-6743. Curator: Beryl K. Smith. Alternative space, located in a college library. Estab. 1970-71. Represents 6-8 artists/year; mid-career and established. Interested in emerging artists, "but not students." Sponsors 6 shows/year. Open during the academic year, September-June. Located on the college campus, 1 mile from downtown; "a library space with long hours, heavily trafficked by the University community as well as the New Brunswick area community. Spots available for lighting, but walls may not be changed (i.e. painted). Work is not noted for sale, although interested persons are put in touch with the artist directly."
Media: Considers oil, acrylic, watercolor, pastel, pen & ink, drawings, mixed media, collage, works on paper, sculpture, photography, and original handpulled prints. "We are most interested in showing work that is innovative and well done."
Terms: "Work is decided upon by jury composed of art historians and studio art faculty." Gallery provides insurance and promotion (press releases and card mailings). Artist pays for shipping (except in New York/Philadelphia corridor). Prefers framed artwork.
Submissions: Send query letter with resume, slides and SASE. "Jury meets in February to plan for next academic year." Replies only if interested within 4 weeks. If does not reply the artist should make a phone inquiry. Files resumes of all submissions; for chosen artists, retain the slides, resume and photos requested.
Tips: "Send 4-6 slides of work representing what is to be shown, in good condition, labelled clearly with size, medium and name of artist. Slides should not show the vast range of which artist is capable, but rather show development within the style, or continuity."

GENEST GALLERY, 121 N. Union St., Lambertville NJ 08530. (609)397-4022. President/Director: Bernard H. Genest. Retail gallery. Estab. 1986. Represents 7-8 artists. Average display time 6 weeks. Interested in emerging and mid-career artists. Overall price range: $300-8,000; most artwork sold at $800-4,000.
Media: Considers oil, acrylic and watercolor. Most frequently exhibits oils, watercolors and acrylics.
Style: Exhibits impressionism, realism and primitivism. Genres include landscapes, florals, still lifes and Americana. Prefers realism and impressionism.
Terms: Accepts work on consignment (50% commission). Retail price set by gallery and artist. Exclusive area representation required. Gallery provides insurance, promotion, contract and shipping costs from gallery. Prefers framed artwork.
Submissions: Send query letter with resume, brochure, business card, slides, photographs, bio and SASE. Call or write to schedule an appointment to show a portfolio, which should include originals and slides, or to schedule a studio visit. Replies in 3-4 weeks or replies only if interested within 2-3 weeks. Files biography and slides (if not returned). All material is returned if not accepted or under consideration.
Tips: "Present a concise presentation that is neat and organized. State your goals, development and consistency of work."

HOLMAN HALL ART GALLERY, Hillwood Lakes, CN 4700, Trenton NJ 08650-4700. (609 771-2189. Chairman, Art Department: Dr. Howard Goldstein. Nonprofit gallery and art consultancy. Estab. 1973. Clientele: students, educators, friends and the general public. Represents 125 artists. Sponsors 7 solo and group shows. Average display time is 5 weeks. Interested in emerging and established artists. Overall price range: $100-5,000.

Media: Considers all media, original handpulled prints and offset reproductions. Most frequently exhibits photography, mixed media, sculpture, prints, paintings and drawings.

Style: Exhibits hard-edge geometric abstraction, painterly abstraction, conceptualism, photorealism and expressionism. Genres include landscapes, Americana and figurative work. "Our gallery specializes in any type, style or concept that will best represent that type, style or concept. Being on a college campus we strive not only to entertain but to educate as well."

Terms: Retail price is set by gallery and artist. Exclusive area representation not required. Gallery provides insurance, promotion and contract; artist pays for shipping.

Submissions: Exhibitions are arranged by invitation only. Open exhibitions are juried. Includes national drawing, national printmaking and county photography exhibitions.

*THE KORBY GALLERY, 479 Pompton Ave., Cedar Grove NJ 07009. (201)239-6789. Owner: Alfred Korby. Retail gallery. Estab. 1958. Clientele: upper income private buyers, upper-end designers; 70% private collectors. Represents 15 artists. Sponsors 18 solo and 4 group shows/year. Average display time 4 weeks-2 months. Interested in emerging and established artists. Overall price range: $200-2,500; most artwork sold at $1,500.

Media: Considers oil, acrylic, watercolor, sculpture, ceramic, fiber, collage, glass and color original handpulled prints. Specializes in lithographs, serigraphs and etchings. Currently looking for oils.

Style: Exhibits contemporary, abstract, landscape, floral, primitive and miniature works. Specializes in contemporary; currently seeking realism.

Terms: Accepts work on consignment (40% commission). Retail price is set by gallery and artist. Exclusive area representation required.

Submissions: Send query letter with resume, slides, photographs and SASE. Call or write to schedule an appointment to show a portfolio.

Tips: Sees a "return to romance and realism."

*PELICAN ART PRINTS, 1 Nasturtium Ave., Glenwood NJ 07418. (914)986-8113 or (201)764-7149. Owner: Tom Prendergast. Art Director: Sean Prendergast. Art consultancy. "Brokers prints, at various locations—restaurants, automobile dealers, galleries, dentist offices, frame shops and banks." Estab. 1986. Represents established artists. Exhibited artists include Doolittle and Bateman. Sponsors 2 shows/year. Average display time 2 months. Open all year. Located "all over NJ and in Port Jervis, NY." Clientele: 50% private collectors, 40% other galleries, 10% corporate clients. Overall price range: $150-1,500; most artwork sold at $350-500.

Media: Considers watercolor and pen & ink, woodcuts, lithographs, serigraphs and etchings. Most frequently exhibits original prints and serigraphs.

Style: Exhibits imagism and realism. Genres include landscapes, Americana, Southwestern, Western, marine, aviation and wildlife. Prefers wildlife, western and Americana.

Terms: Accepts work on consignment (20% commission). Retail price set by the artist. Gallery provides promotion; artist pays for shipping. Prefers unframed artwork.

Submissions: Send query letter with resume and brochure. Call to schedule an appointment to show a portfolio, which should include originals. Replies in 1 week.

Tips: "Have work that shows professional art."

SIDNEY ROTHMAN-THE GALLERY, 21st on Central Ave., Barnegat Light NJ 08006. (609)494-2070. Director-Owner: S. Rothman. Retail gallery. Estab. 1958. Represents 50 artists; emerging, mid-career and established artists. Exhibited artists include John Gable and Gregorio Prestopino. Sponsors 1 show/year. Average display time 14 weeks. Open during summer months. Located in the seashore resort area; 256 sq. ft.; located on the street floor of owner's home. 100% of space for special exhibitions, 100% for gallery artists. Clientele: 100% private collectors. Overall price range: $100-15,000; most artwork sold at $3,000.

Media: Considers oil, acrylic, watercolor, pastel, pen & ink, drawings, mixed media, works on paper, sculpture, craft, original handpulled prints, woodcuts, wood engravings, linocuts, engravings, mezzotints, etchings, lithographs and serigraphs. "We do not want offset lithos." Most frequently exhibits watercolor, hand colored, hand-pulled prints, acrylic and oil.

Style: Exhibits expressionism, neo-expressionism, painterly abstraction, surrealism, conceptualism, minimalism, post modern works, impressionism, realism, hard-edge geometric abstraction. Considers all genres. Prefers expressionism, surrealism and painterly abstraction.

Terms: Accepts work on consignment (33% commission). Retail price set by the gallery and the artist. Gallery provides promotion; shipping costs from gallery.

Submissions: Send query letter with resume, slides and SASE. Call or write to schedule an appointment to show a portfolio, which should include originals and slides. Replies in 1 week. Files bios. "If work is accepted based on slides, however, the final decision is based upon presentation of actual work."

SCHERER GALLERY, 93 School Rd. W., Marlboro NJ 07746. (201)536-9465. Owner: Marty Scherer. Retail gallery. Estab. 1968. Clientele: 80% private collectors, 20% corporate clients. Represents over 40 artists. Sponsors 4 solo and 3 group shows/year. Average display time is 2 months. Interested in mid-career and established artists. Overall price range: $200-25,000; most artwork sold at $1,000-10,000.
Media: Considers oil, acrylic, watercolor, pen & ink, drawings, mixed media, collage, works on paper, sculpture, glass and original handpulled prints. Most frequently exhibits paintings, original graphics and sculpture.
Style: Exhibits hard-edge geometric abstraction, color field, painterly abstraction, minimalism, conceptualism, surrealism, impressionism, expressionism and realism. "Scherer Gallery is looking for artists who employ creative handling of a given medium(s) in a contemporary manner." Specializes in handpulled graphics (lithographs, serigraphs, monotypes, woodcuts, etc.). "Would like to be more involved with original oils and acrylic paintings."
Terms: Accepts work on consignment (50% commission). Retail price is set by gallery and artist. Exclusive area representation required. Gallery provides insurance, promotion and contract; shipping costs are shared.
Submissions: Send query letter, resume, brochure, slides and photographs. Call or write to schedule an appointment to show a portfolio, which should include originals, slides and transparencies.
Tips: Considers "originality and quality of handling the medium."

SERAPHIM FINE ARTS GALLERY, 32 N. Dean St., Englewood NJ 07631. (201)568-4432. Contact: Director. Retail gallery. Clientele: 90% private collectors, 10% corporate clients. Represents 150 artists; emerging and mid-career. Sponsors 6 solo and 3 group shows/year. Overall price range: $700-17,000; most artwork sold at $4,000-7,000.
Media: Considers oil, acrylic, watercolor, drawings, collage, sculpture and ceramic. Most frequently exhibits oil, acrylic and sculpture.
Style: Exhibits impressionism, realism, photorealism, painterly abstraction and conceptualism. Considers all genres. Prefers impressionism, abstraction and photorealism. "We are located in New Jersey, but we function as a New York gallery. We put together shows of artists which are unique. We represent fine contemporary artists and sculptures."
Terms: Accepts work on consignment. Retail price set by gallery and artist. Exclusive area representation required. Gallery provides insurance and promotion. Prefers framed artwork.
Submissions: Send query letter with resume, slides and photographs. Portfolio should include originals, slides and photographs. Replies in 2-4 weeks. Files slides and bios.
Tips: Looking for "artistic integrity, creativity and an artistic ability to express self." Notices a "return to interest in figurative work."

BEN SHAHN GALLERIES, William Paterson College, 300 Pompton Rd, Wayne NJ 07470. (201)595-2654. Director: Nancy Eireinhofer. Nonprofit gallery. Estab. 1968. Clientele: college, local and New Jersey metropolitan-area community. Sponsors 5 solo and 10 group shows/year. Average display time is 6 weeks. Interested in emerging and established artists.
Media: Considers all media.
Style: Specializes in contemporary and historic styles, but will consider all styles.
Terms: Accepts work for exhibition only. Gallery provides insurance, promotion and contract; shipping costs are shared.
Submissions: Send query letter with resume, brochure, slides, photographs and SASE. Write to schedule an appointment to show a portfolio.

*WYCKOFF GALLERY, 210 Everett Ave., Wyckoff NJ 07481. (201)891-7436. Director: Sherry Cosloy. Retail gallery. Estab. 1980. Clientele: collectors, art lovers, interior decorators and businesses; 75% private collectors, 25% corporate clients. Sponsors 1-2 solo and 8-10 group shows/year. Average display time is 1 month. Interested in emerging, mid-career and established artists. Overall price range: $250-10,000; most artwork sold at $500-3,000.
Media: Considers oil, acrylic, watercolor, pastel, pen & ink, pencil, mixed media, sculpture, ceramic, collage and limited edition prints. Most frequently exhibits oil, watercolor and pastel.
Style: Exhibits contemporary, abstract, traditional, impressionistic, figurative, landscape, floral, realistic and neo-expressionistic works.
Terms: Accepts work on consignment. Retail price is set by gallery or artist. Gallery provides insurance and promotion.
Submissions: Send query letter with resume, slides and SASE. Resume and biography are filed.
Tips: Sees trend toward "renewed interest in traditionalism and realism."

New Mexico

THE ALBUQUERQUE MUSEUM, 2000 Mountain Rd. N.W., Albuquerque NM 87104. (505)243-7255. Curator of Art: Ellen Landis. Nonprofit museum. Estab. 1967. Location: Old Town (near downtown). Sponsors mostly group shows. Average display time is 3-6 months. Interested in emerging, mid-career and established artists.

Media: Considers all media.

Style: Exhibits all styles. Genres include landscapes, florals, Americana, Western, portraits, figurative and nonobjective work. "Our shows are from our permanent collection or are special traveling exhibitions originated by our staff. We also host special traveling exhibitions originated by other museums or exhibition services."

Submissions: Send query letter, resume, slides, photographs and SASE. Call or write to schedule an appointment to show a portfolio.

Tips: "Artists should leave slides and biographical information in order to give us a reference point for future work or to consider their work in the future."

ALBUQUERQUE UNITED ARTISTS, INC., Box 1808, Albuquerque NM 87103. (505)243-0531. Nonprofit arts organization. Estab. 1978. Represents over 400 artists. Sponsors 8 group shows/year. Sponsors statewide juried exhibits and performances. Average display time is 4 weeks. Accepts only New Mexico artists. Interested in emerging, mid-career and established artists. Overall price range: $150-2,500; most artwork sold under $500.

Media: Considers oil, acrylic, watercolor, pastel, pen & ink, drawings, mixed media, collage, works on paper, sculpture, ceramic, craft, fiber, glass, installation, photography and original handpulled prints. Most frequently exhibits mixed media, acrylic and ceramics.

Style: Exhibits hard-edge geometric abstraction, color field, painterly abstraction, conceptual works, postmodern, photorealism and expressionism. Genres include landscapes and florals. "Albuquerque United Artists does not specialize in any specific concept as long as the artwork is contemporary."

Terms: Accepts work "only for shows" on consignment (30% commission) or membership fee plus donation of time. Retail price is set by artist. Exclusive area representation not required. AUA provides insurance and contract; shipping costs are shared.

Submissions: Request membership information.

Tips: "We make a special effort to include emerging artists. Part of our mission is to educate and train young and emerging artists. We will look at everything and try to direct artists to the appropriate persons or places where their work is most likely to be shown. Too often artists send slides not labeled properly, works are delivered without wires or otherwise unsuitably prepared for exhibition, miss deadlines, application forms incomplete, fail to follow instructions." Sees trend "in Albuquerque toward more acceptance of contemporary art (non-traditional Southwest). Many new artists moving to this area with fresh ideas."

*BENT GALLERY AND MUSEUM, Box 153, 117 Bent St., Taos NM 87571. (505)758-2376. Owner: O.T. Noeding. Retail gallery and museum. Estab. 1961. Represents 15 established artists. Interested in emerging artists. Exhibited artists include Leal Mack. Open all year. Located 1 block off of the Plaza; "housed in the home of Charles Bent, the first territorial governor of New Mexico." 95% private collectors, 5% corporate collectors. Overall price range: $100-10,000; most work sold at $500-1,000.

Media: Considers oil, acrylic, watercolor, pastel, pen & ink, drawings, sculpture, original handpulled prints, woodcuts, engravings and lithographs.

Style: Exhibits impressionism and realism. Genres include landscapes, florals, Southwestern and Western. Prefers impressionism, landscapes and Western works.

Terms: Accepts work on consignment (33½-50% commission). Retail price set by the gallery and the artist. Artist pays for shipping. Prefers framed artwork.

Submissions: Send query letter with brochure and photographs. Write to schedule an appointment to show a portfolio, which should include originals and photographs. Replies if applicable.

Tips: "It is best if the artist comes in person with examples of his or her work."

*BRUSH FIRE GALLERY, Calle De Parian, Mesilla NM 88046. (505)527-2685. Owner: Pati Bates. Retail gallery. Estab. 1987. Represents 25 artists; emerging, mid-career and established. Exhibited artists include Pati Bates and Steve Hanks. Sponsors 4 shows/year. Average display time 90 days-1 year. Open all year. Located in Old Town Mesilla, a tourist area; 500 sq. ft.; "an old, historical adobe structure." 20% of space for special exhibitions, 80% for gallery artists. Clientele: mostly tourists and local buyers collectors. Overall price range: $3,500-10,000; most artwork sold at $900-1,500.

Media: Considers all media, etchings, offset reproductions and serigraphs. Most frequently exhibits watercolor, pencil and oil.

Style: Exhibits expressionism, painterly abstraction, surrealism, color field, realism, photorealism and all styles. Genres include Southwestern, wildlife, figurative work and all genres. Prefers figurative work and wildlife.

Terms: Accepts work on consignment (30% commission) or buys work outright for 50% of retail price (net 30 days). Retail price set by the artist. Gallery provides insurance and promotion. Artist pays for shipping. Framed and unframed artwork accepted.

Submissions: Send query letter with resume, slides, brochure and SASE. Call or write to schedule an appointment to show a portfolio, which should include slides. Replies in 3 weeks only if interested. Files slides.

BRYANS GALLERY, 121 C. N. Plaza, Taos NM 87571. (505)758-9407. Director: Michael McCormick. Retail gallery. Estab. 1983. "Located in old county courthouse where movie 'Easy Rider' was filmed." Clientele: 90% private collectors; 10% corporate clients. Represents 35 artists. Sponsors 3 solo and 1 group show/year. Average display time: 2-3 weeks. Interested in emerging and established artists. Overall price range: $1,500-85,000; most work sold at $3,500-10,000.

Media: Considers oil, acrylic, watercolor, pastel, pen & ink, drawings, mixed media, collage, works on paper, sculpture, ceramic, craft, photography, woodcuts, wood engravings, linocuts, engravings, mezzotints, etchings, lithographs, pochoir, serigraphs offset reproductions and posters. Most frequently exhibits oil, pottery and sculpture/stone.

Style: Exhibits impressionism, neo-expressionism, surrealism, primitivism, painterly abstraction, conceptualism and post modern works. Genres include landscapes and figurative work. Prefers figurative work, lyrical impressionism and abstraction.

Terms: Accepts work on consignment (50% commission). Retail price set by gallery and artist. Exclusive area representation required. Gallery provides promotion and contract; artist pays for shipping. Prefers artwork framed.

Submissions: Send query letter with resume, brochure, slides, photographs, bio and SASE. Write to schedule an appointment to show a portfolio. Replies in 4-7 weeks.

Tips: "Send a brief, concise introduction with several color photos."

*EL TALLER TAOS GALLERY, 119A Kit Carson Rd., Taos NM 87571. (505)758-4887. Director: Mary Alice Renison. Retail gallery. Estab. 1983. Represents 25 artists; mid-career and established. Exhibited artists include Amado Pena and Katalin Ehling. Sponsors 3 shows/year. Average display time up to 6 months. Open all year. Located downtown; 4,000 sq. ft. 100% of space for gallery artists. Clientele: 80% private collectors, 20% corporate collectors. Overall price range: $35-15,000; most artwork sold at $500-4,000.

Media: Considers oil, acrylic, watercolor, pastel, drawings, mixed media, collage, works on paper, sculpture, ceramic, fiber, glass, original handpulled prints, woodcuts, engravings, lithographs, etchings and serigraphs. Most frequently exhibits paintings, limited edition original graphics and sculpture.

Style: Exhibits primitivism, painterly abstraction, impressionism and realism. Genres include landscapes, Southwestern, Western and figurative work.

Terms: Accepts work on consignment (50% commission). Retail price set by the gallery and the artist. Gallery provides insurance and promotion; artist pays for shipping. Prefers framed artwork.

Submissions: Prefers only Southwest subjects. Send query letter with resume, bio, brochure, photographs, SASE, business card and reviews. Call or write to schedule an appointment to show a portfolio, which should include originals, photographs and transparencies. Replies in 2-3 weeks. Files bio and cover letter.

*FULLER LODGE ART CENTER, Box 790, 2132 Central, Los Alamos NM 87544. (505)662-9331. Director: Connie Poore. Retail gallery, nonprofit gallery, museum and rental gallery for members. Estab. 1977. Represents over 50 artists; emerging, mid-career and established. Has 279 members. Sponsors 11 shows/year. Average display time 3 weeks. Open all year. Located downtown; 1,300 sq. ft.; "gallery housed in the original log building from the Boys School that preceded the town." 98% of space for special exhibitions. Clientele: local, regional and international visitors. 99% private collectors, 1% corporate collectors. Overall price range: $50-1,200; most artwork sold at $200-300.

Media: Considers oil, acrylic, watercolor, pastel, pen & ink, drawings, mixed media, collage, works on paper, sculpture, ceramic, craft, fiber, glass, installation, photography, original handpulled prints, woodcuts, engravings, lithographs, wood engravings, mezzotints, serigraphs, linocuts and etchings.

Style: Exhibits all styles and genres.

Terms: Accepts work on consignment (30% commission). Retail price set by the artist. Gallery provides insurance and promotion; artist pays for shipping. Prefers "exhibition ready" artwork.

Submissions: "Prefer the unique. Not 'Santa Fe' style." Send query letter with resume, slides, bio, brochure, photographs, SASE and reviews. Call to schedule an appointment to show a portfolio, which should include originals, photographs (if a photographer) and slides. Replies in 2 weeks. Files "resumes, etc., slides returned if SASE."

Tips: "Be aware that we never do one person shows—artists will be used as they fit in to scheduled shows." Should show "impeccable craftsmanship."

*GALLERY A, 105 Kit Carson, Taos NM 87571. (505)758-2343. Director: Mary L. Sanchez. Retail gallery. Estab. 1960. Represents 70 artists; emerging, mid-career and established. Exhibited artists include Gene Kloss and Carlos Hall. Sponsors 1 show/year. Average display time 2 months. Open all year. Located one block from the plaza; over 3,500 sq. ft; "Southwestern interior decor." 50% of space for special exhibitions, 100% for gallery artists. Clientele: "from all walks of life." 98% private collectors. Overall price range: $100-12,000; most artwork sold at $500-5,000.

Media: Considers oil, acrylic, watercolor, pastel, original handpulled prints, serigraphs and etchings. Most frequently exhibits oil, watercolor and acrylic.

Style: Exhibits expressionism, impressionism and realism. Genres include landscapes, florals, Southwestern and Western works. Prefers impressionism, realism and expressionism.

Terms: Accepts work on consignment (40% commission). Retail price set by the artist. Gallery provides promotion; artist pays for shipping. Prefers framed artwork.

Submissions: Send query letter with bio and photographs. Call or write to schedule an appointment to show a portfolio, which should include photographs. Replies only if interested within 1 week. Files bios.

*GALLERY G, 111 Romero St. NW, Albuquerque NM 87104. (505)247-4474. Owner-director: Kathy Gallagher. Retail gallery. Estab. 1985. Represents 11 artists; mid-career and established. Exhibited artists include Deborah Christensen and David Drummond. Sponsors 4 shows/year. Average display time 1 month. Open all year. Located in "old town historical area of Albuquerque; 560 sq. ft.; gallery is small and intimate." 100% of space for gallery artists. Clientele: tourists and private collectors. 80% private collectors, 20% corporate collectors. Overall price range: $7,500-200; most artwork sold at $1,200-1,000.

Media: Considers oil, acrylic, watercolor, pastel and pottery. Most frequently exhibits pastel, watercolor and oil.

Style: Exhibits impressionism and realism. Genres include landscapes, florals, Americana, Southwestern and Western. Prefers landscape, Southwestern and floral works.

Terms: Accepts work on consignment (40% commission). Retail price set by the artist. Gallery provides insurance and promotion; artist pays for shipping.

Submissions: Accepts only artists from the Southwest. Send query letter with resume, slides, bio, brochure and SASE. Write to schedule an appointment to show a portfolio, which should include originals and slides. Replies in 3 weeks. Files letter.

*EDITH LAMBERT GALLERY, 707 Canyon Rd., Santa Fe NM 87501. (505)984-2783. Contact: Director. Retail gallery. Estab. 1986. Represents 30 artists; emerging and mid-career. Exhibited artists include Carol Hoy and Margaret Nes. Sponsors 4 shows/year. Average display time 3 weeks. Open all year. Located in "historic 'art colony' area; 1,500 sq. ft.; historic adobe, Southwestern architecture, lush garden compound." 20% of space for special exhibitions. Clientele: 95% private collectors. Overall price range: $100-4,500; most artwork sold at $500-2,600.

Media: Considers oil, acrylic, watercolor, pastel, mixed media, collage, works on paper, ceramic, craft and glass. Most frequently exhibits watercolor/casein, pastel and oil.

Style: Exhibits expressionism, neo-expressionism and painterly abstraction. Genres include landscapes, Southwestern and figurative work. Prefers expressionism and painterly abstraction. No portraits; "animal" paintings.

Terms: Accepts work on consignment (50% commission). Exclusive area representation required. Retail price set by the gallery. Provides insurance, promotion and contract; shipping costs are shared. Prefers framed artwork.

Submissions: Send query letter with resume, slides, bio, SASE and reviews. Call to schedule an appointment to show a portfolio, which should include originals and slides. Replies only if interested within 1 month.

Tips: Looks for "consistency, continuity in the work; artists with ability to interact well with collectors and have a commitment to their career."

THE LEDOUX GALLERY, One Ledoux St., Box 2418, Taos NM 87571. (505)748-9101. Director/Owner: Lawrence Kaplan. Retail gallery. Estab. 1976. Clientele: quality collectors; 90% private collectors, 10% corporate clients. Represents 26 artists. Accepts only Southwest artists. Interested in emerging, mid-career and established artists. Overall price range: $200-7,500; most artwork sold at $500-1,000.

Media: Considers oil, acrylic, watercolor, pastel, mixed media, collage, ceramic and original handpulled prints. Most frequently exhibits oil, watercolor and prints.

Style: Exhibits painterly abstraction, minimalism, impressionism, expressionism and neo-expressionism. Genres include landscapes and figurative work. "I am concerned with all that connects to timelessness."

Terms: Accepts work on consignment (40% commission). Retail price is set by gallery and artist. Exclusive area representation not required. Gallery provides insurance, promotion and contract; artist pays for shipping.

Submissions: Send query letter. Write to schedule an appointment to show a portfolio. Names and addresses of potential artsts are filed. "Artists from Southwest a requisite."

Tips: "Be exciting and have a knowledge of the professional requirements, such as framing." Sees trend toward "too strong reliance on slick—hype and ornate setting."

MAGIC MOUNTAIN GALLERY, INC., 107A N. Plaza, Taos NM 87571. (505)758-9604. Owner: Kay Decker. Retail gallery. Estab. 1980. Represents 45 artists; mid-career and established. Interested in seeing the work of emerging artists. Exhibited artists include Jerry Cajko and John Boomer. Sponsors 3 shows/year. Average display time 1 month for exhibitions, otherwise continuous. Open all year. Located in "the historic plaza area; 1,200 sq. ft; spacious interior." 100% of space for gallery artists. Clientele: 95% private collectors, 5% corporate collectors. Overall price range: $100-15,000.

Media: Considers oil, acrylic, watercolor, pastel, works on paper, sculpture, ceramic, fiber, glass, original handpulled prints, lithographs and serigraphs. Most frequently exhibits sculpture, painting and ceramic.

Style: Exhibits expressionism and impressionism. Genres include landscapes, florals, Southwestern and figurative work. Prefers Southwestern, figurative work and landscapes.

Terms: Accepts work on consignment. Retail price set by the artist. Gallery provides insurance, promotion and contract; artist pays for shipping. Prefers framed artwork.

Submissions: Send query letter with resume, slides, bio, brochure and photographs. Call or write to schedule an appointment to show a portfolio which should include originals, slides, photographs and transparencies. Replies in 2 weeks. "Anything artist wishes to leave with us."

Tips: "Be professional with your presentation. Have everything organized."

*MAYANS GALLERIES, LTD., 601 Canyon Rd., Santa Fe NM 87501; also at 310 Johnson St., Box 1889, Santa Fe NM 87504. (505)983-8068. Director: Maria Martinez. Retail gallery and art consultancy. Estab. 1977. Clientele: 70% private collectors, 30% corporate clients. Represents 25 artists. Sponsors 6 solo and 2 group shows/year. Average display time is 1 month. Interested in emerging and established artists. Overall price range: $450 and up; most artwork sold at $2,500-5,000.

Media: Considers oil, acrylic, watercolor, pastel, pen & ink, drawings, mixed media, sculpture, photography and original handpulled prints. Most frequently exhibits oil, photography, and lithographs.

Style: Exhibits painterly abstraction, post-modernism, impressionism, expressionism, neo-expressionism and realism. Genres include landscapes and figurative work.

Terms: Accepts work on consignment. Retail price is set by gallery and artist. Exclusive area representation required. Gallery provides insurance; shipping costs are shared.

Submissions: Send query letter, resume, business card, slides and SASE. Write to schedule an appointment to show a portfolio, which should include slides and transparencies. Resume and business card are filed.

*OPEN SPACE A COOPERATIVE GALLERY, 103 B E. Plaza, Taos NM 87571. (505)751-1217. Director: Carolyn Thomas. Cooperative gallery. Estab. 1981. Represents 18 established artists. Interested in seeing the work of emerging artists. Has 14 members. Exhibited artists include Elizabeth Jenkins and Carolyn Thomas. Sponsors 9 shows/year. Average display time 6 weeks. Open all year. Located in downtown Taos Plaza; 900 sq. ft. 40% of space for special exhibitions, 100% for gallery artists. Clientele: tourists and local. Overall price range: $15-1,000.

Media: Considers oil, acrylic, watercolor, pastel, pen & ink, drawings, mixed media, collage, works on paper, sculpture, ceramic, craft, fiber, glass, photography and "any works on art form that fits into the contemporary concept."

Style: Exhibits all styles and genres.

Terms: Accepts work on consignment (40-60% commission) or buys outright for 50% of retail price. Co-op membership free plus donation of time (17% commission). Retail price set by the artist. Gallery provides insurance, promotion and contract. "We charge the customer for shipping."

Submissions: Send query letter with resume, slides, bio, photographs and actual work. Call or write to schedule an appointment to show a portfolio, which should include originals and slides. Replies in 3-4 weeks.

*QUAST GALLERIES, TAOS, 229 Kit Carson Rd., Box 1528, Taos NM 87571. (505)758-7160. Director: C. Whitehouse. Retail gallery. Estab. 1986. Represents 26 artists; emerging, mid-career and established. Exhibited artists include Holis Williford and Steve Kestrel. Sponsors 6 shows/year. Average display time 6 months. Open all year. Located a quarter mile east of the town plaza; 1,600 sq. ft.; "old adobe home set under ancient cottonwoods with an outdoor sculpture garden." 100% of space for special exhibitions, 100% for gallery artists. Clientele: collectors from across the country. 80% private collectors, 20% corporate collectors. Overall price range: $500-150,000; most artwork sold at $2,000-15,000.

Media: Considers oil, watercolor, pastel, drawings and sculpture with an emphasis on bronze. Most frequently exhibits bronze, oil and watercolor.

Style: Exhibits impressionism and representational work. Genres include landscapes, florals, Southwestern, Western, wildlife, portraits and figurative work. Prefers wildlife, landscape and Western.

Terms: Accepts work on consignment (50% commission). Buys outright for 40% of retail price. Retail price set by the artist. Gallery provides insurance, promotion and contract; artist pays for shipping. Prefers framed artwork.

Submissions: Send query letter with bio, brochure, photographs, SASE, business card, reviews and prices. Write to schedule an appointment to show a portfolio, which should include originals, slides and photographs. Replies in 6 weeks or within 2 weeks only if interested.

Tips: "Have technical skills and a professional approach to work." Sees trend toward galleries being "more involved in the education and awareness of quality art."

RUTGERS BARCLAY GALLERY, 325 W. San Francisco St., Santa Fe NM 87501. (505)986-1400. Director/ Owner: Rutgers Barclay. Assistant Director: Laurie B. Innes. Retail gallery. Estab. 1988. Clientele: 40% private collectors. Represents 3 or more artists. Sponsors 6-7 solo and 1-2 group shows/year. Average display time 4 weeks. Interested in emerging, mid-career and established artists. Overall price range: $2,000-85,000 and up; most work sold at $3,000-30,000.

Media: Considers oil, acrylic, watercolor, pastel, pen & ink, drawings, mixed media, works on paper, sculpture, ceramic, egg tempera and original handpulled prints. Most frequently exhibits oils, watercolors and monoprints.

Style: Exhibits impressionism, expressionism, neo-expressionism, realism, photorealism, color field and painterly abstraction; considers all styles. Genres include landscapes, florals, wildlife, portraits and figurative work; considers all genres except Southwestern art. Prefers contemporary works, realism and abstraction.

Terms: Accepts work on consignment (50% commission). Retail price set by gallery and artist. Exclusive area representation not required. Gallery provides insurance, promotion and contract; shipping costs are shared. Prefers framed artwork.

Submissions: Send query letter with resume, slides, photographs, bio and SASE. Call to schedule an appointment to show a portfolio, which should include slides, transparencies, photographs and bio. Does not want to see "other people representing them showing their portfolios—prefer to meet with artists themselves whenever possible. Also do not want to see portfolios of *everything* they have *ever* done. Most galleries prefer to see a limited selection of materials, i.e. 20 slides, 3-4 articles, resume/biography." Replies only if interested within 2 weeks. All material is returned if not accepted or under consideration.

SANTA FE EAST GALLERY, 200 Old Santa Fe Trail, Santa Fe NM 87501. Associate Director: Joe Atteberry. Retail gallery. Estab. 1980. Clientele: 98% private collectors, 2% corporate clients. Represents 100 artists. Sponsors 4 solo and 4 group shows/year. Average exhibition length is 1 month. Interested in emerging, mid-career and established artists. Overall price range: $150-35,000; most artwork sold at $900-3,500.

Media: Considers oil, acrylic, watercolor, pastel, mixed media, collage, sculpture and jewelry. Most frequently exhibits oil, sculpture and jewelry.

Style: Exhibits impressionism, expressionism and realism. Genres include landscapes and figurative work. Prefers American impressionism and contemporary realism. "We feature museum quality exhibitions of large nineteenth and early twentieth century American art, contemporary Southwest artists and one-of-a-kind designer jewelry."

Terms: Accepts work on consignment (40-50% commission). Retail price is set by gallery and artist. Exclusive area representation required. Gallery provides insurance, promotion and contract; artist pays for shipping and supplies professional quality photographs.

Submissions: Send query letter, resume, slides, photographs, price information and SASE. Write to schedule an appointment to show a portfolio, which should include originals, slides and resume. Letters and resumes are filed. "Gallery also sponsors juried exhibitions of art and jewelry. Write for information."

*SHELLFISH COLLECTION STUDIO AND GALLERY, Box 370, 212 W. Broadway, Silver City NM 88062. (505)388-3423. Gallery Director: W. Sturgen. Retail and wholesale gallery. Estab. 1988. Represents 5 artists; emerging, mid-career and established. Exhibited artists include Winston Sturgen and Dorothy McCray. Sponsors 3-4 shows/year. Average display time 4 weeks. Open all year. Located downtown; 1,500 sq. ft.; "in restored Victorian storefront." 100% of space for gallery artists. 90% private collectors, 10% corporate collectors. Overall price range: $100-1,000; most artwork sold at $300-500.

Media: Considers oil, acrylic, watercolor, pastel, pen & ink, drawings, mixed media, collage, works on paper, sculpture, ceramic, photography, original handpulled prints only, woodcuts, wood engravings, linocuts, mezzotints, etchings and lithographs. Most frequently exhibits oil, handpulled prints and all other media.

Style: Exhibits painterly abstraction, impressionism and realism.

Terms: Accepts work on consignment (40% commission). Retail price set by the artist. Gallery provides promotion; artist pays for shipping. Prefers framed artwork.

Submissions: Accepts work only from Southwest U.S. Send query letter with resume, slides and bio. Call or write to schedule an appointment to show a portfolio, which should include originals, slides and transparencies. Replies in 3-4 weeks. Files no materials.

Tips: "We are not currently accepting new artists."

*UNIVERSITY ART GALLERY, NEW MEXICO STATE UNIVERSITY, Williams Hall, University Ave. E. of Solano, Las Cruces NM 88003. (505)646-2545. Director: Karen Mobley. Estab. 1972. Represents emerging, mid-career and established artists. Sponsors 6 shows/year. Average display time 6 weeks. Open all year. Located at university; 4,000 sq. ft. 100% of space for special exhibitions.

Media: Considers oil, acrylic, watercolor, paste, pen & ink, drawings, mixed media, collage, works on paper, sculpture, ceramic, craft, fiber, glass, installation and photography.
Style: Exhibits all styles and genres.
Terms: "Work curated for special exhibition." Gallery provides insurance and promotion; sometimes pays shipping costs.
Submissions: Prefers only contemporary work. Send query letter with resume, slides, bio, SASE and reviews. Write to schedule an appointment to show a portfolio, which should include originals and slides. Replies in 2 months.

New York

*ADAMS ART GALLERY, 600 Central, Dunkirk NY 14048. (716)366-7450. Curator: Marvin Bjurlin. Nonprofit gallery. Estab. 1975. Represents 12-16 artists/year in both solos and duos; emerging and mid-career. Sponsors 12 shows/year. Average display time 3 weeks. Open all year. Located near downtown; "a renovated classic revival unitarian church, 18' ceilings, track lights." 100% of space for special exhibitions. Clientele: general public. "There are very few sales." Overall price range: $500-5,000.
Media: Considers oil, acrylic, watercolor, pastel, pen & ink, drawings, mixed media, collage, works on paper, sculpture, ceramic, craft, fiber, glass, installation and photography. No media preferred.
Style: Exhibits all styles and genres. No style preferred. Does not want to see "decorative 'office' art."
Terms: Accepts work on consignment (25% commission). Retail price set by the artist. Gallery provides insurance and promotion; shipping costs are shared. Prefers framed artwork.
Submissions: "Artist's work must represent a strong personal statement." Send query letter with resume, slides and bio. Write to schedule an appointment to show a portfolio, which should include slides.
Tips: "While we have no regional limits, it is hard for us to deal with large artwork which is shipped (limited storage area). Most artists deliver and pick up work. We help with costs." Sees trend toward "diversification of media, more multimedia."

*THE ARTISTS GALLERY, 30 D Essex St., Buffalo NY 14213. (716)883-2303. Contact: Director. Nonprofit gallery and alternative space. Estab. 1976. Represents 185 emerging, mid-career and established artists. Popular artists exhibited include Suzann Denney and Mark Lavatelli. Sponsors 12 shows/year. Average display time 3 weeks. Open September-June. Located on the west side, near Allentown; 2,000 sq. ft.; "in Essex Art Center (complex of residential and studio space); exhibition walls 12' high, available verticle space 20'. Used to be an ice house." 100% of space for special exhibitions. Clientele: wide variety. Overall price range: $250-5,000.
Media: Considers all media. Most frequently exhibits painting, sculpture and photography/video.
Style: Exhibits all styles and genres. Prefers abstraction, expressionism, conceptualism and neo-expressionism.
Terms: Artists encouraged to become members; no commission. Retail price set by the artist. Gallery provides insurance and contract. Artist pays for shipping and exhibition costs are shared. Framed or unframed artwork accepted.
Submissions: Focus on western New York artists. Artists encouraged to become members. Send query letter with resume, slides, SASE, reviews and artist's statement. Call or write to schedule an appointment to show a portfolio, which should include slides and transparencies. Files slides and documentation of show.
Tips: "We are open and receptive to innovative ideas showing thoughtful approach to artistic or social statement, but demand equally thoughtful execution or implementation. Persuade us."

*ARTPARK STORES, Box 371, Lewiston NY 14092. (716)754-9001. Stores Manager: Jean Stopa. Retail gallery. Estab. 1976. Represents 25 artists; emerging, mid-career and established. Exhibited artists include David Tisdale and Ann Jenkins. Sponsors 1 show/year. Average display time 3 months. Not open all year. 3,500 sq. ft; located in 200-acre New York state park. No space for special exhibitions, 70% for gallery artists. Overall price range: $10-500; most artwork sold at $10-50.
Media: Considers craft. Most frequently exhibits jewelry, glass and paper/fiber.
Terms: Accepts work on consignment (40% commission). Retail price set by the artist. Gallery provides promotion and contract; artist pays for shipping.
Submissions: Prefers only craft artists. Send query letter with resume, slides and SASE. Call to schedule an appointment to show a portfolio, which should include originals and slides. Replies in 3 months. Files bio.

KENNETH BERNSTEIN GALLERY, 10-63 Jackson Ave., Long Island NY 11101. (718)784-0591. Owner/Director: Kenneth Bernstein. Retail gallery. Estab. 1983. Clientele: 90% private collectors, 10% corporate clients. Represents 10 artists. Sponsors 2 solo and 2 group shows/year. Average display time is 5 weeks. Accepts only regional artists. Interested in emerging, mid-career and established artists. Overall price range: $300-10,000; most artwork sold at $1,000-3,000.

Media: Considers oil, acrylic, watercolor, pastel, pen & ink, drawings, mixed media, collage, works on paper, sculpture, installation and original handpulled prints. Most frequently exhibits oil, sculpture and water media.
Style: Genres include landscapes, figurative work and abstract styles.
Terms: Accepts work on consignment (50% commission). Retail price is set by gallery and artist. Exclusive area representation not required.
Submissions: Send query letter with resume, slides and SASE. Slides are filed.
Tips: "Show top quality and a strong background."

BOLOGNA LANDI GALLERY, 49 Sag Harbor Rd., East Hampton NY 11937. (516)324-9775. Director: Joseph Landi. Retail gallery and art consultancy. Estab. 1981. Clientele: nationwide; 90% private collectors, 10% corporate clients. Represents 40 artists. Sponsors 6 solo and 4 group shows/year. Average display time is 3 weeks; 1 winter show of gallery artists that lasts 4 months. Interested in emerging artists. Overall price range: $1,200-10,000; most artwork sold at $6,500.
Media: Considers oil, acrylic, watercolor, mixed media, sculpture, fiber, glass and original handpulled prints. Most frequently exhibits oil, acrylic and sculpture.
Style: Exhibits painterly abstraction, impressionism, expressionism, neo-expressionism and realism. Genres include landscapes and figurative work. "Bologna Landi is partial to painterly styles in any category. We are also interested in outdoor sculpture."
Terms: Accepts work on consignment (50% commission). Retail price is set by gallery and artist. Exclusive area representation required. Gallery provides insurance and promotion; artist pays for shipping.
Submissions: Send query letter, resume, brochure, slides, photographs and SASE. Write to schedule an appointment to show actual work. "Slides only O.K. after call. We only file material on the artists that we show."
Tips: Prefers artist to be "educated about their own style, medium and presentation. Be prepared. Make sure your portolio is complete; we would rather see original work because of this problem."

BURCHFIELD ART CENTER, State University College, 1300 Elmwood Ave., Buffalo NY 14222. (716)878-6012. Director: Anthony Bannon. Nonprofit gallery. Estab. 1966. Clientele: urban and suburban adults, college students, corporate clients, all ages in touring groups. Sponsors solo and group shows. Average display time is 4-8 weeks. Interested in emerging, mid-career and established artists who have lived in western New York State.
Media: Considers oil, acrylic, watercolor, pastel, pen & ink, drawings, sculpture, ceramic, fiber, photography, craft, mixed media, performance art, collage, glass, installation and original handpulled prints.
Style: Exhibits contemporary, abstract, impressionistic, figurative, landscape, floral, primitive, non-representational, photorealistic, realistic, neo-expressionistic and post-pop works. "We show both contemporary and historical work by western New York artists, Charles Burchfield and his contemporaries. The museum is not oriented toward sales."
Terms: Accepts work on craft consignment for gallery shop (50% commission). Retail price is set by gallery and artist. Exclusive area representation not required. Gallery provides insurance, promotion and contract; shipping costs are shared.
Submissions: Send query letter, resume, slides and photographs. Call or write to schedule an appointment to show a portfolio. Biographical and didactic materials about artist and work, slides, photos, etc. are filed.
Tips: Sees trend toward "diversity and political ideology."

CEPA GALLERY, 700 Main St., 4th Floor, Buffalo NY 14202. (716)856-2717. Executive Director: Gail Nicholson. Alternative space and nonprofit gallery. Open fall, winter and spring. Clientele: artists and students. Interested in emerging, mid-career and established artists. Sponsors 10 solo and 6 group shows/year. Average display time 4-6 weeks. Prefers only photo, film and installation.
Media: Considers installation and photography. "All work must be photographically oriented or incorporated photography within work or installation."
Style: Exhibits conceptualism and post modern works. Prefers political content. "CEPA is a not-for-profit contemporary arts center, whose raison d'etre is the advancement of photographic related work that engages contemporary issues within the visual arts."
Submissions: Send query letter with resume, slides, SASE, brochure, photographs, bio and artist statement. Call or write to schedule an appointment to show a portfolio, which should include slides and photographs. Replies in 6 months.
Tips: "Have good slides and call first for information regarding suitability for this gallery."

CHAPMAN ART CENTER GALLERY, Cazenovia College, Cazenovia NY 13035. (315)655-9446. Chairman, Center for Art and Design Studies: John Aistars. Nonprofit gallery. Estab. 1978. Clientele: the greater Syracuse community. Sponsors 3 solo and 4 group shows/year. Average display time is 3 weeks. Interested in emerging, mid-career and established artists. Overall price range: $50-3,000; most artwork sold at $100-200.

Media: Considers oil, acrylic, watercolor, pastel, pen & ink, drawings, sculpture, ceramic, fiber, photography, craft, mixed media, collage, glass and prints.

Style: Exhibits all styles. "Exhibitions at the Chapman Art Center Gallery are scheduled for a whole academic year at once. The selection of artists is made by a committee of the art faculty in early spring. The criteria in the selection process is to schedule a variety of exhibitions every year to represent different media and different stylistic approaches; other than that our primary concern is quality. Any artist interested in exhibiting at the gallery is asked to submit to the committee by March 1 a set of slides or photographs and a resume listing exhibitions and other professional activity."

Terms: Retail price is set by artist. Exclusive area representation not required. Gallery provides insurance and promotion; works are usually not shipped.

Submissions: Send query letter, resume, 10-12 slides or photographs.

Tips: A common mistake artists make in presenting their work is that the "overall quality is diluted by showing too many pieces. Call or write and we will mail you a statement of our gallery profiles."

*DARUMA GALLERIES, 554 Central Ave., Cedarhurst NY 11516. (516)569-5221. Owner: Linda. Retail gallery. Estab. 1980. Represents about 15 artists; emerging and mid-career. Interested in seeing the work of emerging artists. Exhibited artists include Kaiko Moti and Claude Gaveau. Sponsors 2-3 shows/year. Average display time 1 month. Open all year. Located on the main street; 1,000 sq. ft. 100% private collectors. Overall price range: $150-5,000; most work sold at $250-1,000.

Media: Considers watercolor, pastel, pen & ink, drawings, mixed media, collage, woodcuts, linocuts, engravings, mezzotints, etchings, lithographs and serigraphs. Most frequently exhibits etchings, lithographs and woodcuts.

Style: Exhibits all styles and genres. Prefers scenic (not necessarily landscapes), figurative and Japanese woodblock prints.

Terms: 33⅓% commission for originals; 50% for paper editions. Retail price set by the gallery (with input from the artist). Artist pays for shipping. Prefers unframed artwork.

Submissions: Send query letter with resume, bio and photographs. Call to schedule an appointment to show a portfolio, which should include originals and photographs. Replies quickly. Files bios and photo examples.

Tips: "Bring good samples of your work and be prepare to be flexible with the time needed to develop new talent. Have a competent bio, presented in a professional way."

DAWSON GALLERY, 349 East Ave., Rochester NY 14604. (716)454-6609. Owners: Beverly McInerny and Shirley Dawson. Retail gallery. Estab. 1982. Clientele: 80% private collectors, 20% corporate clients. Represents 30 artists; emerging, mid-career and established. Sponsors 8 solo and group shows/year. Average display time 1 month. Overall price range: $200-5,000; most artwork sold at $200-3,000.

Media: Considers sculpture, ceramic and glass. Most frequently exhibits metal-sculpture, ceramic-sculpture and wood-sculpture. Specializes in one-of-a-kind sculpture from craft media.

Style: Prefers narrative, surrealist and primitive styles. The gallery was "founded seven years ago to exhibit fine art derived from craft media. It was recently expanded to include paintings when appropriate."

Terms: Accepts work on consignment (50% commission). Gallery provides insurance, promotion, contract and shipping costs from gallery.

Submissions: Send query letter with resume, slides and SASE. All material is returned if not accepted or under consideration.

Tips: "Looks for unique vision and a personal approach to materials. No prints, photography or production-oriented work. We are seeing an expanding market for crafts people through gift shops, department stores and catalog retailing." The most common mistake artists make in presenting their work is showing a "lack of understanding in pricing—studio price and gallery price—this is a disaster!" Sees trend toward "clients who are better informed and willing to pay for work of integrity."

EAST END ARTS COUNCIL, 133 E. Main St., Riverhead NY 11901. (516)727-0900. Visual Arts Coordinator: Patricia Berman. Nonprofit gallery. Estab. 1971. Clientele: 100% private collectors. Exhibits the work of 30 individuals and 7 groups/year. Sponsors 30 solo and 7 group shows/year. Average display time is 6 weeks. Prefers regional artists. Overall price range: $10-10,000; most artwork sold at under $200.

Media: Considers all media and prints.

Style: Exhibits contemporary, abstract, Americana, figurative, landscapes, florals, primitive, non-representational, photorealistic, Western, realistic and post-pop works. "Being an organization relying strongly on community support, we walk a fine line between serving the artistic needs of our constituency and exposing them to current innovative trends within the art world. Therefore, there is not a particular area of specialization. We show photography, fine craft and all art media."

Terms: Accepts work on consignment (30% commission). Retail price is set by gallery and artist. Exclusive area representation not required. Gallery provides insurance, promotion and contract; artist pays for shipping.

Submissions: Send query letter, resume and slides. "All materials will be returned."
Tips: When making a presentation "don't start with 'My slides really are not very good.' Slides should be great! or don't use them."

FOCAL POINT GALLERY, 321 City Island, Bronx NY 10464. (212)885-1403. Artist/Director: Ron Terner. Retail gallery and alternative space. Estab. 1974. Clientele: locals and tourists. Interested in emerging and mid-career artists. Sponsors 7 solo and 1 group show/year. Average display time 3-4 weeks. Overall price range: $175-750; most artwork sold at $300-500.
Media: Most frequently exhibits photography, painting and etching.
Style: Exhibits all styles and genres. Prefers figurative work, landscapes, portraits and abstracts.
Terms: Accepts work on consignment (30% commission). Exclusive area representation required. Gallery provides promotion. Prefers framed artwork.
Submissions: "Artist should please call for information."
Tips: "Do not include resumes. The work should stand by itself."

*GALLERY NORTH, 90 North Country Rd., Setauket NY 11733. (516)751-2676. Director: Elizabeth Goldberg. Nonprofit gallery. Estab. 1965. Represents emerging, mid-career and established artists. Has about 200 members. Sponsors 9 shows/year. Average display time 4-5 weeks. Open all year. (Suburban location) Located near the state university at Stony Brook; approximately 750 sq. ft.; "in a renovated Victorian house." 85% of space for special exhibitions. Clientele: university faculty and staff, Long Island collectors and tourists. 100% private collectors. Overall price range: $100-50,000; most work sold at $5-5,000.
Media: Considers oil, acrylic, watercolor, pastel, pen & ink, drawings, mixed media, collage, works on paper, sculpture, ceramic, craft, fiber, glass, installation, photography, original handpulled prints, woodcuts, wood engravings, linocuts, engravings, mezzotints, etchings, lithographs and serigraphs. Most frequently exhibits paintings, prints and crafts, especially jewelry and patterns.
Style: Exhibits all styles. Prefers realism, abstraction and expressionism.
Terms: Accepts work on consignment (40% commission). Retail price set by the gallery and artist. Gallery provides insurance, promotion and contract; shipping costs are shared.
Submissions: Send query letter with resume, slides, bio, SASE and reviews. Call to schedule an appointment to show a portfolio, which should include originals, slides or photographs. Replies in 2-4 weeks. Files slides and resumes when considering work for exhibition.
Tips: "The artist should visit to determine whether he would feel comfortable exhibiting here."

THE GRAPHIC EYE GALLERY of Long Island, 301 Main St., Port Washington NY 11050. (516)883-9668. President: Olga Poloukhine. Cooperative gallery. Estab. 1974. Represents 25 artists. Sponsors 2 solo and 4 group shows/year. Average display time: 1 month. Interested in emerging and established artists. Overall price range: $35-7,500; most artwork sold at $500-800.
Media: Considers mixed media, collage, works on paper, woodcuts, wood engravings, linocuts, engravings, mezzotints, etchings, lithographs and serigraphs. Most frequently exhibits etchings, mixed graphics and monoprints.
Style: Exhibits impressionism, expressionism, realism, primitivism and painterly abstraction. Genres include figurative works. Considers all genres. Prefers realism, abstraction and figurative work.
Terms: Co-op membership fee plus donation of time. Retail price set by artist. Exclusive area representation not required. Shipping costs are shared. Prefers framed artwork.
Submissions: Send query letter with resume, slides and bio. Portfolio should include originals and slides. Files historical material.
Tips: "Artists must produce their *own* work and be actively involved. We plan to have a competative juried art exhibit in the near future (1991). Open to all artists who are print makers."

HILLWOOD ART GALLERY, Long Island University, C.W. Post Campus, Brookville NY 11548. (516)299-2788. Director: Judy Collischan Van Wagner. Assistant Director: Mary Ann Wadden. Nonprofit gallery. Estab. 1974. Clientele: Long Island residents and university students. Interested in seeing the work of emerging, mid-career and established artists. Sponsors 1-2 solo and 6-7 group shows/year. Average display time is 4-6 weeks. "We prefer metropolitan area artists because of transportation costs." Overall price range: $2,000-80,000.
Media: Considers oil, acrylic, watercolor, pastel, pen & ink, drawings, mixed media, collage, works on paper, sculpture, ceramic, fiber, photography, performance and limited edition prints. Most frequently exhibits sculpture, paintings, drawing and photography.
Style: "Our gallery specializes in work representing the original ideas of artists dedicated to perceiving their world and experiences in a unique and individual manner."
Terms: Accepts work "in the context of invitational/exhibition." Retail price is set by artist. Gallery provides insurance, promotion and contract; shipping costs are shared.
Submissions: Send query letter, resume and slides. Selected slides and resumes are filed.

ISIS GALLERY LTD., 609 Plandome Rd., Manhasset NY 11030. (516)365-8353. President: Dr. Thelma Stevens; Vice President: Dr. Diane Chichura. Retail gallery and art consultancy. Estab. 1982. Clientele: collectors and corporate decorators. Represents 75 artists. Interested in seeing the work of emerging, mid-career and established artists. Sponsors 24 solo shows/year. Average display time 2-6 weeks. Overall price range: $500-10,000; most artwork sold at $2,000.
Media: Considers oil, acrylic, mixed media, sculpture, fiber, glass, lithographs and serigraphs. Most frequently exhibits oil, acrylic and mixed media.
Style: Exhibits impressionism, expressionism, realism, photorealism, surrealism, painterly abstraction and hard-edge geometric abstraction. Genres include landscapes, florals, Americana, portraits and figurative work. Prefers florals, landscapes and abstracts. "Isis Gallery Ltd. is the North Shore's alternative to the art galleries of the Hamptons and Manhattan. It provides the sophisticated consumer with a source for the finest available art at attractive prices to meet the needs of all art buyers."
Terms: Accepts work on consignment (50% commission). Buys outright (50% retail price; net 30 days). Rental fee for space; rental fee covers 2 weeks. Retail price set by gallery and artist. Exclusive area representation not required. Gallery provides insurance, promotion and contract; artist pays for shipping. Prefers framed artwork.
Submissions: Send query letter with resume, brochure, business card, slides, photographs, bio and SASE. Replies in 3 weeks.
Tips: "In your resume show your achievements, exhibits, prizes, reviews and collections your work is in. Do not include rambling personal statements, or commercial or decorative art. Often artists show too many styles and media without a logical transition and without showing growth."

ISLIP ART MUSEUM, 50 Irish Ln., East Islip NY 11730. (516)224-5402. Director: Madeleine Burnside. Nonprofit museum gallery. Estab. 1973. Clientele: contemporary artists from Long Island, New York City and abroad. Sponsors 8 group shows/year. Average display time is 6 weeks. Interested in emerging and established artists.
Media: Considers oil, acrylic, watercolor, pastel, pen & ink, drawings, mixed media, collage, works on paper, sculpture, ceramic, craft, fiber, glass, installation, photography, performance and original handpulled prints. Most frequently exhibits installation, oil and sculpture.
Style: Exhibits all styles. Genres include landscapes, Americana, portraits, figurative work and fantasy illustration. "We consider many forms of modern work by artists from Long Island, New York City and abroad when organizing exhibitions. Our shows are based on themes, and we only present group exhibits. Museum expansion within the next two years will allow for one and two person exhibits to occur simultaneously with the ongoing group shows."
Terms: Retail price is set by artist. Exclusive area representation not required. Gallery provides insurance, promotion, contract and shipping.
Submissions: Send resume, brochure, slides and SASE. Slides, resumes, photos and press information are filed. The most common mistake artists make in presenting their work is that "they provide little or no information on the slides they have sent to the museum for consideration."

KIRKLAND ART CENTER, East Park Row, Clinton NY 13323. (315)853-8871. Director: Dare Thompson. Nonprofit gallery. Estab. 1960. Clientele: general public and art lovers; 95% private collectors, 5% corporate clients. Sponsors 6 solo and 6 group shows/year. Average display time is 3-4 weeks. Interested in emerging, mid-career and established artists. Overall price range: $60-4,000; most artwork sold at $200-600.
Media: Considers oil, acrylic, watercolor, pastel, pen & ink, drawings, mixed media, collage, works on paper, sculpture, ceramic, craft, fiber, glass, installation, photography, performance art and original handpulled prints. Most frequently exhibits watercolor, oil/acrylic, prints, sculpture, drawings, photography and fine crafts.
Style: Exhibits painterly abstraction, conceptualism, impressionism, photorealism, expressionism, realism and surrealism. Genres include landscapes, florals and figurative work.
Terms: Accepts work on consignment (25% commission). Retail price is set by artist. Exclusive area representation not required. Gallery provides insurance, promotion and contract; artist pays for shipping.
Submissions: Send query letter, resume, slides and SASE or write to schedule an appointment to show a portfolio. Resumes are filed.
Tips: Common mistakes artists make are "including slides of all their work, rather than concentrating on one type/style of working that would make a cohesive show. It would be best to call us first for guidance if not sure what to send."

THE LORING GALLERY, 661 Central Ave., Cedarhurst NY 11516. (516)294-1919. President: Rosemary or Arthur Uffner. Retail gallery. Estab. 1952. Represents 9 artists. Sponsors 3 solo shows/year. Average display time is months. Interested in emerging and mid-career artists. Overall price range: $100-10,000; most artwork sold at $1,500-7,000.

Media: Considers oil, acrylic, watercolor, pastel, drawings, mixed media, collage, works on paper and original handpulled prints. Most frequently exhibits oil, pastel and sculpture.

Style: Exhibits color field, painterly abstraction, primitivism, impressionism, photorealism, realism and surrealism. Genres include landscapes, Americana and figurative work. "We handle works from the turn of the century to the present. All must be in the realm of time cut. Wonderful imagery is most important."

Terms: Accepts work on consignment (50% commission) or buys outright. Retail price is set by gallery and artist. Exclusive area representation required. Gallery provides promotion; shipping and insurance costs are shared.

Submissions: Send query letter, resume and slides. Write to schedule an appointment to show a portfolio, which should include originals, slides and transparencies.

MARI GALLERIES OF WESTCHESTER, LTD., 133 E. Prospect Ave., Mamaroneck NY 10543. (914)698-0008. Owner/Director: Carla Reuben. Retail gallery. Estab. 1966. Located in a 200-year-old red barn. Exhibits the work of 30-35 artists. Sponsors 8 solo shows/year. Average display time is 4-5 weeks. Interested in emerging artists.

Media: Considers all media and prints.

Style: Exhibits all contemporary styles.

Terms: Accepts work on consignment (40-50% commission). Retail price is set by gallery and artist. Exclusive area representation required. Gallery provides insurance and promotion; shipping costs are paid by artist to and from gallery.

Submissions: Send query letter with resume, brochure, slides and SASE. Write to schedule an appointment to show a portfolio. "I keep a file on all my artists."

MUSEUM OF STATEN ISLAND/STATEN ISLAND INSTITUTE OF ARTS AND SCIENCES, 75 Stuyvesant Pl., Staten Island NY 10301. (718)727-1135. Curator of Exhibitions: Denise A. Abbate. Museum. Estab. 1881. Clientele: school groups, locals and tourists. Normally sponsors 10-12 shows/year. Currently, an exhibition — *Beyond the Bridge: A Celebration and Exploration of Recent Staten Island History* — is occupying the Museum for two seasons: 1989-1991. Average display time 2-6 weeks. Interested in emerging, mid-career and established artists.

Media: Considers all media. Most frequently exhibits oil, mixed media and photography.

Style: Exhibits all styles and all genres. "The Art collections span 3,500 years of art history and contain more than 250 paintings, 900 drawings, prints, watercolors, and more than 3,800 examples of sculpture, the decorative arts, antiquities, costumes and textiles. It is the mission of the Museum of Staten Island to collect, preserve, exhibit and interpret objects of artistic, scientific and historical interest that constitute an important part of the human heritage, especially with reference to Staten Island."

Terms: Exclusive area representation not required. Gallery provides insurance, promotion and contract. Prefers framed artwork.

Submissions: Send query letter with resume, brochure, photographs and bio. Write to schedule an appointment to show a portfolio, which should include slides. Replies in 1 month. Files query letter, resume and photographs.

Tips: "Artists should not call before introducing themselves through correspondence."

*PETRUCCI GALLERY, 25 Garden Circle at Rt. 9W, Saugerties NY 12477. (914)246-9100. Owner: W.F. Petrucci. Retail gallery. Estab. 1975. Clientele: 98% private collectors, 2% corporate clients. Represents 75 artists. Sponsors 12 solo shows/year. Average display time is 4 weeks. Interested in mid-career and established artists. Overall price range: $1,000-25,000.

Media: Considers all media and original handpulled prints.

Style: Exhibits all styles.

Terms: "Terms are discussed with artist after acceptance." Price set by gallery and artist. Exclusive area representation required. Gallery provides promotion and contract; artist pays for shipping.

Submissions: Send query letter with resume and photographs. Call to schedule an appointment to show a portfolio, which should include originals and slides. Resumes and photographs are filed.

*QUEENS COLLEGE ART CENTER, Benjamin S. Rosenthal Library, Queens College, CUNY, Flushing NY 11367. (718)520-7243. FAX: (718)520-2860. Curator: Deborah Barlow. Nonprofit university gallery. Estab. 1955. Represents emerging, mid-career and established artists. Sponsors 10 shows/year. Average display time 1 month. Open all year. Located in borough of Queens; 1,000 sq. ft. 100% of space for special exhibitions. Clientele: "college and community, some commuters." 100% private collectors. Overall price range: up to $10,000; most artwork sold at $200.

Media: Considers oil, acrylic, watercolor, pastel, pen & ink, drawings, mixed media, collage, works on paper, sculpture, ceramic, craft, fiber, glass, installation, photography, original handpulled prints, woodcuts, wood engravings, linocuts, engravings, mezzotints, etchings, lithographs, pochoir, serigraphs and posters. Most frequently exhibits paintings, prints, drawings and photographs.

Style: Prefers all genres.

Terms: Accepts work on consignment (30% commission). Retail price set by the artist (in consultation with the gallery). Gallery provides promotion; artist pays for shipping.

Submissions: Cannot exhibit large 3d objects. Send query letter with resume, slides, bio, brochure, photographs, SASE and reviews. Write to schedule an appointment to show a portfolio, which should include slides, photographs or transparencies; "originals if presented in person." Replies in 2-3 weeks. Files "resume/bio, publicity materials, photos, etc. if available (any documentation)."

*ROCKLAND CENTER FOR THE ARTS, 27 So. Greenbush Rd., West Nyack NY 10994. (914)358-0877. Executive Director: J. Ramos. Nonprofit gallery. Estab. 1972. Represents emerging, mid-career and established artists. Has 1,500 members. Sponsors 6 shows/year. Average display time 5 weeks. Open September-May. Located in suburban area; 2,000 sq. ft.; "contemporary space." 100% of space for special exhibitions. Clientele: 100% private collectors. Overall price range: $500-50,000; most artwork sold at $1,000-5,000.

Media: Considers oil, acrylic, watercolor, pastel, pen & ink, mixed media, sculpture, ceramic, fiber, glass and installation. Most frequently exhibits painting, sculpture and craft.

Style: Exhibits all styles and genres.

Terms: Accepts work on consignment (33% commission). Retail price set by the artist. Gallery provides insurance, promotion and shipping costs to and from gallery. Prefers framed artwork.

Submissions: "Proposals accepted from curators only. No one person shows. Artists should not apply directly." Replies in 2 weeks.

Tips: "Artist may propose a curated show of 3 or more artists: curator may not exhibit. Request curatorial guidelines. Unfortunately for artists, the trend is toward very high commissions in commercial galleries. Nonprofits like us will continue to hold the line."

SCHWEINFURTH ART CENTER, Box 916, 205 Genesee St., Auburn NY 13021. (315)255-1553. Director: Lisa Pennella. Nonprofit gallery. Estab. 1981. Clientele: local and regional children and adults, specialized audiences for fine art, architecture, photography and folk art. Sponsors 6 solo and 6 group shows/year. Average display time is 2 months. Interested in emerging and established artists. Overall price range: $25-7,500; most artwork sold at $100-500.

Media: Considers oil, acrylic, watercolor, pastel, pen & ink, drawings, sculpture, ceramic, fiber, photography, craft, installations, original handpulled prints and posters.

Style: Exhibits contemporary realism and abstract art.

Terms: Accepts work on consignment (20% commission). Retail price is set by artist. Exclusive area representation not required. Gallery provides insurance, promotion and contract; shipping costs are shared.

Submissions: Send query letter, resume, brochure, slides, photographs and SASE. Call to schedule an appointment to show a portfolio. "Slides, resumes, reviews and promotional materials for past exhibitions, all correspondence and notes" are filed.

New York City

*A.I.R. GALLERY, 63 Crosby St., New York NY 10012. (212)966-0799. Coordinator: Sarah Savidge. Cooperative and nonprofit gallery, alternative space. Estab. 1972. Represents emerging and mid-career artists. Has 17 members. Exhibited artists include Nancy Azara and Elke Solomon. Sponsors 13 shows/year. Average display time 3 weeks. Open September-June. Located in SoHo; 1,670 sq. ft.; "first women's cooperative in the U.S." 10% of space for special exhibitions. Clientele: 80% private collectors, 20% corporate collectors. Price range: $500-5,000; most artwork sold at $1,500-2,000.

Media: Considers oil, acrylic, watercolor, pastel, neon, drawings, mixed media, collage, works on paper, sculpture, glass, installation, photography, original hanpulled prints, woodcuts, linocuts and etchings. Most frequently exhibits paintings, sculpture and mixed media.

Style: Exhibits expressionism, neo-expressionism, primitivism, painterly abstraction, conceptualism, minimalism, post modern works, pattern painting and hard-edge geometric abstraction. Genres include landscapes. Prefers painterly abstraction, primitivism and geometric abstraction.

Terms: Co-op membership fee plus donation of time. Write for details. Retail price set by the artist. Gallery provides promotion; artist pays for shipping. Prefers framed artwork.

Submissions: Women artists only. Send query letter with resume, slides, bio, photographs (optional), SASE and reviews (optional). "We don't do portfolio reviews." Replies in 3-4 weeks. Files "material pertaining to new members accepted in gallery."

Tips: "A common mistake artists make in presenting their work is sending slides without knowledge that A.I.R. is a women's cooperative gallery."

*ACTUAL ART FOUNDATION, 7 Worth St., New York NY 10013. (212)226-3109. Director: Valerie Shakespeare. Nonprofit foundation. Estab. 1981. Represents 10 artists; emerging and mid-career. Sponsors 2 shows/year. Average display time 3 months. Open all year. Located downtown. Clientele: "community business."

Close-up

Connie Butler
Curator
Artists Space

It was in November of 1990 that Artists Space drew national attention for its show "Witnesses: Against Our Vanishing," an exhibition of 23 New York City artists' personal responses to AIDS and the prejudice and apathy of society's reaction to it. It was to be partially funded by the National Endowment for the Arts (NEA). Following the recent congressional restrictions on funding work which is "obscene" and 13 days before the show was due to open, the chairman John Frohnmayer requested that the $10,000 NEA grant be returned. In the wake of outrage from the arts community, Frohnmayer reversed his decision, stipulating that the money was not to be used for the catalog in which Senator Jesse Helms and others were criticized for their positions on homosexuality and AIDS issues. He called it too political.

As this show attests, there is no such thing as "too political" for this nonprofit gallery. Connie Butler, curator at Artists Space, explains it is "all about showing as much work as possible, being as responsive as possible to the artist community." It was founded with the aim of supporting work that is noncommercial, such as installation, film, video, sculpture, experimental painting and photography for artists who do not have a gallery affiliation. Each year there are six six-week exhibitions which are made up of solo, group and audiovisual shows (each of the latter usually showing the work of eight to ten artists). There is a slide archive representing about 3,000 artists who reside in New York, used by arts professionals, curators and gallery directors. There is also an annual regranting program for artists showing in New York who need operating support.

As curator, Butler is responsible for the initial conceptualizing of a show to picking the artist, the art, working on the publication, getting the work to the gallery, working on the installation and getting it up on the wall. She says that often an artist, critic or curator from another institution or space is asked to be the guest curator because Artists Space is unable to do all of the programming and wants to get work from all parts of the country. Butler also goes on a lot of studio visits to see the work of artists who interest her based on the slides they have sent, shows she has seen or the recommendations of other artists and curators.

She says about 50 percent of the artists she chooses are from slide submissions, a slightly lower percentage is of artists she has seen in shows, followed by those who have been recommended to her. Most of the artists whose work is shown in Artists Space have had formal training, have usually exhibited in two to three smaller shows, and "usually try to say something about a particular issue or something that is happening now." She describes the work as "new and raw." When asked what she looks for in an artist's work, she acknowledges the difficulty of divorcing one's personal taste, but says "a lot of times I find work that I don't personally like but find interesting in some way and can see the value of showing. One thing I do look for is work that would probably have trouble being supported by a commercial gallery." She adds, "I would hope that everything we show is conceptually interesting or conceptually rigorous. I think if it's not, the work doesn't stand up very well."

Differences she cites in nonprofit and commercial galleries are based primarily on their approaches to sales. In a nonprofit, she explains, there is an audience rather than a clientele, which tends to be comprised of other artists. She says work is sold, prices ranging from $300-10,000, but it is rare, and that a lot of work they show, because it's installation oriented, doesn't have a price.

She can think of many advantages to showing in a nonprofit. "For emerging artists, it's a very supportive, good way to have a first show. It's a good way for them to get work out, have people see it and get feedback, to get someone to take a chance on it before the galleries or museums will. Because of that, I think a lot of the most interesting work gets shown in nonprofit spaces."

She says she receives 25-30 submissions from artists every two weeks and is usually only interested in one or two of them. She recommends that those submitting be familar with the gallery and the sort of work it shows and emphasizes the importance of including a SASE. When viewing a portfolio, she likes to see a broad selection of the artist's work — slides or photographs — but says a certain amount of editing should take place. "Don't put in 20 years worth of work. Don't inundate whoever you're sending to; send enough to give a feel for what the work is. A sheet of labelled slides is probably the best." She also says she likes to receive biographical information, a written paragraph or resume (clear, concise, without typos) and says write-ups and a small catalog are helpful too.

She says an artist today doesn't have to be in New York or L.A. "What's important," she says, "is for the artist to get his work up on the wall and see it outside of the studio. Even if no one comes to see it, that's still a certain benefit. Even if it's the community center or another artist's studio." And, she says "if you see a gallery that is showing work you like, that has a sensibility you have something in common with, if you have a good feeling about it, that's probably the place to start."

A source of frustration for Butler is the potential weakening of the NEA and the time and effort those at Artists Space must expend to fight this political battle. She fears the repercussions it will have on smaller galleries and institutions that depend directly on the NEA for funding and the possibility of self-censorship that could result if artists don't think their work will be funded because it's too risky, sexually explicit or political.

— Lauri Miller

Reprinted with permission of the artist

Darrel Ellis is one of the artists whose work was part of the show Witnesses: Against Our Vanishing. Ellis' ink on paper portrait portrays the resistance he feels to the frozen images of himself taken by Robert Mappelthorpe and Peter Hujar.

Media: Considers all media.

Style: Exhibits "actual" art. Does not want to see representational art, old-fashioned art or any style of art already established.

Terms: "We arrange for, curate and sponsor exhibitions in off-site spaces." Retail price set by the artist. Gallery provides insurance, promotion and contract; foundation pays for shipping costs to and from site.

Submissions: "Prefers actual artists dealing with effects of time in work." Send query letter with slides, bio and SASE. Call or write to schedule an appointment to show a portfolio, which should include slides. Replies in 1 month. Files "only material requested or interested in."

Tips: "Work should involve effects of time on materials of the work in some way." Sees trends toward "new concerns with time, with questions of conservation, with awareness among artists."

THE ART COLLABORATIVE, 12 White St., New York NY 10013. (212)334-0290. Wholesale gallery and art consultancy. Also has rental gallery. Estab. 1984. Clientele: primarily architects, designers, corporate, some government, 5% private collectors; 95% corporate clients. Represents 300 artists. Sponsors 4 solo and 8 group shows/year. "No erotic, political or religious art." Interested in emerging and established artists. Overall price range: $4,500-20,000; most work sold at $500-5,000.

Media: Considers all media, but no offset reproductions.

Style: "The Art Collaborative was founded on the philosophy that the corporate community was so varied in their art requirements and that artists need someone to market their work effectively to this vast art market. Our role is 'matchmaker' between the two; by interpreting our client's needs correctly as to aesthetic, budget and environmental factors, we make recommendations for artists' works which match those requirements."

Terms: Accepts work on consignment (50% commission). Rental fee for space; rental fee covers 2 weeks-1 month (storefront space only). Retail price set by gallery and artist. Exclusive area representation sometimes required. Gallery provides insurance, promotion and shipping costs from gallery. "Most works on paper, including prints, we prefer unframed; they are either on site or transported to client's space in large portfolio case."

Submissions: Send query letter with slides, brochure, 8 × 10 photographs, bio, price list that relates to visuals sent and SASE. Drop-off policy for portfolios; weekly review. Replies in 3 weeks.

Tips: "Be as professional in your presentation as possible, including all material requested. Pricing info is extremely important! Slides or photos should be top-quality dupes. No originals please. Installation shots are also important for site-specific pieces."

*ARTISTS SPACE, 223 W. Broadway, New York NY 10013. (212)226-3970. FAX: (212)966-1434. Curator: Connie Butler. Alternative space and nonprofit gallery. Estab. 1973. Represents emerging artists. Sponsors 6 visual arts, 6 video and 6 one-person projects/year. Average display time 6 weeks. Open September-June. Located in downtown Manhattan, Tribeca; approximately 5,000 sq. ft.; "a very large space for a Manhattan gallery." 70% of space for special exhibitions. Audience of artists and gallery goers. "We have a very small percentage of sales because we're noncommercial." Overall price range: usually under $10,000.

Media: Considers all media; though deemphasizes craft. Usually does not exhibit prints. Most frequently exhibits installation/video, sculpture and painting.

Style: Exhibits all styles.

Terms: "There is no acquisition or representation. We exhibit artists." Retail price set by the artist. Gallery provides insurance, promotion (in keeping with exhibition) and shipping costs to and from gallery.

Submissions: Exhibits work in all media from all regions. Send letter with resume, slides and SASE. Replies in 4-6 weeks. Files work of New York and New Jersey state artists.

Tips: "Please be familiar with type of work gallery shows; gallery does not represent artists—exhibits work only."

*BOWERY GALLERY, 121 Wooster St., New York NY 10012. (212)226-9543. Director: Carolyn Virgil. Cooperative gallery. Estab. 1969. Represents 32 artists; emerging and mid-career. Exhibited artists include William Plevin-Foust and Patti McManus. Sponsors 12 shows/year. Average display time 3 weeks. Open September-July. Located in Soho; approximately 1,200 sq. ft. 100% of space for gallery artists. 95% private collectors, 5% corporate collectors. Overall price range: $100-10,000.

Media: Considers oil, acrylic, watercolor, pastel, pen & ink, drawings, sculpture, original handpulled prints. Most frequently exhibits paintings, sculpture and drawings.

Style: Exhibits expressionism, painterly abstraction and realism. All genres.

Terms: Co-op membership fee plus donation of time. Retail price set by the artist. Artist pays for shipping. Prefers framed artwork.

Submissions: Accepts only artists from New York region. Send query letter with resume. Call to schedule an appointment to show a portfolio, which should include originals and slides. Replies in 2 weeks. Files resumes.

*BROADWAY WINDOWS, New York University, 80 Washington Square East, New York NY 10003. Viewing address: Broadway at E. 10th St. (212)998-5751. Director or Assistant Director: Marilynn Karp or Ruth D. Newman. Nonprofit gallery. Estab. 1984. Clientele: the metropolitan public. On view to vehicular and pedestrian traffic 24 hours a day. "We do not formally represent any artists. We are operated by New York University as a nonprofit exhibition space whose sole purpose is to showcase artwork and present it to a new ever-growing art interested public." Sponsors 9 solo shows/year. Average display time is 5 weeks. Interested in emerging and established artists.
Media: Considers all media. "We are particularly interested in site specific installations."
Terms: Accepts work on consignment (20% commission). Retail price is set by artist. Exclusive area representation not required. Gallery provides insurance, promotion and contract; artist pays for shipping.
Submissions: Send query letter, resume, slides, photographs and SASE. "Proposals are evaluated once annually in response to an ad calling for proposals. Jurors look for proposals that make the best use of the 24 hour space."
Tips: "Often artists do not provide the visual evidence that they could produce the large scale artwork the Windows' physical structure dictates. And, in general their installation proposals lack details of scale and substance."

FRANK CARO GALLERY, 41 E. 57th St., 2nd floor, New York NY 10022. (212)753-2166. Director: Francis J. Caro. Retail gallery. Estab. 1929. Clientele: collectors, museums, corporations; 85% private collectors; 15% corporate clients. Represents 8 artists. Sponsors 3 solo and 2 group shows/year. Average display time 4 weeks. Overall price range: $1,500-40,000; most artwork sold at $8,000-10,000.
Media: Considers oil, acrylic, watercolor, pastel and egg tempera.
Style: Interested in Chinese and Southeast Asian antiquities only.
Terms: Accepts work on consignment (50% commission). Buys outright (50% retail price; net 30 days). Retail price set by gallery and artist. Exclusive area representation required. Gallery provides insurance, promotion, contract and shipping costs from gallery. Prefers artwork framed.
Submissions: Send query letter with resume, slides, photographs, bio and SASE. Write to schedule an appointment to show a portfolio. Replies in 2-3 weeks. All material is returned if not accepted or under consideration.
Tips: "Don't be pushy or excessively aggressive. Show originality and quality."

CIRCLE GALLERY, 468 W. Broadway, New York NY 10012. (212)677-5100. Contact: Circle Fine Art Corp, Suite 3160, 875 N. Michigan Ave., Chicago IL 60611. Retail gallery. Estab. 1974. Open year round. Clientele: 90% private collectors; 10% corporate clients. Represents 100 artists. Sponsors 3 solo and 5 group shows/year. Average display time 2 weeks. Overall price range: $35-80,000; most artwork sold at $1,500-5,000.
Media: Considers almost all media except photography; also considers woodcuts, wood engravings, linocuts, engravings, mezzotints, etchings, lithographs and serigraphs. Most frequently exhibits graphics, paintings and sculpture.
Style: Exhibits all contemporary styles and genres.
Terms: Buys outright.

*CITY GALLERY, New York City Department of Cultural Affairs, 2 Columbus Circle, New York NY 10019. (212)974-1150. Director: Elyse Reissman. Nonprofit gallery. Estab. 1980. Sponsors 8 group shows/year. Average display time is 4 weeks. Prefers New York City artists. Interested in emerging and established artists.
Media: Considers all media.
Style: Considers all styles and genres. "City Gallery is the official gallery of the City of New York. It presents exhibits that highlight the cultural diversity of New York City's many artistic and ethnic communities. Proposals for group shows from nonprofit arts organizations are reviewed twice each year and selected by a panel of artists and arts administrators."
Terms: Gallery provides promotion and contract.
Submissions: Send proposal, resume, slides and SASE. "Call and request a copy of application guidelines."

DYANSEN GALLERY, 72 Greene St., 3rd Floor, New York NY 10012. (212)925-5550. Director of Merchandising: Ellen Salpeter. Retail gallery. Clientele: 95% private collectors. Represents 20 artists. Average display time is 4 weeks. Interested in emerging and established artists. Overall price range: $1,500-20,000; most artwork sold at $4,000.
Media: Considers oil, acrylic and sculpture, mostly bronze.
Style: Exhibits color field, impressionism and realism. Genres include landscapes, figurative work and fantasy illustration. "Our galleries specialize in beautiful appealing figurative and landscape, architectural imagery."
Terms: Accepts work on consignment (60% commission) or buys outright. Retail price is set by gallery. Exclusive area representation required. Gallery provides insurance, promotion and contract; shipping costs are shared.
Submissions: Send query letter, resume, brochure, slides, photographs and SASE. Resume and brochure are filed.

*FORUM GALLERY, 1018 Madison Ave., New York NY 10021. (212)772-7666. FAX: (212)772-7669. Director: Bella Fishko. Retail gallery. Estab. 1960. Represents 20 artists; emerging, mid-career and established. Exhibited artists include Max Weber and Gregory Gillespie. Sponsors 11 shows/year. Average display time 1 month. Open all year. Located in upper east side; 16,000 sq. ft.; "terrace sculpture garden." 90% of space for special exhibitions, 10% for gallery artists. Clientele: 80% private collectors, 5% corporate clients. Price range: $1,000-250,000; most artwork sold at $20,000-75,000.

Media: Considers oil, acrylic, watercolor, pastel, pen & ink, drawings, mixed media, collage, works on paper, sculpture, ceramic, fiber, glass, original handpulled prints, woodcuts, linocuts, engravings, mezzotints, etchings and lithographs. Most frequently exhibits oil on canvas, bronze and watercolor.

Style: Exhibits all styles. Genres include landscapes, florals, portraits and figurative work. Prefers American Representational and American Modernism.

Terms: Retail price set by the gallery. Gallery provides insurance, promotion and contract. Prefers framed artwork.

Submissions: Accepts only American artists. Send query letter with resume, slides, bio, photographs, SASE and reviews. Replies in 1 month.

Tips: "Only write, do not call first—and be familiar with the type of work we handle."

*GALLERY HENOCH, 80 Wooster, New York NY 10012. (212)966-6360. Director: George Henoch Shechtman. Retail gallery. Estab. 1983. Represents 40 artists; emerging and mid-career. Exhibited artists include Jay Kelly and Max Ferguson. Sponsors 10 shows/year. Average display time 3 weeks. Closed August. Located in SoHo; 4,000 sq. ft. 50% of space for special exhibitions, 50% for gallery artists. Clientele: 90% private collectors, 10% corporate clients. Overall price range: $3,000-40,000; most artwork sold at $10,000-20,000.

Media: Considers oil, acrylic, watercolor, pastel, pen & ink, drawings and sculpture. Most frequently exhibits painting, sculpture, drawing and watercolor.

Style: Exhibits photorealism and realism. Genres include landscapes, figurative work and all genres. Prefers landscapes, cityscapes and still lifes.

Terms: Accepts work on consignment (50% commission). Retail price set by the gallery. Gallery provides insurance and promotion. Shipping costs are shared. Prefers framed artwork.

Submissions: Send query letter with slides, bio and SASE. Portfolio should include slides and transparencies. Replies in 3 weeks.

Tips: "We suggest the artist be familiar with the kind of work we show and be sure their work fits in with our styles."

Director/owner George Henoch Shechtman of Gallery Henoch in New York City purchased "Detour, Doremus Ave./Newark NJ" outright. This watercolor piece by Jay Kelly was exhibited in a one-man show that was completely sold-out. According to Henoch, the work is appropriate for his gallery because it "represents the gallery's aesthetic."

GALLERY INTERNATIONAL 57, 888 Seventh Ave., New York NY 10016. (212)582-2200. Director: Kazuko Hillyer. Retail gallery. Estab. 1987. Seasons for exhibition: September-June. "This gallery features international contemporary artists." Represents 12 artists. Sponsors 5 solo shows/year. Average display time 4 weeks. Interested in established artists. Overall price range: $2,000-10,000.

Media: Considers oil, acrylic, watercolor, and mixed media. Prefers only original oils.
Terms: Accepts artwork on consignment (40% commission). Retail price set by gallery and/or artist. Exclusive area representation not required but preferred. Gallery provides insurance and a contract. Prefers artwork framed.
Submissions: Send query letter with slides and photographs. Replies in 1-2 months only if interested.
Tips: "Please do *not* call or come in. Send in material with SASE."

GALLERY 10, 7 Greenwich Ave., New York NY 10014. (212)206-1058. Director: Marcia Lee Smith Retail gallery. Estab. 1972. Open year round. Clientele: 100% private collectors. Represents approximately 150 artists. Interested in emerging and established artists. Overall price range: $24-1,000; most work sold at $50-300.
Media: Considers ceramic, craft, glass, wood, metal and jewelry.
Style: "The gallery specializes in contemporary American crafts."
Terms: Accepts work on consignment (50% commission). Buys outright (50% retail price; net 30 days). Retail price set by gallery and artist.
Submissions: Call or write to schedule an appointment to show a portfolio, which should include originals, slides, transparencies or photographs.

*STEPHEN GILL GALLERY, 122 E. 57th St., New York NY 10022. (212)832-0800. President: Stephen Gill. Retail gallery. Estab. 1986. Represents 10 artists; emerging and established. Exhibited artists include Peter Max and Robert Rauchenberg. Sponsors 2-3 shows/year. Average display time 1-3 months. Closed July. Located on upper east side; 715 sq. ft. 50% of space for special exhibitions. Clientele: 50% private collectors, 50% corporate collectors. Overall price range: $300-10,000; most artwork sold at $1,000-2,000.
Media: Considers oil, acrylic, mixed media, collage, sculpture (small), photography and original handpulled prints only. Most frequently exhibits acrylic, oil and collage.
Style: Exhibits conceptualism. Looking for "original ideas."
Terms: Accepts work on consignment (50% commission) or buys outright—"names only." New artists must donate 1 piece to gallery if selected ("We have selected 2 new artists in the past years.") Retail price set by the gallery and artist. Gallery provides promotion and contract; artist pays for shipping.
Submissions: Prefers only "paintings on canvas. No watercolor." Send query letter with resume, slides, bio and SASE. Write to schedule an appointment to show a portfolio or send slides and SASE. Portfolio should include slides and transparencies. Replies only if interested within 2 months.
Tips: The most common mistake artists make in presenting their work is "calling me! All I want is SASE with slides. Show me how talented you are with your work."

FOSTER GOLDSTROM GALLERY, #303, 560 Broadway, New York NY 10012 (212)941-9175. Owner: Foster Goldstrom. Retail gallery. Estab. 1970. Located in SoHo. Clientele: 90% private collectors, 10% corporate clients. Represents 8 artists. Sponsors 8 solo and 2 group shows/year. Average display time 3-4 weeks. Interested in emerging and established artists. Overall price range: $650-40,000.
Media: Considers oil, acrylic, drawings, mixed media, collage, works on paper, sculpture, ceramic and photography.
Style: Exhibits all styles and genres. Prefers abstracts.
Terms: Accepts work on consignment (50% commission). Buys outright (50% retail price). Retail price set by gallery and artist. Exclusive area representation not required.
Submissions: Send query letter with slides and SASE. Replies in 2 weeks. All material is returned if not accepted or under consideration.
Tips: "Please come into gallery, look at our stable of artists work, and see first if your work is of our aesthetic."

*JOHN GOOD GALLERY, 532 Broadway, New York NY 10012. (212)941-8066. FAX: (212)274-0124. Director: Carol A. Greene. Retail gallery. Estab. 1984. Represents 10 emerging and mid-career artists. Exhibited artists include David Row and Nancy Haynes. Sponsors 8 shows/year. Average display time 4 weeks. Open all year; summer, by appointment only. Located in SoHo; 3,000 sq. ft. 75-100% of space for special exhibitions, 75-100% for gallery artists. Clientele: private collectors. 80% private collectors, 20% corporate clients. Other clients: museums and art consultants. Overall price range: $500-30,000; most artwork sold at $5,000-15,000.
Media: Considers oil, acrylic, watercolor, pastel, pen & ink, drawings, mixed media, collage, works on paper, sculpture, glass, installation and photography. Does not consider prints. Most frequently exhibits paintings: oil on linen; sculpture: oil on wood; and photography.
Style: Exhibits the development minimalism into new abstract painting.
Terms: Accepts work on consignment (50% commission). Retail price set by the gallery and the artist. Gallery provides insurance, promotion and shipping costs to and from gallery. Prefers unframed artwork.
Tips: "At this time we are not accepting work for review." Notices that in the gallery world there is "less risk taking."

*GRAND CENTRAL ART GALLERIES, 24 W. 57th St., New York NY 10019. (212)867-3344. Contact: Exhibitions Committee. Retail gallery. Estab. 1922. Clientele: private, museum, corporate and industrial; 80% private collectors, 10% corporate clients. Represents 60 artists. Sponsors 5 solo and 5 group shows/year. Interested in emerging and established artists. Overall price range: $1,000-1,000,000; most artwork sold at $10-40,000.

Media: Considers oil, watercolor and pastel.

Style: Exhibits impressionism and realism. Genres include landscapes, portraits and figurative work. "Grand Central Art Galleries exhibits a mix of contemporary realism (oil, watercolor, sculpture) and late 19th- and early 20th-century works." Does not want to see non-representational paintings.

Terms: Accepts work on consignment (40% commission). Retail price is set by gallery and artist. Exclusive area representation required. Gallery provides promotion and contract; shipping costs are shared.

Submissions: Send resume, slides and SASE. Common mistakes artists make are "sending fifty or more slides to view, rather than 10-15 slides and bringing paintings to the gallery without an appointment."

Tips: A trend seems to be "more interest in impressionist painting."

O.K. HARRIS WORKS OF ART, 383 W. Broadway, New York NY 10012. Director: Ivan C. Karp. Commercial exhibition gallery. Estab. 1969. Open fall, winter, spring and early summer. "Four separate galleries for four separate one-person exhibitions and the back room features selected gallery artists which also changes each month." Clientele: 80% private collectors, 20% corporate clients. Represents 65 artists. Sponsors 40 solo shows/year. Average display time 3 weeks. Interested in emerging, mid-career and established artists. Overall price range: $50-$250,000; most artwork sold at $12,500-100,000.

Media: Considers all media. Most frequently exhibits paintings, sculpture and photography.

Style: Exhibits realism, photorealism, minimalism, abstraction, conceptualism, photography and geometric abstraction. Genres include landscapes, Americana and figurative work. "The gallery's main concern is to show the most significant artwork of our time. In its choice of works to be exhibited it demonstrates no prejudice as to style or materials employed. Its criteria demands innovation of concept and maturity of technique. It believes that its exhibitions over the years have proven the soundness of its judgment in identifying important artists and its pertinent contribution to the visual arts culture."

Terms: Accepts work on consignment (50% commission). Retail price set by gallery. Exclusive area representation required. Gallery provides insurance and promotion. Prefers framed artwork.

Submissions: Send query letter with slides "labeled concerning size, medium, top, etc." and SASE. Replies in 1 week.

Tips: "We strongly suggest the artist be familiar with the gallery's exhibitions, i.e. the kind of work we show and be sure their work fits in with our aesthetic. See the exhibitions. Always include SASE."

HELIO GALLERIES, 588 Broadway, New York NY 10012. (212)966-5156/966-5179. FAX: (212)260-1928. Contact: Director. Retail gallery and art consultancy. Estab. 1984. Clientele: 50% private collectors, 50% corporate clients. Represents 12 artists. Sponsors 12 solo and 6 group shows/year. Average display time 3 weeks. Interested in mid-career artists. Overall price range: $150-30,000; most artwork sold at $3,000-6,000.

Media: Considers oil, acrylic, watercolor, pastel, pen & ink, drawings, mixed media, collage, works on paper, ceramic, glass, photography, egg tempera, woodcuts, wood engravings, linocuts, engravings, mezzotints, etchings, lithographs, pochoir and serigraphs. Most frequently exhibits oil, watercolor and acrylic.

Style: Exhibits all styles and all genres. Prefers painterly realism, surrealism and expressionism.

Terms: Retail price set by gallery. Exclusive area representation required. Shipping costs are shared. Prefers framed artwork.

Submissions: Send query letter with resume, slides and SASE. Write to schedule an appointment to show a portfolio, which should include slides. Replies in 3 weeks. Files resume. All material is returned if not accepted or under consideration.

Tips: Wants to see "honesty, commitment, slides labeled with size and title." Feels that realism has been reborn.

HUDSON GUILD ART GALLERY, 441 W. 26th St., New York NY 10001. (212)760-9800. Gallery Director: Haim Mendelson. Nonprofit gallery. Estab. 1948. Clientele: community. Represents 12 artists. Sponsors 2 solo and 6 group shows/year. Average display time is 3 weeks. Interested in emerging, mid-career and established artists. Overall price range: $100-12,000.

Media: Considers oil, acrylic, watercolor, pastel, pen & ink, drawings, collage and original handpulled prints.

Style: Exhibits contemporary, figurative, landscapes and realism. "Our gallery shows the works of talented contemporary artists of professional status. Traditionally the gallery has been the showcase for emerging artists: John Sloan's first one-man show was at Hudson Guild Art Gallery. The gallery continues to exhibit the work of young artists of promise together with seasoned professionals. The exhibits include all media which can be hung on the walls, as well as medium-size free-standing sculpture. Most exhibitors are from the New York City area."

Terms: Accepts work on consignment (20% commission). Retail price is set by artist. Exclusive area representation not required. Gallery provides insurance and contract; artist pays for shipping.
Submissions: Send query letter, resume, brochure, slides, photographs and SASE. Call or write to schedule an appointment to show a portfolio.
Tips: "Would like to see a consistent professional level of work. Don't present a variety of styles and techniques. It is best to present a coherent body of work with a clear impact."

MICHAEL INGBAR GALLERY, 578 Broadway, New York NY 10012. (212)334-1100. Director: Michael Ingbar. Retail gallery and art consultancy. Estab. 1977. Clientele: 10% private collectors, 90% corporate clients. Represents 27 artists. Sponsors 2 solo and 9 group shows a year on a co-op basis with the artists. Average display time is 1 month. Interested in emerging, mid-career and established artists. Overall price range: $600-12,000; most artwork sold at $1,000-2,000.
Media: Considers oil, acrylic, works on paper, fiber and original handpulled prints.
Style: Exhibits hard-edge geometric abstraction, impressionism, realism and surrealism. Genres include landscapes and figurative work. "We feel that we are one of the few solo galleries that show 'pleasing and pretty' works that have a soothing or uplifting effect on the viewer. All works should communicate to the general public we sell to, which is primarily corporations looking for art to be decorative as well as of a high quality." Does not want to see small works.
Terms: Accepts work on consignment (50% commission). Retail price is set by gallery and artist. Exclusive area representation not required.
Submissions: Send query letter and SASE. Slides are filed.
Tips: The most common mistakes artists make in presenting their work are "coming in person, constantly calling, poor slide quality (or unmarked slides)." Sees trend toward "more upbeat art."

JACK GALLERY, 138 Prince St., New York NY 10012. (212)226-1989. Director: Rhoda Epstein. Retail gallery. Estab. 1972. Located in SoHo. Clientele: 70% private collectors, 30% corporate clients. Represents 10 artists. Sponsors 2 solo and 6 group shows/year. Average display time 1 month. Interested in emerging, mid-career and established artists. Overall price range: $3,000-60,000; most artwork sold at $4,500-9,000.
Media: Considers oil, acrylic, mixed media, collage and sculpture. "No prints." Most frequently exhibits acrylics, oils and mixed media.
Style: Exhibits expressionism, neo-expressionism, realism, photorealism, color field, painterly abstraction, hard-edge geometric abstraction and illusionist. Prefers figurative works, abstracts and sculpture.
Terms: Retail price set by gallery. Gallery provides insurance and promotion. Prefers unframed artwork.
Submissions: Send query letter with resume, slides and SASE. Write to schedule an appointment to show a portfolio. Replies in 3 weeks. All material is returned if not accepted or under consideration.

JADITE GALLERIES, 415 W. 50th St., New York NY 10019. (212)315-2740. Director: Roland Sainz. Retail gallery. Estab. 1985. Clientele: 80% private collectors, 20% corporate clients. Represents 30 artists. Sponsors 12 solo and 4 group shows/year. Average display time is 2 weeks. Interested in emerging and established artists. Overall price range: $500-8,000; most artwork sold at $1,000-3,000.
Media: Considers oil, acrylic, watercolor, pastel, pen & ink, drawings, mixed media, collage, sculpture and original handpulled prints. Most frequently exhibited media: oils, acrylics, pastels and sculptures.
Style: Exhibits minimalism, post modern, impressionism, neo-expressionism, realism and surrealism. Genres include landscapes, florals, portraits, Western collages and figurative work. Features "national and international emerging artists dealing with contemporary works."
Terms: Accepts work on consignment (40% commission). Retail price is set by gallery and artist. Exclusive area representation not required. Gallery provides insurance, promotion and contract; exhibition costs are shared.
Submissions: Send query letter, resume, brochure, slides, photographs and SASE. Call or write to schedule an appointment to show a portfolio, which should include originals, slides or photos. Resume, photographs or slides are filed.

*LA MAMA LA GALLERIA, 6 East 1st St., New York NY 10003. (212)505-2476. Director: Lawry Smith. Nonprofit gallery. Estab. 1981. Represents emerging, mid-career and established artists. Sponsors 14 shows/year. Average display time 3 weeks. Open September-June. Located in East Village; 2,500 sq. ft.; "very large and versatile space." 100% of space for special exhibitions. Clientele: 20% private collectors, 20% corporate clients. Overall price range: $1,000-5,000; most artwork sold at $1,000.
Media: Considers oil, acrylic, watercolor, pastel, pen & ink, drawings, mixed media, collage, sculpture, ceramic, craft, installation, photography, original handpulled prints, woodcuts, engraving and lithographs. Most frequently exhibits oil, installation and collage. No performance art.

Style: Exhibits expressionism, neo-expressionism, primitivism, painterly abstraction, imagism, conceptualism, minimalism, post modern works, impressionism, photorealism and hard-edge geometric abstraction.
Terms: Accepts work on consignment (20% commission). Retail price set by the gallery. Gallery provides promotion; artist pays for shipping or shipping costs are shared. Prefers framed artwork.
Submissions: Send query letter with resume, slides and bio. Write to schedule an appointment to show a portfolio, which should include originals, slides, photographs or transparencies. Replies in 3 weeks. Files slides and resumes.

*MARKEL/SEARS FINE ARTS, 40 E. 88th, New York NY 10128. (212)996-7124. President: Kathryn Markel. Private art consultancy. Estab. 1985. Represents 40 artists/year; emerging, mid-career and established. Exhibited artists include Steve Aimone and Madge Willner. Sponsors no exhibitions. Open all year by appointment. Located in Manhattan. 80% corporate clients. Overall price range: $700-5,000.
Media: Considers all original work, unique works on paper. Most frequently sells pastel, watercolor and collage.
Style: Exhibits all styles.
Terms: Accepts work on consignment (50% commission). Retail price set by the gallery and the artist. Gallery provides insurance. Artist pays for shipping. Prefers unframed artwork.
Submissions: Send query letter with slides and SASE. Portfolio should include slides. Replies in 2 weeks.
Tips: "Send 10-15 slides of recent work with SASE."

*MIDTOWN GALLERIES, 11 E. 57th St., New York NY 10022. (212)758-1900. Director: Bridget Moore. Retail gallery. Estab. 1932. Sponsors 6 solo and 4 group shows/year. Interested in emerging and established artists.
Media: Considers painting and sculpture.
Style: Features 20th-century and contemporary American artists.
Terms: Retail price is set by gallery and artist. Exclusive area representation required.
Submissions: Send query letter, resume, brochure, slides, photographs and SASE.

*ALEXANDER F. MILLIKEN INC., 98 Prince St., New York NY 10012. (212)966-7800. Retail gallery. Estab. 1976. Represents 16 artists. Sponsors 6 solo and 2 group shows/year. Average display time is 4-6 weeks. Interested in emerging and established artists. Overall price range: $500-250,000; most artwork sold at $10,000-25,000.
Media: Considers paintings, sculpture and drawings.
Style: Exhibits contemporary, abstract, figurative work and realism.
Submissions: Send query letter, resume, slides and SASE.

*MORNINGSTAR GALLERY, 164 Mercer St., New York NY 10012. (212)334-9330. Director: Jack Krumholz. Retail gallery. Estab. 1979. Represents approximately 20 artists; emerging, mid-career and established. Exhibited artists include Will Barnet and Judith Shahn. Sponsors primarily ongoing group exhibitions. Average display time 1-2 months. Open all year. Located in SoHo section of NYC; 550 sq. ft. 100% of space for gallery artists. Clientele: "retail, decorators, corporations, professionals." 80% private collectors, 20% corporate clients. Overall price range: $50-10,000; most artwork sold at $200-1,000.
Media: Considers oil, acrylic, watercolor, pastel, pen & ink, drawings "preferably on paper," original hand-pulled prints, woodcuts, wood engravings, linocuts, engravings, mezzotints, etchings, lithographs, serigraphs and all limited edition original graphics. Most frequently exhibits etchings/aquatints, serigraphs and lithographs.
Style: Exhibits expressionism, neo-expressionism, surrealism and realism. Considers all genres. Prefers cityscapes, landscapes and still lifes (florals).
Terms: Accepts work on consignment (50% commission). "Gallery may be rented for one- or two-person shows for a period of approximately 3 weeks." Retail price set by the gallery and the artist. Gallery provides insurance and promotion; artist pays for shipping. Prefers unframed artwork, framed for one-person shows.
Submissions: Send query letter with resume, slides, bio, photographs and SASE. Write to schedule an appointment to show a portfolio, which should include originals, slides and photographs. Replies only if interested in 1-2 weeks.
Tips: "Always enclose SASE for return of slides." Sees trend toward "galleries specializing more: media, style, images, etc."

MUSEUM OF CONTEMPORARY HISPANIC ART, 584 Broadway, New York NY 10012. (212)966-6699. Assistant Curator: Rosa Tejada. Museum. Estab. 1986. Open September-July. Located in SoHo. Sponsors 8 solo and 10 group shows/year. Average display time 8 weeks or 3 months. Interested in emerging and established artists.
Style: Exhibits expressionism, neo-expressionism, primitivism, figurative work, painterly abstraction, conceptualism and hard-edge geometric abstraction; considers all styles. Prefers expressionism, realism and abstraction. "The Museum of Contempary Hispanic Art is dedicated to the research, study and presentation of

Hispanic art and artists in the U.S. and abroad. MOCHA offers a year round exhibition season of thematic, group and solo show by artists from South, Central and North America which are of Hispanic origin."
Terms: Exclusive area representation not required. Provides, on special occasions, insurance, promotion and shipping costs; usually shipping costs are shared. Prefers artwork framed.
Submissions: Send query letter with resume, slides and bio. Write to schedule an appointment to show a portfolio, which should include slides, transparencies and photographs. Replies in 6 months. Files slides and resume. Some material is returned if not accepted or under consideration.

MUSEUM OF HOLOGRAPHY, 11 Mercer St., New York NY 10013. (212)925-0581. Curator: Sydney Dinsmore. Nonprofit museum. Estab. 1976. Clientele: 95% private collectors, 5% corporate clients. Sponsors 4 group/theme shows per year and several one-person shows. Average display time is 3-4 months. Accepts only holography. Interested in emerging and established artists. Overall price range: $15-7,000; most artwork sold at $60-200.
Media: Considers only holograms.
Style: "Our museum specializes in all forms of holography, artistic, commercial, scientific and its applications. Style is not a consideration with our institution."
Terms: Accepts work on consignment. Retail price is set by gallery and artist. Exclusive area representation not required. Gallery provides insurance and promotion; shipping costs are shared.
Submissions: Send query letter, resume and slides. Write to schedule an appointment to show a portfolio, which should include originals and slides. Resume and slides are filed.
Tips: "Works are considered for exhibition purposes only. We do not want to represent holographers commercially."

NAHAN GALLERIES, 381 W. Broadway, New York NY 10013. (212)966-9313. Contact: Kenneth Nahan. Retail gallery. Estab. 1960. Represents 10 artists. Sponsors 8-10 solo shows/year. Average display time 3 weeks. Overall price range: $400-40,000.
Media: Considers most media.
Style: Genres include landscapes, florals, Americana, wildlife, portraits and figurative work.
Terms: Buys outright. Retail price set by gallery. Exclusive area representation not required. Gallery provides insurance, promotion and contract; gallery pays for shipping.
Submissions: Send query letter with slides. Write to schedule an appointment to show a portfolio, which should include slides. Replies in a few months. All material is returned if not accepted or under consideration.

NOVO ARTS, 57 E. 11th St., New York NY 10003. (212)674-3093. Fine Art Consultant: Lynda Deppe. Fine arts consultants for private collectors and corporations. Sponsors 5 group shows/year. Average display time is 2 months. Interested in emerging and established artists. Overall price range: $200 and up; most artwork sold at $500 and up. Also sells investment prints by international artists.
Media: Considers all media.
Style: Exhibits all styles.
Terms: Accepts work on consignment. Retail price is set by gallery and artist. Exclusive area representation not required.
Submissions: Send query letter, resume, slides, price the artist would like to receive and SASE. Call or write to schedule an appointment to show a portfolio, which should include originals and slides. Slides, resume and price list are filed.

*OUTER SPACE, INC., 2710 Broadway, New York NY 10025. (212)874-7142. Director: Ernest Acker. Nonprofit gallery and alternative space. Estab. 1984. Represents 20 artists/year; emerging and mid-career. Exhibited artists include Xanda McCagg, Kenneth Agnello, Carol Mahtab and Raphael Collazo. Sponsors 10 shows/year. Average display time 3 weeks. Closed Christmas (2 weeks) and July and August. Located on the upper upper west side in Manhattan; 625 sq. ft.; "in an art deco building on the entire third floor, including two other galleries: Steve Bush Exhibit Room and Fatman Gallery." 20% of space for special exhibitions, 80% for gallery artists. Clientele: 100% private collectors. Prefers only contemporary work. Overall price range: $50-5,000; most artwork sold at $50-500.
Media: Considers oil, acrylic, watercolor, pastel, mixed media, collage, works on paper, sculpture, fiber, glass, installation and photography. "Steve Bush exhibits prints, graphics and photographs." Considers original handpulled prints, offset reproductions, woodcuts, wood engravings, linocuts, engravings, mezzotints, etchings, lithographs, pochoir and serigraphs. Most frequently exhibits oil, acrylic and assemblage/collage.
Style: Exhibits expressionism, neo-expressionism, painterly abstraction, surrealism, post modern works, realism, photorealism. Genres include landscapes, Americana, Southwestern, figurative work and abstraction. Prefers abstract expressionism, neo-expressionism and post modern works.
Terms: Accepts work on consignment (15% commission). Co-op membership fee plus donation of time (15% commission). "Shares are sold and stock certificates issued." Retail price set by the gallery. Gallery provides promotion and contract. Artist pays for shipping. Prefers framed artwork.

Submissions: Prefers only contemporary work. Send query letter with slides. Call or write to schedule an appointment to show a portfolio, which should include originals, slides, photographs and transparencies. Replies in 3 weeks. If interested replies within 3 months. Files member artists' slides.

*THE PHOENIX GALLERY, Suite 607, 568 Broadway, New York NY 10012. (212)226-8711. Director: Linda Handler. Nonprofit gallery. Estab. 1958. Represents 28 artists; emerging, mid-career and established. Has 28 members. Exhibited artists include David Raymond and Margaret Pomfret. Sponsors 10-12 shows/year. Average display time 4 weeks. Open fall, winter and spring. Located in SoHo; 180 linear ft.; "We are in a landmark building in SoHo, the oldest co-op in New York. We have a movable wall which can divide the gallery into two large spaces." 100% of space for special exhibitions, 100% for gallery artists. Clientele: 75% private collectors, 25% corporate clients. Other clients: art consultants, interested in seeing the work of emerging artists. Overall price range: $50-20,000; most artwork sold at $300-10,000.
Media: Considers oil, acrylic, watercolor, pastel, pen & ink, drawings, mixed media, collage, works on paper, sculpture, ceramic, photography, original handpulled prints, woodcuts, engravings, wood engravings, linocuts and etchings. Most frequently exhibits oil, acrylic and watercolor.
Style: Exhibits painterly abstraction, minimalism, realism, photorealism, hard-edge geometric abstraction and all styles. Prefers painterly abstraction, hard-edge geometric abstraction and sculpture.
Terms: Co-op membership fee plus donation of time (25% commission). Retail price set by the gallery. Gallery provides insurance, promotion and contract; artist pays for shipping. Prefers framed artwork.
Submissions: Send query letter with resume, slides and SASE. Call to schedule an appointment to show a portfolio, which should include slides. Replies in 1 month. Only files material of accepted artists. The most common mistakes artists make in presenting their work are "incomplete resumes, unlabeled slides, an application that is not filled out properly."
Tips: "Come and see the gallery—meet the director."

*PRINTED MATTER BOOKSTORE AT DIA, 77 Wooster St., New York NY 10012. (212)925-0325. FAX: (212)925-0464. Director: John Goodwin. Nonprofit bookstore. Estab. 1976. Clientele: international. Represents 2,500 artists. Interested in emerging and established artists. Overall price range: 50 cents-$3,500; most artwork sold at $20.
Media: Considers only artwork in book form in multiple editions.
Terms: Accepts work on consignment (50% commission). Retail price is set by artist. Exclusive area representation not required. Gallery provides promotion and contract; artist pays for shipping.
Submissions: Send query letter and review copy of book.

RAYDON GALLERY, 1091 Madison Ave., New York NY 10028. (212)288-3555. Director: Alexander R. Raydon. Retail gallery. Estab. 1962. Clientele: tri-state collectors and institutions (museums). Sponsors 12 group shows/year. Overall price range: $100-100,000; most artwork sold at $1,800-4,800.
Media: Considers all media. Most frequently exhibits oil, prints and watercolor.
Style: Exhibits all styles and all genres. "We show fine works of arts in all media, periods and schools from the Renaissance to the present with emphasis on American paintings, prints and sculpture."
Terms: Accepts work on consignment or buys outright.
Tips: "Artists should present themselves in person with background back-up material (bios, catalogues, exhibit records and original work, slides or photos)."

*NATHAN SILBERBERG GALLERIES, 382 W. Broadway, New York NY 10012. (212)966-0611. Owner: N. Silberberg. Retail gallery. Estab. 1982. Represents 14 artists; established. Exhibited artists include Joan Miro, Henry Moore and Nada Vitorovic. Sponsors 3-4 shows/year. Average display time 4 weeks. Open all year. Located in SoHo; 1,500 sq. ft. 100% of space for special exhibitions. Clientele: 90% private collectors, 10% corporate clients. Overall price range: $5,000-150,000.
Media: Considers oil, drawings, sculpture, original handpulled prints, woodcuts, engravings, lithographs, pochoir and etchings. Most frequently exhibits oil, drawings and prints.
Style: Exhibits painterly abstraction, surrealism and conceptualism. Prefers surrealism and abstraction.
Terms: Accepts work on consignment (40-60% commission). Retail price set by the gallery. Gallery provides insurance and promotion; shipping costs are shared. Prefers framed artwork.
Submissions: Send query letter with resume, slides and SASE. Write to schedule an appointment to show a portfolio, which should include originals, slides and transparencies. Replies in 4 weeks.
Tips: "First see my gallery and the artwork we show."

SOHO CENTER FOR VISUAL ARTISTS, 114 Prince St., New York NY 10012. (212)226-1995. Director: Bruce Wall. Nonprofit gallery. Estab. 1973. Clientele: 75% private collectors, 25% corporate clients. "We offer one-time group shows to emerging artists." Sponsors 7 group shows/year. Average display time is 5 weeks. Overall price range: $1,000-3,000.

Media: All media.

Style: "The SoHo Center for Visual Artists is a nonprofit exhibition gallery sponsored by the Aldrich Museum of Contemporary Art. Established in 1973, the Center sponsors group exhibitions of emerging artists who are not represented by commercial galleries in New York City."

Terms: Accepts work on consignment (no commission). Retail price is set by artist. Exclusive area representation not required. Gallery provides promotion and contract; artist pays for shipping.

Submissions: Send 20 slides of recent work, resume and SASE. "Contact the Center for times for slide review."

©1990 Rene Lynch

"Sustenance," an oil on linen work by Rene Lynch, was on loan for exhibition at the nonprofit gallery Soho Center for Visual Artists. New York-based Lynch felt the Soho Center was suitable to her needs because "it is a gallery that showcases emerging artists. In addition, it is known for the quality of its exhibitions and the insightfulness of the context (theme)."

STUX GALLERY, 155 Spring St., New York NY 10012. (212)219-0010. Director: Kim Heirston. Retail gallery. Clientele: 80% private collectors, 20% corporate clients. Represents 10 artists. Sponsors 10 solo and 2 group shows/year. Average display time is 3½ weeks. Interested in emerging and established artists. Overall price range: $1,000-50,000; most artwork sold at $2,500-10,000.

Media: Considers oil, acrylic, mixed media, sculpture, photographs and prints.

Terms: Accepts work on consignment (50% commission). Retail price is set by gallery and artist. Exclusive representation required. Gallery provides insurance, promotion and contract.

Submissions: "The Director/Owner views materials with the artist present by appointment. Portfolio should include slides and transparencies. For artist unable to view materials with Director/Owner, send resume, slides, transparencies etc. and SASE."

JOHN SZOKE GRAPHICS, INC., 164 Mercer St., New York NY 10012. (212)219-8300. FAX: (212)966-3064. President: John Szoke. Director: Susan Jaffe. Retail gallery and art publisher. Estab. 1974. Represents 30 artists; emerging, mid-career and established. Exhibited artists include Christo and Dine. Open all year. Located downtown in SoHo; 1,500 sq. ft.; "gallery has a skylight." 50% of space for special exhibitions, 50% for gallery artists. Clientele: other dealers and collectors. 20% private collectors, 20% corporate collectors. Overall price range: $1,000-22,000.

Media: Considers works on paper, sculpture, silkscreen, woodcuts, engravings, lithographs, pochoir, mezzo-tints, serigraphs, linocuts and etchings. Most frequently exhibits etchings and lithographs.

Style: Exhibits surrealism, minimalism and realism. All genres.

Terms: Buys artwork outright. Retail price set by the gallery. Gallery provides insurance and promotion; artist pays for shipping. Prefers unframed artwork.

Submissions: Send query letter with slides and SASE. Write to schedule an appointment to show a portfolio, which should include slides. Replies in 1 week. Files letter, resume, all correspondence and slides unless SASE is enclosed.

TATYANA GALLERY, 6th Floor, 145 East 27th St., New York NY 10016. (212)683-2387. Contact: Director. Retail gallery. Estab. 1980. Open fall, winter, spring and summer. Clientele: 50% private collectors. Sponsors 2 solo and 2 group shows/year. Overall price range: $200-150,000; most artwork sold at $400-16,000.

Media: Considers oil, watercolor, pastel, pen & ink, drawings, mixed media and works on paper. Most frequently exhibits oil, watercolor and drawings.

Style: Exhibits impressionism and realism. Prefers landscapes, figurative work and portraits. "Our gallery specializes in Russian and Soviet Realist Art."

Tips: Looking for "the best Russian Realist paintings I can find in the USA."

JACK TILTON GALLERY, 24 W. 57th St., New York NY 10019. (212)247-7480. Director: Janine Cirincione. Retail gallery. Estab. 1983. Represents 12 artists. Sponsors 6 solo and 5 group shows/year. Average display time 4 weeks. Interested in emerging and established artists.

Media: Considers oil, acrylic, watercolor, pastel, pen & ink, drawings, mixed media, collage, works on paper, sculpture, installation, photography and egg tempera. Most frequently exhibits paintings and sculpture.

Style: Exhibits painterly abstraction, conceptualism, post modern works, hard-edge geometric abstraction and all styles. Prefers abstraction. "Our gallery specializes in contemporary abstract painting and sculpture."

Terms: Accepts artwork on consignment (50% commission). Retail price set by gallery and/or artist. Exclusive area representation not required.

Submissions: Send query letter with slides and SASE. Call or write to schedule an appointment to show a portfolio, which should include slides and small portable works. All material is returned if not accepted or under consideration.

*ALTHEA VIAFORA GALLERY, 568 Broadway, New York NY 10012. (212)925-4422. Director: Althea Viafora. Retail gallery. Estab. 1981. Clientele: 75% private collectors, 25% corporate clients. Represents 10 artists. Sponsors 8 solo and 3 group shows/year. Average display time is 1 month. Interested in emerging and established artists. Overall price range: $2,500-25,000; most artwork sold at $3,000-10,000.

Media: Considers oil, acrylic, watercolor, pastel, pen & ink, drawings, mixed media, collage, works on paper, sculpture, installation, photography and original handpulled prints. Most frequently exhibits acrylic on canvas, oil on canvas and photography.

Style: Exhibits painterly abstraction, conceptualism, surrealism and expressionism. Genres include landscapes and figurative work.

Terms: Accepts work on consignment. Retail price is set by gallery and artist. Gallery provides insurance and promotion.

VIRIDIAN GALLERY, 52 W. 57 St., New York NY 10019. (212)245-2882. Director: Paul Cohen. Cooperative gallery. Estab. 1970. Clientele: consultants, corporations, private collectors; 50% private collectors, 50% corporate clients. Represents 31 artists. Sponsors 13 solo and 2 group shows/year. Average display time is 3 weeks. Interested in emerging, mid-career and established artists. Overall price range: $1,000-15,000; most artwork sold at $2,000-8,000.

Media: Considers oil, acrylic, watercolor, pastel, pen & ink, drawings, mixed media, collage, works on paper, sculpture, installation, photography and limited edition prints. Most frequently exhibits oil, sculpture and mixed media.

Style: Exhibits hard-edge geometric abstraction, color field, painterly abstraction, conceptualism, post modern, primitivism, impressionism, photorealism, expressionism, neo-expressionism and realism. Genres include landscapes, florals, portraits and figurative work. "Eclecticism is Viridian's policy. The only unifying factor is quality. Work must be of the highest technical and aesthetic standards."

Terms: Accepts work on consignment (20% commission). Retail price is set by gallery and artist. Exclusive area representation not required. Gallery provides insurance, shipping, promotion and contract.

Submissions: Send query letter and SASE.

PHILIP WILLIAMS POSTERS, 60 Grand St., New York NY 10013. Contact: Philip Williams. Retail and wholesale gallery. Estab. 1973. Clientele: 70% private collectors, 30% corporate clients. Average display time 2 weeks. Interested in emerging, mid-career and established artists. Overall price range: $10-5,000; most artwork sold at $300-1,500.

Media: Considers posters and original handpulled prints.
Style: Exhibits all styles and all genres. Prefers art deco, art nouveau and contemporary styles.
Terms: Accepts work on consignment or buys outright. Retail price set by gallery. Exclusive area representation not required.
Submissions: Send query letter with brochure, photographs, business card, bio and SASE.

WOLFF GALLERY, 560 Broadway, New York NY 10012. (212)431-7833. Director: Shellee Rudner. Retail gallery. Estab. 1984. Located in SoHo. Represents 10 artists. Interested in emerging, mid-career and established artists. Sponsors 7 or 8 solo and 2 or 3 group shows/year. Average display time 4 weeks.
Media: Considers oil, acrylic, pen & ink, drawings, mixed media, sculpture and installation. Most frequently exhibits paintings and sculpture.
Style: Exhibits abstraction, minimalism and conceptualism.
Submissions: Send query letter with resume, slides and SASE. Replies in 2 weeks.

*YESHIVA UNIVERSITY MUSEUM, 2520 Amsterdam Ave., New York NY 10033. (212)960-5390. Assistant Director: Sylvia A. Herskowitz. Nonprofit gallery. Estab. 1973. Clientele: New Yorkers and tourists. Sponsors 4-6 solo shows/year. Average display time is 3 months. Interested in emerging, mid-career and established artists. "We do not sell except through the gift shop."
Media: Considers oil, acrylic, watercolor, pastel, pen & ink, drawings, mixed media, collage, works on paper, sculpture, ceramic, craft, fiber, glass, installation, photography and original handpulled prints.
Style: Exhibits post-modernism, surrealism, photorealism and realism. Genres include landscapes, florals, Americana, portraits and figurative work. "We only exhibit works of Jewish theme or subject matter but are willing to consider any style or medium."
Terms: Accepts work for exhibition purposes only, no fee. Pieces should be framed. Retail price is set by gallery and artist. Gallery provides insurance, promotion and contract; artist pays for shipping and framing.
Submissions: Send query letter, resume, brochure, slides, photographs and statement about your art. Write to schedule an appointment to show a portfolio, which should include originals. Resumes, slides or photographs are filed "only by special arrangement with artist."

North Carolina

CASE ART GALLERY, Atlantic Christian College, Lee St., Wilson NC 27893. (919)237-3161, ext. 365. Gallery Director: Edward Brown. Nonprofit gallery. Estab. 1965. Clientele: students, faculty, townspeople and area visitors. Sponsors 3 solo and 4 group shows/year. Average display time is 3½ weeks. Interested in mid-career artists. Most artwork sold at $350.
Media: Considers oil, acrylic, watercolor, pastel, pen & ink, drawings, mixed media, collage, works on paper, sculpture, ceramic, craft, fiber, glass, installation, photography and original handpulled prints. Most frequently exhibits fiber, pottery and paintings.
Style: Considers all styles. Genres include landscapes, Americana, figurative work and fantasy illustration. Most frequently exhibits abstraction and photorealism. Looks for "good craftsmanship, professionally presented, strong design, originality and a variety of styles and subjects."
Terms: "We take no commission on possible sales." Retail price is set by artist. Gallery provides insurance, promotion and contract; shipping costs are shared.
Submissions: Send query letter with resume. Write to schedule an appointment to show a portfolio, which should include slides. Resumes are filed.
Tips: "Looks for good design, craftsmanship and exhibition record. Often, however, we exhibit young artists who need exposure but do not have an impressive exhibition record."

*WELLINGTON B. GRAY GALLERY, EAST CAROLINA UNIVERSITY, Jenkins Fine Art Center, Greenville NC 27850. (919)757-6336. Director: Karen L. Churchill. Nonprofit university gallery. Estab. 1977. Represents emerging, mid-career and established artists. Sponsors 12 shows/year. Average display time 4-5 weeks. Open during academic year. Located downtown, in the university; 5,500 sq. ft.; "auditorium for lectures, sculpture garden." 100% of space for special exhibitions. Clientele: 25% private collectors, 75% corporate clients. Overall price range: $1,000-10,000.
Media: Considers all media plus environmental design, architecture, crafts and commercial art, original handpulled prints, relief, intaglio, planography, stencil and offset reproductions. Most frequently exhibits paintings, printmaking and sculpture.
Style: Exhibits all styles and genres.
Terms: There is a 20% suggested donation on sales. Retail price set by the artist. Gallery provides insurance and promotion. Shipping costs are shared. Prefers framed artwork.
Submissions: Send query letter with resume, slides, brochure and SASE. Write to schedule an appointment to show a portfolio, which should include originals, slides and transparencies. Replies in 2-6 months. Files "all mailed information for interesting artists. The rest is returned."

*THE JUDGE GALLERY, 353 W. Main St., Durham NC 27701. (919)688-8893. Director: Chris Rhule. Retail gallery. Estab. 1981. Clientele: "very posh"; 75% private collectors, 25% corporate clients. Represents 50 artists. Sponsors 6 solo shows/year. Interested in mid-career and established artists. Overall price range: $1,000-100,000. Average price: $2,000.
Media: Considers all media. Most frequently exhibits graphics, oil and acrylic.
Style: Considers all styles. Prefers abstraction and figurative work. Does not want to see redundancy and floral watercolors.
Terms: Accepts work on consignment (50% commission). Retail price is set by gallery or artist. Exclusive area representation required. Gallery provides insurance and promotion.
Submissions: Send query letter with resume, slides and SASE. "Include on every slide your name, title, technique, dimensions and retail price." Write to schedule an appointment to show a portfolio. Resumes, brochures and other artist information are filed.

*LITTLE ART GALLERY, North Hills Mall, Raleigh NC 27615. (919)787-6317. President: Ruth Green. Retail gallery. Estab. 1968. Represents 50 artists; emerging, mid-career and established. Exhibited artists include Paul Minnis, Ruth Russell Williams and Holly Brewster Jones. Sponsors 4 shows/year. Average display time 1 month. Open all year. Located in a suburban mall; 2,000 sq. ft.; small balcony for mini-shows. 20% of space for special exhibitions. Clientele: 90% private collectors, 10% corporate clients. Overall price range: $200-2,000; most artwork sold at $500-1,000.
Media: Considers oil, acrylic, watercolor, mixed media, collage, ceramic and all types of original handpulled prints. Most frequently exhibits watercolor, oil and original prints.
Style: Exhibits painterly abstraction, realism and abstracted realism. Genres include landscapes, florals and figurative work. Prefers realism, abstracted realism and abstract.
Terms: Accepts work on consignment (50% commission). "Will buy outright in certain circumstances." Retail price set by the artist. Gallery provides insurance and promotion. Prefers unframed artwork.
Submissions: Send query letter with photographs. Call or write to schedule an appointment to show a portfolio. Include photographs and slides with letter. Replies in 1 week. Files bios and 1 photo.
Tips: Most common mistake artists make is "presenting the whole range of work they have done instead of concentrating on what they are currently doing and are interested in."

*PINEHURST GALLERIES, Magnolia Rd., Pinehurst NC 28374. (919)295-6177. Vice President: Vivien Weller. Retail gallery. Estab. 1990. Represents 100 artists; established. Interested in seeing the work of emerging artists. Exhibited artists include Charles Kapsner and Vivien Weller. Sponsors 5 shows/year. Average display time 6 months. Open all year. Located downtown, in the main village; 4,000 sq. ft.; "the gallery is old Southern brick, covered in colorful flowers." 25% of space for special exhibitions, 75% for gallery artists. 50% private collectors, 50% corporate collectors. Price range: $300-10,000.
Media: Considers oil, acrylic, watercolor, pastel, pen & ink, drawings, mixed media, collage, works on paper, sculpture, ceramic, craft, fiber, glass, installation, photography, original handpulled prints, woodcuts, engravings, lithographs, posters and etchings. Most frequently exhibits oil, ceramic and sculpture.
Style: Exhibits painterly abstraction, impressionism, realism and all styles. Genres include landscapes, florals, portraits and figurative work.
Terms: Accepts work on consignment (40% commission). Retail price set by the artist. Gallery provides insurance, promotion and contract; artist pays for shipping. Prefers framed artwork.
Submissions: Send query letter with resume, slides, bio and reviews. Write to schedule an appointment to show a portfolio, which should include slides. Replies in 2 weeks. Files resumes, correspondence and slides.

THEATRE ART GALLERIES, 220 E. Commerce St., High Point NC 27260. (919)887-3415. Director: Tomi Melson. Nonprofit gallery. Estab. 1976. 4 galleries, with 20 exhibits a year. Clientele: all types from designers to tourists. Represents over 100 artists and fine craftsmen a year. Represents emerging – "with MFA in art as background" – mid-career and established artists. Average display time 6 weeks.
Media: Considers oil, acrylic, watercolor, pastel, pen & ink, drawings, mixed media, collage, works on paper, sculpture, ceramic, craft, fiber, glass, photography and egg tempera.
Style: Exhibits impressionism, expressionism, realism and painterly abstraction. Genres include landscapes, florals, wildlife and figurative work; considers all genres. "In its four galleries, TAG offers up to 20 changing exhibits a year. Open and free to the public, the exhibits present a broad range of topic, style and technique in order to reach our culturally diverse audience."
Terms: Accepts work on consignment (33% commission). Retail price set by artist. Exclusive area representation not required. Gallery provides insurance, promotion, contract and shipping costs from gallery. Prefers framed artwork.
Submissions: Send query letter with resume, brochure, 8×10 slides and bio. Don't send "poor slides and unprofessional materials." Call or write to schedule an appointment to show a portfolio. Replies in 6 weeks to 2 months. "Reply only after slide review and invitation from exhibits committee." Files resume, slides and artist statements.
Tips: It seems there has been "more education on the part of the public that real art is more than decoration."

*UNION COUNTY PUBLIC LIBRARY, 316 E. Windsor St., Monroe NC 28110. (704)283-8184. Director: Barbara M. Johnson. Estab. 1965. Sponsors 8 solo and 6 group shows/year. Average display time is 3 weeks. Interested in emerging and established artists. Overall price range: $50-5,000; most artwork sold at $150-250.
Media: Prefers oil and watercolor; will consider other media.
Style: Exhibits Americana, figurative, landscape, floral and realistic works.
Terms: Accepts work on consignment (10% commission). Retail price is set by gallery and artist. Exclusive area representation not required. Gallery provides promotion and contract.
Submissions: Send query letter with brochure and photographs. Call or write to schedule an appointment to show a portfolio. Artist information and publicity are filed.

WILKES ART GALLERY, 800 Elizabeth St., N. Wilkesboro NC 28659. (919)667-2841. Manager: Ginger Edmiston. Nonprofit gallery. Estab. 1962. Clientele: middle-class. 75% private collectors, 25% corporate clients. Sponsors solo and group shows. Average display time is 3-4 weeks. Interested in emerging and established artists. Overall price range: $200-9,000; most artwork sold at $500-1,500.
Media: Considers all media. Most frequently exhibits paintings, sculpture and photography.
Style: Exhibits conceptual, primitive, impressionistic, photorealistic, expressionistic, realist and surrealist works. Genres include landscapes and figurative work. Most frequently exhibits impressionism, realism and abstraction. Currently seeking impressionism.
Terms: "Exhibition committee meets in January each year to schedule exhibits." Exclusive area representation not required. Gallery provides insurance, promotion and contract; shipping costs are shared.
Submissions: Send query letter with resume, statement, slides and SASE. Resumes are filed.

North Dakota

*ARTMAIN, 13 S. Main, Minot ND 58701. (701)838-4747. Partners/Owners: Beth Kjelson and Becky Piehl. Retail gallery. Estab. 1981. Represents 12-15 artists. Sponsors 6 solo and 2 group shows/year. Average display time is 4-6 weeks. Interested in emerging artists. Overall price range: $100-500; most artwork sold at $100-300.
Media: Considers oil, acrylic, watercolor, pastel, pen & ink, drawings, ceramic, fiber, photography, craft, mixed media, collage, original handpulled prints and posters.
Style: Exhibits contemporary, abstract, Americana, impressionistic, landscapes, primitive, non-representational and realistic works. "We specialize in Native American works."
Terms: Accepts work on consignment (30% commission). Retail price is set by gallery and artist. Exclusive area representation required. Gallery provides insurance, promotion and contract; shipping costs are shared.
Submissions: Send query letter, resume and slides or photographs. May call to schedule an appointment to show a portfolio.

*THE ARTS CENTER, Box 363, 115 2nd St. SW, Jamestown ND 58402. (701)251-2496. Director: Joan Curtis. Nonprofit gallery. Estab. 1981. Sponsors 8 solo and 4 group shows/year. Average display time is 1 month. Interested in emerging artists. Overall price range: $50-600; most artwork sold at $50-350.
Style: Exhibits contemporary, abstract, Americana, impressionistic, figurative, primitive, photorealistic and realistic work; landscapes and florals.
Terms: 20% commission on sales from regularly scheduled exhibitions. Retail price is set by artist. Gallery provides insurance, promotion and contract; shipping costs are shared.
Submissions: Send query letter, resume, brochure, slides, photograph and SASE. Write to schedule an appointment to show a portfolio. Invitation to have an exhibition is extended by Arts Center curator, Kris Storbeck.
Tips: Wants to see "innovative art, but not too avant-garde."

BROWNING ARTS, 22 N. 4th St., Grand Forks ND 58201. (701)746-5090. Director: Mark Browning. Retail gallery. Estab. 1981. Open all year. Clientele: 80% private collectors, 20% corporate clients. Represents 25 artists. Average display time 3 months. Accepts only artists within 200 mile radius. Interested in emerging, mid-career and established artists. Overall price range: $100-2,000; most artwork sold at $200-500.
Media: Considers all media and original prints.
Style: Exhibits all styles and genres. "Our gallery provides a 'showcase' and sales outlet for all media and styles (done within a 200 mile radius generally) by artists consistently producing a professional quality of work."
Terms: Accepts work on consignment (33% commission). Retail price set by artist. Exclusive area representation not required. Gallery provides insurance and promotion.
Submissions: Send query letter with resume, slides, SASE and bio. Call or write to schedule an appointment to show a portfolio, which should include resume, slides, SASE and bio. Replies in 2 weeks.
Tips: Artists should show "A serious dedication to their involvement with their art form; at least one year experience; and only artworks following (not completed during) art instruction. Don't submit old works/slides, art school projects/MFA, etc. To introduce yourself, set up an interview time, appear in person with works or slides and history/bio, then explain current directions/interests."

*HUGHES FINE ART CENTER ART GALLERY, Department of Visual Arts University of North Dakota, Grand Forks ND 58202-8134. (701)777-2257. Director: Brian Paulsen. Nonprofit gallery. Estab. 1979. Represents emerging, mid-career and established artists. Sponsors 5 shows/year. Average display time 3 weeks. Open all year. Located on campus; 96 running ft. 100% of space for special exhibitions.
Media: Considers all media. Most frequently exhibits painting, photographs and jewelry/metal work.
Style: Exhibits all styles and genres.
Terms: Retail price set by the artist. Gallery provides "space to exhibit work and some limited contact with the public and the local newspaper." Gallery pays for shipping costs to and from gallery. Prefers framed artwork.
Submissions: Send query letter with slides. Portfolio should include slides. Replies in 1 week. Files "duplicate slides, resumes."
Tips: "Send slides, and approximate shipping costs."

MIND'S EYE GALLERY, Dickinson State University, Dickinson ND 58601. (701)227-2312. Professor of Art, Director: Katrina Callahan-Dolcater. Nonprofit gallery. Estab. 1972. Clientele: 100% private collectors. Sponsors 5 solo and 6 group shows/year. Average display time is 3 weeks. Interested in emerging and established artists. Overall price range: $10-3,000; most artwork sold at $10-150.
Media: Considers oil, acrylic, watercolor, pastel, pen & ink, drawings, mixed media, collage, works on paper, sculpture, ceramic, craft, fiber, photography and original handpulled prints. Most frequently exhibits oil, watercolor and prints.
Style: Exhibits hard-edge/geometric abstraction, color field, painterly abstraction, post-modernism, surrealism, impressionism, photorealism, expressionism, neo-expressionism and realism. Genres include landscapes, florals, Americana, Western, portraits and figurative work. "We sponsor a biennial 'Emerging Artists National Art Invitational' in which we welcome the opportunity to review slides and professional resumes of any interested artists. 10-15 artists are invited for this group show. Slides are returned within six months of submission and invitations are extended year-round."
Terms: Retail price is set by artist. Exclusive area representation not required. Gallery provides insurance, promotion and contract; shipping costs are shared.
Submissions: Send query letter, resume, brochure, business card and slides. Write to schedule an appointment to show a portfolio, which should include originals and slides. Artist's names and resumes are filed; slides returned.
Tips: Looks for "sophisticated, intelligent images by experienced artists; excellent technique, meaningful images; *curious* images. It is best to start with slides first!"

*MINOT ART GALLERY, Box 325, Minot ND 58702. (701)838-4445. Director: Judith Allen. Nonprofit gallery. Estab. 1970. Represents emerging, mid-career and established artists. Sponsors 24 shows/year. Average display time 1 month. Open all year. Located at North Dakota state fairgrounds; 1,600 sq. ft.; "2-story turn-of-the-century house." 100% of space for special exhibitions. Clientele: 100% private collectors. Overall price range: $50-2,000; most artwork sold at $100-400.
Media: Considers oil, acrylic, watercolor, pastel, pen & ink, drawings, mixed media, collage, works on paper, sculpture, ceramic, fiber, glass, photograpy, woodcuts, engravings, lithographs, serigraphs, linocuts and etchings. Most frequently exhibits watercolor, acrylic and mixed media.
Style: Exhibits all styles and genres. Prefers figurative, Americana and landscapes. No "commercial style work."
Terms: Accepts work on consignment (30% commission). Retail price set by the artist. Gallery provides insurance, promotion and contract; shipping costs from gallery or shipping costs are shared. Prefer framed artwork.
Submissions: Send query letter with resume and slides. Write to schedule an appointment to show a portfolio, which should include photographs and slides. Replies in 1 month. Files "material we are interested in."
Tips: "Send letter with slides/resume. Do not call for appointment. We are seeing many more photographers wanting to exhibit."

Ohio

*ALAN GALLERY, 325 Front St., Berea OH 44017. (216)243-7794. President: Alan Boesger. Retail gallery and arts consultancy. Estab. 1983. Clientele: 20% private collectors, 80% corporate clients. Represents 25-30 artists. Sponsors 4 solo shows/year. Average display time is 6-8 weeks. Interested in emerging, mid-career and established artists. Overall price range: $700-6,000; most artwork sold at $1,500-2,000.
Media: Considers all media and limited edition prints. Most frequently exhibits watercolor, works on paper and mixed media.
Style: Exhibits color field, painterly abstraction and surrealism. Genres include landscapes, florals, Western and figurative work.
Terms: Accepts work on consignment (40% commission). Retail price is set by gallery and artist. Exclusive area representation not required. Gallery provides insurance, promotion and contract; shipping costs are shared.

Submissions: Send resume, slides and SASE. Call or write to schedule an appointment to show a portfolio, which should include originals and slides. All material is filed.

TONI BIRCKHEAD GALLERY, 324 W. 4th St., Cincinnati OH 45202. (513)241-0212. Director: Toni Birckhead. Retail gallery and arts consultancy. Estab. 1979. Clientele: 5% private collectors, 95% corporate clients. Represents 80-110 artists. Sponsors 4 solo and 2 group shows/year. Average display time is 6-7 weeks. Interested in emerging and established artists. Overall price range: $500-5,000; most artwork sold at $500-1,000.
Media: Considers oil, acrylic, watercolor, pastel, pen & ink, drawings, mixed media, collage, works on paper, sculpture, ceramic, installation, photography and original handpulled prints. Most frequently exhibits painting, sculpture and works on paper.
Style: Exhibits hard-edge geometric abstraction, color field, painterly abstraction, minimalism, conceptual post-modernism, neo-expressionism and realism.
Terms: Accepts work on consignment (50% commission). Retail price is set by gallery and artist. Exclusive area representation required. Gallery provides insurance, promotion and contract; shipping expenses are shared.
Submissions: Send query letter, resume, slides and SASE. Call or write to schedule an appointment to show a portfolio, which should include originals and slides. Slides, resumes and reviews are filed.

C.A.G.E., 344 W. 4th St., Cincinnati OH 45202. (513)381-2437. Contact: Programming Committee. Nonprofit gallery. Estab. 1978. Clientele: 99.9% private collectors, .1% corporate clients. Sponsors 7-12 group shows/year. Average display time is 1 month. Interested in emerging and established artists. Overall price range: $100-5,000; most artwork sold at $100-500.
Media: Considers all media. Most frequently exhibits paintings, mixed media and installation.
Style: Considers all styles; "experimental, conceptual, political, media/time art, public art and artists' projects encouraged." Most frequently exhibits figurative, photographic and expressionist. "Proposals from artists are accepted and reviewed in January (deadline December 15) for exhibition 14-20 months from deadline. A panel of peer artists and curators selects the exhibitions."
Terms: Retail price is set by artist. Exclusive area representation not required. Gallery provides insurance, promotion and contract.
Submissions: Send query letter with 10 slides and SASE.

THE CANTON ART INSTITUTE, 1001 Market Ave. N., Canton OH 44702. (216)453-7666. Executive Director: M.J. Albacete. Nonprofit gallery. Estab. 1935. Sponsors 25 solo and 5 group shows/year. Represents emerging, mid-career and established artists. Average display time is 6 weeks. Overall price range: $50-3,000; few sales above $300-500.
Media: Considers all media. Most frequently exhibits oil, watercolor and photography.
Style: Considers all styles. Most frequently exhibits painterly abstraction, post-modernism and realism.
Terms: "While every effort is made to publicize and promote works, we cannot guarantee sales, although from time to time sales are made, at which time a 25% charge is applied." One of the most common mistakes in presenting portfolios is "sending too many materials. Send only a few slides or photos, a brief bio and an SASE."
Tips: There seems to be "a move back to realism, conservatism and support of regional artists."

THE A.B. CLOSSON JR. CO., 401 Race St., Cincinnati OH 45202. (513)762-5564. Director: Phyllis Weston. Retail gallery. Estab. 1866. Clientele: general. Represents emerging, mid-career and established artists. Average display time is 3 weeks. Overall price range: $600-75,000.
Media: Considers oil, watercolor, pastel, mixed media, sculpture, original handpulled prints and limited offset reproductions.
Style: Exhibits all styles and genres.
Terms: Accepts work on consignment or buys outright. Retail price is set by gallery and artist. Exclusive area representation required. Gallery provides insurance and promotion; shipping costs are shared. Portfolio should include originals.

***EASTON LIMITED GALLERY,** 311 Conant, Maumee OH 43537. (419)893-6203. Partner: M.L. Wagener. Retail gallery. Estab. 1984. Represents emerging, mid-career and established artists. Exhibited artists include Heiner Hertling. Sponsors 4 shows/year. Open all year. Located downtown near Main St.; 4,200 sq. ft.; "in a historical section of town." 50% of space for special exhibitions. Clientele: professionals and local businesses. 50% private collectors, 10% corporate clients. Overall price range: $200-3,500.
Media: Considers oil, acrylic, watercolor, pastel and wood carvings. Most frequently exhibits original oils and original watercolors.
Style: Exhibits landscapes and wildlife works.
Terms: Artwork is accepted on consignment (33% commission). Gallery and artist set the retail price. Gallery provides promotion; shipping costs are shared.
Submissions: Write to schedule an appointment to show a portfolio, which should include originals and prints.

*CHARLES FOLEY GALLERY, 973 E. Broad St., Columbus OH 43205. (614)253-7921. Director: Charles Foley. Retail gallery. Estab. 1982. Represents established artists. Interested in seeing the work of emerging artists. Exhibited artists include Tom Wesselmann and Richard Anuszkiewicz. Sponsors 2 shows/year. Average display time 8 weeks. Open all year. Located east of the Columbus Museum of Art; 5,000 sq. ft.; "housed in a turn-of-the-century house, specializing in 20th-century masters." 50% of space for special exhibitions, 50% for gallery artists. Clientele: 90% private collectors, 10% corporate clients. Overall price range: $30-150,000; most artwork sold at $2,500-20,000.

Media: Considers oil, acrylic, watercolor, pen & ink, drawings, mixed media, collage, works on paper, sculpture, ceramic, original handpulled prints, woodcuts, linocuts, engravings, etchings, lithographs, serigraphs and posters. Most frequently exhibits paintings, etchings and drawings.

Style: Exhibits expressionism, color field and hard-edge geometric abstraction. Prefers pop art, op art and expressionism.

Terms: Accepts work on consignment (30% commission). Retail price set by the gallery and the artist. Gallery provides promotion. Gallery pays for shipping costs. Prefers framed artwork.

Submissions: Send query letter with SASE. Call to schedule an appointment to show portfolio, which should include originals and transparencies.

IMAGES GALLERY, 3154 Markway Dr., Toledo OH 43606. (419)537-1400. Owner/Director: Frederick D. Cohn. Retail gallery. Estab. 1970. Clientele: 75% private collectors, 25% corporate clients. Represents more than 40 artists. Sponsors 9 solo and 3 group shows/year. Average display time 3-4 weeks. Accepts American artists usually. Interested in emerging, mid-career and established artists. Most artwork sold at $750-3,000.

Media: Considers oil, acrylic, watercolor, pastel, pen & ink, drawings, mixed media, collage, works on paper, sculpture, glass, color and b&w limited edition prints and posters. Most frequently exhibits paintings, sculpture and graphics.

Style: Exhibits hard-edge geometric abstraction, color field, painterly abstraction, pattern painting, photorealistism and realism. Genres include landscapes, florals, Americana, portraits, figurative.

Terms: Accepts work on consignment (commission varies). Gallery provides insurance and promotion; shipping costs are shared. Will provide contract if required.

Submissions: Send query letter with slides. Call or write for an appointment to show a portfolio, which should include slides.

Tips: Nothing "cutesy and derivative." Most common mistake artists make is presenting "too many directions—no concentration or continuity."

LICKING COUNTY ART ASSOCIATION, 391 Hudson, Newark OH 43055. (614)349-8031. Exibition Coordinator: H. Schneider. Nonprofit gallery. Estab. 1959. Represents 30 artists; emerging and mid-career. Exhibited artists include Marilyn Stocker-Smith and George Arensberg. Sponsors 11 shows/year. Average display time 1 month. Closed during August. Located "6 blocks north of downtown; 784 sq. ft.; in a Victorian brick building." 70% of space for special exhibitions. Clientele: 90% private collectors, 10% corporate clients. Overall price range: $30-6,000; most work sold at $100-500.

Media: Considers oil, acrylic, watercolor, pastel, pen & ink, drawings, mixed media, collage, works on paper, sculpture, ceramic, fiber, glass, installation, photography, original handpulled prints, woodcuts, engravings, lithographs, wood engravings, serigraphs and etchings. Most frequently exhibits watercolor, oil/acrylic and photography.

Style: Exhibits conceptualism, color field, impressionism, realism, photorealism and pattern painting. Genres include landscapes, florals, wildlife, portraits and all genres. Prefers landscape, portraits and floral.

Terms: Artwork is accepted on consignment (30% commission.) Retail price set by artist. Gallery provides insurance, promotion and contract; artist pays for shipping. Prefers framed artwork.

Submissions: Send query letter with resume, brochure and photographs. Write to schedule an appointment to show a portfolio, which should include originals and slides. Replies only if interested within 6 weeks.

THE MIDDLETOWN FINE ARTS CENTER, 130 N. Verity Pkwy., Middletown OH 45042. (513)424-2416. Director: Phyllis A. Short. Nonprofit gallery. Estab. 1975. Clientele: tourists, students, community; 95% private collectors, 5% corporate clients. Sponsors 5 solo and/or group shows/year. Average display time 3 weeks. Overall price range: $100-1,000; most work sold at $150-500.

Media: Considers all media except prints. Most frequently exhibits watercolor, oil, acrylic and drawings.

Style: Exhibits all styles and all genres. Prefers realism, impressionism and photorealism. "Our gallery does not specialize in any one style or genre. We offer an opportunity for artists to exhibit and hopefully sell their work. This also is an important educational experience for the community. Selections are chosen two years in advance by a committee which meets one time a year.

Terms: Accepts work on consignment (30% commission). Retail price set by artist. Exclusive area representation not required. Gallery provides insurance and promotion; artist pays for shipping. Prefers artwork framed and wired.

Submissions: Send query letter with resume, brochure, slides, photographs and bio. Write to schedule an appointment to show a portfolio, which should include originals, slides or photographs. Replies in 3 weeks-3 months (depends when exhibit committee meets.). Files resume or other printed material. All material is returned if not accepted or under consideration.
Tips: "Decisions are made by a committee of volunteers, and time may not permit an on-the-spot interview with the director."

MILLER GALLERY, 2715 Erie Ave., Cincinnati OH 45208. (513)871-4420. Co-Directors: Barbara and Norman Miller. Retail gallery. Estab. 1960. Located in affluent suburb. Clientele: 70% private collectors, 30% corporate clients. Represents about 50 artists. Sponsors 4 solo and 3 group shows/year with display time 3 weeks. Interested in emerging, mid-career and established artists. Overall price range: $25-25,000; most artwork sold at $300-5,000.
Media: Considers, oil, acrylic, mixed media, collage, works on paper, ceramic, fiber, glass and original handpulled prints. Most frequently exhibits oil or acrylic, original etchings, lithographs, blown glass and ceramics.
Style: Exhibits painterly abstraction, impressionism and realism. Genres include landscapes, interior scenes and still lifes. "The ideal artworks for us are those executed in a sure, authoritative technique, not overworked, and not trite. We especially seek both fine realism and nonsubjective paintings; the realism must not include covered bridges or sentiment. Landscapes preferred and must have depth, substance and fine technique. Nonsubjective works must be handled with assurance and not be overworked or busy. We prefer medium to large paintings." Does not want to see "sentiment, barns with old wagons, nudes, purple, mint green, too much orange."
Terms: Accepts artwork on consignment (50% commission); buys outright when appropriate (40% of retail). Retail price set by artist and gallery. Exclusive area representation is required. Gallery provides insurance, promotion and contract; shipping and show costs are shared.
Submissions: Send query letter with resume, brochure, slides or photographs with sizes, wholesale (artist) and selling price and SASE. "All material is filed if we're interested, none if not."
Tips: "Artists often either completely omit pricing info or mention a price without identifying their percentages or selling price."

*SPACES, 1216 W. 6th St., Cleveland OH 44113. (216)621-2314. Alternative space. Estab. 1978. Represents emerging artists. Has 300 members. Sponsors 10 shows/year. Average display time 1 month. Open all year. Located downtown Cleveland; 3,500 sq. ft.; "loft space with row of columns." 100% private collectors.
Media: Considers all media. Most frequently exhibits installation, painting and sculpture.
Style: Exhibits all styles.
Terms: 20% commission. Retail price set by the artist. Gallery provides insurance, promotion and contract.
Submissions: Send query letter with resume, slides and SASE. Annual deadline in spring for submissions.

Oklahoma

DAPHNE ART & FRAME GALLERY, INC., 115 N. Main, Sand Springs OK 74063. (918)245-8005. Secretary-Treasurer: Daphne Loyd. Retail gallery. Estab. 1967. Clientele: 5% private collectors. Represents 20 artists. Sponsors 1 solo and 2 group shows/year. Average display time is 2 months. Interested in emerging, mid-career and established artists. Overall price range: $50-2,500; most artwork sold at $150-250.
Media: Considers oil, acrylic, watercolor, pastel, mixed media, collage, sculpture and limited edition prints. Most frequently exhibits oil, watercolor and acrylics.
Style: Exhibits post modern works and impressionism. Genres include landscapes, florals, Americana, Western and Indian art. Does not want to see "far-out modern."
Terms: Accepts work on consignment (33⅓% commission) or buys outright (50% markup). Retail price is set by gallery and artist. Exclusive area representation required. Gallery provides insurance, promotion and contract; shipping costs are shared.
Submissions: Send query letter, brochure, slides and photographs. Call for an appointment to show a portfolio, which should include originals and slides.
Tips: The most common mistake artists make in presenting their work is "having frames on their works or mattes. Most artists know nothing about framing correctly."

*THE FRAMESMITH GALLERY, 6528-E East 101st St., Tulsa OK 74133. (918)299-6863. Owner: Bob D. McDaniel. Retail gallery, wholesale gallery, art consultancy and consignment gallery. Estab. 1983. Represents 30 emerging, mid-career and established artists. Exhibited artists include S.S. Burris and Troy Anderson. Sponsors 4 shows/year. Average display time 6 months. Open all year. Located in suburbs; 1,500 sq. ft. 33% of space for special exhibitions. Clientele: commercial/walk-in. 2% private collectors, 10% corporate clients. Overall price range: $400-10,000.

Media: Considers oil, acrylic, watercolor, pastel, pen & ink, drawings, mixed media, works on paper, sculpture, glass, installation and photography. Prefers watercolor, oil and pen & ink.
Style: Exhibits all styles. Genres include landscapes, florals, Americana, Southwestern, Western, wildlife, portraits and figurative work. Prefers landscapes, figurative works and western/wildlife.
Terms: Artwork is accepted on consignment and there is a 33% commission. Retail price set by the artist. Gallery provides insurance and promotion. Artist pays for shipping. Prefers framed artwork.
Submissions: Send query letter with resume, slides and photographs. Call or write to schedule an appointment to show a portfolio. Portfolio should include originals, slides and photographs. Replies only if interested within 1 month.
Tips: "Class 'A' neighborhood ($50,000 and up) and very, very conservative." Notices a "return to classical and impressionistic styles."

*GUSTAFSON GALLERY, 9606 N. May, Oklahoma City OK 73120. (405)751-8466. President: Diane. Retail gallery. Estab. 1973. Represents 10 mid-career artists. Exhibited artists include D. Norris Moses and Downey Burns. Sponsors 1 show/year. Average display time 2 months. Open all year. Located in a suburban mall; 1,700 sq. ft. 100% of space for special exhibitions. Clientele: upper and middle income. 60% private collectors, 40% corporate collectors. Prefers contemporary Southwestern art. Overall price range: $4,000 minimum.
Media: Considers oil, acrylic, pastel, mixed media, collage, works on paper, sculpture, ceramic and fiber. Considers offset reproductions, lithographs, posters and serigraphs. Most frequently exhibits acrylic, pastel and serigraphs.
Style: Exhibits primitivism and painterly abstraction. Genres include landscapes, Southwestern and Western.
Terms: Artwork is accepted on consignment (40% commission); or buys outright for 50% of the retail price; net 30 days. Retail price set by the the artist. Gallery provides promotion. Shipping costs are shared.
Submissions: Send query letter with resume, brochure, photographs, business card and reviews. Call to schedule an appointment to show a portfolio, which should include originals and photographs. Replies in 1 month.

PLAINS INDIANS & PIONEERS MUSEUM AND ART GALLERY, 2009 Williams Ave., Woodward OK 73801. (405)256-6813. Director: Frankie A. Herzer. Nonprofit gallery of museum. Estab. 1966. Clientele: 90% private collectors, 10% corporate clients. Represents various number of artists. Sponsors 6 solo and 6 group shows/year. Average display time 1 month. Interested in emerging, mid-career and established artists. Overall price range: $150-5,000; most artwork sold at $150-1,500.
Media: Considers oil, acrylic, watercolor, pastel, pen & ink, drawings, mixed media, collage, works on paper, sculpture, craft, fiber, photography, egg tempera, woodcuts, wood engravings, linocuts, engravings, etchings, lithographs, offset reproductions and posters. Most frequently exhibits oil, watercolor and acrylic.
Style: Exhibits impressionism, expressionism, realism, photorealism, surrealism, primitivism, conceptualism and imagism. Genres include landscapes, florals, Americana, Southwestern, Western, wildlife, portraits and figurative work. Prefers Western themes, wildlife and landscapes. "The Art Gallery is a part of the museum. The museum deals with the history of the Northwest Oklahoma Territory. Although a large range of art is exhibited in the gallery, the public preference leans toward Western art that reflects the history of the area. Decorator art is also a favorite in this area." No "copy art or any interpretation that could be considered in questionable taste."
Terms: Accepts work on consignment (20% commission). Retail price set by artist. Exclusive area representation required. Gallery provides promotion and contract; artist pays for shipping.
Submissions: Send query letter with resume and photographs. Write to schedule an appointment to show a portfolio, which should include originals and photographs. Replies only if interested within 4 weeks. Files photos, resumes and brochures.
Tips: "In our area of the world Western and Indian art still reign supreme."

*THE UNIVERSITY OF OKLAHOMA MUSEUM OF ART, 410 W. Boyd St., Norman OK 73019-0525. (405)325-3272. Director: Tom Toperzer. Museum. Estab. 1936. Represents 10 emerging, mid-career and established artists/year. Exhibited artists include Carolyn Brady and Joseph Glasco. Sponsors 10 shows/year. Average display time 4-6 weeks. Open all year. Located on campus; 13,600 sq. ft.

The asterisk before a listing indicates that the listing is new in this edition. New markets are often the most receptive to freelance submissions.

Media: Considers oil, acrylic, watercolor, pastel, pen & ink, drawings, mixed media, collage, works on paper, sculpture, ceramic, craft, fiber, glass, installation, photography, original handpulled prints, woodcuts, engravings, lithographs, pochoir, posters, wood engravings, mezzotints, serigraphs, linocuts and etchings. Most frequently exhibits paintings, drawings/prints and photographs.

Style: Exhibits all styles and genres.

Terms: Gallery provides insurance and promotion. Prefers framed artwork.

Submissions: Send query letter with resume, slides and bio. Files slides and bio.

*THE WINDMILL GALLERY, Suite 103, 3750 W. Robinson, Norman OK 73072. (405)321-7900. Director/Owner: Andy Denton. Retail gallery. Estab. 1987. Represents 20 emerging, mid-career and established artists. Exhibited artists include Chebon Dacon and Dana Tiger. Sponsors 4 shows/year. Average display time 1 month. Open all year. Located in "northwest Norman (Brookhaven area); 800 sq. ft.; interior decorated Santa Fe style: striped aspen, adobe brick, etc." 30% of space for special exhibitions. Clientele: "middle-class to upper middle-class professionals/housewifes." 100% private collectors. Overall price range $50-15,000; most artwork sold at $100-2,000.

Media: Considers oil, acrylic, watercolor, pastel, pen & ink, drawings, mixed media, works on paper, sculpture and craft. Considers original handpulled prints, offset reproductions, lithographs, posters, cast-paper and serigraphs. Most frequently exhibits watercolor, tempera and acrylic.

Style: Exhibits primitivism and realism. Genres include landscapes, Southwestern, Western, wildlife and portraits. Prefers Native American scenes, portraits and western-southwestern subjects.

Terms: Artwork is accepted on consignment (40% commission). Retail price set by the artist. Gallery provides insurance and promotion. Shipping costs are shared. Prefers framed artwork.

Submissions: Send query letter with slides, bio, brochure, photographs, SASE, business card and reviews. Call to schedule an appointment to show a portfolio. Portfolio should include "whatever best shows their works." Replies only if interested within 1 month. Files brochures, slides, photos, etc.

Tips: Accepts artists from Oklahoma area; Indian art done by Indians only; Western and Southwestern art can be done by Anglo artists. "Call, tell me about yourself, try to set up appointment to view works or to hang your works as featured artist. Fairly casual—but must have bios and photos of works or works themselves! Please, no drop-ins!"

Oregon

*ALDER GALLERY, Suite 107, 767 Willamette, Eugene OR 97401. (503)342-6411. Director: Candy Moffett. Retail gallery, wholesale gallery, art consultancy and rental gallery. Estab. 1985. Represents 52 emerging, mid-career and established artists. Exhibited artists include Mike Leckie and Margaret Coe. Sponsors 6 shows/year. Average display time 6 weeks. Open all year. Located downtown; 1,100 sq. ft. 40% of space for special exhibitions. Clientele: "educated, corporate." 65% private collectors, 35% corporate clients. Accepts only artists from the Pacific Northwest. Overall price range: $100-4,000; most artwork sold at $400-1,200.

Media: Considers oil, acrylic, watercolor, pastel, drawings, mixed media, collage, works on paper, sculpture, ceramic, fiber, glass and photography. Considers original handpulled prints, woodcuts, engravings, lithographs, wood engravings, mezzotints, serigraphs, linocuts and etchings. Most frequently exhibits watercolor, pastel, mixed media, sculpture and handpulled prints.

Style: Exhibits expressionism, painterly abstraction, conceptualism, post modern works, impressionism, realism, photorealism, pattern painting and hard-edge geometric abstraction. Genres include landscapes and florals. Prefers impressionism, realism and post modern works.

Terms: Artwork is accepted on consignment; a variable commission. Retail price set by the gallery and the artist. Gallery provides insurance, promotion and contract. Shipping costs are shared.

Submissions: Send query letter with resume, slides, bio, brochure, photographs, SASE, business card and reviews. Call to schedule an appointment to show a portfolio. Portfolio should include originals, slides, photographs and transparencies. Replies in 3 weeks.

Tips: "Common mistakes artists make in presenting their work are that they don't bring enough to preview and they show-up without an appointment."

*BLACKFISH GALLERY, 420 NW 9th Ave., Portland OR 97209. (503)224-2634. Director: Cheryl Snow. Retail cooperative gallery. Estab. 1979. Represents 24 artists; emerging and mid-career. Exhibited artists include Barry Pelzner and Helen Issifu. Sponsors 12 shows/year. Open all year. Located downtown, in the "Northwest Pearl District; 2,500 sq. ft.; street-level, 'garage-type' overhead wide door, long, open space (100' deep)." 70% of space for feature exhibits, 15-20% for gallery artists. Clientele: 80% private collectors, 20% corporate clients. Overall price range: $250-12,000; most artwork sold at $900-1,400.

Media: Considers oil, acrylic, watercolor, pastel, pen & ink, drawings, mixed media, collage, sculpture, ceramic, photography, original handpulled prints, woodcuts, wood engravings, linocuts, engravings, mezzotints, etchings, lithographs, pochoir and serigraphs. Most frequently exhibits paintings, sculpture and prints.

Style: Exhibits expressionism, neo-expressionism, painterly abstraction, surrealism, conceptualism, minimalism, color field, post modern works, impressionism and realism. Prefers neo-expressionism, conceptualism and painterly abstraction.

Terms: Accepts work on consignment from invited artists (50% commission); co-op membership includes monthly dues fee plus donation of time (40% commission on sales). Retail price set by the artist, with assistance from gallery on request. Gallery provides insurance, promotion, contract and shipping costs from gallery. Prefers framed artwork.

Submissions: Accepts only artists from NW Oregon and SW Washington ("unique exceptions possible"); "must be willing to be an active cooperative member—write for details." Send query letter with resume, slides, SASE, reviews and statement of intent. Write to schedule an appointment to show a portfolio, which should include photographs and slides. "We review 4 times/year." Replies in 1 month. Files material only if exhibit invitation extended.

Tips: "Research first—know who you're approaching!"

WILSON W. CLARK MEMORIAL LIBRARY GALLERY, 5000 N. Willamette Blvd., Portland OR 97203-5798. (503)283-7111. Director: Joseph P. Browne. Nonprofit gallery. Estab. 1959. Clientele: students and faculty. Sponsors 7 solo and 4 group shows/year. Average display time is 1 month. Interested in emerging and established artists. Overall price range: $75-750.

Media: Considers oil, acrylic, watercolor, pastel, pen & ink, drawings, mixed media, collage, photography and prints. Most frequently exhibits watercolor, acrylics and mixed media.

Style: Exhibits all styles and genres. "We are strictly an adjunct to the university library and have sold only one work in the past eight or ten years."

Terms: Accepts work on consignment (10% commission). Retail price is set by artist. Exclusive area representation not required. Gallery provides insurance and promotion.

Submissions: Send query letter, resume, brochure and photographs. Write for an appointment to show a portfolio, which should include photographs.

*COGLEY ART CENTER, 4035 S. 6th St., Klamath Falls OR 97603. (503)884-8699. Owner/Manager: Sue Cogley. Retail gallery. Estab. 1985. Represents 17 artists; emerging, mid-career and established. Exhibited artists include Katheryn Davis, Guy Pederson and Stacy Smith Rowe. Sponsors 10-12 shows/year. Average display time 1 month. Open all year. Located in a suburban area on the main business street; 800 sq. ft.; "contemporary in feeling—all wall space (no windows), movable panels and track lighting." 25% of space for special exhibitions, 75% for gallery artists. Clientele: middle to upper end. 100% private collectors. Overall price range: $150-1,500; most artwork sold at $300-800.

Media: Considers oil, acrylic, watercolor, pastel, pen & ink, drawings, mixed media, collage, works on paper, sculpture, ceramic, fiber, glass, mosaic, original handpulled prints, woodcuts, etchings and serigraphs. Most frequently exhibits watercolor, oil and monotype.

Style: Exhibits all styles, "leaning toward contemporary." Prefers impressionism, painterly abstraction and realism.

Terms: Accepts work on consignment (40% commission). Retail price set by the artist. Gallery provides insurance, promotion and contract. Gallery pays for shipping costs from gallery; artist pays for shipping to gallery. Prefers framed artwork, "but we can work with unframed."

Submissions: Prefers Oregon and Northwest artists. Send query letter with bio, photographs and SASE. Call to schedule an appointment to show a portfolio, which should include originals and slides. Replies in 1-2 weeks. Files bio and photos of artists "which we may be interested in in the future."

Tips: "Have a current bio and photos, slides or originals that are typical of your work; a minimum of 3 pieces."

LANE COMMUNITY COLLEGE ART GALLERY, 4000 E. 30th Ave., Eugene OR 97405. (503)747-4501. Gallery Director: Harold Hoy. Nonprofit gallery. Estab. 1970. Sponsors 7 solo and 2 group shows/year. Average display time is 3 weeks. Interested in emerging, mid-career and established artists. Most artwork sold at $100-1,500.

Media: Considers all media.

Style: Exhibits contemporary works.

Terms: Retail price is set by artist. Exclusive area representation not required. Gallery provides insurance, promotion and contract; shipping costs are shared. "The gallery retains 25% of the retail price on works sold."

Submissions: Send query letter, resume and slides. Resumes are filed.

LAWRENCE GALLERY, Box 187, Sheridan OR 97378. (503)943-3633. Director: Anna Eason. Retail gallery and art consultancy. Estab. 1977. Clientele: tourists, Portland and Salem residents; 80% private collectors, 20% corporate clients. Represents 150 artists. Sponsors 7 two-person and 1 group shows/year. Interested in emerging, mid-career and established artists. Overall price range: $10-10,000; most artwork sold at $250-1,500.

©1989 Dennis Cunningham

"Fishing for the Halibut," a linocut by Dennis Cunningham, is handled by the Jamison/ Thomas Gallery of Portland, Oregon on consignment. It was also shown in the Lane Community College Art Department Gallery in Eugene. The Portland-based artist says he wished to convey "the strong graphic quality of block printmaking" with this piece, as well as "the telling of a story from real life."

Media: Considers oil, acrylic, watercolor, pastel, pen & ink, drawings, mixed media, collage, sculpture, ceramic, fiber, glass, jewelry and original handpulled prints. Most frequently exhibits oil, watercolor, metal sculpture and ceramic.

Style: Exhibits painterly abstraction, impressionism, photorealism and realism. Genres include landscapes, florals and Americana. "Our gallery features beautiful art-pieces that celebrate life."

Terms: Accepts work on consignment (50% commission). Retail price is set by artist. Exclusive area representation required. Gallery provides insurance, promotion and contract; artist pays for shipping.

Submissions: Send query letter, resume, brochure, slides and photographs. Write for an appointment to show a portfolio. Resumes, photos of work, newspaper articles, other informative pieces and artist's statement about his work are filed.

Tips: "Do not bring work without an appointment. Does not want to see colored matts and elaborate frames on paintings."

*LITTMAN GALLERY, Portland State University, Box 751, 1925 SW Broadway, Portland OR 97207. (503)464-4452. Director: Lonnie Feather. Nonprofit gallery. Estab. 1972. Clientele: university students and local businesspeople. Sponsors 8 solo and 2 group shows/year. Average display time is 4 weeks. Interested in emerging and mid-career artists. Overall price range: $200-12,000; most artwork sold at $200-300.

Media: Considers oil, acrylic, watercolor, pastel, pen & ink, drawings, mixed media, collage, works on paper, sculpture, ceramic, craft, fiber, glass, installations, performance art and original handpulled prints. Most frequently exhibits oil and sculpture.

Terms: Accepts work on consignment. Retail price is set by artist. Exclusive area representation not required. Gallery provides insurance and promotion; artist pays for shipping.

Submissions: Send query letter, resume, slides and SASE. Call to schedule an appointment to show a portfolio, which should include slides.

Tips: Sees trend toward "works pricing themselves out of realistic ranges."

*MAVEETY GALLERY, (formerly Lawrence Gallery), 842 S.W. First Ave., Portland OR 97204. (503)224-9442. Director: Billye Turner. Retail gallery and art consultancy. Estab. 1982. Clientele: corporate, tourists and collectors; 50% private collectors, 50% corporate clients. Represents 75 artists. Interested in seeing the work of emerging, mid-career and established artists. Sponsors 11 solo and 1 group shows/year. Average display time is 1 month. "Special shows monthly, always revolving work." Overall price range: $200-10,000; most artwork sold at $1,000-3,000.

Media: Considers oil, acrylic, watercolor, pastel, pen & ink, drawings, mixed media, collage, works on paper, sculpture, ceramic, fiber, glass, photography and original handpulled prints. Most frequently exhibits oils, acrylics, ceramics and glass.

Style: Exhibits painterly abstraction, impressionism and photorealism. Genres include landscapes and figurative work.

Terms: Accepts work on consignment (50% commission). Retail price is set by gallery and artist. Exclusive area representation required. Gallery provides insurance, promotion and contract; artist pays for shipping.

Submissions: Send query letter, slides and photographs. Call to schedule an appointment to show a portfolio, which should include originals, slides and transparencies. All material is filed.

Tips: Feels there is a "movement toward more representative work."

NORTHVIEW GALLERY, 12000 SW 49th, Portland OR 97219. (503)244-6111. Director: Hugh Webb. Nonprofit gallery. Sponsors 6-8 shows/year. Average display time 4 weeks. Interested in emerging and established artists. Overall price range: $100-3,000; most artwork sold at $100-600.

Media: Considers oil, acrylic, watercolor, pastel, pen & ink, drawings, mixed media, collage, sculpture, ceramic, craft, fiber, glass, installation, photography, color and b&w original handpulled prints and posters.

Style: Exhibits all styles and genres. Does not want to see "work done under supervision—calligraphy."

Terms: Accepts work on consignment; no commission. Retail price is set by artist. Exclusive area representation not required. Gallery provides insurance, promotion and contract; shipping costs are shared.

Submissions: Send query letter with resume, slides, photograph and SASE by April 1. Selections for next academic year made in May.

Tips: Looks for a "strong sense of individual direction."

ROGUE GALLERY, 40 S. Bartlett, Medford OR 97501. (503)772-8118. Co-Directors: Billie-Ann Robb and D. Elizabeth Withers. Nonprofit sales and rental gallery. Estab. 1960. Clientele: valley residents and tourists; 95% private collectors, 5% corporate clients. Represents 375 artists. Main gallery sponsors 12 exhibits/year; "rental gallery changes bimonthly." Average display time is 3 months. Interested in emerging, mid-career and established artists. Overall price range in rental shop: $50-1,200; most artwork sold at $300-600.

Media: Considers all media and original handpulled prints.

Style: Exhibits all styles and genres.

Terms: Accepts work on consignment (35% commission) in rental gallery. Retail price is set by artist. Exclusive area representation not required. Gallery provides insurance and promotion; artist pays for shipping.

Submissions: Send resume and slides. Call or write to schedule an appointment to show a portfolio, which should include originals, slides and transparencies. Resumes are filed; slides are returned.

Tips: Likes to see a "wide variety of techniques, styles, etc." Sees trend toward "monotypes Southwest, regional and figurative" work.

Pennsylvania

ALBER GALLERIES, 2004 Pine St., Philadelphia PA 19103. (215)732-0474. Owner: Howard Alber. Wholesale gallery/art consultancy, also Registry of Philadelphia Subjects. Shows Philadelphia subjects plus special commissions. Clientele: 20% private collectors, 80% corporate clients. Represents 30 artists. Average display time 6 months. Accepts primarily artists from the Delaware Valley, with recognizable Philadelphia subjects. Interested in emerging, mid-career and established artists. Overall price range: $25-10,000; most artwork sold at $150-800.

Media: Considers oil, acrylic, watercolor, pastel, pen & ink, drawings, mixed media, collage, works on paper, sculpture, fiber, photography, woodcuts, wood engravings, linocuts, engravings, mezzotints, etchings, lithographs and serigraphs. Most frequently exhibits serigraphs and photos.

Style: Exhibits impressionism, realism, photorealism, minimalism, color field, painterly abstraction, conceptualism. Considers all styles. Genres include landscapes, Americana and figurative work. Prefers landmarks, Philadelphia activities and Philadelphia symbols. "Any artist or photographer whose work includes painting, sculpture, illustration, print editions or photographs can register for the slide registry. Today, we're a major contributor of Philadelphia subject matter to the sales and rental gallery of the Philadelphia Museum of Art."

Terms: Accepts work on consignment (40% commission). Retail price set by gallery and artist. Exclusive area representation not required. Gallery provides some insurance and some promotion. Shipping costs are shared.

Submissions: Send query letter with resume, slides, SASE, brochure, price and bio. Replies in 3 weeks.

Tips: Contact us "only if you have art that shows Philadelphia's recognizable subjects, or if you care to be listed in our general art files for commissions and search reference."

ART INSTITUTE OF PHILADELPHIA, 1622 Chestnut St., Philadelphia PA 19103. (215)567-7080. Gallery Coordinator: Sandra L. Kelly. School gallery. Estab. 1981. Clientele: 50% private collectors, 50% corporate clients. Sponsors 2 solo and 10 group shows/year. Average display time 1 month. We would like artwork to be educational and of interest for our students. Overall price range: $200-1,500.
Media: Considers oil, acrylic, watercolor, pastel, pen & ink, drawings, mixed media, collage, works on paper, photography and lithographs. Most frequently exhibits watercolor, graphics, photography and illustration.
Style: Exhibits impressionism, realism, photorealism and photography. Genres include landscapes, florals, wildlife and portraits. Prefers landscapes, graphics, and illustration. "Our gallery was established as an educational tool for our students. We also are concerned with the community at large. We hope to bring them informative and enlightening exhibits. We deal in many Philadelphia organizations such as the Philadelphia Watercolor Club, Art Alliance, American Institute of Graphic Arts, Interior Design Council, Color Print Society, etc."
Terms: Retail price set by artist. Exclusive area representation not required. Gallery provides insurance. Prefers artwork framed.
Submissions: Send query letter with slides, brochure, and photographs. Schedule a meeting if possible. Artists should call to schedule an appointment to show a portfolio, which should include slides and photographs. Replies in 2 weeks.
Tips: "Artists need to call six months to one year in advance."

*THE BLUE SKY GALLERY, INC., 6022 Penn Circle S., Pittsburgh PA 15232. (412)661-3600. Director: Mimsie Stuhldreher. Retail gallery. Estab. 1972. Represents 22 emerging, mid-career and established artists. Sponsors 9 show/year. Average display time 1 month. Open all year. Located in "East end; 3,000 sq. ft.; contemporary in design." 50% of space for special exhibitions. Clientele: 50% private collectors, 50% corporate clients. Overall price range: $350-10,000.
Media: Considers oil, acrylic, watercolor, drawings, mixed media, collage, works on paper, sculpture, ceramic, fiber, glass, photography, collector-quality craft and original handpulled prints, woodcuts, engravings, lithographs, posters, wood engravings, serigraphs, linocuts and etchings. Most frequently exhibits oil, watercolor and fiber.
Style: Exhibits expressionism, painterly abstraction, minimalism, impressionism, realism and photorealism. Genres include landscapes, florals and Americana. Prefers impressionism, realism and abstract.
Terms: Artwork is accepted on consignment (50% commission). Craft art only is bought for 50% of the retail price. Retail price set by the gallery and the artist. Gallery provides insurance and promotion; gallery pays for shipping costs for craft art only; otherwise artist pays for shipping or shipping costs are shared.
Submissions: Send query letter with resume, slides, bio and SASE. Write to schedule an appointment to show a portfolio, which should include slides and photographs. Replies in 1 month. Files "work we are interested in."

*CARNEGIE MELLON ART GALLERY, 407 S. Craig St., Pittsburgh PA 15213. (412)268-3110. Director: Elaine A. King. Nonprofit Institute of Contemporary Art. Estab. 1985. Exhibits emerging, mid-career and established artists. Exhibited artists include Michael Gitlin, Elizabeth Murray and Jeanne Dunning. Sponsors 6-8 shows/year. Average display time 6 weeks. Open fall through late spring. Located in the "east end of Pittsburgh; two floors of exhibition space."
Media: Considers oil, acrylic, watercolor, pastel, pen & ink, drawings, mixed media, works on paper, sculpture, ceramic, glass, installation and photography. Most frequently exhibits sculpture, drawing, site-specific work.
Style: Exhibits conceptualism, minimalism and a wide range of abstraction.
Terms: "As a nonprofit gallery we exhibit artworks vs. the selling of the art." Retail price set by the artist. Gallery provides insurance. Gallery pays for shipping costs to and from gallery.
Submissions: Prefers only "contemporary works, strong ideas." Send query letter with resume, slides, bio, photographs, SASE and reviews. Call to schedule an appointment to show a portfolio. Portolio should include slides and transparencies. Replies in 2-3 months. Files "everything, unless the artist wishes the return of slides." Will only consider art for exhibition after studio visit.
Tips: "Call to make an appointment. Walking in with a portfolio is not encouraged."

CIRCLE GALLERY, 5416 Walnut St., Pittsburgh PA 15232. (412)687-1336. Director: Beth Evans. Retail gallery. Estab. 1972. Located on a village shopping street. Clientele: 70% private collectors, 30% corporate clients. Represents 250 artists. Sponsors 8-10 solo and 1-2 group shows/year. Average display time 2 weeks. Interested in established artists. Overall price range: $150-125,000; most artwork sold at $700-1,500.
Media: Considers oil, watercolor, pastel, pen & ink, drawings, collage, works on paper, sculpture, fiber, glass, woodcuts, wood engravings, engravings, etchings, lithographs and serigraphs. Most frequently exhibits lithographs, oil paintings and sculpture.
Style: Exhibits impressionism, expressionism, primitivism, painterly abstraction, conceptualism and hard-edge geometric abstraction. Genres include landscapes, florals, portraits and figurative work. Prefers figurative work, landscapes and conceptualism. "We represent established artists—artists whose work we have at

some time published usually, e.g. Rockwell, Erté and Vasarely. We contract with artists such as Calman Shemi and Marcel Salinas to represent them in the States and so we carry their originals and lithographs (if applicable)."

Terms: Accepts work on consignment (1% commission). Retail price set by gallery. Exclusive area representation required. Gallery provides promotion, contract and shipping costs from gallery. Prefers framed artwork.

Submissions: "Contact Jack Solomon, chairman, Circle Fine Art Corporation, Suite 3160, 875 N. Michigan Avenue, Chicago IL 60611."

CONCEPT ART GALLERY, 1031 S. Braddock Ave., Pittsburgh PA 15218. (412)242-9200. Director: Sam Berkovitz. Retail gallery. Estab. 1971. Clientele: 50% private collectors, 50% corporate clients. Represents 40 artists. Sponsors 4 solo and 4 group shows/year. Average display time is 1 month. Interested in emerging and established artists. Overall price range: $50-25,000; most artwork sold at $300-1,000.

Media: Considers oil, acrylic, watercolor, pastel, pen & ink, drawings, mixed media, collage, works on paper, sculpture, ceramic, craft, fiber, glass and limited edition original handpulled prints. Most frequently exhibits watercolor, prints and paintings.

Style: Exhibits geometric abstraction, color field, painterly abstraction, impressionistic, photorealistic, expressionistic and neo-expressionistic works. Genres include landscapes and florals, 19th century European and American paintings.

Terms: Accepts work on consignment (25-50% commission) or buys outright. Retail price is set by gallery. Exclusive area representation required. Gallery provides insurance and promotion; shipping costs are shared.

Submissions: Send query letter with resume, brochure, slides, photographs and SASE. Slides and biographies are filed.

DOLAN/MAXWELL GALLERY, 1701 Walnut St., Philadelphia PA 19103. (215)665-1701. Director: Rachel Robertson Maxwell. Retail gallery. Estab. 1984. Clientele: 60% private collectors, 40% corporate clients. Represents 40 artists. Sponsors 10 solo and 2 group shows/year. Average display time 1 month. Interested in emerging and established artists. Overall price range: $500-50,000; most work sold at $4,000-5,000.

Media: Considers oil, acrylic, watercolor, pastel, pen & ink, drawings, mixed media, collage, sculpture, woodcuts, wood engravings, linocuts, engravings, mezzotints, etchings, lithographs and serigraphs.

Style: Exhibits all styles. "Dolan/Maxwell specializes in contemporary paintings, sculpture, works on paper and contemporary master prints."

Terms: Accepts work on consignment (50% commission). Buys outright (70-80% retail price; net 30 days). Retail price set by gallery and artist. Gallery provides insurance and promotion; shipping costs are shared. Prefers artwork unframed.

Submissions: Send query letter with resume, slides, bio and SASE. Replies in 1 month. All material is returned if not accepted or under consideration.

DREXEL UNIVERSITY DESIGN ARTS GALLERY, Dept. of Interiors and Graphic Design, Philadelphia PA 19104. (215)895-2390. Gallery Coordinator: Stuart Rome. Nonprofit gallery. Clientele: students, artists and Philadelphia community. Sponsors 7 solo and 2 group shows/year. Display time 1 month.

Media: Considers oil, acrylic, watercolor, pastel, pen & ink, drawings, mixed media, collage, works on paper, sculpture, ceramic, craft, fiber, glass, installation and photography.

Style: Exhibits all styles and genres. Prefers narrative, political and design oriented work. "Our gallery is a teaching tool for a design arts gallery whose students are instructed in visual communication. Our shows are designed to be the best examples of these categories."

Terms: Exclusive area representation not required. Gallery provides insurance and promotion. Prefers artwork framed.

Submissions: Send query letter with resume, brochure, slides and SASE. Write to schedule an appointment to show a portfolio, which should include slides. Replies only if interested within 1 month. Files resumes. All material is returned if not accepted or under consideration.

*DORIS FORDHAM GALLERY, INC., 421 S. State St., Clarks Summit PA 18411. (717)586-0088. President: Doris Fordham. Retail gallery and art consultancy. Estab. 1980. Clientele: 50% private collectors, 50% corporate clients. Represents 15 artists/year. Sponsors 6 solo shows/year. Average display time is 3-6 weeks. Interested in established artists only. Overall price range: $250-5,000; most artwork sold at $500-1,500.

Media: Considers oil, acrylic, watercolor, pastel, mixed media, collage and limited edition original handpulled prints. Most frequently exhibits watercolor, oil and pastel.

Style: Exhibits painterly abstraction, impressionistic, expressionistic, neo-expressionistic, realist, surrealist and naif works. Genres include landscapes, florals, portraits, figurative work and still lifes. Most frequently exhibits landscape, floral and still life. Does not want to see sentimentality

Terms: Accepts work on consignment (40% commission). Buys limited edition multiples outright (net 30 days). Retail price is set by gallery or artist. Exclusive area representation not required. Gallery provides insurance, promotion and contract; shipping costs are shared.

Submissions: Send query letter with resume and slides, and "an enlargement of a photo of work is a good idea. Then write for arrangements to show original work." Resume and "my notations concerning the work" are filed.

*PEARL FOX GALLERY, 103 Windsor Ave., Melrose Park PA 19126. (215)635-4586. Owner: Pearl Fox. Retail gallery. Estab. 1948. Clientele: individuals, schools, builders and other corporations. Represents 22 artists. Sponsors 3 solo and 3 group shows/year. Average display time is 2 weeks. Interested in emerging, mid-career and "principally" established artists.
Media: Considers oil, acrylic, watercolor, pastel, pen & ink, drawings, mixed media, collage, works on paper, sculpture, ceramic, craft, fiber, glass and jewelry. Most frequently exhibits oil, polymer tempera and watercolor.
Style: Exhibits hard-edge geometric abstraction, painterly abstraction, primitivism, impressionism, realism and surrealism. Genres include landscapes, florals, portraits, figurative work and fantasy illustration. Most frequently exhibits realism, surrealism and abstraction. Wants museum-quality work.
Terms: Accepts work on consignment (40% commission). Retail price is set by gallery or artist. Exclusive area representation required. Gallery provides insurance, promotion and contract; shipping costs are shared.
Submissions: Send query letter with resume, photographs and SASE. Call to schedule an appointment to show a portfolio, which should include originals. Resumes, catalogs, reviews and photographs are filed.

GALLERY G, 211 9th St., Pittsburgh PA 15222. (412)562-0912. Director: Carol Siegel. Retail gallery and "art resource for design trade." Estab. 1974. Clientele: corporate and commercial, 25% private collectors, 75% corporate clients. Represents 83 artists. Sponsors 2 solo and 2 group shows/year. Interested in mid-career and established artists. Overall price range: $90-10,000; most artwork sold at $500-800.
Media: Considers oil, acrylic, watercolor, pastel, drawings, mixed media, collage, works on paper, sculpture, ceramic, craft, fiber, glass, egg tempera, woodcuts, wood engravings, linocuts, engravings, mezzotints, etchings, lithographs, serigraphs, offset reproductions and posters. Most frequently exhibits oil/acrylic painting, sculpture and handmade paper.
Style: Exhibits impressionism, expressionism, neo-expressionism, realism, photorealism, minimalism, primitivism, color field, painterly abstraction, conceptualism, post modern works, imagism, pattern painting and hard-edge geometric abstraction; considers all styles. Genres include landscapes, florals, Americana, wildlife and figurative work; considers all genres. Prefers realism, impressionism and color field.
Terms: Accepts work on consignment (40% commission) or buys outright (50% retail price; net 30 days). Retail price set by artist. Exclusive area representation required, 150 mile radius. Gallery provides insurance, promotion, contract and shipping from gallery. Prefers framed artwork.
Submissions: Send query letter with resume, brochure, slides, photographs, bio and SASE. Write to schedule an appointment to show a portfolio, which should include complete slide portfolio, transparencies, photographs, "bio and other info." Replies in 3 months. Files materials only of artists accepted for representation. All material is returned if not accepted or under consideration.
Tips: "We are a resource for the design/contract design industry. We are located in the cultural district in the heart of downtown. We show mainly work of established, well-known artists."

*LEN GARON ART STUDIOS, 1742 Valley Greene Rd., Paoli PA 19301. (215)296-3481. Director of Marketing: Phil Hahn. Wholesale gallery. Estab. 1982. Represents 7 emerging, mid-career and established artists. Exhibited artists include Len Garon and Anna Chen. "I sell previously published prints, lithographs, etchings, etc., plus test market original paintings prior to printing the image to press image." Clientele: galleries, frameshops, designers and furniture stores. Most artwork sold at $50-450.
Media: Considers original handpulled prints, offset reproductions, woodcuts, lithographs, posters, mezzotints, serigraphs and etchings.
Style: Exhibits, expressionism, painterly abstraction, impressionism and realism. Genres include landscapes, florals, Americana, Southwestern, Western, wildlife and figurative work. Prefers landscapes, florals and Americana.
Terms: "I sell from samples, then purchase outright." Retail price set by the artist. Gallery pays for shipping costs from gallery. Prefers unframed but matted artwork.
Submissions: Send query letter with photographs, SASE, reviews and samples of prints. Write to schedule an appointment to show a portfolio. Portfolio should include slides, photographs and samples of prints. Replies in 2 weeks.
Tips: "Send prints that are most commercially salable. Painting with the color trends helps sell work to the 3 markets: corporate art, home interior art (decorative) and investor and collectable art."

GROSS MCCLEAF GALLERY, 127 S. 16th St., Philadelphia PA 19102. Director: Estelle Gross. Retail gallery. Estab. 1969. Open all year. Clientele: 40% private collectors, 60% corporate clients. Represents 40-50 artists. Sponsors 9 solo and 6 group shows/year. Average display time 3 weeks. Interested in established artists. Overall price range: $300-10,000; most artwork sold at $1,500-3,000.

Media: Considers oil, acrylic, watercolor, pastel, pen & ink, drawings, mixed media, collage and works on paper. Most frequently exhibits oil/canvas, gouache and pastel.

Style: Exhibits realism and photorealism. Genres include landscapes. Prefers landscapes, still lifes and urban scapes. "Over the years, a wide range of painting style and movements have been shown at Gross McCleaf, but exhibiting the works of painterly realists has been an aesthetic form to which the gallery has been committed for over twenty years."

Terms: Accepts work on consignment. Retail price set by gallery and artist. Exclusive area representation required. Gallery provides insurance, promotion and contract. Artist pays for shipping. Prefers framed artwork.

Submissions: Send query letter with resume, professional slides, SASE, price list and bio. Write to schedule an appointment to show a portfolio. Replies in 1 week.

Tips: "We do not want to see abstract expressionism or neo-expressionism. Common mistakes include not visiting the gallery and knowing the kind of work we carry or the level of expertise we expect or the prices we will consider." Sees trends toward "less interest in investing in so-called 'investment art' and more interest in regional artists. Less interest in 'name' prints. More awareness of art publications and auctions."

*DENE M. LOUCHHEIM GALLERIES, FLEISHER ART MEMORIAL, 709-719 Catharine St., Philadelphia PA 19147. (215)922-3456. Gallery Coordinator: Lanny Bergner. Nonprofit gallery. Sponsors Challenge Exhibitions, 4 juried exhibits per year. Estab. 1978. Clientele: art collectors, curators, dealers, artists. Sponsors 8 shows/year. Average display time is 3 weeks. Accepts regional artists only (50 mile radius of Philadelphia). Interested in emerging artists. Price range: $500-5,000.

Media: Considers oil, acrylic, watercolor, pastel, pen & ink, drawings, mixed media, collage, works on paper, sculpture, ceramic, fiber, glass, installation, photography, performance art and limited edition handpulled prints. Most frequently exhibits painting, sculpture and photography.

Style: Considers all styles. "The work should seek to explore the boundaries of art, not the established norms. Fleisher is an excellent place to show installation sculpture and work that receives little commercial exposure."

Terms: Accepts work on consignment (20% commission). Retail price is set by artist. Exclusive area representation not required. Gallery provides insurance, promotion and contract.

Submissions: Send query letter. "Challenge Exhibitions juried shows brochure sent in January to artists telling how to apply."

MAIN LINE CENTER OF THE ARTS, Old Buck Rd. and Lancaster Ave., Haverford PA 19041. (215)525-0272. Director: Judy Herman. Nonprofit gallery. Clientele: 100% private collectors. Average display time 4 weeks. Accepts only artists from tri-state area (Pennsylvania, New Jersey, Delaware). Interested in emerging and established artists. Overall price range: $20-3,000; most artwork sold at $40-300.

Media: Considers oil, acrylic, watercolor, pastel, pen & ink, drawings, mixed media, collage, works on paper, sculpture, ceramic, craft, fiber, glass and original handpulled prints. Most frequently exhibits works on paper, paintings and sculpture.

Style: Exhibits all styles and all genres. "Main Line Center of the Arts has a varied exhibition schedule to complement its educational mission to serve Montgomery and Delaware counties with classes and a wide range of arts activities as well as to create an active forum for artists in this community. Our annual schedule includes a juried painting and sculpture exhibition, a juried works on paper exhibition, a juried craft exhibition, a faculty exhibition, student and professional members' exhibitions and exhibitions of public school artwork."

Terms: Accepts work on consignment (30% commission). Retail price set by artist. Exclusive area representation not required. Gallery provides promotion and contract; artist pays for shipping.

Submissions: Send query letter with resume, slides and SASE. Call or write to schedule an appointment to show a portfolio, which should include originals and slides. Files resumes. All material is returned if not accepted or under consideration.

THE MORE GALLERY, 1630 Walnut St., Philadelphia PA 19103. (215)735-1827. Director: Charles N. More. Retail gallery. Estab. 1980. Clientele: 70% private collectors, 30% corporate clients. Represents 20 artists. Sponsors 9 solo and 3 group shows/year. Average display time is 4 weeks.

Media: Most frequently exhibits oil, acrylic, drawings and sculpture.

Style: Exhibits contemporary styles.

MUSE GALLERY, 1915 Walnut St., Philadelphia PA 19103. (215)963-0959. Director: Louise Masi. Cooperative and nonprofit gallery. Represents 17 artists. Sponsors 8 solo and 4 group shows/year. Average display time 1 month. Accepts only artists form the tri-state areas. Interested in emerging and established artists. Overall price range: $200-3,000; most work sold at $1,000-1,500.

Media: Considers oil, acrylic, watercolor, pastel, pen & ink, drawings, mixed media, collage, works on paper, sculpture, ceramic, fiber, glass, installation, photography, egg tempera, woodcuts, wood engravings, linocuts, engravings, mezzotints, etchings, lithographs, pochoir, serigraphs and offset reproductions. Most frequently exhibits paintings, sculpture and photography.

Style: Exhibits all styles and genres. Prefers figurative, post-modern and surrealist works. "The Muse Gallery was founded as a women's cooperative to give appropriate opportunities to professional women artists to show their work. We specialize in a diversity of contemporary art pieces."

Terms: Co-op membership fee plus donation of time; 10% commission. Retail price set by artist. Exclusive area representation not required. Prefers artwork framed.

Submissions: Send query letter with resume, 5-21 slides, photographs, bios and SASE. Write to schedule an appointment to show a portfolio, which should include slides. Replies in 1 week. All material is returned if not accepted or under consideration.

Tips: "Send quality slides and show consistency in subject and medium."

NEWMAN GALLERIES, 1625 Walnut St., Philadelphia PA 19103; 850 W. Lancaster Ave., Bryn Mawr PA 19010. (215)563-1779. Vice President: W. Andrews Newman III. Retail gallery. Estab. 1865. Open all year. Located in Center City and in suburbs. "Largest and oldest gallery in Philadelphia." Clientele: 90% private collectors, 10% corporate clients. Represents over 100 artists. Sponsors 8 solo shows/year. Average display time 4 weeks. Interested in emerging and established artists. Overall price range: $250-100,000; most artwork sold at $2,500-25,000.

Media: Considers oil, acrylic, watercolor, pastel, pen & ink, drawings, mixed media, egg tempera, woodcuts, wood engravings, linocuts, engravings, mezzotints, etchings, lithographs and serigraphs. Most frequently exhibits watercolor and oil/acrylic paintings and etchings.

Style: Exhibits impressionism and realism. Genres include landscapes, florals, Americana, wildlife and figurative work. Prefers landscapes, Americana and wildlife/floral works . "We handle many artists, most of whom work in a very traditional or representational style. Our center city gallery specializes in 19th- and early 20th-century American and European painting. We hold our special exhibitions for contemporary American artists at our suburban gallery. Large exhibitions are held at our center city gallery and are promoted."

Terms: Accepts work on consignment (33-40% commission). Retail price set by gallery and artist. Exclusive area representation required. Gallery provides insurance and promotion; shipping costs are shared.

Submissions: Send query letter with resume, slides, SASE, brochure and photographs. Call to schedule an appointment to show a portfolio, which should include originals, slides, transparencies and photographs. Replies in 1 month. All material is returned if not accepted or under consideration.

*OLIN FINE ARTS CENTER GALLERY, Washington and Jefferson College, Washington PA 15301. (412)223-6084. Director: Paul B. Edwards. College gallery. Estab. 1982. Represents emerging, mid-career and established artists. Sponsors 10 shows/year. Average display time 3 weeks. Closed summers. Located near downtown; 1,925 sq. ft.

Style: Does not want to see commercial or clichéd work.

Tips: "Send cover letter and slides, resume, etc. Younger artists are getting more attention."

*PHILADELPHIA ART ALLIANCE, 251 S. 18th St., Philadephia PA 19103. Director: Dr. Marilyn J.S. Goodman. Nonprofit gallery. Estab. 1915. Clientele: members and public; 20% private collectors, 20% corporate clients, 30% artists, performers, actors, etc. Sponsors 14 solo and 7 group shows/year. Average display time is 6 weeks. Interested in emerging, mid-career and established artists. Overall price range: $100 and up; most artwork sold at $500.

Media: Considers all media. Most frequently exhibits oil, acrylic and drawings.

Style: Exhibits contemporary, abstract, primitive and non-representational; small works, jewelry, in display case.

Terms: Accepts work on consignment (40% commission). Retail price is set by gallery or artist. Exclusive area representation not required. Gallery provides insurance, promotion and contract; shipping costs are shared.

Submissions: Send query letter, SASE with resume and 10 slides. One color slides with resume are filed. Slides reviewed in January and June of each year. Must be received at least 3 weeks prior.

Tips: Does not want to see "student work/amateur work."

SAINT JOSEPH'S UNIVERSITY GALLERY, 5600 City Line Ave., Philadelphia PA 19131. Assistant Gallery Director: Timothy W. Shea. Nonprofit gallery. Represents emerging, mid-career and established artists. Sponsors 5 solo and 1 group shows/year. Average display time 1 month.

Media: Considers all media.

Style: Exhibits all styles and genres.

Terms: Retail price set by artist. Exclusive area representation required. Gallery provides insurance and promotion; artist pays for shipping. Prefers framed artwork.

Submissions: Send query letter with resume, slides, bio and SASE. Write to schedule an appointment to show a portfolio. Replies in 4 months. All material is returned if not accepted or under consideration.

THE STATE MUSEUM OF PENNSYLVANIA, 3rd and North St., Box 1026, Harrisburg PA 17108-1026. (717)787-4980. Curator of Fine Arts: Sylvia Laveis. Museum. Estab. 1905. Sponsors 9 group shows/year. Average display time 6 months. Accepts only artists from Pennsylvania. Interested in established artists.
Media: Considers oil, acrylic, watercolor, pastel, pen & ink, drawings, mixed media, collage, works on paper, sculpture, ceramic, craft, fiber, glass, egg tempera, woodcuts, wood engravings, linocuts, engravings, mezzotints, etchings and lithographs.
Style: Exhibits all styles and genres. "The State Museum of Pennsylvania is the official museum of the Commonwealth, to collect, preserve and exhibit Pennsylvania history, culture and natural heritage. The Museum maintains the Pennsylvania Collection of Fine Arts, representing all periods and styles of fine art from the founding of the state to the present. The Museum is also responsible for exhibitions at the Governor's Home and for limited displays of art work in the State Capitol offices of senior officials. The Museum maintains a research file of information on all known Pennsylvania artists."
Submissions: Send query letter with resume, slides and bio. Replies in 1 month. Files resume, bio, exhibit history and photos. All material is returned if not accepted or under consideration.

Rhode Island

ARNOLD ART, 210 Thames, Newport RI 02840. (401)847-2273. President: Bill Rommel. Retail gallery. Estab. 1870. Clientele: tourists and Newport collectors; 95% private collectors, 5% corporate clients. Represents 10-20 artists. Sponsors 6-8 solo or group shows/year. Average display time 2 weeks. Overall price range: $150-12,000; most artwork sold at $150-750.
Media: Considers oil, acrylic, watercolor, pastel, pen & ink, drawings, mixed media, limited edition offset reproductions, color prints and posters. Most frequently exhibits oil, acrylic and watercolor.
Style: Exhibits painterly abstraction, primitivism, photorealism and realism. Genres include landscapes and florals. Specializes in marine art and local landscapes.
Terms: Accepts work on consignment. Retail price is set by gallery or artist. Exclusive area representation not required. Gallery provides insurance, promotion and contract.
Submissions: Send query letter with resume and slides. Call for an appointment to show a portfolio, which should include originals. Resume and slides are filed.

LENORE GRAY GALLERY, INC., 15 Meeting St., Providence RI 02903. (401)274-3900. Director: Lenore Gray. Retail gallery. Estab. about 1970. Sponsors 6 solo and 6 group shows/year. Average display varies. Interested in emerging, mid-career and established artists.
Media: Considers oil, acrylic, watercolor, pastel, drawings, sculpture, photography, mixed media, glass, installation and color and b&w original handpulled prints.
Style: Exhibits contemporary, abstract, Americana, impressionistic, figurative, landscape, primitive, non-representational, photo-realistic, realistic, neo-expressionisitic and post-pop works.
Terms: Accepts work on consignment. Retail price is set by gallery or artist. Exclusive area representation required. Gallery provides insurance.
Submissions: Send query letter with resume, slides, photographs or SASE. Write for an appointment to show a portfolio.

South Carolina

ANDERSON COUNTY ARTS COUNCIL, 405 N. Main St., Anderson SC 29621. (803)224-8811. Executive Director: Diane B. Lee. Program Director: Kimberly Spears. Nonprofit gallery of county art center. Estab. 1972. Clientele: community and tourists. Sponsors about 9 shows/year; local, regional and national. Average display time 4-6 weeks. Interested in emerging and established artists. Overall price range: $100-5,000; most work sold at $100-1,500.
Media: Considers all media. Most frequently exhibits watercolor and 3-dimensional works.
Style: Exhibits all styles and genres. Prefers realism and abstraction. "The Anderson County Arts Council is composed of individuals and organizations interested in the promotion of the visual and performing arts and those wishing to preserve Anderson County cultural growth."
Terms: Accepts work on consignment (30% commission). Retail price set by artist. Gallery provides insurance and promotion; artist pays for shipping.
Submissions: Send query letter with resume, slides and bio. Call or write to schedule an appointment to show a portfolio, which should include originals and slides. Replies in 3 months. All material is returned if not accepted or under consideration.

CECELIA COKER BELL GALLERY, College Ave., Hartsville, SC 29550. (803)332-1381. Director: Kim Chalmers. "The Cecelia Coker Bell Gallery is a campus-located teaching gallery which exhibits a great diversity of media and style to the advantage of exposing students and the community to the breadth of possibility for expression in art. Primarily exhibiting regional artists with an emphasis on quality. Features international shows of emerging artists and sponsors competitions." Estab. 1984. Sponsors 8 solo and 2 group shows/year. Average display time is 3 weeks. Interested in emerging artists.

Media: Considers oil, acrylic, drawings, mixed media, collage, works on paper, sculpture, installation, photography, performance art, graphic design and printmaking. Most frequently exhibits painting, sculpture/installation and mixed media.

Style: Considers all styles. Not interested in conservative/commercial art.

Terms: Retail price is set by artist. Exclusive area representation not required. Gallery provides insurance, promotion and contract; shipping costs are shared.

Submissions: Send query letter with resume, slides and SASE. Write for an appointment to show a portfolio, which should include slides. Resumes are filed.

BROOKGREEN GARDENS, US 17 South, Murrells Inlet SC 29576. (803)237-4218. Director: Gurdon L. Tarbox, Jr. Museum. Estab. 1931. Outdoor garden. Clientele: tourists and local residents. Represents 205 artists. Places permanent installations. Accepts only sculpture by American citizens. Interested in emerging, mid-career and established artists.

Style: Exhibits realism and figurative work. Prefers figurative and wildlife. Gallery shows work by "American sculptor by birth or naturalization; figurative sculpture in permanent materials such as non-ferrous metals or hardstone such as marble, limestone or granite. We suggest you obtain a copy of "A Century of American Sculpture: Treasures from Brookgreen Gardens."

Terms: Buys outright. Retail price set by artist.

Submissions: Send query letter with resume, brochure, slides and photographs. Write to schedule an appointment to show a portfolio, which should include originals, slides, transparencies and photographs. Replies in 6 months. Files all material. All material is returned if requested, if not accepted or under consideration.

Tips: Artists seem to "think Brookgreen Gardens is wealthy. It is not!"

South Dakota

THE HERITAGE CENTER, INC., Red Cloud Indian School, Pine Ridge SD 57770. (605)867-5491. Director: Brother Simon. Nonprofit gallery. Estab. 1984. Clientele: 80% private collectors. Sponsors 6 group shows/year. Represents emerging, mid-career and established artists. Average display time is 10 weeks. Accepts only Native Americans. Price range: $50-1,500; most artwork sold at $100-400.

Media: Considers oil, acrylic, watercolor, pastel, pen & ink, drawings, sculpture and original handpulled prints.

Style: Exhibits contemporary, impressionistic, primitive, Western and realistic works. Specializes in Native American art (works by Native Americans).

Terms: Accepts work on consignment (20% commission). Retail price is set by artist. Exclusive area representation not required. Gallery provides insurance and promotion; artist pays for shipping.

Submissions: Send query letter, resume, brochure and photographs.

Tips: "Show art properly matted or framed. Don't present commercial prints as handpulled prints." Write for information about annual Red Cloud Indian Art Show.

Tennessee

CUMBERLAND GALLERY, 4107 Hillsboro Circle, Nashville TN 37215. (615)297-0296. Director: Carol Stein. Retail gallery. Estab. 1980. Clientele: 60% private collectors; 40% corporate clients. Represents 35 artists. Sponsors 6 solo and 2 group shows/year. Average display time 5 weeks. Interested in emerging and established artists. Overall price range: $450-15,000; most work sold at $1,000-5,000.

Media: Considers oil, acrylic, watercolor, pastel, mixed media, collage, works on paper, sculpture, photography, woodcuts, wood engravings, linocuts, engravings, mezzotints and etchings. Most frequently exhibits paintings, drawings and sculpture.

Style: Exhibits realism, photorealism, minimalism, painterly abstraction, post modernism and hard-edge geometric abstraction. Prefers landscapes, abstraction, realism and minimalism. "Since its inception in 1980, Cumberland Gallery has focused on contemporary art forms including paintings, works on paper, sculpture and multiples. Approximately fifty percent of the artists represented have national reputations and fifty percent are strongly emerging artists. These individuals are geographically dispersed, about half reside in the Southeast."

Tips: "I would hope that an artist would visit the gallery and participate on the mailing list so that he/she has a sense of what we are doing. It would be helpful for the artist to request information with regard to how Cumberland Gallery prefers work to be considered for inclusion. I suggest slides, resume, recent articles and a SASE for return of slides."

*EATON GALLERY, 171 S. Cooper St., Memphis TN 38104. (901)272-9311. FAX: (901)272-9311. Owner/Director: Sandra Saunders. Retail gallery. Estab. 1984. Represents 20 emerging, mid-career and established artists. Exhibited artists include Charles Inzer. Sponsors 10 shows in Gallery I/10 in Gallery II. Average display time 1 month. Open all year. Closed in August for 2 weeks. Located in mid-town; 2,200 sq. ft.; "the interior is spectacular." 800 sq. ft. of space for special exhibitions. Clientele: 80% private collectors, 20% corporate clients. Overall price range: $350-10,000; most artwork sold at $1,500-4,500.

Media: Considers oil, acrylic, watercolor, pastel, drawings, mixed media, works on paper and sculpture. Considers original handpulled prints, woodcuts, engravings, lithographs, mezzotints, serigraphs and etchings. Most frequently exhibits oil, acrylic and watercolor.

Style: Exhibits expressionism, painterly abstraction, color field, impressionism and realism. Genres include landscapes, florals, Americana, Southwestern, portraits and figurative work. Prefers impressionism, expressionism and realism.

Terms: Artwork is accepted on consignment and there is a 50% commission. Retail price set by the artist or both the gallery and the artist. Gallery provides insurance, promotion and contract. Artist pays for shipping. Prefers framed artwork.

Submissions: Send query letter with resume, bio, photographs and reviews. Write to schedule an appointment to show a portfolio. Portfolio should include originals and photographs. Replies in 1 week. Files photos and "anything else the artists will give us."

Tips: "Just contact us—we are here for you."

EDELSTEIN/DATTEL ART INVESTMENTS, 4134 Hedge Hills Ave., Memphis TN 38117. (901)767-0425. Owner/Director: Paul R. Edelstein. Retail gallery. Estab. 1985. Clientele: 80% private collectors, 20% corporate clients. Represents over 30 artists. Sponsors 2 solo and 2 group shows/year. Average display time is 1 month. Interested in emerging, mid-career and established artists. Price range: $300-4,800.

Media: Considers oil, acrylic, watercolor, pastel, pen & ink, drawings, mixed media, collage, works on paper, sculpture, ceramic, fiber, glass, photography and limited edition prints. Most frequently exhibits oil, watercolor and drawings.

Style: Exhibits hard-edge geometric abstraction, color field, painterly abstraction, minimalism, post modern feminist/political works, primitivism, photorealism, expressionism and neo-expressionism. Genres include landscapes, florals, Americana, portraits and figurative work. Most frequently exhibits primitive, painterly abstraction and expressionism. "Especially seeks new folk artists and N.Y. SoHo undiscovered artists." Specializes in contemporary and black folk art; Southern regionalism.

Terms: Accepts work on consignment (40% commission) or buys outright. Retail price is set by gallery. Exclusive area representation required. Gallery provides insurance, promotion and contract.

Submissions: Send query letter with resume, brochure, business card, slides, photographs and SASE. Call or write to schedule an appointment to show a portfolio, which should include originals, slides or transparencies. Biographies and resumes of artists are slides are filed. "Most artists do not present enough slides or their biographies are incomplete. Professional artists need to be more organized when presenting their work."

Tips: "Meet me in person with your original works."

*THE PARTHENON, Centennial Park, Nashville TN 37201. (615)259-6358. Museum Director: Miss Wesley Paine. Nonprofit gallery in a full-size replica of the Greek Parthenon. Estab. 1931. Clientele: general public, tourists; 50% private collectors, 50% corporate clients. Sponsors 8 solo and 6 group shows/year. Average display time is 6 weeks. Interested in emerging and established artists. Overall price range: $300-1,000; most artwork sold at $400.

Media: Considers "nearly all" media.

Style: Exhibits contemporary works, impressionism and American expressionism. Currently seeking contemporary works.

Terms: Accepts work on consignment (20% commission). Retail price is set by artist. Exclusive area representation not required. Gallery provides a contract and limited promotion.

Submissions: Send query letter with resume and slides.

SLOCUMB GALLERY, East Tennessee State University, Department of Art, Box 23740A, Johnson City, TN 37614-0002. (615)929-4247. Director: M. Wayne Dyer. Nonprofit university gallery. Estab. 1960. Sponsors 2-3 solo and 5 group shows/year. Average display time is 1 month. Interested in emerging, mid-career and established artists. Price range: $100-5,000; most artwork sold at $500.

Media: Considers all media.

Style: Exhibits contemporary, abstract, figurative, primitive, non-representational, photorealistic, realistic, neo-expressionistic and post-pop styles and landscapes.

Submissions: Send query letter with resume and slides. Call or write to schedule an appointment to show a portfolio. Slides and resumes are filed.

Texas

*ADAMS-MIDDLETON GALLERY, 3000 Maple Ave., Dallas TX 75201. (214)871-7080. President: Anita Middleton. Retail gallery. Estab. 1980. Clientele: new and seasoned collectors, large and small corporations and interior designers. Represents 25 artists. Sponsors 9 solo and 3 group shows/year. Average display time is 1 month. Interested in emerging, mid-career and established artists. Overall price range: $500-100,000; most artwork sold at $4,000-5,000.

Media: Considers oil, acrylic, pastel, drawings, sculpture, mixed media, collage and original handpulled prints.

Style: Exhibits contemporary, abstract, figurative, landscapes, non-representational, photorealistic, realistic and post-pop works.

Terms: Accepts work on consignment (50% commission). Retail price is set by gallery and artist. Exclusive area representation required. Gallery provides contract; shipping costs are shared.

Submissions: Send query letter, resume, brochure and slides. Write to schedule an appointment to show a portfolio. Slides, resumes, prices "on any artists we might need for presentations or future representation" are filed.

ARCHWAY GALLERY, 2600 Monterose, Houston TX 77006. (713)522-2409. Director: Lyle E. Bates. Cooperative gallery. Estab. 1978. Clientele: 70% private collectors, 30% corporate clients. Represents 14 artists. Sponsors 9 solo and 3 group shows/year. Average display time 4 weeks. Accepts only artists from the Houston area. Interested in emerging artists. Overall price range: $150-4,000; most work sold at $150-1,000.

Media: Considers oil, acrylic, watercolor, pastel, pen & ink, drawings, mixed media, collage, works on paper, sculpture, ceramic, fiber, photography and egg tempera.

Style: Exhibits impressionism, expressionism, realism, surrealism, minimalism, painterly abstraction and constructions/collage. Genres include landscapes, florals and Southwestern works. "Since 1976 this cooperative has shown the works of many regional artists of both local and national acclaim. For the artist Archway provides artistic freedom, individual control of quality and content and a stepping stone on career path. Archway is an active member of the Houston Art Dealers Association."

Terms: Co-op membership fee plus donation of time; (5% commission). Rental fee for space; rental fee per month. Retail price set by artist. Exclusive area representation not required. Gallery provides promotion and contract. Prefers artwork framed.

Submissions: Send query letter with resume, brochure, slides, photographs and SASE. Write to schedule an appointment to show a portfolio, which should include originals, slides and photographs. Replies in 4 weeks. Files resume, brochure and slides. All material is returned if not accepted or under consideration.

Tips: "Don't show poor-quality slides."

ART LEAGUE OF HOUSTON, 1953 Montrose Blvd., Houston TX 77006. (713)523-9530. Executive Director: Barbara Oenbrink. Nonprofit gallery. Estab. 1948. Clientele: general; 60% private collectors. Sponsors 20+ group shows/year. Average display time is 4-5 weeks. Interested in emerging and established artists. Overall price range: $10-10,000; most artwork sold at $100-1,000.

Media: Considers all media and original handpulled prints.

Style: Exhibits contemporary work. Features "high-quality artwork reflecting serious aesthetic investigation and innovation. The work should additionally have a sense of personal vision."

Terms: Accepts work on consignment (20% commission, optional). Retail price is set by artist. Exclusive area representation not required. Gallery provides insurance, promotion and contract; shipping costs are shared.

Submissions: Send query letter, resume and slides. Slides, resumes and brochure are filed.

CONTEMPORARY GALLERY, 4152 Shady Bend Dr., Dallas TX 75244. (214)247-5246. Director: Patsy C. Kahn. Retail gallery. Estab. 1964. Clientele: collectors and retail. Interested in emerging and established artists.

Media: Considers oil, acrylic, drawings, sculpture, mixed media and original handpulled prints.

Style: Contemporary, 20th-century art—paintings, graphics and sculpture.

Terms: Accepts work on consignment or buys outright. Retail price is set by gallery and artist. Gallery provides insurance, promotion and contract; shipping costs are shared.

Submissions: Send query letter, resume, slides and photographs. Write for an appointment to show a portfolio.

*D-ART VISUAL ART CENTER, 2917 Swiss Ave., Dallas TX 75204. (214)821-2522. Manager: Katherine Wagner. Nonprofit gallery. Estab. 1981. Represents emerging, mid-career and established artists. Has 300 members. Sponsors 20 shows/year. Average display time 3 weeks. Open all year. Located "downtown; 24,000 sq. ft.; renovated warehouse."

Media: Considers all media.

Style: Exhibits all styles and genres.

Terms: Rental fee for space. Retail price set by the artist. Gallery provides promotion. Artists pays for shipping. Prefers framed artwork.

Submissions: Supports Dallas area artists. Send query letter with resume, slides, bio and SASE. Call to schedule an appointment to show a portfolio, which should include originals and slides. Files "artist's name, type of work, etc."

GALLERY 1114, 1114 North Big Spring, Midland TX 79701. (915)685-9944. Exhibits Chairman: Carol Bailey. Cooperative gallery. Estab. 1983. Clientele: 95% private collectors, 5% businesses. Represents 15 artists. Sponsors 7 solo and 2 group shows/year. Average display time is 5 weeks. Interested in emerging, mid-career and established artists. Price range: $20-1,000; most artwork sold at $20-200.
Media: Considers oil, acrylic, watercolor, pastel, pen & ink, drawings, sculpture, ceramic, fiber, photography, mixed media and collage.
Style: Exhibits contemporary, abstract, landscape and primitive works. "We are a contemporary artists cooperative. Therefore, we try to present artwork that is new, fresh and non-Southwestern; however, we do handle work that is somewhat traditional but with a contemporary flair." Does not want to see trendiness, lack of direction, commercial exploitation or sloppiness."
Terms: Accepts work on consignment (40% commission) and co-op membership fee plus donation of time. Retail price set by artist. Exclusive area representation not required. Gallery provides promotion and contract; shipping costs are shared.
Submissions: Send query letter, resume, brochure, business card, slides, photographs and SASE. Call or write for an appointment to show a portfolio. Resume and slides are filed.
Tips: "Artists should be fresh, new, innovative and exciting."

GRAHAM GALLERY, 1431 W. Alabama, Houston TX 77006. (713)528-4957. Director: William Graham. Retail gallery. Estab. 1981. Clientele: 70% private collectors, 30% corporate clients. Represents 18 artists. Sponsors 9 solo and 2 group shows/year. Average display time is 1 month. Interested in emerging, mid-career and established artists. Overall price range: $100-15,000; most artwork sold at $500-5,000.
Media: Considers oil, acrylic, watercolor, pastel, pen & ink, drawings, mixed media, collage, works on paper, sculpture, ceramic, craft, fiber, glass, installation, photography and original handpulled prints. Most frequently exhibits oils, photos, sculpture and drawings.
Terms: Accepts work on consignment (50% commission). Retail price is set by gallery and artist. Exclusive area representation required. Gallery provides insurance and promotion.

*HUMMINGBIRD ORIGINALS, INC., 4319-B Camp Bowie Blvd., Ft. Worth TX 76107. (817)732-1549. President: Carole Alford. Retail gallery. Estab. 1983. Represents 50 artists; emerging, mid-career and established. Exhibited artists include Gale Johnson and Mary Ann White. Sponsors 2-5 shows/year. Open all year. Located 2 miles west of downtown in the cultural district; 1,600 sq. ft. 20% of space for special exhibitions, 80% for gallery artists. Clientele: 80% private collectors, 20% corporate collectors. "There is an increasing focus in this area." Price range: $50-10,000; most work sold at $300-700.
Media: Considers oil, acrylic, watercolor, pastel, drawings, mixed media, collage, works on paper, sculpture, ceramic, craft, fiber, glass and original prints. Most frequently exhibits watercolor, oil and acrylic.
Style: Exhibits painterly abstraction, surrealism, conceptualism, minimalism, impressionism, realism and all styles. Genres include landscapes, florals, Americana, Southwestern, Western and wildlife. Prefers impressionism, abstraction and realism.
Terms: Accepts work on consignment (40-50% commission). Retail price set by the gallery and the artist. Gallery provides insurance, promotion and contract; shipping costs are shared. Prefers unframed artwork.
Submissions: Send query letter with resume, slides, bio, brochure, photographs, SASE, business card and reviews. Call or write to schedule an appointment to show a portfolio, which should include originals, slides, photographs and transparencies. Replies only if interested within 2 weeks. Files material useful to clients and future exhibit needs.
Tips: "Be prepared. Know if your work sells well, what response you are getting. Know what your prices are. Also understand a gallery, its role as an agent and its needs."

LAGUNA GLORIA ART MUSEUM, 1809 W. 35th St., Austin TX 78703; Box 5568, Austin TX 78763. (512)458-8191. Assistant Curator: Peter Mears. Museum. Estab. 1961. Clientele: tourists and Austin citizens. Sponsors 2-3 solo and 6 group shows/year. Average display time is 1½ months. Interested in emerging, mid-career and established artists.
Media: Currently exhibit 20th-Century American art with an emphasis on two-dimensional and three-dimensional contemporary artwork to include experimental video, mixed media and site-specific installations."
Style: Exhibits all styles and all genres. No commercial clichéd art.
Terms: Retail price set by artist. Gallery provides insurance and contract; shipping costs are shared.
Submissions: Send query letter with resume, slides and SASE. Write to schedule an appointment to show a portfolio, which should include slides, transparencies and photographs. Replies only if interested within 2-4 weeks. Files slides, resume and bio. All material is returned if not accepted or under consideration. Common mistakes artists make are "not enough information—poor slide quality, too much work covering too many changes in their development."

ROBINSON GALLERIES, #7, 3733 Westheimer, Houston TX 77027. (913)961-5229. Director: Thomas V. Robinson. Retail and wholesale gallery. Estab. 1969. Clientele: 90% private collectors, 10% corporate clients. Represents 10 artists. Sponsors 4 solo and 6 group shows/year. Average display time 5 weeks. Interested in emerging, mid-career and established artists. Overall price range: $100-100,000; most work sold at $1,000-25,000.

Media: Considers oil, acrylic, watercolor, pastel, pen & ink, drawings, mixed media, collages, works on paper, sculpture, ceramic, craft, fiber, glass, installation, photography, egg tempera, woodcuts, wood engravings, linocuts, engravings, mezzotints, etchings, lithographs and serigraphs. Most frequently exhibits oil/acrylic paintings, works on paper and wood.

Style: Exhibits expressionism, realism, photorealism, surrealism, primitivism and conceptualism. Genres include landscapes, Americana and figurative work. Prefers figurative and Americana work and landscapes.

Terms: Accepts work on consignment (50% commission). Buys outright (50% retail price, net 10 days). Retail price set by gallery and artist. Exclusive area representation required. Gallery provides insurance, promotion and shipping costs from gallery. Prefers framed artwork.

Submissions: Send query letter with resume, brochure, slides, photographs, bio and SASE. Write to schedule an appointment to show a portfolio, that includes originals, slides, transparencies and photographs. Replies in 1 week. Files resume and slides. All material is returned if not accepted or under consideration.

*SAN ANTONIO ART INSTITUTE, 6000 N. New Braunfels, San Antonio TX 78209. (512)824-7224. FAX: (512)824-6622. Acting President: Russell A. Cargo. Chair/Gallery Committee: Louis Turner. Nonprofit gallery. Estab. 1939. Represents emerging, mid-career and established artists. Exhibited artists include Larry Bell and Carl Embrey. Sponsors 7 shows/year. Average display time 5 weeks-1½ months. Open all year. Located in northeast San Antonio; 3,008 sq. ft.; "high ceiling, unique lighting; location adjacent to McNay Art Museum; beautiful grounds." 65% of space for special exhibitions. Clientele: college fine arts students, tourists, upscale community. Clientele: 90% private collectors, 10% corporate clients. Overall price range: $25-50,000.

Media: Considers all media.

Style: Exhibits all styles and genres.

Terms: "We follow NEA and Mid-America Arts Alliance guidelines." Retail price set by the artist. Gallery provides insurance, promotion, contract and shipping costs to and from gallery. Prefers framed artwork.

Submissions: NEA guidelines followed. Send query letter with resume and bio. No unsolicited slides. Call or write to schedule an appointment to show a portfolio, which should include slides, photographs and transparencies. Replies in 2 months. Files resume and bio.

Tips: "Send complete information, including social security number. No wildlife art or traditional Western art."

JB TOLLETT GALLERY, 1202 San Antonio St., Austin TX 78701. (512)474-7775. Director: Carole Gollhofer. Retail gallery. Estab. 1977. Represents 35 artists. Sponsors 2-3 solo and 6-8 group shows/year. Average display time is 4 weeks. Interested in emerging and established artists. Overall price range: $200-2,500; most artwork sold at $300-500.

Media: Considers oil, acrylic, watercolor, pastel, pen & ink, drawings, sculpture, ceramic, fiber, craft, mixed media, collage, glass, installation and original handpulled prints.

Terms: Accepts work on consignment (40% commission). Retail price is set by gallery and artist. Exclusive area representation required. Gallery provides insurance, promotion and contract; shipping costs are shared.

Submissions: Send query letter, resume, brochure, slides, photographs and SASE. Write for an appointment to show a portfolio. Resumes, brochures and slides are filed.

JUDY YOUENS GALLERY, 2631 Colquitt St., Houston TX 77098-2117. (713)527-0303. Co-Director: Bruce Wolfe. Retail gallery. Estab. 1981. Clientele 75% private collectors, 25% corporate clients. Represents approximately 30 artists. Sponsors 10 solo and 5 group shows/year. Average display time 5 weeks. Interested in emerging artists. Price range $2,000-20,000; most artwork sold at $2,000-12,000.

Media: Considers oil, acrylic, mixed media, collage, sculpture, glass and installation. Most frequently exhibits glass, paintings and sculpture.

Style: Exhibits expressionism, neo-expressionism, realism, surrealism, minimalism and painterly abstraction.

Terms: Accepts work on consignment. Retail price set by gallery and artist. Exclusive area representation generally not required. Gallery provides insurance, promotion and contract. Prefers unframed artwork.

Submissions: Send query letter with slides, photographs and bio. Write to schedule an appointment to show a portfolio, which should include slides and transparencies. Replies in 3-4 weeks. Files only the work that we accept. All material is returned if not accepted or under consideration.

Tips: "Have good slides that are well marked."

Utah

*APPLE YARD ART, 3096 S. Highland Ave., Salt Lake City UT 84106. (801)467-3621. Manager: Sue Valentine. Retail gallery. Estab. 1981. Clientele: 80% private collectors, 20% corporate clients. Represents 10 artists.

Interested in seeing the work of established artists. Sponsors 3 solo shows/year. Average display time is 6 weeks. Overall price range: $50-750; most artwork sold at $225.

Media: Most frequently exhibits watercolor, serigraphs and handmade paper.

Style: Exhibits impressionisim. Genres include landscapes and florals. Prefers impressionistic watercolors.

Terms: Accepts work on consignment (40% commission). Retail price is set by artist. Exclusive area representation required. Gallery provides insurance, promotion and contract; artist pays for shipping.

Submissions: Send query letter, resume and slides. Write for an appointment to show a portfolio, which should include originals.

Tips: Looks for "fresh, spontaneous subjects, no plagiarism." Most common mistakes artists make in presenting their work are "poorly framed artwork and not knowing a price—wanting me to decide. The public wants more original artwork or limited edition prints—not unlimited prints that can be found in every discount store catalog, etc."

*BRAITHWAITE FINE ARTS GALLERY, 351 West Center, Cedar City UT 84720. (801)586-5432. Director: Valerie Kidrick. Nonprofit gallery. Estab. 1976. Represents emerging, mid-career and established artists. Has "100 friends (donors)." Exhibited artists include Jim Jones and Milford Zornes. Sponsors 17 shows/year. Average display time 3-4 weeks. Open all year. Located on "college campus; 1,500 sq. ft. (275 running wall); historic—but renovated—building." 100% of space for special exhibitions. Clientele: local citizens; visitors for Shakespeare festival during summer. Clientele: 100% private collectors. Overall price range: $100-8,000; most work sold at $100-500.

Media: Considers oil, acrylic, watercolor, pastel, pen & ink, drawings, mixed media, collage, works on paper, sculpture, ceramic, fiber, glass, installation, photography, original handpulled prints, woodcuts, wood engravings, linocuts, engravings, mezzotints, etchings, lithographs, serigraphs. Most frequently exhibits oil, watercolor and ceramic.

Style: Exhibits realism and all styles and genres. Prefers realism (usually landscape), painterly abstraction and surrealism.

Terms: Accepts work on consignment (25% commission). Retail price set by the artist. Gallery provides insurance, promotion and contract (duration of exhibit only); shipping costs are shared. Prefers framed artwork.

Submissions: Send query letter with resume, slides, bio and SASE. Write to schedule an appointment to show a portfolio, which should include slides and transparencies. Replies in 3-4 weeks. Files bios, slides, resume (only for 2 years).

Tips: "Know our audience! Generally conservative; during summer (Shakespeare festival) usually loosens up."

MARBLE HOUSE GALLERY, 44 Exchange Pl. Salt Lake City UT 84111. (801)532-7338. Owner: Dolores Kohler. Retail gallery and art consultancy. Estab. 1987. Clientele 70% private collectors; 30% corporate clients. Represents 20 artists. Sponsors 6 solo or 2-person shows and 2 group shows/year. Average display time 1 month. Interested in emerging and established artists. Overall price range $100-10,000; most work sold at $200-5,000.

Media: Considers oil, acrylic, watercolor, pastel, pen & ink, mixed media, collage, sculpture, ceramic, photography, egg tempera, woodcuts, wood engravings, linocuts, engravings, mezzotints, etchings, lithographs, pochoir and serigraphs. Most frequently exhibits oil, watercolor and sculpture.

Style: Exhibits impressionism, expressionism, realism, surrealism, painterly abstraction and post modern works. Genres include landscapes, florals, Americana Southwestern, Western, portraits and figurative work. Prefers abstraction, landscapes and florals.

Terms: Accepts work on consignment (50% commission); buys outright (net 30 days.) Retail price set by gallery and artist. Exclusive area representation required. Gallery provides promotion and contract; shipping costs are shared. Prefers artwork framed or unframed.

Submissions: Send query letter with resume, slides, photographs, bio and SASE. Call or write to schedule an appointment to show a portfolio, which should include originals, slides, transparencies, and photographs. Replies in 2 weeks. Files slides, resume and price list. All material is returned if not accepted or under consideration.

Vermont

COTTONBROOK GALLERY, RR1, Box 440, Stowe VT 05672. (802)253-8121. Owner: Vera Beckerhoff. Retail gallery and custom frame shop. Estab. 1981. Clientele: upscale second homeowners. Average display time 3 weeks. Prefers New England artists, but will accept work from Northern (West and Canada) artists. Interested in emerging and established artists. Overall price range: $50-3,000; most artwork sold at $100-200.

Media: Considers oil, watercolor, pastel, pen & ink, drawings, mixed media, sculpture, original handpulled prints, limited edition offset reproductions and posters. Most frequently exhibits etchings, watercolor and oil.
Style: Exhibits painterly abstraction, primitivism and impressionism. Genres include landscapes, Americana and figurative work. Most frequently exhibits New England landscapes and winter watercolors. Currently seeking figurative oil and oil landscapes.
Terms: Accepts work on consignment (40% commission); buys outright (net 30 days) or rental fee for space. Retail price is set by gallery or artist. Exclusive area representation not required. Gallery provides promotion and contract; shipping costs are shared.
Submissions: Send query letter with resume, slides and SASE. Write for an appointment to show a portfolio, which should include originals.

*PARADE GALLERY, Box 245, Warren VT 05674. (802)496-5445. Owner: Jeffrey S. Burnett. Retail gallery. Estab. 1982. Clientele: tourist and upper middle class second home owners; 98% private collectors. Represents 15-20 artists. Interested in emerging, mid-career and established artists. Overall price range: $20-2,500; most artwork sold at $50-300.
Media: Considers oil, acrylic, watercolor, pastel, mixed media, collage, works on paper, sculpture and original handpulled prints. Most frequently exhibits etchings, silkscreen and watercolor. Currently looking for oil/acrylic and watercolor.
Style: Exhibits primitivism, impressionistic and realism. "Parade Gallery deals primarily with representational works with country subject matter. The gallery is interested in unique contemporary pieces to a limited degree." Does not want to see "cutesy or very abstract art."
Terms: Accepts work on consignment (⅓ commission) or occasionally buys outright (net 30 days). Retail price is set by gallery or artist. Exclusive area representation required. Gallery provides insurance and promotion.
Submissions: Send query letter with resume, slides and photographs. Write for an appointment to show a portfolio, which should include originals or slides. Biographies and background are filed.

WOODSTOCK GALLERY OF ART, Route 4 E., Woodstock VT 05091. (802)457-1900. Gallery Director: Charles E.H. Fenton. Retail and rental gallery and art consultancy. Estab. 1971. Clientele: knowledgeable collectors; 75% private collectors, 25% corporate clients. Represents 30-40 artists. Sponsors 3 solo and 6 group shows/year. Average display time is 12 weeks. Interested in emerging and established artists. Overall price range: $250-5,000; most artwork sold at $250-2,000.
Media: Considers all media. Most frequently exhibits paint, print and photography. Currently looking for oils and sculpture.
Style: Exhibits painterly abstraction, conceptualism, primitivism, impressionism, expressionism and realism. Genres include landscapes, florals, Americana, figurative work and fantasy illustration. Most frequently exhibits impressionistic, realistic and conceptual works. Currently seeking realistic oils.
Terms: Accepts work on consignment (40% commission). Retail price is set by gallery or artist. Exclusive area representation required, "with exceptions." Gallery provides insurance, promotion and contract.
Submissions: Send query letter with resume, brochure, slides, photographs and SASE. Write for an appointment to show a portfolio, which should include originals, slides and transparencies. Resume and slides are filed if interested.

Virginia

*THE ART LEAGUE, INC., 105 N. Union St., Alexandria VA 22314. (703)683-1780. Gallery Director: Katy Svoboda. Cooperative gallery. Estab. 1953. Clientele: 75% private collectors, 25% corporate clients. Has 700-900 members. Sponsors 10 solo and 16 group shows/year. Average display time is 1 month. Accepts artists from metropolitan Washington area, Northern Virginia and Maryland. Interested in emerging, mid-career and established artists. Overall price range: $50-4,000; most artwork sold at $150-500.
Media: Considers oil, acrylic, watercolor, pastel, pen & ink, drawings, mixed media, collage, works on paper, sculpture, ceramic, fiber, glass, photography and original handpulled prints. Most frequently exhibits watercolor, all print making and oil/acrylic.
Style: Exhibits all styles and genres. Prefers impressionism, painted abstraction and realism. "The Art League is a membership organization open to anyone interested."
Terms: Accepts work on consignment (33⅓% commission) and co-op membership fee plus donation of time. Retail price is set by artist. Exclusive area representation not required.
Tips: A common mistake artists make is "framing that either overwhelms the work or is done in a nonprofessional way with dirty, poorly fitting mattes, etc."

FINE ARTS CENTER FOR NEW RIVER VALLEY, 21 W. Main St., Pulaski VA 24301. (703)980-7363. Director: Lynn Marshall. Nonprofit gallery. Estab. 1978. Clientele: general public, corporate, schools; 80% private collectors, 20% corporate clients. Represents 75 artists and craftspeople (consignment basis only). Sponsors 10 solo and 2 group shows/year. Average display time is 1 month (gallery); 3-6 months (Art Mart). Interested in emerging and established artists. Overall price range: $20-500; most artwork sold at $20-100.

Media: Considers all media. Most frequently exhibits oil, watercolor and ceramic. Currently looking for good quality work—media not important.

Style: Exhibits hard-edge/geometric abstraction, painterly abstraction, minimalism, post-modernism, pattern painting, feminist/political works, primitivism, impressionism, photorealism, expressionism, neo-expressionism, realism and surrealism. Genres include landscapes, florals, Americana, Western, portraits and figurative work. Most frequently exhibits landscapes, abstracts, Americana.

Terms: Accepts work on consignment (25% commission). Retail price is set by gallery or artist. Exclusive area representation not required. Gallery provides insurance (80% of value), promotion and contract.

Submissions: Send query letter with resume, brochure, slides, photographs and SASE. Write for an appointment to show a portfolio, which should include slides. Slides and resumes are filed.

Tips: We do not want to see "unmatted or unframed paintings and watercolors. Don't overprice your works. Label all sample slides."

HERNDON OLD TOWN GALLERY, 720 Lynn St., Herndon VA 22070. (703)435-1888. Membership chairman: Lassie Corbett. Cooperative gallery. Estab. 1984. Clientele: 90% private collectors, 10% corporate clients. Represents 5 member artists and 5 associate artists. Sponsors 4 solo and 8 group shows/year. Average display time 2 months. Interested in emerging artists. Overall price range: $25-1,000; most work sold at $150-350.

Media: Considers oil, acrylic, watercolor, pastel, pen & ink, drawings, mixed media, collage, photography, egg tempera, original handpulled prints and offset reproductions. Most frequently exhibits watercolor, acrylic, oil and drawings.

Style: Exhibits impressionism, realism and oriental brush; considers all styles. Genres include landscapes, florals, Americana, wildlife, figurative work; considers all genres. Prefers impressionism, realism (local scenes) and oriental brush.

Terms: 10% commission. Rental fee for space for artists on consignment; rental fee covers 6 months. Retail price set by artist. Exclusive area representation not required. Gallery provides promotion; artist pays for shipping. Prefers framed artwork.

Submissions: Send query letter with resume, slides and SASE. Call or write to schedule an appointment to show a portfolio, which should include originals, slides or photographs. Replies in 1 week. All material is returned if not accepted or under consideration. Contact for guidelines.

THE PRINCE ROYAL GALLERY, 204 South Royal St., Alexandria VA 22314. (703)548-5151. Director: John Byers. Retail gallery. Estab. 1977. Located in middle of Old Town Alexandria. "Gallery is the ballroom and adjacent rooms of historic hotel." Clientele: primarily Virginia, Maryland & Washington DC residents; 95% private collectors, 5% corporate clients. Sponsors 6 solo and 1 group shows/year. Average display time 3-4 weeks. Interested in emerging, mid-career and established artists. Overall price range: $75-8,000; most artwork sold at $700-1,200.

Media: Considers oil, acrylic, watercolor, pastel, mixed media, sculpture, egg tempera, engravings, etchings and lithographs. Most frequently exhibits oil, watercolor and bronze.

Style: Exhibits impressionism, expressionism, realism, primitivism and painterly abstraction. Genres include landscapes, florals, portraits and figurative work. "The gallery deals primarily in original, representational art. Abstracts are occasionally accepted but are hard to sell in Northern Virginia. Limited edition prints are accepted only if the gallery carries the artist's original work."

Terms: Accepts work on consignment (40% commission). Retail price set by artist. Exclusive area representation required. Gallery provides insurance, promotion and contract. Prefers framed artwork.

Submissions: Send query letter with resume, brochure, slides and SASE. Call or write to schedule an appointment to show a portfolio, which should include originals, slides and transparencies. Replies in 1 week. Files resumes and brochures. All material is returned if requested.

Tips: "Write or call for an appointment before coming. Have at least six pieces ready to consign if accepted. Can't speak for the world, but in Northern Virginia collectors are slowing down. Lower-priced items continue OK, but sales over $3,000 are becoming rare. More people are buying representational rather than abstract art. Impressionist art is increasing."

RESTON ART GALLERY, 11400 Washington Plaza W. Reston VA 22090. (703)481-8156. Publicity: JoAnn Morris-Scott. Nonprofit gallery. Estab. 1988. Clientele: 75% private collectors, 25% corporate clients. Represents 13 artists. Sponsors 10 solo and 2 group shows/year. Average display time 1 month. Interested in emerging artists. Overall price range: $25-1,750; most work sold at $150-350.

Media: Considers all media and prints. Most frequently exhibits oil, acrylic, watercolor, photos and graphics.

Style: Exhibits all styles and genres. Prefers realism and painterly abstraction. The gallery's purpose is to "promote local artist and to educate the public. Gallery sitting and attendance at meetings is required."

Terms: Co-op membership fee plus donation of time; 20% commission. Retail price set by artist. Exclusive area representation not required. Gallery provides promotion; artist pays for shipping. Prefers artwork unframed.

Submissions: Send query letter with resume, slides, photographs, bio and SASE. Call or write to schedule an appointment to show a portfolio, which should include originals, slides and photographs. Replies in 1 week. All material is returned if not accepted or under consideration.

Washington

*VIRGINIA INN, 1937 First Ave., Seattle WA 98101. Partner: Patrice Demombynes. Pub/showcase gallery. Estab. 1981. Exhibits the work of emerging artists. Exhibited artists include Frank Samuelson and Maggie Hanley. Sponsors 12 shows/year. Average display time 1 month. Open all year. Located "downtown, near the Market and the Seattle Art Museum;1,300 sq. ft.; classic corner bar." 100% of space for artists.Clientele: "artsy, yuppie, young and old; 100% private collectors. Overall price range: $600-1,500. Most work sold at $800-1,000.
Media: Considers oil, acrylic, watercolor, pen & ink, drawings, mixed media, collage, works on paper, fiber, photogrpahy, original handpulled prints, woodcuts, wood engravings and linocuts. Most frequently exhibits acrylic, oil and photography. "There is no place for free-form sculpture or schlok."
Style: Exhibits all styles, leaning "more toward abstract; riskier alternative to the typical gallery." No genre artwork shown.
Terms: Artwork is accepted on consignment (20% commision). Retail price set by artist. Gallery provides insurance; artist pays for shipping. Prefers artwork framed.
Submissions: Prefers local and regional artists. Send query letter with resume, SASE, slides or photographs. "Send slides first!" Portfolio should include originals, photographs, slides or transparencies. Replies in 1 month. Does not file material.
Tips: "Drop by."

Wisconsin

*FOSTER GALLERY, 121 Water St., Eau Claire WI 54702. (715)836-2328. Director: Eugene Hood. University gallery. Estab. 1970. Represents emerging, mid-career and established artists. Exhibited artists include Richard Long, Sidney Goodman, Roger Essely, Dorit Cypus and Bruce Charlesworth. Sponsors 9 shows/year. Average display time 3 weeks. Open from September-May. Located on the university campus; 3,250 sq. ft.; "two connected spaces, one with 13′ ceiling and marbelized floor." 95% of space for special exhibitions. Clientele: 75% private collectors, 25% corporate collectors. Overall price range: $35-10,000; most work sold at $200-750.
Media: Considers oil, acrylic, watercolor, pastel, pen & ink, drawings, mixed media, collage, works on paper, sculpture, ceramic, fiber, glass, installation, photography, video, computer and performance art, original handpulled prints, woodcuts, wood engravings, engravings, mezzotints, etchings, lithographs and serigraphs. Most frequently exhibits fiber, drawings and paintings.
Style: Exhibits all styles and genres. Prefers realism, painterly abstraction, conceptualism and photography.
Terms: Accepts work on consignment (10% commission). Retail price set by the artist. Gallery provides insurance and promotion; shipping costs to gallery. Prefers framed artwork.
Submissions: Send query letter with resume, slides, bio, SASE and reviews. "Present an idea of a theme or group show." Portfolio should include slides. Replies only if interested within 2 months.
Tips: Wants to see "quality, works undergraduate students will be inspired by, but can also relate to." Does not want to see "pseudo-naive work, intuitive no-skill work." Notices a "return to skill or craft aesthetic; exhibits that use gallery space not just its walls, to create a total environment."

THE FANNY GARVER GALLERY, 230 State St., Madison WI 53703. (608)256-6755. President: Fanny Garver. Retail gallery and art consultancy. Estab. 1972. Clientele: 80% private collectors, 20% corporate clients. Represents 100 artists. Sponsors 8 solo and 4 group shows/year. Average display time 1 month. Interested in emerging, mid-career and established artists. Overall price range: $40-10,000; most artwork sold at $60-500.
Media: Considers oil, acrylic, watercolor, pastel, pen & ink, drawings, mixed media, collage, works on paper, sculpture, ceramic, craft, fiber, glass, woodcuts, wood engravings, linocuts, engravings, mezzotints, etchings and lithographs. Most frequently exhibits watercolor, oil and pastel. Does not want to see photography.
Style: Exhibits all styles. Genres include landscapes, florals, Americana and portraits.
Terms: Accepts work on consignment or buys outright. Retail price set by gallery and artist. Exclusive area representation required. Gallery provides insurance, promotion and contract; shipping costs are shared.
Submissions: Send query letter with resume, slides, bio and SASE. Call or write to schedule an appointment to show a portfolio, which should include originals and slides. Replies in 2 weeks. Files resume and bio. All material is returned if not accepted or under consideration.
Tips: "Never contact us on Saturday, the busiest day, or during December. Send a SASE if you want slides back." Looking for "direction, maturity, original expression, reliability, consistency of quality, reasonable expectations in pricing, commitment to creating a continuing body of work and a willingness to discuss prices and other marketing strategies with us." As trend sees "interest in emerging artists whose work is still reasonably priced."

KATIE GINGRASS GALLERY, Milwaukee/Santa Fe, 241 N. Broadway, Milwaukee WI 53202. (414)289-0855. Director: Pat Brophy or Elaine Hoth. Retail gallery. Estab. 1984. Clientele: 45% private collectors, 55% corporate clients. Represents 150 artists. Sponsors 6-8 group shows/year. Average display time 6 weeks. Interested in emerging and established artists. Overall price range: $50-10,000; most artwork sold at $100-3,000.
Media: Considers oil, acrylic, watercolor, pastel, drawings, mixed media, collage, works on paper, sculpture, ceramic, craft, fiber, glass, photography, egg tempera, woodcuts, wood engravings, linocuts, engravings, mezzotints, etchings, lithographs, pochoir and serigraphs. Most frequently exhibits paintings, pastel and craft.
Style: Exhibits impressionism, expressionism, realism, photorealism, color field, painterly abstraction, post modern works and imagism. Genres include landscapes, florals and figurative work. Prefers realism, abstraction and impressionism. Specializes in contemporary American paintings, sculptures, drawings and fine crafts.
Terms: Accepts work on consignment (50% commission). Retail price set by gallery and artist. Exclusive area representation required. Gallery provides insurance, promotion, contract and shipping costs from gallery.
Submissions: Send query letter with resume, slides, photographs, bio and SASE. Write to schedule an appointment to show a portfolio, which should include originals, slides and prices. Replies in 2 months. Files resumes, biographies and sildes. All material is returned if not accepted or under consideration.
Tips: Looks for "individualistic and unique thinking in realistic, abstract and craft work."

VALPERINE GALLERY, 1719 Monroe St., Madison WI 53711. (608)256-4040. Director: Valerie Kazamias. Retail gallery and art consultancy. Estab. 1983. Clientele: professionals, corporations and designers; 60% private collectors, 40% corporate clients. Represents 70 artists. Sponsors 2 solo and 4 group shows/year. Interested in emerging, mid-career and established artists. Overall price range: $300-5,000; most artwork sold at $500-2,500.
Media: Considers oil, acrylic, watercolor, pastel, collage, works on paper, sculpture, ceramics, glass and prints. Most frequently exhibits watercolors, prints and acrylics/oils.
Style: Exhibits hard-edge geometric abstraction, post modern, impressionism, realism and surrealism. Genres include landscapes, florals and fantasy illustration.
Terms: Accepts work on consignment (40% commission). Retail price is set by gallery and artist. Exclusive area representation required. Gallery provides return shipping, promotion and contract.
Submissions: Send query letter, resume, brochure, slides and photographs. Write for an appointment to show a portfolio, which should include slides, transparences and photographs. Inventory, contracts, resumes, slides and correspondence are filed.

*CHARLES A. WUSTUM MUSEUM OF FINE ARTS, 2519 Northwestern Ave., Racine WI 53404. (414)636-9177. Director: Bruce Pepich. Museum, rental gallery and museum shop. Represents hundreds of artists; emerging, mid-career and established. Sponsors 7-10 shows/year. Average display time 4 weeks. Open all year. Located northwest of downtown Racine; 3,500 sq. ft.; "100-year-old Victorian farm house." 100% of space for special exhibitions. Clientele: "private collectors from a tri-state area, corporate collectors from Milwaukee, Racine." Clientele: 40% private collectors, 60% corporate collectors. Overall price range: $50-15,000; most artwork sold at $300-7,000.
Media: "We show all media, but specialize in 20th-century works on paper, craft and artists' books." Considers original handpulled prints, woodcuts, wood engravings, linocuts, engravings, mezzotints, etchings, lithographs, pochoir and serigraphs.
Style: Exhibits all styles and genres.
Terms: Annual slide jurying each February (contact Wustum previous November to receive details) for exhibitions. Annual March jurying of actual work for the Art Sales and Rental Gallery (contact Wustum in advance for written materials on this jurying). 30% commission on artworks sold from exhibitions; 40% commission on artworks sold from Art Sales Gallery. For exhibits and sales artist covers delivery. For Gift Shop Wustum pays return postage.
Submissions: Send query letter with resume and slides. Write to schedule an appointment to show a portfolio, which should include slides and resume. Replies in 3 or 4 weeks. Files slides and resumes.
Tips: "Send good quality slides."

Wyoming

BIG RED GALLERY, 2836 U.S. Highway 14-16 East, Clearmont WY 82835. (307)737-2291. Gallery Program Director: Elizabeth Guheen. Nonprofit gallery. Estab. 1983. Open year round. A renovated barn from 1882 on historical register tour. Gallery also houses 4 artist-in-resident studios and a gallery office as well as conference facilities upstairs. Sponsors 1 solo and 7 group shows/year. Average display time 6 weeks. Prefers regional work but not exclusively. Interested in emerging and established artists.
Media: Considers all media and all types of prints. Most frequently exhibits oil/acrylic, clay and bronze.
Style: Exhibits expressionism, realism, post modern works and contemporary art and crafts; all genres. "Our gallery specializes in art produced by, for and about Wyoming and the Rocky Mountin region. We include very contemporary work as well as more traditional treatments. Expanding awareness of all the arts in rural Wyoming is one of our missions."

Terms: Accepts work on consignment (35% commission). Retail price set by artist. Exclusive area representation not required. Gallery provides insurance, promotion, contract and shipping costs to gallery. Prefers artwork framed.
Submissions: Send query letter with resume, slides and SASE. Write to schedule an appointment to show a portfolio, which should include relevant materials. Replies in 2 months.
Tips: "Have patience—Selection Committee meets about 5 times a year. We schedule shows 2 years in advance."

FOUR SEASONS GALLERY, Pink Garter Plaza, Box 2174, Jackson WY 83001. (307)733-4049. Owner: Phillip Shaffer. Retail gallery. Estab. 1970. Clientele: 100% private collectors. Represents 11 emerging, mid-career and established artists. Sponsors 1 solo and 1 group shows/year. Average display time is 6 months. Overall price range: $150-5,000.
Media: Considers oil, acrylic, watercolor, pastel, pen & ink, drawings, sculpture and print. Most frequently exhibits oil, watercolor and pencil.
Style: Genres include landscapes, Westerns and portraits. "Our gallery specializes in Western art of all kinds and Teton landscapes." Does not want to see "abstracts of any kind, run-of-the-mill compositions, poor paint handling."
Terms: Accepts work on consignment (40% commission). Retail price is set by artist. Exclusive area representation required. Gallery provides insurance, promotion and shipping.
Submissions: Send query letter, brochure, slides, photographs and SASE.
Tips: "Looks for quality realism with good paint quality, color and composition. Fewer people with disposable income, so fewer sales."

NICOLAYSEN ART MUSEUM, 400 E. Collins Dr., Casper WY 82601. (307)235-5247. Director: Sam Gappmayer. Museum. Estab. 1967. Open all year. Clientele: 90% private collectors, 10% corporate clients. Sponsors 10 solo and 10 group shows/year. Average display time 2 months. Interested in emerging, mid-career and established artists.
Media: Considers all media.
Style: Exhibits contemporary styles. Does not want to see "wildlife art, cowboy romanticism."
Terms: Accepts work on consignment (30% commission). Retail price set by artist. Exclusive area representation not required. Gallery provides insurance, promotion and shipping costs from gallery.
Submissions: Send query letter with slides. Write to schedule an appointment to show a portfolio, which should include originals or slides. Replies in 2 months.

Puerto Rico

GALERIA BOTELLO INC., 208 Cristo St., Old San Juan Puerto Rico 00901. (809)723-9987. Owner: Juan Botello. Retail gallery. Estab. 1952. Clientele: 60% tourist and 40% local; 75% private collectors, 30% corporate clients. Represents 10 artists. Sponsors 3 solo and 2 group shows/year. Average display time 3 months. Accepts only artists from Latin America. Interested in emerging and established artists. Overall price range: $500-30,000; most artwork sold at $1,000-5,000.
Media: Considers oil, acrylic, watercolor, pastel, drawings, mixed media, collage, sculpture, ceramic, woodcuts, wood engravings, linocuts, engravings, mezzotints, etchings, lithographs and serigraphs. Most frequently exhibits oil on canvas, mixed media and bronze sculpture.
Style: Exhibits expressionism, neo-expressionism and primitivism. Genres include Americana and figurative work. Prefers expressionism and figurative work. "The Botello Gallery exhibits major contemporary Puerto Rican and Latin American artists. We prefer working with original paintings, sculpture and works on paper."
Terms: Accepts work on consignment (40% commission) or buys outright (50% retail price). Retail price set by artist. Exclusive area representation required. Gallery provides insurance and contract; artist pays for shipping. Prefers framed artwork.
Submissions: Send query letter with resume, brochure, slides and photographs. Call to schedule an appointment to show a portfolio, which should include originals. Replies in 2 weeks. Files resumes.
Tips: "Artists have to be Latin American or major European artists."

Canada

*OPEN SPACE, 510 Fort St., Victoria B.C. V8W 1E6 Canada. (604)383-8833. Director: Sue Donaldson. Alternative space and nonprofit gallery. Estab. 1971. Represents emerging, mid-career and established artists. Has 311 members. Sponsors 8-10 shows/year. Average display time 2½ weeks. Open all year. Located downtown; 1,500 sq. ft.; "multi-disciplinary exhibition venue." 100% of space for gallery artists. Overall price range: $300-8,000.
Media: Considers oil, acrylic, watercolor, pastel, pen & ink, drawing, mixed media, collage, works on paper, sculpture, ceramic, installation, photography, video, performance art, original handpulled prints, woodcuts, wood engravings, linocuts, engravings, mezzotints and etchings.

Style: Exhibits all styles. All contemporary genres.

Terms: "No acquisition. Artists selected are paid exhibition fees for the right to exhibit their work." Retail price set by the artist. Gallery provides insurance, promotion, contract and fees; shipping costs are shared. Prefers artwork "ready for exhibition."

Submissions: "Non-Canadian artists must submit by September 30 in order to be considered for visiting foreign artists' fees." Submit by February 28 or September 30. Send query letter with resume, 10-20 slides, bio, SASE, reviews and proposal outline. "No photos or original work." Replies in 1 month.

*WOODLAND NATIVE ART GALLERY, 1 Woodland Dr., Cutler, Ontario P0P 1B0. (705)844-2132. FAX: (705)844-2281. Manager: Tom Duncan. Retail gallery. Estab. 1974. Represents 40-60 artists: emerging, mid-career and established. Exhibited artists include Donald Vann, Leland Bell and J. Gordon Fiddler. Sponsors 4 shows/year. Average display time 1 year. Open all year. Located on the Trans Canada Highway; 1,600 sq. ft. 10% of space for special exhibitions. Clientele: 95% private collectors, 5% corporate clients.

Media: Considers oil, acrylic, deer and moosehide acrylic, watercolor, pastel, pen & ink, drawings, mixed media, sculpture, original handpulled prints, lithographs, etchings, serigraphs, offset reproductions and posters. Most frequently exhibits acrylic, stone lithographs and offset reproductions.

Style: Exhibits conceptualism, primitivism, surrealism, realism and paintings depicting legends. Genres include wildlife and "native."

Terms: Artwork is bought outright for 20-60% of retail price. Retail price set by gallery and artist. Gallery provides promotion; shipping costs are shared. Prefers unframed artwork.

Submissions: Send query letter with resume, bio and slides. Replies only if interested in 1 month. If does not reply, artist should re-write. Files most material.

Galleries/'90-'91 changes

The following galleries appeared in the 1990 edition of *Artist's Market* but are not in the 1991 edition. Those which did not respond to our request for an update of their listings may have done so for a variety of reasons—they may be out of business for example, or they may be overstocked with submissions. If they indicated a reason, it is noted in parentheses after the name.

Aaron Gallery
Art Center of Battle Creek
Berkshire Artisans Community Arts Center
Blackwell St. Center for the Arts
Blue Mountain Gallery
Brent Gallery
Brookfield/Sono Craft Center
Alan Brown Gallery
Cabrillo Gallery
Cade Gallery
Sandy Carson Gallery
Castle Gallery
Cleveland Institute of Art Gallery
Collector's Choice
Core New Art Space
County Art Gallery
Crane Gallery (asked to be deleted)
Cunningham Memorial Art Gallery
The Curtis, Allen, Turner Gallery (asked to be deleted)
Emily Davis Gallery
Debouver Fine Arts

Peter Drew Gallery
Eagles Roose Gallery
Amos Eno Gallery
Fendrick Gallery (not accepting new artists)
Field Art Studio
500X Gallery
Foundry Gallery
Freedman Gallery, Allbright College
Galeric International
Gilman/Gruen Galleries
Helander Gallery
International Images, Ltd.
Janus Gallery (not accepting new artists)
The Jones Gallery
Joslyn Art Museum- Rental & Sales Gallery (out of business)
Kastoriano Shosan (moved; no forwarding address)
The Kling Gallery
Koslow Gallery
Krasl Art Center
Marlboro Gallery
Modernism

Phyllis Needleman Gallery
Ormond Memorial Art Museum and Gardens
Gerald Peters Gallery
Posselt-Baker Gallery
The Print Gallery, Inc.
R-Go International, Inc. Gallery of Fine Art
Running Ridge Gallery
Shidoni Gallery
J.B. Speed Art Museum Rental and Purchase Gallery
Suzanne Galleries, Inc. (moved; no forwarding address)
Swearinger Gallery
T.M. Gallery
Tarble Arts Center Sales/Rental Gallery
Tarbox Gallery
Trachtenberg Gallery
Udinotti Gallery
Vorpal Gallery
Watergate Gallery
The Western Colorado Center for the Arts
Wiesner Gallery

Greeting Cards and Paper Products

In this fast-paced society, in which we often live hundreds of miles away from families and close friends, the greeting card is often our quickest and easiest way of staying in touch. Hence, it continues to be a strong, solid market for freelance artwork. According to the Greeting Card Association, each of us, on the average, buys 33 cards a year. The Association also says that $4.6 billion will have been spent this year on greeting cards, $600 million more than last year. Even though the market remains steady, the industry continues to change as it responds to changes in public taste.

One change in the market, however, comes from the nature of the industry itself. Of the 900 to 1,000 greeting card firms in the United States, most are small operations run by writers and artists. The industry is slowly beginning to reflect this by becoming more sensitive to freelancers' needs, especially in payment policies and terms. Only a few years ago most card companies bought artwork outright—for all rights. This is now changing; more and more firms are willing to negotiate for rights.

More changes

Larger firms, long associated with traditional and rather conservative cards, have now developed their own lines of upbeat, irreverent, humorous cards. The term "studio" had been used to describe slightly off-color, cartoonish vertical cards. Today humorous and risqué cards can be found with other cards, no longer banished to racks at the end of the aisle. The lines between traditional, studio and alternative cards have become so blurred, cards are now described simply as occasion or nonoccasion cards. It is nonoccasion cards that are now the fastest growing segment.

There have been a number of changes that directly influence the type of work greeting card firms will look for this year. One of the largest areas of growth is in the ethnic card area, cards designed to appeal to African-Americans, Hispanics and other cultural and ethnic groups; they are meant to speak to the culture. According to one study, the number of Hispanics in this country has risen by one third, nearly five times faster than the rest of the population. Cards reflect this culture with bright colors, gold foil, bold graphics and sentimental and religious verse. With the unification of Europe in 1992, many in the industry foresee a global increase in their foreign language cards. This has led to a surge in the number of new companies producing these cards and the number of new lines under development by larger firms.

Senior citizens continue to be a strong consumer group. According to U.S. Census Bureau statistics, there are now 64 million people over 50 years old and current projections by the research firm Packaged Facts are that by the year 2000, one in five Americans will be 65 or older with an average life expectancy of 20 more years. Greeting card companies are attempting to cater to this group by offering an array of cards, from lively to sentimental, such as cards for ruby and golden wedding anniversaries, retirement, grandchildren and travel. Other trends this year are cards expressing affirmation and encouragement for those suffering from such maladies as substance abuse and terminal illness, such as AIDs or cancer. The Victorian look is popular—romantic, flowery, elaborate, lacy and pastel—a reflection, some say, of society's desire to return to tradition, family and romance. The population is more environmentally conscious than ever and cards too reflect this.

Christmas cards still account for much of greeting card sales. Designs for Christmas and other holiday cards this year include an emphasis on higher quality cards. Foils, imitation suede, flocking, embossing, die cuts and popups are popular. Such treatments are not just for holiday cards anymore. People are starting to buy expensive cards for a variety of occasions and don't seem to mind paying up to $5 per card, for they often serve as gifts by themselves.

Stationery firms and giftwrap companies are also undergoing changes. Bold colors, colored paper bags and coordinated items are most popular. As with greeting cards, there is a growth in the use of expensive materials and processes.

The need for calendar art continues to grow. Last year there were more then 3,500 varieties with industry sales exceeding $2 billion annually. The biggest seller for the past four years in a row has been "Gary Larson's Off the Wall Page-a-Day," but other cartoon characters sell well too. Other subjects such as florals, landscapes, primitives, wildlife and folk art also promise strong sales. The overall design of calendars will include large writing spaces, and the industry has moved away from 16-month or school year calendars, back to the traditional 12-month type.

Study the market

Research the market carefully before approaching greeting card firms. Small companies are all different. Each has carved out its own specific niche in the field and it is important to be familiar—to know which suits your style and approach. Larger firms may handle a variety of lines, but they are very market-driven and will expand or develop lines according to market research.

One way to research card or stationery firms is, of course, to visit your local card or gift shop. Some firms offer artist guidelines, sample cards or a catalog—usually for a SASE. If you have the opportunity, a visit to one of the regional or national card and stationery shows may be very educational—and a way to meet card editors and publishers.

Once you've chosen a firm, contact the art director or creative director. Since most greeting card work is colorful, send color slides, photos, tearsheets or final reproductions. If you have an idea for a card that requires pop-ups, die cuts or special folds, you may want to include a model card. Note, too, most greeting card designs are still vertical, so most of your samples should also be vertical.

Most card firms buy illustration and verse separately, but if you are a good writer, verse may help sell the idea—and you will be compensated accordingly. Even if you are not a writer, go ahead and include suggested copy, if you have an idea.

Speaking of ideas, think in terms of card lines and related gift items. Many greeting card artists also work with licensing agents to market their ideas to giftware firms. Licensing agents are more interested in ideas or concepts for a line, rather than individual illustrations.

Payment rates for greeting card illustration and design can be as high as for magazine or book illustration. Some card companies pay also for design and concept ideas and for roughs. Although many still pay for all rights, some are willing to negotiate for other arrangements, such as greeting card rights only. This often depends on whether the firm has other plans for the illustration or design, such as use on calendars, stationery, party supplies or even toys. If other uses are anticipated, make sure you are compensated for these in some way upfront.

One other change in the industry is worth special mention. The Greeting Card Create Network (GCCN) is a new organization designed to help writers and artists in the greeting card field. The group provides access to a network of industry professionals, including publishers and licensing agents and acts as a clearinghouse for information on design and marketing trends, legal and financial concerns within the industry. Membership fees in

GCCN ranges from $30 (student) to $50 (professional artist) per year. For more information contact GCCN, Suite 615, 1350 New York Ave., NW, Washington DC 20005.

For more information on illustration and design of greeting cards see *The Complete Guide to Greeting Card Design and Illustration,* by Eva Szela. Magazines such as *HOW, Step by Step Graphics* and *The Artist's Magazine* also include information of greeting card illustration. Industry magazines such as *Greetings* and *Giftware News* are a good source of information on marketing trends and also provide information on upcoming shows. For lists of stationery firms, see the *Thomas Register of Manufacturers.*

ACME GRAPHICS, INC., 201 3rd Ave. SW, Box 1348, Cedar Rapids IA 52406. (319)364-0233. President: Stan Richardson. Estab. 1913. Produces printed merchandise used by funeral directors, such as acknowledgments, register books and prayer cards.
Needs: Approached by 30 freelance artists/year. Considers pen & ink, watercolor and acrylic; religious, floral and nature art.
First Contact & Terms: Send brochure. Samples not filed are returned by SASE. Reports back within 10 days. Call or write to schedule an appointment to show a portfolio, which should include roughs. Original artwork is not returned to the artist after job's completion. Pays by the project. Payment varies. Buys all rights.
Tips: "Send samples or prints of work from other companies. Do not want to see modern art or art with figures. Some designs are too expensive to print."

ADVANCE CELLOCARD CO., INC., 1259 N. Wood St., Chicago IL 60622. (312)235-3403. President: Ron Ward. Estab. 1953. Produces greeting cards.
Needs: Considers watercolor, acrylic, oil and colored pencil. Produces material for Valentine's Day, Mother's Day, Father's Day, Easter, graduation, birthdays and everyday.
First Contact & Terms: Send query letter with brochure. Samples not filed are returned by SASE. Report back within weeks. To show a portfolio, mail original/final art. Original artwork is not returned to the artist after job's completion. Pays average flat fee of $75-150/design. Buys all rights.
Tips: "Make a phone call and follow up with samples or a letter of introduction including photostats or samples of artwork."

*AFRICA CARD CO. INC., Box 91, New York NY 10108. (212)447-5960. President: Vince Jordan. Publishes greeting cards and posters.
Needs: Buys 25 freelance designs/year.
First Contact & Terms: To show a portfolio, mail art or arrange interview. Include SASE. Reports in 6 weeks. Pays $50 minimum, greeting cards and posters. Buys all rights.

*ALASKA MOMMA, INC., 303 Fifth Ave., New York NY 10016. (212)679-4404. President: Shirley Henschel. "We are a licensing company representing artists, illustrators, designers and cartoon characters. We license artwork and design concepts to toy, clothing, giftware, stationery and housewares manufacturers and publishers."
Needs: Approached by 40-50 freelance artists/year. "An artist must have a distinctive and unique style that a manufacturer can't get from his own art department. We prefer art that can be applied to product. We are not successful at licensing cartoon art unless there is a strong central theme."
First Contact & Terms: "Artists may submit work in any way they choose, as long as it is a fair representation of their style." Henschel prefers to see several multiple color samples in a mailable size. No originals. Charges royalties of 7-10% with an advance mandatory. Earned royalties "depend on whether the products sell."
Tips: "We are interested in artists whose work is suitable for licensing program. We do not want to see black and white art drawings. What we need to see are slides or color photographs or color photocopies of finished art. We need to see a consistent style in a fairly extensive package of art. Otherwise, we don't really have a feeling for what the artist can do. The artist should think about products—and determine if the submitted material is suitable for product."

 The asterisk before a listing indicates that the listing is new in this edition. New markets are often the most receptive to freelance submissions.

ALBION CARDS, Box 810, Albion MI 49224. Owners: Maggie and Mike LaNoue. Produces greeting cards, prints, note cards, postcards, catalogs and brochures. Uses b&w, line art, realistic, detailed, old-fashioned, clear; must hold line quality when reduced to "jump out" – high contrast. Directs products to women, older people, tourists, nostalgia buffs and sports enthusiasts.

Needs: Buys approximately 50 designs from freelance artists/year. Considers pen & ink and watercolor. Size of originals 9x12 or proportionate; important elements of design and artist's signature should be one inch from all edges of the drawing. Produces material for Christmas and summer (skiing, golfing, bicycling, boating); other subjects: animals (cats & ducks especially), landscapes, wild flowers and herbs. Catalog $3; art guidelines free for SASE. Theme must be "upbeat" and positive, but not cutesy.

First Contact & Terms: Send query letter with brochure, showing art style and photocopies. Samples not filed are not returned. Reports back within 3 months if interested. Do not send originals. Send color and b&w photographs and photocopies. Pays for illustration by the project, 5% minimum. Payment depends entirely on sales; artists can boost sales and earn sales commission as well. Buys copyright outright to be used for cards only and prints; artist retains some rights for other items. Buys only scenes that have not been published as cards to date. "Looking for artists who seek long-term arrangement not fast cash."

Tips: "We are interested in producing series of cards relating to scenic tourist areas, seascapes, street scenes and landmarks. Please do not send quick sketchy work or designs that display bad taste. Work must reproduce well and give the viewer a good feeling."

AMBER LOTUS, 1241 21st. St., Oakland CA 94607. (415)839-3931. Product Manager: Jerry Horovitz. Estab. 1984. Specializes in calendars, journals and cards. Publishes 12 calendars, 9 journals, and 9 card series.

Needs: Works on assignment only. Works with 2-6 freelance artists/year. Buys 30-50 illustrations/year from freelance artists. Buys artwork mainly for calendars and greeting cards. Prefers local artists, but not necessary. Prefers airbrush, watercolor, acrylic, pastel, calligraphy and computer illustration. Buys approximately 12 computer illustrations from freelancers/year.

First Contact & Terms: Send query letter with brochure or small sampling. Samples are filed or are returned by SASE. Reports back within 6 weeks only if interested. Originals returned to artist at job's completion. Considers skill and experience of artist, project's budget and rights purchased when establishing payment.

Tips: "Show something distinctive, innovative and classy that can be used as a series of images. We are especially looking for work that has not been already over exposed in print. No pets or cartoons."

AMBERLEY GREETING CARD CO., 11510 Goldcoast Dr., Cincinnati OH 45249-1695. (513)489-2775. FAX: (513)489-2857. Vice President: Ned Stern. Estab. 1966. Produces greeting cards. "We are a multi-line company directed toward all ages. Our cards are conventional and humorous."

Needs: Approached by 20 freelance artists/year. Works with 10 freelance artists/year. Buys 200 designs/illustrations/year. Prefers local artists only. Works on assignment only. Uses freelance artists mainly for humorous cards. Considers any media. Looking for humorous styles.

First Contact & Terms: Samples are not filed and are returned by SASE if requested by artist. Reports back to artist only if interested. Call to schedule an appointment to show a portfolio which should include original/final art. Buys all rights. Original artwork is not returned at the job's completion. Pays by the project, $60.

AMERICAN GREETINGS CORPORATION, 10500 American Rd., Cleveland OH 44144. (216)252-7300. Director of Creative Recruitment: Lynne Shlonsky. Estab. 1906. Produces greeting cards, stationery, calendars, paper tableware products, giftwrap and ornaments – "a complete line of social expressions products."

Needs: Prefers artists with experience in illustration, decorative design and calligraphy.

First Contact & Terms: Send query letter with resume. "Send no samples."

ARGUS COMMUNICATIONS, INC., Division of DLM, 1 DLM Park, Allen TX 75002. Managing Art Director: June Boisseau. Produces greeting cards, postcards, calendars, posters, etc.

Needs: Approached by over 100 freelance artists/year. Works with hundreds of freelance artists/year. Must be professional artist. Works on assignment only. Uses artists for roughs, layouts and final art. Particularly interested in new approaches to greeting card illustration, general and humorous, no juvenile. Up-to-date styles – watercolor, pastel, gouache.

First Contact & Terms: Send query letter with resume and samples to be kept on file. Samples not filed are returned by SASE. Reports only if interested. To show a portfolio, mail thumbnails, roughs, tearsheets, photostats and photographs. Payment depends on project. Pays average flat fee of $300 for finished art. Considers complexity of the project and turnaround time when establishing payment.

Tips: "Be familiar with our product line before contacting us. Remember that greeting cards are a consumer product and must meet a consumer need to be successful." Sees trend toward "Southwest themes – humorous art more feminine, lighter touch, than past. Send sample with SASE – indicate what may be retained by art director and what must be returned. Do not want any complete programs or ideas with copy. All art assigned on individual basis. Editorial handled separately by different department."

*THE AVALON HILL GAME CO., 4517 Harford Rd., Baltimore MD 21214. (301)254-9200. FAX: (301)254-0991. Art Director: Jean Baer. Estab. 1958. Produces games for adults. "Primarily produces strategy and sports games, also family and computer games.

Needs: Approached by 30 freelance artists/year. Works with 10 freelance artists/year. Buys 30-50 designs and illustrations from freelance artists/year. Prefers artists with experience in military art. Works on assignment only. Uses freelance artists mainly for cover and interior art. Also uses freelance artists for calligraphy and mechanicals. Considers any media. "The styles we are looking for vary from realistic to photographic, but are sometimes fantasy. We like quality."

First Contact & Terms: Send query letter with tearsheets, slides, SASE and photocopies. Samples are filed or are returned by SASE if requested by artist. Reports back within 2-3 weeks. If does not report back, the artist should "wait. We will contact the artist if we have an applicable assignment." Call to schedule an appointment to show a portfolio or mail appropriate materials. Portfolio should include original/final art and b&w and color photostats and tearsheets. Buys all rights. Original artwork is not returned at the job's completion. Pays by the project, $500 average.

BARNSTABLE ORIGINALS, 50 Harden Ave., Camden ME 04843. (207)236-8162. Art Director: Marsha Smith. Produces greeting cards, posters and paper sculpture cards. Directed toward tourists travelling in New England and sailors or outdoors people—"nature and wildlife lovers."

Needs: Approached by 250 freelance artists/year. Buys 50 designs and illustrations from freelance artists/year. Prefers 5x7 cards, vertical or horizontal. Prefers traditional style; watercolor, acrylic and oil.

First Contact & Terms: Send query letter with brochure, photocopies, slides or photographs showing art style. Samples not filed are returned by SASE. Reports back within 1 month. No originals returned to artist at job's completion. Pays $50 minimum per design/illustration. Pays on acceptance. Buys all rights. Finds most artists through samples received through the mail.

Tips: "We're looking for quality art work—any creative and fresh ideas. The artist must display a sound background in art basics, exhibiting strong draftsmanship in a graphic style. Colors must be harmonious and clearly executed. Do not call. I can't see work over the phone (not yet anyway!) Please enclose postage for return of materials."

BARTON-COTTON INC., 1405 Parker Rd., Baltimore MD 21227. (301)247-4800. Contact: Creative/Art Department. Produces religious greeting cards, commercial Christmas cards, wildlife designs and spring note cards. Free guidelines and sample cards; specify area of interest: religious, Christmas, spring, etc.

Needs: Buys 150-200 illustrations from freelancers/year. Submit seasonal work "any time of the year."

First Contact & Terms: Send query letter with resume, tearsheets, photocopies, photostats, slides and photographs. Previously published work and simultaneous submissions accepted. Reports in 4 weeks. To show a portfolio, mail original/final art, final reproduction/product, and color tearsheets. Submit full-color work only (watercolor, gouache, pastel, oil and acrylic); pays $150-500/illustration; on acceptance.

Tips: "Good draftsmanship is a must, particularly with figures and faces. Spend some time studying market trends in the greeting card industry to determine current market trends. There is an increased need for creative ways to paint traditional Christmas scenes with up-to-date styles and techniques."

BEACH PRODUCTS, 1 Paper Pl., Kalamazoo MI 49001. (616)349-2626. Creative Director: Gabrielle Runza. Publishes paper-tableware products; general and seasonal, birthday, special occasion, invitations, announcements, stationery, wrappings and thank-you notes for children and adults.

Needs: Approached by 200 freelance artists/year. Uses artists for product design and illustration. Sometimes buys humorous and cartoon-style illustrations. Prefers flat 4-color designs; 5¼ wide × 5½ high for luncheon napkins. Produces seasonal material for Christmas, Mother's Day, Thanksgiving, Easter, Valentine's Day, St. Patrick's Day, Halloween and New Year's Day. Submit seasonal material before June 1; everyday (not holiday) material before March.

First Contact & Terms: Send query letter with 9 × 12 SASE so catalog can be sent with response. Disclosure form must be completed and returned before work will be viewed. Call or write to schedule an appointment to show a portfolio, which should include original/final art and final reproduction/product. Previously published work OK. Originals not returned to artist at job's completion; "all artwork purchased becomes the property of Beach Products. Items not purchased are returned." Pays average flat fee of $300 for illustration/design; royalties of 5%. Considers product use when establishing payment.

Tips: "When asking for specifications and catalog, the SASE should be large enough to accommodate the catalog, for example a 9 × 12 SAE. Artwork should have a clean, professional appearance and be the specified size for submissions, as well as a maximum of four flat colors." Trends include "French and Spanish influences in florals, bright graphics (color is everything)."

ANITA BECK CARDS, 3409 W. 44th St., Minneapolis MN 55410. President: Cynthia Anderson. "We manufacture and distribute greeting cards, note cards, Christmas cards and related stationery products through a wholesale and direct mail market." Clients: wholesale and direct mail.

Needs: Uses freelance artists mainly for card designs; note that photographs are not used.
First Contact & Terms: Send query letter with brochure and photographs. Samples are filed or are returned only if requested by artist. Reports back within a month. Call or write to schedule an appointment to show a portfolio. Pays for design by the project, $50 minimum. Buys all rights.
Tips: "Submit design ideas for cards."

*FREDERICK BECK ORIGINALS, 1329 Marster Rd., Burlingame CA 94010. (415)348-1510. FAX: (415)348-1247. Owner: David Bisson. Estab. 1953. Produces greeting cards: silk screen printed Christmas cards, traditional to contemporary.
Needs: Approached by 6 freelance artists/year. Works with 10 freelance artists/year. Buys 25 designs/illustrations/year. Prefers artists with experience in silk screen printing. Uses freelance artists mainly for silk screen Christmas card designs. Considers silk screen printing only. Looking for "artwork compatible with existing line; shape and color are important design elements." Prefers 5⅜×7⅛. Produces material for Christmas. Submit 12 months before holiday.
First Contact & Terms: Send query letter with simple sketches. Samples are filed. Reports back within 2 weeks. Portfolio should include thumbnails. Rights purchased vary according to project. Original artwork is not returned at job's completion "but could be." Pays by the project, $150-200.

*bePUZZLED, A DIVISION OF LOMBARD MARKETING, INC., 45 Wintonbury Ave., Bloomfield CT 06002. (203)286-4222. FAX: (203)286-4229. New Product Development.: Luci Seccareccia. Estab. 1987. Produces games and puzzles for children and adults. "bePUZZLED mystery jigsaw games challenge players to solve an original whodunit thriller by matching clues in the mystery with visual clues revealed in the puzzle."
Needs: Works with 1-3 freelance artists/year. Buys 6-10 designs and illustrations from freelancers/year. Prefers local artists with experience in children's book and adult theme illustration. Uses freelance artists mainly for box cover art and puzzle images. All illustrations are done to spec. Considers acrylic and watercolor. Prefers art 10×12, 25×30 and 21×21.
First Contact & Terms: Send query letter with brochure, resume, SASE, tearsheets, photographs and transparencies. Samples are filed. Reports back within 60 days. Will call to schedule an appointment to show a portfolio, which should include original/final art and photographs. Original artwork is returned at the job's completion. Pays by the project, $100 minimum.

©1989 bePuzzled

Luci Seccareccia, new products developer at bePuzzled in Bloomfield, Connecticut, says the company "uses artists to illustrate box covers and the puzzles the boxes hold." Seccareccia commonly discovers artists through references from other artists and art directors. She looks for "regional accuracy, ability to meet deadlines, enthusiasm and responsiveness" in artists.

*BRAZEN IMAGES INC., 269 Chatterton Parkway, White Plains NY 10606. (914)949-2605. FAX: (914)683-7927. Art Director: Kurt Abraham. Produces greeting cards "for anyone over 18; we make adult sexually oriented cards."

Needs: Approached by 200 freelance artists/year. Works with 5-10 freelance artists/year. Buys 20-50 illustrations from freelance artists/year. Prefers airbrush; but "we like a wide range of styles." Artwork must be proportional to a 5×7 greeting card with extra for trim. Both vertical and horizontal are OK. Produces material for Christmas, Halloween, Valentine's Day, birthdays and weddings. "We look for material all year long—we store it up until press time. If it doesn't make it in one year's printing, it'll make it the next."
First Contact & Terms: Send query letter with brochure, slides, SASE and any clear copy of nonpublished work plus SASE. Samples are filed or are returned by SASE only if requested by artists. Reports back within 1 month. Call or mail original/final art and b&w slides and photographs. Original artwork is "in most cases" returned to the artist after job's completion. Pays average flat fee of $200-300/illustration; by the project, $200-300 average. Buys one-time rights.
Tips: "As our name implies, we expect work to be brazen and very upfront sexually. Subtlety is not for us!" A trend seems to be that "big companies are eating up little companies and destroying them. Also, there is less risk-taking overall (except us of course!)"

BRICKHOUSE PRODUCTIONS, 2505 Amherst Ave., Orlando FL 32804. President/Founder: Michael Houbrick. Estab. 1985. Produces greeting cards. "Publishes hip greeting cards featuring Mr. Brick and other well-known characters. Most cards are geared for the thirty-something crowd."
Needs: Approached by 30 freelance artists/year. Works with 1-3 freelance artists/year. Buys 1-3 designs and illustrations from freelancers/year. Prefers artists with experience in watercolor and cartooning. Works on assignment only. Considers pen & ink and watercolor only. Produces material for all holidays and seasons and the lottery. Submit 12 months before holiday.
First Contact & Terms: Send query letter with brochure, resume and tearsheets. Samples are filed or are not returned. Reports back only if interested. Original artwork is not returned to the artist after job's completion. Pays average flat fee of $100/design; $200/illustration. Buys all rights.
Tips: "Environmental issues are big in the 1990s. Send queries only when established. Many people send out stuff before they are ready to sell artwork."

BRILLIANT ENTERPRISES, 117 W. Valerio St., Santa Barbara CA 93101. Art Director: Ashleigh Brilliant. Publishes postcards.
Needs: Buys up to 300 designs from freelancers/year. Artists may submit designs for word-and-picture postcards, illustrated with line drawings.
First Contact & Terms: Submit 5½×3½ horizontal b&w line drawings and SASE. Reports in 2 weeks. Buys all rights. "Since our approach is very offbeat, it is essential that freelancers first study our line. Ashleigh Brilliant's books include *I May Not Be Totally Perfect, But Parts of Me Are Excellent* and *Appreciate Me Now and Avoid the Rush*. We supply a catalog and sample set of cards for $2." Pays $40 minimum, depending on "the going rate" for camera-ready word-and-picture design.
Tips: "Since our product is highly unusual, freelancers should familiarize themselves with it by sending for our catalog ($2 plus SASE). Otherwise, they will just be wasting our time and theirs."

BURGOYNE, INC., 2030 E. Byberry Rd., Philadelphia PA 19116. (215)677-8000. Art Director: Jon Harding. Publishes greeting cards and calendars; Christmas, winter and religious themes.
Needs: Buys 75-100 designs/year. Prefers artists experienced in greeting card design. Uses freelance artists for product design and illustration and calligraphy. Will review any media; prefers art proportional to 5¼×7⅛. Produces seasonal material for Christmas; will review new work at any time.
First Contact & Terms: Send query letter with original art, published work or actual work. Samples returned by SASE. Simultaneous submissions OK. Reports in 2 weeks. No originals returned to artist at job's completion. To show a portfolio, mail appropriate materials or call to schedule an appointment; portfolio should include original/final art and final reproduction/product. Pays for design by the project, $100-300. Buys all rights; on acceptance.
Tips: "Familiarize yourself with greeting card field. Spend time in card stores."

CAPE SHORE, INC., 42 N. Elm St., Box 1020, Yarmouth ME 04096. Art Director: Anne W. Macleod. Produces notes, stationery products and giftware for year round and Christmas markets. Nautical plus inland in theme. Directs products to gift and stationery stores and shops.
Needs: Buys 25-50 designs and illustrations/year from freelance artists. Prefers watercolor, acrylic, cut paper or gouache. June deadline for finished artwork.
First Contact & Terms: "Please send sample artwork so we can judge if style is compatible. All samples and reports will be returned within several weeks." Pays by the project, $25-200. Pays average flat fee of $125/design. Prefers to buy all rights. Originals returned to artist if not purchased.
Tips: "We do not use black-and-white artwork, greeting cards or photography. Submit samples to see if styles are compatible."

CASE STATIONERY CO., INC., 179 Saw Mill River Rd., Yonkers NY 10701. (914)965-5100. President: Jerome Sudwow. Vice President: Joyce Blackwood. Estab. 1954. Produces stationery, notes, memo pads and tins for mass merchandisers in stationery and housewares departments.

Needs: Approached by 10 freelance artists/year. Buys 50 designs from freelance artists/year. Works on assignment only. Buys design and/or illustration mainly for stationery products. Uses artists for mechanicals and ideas. Produces materials for Christmas; submit 6 months in advance. Likes to see English and French country themes.

First Contact & Terms: Send query letter with resume and tearsheets, photostats, photocopies, slides and photographs. Samples not filed are returned. Reports back. Call or write to schedule an appointment to show a portfolio. Original artwork is not returned. Pays by the project. Buys first rights or one-time rights.

Tips: "Get to know us. We're people who are creative and who know how to sell a product."

H. GEORGE CASPARI, INC., 225 Fifth Ave., New York NY 10010. (212)685-9726. President: Douglas H. Stevens. Publishes greeting cards, Christmas cards, invitations, giftwrap and paper napkins. The line maintains a very traditional theme.

Needs: Buys 80-100 illustrations/year from freelance artists. Prefers watercolor and other color media. Produces seasonal material for Christmas, Mother's Day, Father's Day, Easter and Valentine's Day.

First Contact & Terms: Arrange an appointment with Lucille Andriola to review portfolio. Prefers unpublished original illustrations as samples. Reports within 4 weeks. Negotiates payment on acceptance; pays for design by the project, $300 minimum.

Tips: "Caspari and many other small companies rely on freelance artists to give the line a fresh, overall style rather than relying on one artist. We feel this is a strong point of our company. Please do not send verses."

COLLECTOR'S GALLERY, 2165 Daniels St., Long Lake MN 55356. President: Polly McCrea. Estab. 1980. Produces greeting cards, giftwrap and stationery. Manufactures gift packaging (wrap, boxes and bags), seasonal cards and paper gift products (notepads, filled boxes, stationery sets) with emphasis on children's contemporary design and seasonal products for traditional, yet updated consumer.

Needs: Approached by 50 freelance aritsts/year. Works with 3-4 freelance artists/year. Buys 25 designs and illustrations/year from freelance artists. Prefers local artists with experience in stationery and gift industry. Buys freelance design and illustrations mainly for tote bags, cards and photocards. Consider marker comps, cut paper or black & white with colorbreak. Looking for "simple, bold designs, printing done in solid PMS colors for silkscreen effect. Artwork is simple and slightly stylized rather than realistic or illustrative." Produces material for Christmas, Valentine's Day, Easter, Halloween, birthdays and everyday. Submit 10 months before holiday.

First Contact & Terms: Send query letter with brochure, photocopies and SASE. Samples are filed or are returned by SASE. Reports back within 2 weeks. To show a portfolio, mail roughs, original/final art and final reproduction/product. Original artwork is returned to the artist after job's completion. Pays by the project, $150-500-average. Negotiates rights purchased.

Tips: "Send resume and examples of work with SASE. Examples of printed or produced work are best." Sees trend towards "increase in market—graphics, either simplified or very realistic; ornate, such as florals, Victorian."

CPS CORPORATION, 1715 Columbia Ave., Franklin TN 37065. (615)794-8000. Art Director: Francis Huffman Manufacturer producing Christmas and all-occasion giftwrap.

Needs: Approached by 75 freelance artists/year. Assigns 75-100 freelance jobs/year. Uses freelance artists mainly for giftwrap design.

First Contact & Terms: Send query letter with resume, tearsheets, photostats and slides. Samples are filed or are returned by SASE. Reports back only if interested. Call or write to schedule an appointment to show a portfolio, which should include roughs, original/final art, final reproduction/product, tearsheets and photostats. Pays average flat fee of $400 for illustration/design. Considers complexity of project and skill and experience of artist when establishing payment. Negotiates rights purchased.

Tips: "Designs should be appropriate for one or more of the following categories; Christmas, wedding, baby shower, birthday, masculine/feminine and abstracts." Sees trend toward "giftwrap becoming more high fashion; photography and illustration becoming a larger niche of market."

CREATE-A-CRAFT, Box 330008, Fort Worth TX 76163-0008. (817)292-1855. Editor: Mitchell Lee. Estab. 1967. Produces greeting cards, giftwrap, games, calendars, posters, stationery and paper tableware products for all ages.

Needs: Approached by 500 freelance artists/year. Works with 3 freelance artists/year. Buys 3-5 designs and illustrations from freelance artists/year. Prefers artists with experience in cartooning. Works on assignment only. Buys freelance design and illustration mainly for greetings cards and T-shirts. Also uses freelance artists for calligraphy, P-O-P display, paste-up and mechanicals. Considers pen & ink, watercolor, acrylic and colored pencil. Prefers humor and "cartoons that will appeal to families. Must be cute, apealing, etc. No religious, sexual implications or off-beat humor." Produces material for all holidays and seasons; submit 6 months before holiday.

First Contact & Terms: Contact only through artist's agent. Samples are filed and are not returned. Reports back only if interested. Write to schedule an appointment to show a portfolio, which should include original/final art, final reproduction/product and color and b&w slides and tearsheets. Original artwork is not returned to the artist after job's completion. "Payment depends upon the assignment, amount of work involved, production costs, etc. involved in the project." Buys all rights.

Tips: "Demonstrate an ability to follow directions exactly. Too many submit artwork that has no relationship to what we produce. Sample greeting cards are available for $2.50 and a #10 envelope with SASE. Demonstrate an ability to follow directions exactly. Write, do not call. We can not tell what the artwork looks like from a phone call."

CREATIF LICENSING, 31 Old Town Crossing, Mount Kisco NY 10549. President: Stan Cohen. Licensing Manager. "Creatif is a licensing agency that represents artists and concept people. Creatif Licensing is looking for unique art styles and/or concepts that are applicable to multiple products. The art can range from fine art to cartooning."

First Contact & Terms: "If you have a style that you feel fits our qualifications please send photocopies or slides of your work with a SASE. If we are interested in representing you, we would present your work to the appropriate manufacturers in the clothing, gift, publishing, home furnishings, paper products (cards/gift wrap/party goods, etc.) areas with the intent of procuring a license. We try to obtain advances and/or guarantees against a royalty percentage of the firm's sales. We will negotiate and handle the contracts for these arrangements, show at several trade shows to promote the artist's style and oversee payments to insure that the requirements of our contracts are honored. The artists are responsible for providing us with materials for our meetings and presentations and for copyrights, trademarks and protecting their ownership (which is discretionary). For our services, as indicated above, we receive fifty per cent of all the deals we negotiate as well as renewals. There are no fees if we are not productive."

Tips: Common mistakes illustrators make in presenting samples or portfolios are "sending oversized samples mounted on heavy board; not sending in appropriate material; sending washed out slides."

CREATIVE PAPERS BY C.R. GIBSON, The C.R. Gibson Co., Knight St., Norwalk CT 06856. (203)847-4543. Vice President Creative Papers: Steven P. Mack. Publishes stationery, note paper, invitations and giftwrap. Interested in material for stationery collections or individual notes and invitations. "Two to three designs are sufficient to get across a collection concept. We don't use too many regional designs. Stationery themes are up-to-date, fashion oriented. Designs should be somewhat sophisticated without being limiting. Classic designs and current material from the giftware business do well."

Needs: Buys 100-200 freelance designs/year. Especially needs new 4-color art for note line and invitations; "we need designs that relate to current fashion trends as well as a wide variety of illustrations suitable for boxed note cards. We constantly update our invitation line and can use a diverse selection of ideas." Uses some humorous illustrations but only for invitation line. "We buy a broad range of artwork with assorted themes. The only thing we don't buy is very contemporary or avant-garde." Prefers gouache, watercolor, acrylic, oil and collage. Speculation art has no size limitations. Finished size of notes is $4 \times 5\frac{1}{2}$ and $3\frac{3}{4} \times 5$; folded invitations, $3\frac{3}{4} \times 5$; card style invitations, $4\frac{3}{8} \times 6$; and giftwrap repeat, 9×9 minimum.

First Contact & Terms: Send query letter with brochure showing art style or resume, photocopies, slides and SASE. Prefers 4-6 samples (slides or chromes of work or originals), published or unpublished. Previously published, photocopied and simultaneous submissions OK, if they have not been published as cards and the artist has previous publishers' permissions. Reports in 6 weeks. Call or write to schedule an appointment to show a portfolio, which should include thumbnails, roughs, original/final art and tearsheets. Pays $35-50 for rough sketch. Pays average flat fee of $200, design; $200, illustration; by the hour, $20-25 average; royalties of 6%. Negotiates payment. Usually buys all rights; sometimes buys limited rights.

Tips: "Almost all of the artists we work with or have worked with are professional in that they have a background of other professional assignments and exhibits as well as a good art education. We have been fortunate to make a few 'discoveries,' but even these people have been at it for a number of years and have a very distinctive style with complete understanding of printing specifications and mechanicals. More artists are asking for royalties and are trying to develop licensed characters. Most of the work is not worthy of a royalty, and people don't understand what it takes to make a 'character' sell. Keep your presentation neat and don't send very large pieces of art. Keep the submission as varied as possible. I am not particularly interested in pen & ink drawings. Everything we print is in full color."

THE CROCKETT COLLECTION, Rt. 7, Box 1428, Manchester Center VT 05255. (802)362-2913. FAX: (802)362-5590. President: Sharon Scheirer. Estab. 1929. Publishes mostly traditional, some contemporary, humorous and whimsical Christmas and everyday greeting cards, postcards, note cards and bordered stationery. Christmas themes geared to sophisticated, upper-income individuals. Free artist's guidelines.

Needs: Approached by 225 freelance artists/year. Buys 25-75 designs/year from freelance artists. Produces products by silkscreen method exclusively. Considers gouache, poster paint, cut and pasted paper and acrylic.
First Contact & Terms: Send query letter. Request guidelines which are mailed out once a year in January, one year in advance of printing. Submit unpublished, original designs only. Art should be in finished form. Art not purchased returned by SASE. Buys all rights. Pays $90-140 per design.
Tips: "Designs must be suitable for silkscreen process. Airbrush and watercolor techniques are not amenable to this process. Bold, well-defined designs only. We are seeing more demand for religious themes on Christmas cards. Our look is traditional, mostly realistic and graphic. Request guidelines and submit work according to our instrucitons."

*DALEE BOOK CO., 267 Douglas St., Brooklyn NY 11217. (718)852-6969. Vice President: Charles Hutter. Estab. 1964. Produces stationery accessories. "We manufacture photo albums and telephone address books for the family and the fine arts market.
Needs: Approached by 5 freelance artists/year. Works with 1 feelance artist/year. Buys 1-3 designs and illustrations/year from freelance artists. Prefers local artists only. Works on assignment only. Uses freelance artists mainly for labels and mechanicals. Considers any media.
First Contact & Terms: Send query letter with photocopies. Samples are not filed and are returned by SASE if requested by artist. Reports back to the artist only if interested. Write to schedule an appointment to show a portfolio or mail appropriate materials. Portfolio should include roughs and color samples. Buys all rights. Original artwork is not returned at the job's completion. Pays by the project, $200-500 average.

DECORAL INC., 165 Marine St., Farmingdale NY 11735. (516)752-0076; (800)645-9868. President: Walt Harris. Produces decorative, instant stained glass, plus sports and wildlife decals.
Needs: Buys 50 designs and illustrations from freelance artists/year. Uses artists mainly for greeting cards and decals; also uses artists for P-O-P displays. Prefers watercolor.
First Contact & Terms: Send query letter with brochure showing art style or resume and samples. Samples not filed are returned. Reports back within 30 days. To show a portfolio, call or write to schedule an appointment or mail original/final art, final reproduction/product and photostats. Original artwork is not returned. Pays average flat fee, $200 minimum, illustration or design. Buys all rights.

*DESIGNER GREETINGS, INC., Box 140729, Staten Island NY 10314. (718)981-7700. Art Director: Fern Gimbelman. Produces greeting cards and invitations, and general, informal, inspirational, contemporary, juvenile, soft-line and studio cards.
Needs: Works with 16 freelance artists/year. Buys 100-150 designs and illustrations from freelance artists/year. Works on assignment only. Also uses artists for calligraphy, P-O-P displays and airbrushing. Prefers pen & ink and airbrush. No specific size required. Produces material for all seasons; submit 6 months before holiday.
First Contact & Terms: Send query letter with brochure or tearsheets, photostats or photocopies. Samples are filed or are returned only if requested. Reports back within 3-4 weeks. Call or write to schedule an appointment to show a portfolio, which should include original/final art, final reproduction/product, tearsheets and photostats. Original artwork is not returned after job's completion. Pays average flat fee. Buys all rights.
Tips: "We are willing to look at any work through the mail, (photocopies, etc.). Appointments are given after I personally speak with the artist (by phone)."

*DIEBOLD DESIGNS, Box 236, High Bridge Rd., Lyme NH 03768. (603)795-4592. FAX: (603)795-4222. Principle: Peter Diebold. Estab. 1978. Produces greeting cards. "We produce special cards for special interests and greeting cards for businesses, primarily Christmas."
Needs: Approached by more than 20 freelance artists/year. Works with 5-10 freelance artists/year. Buys 10-20 designs and illustrations/year from freelance artists. Prefers professional caliber artists. Works on assignment only. Uses freelance artists mainly for greeting card design, calligraphy and mechanicals. Also uses freelance artists for paste-up. Considers all media. "We market cards designed to appeal to individual's specific interest—golf, tennis, etc." Looking for an upscale look. "Our cards are all 5×7." Produces material for Christmas and special cards for business people. Submit 6-9 months before holiday.
First Contact & Terms: Send query letter with SASE and brief samples of work. Samples are filed or are returned by SASE. Reports back to artist only if interested. To show a portfolio, mail appropriate materials. "Portfolio should be kept simple." Rights purchased vary according to project. Return of originals at the job's completion is negotiable. Pays by the project, $100 minimum.

*DREAMSCAPE PRESS, Box 389, Northport AL 35476. (205)349-4629. Publisher: Cynthia McConnell. Estab. 1986. Produces greeting cards. "We publish alternative greeting cards, which are primarily watercolor, but not limited as such."

Needs: Approached by 10-15 freelance artists/year. Works with 5 freelance artists/year. Works on assignment only. Also uses freelance artists for original artwork. Considers any media. "We are seeking dreamy, archetypal, somewhat surreal styles. Considers humorous work." Prefers art no larger than 10×14. Produces material for Christmas, birthdays and everyday. Submit 6 months before holiday.

First Contact & Terms: Send query letter with brochure, SASE, photographs, photocopies and slides. Samples are filed. Reports back to the artist only if interested. Rights purchased vary according to project. Original artwork is returned at the job's completion. Pays royalties, which vary.

EARTH CARE PAPER INC., Box 3335, Madison WI 53704. (608)256-5232. Art Director: Barbara Budig. Estab. 1983. Produces greeting cards, giftwrap, note cards and stationery. "All of our products are printed on recycled paper and are targeted toward nature enthusiasts and environmentalists."

Needs: Buys 50-75 illustrations from freelance artists/year. Uses artists for greeting cards, giftwrap, note cards, stationery and postcards. Considers all media. Produces Christmas cards; seasonal material should be submitted 12 months before the holiday.

First Contact & Terms: "For initial contact, artists should submit samples which we can keep on file." Reports back within 2 months. Original artwork is usually returned after publication. Pays 5% royalties plus a cash advance on royalties or a flat fee, $100 minimum. Buys reprint rights.

Tips: "We primarily use a nature theme but will consider anything. We consider graphic, realistic or abstract designs. We would like to develop a humor line based on environmental and social issues. We are primarily mail order. This year we would like to see art with a tree or forest theme. Submit samples we can keep on file."

THE EVERGREEN PRESS, INC., 3380 Vincent Rd., Pleasant Hill CA 94523. (415)933-9700. Art Director: Malcolm K. Nielsen. Publishes greeting cards, giftwrap, stationery, quality art reproductions, Christmas cards and postcards.

Needs: Approached by 750-1,000 freelance artists/year. Buys 200 designs/year from freelance artists. Buys design and/or illustration mainly for greeting cards, Christmas cards and gift wrap and product design. Uses only full-color artwork in any media in unusual designs, sophisticated art and humor or series with a common theme. No super-sentimental Christmas themes, single greeting card designs with no relation to each other, or single color pen or pencil sketches. Roughs may be in any size to get an idea of work; final art must meet size specifications. Would like to see nostalgia, ecology, fine-arts-oriented themes. Produces seasonal material for Christmas, Easter and Valentine's Day; "we examine artwork at any time of the year to be published for the next following holiday."

First Contact & Terms: Send query letter with brochure showing art style or slides and actual work; write for art guidelines. Samples returned by SASE. Reports within 2 weeks. To show a portfolio, mail roughs and original/final art. Originals returned at job's completion. Negotiates rights purchased. "We usually make a cash down payment against royalties; royalty to be negotiated. Pays on publication.

Tips: Sees "trend toward using recycled paper for cards and envelopes and subject matter involving endangered species, the environment and ecology. Spend some time in greeting card stores and become familiar with the 'hot' cards of the moment. Try to find some designs that have been published by the company you approach."

THE FIORI COLLECTION, 710 W. 5th St., Austin TX 78701. (512)328-5881. Art Director: Cheryl Eckholm. Estab. 1983. Produces greeting cards, posters and stationery targeted to high-end sophisticated corporate and consumer markets. Specializes in intricate embossing.

Needs: Works with 12 freelance artists/year. Buys 200 designs/illustrations/year from freelance artists. Works on assignment only. Buys freelance designs/illustrations mainly for corporate custom designs. Also uses artists for calligraphy, paste-up and mechanicals. Considers pen & ink, watercolor, acrylic and colored pencil. Seeks strong graphics. Produces material for Christmas, graduation, New Year, birthdays and everyday; submit 12 months before holiday.

First Contact & Terms: Send query letter with brochure, tearsheets, photocopies and slides. Samples are filed or are returned only if requested by artist. Reports back within 2 weeks. To show a portfolio, mail final reproduction/product, slides, tearsheets and photographs. Original artwork is not returned to the artist after job's completion. Pays by the project, $100-500-average. Buys all rights.

*GORDON FRASER GALLERY, 173 S. Main St., New Town CT 06470. (203)426-8174. FAX: (203)426-3367. Creative Director: Claire Bannister. Estab. 1962. Produces greeting cards, stationery, paper tableware products, giftware and totes. "Our products have realistic designs, are museum reproductions and Victorian.

Needs: Approached by 40 freelance artists/year. Works with 15 freelance artists/year. Buys 150 designs and illustrations/year from freelance artists. Uses freelance artists for all product areas. Produces material for all holidays and seasons: Halloween, Easter, Valentine's Day, Hannukkah, Thanksgiving, Mother's Day, New Year, graduation, birthdays and everyday. Submit 6 months before holiday.

First Contact & Terms: Send query letter with slides. Samples are filed or are returned by SASE if requested by artist. Reports back within 5 days. Call to schedule an appointment to show a portfolio which should include original/final art and slides. Rights purchased vary according to project. Original artwork is not returned at the job's completion unless specifically requested. Pays by the project, $300 minimum.

*FRAVESSI-LAMONT INC., 11 Edison Pl., Springfield NJ 07081. (201)564-7700. Art Director: H. Monahan. Estab. 1934. Produces greeting cards.
Needs: Buys "thousands" of designs and "few" illustrations/year from freelance artists. Uses artists for greeting card design and illustration. Especially needs seasonal and everyday designs; prefers color washes or oil paintings for illustrations.
First Contact & Terms: Send query letter and samples of work. Prefers roughs as samples. Produces seasonal material for Christmas, Mother's Day, Father's Day, Thanksgiving, Easter, Valentine's Day and St. Patrick's Day; submit art 10 months before holiday. Include SASE. Reports in 2-3 weeks. No originals returned to artist at job's completion. Provide samples to be kept on file for possible future assignments. To show a portfolio, mail roughs and some originals. Buys all rights. Negotiates payment; pays $75 minimum; pays on acceptance. Considers product use and reproduction expense when establishing payment. Free artist's guidelines.
Tips: Would like to see "various styles, general and humorous, not cartoons."

FREEDOM GREETINGS, Box 715, Bristol PA 19007. (215)945-3300. Vice President: Jay Levitt. Estab. 1969. Produces greeting cards featuring flowers and scenery.
Needs: Approached by over 100 freelance artists/year. Buys 200 designs from freelance artists/year. Works on assignment only. Considers watercolor, acrylic, etc. Prefers novelty. Call for size specifications. Produces material for all seasons and holidays; submit 14 months in advance.
First Contact & Terms: Send query letter with resume and samples. Samples are returned by SASE. Reports within 10 days. To show a portfolio, mail roughs and original/final art. Originals returned to artist at job's completion. Pays average flat fee of $150-275, illustration/design. Buys all greeting and stationery rights.

GALLANT GREETING CORP., 2654 W. Medill Ave., Chicago IL 60647. (312)489-2000. Creative Director: John Fenwick. Estab. 1965. Produces greeting cards and stationery. Produces everyday and seasonal cards. "Looking for contemporary illustration and graphics with humorous and traditional themes."
Needs: Works with 40 freelance artists/year. Buys 500 designs and illustrations/year. Also uses freelance artists for calligraphy and paste-up. Considers all media. Produces material for all holidays and seasons; submit 9 months before holiday.
First Contact & Terms: Send query letter with photocopies. Samples are filed or are returned only if requested by artist. Reports back within 14 days. Call to schedule an appointment to show a portfolio. Original artwork is sometimes returned to the artist after job's completion. Pays average flat fee of $100-300, illustration. Buys exclusive greeting card rights worldwide.

THE C.R. GIBSON CO., Creative Papers Greeting Cards, 32 Knight St., Norwalk CT 06856. (203)847-4543. Product Manager: John C.W. Carroll. Estab. 1870. Produces greeting cards, photo albums, social books and stationery.
Needs: Approached by over 200 freelance artists/year. Buys 100-200 designs and illustrations from freelance artists/year, mainly for greeting cards, but also for albums, stationery, wrap, gifts, books, baby and wedding collections. Considers most media except collage. Scale work to a minimum of 4 ⅛×6 ¾. Prefers vertical image. Submissions reviewed year-round; submit seasonal material 12 months before the holiday. Will send guidelines on request.
First Contact & Terms: Send query letter and samples showing art style and/or resume and tearsheets, photostats, photocopies, slides, photographs and other materials. Prefers samples, not originals. Samples not filed are returned by SASE. Reports in 2 months. Call or write for appointment to show portfolio, which should include final reproduction/product, tearsheets, photographs and transparencies along with representative originals. Original artwork returned at job's completion. Pays $200 minimum per illustration or design. Negotiates rights purchased.
Tips: "Please consider the appropriateness of an image for an occasion—its 'sendability.' Also, we're happy to consider an artist's suggestions for verse/text. Don't show too many pieces and apologize about some of them; I'd rather see one piece the artist loves than to see ten pieces he or she has to qualify. Our orientation is toward fashion, and "Pretty" as a category has become tremendously important; it includes florals and general styling of a line, by illustration and design. Of particular interest will be work that embodies deluxe production techniques, such as embossing, die-cutting and foil stamping. Our line has grown more traditional, because this is what our customers perceive as appropriate coming from C.R. Gibson/Creative Papers."

*THE GIFT WRAP COMPANY, 28 Spring Ave., Revere MA 02151. (617)284-6000. FAX: (617)284-7007. Sales Coordinator: Wendy Keller. Estab. 1903. Produces giftwrap and invitations; "primarily everyday giftwrap for all occasions, mostly traditional with an emphasis on baby and juvenile designs."

Needs: Approached by 50 freelance artists/year. Works with 10 freelance artists/year. Buys 75 designs/illustrations/year from freelance artists. Prefers artists with experience in giftwrap. Uses freelance artists mainly for giftwrap designs. Also uses freelance artists for P-O-P displays and mechanicals. Size preferred "depends on how the design will be printed—whether in the U.S. or at one of our subsidiary companies in the U.K. or Sweden." Produces material for Christmas, birthdays, Valentine's Day, everyday. Submit 9 months before holiday.
First Contact & Terms: Send query letter with brochure or tearsheets and resume. Samples are not filed and are returned by SASE if requested by artist. Reports back within 2 weeks. Call to schedule an appointment to show a portfolio, which should include roughs, original/final art and color samples. Negotiates rights purchased. Original artwork is not returned at the job's completion. Pays by the project, $250-350.

*GLITTERWRAP, INC., 40 Carver Ave., Westwood NJ 07675. (201)666-9700. FAX: (201)666-5444. President: Melinda Scott. Estab. 1987. Produces giftwrap for contemporary mylar and iridescent wraps and totes.
Needs: Approached by 25 freelance artists/year. Works with 15 freelance artists/year. Buys more than 50 designs/illustrations/year from freelance artists. Uses freelance artists mainly for giftwrap and totebags. Also uses freelance artists for paste-up and mechanicals. Considers designs on acetate. Looking for a contemporary graphic and upscale look. Produces material for all holidays and seasons. Submit 10 months before holiday.
First Contact & Terms: Send query letter with brochure, resume, tearsheets, photostats, resume, photographs, slides, photocopies and transparencies. Samples are not filed and are returned by SASE if requested by artist. Reports back within 2 weeks. To show portfolio, mail thumbnails, roughs and original/final art. Negotiates rights purchased; rights purchased vary according to project. Original artwork is not returned at the job's completion. Pays by the project, $250-600; royalties of 5%.

GRAND RAPIDS CALENDAR CO., 906 S. Division Ave., Grand Rapids MI 49507. (616)243-1732. Art Director: Rob Van Sledright. Publishes calendars; pharmacy, medical and family themes.
Needs: Buys approximately 15 designs/year. Uses artists for advertising art and line drawings.
First Contact & Terms: Send query letter and SASE for information sheet. Reports in 2 weeks. Previously published, photocopied and simultaneous submissions OK. Pays $10 minimum.

THE GREAT NORTHWESTERN GREETING SEED COMPANY, Box 776, Oregon City OR 97045. (503)631-3425. Operations Manager: Norma Rae. Produces greeting cards.
Needs: Approached by 30-40 freelance artists/year. Buys design and/or illustration mainly for greeting cards. Uses artists for calligraphy, P-O-P displays, paste-up and mechanicals. Prefers watercolor. Prefers final size of art to be equal to 150% of product. Would like to see natural themes—botanical, landscapes. Produces material for Christmas, Mother's Day, Father's Day and Valentine's Day. Submit 6 months in advance.
First Contact & Terms: Send query letter with resume and samples to be kept on file. Accepts slides, photostats, photographs, photocopies and tearsheets as samples. Samples not filed are returned by SASE only. No originals returned to artist at job's completion. Pays royalties. Buys all rights.
Tips: "Send examples of work. Express interest and name expectations."

GREETWELL, D-23, M.I.D.C., Satpur, Nasik 422 007 India. Chief Executive: H.L. Sanghavi. Produces greeting cards, calendars and posters.
Needs: Approached by 50-60 freelance artists/year. Buys 50 designs from freelance artists/year. Buys freelance designs/illustrations mainly for greeting cards and calendars. Prefers flowers, landscapes, wildlife and general themes.
First Contact & Terms: Send color photos and samples to be kept on file. Samples not filed are returned only if requested. Reports within 4 weeks. Original art returned after reproduction. Pays flat fee of $50/design. Buys reprint rights.
Tips: "Send color photos."

STUART HALL CO., INC., Box 419381, Kansas City MO 64141. Vice President of Advertising and Art: Judy Riedel. Produces stationery, school supplies and office supplies.
Needs: Buys 40 designs and illustrations from freelance artists/year. Artist must be experienced—no beginners. Works on assignment only. Uses freelance artists for design, illustration, calligraphy, paste-up and mechanicals. Considers pencil sketches, rough color, layouts, tight comps or finished art; watercolor, gouache, or acrylic paints are preferred for finished art. Avoid fluorescent colors. "All art should be prepared on heavy white paper and lightly attached to illustration board. Allow at least one inch all around the design for notations and crop marks. Avoid bleeding the design. In designing sheet stock, keep the design small enough to allow for letter writing space. If designing for an envelope, first consult us to avoid technical problems."
First Contact & Terms: Send query letter with resume, tearsheets, photostats, slides and photographs. Samples not filed returned by SASE. Reports only if interested. To show a portfolio, mail roughs, original/final art, final reproduction/product, color, tearsheets, photostats and photographs. No originals returned to artist at job completion. 'Stuart Hall may choose to negotiate on price but generally accepts the artist's price." Buys all rights.

HALLMARK CARDS, INC., Box 419580, 2501 McGee, Kansas City MO 64141-6580, Mail Drop 276. Contact: Carol King. Produces greeting cards, giftwrap, calendars, partyware, albums, stationery and gift items.

Needs: Buys artwork for a diversified product offering. Works on assignment only with freelance illustrators, designers, calligraphers, cartoonists and needlework artists. "Freelancers must display unique concepts, innovative techniques and good color sense." Send query letter and SASE to request submission guidelines. Do not forward samples with initial query.

Tips: "Hallmark has a large and prolific creative staff. Freelancers must show exceptional skills and originality to interest art directors."

*HARVARD FAIR CORPORATION, Suite 18, 11588 Sorrento Valley Rd., San Diego CA 92121. (619)792-1833. FAX: (619)792-1835. Vice President/Sales/Marketing: Saralyn Englert. Estab. 1984. Produces giftwrap, pull bows, bag enclosures and gift bags for all ages.

Needs: Also uses freelance artists for P-O-P displays. Produces material for all holidays and seasons. Submit 6 months before holiday.

First Contact & Terms: Send query with brochure. Samples are filed. Reports back within 1 week.

INTERCONTINENTAL GREETINGS LTD., 176 Madison Ave., New York NY 10016. (212)683-5830. Creative Marketing Director: Robin Lipner. Sells reproduction rights on a per country per product basis. Licenses and syndicates to 4,500-5,000 publishers and manufacturers in 50 different countries. Industries include greeting cards, calendars, prints, posters, stationery, books, textiles, heat transfers, giftware, china, plastics, toys and allied industries, scholastic items and giftwrap.

Needs: Approached by 500-700 freelance artists/year. Assigns 400-500 jobs and 1,500 designs and illustrations/year from freelance artists. Buys illustration/design mainly for greeting cards and paper products. Also buys illustration for giftwrap, calendars and scholastic products. Uses some humorous and cartoon-style illustrations. Prefers airbrush and watercolor, then colored pencil, acrylic, pastel, marker and computer illustration. Prefers "clean work in series format; all card subjects are considered."

First Contact & Terms: Send query letter and/or resume, tearsheets, slides, photographs and SASE. To show a portfolio, mail appropriate materials or call or write to schedule an appointment; portfolio should include original/final art and color tearsheets and photographs. Pays by average flat fee of $225; design. Pays by the project, design and illustration. Pays 20% royalties upon sale of reproduction rights on all selected designs. Contractual agreements made with artists and licensing representatives; will negotiate reasonable terms. Provides worldwide promotion, portfolio samples (upon sale of art) and worldwide trade show display.

Tips: "More and more of our clients need work submitted in series form, so we have to ask artists for work in a series or possibly reject the odd single designs submitted. Make as neat and concise a presentation as possible with commerical application in mind. Show us color examples of at least one finished piece as well as roughs." Sees trend towards "humorous characters."

*JILLSON & ROBERTS, INC., 5 Watson Ave., Irvine CA 92718. (714)859-8781. Art Director: Lisa Henry. Estab. 1974. Produces giftwrap. "We produce giftwrap and gift bags for adults, teenagers and children. Colorful graphic designs as well as humorous or sophisticated designs are what we are looking for."

Needs: Approached by several freelance artists/year. Works with 10 freelance artists/year. Prefers artists with experience in giftwrap. Buys freelance design and illustration mainly for giftwrap. Also uses freelance artists for paste-up. Considers all media. Prefers elegant, humorous, sophisticated, contemporary styles. Produces material for Christmas, Valentine's Day, Hanukkah, Halloween, graduation, birthdays, baby announcements and everyday. Submit 1 year before holiday.

First Contact & Terms: Send query letter with brochure showing art style, tearsheets and slides. Samples are filed and are returned. Reports back within 3 weeks. To show a portfolio, mail thumbnails, roughs, original/final art, final reproduction/product, color slides and photographs. Original artwork is not returned to the artist after job's completion. Pays by the project. Buys all rights.

KOGLE CARDS, INC., Suite 212, 5575 S. Sycamore St., Littleton CO 80120. President: Patty Koller. Estab. 1982. Produces greeting cards.

Needs: Approached by 300 freelance artists/year. Buys 50 designs and 50 illustrations from freelance artists/year. Works on assignment only. Considers all media for illustration. Prefers 5×7 for final art. Produces material for Christmas and all major holidays plus birthdays; material accepted all year round.

First Contact & Terms: Send slides. Samples not filed are returned by SASE. "No SASE, no return." Reports back within 2 weeks. To show a portfolio, mail original/final art, color and b&w photostats and photographs. Original artwork is not returned. Pays royalties of 8%. Buys all rights.

*LASERCRAFT, 3300 Coffey Ln., Santa Rosa CA 95403. (707)528-1060. FAX: (707)527-8514. Creative Director: David Dyer. Estab. 1975. Produces greeting cards, stationery and desk accessories for men 30 and older and women at the upper end.

Needs: Approached by 50 freelance artists/year. Works with 10 freelance artists/year. Buys 10 designs and illustrations/year from freelance artists. Prefers artists with experience in 4-color production. Works on assignment only. Uses freelance artists mainly for cards and stationery. Also uses freelance artists for calligraphy and mechanicals. Considers watercolor, gouache and pen & ink. Looking for a sophisticated look. Prefers art 8×10. Produces material for Father's Day, Christmas, Valentine's Day, Mother's Day and everyday.

First Contact & Terms: Send query letter with slides. Samples are filed. Reports back within 2 weeks. Call to schedule an appointment to show portfolio which should include thumbnails and color tearsheets and slides. Rights purchased vary according to project. Original artwork is returned at the job's completion. Pays by the project, $200-400.

LOVE GREETING CARDS, INC., 663 N. Biscayne River Dr., Miami FL 33169. (305)685-5683. Vice President: Norman Drittel. Estab. 1984. Produces greeting cards, posters and stationery. "We produce cards for the 40-60 market, complete lines and photography posters."

Needs: Works with 2 freelance artists/year. Buys 60 designs and illustrations/year from freelance artists. Prefers artists with experience in greeting cards and posters. Also buys illustrations for high-tech shopping bags. Uses freelance artwork mainly for greeting cards. Considers pen & ink, watercolor, acrylic, oil and colored pencil. Seeks a contemporary/traditional look. Prefers 5×7 size. Produces material for Hanukkah, Passover, Rosh Hashanah, New Year, birthdays and everyday.

First Contact & Terms: Send query letter, brochure, resume and slides. Samples are filed or are returned. Reports back within 10 days. Call or write to schedule an appointment to show a portfolio, which should include roughs and color slides. Original artwork is not returned to the artist after job's completion. Pays average flat fee of $75/design. Buys first or one-time rights; negotiates rights purchased.

Tips: "Submit designs for our approval. We use 20 designs per year."

*MAID IN THE SHADE, Church Street Station, Box 341, New York NY 10008-0341. (201)659-1269. Art Director: Laird Ehlert. Estab. 1984. Produces greeting cards and postcards. "We are part of the alternative card market. Our largest customer groups are college age, young professional or gay. We are known for sophisticated humor."

Needs: Approached by 20-50 freelance artists/year. Works with 1-20 freelance artists/year. Buys approximately 50 designs and illustrations/from freelance artists/year. Prefers artists with experience in greeting cards and graphic design. Uses freelance artists mainly for greeting cards and postcards; usually finished (concept, artwork, mechanicals); "although our inhouse production staff can do mechanical paste-up if necessary." Considers anything that can be reproduced by the usual printing methods, black & white or color. "We are completely open; however, bear in mind that it should be eye-catching on the display rack." Prefers art for folding cards, prefers 5×7, for postcards, 4¼×6, "which is 100% reproduction size, or else it should be proportional." Produces material for Christmas and birthdays. Submit 9-12 months before holiday.

First Contact & Terms: Send query letter with photocopies. Samples are filed or are returned by SASE if requested by artist. Reports back within 6 weeks. To show a portfolio, mail photocopies. Buys all rights or negotiates rights purchased. Original artwork is not returned at the job's completion. Pays by the project, $100-250 or royalties of 5%.

MAINE LINE COMPANY, Box 947, Rockland ME 04841. (207)594-9418. Contact: Perri Ardman. Estab. 1979. Publishes greeting cards and related products, such as mugs, buttons, magnets and postcards. Most of the products are humorous and deal with contemporary concerns; "also 'sensitive' language cards. Themes for all products revolve around love, support, coping, family, commitment, friendship and birthday."

Needs: Approached by 400-500 freelance artists/year. "Appropriate art styles might include cartooning, pastel washes, watercolor, representational images such as flowers, animals and the like. Calligraphy or type design may also be among the talents needed. Usually the company would commission a series of cards from one artist or designer. Artistic approach should be original, contemporary, but should have wide appeal to the general public. Sensitive, inspirational (with spiritual overtones), inspirational (human potential theme) are secondary, but also needed: punchy, very funny humor. Other products are in the humorous vein and may require expertise in illustration, as well as in lettering or type selection. Strong line work is often required."

First Contact & Terms: "We will review concepts for greeting card and/or postcard series. Artists and designers may also send samples for us to review and evaluate in light of upcoming projects." To show a portfolio, mail final reproduction/product, color tearsheets, photographs, photocopies and/or slides. Also be sure to include SASE when samples, portfolios or concepts are submitted. Each piece sent should have your name, address and phone number on it. Response is usually within 8 weeks. To receive guidelines, send SASE with 45¢ postage. Pays average flat fee of $100-200 for illustration/design; royalties on rare occasions.

Tips: "We are using more and more full-color art and have more need for illustrators and designers. Do not send originals without calling first. Since most of our work is commissioned, we need to see range of abilities. Greeting card illustrations with no words are rarely accepted."

Close-up

Nicole Hollander
Cartoonist

"Sylvia" was born from Nicole Hollander's inclination to do artwork related to social and political issues which were and still are important to her. While a freelance graphic designer doing collateral—brochures, flyers, newsletters, etc.—for nonprofit organizations, she was asked to redesign *The Spokeswoman*, a feminist newsletter. She began to do some illustration for it and before long was creating its monthly comic strip, relating it to various feminist issues. One day out of her pen emerged a character sitting in front of a TV, the precurser of "Sylvia." Hollander says this bold character was modeled after the women she grew up around, her mother and her mother's friends in Chicago.

Sylvia stands out as being so unique in comic strips and greeting cards, according to Hollander, because she is a middle-aged woman, representing the ideas and attitudes of a large section of the population, which have for the most part gone unacknowledged. "When I started out, I thought that because there was 'Doonesbury,' there would be a change in the comic pages. There would begin to be more strips that represented different segments of society. Well, it hasn't really opened up the way I thought it would." She notes the small number of blacks in strips, that there are no gay strips, and that there are many more males and animals than there are women characters. "Women certainly make up more than 50 percent of the newspaper reading population. Just as women buy the most books and greeting cards. So I think they're very under represented."

Hollander's woman characters began to acquire a larger audience when the strip for the newsletter led to her first book, *I'm in Training to be Tall and Blond*, for St. Martin's Press. She was then approached by two syndicates and a greeting card company. She went with a Canadian syndicate, the one that committed first. "I did what you're not supposed to do and what I wouldn't advise people to do. I didn't shop around. I had myself revved up; I wanted to see my strip in the paper. I would advise people to do research." She began to see the strip in fewer and fewer papers and became disenchanted with the syndicate. Utilizing her freelance graphic art skills in business and production, she began to self-syndicate. "Sylvia" now appears in 45 newspapers.

There is a big difference between doing strips and cards for Hollander. "I feel the strips I do for newspapers, within certain limitations, really say what I feel about a lot of different subjects. With a greeting card, there's a reason for that card, an occasion. They're very much less political. The cards are more personal, gentler." She thinks the element of surprise is necessary for a successful greeting card. "You open it up and you ought to be surprised."

She says she chose to go with Recycled Paper Products, which she has been with since 1988, because she thinks it is a company with a humorous and cooperative attitude, respectful of artists. She was also impressed with the artists they worked with, particularly Sandra Boynton. The greeting card process begins with them, she says, when the art director sends out a letter which says it's time to start thinking about a particular holiday or event, encouraging the artists to submit drawings and ideas. For those accepted, she does final drawings and specifies what colors should be used. Hollander also designs mugs, stationery items, notepads and T-shirts.

She begins with the writing, which she enjoys more than doing the artwork, and gets her ideas into a computer, "a lot of stream of consciousness." To keep abreast of what is happening in the world and what people are interested in, a very important part of her job, she listens to National Public Radio and reads the daily paper and numerous magazines. "I love the *Harper's Index*; I also read the *National Enquirer* and the *Star Examiner*. I watch a lot of TV. I try to get as much information as I can."

When she thinks of her greeting card audience she envisions "a woman sending a card to another woman;" whereas, for her strip she envisions a more general audience, which she describes as being educated, politically aware and looking for a laugh. When she draws, she says it is with herself in mind. "I figure there are other people like me out there, so if I do something that I think is funny or interesting, then there's a whole group of people who are also going to think so."

Hollander thinks there is a lot of opportunity within greeting cards but cautions, "It is a slower process than people think. You don't make a lot of money with just one card. You have to do many cards. You have to be patient with the greeting card business." One of her pieces of advice for the cartoonist just starting out is "to do a particular character or situation that you are really interested in. Don't pick something because you think the particular creature or situation is going to sell. If you're successful, you're going to be with it for a long time and you'd better really love it."

For those aspiring to have a strip or a greeting card line, she thinks it is a good idea to work for a greeting card company or as an illustrator or graphic designer. She advises, "Have a regular job and try any way possible to have your work published, even if it's working for organizations or donating work. I don't think donating work should go on for too long, but I really think it's important to draw something and have it published so that you can learn from it and other people can see it."

Commenting further on the fact that there are so few women in the profession, she says that despite all of the funny women out there, "there's still the perception that comedy is a male profession." She adds, "Maybe men are afraid women are going to make fun of them."

— Lauri Miller

Reprinted with permission of the artist

One opens this card and finds, "May all your wildest dreams come true," and gets a sense of Hollander's unique sense of humor. The fact that no attempt is made to squelch this humor is one of the things which appeals to her about Recycled Paper Products. There is "the feeling that you can be trusted to do the very best." Once a piece is accepted, "there's no argument about what you've written."

*MARCEL SCHURMAN CO. INC., 2500 N. Watney Way, Fairfield CA 94533. (707)428-0200. Art Director: Sandra McMillan. Produces greeting cards, giftwrap and stationery. Specializes in "very fine artwork with many different looks: traditional, humorous, graphic, photography, juvenile, etc."

Needs: Buys 800-1000 designs/year from freelance artists. Prefers final art sizes proportionate to 5 × 7, 4 × 6; Produces seasonal material for Valentine's Day, Easter, Mother's Day, Father's Day, graduation, Halloween, Christmas, Hanukkah and Thanksgiving. Submit art by January for Valentine's Day and Easter, May for Mother's and Father's Day, graduation; June for Christmas, Halloween, Thanksgiving and Hanukkah. Interested in all-occasion cards also.

First Contact & Terms: Send query letter with slides, printed material or photographs showing a variety of styles. "No bios, news clippings or original art, please." Reports within 1 month. Returns original art after reproduction. Pays average flat fee of $300/illustration; royalties of 5%.

*DAVID MEKELBURG & FRIENDS, 1222 N. Fair Oaks Ave., Pasadena CA 91103. (818)798-3633. FAX: (818)798-7385. Sales Manager: Richard Crawford or President: Susan Kinney. Estab. 1988. Produces greeting cards, stationery, calendars, posters and giftwrap.

Needs: Approached by 10 freelance artists/year. Works with 2 freelance artists/year. Prefers local artists only. Works on assignment only. Uses freelance artists mainly for design. Produces material for all holidays and seasons, birthdays and everyday. Submit 12 months before holiday.

First Contact & Terms: Send query letter with resume and color photocopies. Samples are filed and are not returned. Reports back only if interested. Write to schedule an appointment to show a portfolio, which should include original/final art, photographs and product renderings. Rights purchased vary according to project. Original artwork returned after publication. Pays royalties of 5%.

THE MICHIGAN STATIONERY CO., 430 Hamilton St., Traverse City MI 49684. (616)941-1372. General Manager: Ardana J. Titus. Estab. 1983. Produces note cards. Seeks "creative, fanciful and humorous designs with one or two subjects. We need colorful and imaginative designs for all-occasion note card line." No landscapes. Sample cards $3.

Needs: Buys 6 designs from freelance artists/year. Uses artists mainly for note cards. Currently working with Michigan artists only. Considers primarily watercolor—bright, distinct colors and designs—no washes. Final art size 8 × 11; allow ¼" on all sides for trim. Prefers vertical designs but will consider horizontal; children, florals and country scenes.

First Contact & Terms: Prefers Michigan artists. Send query letter with samples to be kept on file. Write for art guidelines with SASE. Prefers photographs or originals as samples. Samples not filed are returned by SASE. Reports back within 3 months. Original art returned after reproduction. Pays flat fee of $50 for design. Purchases first rights and/or reprint rights.

Tips: "When submitting material, send bright, colorful designs using imaginative approaches. We will consider a series. We're looking for designs of one or two children as subjects. Designs must be of easily recognizable subjects. Customers want designs of distinct subject work; landscapes don't seem to do well on stationery cards."

MIMI ET CIE, 2925 College Ave. B-5, Costa Mesa CA 92626. Contact: Mary Singleton. Estab. 1981. Manufacturer/distributor. "We are a small giftwrap company catering to high-end retail boutiques and gift stores, designers and manufacturers of giftwrap bags, tote bags, tissue, giftags, etc. Year round designs; baby, wedding, Easter; strong at Christmas."

Needs: Works with 1 freelance artist/year. Assigns various jobs/year. Prefers artists with experience in designing for flexographic printing (flat color—strong design). Uses freelance artists mainly for giftwrap and tote bag design. Also uses freelance artists for product design, rendering of product, P-O-P displays and display fixture design. "For a unique all-occasion collection of cards, we will be buying many designs in all media from watercolor to photography. Please contact Mary for specifics before submitting work to the card collection."

First Contact & Terms: Send query letter with brochure showing art style, tearsheets, photostats, photographs and photocopies. Samples are filed or are returned only if requested by artist. Reports back only if interested. To show a portfolio, mail color and b&w original/final art, final reproduction/product, tearsheets, photostats and photographs. Pays for design by the project, $150-250. Pays for illustration by the project. Considers rights purchased and originality when establishing payment. Buys all rights.

Tips: "Design need not be complicated; color, scale, originality and appropriateness for flexographic printing are the most important qualities. Do not send anything too 'cutesy' like dressed animals. Our market is classic and sophisticated."

MIRAGE IMAGES INC., Box 1222, Angoura Hills CA 91301. President: Caroline Selden. Estab. 1982. Produces postcards and children's books.

Needs: Prefers local artists only. Works on assignment only. Buys freelance designs/illustrations mainly for books. Also uses freelance artists for calligraphy, paste-up and mechanicals. Considers pen & ink, watercolor, colored pencil and photography. Produces material for Christmas; submit 6 months before holiday.

First Contact & Terms: Send query letter with brochure, resume, tearsheets and slides. Samples are not filed and are returned only if requested by artist. Reports back within 2 months. To show a portfolio, mail roughs, original/final art, final reproduction/product, color and b&w slides, tearsheets, photostats and photographs. Original artwork is sometimes returned to the artist after job's completion. Pays royalties of 10%. Buys all rights.
Tips: "Have a good portfolio and professional approach to our business, being punctual on all deadline dates." Would like to see renditions of animals and nature.

MUSEUM GRAPHICS/NEW HEIGHTS, Box 2368, Menlo Park CA 94025. President: Alison Mayhew. Estab. 1952. Produces greeting cards and stationery. "We publish greeting cards from high-quality photographs. We are looking for fun, contemporary and humorous photos to add to our existing line. We are willing to look at other types of art, such as silkscreens, monoprints and collages."
Needs: Works with freelance artists. Looks for contemporary styles. Prefers 8×10 photos. Produces material for all holidays and seasons; submit 6 months before holiday.
First Contact & Terms: Send query letter with brochure showing art style, photostats, slides and SASE. Samples are not filed and are returned by SASE. Reports back regarding query/submission within 1 month. To show a portfolio, mail color and b&w original/final art, final reproduction/product, slides, tearsheets, photostats and photographs. Original artwork is returned to the artist after job's completion. Pays royalties of 10%.

NATIONAL ANNOUNCEMENTS INC., 34-24 Collins Ave., Flushing NY 11753. (718)353-4002. Vice President: David Rosner. Estab. 1960. Produces wedding invitations (blank stock, ready for printing) for women ages 18 up.
Needs: Prefers local artists with greeting card background. Buys illustrations mainly for wedding invitations. Prefers half-tone florals.
First Contact & Terms: Send query letter with brochure. Samples are not filed and are returned only if requested by artist. Reports back only if interested. Call or write to schedule an appointment to show a portfolio, which should include final reproduction/product. Original artwork is not returned to the artist after job's completion. Pays average flat fee of $50-250. Buys all rights.
Tips: "Greeting card experience is necessary, plus it's helpful to understand the graphic arts process."

*NEW BOUNDARY DESIGNS, INC., 1453 Park Rd., Chanhassen MN 55317. (612)474-0924. FAX (612)474-9525. President: M. Melgaard. Estab. 1979. Produces greeting cards, stationery and giftware. "Our greeting cards and stationery are for the Christian market and our support and encouragement cards are for the recovery market."
Needs: Approached by 10-12 freelance artists/year. Works with 2-3 freelance artists/year. Prefers artists with experience in sensitive design. Uses freelance artists mainly for graphics and verse. Also uses freelance artists for calligraphy and "state-oriented designs. We are looking for a 'songs from the heart' look: soft, positive, sensitive and affirming." Produces material for Father's Day, Christmas, Easter, birthdays, Valentine's Day, Mother's Day and everyday. Submit 6 months before holiday.
First Contact & Terms: Send query letter with brochure and resume. Samples are not filed and are returned. Reports back within 2 weeks. To show a portfolio, mail roughs and photographs. Rights purchased vary according to project. Original artwork is not returned at the job's completion. Pays $240 per design.
Tips: Sees trend towards "clarity, color, non-traditional occasions."

NEW DECO, INC., 6401 E. Rogers Circle, Boca Raton FL 33487. (407)241-3901. President: Brad Hugh Morris. Estab. 1984. Produces greeting cards, posters, fine art prints and original paintings.
Needs: Approached by 10-20 freelance artists/year. Works with 5-10 freelance artists/year. Buys 8-10 designs and 5-10 illustrations from freelance artists/year. Buys artwork for greeting cards, giftwrap, calendars, paper tableware, poster prints, etc.
First Contact & Terms: Send query letter with brochure, resume, tearsheets, slides and SASE. Samples not filed are returned by SASE. Reports back within 10 days only if interested. To show a portfolio, mail color slides. Original artwork is returned after job's completion. Pays royalties of 10%. Negotiates rights purchased.
Tips: "Do not send original art at first."

*NEW ENGLAND CARD CO., Box 228, Route 41, West Ossipee NH 03890. (603)539-5200. Manager: Harold Cook. Estab. 1980. Produces greeting cards and prints of New England scenes.
Needs: Approached by 75 freelance artists/year. Works with 10 freelance artists/year. Buys more than 24 designs and illustrations/year. Prefers artists with experience in New England art. Considers oil, acrylic and watercolor. Looking for realistic styles. Prefers art in multiples of 5×7. Produces material for all holidays and seasons. Submit 6 months before holiday.
First Contact & Terms: Send query letter with photographs, slides and transparencies. Samples are filed or are returned. Reports back within 2 months. Call or write to schedule an appointment to show a portfolio of mail appropriate materials: original/final art, photographs and slides. Rights purchased vary according to project; but "we prefer to purchase all rights." Payment negotiable.

*THE NEXT TREND, 11385 Landan Ln., Cincinnati, OH 45246. (513)771-NEXT. FAX: (513)771-6419. Director: Craig Signer. Estab. 1987. Produces greeting cards, stationery and giftwrap. "We design and manufacture social greetings sold to specialty card and Hallmark stores."

Needs: Approached by 20 freelance artists/year. Works with 5 freelance artists/year. Buys 50 freelance designs and illustrations/year. Prefers local artists with experience. Works on assignment only. Uses freelance artists mainly for graphic design and sales literature. Also uses freelance artists for P-O-P displays, paste-up, mechanicals and product design. Looking for contemporary, trendy and bold graphics. Produces material for all holidays and seasons. Submit 6-8 months before holiday.

First Contact & Terms: Send query letter with brochure, resume, tearsheets, photocopies and slides. Samples are filed and are not returned. Reports back to the artist only if interested. To show a portfolio, mail color photostats and dummies. Rights purchased vary according to project. Original artwork is not returned at the job's completion. Pays by the hour, $10-17; by the project, $25-300.

*NORTH EAST MARKETING SYSTEM (NEMS), 4818 Toftrees Dr., Allison Park PA 15101. (412)443-2976. FAX: (412)935-5020. Managing Director: Mark Von Zierenberg. Estab. 1985. Produces rock 'n' roll games for 20-45 year olds, posters and baby products for new parents.

Needs: Approached by 1 freelance artist/year. Works with 6 freelance artists/year. Buys 3 designs and illustrations/year from freelance artists. Prefers artists with experience in baby goods and music. Works on assignment only. Uses freelance artists mainly for product design and catalog sheets. Also uses freelance artists for P-O-P displays, paste-up and mechanicals. Looking for contemporary styles and music-related themes.

First Contact & Terms: Send query letter with brochure, resume and SASE; the best representation of the artist's work. Samples are filed. Reports back to the artist only if interested. To show a portfolio, mail original/final art and photographs. Rights purchased vary according to project. Original artwork is not returned at the job's completion. Payment is "greatly dependent upon the assignment." Pays by the project, $100-250.

*NOVA GREETINGS, INC., Box 517, St. Clair MI 48079. (313)329-3422. FAX: (313)329-2866. Vice President: Doug Bryant. Estab. 1988. Produces greeting cards and giftwrap. "We produce a diverse group of cards from risqué photos to high-end artwork."

Needs: Approached by more than 100 freelance artists/year. Works with 40 freelance artists/year. Buys 300-400 designs/illustrations/year. Uses freelance artists mainly for greeting cards. Considers any media. Looking for "cute to serious detailed artwork for all occasions." Prefers 7½ × 10½ with ¼ bleed. Produces material for all holidays and seasons. Submit 9 months before holiday.

First Contact & Terms: Send query letter with brochure, resume, SASE, photocopies and slides. Samples are not filed and are returned. Reports back within 4 weeks. Call to schedule an appointment to show a portfolio, which should include roughs, color tearsheets and slides. Negotiates rights purchased. Original artwork returned after publication. Pays by the project, $250-500; will negotiate.

OATMEAL STUDIOS, Box 138, Rochester VT 05767. (802)767-3171. FAX: (802)767-9890. Creative Director: Helene Lehrer. Estab. 1979. Publishes humorous greeting cards and notepads, creative ideas for everyday cards and holidays.

Needs: Approached by approximately 300 freelance artists/year. Buys 100-150 designs/illustrations per year from freelance artists. Uses artists for greeting card design and illustration. Considers all media; prefers 5 × 7, 6 × 8½, vertical composition. Produces seasonal material for Christmas, Mother's Day, Father's Day, Easter, Valentine's Day and Hanukkah. Submit art in May for Christmas and Hanukkah, in January for other holidays.

First Contact & Terms: Send query letter with slides, roughs, printed pieces and brochure/flyer to be kept on file; write for artists' guidelines. "If brochure/flyer is not available, we ask to keep one slide or printed piece." Samples returned by SASE. Reports in 3-6 weeks. "We do not hold portfolio reviews." Negotiates payment arrangement with artist.

Tips: "We're looking for exciting and creative humorous (not cutesy) illustrations. If you can write copy and have a humorous cartoon style all your own, send us your ideas! We do accept work without copy too. Our seasonal card line includes traditional illustrations, so we do have a need for non-humorous illustrations as well."

*OPEN END STUDIOS, Box 620309, Littleton CO 80162-0309. Creative Director: Susanne Meis. Estab. 1990. "We produce alternative and humorous, seasonal and all-occasion cards, posters and artistic buttons. We are especially interested in humorous illustration and cartoon art appealing to a contemporary market. Will consider some not-too-cutsey whimsical art. We would like to see original new looks and ideas."

Needs: Works with 6-10 freelance artists/year. Buys about 30-40 designs/illustrations/year from freelance artists. Uses freelance artists mainly for greeting cards and artistic buttons. Also uses freelance artists for P-O-P displays, paste-up and mechanicals. Considers all media. Looking for simple, clean and contemporary art styles. Produces material for all holidays and seasons, graduation, birthdays, get well, congratulations, thank you, anniversary, wedding, baby and everyday. Material may be submitted anytime.

First Contact & Terms: Send query letter with brochure, resume, SASE, tearsheets, photographs, photocopies and slides. Samples are filed "if we're interested," or are returned by SASE. Reports back within 4 weeks. To show a portfolio, mail SASE, b&w and color tearsheets, photographs, slides and dummies. Buys all rights. Original artwork is not returned at the job's completion. Pays by the project, $50-150. "We consider the complexity of the project."

*OUT OF THE WEST, 1857 Discovery Way, Sacramento CA 95819. (916)739-8283. Marketing Director: Tom Fay. Estab. 1986. Produces greeting cards, calendars and postcards. "Our postcards are nostalgic. Our notecards are for a mass audience."
Needs: Approached by 6 freelance artists/year. Works with 1 freelance artist/year. Buys 12 designs and illustrations/year. Prefers artists with experience in satire and advertising illustration. Uses freelance artists mainly for card designs. Also uses freelance artists for P-O-P displays and future lines. Considers all media. Looking for "satire on famous celebrities in nostalgic settings." Prefers art 9×12, 10×11, 18×24 and 20×22. Produces material for Halloween and Christmas. Submit 1 year before holiday.
First Contact & Terms: Send query letter with resume and photocopies. Samples are filed or are returned by SASE if requested by artist. Reports back within 90 days. To show a portfolio, mail b&w photostats and photographs. Buys all rights. Original artwork is returned at the job's completion. Pays by the project, $150-200.

*OUTREACH PUBLICATIONS, Box 1010, Siloam Springs AR 72761. (501)524-9381. Creative Art Director: Darrell Hill. Produces greeting cards, calendars and stationery. Produces announcements, invitations; general, informal, inspirational, contemporary, soft line and studio.
Needs: Works with 12 freelance artists/year. Buys 30 designs from freelance artists/year. Works on assignment only. Also uses artists for calligraphy. Prefers designers' gouache colors and watercolor. "Greeting card sizes range from $4\frac{1}{2} \times 6\frac{1}{2}$ to $5\frac{1}{2} \times 8\frac{1}{2}$; prefer same size, but not more than 200% size." Produces material for Valentine's, Easter, Mother's Day, Father's Day, Confirmation, Graduation, Thanksgiving, Christmas; submit 1 year before holiday.
First Contact & Terms: Send query letter with brochure or photocopies, slides and SASE. Samples are not filed and are returned by SASE. Reports back within 4-6 weeks. To show a portfolio, mail color original/final art, final reproduction/product, slides and photographs. Original artwork is not returned after job's completion. Pays average flat fee of $100-325/design. Buys all rights.
Tips: "Outreach Publications produces Dayspring Greeting cards, a Christian card line. Suggest interested artists request our guidelines for freelance artists. Experienced greeting cards artists preferred. Submissions should include no more than 12 selections."

*P.S. GREETINGS, INC., 4459 W. Division St., Chicago IL 60651. Art Director: Kevin Lahvic. Produces greeting cards.
Needs: "Receives submissions from 300-400 freelance artists/year. Works with 20-25 designers, greeting cards. Prefers illustrations be 5×7 cropped. Publishes greeting cards for everyday and Christmas.
First Contact & Terms: Send query letter requesting artist's guidelines. All requests as well as submissions must be accompanied by SASE. Reports within 1 month. Pays $100-200. Buys exclusive worldwide rights for greeting cards only.
Tips: "Include your name and address on each piece. Our needs are varied: florals, roses, feminine, masculine, pets (dogs and cats), photos. Also, ideas for foil stamping and embossing images. We also print Christmas cards with various types of treatments. We will be moving soon."

PACIFIC PAPER GREETINGS, INC., Box 2249, Sidney British Columbia V8L 3S8 Canada. (604)656-0504. President: Louise Rytter. Produces greeting cards, stationery, bookmarks, enclosure cards and wrapping paper for men and women ages 20-60. "Artwork is refined, realistic and romantic, incorporating nostalgia."
Needs: Works with 4 freelance artists/year. Buys 16 designs/year from freelance artists. "Prefers artists that will develop a theme to their artwork, thus creating a series for greeting cards." Uses artists for paste-up and also verse writing. Prefers romantic style, fantasy and humor. Prefers watercolor and acrylic. Prefers greeting cards 10×14. Produces material for Christmas, Mother's Day, Easter, Father's Day, Valentine's Day and all general occasions; submit 10 months before holiday.
First Contact & Terms: Send query letter with brochure showing art style or slides and SASE. Samples not filed returned by SASE. "Please make sure Universal Postal Coupon is used for returned work—available at the post office." Reports within 1 month. To show a portfolio, mail color original/final art and slides. Negotiates payment and rights purchased.
Tips: "Send slides of work sold. List experience in the greeting card track. List how you prefer to be paid."

PAPEL/FREELANCE, INC., Box 7094, North Hollywood CA 91609. (818)765-1100. Art Department Manager: Helen Scheffler. Estab. 1955. Produces souvenir and seasonal ceramic giftware items: mugs, photo frames, greeting plaques.

Needs: Approached by about 125 freelance artists/year. Buys 250 illustrations from freelance artists/year. Artists with minimum 3 years of experience in greeting cards only; "our product is ceramic but ceramic experience not necessary." Uses artists for product and P-O-P design, illustrations on product, calligraphy, paste-up and mechanicals. Produces material for Christmas, Valentine's Day, Easter, St. Patrick's Day, Mother's and Father's Day; submit 1 year before holiday.

First Contact & Terms: Send query letter with brochure, resume, photostats, photocopies, slides, photographs and tearsheets to be kept on file. Samples not kept on file are returned by SASE if requested. Reports within one month. No originals returned to artist at job's completion. To show a portfolio, mail final reproduction/product and b&w and color tearsheets, photostats and photographs. Pays by the project, $125-450. Buys all rights.

Tips: "I look for an artist who has realistic drawing skills but who can temper everything with a decorative feeling. I look for a 'warm' quality that I think will be appealing to the consumer. We still depend a tremendous amount on freelance talent. Send samples of as many different styles as you are capable of doing well. Versatility is a key to having lots of work. Update samples sent over time as new work is developed." Sees trends toward "risqué humor or black comedy humor — not necessarily positive sayings; drifting away from regimentation and straight lines. Type is all hand-written looking; there is a frenetic quality and uneveness to a lot of drawings; items for adults are looking less juvenile than the last few years."

PAPER ART COMPANY INC., Suite 300, 7240 Shadeland Station, Indianapolis IN 46256. (800)428-5017. Creative Director: Shirley Whillhite. Estab. 1934. Produces paper-tableware products, invitations and party decor.

Needs: Approached by 50 freelance artists/year. Buys 40% of line from freelance artists/year. Prefers flat watercolor, designer's gouache for designs. Prefers 4×5 design area for invitations; 9¼ for plate design. Produces general everyday patterns for birthday, weddings, casual entertaining, baby and bridal showers; St. Patrick's Day, Easter, Valentine's Day, Fall, Halloween, Thanksgiving, Christmas and New Year.

First Contact & Terms: Send query letter with photocopies of artwork, printed samples and SASE. Samples are not returned. Original artwork is not returned if purchased. Pays by the project, $250-500.

Tips: "Color coordinating and the mixing and matching of patterns are prevalent. Need sophisticated designs. We require professional, finished art that would apply to our product."

THE PAPER COMPANY, 731 S. Fidalgo, Seattle WA 98108. (206)762-0982. Vice President: Tom Boehmer. Estab. 1979. Produces stationery. "Produces contemporary stationery (fine writing papers) whose primary market is females from ages 16 to 60. Wide range of themes from sexy and sophisticated to fun and silly (but not juvenile)."

Needs: Approached by 20 freelance artists/year. Works with 4-6 freelance artists/year. Buys 45 designs and illustrations/year from freelance artists. Prefers artists whose work is adaptable to stationery (writing paper). Buys freelance designs and illustrations mainly for writing papers. Considers airbrush and pastel (open to whatever works). Prefers fun, silly or sophisticated, upscale themes. "We do not use cartoons." Prefers 6¼×9. Produces material for Christmas and everyday; "limitless subjects"; submit 9 months before holiday.

First Contact & Terms: Send query letter with brochure, photostats and rough sketches suitable for writing papers. Samples are filed or are returned only if requested by artist. Reports back within 1 month. To show a portfolio, mail thumbnails, roughs and photostats. Original artwork is sometimes returned to the artist after job's completion. Pays average flat fee of $400/illustration.

Tips: "Submit rough sketches of artwork in a format suitable for writing paper (i.e. there must be enough space left on sheet for writing space.) We do not do greeting cards. Write a query letter with b&w photocopies for artist's file. Black and white photocopies not returned. Most of our artwork is on a commissioned basis."

PAPER MAGIC GROUP INC., 347 Congress St., Boston MA 02210. Art Director: Mel Nieders. Estab. 1984. Produces greeting cards, stationery, paper wall decorations and 3-D paper decorations. "We are primarily publishing seasonal cards and decorations for the mass market. Design is traditional to contemporary, with an emphasis on Christmas."

Needs: Approached by 150 freelance artists/year. Works with 50 freelance artists/year. Buys 800 designs and illustrations/year from freelance artists. Prefers artists with experience in greeting cards. Works on assignment only. Also uses freelance artists for calligraphy. Considers gouache, acrylic, watercolor and pastel. Produces material for Christmas, Valentine's Day, Easter, Halloween and birthdays.

First Contact and Terms: Send query letter with brochure, resume, slides and SASE. "A 4-color printed brochure is nicest." Samples are filed or are returned by SASE only if requested by artist. Reports back within 30 days. Original artwork is not returned to the artist after job's completion. Pays by the project, $275-800. Buys all rights.

Tips: "Send samples of work by mail, especially Christmas ideas. We assign all freelance work by the project. If we decide to assign, please meet the deadlines." A common mistake illustrators make in presenting samples or portfolios is "handwritten or sloppy letters. Make only one phone inquiry to see if it was received, no others."

PAPER MOON GRAPHICS, INC., Box 34672, Los Angeles CA 90034. (213)645-8700. Creative Director: Michael Conway or Robert Fitch. Estab. 1977. Produces greeting cards and stationery. "We publish greeting cards with a friendly, humorous approach – dealing with contemporary issues for an audience 20-35 year old, mostly female."
Needs: Works with 20 freelance artists/year. Buys 400 designs/illustrations/year. "Looking for a new cartoon style with bright, friendly color." Buys freelance illustrations mainly for greeting cards and card concepts. Prefers 10×14. Produces material for all holidays and seasons, Valentine's Day and Birthdays. Submit 12 months before holiday.
First Contact & Terms: Send query letter with brochure, tearsheets, photostats, photocopies, slides and SASE. Samples are filed or are returned only if requested by artist. Reports back within 6 weeks. To show a portfolio, mail color roughs, slides and tearsheets. Original artwork is returned to the artist after job's completion. Pays average flat fee of $350/design; $350/illustration. Negotiates rights purchased.
Tips: "We're looking for bright, fun cartoon style with contemporary look. Artwork should have a young 20's and 30's appeal."

*PAPER PEDDLER, INC., 1201 Pennsylvania Ave., Richmond CA 94801. Produces postcards. "Our postcards have a variety of subject matter. Off the wall, humor, fine arts, political comment and slice of life. The postcards are generally directed towards younger people."
Needs: Buys 15-20 b&w photos from freelance artists/year. Prefers 4⅛×5⅞ or proportional for postcards.
First Contact & Terms: Send query letter with slides or originals. Samples are filed. "Please include SASE." Reports back within 4-6 weeks. To show a portfolio, mail original/final art, photographs or slides. Original artwork is returned after job's completion. Pays average of $50-150/photo; advance against royalties of 5%.
Tips: "Paper Peddler, Inc. is largely an importer of postcards. However, we also do our own publishing. Our publishing attempts to give a more Americana 'feel; to the rest of the line."

PAPERPOTAMUS PAPER PRODUCTS INC., Box 35008, Station E, Vancouver BC V6M 4G1 Canada. (604)270-4580. FAX: (604)270-1580. Director of Marketing: George Jackson. Estab. 1988. Produces greeting cards for women ages 18 to 55.
Needs: Works with 6-10 freelance artists/year. Buys 48-96 illustrations from freelance artists/year. Also uses artists for P-O-P displays, paste-up and inside text. Prefers watercolor, but will look at all media that is colored; no b&w except photographic. Seeks detailed humorous cartoons and detailed nature drawings i.e. flowers, cats. "No studio card type artwork." Prefers 5⅛×7 finished art work. Produces material for Christmas; submit 18 months before holiday.
First Contact and Terms: Send query letter with brochure, resume, photocopies and SASE. Samples are not filed and are returned by SASE only if requested by artist. Reports back within 2 months. Call or write to schedule an appointment to show a portfolio, or mail roughs and color photographs. Original artwork is not returned to the artist after job's completion. Pays average flat fee of $100/illustration or royalties of 3-5%. Prefers to buy all rights, but will negotiate rights purchased.
Tips: "Have a good sense of what the greeting card market is about. Know what the best selling humorous card lines are and what the market is buying. Understand the time frame necessary to produce a properly done card line."

*PARTHENON WEST, Box 5, Boulder CO 80306. (303)444-7662. President: Clark Ummel. Estab. 1985. Produces stationery, calendars and greeting cards. "We are a publisher of bold, hip greeting cards and note cards, mainly appealing to young creative urbanites."
Needs: Approached by 10-30 freelance artists/year. Works with 0-10 freelance artists/year. Buys 0-50 designs/illustrations/year from freelance artists. "We prefer artists able to create non-traditional and wild designs suitable for greeting cards." Uses freelance artists mainly for new lines of greeting cards. Also uses freelance artists for mechanicals. Considers "any media as long as it reproduces well." Looking for "bold, contemporary, new and very graphic styles." Produces material for Father's Day, Mother's Day, Christmas, Valentine's Day, birthdays, everyday and blank note cards. Submit 1 year before holiday.
First Contact & Terms: Send query letter with resume, SASE, photographs and slides. Samples are filed for 18 months or are returned by SASE if requested by artist. Reports back within 30 days. "We will call if we are interested in reviewing a portfolio." Negotiates rights purchased. Original artwork is returned at the job's completion. Pay by the project, $100-350; royalties of 5-10%.
Tips: Sees trend toward "independent companies capturing more and more of the market."

PAWPRINTS GREETING CARDS, Pierce Crossing Rd., Jaffrey NH 03452. President: Marcy Tripp. Estab. 1972. Produces greeting cards and magnets. "Publishes greeting cards for all ages with an emphasis on family humor, puns and strong art. Looking for children's book illustrators and designers with good grasp of anatomy, color and line."
Needs: Works with 4 freelance artists/year. Buys 40 freelance designs/illustrations/year. Prefers strong, individual style. Buys freelance designs/illustrations mainly for everyday and Christmas. Also uses artists for calligraphy. Considers all media. Seeks strong line, good drawing, warm and humorous style. Cards are

4¾ × 7, use any multiple of that. Produces material for all holidays and seasons; submit 12 months before holiday.

First Contact & Terms: Send query letter with photocopies, slides and SASE. Samples are filed or are returned by SASE. Reports back within 1 month only if interested. To show a portfolio, mail thumbnails, color slides, photostats and photographs. Original artwork is sometimes returned to the artist after job's completion. Pays royalties of 5%. Buys all rights.

Tips: "Show us what you like to do best; if it's right for us, we'll both be happy. Look for Pawprints in stores; see how you'd fit in. We like warm humor, off-the-wall wit and good solid art. We publish the best illustrators in the country. If you're good, we'll know it."

*PEACHTREE COMMUNICATIONS, INC., Box 3146, Pompano Beach FL 33072. (305)941-2926. FAX: (305)941-2926. Art Director: George Spencer. Estab. 1988. Produces greeting cards, stationery, calendars, posters and T-shirts; family-oriented with family appeal—"nothing X-rated."

Needs: Approached by 100 freelance artists/year. Works with 20 freelance artists/year. Buys 100 designs and illustrations/year from freelance artists. Prefers artists with experience in humorous illustrations and captions for greeting cards, get-well and general cards. Also for calendars and stationery, humorous illustrations and captions for posters and T-shirts. Works on assignment only. Also uses freelance artists for paste-up, mechanicals, design and layout. Media determined by job requirements. Size to be determined by job. Produces material for all holidays and seasons.

First Contact & Terms: Send query letter with resume, SASE and photocopies. Samples are filed or are returned by SASE if requested by artist. Reports back to the artist only if interested. To show a portfolio, mail roughs and b&w tearsheets. Negotiates rights purchased. Original artwork is not returned at the job's completion. Payment to be determined by job.

PINEAPPLE PRESS, Box 461334, Los Angeles CA 90046. (818)972-9239. President: S. A. Piña. Estab. 1986. Produces posters and limited editions.

Needs: Approached by 200 freelance artists/year. Works with 8 freelance artists/year. Buys 5 designs from freelance artists/year. Buys 20 illustrations from freelance artists/year. Prefers "artists who understand a deadline." Works on assignment only. Also uses freelance artists for paste-up, mechanicals and lettering. Prefers acrylic and airbrush technique. Prefers contemporary look.

First Contact & Terms: Send query letter with resume, slides and SASE. Samples are filed or are returned by SASE. Reports back within 2 months. Original artwork is returned to artist after job's completion. Pays by the project, $200-1,000 average; royalties of 5-10%. Negotiates rights purchased.

Tips: "Be persistent and professional. New emerging artists should not be afraid to submit their work. Send a bio or a resume. Do not send black-and-white photocopies as color samples. Sees trend toward more contemporary prints/patterns."

*PIONEER BALLOON COMPANY, 555 N. Woodlawn, Wichita KS 67208. (316)685-2266. FAX: (316)685-2409. Art Directors: Stan Weir and Rob Braselton. Estab. 1918. Produces "microfoil and latex balloons with holiday, general message and specialty-advertising themes, intended for all ages."

Needs: Approached by 10 freelance artists/year. Works with 5 freelance artists/year. Buys 10-20 designs and illustrations/year from freelance artists. Prefers artists with experience. Works on assignment only. Uses freelance artists mainly for illustration and calligraphy. Also uses freelance artists for P-O-P displays and paste-up. Considers all media. Produces material for all holidays and seasons: Father's Day, Halloween, Christmas, Easter, graduation, birthdays, Valentine's Day, Thanksgiving, Mother's Day, New Year and anniversary. Submit 6 months before holiday.

First Contact & Terms: Send query letter with brochure, tearsheets, photostats, photographs, slides and transparencies. Samples are filed or are returned. Reports back to the artist only if interested. Call to schedule an appointment to show a portfolio, which should include b&w and color tearsheets, photographs and slides. Rights purchased vary according to project. Original artwork is returned at the job's completion. Pays by the project, $500-2,000.

PIONEER GIFT WRAP, 2939 Vail Ave., Los Angeles CA 90040. (213)726-2473. Vice President, Marketing Services: Bill Lake III. Estab. 1928. Produces giftwrap.

Needs: Approached by around 20 freelance artists/year. Works with 20-30 freelance artists/year. Buys 50-75 designs and illustrations/year. Prefers artists with experience in giftwrap and greeting cards. Considers acrylic. Seeks upscale traditional and downscale contemporary styles. Prefers 15″ cylinder circumference. Produces material for Christmas, Valentine's Day, Mother's Day, Father's Day, Easter, Hanukkah, birthdays and everyday; "all art to be finalized 2/15."

First Contact & Terms: Send query letter with brochure, tearsheets and slides. Samples are not filed and are returned only if requested by artist. Reports back within 3 weeks. To show a portfolio, mail thumbnails, roughs, original/final art, slides and photographs. Original artwork is not returned to the artist after job's completion. Pays average flat fee of $250/design. Buys all rights.

Tips: "Know the giftwrap market and be professional. Know flexographic printing process."

PLUM GRAPHICS INC., Box 136, Prince Station, New York NY 10012. (212)966-2573. Contact: Kirsten Coyne. Estab. 1983. Produces greeting cards. "They are full-color, illustrated, die-cut; fun images for young and old."
Needs: Buys 12 designs and illustrations/year from freelance artists. Prefers local artists only. Works on assignment only. Uses freelance artists for greeting cards only. Considers oil, acrylic, airbrush and watercolor (not the loose style.) Looking for representational and tight-handling styles. Prefers animal themes. "I suggest that artists look for the cards in stores to have a better idea of the style."
First Contact & Terms: Send query letter with photocopies or tearsheets. Samples are filed or are returned by SASE if requested by artist. Reports back to the artist only if interested. "We'll call to view a portfolio." Portfolio should include original/final art and color tearsheets. Buys all rights. Original artwork is returned at the job's completion. Pays by the project, $200 minimum.

PLYMOUTH INC., 361 Benigno Blvd., Bellmawr NJ 08031. Art Director: Alene Sirott-Cope. Produces posters, stationery and paper products, such as 3×5 wire-bound memo books, wire-bound theme books, portfolios, scribble pads, book covers, pencil tablets, etc., all with decorative covers for school, middle grades and high school. "We use contemporary illustrations. Some of our work is licensed. We are expanding into the gift trade with various paper products aimed toward an older age group, 19 and up."
Needs: Approached by 200 freelance artists/year. Buys 300 designs and 300 illustrations from freelance artists/year. Works on assignment only. Uses artists for illustration, logo design, design, paste-up and mechanicals. Prefers full-color and airbrush. Prefers "very graphic designs and illustration." Looking for "contemporary styles and fads."
First Contact & Terms: Send query letter with brochure showing art style or resume, tearsheets, photostats, photocopies, slides and photographs. Samples returned by SASE. Reports only if interested. Mail appropriate materials or write to schedule an appointment to show a portfolio, which should include final reproduction/product and color tearsheets. Pays by the project, $300-500. Considers experience of artist when establishing payment. Buys all rights or negotiates rights purchased.
Tips: "Plymouth is looking for professional illustrators and designers. The work must be top notch. It is the art that sells our products. We use many different styles of illustration and design and are open to new ideas. Portfolio should include color print samples (approximately postcard size); we do not use black-and-white illustration or cartoons." The most common mistake freelancers make in presenting samples or portfolios is "presenting everything instead of a few choice pieces."

*POPSHOTS, INC., 472 Riverside Ave., Westport CT 06880. (203)454-9700. FAX: (203)454-4955. Vice President, Creative: Paul Zalon. Estab. 1978. Produces greeting cards that pop-up for customers aged 13-60.
Needs: Works with 40 freelance artists/year. Commissions 50 designs and illustrations/year from freelance artists. Works on assignment only. Uses freelance artists mainly for camera ready art and concepts. Considers all media. Looking for "very contemporary designs, as well as period reproduction styles (Victorian, 1940s and 1950s etc.)" Produces material for Christmas, graduation, birthdays, Valentine's Day, Mother's Day and get well. Submit 1 year before holiday.
First Contact & Terms: Send query letter with tearsheets, slides and transparencies. Samples are filed or are returned by SASE. Reports back within 1 month to the artist only if interested. Write to schedule an appointment to show a portfolio or mail appropriate materials." Buys all rights. Pays by the project, $100-2,500.

POTPOURRI PRESS, 6210 Swiggett Rd., Greensboro NC 27410; mailing address: Box 19566, Greensboro NC 27419. (919)852-8961. Director of New Product Development: Janet Pantuso. Estab. 1968. Produces paper products including bags, boxes, stationery and tableware; tins; stoneware items; fragrance and fabric items for giftshops, the gourmet shop trade and department stores.
Needs: Buys 10-20 designs from freelance artists/year; buys 10-20 illustrations from freelance artists/year. Works on assignment only. Uses artists for calligraphy, mechanicals and art of all kinds for product reproduction. Prefers watercolor, acrylic, marker and mechanical work. Produces everyday and seasonal products; submit material 1-2 years in advance.
First Contact & Terms: Send query letter with resume and tearsheets, photostats, photocopies, slides and photographs. Samples not filed are returned by SASE. Reports back as soon as possible. Call or write to schedule an appointment to show a portfolio, which should include anything to show ability. "Artist must have good portfolio showing styles the artist is comfortable in." Pays for illustration by the project $150-2,500. Buys all rights.
Tips: "Business is booming. Our art needs are increasing. We need artists who are flexible and willing to meet deadlines. Provide references that can tell us if you meet deadlines, are easy, medium or tough to work with, etc."

THE PRINTERY HOUSE OF CONCEPTION ABBEY, Conception MO 64433. Art Director: Rev. Norbert Schappler. Estab. 1950. A publisher of religious greeting cards; religious Christmas and all-occasion themes for people interested in religious yet contemporary expressions of faith. "Our card designs are meant to touch the heart and feature strong graphics, calligraphy and other appropriate styles."

Needs: Approached by 75 freelance artists/year. Works with 25 freelance artists/year. Uses artists for product illustration. Prefers acrylic, pastel, cut paper, silk-screen, oil, watercolor, line drawings; classical and contemporary calligraphy. Prefers contemporary and dignified styles and solid religious themes. Produces seasonal material for Christmas and Easter.

First Contact & Terms: Send query with brochure showing art style or resume, tearsheets, photostats, photocopies, slides and photographs. Samples returned by SASE. Reports within 3 weeks. To show a portfolio, mail appropriate materials only after query has been answered. Portfolio should include final reproduction/product and color tearsheets and photographs. "In general, we continue to work with artists year after year once we have begun to accept work from them." Pays flat fee of $150-250 for illustration/design. Usually purchases exclusive reproduction rights for a specified format; occasionally buys complete reproduction rights.

Tips: "Abstract or semi-abstract background designs seem to fit best with religious texts. Color washes and stylized flowers are sometimes appropriate. Computerized graphics are beginning to have an impact in our field; multi-colored calligraphy is a new development. Remember our specific purpose of publishing greeting cards with a definite Christian/religious dimension but not piously religious i.e. wedded with religious dimension; it must be good quality artwork. We sell mostly via catalogs so artwork has to reduce well for catalog." Sees trend towards "more personalization and concern for texts."

PRODUCT CONCEPT, INC, 209 Sutton Lane, Colorado Springs CO 80907. (719)632-1089. Creative Director: Cliff Sanderson. President: Susan Ross. Estab. 1986. New product development agency. "We work with a variety of companies in the gift and greeting card market in providing design, new-product development and manufacturing services."

Needs: Works with 20-25 freelance artists/year. Buys 400 designs and illustrations/year from freelance artists. Prefers artists with 3 - 5 years of experience in gift and greeting card design. Works on assignment only. Buys freelance designs and illustrations mainly for new product programs. Also uses freelance artists for calligraphy, P-O-P display and paste-up. Considers all media. Produces material for all holidays and seasons.

First Contact & Terms: Send query letter with resume, tearsheets, photostats, photocopies, slides and SASE. Samples are filed or are returned by SASE only if requested by artist. Reports back within 7 days. To show a portfolio, mail color and b&w roughs, original/final art, final reproduction/product, slides, tearsheets, photostats and photographs. Original artwork is not returned after job's completion. Pays by the project, $250-2,000. Buys all rights.

Tips: "Be on time with assignments."

*RAINBOW ZOO DESIGNS, Suite #215, 2132 Century Park Lane, Los Angeles CA 90067. (213)551-3034. President/Owner: S. Steier. Estab. 1981. Produces greeting cards, stationery and children's novelties; a traditional and contemporary mix geared toward children 8-18, as well as schoolteachers."

Needs: Approached by 15 freelance artists/year. Works with 3 freelance artists/year. Buys varying number of designs and illustrations/year. Prefers local artists only. Sometimes works on assignment basis only. Uses freelance artists mainly for new designs, new concepts and new mediums. Also uses freelance artists for P-O-P displays, paste-up and mechanicals. Looking for "contemporary, trendy, bright, crisp colors." Produces material for all holidays and seasons. Submit 12 months before holiday.

First Contact & Terms: Send query letter with any and all types of samples. Samples are not filed and are returned. Reports back within 1 month. To show a portfolio, mail appropriate materials. Rights purchased vary according to project. Original artwork returned at the request of the artist. Pays royalties of 3-10%.

RECYCLED PAPER PRODUCTS INC., 3636 N. Broadway, Chicago IL 60613. Art Director: Melinda Gordon. Publishes greeting cards, postcards, Post-It Notes, buttons and mugs. Artist's guidelines available.

Needs: Buys 1,000-2,000 and up designs and illustrations/year from freelance artists. Considers b&w line and color—"no real restrictions." Looking for "great ideas done in your own style." Prefers 5×7 vertical format for cards, 10×14 maximum. "Our primary concern is greeting cards." Produces seasonal material for all major and minor holidays including Jewish holidays. Submit seasonal material 18 months in advance; everyday cards are reviewed throughout the year.

First Contact & Terms: Send SASE for artist's guidelines. Reports in 2 months. Original work usually not returned at job's completion, but "negotiable." Buys all rights. Average flat fee is currently under review. Some royalty contracts."

Tips: "Remember that a greeting card is primarily a message sent from one person to another. The art must catch the customer's attention, and the words must deliver what the front promises. We are looking for unique points of view and manners of expression whether the themes are traditional or very contemporary. Our artists must be able to work with a minimum of direction and meet deadlines."

Let's
dance
It's
Spring
new
life
new
beginnings

© 1989 Recycled Paper Products, Inc.

This calligraphy/watercolor illustration was submitted to Recycled Paper Products on speculation by Olympia, Washington artist Beverly Frost McKinney. Art director Melinda Gordon says the Easter greeting card is successful because it is "light and airy—a perfect spring piece."

RED FARM STUDIO, 334 Pleasant St., Box 347, Pawtucket RI 02862. (401)728-9300. Executive Vice President: Steven P. Scott. Chairman of the Board: J. Parker Scott. Produces greeting cards, giftwrap, coloring books, paper dolls, story-coloring books, paper party ware, playing cards, Christmas cards, gift enclosures, notes, invitations, postcards and paintables. Specializing in nautical and country themes and fine watercolors. Art guidelines available upon request if SASE is provided.
Needs: Buys approximately 200 designs and illustrations/year from freelance artists. Considers watercolor. Submit Christmas artwork 1 year in advance.
First Contact & Terms: Send query letter with printed pieces, photographs, or original art. Call for appointment to show portfolio, which should include "good examples, either printed or originals of finished product. Do not send sketches. Important—always include an SASE." Samples not filed are returned by SASE. Reports within 2 weeks. Original artwork not returned after reproduction. "Pays for illustration by the project, $175 minimum. Buys all rights. Finds most artists through references/word-of-mouth, samples received through the mail and portfolio reviews.
Tips: "We are interested in realistic, fine art watercolors of traditional subjects like country and nautical scenes, flowers, birds, shells and baby animals. We do not reproduce photography."

*REEDPRODUCTIONS, Suite 650, 123 Townsend St., San Francisco CA 94107. (415)974-5767. Partner/Art Director: Susie Reed. Estab. 1978. Produces celebrity postcards, key rings, notebooks, address books, etc.
Needs: Approached by 20 freelance artists/year. Works with few freelance artists/year. Prefers local artists with experience. Works on assignment only. Artwork used for paper and gift novelty items. Also uses artists for paste-up and mechanicals. Prefers color or b&w photorealist illustrations of celebrities.
First Contact & Terms: Send query letter with brochure or resume, tearsheets, photostats, photocopies or slides and SASE. Samples are filed or are returned by SASE. Reports back within 1 month only if interested. Call or write to schedule an appointment to show a portfolio, which should include color or b&w original/ final art, final reproduction/product, slides, tearsheets and photographs. Original artwork is returned after job's completion. Payments negotiated at time of purchase.
Tips: "We specialize in products related to Hollywood memorabilia."

REGENCY & CENTURY GREETINGS, 1500 W. Monroe St., Chicago IL 60607. (312)666-8686. Art Director: David Cuthbertson. Estab. 1921. Publishes Christmas cards; traditional and some religious.
Needs: Approached by 300 freelance artists/year. Buys 200 illustrations and designs/year from freelance artists. Prefers pen & ink, airbrush, watercolor, acrylic, oil, collage and calligraphy. Prefers traditional themes.
First Contact & Terms: Send query letter with samples. Submit seasonal art 8 months in advance. Reports in 6 weeks. Previously published work OK. Buys exclusive Christmas card reproduction rights. Originals can be returned to artist at job's completion. Pays $150 minimum, b&w; $200, color design. Pays on acceptance. Finds most artists through references/word-of mouth and samples received through the mail and galleries.

Tips: "Artist should visit stationery shops for ideas and request artist's guidelines to become familiar with the products. Portfolio should include published samples." Does not want to see college projects. "Traditional still sells best in more expensive lines but will review contemporary designs for new lines. Present a wide range of styles."

RENAISSANCE GREETING CARDS, Box 845, Springvale ME 04083. (207)324-4153. FAX: (207)324-9564. Art Director: Janice Keefe. Estab. 1977. Publishes greeting cards; "current approaches" to all-occasion cards, seasonal cards, Christmas cards and nostalgic Christmas themes. "Alternative card company with unique and interesting cards of all captions for all ages."
Needs: Approached by 400-500 freelance artists/year. Buys 200 illustrations/year from freelance artists. Full-color illustrations only. Produces everyday occasions – Birthday, Get Well, Friendship, etc., and seasonal material for Christmas, Valentine's Day, Mother's Day, Father's Day, Easter, graduation, St. Patrick's Day, Halloween, Thanksgiving, Passover, Jewish New Year and Hanukkah; submit art 18 months in advance for Christmas material; approximately 1 year for other holidays. "Currently interested in humorous concepts and illustration."
First Contact & Terms: To request artists' guidelines, include a SASE with 45¢ postage. To show a portfolio, mail original/final art, color tearsheets, slides or transparencies. Packaging with sufficient postage to return materials should be included in the submission. Reports in 2 months. Originals returned to artist at job's completion. Pays for design by the project, $125-300 with an advance on royalties.
Tips: "Start by sending a small (10-12) sampling of 'best' work, preferably printed samples or slides of your best work (with SASE for return). This allows a preview for possible fit, saving time and expense. In traditional themes, Victorian, fine art and classical styles are strong as ever; in contemporary – bright colors textures."

SCOTT CARDS INC., Box 906, Newbury Park CA 91320. (818)998-8617. President: Larry Templeman Estab. 1985. Produces greeting cards for contemporary adults of all ages.
Needs: Approached by 100 freelance artists/year. Works with 15 freelance artists/year. Buys 75 designs from freelance artists/year. "We will double that amount this year if submissions warrant." Prefers pen & ink. Looking for "hard-edged cartoons appealing to sophisticated adults. We like humorous, sensitive and romantic messages aimed at modern adult relationships: single, married, friends, work, etc. No ryhmed verse." No seasonal material.
First Contact & Terms: Send query letter with brochure or photocopies. Samples are filed or are returned by SASE. Reports back within 3 months. To show a portfolio, mail photocopies only, no original artwork. Pays average flat fee of $50, design/illustration or royalties of 5% "after first 10 designs purchased." Buys all rights.
Tips: "New ways to say 'I love you' always sell if they aren't corny or too obvious. Humor helps, especially if it twists. We are looking for non-traditional sentiments that are sensitive, timely and sophisticated. Our cards have a distinct flavor, so before submitting your work, write for our guidelines and samples brochure."

***SON MARK, INC.**, 184 Quigley Blvd., New Castle DE 19720. (302)322-2143. FAX: (302)322-2163. Executive Assistant: Gladys King. Estab. 1986. Produces greeting cards that "target market of up-scale 25 year olds and up. Standard cards are 5×7 for everyday use. Verses are chosen separately at P-O-P and inserted into cards; secular and Christian."
Needs: Approached by more than 30 freelance artists/year. Works with 5-10 freelance artists/year. Works on assignment only. Uses freelance artists mainly for greeting card illustration and concept. Produces material for Christmas, Valentine's Day, Mother's Day, graduation, birthdays and everyday. Submit 9 months before holiday.
First Contact & Terms: Send query letter with photocopies. Samples are filed. Reports back to the artist if interested. To show a portfolio, mail photostats and photographs. Rights purchased vary according to project. Pays royalties of 5% minimum.
Tips: "Note that Son Mark, Inc. is not currently accepting new material."

***SUNSHINE ART STUDIOS, INC.**, 45 Warwick St., Springfield MA 01077. (413)781-5500. Assistant Art Director: Midge Stark. Estab. 1921. Produces greeting cards, stationery, calendars and giftwrap which are sold in own catalog, appealing to all age groups.
Needs: Approached by 100 freelance artists/year. Works with 100-125 freelance artists/year. Buys 100-125 designs and illustrations/year from freelance artists. Prefers artists with experience in greeting cards. Works on assignment only. Uses freelance artists mainly for greeting cards, giftwrap and stationery. Also uses freelance artists for calligraphy. Considers gouache, watercolor and acrylic. Looking for "cute animals, florals and traditional motifs." Prefers art 4½×6½ or 5×7. Produces material for Christmas, Easter, birthdays and everyday. Submit 6-8 months before holiday.
First Contact & Terms: Send query letter with brochure, resume, SASE, tearsheets and slides. Samples are filed or are returned by SASE if requested by artist. Reports back to the artist only if interested. Portfolio should include original/final art and color tearsheets and slides. Buys all rights. Original artwork is not returned at the job's completion. Pays by the project, $250-400.

*T.E.E.M., 343 Beinoris Dr., Wood Dale IL 60191. (708)860-0323. FAX: (708)860-0382. Vice President: Margot A. Fraisl. Estab. 1985. Produces ribbon, tags and enclosure cards, for a Narrow Web Printer-Converter of highly decorative ribbons, seals, tags and enclosure cards, directed towards craft, floral and gift markets; all ages.
Needs: Approached by more than 10 freelance artists/year. Works with 3-4 freelance artists/year. Buys more than 300 designs and illustrations/year from freelance artists. Prefers local artists with some understanding of pre-press artwork. Works on assignment basis only. Uses freelance artists mainly for concept designs for seasonal events and collections, particularly for ribbon and gift tags. Also uses freelance artists for illustration. Considers pencil and marker. Looking for all styles, except airbrush. For size, contact at company will give specific directions. Produces material for all holidays and seasons and everyday. Submit 6-12 months before holiday.
First Contact & Terms: Send query letter with resume and SASE. Samples are filed or are returned by SASE if requested by artist. Reports back within 1 month. To show a portfolio, mail roughs, original/final art and b&w and color samples. Rights purchased vary according to project. Original artwork is not returned at job's completion. Pays by the project, $35-75. Payment is based on the complexity of the design.

*TEXAN HOUSE, INC., Box 1487, 40214 Industrial Park Circle, Georgetown TX 78626. (512)863-9460. President: Joan K. Davis. Produces greeting cards, giftwrap and stationery. Publishes general cards and invitations.
Needs: Approached by 30 freelance artists/year. Works with 40 freelance artists/year. Works on assignment only. Uses freelance artists for greeting cards, Christmas cards and invitations. Also uses artists for calligraphy. Prefers Southwestern styles. Produces material for Christmas; submit 15 months before holiday.
First Contact & Terms: Send query letter with brochure or photostats and photocopies. Samples are returned. Reports back within 4 weeks. Call or write to schedule an appointment to show a portfolio, which should include thumbnails, original/final art and photographs. Original artwork is not returned after job's completion. Pays flat fee. Buys all rights.

ARTHUR THOMPSON & COMPANY, 4700 F St., Omaha NE 68117-1482. (402)731-0411. Contact: Jeanie Sturgeon. Publishes greeting cards and letterheads; holiday (Christmas and Thanksgiving) and special occasion designs.
Needs: Approached by 50 or so freelance artists/year. Uses freelance artists for product illustration and freelance photographers for photos. Accepts art in any media. Prefers clean, corporate-type designs or traditional work.
First Contact & Terms: Write and send samples if possible. Prefers transparencies or slides of original art. Reports in 6 weeks. Provide samples and tearsheets to be kept on file for possible future assignments. Negotiates payment. Pays by the project, $200-350. Considers product use and rights purchased when establishing payment. Artist guidelines available upon request.
Tips: "Remember that we are a business-to-business greeting card company. We try to keep our cards oriented toward business themes, but will also look at ideas for our special occasion line."

TLC GREETINGS, 615 McCall Rd., Manhattan KS 66502. Creative Director: Michele Johnson. Estab. 1986. Produces greeting cards for women 18-40.
Needs: Works with 9 freelance artists/year. Buys 20 designs from freelance artists/year. Works on assignment only. Open to any media. Prefers cartoon-type characters, humorous illustrations. "Our cards are 5×7; can work with larger size."
First Contact & Terms: Send query letter with brochure, photocopies and SASE. Samples are filed or are returned by SASE. Reports back within 4-6 weeks. To show a portfolio, mail slides, tearsheets and photostats. Pays average flat fee of $100-200. Negotiates rights purchased.
Tips: "Keep in mind positive, humorous designs. I see a trend away from so much risqué and cutting humor—see more fun, cleaner humor."

*TRISAR, INC., 2231 S. DuPont Dr., Anaheim CA 92806. (714)978-1433. FAX: (714)978-3788. Creative Director: Randy Harris. Estab. 1979. Produces greeting cards, buttons, balloons, T-shirts and mugs. "There is a strong emphasis on age-related concepts, i.e. 'over the hill' etc., also on seasonal shirts, mugs, etc."
Needs: Approached by 10 freelance artists/year. Works with 5 freelance artists/year. Buys 6 designs and illustrations/year from freelance artists. Prefers local artists with experience in silk screening, shirts and hats and mug designs. Works on assingment only. Uses freelance artists mainly for specific projects. Considers torn paper, acrylic, graphic design, combination of phrase and art. Produces material for Father's Day, Halloween, Christmas, graduation, birthdays, Valentine's Day, Mother's Day and everyday. Submit 9 months before holiday.
First Contact & Terms: Send query letter with SASE, photographs, photocopies, photostats and slides. Samples are filed or are returned by SASE if requested by artist. Reports back to the artist only if interested. Call to schedule an appointment to show a portfolio, which should include roughs, original/final art and color photographs. Negotiates rights purchased. Original artwork is not returned at the job's completion. Pays by the project, $200-400.

UNIQUE INDUSTRIES, INC., 2400 S. Weccacoe Ave., Philadelphia PA 19148. (215)336-4300. Director of New Products: Martin Moshel. Estab. 1962. Manufacturer. "We publish a complete line of party supplies aimed primarily at the children's market." Products include paper party plates, party napkins, tablecovers, giftwrap, party hats, blowouts, invitations, party games, hanging decorations, etc.

Needs: Approached by 30-50 freelance artists/year. Works with 15-20 freelance artists/year. "We purchase birthday and party graphics for our products. We do not print full-color reflective art. Art must be prepared as 'line art' to be printed in four flat colors (plus screens). Frequently after reviewing an artist's style and capabilities, Unique offers assignments utilizing the artist's specific style or technique. Unique uses freelance artists for design concepts and finished art. *New* designs created for our party supplies must be presented as it would appear on a plate (in a 9⅜ inch circle). *Existing* art can be presented in any size or shape."

First Contact & Terms: Send query letter, tearsheets, photostats and/or photographs. Do not send original art. "We report back within 4-6 weeks. To show a portfolio, call to schedule an appointment." Pays $50 minimum for design sketches. Payment for finished art ranges between $75-250 depending on the complexity of the project. Buys all rights. "All art becomes the exclusive property of Unique Industries, Inc., for use on any and all products we market."

Tips: "Visit large party goods stores and major toy chains (which have large party departments). Artwork submitted to us must be colorful and upbeat. Our catalog is available upon request."

*U.S. PIZAZZ, INC., Suite 5G, 1440 S. State College, Anaheim CA 92806. (714)778-6871. FAX (714)778-6874. Marketing Director: Stephen R. Meeks. Estab. 1984. Produces giftwrap and tote bags. "U.S. Pizazz concentrates on the production of fun, colorful gift bags and giftwrap. Designs are contemporary and the quality of the design and material is of the utmost importance."

Needs: Approached by 20 freelance artists/year. Works with 2-6 freelance artists/year. Buys 10-30 designs and illustrations/year from freelance artists. Uses freelance artists mainly for tote bags. Also uses freelance artists for P-O-P displays. Looking for a contemporary yet sophisticated style. We are also willing to consider new concepts for traditional design. Produces material for Christmas, birthdays and Valentine's Day. Submit 10 months before holiday.

First Contact & Terms: Send query letter with brochure, resume, SASE, tearsheets, photographs, photostats and slides. Samples are filed. Reports back within 4-6 weeks. Call to schedule an appointment to show a portfolio or mail appropriate materials. Portfolio should include original/final art, tearsheets and slides. Rights purchased vary according to project. Original artwork is not returned at the job's completion. Pays by the project, $250-500.

VAGABOND CREATIONS INC., 2560 Lance Dr., Dayton OH 45409. (513)298-1124. Art Director: George F. Stanley, Jr. Publishes stationery and greeting cards with contemporary humor. 99% of artwork used in the line is provided by staff artists working with the company.

Needs: Works with 4 freelance artists/year. Buys 120 finished illustrations from freelance artists/year. Prefers local artists; line drawings, washes and color separations; material should fit in standard size envelope.

First Contact & Terms: Query. Samples returned by SASE. Reports in 2 weeks. Submit Christmas, Mother's Day, Father's Day, Valentine's Day, everyday and graduation material at any time. Originals only returned upon request. Payment negotiated.

Tips: "Important! Important! Currently we are *not* looking for additional freelance artists because we are very satisfied with the work being submitted by those individuals working directly with us. We do not in any way wish to offer false hope to anyone, but it would be foolish on our part not to give consideration. Our current artists are very, very experienced and have been associated with us for many years, in some cases over 30 years."

*VINTAGE IMAGES, Box 228, Lorton VA 22199. (703)550-1881. (703)207-9891. Art Director: Brian Smolens. Estab. 1985. Produces greeting cards, games and posters. "We produce social stationery and prints using sophisticated humor."

Needs: Approached by 10 freelance artists/year. Works with 3 freelance artists/year. Buys 36 designs and illustrations/year from freelance artists. Uses freelance artists for whole card lines. Also uses freelance artists for calligraphy and P-O-P displays. Considers "any media that can be accurately reproduced." Looking for sophisticated humor. "We will also consider a bold, elegant personal style." Produces material for Christmas, Valentine's Day and everyday.

First Contact & Terms: Send query letter with brochure, SASE and photographs. Samples are filed or are returned by SASE. Reports back within 2 months. To show a portfolio, mail photostats, photographs and slides. Buys all rights. Original artwork is returned at the job's completion. Pays by the hour, $20-50; by the project, $200-500; royalties of 5%.

*ALFRED J. WALKER TOWNHOUSE PRESS, 319 Dartmouth St., Boston MA 02116. (617)262-0188. Vice President: Jim Duffy. Estab. 1978. Produces greeting cards. "We produce fine art greeting cards, notecards and Christmas cards."

Needs: Approached by 15-20 freelance artists/year. Works with 6-8 freelance artists/year. Buys 10-20 designs and illustrations/year. "We are presently looking for Christmas images." Uses freelance artists mainly for reproducing fine art as note cards and greeting cards, sometimes illustrations. Considers oil, acrylic, watercolor and pastel. Produces material for Christmas. Submit 1 year before holiday.

First Contact & Terms: Send query letter with SASE, tearsheets, photographs, photocopies, slides and transparencies. Samples are filed and returned by SASE if requested by artist. Reports back within 60 days. Call to schedule an appointment to show a portfolio, which should include original/final art, photographs and slides. Negotiates rights purchased. Original artwork is returned at job's completion. Pays royalties of 5%. "There is initial payment of $150, then royalties."

*WANDA WALLACE ASSOCIATES, Box 436, Inglewood CA 90306. (213)419-0376. President: Wanda. Estab. 1980. Produces greeting cards and posters for general public appeal. "We produce black art prints, posters, originals and other media."

Needs: Approached by 10-12 freelance artists/year. Works with varying number of freelance artists/year. Buys varying number of designs and illustrations/year from freelance artists. Prefers artists with experience in black art subjects. Uses freelance artists mainly for production of originals and some guest appearances. Considers all media. Produces material for Christmas. Submit 4-6 months before holiday.

First Contact & Terms: Send query letter with any visual aid. Some samples are filed. Policy varies regarding answering queries and submissions. Call or write to schedule an appointment to show a portfolio. Rights purchased vary according to project. Original artwork is returned at the job's completion. Pays by the project.

*WATERLINE PUBLICATIONS, INC., 60 K St., Boston MA 02127. (617)268-8792. FAX: (617)268-4868. Contact: Brooke DeHaven. Estab. 1984. Produces greeting cards, calendars and posters for all markets.

Needs: Approached by 50-100 freelance artists/year. Works with 10-20 freelance artists/year. Considers any media.

First Contact & Terms: Send query letter with slides. "No originals." Samples are filed or are returned by SASE if requested by artist. Reports back within 4 weeks. Write to schedule an appointment to show a portfolio, which should include original/final art and color slides. Rights purchased vary according to project. Original artwork returned at the job's completion. Pays royalties of 5-10%.

WEST GRAPHICS, 238 Capp St., San Francisco CA 94110. (415)621-4641. FAX: (415)621-8613. Art Director: Tom Drew. Estab. 1979. Produces greeting cards, calendars, satirical books and gift bags. "We publish greeting cards of a humorous and satirical nature targeting women between the ages of 30-40."

Needs: Approached by 100 freelance artists/year. Works with 40 freelance artists/year. Buys 150 designs and illustrations/year from freelance artists. Works on assignment only. Uses freelance artists mainly for illustration. "All other work is done inhouse." Considers all media. Looking for outrageous contemporary illustration; images that are on the cutting edge. Prefers art proportionate to finished size of 5×7, no larger than 10×14. Produces material for Father's Day, Halloween, Christmas, Easter, graduation, birthdays, Valentine's Day, Hanukkah, Thanksgiving, Mother's Day, New Year and everyday. Submit 1 year before holiday.

First Contact & Terms: Send query letter with resume, SASE, tearsheets, photocopies, photostats, slides and transparencies. Samples are filed or are returned by SASE if requested by artist. Reports back within 6 weeks. To show a portfolio, mail thumbnails, roughs, color photostats, tearsheets, photographs, slides, dummies and samples of printed work if available. Rights purchased vary according to project. Pays by the project, $200-350.

Tips: "Art and concepts should be developed with an occasion in mind such as birthday, belated birthday etc. Humor sells the best. Submit your work for "Off the Wall" as transparencies. We will also review published samples and roughs. Your target should be issues that women care about: relationships, safe sex, religion, aging, success, money, crime, health, weight, etc. Alternative greeting cards are on the increase." Also there is a "younger market and more cerebral humor."

WESTERN GREETING, INC., Box 81056, Las Vegas NV 89180. (702)733-3921. President: Barbara Jean Sullivan. Estab. 1986. Produces greeting cards. Publishes American Western themes and Southwest designs. "For people who love the West, the outdoors and the history of the West."

Needs: Prefers artists with experience in painting the West. Prefers oil; considers watercolor, acrylic and dye. "For the Western cards, we are looking for humorous artwork as well as artwork describing sensitive and real situations. Southwest may include desert and cactus. Artwork must reduce to 5×7 with allowance for bleed. Prefers vertical for everyday cards, but will look at horizontal." Produces material for Christmas, all occasions, friendship and blank note cards; submit 18 months before holiday.

First Contact & Terms: Send query letter with brochure, tearsheets, duplicate slides and SASE. Send duplicate transparencies of completed work relating to Western and Southwestern design and illustration upon request. Samples are filed or are returned by SASE. Reports back within 3-4 weeks. "If in the area," call or write to schedule an appointment to show a portfolio, which should include original/final art, final reproduction/product, slides or tearsheets. Original artwork is returned to the artist after job's completion. Pays average flat fee of $75/design; $125/illustration. Buys all rights.

OFF The Wall GReeTiNG CArds

Humor For The 90's

WEST GRAPHICS PUBLISHING · SAN FRANCISCO · CA

© 1989 West Graphics Publishing

West Graphics' art director Tom Drew says he looks for artists with a "unique, individual style. In greeting cards there is a mainstream, such as Hallmark and Gibson, and we try to stay away from it." Drew says the company's largest purchase category is birthdays, and they are always looking for a new twist. The artwork they purchase is commonly done in pen and ink, watercolor, gouache and colored pencil.

Tips: "Well-executed drawings and composition a must. We are looking for artists that know how to use the dramatic use of light as well as color. Striking is the word. Looking for ideas that are unique and different."

WILLIAMHOUSE-REGENCY, INC., 28 West 23rd St., New York NY 10010. Executive Art Director: Nancy Boecker. Estab. 1955. Produces Christmas cards, stationery, invitations and announcements.
Needs: Approached by 20 freelance artists/year. Works with 5 freelance artists/year. Buys 20 designs and illustrations/year. "Prefers artists with experience in our products and techniques (including foil and embossing)." Buys freelance designs and illustrations mainly for Christmas cards and wedding invitations. Also uses freelance artists for calligraphy. Considers all media. "In wedding invitations, we seek a non-greeting card look. Have a look at what is out there." Produces material for personalized Christmas, Rosh Hashanah, New Year, invitations and announcements. Submit seasonal material 12 months before holiday.
First Contact & Terms: Send query letter with SASE. Samples are not filed and are returned by SASE. Reports back within 3 weeks. Call or write to schedule an appointment to show a portfolio or mail roughs, original/final art and dummies. Pays average flat fee of $150/design. Buys reprint rights or all rights.
Tips: "Send in any roughs or copies of finished ideas you have, and we'll take a look. Write for specs on size first with SASE or write to show portfolio."

CAROL WILSON FINE ARTS, INC., Box 17394, Portland OR 97217. (503)283-2338 or 281-0780. Contact: Gary Spector. Estab. 1983. Produces greeting cards, postcards, posters and stationery that range from contemporary to nostalgic. "At the present time we are actively looking for unusual humor to expand our contemporary humor line. We want cards that will make people laugh out loud! Another category we also wish to expand is fine arts."
Needs: Approached by hundreds of freelance artists/year. Uses artists for product design and illustration of greeting cards and postcards. Considers all media. Prefers humorous cartoons and fine art. Produces seasonal material for Christmas, Valentine's Day and Mother's Day; submit art preferably 1 year in advance.
First Contact & Terms: Send query letter with resume, business card, tearsheets, photostats, photocopies, slides and photographs to be kept on file. No original artwork on initial inquiry. Write for an appointment to show portfolio or for artists' guidelines. "All approaches are considered but, if possible, we prefer to see ideas that are applicable to specific occasions, such as birthday, anniversary, wedding, new baby, etc. We look for artists with creativity and ability." Samples not filed are returned by SASE. Reports within 2 months. Negotiates return of original art after reproduction. Payment ranges from flat fee to royalties. Buys all rights.
Tips: "We have noticed an increased emphasis on humorous cards for specific occasions, specifically, feminist and 'off-the-wall' humor. We are also seeing an increased interest in romantic fine-arts cards."

WIZWORKS, Box 240, Masonville CO 80541-0240. Contact: Director, Creative Recruitment. Estab. 1988. "Our company distributes greeting cards through supermarkets using vending machines which print cards on site using a high-resolution color printer. Card designs are stored as digitized images in the computer memory. Each vending machine has 5,000 card designs which are revised quarterly to accommodate seasonal and holiday requirements. We are seeking card designs which are specific to age, sex, lifestyle, life event, etc.; holiday, birthday and all types of non-occasion cards are needed. We prefer bold, well-defined graphic designs, line drawings and simple illustrations using no more than four colors. Artists with Macintosh computer capability are of special interest." Submit holiday material 6 months before holiday.
First Contact & Terms: Send 4-6 photocopies, slides or tearsheets. Samples are filed and are not returned. Reports back within 6 weeks. Original card concepts are returned by SASE. Pays royalties of 1-2% on retail sales "depending on contribution and complexity. Payments made quarterly. Small advance will be considered for complex designs." Buys greeting card rights for electronic distribution.
Tips: "We rely almost exclusively on freelance graphic designers and artists for card concepts and finished art. Need illustrations for our copy."

*XSEND-TRIX CARDS, Box 470307, Fort Worth TX 76147. (817)737-9912. Contact: Pam Pace. Estab. 1986. Produces greeting cards for all occasions for ages 25-60.
Needs: Approached by 25 freelance artists/year. "We will work with unpublished artists and writers. We are always looking for new and different line ideas, artwork and writers." Uses freelance artists mainly for "artwork and greetings; both individual card ideas and *line* ideas." Considers "two-dimensional works only: watercolor, tempera, marker, anything! We are looking for a bright, contemporary feeling paired with brief greetings." Prefers art no larger than 11×14; not smaller than 5×5. Produces material for Mother's Day, Father's Day, birthdays, everyday and blank cards. Submit 1 year before holiday.
First Contact & Terms: Send query letter with resume, SASE, tearsheets and slides. Samples are filed if interested or returned by SASE. Reports back within 2 months. To show a portfolio, mail original/final art, tearsheets, slides and dummies. Rights purchased vary according to project. Pays royalties of 4-8%.
Tips: The market for alternative card lines is getting tougher due to rack/buy-back programs of the 'big boys'. Small alternative lines must maintain quality and a unique look to compete. We like to buy groups of art from the same artist, which are then featured with his/her own credit line. Also, line ideas msut be well roughed out."

Greeting Card and Paper Products/'90-'91 changes

The following greeting card and paper product companies appeared in the 1990 edition of *Artist's Market* but are not in the 1991 edition. Those which did not respond to our request for an update of their listings may have done so for a variety of reasons—they may be out of business for example, or they may be overstocked with submissions. If they indicated a reason, it is noted in parentheses after their name.

Agent Andy Inc. (overstocked)
Amcal
Athena International
Caring Card Co. (moved; no forwarding address)
Eldercards, Inc. (moved; no forwarding address)
Kristen Elliott, Inc.
G.N.I. Inc. (asked to be deleted)
Gibson Greeting Cards
The Graphic Artisan, Ltd.
HOS International
Joli Greeting Card Co.
KEM Plastic Playing Cards,

Inc.
The Stephen Lawrence Co. (asked to be left out this year)
Leaverly Greeting (asked to be deleted)
Paul Levy- Designer (moved; no forwarding address)
Mark I Inc.
Me To You! Greetings, Inc. (asked to be deleted)
Robert Mulligan Graphics (moved; no forwarding address)
Papercraft Co.

Paramount Cards Inc.
Peck Inc.
Produce Centre-S.W. Inc./The Texas Postcard Co.
Rainboworld Cards
C.A. Reed, Inc. (asked to be deleted)
Reed Starline Card Co.
Scandecor Inc.
Stoneway Ltd.
Sunrise Publications, Inc.
These Three, Inc.
To Coin a Phrase
Wild Card

The magazine industry may have difficult times ahead. There was a 3.5 percent decline in advertising pages in the first quarter of this year, according to the Magazine Publishers of America. The most significant cutbacks came from the automobile, cigarette and liquor industries. And while six years ago 171 new magazines were started, last year the number rose to 584, according to *Samir Husni's Guide to New Magazines*. As Owen J. Lipstein, owner of *The Mother Earth News* and two other magazines, was quoted as saying in *The New York Times*, "There are too many magazines and not enough advertising dollars. The only defense is to put out good, original magazines."

In order to do this, many editors, art directors and publishers have begun to rethink their magazines and have taken innovative steps in redesigning or completely making over their publications. These magazines are attuned to contemporary tastes and have a slicker look, with shorter articles, bolder graphics and more open space. A few such examples found in the following listings are *The New Republic*, *Modern Maturity* and *The Mother Earth News*. Magazine publishers also realize they must reduce costs. As Owen Lipstein says, "In the era of fax machines and Macintoshes, you don't need large magazine staffs. With a network of freelancers, it's irrelevant. The money goes into paper, printing, distribution and talent." Thus, the magazine market presents stronger opportunities than ever for freelance illustrators and cartoonists. Encompassing an assortment of consumer, trade and special interest publications, this market can be quite lucrative for skillful, persistent artists. Magazines are generally published on a monthly or bimonthly basis, requiring art directors to constantly be on the lookout for dependable artists who can deliver quality artwork with a particular style and focus.

Here lies the key to success in the magazine arena—matching and adapting your style and subject matter to those of a specific publication. Art directors want to achieve a "chemistry" between artist and magazine, creating a relationship in which the artwork and editorial content complement each other. Every magazine caters to a different audience and, as mentioned, changes its look from time to time, so before approaching any of the magazines listed in this section, be sure to do your homework. By examining magazines at your local newsstand or library, you'll find that nearly all publications utilize cartoons or illustrations of some kind. Following this route will also prevent mistargeting—such as sending cartoons depicting housekeeping routines to a women's career publication, or submitting countryside illustrations to a sophisticated city magazine.

Keep in mind that consumer magazines, in the broadest sense of the term, appeal to the public at-large. But these are often broken down into less generic categories such as women's publications, product information and news magazines. Illustrations here are commonly used as teasers to draw readers into an article, to supplement the editorial message or, in children's magazines especially, for narrative clarity. Trade or business publications focus on an audience involved in a particular profession, and their busy readers require attention-grabbing, graphic images which convey an instant message; airbrush illustration, as well as conventional pen and ink and pencil, tend to be popular media. In addition, approximately 8,000 house organs or company magazines serve businesses throughout the country, heralding employee activities, company achievements and industry news. Finally, special interest magazines appeal to individualized groups. Literary publications are ideal for experimental abstract and lithographic work, while the recent upswing in travel magazines has created a growing market for artwork with leisure and recreational themes.

Before submitting any samples, read the guidelines for each magazine listed here carefully. Some publications have special submission requirements. It is, however, fairly standard practice to mail nonreturnable samples along with a brief cover letter of introduction and a resume. Always include a self-addressed, stamped envelope large enough to accomodate your samples, but indicate that the director is welcome to keep samples on file.

Persistence pays off in this field if your work is good, your attitude professional and your target market appropriate. Several weeks after your initial submission, mail another sample package accompanied by a "reminder" letter, another copy of your resume and an SASE. Regardless of the response you receive, follow-up again in a few months to remind the art director that you are still interested in the publication and are available for assignments. Art directors and editors often offer tips if they think your work is promising, and making changes based upon these suggestions can sometimes result in sales as well as helpful tips for future ventures. Remember, however, to check the magazine's masthead before resubmitting any material. A staff change, especially in a top editing or art directing position, can mean that you are dealing with a whole new ballgame.

Payment for cartoons and illustrations varies and is determined by the assignment, your skill, experience, rights purchased and the magazine's budget. Widely circulated publications usually boast large pay scales, but small, fledgling magazines, even nonpaying ones, should not be discounted if you are starting out. These publications, which tend to be more open to experimentation, can also provide a valuable testing ground for your potential in the market.

To supplement the listings in this section, look for the following resources in your library: the *Standard Periodical Directory*, the *Internal Publications Directory*, *The Gebbie Press All-in-One Directory*, and *Ulrich's International Periodical Directory*. *Folio*, *Print*, *HOW*, *Communication Arts*, *Magazine Design and Production*, and *Design Quarterly* are good sources for industry updates. Cartoonists can consult *Cartoon World*, *Witty World*, and *The Gag Recap* for trends; Writer's Digest Books has published a new market book just for cartoonists, *Humor and Cartoon Markets*.

A&M MAGAZINE, 4041 N. Central Ave., Phoenix AZ 85012. (602)234-0840. Art Director: Linda Longmire. Estab. 1985. Trade journal. "Arizona's only advertising and marketing magazine presenting industry news in the fields of advertising, marketing, communications and business with a monthly circulation of 5,300 split equally between executives in the advertising and marketing industry and top marketing decision-makers in business." Monthly. Circ. 5,300. Accepts previously published artwork. Original artwork is returned after publication. Sample copies free for SASE with first-class postage. Art guidelines available.
Illustrations: Buys illustrations mainly for covers and feature spreads. Buys 1-3 illustrations/issue, 6-12 illustrations/year from freelancers. Works on assignment only. Considers pen & ink, airbrush, mixed media, colored pencil, watercolor, acrylic, oil and pastel. Send query letter with resume, tearsheets, slides and transparencies. "I look for unique styles with a national level of quality." Samples are filed or are returned by SASE. Does not report back. Write to schedule an appointment to show a portfolio. Buys one-time rights. Pays $75, b&w, cover and inside; on publication.
Tips: "We are not accepting any artwork at this time."

ABORIGINAL SF, Box 2449, Woburn MA 01888-0849. Editor: Charles C. Ryan. Estab. 1986. Science fiction magazine for adult science fiction readers. Bimonthly. Circ. 30,000. Sample copy $3.50; art guidelines for SASE with 1 first-class stamp.
Cartoons: Buys 2-8 cartoons/year from freelancers. Prefers science fiction, science and space themes. Prefers single panel or double panel with or without gagline; b&w line drawings, b&w washes and color washes. Send finished cartoons. Samples are filed or are returned by SASE. Reports back within 2 months. Buys first rights and nonexclusive reprint rights. Pays $20, b&w; $20, color.
Illustrations: Works with 10-15 illustrators/year. Buys 8-16 illustrations/issue from freelancers. Works on assignment only. Prefers science fiction, science and space themes. "Generally, we prefer art with a realistic edge, but surrealistic art will be considered." Prefers watercolor, acrylic, oil and pastel. Send query letter with photocopies and slides. Samples not kept on file are returned by SASE. Reports back within 2 months. To show a portfolio, mail photocopied samples and/or color slides. Buys first rights and nonexclusive reprint rights. Pays $300, color, cover; $250, color, inside; on publication.
Tips: "Show samples of color art showing a range of ability. The most common mistake freelancers make is failure to include a SASE."

ABYSS, 3716 Robinson Ave., Austin TX 78722. Editor: David F. Nalle. Estab. 1979. Full-sized magazine emphasizing fantasy and adventure games for adult game players with sophisticated and varied interests. Bimonthly. Circ. 1,800. Does not accept previously published material. Returns original artwork after publication. Sample copy for $3. Art guidelines free for SASE with first-class postage.

Cartoons: Approached by 25 cartoonists/year. Buys 8-10 cartoons/year from freelancers. Prefers humorous, game or fantasy-oriented themes. Prefers single, double or multiple panel with or without gagline; b&w line drawings. Send query letter with roughs. Write for appointment to show portfolio. Material not filed is returned by SASE. Reports in 6 weeks. Buys first rights. Pays $15, b&w; on publication.

Illustrations: Approached by 100 illustrators/year. Works with 3-5 illustrators/year. Buys 50-70 illustrations/year from freelancers. Uses freelance artists mainly for covers and spots. Prefers science fiction, fantasy, dark fantasy, horror or mythology themes. Send query letter with samples. Write for appointment to show portfolio. Prefers photocopies or photographs as samples. Samples not filed are returned by SASE. Reports within 1 month. Buys first rights. Pays $20-30, b&w, $50-75, color, cover; $3-8, b&w, inside; on publication.

Tips: Does not want to see "Dungeons and Dragons oriented cartoons or crudely-created computer art." Notices "more integration of art and text through desktop publishing."

ACCENT ON LIVING, Box 700, Bloomington IL 61702. Editor: Betty Garee. Estab. 1956. Emphasis on success and ideas for better living for the physically handicapped. Quarterly. Original artwork returned after publication, if requested. Sample copy $2.

Cartoons: Approached by 30 cartoonists/year. Buys approximately 12 cartoons/issue, 50 cartoons/year from freelancers. Receives 5-10 submissions/week from freelancers. Interested in seeing people with disabilities in different situations. Send finished cartoons and SASE. Reports in 2 weeks. Buys first-time rights (unless specified). Pays $20 b&w; on acceptance.

Illustrations: Approached by 20 illustrators/year. Uses 3-5 illustrations/issue from freelancers. Interested in illustrations that "depict articles/topics we run." Works on assignment only. Provide samples of style to be kept on file for future assignments. Samples not kept on file are returned by SASE. Reports in 2 weeks. To show a portfolio, mail color and b&w samples. Buys all rights on a work-for-hire basis. Pays $50 and up, color, cover; $20 and up, b&w; on acceptance.

Tips: "Send a sample and be sure to include various styles of artwork that you can do."

AIM, Box 20554, Chicago IL 60620. (312)874-6184. Editor-in-Chief: Ruth Apilado. Managing Editor: Dr. Myron Apilado. Art Director: Bill Jackson. Estab. 1973. Readers are those "wanting to eliminate bigotry and desiring a world without inequalities in education, housing, etc." Quarterly. Circ. 16,000. Sample copy $3.50; artist's guidelines for SASE. Reports in 3 weeks. Previously published, photocopied and simultaneous submissions OK. Receives 12 cartoons and 4 illustrations/week from freelance artists. Finds most artists through references/word-of-mouth and samples received through the mail.

Cartoons: Buys 10-15 cartoons/year. Uses 1-2 cartoons/issue; all from freelancers. Interested in education, environment, family life, humor through youth, politics and retirement; single panel with gagline. Especially needs "cartoons about the stupidity of bigotry." Mail finished art. SASE. Reports in 3 weeks. Buys all rights on a work-for-hire basis. Pays $5-15, b&w line drawings; on publication.

Illustrations: Uses 4-5 illustrations/issue; half from freelancers. Prefers pen & ink. Interested in current events, education, environment, humor through youth, politics and retirement. Provide brochure to be kept on file for future assignments. No samples returned. Reports in 4 weeks. Prefers b&w for cover and inside art. Buys all rights on a work-for-hire basis. Pays $25, b&w illustrations, cover; on publication.

Tips: "For the most part, artists submit material omitting African-American characters. We would be able to use more illustrations and cartoons with people from all ethnic and racial backgrounds in them. We also use material of general interest. Artists should show a representative sampling of their work and target their samples magazine's specific needs; nothing on religion."

AMAZING HEROES, 7563 Lake City Way, Seattle, WA 98115. Art Director: Mark Thompson. Estab. 1981. Magazine emphasizing news and features on popular comic books. Circ. 20,000. Original artwork, photocopies or photostats are returned to the artist after publication with SASE. Sample copy $3.50.

Cartoons: Approached by over 50 cartoonists/year. Prefers "black & white cartoons, serious or humorous, about comic book characters and super-heroes." Pays $5, b&w.

Illustrations: Prefers b&w spot illustrations and gags dealing with comics. Buys one-time North American rights. Pays $5 or Fantagraphics merchandise; b&w; inside; on publication.

AMELIA, 329 "E" St., Bakersfield CA 93304. (805)323-4064. Editor: Frederick A. Raborg, Jr. Estab. 1983. Magazine; also publishes 2 supplements—*Cicada* (haiku) and *SPSM&H* (sonnets) and illustrated postcards. Emphasizes fiction and poetry for the general review. Quarterly. Circ. 1,250. Accepts some previously published material from illustrators. Original artwork returned after publication if requested with SASE. Sample copy $7.95; art guidelines for SASE.

Cartoons: Buys 3-5 cartoons/issue from freelancers for *Amelia*. Prefers sophisticated or witty themes (see Cynthia Darrow's or Jessica Finney's work). Prefers single panel with or without gagline (will consider multi panel on related themes); b&w line drawings, b&w washes. Send query letter with finished cartoons to be kept on file. Material not filed is returned by SASE. Reports within 1 week. Buys first rights or one-time rights; prefers first rights. Pays $5-25, b&w; on acceptance.

Ilustrations: Buys 80-100 illustrations and spots annually from freelancers for *Amelia;* 24-30 spots for *Cicada*; 15-20 spots for *SPSM&H* and 50-60 spots for postcards. Considers all themes; "no taboos, except no explicit sex; nude studies in taste are welcomed, however." Prefers pen & ink, pencil, watercolor, acrylic, oil, pastel, mixed media and calligraphy. Send query letter with resume, photostats and/or photocopies to be kept on file; unaccepted material returned immediately by SASE. Reports in 1 week. Portfolio should contain "one or two possible cover pieces (either color or black and white), several b&w spots, plus several more fully realized b&w illustrations." Buys first rights or one-time rights; prefers first rights; Pays $25, b&w, $100, color, cover; $5-25, b&w, inside; on acceptance, "except spot drawings which are paid for on assignment to an issue."

Tips: "Wit and humor above all in cartoons. In illustrations, it is very difficult to get excellent nude studies (such as one we used by Carolyn G. Anderson to illustrate a short story by Judson Jerome in our Fall 1986 issue.) Everyone seems capable of drawing an ugly woman; few capture sensuality, and fewer still draw the nude male tastefully."

AMERICA WEST AIRLINES MAGAZINE, #240, 7500 N. Dreamy Draw Dr., Phoenix AZ 85020. Art Director: Elizabeth Krecker. Estab. 1986. Inflight magazine for fast-growing national airline. Appeals to an upscale audience of travelers reflecting a wide variety of interests and tastes. Monthly. Circ. 125,000. Original artwork is returned after publication. Sample copy $2.

Illustrations: Approached by 100 illustrators/year. Buys illustrations mainly for spots, columns and feature spreads. Buys 5-10 illustrations/issue, 60-100 illustrations/year from freelancers. Uses freelance artwork mainly for features and columns. Works on assignment only. Prefers pen & ink, airbrush, mixed media, colored pencil, watercolor, acrylic, oil, pastel, collage and calligraphy. Send query letter with color brochure showing art style and tearsheets. Looks for the "ability to intelligently grasp idea behind story and illustrate it. Likes crisp, clean colorful styles." Samples are filed. Does not report back. Does not review portfolios. Buys one-time rights. Pays $75-250, b&w; $150-500, color, inside; on publication. "Send lots of good-looking color tearsheets that we can keep on hand for reference. If your work interests us we will contact you."

Tips: "In your portfolio show examples of editorial illustration for other magazines, good conceptual illustrations and a variety of subject matter. Often artists don't send enough of a variety of illustrations; it's much easier to determine if an illustrator is right for an assignment if I have a complete grasp of the full range of their abilities. Send high-quality illustrations and show specific interest in our publication." Does not want to see "black & white Xerox's—makes artwork and artist look sloppy and unprofessional."

THE AMERICAN ATHEIST, Box 140195, Austin TX 78714-0195. (512)458-1244. Editor: R. Murray-O'Hair. Estab. 1958. For atheists, agnostics, materialists and realists. Monthly. Circ. 30,000. Simultaneous submissions OK. Free sample copy; send 9x12 envelope or label.

Cartoons: Buys 5 cartoons/issue from freelancers. Especially needs 4-seasons art for covers and greeting cards. Send query letter with resume and samples. Pays $15 each.

Illustrations: Buys 1 illustration/issue from freelancers. "Illustrators should send samples to be kept on file. We do commission artwork based on the samples received. All illustrations must have bite from the atheist point of view and hit hard." Prefers pen & ink, then airbrush, charcoal/pencil and calligraphy. To show a portfolio, mail original/final art, final reproduction/product, and b&w photographs. Pays $75-100, cover; $25, inside; on acceptance.

Tips: "*The American Atheist* looks for clean lines, directness and originality. We are not interested in side-stepping cartoons and esoteric illustrations. Our writing is hard-punching and we want artwork to match. The mother press of the *American Atheist*, the American Atheist Press, buys book cover designs and card designs. I would like to see a sample of various styles, but since we can't print in color, I need to know if the artist can design/illustrate for offset printing."

AMERICAN BANKERS ASSOCIATION-BANKING JOURNAL, 345 Hudson St., New York NY 10014. (212)620-7256. Art Director: Bob Supina. Estab. 1908. Emphasizes banking for middle and upper level-banking executives and managers. Monthly. Circ. 42,000. Accepts previously published material. Returns original artwork after publication.

Illustrations: Approached by 24 illustrators/year. Buys 4 illustrations/issue from freelancers. Themes relate to stories, primarily financial; styles vary, realistic, cartoon, surreal. Works on assignment only. Send query letter with brochure and samples to be kept on file. Prefers tearsheets, slides or photographs as samples. Samples not filed are returned by SASE. Negotiates rights purchased. Pays $500, color, cover; $100-300, b&w or color, inside; on acceptance.

THE AMERICAN BAPTIST MAGAZINE, Box 851, Valley Forge PA 19482-0851. (215)768-2441. Executive Editor: Philip Jenks. Managing Editor: Ronald Arena. News Editor: Richard Schramm. Estab. 1803. National publication of American Baptist Churches in the USA. Contains feature articles, news, and commentary of interest to the American Baptist (1.6 million) constituency. Circ. 50,000. Published 10 times/year. Guidelines available.
Cartoons: Buys 4-6 cartoons/year from freelancers. Pays $35, b&w; $75, color.
Illustrations: Works with 3-5 illustrators/year. Buys 12-15 illustrations/year from freelancers. All artwork on assignment for specific themes/subjects. (May make occasional use of freelance line art and cartoons.) Pays $400, color, cover; $150, b&w, $250, color, inside. Portfolio samples and resume welcomed; enclose SASE for material to be returned.
Tips: "Artists should be willing to work promptly and creatively within stated guidelines for both specific and thematic art work. Target your samples to American Baptist or church audience, show that you can work within a given budget and meet deadlines."

*AMERICAN BREWER MAGAZINE, Box 510, Hayward CA 94541. (415)538-9500 (mornings). Publisher: Bill Owens. Estab. 1985. Trade journal; magazine format. "We focus on the micro-brewing industry." Quarterly. Circ. 4,000. Accepts previously published artwork. Original artwork returned after publication. Sample copies for $5. Art guidelines available.
Cartoons: Approached by 6-8 cartoonists/year. Buys 2 cartoons/issue, 8 cartoons/year from freelancers. Prefers themes "related to drinking or brewing handcrafted beer"; single panel. Send query letter with roughs. Samples not filed and are returned. Reports back within 2 weeks. Buys reprint rights. Pays $50, b&w.
Illustration: Approached by 6-10 illustrators/year. Buys 2 illustrations/issue, 10 illustrations/year from freelancers. Works on assignment only. Prefers themes relating to "beer, brewing, or drinking." Considers pen & ink. Send query letter with photocopies. Samples are not filed and are returned. Reports back within 2 weeks. To show a portfolio mail appropriate materials, which should include photocopies. Buys reprint rights.

*AMERICAN FITNESS, Suite 310, 15250 Ventura Blvd., Sherman Oaks CA 91403. (818)905-0040. Editor-at-Large: Peg Jordan. Managing Editor: Rhonda Jo Wilson. Magazine emphasizing fitness, health and exercise for sophisticated, college-educated, active lifestyles. Bimonthly. Circ. 25,000. Accepts previously published material. Original artwork returned after publication. Sample copy $1.
Cartoons: Approached by 12 cartoonists/month. Buys 1 cartoon/issue from freelancers. Material not kept on file is returned if requested. Buys one-time rights. Pays $35.
Illustrations: Approached by 12 illustrators/month. Buys 1-2 illustrations/issue from freelancers. Works on assignment only. Prefers very sophisticated 4-color line drawings. Send query letter with brochure showing art style and tearsheets. Wants to see "previously published work featuring material geared toward our magazine." Reports back within 2 months. To show a portfolio, mail thumbnails and roughs. Buys one-time rights. Pays $50; on publication.

*AMERICAN HORTICULTURIST, 7931 E. Boulevard Dr., Alexandria VA 22308. (703)768-5700. Editor: Kathleen Fisher. Estab. 1922. Consumer magazine for advanced and amateur gardeners and horticultural professionals who are members of the American Horticultural Society. Monthly. Circ. 20,000. Accepts previously published artwork. Original artwork is returned at job's completion. Sample copies for $2.50. Art guidelines not available.
Illustrations: Buys 15-20 illustrations/year from freelancers. Works on assignment only. "Botanical accuracy is important for many assignments." Considers pen & ink, colored pencil, watercolor and charcoal. Send query letter with tearsheets, slides and photocopies. Samples are filed. "We will call artist if their style matches our need." To show a portfolio mail b&w and color tearsheets and slides. Buys one-time rights. Pays $50-150, b&w, $100-300, color, inside; on publication.

THE AMERICAN LEGION MAGAZINE, Box 1055, Indianapolis IN 46206. Contact: Cartoon Editor. Emphasizes the development of the world at present and milestones of history; general-interest magazine for veterans and their families. Monthly. Original artwork not returned after publication.

The asterisk before a listing indicates that the listing is new in this edition. New markets are often the most receptive to freelance submissions.

Cartoons: Uses 2-3 cartoons/issue, all from freelancers. Receives 100 submissions/week from freelancers. Especially needs general humor in good taste. "Generally interested in cartoons with broad appeal. Prefer action in the drawing, rather than the illustrated joke-type gag. Those that attract the reader and lead us to read the caption rate the highest attention. No-caption gags purchased only occasionally. Because of tight space, we're not in the market for the spread or multipanel cartoons but use both vertical and horizontal single-panel cartoons. Themes should be home life, business, sports and everyday Americana. Cartoons that pertain only to one branch of the service may be too restricted for this magazine. Service-type gags should be recognized and appreciated by any ex-service man or woman. Cartoons that may offend the reader are not accepted. Liquor, sex, religion and racial differences are taboo. Ink roughs not necessary but desirable. Finish should be line, Ben Day." Usually reports within 30 days. Buys first rights. Pays $125-150; on acceptance.

Tips: "Artists should submit their work as we are always seeking new slant and more timely humor. Black-and-white art is primarily what we seek. Note: Cartoons are separate from the art department."

*AMERICAN LIBRARIES, 50 E. Huron St., Chicago IL 60611. (312)280-4216. FAX: (312)440-0901. Senior Editor: Edie McCormick. Estab. 1907. Professional journal; magazine format; "published by the American Library Association for its 50,000 members, providing independent coverage of news and major developments in and related to the library field." Monthly. Circ. 50,554. Original artwork is returned at job's completion. Sample copy $5. Art guidelines available.

Cartoons: Approached by 20 cartoonists/year. Buys 2-3 cartoons/issue, 20 cartoons/year from freelancers. Prefers themes related to libraries. Send query letter with brochure and finished cartoons. Samples are filed. Does not report back, in which case the artist should "do nothing." Buys first rights. Pays $25, b&w, $100, color.

Illustrations: Approached by 20 illustrators/year. Buys 2 illustrations/issue, 20 illustrations/year from freelancers. Works on assignment only. Send query letter with brochure, tearsheets and resume. Samples are filed. Does not report back, in which case the artist should "do nothing." To show a portfolio, mail tearsheets, photostats, photographs and photocopies. Buys first rights. Pays $150, color, cover; $25-75, color, inside; on acceptance.

Tips: "I suggest inquirer go to a library and take a look at the magazine first."

AMERICAN MOTORCYCLIST, American Motorcyclist Association, Box 6114, Westerville OH 43081-6114. (614)891-2425. Executive Editor: Greg Harrison. Managing Editor: Bill Wood. Associate Editor: Roger T. Young. Monthly. Circ. 150,000. For "enthusiastic motorcyclists investing considerable time and money in the sport." Sample copy $1.50.

Cartoons: Buys 1-2 cartoons/issue from freelancers. Receives 5-7 submissions/week from freelancers. Interested in motorcycling; "single panel gags." Prefers to receive finished cartoons. Include SASE. Reports in 3 weeks. Buys all rights on a work-for-hire basis. Pays $15 minimum, b&w washes; on publication.

Illustrations: Buys 1-2 illustrations/issue, almost all from freelancers. Receives 1-3 submissions/week from freelancers. Interested in motorcycling themes. Send query letter with resume and tearsheets to be kept on file. Prefers to see samples of style and resume. Samples returned by SASE. Reports in 3 weeks. Buys first North American serial rights. Pays $100 minimum, color, cover; $30-100, b&w and color, inside; on publication.

AMERICAN MUSIC TEACHER, Suite 1432, 617 Vine St., Cincinnati OH 45202-2434. Art Director:Diane M. DeVillez. Estab. 1951. Trade journal emphasizing music teaching. Features historical and how-to articles. "*AMT* promotes excellence in music teaching and keeps music teachers informed. It is the official journal of the Music Teachers National Association, an organization which includes concert artists, independent music teachers and faculty members of educational institutions." Bimonthly. Circ. 26,424. Accepts previously published material. Original artwork returned after publication. Sample copies available.

Illustrations: Buys 1 illustration/issue from freelancers. Buys 6 illustrations/year from freelancers. Uses freelance artwork mainly for diagrams and illustrations. Prefers musical theme. "No interest in cartoon illustration." Send query letter with brochure or resume, tearsheets, slides and photographs. Samples are filed or are returned only if requested. Reports back within 3 months. To show a portfolio, mail original/final art, color and b&w tearsheets, photographs and slides. Buys one-time rights. Pays $50-150, b&w and color, cover; on publication.

Tips: "In a portfolio show silhouettes and classical music subject matter."

*THE AMERICAN SPECTATOR, Box 10448, Arlington VA 22210. Managing Editor: Wladyslaw Pleszczynski. Concerns politics and literature. Monthly. Circ. 43,000. Original artwork returned after publication.

Illustrations: Uses 2-3 illustrations/issue, all from freelancers. Interested in "caricatures of political figures (or portraits with a point of view)." Works on assignment only. Samples returned by SASE. Reports back on future assignment possibilities. Provide resume, brochure and tearsheets to be kept on file for future assignments. Prefers to see portfolio and samples of style. Reports in 2 weeks. Buys first North American serial rights. Pays $150 minimum, b&w line drawings, cover; $35 minimum, b&w line drawings, inside; on publication.

AMERICAN SQUAREDANCE, Box 488, Huron OH 44839. Editors: Stan and Cathie Burdick. For squaredancers, callers and teachers. Emphasizes personalities, conventions and choreography. Monthly. Original artwork returned after publication if requested. Free sample copy.
Cartoons: Buys 1 cartoon/issue, 6 cartoons/year from freelancers. Interested in dance theme; single panel. Send finished cartoons. SASE. Reports in 1 week. Buys all rights on a work-for-hire basis. Pays $10-20, halftones and washes; on publication.
Illustrations: Uses 5 illustrations/issue; buys 1 illustration/issue from freelancers. Interested in dance themes. Send finished art and SASE. Reports in 1 week. Buys all rights on a work-for-hire basis. Pays $25-50, b&w line drawings, washes and color-separated art, cover; $5-15, b&w line drawings and washes inside; on publication.

*ANEMONE, Box 369, Chester VT 05743. Contact: Bill Griffin. Estab. 1984. Literary magazine. "Our readership is the man on the street, women in the house to the unviersity intellectual. A literary publication of social and political impact; from the other side of the fence." Quarterly. Circ. 5,000. Original artwork is returned after publication. Sample copy $2. Art guidelines not available.
Cartoons: Send query letter with finished cartoons. Samples are returned if requested. Reports back within 2 months. Buys one-time rights. Pays $5 and up on publication.
Illustration: Considers pen & ink, airbrush, mixed media, watercolor, collage and marker. Send query letter with photostats and photographs. Samples are returned only if requested. Reports back in 2 months. Pays $5 and up; on publication.

ANIMALS, 350 S. Huntington Ave., Boston MA 02130. Photo Researcher: Laura Ten Eyck. Estab. 1868. "*Animals* is a national full-color, bimonthly magazine published by the Massachusetts Society for the Prevention of Cruelty to Animals. We publish articles on and photographs of wildlife, domestic animals, conservation, controversies involving animals, animal-welfare issues, pet health and pet care." Circ. 70,000. Original artwork usually returned after publication. Sample copy $2.50.
Illustrations: Approached by 1,000 illustrators/year. Works with 3 illustrators/year. Buys 5 or less illustrations/year from freelancers. Uses artists mainly for spots. Prefers pets or wildlife illustrations relating to a particular article topic. Prefers pen & ink, then airbrush, charcoal/pencil, colored pencil, watercolor, acrylic, oil, pastel and mixed media. Send query letter with brochure or tearsheets. Samples are filed or are returned by SASE. Reports back within 1 month. Write to schedule an appointment to show a portfolio, which should include color roughs, original/final art, tearsheets and final reproduction/product. Negotiates rights purchased. Pay varies; on acceptance.
Tips: "In your samples, include work showing animals, particularly dogs and cats or humans with cats or dogs. Show a representative sampling."

APPALACHIAN TRAILWAY NEWS, Box 807, Harpers Ferry WV 25425. (304)535-6331. Editor: Judith Jenner. Emphasizes the Appalachian Trail for members of the Appalachian Trail Conference. 5 issues/year. Circ. 26,000. Sometimes accepts previously published material. Returns original artwork after publication. Sample copy $3 for serious inquiries; art guidelines for SASE with first-class postage. Finds most artists through references/word-of-mouth and samples received through the mail.
Illustrations: Buys 2-5 illustrations from freelancers. Prefers pen & ink, charcoal/pencil, colored pencil, watercolor, acrylic, oil, pastel and calligraphy. Original artwork must be related to the Appalachian Trail. Send query letter with samples to be kept on file. Prefers photostats, photocopies or tearsheets as samples. Samples not filed are returned by SASE. Reports within 1 month. Negotiates rights purchased. Pays $25-150, b&w, occasional color; on acceptance.

*ARARAT, 585 Saddle River Rd., Saddle Brook NJ 07662. Contact: Leo Hamalian. For those interested in Armenian life and culture, for Americans of Armenian descent, and Armenian immigrants. Quarterly. Circ. 2,000.
Illustrations: Include SASE. Pays on publication.

*ARCHIE COMIC PUBLICATIONS INC., 325 Fayette Ave., Mamaroneck NY 10543. (914)381-5155. Editor: Victor Gorelick. Estab. 1942. Publishes comic books and graphic novels. Various titles: Archie Jughead, Betty and Veronica, Pep, Little Archie, etc. also a syndicated newspaper strip. Genres include humor. Themes geared toward social commentary, family situations and teenage exploits. "The Archie reader is 11 years old. We entertain through the medium of believable humor." Bi-monthly. Circ. 13 million+ per year. Original artwork is sometimes returned to the artist after publication. Sample copies and art guidelines available.
Illustrations: Prefers three-tier page of 6 panels. Freelance artists are used for inking, lettering, pencilling, color work, paste-up, posters and covers. Send query letter with samples, which should include teenage art. Samples are not filed and are returned by SASE. Reports back to the artist within 6 weeks. Call or write to schedule an appointment to show a portfolio, which should include 12 pages of pencil or ink drawings, twice

up, photocopies of original pencil art or inking and pages of lettering, twice up. Negotiates payment; considers experience of artist. Pays on acceptance.

ARCHITECTURAL DIGEST, 140 E. 45th, New York NY 10017. Art Director: Marino M. Zullich. Estab. 1965. Interior design magazine emphasizing design, architecture, art, etc. Monthly. Circ. 625,000. Does not accept previously published artwork. Original artwork is sometimes returned after publication. Sample copies $4.50. Art guidelines not available.
Cartoons: Buys 6 cartoons/year. Send query letter with samples of style. Samples are filed or are returned if requested by SASE. Reports back regarding queries/submissions only if interested. Negotiates rights purchased. Pays $400, b&w; $600, color; on publication.
Illustrations: Buys illustrations mainly for promotion. Buys 6 illustrations/year. Works on assignment only. Prefers mixed media. Considers pen & ink, airbrush, colored pencil, watercolor, acrylic, oil, pastel, collage, marker, charcoal pencil and calligraphy. Send query letter. Interested in any style or subject. Samples are filed or are returned only if requested by SASE. Reports back about queries/submissions only if interested. Negotiates rights purchased. Pays $400, b&w; $600, color, cover and $150, b&w; $250, color, inside; on publication.

*ART BUSINESS NEWS, Box 3837, Stamford CT 06905. (203)356-1745. Editor: Jo Yanow-Schwartz. Trade journal emphasizing the business of selling art and frames, trends, new art editions, limited editions, posters and framing supplies. Features general interest, interview/profile and technical articles. Monthly. Circ. 30,000. Original artwork returned after publication. Sample copy $3.50. Uses freelance artists mainly for big features.
Cartoons: Approached by 10 cartoonists/year. Buys some cartoons/issue from freelancers. Prefers "sophisticated, light business orientation." Prefers single panel, b&w line drawings and b&w washes. Send query letter with samples of style. Samples are filed or are returned. Reports back within weeks. Pays $35-50, b&w.
Illustrations: Approached by 5 illustrators/year. Works on assignment only. Send query letter with brochure showing art style, tearsheets and slides. Samples are filed (excluding slides) or are returned. Reports back within weeks. Write to schedule an appointment to show a portfolio or mail color and b&w tearsheets and photographs. Buys one-time rights. Pays $100, b&w, cover; $200, color, inside.

ART DIRECTION, 10 E. 39th St., 6th Floor, New York NY 10016. (212)889-6500. Editor: Dan Barron. Estab. 1949. Emphasizes advertising for art directors. Monthly. Circ. 12,000. Original work not returned after publication. Sample copy $3.50. Art guidelines available.
Illustrations: Receives 7 illustrations/week from freelancers. Uses 2-3 illustrations/issue; all from freelancers. Works on assignment only. Interested in themes that relate to advertising. Send query letter with brochure showing art styles. Samples are not filed and are returned only if requested. Reports in 3 weeks. Write to schedule an appointment to show a portfolio, which should include tearsheets. Negotiates rights purchased. Pays $350, color, cover; on publication.
Tips: "Must be about current advertising."

THE ARTIST'S MAGAZINE, 1507 Dana Ave., Cincinnati OH 45207. Editor: Mike Ward. Emphasizes the techniques of working artists for the serious beginning, amateur and professional artist. Published 12 times/year. Circ. 250,000. Occasionally accepts previously published material. Returns original artwork after publication. Sample copy $2 with SASE and 50¢ postage.
Cartoons: Contact Mike Ward, editor. Buys 2-3 "top-quality" cartoons/issue from freelancers. Most cartoons bought are single panel finished cartoons with or without gagline; b&w line drawings, b&w washes. "We're also on the lookout for color, multi panel (4-6 panels) work with a theme to use on our 'P.S.' page. Any medium." All cartoons should be artist-oriented, appeal to the working artist and should not denigrate art or artists. Avoid cliché situations. For single panel cartoon submissions, send cover letter with 4 or more finished cartoons. For "P.S." submissions, query first with roughs and samples of your artwork. Material not filed is returned only by SASE. Reports within 1 month. Pays $50 and up, b&w single panels; $200 and up, "P.S." work. Buys first North American serial rights. Pays on acceptance.
Illustrations: Contact Carol Winters, Art Director. Buys 2-3 illustrations/issue from freelancers. Works on assignment only. Send query letter with brochure, resume and samples to be kept on file. Prefers photostats or tearsheets as samples. Samples not filed are returned by SASE. Buys first rights. Pays on acceptance. "We're also looking for black-and-white spots of art-related subjects. We will buy all rights, $15-25 per spot."

ISAAC ASIMOV'S SCIENCE FICTION MAGAZINE, 380 Lexington Ave., New York NY 10017. (212)557-9100. FAX: (212)986-7313. Art Director: Terri Czeczko. Estab. 1977. Consumer magazine of science fiction and fantasy. Monthly. Circ. 100,000. Accepts previously published artwork. Original artwork returned at job's completion. Sample copies available. Art guidelines free for SASE with first-class postage.
Illustrations: Approached by 60 illustrators/year. Buys 10 illustrations/issue, 130 illustrations/year from freelancers. Works on assignment only. Considers pen & ink, airbrush, watercolor, acrylic and oil. Send query letter with tearsheets "I view portfolios on Tuesdays of each week." Samples are sometimes filed or are

returned by SASE if requested by artist. Reports back only if interested. Portfolio should include tearsheets. Buys one-time rights; rights purchased vary according to project. Pays $600, color, cover. Pays $100, b&w.

ATLANTIC CITY MAGAZINE, Suite 100, 1270 W. Washington Ave., Pleasantville NJ 08232-1324. (609)348-6886. Art Director: Michael L. B. Lacy. Estab. 1979. Emphasizes the growth, people and entertainment of Atlantic City for residents and visitors. Monthly. Circ. 50,000.

Cartoons: Approached by 250 cartoonists/year. Pays $50, b&w, $150, color cartoons.

Illustrations: Approached by 1,000 illustrators/year. Works with 20 illustrators/year. Buys 36 illustrations/year from freelancers. Uses artists mainly for spots. Mainly b&w, some 4-color. Works on assignment only. Send query letter with brochure showing art style and tearsheets, slides and photographs to be kept on file. Call or write to schedule an appointment to show a portfolio, which should include original/final art, final reproduction/product, color and b&w tearsheets and photographs. Buys first rights. Pays $500, b&w and color, cover; $75, b&w, $225, color, inside; on publication.

Tips: "We are looking for intelligent, reliable artists who can work within the confines of our budget and time frame. Deliver good art and receive good tearsheets." Believes that in the future "artists will regain interest in the Renaissance and its styles, some artists/designers will rebel against computer aided art and design and work towards a consciously recognized style that reflects the hand at work, not the computer."

ATLANTIC SALMON JOURNAL, Suite 1030, 1435 St. Alexandre, Montreal, Quebec H3A 2G4 Canada. (514)842-8059. Managing Editor: Terry Davis. Estab. 1952. Emphasizes conservation and angling of Atlantic salmon; travel, biology and cuisine for educated, well-travelled, affluent and informed anglers and conservationists, biologists and professionals. Quarterly. Circ. 20,000. Does not accept previously published material. Returns original artwork after publication. Sample copy free for SAE. Art guidelines available.

Cartoons: Buys 1-2/issue from freelancers. Prefers environmental or political themes, specific to salmon resource management, travel and tourism—light and whimsical. Prefers single panel with or without gagline; b&w line drawings. Send query letter with samples of style to be kept on file. Material not filed is returned. Reports within 8 weeks. Buys first rights and one-time rights. Pays $25-50, b&w; on publication.

Illustrations: Buys 1-2/issue from freelancers. Prefers themes on angling, environmental scenes and biological drawings. Prefers spot pencil sketches, watercolor and acrylic. Send query letter with samples to be kept on file. Prefers photostats, tearsheets, slides or photographs as samples. Include SAE and IRC. Samples not filed are returned. Reports within 8 weeks. Buys first rights and one-time rights. Pays $150-225, b&w; and $350-500, color, cover; on publication.

© 1989 Kathleen Merritt

This watercolor-cover illustration for The Atlantic Salmon Journal was done by Kathleen Merritt of Council, Iowa. After seeing her resume and portfolio, publications editor Terry David asked her to reproduce a photograph, using her creative imagination. Davis says Merritt has captured "the excitement and passion of hooking and playing an Atlantic salmon on a fly rod. The subjects are realistic, and there is a certain tension throughout the work."

THE AUTOGRAPH COLLECTOR'S MAGAZINE, Box 55328, Stockton CA 95205. (209)473-0570. Editor: Joe Kraus. Estab. 1986. Consumer magazine. "We cover world of collecting autographs, signed photos, letters, and historical documents. Subscribers throughout the world range in age from 8 to 80. All fields covered: entertainment, sports, military, literary, science, political, etc." Published 8 times a year. Circ. 4,000. Original artwork is returned after publication. Sample copies $3.

Cartoons: Buys 1-2 cartoons/issue. Buys 8-16 cartoons/year. Prefers material in good taste, to appeal to all ages on the subject of in-person, through-the-mail or historical autograph collecting." Prefers single, double or multiple panel with gagline; b&w line drawings. Send query letter with finished cartoons. Samples are filed. Samples not filed are returned by SASE. Reports back within 2 weeks. Buys first rights. Pays $25 on publication.

Illustrations: Buys illustrations mainly for feature spreads. Buys 1-2 illustrations/issue. Works on assignment only. Prefers pen & ink. Send query letter with photostats. Samples are filed. Samples not filed are returned by SASE. Reports back within 2 weeks. To show a portfolio, mail photostats. Buys first rights. Pays $25-50, b&w; on publication.

Tips: "We are open to all illustrators regardless of past experience. All departments of the magazine are open. Our goal is to use a great deal more art work than we have in the past."

AUTOMOBILE MAGAZINE, 120 East Liberty, Ann Arbor MI 48104. (313)994-3500. Art Director: Lawrence C. Crane. Estab. 1986. An "automobile magazine" for up-scale life styles. Monthly. Circ. 450,000. Original artwork is returned after publication. Art guidelines specific for each project.

Illustrations: Buys illustrations mainly for spots and feature spreads. Works with 5-10 illustrators/year. Buys 20-30 illustrations/year. Buys 2-5 illustrations/issue from freelancers. Works on assignment only. Considers airbrush, mixed media, colored pencil, watercolor, acrylic, oil, pastel and collage. Send query letter with brochure showing art style, resume, tearsheets, slides, photographs and transparencies. Show automobiles in various styles and media. "This is a full-color magazine, illustrations of cars and people must be accurate." Samples are returned only if requested. "I would like to keep something in my file." Reports back about queries/submissions only if interested. To show a portfolio mail appropriate materials, then call. Portfolio should include original/final art, and color tearsheets, slides and transparencies. Buys first rights and one-time rights. Pays $900, color, cover; $200 and up, color, inside.

Tips: "Send samples that show cars drawn accurately with a unique style and imaginative use of medium."

*AXIOS, The Orthodox Journal, 800 S. Euclid Ave., Fullerton CA 92632. (714)526-4952. Editor: Daniel Gorham. Emphasizes "challenges in ethics and theology, some questions that return to haunt one generation after another, old problems that need to be restated with new urgency. *Axios* tries to present the 'unthinkable.' " From an Orthodox Catholic viewpoint. Monthly. Circ. 8,478. Accepts previously published material and simultaneous submissions. Original artwork returned after publication. Sample copy $2.

Illustrations: Buys 5-10 illustrations/issue from freelancers. Prefers bold line drawings, seeks icons, b&w; "no color *ever*; uses block prints—do not have to be religious, but must be *bold*!" Send query letter with brochure, resume, business card or samples to be kept on file. Samples not filed are returned by SASE. Reports within 5 weeks. To show a portfolio, mail final reproduction/product and b&w. Buys one-time rights. Pays $50, b&w cover and $20-50, b&w inside; on acceptance.

Tips: "Realize that the Orthodox are *not* Roman Catholics, nor Protestants. We do not write from those outlooks. Though we do accept some stories about those religions, be sure *you* know what an Orthodox Catholic is. Know the traditional art form—we prefer line work, block prints, lino-cuts."

BAJA TIMES, Box 5577, Chula Vista CA 92012. (706)612-1244. Editor: John W. Utley. Emphasizes Baja California, Mexico for tourists, other prospective visitors and retirees living there. Monthly. Circ. 60,000. Accepts previously published material. Original artwork returned after publication. Sample copy for 9x12 or larger SASE with $1 postage.

Cartoons: All must be Baja California-oriented. Prefers single panel with gagline; b&w line drawings. Send query letter with sample of style to be kept on file. Material not filed returned by SASE. Reports within 1 month. Buys one-time rights. Pays $5-10, b&w; on publication.

Illustrations: Theme: Baja California. Send query letter with samples, tearsheets or photocopies to be kept on file. Samples not filed are returned by SASE. Reports within 1 month. Buys one-time rights. Pays $15, b&w, inside; on publication.

Tips: "We have not used art, mostly because it has not been offered to us. If properly oriented to our theme (Baja California), we would consider on an occasional basis."

BALLOON LIFE MAGAZINE, 3381 Pony Express Dr., Sacramento CA 95834. (916)922-9648. Editor: Glen Moyer. Estab. 1985. Monthly magazine emphasizing the sport of ballooning. This is a "four-color magazine covering the life of sport ballooning, contains current news, feature articles, a calendar and more. Audience is sport balloon enthusiasts." Circ. 3,500. Accepts previously published material. Original artwork returned after publication. Sample copy for SASE with $1.65 postage.

Cartoons: Approached by 20-30 cartoonists/year. Buys 1-2 cartoons/issue, 10-15 cartoons/year from freelancers. Prefers gag cartoons, editorial or political cartoons, caricatures and humorous illustrations. Prefers single panel with or without gaglines; b&w line drawings. Send query letter with samples, roughs and finished cartoons. Samples are filed or are returned. Reports back within 2 weeks. Buys first rights. Pays $25, b&w; on publication.

Illustrations: Approached by 10-20 illustrators/year. Buys 1-3 illustrations/year from freelancers. Send query letter with business card and samples. Samples are filed or are returned. Reports back within 2 weeks. Buys first rights. Pays $25-50, color, cover; $25-40, color, inside; on publication.
Tips: "The magazine files samples. When we identify a need, we look at our files to see whose style would best fit the project."

BALTIMORE JEWISH TIMES, 2104 North Charles St., Baltimore MD 21218. (301)752-3504. Creative Director: Kim Muller-Thym. Tabloid emphasizing special interest to the Jewish community for largely local readership. Weekly. Circ. 20,000. Returns original artwork after publication, if requested. Sample copy available.
Illustrations: Approached by 50 illustrators/year. Buys 4-6 illustrations/issue from freelancers. Works on assignment only. Prefers high-contrast, b&w illustrations. Send query letter with brochure showing art style or tearsheets and photocopies. Samples not filed are returned by SASE. Reports back if interested. To show a portfolio, mail appropriate materials or write to schedule an appointment; portfolio should include original/final art, final reproduction/product and color tearsheets and photostats. Buys first rights. Pays $200, b&w, cover and $300, color, cover; $50-100, b&w, inside; on publication.
Tips: Sees trend toward "more freedom of design integrating visual and verbal."

*BARTENDER MAGAZINE, Box 158, Liberty Corner NJ 07938. (201)766-6006. FAX: (201)766-6607. Estab. 1979. Trade journal emphasizing restaurants, taverns, bars, bartenders, bar managers, owners, etc. Quarterly. Circ. 130,000.
Cartoons: Approached by 10 cartoonists/year. Buys 3 cartoons/issue from freelancers. Prefers bar themes; single panel. Send query letter with finished cartoons. Samples are filed. Reports back within 2 weeks. Buys first rights. Pays $500, color.
Illustrations: Approached by 5 illustrators/year. Buys 1 illustration/issue from freelancers. Works on assignment only. Prefers bar themes. Considers any media. Send query letter with brochure. Samples are filed. Reports back within 2 weeks. Mail appropriate materials. Negotiates rights purchased. Pays $500, color, cover; on publication.

*BASEBALL CARDS MAGAZINE, 700 E. State St., Iola WI 54990. (715)445-2214. FAX: (715)445-4087. Editorial Assistant: Greg Ambrosius. Estab. 1981. Consumer magazine. "We publish the nation's largest magazine for collectors of sports cards and other sports memorabilia." Monthly. Circ. 305,000. Accepts previously published artwork. Original artwork returned after publication. Sample copy for 8½ × 11 envelope and $1.25 postage. Art guidlines free for SASE with first-class postage.
Cartoons: Approached by 1 cartoonist/year. Buys 6 cartoons/issue, 48 cartoons/year from freelancers. Prefers cartoons "done in the style of Topps' cartoon backs for its baseball and football cards"; single panel, b&w line drawings. Send query letter with roughs. Samples are filed. Reports back within 2 weeks. Buys one-time rights. Pays $35, b&w, $50, color.
Illustrations: Approached by 8-10 illustrators/year. Buys 2 illustrations/issue; 24 illustrations/year from freelancers. Prefers baseball themes. Considers collage, airbrush, acrylic, marker and colored pencil. Send query letter with SASE, photostats and slides. Samples are filed. Reports back within 2 weeks. Call to schedule an appointment to show a portfolio, which should include b&w, roughs, color, photostats, photocopies, original/final art and photographs. Rights purchased vary according to project. Pays $35, b&w, $50, color, inside.
Tips: The best way for a cartoonist or illustrator to break in is "by showing the ability to render usual faces and images in a slightly unusual manner."

*BASSMASTER MAGAZINE, 1 Bell Rd., Montgomery AL 36117. (205)272-9530. Art Director: Scott W. Hughes. Estab. 1968. Membership only publication with 2 newstand issues a year; magazine format. Monthly. Circ. 550,000. Original artwork returned at job's completion. Sample copies available. Art guidelines not available.
Illustrations: Approached by 10-20 illustrators/year. Buys 5 illustrations/issue, 50 illustrations/year from freelancers. Works on assignment only. Preferred subjects are bass fish, fishing techniques and maps. Considers pen & ink, watercolor, mixed media and Macintosh computer created diagrams such as maps. Send query letter with brochure, tearsheets and resume. Samples are not filed and are returned by SASE if requested by artist. Reports back within 1 week. Write to schedule an appointment to show a portfolio. Portfolio should include original/final art and b&w tearsheets and slides. Rights purchased vary according to project. Payment varies. "We do not use art for the cover."
Tips: "Artists should have a basic knowledge of bass fish, fishing techniques, etc." Does not want to see "illustrious oil, pastel, or acrylic paintings (we just don't use them)." Macintosh experience on Adobe Illustrator is a definite plus."

B.C. OUTDOORS, 202-1132 Hamilton St., Vancouver, British Columbia V6B 2S2 Canada. (604)687-1581. Editor: George Will. Emphasizes fishing, hunting, RV camping, wildlife/conservation. Published 10 times/year. Circ. 55,000. Original artwork returned after publication unless bought outright. Free sample copy.

Cartoons: Approached by more than 10 cartoonists/year. Buys 1-2 cartoons/issue; all from freelancers. Cartoons should pertain to outdoor recreation: fishing, hunting, camping and wildlife in British Columbia. Format: single panel, b&w line drawings with or without gagline. Prefers finished cartoons. Include SAE (nonresidents include IRC). Pays on acceptance. Reports in 2 weeks. Buys one-time rights.

Illustrations: Approached by more than 10 illustrators/year. Buys 12 illustrations/year from freelancers. Interested in outdoors, creatures and activities as stories require. Freelancers selected "generally because I've seen their work." Format: b&w line drawings for inside, rarely for cover; b&w washes for inside and color washes for inside and cover. Works on assignment only. Samples returned by SAE (nonresidents include IRC). Reports back on future assignment possibilities. Arrange personal appointment to show portfolio or send samples of style. When reviewing samples, especially looks at how their subject matter fits the publication and the art's quality. Reports in 2-6 weeks. Buys first North American serial rights or all rights on a work-for-hire basis. Payment negotiable, depending on nature of assignment. Pays on acceptance.

BEND OF THE RIVER® MAGAZINE, 143 W. Third St., Box 239, Perrysburg OH 43551. Editors-in-Chief: Christine Raizk Alexander and R. Lee Raizk. For local history enthusiasts. Monthly. Circ. 3,400. Previously published and photocopied submissions OK. Original artwork returned after publication. Sample copy $1.
Cartoons: Approached by 5-10 cartoonists/year. Buys 12 cartoons/issue from freelancers. Interested in early Americana; single panel with gagline. SASE. Buys first North American serial rights or all rights on a work-for-hire basis. Pays $2-5, b&w line drawings. Wants to see "cartoons that are funny."
Tips: Query if sending anything, except cartoons. Needs cartoons. A common mistake is that the "artwork is good, but the gagline's not funny."

BEVERAGE WORLD MAGAZINE, 150 Great Neck Rd., Great Neck NY 11021. (516)829-9210. Art Director: Ingrid Atkinson. Editor: Alan Wolf. Emphasizes beverages (beers, wines, spirits, bottled waters, soft drinks, juices) for soft drink bottlers, breweries, bottled water/juice plants, wineries and distilleries. Monthly. Circ. 33,000. Accepts simultaneous submissions. Original artwork returned after publication if requested. Sample copy $2.50.
Illustrations: Uses 5 illustrations/issue; buys 3-4 illustrations/issue from freelancers. Works on assignment only. Send query letter with photostats, slides or tearsheets to be kept on file. Write for appointment to show portfolio. Reports only if interested. Negotiates rights purchased. Pays $350 color, cover; $50-100, b&w, inside; on acceptance. Uses color illustration for cover, usually black-and-white for spot illustrations inside.

BICYCLING MAGAZINE, 33 East Minor St., Emmaus PA 18098. Art Director: John Pepper. Magazine. 10 published/year. Original artwork is returned after publication.
Illustrations: Buys illustrations mainly for spots, feature spreads, technical and maps. Buys 8 illustrations/issue from freelancers. Works on assignment only. Send query letter with tearsheets, photocopies, slides, photographs and transparencies. Samples are filed or are returned only if requested. Reports back about queries/submissions only if interested. Call to schedule an appointment to show a portfolio. Buys one-time rights.

BIRD TALK, Box 6050, Mission Viejo CA 92690. (714)855-8822. Editorial Director: Karyn New. Estab. 1983. Consumer magazine publishing "informative material to help pet bird owners care for their birds." Monthly. Circ. 175,000. Accepts previously published artwork. Original artwork is returned after publication. Sample copies $3.50. Art guidelines free for SASE with first-class postage.
Cartoons: Buys about 6 cartoons/issue, about 72 cartoons/year from freelancers. Prefers clear line drawings of humorous pet bird situations. "No 'Polly want a cracker' or pirate jokes!" Prefers single panel with gagline; b&w line drawings. Send finished cartoons. Samples not filed and are returned by SASE. Reports back within 4 weeks. Buys one-time rights. Pays $35, b&w; after publication.
Illustrations: Buys illustrations mainly for spot use and feature spreads. Buys 0-3 illustrations/issue, 30 illustrations/year from freelancers. Works on assignment only. Prefers line drawings. Samples are not filed and are returned by SASE. Reports back within 4 weeks. "We work only with someone who can send good original spot art." Buys one-time spot rights, when assigned all rights. Pays $20, b&w; after publication.
Tips: "We accept finished spot art as fillers. If we like the artist's style, we will contact him/her for assignments."

BIRD WATCHER'S DIGEST, Box 110, Marietta OH 45750. (614)373-5285. Editor: Mary B. Bowers. Emphasizes birds and bird watching for "bird watchers and birders (backyard and field; veteran and novice)." Bimonthly. Circ. 80,000. Previously published material OK. Original work returned after publication. Sample copy $3.
Cartoons: Buys 1-3 cartoons/issue; all from freelancers. Interested in themes pertaining to birds and/or bird watchers. Single panel with or without gagline; b&w line drawings. Send roughs. Samples returned by SASE. Reports in 2 months. Buys one-time rights and reprint rights. Pays $20, b&w; on publication.

BLACK BEAR PUBLICATIONS, 1916 Lincoln St., Croydon PA 19020-8026. (215)788-3543. Editor: Ave Jeanne. Associate Editor: Ron Zettlemoyer. Estab. 1984. Magazine emphasizing social, political, ecological and environmental subjects for a mostly well-educated audience, any age group. Semiannual. Circ. 500. Accepts previously published material. Original artwork returned after publication with SASE. Sample copy $3 (for back issues); art guidelines for SASE with first-class postage. Current copy $4 postpaid in U.S. and Canada.
Illustrations: Works with 12 illustrators/year. Buys 20 illustrations/issue from freelancers. Prefers collage, woodcut, pen & ink. Send samples with SASE, resume and photocopies. Samples not filed returned by SASE. Reports within 10 days. To show a portfolio, mail photocopies. Buys one-time rights or reprint rights. Pays in copies; on publication, for the magazine. Pays cash on acceptance for chapbook illustrators. Average pay for chapbook illustrators is $35 for one time rights.
Tips: A common mistake freelancers make in presenting their work is that they have "no idea what we publish."

*BLACK WARRIOR REVIEW, Box 2936, University of Alabama, Tuscaloosa AL 35487. (205)348-4518. Editor: Alicia Griswold. Literary magazine; publishes contemporary poetry, fiction and non-fiction by new and established writers. "It is known for its unique covers." Biannual. Circ. 2,000. Accepts previously published artwork. Original artwork is returned at job's completion. Sample copy $3.50. Art guidelines not available.
Illustrations: Approached by 4 freelance illustrators/year. Buys 2 illustrations/issue from freelancers. Themes and styles vary. Considers pen & ink, airbrush, watercolor, acrylic, oil, collage and marker. Send query letter with photocopies. Samples are not filed and are returned. Reports back in 1 month. Pays on publication.
Tips: "Look at the magazine."

*BLUE COMET PRESS, 1708 Magnolia Ave., Manhattan Beach CA 90266. (213)545-6887. President/Publisher: Craig Stormon. Estab. 1986. Publishes limited edition comic books. Genres: adventure, fantasy, science fiction, animal parodies and social parodies. Themes: outer space, future science and social commentary. "Our comics are for everybody—for kids and grown ups. We have PG rating." Bimonthly and quarterly. Circ. 2-20,000. Original artwork returned after publication. Sample copy $2.50. Art guidelines for SASE with 1 first-class stamp.
Illustrations: Uses freelance artists for inking, lettering, pencilling, color work, posters and covers. Send query letter with resume and photocopies of work, story form 4-8 pages. Samples not filed are returned by SASE if requested. Reports back within 1 month. Call or write to schedule an appointment to show a portfolio, or mail 4-8 pages of pencil or ink drawings, 4-8 pages of action continuity, 4-8 photocopies of original pencil art or inking and 4-8 pages of lettering. Rights purchased vary. Pays $10-35/page for pencilling, $15-25/page for inking and $5-10 for lettering. Pays on publication "or after."Also pays percentage.
Tips: "I don't need cartoony art. Need realistic art, good anatomy. Must be top quality."

THE B'NAI B'RITH INTERNATIONAL JEWISH MONTHLY, B'nai B'rith, 1640 Rhode Island Ave. NW, Washington DC 20036. (202)857-6645. Editor: Jeff Rubin. Emphasizes a variety of articles of interest to the Jewish family. Published 10 times/year. Circ. 200,000. Original artwork returned after publication. Sample copy $1. Also uses artists for "design, lettering, calligraphy on assignment. We call or write the artist, pay on publication."
Illustrations: Approached by 20 illustrators/year. Buys 2 illustrations/issue from freelancers. Theme and style vary, depending on tone of story illustrated. Works on assignment only. Write or call for appointment to show portfolio, which should include tearsheets, slides or photographs. Reports within 3 weeks. Samples returned by SASE. Buys first rights. Pays $500, color, cover; $50, b&w, $100, color, inside; rates vary according to size of illustration; on publication.

*BOAT JOURNAL (formerly *Small Boat Journal*), 2100 Powers Ferry Rd., Atlanta GA 30339. (404)955-5656. Editor: Richard Lebovitz. Managing Editor: John Weber. Magazine emphasizing boats and boating for recreation boaters of all types—sailors, powerboaters and rowers. Bimonthly.
Illustrations: Works with 4-6 artists/year. Uses artists for illustrating technical details, boat building and repair techniques, perspective and profile views of boats and maps. Prefers illustration of small craft, technical/representative illustration. Prefers pen & ink, charcoal/pencil, watercolor, acrylic and oil. Cartoon ideas also welcomed. Send query letter with brochure or samples. Reports back only if interested. Call to schedule an appointment to show a portfolio, which should include roughs and original/final art. Pays by the piece, $25-350.
Tips: "Ability to render people is a plus. Familiarity with boats and nautical subjects is necessary."

BODY, MIND AND SPIRIT MAGAZINE, Box 701, Providence RI 02901. (401)351-4320. Publisher and Editor-in-Chief: Paul Zuromski. Editor: Carol Kramer. Estab. 1982. Magazine emphasizing New Age, natural living and metaphysical topics for people looking for tools to improve body, mind and spirit. Bimonthly. Circ. 150,000. Original artwork returned after publication. Sample copy for 9x12 SASE with $1.07 postage.

Cartoons: Approached by 10 cartoonists/year. Buys 6 cartoons/year from freelancers. Prefers New Age, natural living and metaphysical themes. Prefers single panel with gagline; b&w line drawings. Send query letter with samples of style and roughs to be kept on file. Write to show a portfolio. Material not filed is returned by SASE. Reports within 3 months. Buys one-time or reprint rights. Pays $25, b&w.

Illustrations: Approached by 40 illustrators/year. Works with 3 illustrators/year. Buys 25 illustrations/year from freelancers. Works on assignment only. Prefers line art with New Age, natural living and metaphysical themes. Send query letter with resume, tearsheets, photostats, photocopies, slides and photographs. Samples not filed are returned by SASE. Reports within 3 months. To show a portfolio, mail original/final art and tearsheets. Buys one-time reprint rights. Pays $75, b&w, $250, color, inside; on publication.

BOSTONIA MAGAZINE, 10 Lenox St., Brookline MA 02146. (617)353-9711. Art Director: Douglas Parker. Estab. 1900.Magazine emphasizing "innovative ideas and profiles of creative people" for graduates of the university and residents of New England. Bimonthly. Circ. 145,000. Original artwork is returned to the artist after publication. Sample copies $2.50.

Cartoons: "Haven't used but would be interested in creative ideas." Send query letter with samples of style. Samples are filed. Reports back within weeks only if interested. Buys first rights.

Illustrations: Buys 25 illustrations/issue from freelancers. Buys 200 illustrations/year from freelancers. Works with 150-200 illustrators/year. Works on assignment only. Send resume, tearsheets, photostats, photocopies, slides and photographs. Samples are filed. Reports back within weeks only if interested. To show a portfolio, mail color and b&w thumbnails, roughs, original/final art, tearsheets, final reproduction/product, photostats, photographs and slides. Buys first rights. "Payment depends on final use and size." Pays on acceptance.

Tips: "Portfolio should include plenty of tearsheets/photocopies as handouts. Don't phone; it disturbs flow of work in office. No sloppy presentations. Show intelligence and uniqueness of style."

BOUNDARY MAGAZINE, 23 Kingsley Rd., Runcorn Cheshire, WA7 5PL England. Phone 563889. Contact: Raymond Darlington. Estab. 1984. Literary magazine. Published 3 times per year. Circ. 250+. Accepts previously published artwork. Original artwork is returned after publication. Sample copies free for SASE with first-class postage. Art guidelines free for SASE with first-class postage.

Cartoons: Prefers b&w line drawings. Send finished cartoons. Samples not filed are returned by SASE. Reports back within weeks. Pays 1 free issue.

Illustrations: Prefers pen & ink. Send photocopies. Samples not filed are returned by SASE. Reports back within weeks. Portfolio should include photostats and b&w. Pays 1 free issue; on publication.

*BOW & ARROW MAGAZINE, Box HH, Capistrano Beach CA 92624. (714)493-2101. Editorial Director: Roger Combs. Emphasizes bowhunting and bowhunters. Bimonthly. Original artwork not returned after publication.

Cartoons: Buys 2-3 cartoons/issue; all from freelancers. Prefers single panel, with gag line; b&w line drawings. Send finished cartoons. Material not kept on file returned by SASE. Reports within 2 months. Buys all rights. Pays $7.50-$10, b&w; on acceptance.

Illustrations: Buys 1-2 illustrations/issue; all from freelancers. Prefers live animals/game as themes. Send samples. Prefers photographs or original work as samples. Especially looks for perspective, unique or accurate use of color and shading, and an ability to clearly express a thought, emotion or event. Samples returned by SASE. Reports in 2 months. Buys all rights or negotiates rights purchased. Pays $100-150, color, cover; payment for inside b&w varies; on acceptance.

BOY'S LIFE, 1325 Walnut Hill Ln., Irving TX 75038-3096. (214)580-2352. Design Director: Joseph Connolly. Magazine emphasizing fiction and articles on scout-related topics such as camping, nature lore, history and science. Monthly. Circ. 1,400,000.

Cartoons: Buys 5 cartoons/issue from freelancers.

Illustrations: Buys 6 b&w and 5 color illustrations/issue from freelancers. Prefers b&w work. Send query letter with photocopies and slides. Reports back within 10 days. Buys first rights. Pays $1,250-1,500 color, cover; $175-200, b&w, $950, color, inside.

Tips: "Artwork for this magazine should not be simplistic or crude and should not be geared down to kids."

BRIDAL GUIDE, 441 Lexington Ave., New York NY 10017. (212)949-4040. Design Director: Jeannie Oberholtzer. Estab. 1984. "Magazine for 'Brides to Be', advice on wedding gowns, wedding ceremonies, receptions, showers and married life including finance, sex, consumer tips, decorating your first home and registering for china and tableware." Bimonthly. Circ. 500,000. Accepts previously published artwork. Original artwork is returned after publication (unless bought outright). Samples copies available. Art guidelines available.

Cartoons: Buys 1-2 cartoons/issue, 6-12/year from freelancers. Prefers single panel with or without gagline; b&w line drawings and washes and color washes. Send query letter with samples of style. Samples are filed and are not returned. Reports back within 2 weeks only if interested. Negotiates rights purchased. Pays $120-250, color; on acceptance.

Illustrations: Buys illustrations mainly for spots and feature spreads. Buys 5 illustrations/issue, 30/year from freelancers. Works on assignment only. Prefers pastel. Considers pen & ink, mixed media, colored pencil, watercolor, charcoal pencil and calligraphy. Send query letter with tearsheets, photostats and photocopies. Samples are filed or are returned only if requested. Reports back only if interested. Call to schedule an appointment to show a portfolio which should include tearsheets and transparencies. Negotiates rights purchased. Pays $120, b&w; $250, color, inside.
Tips: "Best to send promo piece and follow up with a call to send portfolio if we're interested."

BRIDE'S MAGAZINE, Condé-Nast Publications, 350 Madison Ave., New York NY 10017. (212)880-8530. Art Assistant: Jacqueline Savetsky. Estab. 1934. Magazine. Bimonthly. Original artwork is returned after publication. Sample copies free for SASE with first-class postage.
Cartoons: "No cartoons at this time. Possibly in the future." Send query letter with samples of style.
Illustrations: Buys illustrations mainly for spots and feature spreads. Buys 10 illustrations/issue from freelancers. Works on assignment only. Considers pen & ink, airbrush, mixed media, colored pencil, watercolor, acrylic, collage and calligraphy. Send query letter with brochure, tearsheets, photocopies and slides. In samples or portfolio, look for "graphic quality, conceptual, skill, good 'people' style; lively, young, but sophisticated work." Samples are filed. Reports back only if interested. Call to schedule an appointment to show a portfolio, or mail color and b&w original/final art, tearsheets, slides, photostats, photographs and transparencies. Buys one-time rights or negotiates rights purchased. Pays $100-300, b&w; $100-500, color, inside; on publication.
Tips: Sectons most open to illustrators are "Something New" (a short subject page with 4-color art); special sections (pulp paper 2-color), travel section features (black and white)."

BRIGADE LEADER, Box 150, Wheaton IL 60189. (708)665-0630. Estab. 1960. For Christian laymen and adult male leaders of boys enrolled in the Brigade man-boy program. Circ. 12,000. Published 4 times/year. Original artwork returned after publication. Sample copy for $1.50 and large SASE; artist's guidelines for SASE.
Cartoons: Contact: Cartoon Editor. Approached by 30 cartoonists/year. Buys 1 cartoon/issue, all from freelancers. Receives 3 submissions/week from freelancers. Interested in sports, nature and youth; single panel with gagline. SASE. Buys first rights only. Pays $35, b&w line drawings; on publication.
Illustrations: Art Director: Robert Fine. Approached by 45 illustrators/year. Buys 2 illustrations/issue from freelancers. Uses freelance artists mainly for illustrations for articles. Prefers clean line & wash. Uses pen & ink, airbrush, charcoal/pencil and watercolor. Interested in man and boy subjects, sports, camping—out of doors, family. Works on assignment only. Samples returned by SASE. Reports back on future assignment possibilities. Provide resume and flyer to be kept on file for future assignments. Prefers to see portfolio and samples of style. Pays $150 and up, b&w, cover and $120-150, for inside use of b&w line drawings and washes; on publication.
Tips: Looks for "good crisp handling of black & white line work, clean washes and skill in drawing. Portfolios should have printed samples of work. We like to see original concepts and well-executed drawings. We need more work on sports and father-son activities."

BRUM BEAT, Box 944, Edgbaston, Birmingham B16 8UT England. (021)454-7020. Editor: Steve Morris. Magazine emphasizing music and entertainment for ages 16 to 35 interested in music and music-related activities. Monthly. Circ. 40,000. Accepts previously published material. Original artwork returned after publication. Sample copy for SASE with 31 pence postage.
Cartoons: Approached by 4-6 cartoonists/year. Currently buys no cartoons but will consider music-related ones. Send samples of style to be kept on file. Material not kept on file is returned by SASE. Reports only if interested. Buys one-time rights. Payment varies.
Illustrations: Approached by 10-12 illustrators/year. Buys few illustrations. Prefers music-related themes. Send samples. Samples not filed are returned by SASE. Reports only if interested. Pays on publication. Does not want to see political work.

BULLETIN OF THE ATOMIC SCIENTISTS, 6042 S. Kimbark, Chicago IL 60637. (312)702-2555. Production Artist: Paula Lang. Emphasizes arms control; science and public affairs for audience of 40% scientists, 40% politicians and policy makers, and 20% interested, educated citizens. Monthly. Circ. 25,000. Original artwork returned after publication. Sample copy $3; free artist's guidelines for SASE.
Cartoons: Buys about 5-10 cartoons/issue, including humorous illustrations, from freelancers. Considers arms control and international relations themes. "We are looking for new ideas. Please, no mushroom clouds or death's heads." Prefers single panel without gagline; b&w line drawings. Send finished cartoons. Cartoon portfolios are not reviewed. Material returned by SASE. Reports within 1 month. Buys first rights. Pays $25, b&w; on acceptance.
Illustrations: Buys 2-8 illustrations/issue from freelancers. Prefers serious conceptual b&w art with political or other throughtful edtional themes; pen & ink, airbrush, charcoal/pencil, acrylic, oil, and collage. "Do not even consider sending work until you have viewed a few issues. The name of the magazine misleads artists who don't bother to check; they wind up wasting time and postage." Works on assignment only. Send query

letter with brochure and tearsheets or photostats to be kept on file, "except for completely unsuitable work which is returned promptly by SASE." Artist may write or call for appointment to show portfolio but prefers mailed samples. Reports within 1 month. Buys first world-wide rights. Pays $300, b&w, $400, color cover; $100/¼ page, $150/½ page, $250/full page, b&w, inside; on acceptance.

Tips: "Don't show design, advertising, calligraphy samples—just editorial illustration. It helps to show printed pieces within the published text so I can see how the artist interpreted the article. Also, don't bother with nude figure studies. Come on, look at the titles of the magazines you send to! A representative sampling of work is OK. Our needs are so specific that artists usually try too hard to match them—with little success."

BUSINESS & COMMERCIAL AVIATION, (Division of McGraw Hill), Hangar C-1, Westchester County Airport, White Plains NY 10604. (914)948-1912. Art Director: Mildred Stone. Technical publication for corporate pilots and owners of business aircraft. Monthly. Circ. 55,000.

Illustrations: Works with 12 illustrators/year. Buys 12 illustrations/year from freelancers. Uses artists mainly for editorials and some covers. Especially needs full-page and spot art of a business-aviation nature. "We generally only use artists with a fairly realistic style. This is a serious business publication—graphically conservative. We have a monthly section for the commuter industry and another for the helicopter industry. These magazines will have a more consumer-magazine look and will feature more four-color illustration than we've used in the past. Need artists who can work on short deadline time." Query with samples and SASE. Reports in 4 weeks. Photocopies OK. Buys all rights, but may reassign rights to artist after publication. Negotiates payment. Pays $350, inside illustration and $800-1,000, color, cover; on acceptance.

Tips: "Send or bring samples. I like to buy based more on style than whether an artist has done aircraft drawings before."

BUTTER FAT MAGAZINE, Box 9100, Vancouver British Columbia, V6B 4G4 Canada. (604)420-6611. Executive Editor: Carol A. Paulson. Editor: Grace Chadsey. Emphasizes dairy farming, dairy product processing, marketing and distribution for dairy cooperative members and employees in British Columbia. Monthly. Circ. 3,500. Free sample copy and art guidelines. Finds most artists through references/word-of-mouth and portfolio reviews.

Cartoons: Buys 2 cartoons/issue; all from freelancers. Receives 10 submissions/week from freelancers. Interested in agriculture, dairy farming, farming families and Canadian marketing systems. No cartoons unrelated to farming, farm family life or critical of food prices. Prefers single panel, b&w line drawings or washes with gagline. Send query letter with finished cartoons. Reports in 2 weeks. Negotiates rights purchased. Pays $10, b&w; on acceptance.

Illustrations: Buys 1 illustration/issue; mostly from freelancers. Prefers charcoal/pencil, watercolor, pastel, marker and mixed media. Interested in making assignments for specific issues—variable technical, food. Works on assignment only. Send brochure. Samples not kept on file are returned. Provide resume and samples to be kept on file for possible future assignments. Reports in 2 weeks. To show a portfolio, mail original/final art. Portfolio should include color work. Negotiates rights purchased. Pays $75-150 minimum, b&w inside; on acceptance.

Tips: "We prefer to meet artists as well as see their work. Target your samples to our need—dairying. Most assignments are short notice: 10-14 days." Prefers "gentle, nostalgic" style.

***CALIFORNIA APPAREL NEWS**, 945 S. Wall St., Los Angeles CA 90015. (213)626-0411. Art Director: Jim Yousling. Trade publication emphasizing women's fashion. Weekly. Circ. 720,000. Accepts previously published material. Original artwork is returned to the artist after publication. Sample copy available.

Illustrations: Approached by 100 or more freelance artists each year. Works with 10 freelance illustrators and 3 freelance designers/year. Buys 2,000 illustrations/year from freelancers. Works on assignment only. Send query letter with brochures, resume, tearsheets and photocopies. Samples are filed or returned only if requested by artist. Reports back only if interested. Call or write to schedule an appointment to show a portfolio, which should include roughs, original/final art, tearsheets and color and b&w photostats and photographs. Negotiates rights purchased. Pays $35-175 color, cover; on publication.

***CALIFORNIA QUARTERLY**, 100 Sproul Hall, UC Davis, Davis CA 96616. (916)752-2272. Editor: Elliot Gilbert. Estab. 1971. Literary magazine. "We publish serious literary works of short fiction and poetry, as well as black & white graphics." Quarterly. Circ. 700. Original artwork returned at job's completion. Sample copies are available. Art guidelines available for SASE with first-class postage.

Cartoons: "We haven't used cartoons, but would consider classy, intelligent ones." Prefers single panel, without gagline and b&w line drawings. Send query letter with finished cartoons. Samples are filed or are returned by SASE if requested by artist. Reports back within 1 month. Buys first rights. Pays $5, b&w.

Illustrations: Approached by 12 illustrators/year. Buys 15 illustrations/issue, 60 illustrations/year from freelancers. Considers pen & ink, and any b&w graphic. Send query letter with SASE. Samples are filed or are returned by SASE. Reports back within 1 month. Mail appropriate materials. Portfolio should include original/final art. Buys first rights. Pays $5, b&w, cover and inside; on publication.

CAMPUS LIFE, 465 Gundersen Dr., Carol Stream IL 60188. Art Director: Jeff Carnehl. For high school and college students. "Though our readership is largely Christian, *Campus Life* reflects the interests of all kids — music, activities, photography and sports." Monthly. Circ. 120,000. Original artwork returned after publication. "No phone calls, please. Show us what you can do." Uses freelance artists mainly for illustration.

Cartoons: Approached by 50 cartoonists/year. Buys 100 cartoons/year from freelancers. Uses 3-8 single-panel cartoons/issue plus cartoon features (assigned) on high school and college education, environment, family life, humor through youth, and politics; applies to 13-23 age groups; both horizontal and vertical format. Prefers to receive finished cartoons. Reports in 4 weeks. Pays $50 minimum, b&w; on acceptance.

Illustrations: Approached by 100 illustrators/year. Works with 10-15 illustrators/year. Buys 2 illustrations/issue, 50 illustrations/year from freelancers. Styles vary from "literal traditional to very conceptual." Works on assignment only. "Show us what you can do, send photocopies, promos, or tearsheets. Please no original art transparencies or photographs. Samples returned by SASE." Reporting time varies. Buys first North American serial rights; also considers second rights. Pays $50-300, b&w, $125-400 for color, inside; on acceptance.

Tips: "I do like to see a variety in styles, but I don't want to see work that 'says' grade school. Keep sending a reminder every couple of months."

CANADIAN FICTION MAGAZINE, Box 946, Station F, Toronto, Ontario M4Y 2N9 Canada. Editor: Geoffrey Hancock. Anthology devoted exclusively to contemporary Canadian fiction. Quarterly. Canadian artists or residents only. Sample copy $5.50.

Illustrations: Buys 16 pages of art/issue; also cover art. Include SAE (nonresidents include IRC). Reports in 4-6 weeks. Pays $10/page; $25, cover. Uses b&w line drawings and photographs.

Tips: "Portraits of contemporary Canadian writers in all genres are valuable for archival purposes."

CANOE MAGAZINE, Box 3146, Kirkland WA 98083. (206)827-6363. Art Director: Ray Weisgerber. Estab. 1973. Magazine dealing with all types of paddle sports. Bimonthly. Circ. 44,000. Accepts previously published artwork. Original artwork is returned after publication. Sample copies free for SASE with first-class postage. Art guidelines not available.

Illustrations: Buys illustrations mainly for spots. Buys 2-5 illustrations/issue, 14-21 illustrations/year from freelancers. Works on assignment only. Prefers pen & ink. Considers colored pencil, watercolor and acrylic. Send query letter with brochure showing art style, tearsheets and photocopies. When reviewing a portfolio looks for knowledge of paddle sports. Samples are filed. Does not report back. Write to schedule an appointment to show a portfolio. Buys one-time rights. Pays $75, b&w, $600, color, inside; on publication.

CAR CRAFT, Petersen Publishing Co., 8490 Sunset Blvd., Los Angeles CA 90069. (213)657-5100. Editor: Jim McGowan. Managing Editor: Anne Lubow. Art Director: Greg Hollobaugh. "We feature articles on automotive modifications and drag racing." Monthly. Circ. 425,000. Original artwork not returned unless prior arrangement is made. Free sample copy and artist's guidelines.

Illustrations: Buys 1 or more illustrations/issue from freelancers. Interested in "automotive editorial illustration and design with a more illustrative and less technical look." Works on assignment only. Query with business card, brochure, flyer and tearsheet to be kept on file for future assignments. Include SASE. Reports in 2 weeks. Pays for design and illustration by the project, $100-1,000. Buys all rights on a work-for-hire basis.

CARENETWORK, Box 215, Westminster CO 80030. (303)426-6000. Editor: Tom Aver. Estab. 1986. A bimonthly news magazine serving the Colorado mental health community. Readership consists of professionals from all the disciplines (psychiatrists to school counselors). Bimonthly. Circ. 5,000. Original artwork is returned after publication. Sample copies $5.

Cartoons: Approached by 50 cartoonists/year. Buys 2 cartoons/issue, 12 cartoons/year from freelancers. Themes or styles must be related to mental health. Prefers b&w line drawings and b&w washes with gagline. Send query letter with roughs. Samples are filed. Reports back regarding queries/submissions within 2 weeks. Buys first rights. Pays $25, b&w; on publication.

Illustrations: Approached by 25 illustrators/year. Buys 1 illustration/issue; 6 illustrations/year from freelancers. Works on assignment only. Prefers pen & ink. Considers airbrush, mixed media, watercolor, acrylic, oil, pastel, marker and charcoal pencil. Send query letter with brochure showing art style and resume. Samples are returned by SASE. Reports back about queries/submissions within 2 weeks. Mail appropriate materials to show a portfolio. Buys first rights. Pays $100, b&w; on publication.

*CARTOON WORLD, Box 30367, Lincoln NE 68503. (402)435-3191. Editor/publisher: George Hartman. Estab. 1936. Trade journal; newsletter format; "for artists, cartoonists and hobbyists. I find new cartoon markets, print news about cartoon markets as to folding, being stocked, new markets, etc." Monthly. Circ. 200. Accepts previously published artwork. Original artwork returned at job's completion if SASE is enclosed. Sample copy $5 and SASE with first-class postage.

Cartoons: Approached by 15 cartoonists/year. Buys 2 cartoons/issue, 24 cartoons/year from freelancers. Prefers cartoons about "ways a tooner can make money"; single panel. Send query letter with $5 for sample. Samples are not filed and are returned by SASE. Reports back in 1 month. Buys all rights. Pays $5 or sample copies.
Illustrations: Approached by 10 illustrators/year. Buys 2 illustrations/issue from freelancers. Works on assignment only. Send query letter with SASE. Samples are not filed and are returned by SASE if requested by artist. Reports back in 1 month. Portfolio should include roughs. Rights purchased vary according to project. Pays $5, b&w, cover and inside.
Tips: "Get a sample for $5 and study it. If you send anything it has to be on ways to help other artists and tooners in some way. We find new cartoon markets—145 in the last 6 months. We print tips on tooning, gagwriting, etc. We are the clearinghouse for all freelance artists and tooners. Its only purpose is to help artists in some way or other."

CARTOONS, 8490 Sunset Blvd., Los Angeles CA 90069. Contact: Dennis Ellefson. For young males who like cars and bikes.
Cartoons: Buys 150 pages of cartoon stories and 60 single panel cartoons/year from freelancers. Should be well-drawn, identifiable, detailed cars. Prefers to see roughs. Include SASE. Reports in 2-4 weeks. Pays $100 minimum, page; $25, single panel; $25, spot drawings.
Tips: "Check out the automotive scene in *Hot Rod* and *Car Craft* magazines. And then look at *Cartoons*." Remember to include "return address and phone number."

CAT FANCY, Fancy Publications Inc., Box 6050, Mission Viejo CA 92690. (714)855-8822. Editor: K.E. Segnar. For cat owners, breeders and fanciers. Readers are men and women of all ages interested in all phases of cat ownership. Monthly. Circ. 332,000. Simultaneous submissions and previously published work OK. Sample copy $3; free artist's guidelines.
Cartoons: Buys 12 cartoons/year from freelancers; single, double and multi panel with gagline. "Central character should be a cat." Send query letter with photostats or photocopies as samples. Send SASE. Reports in 6 weeks. Pays $20-50, b&w line drawings; on publication. Buys first rights.
Illustrations: Buys 2-5 b&w spot illustrations per issue. Article illustrations assigned. Prefers to work with local artists. Pays $20, spots; $50-100, b&w illustrations.
Tips: "We need good cartoons."

CATHOLIC FORESTER, 425 W. Shuman Blvd., Naperville IL 60566. (312)983-4920. Editor: Barbara Cunningham. Estab. 1883. Magazine. "We are a fraternal insurance company but use general interest art and photos. Audience is middle-class, many small town as well as big city readers, patriotic, somewhat conservative. We are distributed nationally." Bimonthly. Circ. 150,000. Accepts previously published material. Original artwork returned after publication if requested. Sample copy for 9 × 12 SASE with 73¢ postage.
Cartoons: Approached by more than 50 cartoonists/year. Buys 6-7 cartoons/issue from freelancers. Considers "anything *funny* but it must be clean." Prefers single panel with gagline; b&w line drawings. Material returned by SASE if requested. Reports within 3 months; "we try to do it sooner." Buys one-time rights or reprint rights. Pays $25, b&w; on acceptance.
Illustrations: Approached by more than 20 illustrators/year. Works with 4-5 illustrators/year. Buys 145 illustrations/year from freelancers. Prefers watercolor, pen & ink, airbrush, oil and pastel. Send query letter with photostats, tearsheets, photocopies, slides, photographs, etc. to be kept on file. Samples not filed are returned by SASE. Reports within 3 months. Write for appointment to show portfolio. Does not want to see "weird, off-beat illustrations." Buys one-time rights or reprint rights. "Payment depends on difficulty of art." Pays $40-50, b&w, cover; $30-50, simple spot; $70 larger, $300-400 cover; on acceptance. "We have large and small needs, so it's impossible to say."
Tips: "A list of what artist expects to be paid would be a big help—some I've contacted after receiving their samples wanted *much* more money than I can pay."

CATHOLIC SINGLES MAGAZINE, Box 1920, Evanston IL 60204. (312)731-8769. Founder: Fred C. Wilson. Magazine for single, widowed, separated and divorced Catholic persons. Circ. 10,000. Accepts previously published material. Original artwork returned after publication by SASE. Sample copy $3. Art guidelines free for SASE with first-class postage.
Cartoons: Approached by 50 cartoonists/year. Buys variable amount of cartoons/issue from freelancers. Prefers anything that deals with being single (no porn) as themes. Considers all media. Send query letter with finished cartoons to be kept on file. Write or call to schedule an appointment to show a portfolio. Material not filed returned by SASE only if requested. Reports only if interested. Buys one-time rights. Pays $10, b&w; $13, color.
Illustrations: Approached by 60 illustrators/year. Works on assignment only. Prefers anything dealing with singledom as theme. Send query letter with samples. Samples not filed returned by SASE. Reports only if interested. To show a portfolio, mail original/final art. Buys one-time rights. Pays $15, b&w, $20, color, cover; $12, b&w; $14, color inside; on publication.

Tips: "We would like to go four-color. We review everything but smut! Show a representation sampling of your work. In 1991 we'll switch from being a singles service to an educational journal."

*CATS MAGAZINE, Box 290037, Port Orange FL 32129. (904)788-2770. FAX: (904)788-2710. Editor: Linda J. Walton. Estab. 1945. Consumer magazine. "*Cats* is edited for those with an active involvement with cats, whether as owners or breeders." Monthly. Circ. 149,000. Original artwork returned after publication. Sample copies free for SASE with $1.25 first-class postage. Art guidelines not available. Uses freelance artists mainly for inside art.
Cartoons: Approached by 3-5 cartoonists/year. Buys 2 cartoons/issue, 12-15 cartoons/year from freelancers. Prefers "humorous cat themes. No dead-cat or cruel-to-cats themes." Prefers single panel, with gagline, b&w washes and b&w line drawings. Send query letter with finished cartoons. Most samples are filed. Those not filed are returned by SASE if requested by artist. Reports back within 5 days. Buys one-time rights. Pays $15, b&w.
Illustration: Approached by 5-15 illustrators/year. Buys 10-12 illustrations/year. Prefers "cats" themes. Considers pen & ink, watercolor and oil. Send query letter with SASE and transparencies. Samples are filed. Reports back within 5 days. Mail appropriate materials. Pays $150, color, cover.
Tips: "Funny, well-drawn cartoons usually hit the spot with our readers. Make sure the gaglines aren't stupid. Artwork should show cats in a realistic manner." Does not want to see "cutesey cats."

CAVALIER, 2355 Salzedo St., Coral Gables FL 33134. (305)443-2378. Managing editor: Nye Willden. Estab. 1952. Consumer magazine. "Sophisticated adult men's magazine, sexually oriented." Monthly. Circ. 200,000. Original artwork returned after publication on request. Sample copy $3. Art guidelines available.
Cartoons: Approached by 30-50 cartoonists/year. Buys 6-7 cartoons/issue, 70-80 cartoons/year from freelancers. Prefers "traditional, funny sex cartoons." Prefers single panel, with gagline; b&w washes. Send query letter with finished cartoons. Samples are not filed and are returned by SASE. Reports back within 2 weeks. Buys first rights. Pays $50, b&w, $150, color.
Illustrations: Approached by 20-30 illustrators/year. Buys 2 illustrations/issue, 24 illustrations/year from freelancers. Works on assignment only. Prefers sexual themes. Considers watercolor, airbrush, acrylic, oil and mixed media. Send query letter with SASE, tearsheets, photographs, slides and transparencies. Most samples are filed. Those not filed are returned by SASE if requested. Reports back within 10 days. Call to schedule an appointment to show a portfolio, which should include color tearsheets, photocopies, original/final art and photographs. Buys first rights. Pays $200, b&w, $300, color, inside; on publication.
Tips: "Study our magazine for our style and format."

*CENTRAL FLORIDA MAGAZINE, 541 N. Maitland Ave., Maitland FL 32794-8439. (407)539-3939. FAX: (407)539-0533. Design Director: Mike Havekotte. Estab. 1973. Consumer magazine. "Regional lifestyle magazine—upper middle to upper class." Monthly. Circ. 25,000. Accepts previously published artwork. Original artwork returned after publication if requested. Art guidelines not available.
Illustrations: Approached by 50 illustrators/year. Buys 2 illustrations/issue, 25 illustrations/year from freelancers. Works on assignment only. "Occasionally use stock or submission." Prefers "modern, graphics styles—rarely realistic." Any media considered. Send tearsheets and printed promotion. Samples are filed. Reports back to the artist only if interested. Call to schedule an appointment to show a portfolio, which should include tearsheets, slides, roughs, color, photocopies and original/final art. Buys one-time rights "usually." Rights purchased vary according to project. Pays $400, color, cover. Pays $25-75, b&w, $25-350, color, inside; on publication.
Tips: "Subject matter illustrated—usually health and medicine, shopping, homeowners' issues, summer pleasures, financial advice and topical or controversial events or issues."

*CHANNELS MAGAZINE, 401 Park Avenue South, New York NY 10016. (212)545-5100. Contact: Art Director. "Controlled circulation for the decision makers in the television and cable business." Monthly. Circ. 32,000. Original artwork is returned to the artist after publication.
Illustrations: Send query letter with brochure showing art style or tearsheets, other "business magazine illustrations" and conceptual problem solving. Samples are filed. Does not report back. Call to schedule an appointment to show portfolio. Negotiates rights purchased. Payment varies. Pays on acceptance.

*CHARLESTON MAGAZINE, Box 10343, Charleston SC 29411-0343. (803)747-0025. Editor/Art Director: Paula Borgstedt. City magazine. "Ours is a city magazine that conveys the lifestyle of Charleston. Our audience is middle to upper-middle income, primarily between the ages of 25 and 45, interested in arts, architecture and history." Bimonthly. Circ. 20,000. Accepts previously published artwork. Original artwork returned after publication. Sample copies available.
Cartoons: Approached by 2 cartoons/year. Buys 2-3 cartoons/year from freelancers. Prefers local political, humorous illustrations; single panel, b&w washes, color washes and b&w line drawings. Send query letter with brochure, finished cartoons or copies of published work. Samples not filed or returned by SASE. Reports back within 3 weeks. Buys first rights, one-time rights or reprint rights. Pays $50, b&w, $75, color.

Illustration: Approached by 6 illustrators/year. Buys 2 illustrations/issue, 12-18 illustrations/year from freelancers. Considers pen & ink, watercolor, collage, airbrush, acrylic, colored pencil and oil. Send query letter with brochure, resume, SASE, tearsheets, photocopies, photostats, slides and transparencies. Samples not filed and are returned by SASE. Reports back within 2 weeks on an assignment. To show a portfolio mail appropriate materials. Portfolio should include b&w and color tearsheets and photocopies. Buys first rights, one-time right or reprint rights. Pays $50-75.
Tips: "When he or she takes an assignment, it should be completed according to specifications and by deadline."

CHATTANOOGA LIFE & LEISURE, 1085 Bailery Ave., Chattanooga TN 37404. (615)629-5375. Art Director: Wes Spencer. "We are a city magazine that serves the greater Chattanooga area. Our readers are newcomers and natives who have an interest in the region and want the inside story." Monthly. Accepts previously published material. Original artwork is returned to the artist after publication. Sample copies $2.50.
Cartoons: Approached by 15-20 cartoonists/year. Buys some cartoons/year from freelancers. Prefers creative, colorful and detailed cartoons, although we use some b&w line drawings. Prefers b&w line drawings, b&w and color washes. Samples are not filed and are returned by SASE. Reports back within 3 months. Buys first rights or one-time rights. Pays $20 minimum, b&w; $50 minimum, color.
Illustrations: Approached by 20-25 illustrators/year. Buys 1-2 illustrations/issue, 12-24 illustrations/year from freelancers. Uses freelance artists mainly for illustration for columns or feature stories. Works on assignment only. Prefers architectural, creative, and thematic illustration plus portraits. Send query letter with brochure, resume and tearsheets. Samples are not filed and are returned by SASE. Reports back within 3 months. Call to schedule an appointment to show portfolio, or mail color and b&w original/final art, tearsheets, final reproduction/product. Buys first rights and one-time rights. Negotiates rights purchased. Pays $100 minimum, b&w; $150, minimum, color, cover; $25, minimum, b&w; $60, minimum, color, inside; on publication.
Tips: "Have a decent portfolio. It should be complete. Don't say, 'I did this but don't have it with me.' Be confident that you are able to meet the deadlines. Remember, we are a regional magazine that covers Chattanooga. I do not need sunsets over Miami. Be creative. Too many artists do landscapes that don't interest us."

***CHESAPEAKE BAY MAGAZINE,** 1819 Bay Ridge Ave., Annapolis MD 21403. (301)263-2662. Art Director: Christine Gill. Estab. 1972. Consumer magazine. "The magazine focuses on the boating environment of the Chesapeake Bay—including its history, people, places, and ecology." Monthly. Circ. 35,000. Original artwork returned after publication. Sample copies free for SASE with first class postage. Art guidelines available. "Please call."
Cartoons: Approached by 12 cartoonists/year. Prefers boating themes; single panel, with gagline, b&w washes and line drawings. Send query letter with finished cartoons. Samples are filed. Reports back to the artist only if interested. Buys one-time rights. "Please inquire about payment."
Illustrations: Approached by 12 illustrators/year. Buys 2-3 illustrations/issue from freelancers. Considers pen & ink, watercolor, collage, acrylic, marker, colored pencil, oil, charcoal, mixed media and pastel. Send query letter with resume, tearsheets and photographs. Samples are filed. Reports back only if interested. Call to schedule an appointment to show a portfolio, which should include b&w and color thumbnails, tearsheets, slides, roughs, photostats, photocopies, original/final art and photographs. "Anything they've got." Does not want to see "b&w Xeroxes." Buys one-time rights. "Price decided when contracted."
Tips: "Style seems to be loosening up. Colors brighter, more computer-friendly artists available. Send tearsheets or call for an interview—we're always looking."

CHESS LIFE, 186 Route 9W, New Windsor NY 12550. (914)562-8350. Art Director: Jami Anson. Estab. 1939. Official publication of the United States Chess Federation. Contains news of major chess events with special emphasis on American players, plus columns of instruction, general features, historical articles, personality profiles, cartoons, quizzes, humor and short stories. Monthly. Circ. 60,000. Accepts previously published material and simultaneous submissions. Sample copy for SASE with $1.07 postage; art guidelines for SASE with first-class postage.
Cartoons: Approached by 100-150 cartoonists/year. Buys 48 cartoons/year from freelancers. All cartoons must have a chess motif. Prefers single panel with gagline; b&w line drawings. Send query letter with brochure showing art style. Material not kept on file returned by SASE. Reports within 2-4 weeks. Negotiates rights purchased. Pays $25, b&w; $40, color; on publication.
Illustrations: Approached by 75-100 illustrators/year. Works with 4-5 illustrators/year. Buys 8-10 illustrations/year from freelancers. Uses artists mainly for covers and cartoons. All must have a chess motif; uses some humorous and occasionally cartoon-style illustrations. "We use mainly b&w." Works on assignment, but will also consider unsolicited work. Send query letter with photostats or original work for b&w; slides for color, or tearsheets to be kept on file. Reports within 4 weeks. Call to schedule an appointment to show a portfolio, which should include roughs, original/final art, final reproduction/product and tearsheets. Negotiates rights purchased. Pays $100, b&w; $200, color, cover; $25, b&w; $35-50, color, inside; on publication.
Tips: "Include a wide range in your portfolio."

CHIC, Larry Flynt Publications, Suite 300, 9171 Wilshire Blvd., Beverly Hills CA 90210. (213)858-7100. Cartoon/Humor Editor: Dwaine and Susan Tinsley. For affluent men, 25-30 years of age, college-educated and interested in current affairs, luxuries, investigative reporting, entertainment, sports, sex and fashion. Monthly. Returns original art.

Cartoons: Publishes 20/month; 10 full-page color, 4 color spots and 6 b&w spots. Receives 300-500 cartoons from freelancers. Especially needs "outrageous material. Mainly sexual, but politics, sports OK. Topical humor and seasonal/holiday cartoons good." Mail samples. Prefers 8½x11" size; avoid crayon, chalk or fluorescent color. Also avoid, if possible, large, heavy illustration board. Samples returned by SASE only. Place name, address and phone number on back of each cartoon. Reports in 3 weeks. Buys first rights with first right to reprint. Pays $200, full page, color; $100 spot, color; $75 spot, b&w; on acceptance.

Tips: Especially needs more cartoons, cartoon breakaways or one-subject series. "Send outrageous humor— work that other magazines would shy away from. Pertinent, political, sexual, whatever. We are constantly looking for new artists to complement our regular contributors and contract artists. An artist's best efforts stand the best chance for acceptance!"

CHICAGO, 414 N. Orleans, Chicago IL 60610. (312)222-8999. Editor: Hillel Levin. Art Director: Kathy Kelley. "For active, well-educated, high-income residents of Chicago's metropolitan area concerned with quality of life and seeking insight or guidance into diverse aspects of urban/suburban life." Monthly. Circ. 204,000. Original artwork returned after publication.

Illustrations: Buys 7-8 editorial illustrations/issue from freelancers. Interested in "subjective approach often, but depends on subject matter." Works on assignment only. Query with brochure, flyer and tearsheets, photostats, photocopies, slides and photographs to be kept on file. Accepts finished art, transparencies or tearsheets as samples. Samples not filed are returned by SASE. Reports in 4 weeks. Call to schedule an appointment to show a portfolio, which should include original/final art, tearsheets and photostats. Buys first North American serial rights. Negotiates pay for covers, color-separated and reflective art. Pays $600, color, $400 minimum, b&w ($100-200 for spot illustrations); inside. Usually pays on publication.

*CHICAGO LIFE MAGAZINE, Box 11311, Chicago IL 60611-0311. Publisher: Pam Berns. Estab. 1984. Consumer magazine emphasizing lifestyle. Bimonthly. Circ. 60,000. Accepts previously published artwork. Original artwork returned at job's completion. Sample copy free for SASE with $1.75 postage. Art guidelines not available.

Cartoons: Approached by 25 cartoonists/year. Buys 1 cartoon/issue, 6 cartoons/year from freelancers. "Prefers sophisticated humor"; b&w line drawing. Send query letter with photocopies of finished cartoons. Samples are filed or are returned by SASE if requested. Reports back only if interested. Buys one-time rights. Pays $20 for cartoons.

Illustration: Approached by 30 freelance illustrators/year. Buys 3 freelance illustrations/issue. Buys 18 illustrations/year from freelancers. Prefers "sophisticated, avant-garde or fine art. No 'cute' art, please." Considers all media. Send SASE, slides and photocopies. Samples are filed or are returned by SASE. Reports back within 3 weeks. To show a portfolio, mail appropriate material with SASE. Portfolio should include slides and photocopies. Buys one-time rights. Pays $30 for b&w, $30 for color, inside. Pays on acceptance.

CHILD LIFE, 1100 Waterway Blvd., Box 567, Indianapolis IN 46206. (317)636-8881. Art Director: Janet K. Moir. Estab. 1921. For children 9-11. Monthly except bimonthly January/February, March/April, May/June and July/August. Sample copy 75¢.

Illustrations: Approached by 200 illustrators/year. Works with 20 illustrators/year. Buys approximately 50 illustrations/year from freelancers on assigned themes. Especially needs health-related (exercise, safety, nutrition, etc.) themes, and stylized and realistic styles of children 9-11 years old. Uses freelance artwork mainly for stories, recipes and poems. Send query letter with brochure showing art style or resume and tearsheets, photostats, photocopies, slides, photographs and SASE. Especially looks for an artist's ability to draw well consistently. Reports in 4 weeks. To show a portfolio, mail appropriate materials or call or write to schedule an appointment; portfolio should include original/final art, b&w and 2-color and/or 4-color preseparated art. Buys all rights. Pays $250/illustration, color, cover. Pays for illustrations inside by the job, $65-140 (4-color), $55-110 (2-color), $30-70 1 page (b&w); thirty days after completion of work. "All work is considered work for hire."

Tips: "Artists should obtain copies of current issues to become familiar with our needs. I look for the ability to illustrate children in group situations and interacting with adults and animals, in realistic or cartoony styles. Also use unique styles for occasional assignments—cut paper, collage or woodcut art. We do not purchase cartoons at this time. I do not want to see cartoons, portraits of children or slick airbrushed advertising work. It's a good idea to send out mailings of your current work—it keeps your name in the art director's mind. Often I like someone's work but won't get an appropriate assignment for some time; be patient."

CHILDREN'S DIGEST, Box 567, Indianapolis IN 46206. (317)636-8881. Art Director: Lisa A. Nelson. Special emphasis on health, nutrition, safety and exercise for preteen children. Monthly except bimonthly January/February, March/April, May/June and July/August. Accepts previously published material and simultaneous submissions. Sample copy 75¢; art guidelines free for SASE.
Illustrations: Approached by 200 illustrators/year. Works with 50 illustrators/year. Buys 23-35 illustrations/issue, 230 illustrations/year from freelancers. Uses freelance artwork mainly for stories, articles and recipes. Works on assignment only. Send query letter with brochure, resume, samples and tearsheets to be kept on file. Write for appointment to show portfolio. Prefers photostats, slides and good photocopies as samples. Samples returned by SASE if not kept on file. Reports within 4 weeks. Buys all rights. Pays $250, color, cover; $30-70, b&w; $55-110, 2-color; $65-140, 4-color, inside; on acceptance. "All artwork is considered work for hire."
Tips: Likes to see situation and story-telling illustrations with more than 1 figure. When reviewing samples, especially looks for artists' ability to bring a story to life with their illustrations. "We welcome the artist who can illustrate a story that will motivate a casual viewer to read. I do not want to see samples of graphic design (menus, logos, etc.). To break in, pick a story already illustrated and re-illustrate it the way you would have."

CHILDREN'S PLAYMATE, Box 567, Indianapolis IN 46206. (317)636-8881. Art Director: Steve Miller. For ages 6-8; special emphasis on health, nutrition, exercise and safety. Published 8 times/year. Sample copy sent if artist's work might be used.
Illustrations: Uses 25-35 illustrations/issue; buys 10-20 from freelancers. Interested in "stylized, humorous or realistic themes; also nature and health." Prefers pen & ink, airbrush, charcoal/pencil, colored pencil, watercolor, acrylic, oil, pastel, collage and computer illustration. Especially needs b&w and 2-color artwork for line or halftone reproduction; text and full-color cover art. Works on assignment only. Prefers to see portfolio and samples of style; include illustrations of children, families, animals—targeted to children. Provide brochure or flyer, tearsheet, stats or good photocopies of sample art to be kept on file. Send SASE. Buys all rights on a work-for-hire basis. Will also consider b&w art, camera-ready for puzzles, such as dot-to-dot, hidden pictures, crosswords, etc. Payment will vary. "All artwork is considered work for hire."
Tips: "Look at our publication prior to coming in; it is for *children*. Also, gain some experience in preparation of two-color and four-color overlay separations."

THE CHRISTIAN CENTURY, 407 S. Dearborn St., Chicago IL 60605. (312)427-5380. Production Coordinator: Matthew Giunti. Emphasizes religion and comments on social, political and religious subjects; includes news of current religious scene, book reviews, humor. Weekly. Circ. 38,000. Original artwork returned after publication if requested. Sample copy free for SASE.
Cartoons: Occasionally uses cartoons. Prefers social, political, religious (non-sexist) issues. Prefers single panel with gagline; b&w line drawings. Send query letter with finished cartoons to be kept on file unless "we can't possibly use them." Material not filed is returned only if requested. Reports only if interested. Buys one-time rights. Pays $20, b&w; on publication.
Illustrations: Uses 4 illustrations/issue; buys 1-2 from freelancers. Prefers pen & ink, charcoal/pencil, colored pencil and collage. Prefers religious and general scenes, people at various activities, books. Send query letter with resumes and photocopies to be kept on file. Samples not filed are returned by SASE. Reports only if interested. Buys one-time rights. Pays $75, cover and $25, inside b&w; on publication.
Tips: "Because of our newsprint, bold, uncluttered styles work the best. Too much detail gets lost. We need more inclusive illustrations—non-sexist."

CHRISTIAN HERALD, 40 Overlook Dr., Chappaqua NY 10514. (914)769-9000. Managing Editor: Bob Chuvala. Grassroots magazine for Christian adults (30 and up); specializes in people stories, real-life examples. Bimonthly. Circ. 180,000. Original artwork returned after publication. Receives 3 illustrations/week from freelancers. Sample copy $3.
Cartoons: Should have religious flavor.
Illustrations: Buys 2-3 illustrations/issue from freelancers. Prefers "more realistic and figurative styles due to the 'real people in action' format of our publication." Prefers colored pencil, then collage, mixed media, calligraphy, pen & ink, airbrush, wash, oil, acrylic. Works on assignment only. Send query letter with resume and tearsheets, photostats and slides. Samples not kept on file are returned by SASE. Reports in 4 weeks or less. Negotiates rights purchased. Pays $75-200, b&w line drawings or b&w washes, $100-350, color washes; inside, on publication.
Tips: "I want to see work that shows the artist's ability to interpret. Show a variety of work, but include a couple of pieces geared especially to our needs."

CHRISTIAN HOME & SCHOOL, 3350 E. Paris Ave. SE, Grand Rapids MI 49512. (616)957-1070. Associate Editor: Judy Zylstra. Emphasizes current, crucial issues affecting the Christian home for parents who support Christian education. Published 6 times/year. Circ. 50,000. Original artwork returned after publication. Sample copy for 9 × 12 SASE with $1.00 postage; art guidelines for SASE with first-class postage. Finds most artists through references/word-of-mouth, portfolio reviews, samples received through the mail and artist reps.

Illustrations: Buys approximately 2 illustrations/issue from freelancers. Prefers pen & ink, charcoal/pencil, colored pencil, watercolor, collage, marker, mixed media and calligraphy. Prefers family or school life themes. Works on assignment only. Send query letter with resume, tearsheets, photocopies or photographs. Show a representative sampling of work. Samples returned by SASE. Reports only if interested. Buys first rights. Pays on publication.

*THE CHRISTIAN MINISTRY, 407 S. Dearborn St., Chicago IL 60605. (312)427-5380. Production Coordinator: M. Giunti. Estab. 1969. For the professional clergy (primarily liberal Protestant). Bimonthly. Circ. 12,000.
Cartoons: Buys 3 cartoons/issue from freelancers on local church subjects. Send query letter with brochure showing art style or resume, tearsheets, photostats, photocopies, photographs and SASE. Reports in 2 weeks. Pays $20 minimum, b&w; on publication.
Illustrations: Buys 4 spot drawings/issue from freelancers on local church issues; preaching, counseling, teaching, etc. Illustrations and cartoons should reflect the diversity of professional clergy—male, female, black, white, young, old, etc. To show a portfolio, mail thumbnails, original/final art, final reproduction/product and b&w photostats and photographs. Pays $50, b&w, cover; $25, b&w, inside; on publication.
Tips: "We tend to use more abstract than concrete artwork. We insist on a balance between portrayals of male and female clergy."

THE CHRONICLE OF THE HORSE, Box 46, Middleburg VA 22117. Editor: John Strassburger. Estab. 1937. Emphasizes horses and English horse sports for dedicated competitors who ride, show and enjoy horses. Weekly. Circ. 23,000. Sample copy and guidelines available for $2.
Cartoons: Approached by 25 cartoonists/year. Buys 1-2 cartoons/issue, 50-75 cartoons/year from freelancers. Considers anything about English riding and horses. Prefers single panel with or without gagline; b&w line drawings or washes. Send query letter with finished cartoons to be kept on file if accepted for publication. Material not filed is returned. Reports within 3 weeks. Buys first rights. Pays $20, b&w; on publication.
Illustrations: Approached by 25 illustrators/year. "We use a work of art on our cover every week. The work must feature horses, but the medium is unimportant. We do not pay for this art, but we always publish a short blurb on the artist and his or her equestrian involvement, if any." Send query letter with samples to be kept on file until published. If accepted, insists on high-quality, b&w 8x10 photographs of the original artwork. Samples are returned. Reports within 3 weeks.
Tips: Does not want to see "current horse show champions."

CHRONICLES, A MAGAZINE OF AMERICAN CULTURE, 934 N. Main St., Rockford IL 61103. (815)964-5813. Art Director: Anna Mycek-Wodecki. Literary magazine. Monthly. Original artwork is returned to the artist after publication. Sample copy $3.50.
Illustrations: Buys 6-7 illustrations/issue from freelancers. Prefers fine art drawings pen & ink, airbrush, colored pencil, watercolor, acrylic, oil and pastel. Send query letter with portfolio. Samples are filed or are returned by SASE. Reports back only if interested. Write to schedule an appointment to show a portfolio, or mail color and b&w original/final art, slides. Buys first rights. Pays $250, 7-9 b&w drawings; $400, color cover; on publication.
Tips: "Familiarize yourself with our magazine before sending samples."

CHURCH MANAGEMENT—THE CLERGY JOURNAL, Box 162527, Austin TX 78716. (512)327-8501. Editor: Manfred Holck Jr. For professional clergy and church business administrators. Circ. 30,000. Original artwork returned after publication if requested. Monthly (except June and December).
Cartoons: Buys 4 single panel cartoons/issue from freelancers on religious themes. Send SASE. Reports in 2 months. Pays $10, b&w; on publication.

THE CHURCHMAN'S HUMAN QUEST, (formerly *The Churchman*), 1074 23rd Ave. N., St. Petersburg FL 33704. (813)894-0097. Editor: Edna Ruth Johnson. Published 6 times/year. Circ. 10,000. Original artwork returned after publication. Sample copy available.
Cartoons: Buys 2-3 cartoons/issue from freelancers. Interested in religious, political and social themes. Prefers to see finished cartoons. SASE. Reports in 1 week. Pays on acceptance.
Illustrations: Buys 2-3 illustrations/issue from freelancers. Interested in themes with "social implications." Prefers to see finished art. Provide tearsheet to be kept on file for future assignments. SASE. Reports in 1 week. Pays $5, b&w spot drawings; on acceptance.
Tips: "Read current-events news so you can apply it humorously."

*CINCINNATI MAGAZINE, 409 Broadway, Cincinnati OH 45202. (513)421-4300. Art Director: Tom Hawley. Estab. 1960. Consumer magazine; emphasizing the city of Cincinnati. Monthly. Circ. 30,000. Accepts previously published artwork. Original artwork returned at job's completion. Sample copies free for SASE with first-class postage. Art guidelines not available.

Cartoons: Approached by 20 cartoonists/year. Buys 4 cartoons/issue, 48 cartoons/year from freelancers. "There are no thematic or stylistic restrictions." Prefers single panel; b&w line drawings. Send query letter with finished cartoons. Samples are filed or returned by SASE. Reports back within 2 months. Buys one-time rights or reprint rights. Pays $25, b&w.

Illustrations: Approached by 20 illustrators/year. Buys 6 illustrations/issue, 72 illustrations/year from freelancers. Works on assignment only. Send query letter with tearsheets and photocopies. Samples should be 8½ × 11. Samples are filed or returned by SASE if requested by artist. Reports back only if interested. Call to schedule an appointment to show a portfolio. Buys one-time rights or reprint rights. Pays $250, color, cover; $85, b&w; $135, color, inside; on acceptance.

© 1990 M. Streff

Illustrator Michael Streff created this article illustration in mixed media collage for Cincinnati Magazine. The Cincinnati artist wanted to convey "the basic idea of the article, which was how Cincinnati was improving itself to attract convention business. The 'old' elements (cleaning products and the crew busy at work) add humor and offer a contrast to the geometric, somewhat staid skyline." The assignment was a result of a "regular portfolio showing."

*CIRCLE K MAGAZINE, 3636 Woodview Trace, Indianapolis IN 46268. (317)875-8755. FAX: (317)879-0204. Art Director: Vicki Jonak. Estab. 1968. Kiwanis International's youth magazine for (college age) students emphasizing service, leadership, etc. 5/year. Circ. 12,000. Original artwork is returned to the artist at the job's completion. Sample copies are available.

Illustrations: Approached by more than 30 illustrators/year. Buys 1-2 illustrations/issue, 5-10 illustrations/year from freelancers. Works on assignment only. No preferred themes, styles or media. "We look for variety." Send query letter with tearsheets. Samples are filed. Reports back to the artist only if interested. Mail appropriate materials: tearsheets and slides. Pays $100, b&w, $250, color, cover; $50, b&w, $150, color, inside; on acceptance.

*CITY GUIDE MAGAZINE, 853 Seventh Ave., New York NY 10019. FAX: (212)315-0800. (212)397-9513. Associate Publisher: Joyce Snadecky. Estab. 1982. Visitor's guide to New York City; magazine. Weekly. Circ. 42,500. Accepts previously published artwork. Original artwork returned after publication. Sample copy $2. Art guidelines available.

Illustrations: Approached by 10 illustrators/year. Buys 3 illustrations/year from freelancers. Works on assignment only. Prefers all media. Send query letter with tearsheets and photostats. Samples are not filed and are returned. Reports back to the artist only if interested. Mail appropriate materials. Portfolio should include color, photostats, photocopies and photographs. Pays on acceptance.

CLASSIC TOY TRAINS, 1027 N. Seventh St., Milwaukee WI 53233. Art Director: Lawrence Luser. Estab. 1987. Magazine emphasizing collectible toy trains. Quarterly. Circ. 73,000. Accepts previously published material. Original artwork is sometimes returned to the artist after publication. Sample copies available.

Illustrations: Buys various illustrations/issue from freelancers. Send query letter with brochure. Samples are filed or are returned only if requested. Reports back only if interested. Write to schedule an appointment to show a portfolio, or mail original/final art, final reproduction/product and color and b&w photographs. Negotiates rights purchased.

*CLAVIER, 200 Northfield Rd., Northfield IL 60093. Editor: Kingsley Day. For teachers and students of keyboard instruments. Published 10 times/year. Buys all rights. Sample copy available with magazine-sized SASE. Uses freelancers mainly for cover photos and cartoons.
Cartoons: Approached by 10 cartoonists/year. Buys 10-20 cartoons/year on music, mostly keyboard music. Pays $20 on acceptance.

CLEARWATER NAVIGATOR, 112 Market St., Poughkeepsie NY 12603. (914)454-7673. Graphics Coordinator: Nora Porter. Emphasizes sailing and environmental matters for middle-upper income Easterners with a strong concern for environmental issues. Bimonthly. Circ. 8,000. Accepts previously published material. Original artwork returned after publication. Sample copy free with SASE.
Cartoons: Buys 1 cartoon/issue from freelancers. Prefers editorial lampooning—environmental themes. Prefers single panel with gaglines; b&w line drawings. Send query letter with samples of style to be kept on file. Material not filed is rturned only if requested. Reports within 1 month. Buys first rights. Pays negotiable rate, b&w; on publication.

CLEVELAND MAGAZINE, Suite 730, 1422 Euclid Ave., Cleveland OH 44115. (216)771-2833. City magazine emphasizing local news and information. Monthly. Circ. 50,000.
Illustrations: Approached by 100 illustrators/year. Buys 5-6 editorial illustrations/issue from freelancers on assigned themes. Sometimes uses humorous illustrations. Send query letter with brochure showing art style or samples. Call or write to schedule an appointment to show a portfolio, which should include original/final art, final reproduction/product, color tearsheets and photographs. Pays $300, b&w, $400, color, cover; $200, b&w, $350, color, inside.
Tips: "Artists used on the basis of talent. We use many talented college graduates just starting out in the field. We do not publish gag cartoons but do print editorial illustrations with a humorous twist. Full page editorial illustrations usually deal with local politics, personalities and stories of general interest. Generally, we are seeing more intelligent solutions to illustration problems and better techniques."

*CLIFTON MAGAZINE, 204 Tangeman University Center, University of Cincinnati, Cincinnati OH 45221. (513)556-6379. Editor-in-Chief: Rich Roell. General interest publication for the University community and neighborhood. Published 3 times/academic year. Circ. 10,000. Copy available for SASE.
Illustrations: Contact Art Director. Uses illustrations and photography for feature stories; art photos published. Reports in 6-8 weeks. Acquires first serial rights.

CLUBHOUSE, Box 15, Berrien Springs MI 49103. (616)471-9009. Editor: Elaine Trumbo. Art Director: Kris Hackleman. Magazine emphasizing stories, puzzles and illustrations for children ages 9-15. Published 6 times/year. Circ. 18,000. Accepts previously published material. Returns original artwork after publication if requested. Sample copy for SASE with postage for 3 oz. Finds most artists through references/word-of-mouth and mailed samples received.
Cartoons: Approached by over 100 cartoonists/year. Buys 2 cartoons/issue from freelancers. Prefers animals, kids and family situation themes; single panel with gagline, vertical format; b&w line drawings. Accepts previously published material. Pays $12 b&w, inside; on acceptance.
Illustrations: Approached by over 100 illustrators/year. Buys 19-20 illustrations/issue from freelancers on assignment only. Prefers pen & ink, charcoal/pencil and all b&w media. Assignments made on basis of samples on file. Send query letter with resume and samples to be kept on file. Samples returned by SASE within 1 month. Portfolio should include b&w final reproduction/product, tearsheets and photostats. Usually buys one-time rights. Pays according to published size: $30 b&w, cover; $25 full page, $18 half page, $15 third page, $12 quarter page, b&w inside; on acceptance.
Tips: Prefers "natural, well-proportioned, convincing expressions for people, particularly kids. Children's magazines must capture the attention of the readers with fresh and innovative styles—interesting forms. I continually search for new talents to illustrate the magazine and try new methods of graphically presenting stories. Samples illustrating children and pets in natural situations are very helpful. Tearsheets are also helpful. I do not want to see sketchbook doodles, adult cartoons, or any artwork with an adult theme. No fantasy, dragons or mystical illustrations."

COBBLESTONE MAGAZINE, 30 Grove St., Peterborough NH 03458. (603)924-7209. Editor: Carolyn Yoder. Emphasizes American history; features nonfiction, supplemental nonfiction, fiction, biographies, plays, activities, poetry for children between 8 and 14. Monthly. Circ. 45,000. Accepts previously published material and simultaneous submissions. Sample copy $3.95. Material must relate to theme of issue; subjects and topics published in guidelines which are available for SASE.
Illustrations: Uses variable number of illustrations/issue; buys 1-2 illustrations/issue from freelancers. Prefers historical theme as it pertains to a specific feature. Works on assignment only. Send query letter with brochure, resume, business card and b&w photocopies or tearsheets to be kept on file or returned by SASE. Write for appointment to show portfolio. Buys all rights. Payment varies. Artists should request illustration guidelines. Pays on publication.

Tips: "Study issues of the magazine for style used. Send samples and update samples once or twice a year to help keep your name and work fresh in our minds."

COLLISION® MAGAZINE, Box M, Franklin MA 02038. (508)528-6211. Editor: Jay Kruza. Has an audience of new car dealers, auto body repair shops, and towing companies. Articles are directed at the managers of these small businesses. Monthly. Circ. 16,000. Prefers original material but may accept previously published material. Sample copy $4. Art guidelines free for SASE with first-class postage.
Cartoons: Cartoon Editor: Brian Sawyer. Buys 3 cartoons/issue from freelancers. Prefers themes that are positive or corrective in attitude. Prefers single panel with gagline; b&w line drawings. Send rough versions or finished cartoons. Reports back in 2 weeks or samples returned by SASE. Buys all rights and reprint rights. Pays $10/single panel b&w line cartoon.
Illustrations: Buys about 2 illustrations/issue from freelancers based upon a 2-year advance editorial schedule. Send query letter with brochure, tearsheets, photostats, photocopies, slides and photographs. Samples are returned by SASE. Reports back within 15-30 days. "Payment is for assigned artwork ranging form $25 for spot illustrations up to $200 for full page material" on acceptance.
Tips: "Show us your style and technique on a photocopy. Include phone number and time to call. We'll suggest material we need illustrated if your work seems appropriate. We prefer clean pen and ink work but will use color."

COLUMBIA, Drawer 1670, New Haven CT 06507. (203)772-2130, ext. 263-64. Editor: Richard McMunn. Fraternal magazine of the Knights of Columbus; features articles on family life, social problems, education, current events and apostolic activities as seen from the Catholic viewpoint. Monthly. Circ. 1,405,411. Sample copy available.
Cartoons: Buys cartoons from freelancers. Interested in pungent humor. Send roughs or finished cartoons and SASE to be kept on file. Reports in 2 weeks. Pays $50; on acceptance.
Tips: "Columbia's focus has changed. We use illustration rarely now, relying instead on photography."

COLUMBUS SINGLE SCENE, Box 30856, Gahanna OH 43230. (614)476-8802. Publisher: Jeanne Marlowe. Estab. 1985. A literary magazine and consumer publication for singles. Emphasis on activities for single living, dating and relationships for people in central Ohio. Readers range from 18-80, most college educated. Monthly. Circ. 5,000. Original artwork is returned to the artist after publication if requested. Sample copies $1.
Cartoons: Prefers modern and bold "since fine lines wash out on newsprint." Prefers single panel and double panel. Send finished cartoons. Samples are not filed and are returned by SASE. Reports back regarding query/submission within weeks. Buys one-time rights. Pays $0-15, b&w cartoon.
Illustration: Buys 12 illustrations/year from freelancers. Uses artwork mainly for covers and story illustration. Prefers modern and bold styles. Send tearsheets if reprint OK and photographs. Samples are filed or are returned by SASE. Reports back regarding query/submission within 2 weeks. Does not review portfolios. Buys one-time rights. Byline given. Pays $5-25, b&w cover and inside illustration on publication. Payment includes ad trade and copies.
Tips: "Although 40% of the population is single, there are few good cartoons dealing with singles over age 25. It's possible a good cartoonist would be picked up by all publishers in the Singles Press Association."

COMICO THE COMIC COMPANY, 1547 DeKalb St., Norristown PA 19401. (215)277-4305. FAX: (215)277-5651. Art Director: Rick Taylor. Estab. 1981. Publishes monthly comics line (roughly 6 titles per month). Target audience: college level and above. Titles include *Elementals, E-Man, Grendel, Star Blazers, Silverbacks, Rocketeer Adventure Magazine, The World of Ginger Fox, Night and the Enemy* and *Rio.* "Comico is presently publishing an eclectic assortment of comic book titles, with a wide audience appeal." Circ. 30,000. Original artwork returned 120 days after publication.
Cartoons: Approached by 800-1,000 cartoonists/year. Prefers heroic fiction, mystery, science fiction, humor and horror. Prefers b&w line drawings; pages (stories) only. Send SASE for submissions guidelines. Samples are filed or are returned by SASE. Buys first rights, reprint rights, negotiates rights purchased. Payment negotiable.
Illustrations: Approached by 800-1,000 freelance illustrators/year. Buys approximately 24 pages of illustration/issue from freelancers for each title. Uses vertical, horizontal, inset, borderless, circular panels, double-page spreads and sequential narrative (any form). Uses freelance artists for inking, lettering, pencilling, color work, posters, covers, cover paintings and pin-ups. Prefers pen & ink, airbrush, watercolor, oil, collage and marker. Send query letter with resume and samples. Samples are filed or are returned by SASE. Reports back within 6 weeks. To show a portfolio, mail photocopies of original pencil art or inking. Rights purchased vary. Negotiates payment. Pays on acceptance.
Tips: "We are looking for the artist's ability to tell a story through pictures. We want to see storytelling samples, not single illustrations. Due to the comic book market's preference for realism coupled with highly detailed renderings, we also look for the artist's abilities in anatomy, perspective, proportion, composition, good use of negative space. Artists should never send original art, unless they want to risk losing it. We are

not responsible for unsolicited submissions. Generally, the thicker a submissions package is, the longer it takes the editor to get around to looking at it."

*COMMON LIVES/LESBIAN LIVES, Box 1553, Iowa City IA 52244. Contact: Editorial Collective. Magazine emphasizing lesbian lives for lesbians of all ages, races, nationalities and sizes. Quarterly. Circ. 2,000. Original artwork returned if requested and SASE provided. "Otherwise, all submissions sent to the Lesbian Herstory Archives." Sample copy $5.
Cartoons: Approached by 5-8 cartoonists/year. Prefers lesbian themes. Prefers vertical format 5½×8½ page. Send finished cartoons to be kept on file. Material not kept on file is returned only if SASE provided. Reports within 4 months.
Illustrations: Approached by 30-40 illustrators/year. Prefers lesbian themes. Prefers vertical format 5½×8½ page. Samples not filed are returned only if SASE provided. Reports back within 4 months.

*COMMONWEAL, 15 Dutch St., New York NY 10038. (212)732-0800. Contact: Editor. Estab. 1924. Public affairs journal. "Journal of opinion edited by Catholic lay people concerning public affairs, religion, literature and all the arts." Bi-weekly. Circ. 20,000. Original artwork is returned at the job's completion. Sample copies free for SASE with first-class postage. Guidelines free for SASE with first-class postage.
Cartoons: Approached by 20-40 cartoonists/year. Buys 3-4 cartoons/issue, 60 cartoons/year from freelancers. Prefers simple lines and high contrast styles. Prefers single panel, with or without gagline; b&w line drawings. Send query letter with finished cartoons. Samples are filed or are returned by SASE is requested by artist. Reports back within 5 days. Buys first rights. Pays $8.50, b&w.
Illustrations: Approached by 20 illustrators/year. Buys 3-4 illustrations/issue, 60 illustrations/year from freelancers. Prefers high contrast, illustrations that "speak for themselves." Prefer pen & ink and marker. Send query letter with tearsheets, photographs, SASE and photocopies. Samples are filed or are returned by SASE if requested by artist. Reports back within 5 days. Mail appropriate materials: b&w tearsheets, photographs and photocopies. Buys first rights. Pays $25, b&w cover; $10, b&w inside; on publication.

*COMMUNICATION WORLD, Suite 600, One Hallidie Plaza, San Francisco CA 94102. (415)433-3400. Editor: Gloria Gordon. Emphasizes communication, public relations (international) for members of International Association of Business Communicators: corporate and nonprofit businesses, hospitals, government communicators, universities, etc. who produce internal and external publications, press releases, annual reports and customer magazines. Monthly except June/July combined issue. Circ. 14,000. Accepts previously published material. Original artwork returned after publication. Art guidelines available.
Cartoons: Approached by 6-10 cartoonists/year. Buys 6 cartoons/year from freelancers. Considers public relations, entrepreneurship, teleconference, editing, writing, international communication and publication themes. Prefers single panel with gagline; b&w line drawings or washes. Send query letter with samples of style to be kept on file. Material not filed is returned by SASE only if requested. Reports within 2 months only if interested. Write or call for appointment to show portfolio. Buys first rights, one-time rights or reprint rights; negotiates rights purchased. Pays $25-50, b&w; on publication.
Illustrations: Approached by 20-30 illustrators/year. Buys 6-8 illustrations/issue from freelancers. Theme and style are compatible to individual article. Send query letter with samples to be kept on file; write or call for appointment to show portfolio. Accepts tearsheets, photocopies or photographs as samples. Samples not filed are returned only if requested. Reports back within 1 year only if interested. Buys first rights, one-time rights or reprint rights; negotiates rights purchased. Pays $100, b&w and $300, color, cover; $100 maximum, b&w and $275, color, inside; on publication.
Tips: Sees trend toward "more sophistication, better quality, less garish, glitzy—subdued, use of subtle humor."

*CONFIDENT LIVING, Box 82808, Lincoln NE 68501. (402)474-4567. Contact: Managing Editor. Estab. 1944. Company magazine for Back to the Bible. Readers are religious, conservative, mostly protestant, adults, primarily over 50. Monthly except July-August is combined. Circ. 85,000. Accepts previously published artwork. Original artwork is returned to the artist at the job's completion. Sample copy $1.75.
Illustrations: Approached by 10-15 illustrators/year. Buys 3-4 illustrations/issue, 35-40 illustrations/year from freelancers; on assignment only. Send query letter with resume, SASE, photostats and slides. Samples are filed or are returned by SASE if requested by artist. Mail appropriate materials: b&w and color tearsheets and slides. Buys first rights. Pays $275 and up for color cover; $75-100, b&w, $185 and up for color inside; on acceptance.

CONSERVATORY OF AMERICAN LETTERS, Box 123, South Thomaston ME 04858. (207)354-6550. Editor: Bob Olmsted. Estab. 1986. Newsletter emphasizing literature for literate, cultured adults. Quarterly. Original artwork returned after publication. Sample copy for SASE with first-class postage.
Illustrations: Approached by 30-50 illustrators/year. "Find out what is coming up, then send something appropriate. Unsolicited 'blind' portfolios are of little help." Buys first rights, one-time rights or reprint rights. Pays $150, color, cover; on acceptance.

CONSTRUCTION EQUIPMENT OPERATION AND MAINTENANCE, Construction Publications, Inc., Box 1689, Cedar Rapids IA 52406. (319)366-1597. Editor-in-Chief: C.K. Parks. Estab. 1948. Concerns heavy construction and industrial equipment for contractors, machine operators, mechanics and local government officials involved with construction. Bimonthly. Circ. 67,000. Original artwork not returned after publication. Free sample copy.
Cartoons: Buys 75 cartoons/year. Buys 8-10 cartoons/issue, all from freelancers. Interested in themes "related to heavy construction industry" or "cartoons that make contractors and their employees 'look good' and feel good about themselves"; multiple panel. Send finished cartoons and SASE. Reports within 2 weeks. Buys all rights but may reassign rights to artist after publication. Pays $10-15, b&w.
Illustrations: Buys more than 20 illustrations/issue; "very few" are from freelancers. Works with 2 illustrators/year. Pays $80-125; on acceptance.

THE CONSTRUCTION SPECIFIER, 601 Madison St., Alexandria VA 22314. (703)684-0300. Editor: Kimberly C. Young. Estab. 1949. Emphasizes commercial (*not* residential) design and building for architects, engineers and other A/E professionals. Monthly. Circ. 19,000. Returns original artwork after publication if requested. Sample copy for SASE.
Illustrations: Works with 2-3 illustrators/year. Buys 1-2 illustrations/issue; 10-20 illustrations/year from freelancers on assignment only. Send query letter with photostats, tearsheets, photocopies, slides or photographs. Samples not filed are returned by SASE. Reports back only if interested. Buys one-time rights. Pays $200, color, cover; $50-125, b&w, inside; on publication.
Tips: Does not want to see cartoons.

DAVID C. COOK PUBLISHING CO., 850 N. Grove Ave., Elgin IL 60120. (312)741-2400. Director of Design Services: Randy R. Maid. Publisher of magazines, teaching booklets, visual aids and film strips. For Christians, "all age groups."
Cartoons: Approached by 250 cartoonists/year. Pays $50, b&w; $65, color.
Illustrations: Buys about 30 full-color illustrations/week from freelancers. Send tearsheets, slides or photocopies of previously published work; include self-promo pieces. No samples returned unless requested and accompanied by SASE. Reports in 2-4 weeks to personal queries only. Works on assignment only. Pays $550, color, cover; $350, color, inside; on acceptance. Considers complexity of project, skill and experience of artist and turnaround time when establishing payment. Buys all rights. Originals can be returned in most cases.
Tips: "We do not buy illustrations or cartoons on speculation. We welcome those just beginning their careers, but it helps if the samples are presented in a neat and professional manner. Our deadlines are generous but must be met. We send out checks as soon as final art is approved, usually within 2 weeks of our receiving the art. We want art radically different from normal Sunday School art. Fresh, dynamic, the highest of quality is our goal; art that appeals to preschoolers to senior citizens; realistic to humorous, all media."

*COUNTRY AMERICA, 1716 Locust St., Des Moines IA 50336. (515)284-3031. FAX: (515)284-2700. Art Director: Jerry J. Rank. Estab. 1989. Consumer magazine "emphasizing entertainment and lifestyle for people who enjoy country life and country music." Monthly. Circ. 600,000. Original artwork sometimes returned at job's completion. Art guidelines not available.
Cartoons: Approached by 5-10 cartoonists/year. Buys 1-2 cartoons/issue; 10-15 cartoons/year from freelancers. Prefers descriptive, literal and clean styles; without gagline. Contact through artist rep or send query letter with portfolio or sample sheets. Samples are filed. Reports back only if interested. Rights purchased vary according to project, but all rights preferred. Payment negotiable.
Illustrations: Approached by 10-20 illustrators/year. Buys 1-2 illustrations/issue, 10-15 illustrations/year from freelancers on assignment only. Contact through artist rep or send query letter with brochure, tearsheets, slides and transparencies. Samples are filed. Reports back only if interested. Call or write to schedule an appointment to show a portfolio, which should include roughs, original/final art, tearsheets and slides. Rights purchased vary according to project. Pays on acceptance.

THE COVENANT COMPANION, 5101 N. Francisco Ave., Chicago IL 60625. (312)784-3000. Editor: James R. Hawkinson. Emphasizes Christian life and faith. Monthly. Circ. 24,500. Original artwork returned after publication if requested. Sample copy $2.
Illustrations: Uses b&w drawings or photos about Easter, Advent, Lent, and Christmas. Works on submission only. Write or submit art 10 weeks in advance of season. Send SASE. Reports "within a reasonable time." Buys first North American serial rights. Pays $15, b&w, $25, color, cover. Pays 1 month after publication.
Tips: "We usually have some rotating file, if we are interested, from which material may be selected."

CREATIVE CHILD & ADULT QUARTERLY, The National Association for Creative Children and Adults, 8080 Spring Valley, Cincinnnati OH 45236. Publisher: Anne Fabe Isaacs. Editor: Dr. Wallace D. Draper. Emphasizes creativity in *all* its applications for parents, teachers, students, administrators in the professions. Quarterly. Original artwork returned after publication if SASE is enclosed. Sample copy $10.

Cartoons: Uses 1 cartoon/issue. Prefers single panel; b&w line drawings. Send samples of style or finished cartoons to be kept on file. Material not kept on file is returned by SASE. Reports within weeks. Pays in copies of publication.

Illustrations: Uses various number of illustrations/issue from freelancers, including some humorous and cartoon-style illustrations. Send query letter and original work. Samples returned by SASE. Reports within weeks. Pays in copies of publication.

CRICKET, The Magazine for Children, Box 300, Peru IL 61354. Art Director: Ron McCutchan. Estab. 1973. Emphasizes children's literature for children, ages 6-14. Monthly. Circ. 140,000. Accepts previously published material. Original artwork returned after publication. Sample copy $1; art guidelines free for SASE.

Illustrations: Approached by 300-400 illustrators/year. Works with 75 illustrators/year. Buys 600 illustrations/year from freelancers. Uses artists mainly for cover and interior illustration. Prefers realistic styles (animal or human figure); occasionally accepts caricature. Works on assignment only. Send query letter with brochure, samples and tearsheets to be kept on file, "if I like it." Prefers photostats and tearsheets as samples. Samples are returned by SASE if requested or not kept on file. Reports within 6-8 weeks. Portfolio should include "several pieces that show an ability to tell a continuing story or narrative." Does not want to see "overly slick, cute commercial art (i.e. licensed characters and overly sentimental greeting cards)." Buys reprint rights. Pays $500, color, cover; $150/full page, b&w; on publication.

Tips: Freelancers have "a tendency to throw in the kitchen sink—I notice a lack of editing, which is helpful for me actually, since I can see what they've done that doesn't work. Of course, it's usually to their detriment." Today the "emphasis seems to be moving away from realism in illustration—and there is a lack of good realists who know anatomy and how the body works in movement."

*CROSSCURRENTS, 2200 Glastonbury Rd., Westlake Village CA 91361. (818)991-1694. Graphic Arts Editor: Michael Hughes. "A literary quarterly that uses graphic art as accompaniment to our fiction and poetry. We are aimed at an educated audience." Circ. 3,000. Original artwork returned after publication. Sample copy $5; art guidelines available for SASE.

Illustrations: Uses 5-7 illustrations/issue; buys 75% from freelancers. Considers "any work of high quality and in good taste that will reproduce b&w, 5x7", with clarity, including but not limited to line drawings, charcoal sketches, etchings, lithographs, engravings; vertical format. No pornography." Send brochure, resume, tearsheets, photostats, slides, photographs and SASE. No simultaneous submissions or previously published material. Reports in 3 weeks. To show a portfolio, mail appropriate material. Buys first rights. Pays $10 minimum cover or inside, b&w line drawings and b&w washes; $15 minimum cover, color washes; on publication.

Tips: "We only use work in vertical format. I receive a tremendous amount of work in horizontal format; this work does not fit the proportions of our picture boxes, and is therefore unusable. A professional, neat submission is a must, of course."

CURRENTS, Box 6847, 314 N. 20th St., Colorado Springs CO 80904. Editor: Eric Leaper. Estab. 1979. Magazine emphasizing whitewater river running for kayakers, rafters and canoeists; from beginner to expert; middle-class, college-educated. Bimonthly. Circ. 10,000. Accepts previously published material. Original artwork returned after publication. Sample copy $1. Art guidelines for SASE with first-class postage.

Cartoons: Buys 0-1 cartoon/issue from freelancers. Themes *must* deal with whitewater rivers or river running. Prefers single panel with gagline; b&w line drawings. Send query letter with roughs of proposed cartoon(s) to be kept on file. Samples not kept on file are returned by SASE. Reports within 6 weeks. Buys one-time rights. Pays $10-35, b&w.

Illustrations: Buys 0-2 illustrations/issue from freelancers. Prefers pen & ink. Works on assignment only. Themes must deal with rivers or river running. Send query letter with proposed illustrations. Samples not filed returned by SASE. Reports within 6 weeks. To show a portfolio, mail "whatever artists feel is necessary." Buys one-time rights. Pays $10-35, b&w; inside. Pays on publication.

Tips: "Make sure you have seen a sample copy of *Currents* and our guidelines. Be sure you know about rivers and whitewater river sports. Art must pertain to whitewater river running." Don't send sketches that are too rough to tell if you're any good."

*CWC/PETERBOROUGH, 80 Elm St., Peterborough NH 03458. (617)924-9471. Creative Director: Christine Destrempes. "We publish 5 microcomputing monthlies and various quarterlies: *AmigaWorld, Computers in Science, CD-ROM Review, 80 Micro, RUN,* and *inCider*." Circ. 100,000-550,000. Accepts previously published material. Returns original artwork after publication. Sample copy for SASE.

Cartoons: Minimal number of cartoons purchased from freelancers. Prefers single panel without gaglines; b&w line drawings and washes or color washes. "I don't use light cartoons." Send query letter with samples of style or finished cartoons to be kept on file. Material not filed is returned only if requested. Reports within 5 weeks. Rights purchased and payment varies; pays within 30 days.

Illustrations: Buys 8-20 illustrations/issue from freelancers. Uses airbrush, charcoal/pencil, watercolor, acrylic, oil, collage and computer illustration. Buys 2-3 computer illustrations/year from freelancers. Works on assignment only. Send query letter with resume and tearsheets to be kept on file. Samples not filed are returned only if requested. Reports within 5 weeks. To show a portfolio, mail color and b&w final reproduction/product or call or write to schedule an appointment. Rights purchased and payments vary; pays on acceptance.

Tips: "Artists must understand technical manuscripts. They must be very creative and must do excellent work. I like to see what artists perceive as their best work, but samples targeted to our specific needs are most helpful."

*CYCLE WORLD, 1499 Monrovia Ave., Newport Beach CA 92663. (714)720-5300. For active motorcyclists who are "young, affluent, educated, very perceptive." Monthly. Circ. 375,000. "Unless otherwise noted in query letter, we will keep spot drawings in our files for use as future fillers." Free sample copy and artist's guidelines.

Illustrations: Art Director: Elaine Anderson. Uses 5 illustrations/issue, all from freelancers. Interested in motorcycling and assigned themes. Works on assignment only. Prefers to see resume and samples. Samples returned, if originals; kept if photocopies. Reports back on future assignment possibilities to artists who phone. Does not report back to artists who contact through mail. Call or write to schedule an appointment to show a portfolio, which should include original/final art, final reproduction/product, color and b&w tearsheets. Provide brochure, tearsheet, letter of inquiry and business card to be kept on file for future assignments. Buys all rights. Pays $750, cover; $150, b&w, $500, color, inside; $75, spot drawings; on publication.

Tips: "We use a lot of spot drawings as fillers. Black-and-white motorcycle illustrations used mostly. Call or write. Do not send original art or unsolicited art."

DC COMICS INC., 666 Fifth Ave., New York NY 10103. (212)484-2800. Executive Editor: Dick Giordano. Super-hero and adventure comic books for mostly boys 7-14, plus an older audience of high school and college age. Monthly. Circ. 6,000,000. Original artwork is returned after publication.

Illustrations: Buys 22 comic pages/year. Works on assignment only. Send query letter with resume and photocopies. Do not send original artwork. Samples not filed are returned if requested and accompanied by SASE. Reports back within 2 months. Write to schedule an appointment to show a portfolio, which should include thumbnails and original/final art. Buys all rights. Payment varies on acceptance.

Tips: "Work should show an ability to tell stories with sequential illustrations. Single illustrations are not particularly helpful, since your ability at story telling is not demonstrated."

*DECORATIVE ARTIST'S WORKBOOK, 1507 Dana Ave., Cincinnati OH 45207. Art Director: Carole Winters. Estab. 1987. Magazine. "A step-by-step decorative painting workbook. The audience is primarily female; slant is how-to." Bimonthly. Circ. 120,000.Does not accept previously published artwork. Original artwork is returned at job's completion. Sample copy available for $4.65. Art guidelines not available.

Cartoons: Approached by 5-10 cartoonists/year. Buys 10-15 cartoons/year. Prefers themes and styles related to the decorative painter; single panel with and without gagline; b&w line drawings. Send query letter with finished cartoons. Samples are not filed and are returned by SASE if requested by artist. Reports back within 1 month. Buys first rights. Pays $50, b&w.

Illustrations: Approached by 100 freelance illustrators/year. Buys 1 illustration/issue; 6-7/year from freelance artists. Works on assignment only. Prefers realistic and humorous themes and styles. Prefers pen & ink, watercolor, airbrush, acrylic, colored pencil, mixed media and pastel. Send query letter with brochure, tearsheets and photocopies. Samples are filed. Reports back to the artist only if interested. To show a portfolio, mail slides. Buys first rights or one-time rights. Pays $50, b&w, $150, color, inside. Pays on publication.

DELAWARE TODAY MAGAZINE, 120A Senatorial Dr., Wilmington DE 19807. (302)656-1809. Art/Design Director: Ingrid Hansen-Lynch. Magazine emphasizing regional interest in and around Delaware. Features general interest, historical, humorous, interview/profile, personal experience and travel articles. "The stories we have are about people and happenings in and around Delaware. They are regional interest stories. Our audience is middle-aged (40-45) people with incomes around $79,000, mostly educated." Monthly. Circ. 25,000. Accepts previously published material. Original artwork returned after publication. Sample copy available.

Cartoons: Buys approximately 1 cartoon every other month from freelancers. Open to all styles. Works on assignment only. Prefers no gagline; b&w line drawings, b&w and color washes. Send query letter with samples of style. Do not send folders of pre-drawn cartoons. Samples are filed. Reports back only if interested. Buys first rights or one-time rights. Pays $75, small; $100, large.

Illustrations: Buys approximately 3-4 illustrations/issue from freelancers. Works on assignment only. Open to all styles. Send query letter with resume, tearsheets, slides and whatever pertains. Samples are filed. Reports back only if interested. Call to schedule an appointment to show a portfolio, which should include original/final art and color and b&w tearsheets and final reproduction/product. Buys first rights and one-time rights. Pays $75, small b&w and color; $100, large b&w and color, inside; $250, cover; on publication.

*DENVER MAGAZINE/DENVER BUSINESS MAGAZINE, Suite 108, 10394 W. Chatfield, Littleton CO 80127. (303)979-6660. FAX: (303)973-0974. Art/Production Director: Bernadette Feng. Estab. 1970. Consumer magazine; emphasizes Denver metro area interests and business interests. Monthly. Circ. 20,000. Original artwork returned at job's completion. Sample copies available. Art guidelines available.

Illustrations: Approached by 12 freelance illustrators/year. Buys 4 illustrations/year from freelancers. Works on assignment only. Considers all media. Send query letter with tearsheets, resume and other samples. Samples are filed. Reports back only if interested. Call to schedule an appointment to show a portfolio, which should include thumbnails, roughs, original/final art and b&w tearsheets. Rights purchased vary according to project. Pays $300 color, cover; $75 b&w, $150 color, inside. Pays on acceptance.

DETROIT MAGAZINE, 321 W. Lafayette, Detroit MI 48231. (313)222-6446. Art Director: Deborah Withey. Sunday magazine of major metropolitan daily newspaper emphasizing general subjects. Weekly. Circ. 1.3 million. Original artwork returned after publication; "the fourth largest magazine in the country." Sample copy available.

Illustrations: Buys 1-2 illustrations/issue from freelancers. Uses a variety of themes and styles, "but we emphasize fine art over cartoons." Works on assignment only. Send query letter with samples to be kept on file unless not considered for assignment. Send "whatever samples best show artwork and can fit into 8½ × 11 file folder." Samples not filed are not returned. Reports only if interested. Buys first rights. Pays $350-600, color, cover; $350-600, color and $250-350, b&w, inside; on publication.

New York City artist Ellen Weinstein created this cover illustration for Detroit Monthly magazine in monotype, pastel and collage. Weinstein, along with other artists, did the sketch on spec. Once she was selected, she had a month for completion. She wanted to convey "a lively and fun mood, similar to posters of the jazz age." First rights to the piece were purchased for $600.

© 1990 Ellen Weinstein

DETROIT MONTHLY MAGAZINE, 1400 Woodbridge, Detroit MI 48207. Design Director: Michael Ban. Emphasizes "features on political, economic, style, cultural, lifestyles, culinary subjects, etc., relating to Detroit and region" for "middle and upper-middle class, urban and suburban, mostly college-educated professionals." Monthly. Circ. approximately 100,000. "Very rarely" accepts previously published material. Sample copy for SASE.

Cartoons: Approached by 25 cartoonists/year. Pays $150, b&w; $200, color.

Illustrations: Approached by 1,300 illustrators/year. Buys 10/issue from freelancers. Works on assignment only. Send query letter with samples and tearsheets to be kept on file. Write for appointment to show portfolio. Prefers anything *but* original work as samples. Samples not kept on file are returned by SASE. Reports only if interested. Pays $1,000, color, cover, $300-400, color, full page, $200-300, b&w, full page, $100, spot illustrations; on publication.

Tips: A common mistake freelancers make in presenting their work is to "send too much material or send badly printed tearsheets." Sees trends toward Russian/European poster style illustrations, post modern "big type" designs.

DISCOVER, 3 Park Ave., New York NY 10016. (212)779-6200. Art Director: C. Warre. Estab. 1980. A science magazine. Monthly. Circ. 1 million.
Cartoons: Buys 1 cartoon/issue. Buys 40 cartoons/year. Prefers science as a theme. Prefers single panel b&w line drawings. Send query letter with samples of style. Samples are filed or are returned. Reprts back regarding queries/submissions within 1 month. Buys first rights. Pays on acceptance.
Illustrations: Buys illustrations mainly for covers, spots and feature spreads. Buys 20 illustrations/issue, 300/year from freelancers. Prefers watercolor. Considers pen & ink, airbrush, mixed media, colored pencil, acrylic, oil, pastel, collage, marker, charcoal pencil, photo engraving, scraperboard and silkscreen. Send query letter with brochure showing art style, or nonreturnable tearsheets. Samples are filed or are returned only if requested. Reports back within 1 month. Mail appropriate materials to show a portfolio. Buys first rights. Pays on acceptance.
Tips: Would like to see technical, anatomical, science maps, schematic diagrams, astronomical, geological and archeological illustrations.

*DISCOVERIES, 6401 The Paseo, Kansas City MO 64131. (816)333-7000. Editor: Molly Mitchell. Estab. 1974. Story paper "for 8-12 year olds of the Church of the Nazarene and other holiness denominations; material is based on everyday situations with Christian principles applied." Weekly. Circ. 68,000. Originals are not returned at job's completion unless prior arrangements are made with artist. Sample copies free for SASE with first-class postage. Art guidelines not available.
Cartoons: Approached by 15 cartoonists/year. Buys 1 cartoon/issue, 55 cartoons/year from freelancers. Prefers artwork with children and animals; single panel. Send query letter with finished cartoons. Samples not filed are returned by SASE. Reports back in 6 weeks. Buys first rights or reprint rights. Pays $15, b&w.
Illustrations: Approached by 30-40 illustrators/year. Buys 1 illustration/issue, 30 illustrations/year from freelancers. Works on assignment only. Considers watercolor, acrylic and other mediums on request. Send query letter with brochure and resume. Samples are filed. Reports back only if interested. Mail appropriate materials: tearsheets. Buys all rights. Pays $75-85, color, cover; on acceptance.
Tips: Does not want to see "fantasy or science fiction situations, children in situations not normally associated with Christian attitudes or actions. Our publications require more full-color artwork than in the past."

DOG FANCY, Box 6050, Mission Viejo CA 92690. (714)240-6001. Editor: Kim Thornton. Estab. 1969. For dog owners and breeders of all ages, interested in all phases of dog ownership. Monthly. Circ. 150,000. Simultaneous submissions and previously published work OK. Sample copy $3.; free artist's guidelines with SASE.
Cartoons: Buys 24 cartoons/year from freelancers; single, double or multiple panel. "Central character should be a dog." Mail finished art. Send SASE. Prefers photostats or photocopies as samples. Reports in 6 weeks. Buys first rights. Pays $35, b&w line drawings; on publication.
Illustrations: Buys 10 illustrations/year from freelancers, mainly for spot art and article illustration. Prefers local artists. Works on assignment only. Buys one-time rights. Pays $20, spot, $50-100, b&w illustrations; on publication.
Tips: "Spot illustrations are used in nearly every issue. I need dogs in action (doing just about anything) and puppies. Please send a selection that we can keep on file. We pay $20 for each spot drawing used. Drawings should be scaled to reduce to column width (2¼)"."

THE DOLPHIN LOG, The Cousteau Society, 8440 Santa Monica Blvd., Los Angeles CA 90069. (213)656-4422. Editor: Pamela Stacey. Educational magazine covering "all areas of science, history and the arts related to our global water system, including marine biology, ecology, the environment and natural history" for children ages 7-15. Bimonthly. Circ. 100,000. Original artwork returned after publication. Sample copy for $2 and SASE with 65¢ postage; art guidelines for SASE with first-class postage.
Cartoons: Buys 2 cartoons/year from freelancers. Considers themes or styles related to magazine's subject matter. Prefers single panel with or without gagline; b&w line drawings. Send query letter with samples of style. Samples are not filed and are returned by SASE. Reports within 1 month. Buys one-time rights, reprint rights and translation rights. Pays $25-75, b&w and color; on publication.

The asterisk before a listing indicates that the listing is new in this edition. New markets are often the most receptive to freelance submissions.

Illustrations: Approached by 10 illustrators/year. Buys 4-6 illustrations/year from freelancers. Uses simple, biologically and technically accurate line drawings and scientific illustrations. Subjects should be carefully researched. Prefers pen & ink, airbrush and watercolor. Send query letter with tearsheets and photocopies or brochure showing art style. "No portfolios. We review only tearsheets and/or photocopies. No original artwork, please." Samples are not filed and are returned by SASE. Reports within 1 month. Buys one-time rights and worldwide translation rights. Pays $25-200 on publication.

Tips: "Artists should first request a sample copy to familiarize themselves with our style. Do not send art which is not water-oriented."

DRAGON MAGAZINE, TSR, Inc., Box 111, Lake Geneva WI 53147. (414)248-3625. Editor: Roger Moore. Art Director: Larry Smith. For readers interested in role-playing games, particularly Dungeons & Dragons. Circ. 90,000. Query with samples and SASE. Usually buys first rights only. Pays within 60 days after acceptance.

Cartoons: Approached by 100 cartoonists/year. Buys 80 cartoons/year from freelancers on fantasy role-playing. Pays $35-80, b&w only.

Illustrations: Approached by 100 illustrators/year. Buys at least 100 illustrations/year from freelancers on fantasy and science fiction subjects. Wants to see "samples that show complete compositions—not spot drawings or portrait style work." Does not want to see "single figure drawings, morbid subjects, bad taste in general." Pays $250, b&w, $500 and up, color, inside; $800 and up, color, cover.

Tips: "Commissions are not likely unless the artist provides a sampling of work which demonstrates his ability to render realistic fantasy art. The more particular the work is to the Dungeons & Dragons game the better. Please send slides, b&w or color photocopies. Do not send any material larger than 8½×11."

ECLIPSE COMICS, Box 1099, Forestville CA 95436. Editor-in-Chief: Catherine Yronwode. Estab. 1978. Publishes comic books and graphic albums. "Most of our comics feature fictional characters in action-adventures. Genres include super-heroes, science fiction, weird horror, detective adventure, literary adaptations, etc. We also publish a line of nonfiction comics (graphic journalism) dealing with current and historic political and social subjects. The emphasis is on drawing the human figure in action. Audience is adolescent to adult. Publishes 20 comics/month on average. Some are monthlies, some bi-monthly; others are one-shots or mini-series. Circ. 30,000-100,000, depending on title. Does not accept previously published material except for reprint collections by famous comic book artists. Original artwork returned after publication. Sample copy $2; art guidelines for SASE.

Cartoons: "We buy entire illustrated stories, not individual cartoons. We buy approximately 6,250 pages of comic book art by freelancers/year—about 525/month." Interested in realistic illustrative comic book artwork—drawing the human figure in action; good, slick finishes (inking); ability to do righteous 1-, 2- and 3-point perspective required. Formats: b&w line drawings or fully painted pages with balloon lettering on overlays. Send query letter with samples of style to be kept on file. "Send minimum of 4-5 pages of full-size (10×15) photocopies of pencilled *storytelling* (and/or inked too)—no display poses, just typical action layout continuities." Material not filed is returned by SASE. Reports within 2 months by SASE only. Buys first rights and reprint rights. Pays $100-200/page, b&w; "price is for pencils plus inks; many artists do only pencil for us, or only ink."; on acceptance (net 30 days). Pays $25-35/page for painted or airbrushed coloring of greylines made from line-art; on acceptance (net 30 days).

Illustrations: "We buy 12-15 cover paintings for science fiction and horror books per year." Science fiction paintings: fully rendered science fiction themes (e.g. outer space, aliens); horror paintings: fully rendered horror themes (e.g. vampires, werewolves, etc.). Send query letter with business card and samples to be kept on file. Prefers slides, color photos or tearsheets as samples. Samples not filed are returned by SASE. Reports within 2 months by SASE only. Buys first rights or reprint rights. Pays $200-500, color; on acceptance (net 30 days). "We also buy paintings for our popular political trading card sets; each set consists of 36 small painted caricatures of politically or socially prominent people (dictators, indicted officials, etc.), backed by researched text matter. Trading card art pays $3,700 per set of paintings; on acceptance (net 30 days)."

EIDOS MAGAZINE: Erotic Entertainment for Women, Men and Couples, Box 96, Boston MA 02137-0096. (617)262-0096. Editor: Brenda L. Tatelbaum. Estab. 1984. Magazine emphasizing erotica and erotic entertainment for women and men. Quarterly. Original artwork returned after publication.

Cartoons: Approached by 6 cartoonists/year. "Standard payment terms."

Illustrations: Approached by 30 illustrators/year. Works with 12-15 artists/year. Buys 12-15 illustrations/year from freelancers. Use freelancers for editorial art and photography; pasteup/design. Send query letter with resume, tearsheets, photostats and photographs. Samples are filed or are returned by SASE. Reports back within 2 months. Write first before sending a portfolio, which should include original/final art, photostats and photographs. Buys first rights. "We have standard payment terms."

Tips: "We look for sensuous, sensitive, sophisticated erotica depicting mutually respective sexuality and images of the human form. Alternative to commercial mainstream men's and women's magazines. More images of men and couples are published in *Eidos* than female images." We do not want to see "stereotypical

Artist David Wenzel did these illustrations for the graphic album adaptation of Tolkien's The Hobbit, *published by Eclipse Enterprises, Inc. Publisher Dean Mullaney chose Wenzel for this assignment because "his use of clear, bright colors is something we look for in the comics medium. In addition, his background and detailed work is above average, and that is necessary for the fantasy-world's reality." Wenzel sold reprint rights to the illustrations, which were done in ink and watercolor.*

images and language (cartoons); lack of sexually—explicit detail (art and photography); lack of bold b&w contrast."

ELECTRICAL APPARATUS, Barks Publications, Inc., Suite 1016, 400 N. Michigan Ave., Chicago IL 60611-4198. (312)321-9440. Contact: Cartoon Editor. Estab. 1948. Trade journal; magazine format; emphasizing industrial electrical mechanical maintenance. Monthly. Circ. 16,000. Original artwork not returned at job's completion. Sample copy $4. Art guidelines not available.
Cartoons: Approached by several cartoonists/year. Buys 3-4 cartoons/issue, 35-40 cartoons/year from freelancers. Prefers themes relevant to magazine content; with gagline. "Captions are typeset in our style." Send query letter with roughs and finished cartoons. "Anything we don't use is returned." Reports back within 2-3 weeks. Buys all rights. Pays $15-20, b&w and color.
Illustrations: "We have staff artists so there is little opportunity for freelance illustrators, but we are always glad to hear from anyone who believes he or she has something relevant to contribute."

*ELECTRICAL CONTRACTOR, 7315 Wisconsin Ave., Bethesda MD 20814. (301)657-3110. Managing Editor: Walt Albro. Trade journal emphasizing management of electrical construction businesses. "We are a controlled-circulation magazine distributed to the owners and key employees of all electrical construction businesses in the U.S. We publish features and news of interest to the entire electrical construction industry." Monthly. Circ. 66,000. Original artwork is sometimes returned to the artist after publication. Sample copies available.
Cartoons: Approached by 2-4 cartoonists/year. Pays $100.
Illustrations: Approached by 10-12 illustrators/year. Buys 6-8 illustrations/year from freelancers. Mainly uses freelancers for inside illustrations, charts and graphs. Works on assignment only. Prefers "a sophisticated look, suitable for a management magazine." Send query letter with resume. Samples are filed. Reports back only if interested. Call or write to schedule an appointment to show a portfolio, which should include "previously published magazine art. (We prefer working with artists in the metropolitan Washington area.)" Buys one-time rights or reprint rights. Pays $100, b&w; $150, color, inside; on acceptance.

EMERGENCY MEDICINE MAGAZINE, Cahners Publishing Company, 249 W. 17th St., New York NY 10011. (212)645-0067. Art Director: Lois Erlacher. Estab. 1969. Emphasizes emergency medicine for primary care physicians, emergency room personnel, medical students. Bimonthly. Circ. 129,000. Returns original artwork after publication.

Cartoons: "We rarely use cartoons."
Illustrations: Works with 70 illustrators/year. Buys 3-12 illustrations/issue, 100-200 illustrations/year from freelancers. Prefers all media except marker and computer illustration. Works on assignment only. Send tearsheets, transparencies, original art or photostats to be kept on file. Samples not filed are not returned. To show a portfolio, mail appropriate materials. Reports only if interested. Buys first rights. Pays $750, color, cover; $100-500, b&w and $250-600, color, inside; on acceptance.
Tips: "Portfolios may be dropped off Tuesdays only and picked up Thursdays. All portfolios will be reviewed by art directors from other Cahners publications as well. Contact Annabell Carter. Do not show marker comps. Show a minimum of 4×5 transparencies; 8×10's are much better. In general, slides are too small to see in a review."

*EMPLOYEE SERVICES MANAGEMENT MAGAZINE, NESRA, 2400 S. Downing Ave., Westchester IL 60154. (312)562-8130. Editor: Elizabeth D. Grumbine. Emphasizes the field of employee services and recreation for human resource professionals, employee services and recreation managers and leaders within corporations, industries or units of government. Published 10 times/year. Circ. 5,000. Accepts previously published material. Returns original artwork after publication. Sample copy for SASE with 56¢ postage; art guidelines for SASE with first-class postage.
Illustrations: Approached by 5-10 illustrators/year. Buys 0-1 illustration/issue from freelancers. Works on assignment only. Send query letter with resume and tearsheets or photographs to be kept on file. Samples not filed are returned only if requested. Reports within 1 month. Buys one-time rights. Pays $100-200, b&w and $300-400, color, covers; on acceptance.
Tips: Looking for "illustrations with clean lines in bright colors pertaining to human resources issues. I like to be suprised; 'typical' illustrations bore me." Sees as trend "the use of computer graphic programs to enhance, create or 'play with' an illustration."

*ENDLESS VACATION MAGAZINE, 3502 Woodview Trace, Indianapolis IN 46268. (317)871-9417. FAX: (317)871-9507. Designer: Robert Allen. Estab. 1975. Consumer magazine; "we are a travel magazine published for people dedicated to vacationing." Monthly. Circ. 750,000. Original artwork returned at job's completion. Sample copies available. Art guidelines not available.
Illustrations: Buys 2-3 illustrations/issue, 20 illustrations/year from freelancers. Works on assignment only. Usually prefers "positive and fun" themes and styles. Considers mixed media, watercolor, pastel and collage. Send query letter with tearsheets. Samples are filed or are returned by SASE if requested by artist. Reports back only if interested. Mail appropriate materials: tearsheets and slides. "If sending slides, send SASE for their return." Buys first rights. Pays $300, color, inside; on acceptance.
Tips: "Send non-returnable samples of work for our files. Be sure to send enough to give us an idea of your style. No phone calls please."

*ENTREPRENEUR MAGAZINE, 2392 Morse Ave., Box 19787, Irvine CA 92714-6234. Editor: Rieva Lesonsky. Design Director: Richard R. Olson. Magazine offers how-to information for starting a business, plus ongoing information and support to those already in business. Monthly. Circ. 325,000. Original artwork returned after publication.
Illustrations: Approached by 36 illustrators/year. Uses varied number of illustrations/issue; buys varied number/issue from freelancers. Works on assignment only. Send query letter with resume, samples and tearsheets to be kept on file. Does not want to see Xeroxes. Write for appointment to show portfolio. Buys first rights. Pays $800, color, cover; $200-600, color, inside; on acceptance.
Tips: Freelancers should "have a promo piece to leave behind." A developing trend is the "use of a combination of different media—going away from airbrush to a more painterly style."

ENVIRONMENT, 4000 Albemarle St. NW, Washington DC 20016. (202)362-6445. Production Graphics Editor: Ann Rickerich. Estab. 1958. Emphasizes national and international environmental and scientific issues. Readers range from "high school students and college undergrads to scientists, business and government leaders and college and university professors." Circ. 12,500. Published 10 times/year. Original artwork returned after publication if requested. Sample copy $4.50; cartoonist's guidelines available.
Cartoons: Buys 1-2 cartoon/issue; all from freelancers. Receives 5 submissions/week from freelancers. Interested in single panel b&w line drawings or b&w washes with or without gagline. Send finished cartoons and SASE. Reports in 2 months. Buys first North American serial rights. Pays $35, b&w cartoon; on publication.
Illustrations: Buys 0-10/year from freelance artists. Uses illustrators mainly for cover design, promotional work and occasional spot illustrations. Send query letter, brochure, tearsheets and photocopies. To show a portfolio, mail original/final art or reproductions. Pays $300 color, cover; $100 b&w, $200, color, inside; on publication.
Tips: "Regarding cartoons, we prefer witty or wry comments on the impact of humankind upon the environment." For illustrations, "we are looking for an ability to communicate complex environmental issues and ideas in an unbiased way. Send samples of previously published work and samples of different styles."

EVANGEL, 901 College Ave., Winona Lake IN 46590. (219)267-7656. Contact: Vera Bethel. Readers are 65% female, 35% male; ages 25-31, married, city-dwelling, mostly non-professional high school graduates. Circ. 35,000. Weekly.
Cartoons: Approached by 20 cartoonists/year. Buys 1 cartoon/issue from freelancers on family subjects. Pays $10, b&w; on publication. Mail finished art.
Illustrations: Approached by 10 illustrators/year. Buys 1 illustration/issue from freelancers on assigned themes. Pays $50, 2-color; on acceptance. Query with samples or slides and SASE. Reports in 1 month.

EVENT, Douglas College, Box 2503, New Westminster, British Columbia V3L 5B2 Canada. (604)527-5298. Editor: Dale Zieroth. Estab. 1971. For "those interested in literature and writing." Published 3 times/year. Circ. 1,000. Original artwork returned after publication. Sample copy $4.
Illustrations: Buys approximately 3 illustrations/year from freelancers. Uses freelancers mainly for covers. "Interested in drawings and prints, b&w line drawings, photographs and lithographs for cover and inside, and thematic or stylistic series of 12-20 works. Work must reproduce well in one color." SAE (non residents include IRC). Reporting time varies; at least 2 months. Buys first North American serial rights. Pays honorarium plus complimentary copy on publication.

*EXCLUSIVELY YOURS MAGAZINE, 161 W. Wisconsin Ave., Milwaukee WI 53203. (414)271-4270. Art Director: Jan Lawrenz. Estab. 1949. Consumer magazine. "Advertising tool catering to upper income readers." Monthly publication. Circ. 50,000. Accepts previously published artwork. Original artwork is returned at the job's completion. Sample copy $3.15. Art guidelines available.
Illustrations: Approached by 3-4 illustrators/year. Buys 12 illustrations/year from freelancers. Usually works on assignment only. Prefers homes, portraits, tabloid issues. Considers all media. Send query letter with letter and samples (any format). Samples sometimes filed, "depending on project" or are returned by SASE if requested by artist. Does not report back, in which case the artist should call. Call to schedule an appointment to show a portfolio. Rights purchased vary according to project. Pays $100, b&w, $150, color, cover; $100, b&w, $150, color, inside.
Tips: "Call (for appointment or information)."

EXECUTIVE FEMALE, 127 W. 24th St., New York NY 10011. (212)645-0770. Editor-in-Chief: Diane Burley. Estab. 1978. Association magazine NAFE. "Get ahead guide for women executives, which includes articles on managing employees, personal finance, starting and running a business." Circ. 250,000. Accepts previously published artwork. Original artwork is returned after publication.
Cartoons: Send query letter with roughs. Samples are filed. Responds only if interested. Buys first or reprint rights. Pays $25-50, b&w; $250, color (4 panels).
Illustrations: Buys illustrations mainly for spots and feature spreads. Buys 7 illustrations/issue. Works on assignment only. Send query letter with brochure, resume and tear sheets. Samples are filed. Responds only if interested. Call to schedule an appointment to show a portfolio. Buys first or reprint rights. Pays $50-200, b&w; $75-300, color, inside; on publication.

EXPECTING MAGAZINE, 685 Third Ave., New York NY 10017. (212)878-8700. Art Director: Robin Zachary. Estab. 1967. Emphasizes pregnancy, birth and care of the newborn; for pregnant women and new mothers. Quarterly. Circ. 1.2 million, distributed through obstetrician and gynecologist offices nationwide. Original artwork returned after publication.
Cartoons: Approached by 40-50 cartoonists/year. Buys 12 cartoons/year from freelancers. Pay varies.
Illustrations: Approached by 40-50 illustrators/year. Buys approximately 6 illustrations/issue. Color only. Works on assignment. "We have a drop-off policy for looking at portfolios; I make appointments if time permits. Include a card to be kept on file." Buys one-time rights. Pays $200 and up for color, inside. Pays within 30 days after publication.
Tips: "I need examples of 'people' illustrations. Bright colors. Very stylized work. Almost all of the illustrations I assign are about moms, dads, babies and sometimes I need a still life."

THE EYE MAGAZINE, 11th & Washington Sts., Wilmington DE 19801. (302)571-6978. Art Director: Paul A. Miles. Estab. 1978. Tabloid for high school students; all writing, cartoons, photographs, etc. are produced by high-school age cartoonists and artists. Monthly, October through May. Circ. 25,000. Accepts previously published material. Original artwork returned after publication. Sample copy for SASE with 37¢ postage.
Cartoons: Uses 1 cartoon/issue. Prefers single panel with gagline; b&w line drawings. Prefers themes showing resourcefulness of young people. "We prefer ones that do not show teens in a derogatory manner." Send query letter with samples of style to be kept on file. Material not kept on file is returned by SASE. Reports within 30 days. Buys one-time rights.
Illustrations: Buys 1 illustration/issue from freelancers. Works on assignment only. Primary theme is teenagers; artist must be 14-19 years old. Prefers b&w high-contrast or pen & ink drawing; or charcoal/pencil, markers and computer illustration. Send query letter with resume and photocopies. Samples not filed are returned by SASE. Reports within 30 days. "We do not see portfolios." Buys one-time rights. Pays $25, b&w,

cover; $10, b&w, inside. "Our publication is produced by a nonprofit agency to give students a voice to their peers and adults. We are a training ground and as such do not pay very much for editorial or artwork. We will gladly give copies of publication and letters of recommendations to high school students interested in getting something published."
Tips: "Don't expect very much from us. We are small and like to help artists; not monetarily, but by giving them a chance to be published."

FAMILY CIRCLE, 110 5th Ave., New York NY 10011. Art Director: Doug Turshen. Circ. 7,000,000. Supermarket-distributed publication for women/homemakers covering areas of food, home, beauty, health, child care and careers. 17 issues/year. Does not accept previously published material. Original artwork returned after publication. Sample copy and art guidelines not available.
Cartoons: No unsolicited cartoon submissions accepted. Reviews in office first Wednesday of each month. Buys 1-2 cartoons/issue. Prefers themes related to women's interests from a feminist viewpoint. Uses limited seasonal material, primarily Christmas. Prefers single panel with gagline, b&w line drawings or washes. Buys all rights. Pays $325 on acceptance. Contact Christopher Cavanaugh, (212)463-1000, for cartoon query only.
Illustrations: Buys 20 illustrations/issue from freelancers. Works on assignment only. Reports only if interested. Provide query letter with samples to be kept on file for future assignments. Prefers slides or tearsheets as samples. Samples returned by SASE. Prefers to see finished art in portfolio. Submit portfolio on "portfolio days," every Wednesday. All art is commissioned for specific magazine articles. Reports in 1 week. Buys all rights on a work-for-hire basis. Pays on acceptance.

FANTAGRAPHIC BOOKS, 7563 Lake City Way, Seattle WA 98115. (206)524-1967. FAX: (206)524-2104. Contact: Gary Groth or Kim Thompson. Publishes comic books and graphic novels. Titles include *Love and Rockets*, *Amazing Heroes*, *Los Tejanos*, *Hate*, *Eightball*, *Graphic Story Monthly*, *Sinner*, *Yahoo* and *Unsupervised Existence*. All genres except superheroes. Monthly and bimonthly depending on titles. Circ. 8-30,000. Sample copy $2.50.
Cartoons: Approached by 500 cartoonists/year. Fantagraphic is looking for artists who can create an entire product or who can work as part of an established team. Most of the titles are black and white. Send query letter with photocopies which display storytelling capabilities, or submit a complete package. All artwork is creator-owned. Buys one-time rights usually. Payment terms vary. Creator receives an advance upon acceptance and then royalties after publication.
Tips: "We prefer not to see illustration work unless there is some accompanying comics work. We also do not want to see unillustrated scripts." A common mistake freelancers make is that they "sometimes fail to include basic information like name, address, phone number, etc. They also fail to include SASE. In comics, I see a trend away from 'classical' representation towards more personal styles. In illustration in general, I see more and more illustrators who got their starts in comics appearing in national magazines."

*FASHION ACCESSORIES, 65 W. Main St., Bergenfield NJ 07630. (201)384-3336. FAX: (201)384-6776. Publisher: Sam Mendelson. Estab. 1951. Trade journal; tabloid; emphasizes costume jewelry and accessories—wholesale level. Monthly publication. Circ. 8,000. Accepts previously published artwork. Original artwork is returned to the artist at the job's completion. Sample copies for $2. Art guidelines not available.
Illustrations: Works on assignment only. Prefers mixed media. Send query letter with brochure and photocopies. Samples are filed. Reports back within 2 weeks. Mail appropriate materials: photocopies. Rights purchased vary according to project. Pays $150, b&w, $250, color, cover; $75, b&w, $125, color, inside; on acceptance.

*FATE MAGAZINE, Box 64383, St. Paul MN 55164. (612)291-1970. FAX: (612)291-1908. Art Director: Terry Buske. Estab. 1948. Consumer magazine; "true reports of the strange and unknown; focus on parapsychology, UFOs, the paranormal, monsters, archaeology, lost civilizations, new science, ghosts, etc." Monthly. Circ. 100,000. Accepts previously published artwork. Original artwork returned after publication. Sample copies are available. Art guidelines free for SASE with first-class postage.
Illustrations: Approached by 75-100 illustrators/year. Buys 1 illustration/issue, 12-20 illustrations/year from freelancers. Works on assignment only. Prefers very professional and modern pulp styles and a knowledge of the subject. Considers airbrush, acrylic, and oil. Send query letter with brochure, tearsheets, photographs, slides and SASE. Samples are filed or returned by SASE if requested. Reports back within 1-1½ months. Mail appropriate materials: b&w and color tearsheets, photographs and slides. Negotiates rights purchased. Pays $200-400, color, cover. Pays net 30 after acceptance.
Tips: "Have a good knowledge of the subject matter and pulp magazine style. Not all of our covers are pulp, however. We also use very nice modern paintings and a variety of styles. We want the artist to have fun."

FFA NEW HORIZONS, (formerly National Future Farmer), Box 15160, Alexandria VA 22309. (703)360-3600. Editor-in-Chief: Wilson W. Carnes. For members of the Future Farmers of America who are students of vocational agriculture in high school, ages 14-21. Emphasizes careers in agriculture/agribusiness and topics of general interest to youth. Bimonthly. Circ. 396,536. Reports in 3 weeks. Buys all rights. Pays on acceptance. Sample copy available.

Cartoons: Approached by 25 cartoonists/year. Buys 15-20 cartoons/year from freelancers on Future Farmers of America or assigned themes. Receives 10 cartoons/week from freelance artists. Pays $20, cartoons; more for assignments.

Illustrations: Approached by 10 illustrators/year. "We buy a few illustrations for specific stories; almost always on assignment." Send query letter with tearsheets or photocopies. Write to schedule an appointment to show a portfolio, which should include final reproduction/product, tearsheets and photostats. Negotiates payment.

Tips: Wants to see "b&w line art; several pieces to show style and general tendencies; printed pieces." Does not want to see "slides of actual 4-color original art." Sees a glut of poor computer graphics. It all looks the same. Good computer graphic designers are great—why does everyone copy?"

*FICTION INTERNATIONAL, San Diego State University, San Diego CA 92182-0295. Art Editors: M. Jaffe/ D. Small. Estab. 1970. Literary magazine with "twin interests: left politics and experimental fiction and art." Biannual. Accepts previously published artwork. Original artwork is returned to the artist at the job's completion. Sample copies are available. Art guidlines are not available.

Illustrations: Prefers political artwork. Prefers pen & ink and photos. Send query letter with photographs and slides. Samples are not filed and are returned. Reports back within 1 month. Mail appropriate materials: b&w tearsheets, slides and photographs. Pays $25, b&w, cover; $25, b&w, inside; on publication.

FIELD & STREAM MAGAZINE, 2 Park Ave., New York NY 10016. (212)779-5294. Art Director: Victor J. Closi. Magazine emphasizing wildlife hunting and fishing. Monthly. Circ. 2 million. Original artwork returned after publication. Sample copy and art guidelines for SASE.

Illustrations: Approached by 200-250 illustrators/year. Buys 9-12 illustrations/issue from freelancers. Works on assignment only. Prefers "good drawing and painting ability, realistic style, some conceptual and humorous styles are also used depending on magazine article." Wants to see "emphasis on strong draftsmanship, the ability to draw wildlife and people equally well. Artists who can't, please do not apply." Send query letter with brochure showing art style or tearsheets and slides. Samples not filed are returned only if requested. Reports only if interested. Call or write to schedule an appointment to show a portfolio, which should include roughs, original/final art, final reproduction/product and tear sheets. Buys first rights. Payment varies: $75-300 simple spots; $500-1,000, single page, $1,000 and up, spreads, and $1,500 and up, covers; on acceptance.

Tips: Wants to see "more illustrators who can handle simple pen & ink and 2-color art besides 4-color illustrations, who are knowledgeable about hunting and fishing."

THE FINAL EDITION, Box 294, Rhododendron OR 97049. (503)622-4798. Editor: Michael P. Jones. Estab. 1985. Investigative journal that deals "with a variety of subjects—environment, wildlife, crime, etc. for professional and blue collar people who want in-depth reporting." Monthly. Circ. 1,500. Accepts previously published material. Original artwork is returned after publication. Art guidelines for SASE with 1 first-class stamp.

Cartoons: Buys 1-18 cartoons/issue, 260/year from freelancers. Prefers single panel, double panel, multi panel, with or without gagline; b&w line drawings, b&w or color washes. Send query letter with samples of style, roughs or finished cartoons. Samples are filed or are returned by SASE. Reports back within 2 weeks. Buys one-time rights. Pays in copies.

Illustrations: Buys 10 illustrations/issue, 390/year from freelancers. Works with 29 illustrators/year. Prefers pen & ink, aribrush, pencil, marker, calligraphy and computer illustration. Send query letter with brochure showing art style or resume and tearsheets, photostats, photocopies, slides or photographs. Samples not filed are returned by SASE. Reports back within 2 weeks. To show a portfolio, mail thumbnails, roughs, original/ final art, final reproduction/product, color or b&w tearsheets, photostats and photographs. Buys one-time rights. Pays in copies.

Tips: "We have a real need for nonfiction illustrations. *The Final Edition* deals with real things and real events, not science fiction. Subject matter may be on bison, wolves, wild horses, wiretapping, enviromental, social jutice issues, or profiling the life history of an individual. We are really looking for artists who can sketch covered wagons, pioneers, Native Americans, and Mountain Men."

FINESCALE MODELER, 1027 N. Seventh St., Milwaukee WI 53233. Art Director: Lawrence Luser. Estab. 1972. Magazine emphasizing plastic modeling. Circ. 73,000. Accepts previously published material. Original artwork is sometimes returned to the artist after publication. Sample copy and art guidelines available.

Illustrations: Prefers technical illustration "with a flair." Send query letter with brochure. Samples are filed or returned only if requested by artist. Reports back only if interested. Write to schedule an appointment to show portfolio or mail color and b&w tearsheets, final reproduction/product, photographs and slides. Negotiates rights purchased.

Tips: "Show black-and-white and color technical illustration. I want to see automotive, aircraft and tank illustrations."

FIRST HAND LTD., 310 Cedar Ln., Teaneck NJ 07666. (201)836-9177. Art Director: Laura Patricks. Emphasizes homoerotica for a male audience. Monthly. Circ. 60,000. Sample copy $3; art guidelines available for SASE.
Cartoons: Buys 5 cartoons/issue from freelancers. Prefers single panel with gagline; b&w line drawings. Send finished cartoons to be kept on file. Material not filed is returned by SASE. Reports back within 2 weeks. Buys first rights. Pays $15, b&w; on acceptance.
Illustrations: Buys 20 illustrations/issue from freelancers. Prefers "nude men in a realistic style; very basic, very simple." Send query letter with photostats or tearsheets to be kept on file or are returned. Reports within 2 weeks. Call or write for appointment to show portfolio. Buys all magazine rights. Pays for design by the hour, $10. Pays $25-50, b&w, inside; on acceptance.
Tips: "I like to see current work, not work that is too old. And I prefer to see printed samples if that is possible."

*FIRST PUBLISHING, 435 N. LaSalle, Chicago IL 60610. (312)670-6770. Art Director: Alex Wald. Publishes comic books and graphic novels including *Badger*, *Nexus* and *Dreadstar*.
Illustrations: Prefers comic storytelling with well-realized figures. Uses freelance artists for inking, lettering, pencilling, color work and covers. Send query letter with photocopies of original art, which should be proportional to 10x15; include your name, address and phone number on every sample page. Samples are sometimes filed. Call to schedule an appointment to show a portfolio. Negotiates rights purchased and payment. All material is invoiced. Pays $200 and up, cover; $50 and up, pencil and ink, $20 and up, color, $15 and up, letters; inside. Payment is 30-60 days after acceptance.
Tips: "I'd rather see what the artist considers his strongest work, rather than his attempt to imitate the current editorial product."

FLORIDA LEADER MAGAZINE, Box 14081, Gainesville FL 32604-2081. (904)373-6907. Art Director: Jeffrey L. Riemersma. Estab. 1983. "Florida Leader Magazine is a college-oriented publication that blends trendy feature articles, news from Florida schools, plus hard-hitting investigative reporting and interviews that debate important student issues." Quarterly. Circ. 27,000. Accepts previously published artwork. Original artwork is not returned after publication. Sample copies free for SASE with first-class postage. Art guidelines available. "We use freelancers for all inside illustrations and often for the cover."
Cartoons: Approached by 10-20 cartoonists/year. Buys 1-2 cartoons/issue, 4-8 cartoons/year from freelancers. Works on assignment only. Prefers student-oriented situations, political cartoons (Florida-related). Prefers single panel with or without gagline and multiple panel with gagline; color drawings. Send query letter with samples of style and finished cartoons. Samples are filed or returned by SASE. Reports back regarding queries/submissions only if interested. Negotiates rights purchased. Pays $30, b&w; $50, color; on publication.
Illustrations: Approached by 10-20 illustrators/year. Buys illustrations mainly for, spots and feature spreads. Buys 4-5 illustrations/issue, 12 illustrations/year from freelancers. Works on assignment only. Considers pen & ink, airbrush, mixed media, colored pencil, acrylic, oil, pastel and collage. Send query letter with brochure showing art style and tearsheets. Looks for originality, technique, use of color, ability to draw human figure and caricatures. Samples are filed or returned by SASE. Reports back about queries/submissions only if interested. Negotiates rights purchased. Call or write to schedule an appointment to show a portfolio, mail color and b&w original/final art or tearsheets. Pays $30, b&w; $50, color, inside; on publication.
Tips: "Mistakes freelancers make in presenting their work are not describing the project and media used in enough detail and sending only black and white examples—we use color far more than b&w currently."

FLOWER & GARDEN, 4251 Pennsylvania, Kansas City MO 64111. (816)531-5730. Editor: Kay M. Olson. Estab. 1954. "The Home Gardening Magazine." Bimonthly. Circ. 630,000. Sample copy $2.
Cartoons: Receives about 10 submissions/week. Buys 1 cartoon/issue from freelancers. Needs cartoons related to "indoor or outdoor home gardening." Format: single panel b&w line drawings or washes with gagline. Prefers to see finished cartoons. Send SASE. Reports in 4 weeks. Buys one-time rights. Pays $20, b&w cartoon; on acceptance.
Illustrations: Works with 4 illustrators/year. Buys 50 illustrations/year from freelancers. Send samples that show range of style. "Query first, send good samples, then follow up with a phone call." Pays $75, b&w, inside.

FLY FISHERMAN MAGAZINE, 2245 Kohn Rd., Harrisburg PA 17110. (717)540-8175. Art Director: Rod Bond. Estab. 1969. Magazine covering all aspects of fly fishing including how to, where to, new products, wildlife and habitat conservation, and travel through top-of-the-line photography and artwork. In-depth editorial. Readers are upper middle class subscribers. Bimonthly. Circ. 144,000. Sample copies free for SASE with first-class postage. Art guidelines free for SASE with first-class postage.
Cartoons: Buys 1 cartoon/issue, 6-10 cartoons/year from freelancers. Prefers fly fishing related themes only. Prefers single panel with or without gagline; b&w line drawings and washes. Send query letter with samples of style. Samples are filed or returned by SASE. Reports back regarding queries/submissions within 3 weeks. Buys one-time rights. Pays on publication.

Illustrations: Buys illustrations to illustrate fishing techniques and for spots. Buys 4-10 illustrations/issue, 50 illustrations/year from freelancers. Prefers pen & ink. Considers airbrush, mixed media, watercolor, acrylic, pastel and charcoal pencil. Send query letter with brochure showing art style, resume, tearsheets, photostats, photocopies, slides, photographs and transparencies. Samples are filed or returned by SASE. Call or write to schedule an appointment to show a portfolio or mail appropriate materials. Buys one-time rights and occasionally all rights. Pays on publication. Spot art for front and back of magazine is most open to illustrators.

*FLYING MAGAZINE, 1633 Broadway, New York NY 10019. (212)767-6963. FAX: (212)767-5620. Art Director: Nancy Bink. Consumer magazine; emphasizing airplanes and pilots. "We use lots of 4-color photography and illustrations." Monthly. Circ. 325,000. Original artwork returned after publication. Sample copies are available. Art guidelines not availble.
Illustrations: Approached by 50-100 illustrators/year. Buys 2-3 illustrations/issue, 24-36 illustrations/year from freelancers. Works on assignment only. Theme preferred is "airplanes." Any media is acceptable. Contact through artist rep or send query letter with tearsheets. Samples are filed. Reports back only if interested. Write to schedule an appointment to show portfolio which should include roughs, original/final art, and tearsheets. Buys one-time rights. Pays $150, b&w, $500, color; inside "more depending on the size and complexity." Pays on acceptance.
Tips: "Understand and love airplanes and flying."

FOOD & SERVICE, Box 1429, Austin TX 78767. (512)444-6543. Editor: Steve Greenhow. Art Director: Neil Ferguson. Estab. 1940. Official trade publication of Texas Restaurant Association. Seek illustrations (but not cartoons) dealing with business problems of restaurant owners and food-service operators, primarily in Texas, and including managers of clubs, bars and hotels. Published 11 times/year. Circ. 5,000. Simultaneous submissions OK. Sample copy for SASE.
Illustrations: Works with 15 illustrators/year. Buys 36-48 illustrations/year from freelancers. Uses artwork mainly for covers and feature articles. Seeks high-quality b&w or color artwork in variety of styles (airbrush, watercolor, pastel, pen & ink, etc.). Seeks versatile artists who can illustrate articles about food-service industry, particularly business aspects. Works on assignment only. Query with resume, samples and tearsheets. Call for appointment to show portfolio. Pays for illustration $175-250, color, cover; $50-100, b&w; $125-200, color, inside. Negotiates rights and payment upon assignment. Originals returned after publication.
Tips: "In a portfolio, show samples of color work and tearsheets. Common mistakes made in presenting work include sloppy presentation and typos in cover letter or resume. Request a sample of our magazine (include a 10x13 SASE), then send samples that fit the style or overall mood of our magazine."

*FORBES MAGAZINE, 60 Fifth Ave., New York NY 10011. (212)620-2200. Art Director: Everett Halvorsen. Deputy Art Director: Roger Zapke. Estab. 1917. Business magazine; for adults "usually over 40; witty intelligent, no cartoons." Biweekly. Circ. 770,000. Does not accept previously published material "except stock material." Original artwork returned after publication. Sample copies available. Art guidelines not available.
Illustrations: Approached by 100 illustrators/year. Buys 5-6 illustrations/issue, 200 illustrations/year from freelancers. Works on assignment only. Prefers witty, intelligent, not too avant-garde. Considers pen & ink, airbrush, watercolor, acrylic and oil; "it doesn't really matter if it's well done." Send query letter with photocopies. Samples are filed "if they're interesting; otherwise they are discarded" or returned by SASE if requested. Reports back within 2 weeks only if interested. If does not report back, "forget it or wait until we have an assignment. Generally, we don't report back unless we have an assignment." Call to schedule an appointment to show a portfolio, which should include thumbnails, original/final art, tearsheets and slides. Buys one-time rights. Pays $1,700, b&w, $2,000, color, cover; $400, b&w, $450, color, inside; on acceptance.
Tips: "We recommend sending samples a few times only. Call Roger Zapke, Deputy Art Director for portfolio reviews. Also look at the masthead. There are a total of 4 associates who make the assignments. The artist should at least know the names and titles of those they wish to contact."

FOREIGN SERVICE JOURNAL, 2101 E St. NW, Washington DC 20037. (202)338-4045. Contact: Managing Editor. Estab. 1924. Emphasizes foreign policy for foreign service employees. Monthly. Circ. 11,000. Accepts previously published material. Returns original artwork after publication.
Cartoons: Buys 6 cartoons/year from freelancers. Write or call for appointment to show portfolio. Buys first rights. Pays $100 and up, b&w; on publication.
Illustrations: Works with 6-10 illustrators/year. Buys 20 illustrations/year from freelancers. Uses artists mainly for covers and article illustration. Works on assignment only. Write or call for appointment to show portfolio. Buys first rights. Pays $100 and up, b&w, cover; $100 and up, b&w, inside; on publication.
Tips: Portfolio should include "political cartoons and conceptual ideas/themes."

*FOUNDATION NEWS, 1828 L St. NW, Washington DC 20036. (202)466-6512. Associate Editor: Jody Curtis. Estab. 1959. Nonprofit association magazine which "covers news and trends in the nonprofit sector, with an emphasis on foundation grantmaking and grant-funded projects." Bimonthly. Circ. 15,000. Accepts previously

FOREIGN SERVICE JOURNAL

Are
Diplomats
Patriotic?
by David D. Newsom

Short-order
Intelligence
by Frank McNeil

Plus:
Farewell Interview with
George P. Shultz

Freelance illustrator Ruth Sofair Ketler created this cover illustration for Foreign Service Journal in pen and ink, watercolor and india ink. Working with a two-week deadline, she needed to convey the idea that "diplomats were torn in a balancing act between U.S. needs and the needs of the country in which they were serving." Ketler says she was able to "use this image later in a promotional piece and get subsequent work from it." She was paid $300 for the illustration.

© 1989 Ruth Sofair Ketler

published artwork. Original artwork returned after publication. Sample copy available. Art guidelines not available.

Cartoons: Approached by 3 cartoonists/year. Buys 3 cartoons/year from freelancers. Prefers single panel; b&w line drawings. Send query letter with brochure, finished cartoons and other samples. Samples are filed "if good"; otherwise returned by SASE if requested. Reports back within weeks. Buys one-time rights. Pays $100, b&w, minimum; $300, color, minimum.

Illustrations: Approached by 10 freelance illustrators/year. Buys 3 illustrations/issue, 18 illustrations/year from freelancers. Considers pen & ink, line drawings and charcoal. Send query letter with tearsheets, photostats, slides and photocopies. Samples are filed "if good"; otherwise returned by SASE if requested. Reports back in weeks. Call or write to schedule an appointment to show a portfolio, which should include thumbnails, roughs and b&w and color tearsheets, photostats, photographs, slides and photocopies. Buys first rights. Pays $750, color, cover; $250, b&w; on acceptance.

FUTURIFIC MAGAZINE, Suite 1210, 280 Madison Ave., New York NY 10016. Publisher: B. Szent-Miklosy. Emphasizes future-related subjects for highly educated, upper income government, corporate leaders of the community. Monthly. Circ. 10,000. Previously published material and simultaneous submissions OK. Original artwork returned after publication. Free sample copy for SASE with $3 postage and handling.

Cartoons: Buys 5 cartoons/year from freelancers. Prefers positive, upbeat, futuristic themes; no "doom and gloom." Prefers single, double or multiple-panel with or without gagline, b&w line drawings. Send finished cartoons. Samples returned by SASE. Reports within 4 weeks. Will negotiate rights and payment. Pays on publication.

Illustrations: Buys 5 illustrations/issue from freelancers. Prefers positive, upbeat, futuristic themes; no "doom and gloom." Send finished art. Samples returned by SASE. Reports within 4 weeks. Walk in to show a portfolio. Negotiates rights and payment. Pays on publication.

Tips: "Only optimists need apply. Looking for good, clean art. Interested in future development of current affairs, but not sci-fi."

THE FUTURIST, 4916 St. Elmo Ave., Bethesda MD 20814. (301)598-6414. Art Director: Cynthia Fowler. Managing Editor: Timothy H. Willard. Emphasizes all aspects of the future for a well-educated, general audience. Bimonthly. Circ. 30,000. Accepts simultaneous submissions. Return of original artwork following publication depends on individual agreement.

Cartoons: Approached by 1-2 cartoonists/year. Pays $125, b&w; $175, color.

Illustrations: Approached by 5-10 freelance illustrators/year. Buys 3-4 illustrations/issue from freelancers. Uses a variety of themes and styles "usually line drawings, often whimsical. We like an artist who can read an article and deal with the concepts and ideas." Works on assignment only. Send query letter with brochure, samples or tearsheets to be kept on file. Call or write for appointment to show portfolio. "Photostats are fine as samples; whatever is easy for the artist." Reports only if interested. Rights purchased negotiable. Pays $500, color, cover; $125, b&w, $300, color, inside; on acceptance.

Tips: "When a sample package is poorly organized, poorly presented—it says a lot about how the artists feel about their work." Sees trend toward "moving away from realism; highly stylized illustration with more color."

GALLERY MAGAZINE, 401 Park Ave., South, New York NY 10016. Creative Director: Michael Monte. Emphasizes sophisticated men's entertainment for the middle-class, collegiate male. Monthly. Circ. 375,000.
Cartoons: Approached by 100 cartoonists/year. Buys 3-8 cartoons/issue from freelancers. Interested in sexy humor; single, double, or multiple panel with or without gagline, color and b&w washes, b&w line drawings. Send finished cartoons. Reports in 1 month. Buys first rights. Pays $70, b&w, $100, color; on publication. Enclose SASE. Contact: J. Linden.
Illustrations: Approached by 300 illustrators/year. Buys 60 illustrations/year from freelancers. Works on assignment only. Interested in the "highest creative and technical styles." Especially needs slick, high quality, 4-color work. Send flyer, samples and tearsheets to be kept on file for possible future assignments. Send samples of style or submit portfolio. Prefers prints over transparencies. Samples returned by SASE. Reports in several weeks. Negotiates rights purchased. Pays $800-1,500, inside color washes; on publication.
Tips: A common mistake freelancers make is that "often there are too many samples of literal translations of the subject. There should also be some conceptual pieces."

GAME & FISH PUBLICATIONS, 2250 Newmarket Parkway, Marietta GA 30067. (404)953-9222. Graphic Artist: Allen Hansen. Estab. 1975. Consumer magazine. Monthly. Circ. 400,000 for 34 state-specific magazines. Original artwork is returned after publication. Sample copies available. Uses freelancers mainly for spot illustrations and leads for feature articles.
Illustrations: Approached by 50 illustrators/year. Buys illustrations mainly for spots and feature spreads. Buys 1-8 illustrations/issue, 30-60 illustrations/year from freelancers. Considers pen & ink, watercolor, acrylic and oil. Send query letter with photostats and photocopies. "We look for an artist's ability to realistically depict North American game animals and game fish." Samples are filed or returned only if requested. Reports back only if interested. Buys first rights. Pays $25 and up, b&w, $75-100, color, inside; 2½ months prior to publication.
Tips: "We prefer that illustrators send a few samples of their work, particularly pieces that depict wild game or fish, or hunting and fishing scenes. If we think a particular artist is well-suited for a certain illustration need, we'll assign it." Does not want to see cartoons.

*GAMES, 810 Seventh Ave., New York NY 10019. (212)246-4640. Contact: Art Director. Emphasizes games, puzzles, mazes, brain teasers, etc. for adults interested in pop culture trivia and pencil games. Bimonthly. Circ. 600,000.
Cartoons: Approached by 300 cartoonists/year. Buys 1 cartoon/issue from freelancers. Pays $100 b&w and $200 color.
Illustrations: Approached by 500 illustrators/year. Buys 5-15 illustrations/issue from freelancers. Illustrations should be lighthearted but not childish. Send query letter with brochure showing art style or tearsheets. Buys one-time rights. Pays $300 b&w; $1,500 color, inside.
Tips: "We encourage artists to *create games or puzzles* that they can execute in their own style after editorial approval. Illustrations are often required to be based on specific puzzles but can also be conceptual in nature."

*GBH, THE MEMBERS' MAGAZINE, 420 Boylston St., Boston MA 02116-4000. (617)424-7700. FAX: (617)437-8424. Art Director: Linda Koury. Estab. 1987. Consumer magazine for Channel 2 members in Boston; contains feature articles, departments and members perks and listings." Monthly. Circ. 180,000. Accepts previously published artwork. Original artwork returned after publication. Sample copy available. Art guidelines not available.
Illustrations: Approached by freelance 100 illustrators/year. Buys 4 illustrations/issue, 50 illustrations/year from freelancers. Works on assignment only. "Themes are all editorially related." Considers pen & ink, airbrush, acrylic, collage, oil and mixed media. Send query letter with tearsheets and slides. Samples are filed or are returned. Reports back within 1 week. To show a portfolio, call or mail appropriate materials. Portfolio should include original/final art and color tearsheets, photographs and slides. Rights purchased vary according to project. Pays $750, color, cover; $100, b&w, $250, color, inside; on acceptance.
Tips: "Send samples or promo pieces, then follow up with a phone call a few days later. We're always looking for new illustrators."

*GENERAL LEARNING CORPORATION, 60 Revere Dr., Northbrook IL 60062-1563. (312)564-4070. Photo and Graphics Editor: Terese Noto. Produces *Current Health 1, Current Health 2, Career World, Writing!* and *Current Consumer & Lifestudies* published monthly during the school year. Readership is 7-12th grade students. *Your Health & Fitness* is published bimonthly, *Health Reports* are quarterly. The readership is a general audience. Accepts previously published material. Original artwork returned after publication. Sample copy for 8×10 SASE. *Your Health & Fitness* magazine uses 4-color art plus photos. School magazines use b&w photos only.

Cartoons: Approached by 12 cartoonists/year. Pays $200, b&w; $400, color.

Illustrations: Occasionally commissions original illustration. Prefers pen & ink, airbrush, watercolor, acrylic, oil, pastel, collage, marker, mixed media and computer illustration. Medical illustrator sought. Wants to see "healthy looking people—lots of exercising pieces, medical photos and/or illustrations." Pays $200, b&w, $800, color, cover; $200, b&w, $400, color, inside; on publication. Negotiates rights purchased and payment for general magazines; on acceptance.

Tips: "Target your samples around medical illustration or on the topic of safe exercising. I do not want to see fashion pieces or anything sexy."

*GENT, Dugent Publishing Corp., 2355 Salzedo St., Coral Gables FL 33134. Publisher: Douglas Allen. Editor: Bruce Arthur. Managing Editor: Nye Willden. For men "who like big-breasted women." Sample copy $3.

Cartoons: Buys humor and sexual themes; "major emphasis of magazine is on large D-cup-breasted women. We prefer cartoons that reflect this slant." Mail cartoons. Buys first rights. Pays $50, b&w spot drawing; $100, page.

Illustrations: Buys 3-4 illustrations/issue from freelancers on assigned themes. Submit illustration samples for files. Portfolio should include "b&w and color, with nudes/anatomy." Buys first rights. Pays $125-150, b&w; $200, color.

Tips: "Send samples designed especially for our publication. Study our magazine. Be able to draw erotic anatomy. Write for artist's guides and cartoon guides *first*, before submitting samples, since they contain some helpful suggestions."

*GLASS FACTORY DIRECTORY, Box 7138, Pittsbrugh PA 15213. (412)362-5136. Manager: Liz Scott. Lists glass manufacturers in U.S., Canada and Mexico. Annual.

Cartoons: Buys 5-10 cartoon/issue from freelancers. Receives an average of 1 submisson/week from freelancers. Cartoons should pertain to glass manufacturing (flat glass, fiberglass, bottles and containers; no mirrors). Prefers single and multiple panel b&w line drawings with gagline. Prefers roughs or finished cartoons. Send SASE. Reports in 1-3 months. Buys all rights. Pays $25; on acceptance.

Tips: "Learn about making glass of all kinds."

*GLENFED TODAY, 700 N. Brand Blvd., 11th floor, Box 1709, Glendale CA 91209. (818)500-2732. Editor-in-Chief: Charles Coleman. Emphasizes the savings and loan industry and company events for employees of Glendale Federal. Monthly. Circ. 8,000.

Illustrations: Buys 1 illustration/issue from freelancers. Interested in conservative themes. No anti-establishment themes. Prefers conceptual art addressing serious subjects. Prefers pen & ink, airbrush, charcoal/pencil and computer illustration. Works on assignment only; reports back on whether to expect possible future assignments. Send query letter "that we can keep. Do not phone. Do not send unsolicited photos. We cannot return them." Reporting time "depends on work load." Buys all rights. Negotiates pay; pays on publication.

Tips: "We are becoming comprehensive family financial centers with a housing orientation. Changes within our operation include the introduction of interest-bearing checking accounts, credit cards, etc. Freelance artists should be sure to query first and send SASE. We prefer to deal with local artists as we do not usually buy pre-made art. We usually conceptualize and hire an artist to meet our needs. Close locations allows for quick and easy revision."

GOLF ILLUSTRATED, 3 Park Ave., New York NY 10016. (212)340-4803. Art Director: Ellen Oxild. Estab. 1914. "First full-service golf magazine. It helps readers improve their game and stay on top of events on the pro tour. Also additional coverage of travel, fitness and fashion." Published 10 times a year. Circ. 450,000. Original artwork is usually returned to the artist after publication. Sample copies free for SASE with first-class postage.

Cartoons: Buys 5-10 cartoons/year from freelancers. Prefers "not your typical golf cartoon." Prefers single or double b&w panel with gagline. Send query letter with finished cartoons. Samples are filed or are returned by SASE. Returns unusable cartoons within 2 weeks. Does not report back on kept cartoons until used. Buys first rights. Pays $50, b&w.

Illustrations: Buys 5-10 illustrations/issue from freelancers. Works on assignment only. Send query letter with samples. Call or write to schedule an appointment to show a portfolio, which should include color and b&w tearsheets or final reproduction/product. Buys first rights. Pays $300 and up, b&w; $400 and up, color, inside; on publication.

Tips: "Send tearsheets of current work. Color and black-and-white samples should have client's name present. Send samples that are the same size."

GOLF JOURNAL, Golf House, Far Hills NJ 07931. (201)234-2300. Managing Editor: George Eberl. Readers are "literate, professional, knowledgeable on the subject of golf." Published 8 times/year. Circ. 251,000. Original artwork not returned after publication. Free sample copy.

Cartoons: Approached by 50-60 cartoonists/year. Buys 2-3 cartoons/issue, 20 cartoons/year from freelancers. Receives 50 submissions/week from freelancers. "The subject is golf. Golf must be central to the cartoon. Drawings should be professional, and captions sharp, bright and literate, on a par with our generally sophisticated readership." Formats: single or multiple panel, b&w line drawings with gagline. Prefers to see finished cartoons. Send SASE. Reports in 1 month. Buys one-time rights. Pays $25-50, b&w cartoons; on acceptance.

Illustrations: Approached by 20 illustrators/year. Buys several illustrations/issue from freelancers. "We maintain a file of samples from illustrators. Our needs for illustrations — and we do need talent with an artistic light touch — are based almost solely on assignments, illustrations to accompany specific stories. We would assign a job to an illustrator who is able to capture the feel and mood of a story. Most frequently, they are light-touch golf stories that beg illustrations. A sense of humor is a useful quality in the illustrator, but this sense shouldn't lapse into absurdity." Uses color washes. Send samples of style to be kept on file for future assignments and SASE. Reports in 1 month. Buys all rights on a work-for-hire basis. Payment varies, "usually $300/page, $500, color, cover."

Tips: "We often need illustrations supporting a story." Wants to see "a light touch, identifiable, relevant; rather than nitwit stuff showing golfballs talking to each other." Does not want to see "willy-nilly submissions of everything from caricatures of past presidents to meaningless art you'd be embarrassed to hang on your laundryroom wall. They should know their market; we're a golf publication, not an art gazette."

GOOD OLD DAYS, 306 E. Parr Rd., Berne IN 46711. (219)589-8741. Editor: Rebekah Montgomery. Estab. 1964. Literary magazine covering American oral history 1900-1949. Monthly. Circ. 125,000. Accepts previously published artwork. Original artwork is sometimes returned after publication. Sample copies available for $2. Art guidelines not available.

Cartoons: Buys 1 or more cartoons/issue, 12 or more cartoons/year from freelancers. Prefers nostalgic themes. Prefers single panel or double panel with or without gagline; b&w line drawings. Send finished cartoons. Samples are filed. Reports back regarding queries/submissions within 14 days. Buys first rights, one-time or all rights. Pays $15-75, b&w; on publication.

Illustration: Buys illustrations mainly for covers, spots and feature spreads. Buys 4 illustrations/issue, 45 illustrations/year from freelancers. Works on assignment only. Prefers pen & ink. Considers mixed media, watercolor, acrylic, oil and pastel. Send query letter with photostats, photocopies, photographs and transparencies. Looks for realism and authenticity in subject matter. Reports back about queries/submissions within 14 days. Call or write to schedule an appointment to show a portfolio which should include color and b&w original/final art, tearsheets, slides, photostats and transparencies. Buys first rights, one-time rights, reprint rights or all rights. Will negotiate rights purchased. Pays $500-800, color, cover; $35-75, b&w, inside; on publication.

Tips: "Show realistic, historically accurate portrayals. I do not want to see cartoony drawings."

*GOOD READING MAGAZINE, Box 40, Litchfield IL 62056. (217)324-3425. "Nonfiction magazine which emphasizes travel, business, human interest and novel occupations." Monthly. Circ. 8,000. Original artwork returned after publication, only if requested.

Cartoons: Approached by 200 cartoonists/year. Buys 1 cartoon/issue from freelancers. Receives 10 submissions/week from freelancers. Interested in "business, points of interest, people with unusual hobbies and occupations and wholesome humor." Prefers to see finished cartoons; black & white only. Send SASE. Reports in 6-8 weeks. To show a portfolio, mail original/final art. Buys first North American serial rights. Pays $20 b&w; on acceptance.

GOURMET, Conde Nast Publications, Inc., 560 Lexington Ave., New York NY 10022. (212)371-1330. Art Director: Irwin Glusker. Magazine "for those interested in all aspects of good living, preparation of food, wine, dining out and travel." Monthly. Circ. 700,000. Sample copies $2.50 and SASE.

Cartoons: Buys one-time rights. Pays $300, b&w.

Illustrations: "Larger issues include work from 15 artists. We are open to new artists, especially for black-and-white work." Columns are illustrated by regular freelancers, but restaurants in other cities are sometimes featured, and those areas' local artists are generally used. Send query letter with photocopies and SASE. Samples are filed. Reports "as soon as possible." Buys one-time rights. Pays $200-400, b&w.

*GRAPHIC ARTS MONTHLY, 249 W. 17th St., New York NY 10011. (212)463-6834. Editor: Roger Ynostroza. Managing Editor: Michael Karol. For management and production personnel in commercial and specialty printing plants and allied crafts. Monthly. Circ. 94,000. Sample copy $10.

Cartoons: Approached by 25 cartoonists/year. Buys 15 cartoons/year from freelancers on printing, layout, paste-up, typesetting and proofreading; single panel. Mail art. Send SASE. Reports in 3 weeks. Buys first rights. Pays on acceptance.

Illustrations: Approached by 120 illustrators/year. Pays $125-1,200, cover. Portfolio should include good, recent work. Also any printed cards to keep for our files.

*GRAPHIC STORY MONTHLY, (formerly Prime Cuts), 7563 Lake City Way, Seattle WA 98115. (206)524-1967. FAX: (206)524-2104. Editor: Gary Groth. Art Director: Dale Yarger. A comic magazine aimed at thinking adults and devoted to "the work of the new breed of sophisticated comic artists. Any and all subjects considered (drama, humor, satire, etc.)." Stories consist of 1-10 b&w pages. Circ. 10,000. Sample copy $3.50.
Illustrations: Send query letter with samples. Buys one-time North American rights. "Creator retains copyright." Pays $30/page; on publication.

*GRAY'S SPORTING JOURNAL, On The Common, Box 130, Lyme NH 03768. (603)795-4757. Editor: Ed Gray. Art Director: DeCourcy Taylor. Concerns the outdoors, hunting and fishing. Published 6 times/year. Circ. 35,000. Sample copy $6.95; artist's guidelines for SASE.
Illustrations: Buys 2-6 illustrations/issue, 10 illustrations/year from freelancers on hunting and fishing. Send query letter with tearsheets, slides and SASE. Reports in 4 weeks. To show a portfolio, mail tearsheets and photographs. Buys one-time rights. Pays $350, color art; $75-200, b&w line drawings, inside.
Tips: "Will definitely not accept unsolicited original art."

GREEN FEATHER MAGAZINE, Box 770604, Lakewood OH 44107. Editor: Gary S. Skeens. Emphasizes fiction and poetry for general audience. Published 4 times a year (March, June, September, December). Circ. 150-200. Accepts previously published material. Original artwork returned after publication. Sample copy $1.50; art guidelines for SASE.
Cartoons: Buys 1 cartoon/issue from freelancers. Prefers single panel with gagline; b&w line drawings. Send query letter with samples of style to be kept on file. Material not filed is returned by SASE. Reports in 1 month. Buys first rights or reprint rights. Negotiates payment, $5 maximum; on publication.
Illustrations: Buys 1 illustration/issue from freelancers. Send query letter with resume, tearsheets or photocopies to be kept on file. Samples not filed are returned by SASE. Reports within 1 month. To show a portfolio, mail b&w tearsheets. Buys first rights or reprint rights. Negotiates payment. Pays on publication.

GROUP PUBLISHING, 2890 N. Monroe, Loveland CO 80538. (303)669-3836. Senior Art Director: Jean Bruns. Publishes *Group Magazine* (8 issues/year; circ. 62,000) and *Group's Jr. High Ministry Magazine* (5 issues/year) for adult leaders of Christian youth groups and *Parents & Teenagers Magazine* (bimonthly) for families with teenagers. Also books for adults and teenagers (many with cover and interior illustration), clip-art resources, audiovisual material and printed marketing material. Previously published, photocopied and simultaneous submissions OK. Original artwork returned after publication, if requested. Sample copy $1.
Cartoons: Occasionally uses spot cartoons in publications.
Illustrations: Buys 2-5 illustrations/issue from freelancers. Prefers a loose, lighthearted pen & ink and/or color style. Send query letter with brochure showing art style or samples to be kept on file for future assignments. Reports only if interested. To show a portfolio, mail, color and b&w photostats and slides. Cover: Pays $350 minimum, color (negotiable). Pays $25-400, b&w/spot illustrations (line drawings and washes) to full-page color illustrations, inside; on acceptance. Buys first publication rights and sometimes reprint rights.
Tips: "We seek black-and-white illustrations of a serious, more conceptual nature as well as humorous illustrations in styles appropriate to our Christian adult and teenage audience (mature and contemporary, not childish). We look for evidence of maturity and a well-developed style in the illustrator. We are also attracted to good, artistically-sound renderings, particularly of people and the ability to conceptualize well and approach subjects in an unusual way. We do not want to see amateurish work nor work that is crude, gross, deliberately offensive, or puts down any ethnic or religious group. We want to see work that shows thought, care, good technique and craftsmanship."

*GTE DISCOVERY PUBLICATIONS, INC., Box 3007, Bothell WA 98118. (206)487-6172. Creative Director: Kate Thompson. Consumer magazines; "annual state tourism magazines for various areas throughout the nation including the Pacific NW, Alaska, California, Hawaii, and Massachussetts." Annual combined circ. 2 million. Accepts previously published artwork. Original artwork returned after publication. Sample copies available. Art guidelines not available.
Illustrations: Approached by 8-10 illustrators/year. Buys 10 illustrations/year from freelancers. Works on assignment only. Considers pen & ink, airbrush, acrylic, collage, color pencil and computer generated art. Send query letter with brochure, tearsheets and resume. Samples are filed. Reports back only if interested. Mail appropriate materials: original/final art, b&w tearsheets, slides and photocopies. Rights purchased vary according to project. Pays on acceptance.

GULFSHORE LIFE MAGAZINE, Suite 800, 2975 S. Horseshoe Dr., Naples FL 33942. (813)643-3933. Creative Director: Mark May. Estab. 1970. "Consumer magazine emphasizing lifestyle of southwest Florida for an affluent, sophisticated audience." Monthly. Circ. 20,000. Accepts previously published material. Original artwork returned after publication. Sample copy $3.
Cartoons: Approached by 4 cartoonists/year. Buys 1 cartoon/issue, 10 cartoons/year from freelancers. Prefers pen & ink. Send query letter with brochure, finished cartoons and tearsheets. Samples are filed. Reports back to the artist only if interested. Buys one-time rights "usually." Rights purchased vary according to project. Pays $75, b&w.

Illustrations: Approached by 15-20 freelance illustrators/year. Buys 1 illustration/issue from freelancers. Prefers watercolor, collage, airbrush, acrylic, colored pencil, mixed media and pastel. Send query letter with brochure, resume, tearsheets, photostats and photocopies. Samples not filed are returned by SASE. Reports back only if interested. Write to schedule appointment to show a portfolio, which should include thumbnails, original/final art, final/reproduction/product and tearsheets. Negotiates rights purchased. Buys one-time rights. Pays $50-2,000, color, inside and cover; on publication.

*GUN WORLD, Box HH, Capistrano Beach CA 92624. Contact: Managing Editor. For shooters and hunters. Monthly. Circ. 136,000. Mail art. SASE. Reports in 8 weeks. Buys all rights, but may reassign rights to artist after publication. Pays on acceptance.
Cartoons: Approached by 30-40 cartoonists/year. Buys 3-4 cartoons/issue from freelancers on shooting and hunting. Pays $10-15, halftones.
Illustrations: Buys assigned themes.
Tips: Do not want to see "any anti-gun or anti-hunting stuff."

*HARVARD MAGAZINE, 7 Ware St., Cambridge MA 02138. Managing Editor: Christopher Reed. Estab. 1898. General interest university magazine "mining the resources of a great university, aiming to bring the world of ideas to thoughtful readers." Bimonthly. Circ. 150,000. Original artwork returned after publication. Sample copy available. Art guidelines not available.
Illustrations: Approached by 30 freelance illustrators/year. Buys 4 illustrations/issue, 24 illustrations/year from freelancers. Works on assignment only. Send query letter with tearsheets, photostats, photographs, photocopies. Samples are filed. Does not report back, in which case artist should "do nothing except be patient." To show a portfolio, call or mail appropriate materials. Buys first rights or one-time rights. Pays $350, color, cover; $75, b&w, $125, color, inside; on acceptance.

HAWAII – Gateway to the Pacific, Box 6050, Mision Viejo CA 92690. (714)855-8822. Editor: Dennis Shattuck. Estab. 1984. Consumer magazine "written for and directed to the frequent visitor to the Hawaiian Islands. We try to encourage people to discover the vast natural beauty of these Islands." Bimonthly. Circ. 50,000. Original artwork is returned after publication. Sample copies $3.95. Art guidelines not available.
Cartoons: Prefer single panel with gagline; b&w line drawings. Send query letter with finished cartoons. Samples not filed are returned. Reports back within 3 weeks. Buys first rights. Pays $35, b&w; $50, color; on publication.
Illustrations: Buys illustrations mainly for spots and feature spreads. Buys 1-2 illustrations/issue, 6 illustrations/year from freelancers. Works on assignment only. Considers pen & ink, airbrush, watercolor, acrylic, oil, charcoal pencil and calligraphy. Send query letter with photocopies. Samples are not filed and are returned. Reports back about queries/submissions within 4 weeks. To show a portfolio mail original/final art and tearsheets. Buys first rights. Pays $75, b&w; $150, color, inside.

HEALTH EDUCATION, 1900 Association Dr., Reston VA 22091. Editor: Patricia Steffan. Estab. 1970. "For school and community health professionals, keeping them up-to-date on issues, trends, teaching methods, and curriculum developments in health." Bimonthly. Circ. 10,000. Original artwork is returned to the artist after publication if requested. Sample copies available. Art guidelines not available.
Illustrations: Approached by 15 illustrators/year. Works with 6 illustrators/year. Buys 6 illustrations/year from freelancers. Uses artists mainly for covers. Wants health-related topics, any style. Prefers watercolor, pen & ink, airbrush, acrylic, oil and computer illustration. Works on assignment only. Send query letter with brochure showing art style or photostats, photocopies, slides or photographs. Samples are filed or are returned by SASE. Reports back within weeks only if interested. Write to schedule an appointment to show a portfolio, which should include color and b&w thumbnails, roughs, original/final art, photostats, photographs and slides. Negotiates rights purchased. Pays $45, b&w; $250-500, color, cover; on acceptance.

*HEALTH WORLD, 1477 Rollins, Burlingame CA 94010. (415)343-1637. FAX: (415)343-0503. President: Kumar Pati. Estab. 1986. Magazine emphasizing health and nutrition. *"Health World* is an open forum for discussion of a wide variety of health sciences, news, and health products available around the world." Bimonthly. Circ. 80,000. Accepts previously published material. Original artwork is returned to the artist after publication. Samples copies $2.50. Art guidelines available.
Cartoons: Prefers b&w line drawings and b&w and color washes. Send samples of style. Samples not filed are returned. Pay is negotiable.
Illustrations: Works on assignment only. Send query letter with brochure or tearsheets, photocopies and photographs. Call or write to schedule an appointment to show a portfolio. "Bill proper invoice." Pays on publication.

*HEARTLAND JOURNAL, by Older Writers for Readers of all Ages, Box 55115, Madison WI 53705. (608)524-4557. Art Editor: Shirley Groy. Literary magazine. "Our objective is to provide an opportunity for publishing quality articles, stories, poetry and visual arts created by people over 60. Our content is varied and we aim at a wide audience." Quarterly. Circ. 2,000. Accepts previously published artwork. Original artwork returned to the artist at the job's completion with SASE. Sample copy $4 with $1 postage. Art guidelines not available.

Illustrations: "We prefer fairly representational work." Prefers pen & ink, collage, marker and charcoal; "we are willing to consider a wide variety of media." Send query letter with photographs, slides, SASE and photocopies. Samples are filed or are returned by SASE if requested by artist. Reports back within weeks. Mail appropriate materials: b&w and color slides, photostats, photographs and photocopies. Buys one-time rights.

Tips: "We are interested in a wide variety of visual work both in subject matter and media. Submissions must be made by people over 60. Looking at an issue of the *Journal* is the best way to understand what we are interested in."

HEAVEN BONE, Box 486, Chester NY 10918. (914)469-9018. Editor: Steve Hirsch. Estab. 1987. Literary magazine emphasizing poetry, fiction, essays reflecting spiritual/mystical and transformational concerns. Bi-annual. Circ. 500. Accepts previously published artwork. Original artwork is returned after publication if requested. Sample copies $4.50. Art guidelines free for SASE with first-class postage.

Cartoons: Approached by 2-3 cartoonists/year. We have never used any cartoons but we will consider. Pays 2 copies of magazine, b&w.

Illustrations: Approached by 5-7 illustrators/year. Buys illustrations mainly for covers and feature spreads. Buys 2-7 illustrations/issue, 4-14 illustrations/year from freelancers. Considers pen & ink, mixed media, watercolor, acrylic, oil, pastel, collage, markers, charcoal, pencil and calligraphy. Send query letter with brochure showing art style, tearsheets, photostats, photocopies and photographs. Samples should be esoteric, spiritual, Buddhist/Hindu and expansive. Samples are not filed and are returned by SASE. Reports back about queries/submissions within 3 months. To show a portfolio, mail b&w tearsheets, slides, photostats and photographs. Buys first rights. Pays 2 copies of magazine, b&w.

Tips: "Please see sample issue before sending unsolicited portfolio."

*THE HERB QUARTERLY, Box 548, Boiling Springs PA 17007. (717)245-2764. Editor and Publisher: Linda Sparrowe. Magazine emphasizing horticulture for middle to upper class men and women with an ardent enthusiasm for herbs and all their uses—gardening, culinary, crafts, etc. Most are probably home owners. Quarterly. Circ. 30,000. Accepts previously published material. Original artwork returned after publication if requested. Sample copy $5.

Illustrations: Prefers pen & ink illustrations, heavily contrasted. Illustrations of herbs, garden designs, etc. Artist should be able to create illustrations drawn from themes of manuscripts sent to them. Send query letter with brochure showing art style or resume, tearsheets, photocopies, slides and photographs. Samples not filed are returned by SASE only if requested. Reports within weeks. To show a portfolio, mail original/final art, final reproduction/product or b&w photographs. Buys reprint rights. Pays $200, full page; $100, half page; $50, quarter page and spots; on publication.

HIBISCUS MAGAZINE, Box 22248, Sacramento CA 95822. Editor: Margaret Wensrich. Estab. 1985. Magazine for "people who like to read poetry and short stories." Published three times/year. Circ. 2,000. Original artwork returned after publication if requested. Sample copy $4; art guidelines for SASE with first class postage for 3 ounces.

Cartoons: Uses all subjects. Pays $3 on acceptance.

Illustrations: Buys 3-4 illustrations/issue from freelancers. Uses freelance artists mainly for story illustrations. Works on assignment only. Send query letter with resume and samples. Samples not filed are returned by SASE. Reports back only if interested. To show a portfolio, mail original/final art or photocopy of finished work. "We use pen & ink drawings only. No color, slides, etc." Buys first rights. Pays for design and illustration by the project, $20; on acceptance.

Tips: "We need clean pen & ink or pencil that can be reproduced exactly by printer. We can tell from 4 to 6 samples if artist is appropriate for us. Subjects are assigned. The portfolio gives us an idea of artist's work."

HIGHLIGHTS FOR CHILDREN, 803 Church St., Honesdale PA 18431. (717)253-1080. Art Director: Rosanne Guararra. Cartoon Editor: Kent Brown. For ages 2-12. Monthly, bimonthly in July/August. Circ. 2,300,000.

Cartoons: Buys 2-4 cartoons/issue from freelancers. Receives 20 submissions/week from freelancers. Interested in upbeat, positive cartoons involving children, family life or animals; single or multiple panel. Send roughs or finished cartoons and SASE. Reports in 4-6 weeks. Buys all rights. Pays $20-40, line drawings; on acceptance. "One flaw in many submissions is that the concept or vocabulary is too adult, or that the experience necessary for its appreciation is beyond our readers. Frequently, a wordless self-explanatory cartoon is best."

Illustrations: Uses 30 illustrations/issue; buys 25 from freelancers. Works with freelancers on assignment only. "We are always looking for good hidden pictures. We require a picture that is interesting in itself and has the objects well hidden. Usually an artist submits pencil sketches. In no case do we pay for any preliminaries to the final hidden prictures." Also needs "original ideas and illustrations for covers and 'What's Wrong'

illustrations for back cover. Prefers "realistic and stylized work, very little cartoon." Prefers pen & ink, colored pencil, watercolor, marker and mixed media. Send samples of style and flyer to be kept on file. Send SASE. Reports in 4-6 weeks. Buys all rights on a work-for-hire basis. Pays on acceptance.
Tips: "I want to see if and how an illustrator can draw people, especially children. We have a wide variety of needs, so I would prefer to see a representative sample of an illustrator's style or styles."

*HISTORIC PRESERVATION MAGAZINE, 1785 Massachusetts Ave. NW, Washington DC 20036. (202)673-4042. FAX: (202)673-4172. Art Director: Jeff Roth. Estab. 1952. Association magazine; "a benefit of membership in the National Trust for Historic Preservation." Bimonthly. Circ. 225,000. Original artwork returned after publication. Sample copies available for $2 plus SASE. Art guidelines not available.
Illustrations: Approached by more than 100 illustrators/year. Buys 1-3 illustrations/issue, 6-18 illustrations/year from freelancers. Works on assignment only. Considers all media. Send query letter with brochure, tearsheets and photostats. Samples are filed. Reports back to the artist only if interested. Mail appropriate materials: thumbnails, tearsheets, slides, roughs and photographs. Buys one-time rights. Pays $200, b&w, $300, color, cover. Pays $100, b&w, $150, color, inside; on acceptance.
Tips: "Do not show us a variety of styles or techniques; show us the style or technique that you do best."

*HOME & CONDO, Suite 800, 2975 S. Horseshoe Dr., Naples FL 33942. (813)643-3933. FAX: (813)953-9899. Art Director: Susan Donolo. Estab. 1980. Consumer magazine; "a homebuyers guide to Gulf Coast living." Monthly. Circ. 2,500. Accepts previously published artwork. Original artwork is returned at the job's completion. Sample copies $2.50. Art guidelines free for SASE with first class postage.
Illustrations: Buys 1 illustration/issue, 10 illustrations/year from freelancers. Works on assignment only. Considers pen & ink, colored pencil, watercolor and marker. Send query letter with brochure, tearsheets, photostats, resume, photocopies and transparencies. Samples are filed. Reports back to the artist only if interested. Call to schedule an appointment to show a portfolio. Portfolio should include original/final art and tearsheets. Buys one-time rights. Pays on publication.

HOME EDUCATION MAGAZINE, Box 1083, Tonasket WA 98855. (509)486-1351. Managing Editor: Helen Hegener. Estab. 1983. "We publish one of the largest magazines available for home schooling families." Bimonthly. Circ. 5,500. Accepts previously published artwork. Original artwork is returned after publication upon request. Sample copy $4.50. Art guidelines free for SASE with first-class postage.
Cartoons: Approached by 10-15 cartoonists/year. Buys 2-4 cartoons/issue, 12-24 cartoons/year from freelancers. Style preferred is open, but theme must relate to home schooling. Prefers single, double or multiple panel with or without gagline; b&w line drawings and washes. Send query letter with samples of style, roughs and finished cartoons "any format is fine with us." Samples are filed or are returned by SASE if requested. Reports back regarding queries/submissions within 10 days. Buys reprint rights, one-time rights or negotiates rights purchased. Pays $5-10, b&w; on acceptance.
Illustration: Approached by 20-30 illustrators/year. Buys illustrations mainly for cover, spots and feature spreads. Buys 12-20 illustrations/issue. Buys 150-200 illustrations/year from freelancers. Works with 4-6 illustrators/year. Consider pen & ink, mixed media, markers, charcoal pencil or any good sharp black & white or color media. Send query letter with tearsheets, photocopies or photographs. "We're looking for originality, clarity, warmth, children, families, and parent-child situations are what we need." Samples are filed or are returned by SASE if requested. Reports back about queries/submissions within 10 days. Call or write to schedule an appointment to show a portfolio or mail appropriate materials, which should include tearsheets. Buys one-time rights, reprint rights or negotiates rights purchased. Pays $15-40, b&w, $20-100 color, cover and $2-40, b&w; $10-50 color inside; on acceptance.
Tips: "We always need good 'filler' artwork for our publications. We're very willing to work with new artists."

HONOLULU MAGAZINE, 36 Merchant St., Honolulu HI 96813. (808)524-7400. Art Director: Teresa J. Black. "City/regional magazine reporting on current affairs and issues, people profiles, lifestyle. Readership is generally upper income (based on subscription)." Monthly. Circ. 45,000. Original artwork is returned after publication. Sample copies free for SASE with first-class postage.
Cartoons: Buys 2-5 cartoons/issue from freelancers. Prefers local (Hawaii) themes. Prefers single or double panel without gagline; b&w line drawings, b&w and color washes. Send query letter with samples of style. Samples are filed or are returned if requested. Reports back only if interested. Buys first rights or one-time rights. Pays $35, b&w; $50, color; on publication.
Illustrations: Buys illustrations mainly for spots and feature spreads. Buys 1-3 illustrations/issue from freelancers. Works on assignment only. Prefers airbrush, colored pencil and watercolor. Considers pen & ink, mixed media, acrylic, pastel, collage, charcoal pencil and calligraphy. Send query letter with brochure showing art style. Looks for local subjects, conceptual abilities for abstract subjects (editorial approach)—likes a variety of techniques. Looks for strong black-and-white work. Samples are filed or are returned only if requested. Reports back only if interested. Write to schedule an appointment to show a portfolio which should include original/final art and color and b&w tearsheets. Buys first rights or one-time rights. Pays $75, b&w; $200, color, inside; on publication.

Tips: "Needs both feature and department illustration—best way to break in is with small spot illustration."

HOSPITAL PRACTICE, 10 Astor Place, New York NY 10003. (212)477-2727. Design Director: Robert S. Herald. Estab. 1966. Emphasizes clinical medicine and research for practicing physicians throughout the U.S. 18 issues/year. Circ. 200,000. Original artwork returned after publication if requested.
Illustrations: Approached by 30 illustrators/year. Works with 6-10 illustrators/year. Buys about 400 illustrations/year from freelancers. Uses only non-symbolic medical and scientific (conceptual) illustrations in a style similar to *Scientific American*. Also charts and graphs. Prefers "an elegant, if traditional, visual communication of biomedical and clinical concepts to physicians." Prefers pen & ink, airbrush, watercolor and acrylic. Works on assignment only. Send query letter with brochure showing art style, resume, photostats, photographs/slides and/or tearsheets to be kept on file. Does not report unless called. Call for appointment to show portfolio, which should include b&w and color original/final art, tearsheets and photostats. Returns material if SASE included. Negotiates rights purchased. Pays $950, color, cover; $100 and up, b&w, inside; on publication.
Tips: "Our specific editorial approach limits our interest to physician-oriented, 'just-give-us-the-facts' type of medical and scientific illustrations, though they, too, can be done with creative imagination."

HOUSE & GARDEN, 350 Madison Ave., New York NY 10017. (212)880-6693. Art Director: Gail Towey. Readers are upper income home owners or renters. Monthly. Circ. 500,000.
Illustrations: Uses minimum number of illustrations/issue, all of which are commissioned by the magazine. Selection based on "previous work, samples on file, and from seeing work in other publications. Illustrations are almost always assigned to fit specific articles." Themes "vary with our current format and with article we want illustrated." Format: b&w line drawings or washes. Portfolios viewed on first Tuesday of every month. Send samples of style and SASE to art director. Reports "from immediately to 4 weeks." Payment on acceptance "varies depending on artist, size and type of illustration." Buys one-time rights.

***HOW MAGAZINE**, 1507 Dana Ave., Cincinnati OH 45207. Art Director: Carole Winters. Estab. 1985. Trade journal; magazine format; "how-to and business techniques magazine for graphic design professionals." Bimonthly. Circ. 35,000. Does not accept previously published artwork. Original artwork return at job's completion. Sample copy available for $8.50. Art guidelines not available.
Illustrations: Approached by 100 freelance illustrators/year. Buys 2 illustrations/issue, 12 illustrations/year from freelancers. Works on assignment only. Considers all media, including photography. Send query letter with brochure, teasheets, photocopies and transparencies. Samples are filed or are returned by SASE if requested by artist. Reports back only if interested. To show a portfolio, mail slides. Buys first rights, one-time rights or reprint rights. Pays $500, color, cover; $50, b&w, $150, color, cover. Pays on publication.

HUDSON VALLEY, Box 429, 297 Main Mall, Poughkeepsie NY 12602. (914)485-7844. Art Director: Felicia T. Webster. Estab. 1971. Regional magazine with a broad range of subjects-Hudson Valley from Saratoga north to Westchester south. Average income of well educated reader is $88,000. "We have national advertising and special features. The Hudson Valley area has rural charm, jet city savvy, history, environmental concern and business sense." Monthly. Circ. 26,000. Accepts previously published artwork. Original artwork is returned after publication. Sample copies free for SASE with first-class postage.
Illustrations: Approached by 200 illustrators/year. Buys humorous and serious editorial illustrations for covers, spots, and feature spreads. Buys 15 illustrations/year from freelancers. Works on assignment only. Considers pen & ink, airbrush, mixed media, colored pencil, watercolor, acrylic, oil, pastel, collage, markers, charcoal pencil and calligraphy. Send query letter with samples. Samples are filed. Reports back within 2 months only if interested. Write or call to schedule an appointment to show a portfolio. Buys one-time rights; negotiates rights purchased. Pays $300, color, cover; up to $150, b&w; up to $250, color, inside; on publication.
Tips: "Submit a sample promotional piece for review with name, telephone number and address."

HUMPTY DUMPTY'S MAGAZINE, Box 567, Indianapolis IN 46206. (317)636-8881. Art Director: Lawrence Simmons. Special emphasis on health, nutrition, safety and exercise for girls and boys, ages 4-6. Monthly except bimonthly January/February, March/April, May/June, July/August. Sample copy 75¢; art guidelines for SASE.
Illustrations: Buys 25-35 illustrations/issue from freelancers. Works on assignment only. Send query letter with resume, photostats, slides, good photocopies or tearsheets to be kept on file. Samples returned by SASE if not kept on file. Reports within 8-12 weeks. Buys all rights. To show a portfolio, mail b&w, color and 2-color original/final art and final reproduction/product. Include SASE for return. Pays $250, cover; $30-70, b&w; $55-110, 2-color; $65-140, 4-color, inside; on publication.
Tips: Illustrations should be figurative and composed of story-telling situations. "Be familiar with the magazine before submitting artwork or samples that are inappropriate."

MACLEAN HUNTER PUBLISHING COMPANY, 29 North Wacker Dr., Chicago IL 60606. (312)726-2802. Art Director: Raymond Kohl. Estab. 1920. Publishes magazine, consumer magazine and trade journals. "Company prepares and produces 11 magazines—all of which except one are trade books. Coverage is of printing, packaging, mining of metals, non-metals, construction and pure bred dogs." Monthly. Circ. 20,000. Accepts previously published artwork. Original artwork is sometimes returned after publication. Sample copies available. Art guidelines available.

Cartoons: Buys few cartoons/issue from freelancers. Send query letter with samples of style. Samples are filed. Does not report back. Negotiates rights purchased. Pays $50, b&w; on publication.

Illustrations: Buys illustrations mainly for covers and spots. Works on assignment only. Considers pen & ink, airbrush, mixed media, colored pencil, watercolor, acrylic, oil, pastel, collage, marker and charcoal pencil. Send query letter with tearsheets. Looks for "creative approach in answering problems, not just mechanical ability. Interesting solutions to everyday subjects." Call to schedule an appointment to show a portfolio. Negotiates rights purchased. Pays $300, b&w, $500, color, cover; $100, b&w, $200, color, inside; on acceptance.

Tips: "Most illustration work, especially color work is for covers. Interview with leave behind samples for future referals."

HUSTLER, Larry Flynt Publications, Suite 300, 9171 Wilshire Blvd., Beverly Hills CA 90210. (213)858-7100. Cartoon/Humor Editor: Dwaine and Susan Tinsley. For middle-income men, 18-35 years of age, interested in current affairs, luxuries, investigative reporting, entertainment, sports, sex and fashion. Monthly. Original artwork returned after publication.

Cartoons: Publishes 23 cartoons/month; 10 full-page color, 4-color spots, 8 b&w and 1 "Most Tasteless." Receives 300-500 cartoons/week from freelance artists. Especially needs "outrageous material, mainly sexual, but politics, sports acceptable. Topical humor and seasonal/holiday cartoons good." To show a portfolio mail samples. Prefers 8½x11" size; avoid crayon, chalk or fluorescent color. Prefers original art submissions to roughs. Avoid, if possible, large, heavy illustration board. Samples returned by SASE only. Place name, address and phone number on back of each cartoon. Reports in 3 weeks to 1 month. Adheres to Cartoonists Guild guidelines. Pays $350, full- page, $150 ¼-page, color; $125 ¼-page b&w; $150, ¼-page "Most Tasteless." Pays on acceptance.

Tips: Especially needs more cartoons, cartoon breakaways or one-subject theme series. "Send outrageous humor—work that other magazines would shy away from. Pertinent, political, sexual, whatever. We are constantly looking for new artists to compliment our regular contributors and contract artists. Let your imagination and daring guide you. We will publish almost anything as long as it is funny. Remember, we are 'equal-opportunity offenders'."

HUSTLER HUMOR MAGAZINE, Larry Flynt Publications, Suite 300, 9171 Wilshire Blvd., Beverly Hills CA 90210. (213)858-7100. Cartoon/Humor Editor: Dwaine and Susan Tinsley. Monthly. Circ. 150,000.

Cartoons: Uses 150-180 cartoons/issue; buys 30% from freelancers. Prefers "outrageous sexual, social, political" themes. Prefers single or multiple panel, with or without gag line; b&w line drawings and washes. Send finished cartoons to be kept on file. Material not kept on file returned by SASE. Reports within 1 month. Buys first rights. Pays $10, b&w spot, $75, b&w strips/page. Original artwork returned after publication. Pays on acceptance.

Illustrations: Uses 2 covers, full-color sight gags. Prefers soft sexual themes; realistic cartoon styles. Send samples and tearsheets to be kept on file. Reports within 2 weeks. Pays $500, front; $200, back. Pays on acceptance.

Tips: This is a "humor magazine consisting of jokes and cartoons exclusively. The material is primarily sexual in nature—but the scope is wide-ranging. We need work *badly* to build our inventory."

*IDEALS MAGAZINE, Box 140300, Nashville TN 37214. (615)885-8270. Editor: Nancy Skarmeas. Magazine emphasizing poetry and light prose. Published 8 times/year. Accepts previously published material. Sample copy $4.95.

Illustrations: Approached by 25-30 illustrators/year. Buys 6-8 illustrations/issue from freelancers. Uses freelance artists mainly for spot art. Prefers seasonal themes rendered in a realistic style. Prefers pen & ink, airbrush, charcoal/pencil, watercolor and pastel. Send query letter with brochure showing art style or tearsheets and slides. Samples not filed are returned by SASE. Reports within 12-15 weeks. To show a portfolio, mail appropriate materials; portfolio should include final reproduction/product and tearsheets. Do not send originals. Buys artwork outright. Pays on publication.

Tips: "In portfolios, target our needs as far as style is concerned, but show representative subject matter. Artists should be familiar with our magazine before submitting samples of work."

*IMPULSE MAGAZINE, 16 Skey Lane, Toronto, Ontario M6J 3S4 Canada. (416)537-9551. Administrator: Lisa Henderson. Estab. 1971. Literary magazine; "an eclectic look into the arts, culture and literary milieus in Canada, the U.S. and overseas." Quarterly. Circ. 5,000. Accepts previously published artwork. Original artwork returned by SASE. Sample copy $10. Art guidelines not available.

Cartoons: Approached by 5 cartoonists/year. Buys 2 cartoons/year from freelancers. Prefers 'alternative' themes and styles which depend on the nature of the issue. Prefers single and double panel with and without gagline; b&w line drawings. Send query letter with brochure and finished cartoons. Samples are filed or are returned by SASE if requested by artist. Reports back only if interested. Rights purchased vary according to project. Payment negotiated. "This is a nonprofit magazine."

Illustrations: Approached by 5 freelance illustrators/year. Considers pen & ink, airbrush, colored pencil, mixed media, pastel, collage, marker and charcoal. Send query letter with brochure, photostats, resume, photographs, slides, photocopies and transparencies. Samples are filed or are returned by SASE if requested by artist. Reports back within months. If does not report back, the artist should "contact office for update." Call or write to schedule an appointment to show a portfolio, which should include b&w and color tearsheets, photostats, slides, original/final art and photographs. Rights purchased vary according to project. Payment negotiated. "We are a nonprofit organization."

inCIDER MAGAZINE, 80 Elm St., Peterborough NH 03458. Art Director: Roger Goode. Estab. 1984. Magazine. "*InCider* covers the Apple II, Apple II GS computer market. The magazine reviews new products, software, hardware and peripherals and teaches basic programs in support of those computers. Monthly. Circ. 124,000. Original artwork is returned after publication. Sample copies free for SASE with $1.25 postage.

Illustrations: Approached by over 100 illustrators/year. Buys illustrations mainly for covers, spots and feature spreads. Works with 24 illustrators/year. Buys 2-3 illustrations/issue, 24 illustrations/year from freelancers. Uses freelance artists mainly for full-page, 4-color illustration for feature articles and covers, spot art. Works on assignment only. Considers airbrush, mixed media, watercolor, acrylic, oil, collage and charcoal/pencil. Send brochure and tearsheets. "Illustrator must understand technical aspects of our computer." Samples are filed or returned only if requested. Wants to see "examples of Mac generated work for use with DTP." Reports back only if interested. Write to schedule an appointment to show a portfolio, or mail original/final art, tearsheets, slides and transparencies. Buys first rights. Pays $800-1,000, b&w; $1,000-1,200, color, cover; $400-700, b&w; $750-900, color, inside; on acceptance.

Tips: "Know our magazine. You must be creative, be able to work with our budget and hold deadlines. All illustrations must be well executed." Common mistakes freelancers make in presenting their work is "sending b&w representations of color work, not researching the type of manager they are contacting. As trend sees illustration moving closer to fine art, further blurring any distinction between the two . . . anything goes."

INSIDE, 226 S. 16th St., Philadelphia PA 19102. (215)893-5797. Editor: Jane Biberman. Estab. 1979. Quarterly. Circ. 70,000. Original artwork returned after publication.

Illustrations: Buys several illustrations/issue from freelancers. Buys 40 illustrations/year. Prefers color and b&w drawings. Works on assignment only. Send samples and tearsheets to be kept on file; call for appointment to show portfolio. Samples not kept on file are not returned. Reports only if interested. Buys first rights. Pays from $125, b&w, and from $300, full-color; on acceptance. Prefers seeing sketches.

*INSIDE INTERNATIONAL, Box 33696, Denver CO 80233-0696. (303)450-4774. FAX: (303)450-5127. Editor: Elizabeth Lenell. Estab. 1985. Magazine of the International Arabian Horse Association; "for youth adult members and all others interested in Arabian and registered part Arabian horses." Bimonthly. Circ. 30,000. Accepts previously published artwork. Returns originals after publication if requested. Sample copies available. Art guidelines not available.

Cartoons: Approached by 2-5 cartoonists. "We only occasionally use cartoons." Prefers single panel, double panel and multiple panel; with gagline. Send query letter. Samples are filed. Reports back only if interested. Rights purchased vary according to project. No payment. "We occasionally profile the artist or trade ads."

Illustrations: Send query letter. Call or write to schedule an appointment to show a portfolio. Rights purchased vary according to project. Pays on publication.

Tips: "Contact us by phone or letter. We are always looking for cover art (no identifiable horses or people, please). Because of the prestige of the magazine we never pay or negotiate rights (artist keeps all rights except for exclusives during issue date.) Art must be clearly related to Arabian horses. We occasionally need cartoons for the youth newsletter."

INSIDE TEXAS RUNNING, 9514 Bristlebrook, Houston TX 77083. Estab. 1977. "Information, features and calendar for runners, triathletes and bicyclists in the state of Texas. Slant is on healthy competition and exercise." Monthly. Circ. 10,000. Accepts previously published material. Original artwork is returned to the artist after publication with SASE. Sample copy $1.50. Finds most artists through references/word-of-mouth and samples received through the mail.

Cartoons: Approached by 2 cartoonists/year. Buys 6 cartoons/year from freelancers. Prefers single panel with gagline; b&w line drawings. Send roughs and finished cartoons. Samples are not filed and not returned. Reports back within 6 weeks. Buys reprint rights, one-time rights or all rights. Pays $10, b&w; $25, color.

Illustrations: Approached by 2 illustrators/year. Buys 6 illustrations/year from freelancers. Prefers pen & ink. Send query letter with brochure showing art style or tearsheets, photostats, photocopies or photographs. Samples are not filed, but returned by SASE. Reports back within 6 weeks. To show a portfolio, mail appropriate materials. Buys one-time rights, reprint rights or all rights. Negotiates rights purchased. Pays $10, b&w; $25, color, cover.

Tips: "Submit cartoons and illustrations for our 'Texas Roundup' section. These would complement short items (newsy and/or humorous) about happenings in *Texas Running*. We could use artists we can call on with 'scenarios' for timely use. Also looking for runners, triathletes, walkers, cyclists, etc."

INSIGHT MAGAZINE, 3600 New York Ave. NE, Washington DC 20002. (202)636-8800. Design Director: Roberta Morcone. Art Director: Sharon Roy Finch. Estab. 1985. "*Insight* is a newsweekly put together by some of the most talented people in the business today. It is always refreshing in its reporting and presentation of the news, never following others' standards but creating and following its own. Being directed to a more educated group, *Insight* aims not only to inform readers but to stimulate them to come to conclusions or even solutions to today's problems, whether at home or abroad." Weekly. Circ. ½ million. Sometimes accepts previously published artwork. Original artwork is not returned after publication. Sample copies $3. Art guidelines not available.
Cartoons: Buys 1 to 2 cartoons/issue, 56/year from freelancers. Prefers political and character themes. Send samples of style. Samples are filed or are returned if requested. Reports back regarding queries/submissions only if interested. Buys all rights or negotiates rights purchased. Pays $200, color; on acceptance.
Illustrations: Buys illustrations mainly for covers, spots and feature spreads. Buys 0-1 illustration/issue, 40/year from freelancers. Works on assignment only. Considers pen & ink, airbrush, mixed media, colored pencil, watercolor, acrylic, oil, pastel, collage, marker, charcoal pencil and calligraphy. Send query letter with something to show example of your style. "We are interested in medical illustrations and informational charts and graphs." Samples are returned only if requested. Reports back about queries/submissions only if interested. For a portfolio review, send samples first then follow up with a call. Pays $1,000, color, cover; $200, color, inside; on acceptance.
Tips: The section most open to illustrators is "the back of our book, which for our magazine is our feature section. Categories like Art, Business, Media, TV, Science, Health, Film, People, Law, etc. can be found there."

THE INSTRUMENTALIST, 200 Northfield Rd., Northfield IL 60093. (708)446-5000. Managing Editor: Judy Nelson. Emphasizes music education for "school band and orchestra directors and teachers of the instruments in those ensembles." Monthly. Circ. 20,000. Original artwork may be returned after publication. Sample copy $2.50
Cartoons: Approached by 3-4 cartoonists each year. Buys 3 cartoons/issue, 36 cartoons/year, all from freelancers. Interested in positive cartoons; no themes stating "music is a problem"; single panel with gagline, if needed; b&w line drawings. Send finished cartoons. Samples not returned. Reports in 1-2 months. Buys all rights. Pays $25, b&w; on acceptance.
Illustrations: Uses freelance artwork mainly for covers. Buys Kodachrome transparencies or slides for covers. Query about suitable subjects. Pays $50-100 on acceptance.
Tips: Looks for "realistic or abstract closeups of performers and musical instruments. Style should be modern, with clean lines and sharp focus that will reproduce well. Black-and-white glossy photos are best; color slides for covers should be Kodachrome film. Artwork that does not pertain to music can help show your style, but it is best to see what you can do within musical themes. Include music-related cartoons—instrumentalists, conductors, music teachers that do not make fun of the profession."

INTERNATIONAL DOLL WORLD, (formerly *National Doll World*), 306 E. Parr Rd., Berne IN 46711. (219)589-8740. Editor: Rebekah Montgomery. A trade journal which provides information on doll collecting, restoration and crafting. Bimonthly. Circ. 85,000. Accepts previously published artwork. Original artwork is sometimes returned after publication. Sample copies $2.50. Art guidelines not available.
Cartoons: Approached by 2-3 cartoonists/year. Buys 2-3 cartoons/year from freelancers. Prefers themes on doll collecting. Prefers single panel with gagline. Send finished cartoons. Samples are filed. Samples not filed are returned by SASE. Reports back regarding queries/submissions only if interested. Negotiates rights purchased. Pays $20, b&w; on publication.
Illustrations: Approached by 14-15 illustrators/year. Buys illustrations mainly for feature spreads and paper dolls. Buys 2 illustrations/issue, 12 illustrations/year from freelancers. Considers mixed media, colored pencil, watercolor, acrylic, oil and pastel. Send query letter with tearsheets, slides, photographs and transparencies. Looks for realistic technique. Samples are filed or are returned by SASE if requested. Reports back about queries/submissions within 14 days. Call or write to schedule an appointment to show a portfolio which should include color original/final art, slides, photographs and transparencies Negotiates rights purchased. Pays $35-150, color, inside; on publication.
Tips: "The best way for an illustrator to break into our publication is to send paper dolls." The most common mistake freelancers make in presenting their work is "sending it on paper that produces a blurry line."

*ISLANDS, 3886 State St., Santa Barbara CA 93105. (805)682-7177. FAX: (805)569-0349. Art Director: Albert Chiang. Estab. 1981. Consumer magazine of "international travel with an emphasis on islands." Bimonthly. Circ. 150,000. Original artwork returned after publication. Sample copies available. Art guidelines free for SASE with first-class postage.

Illustrations: Approached by 20-30 illustrators/year. Buys 1-2 illustrations/issue, 6-8 illustrations/year from freelancers. Uses freelance artists mainly for production on computer and editorial illustration. No theme or style preferred. Considers pen & ink, watercolor, collage, colored pencil, charcoal, mixed media, and pastel. Send query letter with brochure, tearsheets, photographs and slides. "We prefer samples of previously published tearsheets." Samples are filed. Reports back only if interested. Write to schedule an appointment to show a portfolio or mail appropriate materials. Portfolio should include original/final art and color tearsheets. Buys first rights or one-time rights. Pays $100-250, b&w, $500-1,000, color, cover or inside; on acceptance.

Tips: A common mistake freelancers make is that "they show too much, not focused enough. Specialize!" Notices "no real stylistic trends, but desktop publishing is affecting everything in terms of how a magazine is produced."

JACK AND JILL, Box 567, 1100 Waterway Blvd., Indianapolis IN 46206. (317)636-8881. Art Director: Edward F. Cortese. Emphasizes entertaining articles written with the purpose of developing the reading skills of the reader. For ages 7-10. Monthly except bimonthly January/February, March/April, May/June and July/August. Buys all rights. Original artwork not returned after publication (except in case where artist wishes to exhibit the art. Art must be available to us on request.) Sample copy 75¢.

Illustrations: Approached by more than 100 illustrators/year. Buys 25 illustrations/issue; 10-15/issue from freelancers. Uses freelance artists mainly for cover art, story illustrations and activity pages. Interested in "stylized, realistic, humorous illustrations for mystery, adventure, science fiction, historical and also nature and health subjects." Prefers mixed media. Works on assignment only. Send query letter with brochure showing art style or resume, tearsheets, photostats, photocopies, slides and photographs to be kept on file; include SASE. Reports in 1 month. To show a portfolio, mail appropriate materials or call or write to schedule an appointment; portfolio should include original/final art, color, tearsheets, b&w and 2-color pre-separated art. Buys all rights on a work-for-hire basis. Pays $250 cover, $140 full page, $90 ½ page, $65 spot for 4-color. For 4-color pre-separation art pays $175 full page, $105 ½ page and $70 spot. Pays $110 full page, $80 ½ page, $55 spot for 2-color. Pays $70 full page, $55 ½ page, $30 spot for b&w. On publication date, each contributor is sent two copies of the issue containing his or her work.

Tips: Portfolio should include "illustrations composed in a situation or storytelling way, to enhance the text matter. I do not want to see samples showing *only* single figures, portraits or landscapes, sea or air."

JAPANOPHILE, Box 223, Okemos MI 48864. (517)349-1795. Editor: Earl R. Snodgrass. Emphasizes cars, bonsai, haiku, sports, etc. for educated audience interested in Japanese culture. Quarterly. Circ. 500. Accepts previously published material. Original artwork not returned after publication. Sample copy $4; art guidelines free for SASE.

Cartoons: Approached by 7-8 cartoonists/year. Buys 1 cartoon/issue from freelancer. Prefers single panel with gagline; b&w line drawings. Send finished cartoons. Material returned only if requested. Reports only if interested. Buys all rights. Pays $10, b&w and color; on publication.

Illustrations: Buys 1-5 illustrations/issue from freelancers. Prefers sumie or line drawings. Send photostats or tearsheets to be kept on file if interested. Samples returned only if requested. Reports only if interested. Buys all rights. Pays $10, b&w and color, cover and $10, inside, b&w; on publication.

Tips: Does not want to see cartoons or illustrations which depict conflict between Americans and Japanese cultures.

JOURNAL OF ACCOUNTANCY, 1211 Avenue of the Americas, New York NY 10036. (212)575-5268. Art Director: Jeryl Costello. Magazine emphasizing accounting for certified public accountants. Monthly. Circ. 300,000. Original artwork returned after publication.

Illustrations: Approached by 200 freelance illustrators/year. Buys 2-6 illustrations/issue from freelancers. Prefers business, finance and law themes. Prefers mixed media, then pen & ink, airbrush, colored pencil, watercolor, acrylic, oil and pastel. Works on assignment only. Send query letter with brochure showing art style. Samples not filed are not returned. Reports only if interested. Call to schedule an appointment to show a portfolio, which should include original/final art, color and b&w tearsheets. Buys first rights. Pays $1,200, color, cover; $150-600, color (depending on size), inside; on publication.

Tips: "I look for indications that an artist can turn the ordinary into something extraordinary, whether it be through concept or style. In addition to illustrators, I also hire freelancers to do charts and graphs. In portfolios, I like to see tearsheets showing how the art and editorial worked together." Does not want to see "too many different styles in subject matter not relative to accounting, business or government."

THE JOURNAL OF LIGHT CONSTRUCTION, RR #2, Box 146, Richmond VT 05477. (802)864-5495. Art Director: Theresa Sturt. Tabloid, trade journal emphasizing residential and light commercial building and remodeling. Emphasizes the practical aspects of building technology and small-business management. Monthly. Circ. 60,000. Accepts previously published material. Original artwork is returned to the artist after publication. Sample copy $3.

Illustrations: Buys 10 illustrations/issue, 120 illustrations/year from freelancers. "Lots of how-to illustrations are assigned on various construction topics." Send query letter with brochure, resume, tearsheets, photostats and photocopies. Samples are filed or are returned only if requested by artist. Reports back within 2 weeks. Call or write to schedule an appointment to show a portfolio, which should include original/final art, final reproduction/product and b&w tearsheets. Buys one-time rights. Pays $400, color, cover; $60 b&w, inside; on acceptance.

Tips: "Write for a sample copy. We are unusual in that we have drawings illustrating construction techniques. We prefer artists with construction and/or architectural experience."

JOURNAL OF THE WEST, 1531 Yuma, Box 1009, Manhattan KS 66502. (913)532-6733. Editor: Robin Higham. Estab. 1962. Emphasizes Western History and culture for readers in public libraries and classrooms. Quarterly. Circ. 4,500 (readership). Original artwork returned after publication. Sample copy available.

Illustrations: Approached by 3-4 illustrators/year. Uses cover illustrations only; artist supplies 4-color separations. Works with 4 illustrators/year. Send query letter with brochure or samples and/or tearsheets to be kept on file. Prefers either photographs, prints or preferably duplicate slides as samples. Samples not filed are returned only if requested. Reports within 4 days. Negotiates rights purchased. Payment: exchange cover art for advertising space.

Tips: There is a trend toward "pastel with sometimes interesting and eye-catching results in Western scenes." Looks for work that is "original and not copied from a photograph; and is evidence of artistic talent and ability. We also are attempting to concentrate on the twentieth century, but other material will be considered. Please ask for a sample issue before submitting."

JUDICATURE, Suite 1600, 25 E. Washington, Chicago IL 60602. Contact: David Richert. Estab. 1917. Journal of the American Judicature Society. Published 6 times/year. Circ. 20,000. Accepts previously published material. Original artwork returned after publication. Sample copy for SASE with $1.25 postage.

Cartoons: Approached by 10 cartoonists/year. Buys 1-2 cartoons/issue from freelancers. Interested in "sophisticated humor revealing a familiarity with legal issues, the courts and the administration of justice." Send query letter with samples of style and SASE. Reports in 2 weeks. Buys one-time rights. Pays $35 for unsolicited cartoons.

Illustrations: Approached by 20 illustrators/year. Buys 2-3 illustrations/issue. Works on assignment only. Interested in styles from "realism to light cartoons." Prefers subjects related to court organization, operations and personnel. Send query letter with brochure showing art style and SASE. Reports within 2 weeks. Write to schedule an appointment to show a portfolio, which should include roughs and original/final art. Wants to see "b&w and the title and synopsis of editorial material the illustration accompanied." Buys one-time rights. Negotiates payment. Pays $250, b&w, cover; $175, b&w, inside.

Tips: "Show a variety of samples, including printed pieces and roughs."

KALEIDOSCOPE: International Magazine of Literature, Fine Arts, and Disability, 326 Locust St., Akron OH 44302. (216)762-9755. Editor-in-Chief: Darshan Perusek. Estab. 1979. Magazine. "We address the experience of disability through literature and the fine arts. Avoid the trite and sentimental. Treatment of subject should be fresh, original and imaginative." Semiannual. Circ. 1,500. Accepts previously published artwork. Original artwork is returned after publication. Sample copies $2. Art guidelines available.

Illustrations: Approached by 10 illustrators/year. Considers pen & ink, watercolor and acrylic. Send query letter with photocopies, slides and photographs. Samples are not filed. Samples not filed are returned by SASE. Reports back within 6 weeks. "Final acceptance or rejection can take up to six months." Buys first rights. Pays $25-100; on publication.

Tips: "Inquire about future theme of upcoming issues. Become familiar with *Kaleidoscope*. Sample copy very helpful. We are actively seeking high quality art. We welcome freelance submissions of art (35mm, 3×5, 5×7 black/white and color prints)."

*KALLIOPE, a journal of women's art, 3939 Roosevelt Blvd., Jacksonville FL 32205. (904)387-8211. Contact: Art Director. Estab. 1978. Literary magazine which publishes an average of 18 pages of art by women in each issue. (Reproductions are published in black and white). "Publishes poetry fiction, reviews and visual art by women and about women's concerns." Triannual. Circ. 1,200. Original artwork is returned at the job's completion. Sample copy $7. Art guidelines available.

Cartoons: Approached by 1 cartoonist/year. Uses 1 cartoon/issue from freelancers. Send query letter with roughs. Samples are not filed and are returned by SASE. Reports back within 2 months. Rights purchased vary according to project. Pays one year subscription of 3 complimentary copies for b&w.

Illustrations: Approached by 100 illustrators/year. Uses 18 illustrations/issue, 54 illustrations/year from freelancers. Looking for "excellence in visual art by women (nothing pornographic)." Send query letter with resume, SASE, photographs and artist's statement (50-75 words). Samples are not filed and are returned by SASE. Reports back within 2 months. Mail appropriate material: b&w photographs, resume and artist's statement. Rights purchased vary according to project. Pays one year subscription or 3 complimentary copies for b&w, cover and inside.

Tips: Seeking "Excellence in theme and execution and submission of materials. Previous artists have included: Louise Fishman, Nancy Azara, Lorraine Bodger, Genna Watson, Betty LaDuke, Grace Graupe-Pillard, Anna Tomczak."

KASHRUS Magazine—The Periodical for the Kosher Consumer, Box 204, Brooklyn NY 11204. (718)998-3201. Editor: Rabbi Wikler. Estab. 1980. Consumer magazine which updates consumer and trade on issues involving the kosher food industry, especially mislabeling, new products and food technology. Bimonthly. Circ. 10,000. Accepts previously published artwork. Original artwork is returned after publication. Sample copy $1.
Cartoons: Buys 5 cartoons/year. Buys 1 cartoon/issue from freelancers. Pays $50, b&w.
Illustrations: Buys illustrations mainly for covers. Works on assignment only. Prefers pen & ink. Send query letter with photocopies. Reports back about queries/submissions within 7 days. To show a portfolio, mail appropriate materials, which should include tearsheets and photostats. Pays $150, b&w, cover; $100, b&w, inside.
Tips: "Send food- and travel-related material. Do not send off-color material."

KENTUCKY LIVING, Box 32170, Louisville KY 40232. Editor: Gary Luhr. Magazine emphasizing Kentucky-related and general feature material for Kentuckians living outside metropolitan areas. Monthly. Circ. 330,000. Accepts previously published material. Original artwork returned after publication if requested. Sample copy available. All artwork is solicited by the magazine to illustrate upcoming articles.
Cartoons: Approached by 10-12 cartoonists/year. Pays $30, b&w.
Illustrations: Buys occasional illustrations/issue from freelancers. Works on assignment only. Prefers b&w line art. Send query letter with resume and samples. Samples not filed are returned only if requested. Reports within 2 weeks. Buys one-time rights. Pays $30-50 b&w, inside: on acceptance.

KEYNOTER, Kiwanis International, 3636 Woodview Trace, Indianapolis IN 46268. (317)875-8755. Executive Editor: Tamara P. Burley. Art Director: Jim Patterson. Official publication of Key Club International, non-profit high school service organization. Published 7 times/year. Copyrighted. Circ. 130,000. Previously published, photocopied and simultaneous submissions OK. Original artwork returned after publication. Free sample copy.
Illustrations: Buys 3 illustrations/issue from freelancers. Works on assignment only. SASE. Reports in 2 weeks. "Freelancers should call our Production and Art Department for interview." Buys first rights. Pays by the project, $100-500. Pays on receipt of invoice.

*KID CITY MAGAZINE, 1 Lincoln Plaza, New York NY 10023. (212)595-3456, ext. 512. Art Director: Michele Weisman. For ages 6-10.
Illustrations: Approached by 100 illustrators/year. Buys 60 illustrations/year from freelancers. Query with photocopied samples and SASE. Buys one-time rights. Pays $300 minimum, page, b&w; $400, page, $600, spread, color; on acceptance.
Tips: A common mistake freelancers make in presenting their work is "sending samples of work too babyish for our acceptance."

*KIDS! MAGAZINE, Suite 2E, 107 W. Front St., Wheaton IL 60187. Designer/Art Director: Larry Taylor. Estab. 1988. "A magazine for kids ages 8-13 years old with a Christian message." Published 9 times a year. Circ. 50,000. Accepts previously published artwork. Original artwork returned to the artist at the job's completion. Sample copies available. Art guidelines available.
Cartoons: Approached by 5-10 cartoonists/year. Buys 5 cartoons/issue, 100 cartoons/year from freelancers. Prefers all types of styles, Christian themes. Prefers format without gagline. Send query letter with brochure and samples. Samples are filed or are returned. Reports back to the artist only if interested. Rights purchased vary according to project. Pays $50, b&w; $100, color.
Illustrations: Approached by 10-20 illustrators/year. Buys 5-10 illustrations/issue, 200 illustrations/year from freelancers. Works on assignment only. Interested in all themes and styles. Prefers pen & ink, watercolor, collage, airbrush, acrylic, colored pencil, oil, charcoal and mixed media. Send query letter with brochure, tearsheets, photographs, slides and transparencies. Samples are filed or are returned. Reports back to the artist only if interested. Mail appropriate materials: b&w tearsheets, slides and photographs. Rights purchsed vary according to project. Pays $100, b&w; $250, color, cover; $75, b&w, $200, color, inside; on publication.
Tips: "Send a cover letter and a sample sheet or tearsheets. These will be filed until a project comes along. The illustrator will then be contacted by phone for the assignment."

*KIDSPORTS MAGAZINE, Suite 1800, 1101 Wilson Blvd., Arlington VA 22209. (703)276-4126. FAX: (703)276-3090. Art Director: John Herne. Estab. 1989. Consumer magazine; a sports publication for children; editorial written by professional athletes with an educational slant. Quarterly. Circ. 100,000. Accepts previously published artwork. Original artwork not returned, "but we can return them for special requests." Sample copies available. Art guidelines not available.

Cartoons: Approached by 3-4 cartoonists/year. Buys 4-5 cartoon/issue. Buys 16-20 cartoons/year. Prefers sports related, athlete, etc. themes. Send query letter with brochure and finished cartoons. Samples are filed. Reports back only if interested. Buys one-time rights.

Illustrations: Approached by 4-5 illustrators/year. Buys 5 illustration/issue. Buys 20 illustrations/year. Works on assignment. Prefers sports themes, fun and bright styles. Considers pen & ink and colored pencil. Send query letter with brochure, tearsheets, and resume. Samples are filed. Reports back only if interested. Write to schedule an appointment to show a portfolio or mail appropriate materials. Portfolio should include original/final art and b&w and color tearsheets. Buys one-time rights.

KITE LINES, Box 466, Randallstown MD 21133-0466. Publisher/Editor: Valerie Govig. Magazine emphasizing kites for the adult enthusiast only. Quarterly. Circ. 13,000. Original artwork returned after publication. Sample copy $3.50. Art guidelines available.

Cartoons: Buys 1 cartoon/year from freelancers. Prefers single panel; b&w line drawings—kites only. Send finished cartoons. Samples are filed or are returned by SASE. Reports back within 1 month only if interested. Buys first rights. Pays $15-20, b&w.

Illustrations: Buys 2-3 illustrations/year from freelancers. Works on assignment primarily. Send query letter with brochure showing art style or photocopies. Samples are filed are returned by SASE. Reports back within 1 month only if interested. To show a portfolio, mail final reproduction/product. Buys first rights. Pays $30-100, b&w; $30-100, color, inside. "We often pay in the form of subscriptions, kite books, etc."

Tips: "We use very little outside art anyway, and our rates are embarrassingly low—although we'd use more and pay more if we could get the kind of work we really need. We're talking working drawings here. No 'fine' art, no pretty for pretty's sake. You must be intensely interested in kites, enter into the life of our magazine and subordinate your skills to helping people who want to make and fly interesting kites. Choice of subject kites and style of drawing are both extremely circumscribed."

KIWANIS, 3636 Woodview Trace, Indianapolis IN 46268. (317)875-8755. Executive Editor: Chuck Jonak. Art Director: Jim Patterson. Estab. 1918. Magazine emphasizing civic and social betterment, business, education, religion and domestic affairs for business and professional persons. Uses cartoons, illustrations, and photos from freelancers. Original artwork returned after publication. Published 10 times/year. Finds artists through talent sourcebooks, references/word-of-mouth and portfolio reviews.

Cartoons: Buys 30 cartoons/year. Buys 3 cartoons/issue, all from freelancers. Interested in "daily life at home or work. Nothing off-color, no silly wife stuff, no blue-collar situations." Prefers finished cartoons. Send query letter with brochure showing art style or tearsheets, slides, photographs and SASE. Reports in 3-4 weeks. Pays $50, b&w; on acceptance.

Illustrations: Works with 20 illustrators/year. Buys 6-8 illustrations/issue, 30 illustrations/year from freelancers. Prefers pen & ink, airbrush, colored pencil, watercolor, acrylic, mixed media, calligraphy and paper sculpture. Interested in themes that correspond to themes of articles. Works on assignment only. Keeps material on file after in-person contact with artist. Include SASE. Reports in 2 weeks. To show a portfolio, mail appropriate materials (out of town/state) or call or write to schedule an appointment; portfolio should include roughs, original/final art, final reproduction/product, color and b&w tearsheets, photostats and photographs. Buys first North American serial rights or negotiates. Pays $1,000, full-color, cover; $400-800, full-color, inside; $50-75, spot drawings; on acceptance.

Tips: "We deal direct—no reps. Have plenty of samples, particularly those that can be left with us. I see too much student or unassigned illustration in many portfolios."

*LACMA PHYSICIAN, Box 3465, Los Angeles CA 90054. (213)483-1581. Managing Editor: Michael Villaire. "Membership publication for physicians who are members of the Los Angeles County Medical Association; covers association news and medical issues." Published 20 times/year, twice monthly except once in January, July, August and December. Circ. 11,000. Does not accept previously published material. Original artwork returned after publication "if requested." Sample copy for SASE with check for $2 payable to LACMA.

Illustrations: "Occasionally use illustrations for covers." These are "generally medical, but can relate to a specific feature story topic." Works on assignment only. Send query letter with business card and samples to be filed. Samples not kept on file are returned by SASE. Reports only if interested. Call or write for appointment. Negotiates payment; pays on acceptance. Buys all rights.

LADY'S CIRCLE MAGAZINE, 111 East 35th St., New York NY 10016. (212)689-3933. Editor: Mary F. Bemis. Art Director: Mike Gaynor. Estab. 1963. We are a mid- to low-income homemaker's magazine that specializes in cooking, crafts, psychology and how-to articles. We have a special section devoted to an older audience entitled "The Over-50 Section" that's very popular. We publish humor and fiction, both needing illustration. Bimonthly. Circ. 250,000. Accepts previously published artwork. Original artwork is sometimes returned after publication. Sample copy $1.95. Art guidelines not available. Prefers single panel with gagline; b&w line drawings. Send query letter with samples of style. Samples are filed. Samples not filed are returned. Reports back regarding queries/submissions within 3 months. Negotiates rights purchased. Pays $10-50, b&w; on publication.

Illustrations: Buys illustrations mainly for spots and feature spreads. Buys 3 illustrations/issue, 30 illustrations/year from freelancers. Works on assignment only. Prefers pen & ink. Considers watercolor, collage, markers and calligraphy. Send query letter with brochure showing art style, tearsheets and photostats. Samples are filed. Samples not filed are returned only if requested. Reports back about queries/submissions within 3 months. Call or write to schedule an appointment to show a portfolio or mail appropriate materials which should include tearsheets, photostats, photographs and b&w. Negotiates rights purchased. Pays $50-150, b&w; on publication.

*LAKELAND BOATING, Suite 500, 1600 Orrington Ave., Evanston IL 60201. (708)865-5400. FAX: (708)869-5989. Art Director: Allen Landsberger. Estab. 1945. Consumer magazine for Great Lakes boaters. Monthly. Accepts previously published artwork. Original artwork returned after publication. Sample copies and art guidelines available.
Cartoons: Prefers boating oriented theme (i.e. safety, pleasure, satire). Send query letter with brochure. Samples are filed. Reports back within 1 month. Rights purchased vary according to project. Negotiates payment.
Illustrations: Approached by 5-6 illustrators/year. Prefers "boating oriented themes (i.e. safety, pleasure, skiing—Great Lake images)." Considers any media. Send query letter with samples. Samples are filed or are returned by SASE if requested. Does not report back, in which case the artist should call. Call to schedule an appointment to show portfolio. Rights purchased vary according to project. Negotiates payment. Pays $25-35/¼ page, b&w; $50-65/¼ page, color, inside.
Tips: "We are interested in first-class images pertaining to the Great Lakes region as well as illustrating 'life on the water.' "

*LANDSCAPE TRADES, 1293 Matheson Blvd., Mississauga, Ontario Canada. (416)629-1184. Kevin Press. Readers are landscapers, nursery garden centers, grounds maintenance firms, wholesale growers, suppliers of goods to the landscaping industry, parks and recreation officials, horticulturists and others. Monthly. Circ. 5,086. Free sample copy.
Cartoons: Buys 1 cartoon/issue from freelancers which should relate to the industry and have appeal to readers mentioned above. Prefers single or multiple panel b&w line drawings or washes with or without gag line but will also consider color cartoons. Send finished cartoons or samples of style. Buys one-time rights. Pays $20 (Canadian), b&w; on publication. "Please include phone number when writing."
Illustrations: Buys 1 illustration/issue; 0-1 from freelancers. "I'd be happy to keep samples on file and request illustrations when a particular need or idea comes up." Prefers b&w line drawings or washes for inside. Send finished art or samples of style. Pays $20 (Canadian) for inside b&w; on publication. "Please include phone number when writing."

LAW PRACTICE MANAGEMENT, (formerly *Legal Economics*), Box 11418, Columbia SC 29211. (803)754-3563 or 359-9940. Managing Editor/Art Director: Delmar L. Roberts. For the practicing lawyer. Published 8 times/year. Circ. 23,113. Previously published work rarely used.
Cartoons: Primarily interested in cartoons "depicting situations inherent in the operation and management of a law office, e.g., operating word processing equipment and computers, interviewing, office meetings, lawyer/office staff situations, and client/lawyer situations. We are beginning to use 1-2 cartoons/issue. We never use material about courtroom situations." Send query letter with resume. Reports in 90 days. Usually buys all rights. Pays $50 for all rights; on acceptance.
Illustrations: Uses inside illustrations and, infrequently, cover designs. Pen & ink, charcoal/pencil, watercolor, acrylic, oil, collage and mixed media used. Send query letter with resume. Reports in 90 days. Usually buys all rights. Pays $75-125; $150-200 for 4-color; on publication.
Tips: "There's an increasing need for artwork to illustrate high-tech articles on technology in the law office. We're also interested in computer graphics for such articles."

*LEGION, Suite 504, 359 Kent St., Ottawa, Ontario K2P 0R6 Canada. (613)235-8741. Art Director: J. Morse. For Royal Canadian Legion members. Published 10 times/year. Circ. 528,908. Free sample copy.
Cartoons: Approached by 12 cartoonists/year. Pays $250, b&w; $350, color.
Illustrations: Approached by more than 30 illustrators/year. Buys 6-8 illustrations/issue from freelancers. Interested in "various techniques." Works on assignment only. "Because of the invariable loss of time clearing illustrations through Canada Customs, Canadian artists are used to illustrate most stories." Provide tearsheets to be kept on file. Prefers to see portfolio, which should include 4-color illustration, life drawing, as opposed to still life. "I need to see how an artist handles the human form." Looking for innovative style and mixed media. Buys various rights. Cover: Pays $400-800, color, cover, inside $300-600, b&w or color, cover; on acceptance.
Tips: A common mistake freelancers make in presenting their work is that "the work is not neatly arranged and not applicable. They haven't taken the time to look at our publication and tailor their portfolio accordingly."

*LEISURE WORLD, 1215 Ouellette Ave., Windsor, Ontario N8X 1J3 Canada. (519)971-3208. FAX: (519)255-7379. Managing Editor: Carmel Ravannello. Estab. 1988. Consumer magazine. Reflects the leisure time activities of members of the Canadian Automobile Association. Bimonthly. Circ. 250,000. Accepts previously pubished artwork. Original artwork returned at the job's completion. Sample copy free for SASE with first class stamp. Art guidelines available.
Cartoons: Reports back within 1 month. Pays $25, b&w; $50, color.
Illustrations: Send query letter with photographs, photocopies, photostats, slides and transparencies. Most samples are filed. Those not filed are returned. Reports back in 1 month. Call or write to schedule an appointment to show a portfolio or mail appropriate materials: thumbnails, roughs, original/final art, b&w or color tearsheets, photostats, photographs, slides and photocopies. Pays $25, b&w, $200, color, cover. "Negotiable."
Tips: "Send material for us to view."

THE LOOKOUT, 8121 Hamilton Ave., Cincinnati OH 45231. (513)931-4050. Editor-in-Chief: Mark A. Taylor. For conservative Christian adults and young adults. Weekly. Circ. 140,000. Original artwork not returned after publication, unless requested. Sample copy and artists' guidelines available for 50¢.
Cartoons: Uses 1 cartoon/issue; buys 20 cartoons/year from freelancers. Interested in church, Sunday school and Christian family themes. Currently overstocked.
Illustrations: Buys 3-4 illustrations/issue from freelancers. Interested in "adults, families, interpersonal relationships; also, graphic treatment of titles." Works on assignment only. Send query letter with brochure, flyer or tearsheets to be kept on file for future assignments to Frank Sutton, Art Director, at above address. Reporting time varies. Buys all rights but will reassign. Pays $125, b&w, $150, full-color illustrations, inside, firm; on acceptance. "Sometimes more for cover work."

LOS ANGELES, 1888 Century Park E, Los Angeles CA 90067. (213)557-7592. Design Director: William Delorme. Emphasizes lifestyles, cultural attractions, pleasures, problems and personalities of Los Angeles and the surrounding area. Monthly. Circ. 170,000. Especially needs very localized contributors—custom projects needing person-to-person concepting and implementation. Previously published work OK. Pays on publication. Sample copy $3.
Cartoons: Contact Geoff Miller, Editor-in-Chief. Buys 5-7 cartoons/issue on current events, environment, family life, politics, social life and business; single, double or multi panel with gagline. To show a portfolio mail roughs. Pays $25-50, b&w line or tone drawings.
Illustrations: Buys 10 illustrations/issue on assigned themes. Send or drop off samples showing art style (tearsheets, photostats, photocopies and dupe slides). Pays $300-500, color, cover; $150-500, b&w, $200-800, color, inside; on publication.
Tips: "Show work similar to that used in the magazine—a sophisticated style. Study a particular publication's content, style and format. Then proceed accordingly in submitting sample work." There is a trend toward "imaginative imagery and technical brilliance with computer-enhanced art being a factor. Know the stylistic essence of a magazine at a gut level as well as at a perceptive level. Identify with Los Angeles or Southern California."

LOST TREASURE, Box 1589, Grove OK 74344. (918)786-2182. Managing Editor: Debi Williams. Emphasizes treasure hunting for treasure hunters, coinshooters, metal detector owners. Monthly. Circ. 50,000. Sample copy for 9×12 SASE.
Cartoons: Buys "some horizontal cartoons;" all from freelancers. Receives 10 cartoons from freelancers/month. Cartoons should pertain to treasure hunting, people using metal detectors, prospecting, etc. Prefers single panel b&w line drawings or b&w washes with gagline. Send query letter with finished cartoons and SASE. Reports in 6-8 weeks. Pays $5 on publication. Buys first North American serial rights.
Tips: "Cartoon should be very treasure hunting-oriented and funny. Prefer irony to slapstick."

*LOUISIANA LIFE MAGAZINE, Box 308, Metairie LA 70004. (504)456-2220. Art Director: Julie Dalton Gourgues. Estab. 1981. Consumer magazine; "general interest; covering all aspects of life in Louisiana—from music and food to politics and business." Bimonthly. Circ. 35,000. Accepts previously published artwork. Original artwork returned after publication. Sample copy $3.50. Art guidelines not available.
Illustrations: Approached by 3-5 illustrators/year. Buys 1-2 illustrations/issue, 8-10 illustration/year from freelancers. Works on assignment only. Prefer themes and styles which are not traditional and are those of the individual artist. Prefers collage, colored pencil, oil, charcoal, mixed media, scratchboard and pencil. Send query letter with brochure, tearsheets, resume, SASE and transparencies. Samples are filed. Reports back within 2 months. Call or mail appropriate materials. Portfolio should include original/final art and b&w tearsheets and slides. Buys first rights. Pays $225, color or b&w, cover. Pays $85-200, color or b&w, inside; on publication.
Tips: "Since we use minimal illustration, it's best to submit examples of your best work. When we desire an illustration that fits your style, we'll contact you."

*LUNA VENTURES, Box 398, Suisun CA 94585. Editor: Paul Doerr. Publishes *Backwoods*, emphasizing mountainmen, muzzleloading, subsistence farming; *SCIFANT*, on microfiche only, emphasizing science fiction, fantasy, horror and fandom. Accepts previously published material. Original artwork not necessary. Sample copy $3 for microfiche, $2 for paper. Art guidelines available for SASE with first class postage. Pays in copy of issue and percentage of sales.
Tips: "New or nonprofessional artists welcomed."

THE LUTHERAN, 8765 W. Higgins Rd., Chicago IL 60631. (312)380-2540. Art Director: Jack Lund. Estab. 1988. General interest magazine of the Evangelical Lutheran Church in America. Published 17 times a year. Circ. 1.2 million. Previously published work OK. Original artwork returned after publication on request. Free sample copy.
Cartoons: Approached by 300 cartoonists/year. Buys 1 cartoon/issue from freelancers. Receives 30 submissions/week from freelancers. Interested in humorous or thought-provoking cartoons on religion or about issues of concern to Christians; single panel. Prefers finished cartoons. Send SASE. Reports usually within a week. Buys first rights. Pays $25-100, b&w line drawings and washes; on publication.
Illustrations: Buys 6 illustrations/year from freelancers. Works on assignment. Send samples of style to keep on file for future assignments. Buys all rights on a work-for-hire basis. Samples returned by SASE if requested. Pays $500, 2-color and 4-color, cover; $25-300, b&w, $400, color, inside; on publication.
Tips: Include your phone number with submission.

THE LUTHERAN JOURNAL, 7317 Cahill Rd., Edina MN 55435. Contact: J.W. Leykom. Family magazine for Lutheran Church members, middle aged and older. Previously published work OK. Free sample copy.
Illustrations: Seasonal 1-, 2- or full-color covers. Mail art with price. Buys one-time rights. Pays on publication.

MADE TO MEASURE, 600 Central Ave., Highland Park IL 60035. (312)831-6678. Publisher: William Halper. Emphasizes manufacturing, selling of uniforms, career clothes, men's tailoring and clothing. Magazine distributed to retailers, manufacturers and uniform group purchasers. Semiannual. Circ. 24,000. Art guidelines available.
Cartoons: Buys 15 cartoons/issue from freelancers. Prefers themes relating to subject matter of magazine; also general interest. Prefers single panel with or without gagline; b&w line drawings. Send query letter with samples of style or finished cartoons. Any cartoons not purchased are returned to artist. Reports back. Buys first rights. Pays $30-40 b&w; on acceptance.

MAGIC CHANGES, 2S424 Emerald Green Dr., Unit F, Warrenville IL 60555. (312)393-7856. Editor: John Sennett. Estab. 1978. Emphasizes fantasy and poetry for college students, housewives, teachers, artists and musicians: "People with both an interesting and artistic slant." Annually. Circ. 500. Accepts previously published material. Original artwork returned after publication. Sample copy $5; make check payable to John Sennett. Art guidelines for SASE. Uses freelance artists mainly for cover art.
Cartoons: Approached by 20 cartoonists/year. Buys 2 cartoons/issue from freelancers. Considers space, art, animals and street activity themes. Single, double, or multi-panel with or without gagline; b&w line drawings. Send query letter with finished cartoons. Material returned by SASE. Reports within 2-4 weeks. Acquires first rights. Pays $0-10.
Illustrations: Approached by 50 illustrators/year. Buys 10 illustrations/year from freelancers. Considers city, wilderness, bird, space and fantasy themes. Prefers pen & ink, then charcoal/pencil and computer illustration. Send query letter with samples. Samples returned by SASE. Reports within 1 month. To show a portfolio, mail original/final art, final reproduction/product or b&w. Acquires first rights. Pays $0-10.
Tips: "I want to see black-and-white drawings, no larger than 8½×11. I do not want to see slides. Target your samples to our needs."

MAGICAL BLEND, Box 11303, San Francisco CA 94101. Art Director: Matthew Courtway. Estab. 1980. Emphasizes spiritual exploration, transformation and visionary arts. Quarterly. Circ. 75,000. Original artwork returned after publication. Sample copy $4; art guidelines for SASE.
Illustrations: Works with 20 illustrators/year. Uses 65 illustrations/year from freelancers. Also publishes 2-3 portfolios on individual artists per issue. "We keep samples on file and work by assignment according to the artists and our time table and workability. We prefer color work. We look for pieces with a positive, inspiring, uplifting feeling." Send photographs, slides and SASE. Reports in 1 week to 6 months. Buys first North American serial rights. Rights revert to artist. Pays in copies.
Tips: "We want work that is energetic and thoughtful, and that has a hopeful outlook on the future. Our page size is 8½×11. High-quality, camera-ready reproductions are preferable over originals. The best way to see what we need is to send $4 for a sample copy of *Magical Blend*. We like to print quality art by people who have talent, but don't fit into any catagory and are usually unpublished. Since we can't afford to pay them, we can at least give them a break and get them some exposure."

*THE MAINE SPORTSMAN, Box 365, Augusta ME 04332. Editor: Harry Vanderweide. Emphasizes Maine outdoors for hunters and fishermen. Monthly tabloid. Circ. 30,000. Original work returned after publication.
Cartoons: Approached by 20 cartoonists/year. Buys 1-3 cartoons/month from freelancers. Prefers to buy 10-12 at a time. Samples returned by SASE. Reports in one week. B&w only. Pays $10 on acceptance.
Illustrations: Approached by 2-4 illustrators/year. Buys 1-3 illustrations/month from freelancers. Especially wildlife scenes. Most issues feature drawing on cover. Send query letter with brochure showing art style and samples. Samples returned by SASE. Reports in one week. Buys first rights, pays when illustration is published. Black and white only. Pays $100, cover drawing, $20-50, illustrations used inside.
Tips: "We prefer cartoons that are actually humorous, especially if they don't require a caption line. Currently we are in need of high quality, pen & ink wildlife drawings. We need dynamic, single image drawings with minimal background image size two to three or actual size of 6×9. Subjects needed are trout, salmon, bass, bluefish, striped bass, whitetail bucks, moose, bear, coyote, bobcat."

MANAGEMENT ACCOUNTING, 10 Paragon Dr., Montvale NJ 07645. (201)573-6269. Editor: Robert F. Randall. Estab. 1919. Emphasizes management accounting for management accountants, controllers, chief accountants and treasurers. Monthly. Circ. 85,000. Accepts simultaneous submissions. Original artwork not returned after publication. Sample copy free for SASE.
Cartoons: Approached by 15 cartoonists/year. Buys 12 cartoons/year from freelancers. Prefers single panel with gagline; b&w line drawings. Send finished cartoons. Material not kept on file is returned by SASE. Reports within 2 weeks. Buys one-time rights. Pays $25, b&w; on acceptance.
Illustrations: Approached by 6 illustrators/year. Buys 1 illustration/issue from freelancers.
Tips: Does not want to see sexist cartoons.

*MANAGEMENT REVIEW, 135 West 50th St., New York NY 10020. (212)903-8058. FAX: (212)903-8168. Art Director: Seval Newton. Estab. 1921. Company magazine; "a business magazine for senior managers. A general, internationally focused audience." Monthly. Circ. 150,000. Original artwork returned after publication. Tearsheets available.
Cartoons: Approached by 10-20 cartoonists/year. Buys 1-2 cartoons/issue, 10-12 cartoons/year from freelancers. Prefers "business themes and clean drawings of minority women as well as men." Prefers double panel; b&w washes and line drawings. Send query letter with finished cartoons and SASE. Samples are filed. Reports back within 2 months. Buys first rights. Pays $100, b&w, $200, color.
Illustrations: Approached by 50-100 illustrators/year. Buys 4-8 illustrations/issue, 70-80 illustrations/year from freelancers. Works on assignment only. Prefers business themes and strong colors. Considers airbrush, watercolor, collage, acrylic, and oil. Send query letter with tearsheets, photographs and slides. Samples are filed. Reports back only if interested. To show a portfolio, mail original/final art and b&w tearsheets, photographs and slides. Buys first rights. Pays $800, color, cover; $250, b&w, $350, color, inside; on acceptance.
Tips: "Send tearsheets; periodically send new printed material."

MARRIAGE PARTNERSHIP, 465 Gundersen Dr., Carol Stream IL 60188. Art Director: Gary Gnidovic. Trade journal. Quarterly magazine. Circ. 60,000. Accepts previously published artwork. Original artwork is returned after publication.
Cartoons: Buys 12 cartoons/issue, 48 cartoons/year from freelancers. Prefers single panel with or without gagline; b&w line drawings or b&w washes. Send query letter with finished cartoons. Reports back within weeks.
Illustrations: Buys illustrations mainly for spots and feature spreads. Buys 16 illustrations/issue, 64 illustrations/year from freelancers. Works on assignment only. Considers pen & ink, mixed media, colored pencil, watercolor, acrylic, oil, pastel and charcoal pencil. Send query letter with brochure, resume and tearsheets. "Show an ability to conceptualize appropriately." Prefers contemporary styles. Reports back only if interested. To show a portfolio, mail b&w and color tearsheets and slides. Buys first rights. Pays $400-500, color, inside (full page), $200-250 for spots; on acceptance.

MEDICAL ECONOMICS MAGAZINE, 680 Kinderkamack Rd., Oradell NJ 07649. (201)599-8442. Art Administrator: Mrs. Donna DeAngelis. Estab. 1909. Magazine for those interested in the financial and legal aspects of running a medical practice. Bimonthly. Circ. 182,000. Accepts previously published material. Original

The asterisk before a listing indicates that the listing is new in this edition. New markets are often the most receptive to freelance submissions.

artwork returned after publication. Uses freelance artists mainly for "all editorial illustration in the magazine."

Cartoons: Approached by more than 50 cartoonists/year. Buys 10-12 cartoons/issue from freelancers. Prefers medically-related themes. Prefers single panel, with gagline; b&w line drawings and b&w washes. Send query letter with finished cartoons. Material not filed is returned by SASE. Reports within 8 weeks. Buys all rights. Pays $100, b&w.

Illustrations: Approached by more than 100 illustrators/year. Works with more than 30 illustrators/year. Buys 100 illustrations/year from freelancers. Prefers pen & ink, airbrush, charcoal/pencil, colored pencil, watercolor, acrylic, oil, pastel, collage, mixed media and 3-D illustration. Works on assignment only. Send query letter with resume and samples. Samples not filed are returned by SASE. Reports only if interested. Call to schedule an appointment to show a portfolio, which should include original/final art (if possible) and tearsheets. Buys one-time rights. Pays $400-1,200, color, cover; $125-400, b&w and $400-1,000, color, inside; on acceptance.

Tips: "In a portfolio, include original art and tearsheets, showing conceptualization. I do not want to see work copied from another source." Would like to see "promo pieces or leave behinds—how else do we remember an illustrator's work?" A common mistake freelancers make in presenting their work is "self-deprecation—they'll show a piece, then say 'Oh that's just leftover from my old style (days, school, whatever)' if they feel it's not up to par, they should get rid of it, or at least get it out of their portfolio."

MEDICAL TIMES, 80 Shore Rd., Port Washington NY 11050. Executive Editor: Anne Mattarella. Emphasizes clinical medical articles. Monthly. Circ. 120,000. Sample copy $5.

Cartoons: Buys 5-6 cartoons/year from freelancers. Prefers medical themes, "but nothing insulting to our audience. Jokes about doctors' fees are *not* funny to doctors." Accepts single panel with gagline; b&w line drawings. Send query letter with finished cartoons; "we'll either accept and pay or return them within one month." Negotiates rights purchased. Pays $25, b&w; on acceptance.

Illustrations: Buys 2 or 3 illustrations/issue, 24-36/year from freelancers. Works on assignment only. Send query letter with resume and medical art samples such as tearsheets, photostats, photocopies, slides and photographs. Samples not filed are returned. Reports within 1 month. Write to schedule an appointment to show a portfolio, which should include original art (1 or 2 pieces only) and printed material "so we can see how the artist's work reproduces. Most of the portfolio should consist of printed pieces." Negotiates rights purchased. Payment varies; pays on acceptance.

Tips: "With the ever-increasing number of medical journals competing for the same ad budgets, competition and cost controls are becoming fierce. This may mean a cutback in the amount of artwork purchased by some of the marginally successful journals."

MEMCO NEWS, Box 1079, Appleton WI 54912. Editor: Richard F. Metko. Emphasizes "welding applications performed with Miller Electric equipment. Readership ranges from workers in small shops to metallurgical engineers." Quarterly. Circ. 44,000. Previously published material and simultaneous submissions OK. Original artwork not returned after publication.

THE MERCEDES-BENZ STAR, 1235 Pierce St., Lakewood CO 80214. (303)235-0116. Editor: Frank Barrett. Estab. 1956. Magazine emphasizing new and old Mercedes-Benz automobiles for members of the Mercedes-Benz Club of America and other automotive enthusiasts. Bimonthly. Circ. 25,000. Does not usually accept previously published material. Returns original artwork after publication. Sample copy for SASE with $2 postage.

Illustrations: Works with 3+ illustrators/year. Buys 20+ illustrations/year from freelancers. Uses freelancers mainly for technical illustration. Prefers Mercedes-Benz related themes. Looks for authenticity in subject matter. Prefers pen & ink, airbrush and oil. Send query letter with resume, slides or photographs to be kept on file except for material requested to be returned. Write for appointment to show portfolio. Samples not filed are returned by SASE. Buys first rights. Pays $100-1,500; on publication.

Tips: " In a portfolio, include subject matter similar to ours."

*MICHIGAN WOMAN MAGAZINE, Suite 370, 30400 Telegraph, Birmingham MI 48010. (313)646-5575. FAX: (313)646-0208. Art Director: Andrea Stork. Estab. 1984. Consumer magazine emphasizing women's lifestyle. Bimonthly. Circ. 35,000. Accepts previously published artwork. Original artwork returned after publication. Sample copies available; art guidelines free for SASE with first-class postage.

Cartoons: Prefers single panel; color washes and b&w line drawings. Send query letter with roughs, finished cartoons and non-returnable samples. Samples are filed or are returned by SASE if requested by artist. Reports back only if interested. Buys one-time rights. Pays $50, b&w, $75, color.

Illustrations: Approached by 30 illustrators/year. Buys 10 illustrations/issue, Buys 60 illustrations/year from freelancers. Works on assignment only. No particular theme or style preferred. Considers pen & ink, collage, oil, charcoal, mixed media and pastel. Send query letter with brochure, tearsheets, photocopies, photostats and non-returnable samples. Samples are filed. Reports back only if interested. Call to schedule an appointment to show a portfolio, which should include thumbnails, roughs, original/final art and b&w and color tearsheets, photostats, photographs, slides and photocopies. Buys first rights. Pays $50, b&w, and $100, color, inside. Pays on publication.

Tips: "Supply samples of very creative (new approaches to old problems), good artwork. There is an emphasis on women." Sees trend toward "Things that are obviously hand drawn. The computer is making a real need for the intimacy of handwork."

MID ATLANTIC COUNTRY MAGAZINE, Suite 305, 300 N. Washington St., Alexandria VA 22314. (703)548-6177. Art Director: Randy Clark. Estab. 1980. Magazine emphasizing travel/leisure, home/entertaining and gardening. "We are a travel/leisure magazine for the Mid-Atlantic region, the only magazine of this kind in this market. We use illustrations in our feature stories as well as regular columns such as our gardening column." Monthly. Accepts previously published material. Art guidelines free for SASE with first-class postage.
Illustrations: Works with 10-20 illustrators/year. Buys 24-36 illustrations/year from freelancers. Uses artists mainly for spots and departments. Works on assignment only. Prefers New Yorker style. Samples are filed and are not returned. Does not report back. Write to schedule an appointment to show a portfolio, which should include color and b&w tearsheets. Buys one-time rights. Pays $75, b&w, $150+, color, inside; on publication.
Tips: "Interested in all media. Art direction varies from very tight to total reliance on illustrator for creative ideas."

MIDDLE EASTERN DANCER, Box 181572, Casselberry FL 32718-1572. (407)831-3402. Editor/Publisher: Karen Kuzsel. Associate Editor: Tracie Harris. Estab. 1979. Magazine, trade journal that is "informative and entertaining guide for the Middle Eastern dance and culture professional and enthusiast. Offers current news on international scale." Monthly. Circ. more than 2,500. Original artwork is returned after publication if requested. Samples copies free for SASE with first-class postage. Art guidelines not available.
Cartoons: Approached by 2 cartoonists/year. Buys 1-2 cartoons/issue, 15-20 cartoons/year from freelancers. Themes or style must relate to M.E. dance/culture. Prefers single panel with gagline; b&w line drawings and washes. Send query letter with samples of style, roughs, finished cartoons and SASE. Samples not filed are returned by SASE. Reports back regarding queries/submissions within 2 weeks. Buys first rights. Pays $10, b&w; on acceptance.
Illustrations: Approached by 5 illustrators/year. Buys illustrations mainly for spots and feature spreads. Buys 5-10 illustrations/issue, 60-100 illustrations/year from freelancers. Prefers pen & ink. considers marker, charcoal pencil and calligraphy. Send query letter with brochure showing art style, tearsheets, photocopies, photographs and roughs. Samples must relate to M.E. dance and/or culture. Reports back about queries/submissions within 2 weeks. To show a portfolio, mail appropriate materials which should include original/final art, tearsheets, slides, photostats and photographs. Buys first rights. Pays $10, b&w; on acceptance.
Tips: "Know the subject matter and include SASE." As a trend sees "artists going for more special interest; more open space; unbalanced, but flowing layouts."

MILITARY LIFESTYLE MAGAZINE, 1732 Wisconsin Ave. NW, Washington DC 20007. Art Director: Judi Connelly. Estab. 1969. Emphasizes active-duty military lifestyles for military families. Published 10 times/year. Circ. 530,000. Original artwork returned after publication.
Illustrations: Approached by 30-35 illustrators/year. Buys 2-6 illustrations/issue, 60-65 illustrations/year from freelancers. Uses artists mainly for features, no covers. Theme/style depends on editorial content. Works on assignment only. Send brochure and business card to be kept on file. Accepts photostats, recent tearsheets, photocopies, slides, photographs, etc., as nonreturnable samples. Samples returned only if requested. Reports only if interested. Buys first rights. Payment depends on size published, cover and inside; pays on publication.
Tips: "Request copy of magazine with guidelines. Include $1.50 per issue for postage and handling."

MILITARY MARKET MAGAZINE, Springfield VA 22159-0210. (703)750-8676. Editor: Nancy M. Tucker. Emphasizes "the military's PX and commissary businesses for persons who manage and buy for the military's commissary and post exchange systems; also manufacturers, brokers and distributors." Monthly. Circ. 9,500. Simultaneous submissions OK. Original artwork not returned after publication.
Cartoons: Approached by 25 cartoonists/year. Buys 3-4 cartoons/issue from freelancers. Interested in themes relating to "retailing/buying of groceries or general merchandise from the point of view of the store managers and workers"; single panel with or without gagline, b&w line drawings. Send finished cartoons. Samples returned by SASE. Reports in 6 months. Buys all rights. Pays $25, b&w; on acceptance.
Tips: "We use freelance cartoonists only—*no* other freelance artwork." Do not "send us military oriented cartoons. We want retail situations ONLY."

MODERN DRUMMER, 870 Pompton Ave., Cedar Grove NJ 07009. (201)239-4140. Editor-in-Chief: Ronald Spagnardi. Art Director: Scott Bienstock. For drummers, all ages and levels of playing ability with varied interests within the field of drumming. Monthly. Circ. 85,000. Previously published work OK. Original artwork returned after publication. Sample copy $3.95.
Cartoons: Buys 3-5 cartoons/year. Buys 1 cartoon/every other issue from freelancers. Interested in drumming themes; single and double panel. Prefers finished cartoons or roughs. Include SASE. Reports in 3 weeks. Buys first North American serial rights. Pays $5-25; on publication.
Tips: "We want strictly drummer-oriented gags."

*MODERN LITURGY, Suite 290, 160 E. Virginia St., San Jose CA 95112. Editor: John Gallen. For religious artists, musicians and planners of worship services for Catholic and Protestant liturgical traditions. Published 9 times/year. Circ. 15,000. Sample copy $4.
Illustrations: Holds two contests each year for liturgical artists. Features liturgical art and artists in every issue. Send query letter with samples and SASE. Reports in 4-6 weeks. Buys all rights but may reassign rights to artist after publication. Pays with subscription, copies and advertising credit.

MODERN MATURITY, 3200 East Carson, Lakewood CA 90712. (213)496-2277. Art Director: James H. Richardson. Estab. 1956. Emphasizes health, lifestyles, travel, sports, finance and contemporary activities for members 50 years and over. Bimonthly. Circ. 21,000,000. Previously published work OK. Original artwork returned after publication. Sample copy available.
Illustrations: Approached by 200 illustrators/year. Buys 8 illustrations/issue, 48 illustrations/year from freelancers. Works on assignment only. Considers watercolor, collage, oil, mixed media and pastel. Samples are filed "if I can use the work." Reports back to the artist only if interested. Call to schedule an appointment to show a portfolio. Portfolio should include original/final art, tearsheets, slides and photocopies. Buys first rights. Pays $1,000, b&w; $2,000, color, cover; $2,000, color, inside, full page; on acceptance.
Tips: "We generally use people with a proven publications editorial track record. I request tearsheets of published work when viewing portfolios."

MONEY MAKER MAGAZINE, 5705 N. Lincoln Ave., Chicago IL 60659. (312)275-3590. Art Director: Debora Clark. Estab. 1980. Consumer magazine. Bimonthly. Circ. 350,000. Accepts previously published artwork. Original artwork returned after publication. Sample copies available. Art guidelines free for SASE with first-class postage.
Illustrations: Approached by 100 illustrators/year. Buys 8 illustrations/issue, 50 illustrations/year from freelancers. Works on assignment only. Considers pen & ink, airbrush, mixed media, acrylic, oil and collage. Send query letter with brochure, tearsheets, photographs, slides, SASE, photocopies and transparencies. Samples are filed or returned by SASE. Reports back within 2 weeks. Call or write to schedule an appointment to show a portfolio or mail appropriate materials. Portfolio should include b&w and color tearsheets and photostats. Buys first rights and one-time rights. Pays $1,000 for b&w, $2,000 for color, cover; $400 for b&w, $1,000 for color, inside; on acceptance.

*THE MORGAN HORSE, Box 960, Shelburne VT 05482. (802)985-4944. Art Director: Dorian Scotti. Emphasizes all aspects of Morgan horse breed including educating Morgan owners, trainers and enthusiasts on breeding and training programs; the true type of the Morgan breed, techniques on promoting the breed, how-to articles, as well as preserving the history of the breed. Monthly. Circ. 10,000. Accepts previously published material and simultaneous submissions. Original artwork returned after publication. Sample copy $4.
Illustrations: Approached by 10 illustrators/year. Buys 2-5 illustrations/issue from freelancers. Uses freelance artists mainly for editorial illustration and mechanical production. "Line drawings are most useful for magazine work. We also purchase art for promotional projects dealing with the Morgan horse—horses must look like *Morgans*." Send query letter with samples and tearsheets. Accepts "anything that clearly shows the artist's style and craftsmanship" as samples. Samples are returned by SASE. Reports within 6-8 weeks. Call or write for appointment to show portfolio. Buys all rights or negotiates rights purchased. Pays $25-100, b&w; $200-400, color, inside on acceptance.
Tips: As trend sees "more of an effort on the part of art directors to utilize a broader style. Magazines seem to be moving towards more interesting graphic design."

THE MOTHER EARTH NEWS, 80 Fifth Ave., 5th Fl., New York NY 10010. (212)242-2460. Art Director: Roger Black. Magazine emphasizing self-reliant living, do-it-yourself products, natural foods, organic gardening, etc. for suburban, rural, small town, upper-middle income, family folks. Bimonthly. Circ. 700,000. Accepts previously published material. Original artwork returned after publication.
Illustrations: Buys 1-4 illustrations/issue from freelancers. Works on assignment only. Send query letter with brochure showing art style or tearsheets, photostats and photocopies. Samples not filed are returned by SASE. Reports only if interested. Negotiates rights purchased. Pays $200-400, b&w; $300-500, color, inside; on acceptance.

*MOTOR MAGAZINE, 645 Stewart Ave., Garden City NY 11530. (516)227-1303. Art Director: Harold A. Perry. Estab. 1903. Emphasizes automotive technology, repair and maintenance for auto mechanics and technicians. Monthly. Circ. 135,000. Accepts previously published material. Original artwork returned after publication if requested. Never send unsolicited original art.

Illustrations: Buys 5-15 illustrations/issue from freelancers. Works on assignment only. Prefers realistic, technical line renderings of automotive parts and systems. Send query letter with resume and photocopies to be kept on file. Will call for appointment to see further samples. Samples not filed are not returned. Reports only if interested. Buys one-time rights. Write to schedule an appointment to show a portfolio, which should include final reproduction/product and color tearsheets. Payment negotiable for cover, basically $300-1,500; $50-500, b&w, inside; on acceptance.

Tips: *"Motor* is an educational, technical magazine and is basically immune to illustration trends because our drawings *must* be realistic and technical. As design trends change we try to incorporate these into our magazine (within reason). Though *Motor* is a trade publication, we approach it, design-wise, as if it were a consumer magazine. We make use of white space when possible and use creative, abstract and impact photographs and illustration for our opening pages and covers. But we must always retain a 'technical look' to reflect our editorial subject matter. There are more and more design clones entering the market. A few of the elite say what is good and the rest fall into line. Publication graphics is becoming like TV programming, more calculating and imitative and less creative."

*MTL MAGAZINE, Suite 201, 8270 Mountain Sights, Montreal, Quebec H4P 2B7 Canada. (514)731-9449. FAX: (514)731-7459. Art Director: Hamo Abdalian. Estab. 1986. Consumer magazine; "an informative and entertaining approach to the interests, activities and lifestyle of Montrealers." Monthly. Circ. 65,000. Original artwork returned after publication. Sample copies available. Art guidelines not available.

Illustrations: Approached by 15 illustrators/year. Buys 5 illustrations/issue, 55 illustrations/year from freelancers. Works on assignment only. Prefers themes appropriate to the Montreal lifestyle. Considers acrylic and mixed media. Send query letter with photocopies. Samples are filed. Reports back within 2 weeks. Call to schedule an appointment to show a portfolio, which should include tearsheets. Buys first rights. Pays $350, b&w, $450, color, cover; $200, b&w, $250, color, inside; on publication.

Tips: "We are looking for good technique and originality."

MUSCLE MAG INTERNATIONAL, Unit 2, 52 Bramsteele Rd., Brampton, Ontario L6W 3M5 Canada. (416)457-3030. Editor-in-Chief: Robert Kennedy. Estab. 1972. For 16- to 50-year-old men and women interested in physical fitness and overall body improvement. Published 12 times/year. Circ. 210,000. Previously published work OK. Original artwork not returned after publication. Sample copy $4. Uses freelance artists mainly for T-shirt design.

Cartoons: Approached by 30 cartoonists/year. Buys 6 cartoons/issue, 20 cartoons/year from freelancers. Receives 30 submissions/week from freelancers. Interested in weight training and body building; single panel; "well-drawn work—professional." Send finished cartoons. SAE (nonresidents include IRC). Send $3 for return postage. Reports in 3 weeks. Buys all rights on a work-for-hire basis. Pays $85, color; $50, b&w; on acceptance. More for superior work.

Illustrations: Approached by 50 illustrators/year. Works with 6 illustrators/year. Uses 2 illustrations/issue; buys 1/issue from freelancers. Receives 20 submissions/week from freelancers. Interested in "professionally drawn exercise art of body builders training with apparatus." Prefers pen & ink, pastel and collage. Send query letter with tearsheets, photocopies, slides, photographs, and preferably finished art. SAE (nonresidents include IRC). Send $4 for return postage. Reports in 2 weeks. Call to schedule an appointment to show a portfolio, which should include original/final art. Buys all rights on a work-for-hire basis. Pays $350, color, cover; $250, color and $185, b&w, inside; on acceptance. "Pay can be triple for really professional or outstanding artwork."

*MUSCLE MAGAZINE, Box 6100, Rosemead CA 91770. Art Director: Michael Harding. Magazine emphasizing bodybuilding, exercise and professional fitness. Features general interest, historical, how-to, inspirational, interview/profile, personal experience, travel articles and experimental fiction (all sports-related). Monthly. Circ. 340,120. Accepts previously published material. Original artwork returned after publication.

Illustrations: Buys 5 illustrations/issue, 60 illustrations/year from freelancers. Send query letter with resume, tearsheets, slides and photographs. Samples are filed or are returned. Reports back within 1 week. To show a portfolio mail color and b&w tearsheets, final reproduction/product, photographs and slides. Buys first rights, one-time rights, reprint rights and all rights. Pays on acceptance.

Tips: "Be consistent in style and quality."

THE NATION, 72 Fifth Ave., New York NY 10011. (212)242-8400. Assistant Editor: Micah Sifry. Estab. 1865. "We are a journal of left/liberal political opinion, covering national and international affairs, literature and culture" in magazine format. Weekly. Circ. 85,000. Original artwork is returned after publication upon request. Sample copies available. Art guidelines not available.

Illustrations: Approached by 50 freelance illustrators/year. Buys illustrations mainly for spots and feature spreads. Buys 3-4 illustrations/issue. Buys 150-200 illustrations/year. Works with 25 illustrators/year. Works on assignment only. Considers pen & ink, airbrush, mixed media and charcoal pencil. No color, b&w only. Send query letter with tearsheets and photocopies. "On top of a defined style, artist must have a strong and original political sensibility." Samples are filed or are returned by SASE. Reports back about queries/submissions only if interested. Call to schedule a portfolio review or mail appropriate materials. Portfolio should include tearsheets and photostats. Buys first rights. Pays $150, b&w, cover; $75, b&w, inside.

NATIONAL AUDUBON SOCIETY, 950 3rd Ave., New York NY 10022. (212)546-9189. Contact: Photo Editor. Publishes *American Birds*. Emphasizes ornithology—migration, distribution, breeding and behavior of North and Middle American birds, including Hawaii and the West Indies, for amateur and professional birders, scientists, researchers, schools and libraries. Published 5 times/year (seasonal and Christmas Bird Count issue). Circ. 11,000. Original artwork returned after publication. Sample copy $5. Art guidelines for SASE with 1 first-class stamp.
Needs: Approached by over 30 freelance illustrators/year. Buys freelance art mainly for fillers, "but placed in important positions throughout magazine." Prefers "detailed drawings of birds of the Americas; drawings to aid in identification (anatomically correct a must)"; black & white line drawings, paintings, etchings, engravings and sketches.
First Contact & Terms: Send query letter with good quality photostats and slides. Samples will be kept on file for one year unless otherwise requested.
Tips: "I do not want to see anatomically incorrect birds. We are using more and more freelance art. We are not printing color artwork at this time."

*NATIONAL GARDENING, 180 Flynn Ave., Burlington VT 05401. (802)863-1308. FAX: (802)863-5962. Art Director: Linda Provost. Estab. 1980. Consumer magazine "specializing in home vegetable gardening; environmentally conscious; fun and informal but accurate; a gardener-to-gardener network." Monthly. Circ. 200,000. Sometimes accepts previously published artwork. Original artwork returned after publication. Sample copies available. Art guidelines not available.
Illustrations: Approached by 50 illustrators/year. Buys 10 illustrations/issue, 220 illustrations/year from freelancers. Works on assignment only. Preferred themes or styles "range from botanically accurate how-to illustrations to less literal, more interpretive styles. See the magazine. We use all media." Send query letter with brochure, SASE, tearsheets, photostats and slides. "I prefer something to keep on file, and SASE if I must return anything." Samples are filed or returned by SASE if requested. Reports back only if interested "and when interested, i.e. ready to assign work." Call to schedule an appointment to show a portfolio, which should include "your best work in your best form." Buys one-time rights. Pays $50-200, b&w; $125, spot; $350 (average), full page for color, inside; within 30 days of acceptance.

NATIONAL GEOGRAPHIC, 17th and M Sts. NW, Washington DC 20036. (202)857-7000. Art Director: Howard E. Paine. Estab. 1888. Monthly. Circ. 10,500,000. Original artwork sometimes returned after publication.
Illustrations: Works with 20 illustrators/year. Buys 50 illustrations/year from freelancers. Interested in "full-color, representational renderings of historical and scientific subjects. Nothing that can be photographed is illustrated by artwork. No decorative, design material. We want scientific geological cut-aways, maps, historical paintings." Works on assignment only. Prefers to see portfolio and samples of style. Samples are returned by SASE. "The artist should be familiar with the type of painting we use." Provide brochure, flyer or tearsheet to be kept on file for future assignments. Pays $3,500, color, $750, b&w, inside; on acceptance.
Tips: "Send historical and scientific illustrations, ones that are very informative and very accurate. I do not want to see decorative, abstract portraits."

THE NATIONAL NOTARY, 8236 Remmet Ave., Box 7184, Canoga Park CA 91304-7184. (818)713-4000. Contact: Production Editor. Emphasizes "notaries public and notarization—goal is to impart knowledge, understanding, and unity among notaries nationwide and internationally." Readers are notaries of varying primary occupations (legal, government, real estate and financial), as well as state and federal officials and foreign notaries. Bimonthly. Circ. 80,000. Original artwork not returned after publication. Sample copy $5.
Cartoons: Approached by 5-8 cartoonists/year. Cartoons "must have a notarial angle"; single or multi panel with gagline, b&w line drawings. Send samples of style. Samples not returned. Reports in 4-6 weeks. Call to schedule an appointment to show a portfolio. Buys all rights. Negotiates pay; on publication.
Illustrations: Approached by 3-4 illustrators/year. Uses about 3 illustrations/issue; buys all from local freelancers. Works on assignment only. Themes vary, depending on subjects of articles. Send business card, samples and tearsheets to be kept on file. Samples not returned. Reports in 4-6 weeks. Call for appointment. Buys all rights. Negotiates pay; on publication.
Tips: "We are very interested in experimenting with various styles of art in illustrating the magazine. We generally work with Southern California artists, as we prefer face-to-face dealings."

Close-up

Victoria Leidner
Managing Editor, American Birds
The Audubon Society

"One artist constantly sends me material, one or two drawings at a time," says Victoria Leidner, managing editor of *American Birds*, a quarterly journal published by the National Audubon Society. "He's a baker by profession, in Arizona, very hard to get in touch with. Finally I got hold of him, and he was so pleased that we were using his work." This situation is quite common, Leidner says; much of the artwork she uses is not done by professional artists, but by people who earn their living in other fields, who nevertheless have become interested in illustration.

American Birds, she says, unlike the Society's consumer magazine on ecological and nature-related issues, *Audubon*, is really a journal for amateur and professional birders. Although the feature articles, especially those in the front part of the magazine, are accessible to anybody, she says, "It does become technical in nature. The back part is very technical data, which pertains to regions throughout the American states. It's a magazine that you won't generally see around; it's not on the newsstands.

"I'm always looking for new artists," Leidner emphasizes. "There are a certain few that I tap constantly, but there's no reason why I don't go to other people." She stresses that the National Audubon Society is a very pleasant, low-key organization to work for: "It's not an ad agency, not a corporation." Many authors and researchers arrive at the Society's offices at Fifty-seventh Street and Third Avenue right in from the field, in fact, with their field drawings, photographs, and knapsacks in tow.

In choosing artwork for *American Birds*, Leidner looks for "very succinct, good, clear drawings" of birds, as well as etchings and wood and block prints. Line art, she says, reproduces best, including black-and-white washes, prints and black-and-white tone. She asks that artists send clear photocopies or photostats (labeled with name and phone number) rather than originals, "simply because I can't be responsible for their artwork."

"Art should be as detailed as possible," she says, adding that drawings with a "pretty basic" rendering style are unlikely to be accepted. Leidner keeps the work she receives on file for a year, to be used mainly as fillers in *American Birds*, although drawings often stretch to half or three quarters of a page.

Leidner does not normally review portfolios and seldom finds herself looking for a particular species of bird. "I would love to see what they like to do," she says, adding that some artists do send lists of the bird species for which they have drawings on hand; Leidner files these lists and will get in touch with an artist in case a certain unfamiliar type of bird — "like a vireo or a shrike" — is needed. "What we do," she says, "is develop a library of pen-and-inks and etchings.

"Being a nonprofit organization, we do not pay artists for their work," Leidner says, adding, however, that artists do receive bylines and valuable exposure — and that cover photographs of birds are paid for. She hopes that the magazine's growing circulation rate — it's now over 13,500 — will someday enable her to pay artists for their work, and she would also like to be able to use color drawings in the magazine in the future.

— Laurie Henry

NATIONAL REVIEW, 150 E. 35th St., New York NY 10016. (212)679-7330. Art Director: Paul Hebert. Emphasizes world events from a conservative viewpoint. Bimonthly. Original artwork returned after publication. Uses freelance artists mainly for illustrations of articles and book reviews, also covers.

Cartoons: Buys 15 cartoons/issue from freelancers. Interested in "political, social commentary." Prefers to receive finished cartoons. Send SASE. Reports in 2 weeks. Buys first North American serial rights. Pays $60 b&w; on publication.

Illustrations: Buys 15 illustrations/issue from freelancers. Especially needs b&w ink illustration, portraits of political figures and conceptual editorial art (b&w line plus halftone work). "I look for a strong graphic style; well-developed ideas and well-executed drawings." Works on assignment only. Send query letter with brochure showing art style or tearsheets and photocopies. No samples returned. Reports back on future assignment possibilities. Call to schedule an appointment to show a portfolio, which should include original/final art, final reproduction/product and b&w tearsheets. SASE. Also buys small decorative and humorous spot illustrations in advance by mail submission. Buys first North American serial rights. Pays $85-100 b&w, inside; $500 color, cover; on publication.

Tips: "Tearsheets and mailers are helpful in remembering an artist's work. Artists ought to make sure their work is professional in quality, idea and execution. Recent printed samples alongside originals help. Changes in art and design in our field include fine art influence and use of more halftone illustration." A common mistake freelancers make in presenting their work is "no uniformed style, i.e. a cross sample of too many different styles by one illustrator so that I am unsure about what type of illustration I'll be getting."

Freelance illustrator Shannon Jeffries of Brooklyn, New York designed this illustration in acrylic paint for **National Review** *magazine. Jeffries says she benefited from the publication of the piece because it allowed her the opportunity to develop a strong black-and-white piece for her portfolio.*

NATIONAL RURAL LETTER CARRIER, Suite 100, 1448 Duke St., Alexandria VA 22314. (703)684-5545. Managing Editor: RuthAnn Saenger. Emphasizes news and analysis of federal law and current events for rural letter carriers and family-oriented, middle-Americans; many are part-time teachers, businessmen and farmers. Weekly. Circ. 75,000. Mail art and SASE. Reports in 4 weeks. Original artwork returned after publication. Previously published, photocopied and simultaneous submissions OK. Buys first rights. Sample copy 24¢. Receives 1 cartoon and 2 illustrations/month from freelance artists.

Illustrations: Buys 12 covers/year on rural scenes, views of rural mailboxes and rural people. Buys 1 illustration/issue from freelancers. Interested in pen & ink or pencil on rural, seasonal and postal matter. Especially needs rural mailboxes and sketches of scenes on rural delivery. Works on assignment only. Send query letter with brochure showing art style or resume, tearsheets, photocopies, slides and photographs. Samples returned by SASE. Reports in 1 week, if accepted; 1 month if not accepted. Write to schedule an appointment to show a portfolio, which should include original/final art, final reproduction/product, color and b&w tearsheets, photostats and photographs. Buys all rights on a work-for-hire basis. Pays by the project, $60-150; on publication.

Tips: "Please send in samples when you inquire about submitting material." Has a definite need for "realistic painting and sketches. We need a clean, crisp style. Subjects needed are rural scenes, mailboxes, animals and faces. We need fine black-and-white, pen-and-ink and watercolor."

NATURAL HISTORY, American Museum of Natural History, Central Park W. and 79th St., New York NY 10024. (212)769-5500. Editor: Alan Ternes. Designer: Tom Page. Emphasizes social and natural sciences. For well-educated professionals interested in the natural sciences. Monthly. Circ. 500,000. Previously published work OK.

Illustrations: Buys 23-25 illustrations/year; 25-35 maps or diagrams/year. Works on assignment only. Query with samples. Samples returned by SASE. Provide "any pertinent information" to be kept on file for future assignments. Buys one-time rights. Pays $200 and up, color inside; on publication.

Tips: "Be familiar with the publication. Always looking for accurate and creative scientific illustrations, good diagrams and maps."

NEW AGE JOURNAL, 342 Western Ave., Brighton MA 02135. (617)787-2005. Art Director: Dan Mishkind. Emphasizes alternative lifestyles, holistic health, ecology, personal growth, human potential, planetary survival. Bimonthly. Circ. 150,000. Accepts previously published material and simultaneous submissions. Original artwork returned after publication by request. Sample copy $3.

Illustrations: Approached by 500 illustrators/year. Uses 8 illustrations/issue from freelancers. Illustrations accompany specific manuscripts. Send query letter with samples or tearsheets to be kept on file. Prefers photostats, photocopies or slides as samples. Samples returned by SASE if not kept on file. Buys one-time rights. Pays $600, color, cover; $300, color, inside.

Tips: Wants to see "name and phone number printed on each sample."

Dan Mishkind, art director of **New Age Journal,** *learned of* **New York** *artist Amy Guip through a self-promotional piece. This black-and-white photography and paint illustration creates just the haunting mood Mishkind was looking for, a sense of the emotional anguish reported by victims of therapist/patient abuse. Jonathon Adolph of the Journal says, "Guip's skillful use of color and contrast powerfully evokes the victim's sense of isolation and betrayal."*

© 1989 New Age Journal

*NEW BLOOD MAGAZINE, 1843 E. Venton St., Covina CA 91724. Editor: Chris B. Lacher. Estab. 1987. Magazine emphasizing "fiction, features, art and cartoons considered too strong or bizarre for any ordinary periodical." Quarterly. Circ. 15,000. Accepts previously published artwork. Originals returned at job's completion if SASE is enclosed. Sample copy $4. Art guidelines not available. "I'm not too picky about style or sizes."

Cartoons: Approached by 25 cartoonists/year. Buys 20-30 cartoons/issue, 100-150 cartoons/year from freelancers. "It just has to be a bit 'off,' unique. I am not adverse to controversial themes." Prefers single panel and multiple panel with gagline. Send query letter with samples available for purchase. Reports back within 3 weeks. Buys first rights. Average payment is $10-25, single panel; multiple panel is negotiable. Pays $5, b&w.

Illustrations: Approached by 25 illustrators/year. Buys 5 illustrations/issue, 15 illustrations/year from freelancers. Prefers horror themes and styles. Considers pen & ink, airbrush and mixed media. Send query letter with SASE and photocopies. Samples are filed. Reports back within 3 weeks. Mail appropriate materials: thumbnails, roughs, original/final art and b&w tearsheets and photocopies. Buys first rights. Pays $5, b&w.

Tips: "We don't do 'Chester the Molester' type of cartoons. The work I purchase is usually very different from what a contributor would assume."

NEW ENGLAND MONTHLY, 132 Main St., Haydenville MA 01039. (413)268-7262. Art Director: Tim Gabor. Design Director: Mike Grinley. Estab. 1984. A general interest magazine focusing on contemporary matters that affect the lives of the residents of New England. Covers all subjects—people, politics, recreation, arts, the outdoors, business, food, and often a photo-heavy article or portfolio. Monthly. Circ. 115,000. Original artwork is returned after publication. Art guidelines available.

Illustrations: Buys 60-80 illustrations/year from freelancers. Works on assignment only. Send query letter with brochure, tearsheets, slides and photographs. Samples are filed or are returned only if requested by artist. Reports back within weeks. Call to schedule an appointment to show a portfolio, which should include tearsheets, final reproduction/product, photographs and slides. Pays $700, color, cover; $300, b&w; $400, color, inside; on acceptance or publication.

Tips: "I prefer to see tearsheets or printed art. Develop originality and a fresh style. Keep sending cards to update our files."

*NEW HOME MAGAZINE, Box 2008, Laconia NH 03247. (603)528-4285. FAX: (603)524-0643. Art Director: Kevin Wells. Estab. 1986. Consumer magazine "targeted to people who have recently purchased a home. *New Home* concentrates on the issues and needs of the new homeowner with service based articles and departments." Bimonthly. Circ. 300,000. Accepts previously published artwork. Original artwork is returned at job's completion. Samples copies available. Art guidelines free for SASE with first-class postage.

Illustrations: Approached by 100-150 illustrators/year. Buys 5-10 illustrations/issue, 35-75 illustrations/year from freelancers. Works on assignment only. Considers various styles. Considers pen & ink, airbrush, colored pencil, watercolor, acrylic, oil, pastel and collage. Send query letter with tearsheets. Samples are filed. Reports back to the artist only if interested. Write to schedule an appointment to show a portfolio, which should include b&w and color tearsheets. Rights purchased vary according to project. Pays $100, color, inside; on publication.

NEW LETTERS, 5216 Rockhill Rd., University of Missouri, Kansas City MO 64110. "Innovative" small magazine with an international scope. Quarterly. Sample copy $4.

Illustrations: Uses camera-ready spot drawings, line drawings and washes; "any medium that will translate well to the 6x9″ b&w printed page." Also needs cover designs. Submit art. Reports in 2-8 weeks. Buys all rights. Pays $5 maximum, pen & ink, line drawings and washes. Must include SASE for return of work.

Tips: "Fewer pieces of freelance art being accepted; we consider only work of the highest quality. Artwork does not necessarily have to relate to content."

NEW MEXICO MAGAZINE, 1100 St. Francis Dr., Santa Fe NM 87503. (505)827-0220. Art Director: John Vaughan. Emphasizes the state of New Mexico for residents and visiting vacationers. Monthly. Circ. 100,000. Accepts previously published material and simultaneous submissions. Original artwork returned after publication. No printed artists' guidelines, but may call for information. Also interested in calligraphers.

Cartoons: Buys 1-2 cartoons/issue, 12 cartoons/year from freelancers. Prefers single panel; b&w line drawings, b&w washes. Send resume, tearsheets, photostats, photocopies and slides. Call to schedule an appointment to show a portfolio, which should include color and b&w original/final art, final reproduction/product, tearsheets and photographs. Material not kept on file is returned only if requested. Reports only if interested. Buys one-time rights. Pays $50-100, b&w; $50-100, color; two weeks after acceptance, on publication for stock material.

Illustrations: Works with 10-20 illustrators/year. Buys 15-25 illustrations/year from freelancers. Works on assignment only. Send query letter with samples to be filed. Samples not filed are returned only if requested. Reports only if interested. Buys one-time rights. Pays for design $7-15; $40 for small illustrations to $300 for 4-color work, usually all inside; on acceptance.

Tips: Contact verbally or with written material first. Send appropriate materials and samples. "Don't present too much. Show what you do best."

NEW ORLEANS REVIEW, Box 195, Loyola University, New Orleans LA 70118. (504)865-2294. Editor: John Mosier. Journal of literature and film. Published 4 times/year. Sample copy $9.
Illustrations: Uses 5-10 illustrations/issue. Cover: uses color, all mediums. Include SASE. Reports in 4 months. Inside: uses b&w line drawings, photos/slides of all mediums.

*THE NEW PHYSICIAN, 1890 Preston White Dr., Reston VA 22091. Contact: Art Director: Mary Ellen Vehlow. For physicians-in-training; concerns primary medical care, political and social issues relating to medicine. Published 9 times/year. Circ. 42,000. Original artwork returned after publication. Buys one-time rights. Pays on publication.
Cartoons: Approached by 2-6 cartoonists/year. Cartoon submissions welcome. Interested in medical education. Send finished artwork. Reports in 2 weeks.
Illustrations: Approached by 100-200 illustrators/year. Buys 5 illustrations/issue from freelancers. Usually commissioned. Samples returned by SASE. Submit resume and samples of style. Reports in 2 weeks. Provide resume, letter of inquiry, brochure and flyer to be kept on file for future assignments. Buys one-time rights. Pays $600, color, cover; $100, b&w, $300, color, inside.

the new renaissance, 9 Heath Rd., Arlington MA 02174. Editor: Louise T. Reynolds or Art Editor: Olivera Sajkovic. Estab. 1968. Magazine emphasizing literature, arts and opinion for "the general, literate public an aesthetic sensibility and which has an interest in provocative idea and opinion pieces." Bi-annual (spring and fall). Size: 6×9. Circ. 1,600. Returns original artwork after publication if SASE is enclosed. Sample copy $6.30, U.S.; $6.60, foreign.
Cartoons: Approached by 15-18 cartoonists/year. Pays $20, b&w.
Illustrations: Buys 6-8 illustrations/issue from freelancers and "occasional supplementary artwork (2-4 pp)." Works mainly on assignment. Send resume, samples, photos and SASE. No slides. Samples not filed are returned by SASE. Reports within 1-3 months. To show a portfolio, mail roughs, b&w photographs and SASE. Buys one-time rights. Pays $25, b&w; after publication.
Tips: "We have never been an "anything goes" litmag but we are receiving a good deal of alternative-press style cartoons and drawings as well as much populist and ash can artwork that is, at best, a long-shot. We are also receiving, despite what we thought was our emphasis on b&w, a surprising large number of colour pieces—and these are absolutely no good to us as we always reproduce in b&w. We want artists who have an understanding of what is involved in illustrating a "quality" (or "serious" or "literary") piece of fiction (or, occasionally, a poem) and for this they should be studying the illustrations that we have used in the past. We are receiving work that is more appropriate for a newsletter or newsprint or alternative-press kinds of magazines. *tnr* takes a classicist position in the arts—we want our work to stand up, not only to casual glances, but to decades and generations of examination.

THE NEW REPUBLIC, 1220 19th St. NW, Washington DC 20036. (202)331-7494. Assistant Editor: Leona Hiraoka Roth. Estab. 1914. Political/literary magazine; political journalism, current events in the front section, book reviews and literary essays in the back. Weekly. Circ. 100,000. Original artwork returned after publication. Sample copy $3.
Illustrations: Approached by 300 illustrators/year. Buys 1-2 illustrations/issue, 48 illustrations/year from freelancers. Uses freelance illustration mainly for cover art. Works on assignment only. Prefers caricatures, portraits, 4-color, "no cartoons." Considers airbrush, colored pencil, watercolor, acrylic and oil. Send query letter with tearsheets. Samples are filed "if we think we may work together," or returned by SASE. Reports back within 1 month. "We'll contact you after seeing tearsheets." Portfolio should include roughs, tearsheets and "whatever the artist thinks matches our style best." Rights purchased vary according to project. Pays $500 for color, cover. Pays on publication.

NEW WOMAN MAGAZINE, 215 Lexington Ave., New York NY 10016. (212)685-4790. Magazine emphasizing emotional self-help for women ages 25-34, 50% married. Most have attended college. Published monthly. Circ. 1.2 million. Accepts previously published material. Returns original artwork to the artist upon request.
Cartoons: Approached by 1,500 cartoonists/year. Buys approximately 4-6 freelance cartoons/issue from freelancers. Prefers single panel, with gagline; b&w line drawings. "We have changed quite a bit. We are still pro-women, but not as hard-hitting or as sexist in putting men down. We need cartoons every month for our word power quiz, pin-ups and letters to the editor column. Look at recent issues of the magazine." Contact Yvonne Stender, Cartoon Editor, for more information or to be added to the monthly mailing list, which tells which articles in upcoming issues will require cartoons. Cartoons are not matched with editorial. Send finished cartoon and SASE. Purchases all serial rights. Pays $225; on acceptance.
Illustrations: Uses 6-10 freelance illustrations/issue. Works on assignment only. Send tearsheets and photocopies to be kept on file to Catherine Caldwell, Art Director. Samples not kept on file are not returned. Reports only if interested. Payment varies. Pays on acceptance.

*NEW WRITER'S MAGAZINE, Box 5974, Sarasota FL 34277. (813)953-7903. Editor/Publisher: George J. Haborak. Estab. 1986. Literary magazine; "in a format where all writers can exchange thoughts, ideas and their own writing. It is focused on the needs of the aspiring or new writer." Bimonthly. Rarely accepts previously published artwork. Original artwork returned after publication if the artist requests it. Sample copies for $2. Art guidelines not available.

Cartoons: Approached by 2-3 cartoonists/year. Buys 1 cartoon/issue; 6-8 cartoons/year from freelancers. Prefers cartoons "that reflect the joys or frustrations of being a writer/author." Prefers single panel with gagline; b&w line drawings. Send query letter with samples of style. Samples are sometimes filed or returned if requested. Reports back within 1 month. Buys first rights. Pays $25, b&w; on publication.

Illustration: Buys 1 illustration/issue, 6 illustrations/year from freelancers. Works on assignment only. Prefers line drawing. Considers watercolor, mixed media, colored pencil and pastel. Send query letter with brochure showing art style. Samples are filed or returned if requested by SASE. Reports within 1 month. Portfolio should include tearsheets. Buys first rights and negotiates rights purchased. Payment negotiated. Pays on publication.

NEW YORK HABITAT MAGAZINE, 928 Broadway, New York NY 10010. Managing Editor: Lloyd Chrein. Estab. 1982. "We are a how-to magazine for cooperative and condominium boards of directors in New York City and Westchester." 8 times a year. Circ. 10,000. Original artwork is returned after publication. Sample copy $5. Art guidelines free for SASE with first-class postage.

Illustrations: Approached by 50 freelance illustrators/year. Buys illustrations mainly for spots and feature spreads. Buys 1-3 illustrations/issue, 8-20 illustrations/year from freelancers. Works on assignment only. Prefers pen & ink. Considers marker. Send query letter with brochure showing art style, resume, tearsheets, photostats, photocopies, slides, photographs and transparencies (fee requirements). Looks for "clarity in form and content." Samples are filed or are returned by SASE. Reports back about queries/submissions only if interested. For a portfolio review mail original/final art and b&w tearsheets. Pays $75-125, b&w.

Tips: "Read our publication, understand the topic. Look at the 'Habitat Hotline' and 'Case Notes' sections." Does not want to see "tired cartoons about Wall Street board meetings and cute street beggars."

*NEW YORK MAGAZINE, 755 Second Ave., New York NY 10017. (212)880-0700. Design Director: Robert Best. Art Director: Syndi Becker. Emphasizes New York City life; also covers all boroughs for New Yorkers with upper-middle income and business people interested in what's happening in the city. Weekly. Original artwork returned after publication.

Illustrations: Works on assignment only. Send query letter with tearsheets to be kept on file. Prefers photostats as samples. Samples returned if requested. Call or write for appointment to show portfolio (drop-offs). Buys first rights. Pays $1,000, b&w and color, cover; $800, 4-color, $400, b&w full page, inside; $225, 4-color, $150, b&w spot, inside; on publication.

THE NEW YORKER, 25 W. 43rd St., New York NY 10036. (212)840-3800. Contact: Art Editor. Emphasizes news analysis and lifestyle features.

Needs: Buys cartoons and cover designs. Receives 3,000 cartoons/week. Mail art or deliver sketches on Wednesdays. Include SASE. Strict standards regarding style, technique, plausibility of drawing. Especially looks for originality. Pays $500 minimum, cartoons; top rates for cover designs. "Not currently buying spots."

Tips: "Familiarize yourself with your markets."

NORTH AMERICAN HUNTER, Box 3401, Minnetonka MN 55343. (612)936-9333. FAX: (612)944-2687. Editor: Bill Miller. Estab. 1978. Publishes hunting material only, for avid hunters of both small and big game in North America. Bimonthly. Circ. 250,000. Accepts previously published material. Original artwork returned after publication unless all rights are purchased. Sample copy $5; art guidelines available.

Cartoons: Approached by 50 cartoonists/year. Buys 15-20 cartoons/year from freelancers. Considers humorous hunting situations. "Must convey ethical, responsible hunting practices; good clean fun; not too detailed, but logically accurate." Prefers single panel with gagline; b&w line drawings or washes; 8½×11 vertical or horizontal format. Send query letter with roughs or finished cartoons. Returns unpurchased material immediately. Reports within 2 weeks. Buys all rights. Pays $35, b&w; on acceptance.

Illustrations: Approached by 100 illustrators/year. Buys 2 illustrations/issue from freelancers; usually includes 1 humorous illustration. Works with 5-7 illustrators/year. Prefers line art, mostly b&w, occasionally color. "Work should be close to being photographically real in most cases." Works on assignment only. Send query letter with samples. Samples not filed are returned. Reports within 2 weeks. Buys one-time rights. Pays up to $250, color, cover; up to $100, b&w or color, inside; on acceptance.

Tips: "Send only art that deals with hunting, hunters, wildlife or hunting situations. North American big and small game only. We accept only detailed and realistic-looking pieces—no modern art."

NORTHERN CALIFORNIA HOME & GARDEN, WESTAR MEDIA, 656 Bair Island Rd., Redwood City CA 94063. Art Director: Dana Irwin. Estab. 1987. "We are a regional home & garden consumer magazine with emphasis on design in architecture (interior and exterior), interior design and design in landscaping and gardens. Readership is upscale (middle to high income level)." Monthly. Circ. 50,000. Original arwork is returned after publication. Sample copy $2. Art guidelines available.

Illustrations: Approached by 30-50 illustrators/year. Works with 5-10 illustrators/year. Buys 3 illustrations/issue, 36 illustrations/year from freelancers. Buys illustrations mainly for spots. Works on assignment only. Considers pen & ink, mixed media, colored pencil, pastels and scratchboard. Send query letter with tearsheets, photocopies and transparencies. Samples are filed. Samples not filed are returned by SASE. Reports back about queries/submissions within 1 month. To show a portfolio mail color and b&w tearsheets, slides, photographs and transparencies, or drop off portfolio for 2-day review. Buys one-time rights. Pays $100, b&w, $150-200, color, inside.

Tips: Sections most open to illustrators are four-color gardening articles and b&w how to and money departments. Does not want to se "history—past work that is outdated with the artist's current style."

THE NORTHERN LOGGER & TIMBER PROCESSOR, Northeastern Loggers Association Inc., Box 69, Old Forge NY 13420. (315)369-3078. Editor: Eric A. Johnson. Emphasizes methods, machinery and manufacturing as related to forestry. "For loggers, timberland managers and processors of primary forest products." Monthly. Circ. 13,000. Previously published material OK. Free sample copy; guidelines sent upon request.

Cartoons: Buys 1 cartoon/issue, all from freelancers. Receives 1 submission/week from freelancers. Interested in "any cartoons involving forest industry situations." Send finished cartoons with SASE. Reports in 1 week. Pays $15 minimum, b&w line drawings; on acceptance.

Tips: "Keep it simple and pertinent to the subjects we cover. Also, keep in mind that on-the-job safety is an issue that we like to promote."

NORTHWEST REVIEW, 369 PLC, University of Oregon, Eugene OR 97403. (503)686-3957. Editor: John Witte. Art Editor: George Gessert. Emphasizes literature. "We publish material of general interest to those who follow the American world of poetry and fiction." Original artwork returned after publication. Published 3 times/year. Sample copy $3.

Illustrations: Uses b&w line drawings, graphics and cover designs. Receives 20-30 portfolios/year from freelance artists. Arrange interview or mail slides. Send SASE. Reports as soon as possible. Acquires one-time rights. Pays in contributor's copies. Especially needs high-quality graphic artwork. "We run a regular art feature of the work of one artist, printed in b&w, 133-line screen on quality coated paper. A statement by the artist often accompanies the feature."

Tips: "We are currently committed to an ongoing feature on *artists' books*, publishing in each issue reviews of artists' books and reproducing one artists' book in its entirety."

NOTRE DAME MAGAZINE, 415 Main Bldg., Notre Dame IN 46556. (219)239-5336. Art Director: Don Nelson. Estab. 1971. General interest university magazine for Notre Dame alumni and friends. Quarterly. Circ. 115,000. Accepts previously published artwork. Original artwork returned after publication. Sample copies and/or art guidelines not available.

Illustrations: Approached by 40 illustrators/year. Buys 5 illustrations/issue from freelancers. Works on assignment only. Looking for experienced editorial artists only. Send query letter with tearsheets, photostats, photographs, slides and photocopies. Samples are filed "if they are good" or are returned by SASE if requested. "Don't send submissions—only tearsheets and samples." Mail appropriate materials. Portfolio should include published editorial art. Buys first rights. Payment negotiated.

Tips: "Send accomplished, professional editorial samples."

NUCLEAR TIMES MAGAZINE, Suite 300, 1601 Connecticut Ave., NW, Washington DC 20009. (202)332-9222. Art Director: Elliott Negin. Provides straight news coverage of U.S.-Soviet relations, U.S. foreign policy, and the anti-nuclear weapons movement. Bimonthly. Circ. 40,000. Accepts previously published material. Returns original artwork after publication. Sample copy $3.

Cartoons: Approached by 20 cartoonists/year. Pays $200, b&w.

Illustrations: Buys 4-10 illustrations/issue from freelancers. Primarily works on assignment. Write for appointment to show portfolio. Prefers to review photocopies and tearsheets in mail submissions. Samples not filed are returned by SASE only if requested. Reports within 4 weeks. Buys one-time rights. Pays $500, four-color cover; $50-300, b&w and color, inside; within 30 days of acceptance.

Tips: "I like to see printed pieces. I don't want to see any work from more than three years before. Gear your samples to our specific needs, such as samples of work published in periodicals or illustrations sympathetic to the topics covered by our magazine. I don't want to see children's book illustrations, for example."

NUGGET, Dugent Publishing Co., 2355 Salzedo St., Coral Gables FL 33134. Editor: Jerome Slaughter. Illustration Assignments: Nye Willden. For men and women with fetishes.

Cartoons: Buys 10 cartoons/issue, all from freelancers. Receives 50 submissions/week from freelancers. Interested in "funny fetish themes." Black-and-white only for spots, b&w and color for page. Prefers to see finished cartoons. SASE. Reports in 2 weeks. Buys first North American serial rights. Pays $75, spot drawings; $100, page.

Illustrations: Buys 4 illustrations/issue from freelancers. Interested in "erotica, cartoon style, etc." Works on assignment only. Prefers to see samples of style. No samples returned. Reports back on future assignment possibilities. Send brochure, flyer or other samples to be kept on file for future assignments. Buys first North American serial rights. Pays $100-200, b&w.

Tips: Especially interested in "the artist's anatomy skills, professionalism in rendering (whether he's published or not) and drawings which relate to our needs." Current trends include "a return to the 'classical' realistic form of illustration, which is fine with us because we prefer realistic and well-rendered illustrations."

*OCEANUS, 9 Maury Ln., Woods Hole MA 02540. (508)548-1400, ext 2386. FAX: (508)548-1400, ext. 6016. Assistant Editor: Timothy Hawley. Estab. 1952. Consumer magazine. "*Oceanus* features articles by the world's foremost oceanographic researchers and marine science experts, edited for lay readers with high-school education." Quarterly. Circ. 15,000. Accepts previously published artwork. Original artwork is returned at job's completion. Sample copies free for SASE with first-class postage. Art guidelines availble.

Cartoons: Approached by less than 10 cartoonists/year. Buys 2 cartoons/issue, 10 cartoons/year from freelancers. Prefers "scientific/political humorous cartoons; must relate to the marine environment;" single panel and b&w line drawing. Send query letter with finished cartoons. Samples are filed. Buys all rights. Pays $50, b&w, $300, color.

Illustrations: Approached by 5 illustrators/year. Buys 10 illustrations/issue, 50 illustrations/year from freelancers. Works on assignment only. Prefers scientific/technical illustration, maps. Considers whatever medium is most appropriate to the subject. Send query letter with resume, SASE and tearsheets. Samples are filed. Call or write to schedule an appointment to show a portfolio, which should include original/final art, tearsheets and photographs. Buys all rights. Pays $300, b&w, $500, color, cover; $50, b&w, $100, color, inside; on acceptance.

Tips: "Illustrations must capture the essence and nuances of very technical and sometimes esoteric ideas. Artists must not only be very skilled technically, but also be able to understand and work with scientists."

*OHIO BUSINESS MAGAZINE, 1720 Euclid, Cleveland OH 44115. (216)621-1644. FAX: (216)621-5918. Editor: Robert Gardner. Estab. 1976. Business magazine for the state of Ohio. Monthly. Circ. 50,000. Accepts previously published artwork. Original artwork is returned at job's completion. Sample copies available. Art guidelines available.

Illustrations: Works on assignment only. Send query letter with brochure. Samples are filed. Write to schedule an appointment to show a portfolio. Buys one-time rights. Payment is negotiable.

OHIO MAGAZINE, 40 S. Third St., Columbus OH 43215. (614)461-5083. Designer: Brooke Wenstrup. Emphasizes feature material of Ohio for an educated, urban and urbane readership. Monthly. Circ. 110,000. Previously published work OK. Original artwork returned after publication. Sample copy $3.

Illustrations: Buys 1-3/issue from freelancers. Interested in Ohio scenes and themes. Prefers fine art versus 'trendy' styles. Prefers pen & ink, charcoal/pencil, colored pencil, watercolor, acrylic, oil, pastel, collage, marker, mixed media and calligraphy. Works on stock and assignment. Send query letter with brochure showing art style or tearsheets, dupe slides and photographs. SASE. Reports in 4 weeks. On assignment: pays $75-150, b&w; $100-250, color, inside; on publication. Buys one-time publication rights.

Tips: "It helps to see one work in all its developmental stages. It provides insight into the artist's thought process. Some published pieces as well as non-published pieces are important. A representative sampling doesn't hurt, but it's a waste of both parties' time if their work isn't even close to the styles we use."

OLD WEST, Box 2107, Stillwater OK 74076. (405)743-0130. Editor: John Joerschke. Emphasizes American western history from 1830 to 1910 for a primarily rural and suburban audience, middle-age and older, interested in Old West history, horses, cowboys, art, clothing and all things western. Quarterly. Circ. 30,000. Accepts previously published material and considers some simultaneous submissions. Original artwork returned after publication. Sample copy $2. Art guidelines for SASE.

Illustrations: Buys 5-10 illustrations/issue, including 2 or 3 humorous illustrations; buys all from freelancers. "Inside illustrations are usually, but need not always be, pen & ink line drawings; covers are western paintings." Send query letter with samples to be kept on file; "we return anything on request." Call or write for appointment to show portfolio. "For inside illustrations, we want samples of artist's line drawings. For covers, we need to see full-color transparencies." Reports within 1 month. Buys one-time rights. Pays $100-150 for color transparency for cover; $20-50, b&w, inside. "Payment on acceptance for new artists, on assignment for established contributors."

Tips: "We think the mainstream of interest in Western Americana has moved in the direction of fine art, and we're looking for more material along those lines." Wants to see any "work related directly to history of the Old West."

*OPHTHALMOLOGY MANAGEMENT, 1515 Broadway, New York NY 10036. (212)869-1300. FAX: (212)302-6273. Art Director: Mark Tuchman. Estab. 1965. Trade journal; magazine format; business management magazines for the vision-care professional. Monthly. Circ. 18,000. Original artwork is returned at job's completion. Sample copies are available. Art guidelines not available.

Illustrations: Approached by 75 illustrators/year. Buys 6 illustrations/issue, 72 illustrations/year from freelancers. Works on assignment only. "We use illustrations presented in a variety of styles and media throughout the journal." Considers pen & ink, airbrush, colored pencil, mixed media, watercolor, acrylic, oil, pastel, collage and marker. Send query letter with tearsheets. Samples are filed. Reports back only if interested. Call to schedule an appointment to show a portfolio, which should include original/final art and tearsheets. Buys all rights. Pays $450, color, cover; $160, b&w, $220, color, inside; on publication.

Tips: "Let your work speak for itself; send samples on occasion but don't call. We'll call when and if we have something for you."

*THE OPTIMIST MAGAZINE, 4494 Lindell Blvd., St. Louis MO 63108. (314)371-6000. Editor: Gary S. Bradley. Emphasizes activities relating to Optimist clubs in U.S. and Canada (civic-service clubs). "Magazine is mailed to all members of Optimist clubs. Average age is 42, most are management level with some college education." Circ. 170,000. Accepts previously published material. Sample copy for SASE.

Cartoons: Buys 3 cartoons/issue from freelancers. Prefers themes of general interest; family-orientation, sports, kids, civic clubs. Prefers single panel, with gagline. No washes. Send query letter with samples. Submissions returned by SASE. Reports within 1 week. Buys one-time rights. Pays $30, b&w; on acceptance.

*OPTOMETRIC MANAGEMENT, 1515 Broadway, New York NY 10036. (212)869-1300. Art Director: Mark Tuchman. Estab. 1965. "We are a national business management magazine for optometrists. 70% of our readers are in private practice. Recent articles include 'Computerizing the Office' and 'Income Survey.'" Monthly. Circ. 25,000. Original artwork is sometimes returned after publication. Sample copies available. Art guidelines not available.

Illustrations: Buys illustrations mainly for spots and feature spreads. Buys 3-4 illustrations/issue, 36 illustrations/year from freelancers. Works on assignment only. Considers pen & ink, mixed media, watercolor, acrylic, oil, pastel, collage and marker. Uses pen & ink most. Send query letter with brochure showing art style, tearsheets, photocopies and "send in any format that will best represent your work. We are looking for an ability to conceptualize an idea and execute it with style." Samples are filed. Reports back only if interested. Call to schedule an appointment to show portfolio, which should include anything the artist thinks appropriate. Buys one-time rights. Pays $400, color, cover; $120, b&w, $200, color, inside; on publication.

Tips: "We usually use illustrations inside the magazine, not on the cover. Send samples and we will look at everything." Common mistakes freelancers make in presenting their work are having "inconsistent portfolios or not letting the Art Director look through portfolio uninterrupted by conversation or explanation." Sees trend toward "more mixed media using collage elements and more graphic illustrations."

ORANGE COAST MAGAZINE, Suite 8, 245-D Fischer Ave, Costa Mesa CA 92626. (714)545-1900. Art Director: Sarah McNeill. General interest regional magazine. Monthly. Circ. 40,000. Returns original artwork after publication. Sample copy and art guidelines available. Contact Brigid Madaris, Associate Art Director for guidelines.

Illustrations: Works with several illustrators and assigns 24-30 illustration jobs/year. Considers airbrush. Works on assignment only. Send brochure showing art style or tearsheets, slides or transparencies to be kept on file. Samples not filed are returned only if requested. Reports only if interested. To show a portfolio, mail color original/final art, final reproduction/product, tearsheets and photographs. Acquires one-time rights. Works on byline–basis only–there is no budget for monetary payment. Illustrator receives full credit and tearsheets in trade for artwork.

Tips: There is a need for "fluid free-style illustration and for more photojournalistic expression within an artists mode–i.e., the art meets needs to express a story exactly, yet in a creative manner and executed well. Please send samples soon."

ORGANIC GARDENING, 33 E. Minor St., Emmaus PA 18098. (212)967-5171 ext. 1582. Art Director: Emilie Whitcomb. Magazine emphasizing gardening. Published 10 times/year. Circ. 1.2 million. Original artwork is returned to the artist after publication unless all rights are bought. Sample copies free for SASE with first-class postage.

Illustrations: Buys 10 illustrations/issue, 100 illustrations/year from freelancers. Works on assignment only. Prefers botanically accurate plants and, in general, very accurate drawing and rendering. Send query letter with brochure, tearsheets, slides and photographs. Samples are filed. Samples not filed are returned by SASE only. Reports back within 1 month. Call or write to schedule an appointment to show a portfolio, which should include color or b&w final reproduction/product. Buys first rights or one-time rights.

THE OTHER SIDE, 300 W. Apsley St., Philadelphia PA 19144. (215)849-2178. Editor: Mark Olson. Art Director: Cathleen Boint. "We are read by Christians with a radical commitment to social justice and a deep allegiance to Biblical faith. We try to help readers put their faith into action." Published 6 times/year. Circ. 13,000. Sample copy $4.

© Rene Lausen

This acrylic paint and Prismacolor pencil illustration was designed by Costa Mesa, California artist Rene Lausen for **Orange Coast Magazine.** *Art director Sarah McNeill says, "We wanted an illustration that conveyed the cutback of defense spending in Orange County. Lausen has great concepts, and his talent lies in acrylics for achieving mood/depth." Lausen completed the assignment in ten days and sold all rights to the piece.*

Cartoons: Approached by 20-30 cartoonists/year. Receives 3 cartoons and 1 illustration/week from freelance artists. Buys 12 cartoons/year from freelancers on current events, environment, economics, politics and religion; single and multiple panel. Pays $25, b&w line drawings; on publication. "Looking for cartoons with a radical political perspective."

Illustrations: Approached by 40-50 illustrators/year. Especially needs b&w line drawings illustrating specific articles. Send query letter with tearsheets, photocopies, slides, photographs and SASE. Reports in 6 weeks. Photocopied and simultaneous submissions OK. To show a portfolio, mail appropriate materials or call to schedule an appointment; portfolio should include roughs, original/final art, final reproduction/product and photographs. Pays "within 4 weeks of publication." Pays $125-200, 4-color; $40-150, b&w line drawings inside; on publication.

OTTAWA MAGAZINE, 192 Bank St., Ottawa, Ontario K2P 1W8 Canada. (613)234-7751. Art Director: Peter de Gannes. Emphasizes lifestyles for sophisticated, middle and upper income, above average education professionals; ages 25-50. Monthly. Circ. 50,000. Accepts previously published material. Sample copy available; include $2 Canadian funds to cover postage (nonresidents include 4 IRCs).

Cartoons: Approached by 10 cartoonists/year. Pays $75, b&w; $125, color.

Illustrations: Buys 6-8 illustrations/issue from freelancers. Receives 3-4 submissions/week from freelancers. "Illustrations are geared to editorial copy and run from cartoon sketches to *Esquire, New York* and *D* styles. Subjects range from fast-food franchising to how civil servants cope with stress. Art usually produced by local artists because of time and communication problems." Open to most styles including b&w line drawings, b&w and color washes, collage, photocopy art, oil and acrylic paintings, airbrush work and paper sculpture for inside. Also uses photographic treatments. Send query letter with resume and photocopies. "Do not send original artwork." No samples returned. Reports in 2 months. To show a portfolio, mail appropriate materials, which should include tearsheets and photostats. Buys first-time rights, or by arrangement with artist. Pays $450, b&w; $600, color, cover; $200, b&w; $400-500, color, inside; on acceptance.

Tips: Prefers "work that shows wit, confidence in style and a unique approach to the medium used. Especially in need of artists who can look at a subject from a fresh, unusual perspective. There is a trend toward more exciting illustration, use of unusual techniques like photocopy collages or collages combining photography, pen & ink and watercolor. Freedom is given to the artist to develop his treatment. Open to unusual techniques. Have as diversified a portfolio as possible."

OUTDOOR AMERICA MAGAZINE, 1401 Wilson Blvd., Level B, Arlington VA 22209. Editor: Kristin Merriman. Estab. 1922. Emphasizes conservation and outdoor recreation (fishing, hunting, etc.) for sportsmen and conservationists. Quarterly. Circ. 55,000. Accepts previously published material. Original artwork returned after publication. Sample copy $1.50.
Cartoons: Approached by 100 cartoonists/year. Payment for cartoons varies.
Illustrations: Approached by 150 illustrators/year. Buys 10+ illustrations/year from freelancers. Often commissions original work from non-local artists, and will occasionally purchase one-time or reprint rights to existing wildlife or recreation illustrations. Send query letter with resume, Xeroxed samples or tearsheets, list of where previously published, to be kept on file. Samples not filed are returned. Reports within 2 months. Buys one-time rights or reprint rights. Pays, $250, color, cover; $15-75, b&w; $35-100, color, inside. Pays on publication.
Tips: "Send samples and resume, then call us later if you don't hear from us in a month or so."

OUTDOOR CANADA MAGAZINE, 801 York Mills Rd., Don Mills, Ontario M3B 1X7 Canada. Editor: Teddi Brown. For the Canadian sportsman and his family. Stories on fishing, camping, hunting, canoeing, wildlife and outdoor adventures. Readers are 81% male. Publishes 8 regular issues a year, a fishing special in February. Circ. 150,000. Finds most artists through references/word-of-mouth.
Illustrations: Approached by 12-15 illustrators/year. Buys approximately 10 drawings/issue from freelancers. Uses freelance artists mainly for illustrating features and columns. Prefers pen & ink, airbrush, acrylic, oil and pastel. Buys first rights. Pays up to $400. Artists should show a representative sampling of their work, including fishing illustrations.

*OUTSIDE MAGAZINE, 1165 N. Clark St., Chicago IL 60610. (312)951-0990. FAX: (312)951-6136. Design Director: John Askwith. Estab. 1977. Consumer magazine. "America's leading active lifestyle magazine." Monthly. Circ. 325,000. Sample copies available. Art guidelines free for SASE with first-class postage.
Illustrations: Approached by 150-200 illustrators/year. Buys 150 illustrations/year from freelancers. Works on assignment only. Prefers contemporary editorial styles. Considers watercolor, collage, airbrush, acrylic, colored pencil, oil, mixed media and pastel. Send query letter with brochure, tearsheets and slides. Most samples are filed. Those not filed are returned by SASE. Call to schedule an appointment to show a portfolio, which should include original/final art, tearsheets and slides. Buys one-time rights. Pays $750 for color, inside; on publication.
Tips: "Establish target publications. Maintain contact through update mailings until assignment is received. Always get as many tearsheets from a job that you can."

OVERSEAS!, Kolpingstr 1, 6906 Leimen, West Germany. Editorial Director: Charles L. Kaufman. Managing Editor: Greg Ballinger. Estab. 1973. "*Overseas!* is the leading lifestyle magazine for the U.S. military stationed throughout Europe. Primary focus is on European travel, with regular features on music, sports, video, audio and photo products." Sample copy for SAE and 4 IRCs; art guidelines for SAE and 1 IRC.
Cartoons: Buys 5+ cartoons/issue, 60+ cartoons/year from freelancers. Prefers single and multiple panel cartoons. "Always looking for humorous cartoons on travel, being a tourist in Europe and working in the U.S. military. Looking for more *National Lampoon* or *New Yorker*-style cartoons/humor than a *Saturday Evening Post*-type cartoon. Anything new, different or crazy is given high priority." On cartoons or cartoon features don't query, send nonreturnable photocopies. Pay is negotiable, $15-50/cartoon.
Illustrations: Works with 20+ illustrators/year. Buys 50-75 illustrations/year from freelancers. Prefers pen & ink, pencil and mixed media. Send query letter with nonreturnable photocopies. "We will assign when needed." Pays $50-100, b&w; $150, color, inside.
Tips: "We are very interested in publishing new young talent. Previous publication is not necessary."

*PACIFIC NORTHWEST, 222 Dexter Ave. N, Seattle WA 98109. Editor: Ann Naumann. Emphasizes regional interests. Published 12 times/year. Circ. 90,000. Previously published material and simultaneous submissions OK if so indicated. Original artwork returned after publication. Free art guidelines for SASE.
Illustrations: Uses 6-10 illustrations/issue. Uses illustrations for specific articles. Send query letter, roughs and samples of style. Provide samples to be kept on file for possible future assignments. Samples returned by SASE if not kept on file. Buys one-time rights.

PAINT HORSE JOURNAL, Box 961023, Fort Worth TX 76161-0023. (817)439-3412. Editor: Bill Shepard. Art Director: Vicki Day. Official publication of breed registry for Paint horses. For people who raise, breed and show Paint horses. Monthly. Circ. 14,000. Original artwork returned after publication if requested. Sample copy $2; artist's guidelines free for SASE.

Cartoons: Approached by 10 or so cartoonists/year. Receives 8-10 cartoons/week from freelance artists. Buys 10-20 cartoons/year from freelancers. Interested in *Paint* horses; single panel with gagline. Material returned by SASE only if requested. Reports in 1 month. Buys first rights. Pays $10-20, b&w line drawings; on acceptance.

Illustrations: Approached by 25-30 illustrators/year. Receives 4-5 illustrations/week from freelancers. Uses 1-3 illustrations/issue; buys few illustrations/issue from freelancers. Send business card and samples to be kept on file. Prefers snapshots of original art or photostats as samples. Samples returned by SASE if not kept on file. Reports within 1 month. Send query letter with brochure showing art style or photocopies and finished art. Buys first rights. Pays $10-15, b&w, inside; $50 color, cover; on publication.

Tips: "We use a lot of different styles of art, but no matter what style you use-you *must* include Paint horses with acceptable (to the APHA) conformation. As horses are becoming more streamlined – as in race-bred Paints, the older style of horse seems so out dated. We get a lot of art with Arabian-type conformation, which also is incorrect. Action Art and performance events are very nice to have."

*PALM BEACH LIFE, 265 Royal Poinciana Way, Palm Beach FL 33480. (305)837-4762. Design Director: Anne Wholf. Emphasizes culture, cuisine, travel, fashion, decorating and Palm Beach County lifestyle. Readers are affluent, educated. Monthly. Circ. 32,000. Sample copy $4.18; art guidelines for SASE.

Illustrations: Buys 3-4 illustrations/issue; all from freelancers. Only assigned work. Uses line drawings to illustrate regular columns as well as features. Format: color washes for inside and cover; b&w washes and line drawings for inside. "Any technique that can be reproduced is acceptable." Send samples or photocopies and/or arrange appointment to show portfolio. Send SASE. Reports in 4-6 weeks. Pays $300-600, color cover; $100-400, inside color; $60-200, inside b&w; on acceptance. Top price on covers only paid to established artists; "the exception is that we are looking for super-dramatic covers." Looking for subjects related to Florida and lifestyle of the affluent. Price negotiable. Send slides or prints; do not send original work. *Palm Beach Life* cannot be responsible for unsolicited material.

Tips: "Look at magazines to see what we are like – make an appointment."

PANDORA, 2844 Grayson, Ferndale MI 48220. Editor: Meg MacDonald. Art Editor: Polly Vedder. Emphasizes science fiction and fantasy. Biannual. Circ. 1,000. Accepts previously published material. Original artwork returned after publication if requested but prefers photostat. Sample copy $5.

Cartoons: Buys 12-15 cartoons/year from freelancers. Considers science fiction themes. Prefers single panel; b&w line drawings. Send query letter with samples to be kept on file. "Always send SASE. We will not return or respond to work without return postage, postcard, etc." Reports within 8 weeks. Rights negotiated individually; prefers all rights on in-house generated ideas. Pays $3.50 and up, b&w; on publication.

Illustrations: Buys 8-12 illustrations/issue from freelancers. Style should suit story. Prefers pen & ink. Will consider unsolicited work for art portfolio section and cover art as well. Send query letter with tearsheets or photocopies to be kept on file. Samples not filed are returned by SASE. Reports in 8 weeks. Buys first North American serial rights; buys all rights on cover (if available). Pays $7 and up, b&w, cover and inside; on publication. Covers usually start at $10 and often go much higher.

Tips: "We lean somewhat more toward fantasy art than hard sf – we're not about hardware; we're about people of all races and biological makeup. As a digest-sized magazine, we cannot use extremely detailed or busy work; consider final size when sending samples. We highly recommend artists study issues before submitting. Tell us you want a good representation of our current art needs when you order back issues. We like to see versatility of content and style in samples, as well as a good grasp of anatomy, contrast, and composition. We use anything from action scenes to portraits (usually for story illustrations) to cartoons, border designs, and filler doodles. No horror!"

PARADE MAGAZINE, 750 Third Ave., New York NY 10017. (212)573-7187. Director of Design: Ira Yoffe. Photo Editor: Miriam White. Emphasizes general interest subjects. Weekly. Circ. 36 million (readership is 65 million). Original artwork returned after publication. Sample copy and art guidelines available.

Illustrations: Uses varied number of illustrations/issue. Works on assignment only. Send query letter with brochure, resume, business card and tearsheets to be kept on file. Call or write for appointment to show portfolio. Reports only if interested. Buys first rights, and occasionally all rights.

Tips: "Provide a good balance of work."

*PARENTING MAGAZINE, 501 2nd St., San Francisco CA 94107. (415)546-7575. FAX: (415)546-0578. Contact: Art Director. Estab. 1987. Consumer magazine emphasizing "child-rearing, health, and other general topics related to parents, children and parenting. Directed at first time parents or parents with children 0-10 years." Monthly. Circ. 600,000. Accepts previously published artwork. Original artwork is returned at job's completion. Sample copies are free for SASE with first-class postage. Art guidelines not available.

Cartoons: Approached by more than 100 cartoonists/year. Buys 1 cartoon/issue, 20-30 cartoons/year from freelancers. Prefers parenting and children themes; single panel, with gagline; b&w washes. Send query letter with roughs or finished cartoons. Samples are filed or are returned by SASE if requested by artist. Reports back to the artist only if interested. Buys first rights or one-time rights. Pays $200, b&w; $200, color.

Illustrations: Approached by 500-600 illustrators/year. Buys 4-10 illustrations/issue, 100 illustrations/year from freelancers. Works on assignment only. Prefers parenting, children and mothers theme. Send query letter with brochure, SASE, tearsheets, photocopies, slides and transparencies. Samples are filed or are returned by SASE if requested by artist. Reports back to the artist only if interested. Call or mail appropriate materials: original/final art and b&w and color tearsheets, photographs, slides and photocopies. Buys first rights or one-time rights. Pays $300-500, b&w, $300-500, color, inside; on publication.

Tips: "Do good and interesting work. Don't try to interest us in overly commercial or 'illustrative' work. We're more interesting in work with strong emotional content."

PARENT'S CHOICE, Box 185, Waban MA 02168. (617)965-5913. Editor: Diana Huss Green. Reviews children's media. Designed to alert parents to the best books, TV, records, movies, music, toys, computer software, rock-n-roll and home video cassettes. Quarterly. Original artwork returned after publication. Sample copy $2.50.

Illustrations: Approached by 20 illustrators/year. Uses 4 illustrations/issue, 2 from freelancers. Uses "work of exceptional quality." Format: b&w line drawings for inside and cover; no pencil. Works on assignment only. Send samples or arrange appointment to show portfolio. Samples returned. Prefers to see portfolio. Send SASE. Reports in 4-6 weeks. Pays on publication.

PARIS PASSION, 23 Rue Yves Toudic, Paris 75010 France. (01)42-39-15-80. Editor/Art Director: Robert Sarner. Estab. 1981. "A city magazine in English focusing on all current events in Paris, cultural, political, reviews, listings, profiles, etc." Monthly. Circ. 50,000. Original artwork is returned after publication. Sample copies $5.

Cartoons: Approached by 10 cartoonists/year. Pays $50, profiles, etc., b&w.

Illustrations: Approached by 50 illustrators/year. Works with 12-15 illustrators/year. Buys illustrations mainly for spots and feature spreads. Buys 3-4 illustrations/issue from freelancers. Works on assignment only. Considers pen & ink, airbrush, mixed media, acrylic, marker and charcoal pencil. Send query letter with tearsheets and photocopies. Seeks "originality, expressiveness and boldness." Samples are filed. Reports back only if interested. Call to schedule an appointment to show a portfolio which should inlcude original/final art, tearsheets and photostats. Buys one-time rights. Pays $250, color, cover; $100, b&w, inside; on publication.

Tips: "Preference is given to those living in Paris or on extended stay. Require proof of tax status for country of residence."

PC RESOURCE, IDG/Peterborough, 80 Elm St., Peterborough NH 03458. (603)924-9471. Art Director: Erik Murphy. Emphasizes computing for small-medium size businesses who own and operate MS-DOS computers. Monthly. Circ. 200,000. Original artwork returned after publication.

Illustrations: Approached by 25 illustrators/year. Prefers exciting, creative styles and computer generated artwork. Works on assignment only. Send tearsheets, photographs or promotional material. Reports only if interested. Negotiates rights purchased. Pays $150-500, b&w, $300-500, color, cover; $300-600 b&w, $500-1,000, color, inside; on acceptance.

Tips: "Would prefer to see a few very good samples rather than a large quantity of mediocre samples."

*PENINSULA MAGAZINE, Suite 200, 656 Bair Island Rd., Redwood City CA 94063. (415)368-8800. FAX: (415)368-6251. Art Director: Ellen Zaslow. Estab. 1986. Consumer regional magazine for upscale audience. Monthly. Circ. 35,000. Original artwork is returned at job's completion. Samples copies available. Art guidelines not available.

Illustrations: Approached by 40 illustrators/year. Buys 2-10 illustrations/issue, 40 illustrations/year from freelancers. Works on assignment only. Preferred themes or styles vary. Interested in any media. Send query letter with tearsheets and samples of range of styles/media. Samples are filed. Reports back to the artist only if interested. Call or mail appropriate materials. Portfolio should include tearsheets and "whatever format best displays your work." Buys first rights. Pays $150 for color, inside; 30 days after acceptance.

Tips: "Send samples then follow up with a call."

PENNSYLVANIA MAGAZINE, Box 576, Camp Hill PA 17011. (717)761-6620. Editor-in-Chief: Albert Holliday. Estab. 1981. For college-educated readers, ages 35-60+, interested in self-improvement, history, travel and personalities. Bimonthly. Cir. 40,000. Query with samples. SASE. Reports in 3 weeks. Previously published, photocopied and simultaneous submissions OK. Buys first serial rights. Pays on publication or on acceptance for assigned articles/art. Sample copy $2.95.

Cartoons: Buys 5-10 cartoons/year from freelancers. Must be on Pennsylvania topics. Pays $25-50.

Illustrations: Buys 25 illustrations/year from freelancers on history and travel-related themes. Minimum payment for cover, $100, inside color, $25-50; inside b&w, $5-50. "I would like to see small *New Yorker*-type pen & ink sketches for spot art."

*PENNWELL PUBLISHING CO., 1421 S. Sheridan, Tulsa OK 74112. (918)835-3161. Art Director: Mike Reeder. Emphasizes dental economics for practicing dentists; 24-65 years of age. Monthly. Circ. 100,000. Sample copy for SASE; art guidelines available.
Cartoons: Approached by 6-12 cartoonists/year. Buys about 1 cartoon/2 issues from freelancers. Prefers dental-related themes. Prefers single panel, with or without gagline; b&w line drawings. Send up to 12 cartoons in a batch. Material is returned by SASE only. Reports if interested. Pays $40, b&w; on acceptance.

*PENSIONS AND INVESTMENTS, 740 N. Rush St., Chicago IL 60611. (312)649-5388. FAX: (312)649-5228. Art Director: Kristina Schramm. Estab. 1973. Trade journal; tabloid format; "a newspaper of corporate and institutional investing." Biweekly. Circ. 50,000. Original artwork returned if requested. Sample copies and art guidelines available.
Cartoons: Approached by 5-6 cartoonists/year. Buys 12 cartoons/year from freelancers. Prefers color washes and b&w line drawings. Send brochure, "no originals." Samples are filed. Reports back only if interested. Buys first rights or negotiates rights purchased. Pays $150, b&w and $300, color.
Illustrations: Approached by 25 illustrators/year. Buys 12-20 illustrations/year from freelancers. Works on assignment only. All media are acceptable. Send query letter with brochure and tearsheets. Samples are filed. Reports back only if interested. Call to schedule an appointment to show a portfolio, which should include original/final art and b&w and color tearsheets, slides and "whatever is appropriate to the media." Rights purchased vary according to project. Pays $300, b&w and $600, color, cover; $300, b&w and $300, color, inside; on acceptance.
Tips: "Send a really fine mailing piece that is an accurate example of your preferred style. They are expensive, but all the art directors here share mailings. Portfolios from out of state artists are rarely seen. Contact by recommendation or solely through mailing."

*PERINATOLOGY-NEONATOLOGY, Macmillan Professional Journals, 1640 5th St., Santa Monica CA 90401. Publisher: Curt Pickelle. Art Director: Ron Tammerillo. Emphasizes technological, medical and professional news.
Illustrations: Submit brochure/flyer to be kept on file for possible future assignments. Reports only when assignment available. Buys all rights. Pays $60 and up, spot art; $400, full-color cover; on acceptance.

*PERSIMMON HILL, 1700 NE 63rd St., Oklahoma City OK 73111. (405)478-2250. FAX: (405)478-4714. Director of Publications: M.J. Van Deventer. Estab. 1963. "A journal of western heritage focusing on both historical and contemporary themes. It features nonfiction articles on notable persons connected with pioneering the American West; western art, rodeo, cowboys, western flora and animal life; or other phenomena of the West of today or yesterday. Lively articles, well written, for a popular audience." Quarterly. Circ. 15,000. Accepts previously published artwork. Original artwork returned after publication. Sample copy $5. Art guidelines free for SASE with first-class postage.
Illustrations: Approached by 75-100 illustrators/year. Buys 5 illustrations/issue, 20-25 illustrations/year from freelancers. Works on assignment only. Prefers western-related themes and pen & ink sketches. Considers pen & ink. Send query letter with resume, SASE, photographs or slides and transparencies. Samples are filed or returned by SASE if requested. Reports back within 2-3 weeks. Call to schedule an appointment to show a portfolio, which should include original/final art, photographs or slides. Buys first rights. Pays $50, b&w, $200, color, cover; $150, color, inside (negotiable).
Tips: "Most illustrations are used to accompany articles. Work with our writers, or suggest illustrations to the editor that can be the basis for a freelance article on a companion story." Sees trends toward "bold colorations/magazine illustration; design borders on geometric design themes."

*PETERSEN'S FISHING, 8480 Sunset Blvd., Los Angeles CA 90069. (213)854-2176. Art Director: Michael Vannatter. Estab. 1984. Consumer magazine; "a national, newsstand magazine about fresh and salt water fishing." Monthly. Circ. 120,000. Original artwork not returned. Sample copies free for SASE with first-class postage. Art guidelines not available.
Cartoons: Buys 1 cartoon/issue, 12 cartoons/year from freelancers. Prefers simple, clever theme and styles. Prefers b&w washes and b&w line drawings. Send query letter with samples. Samples are filed. Reports back within 3 weeks only if interested. Buys all rights. Pays $100, b&w.
Illustration: Approached by 5-6 illustrators/year. Buys 10-15 illustrations/issue, 120 illustrations/year from freelancers. Works on assignment only. Prefers realistic adventure and outdoor themes and styles. Prefers pen & ink, pencil and watercolor. Send query letter with tearsheets and photocopies. Would like to see published samples. Samples are filed. Reports back within 3 weeks only if interested. Call to schedule an appointment to show a portfolio, which should include original/final art and b&w tearsheets and photocopies. Buys all rights. Pays $200, b&w, cover; $100, b&w, $300, color, inside, on publication.
Tips: Sees trend toward "more design to the illustration, bizarre or distorted images, lots of creativity."

PHI DELTA KAPPAN, Box 789, Bloomington IN 47402. Editor-in-Chief: Pauline Gough. Contact: Editor. Emphasizes issues, policy, research findings and opinions in the field of education. For members of the educational organization Phi Delta Kappa and subscribers. Published 10 times/year. Circ. 150,000. SASE.

Reports in 8 weeks. "We return cartoons after publication." Sample copy $3—"the journal is available in most public and college libraries." Uses freelance artists mainly for cartoons, assigned illustrations.

Cartoons: Approached by over 100 cartoonists/year.

Illustrations: Approached by over 100 illustrators/year. Uses 5 b&w illustrations/issue, all from freelancers, who have been given assignments from upcoming articles. Most illustrations depict teachers or kids. Samples returned by SASE. To show a portfolio, mail a few slides or photocopies with SASE. Buys one-time rights. Payment varies.

Tips: "Illustration seemed to be moving toward the bizarre the past few years—now there seems to be more of a synthesis—with the good, free energy of the 'bizarre' being channeled into more accessible vocabularies."

*PHOENIX HOME & GARDEN MAGAZINE, 3136 N. 3rd Ave., Phoenix AZ 85013. (602)234-0840. Art Director: Barbara Denney. Estab. 1980. Consumer magazine. "Phoenix Home & Garden is a consumer home and garden publication, serving an affluent Southwest audience. While the central focus is on the home, its interiors design and architecture, other featuers highlight gardening, landscaping, gourmet cuisine, art, community events, travel and health. Monthly. Circ. 35,000. Accepts previously published artwork. Original artwork is returned after publication. Sample copies free for SASE with first-class postage. Art guidelines available.

Illustrations: Buys illustrations mainly for spots, feature spreads. Buys 5 illustrations/year. Prefers pen & ink; considers mixed media, colored pencil, watercolor, acrylics, oils, pastels, collage, markers, charcoal/pencil and calligraphy. Send query letter with brochure, tear sheets, photostats, photocopies, slides, photographs, and transparencies. Samples are filed. Samples not filed are returned only if requested. Reports back only if interested. To show a portfolio, mail tearsheets, slides, photostats, photographs, transparencies, color and b&w. Buys one-time rights. Pays $35, b&w; $250, color, inside; on publication.

Tips: "What is the section most open to illustrators? Food and gardening. I'm looking for imeediate use of some black and white spot illustrations for either section, especially gardening á la The New Yorker. They can be stock."

PHYSICIAN'S MANAGEMENT, 7500 Old Oak Blvd., Cleveland OH 44130. (216)243-8100, ext. 808. Editor: Robert A. Feigenbaum. Art Director: David Komitau. Published 12 times/year. Circ. 110,000. Emphasizes business, practice management and legal aspects of medical practice for primary care physicians.

Cartoons: Receives 50-70 cartoons/week from freelancers. Buys 10 cartoons/issue from freelancers. Themes typically apply to medical and financial situations "although we do publish general humor cartoons." Prefers single and double panel; b&w line drawings with gagline. Uses "only clean-cut line drawings." Send cartoons with SASE. Pays $80 on acceptance.

Illustrations: Approached by 5 illustrators/year. Buys 5 illustrations/issue from freelancers. Accepts b&w and color illustrations. All work done on assignment. Send a query letter to editor or art director first or send examples of work. Fees negotiable. Buys first rights. No previously published and/or simultaneous submissions.

Tips: "First, become familiar with our publication; second, query the art director. Cartoons should be geared toward the physician—not the patient. No cartoons about drug companies or medicine men. No sexist cartoons. Illustrations should be appropriate for a serious business publication. We do not use cartoonish or comic book styles to illustrate our articles. We work with artists nationwide."

PIG IRON, Box 237, Youngstown OH 44501. (216)783-1269. Editors-in-Chief: Jim Villani, Rose Sayre and Naton Leslie. Emphasizes literature/art for writers, artists and intelligent lay audience with emphasis in popular culture. Annually. Circ. 1,000. Previously published and photocopied work OK. Original artwork returned after publication. Sample copy $2.50.

Cartoons: Uses 1-15 cartoons/issue, all from freelancers. Receives 1-3 submissions/week from freelancers. Interested in "the arts, political, science fiction, fantasy, alternative lifestyles, psychology, humor"; single and multi panel. Especially needs fine art cartoons. Prefers finished cartoons. SASE. Reports in 1 month. Buys first North American serial rights. Pays $2 minimum, b&w halftones and washes; on acceptance.

Illustrations: Uses 15-30 illustrations/issue, all from freelancers. Receives 1-3 submissions/week from freelancers. Interested in "any media: pen & ink washes, lithographs, silk screen, charcoal, collage, line drawings; any subject matter." B&w only. Prefers finished art or velox. Reports in 2 months. Buys first North American serial rights. Minimum payment: Cover: $4, b&w. Inside: $2; on publication.

Tips: "*Pig Iron* is a publishing opportunity for the fine artist; we publish art in its own right, not as filler or story accompaniment. The artist who is executing black-and-white work for exhibit and gallery presentations can find a publishing outlet with *Pig Iron* that will considerably increase that artist's visibility and reputation." Current themes: Labor in the Post-Industrial Age and Epistolary Fiction and the Letter as Artifact.

*PITTSBURGH MAGAZINE, 4802 5th Ave., Pittsburgh PA 15213. (412)622-1360. Art Director: Michael Maskarinec. Emphasizes culture, feature stories and material with heavy Pittsburgh city emphasis; public broadcasting television and radio schedule. Monthly. Circ. 58,000. Sample copy $2.

Illustrations: Uses 5-10 illustrations/issue; all from freelancers; inside b&w and 4-color illustrations. Works on assignment only. Prefers to see roughs. Send SASE. Buys one-time rights on a work-for-hire basis. Pays on publication.

*PLAINSWOMAN, Box 8027, Grand Forks ND 58202. (701)777-8043. Editor: Elizabeth Hampsten. Estab. 1977. "A regional monthly journal, focused on progressive ideas, often with rural emphasis; interest in women's issues." Monthly except February and August. Circ. 500. Original artwork is returned after publication. Sample copies free for SASE with first-class postage. Art guidelines free for SASE with first-class postage. Send query letter with samples of style. Samples are filed. Samples not filed are returned by SASE. Reports back regarding queries/submissions within 6 weeks. Buys one-time rights. Pays $5+, b&w. Pays on publication.
Illustrations: Buys illustrations mainly for covers and spots. Buys 2 illustrations/issue. Buys 10 illustrations/year. Prefers pen & ink. Send query letter with tear sheets and photographs. "We print in brown ink on cream paper." No color. Samples are filed. Samples not filed are returned by SASE. Reports back about queries/submissions within 6 weeks. To show a portfolio, mail appropriate material which should include tear sheets and photographs. Buys first rights. Pays $5+, b&w. Pays on publication.

PLANNING, American Planning Association, 1313 E. 60th St., Chicago IL 60637. (312)955-9100. Editor-in-Chief: Sylvia Lewis. Art Director: Richard Sessions. For urban and regional planners interested in land use, housing, transportation and the environment. Monthly. Circ. 25,000. Previously published work OK. Original artwork returned after publication, upon request. Free sample copy and artist's guidelines available.
Cartoons: Buys 2 cartoons/year from freelancers on the environment, city/regional planning, energy, garbage, transportation, housing, power plants, agriculture and land use. Prefers single panel with gaglines ("provide outside of cartoon body if possible"). Include SASE. Reports in 2 weeks. Buys all rights. Pays $50 minimum, b&w line drawings; on publication.
Illustrations: Buys 20 illustrations/year from freelancers on the environment, city/regional planning, energy, garbage, transportation, housing, power plants, agriculture and land use. Prefers to see roughs and samples of style. Include SASE. Reports in 2 weeks. Buys all rights. Pays $250 maximum, b&w drawings, cover, $100 minimum, b&w line drawings inside; on publication.
Tips: "Don't send portfolio." Does not want to see "corny cartoons. Don't try to figure out what's funny to *Planners.* All attempts seen so far are way off base."

POCKETS, Box 189, 1908 Grand Ave., Nashville TN 37202. (615)340-7333. Editor: Janet Bugg. Devotional magazine for children 6 to 12. Monthly magazine except January/February. Circ. 68,000. Accepts previously published material. Original artwork returned after publication. Sample copy for SASE with 73¢ postage.
Illustrations: Approached by 50-60 illustrators each year. Uses variety of styles; 4-color, 2-color, flapped art appropriate for children. Realistic fable and cartoon styles. We will accept tearsheets, photostats and slides. Samples not filed are returned by SASE. Reports only if interested. Buys one-time or reprint rights. Pays $50-500 depending on size; on acceptance. Decisions made in consultation with out-of-house designer.
Tips: "We forward artists' samples to our out-of-town designer. He handles all contacts with illustrators."

*POPULAR ELECTRONICS, (formerly Hands-On Electronics), 500 B Bi-County Blvd., Farmingdale NY 11735. (516)293-3000. Editor: Carl Laron. Magazine emphasizing hobby electronics for consumer and hobby-oriented electronics buffs. Monthly. Circ. 80,000. Original artwork not returned after publication. Sample copy free.
Cartoons: Approached by over 20 cartoonists/year. Buys 3-5 cartoons/issue from freelancers. Prefers single panel with or without gagline; b&w line drawings and b&w washes. Send finished cartoons; "we purchase and keep! Unused ones returned." Samples are returned. Reports within 2 weeks. Buys all rights. Pays $25, b&w.

POPULAR SCIENCE, Times Mirror Magazines, Inc., 2 Park Ave., New York NY 10016. (212)779-5000. Art Director: David Houser. For the well-educated adult male, interested in science, technology, new products. Original artwork returned after publication.
Illustrations: Uses 30-40 illustrations/issue; buys 30/issue from freelancers. Works on assignment only. Interested in technical 4-color art and 2-color line art dealing with automotive or architectural subjects. Especially needs science and technological pieces as assigned per layout. Samples returned by SASE. Reports back on future assignment possibilities. Provide tearsheet to be kept on file for future assignments. "After seeing portfolios, I photocopy or photostat those samples I feel are indicative of the art we might use." Reports whenever appropriate job is available. Buys first publishing rights.
Tips: "More and more scientific magazines have entered the field. This has provided a larger base of technical artists for us. Be sure your samples relate to our subject matter, i.e., no rose etchings, and be sure to include a tearsheet for our files."

*PRACTICAL HOMEOWNER MAGAZINE, 27 Unquowa Rd., Fairfield CT 06430. (203)259-9877. FAX: (203)259-2361. Contact: Art Director. Estab. 1980. Consumer magazine emphasizing home design, building and remodeling. 9 issues/year. Circ. 740,000. Original artwork returned after publication. Sample copies and/or art guidelines not available.
Illustrations: Approached by 50 illustrators/year. Buys 8 illustrations/issue, 70 illustrations/year from freelancers. Works on assignment only. Prefers "technical and architectural/whimsical themes and styles." Prefers pen & ink, watercolor, airbrush and colored pencil. Send tearsheets. Samples are filed. Reports back only if interested. Mail appropriate materials: tearsheets and slides. Buys one-time rights. Pays $150 for b&w, $300 for color, inside; on publication.

PRAIRIE SCHOONER, 201 Andrews Hall, University of Nebraska, Lincoln NE 68588-0334. (402)472-3191. Editor: Hilda Raz; Business Manager: Pam Weiner. Estab. 1927. Literary magazine. *"Prairie Schooner,* now in its sixty-fourth year of continuous publication, is called 'one of the top literary magazines in America,' by *Literary Magazine Review.* Each of the four annual issues contains short stories, poetry, book reviews, personal essays, interviews or some mix of these genres. Contributors are both established and beginning writers. Readers live in all states in the U.S. and in most countries outside the U.S." Quarterly. Circ. 2,000. Original artwork is returned after publication. "We rarely have the space or funds to reproduce artwork in the magazine but hope to do more in the future." Sample copies $2.
Illustrations: Approached by 1-5 illustrators/year. Uses freelance artists mainly for cover art. "Before submitting, artist should be familiar with our cover and format, $6\times9"$, black and one color or b&w, vertical images work best; artist should look at previous issues of *Prairie Schooner.* We are rarely able to pay for artwork; have paid $50 to $100."

PRAYING, Box 419335, Kansas City MO 64141. (816)531-0538. Editor: Arthur N. Winter. Estab. 1984. Emphasizes spirituality for everyday living for lay Catholics and members of mainline Protestant churches; primarily Catholic, non-fundamentalist. "Starting point: The daily world of living, family, job, politics, is the stuff of religious experience and Christian living." Bimonthly. Circ. 20,000. Accepts previously published material. Original artwork not returned after publication. Sample copy and art guidelines available.
Cartoons: Approached by about 24 cartoonists/year. Buys 1-2 cartoons/issue from freelancers. Especially interested in cartoons that spoof fads and jargon in contemporary spirituality, prayer and religion. Prefers single panel with gagline; b&w line drawings. Send query letter with samples of style to be kept on file. Material not filed is returned by SASE. Reports within 2 weeks. Buys one-time rights. Pays $58, b&w; on acceptance.
Illustrations: Approached by about 24 illustrators/year. Works with 6 illustrators/year. Buys 2-3 illustrations/issue, 12-15 illustrations/year from freelancers. Prefers contemporary interpretations of traditional Christian symbols to be used as incidental art; also drawings to illustrate articles. Send query letter with samples to be kept on file. Prefers photostats, tearsheets and photocopies as samples. Samples returned if not interested or return requested by SASE. Reports within 2 weeks. Buys one-time rights. Pays $50, b&w; on acceptance.
Tips: "I do not want to see old-fashioned church cartoons centering on traditional church humor — windy sermons, altar boy jokes, etc. Know our content. We'd like cartoons making fun of contemporary Catholic spirituality."

*PRELUDE MAGAZINE, Box 4628, Carmel CA 93921. (408)375-5711. Art Director: Johathan Drake. Magazine emphasizing fine arts, classical music and entertainment for the northwestern United States. Monthly. Circ. 25,000. Accepts previously published material. Original artwork is returned to the artist after publication. Sample copy free for SASE with first-class postage. Art guidelines free for SASE with first-class postage.
Cartoons: Cartoon Editor: Jeffrey Parks. Buys 3 cartoons/issue; 40 cartoons/year from freelancers. Prefers single, double or multiple panel with gagline; b&w line drawings. Send roughs. Samples are filed or are returned. Reports back within 6 weeks. Pays $15 and up, b&w.
Illustrations: Buys 3-6 illustrations/issue; 30-60 illustrations/year from freelancers. Prefers b&w editorial illustrations in all media. Works on assignment only. Send query letter with brochure, resume, tearsheets, photocopies, slides and photographs. Samples are filed or are returned. Reports back within 6 weeks. To show a portfolio, mail thumbnails, roughs, color and b&w tearsheets, photostats, photographs and slides. Buys first rights. Pays $50, b&w, cover; on publication.

PREMIERE MAGAZINE, 2 Park Ave., New York NY 10016. (212)725-5846. Art Director: David Walters. Estab. 1987. "Popular culture magazine about movies and the movie industry, both in the U.S. and international. Of interest to both a general audience and people involved in the film business." Monthly. Circ. 500,000. Original artwork is returned after publication. Sample copy $2.50. Art guidelines not available.
Illustrations: Approached by 250+ illustrators/year. Works with 150 illustrators/year. Buys 15-25 illustrations/issue, 180-200+ illustrations/year from freelancers. Buys illustrations mainly for spots and feature spreads. Works on assignment only. Considers all styles depending on needs. Send query letter with tearsheets, photostats and photocopies. Samples are filed. Samples not filed are returned by SASE. Reports back about queries/submissions only if interested. Call to schedule an appointment to show a porfolio which should

include tearsheets. Buys first rights or one-time rights. Pays $350, b&w; $375-1,200, color, inside.
Tips: "I do not want to see originals or too much work. Show only your best work."

*THE PRESBYTERIAN RECORD, 50 Wynford Dr., Don Mills, Ontario M3C 1J7 Canada. (416)441-1111. Production and Design: Valerie Dunn. Published 11 times/year. Deals with family-oriented religious themes. Circ. 68,000. Original artwork returned after publication. Simultaneous submissions and previously published work OK. Free sample copy and artists' guidelines.
Cartoons: Approached by 12 cartoonists/year. Buys 1-2 cartoons/issue from freelancers. Interested in some theme or connection to religion. Send roughs and SAE (nonresidents include IRC). Reports in 1 month. Pays $25-50, b&w; on publication.
Illustrations: Approached by 6 illustrators/year. Buys 1 illustration/year from freelancers on religion. "We use freelance material, and we are interested in excellent color artwork for cover." Any line style acceptable— should reproduce well on newsprint. Works on assignment only. Send query letter with brochure showing art style or tearsheets, photocopies and photographs. Samples returned by SAE (nonresidents include IRC). Reports in 1 month. To show a portfolio, mail original/final art and color and b&w tearsheets. Buys all rights on a work-for-hire basis. Pays $50-100, color washes and opaque watercolors, cover; pays $30-50, b&w line drawings, inside; on publication.
Tips: "We don't want any 'cute' samples (in cartoons). Prefer some theological insight in cartoons; some comment on religious trends and practices."

*PRESBYTERIAN SURVEY, 100 Witherspoon, Louisville KY 40202. (502)569-5636. FAX: (501)596-5018. Art Director: Lee Jenkins. Estab. 1830. Official church magazine emphasizing religious world news and inspirational features. Monthly. Circ. 250,000. Originals are sometimes returned after publication. Sample copies free for SASE with first-class postage. Art guidelines not available.
Cartoons: Approached by 20-30 cartoonists/year. Buys 1 cartoon/issue, 20 cartoons/year from freelancers. Prefers general religious material; single panel. Send query letter with brochure, roughs and/or finished cartoons. Samples are filed or are returned. Reports back within 3 weeks. Rights purchased vary according to project. Payment depends on cover and/or size.
Illustrations: Approached by more than 50 illustrators/year. Buys 2-6 illustrations/issue, 50 illustrations/year from freelancers. Works on assignment only. Prefers ethnic, mixed groups and symbolic world unity themes. Media varies according to need. Send query letter with slides. Samples are filed or are returned by SASE. Reports back only if interested. Call or write to schedule an appointment to show a portfolio, which should include original/final art, tearsheets and photographs. Buys one-time rights. Pays $100, b&w, $350, color, cover; $150, b&w, $100, color, inside.
Tips: "The artist's work should represent the tasteful, representative style of Presbyterianism."

*PRESERVATION NEWS, 1785 Massachusetts Ave., NW, Washington DC 20036. (202)673-4164. Editor: Arnold Berke. Estab. 1964. Trade journal; tabloid format; "covers news stories of interest to the historic preservation community; a publication of the National Trust for Historic Preservation." Monthly. Circ. 300,000. Accepts previously published artwork. Sample copy for $1 plus 56¢ postage. Art guidelines available.
Cartoons: Approached by 2 cartoonists/year. Buys 1 cartoon/issue 10 cartoons/year from freelancers. Prefers political commentary and historic preservation themes. Send query letter with roughs, clips and examples of other published material. Samples are filed. Reports back within 5 days. Rights purchased vary according to project. Pays $25, b&w.
Illustrations: Approached by 1 illustrator/year. Buys 2-5 illustrations/issue, 30-40 illustrations/year from freelancers. Prefers pen & ink. Send query letter with resume, SASE and tearsheets. Sample are not filed and are returned. Reports back within 5 days. Write to schedule an appointment to show a portfolio. Portfolio should include thumbnails, roughs, original/final art, tearsheets and photographs. Rights purchsed vary according to project. Pays $25, b&w, inside; on publication.
Tips: "Examine several back issues, ask for writer's guidelines, and then make a *written* proposal."

PREVENTION MAGAZINE, 33 E. Minor St., Emmaus PA 18098. (215)967-5171. Executive Art Director: Wendy Ronga. Estab. 1940. Emphasizes health, nutrition, fitness and cooking. Monthly. Circ. 3,200,000. Accepts previously published artwork. Returns original artwork after publication. Art guidelines available.

The asterisk before a listing indicates that the listing is new in this edition. New markets are often the most receptive to freelance submissions.

Cartoons: Approached by more than 50 cartoonists/year. Buys 2 cartoons/issue, 24 cartoons/year from free-lancers. Prefers themes of health, pets and fitness. Considers single panel with or without gagline; b&w line drawings, b&w washes. Send finished cartoons. Samples are not filed and are returned by SASE within 2 weeks. Reports back within 1 month. Buys first rights. Pays $250, b&w; on acceptance.

Illustrations: Approached by more than 70 freelance illustrators/year. Buys about 5 illustrations/issue from freelancers. Uses freelance artwork mainly for inside editorial. Themes are assigned on editorial basis. Works on assignment only. Send samples to be kept on file. Prefers tearsheets or slides as samples. Samples not filed are returned by SASE only if requested. Reports back only if interested. Call to schedule an appointment to show a portfolio which should include b&w and color tearsheets, slides and transparencies. Buys one-time rights. Pays $100-2,500.

Tips: "Send me tearsheets to be kept on file. Artists too often don't see a current issue to see the kind of work I use. They think since this is a health magazine that I want just medical art, or they saw the magazine ten years ago." Looking for "health-related, stylized" work.

PRIMAVERA, University of Chicago, 1212 E. 59th St., Chicago IL 60637. (312)324-5920. Contact: Editorial Board. Estab. 1974. Emphasizes art and literature for readers interested in contemporary literature and art which reflects the experiences of women. Annual. Circ. 800. Original artwork returned after publication. Sample copy $4; art guidelines available for SASE.

Illustrations: Works with 5 illustrators/year. Buys 15 illustrations/year from freelancers. Receives 5 illustrations/week from freelance artists. "We are open to a wide variety of styles and themes. Work must be in b&w with strong contrasts and should not exceed 7" high x 5" wide." Send finished art. Reports in 1-2 months. "If the artist lives in Chicago, she may call us for an appointment." Acquires first rights. "We pay in 2 free copies of the issue in which the artwork appears"; on publication.

Tips: "It's a good idea to take a look at a recent issue. Artists often do not investigate the publication and send work which may be totally inappropriate. We publish a wide variety of artists. We have increased the number of graphics per issue. Send us a *variety* of prints. It is important that the graphics work well with the literature and the other graphics we've accepted. Our decisions are strongly influenced by personal taste and the work we know has already been accepted. Will consider appropriate cartoons and humorous illustrations."

*PRISM INTERNATIONAL, Department of Creative Writing, U.B.C., Buch E462 – 1866 Main Mall, Vancouver, B.C. V6T 1W5 Canada. (604)228-2514. Executive Editor: Heidi Neufeld Raine. Estab. 1959. Literary magazine. "We use cover art for each issue." Quarterly. Circ. 1,000. Original artwork is returned to the artist at the job's completion. Sample copies free for SASE with first class postage.

Illustrations: Approached by 20 illustrators/year. Buys 1 illustration/issue, 4 illustrations/year from freelancers. "Most of our covers are monochrome; however, we try to do at least 1 color cover/year." Send query letter with photographs. Most samples are filed. Those not filed are returned by SASE is requested by artist. Reports back within 10-12 weeks. Mail appropriate materials: original/final art and photographs. Buys first rights. Pays $150; on publication.

PRIVATE PILOT, Box 6050, Mission Viejo CA 92690. (714)855-8822. Contact: Editor. Estab. 1965. For owners/pilots of private aircraft, student pilots and others aspiring to attain additional ratings and experience. Circ. 105,000. Monthly. Receives 5 cartoons and 3 illustrations/week from freelance artists.

Cartoons: Buys 15-20 cartoons/year. Buys 1-2 cartoons/issue from freelancers on flying. Send finished artwork and SASE. Reports in 3 months. Pays $35, b&w; on publication.

Illustrations: Works with 2-3 illustrators/year. Buys 12-18 illustrations/year from freelancers. Uses artists mainly for spot art and layout. Send query letter with samples and SASE. Reports in 3 months. Pays $75-150, color. "We also use spot illustrations as column fillers; buys 1-2 spot illustrations/issue. Pays $25/spot."

Tips: "Know the field you wish to represent; we get tired of 'crash' gags submitted to flying publications."

PRIVATE PRACTICE, Suite 470, 3535 NW 58th St., Oklahoma City OK 73112. (405)943-2318. Art Director & Design Director: Rocky C. Hails. Estab. 1968. Editorial features "maintenance of freedom in all fields of medical practice and the effects of socioeconomic factors on the physician." Monthly. Circ. 180,000. Artists' guidelines available.

Cartoons: Approached by 5-10 cartoonists/year. Buys 1 cartoon/issue, 12 cartoons/year from freelancers. Pays $30, b&w; on acceptance. SASE for returns.

Illustrations: Approached by 50 illustrators/year. Buys 20 illustrations/year from freelancers on politics, medicine and finance. Also uses artists for 4-color cover illustration. Uses some humorous illustrations and occasionally cartoon-style illustrations. Especially looks for "craftsmanship, combined with an ability to communicate complex concepts." Send a brochure showing art style or tearsheets, photostats, slides and photographs. Call to schedule an appointment to show a portfolio, which should include color original/final art, final reproduction/product, tearsheets, photostats and photographs. Buys first and reprint rights. Pays $200-400, unlimited to media, all forms, cover. Pays 100, b&w line drawings and washes inside; on acceptance.

Tips: "Provide reproductions of several illustrations (that demonstrate the uniqueness of your style) to leave with the art director. Include a postcard requesting my response to the applicability of your work to *Private Practice*. This is efficient for both the art director and artist."

PROCEEDINGS, U.S. Naval Institute, Annapolis MD 21402. (301)268-6110. Art Director: LeAnn Bauer. Magazine emphasizing naval and maritime subjects. "*Proceedings* is an independent forum for the sea services." Monthly. Circ. 110,000. Accepts previously published material. Sample copies and art guidelines available.

Cartoons: Buys 1 cartoon/issue, 23 cartoons/year from freelancers. Prefers cartoons assigned to tie in with editorial topics. Send query letter with samples of style to be kept on file. Material not filed is returned if requested by artist. Reports within 1 month. Negotiates rights purchased. Payment varies.

Illustrations: Buys 1 illustration/issue, 12 illustrations/year from freelancers. Works on assignment only. Prefers illustrations assigned to tie in with editorial topics. Send query letter with brochure, resume, tearsheets, photostats, photocopies and photographs. Samples are filed or are returned only if requested by artist. Reports within 1 month. Write to schedule an appointment to show a portfolio or mail appropriate materials. Negotiates rights purchased. Payment varies. "Contact us first to see what our needs are."

PROFIT, Box 1132, Studio City CA 91604. (818)789-4980. Associate Editor: Marjorie Clapper. Magazine emphasizing business news for the business community. Circ. 10,000. Monthly. Original artwork not returned after publication. Sample copy $1.

Cartoons: Prefers single panel; b&w line drawings or b&w washes. Send query letter with samples of style to be kept on file if acceptable. Samples not filed are returned by SASE. Reports only if interested. Buys all rights. Payment varies.

Illustrations: Buys 0-5 illustrations/issue from freelancers. Works on assignment only. Send query letter with brochure showing art style or resume and samples. Samples returned by SASE. Reports only if interested. To show a portfolio, mail thumbnails, original/final art, final reproduction/product, tear sheets, b&w photographs and as much information as possible. Buys all rights. Payment varies. Pays on publication.

THE PROGRESSIVE, 409 E. Main St., Madison WI 53703. Art Director: Patrick JB Flynn. Estab. 1909. Monthly. Circ. 40,000. Free sample copy and artists' guidelines.

Illustrations: Works with 50 illustrators/year. Buys 12 b&w illustrations/issue, 150 illustrations/year from freelancers. Works on assignment only. Send query letter with tear sheets and/or photocopies. Samples returned by SASE. Reports in 2 months. Cover pays $250-300. Inside pays $100-200, b&w line or tone drawings/paintings. Buys first rights.

Tips: Do not send original art. Send direct mail samples, a postcard or photocopies and appropriate return postage. "The successful art direction of a magazine allows for personal interpretation of an assignment."

PUBLIC CITIZEN, Suite 605, 2000 P St., Washington DC 20036. (202)293-9142. Editor: Ann Radelat. Emphasizes consumer issues for the membership of Public Citizen, a group founded by Ralph Nader in 1971. Bimonthly. Circ. 42,000. Accepts previously published material. Returns original artwork after publication. Sample copy available with 9×12″ envelope, SASE with first-class postage.

Illustrations: Buys up to 10 illustrations/issue. Prefers contemporary styles. Prefers pen & ink; uses computer illustration also. "I use computer art when it is appropriate for a particular article." Send query letter with samples to be kept on file. Samples not filed are returned by SASE. Reports only if interested. Buys first rights or one-time rights. Pays $300, 3-color, cover; $50-200, b&w or 2-color, inside; on publication.

Tips: "Frequently commissions more than one spot per artist. Also, send several keepable samples that show a range of styles and the ability to conceptualize."

PUBLIC RELATIONS JOURNAL, 33 Irving Place, New York NY 10003. (212)995-2230. Art Director: Susan Yip. Emphasizes issues and developments, both theory and practice, for public relations practitioners, educators and their managements. Monthly. Circ. 15,733. Accepts previously published material. Returns original artwork after publication.

Illustrations: Preferred themes and styles vary. Send brochure and samples to be kept on file. Samples not filed are returned only if requested. Reports back only if interested. Negotiates rights purchased. Pays $500, color, cover; $75, b&w, $100, color, inside; on publication.

PUBLISHER'S WEEKLY, 249 W. 17th St., 4th Floor, New York NY 10011. (212)645-9700. Art Director: Karen E. Jones. Magazine emphasizing book publishing for "people involved in the creative or the technical side of publishing." Weekly. 51 issues /year. Circ. 50,000. Original artwork is returned to the artist after publication. Sample copy available.

Illustrations: Buys 75 illustrations/year from freelancers. Works on assignment only. "Open to all styles, with book-oriented themes." Send query letter with brochure or resume, tearsheets, photostats, photocopies, slides and photographs. Samples are filed or are returned by SASE. Reports back only if interested. To show

a portfolio, mail appropriate materials. Generally buys reprint rights. Pays $100, b&w, $200, color, inside; on acceptance.
Tips: "Send promotional pieces and follow up with a phone call."

*QUANTUM—Science Fiction & Fantasy Review, (formerly *Thrust*), 8217 Langport Terrace, Gaithersburg MD 20877. Publisher/Editor: D. Douglas Fratz. Emphasizes science fiction and fantasy literature for highly knowledgeable science fiction professionals and well-read fans. Quarterly. Circ. 1,800. Accepts previously published material. Returns original artwork after publication. Sample copy $3. Art guidelines for SASE with first-class postage.
Cartoons: Approached by 25 cartoonists/year. Buys 1-2 cartoons/issue, 6-8 cartoons/year from freelancers. Themes must be related to science fiction or fantasy. Prefers single panel; b&w line drawings. Send query letter with samples of style to be kept on file unless SASE included. Reports within 2 months. Buys one-time rights. Pays $15/page, b&w; on publication.
Illustrations: Approached by 40 illustrators/year. Works with 20 illustrators/year. Buys 9-10/issue from freelance artists. Prefers "sharp, bold b&w art." Science fiction or fantasy themes only. Prefers pen & ink, then airbrush and charcoal/pencil. Send query letter with tearsheets, photostats or photocopies to be kept on file unless SASE included. Accepts any style. Samples not filed are returned by SASE. Reports within 4 weeks. To show a portfolio, mail appropriate materials, which should include b&w original/final art, final reproduction/product and tearsheets. Buys one-time rights. Pays $25, b&w, cover; $15/page, b&w, inside; on publication.
Tips: "Show us only science fiction or fantasy work. Do not send color samples, slides or original art. Send black-and-white samples."

QUARRY MAGAZINE, Box 1061, Kingston, Ontario K7L 4Y5 Canada. (613)548-8429. Editor: Steven Heighton. Emphasizes poetry, fiction, short plays, book reviews—Canadian literature. Audience: Canadian writers; libraries (public, high school, college, university); persons interested in current new writing. Quarterly. Circ. 1,000. Original artwork returned after publication. Sample copy $5.
Illustrations: Buys 3-5 illustrations/issues from freelancers. Uses freelance artists mainly for cover of magazine. No set preference on themes or styles; "we need high quality line drawings." Send query letter with originals or good photostats to be kept on file. Contact only by mail. Reports within 12 weeks. Buys first rights. Pays $100, b&w, cover; on publication.

*QUILT WORLD, 306 E. Parr Rd., Berne IN 46711. Editor: Sandra L. Hatch. Concerns patchwork and quilting. Bimonthly. Previously published work OK. Original artwork not returned after publication. Sample copy with 9 × 12 SASE with 66¢ postage.
Cartoons: Approached by 10 cartoonists/year. Buys 2 cartoons/issue from freelancers. Receives 25 submissions/month from freelancers. Uses themes "poking gentle fun at quilters." Send finished cartoons. Reports in 3 weeks if not accepted. "I hold cartoons I can use until there is space." Buys all rights. Pays $15; on acceptance and/or publication.

R-A-D-A-R, 8121 Hamilton Ave., Cincinnati OH 45231. Editor: Margaret Williams. For children 3rd-6th grade in Christian Sunday schools. Original artwork not returned after publication.
Cartoons: Buys 1 cartoon/month from freelancers on animals, school and sports. Prefers to see finished cartoons. Reports in 1-2 months. Pays $10-15; on acceptance.
Illustrations: Buys 5 or more illustrations/issue from freelancers. "Art that accompanies nature or handicraft articles may be purchased, but almost everything is assigned." Send tearsheets to be kept on file. Samples returned by SASE. Reports in 1-2 months. Buys all rights on a work-for-hire basis. Pays $150, full-color cover; $70, inside.

RADIO-ELECTRONICS, 500-B Bi-County Blvd., Farmingdale NY 11735. (516)293-3000. FAX: (516)293-3115. Editor: Brian Fenton. Estab. 1939. Monthly. Consumer magazine emphasizing electronic and computer construction projects and tutorial articles; practical electronics for technical people including service technicians, engineers and experimenters in TV, hi-fi, computers, communications and industrial electronics. Circ. 210,000. Previously published work OK. Free sample copy.
Cartoons: Approached by 20-25 cartoonists/year. Buys 70-80 cartoons/year on electronics, computers, communications, robots, lasers, stereo, video and service; single panel. Send query letter with finished cartoons. Samples are filed or are returned by SASE. Reports in 1 week. Buys first or all rights. Pays $25 minimum, b&w washes; on acceptance.
Illustrations: Approached by 10 illustrators/year. Buys 3 illustrations/year from freelancers. Works on assignment only. Preferred themes or styles depend on the story being illustrated. Considers airbrush, watercolor, acrylic and oil. Send query letter with tearsheets and slides. Samples are filed or are returned by SASE. Reports back within 2 weeks. Mail appropriate materials: roughs, tearsheets, photographs and slides. Buys all rights. Pays $300, color, cover; $100, b&w, $300, color, inside; on acceptance.
Tips: Artists approaching Radio-Electronics should have an innate interest in electronics and technology that shows through in their work."

Close-up

Anita Kunz
Illustrator

Rolling Stone readers regularly see the Toronto-based Anita Kunz's work on the "History of Rock and Roll" page which she and illustrator Chris Payne take turns doing. Her illustrations include Jim Morrison dressed as a boy scout rubbing two sticks together, "Jim Morrison Lights His First Fire"; a little Jimi Hendrix in a highchair putting a toy guitar into his mouth, "Jimi Hendrix: Foxy Baby"; and David Bowie with the face of a chameleon framed by foliage entitled "Ch-ch-ch-ch-changes." Other magazines she illustrates for include *The New York Times Magazine, Spy, Atlantic Monthly, Esquire, Playboy* and *Newsweek.*

Each of her multi-layered watercolor paintings is true to Kunz, a unique expression of how she views the subject at hand. They are clever and often provocative comments, conveyed with playfulness, passion, thoughtfulness and skill. "For me," she says, "all art should have a point, come from somewhere, not just be something decorative."

The earliest contributer to this perspective was her uncle, a textbook and education materials illustrator. Later she studied illustration at the Ontario College of Art and upon graduating did some work in advertising, which she found was not for her. "For me it was restrictive. The nature of advertising seemed to be too much of a formula. And at an ad agency the illustrator is the last person down the line; everything is already figured out. So basically it's just rendering and that's not the aspect of illustration that I've always been interested in. I'm much more interested in the concept and creative process.

"The fine art field seemed too introspective and advertising seemed too cold and commercial, so somewhere in between is editorial where I can still earn a living and have creative freedom to comment on social and political issues." With editorial illustration, she says, an illustration can work in conjunction with what is written or it can set out to prove an alternate viewpoint. "I think there's just much more room for exploration, more room to play. I really dislike the kind of work that only attempts to duplicate what's said in print."

She often compares illustrating to speaking, as much a natural extension of herself as are the things she says, the words she uses. She says she absolutely has a viewer in mind when she conceptualizes, sketches and paints. "It's like a language. You're always aware of who you're talking to." She uses the same analogy when she speaks of the evolution of her style. "It's something that comes out of you naturally. It's like the way you construct sentences, the way you speak. It's really hard to figure out how your vocabulary has changed over the years. Every illustrator has a unique viewpoint."

Two frustrations she sometimes feels are due to the nature of this mode of communication, which can be one-sided. She says, "there is a response but not as much as I would like." Also because of the desire to communicate with a still somewhat mysterious audience, she wonders whether she is yielding to it too much.

When she illustrated an announcement poster for a talk she gave in Dallas, a nude rendition of herself with horns and tail, it didn't garner a very favorable response. She says, "I guess I don't really understand how I'm perceived a lot of the time. I mean that poster seemed the perfectly natural thing to do. It wasn't that well received. But I guess it's important to try to be true to yourself and not always try to accomodate every single person, because you could drive yourself crazy. I don't think it's anything precious or special. It just seems natural to me."

Whereas now most of her assignments come from those art directors she works with on a regular basis, referrals and her rep in England, when she first started out her biggest problem was finding work. "I basically knocked on doors. Then in 1981 I lived in London for six months and basically did the same thing there. I called up every art director that I'd been told of or whose work I'd seen and I went around and tried to promote my work. When I came back to Canada, I tried to make myself as visible as I could for as little money as I could. At one point I went to see Marshall Arisman (one of her favorite illustrators and biggest influences), and he was extremely helpful and gave me all sorts of advice on whom to contact. Basically I tried to educate myself on what was out there and then target it."

Her advice to one just starting out is to "work toward finding your own voice. Try to get work accordingly. Move in the direction that's appropriate for you and the way that you live. And the way that you look at the world."

Her biggest problem now is that she has to turn down so much work, which makes her feel badly. She tries not to work on any more than six projects at a time. "I find that if I get above six, I turn into a monster. The pressure starts getting to me. There are too many things to think about." Another difficult feature of her profession for her is the business side. "It's the worst aspect of it for me," she says, "because I'm not very good at it. It's really something you have to work at. I have a terrible time quoting prices. I never know how much to charge. It just seems so alien to the creative process." Her rates range from $300-3,000 and, she says, often times this is up to the magazine. Magazines with very high circulations can afford to pay the most, but she often does work for what she considers to be worthwhile magazines that don't have the same budget. She finds with publications such as these, she is given a greater freedom, which along with respect for her work, are what she holds most dear in an assignment.

— Lauri Miller

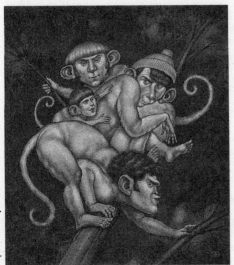

"Talkin' 'Bout an Evolution" portrait of the Monkees was done for the *"History of Rock and Roll"* page of Rolling Stone and was influenced by the fact that Kunz is no fan. About illustration she says, "I love doing it and feel compelled to do it and so I don't consider it like work. I mean when I was really young to supplement my income, I worked at Seagram in an assembly line. I was waiting for the break and then I was waiting for lunch. I mean I was just waiting for the whole time to pass. But this is so different."

RAG MAG, Box 12, Goodhue MN 55027. Contact: Beverly Voldseth. Estab. 1982. Emphasizes poetry, graphics, fiction and reviews for small press, writers, poets and editors. Semiannually: fall and spring. Circ. 300. Accepts previously published material. Send no original work. Sample copy $4.50; art guidelines free for SASE.

Cartoons: Approached by 4-5 cartoonists/year. Acquires 2 cartoons/issue from freelancers. Any theme or style. Prefers single panel or multiple panel with gagline; b&w line drawings. Send samples of styles or finished cartoons. Material returned in 2 months by SASE if unwanted. Reports within 2 months. Acquires first rights. Pays in copies only.

Illustrations: Approached by up to 12 illustrators/year. Acquires 6 illustrations/issue from freelancers. Any style or theme. Send camera-ready copy. Samples returned by SASE. Reports within 1 month. Acquires first rights. Pays in copies for b&w cover and inside.

Tips: "Realize I publish only 2 issues per year. I can use only 10-12 art pieces per year. I only take what's ready to be used on receipt. I return what I don't want. I don't hold a lot in my files because I think artists should be sending their art work around. And even if I like someone's art work very much, I like to use new people. I do not want to see anything portraying violence or putting down a group."

*RAINBOW CITY EXPRESS, Box 8447, Berkeley CA 94707-8447. "We do not accept query calls." Editor/ Publisher: Helen B. Harvey. Estab. 1988. "Journal/newsletter/creative forum"; magazine format emphasizing adventures on the spiritual path, true experiences and insights of spiritual awakening, evolving consciousness, women's issues, creativity and related topics." Quarterly. Circ. 500-1,000. Sometimes accepts previously published artwork. Whether originals returned to the artist at the job's completion depends on rights purchased. Back issues $6. Art guidelines free for SASE with first class postage.

Illustrations: "We have a commissioned artist but are branching out." Buys 1-5 illustrations/issue, 4-20 illustrations/year from freelancers. "We also purchase completed art." Prefers "sophisticated, delicate renderings with ethereal , spiritual, aesthetic qualities." Prefers pen & ink. Send query letter with SASE tearsheets and photocopies. Samples not filed and are returned by SASE if requested by artist. Reports back within 1-3 months, only if accompanied by SASE. Mail appropriate materials: b&w photocopies. Rights purchased vary according to project. Pays $75-100, b&w, cover; $20-50, b&w, inside.

Tips: "Buy a sample copy and read and study it. To draw or write for RCE, one must read RCE. We are very unique. We wish to convey the beauty and joy of the creative/spiritual life. Artwork reflects the contents of our essays/poetry, etc. Most issues feature a concept or theme and artwork is tailored for that theme. Example: Autumn issues feature 'Harvests in the Feminine Realm'; our Summer '90 issue features 'Kunalini & Transcendent Energy.' "

*READ ME, 1118 Hoyt Ave., Everett WA 98201. (206)259-0804. Editor/Publisher: Ron Fleshman. Estab. 1988. Literary magazine; tabloid format. Quarterly. Circ. 2,000. Accepts previously published artwork. Sample copy $1.50. Art guidelines not available.

Cartoons: Approached by 10 cartoonists/year. Buys 10-12 cartoons/issue, 40-50 cartoons/year from freelancers. Prefers themes relating to reading, books, libraries, general." Prefers single panel. Send query letter with finished cartoons. Samples not filed are returned by SASE. Reports back within 3 weeks. Buys one-time rights. Pays $5, b&w; $15, b&w cover.

Illustrations: Approached by 6 illustrators/year. Buys 1 illustration/issue, 4 illustrations/year from freelancers. Works on assignment only. Prefers pen & ink. SASE. Samples not filed are returned by SASE. Reports back within 3 weeks. Mail appropriate materials: original/final art and b&w photocopies. Buys first rights. Pays $15, b&w.

Tips: "Be familiar with what we're doing."

*REAL ESTATE CENTER JOURNAL, (formerly Tierra Grande), Real Estate Center, Texas A&M University, College Station TX 77843. (409)845-0369. Art Director: Bob Beals. Emphasizes real estate; "primarily for real estate practitioners, with a smattering of investors, attorneys, CPAs, architects and others interested in real estate." Quarterly. Circ. 65,000. Previously published material and simultaneous submissions OK. Free sample copy.

Illustrations: Uses 1-3 illustrations/issue; buys 1-3 from freelancers. Interested in "anything relating directly or indirectly to real estate." Works on assignment only. Send query letter. Provide samples and tearsheets to be kept on file for possible future assignments. Reports in 2 months. Negotiates rights purchased. Pays $150-200, inside b&w line drawings and b&w washes; on acceptance.

Tips: "There are a great many talented artists, making it unnecessary to consider the marginally talented or those with less than professional presentation of their material. I especially like the artist to know printing production, and I want to know how well the artist works in 1 or 2 colors."

*REAL PEOPLE MAGAZINE, 950 Third Ave., 16th Floor, New York NY 10022. (212)371-4932. FAX: (212)838-8420. Editor: Alex Polner. Estab. 1988. Consumer magazine; "general interest featuring celebrities and self-help articles and profiles for men and women ages 35 and up, a middle brow audience." Bimonthly.

Circ. 165,000. Original artwork returned after publication. Sample copy $3.50 plus postage. Art guidelines not available.

Illustrations: Approached by 5-10 illustrators/year. Buys 1-2 illustrations/issue, 6-12 illustrations/year from freelancers. Works on assignment only. Theme or style depends on the article. Prefers pen & ink, watercolor or acrylic. Send query letter with tearsheets. Samples are filed. Reports back only if interested. Call to schedule an appointment to show a portfolio, which should include tearsheets. Buys one-time rights. Pays $100, b&w, $200, color, inside; on publication.

Tips: "There is no secret. We select the artist that best matches the story we want illustrated."

*REDBOOK MAGAZINE, 224 W. 57th St., New York NY 10019. (212)649-3438. Art Director: Patti Ratchford. Consumer magazine "geared to baby boomers with busy lives. Interests in fashion, food, beauty, health, etc." Monthly. Circ. 7 million. Accepts previously published artwork. Original artwork returned after publication with additional tearsheet if requested. Art guidelines not available.

Illustrations: Buys 3-4 illustrations/issue. "We prefer photo illustration for fiction and more serious articles, loose or humorous illustrations for lighter articles; the only thing we don't use is high realism. Illustrations can be in any medium. Book drop off any day, pick up the next day. Work samples are accepted in the mail; should include anything that will represent the artist and should not have to be returned. This way the sample can remain on file, and the artist will be called if the appropriate job comes up." Buys reprint rights or negotiates rights. Payment for accepted work only: $150-600, b&w, $400-1,200, color.

Tips: "Look at the magazine before you send anything, we might not be right for you. Generally, illustrations should look new, of the moment, intelligent."

RESIDENT AND STAFF PHYSICIAN, 80 Shore Rd., Port Washington NY 11050. (516)883-6350. Executive Editor: Anne Mattarella. Emphasizes hospital medical practice from clinical, educational, economic and human standpoints. For hospital physicians, interns and residents. Monthly. Circ. 100,000.

Cartoons: Buys 3-4 cartoons/year from freelancers. "We occasionally publish sophisticated cartoons in good taste dealing with medical themes." Interested in "inside" medical themes. Send query letter with brochure showing art style or resume, tearsheets, photostats, photocopies, slides and photographs. Call or write to schedule an appointment to show a portfolio, which should include color and b&w final reproduction/product and tearsheets. Reports in 2 weeks. Buys all rights. Pays $25; varies for color; also buys spots; pays $10-50; on acceptance.

Illustrations: "We commission qualified freelance medical illustrators to do covers and inside material. Artists should send sample work." Pays $700, color, cover; payment varies for inside work; on acceptance.

Tips: "We like to look at previous work to give us an idea of the artist's style. Since our publication is clinical, we require highly qualified technical artists who are very familiar with medical illustration. Sometimes we have use for nontechnical work. We like to look at everything. We need material from the *doctor's* point of view, *not* the patient's."

*RESTAURANT BUSINESS MAGAZINE, 633 Third Ave., New York NY 10017. Art Director: Lisa Powers. Emphasizes restaurants/food/business and management for restaurateurs. Monthly. Circ. 110,000. Original artwork returned after publication. Uses freelance artists mainly for photography.

Illustrations: Buys 2-5 illustrations/issue from freelancers. Works on assignment only. Drop off portfolio. Negotiates rights purchased and payment. Pays $800-1,000 color, cover; $125 b&w inside; within 60 days.

Tips: Wants to see "food oriented illustration with concepts or pictures dealing with business/management subjects."

RESTAURANT HOSPITALITY, 1100 Superior Ave., Cleveland OH 44114. (216)696-7000. Features Editor: David Farkas. Emphasizes commercial food service industry for owners, managers, chefs, etc. Circ. 141,000. Original artwork returned after publication. Sample copy $4.

Illustrations: "We have a file of freelance illustrators but want to see the work of others to whom we can assign projects." Works on assignment only. Send query letter with brochure, resume, business card, samples or tearsheets. Prefers photographs as samples, 5x7 or larger, but will accept photostats. Does not report back to the artist.

THE RETIRED OFFICER, 201 N. Washington St., Alexandria VA 22314. (703)549-2311. Art Director: M.L. Woychik. Estab. 1945. For retired officers of the uniformed services; concerns current military/political affairs; recent military history, especially Vietnam and Korea; holiday anecdotes; travel; human interest; humor; hobbies; second-career job opportunities and military family lifestyle.

Illustrations: Approached by 24 illustrators/year. Works with 9-10 illustrators/year. Buys 15-20 illustrations/year from freelancers. Buys illustrations on assigned themes. (Generally uses Washington DC area artists.) Uses freelance artwork mainly for features and covers. Send query letter with resume and samples. Pays $300, b&w; $400+, color, cover; $250, full page b&w; $300, full page color, inside.

Tips: "Send pieces showing your style and concepts in a few different mediums. I do not want to see a different style for every piece of art." Common mistakes freelancers make in presenting their work are "talking negatively about their work or experiences.and not showing any published pieces."

RIP OFF PRESS, INC., Box 4686, Auburn CA 95604. (916)885-8183. Chief Copy Editor: Kathe Todd. Estab. 1969. Quarterly. Publishes comic books including *Fabulous Furry Freak Brothers*, *Rip Off Comix* and *Strips*. Genres: social parodies. Themes: social commentary and alternative lifestyles. "We publish 'underground' comix. Prefer submissions to be intelligent, funny and well-drawn, rather than heavily violent, graphically sexual or New Wave." Circ. 5-50,000. Original artwork returned after publication. Send $1 for catalog listing retail prices. Art guidelines for SASE with first-class postage.
Cartoons: Works with 30-40 cartoonists/year. Buys 300 comic pages/year from freelancers. Prefers three-tier page of 6 panels or format 2 wide by 3 tall. Send query letter with photocopies of representative pages or stories. Samples are filed "depending on merit." Samples not filed are returned by SASE if requested. Call or write to schedule an appointment to show a portfolio, which should include 4-5 photocopies of original inking. Buys U.S. comic rights and first refusal on subsequent collections. "Our advance ranges $40-75 per b&w finished page against 10% of cover price on net copies sold (divided by number of pages on multi-contributor publications)." Pays $100-200, color; on acceptance and publication when earned royalties exceed advance.
Tips: Looks for "knowledge of successful techniques for b&w reproduction; ability to use comic narrative techniques well; knowledge of and facility with anatomy and perspective." Does not want to see "uncompleted comic pages or 350-page manuscripts, work which shows a complete ignorance of repo techniques."

RISK MANAGEMENT, 205 E. 42nd St., New York NY 10017. (212)286-9292. Graphic Design Manager: Linda Golden. Emphasizes the risk management and insurance fields. Monthly. Circ. 11,500.
Illustrations: Approached by 15-20 illustrators/year. Buys 3-5 illustrations/issue, 48 illustrations/year from freelancers. Uses artists mainly for covers, 4-color inside and spots. Prefers color illustration or stylized line; no humorous themes. Works on assignment only. Send card showing art style or tearsheets. Call for appointment to show portfolio, which should include original art and tearsheets. Prefers printed pieces as samples; original work will not be kept on file after 1 year. Samples not kept on file are returned only if requested. Buys one-time rights. Pays $385, 4-color, inside and $500, 4-color cover; on acceptance.
Tips: When reviewing an artist's work, looks for "neatness, strong concepts, realism with subtle twists and sharply-defined illustrations."

ROAD KING MAGAZINE, Box 250, Park Forest IL 60466. (312)481-9240. Editor: George Friend. Estab. 1963. Emphasizes services for truckers, news of the field, CB radio and fiction; leisure-oriented. Readers are "over-the-road truckers." Quarterly. Circ. 224,000.
Cartoons: Approached by 10 cartoonists/year. Buys 1-2 cartoons/issue; all from freelancers. Interested in over-the-road trucking experiences. Prefers single panel b&w line drawings with gagline. Send finished cartoons and SASE. "Gag lines and cartoon must be legible and reproduceable." Reports in 2-4 months. Buys first North American serial rights. Pays $25 and up, b&w; on acceptance.
Illustrations: Approached by 10 illustrators/year. Works with 4-5 illustrators/year. Uses artwork mainly for spots and cartoons. Pays $100-300, color, cover; $25-50 b&w, $75-100 color, inside.
Tips: "Stick to our subject matter. No matter how funny the cartoons are, we probably won't buy them unless they are about trucks and trucking."

THE ROTARIAN, 1560 Sherman Ave., Evanston IL 60201. Editor: Willmon L. White. Associate Editor: Jo Nugent. Art Director: P. Limbos. Estab. 1911. Emphasizes general interest and business and management articles. Service organization for business and professional men and women, their families, and other subscribers. Monthly. Sample copy and editorial fact sheet available.
Cartoons: Approached by 14 cartoonists/year. Buys 5-8 cartoons/issue from freelancers. Interested in general themes with emphasis on business. Avoid topics of sex, national origin, politics. Send query letter to Cartoon Editor, Charles Pratt, with brochure showing art style. Reports in 1-2 weeks. Buys all rights. Pays $75 on acceptance.
Illustrations: Approached by 8 illustrators/year. Buys 10-20 illustrations/year; 7 or 8 humorous illustrations year from freelancers. Uses freelance artwork mainly for covers and feature illustrations. Buys assigned themes. Most editorial illustrations are commissioned. Send query letter to Art Director with brochure showing art style. Reports within 10 working days. Buys all rights. Call to schedule an appointment to show a portfolio, which should include keyline paste-up, original/final art, final reproduction/product, color and photographs. Pays on acceptance; payment negotiable, depending on size, medium, etc.
Tips: "Artists should set up appointments with art director to show their portfolios. Preference given to area talent." Conservative style and subject matter.

ROUGH NOTES, 1200 N. Meridian, Indianapolis IN 46204. Assistant Editor: Nancy Doucette. Estab. 1878. **Cartoons:** Buys 3-5 cartoons/issue on property and casualty insurance, automation, office life (manager/subordinate relations) and general humor. No risque material. Receives 30-40 cartoons/week from freelance artists. Submit art the third week of the month. SASE. Reports in 1 month. Buys all rights. Prefers 5×8 or 8×10 finished art. Pays $20, line drawings and halftones; on acceptance.
Tips: "Do not submit sexually discriminating materials. I have a tendency to disregard all of the material if I find any submissions of this type. Send several items for more variety in selection. We would prefer to deal only in finished art, not sketches."

RUNNER'S WORLD, 33 E. Minor St., Emmaus PA 18098. (215)967-5171. Art Director: Ken Kleppert. Estab. 1965. Emphasizes serious, recreational running. Monthly. Circ. 470,000. Returns original artwork after publication. Sample copy available.
Illustrations: Approached by hundreds of illustrators/year. Works with 25 illustrators/year. Buys average of 90 illustrations/year, 6/illustrations/issue from freelancers. "Styles include tightly rendered human athletes, caricatures and cerebral interpretations of running themes. Also, *RW* uses medical illustration for features on biomechanics." Prefers pen & ink, airbrush, charcoal/pencil, colored pencil, watercolor, acrylic, oil, pastel, collage and mixed media. Works on assignment only. Send samples to be kept on file. Prefers tearsheets or slides as samples. Samples not filed are returned by SASE. Reports back only if interested. Pays $300 and up. Buys one-time rights. "No cartoons or originals larger than 11×14."
Tips: Portfolio should include "a maximum of 12 images. Show a clean presentation, lots of ideas and few samples. Don't show disorganized thinking. Portfolio samples should be uniform in size."

RUTGERS MAGAZINE, Alexander Johnston Hall, New Brunswick NJ 08903. Art Director: Joanne Dus-Zastrow. Estab. 1987. General interest magazine covering research, events, art programs, etc. that relate to Rutgers University. Readership consists of alumni, parents of students and University staff. Published 4 times/year. Circ. 130,000. Accepts previously published artwork. Original artwork is returned after publication. Sample copies available.
Illustrations: Approached by 40 illustrators/year. Buys illustrations mainly for covers and feature spreads. Buys 2 illustrations/issue, 8 illustrations/year from freelancers. Considers mixed media, watercolor, pastel and collage. Send query letter with brochure. "Show a strong conceptual approach." Samples are filed. Does not report back. Write to schedule an appointment to show a portfolio. Buys one-time rights. Pays $500-800, color, cover; $300, b&w; $350-500, color, inside; on publication.
Tips: "Open to new ideas. See a trend away from perfect realism in illustration. See a willingness to experiment with type in design."

SAFE & VAULT TECHNOLOGY, 5083 Danville Rd., Nicholasville KY 40356. Editor: April Truitt. Estab. 1986. "Our subscribers maintain, service and sell safes and vaults for everyone from individual homeowners to banks, institutions and government installations." Monthly. Circ. 5,000. Accepts previously published material. Original artwork is not returned to the artist after publication unless requested. Sample copy $7. Art guidelines not available. Uses freelance artists mainly for cartoons, cover art.
Cartoons: Approached by 25-30 cartoonists/year. Prefers single panel with or without gagline; b&w line drawings and b&w washes. Send query letter with finished cartoons. Samples are not filed, but returned by SASE if requested. Reports back only if interested. Buys one-time rights. Pays $50, b&w.
Illustrations: Approached by 5 illustrators/year. Send query letter with brochure showing art style or tearsheets, photostats or photocopies. Samples are not filed and returned only if requested. Reports back only if interested. To show a portfolio, mail appropriate materials. Payment "depends on quality." Buys reprint rights.
Tips: "We're interested in full-color cover illustrations. Show us your style—we'll suggest the theme."

SAFETY & HEALTH, National Safety Council, 444 N. Michigan Ave., Chicago IL 60611-3991. (312)527-4800. Editor: Austin Weber. For those responsible for developing and administering occupational and environmental safety and health programs. Monthly. Circ. 56,000. Original artwork returned after publication. Free sample copy and artist's guidelines. Also uses artists for 4-color cover design, publication redesign and layout mock-ups.
Cartoons: Approached by 15-20 cartoonists/year. Prefers to see tearsheets, Xeroxes or transparencies of 4-color work. Include SASE. Reports in 4 weeks. Buys first North American serial rights or all rights on a work-for-hire basis. Pay negotiable.

THE ST. LOUIS JOURNALISM REVIEW, 8380 Olive Blvd., St. Louis MO 63132. (314)991-1699. Contact: Charles L. Klotzer. Features critiques of primarily St. Louis but also national media—print, broadcasting, TV, cable, advertising, public relations and the communication industry. Monthly. Circ. 6,900.
Cartoons: Subject should pertain to the news media; preferably local. Query with samples. SASE. Reports in 4-7 weeks. Pays $15-25; on publication.
Illustrations: Query with samplescv and SASE. Reports in 4-6 weeks. Pays $15-25 each (negotiable) for b&w illustrations pertaining to the news media (preferably local); on publication.

*SALT LICK PRESS, 1804 E. 38½ St., Austin TX 78722. Editor/Publisher: James Haining. Published irregularly. Circ. 1,500. Previously published material and simultaneous submissions OK. Original artwork returned after publication. Sample copy $5.
Illustrations: Uses 12 illustrations/issue; buys 2 from freelancers. Receives 2 illustrations/week from freelance artists. Interested in a variety of themes. Send brochure showing art style or tearsheets, photostats, photocopies, slides and photographs. Samples returned by SASE. Reports in 6 weeks. To show a portfolio, mail roughs and b&w photostats and photographs. Negotiates payment; on publication. Buys first rights.

SAN JOSE STUDIES, San Jose State University, San Jose CA 95192. (408)277-2841. Editor: Fauneil J. Rinn. Estab. 1974. Emphasizes the arts, humanities, business, science, social science; scholarly. Published 3 times/ year. Circ. 500. Original artwork returned after publication. Sample copy $5.
Cartoons: Acquires 3-4 cartoons. Interested in "anything that would appeal to the active intellect." Prefers single panel b&w line drawings. Send photocopies and SASE. Reports in 2 weeks. Acquires first North American serial rights. Pays in 2 copies of publication, plus entry in $100 annual contest.
Illustrations: Approached by 3-4 illustrations/year. "We have used several pieces of work in a special section and have used details of work on our covers."
Tips: "We are interested in cartoons and other drawings whose detail is still visible even if reduced in size. We like art that relieves the reader faced with type-filled pages."

SANTA BARBARA MAGAZINE, 216 E. Victoria St., Santa Barbara CA 93101. (805)965-5999. Art Director: Kimberly Kavish. Estab. 1975. Magazine emphasising Santa Barbara culture and community. Bimonthly. Circ. 11,000. Original artwork returned after publication if requested. Sample copy $2.95.
Illustrations: Approached by 20 illustrators/year. Works with 2-3 illustrators/year. Buys about 3 illustrations/ issue, 12-15 illustrations/year from freelance artists. Uses freelance artwork mainly for departments. Works on assignment only. Send query letter with brochure, resume, tearsheets and photocopies. Reports back within 6 weeks. To show a portfolio, mail b&w and color original/final art, final reproduction/product and tearsheet; will contact if interested. Buys first rights. Pays $275, color, cover; $175, color, inside; on acceptance. "Payment varies."
Tips: "Be familiar with our magazine."

*SATELLITE ORBIT, Suite 600, 8330 Boone Blvd., Vienna VA 22182. (703)827-0511. FAX: (703)356-6179. Contact: Art Director. Magazine emphasizing satellite television industry for home satellite dish owners and dealers. Monthly. Circ. 350,000. Accepts previously published material. Original artwork returned after publication.
Illustrations: Buys 2-5 illustrations/issue from freelancers. Works on assignment only. Send query letter with tearsheets, photocopies, slides and photographs. Samples not filed are returned only if requested. Reports within 1 month. To show a portfolio, mail color and b&w tearsheets and photographs. Negotiates rights purchased. Negotiates payment. Pays $450, b&w; $1,500, color, cover; $150, b&w; $200, color, inside; on publication.
Tips: "I usually only use spot illustration work. Black and white stuff usually gets overlooked and I don't like to see uninventive poorly-drawn stuff." Notices "more spot illustration. As for design—the trend seems to be copying 40's and 50's styles."

THE SATURDAY EVENING POST, The Saturday Evening Post Society, 1100 Waterway Blvd., Indianapolis IN 46202. (317)636-8881. Estab. 1897. General interest, family-oriented magazine. Published 9 times/year. Circ. 600,000. Sample copy $1.
Cartoons: Cartoon Editor: Steven Pettinga. Buys about 300 cartoons/year, 35 cartoons/issue. Uses freelance artwork mainly for humorous ficiton. Prefers single panel with gaglines. Receives 100 batches of cartoons/ week from freelance cartoonists. "We look for cartoons with neat line or tone art. The content should be in good taste, suitable for a general-interest, family magazine. It must not be offensive while remaining entertaining. We prefer that artists first send SASE for guidelines and then review recent issues. Political, violent or sexist cartoons are not used. Need all topics, but particularly medical, health, travel and financial." SASE. Reports in 1 month. Buys all rights. Pays $125, b&w line drawings and washes, no pre-screened art; on publication.
Illustrations: Art Director: Chris Wilhoite. Uses average of 3 illustrations/issue; buys 90% from freelancers. Send query letter with brochure showing art style or resume and samples. To show a portfolio, mail original/ final art. Buys all rights, "generally. All ideas, sketchwork and illustrative art are handled through commissions only and thereby controlled by art direction. Do not send original material (drawings, paintings, etc.) or 'facsimiles of' that you wish returned." Cannot assume any responsibility for loss or damage. "If you wish to show your artistic capabilities, please send nonreturnable, expendable/sampler material (slides, tearsheets, photocopies, etc.)." Pays $1,000, color, cover; $175, b&w, $450, color, inside.
Tips: "Send samples of work published in other publications. Do not send racy or too new wave looks. Have a look at the magazine. It's clear that fifty percent of the new artists submitting material have not looked at the magazine."

SCHOOL SHOP/TECH DIRECTIONS, 416 Longshore Dr., Ann Arbor MI 48105. Managing Editor: Susanne Peckham. Estab. 1941. Magazine emphasizes industrial technology and vocational-technical education. Audience is administrators and teachers in industrial arts, technology education and vo-tech education. Articles cover projects, tips, and new information in the field. Monthly. Circ. 45,000. Original artwork not returned to the artist after publication. Sample copies $2.
Cartoons: Buys 20 cartoons/year. Buys 2 cartoons/issue; buys all from freelancers. Prefers industrial/technology and vocational-technical education themes. Prefers single panel with or without b&w line drawings. Send query letter with finished cartoons. Samples are not filed and are returned if requested by artist. Reports back within 4-6 weeks. Pays $20, b&w.
Tips: "All cartoons submitted must be educationally oriented in the fields mentioned."

*SCIENCE NEWS, 1719 N St. NW, Washington DC 20036. (202)785-2255. Art Director: Janice Rickerich. Emphasizes all sciences for teachers, students and scientists. Weekly. Circ. 235,000. Accepts previously published material. Original artwork returned after publication. Sample copy for SASE with 39¢ postage.
Illustrations: Buys 6 illustrations/year from freelancers. Prefers realistic style, scientific themes; uses some cartoon-style illustrations. Works on assignment only. Send query letter with photostats or photocopies to be kept on file. Samples returned by SASE. Reports only if interested. Buys one-time rights. Write to schedule an appointment to show a portfolio, which should include original/final art. Pays $50-200; on acceptance.
Tips: Uses some cartoons and cartoon-style illustrations.

*SCREAM MAGAZINE, Box 10363, Raleigh NC 27605. (919)834-7542. Managing Editor: Katie Boone. Estab. 1985. Literary magazine; magazine format, publishes a wide range of fiction, poetry, nonfiction—all illustrated; emphasize comics as art; specialize in fine art illustrations. Biennial. Circ. 1,500. Original artwork returned to artist at the job's completion. Sample copy $5. Art guidelines free for SASE with first class postage.
Cartoons: Approached by 20 cartoonists/year. Acquires 10 cartoons/issue, 20 cartoons/year from freelancers. We publish a comics section called the *Rollywood Funny Papers* (about 20 pages of multi panel strips) underground, no traditional superheros, continuing story lines OK. Will consider political and one-panel. Prefers multiple panel and b&w line drawings. Send query letter with photocopies only. Samples are filed and returned by SASE if requested by artist. Reports back within 2 months. Write to schedule an appointment to show a portfolio or mail appropriate materials: b&w photostats and photocopies. Rights purchased vary according to project. Pays in contributor's copies of Scream.
Illustrations: Approached by 20 illustrators/year. Acquires 12 illustrations/issue, 25 illustrations/year from freelancers. Prefers work to "accompany fiction and poetry with dark themes and investigative nonfiction (Hemingway, Vietnam, FBI files)." Considers pen & ink, oil, charcoal and mixed media. Send a query letter with photostats or photocopies and SASE. Samples are filed or returned by SASE if requested by artist. Reports back within 2 months. Write to schedule an appointment to show a portfolio or mail appropriate materials: b&w photostats or photocopies. Rights purchased vary according to project. Pays in contributors copies.
Tips: "We have been publishing for five years and are publishing cartoonists such as Matt Feazell and William Nealy and Ace Backwords. If we like your illustrations, we will send you an assignment story. Comics published every issue in."

SEA MAGAZINE, Box 1579, Newport Beach CA 92663. Art Director: Jeffrey Fleming. Estab. 1908. Consumer magazine. Emphasizes recreational boating for owners or users of recreational boats, both power and sail, primarily for cruising and general recreation; some interest in boating competition; regionally oriented to 13 western states. Monthly. Circ. 70,000. Accepts previously published artwork. Return of original artwork depends upon terms of purchase. Sample copy for SASE with first-class postage.
Illustrations: Approached by 20 illustators/year. Buys illustrations mainly for editorial. Buys 10 illustrations/ year from freelancers. Prefers pen & ink. Considers airbrush, watercolor, acrylic and calligraphy. Send query letter with brochure showing art style. Samples are returned only if requested. Reports only if interested. Call to schedule an appointment to show a portfolio, which should include tearsheets and cover letter indicating price range. Negotiates rights purchased. Pays $50, b&w; $250, color, inside; on publication (negotiable).
Tips: "We will accept students for portfolio review with an eye to obtaining quality art at a reasonable price. We will help start career for illustrators and hope that they will remain loyal to our publication."

SEACOAST LIFE MAGAZINE, Box 594, North Hampton NH 03862. (603)964-9898. Art Director: Heidi Illingworth. Estab. 1985. A regional lifestyle magazine. Bimonthly. Circ. 20,000. Original artwork is not returned after publication. Sample copies $2.50.
Cartoons: Approached by 25 cartoonists/year. Buys 1 cartoon/year from freelancers. Prefers b&w line drawings or color washes. Send query letter with samples of style. Samples are filed. Reports back within 2 weeks only if interested. Buys first rights. Pays $30, b&w; $100, color; on publication.

Illustrations: Approached by 100 illustrators/year. Buys 1 illustration/issue, 6 illustrations/year from free-lancers. Buys illustrations mainly for feature spreads. Works on assignment only. Prefers watercolor. Considers pen & ink, colored pencil and pastel. Send query letter with brochure, resume, tearsheets, photostats and photocopies. Looks for "traditional and realistic drawing styles." Samples are filed or are returned by SASE. Reports back within 2 weeks. Write to schedule an appointment to show a portfolio which should include color and b&w original/final art, tearsheets and photostats. Pays $30, b&w; $100, color, inside; on publication.
Tips: "The fiction story is illustrated in each issue." Does not want to see "any subject matter that is not regional to New England."

SEEK, 8121 Hamilton Ave., Cincinnati OH 45231. (513)931-4050, ext. 365. Emphasizes religion/faith. Readers are young adult to middle-aged adults who attend church and Bible classes. Quarterly in weekly issues. Circ. 45,000. Free sample copy and guidelines; SASE.
Cartoons: Editor: Eileen H. Wilmoth. Approached by 6 cartoonists/year. Buys 8-10 cartoons/year from freelancers. Buys "church or Bible themes—contemporary situations of applied Christianity." Prefers single panel b&w line drawings with gagline. Send finished cartoons, photocopies and photographs. SASE. Reports in 3-4 months. Buys first North American serial rights. Pays $15-18; on acceptance.
Illustrations: Art Director: Frank Sutton. Approached by 24-36 illustrators/year. Buys 20 illustrations/year from freelancers. Works with several illustrators/year. Uses cover and inside b&w line drawings and washes. Works on assignment only; needs vary with articles used. Arrange appointment to show portfolio "2-color work; attractive yet realistic; detail, shading and realism important." Reports in 1 week. Pays $60, cover or full page art; $40, inside pieces; on acceptance. Buys first North American serial rights.
Tips: "We use only 2-color work. The art needs to be attractive as well as realistic. I look for detail, shading and realism. Send sample with cover letter."

SERVICE BUSINESS, Suite 345, 1916 Pike Pl., Box 1273, Seattle WA 98111. (206)622-4241. Publisher: Bill Griffin. Submissions Editor: Gerri LaMarch. Technical, management and human relations emphasis for self-employed cleaning and maintenance service contractors. Quarterly. Circ. 6,000. Prefers first publication material, simultaneous submissions OK "if to non-competing publications." Original artwork returned after publication if requested by SASE. Sample copy $3.
Cartoons: Buys 1-2 cartoons/issue from freelancers. Must be relevant to magazine's readership. Prefers b&w line drawings.
Illustrations: Buys approximately 12 illustrations/issue including some humorous and cartoon-style illustrations from freelancers. Send query letter with samples. Samples returned by SASE. Buys first publication rights. Reports only if interested. Pays for design by the hour, $10-15. Pays for illustration by the project, $3-15; on publication.
Tips: "Our budget is extremely limited. Those who require high fees are really wasting their time. However, we are interested in people with talent and ability who seek exposure and publication. Our readership is people who work for/and own businesses in the cleaning industry. If you have material relevant to this specific audience, we would definitely be interested in hearing from you. Better yet, send samples."

SESAME STREET, Children's Television Workshop, One Lincoln Plaza, New York NY 10023. (212)595-3456. Art Director: Paul Richer. Aimed at pre-schoolers. Articles use Muppet characters to teach pre-reading skills to 2-6 year olds. Published 10 times/year. Circ. 1.3 million.
Illustrations: Works with 30 illustrators/year. Buys 120 illustrations/year. Uses freelancers mainly for 95% of all visuals. Works on assignment only. Does not accept Muppet illustrations. Interested in non-Muppet illustrations mostly. Send query letter with samples and SASE. Reports back within 1 week. Pays $600-900/spread; within 30 days of completion of work; $750, color, cover.

*73 MAGAZINE, Hancock NH 03449. Publisher: Wayne Green. For amateur radio operators and experimenters. Sample copy $2.50. Especially needs work for covers.
Cartoons: Approached by 8 cartoonists/year. Pays $25, b&w.
Illustrations: Approached by 2 illustrators/year. Buys 15 illustrations/issue. Receives 3 illustrations/week from freelance artists. Works on assignment only. Does not return samples. Does not report back on possible future assignments. Send query letter with resume to be kept on file. Buys all rights on a work-for-hire basis. Submit rough line drawings for assignment as oil, watercolor or pastel covers. Pays $5-20, spot art; $75/page, finished art; $400, color, cover; on acceptance.

*SHAREWARE MAGAZINE, 1030 D East Duane Ave., Sunnyvale CA 94086. (408)730-9291. FAX: (408)730-2107. Art Director: Dave Titus. Estab. 1988. Consumer magazine featuring software (called Shareware) for the IBM PC and compatible computers: reviews, new releases, author interviews, for beginners to programmers. Bimonthly. Circ. 65,000. Accepts previously published artwork. Original artwork is returned to the artist at the job's completion. Sample copies available. Art guidelines not available.

Cartoons: Approached by 5 cartoonists/year. Buys 6 cartoons/year from freelancers. Prefers "anything on computer or software usage." Prefers single panel, b&w line drawings and washes. Send a query letter to be kept on file. Reports back only if interested. Buys first rights or reprint rights. Pays $50, b&w.

Illustrations: Approached by 10-20 illustrators/year. Buys 1 illustration/issue, up to 6 illustrations/year from freelancers. Work is on assignment only. Considers watercolor, collage, airbrush, acrylic, oil and mixed media. Send a query letter with brochure and tearsheets to be kept on file. Reports back only if interested. mail appropriate materials: artist's best work. Buys first rights or reprint rights. Pays $500, color, cover; $150, b&w, $300, color, inside; on acceptance.

Tips: "Be able to work on a tight budget."

*SHOFAR, 43 Northcote Dr., Melville NY 11747. (516)643-4598. Publisher/Editor: Gerald H. Grayson. Estab. 1984. Consumer magazine for Jewish children ages 9-13. Monthly (October through May). Circ. 10,000. Accepts previously pubilshed artwork. Original artwork is returned to the artist at the job's completion. Sample copy for 9×12 SASE with first class postage. Art guidelines not available.

Illustrations: Approached by 3-4 illustrators/year. Buys 4-6 illustrations/issue, 24-35 illustrations/year from freelancers. Works on assignment only. Preferred themes or styles varies. Prefers pen & ink, airbrush and marker. Send query letter with tearsheets. Samples are filed. Reports back to the artist only if interested. Mail appropriate materials. Buys one-time rights. Pays $75, b&w; $150, color, cover; $25, b&w, $100, color, inside; on publication.

Tips: "If samples of work are on file and it seems appropriate for the story, we will give an assignment."

SIGN OF THE TIMES—A CHRONICLE OF DECADENCE IN THE ATOMIC AGE, Box 70672, Seattle WA 98107-0672. (206)323-6779. Contact: M. Souder. Magazine emphasizing fiction, photography and graphics for sleazy upscale college educated readers. Biannual. Circ. 750. Accepts previously published material. Original artwork returned after publication if requested. Sample copy $4. Art guidelines available.

Cartoons: Approached by 15 cartoonists/year. Buys 1-2 cartoons/issue from freelancers. Prefers single or multiple panels with or without gagline; b&w line drawings. Send query letter to be kept on file. Material not kept on file is returned by SASE. Reports within 6 weeks. Buys reprint rights. Pays in lifetime subscription and copies.

Illustrations: Approached by 15 illustrators/year. Buys 1-2 illustrations/issue from freelancers. Prefers decadent themes. Send query letter with photocopies. Samples not filed are returned by SASE. Reports within 6 weeks. To show a portfolio, mail original/final art. Buys reprint rights. Pays in lifetime subscription and copies.

SIGNS OF THE TIMES MAGAZINE, 1350 North King's Rd., Nampa ID 83687. (208)465-2591 or 465-2500. Art Director/Designer: Ed Guthero. Magazine emphasizing Christian lifestyle. "Looks at contemporary issues, from a Christian viewpoint—news, health, self-help, etc., covers a wide variety of topics. We attempt to show that Biblical principles are relevant to all of life. Our audience is the general public." Monthly. Circ. 370,000. Accepts previously published material. Original artwork is returned to the artist after publication.

Cartoons: Buys when applicable. Prefers "any contemporary style, also,—airbrush, and "David-Levine" type of editorial style for black & white. We don't use a lot of cartooning, but we use some." Send query letter with samples. Samples are filed. Reports back only if interested. Buys one-time rights. Pays approximately $300-450, color, full page.

Illustrations: Buys 6-10 illustration/issue, 72-120/year from freelancers. Works on assignment only. Prefers contemporary editorial illustration, "conceptual in approach as well as contemporary realism." Prefers mixed media, then pen & ink, airbrush, colored pencil, watercolor, acrylic, oil, pastel, collage and calligraphy. Call or send query letter with tear sheets and slides. Samples are filed or are returned only if requested by artist. Reports back only if interested. Call or write to schedule an appointment to show a portfolio or mail final reproduction/product, color or b&w slides. Buys one-time rights. Pays approximately $500+, color, cover; $80-300, b&w, (1 page) $450+ average, color, inside. Pays on acceptance (30 days). Fees negotiable depending on needs and placement, size, etc. in magazine.

Tips: "Many young illustrators show work using popular movie stars, photos, etc, as reference-I like to see the techniques done using their own original reference; it's better to show their ability to do original work."

THE SINGLE PARENT, 8807 Colesville Rd., Silver Spring MD 20910. (301)588-9354. Editor: Allan Glennon. Estab. 1958. Emphasizes family life in all aspects—raising children, psychology, divorce, remarriage, etc.— for all single parents and their children. Bimonthly. Circ. 120,000. Accepts simultaneous submissions and occasionally accepts previously published material. Original artwork returned after publication. Sample copy available for 10×12 SASE with postage for 3 oz. or for $1 without SASE.

Cartoons: Rarely uses cartoons.

Illustrations: Works with 3-6 illustrators/year. Buys 25-30 illustrations/year; buys all from freelancers, mainly article and story illustration. Works on assignment for all stories. Assignments based on artist's style. Send query letter with brochure, samples to be kept on file. Write or call for appointment to show portfolio. Prefers photostats, photographs, tearsheets as samples. Reports within 6 weeks. Purchases one-time rights. Pays

$250, color, cover; $75-150, b&w; $75-150, color, inside (2-color mechanicals); on publication.
Tips: "Send line art and one- or two-color illustrations of parent-child interaction or children. Bring your portfolio by if you are in the vicinity. *The Single Parent* uses more realistic illustrations than before, though an occasional 'mood piece' or symbolic image is used."

SKI MAGAZINE, 380 Madison Ave., New York NY 10016. Art Director: Steve Wierzbicki. Estab. 1936. Emphasizes instruction, resorts, equipment and personality profiles. For new, intermediate and expert skiers. Published 8 times/year. Circ. 600,000. Previously published work OK "if we're notified."
Cartoons: Approached by approximately 12 cartoonists/year. Buys 40-50 cartoons/year from freelancers. Especially needs cartoons of skiers with gagline. "Artist/cartoonist must remember he is reaching experienced skiers who enjoy 'subtle' humor." Mail art and SASE. Reports immediately. Buys first serial rights. Pays $50, b&w and color; on publication.
Illustrations: Approached by 30-40 freelance illustrators/yaer. Buys 40-50 illustrations/year from freelancers. Mail art and SASE. Reports immediately. Buys one-time rights. Pays $1,000, color, cover; $150, b&w and color, inside; on acceptance.
Tips: "The best way to break in is an interview and showing a consistent style portfolio. Then, keep us on your mailing list."

*SKY AND TELESCOPE, Box 9111, Belmont MA 02178-9111. Editor: Leif V. Robinson. Art Director: Steven Simpson. Concerns astronomy, telescopes and space exploration for enthusiasts and professionals. Monthly. Circ. 110,000. Buys one-time rights.
Cartoons: Buys 4 cartoons/year from freelancerson astronomy, telescopes and space exploration; single panel preferred. Pays $25-50, b&w line drawings, washes and gray opaques; on publication. Send query letter with samples.
Illustrations: Buys assigned themes. Send query letter with previously published work. Pays $50-200; on publication.

*SKYLANDER MAGAZINE, 202 Church St., Hackettstown NJ 07840. (201)850-6688. FAX: (201)850-8258. Art Director: Darren Westley. Estab. 1986. Consumer magazine "addressing the people, places and progress of the 5 counties (Skylands) of northwestern New Jersey." Quarterly, "soon to be bimonthly." Circ. 20,000. Accepts previously published artwork. Original artwork returned after publication. Sample copies free for SASE with first-class postage. Art guidelines available.
Illustrations: Approached by 20 illustrators/year. Buys 2 illustrations/issue, 15 illustrations/year from freelancers. Works on assignment only. "75% of the artwork is b&w spot illustration; 25% is color illustration. The theme depends on the story." Considers pen & ink, watercolor, airbrush and acrylic. Send query letter with resume, tearsheets and photocopies. Samples are filed or are returned by SASE if requested by artist. Reports back only if interested. Call or write to schedule an appointment to show a portfolio, which should include roughs and original/final art and b&w and color tearsheets, photographs and printed pieces. Rights purchased vary according to project. Pays $50, b&w, $100, color, cover; $10, b&w, $25, color, inside.
Tips: "We are looking for artists with the ability to come up with creative concepts."

THE SMALL POND MAGAZINE OF LITERATURE, Box 664, Stratford CT 06497. Editor: Napoleon St. Cyr. Estab. 1964. Emphasizes poetry and short prose. Readers are people who enjoy literature—primarily college-educated. Published 3 times/year. Circ. 300. Sample copy $2.50; current issue $5; art guidelines for SASE.
Illustrations: Receives 50-75 illstrations/year. Acquires 1-5 illustrations/issue, 10-15/year from freelancers. Uses freelance artwork mainly for covers, centerfolds and spots. Uses "line drawings (inside and on cover) which generally relate to natural settings, but have used abstract work completely unrelated." Especially needs line drawings; "fewer wildlife drawings and more unrelated-to-wildlife material." Send query letter with finished art or production-quality photocopies, 2×3 minimum, 8×11 maximum. SASE. Reports in 1-2 months. Pays 2 copies of issue in which work appears on publication. Buys copyright in convention countries.
Tips: "Need cover art work, but inquire first or send for sample copy." Especially looks for "smooth clean lines, original movements, an overall impact. Don't send a heavy portfolio, but rather 4-6 black-and-white representative samples with SASE. Better still, send for copy of magazine. Don't send your life's history and/ or a long sheet of credits. Work samples are worth a thousand words."

SOAP OPERA DIGEST, 45 W. 25th St., New York NY 10010. (212)645-2100. Art Director: Catherine Connors. Estab. 1976. Emphasizes soap opera and prime-time drama synopses and news. Biweekly. Circ. 1,100,000. Accepts previously published material. Returns original artwork after publication upon request. Sample copy available with SASE.
Cartoons: Buys 50 cartoons/year. Publishes 2/issue. Seeks humor on soaps, drama or TV. Accepts single or double panel with gagline; b&w line drawings, b&w washes. Send query letter to Lynn Davey, Managing Editor with samples of style to be kept on file. Material not filed is returned by SASE. Pays $50, b&w; on publication.

Illustrations: Works with 2 illustrators/year. Buys 25 illustrations/year from freelancers. Works on assignment only. Prefers humor; pen & ink, airbrush and watercolor. Send query letter with brochure showing art style or resume, tear sheets and photocopies to be kept on file. Negotiates rights purchased. Pays $50-100, b&w, $150, color, inside; on publication. All original artwork is returned after publication.
Tips: "Cartoons should be light-hearted and fun, not put-downs on the soaps. I'm not interested in keeping illustrations on file that do not fit in with our look. Review the magazine before submitting work."

SOCIAL POLICY, 25 W. 43rd St., New York NY 10036. (212)642-2929. Managing Editor: Audrey Gartner. Estab. 1970. Emphasizes the human services—education, health, mental health, self-help, consumer action, voter registration, employment. For social action leaders, academics, social welfare practitioners. Quarterly. Circ. 5,000. Accepts simultaneous submissions. Original artwork returned after publication. Sample copy $2.50.
Cartoons: Approached by 6 cartoonists/year. Accepts b&w only, "with social consciousness." Sometimes uses humorous illustrations; often uses cartoon-style illustrations. Call for appointment to show portfolio. Reports only if interested. Buys one-time rights. Pays $25, b&w; on publication.
Illustrations: Approached by 12 illustrators/year. Works with 6+ illustrators/year. Buys 6-8 illustrations/issue from freelancers. Uses artists mainly for articles. Accepts b&w only, "with social consciousness." Prefers pen & ink and charcoal/pencil. Send query letter and tearsheets to be kept on file. Call for appointment to show portfolio, which should include b&w original/final art, final reproduction/product and tearsheets. Reports only if interested. Buys one-time rights. Pays $100, b&w, $100, b&w, cover; $25, b&w, inside; on publication.
Tips: When reviewing an artist's work, looks for "sensitivity to the subject matter being illustrated."

*SOFTWARE MAINTENANCE NEWS, Suite 5F, 141 St. Marks Pl., Staten Island NY 10301. (718)816-5522. Editor: Nicholas Zvegintzov. Estab. 1983. Magazine "that talks directly to the experience of software professionals who maintain existing software." Monthly. Circ. 8,000. Accepts previously published artwork. Original artwork may be returned after publication. Sample copies available. Art guidelines not available.
Cartoons: Approached by 5 cartoonists/year. Buys 1 cartoon/issue, 12 cartoons/year from freelancers. "Cartoons must be about software; prefers wild styles." Any format is acceptable. Send query letter with roughs. Samples are returned. Reports back in 1 week. Buys one-time rights. Pays $20 and up, b&w; $50 and up, color; on publication.
Illustrations: Approached by 5 illustrators/year. Buys illustrations mainly for covers. Buys 1 illustration/issue, 12 illustrations/year from freelancers. Works on assignment only. We are looking for sci-fi type, imaginative illustration. Considers pen & ink, airbrush, mixed media, colored pencil, watercolor, acrylic, oil, pastel, collage, marker, charcoal pencil and calligraphy. Send query letter with brochure showing art style and photocopies. Samples are filed; "don't send something you want back." Reports within 1 week. Call to schedule an appointment to show a portfolio. Buys one-time rights. Pays $125 and up, b&w, $125 and up, color, cover; $25, b&w, $50, color, inside; on publication.

SOLDIERS MAGAZINE, Cameron Station, Alexandria VA 22304-5050. (202)274-6671. Editor-in-Chief: Lt. Col. Donald Maple. Lighter Side Compiler: Steve Harding. Provides "timely and factual information on topics of interest to members of the Active Army, Army National Guard, Army Reserve and Department of Army civilian employees." Monthly. Circ. 250,000. Previously published material and simultaneous submissions OK. Samples available upon request.
Cartoons: Approached by 15 cartoonists/year. Purchases approximately 60 cartoons/year from freelancers. Should be single panel with gagline. Prefers military and general audience humor. Reports within 3 weeks. Buys all rights. Pays $25/cartoon on acceptance.
Tips: "We are actively seeking new ideas, fresh humor and looking for new talent—people who haven't been published before. We recommend a review of back issues before making a submission. Issues available upon request. Remember that we are an inhouse publication—anti-Army humor, sexist or racist material is totally unacceptable."

SONOMA BUSINESS MAGAZINE AND 101 NORTH MAGAZINE, Box 11009, Santa Rosa CA 95406. Art Director: Laura Garvey. Both are monthly. *Sonoma Business:* tabloid emphasizing business with very local editorial content. Relates to business owners in Sonoma County. Circ. 10,000. *101 North:* tabloid emphasizing people and pleasures of the North Bay. Relates to residents of Marin and Sonoma Counties. Accepts previously published material. Returns original artwork after publication. Sample copy $3.50 with 9×12 SASE. Art guidelines not available.
Illustrations: Approached by 25 illustrators/year. Works with 5-6 illustrators/year. Buys 20 illustrations/year from freelancers. Uses artists mainly for showing concepts a photo can't manage. Works on assignment only. Send query letter with brochure. Samples are filed. Reports back only if interested. Write to schedule an appointment to show a portfolio, which should include b&w and color original/final art, tearsheets and final reproduction/product. Buys one-time rights. Pays $75 b&w, cover and inside; $75, color, inside; $150, color, cover; on acceptance.

Tips: "Must be well-drawn, clever, and we usually buy b&w."

*SOUTH COAST POETRY JOURNAL, English Department, California State University, Fullerton CA 92634. (714)773-3163. Editor: John Brugaletta. Estab. 1986. Literary magazine; "we publish some of the best poetry being written today. Among our subscribers are some of the finest libraries in the U.S. Readership tends to be active in all of the arts." Biannual. Circ. 300. Accepts previously published artwork. Original artwork returned after publication. Sample copy $3.50. Art guidelines free for SASE with first-class postage.
Illustrations: Approached by 4-5 illustrators/year. Buys 12-15 illustrations/issue, 24-30 illustrations/year from freelancers. Prefers sketches of objects and details from everyday life. Considers pen & ink, charcoal, colored pencil and any line art in black & white. Send query letter with photocopies, slides and photographs. "We are mainly interested in fillers, but are happy to look at work as large as 3×5 or work that can be reduced to that." Samples are not filed and are returned by SASE. Reports back within 6 weeks. Buys one-time rights. Pays one copy of magazine on publication.
Tips: "Send 4 to 6 photocopies of pages from your sketch book." Does not want to see "Any work that will not photocopy well."

*SOUTH FLORIDA MAGAZINE, 600 Brickell Ave., Miami FL 33131. (305)374-5011. FAX: (305)374-7691. Art Director: Barbara Bose. Consumer magazine. "Regional lifestyle monthly magazine. Readers are sophisticated, generally affluent, mobile, have taste." Monthly. Circ. 40,000. Original artwork returned to the artist at the job's completion.
Cartoons: Approached by 10 cartoonists/year. Buys 5 cartoons/year from freelancers. Prefers "political, satirical, charactature" themes. Send query letter with brochure. Samples are filed. Reports back to the artist only if interested. Buys one-time rights. Pays $100, b&w; $2-500, color.
Illustrations: Approached by 25 illustrators/year. Buys 20 illustrations/year from freelancers. Works on assignment only. Prefers pen & ink, watercolor, collage, airbrush, colored pencil, oil, charcoal, mixed media and pastel. Send query letter with brochure, tearsheets, photographs, photocopies and photostats. Samples are filed. Reports back to the artist only if interested. Call to schedule an appointment to show a portfolio. Portfolio should include roughs, tearsheets and slides. Buys first rights. Pays $100, b&w, $200+, color, inside; on acceptance.

SOUTHERN ACCENTS, 2100 Lakeshore Dr., Birmingham AL 35209. (205)877-6347. Art Director: Lane Gregory. Magazine emphasizing high-style interiors. Monthly. Circ. 800,000. Original artwork returned after publication. Sample copy for a large manila SASE.
Illustrations: Approached by 30-40 illustrators/year. Buys 2 illustrations/issue from freelancers. Uses freelance artists mainly for illustrating monthly columns. Works on assignment only. Prefers watercolor, colored pencil or pen & ink. Send query letter with brochure showing art style or resume and samples. Samples returned only if requested. Reports only if interested. Call or write to schedule an appointment to show a portfolio, which should include b&w and color tearsheets and slides. Buys one-time rights. Pays $300, b&w; $500 color, inside; on acceptance.
Tips: In a portfolio include "four to five best pieces to show strengths and/or versatility. Smaller pieces are much easier to handle than large. Its best not to have to return samples but to keep them for reference files." Don't send "too much. It's difficult to take time to plow through mountains of examples." Notices trend toward "lighter, fresher illustration."

SPORTS CAR INTERNATIONAL, Suite 120, 3901 Westerly Place, Newport Beach CA 92660. (714)851-3044. Art Director: Keith May. Estab. 1986. Entertainment for the exotic and classic sports car enthusiast. Printed "four-color on glossy stock, we are America's premier sports car magazine." Monthly. Circ. 75,000. Original artwork is returned after publication. Sample copy and art guidelines available.
Illustrations: Works with 6-8 illustrators/year. Buys 48-60 illustrations/year from freelancers. Buys illustrations mainly for spots and feature spreads. Works on assignment only. Prefers pen & ink, airbrush and watercolor. Send query letter with brochure showing art style. Looks for originality, movement and color. Samples are filed. Reports back about queries/submissions only if interested. Call to schedule an appointment to show a portfolio which should include tearsheets, slides, photographs and transparencies. Buys first rights. Pays $400, b&w, $600, color, full page; $200, color, spots; on publication.

STARWIND, Box 98, Ripley OH 45167. Contact: Editor. Estab. 1974. Emphasizes science fiction, fantasy and nonfiction of scientific and technological interest. Quarterly. Circ. 2,500. Sample copy $3.50; art guidelines for SASE.
Cartoons: Approached by 10-12 cartoonists/year. Buys 17-20 cartoons/year from freelancers. Interested in science fiction and fantasy subjects. Format: single and multi-panel b&w line drawings. Prefers finished cartoons. SASE. Reports in 2-3 months. Buys first North American serial rights. Pays $5; on publication.
Illustrations: Approached by 20-30 illustrators/year. Buys 35 illustrations/year from freelancers. Works with 15 illustrators/year. Sometimes uses humorous and cartoon-style illustrations depending on the type of work being published. Works on assignment only. Samples returned by SASE. Reports back on future assignment

possibilities. Send resume or brochure and samples of style to be kept on file for future assignments. Illustrates stories rather extensively (normally an 8x11 and an interior illustration). Format: b&w line drawings (pen & ink and similar media). Send SASE. Reports in 2-3 months. Buys first North American rights. Pays up to $50, b&w, cover; up to $25, b&w, inside; on publication.

Tips: "We first of all look for work that falls into science fiction genre; if an artist has a feel for and appreciation of science fiction he/she is more likely to be able to meet our needs. We look to see that the artist can do well what he/she tried to do—for example, draw the human figure well. We are especially attracted to work that is clean and spare, not cluttered, and that has a finished, not sketchy quality. If an artist also does technical illustrations, we are interested in seeing samples of this style too. Would specifically like to see samples of work that we'd be capable of reproducing and that are compatible with our magazine's subject matter. We prefer to see photocopies rather than slides. We also like to be able to keep samples on file, rather than have to return them."

*STERLING MAGAZINE, 355 Lexington Ave., New York NY 10017. Executive Art Director: Larry Matthews. Magazine emphasizing sports, music and black romance for people interested in sports, ages 13-30; music, ages 13-17; black romance, ages 16-20. Monthly. Circ. 160,000. Original artwork returned after publication. Sample copy and art guidelines available.

Cartoons: Write for appointment to show a portfolio. Material not kept on file is returned by SASE. Buys all rights.

Illustrations: Approached by 5 illustrators/year. Send query letter with brochure showing art style or samples. Samples not filed are returned by SASE. Reports only if interested. Call or write to schedule an appointment to show a portfolio, which should include roughs, original/final art, final reproduction/product and color. Buys first or one-time rights. Pays $250, color, cover; on acceptance.

Tips: Sees trend towards "computer-enhanced images."

*STOCK CAR RACING MAGAZINE, Box 715, Ipswich MA 90138. Editor: Dick Berggren. For stock car racing, fans and competitors. Monthly. Circ. 120,000.

Cartoons: Buys 4 cartoons/issue from freelancers. Receives 4 cartoons from freelancers/week. Interested in cartoons pertaining to racing. Format: single or multipanel with gag line; b&w line drawings. Prefers samples of style or finished cartoons include SASE. Reports in 2 weeks. Buys all rights. Pays $20-35 on publication.

Illustrations: Number of illustrations/issue varies. Format: b&w line drawings. Prefers finished art. Include SASE. Buys all rights. Pays on publication.

STONE SOUP, The Magazine by Children, Box 83, Santa Cruz CA 95063. (408)426-5557. Editor: Gerry Mandel. Literary magazine emphasizing writing and art by children through age 13. Features adventure, ethnic, experimental, fantasy, humorous and science fiction articles. "We publish writing and art by children through age 13. We look for artwork that reveals that the artist is closely observing his or her world." Bimonthly. Circ. 12,000. Original artwork is sometimes returned after publication. Sample copies available. Art guidelines for SASE with first-class postage.

Illustrations: Buys 8 illustrations/issue from freelancers. Prefers complete and detailed scenes from real life. Send query letter with photostats, photocopies, slides and photographs. Samples are filed or are returned by SASE. Reports back within 1 month. Buys all rights. Pays $10, b&w; $10, color, inside; on acceptance.

Tips: "We accept artwork by children only, through age 13."

*THE STRAIN, Box 330507, Houston TX 77233-0507. (713)733-6042. Articles Editor: Alicia Adler. Estab. 1987. Literary magazine and interactive arts publication. "The purpose of our publication is to encourage the interaction between diverse fields in the arts and (in some cases) science." Monthly. Circ. 1,000. Accepts previously published artwork. Original artwork is returned to the artist at the job's completion. Sample copy for $5 plus 9×12 SAE and 7 first class stamps.

Cartoons: "We are considering an opening for currently unsyndicated cartoonists." Send copies of finished cartoon with SASE. Samples not filed and are returned by SASE. Reports back within "1 year on submissions—queries will be returned unread." Buys one-time rights or negotiates rights purchased.

Illustrations: "We are just expanding from the use of staff illustrators." Buys 2-10 illustrations/issue, 45 illustrations/year. "We look for works that inspire creation in other arts." Send work that is complete in any format other than computer. Samples are filed "if we think there's a chance we'll use them." Those not filed are returned by SASE. Reports back within 1 year. Mail appropriate materials: original/final art. Negotiates rights purchased. Pays $10, b&w, $5, color, cover; $10, b&w, $5, color, inside, on publication.

Tips: "Find out about the particular thematic bent of upcoming issues after submitting samples of completed works."

STUDENT LAWYER, 750 N. Lake Shore Dr., Chicago IL 60611. (312)988-6049. Editor: Sarah Hoban. Art Director: Robert Woolley. Estab. 1972. Trade journal emphasizing legal education and social/legal issues. "*Student Lawyer* is a monthly legal affairs magazine published by the Law Student Division of the American Bar Association. It has a circulation of approximately 40,000, most of whom are law students. It is not a legal journal. It is a features magazine, competing for a share of law students' limited spare time—so the articles we publish must be informative, lively good reads. We have no interest whatsoever in anything that resembles a footnoted, academic article. We are interested in professional and legal education issues, sociolegal phenomena, legal career features, profiles of lawyers who are making an impact on the profession and the (very) occasional piece of fiction." Monthly (September-May). Circ. 35,000. Accepts previously published material. Original artwork is returned to the artist after publication. Samples copies $3. Art guidelines free for SASE with first-class postage.

Illustrations: Approached by 20 illustrators/year. Buys 8 illustrations/issue, 75 illustrations/year from freelancers. Uses freelance art mainly for covers and inside art. Works on assignment only. Send query letter with brochure, tearsheets and photographs. Samples are filed or returned by SASE. Reports back within 3 weeks only if interested. Call to schedule an appointment to show a portfolio, which should include original/final art and tearsheets. Buys one-time rights. Pays $450, b&w; $500, color,cover; $250, b&w; $350, color, inside; on acceptance.

Tips: "In your portfolio, show a variety of color and black and white, plus editorial work."

SUDS 'N' STUFF, Box 586402, Oceanside CA 92058. (619)724-4447. Publisher: Michael J. Bosak, III. Estab. 1978. Bimonthly newsletter emphasizing beer. "Interested in new beers on the market, interesting stories regarding old breweries, mini-breweries, national and international events concerning beer, interesting people in the beer industry, historical events concerning beer. Example: Why did the Pilgrims land at Plymouth Rock? They ran out of beer. Readers are all ages, mostly college graduates." Circ. 10,000. Accepts previously published material. Original artwork is returned to artist after publication. Sample copies free for SASE with 50¢ postage.

Cartoons: Buys 4-6 cartoons/issue, 30 cartoons/year from freelancers. Prefers multiple panels without gagline; b&w line drawings. Send query letter. Samples not filed are not returned. Reports back within 1 month. Pays $10 and up, b&w. Negotiates rights purchased.

Illustrations: Buys 6 illustrations/year from freelancers. Send query letter with brochure. Pays $25, b&w.

THE SUN, 107 N. Roberson, Chapel Hill NC 27516. (919)942-5282. Editor: Sy Safransky. Magazine of ideas. Monthly. Circ. 12,000. Accepts previously published material. Original artwork returned after publication. Sample copy $3. Art guidelines free for SASE with first-class postage.

Cartoons: Buys various cartoons/issue from freelancers. Send finished cartoons. Material not kept on file is returned by SASE. Reports within 2 months. Buys first rights. Pays $25 and up b&w and color; plus copies and subscription.

Illustrations: Buys various illustrations/issue from freelancers. Send query letter with samples. Samples not filed are returned by SASE. Reports within 2 months. To show a portfolio, mail appropriate materials. Buys first rights. Pays $25 and up; plus copies and subscription. Pays on publication.

*SUN DOG: THE SOUTHEAST REVIEW, English Department, Florida State University, Tallahassee FL 32306. Editors: Susan Underwood and Jamie Granger. Biannual. Circ. 2,000. Emphasizes literature for college students, faculty and educated readers. Sample copy $4.

Illustrations: Approached by 7 freelance illustrators/year. Interested in b&w line drawings and photographs. Also occasionally features one artist in an issue. Send query letter and b&w samples. Samples returned by SASE. Reports within 3 months. Pays in copies.

THE SUNDAY OREGONIAN'S NORTHWEST MAGAZINE, 1320 SW Broadway, Portland OR 97201. (503)221-8235. Graphic Coordinator: Kevin Murphy. Magazine emphasizing stories with Northwest orientation for aged 25-45 and upwardly mobile people. Weekly. Circ. 430,000. Original artwork returned after publication. Sample copy for SASE.

Illustrations: Buys 2 illustrations/issue from freelancers. Preference given to Northwest illustrators. Works on assignment only. Send query letter with brochure showing art style or resume and slides. Samples not filed are returned only if requested. Reports only if interested. Call or write to schedule an appointment to show a portfolio, which should include original/final art, color, photographs and slides. Buys first or one-time rights. Negotiates payment. Pays on publication.

*SUNSHINE MAGAZINE, 101 N. New River Dr., Ft. Lauderdale FL 33301. (305)761-4020. Art Director: Kent Barton. Estab. 1983. Consumer magazine; the Sunday Magazine for the Sun Sentinel Newspaper; featuring anything that would interest an intelligent adult reader living on South Florida's famous 'gold goast.' " Circ. 350,000. Accepts previously pubished artwork. Original artwork returned to artist at the job's completion. Sample copies and art guidelines available.

Illustrations: Approached by 12-25 illustrators/year. Buys 1 illustration/issue, 60-70 illustrations/year from freelancers. Works on assignment only. Preferred themes and styles vary. Considers all color media. Send query letter with any available samples. Samples are filed or are returned by SASE. Reports back to the artist only if interested. Mail approprite materials: original/final art and color tearsheets, photostats, slides and photocopies. Buys first rights, one-time rights. Pays $650, color, cover; $550, color, inside; on acceptance.

TENNIS, 5520 Park Ave., Trumbull CT 06611. (203)373-7000. Art Director: Kathleen Burke. For young, affluent tennis players. Monthly. Circ. 500,000.
Cartoons: Buys 12 cartoons/year from freelancers. Receives 6 submissions/week from freelancers on tennis. Prefers finished cartoons, single panel. Reports in 2 weeks. Pays $75, b&w.
Illustrations: Works with 15-20 illustrators/year. Buys 50 illustrations/year from freelancers. Uses artists mainly for spots and openers. Works on assignment only. Send query letter with tearsheets. To show a portfolio, mail appropriate materials or call to schedule an appointment. Pays $200-800 for color; on acceptance.
Tips: "Prospective contributors should first look through an issue of the magazine to make sure their style is appropriate for us."

THE TEXAS OBSERVER, 307 W. 7th., Austin TX 78701. (512)477-0746. Contact: Editor. Estab. 1954. Emphasizes Texas political, social and literary topics. Biweekly. Circ. 12,000. Accepts previously published material. Returns original artwork after publication. Sample copy for SASE with postage for two ounces; art guidelines for SASE with first class postage.
Illustrations: Buys 2 illustrations/issue, 24-30 illustrations/year from freelancers. "We only print black and white, so pen & ink is best; washes are fine." Send photostats, tearsheets, photocopies, slides or photographs to be kept on file. Samples not filed are returned by SASE. Reports within 1 month. Write or call for appointment to show portfolio. Buys one-time rights. Pays $35, b&w cover; $20, inside; on publication.
Tips: "I don't want to see unsolicited cartoons or color. We use a few pen-and-ink line drawings, mainly from local artists.

***THEDAMU ARTS MAGAZINE**, 13217 Livernois, Detroit MI 48238. (313)931-3427. Publisher: David Rambeau. Estab. 1970. Literary magazine; tabloid format; "general adult multi-disciplinary urban arts magazine." Monthly. Circ. 4,000. Accepts previously published artwork. "Send copies only." Sample copies free for SASE with first-class postage. Art guidelines free for SASE with first-class postage.
Cartoons: Approached by 5-10 cartoonists/year. "We do special cartoon issues featuring a single artist like a comic book except with adult, urban themes. That would run 7 tab pages and a cover." Prefers b&w line drawings. Send query letter with 3-6 b&w cartoons. Samples are filed. Reports back within 2-3 months only if interested. Buys one-time rights usually, but rights purchased vary according to project. Pays $25-200 for b&w.
Illustrations: Approached by 5-10 illustrators/year. Buys 2-3 illustrations/issue, 20 illustrations/year from freelancers. Prefers urban contemporary themes and styles. Prefers pen & ink. Send query letter with resume and 3-6 photocopies. Samples are filed. Reports back within 2-3 months. "We're a small magazine so we're not interested in a full portfolio." Pays $25-200 for b&w, cover; on publication.
Tips: "We're the first or second step on the publishing ladder for artists and writers. Submit same work to others also. Be ready to negotiate."

***THIRD WORLD**, Rua da Gloria, 122, Sala 105, Rio de Janeiro, RJ, CEP 20241 Brazil. (021)222-1370 or 242-1957. Editor: Bill Hinchberger. Estab. 1986. Magazine "which presents world affairs from a Third World perspective, focusing on politics, economics, culture and the environment. Our circulation is worldwide." Bimonthly. Circ. 5,000. Accepts previously published artwork. Original artwork not returned after publication. Sample copies are free. Art guidelines not available.
Cartoons: Approached by 10 cartoonists/year. Buys 0-2 cartoons/issue from freelancers. Number of cartoons bought varies each year. Prefers "work by Third World artists and work which is devoid of stereotypes. We don't want to see a Bolivian peasant on the 'drug trail,' for example." Prefers single, double and multiple panels; b&w line drawings. Send query letter with samples of style and roughs. Samples are not returned. Reports back within 2 weeks. "Please leave time for international mail." Buys reprint rights or one-time rights. Pays $7, b&w; $12, color; on publication. "This is Brazilian union scale. Dollar figures depend on exchange rate."
Illustrations: Approached by 10 illustrators/year. Buys illustrations mainly for covers and spots. Buys 0-5 illustrations/issue, approx. 20-25 illustrations/year from freelancers. Considers pen & ink, colored pencil and watercolor. Send query letter with photocopies. "Looking for versatility, clarity and an understanding of the Third World." Samples are filed and are not returned. Reports back in 2 weeks. Mail appropriate materials: tearsheets and color and b&w samples. Buys one-time rights or reprint rights. Pays $12, b&w; $12, color, cover. Pays $7, b&w, inside.
Tips: "Our illustrations either accompany articles or are used on the cover. The best way to break in is to contact us and discuss specific themes." Would like to see "clarity with sophistication. Challenge the reader without trying to fool him or her."

***TIKKUN MAGAZINE**, 5100 Leona St., Oakland CA 94619. (415)482-0805. Publisher: Michael Lerner. Estab. 1986. "A Jewish critique of politics, culture and society. Includes articles regarding Jewish and non-Jewish issues, left of center politically." Bimonthly. Circ. 40,000. Accepts previously published material. Original artwork is returned to the artist after publication. Sample copies $5 plus $1.20 postage or "call our distributor

for local availability at (800)221-3148. If unavailable in your area, free with SASE."
Illustrations: Approached by 50-100 illustrators/year. Buys 0-8 illustrations/issue from freelancers. Prefers line drawings: (filed, payment on use). Send brochure, resume, tearsheets, photostats, photocopies. Slides and photographs for color artwork only. Buys one time rights. Slides and photographs returned if not interested. Often we hold onto line drawings for last-minute use. Pays $25 b&w, inside; $250 color; on publication.
Tips: Does not want to see "computer graphics, sculpture, heavy religious content."

TODAY'S FIREMAN, Box 875108, Los Angeles CA 90087. Editor: Don Mack. Estab. 1960. Trade journal emphasizing the fire service. Features general interest, humor and technical articles. "Readers are firefighters—items should be of interest to the fire service." Quarterly. Circ. 10,000. Accepts previously published material. Original artwork is not returned after publication.
Cartoons: Buys 12 cartoons/year from freelancers. Prefers single panel with gagline; b&w line drawings. Send query letter with samples of style, roughs or finished cartoons. Reports back only if interested. Buys one-time rights. Pays $4.

TODAY'S POLICEMAN, Box 875108, Los Angeles CA 90087. Editor: Don Mack. Estab. 1960. For persons employed in and interested in police services. Semiannual. Circ. 10,000.
Cartoons: Buys 8 cartoons/issue, 16 cartoons/year from freelancers dealing with law enforcement and politics. Send finished art and SASE. Pays $2.50, b&w.

TRADITION, Box 438, Walnut IA 51577. (712)366-1136. Editor-in-Chief/Art Director: Robert Everhart. "For players and listeners of traditional and country music. We are a small, nonprofit publication and will use whatever is sent to us. A first time gratis use is the best way to establish communication." Monthly. Circ. 2,500. Previously published work OK. Buys one-time rights. Sample copy $1 to cover postage and handling.
Cartoons: Buys 1 cartoon/issue from freelancers on country music; single panel with gagline. Receives 10-15 cartoons/week from freelance artists. Mail roughs. Pays $5-15, b&w line drawings; on publication.
Illustrations: Buys 1 illustration/issue from freelancers on country music. Query with resume and samples. Send SASE. Pays $5-15, b&w line drawings, cover; $5-15, b&w line drawings, inside; on publication. Reports in 4 weeks.
Tips: "We'd like to see an emphasis on traditional country music."

*TRAINING MAGAZINE, The Magazine of Human Resources Development, 50 South Ninth St., Minneapolis MN 55402. (612)333-0471. FAX: (612)333-0471 ext. 398. Art Director: Jodi Boren Scharff. Estab. 1964. Trade journal; magazine format; "covers job-related training and education in business and industry, both theory and practice." Audience: "training directors, personnel managers, sales and data processing managers, general managers, etc." Monthly. Circ. 51,000. Sample copies free for SASE with first-class postage. Art guidelines not available.
Cartoons: Approached by 20-25 cartoonists/year. Buys 2-4 cartoons/issue, varying number of cartoons/year from freelancers. "We buy a wide variety of styles. The themes relate directly to our editorial content, which is training in the workplace." Prefers single panel, with and without gagline; b&w line drawings; b&w washes. Send query letter with brochure and finished cartoons. Samples are filed or are returned by SASE if requested by artist. Reports back within 1 month. Buys first rights or one-time rights. Pays $25, b&w.
Illustrations: Buys 6-8 illustrations/issue, 90-100 illustrations/year from freelancers. Works on assignment only. Prefers "themes that relate directly to editorial content. Styles are varied." Considers pen & ink, airbrush, mixed media, watercolor, acrylic, oil, pastel and collage. Send query letter with brochure, resume, tearsheets, photocopies and photostats. Samples are filed or are returned by SASE if requested by artist. Reports back to the artist only if interested. Call or write to schedule an appointment to show a portfolio, which should include original/final art and b&w and color tearsheets, photostats, photographs, slides and photocopies. Buys first rights or one-time rights. Pays $500 and up, color, cover; $75-200, b&w, $200-250, color, inside; on acceptance.
Tips: "Show a wide variety of work in different media and with different subject matter. Good renditions of people are extremely important."

TRANSITIONS ABROAD: The Magazine of Overseas Opportunities, 18 Hulst Rd., Box 344, Amherst MA 01004. Editor: Clayton A. Hubbs. Emphasizes "educational, low-budget and special interest overseas travel for those who travel to learn and to participate." Bimonthly. Circ. 10,000. Original artwork returned after publication. Sample copy $3.50; art guidelines for SASE.
Illustrations: Buys 3 illustrations/issue from freelancers. Especially needs illustrations of American travelers and natives in overseas settings (work, travel and study). Send roughs to be kept on file. Samples not kept on file are returned by SASE. Reports in 4 weeks. Buys one-time rights. Pays $25-100, b&w line drawings, $30-100, b&w washes, cover; on publication.
Tips: The trend is toward "more and more interest in travel which involves interaction with people in the host country, with a formal or informal educational component. We usually commission graphics to fit specific features. Inclusion of article with graphics increases likelihood of acceptance. Artists should study the publication and determine its needs."

TRAVEL & LEISURE, 1120 6th Ave., New York NY 10036. (212)382-5600. Design/Art Director: Bob Ciano. Associate Art Directors: Joseph Paschke and Daniela Maioresco. Emphasizes travel, resorts, dining and entertainment. Monthly. Circ. 1,300,000. Original artwork returned after publication. Art guidelines for SASE.
Illustrations: Approached by 250-350 illustrators/year. Buys 1-15 illustrations/issue, all from freelancers. Interested in travel and leisure-related themes. Prefers pen & ink, airbrush, colored pencil, watercolor, acrylic, oil, pastel, collage, mixed media and calligraphy. "Illustrators are selected by excellence and relevance to the subject." Works on assignment only. Provide business card to be kept on file for future assignment; samples returned by SASE. Reports in 1 week. Buys world serial rights. Pays a minimum of $250 inside b&w and $800-1,500 maximum, inside color; on publication.

TROUT, Box 6225, Bend OR 97708. (503)382-2327. Editor: Thomas R. Pero. Estab. 1959. High-calibre quarterly magazine aimed at sophisticated trout and salmon anglers. Theme is conservation of fisheries habitat and a quality outdoor environment. Quarterly. Circ. 70,000. Original artwork is returned after publication. Sample copy $4. Art guidelines free for SASE with first-class postage.
Cartoons: Buys 1 cartoon/issue, 4 cartoons/year from freelancers. Prefers single panel b&w line drawings, b&w washes and color washes. Send query letter. Samples are filed. Samples not filed are returned. Reports back regarding queries/submissions within 1 month. Buys first rights. Pays $50, b&w; on acceptance.
Illustrations: Buys illustrations mainly for spots and feature spreads. Buys 6 illustrations/issue, 24 illustrations/year from freelancers. Considers watercolor, acrylic, oil and charcoal pencil. Send query letter with brochure showing art style, tearsheets and photographs. Samples are filed. Samples not filed are returned. Reports back about queries/submissions within 1 month. For a portfolio review mail appropriate materials, which should include photographs. Buys first rights. Pays $50, b&w; $200, color, inside; on acceptance.

TRUE WEST, Box 2107, Stillwater OK 74076. Editor: John Joerschke. Emphasizes American western history from 1830 to 1910 for a primarily rural and suburban audience, middle-age and older, interested in Old West history, horses, cowboys, art, clothing and all things western. Monthly. Circ. 30,000. Accepts previously published material and considers some simultaneous submissions. Original artwork returned after publication. Sample copy $2. Art guidelines for SASE.
Illustrations: Approached by 75 illustrators/year. Buys 5-10 illustrations/issue from freelancers. "Inside illustrations are usually, but not always, pen & ink line drawings; covers are Western paintings." Send query letter with samples to be kept on file; "we return anything on request." "For inside illustrations, we want samples of artist's line drawings. For covers, we need to see full-color transparencies." Reports within 30 days. Call or write for appointment to show portfolio. Buys one-time rights. Pays $100-150, for color transparency for cover; $20-50, b&w, inside. "Payment on acceptance for new artists, on assignment for established contributors."

TURTLE MAGAZINE FOR PRESCHOOL KIDS, 1100 Waterway Blvd., Box 567, Indianapolis IN 46206. (317)636-8881. Art Director: Bart Rivers. Estab. 1979. Emphasizes health, nutrition, exercise and safety for children 2-5 years. Monthly except bimonthly January/February, March/April, May/June and July/August. Original artwork not returned after publication. Sample copy 75¢; art guidelines for SASE. Finds most artists through samples received in mail.
Illustrations: Approached by 100 illustrators/year. Works with 20 illustrators/year. Buys 15-30 illustrations/issue from freelancers. Interested in "stylized, humorous, realistic and cartooned themes; also nature and health." Works on assignment only. Send query letter with resume, photostats or good photocopies, slides and tearsheets to be kept on file. Samples not kept on file returned by SASE. Reports only if interested. Buys all rights. To show a portfolio, mail tearsheets or slides. Pays $250, cover; $70-175, pre-separated 4-color; $65-140, 4-color, $55-110, 2-color; $30-70, b&w; inside; on publication.
Tips: "Familiarize yourself with our magazine and other children's publications before you submit any samples. The samples you send should demonstrate your ability to support a story with illustration."

*UNMUZZLED OX, 105 Hudson St., New York NY 10013. (212)226-7170. Editor: Michael Andre. Emphasizes poetry, stories, some visual arts (graphics, drawings, photos) for poets, writers, artists, musicians and interested others. Circ. 18,000. Whether original artwork is returned after publication "depends on work—artist should send SASE." Sample copy $4.95 plus $1 postage.
Cartoons: Number used/issue varies. Send query letter with copies. Reports within 10 weeks. No payment for cartoons.
Illustrations: Uses "several" illustrations/issue. Themes vary according to issue. Send query letter and "anything you care to send" to be kept on file for possible future assignments. Reports within 10 weeks.
Tips: Magazine readers and contributors are "highly sophisticated and educated"; artwork should be geared to this market. "Really, *Ox* is part of New York art world. We publish art not 'illustration.'"

© 1990 Risko

© 1990 Daniel Kirk

These illustrations for VARBusiness magazine were designed by artists Robert Risko and Daniel Kirk, both of New York City. Risko's cover illustration, done in gouache, was designed, he says, to convey "the subject choreographing a basketball shot with himself in an upbeat manner." Kirk's illustration, painted in oil on canvas, was intended to convey a "gentle, nostalgic, atmospheric look." Both artists sold first rights to their works.

VARBUSINESS, 600 Community Dr., Manhasset NY 11030. (516)365-4600. Art Director: David Loewy. Estab. 1985. Emphasizes computer business. "Aimed to and about people; hardware and technology is downplayed. The art is in a lighter, less technical vein." Monthly. Circ. 75,000. Original artwork is returned to the artist after publication. Art guidelines not available.
Illustrations: Approached by 100+ illustrators/year. Works with 30-50 illustrators/year. Buys 150 illustrations/year from freelancers. Uses artists mainly for covers, full and single page spreads and spots. Works on assignment only. Prefers pop, illustrative style. Prefers airbrush, then pen & ink, colored pencil, acrylic, pastel and computer illustration. Send query letter with tearsheets. Samples are filed or are returned only if requested. Reports back only if interested. Call or write to schedule an appointment to show a portfolio, which should include tearsheets, final reproduction/product and slides. Buys one-time rights. Pays $2,000, color, cover; $500, color, inside; on publication.
Tips: "Show printed pieces or suitable color reproductions, no photocopies, stats or original art. Artists should have a pop, illustrative style. Concepts should be imaginative not literal. Sense of humor is important." Sees trend toward "more computer illustration." Emphatically says, "I do not use editorial cartoons."

VEGETARIAN TIMES, Box 570, Oak Park IL 60303. (708)848-8120. Art Director: Gregory Chambers. Consumer food magazine with emphasis on fitness and health for readers ages 30-50, 75% women. Monthly. Circ. 100,000. Accepts previously published material. Artwork returned after publication. Sample copy $2.
Illustrations: Buys 4 illustrations/issue from freelancers. Send query letter with samples showing art style. To show a portfolio, mail appropriate materials or call to schedule an appointment; portfolio should include roughs, original/final art, color and b&w tearsheets and photographs. Pays $30-300, inside; on publication.
Tips: "I work primarily with food/health-related topics, and look for someone who is familiar with or sympathetic to vegetarianism and whole foods cuisine."

VENTURE, Box 150, Wheaton IL 60189. (708)665-0630. Art Director: Robert Fine. Estab. 1959. For boys 10-15. "We seek to promote consciousness, acceptance of and personal commitment to Jesus Christ." Published 6 times/year. Circ. 25,000. Simultaneous submissions and previously published work OK. Original artwork returned after publication. Sample copy $1.50 with large SASE; artists' guidelines with SASE.
Cartoons: Send to attention of cartoon editor. Approached by 20 cartoonists/year. Buys 1-3 cartoons/issue; all from freelancers. Receives 2 submissions/week from freelancers, on nature, sports, school, camping, hiking; single panel with gagline. "Keep it clean." Prefers finished cartoons. SASE. Reports in 2-4 weeks. Buys first-time rights. Pays $30 minimum, b&w line drawings; on acceptance.

Illustrations: Approached by 35 illustrators/year. Contact art director. Works with 3-4 illustrators/issue. Buys 2 illustrations/issue, 15-20 illustrations/year from freelancers, on education, family life and camping; b&w only. Works on assignment only. Send business card, tearsheets and photocopies of samples to be kept on file for future assignments. Samples returned by SASE. Reports back on future assignment possibilities. SASE. Reports in 2 weeks. Buys first time rights. Pays $100+ for b&w, cover; $85+ for b&w; inside; on publication.

VETTE MAGAZINE, 299 Market St., Saddle Brook NJ 07662. (201)488-7171. Editor-in-Chief: D. Randy Riggs. Estab. 1976. Magazine "devoted exclusively to the Corvette automobile and the hobby of Corvetting." Monthly. Circ. 60,000. Original artwork is returned after publication. Sample copies $2.50. Art guidelines not available.
Cartoons: Approached by 5 cartoonists/year. Pays $50-75 b&w.
Illustrations: Buys illustrations mainly for spots and feature spreads. Buys 1-2 illustrations/issue, 20 illustrations/year from freelancers. Works on assignment only. Consider pen & ink, airbrush, colored pencil, watercolor, acrylic, oil, pastel, marker and charcoal/pencil. Send query letter with brochure, tearsheets, photostats and photocopies. Samples not filed are returned only if requested. Reports back within 2 weeks. Call to schedule an appointment to show a portfolio, or mail tearsheets and photostats. Buys first rights. Pays $35-150, b&w; $50-800, color, inside; on acceptance.
Tips: The best way to break in is to send "spot illustrations for fillers. Major art is assigned according to articles. Label back of art with name and address."

*VIDEOMAKER MAGAZINE, Box 4591, Chico CA 95927. (916)891-8410. FAX: (916)891-8443. Designer: Tara Wilkins. Art Director: Stephanie Geller. Consumer magazine for video camera users. Monthly. Circ. 50,000. Accepts previously published artwork. Original artwork returned at job's completion. Sample copies are available. Art guidelines not available.
Cartoons: Approached by 30 cartoonists/year. Buys 3 cartoons/issue, 32 cartoons/year from freelancers. "We will assign themes or styles." Prefers b&w line drawings, color washes. Send query letter with photocopies. Samples are filed. Reports back to the artist only if interested. Rights purchased vary according to project. Pays $35-100, b&w, $50, color.
Illustrations: Approached by 30 illustrators/year. Buys 3 illustrations/issue, 36 illustrations/year from freelancers. Works on assignment only. Preferred themes are camcorders. Considers pen & ink, airbrush, colored pencil, mixed media, watercolor, acrylic, oil, pastel, collage, marker and charcoal. Send query letter with photocopies. Samples are filed. Reports back to the artist only if interested. Call to schedule an appointment to show a portfolio, which should include thumbnails, tearsheets and photographs. Negotiates rights purchased. Pays $30, b&w, $125, color, inside; on publication.
Tips: "Come up with ideas (cartoons) drawn out (something to do with camcorder) then write or call. Send a sample of previous work."

VISIONS—INTERNATIONAL, THE WORLD OF ILLUSTRATED POETRY, Black Buzzard Press, 1110 Seaton Lane, Falls Church VA 22046. Editors: Bradley R. Strahan, Ursula Gill and Shirley Sullivan. Emphasizes literature and the illustrative arts for "well educated, very literate audience, very much into art and poetry." Published 3 times/year. Circ. 700. Only accepts previously published material under very special circumstances. Original artwork returned after publication *only if requested*. Sample copy $3.50 (latest issue $4); art guidelines for SASE.
Illustrations: Approached by 40-50 illustrators/year. Acquires approximately 21 illustrations/issue, 60 illustrations/year from freelancers. Works on assignment only. Representational to surrealistic and some cubism. B&w only. Send query letter with SASE and samples to be kept on file. Samples should clearly show artist's style and capability; no slides or originals. Samples not filed are returned by SASE. Reports within 2 months. Acquires first rights. "For information on releases on artwork, please contact the editors at the above address." Pays by the project, in copies or up to $10.
Tips: "Don't send slides. We might lose them. We don't use color, anyway."

VOLKSWAGEN WORLD, Volkswagen of America, Inc., Troy MI 48007. (313)362-6770. Editor: Marlene Goldsmith. For Volkswagen owners. Quarterly. Circ. 300,000.
Illustrations: Approached by 10 illustrators/year. Send query letter with samples. SASE. Reports in 6 weeks. Buys First North American rights. Pays $500 minimum, color, cover; $150 minimum, per printed page, color, cover; on acceptance.
Tips: "We're happy to send sample issues to prospective contributors. It's the best way of seeing what our needs are. I'm looking for contemporary illustration."

*THE WAR CRY, Magazine of The Salvation Army, 799 Bloomfield Ave., Verona NJ 07044. Art Director: Warren L. Maye. Emphasizes the work of The Salvation Army worldwide, inspirational fiction and nonfiction with a "Christian-oriented, social service focus: helping others in need, homeless, disaster victims, etc., food, shelter, and other resources." Biweekly. Circ. 350,000. Accepts previously published material. Original artwork is sometimes returned to the artist after publication. Sample copies for SASE with first-class postage. Art guidelines available. Uses freelance artists mainly for editorial illustration.

Illustrations: Approached by 5 illustrators/year. Buys 0-1 illustration/issue, 8-10 illustrations/year from freelancers. Prefers realistic, color illustration. Send query letter with brochure showing art style or resume, tearsheets, slides and photographs. Wants to see "Salvation Army subjects, scenic illustrations and Biblical environments and characters. "Does not want to see "church buildings or crosses." Samples are filed or are returned by SASE. Reports back within 2 weeks. To show a portfolio, mail color and b&w tearsheets, photographs and slides. Buys reprint rights or all rights. Pays $50-100, b&w and $300-400, color, cover; $50-100, b&w and $150-200, color, inside; on acceptance.

Tips: "Read an issue first. Gain an understanding of the organization through a local corps, hospital, recreation or rehabilitation center."

*WASHINGTON FLYER MAGAZINE, Suite 111, 11 Canal Center Plaza, Alexandria VA 22314. (703)739-9292. FAX: (703)683-2848. Editorial Assistant: Laurie McLaughlin. Estab. 1989. Consumer magazine. "In-airport publication focusing on travel, transportation, trade and communications for frequent business and pleasure travelers." Bimonthly. Circ. 160,000. Accepts previously published artwork. Original artwork is returned to the artist at the job's completion. Sample copies available. Art guidelines available.

Illustrations: Buys 2 illustrations/issue, 12 illustrations/year from freelancers. Works on assignment only. Considers all media. Send query letter with brochure, tearsheets, photostats, photographs, slides, SASE, photocopies and transparencies. Samples are filed. Reports back to the artist only if interested. Call or write to schedule an appointment to show a portfolio. Portfolio should include color tearsheets, photostats, photographs, slides and photocopies. Buys reprint rights or all rights. Pays $700, color, cover; $50, color, inside; on acceptance.

Tips: "We are very interested in reprint rights."

*THE WASHINGTON POST MAGAZINE, 1150 15th St. NW, Washington DC 20071. (202)334-6185. FAX: (202)334-5693. Art Director: Mark Danzig. Estab. 1986. Consumer magazine; general interest. Weekly. Circ. 1,200,000. Original artwork returned after publication. Art guidelines not available.

Illustrations: Approached by 500 illustrators/year. Buys 3 illustrations/issue, 200 illustrations/year from freelancers. Works on assignment only. Prefers any media. Send query letter with tearsheets. Samples are filed. Reports back only if interested. Mail appropriate materials: tearsheets and slides. Buys one-time rights. Pays $1,500, color, cover; $350, color, inside; on acceptance.

*WEDDINGS WEST, 1685 Lincoln Ave., San Jose CA 95125. (408)292-5100. FAX: (408)292-5778. Art Director: Alex von Wolff. Consumer magazine emphasizing West Coast weddings. Quarterly. Circ. 50,000. Accepts previously published artwork. Returns originals upon completion. Sample copies available. Art guidelines not available.

Cartoons: Prefers cartoons which revolve around West Coast professional women getting married; single or double panel, with or without gagline, b&w and color washes. Send query letter with brochure, roughs and finished cartoons. Samples are filed. Reports back within 1 month. Negotiates rights purchased. Rights purchased vary according to project.

Illustrations: Prefers themes relating to "weddings, bridal gowns, china and bridal products." Considers airbrush, watercolor and charcoal. Send query letter with brochure, tearsheets, resume, photographs, slides, SASE and transparencies. Samples are filed. Reports back within 1 month. Call to schedule an appointment to show a portfolio or mail appropriate materials: thumbnails, roughs, original/final art, b&w and color tearsheets, photographs and slides. Negotiates rights purchesed. Rights purchased vary according to project.

Tips: "Cartoonists should gear themselves to females, 25-35 years old, and professional careers. First, second and third marriages, step-children, etc."

*WEEKLY READER (PRE-K THRU 6)/U.S. KIDS MAGAZINE C/C Field Publications, 245 Long Hill Rd., Middletown CT 06457. (203)638-2757. FAX: (203)638-2787 or 638-2609. Senior Illustrator: Vickey Bolling. Estab. 1928. Educational newspaper, magazine, posters and books. U.S. Kids has a magazine format and *Weekly Reader* has a newspaper format. The *Weekly Reader* emphasizes news and education life for children 5-14. The philosophy is to connect students to the world. *U.S. Kids* magazine features educational fun. Accepts previously published artwork. Original artwork is returned the artist at the job's completion. Sample copies are available.

Cartoons: Approached by 10 cartoonists/year. Preferred themes and styles vary according to the needs of the story/articles; single panel. Send query letter with printed samples. Samples filed or are returned by SASE if requested by artist. Reports back within 3-4 weeks. Rights purchased vary according to project. Pays $50, b&w; $250-300, color (full page).

Illustrations: Approached by 50-60 illustrators/year. Buys more than 50/week, 2,300 illustrations/year from freelancers. Works on assignment only. Prefers pen & ink, airbrush, colored pencil, mixed media, watercolor, acrylic, pastel, collage and charcoal. Send query letter with brochure, tearsheets, slides, SASE and photocopies. Samples are filed or are returned by SASE if requested by artist. Reports back within 3-4 weeks. Mail appropriate materials: original/final art, tearsheets, slides and photocopies. Pays $250, b&w, $300, color, cover; $250, b&w, $300, color, inside.

Tips: "Our primary focus is the children's marketplace; figures are drawn well if style is realistic. Art should reflect creativity and knowledge of audience's sophistication needs."

*WEST COAST REVIEW OF BOOKS, 5265 Fountain Ave., Los Angeles CA 90029. (213)660-0433. Managing Editor: Crane Jackson. Estab. 1974. Consumer magazine of book reviews and feature articles. Bimonthly. Circ. 80,000. Accepts previously published artwork. Original artwork not returned to the artist at the job's completion. Sample copies available. Art guidelines not available.

Cartoons: Approached by 2 cartoonists/year. Buys 12 cartoons/year from freelancers. Prefers business-oriented cartoons; single panel, with gagline. Send query letter with brochure. Samples are filed. Reports back to the artist only if interested. Buys all rights. Pays $100, b&w, $200, color.

Illustrations: Approached by 12 illustrators/year. Buys 4 illustrations/issue, 24 illustrations/year from free-lancers. Works on assignment only. "The kind of artist we like to work with is one who knows airbrush and ink. We *occasionally* buy pen & ink and wash illustrations." Prefers airbrush and marker. Send query letter with brochure and transparencies. Samples are filed. Reports back to the artist only if interested. Call to schedule an appointment to show a portfolio. Portfolio should include original/final art and slides. Buys all rights. Pays $50, b&w, $200, color, cover; $50, b&w, $100, color, inside; on acceptance.

THE WESTERN PRODUCER, Box 2500, Saskatoon, Saskatchewan S7K 2C4 Canada. (306)665-3500. For farm families in western Canada. Weekly. Circ. 140,000.

Cartoons: Approached by 25 cartoonists/year. Uses 3-6 cartoons/week from freelance artists. Uses only cartoons about rural life. SASE (nonresidents include IRC). Reports in 2 weeks. Buys first Canadian rights. Pays $15, b&w line drawings; on acceptance.

Illustrations: Approached by 15-20 illustrators/year. Buys about 12 illustrations/year from freelancers. Send "about 6 illustrations of people interacting; no logos or typesettings." Pays $50-140 – depending on quality.

WESTERN SPORTSMAN, Box 737, Regina, Saskatchewan S4P 3A8 Canada. (306)352-2773. Editor-in-Chief: Roger Francis. For fishermen, hunters, campers and outdoorsmen. Bimonthly. Circ. 32,000 ABC audited. Original artwork returned after publication. Sample copy $4; artist's guidelines for SASE (nonresidents include IRC).

Cartoons: Approached by 20 cartoonists/year. Buys 90 cartoons/year on the outdoors; single panel with gaglines. Send art or query with samples. SASE (nonresidents include IRC). Reports in 3-8 weeks. Buys first North American serial rights. Pays $20, b&w line drawings; on acceptance.

Illustrations: Approached by 15 illustrators/year. Buys 8 illustrations/year from freelancers on the outdoors. Mail art or query with samples. SASE (nonresidents include IRC). Reports in 3-8 weeks. Buys first North American serial rights. Pays $50-250, b&w line drawings, inside; on acceptance.

Tips: "Send animal samples to judge for accurate depiction."

WESTWAYS, Terminal Annex, Box 2890, Los Angeles CA 90051. (213)741-4760. Editor: Mary Ann Fisher. Art Director: Paul Miyamoto. Production Manager: Vincent J. Corso. Estab. 1909. For the people of the Western U.S. Emphasizes current and historical events, culture, art, travel and recreation. Monthly. Circ. 478,000.

Illustrations: Works with 3 illustrators/year. Buys 3 illustrations/year from freelancers. Buys assigned themes on travel, history, and arts in the West. Send resume to be kept on file. Do not call. Buys first rights, based on decision of the editor. Pays $400, cover; $50-150, drawings, inside; $150, 4-color illustrations, inside; on publication.

*WHERE VICTORIA, 1001 Wharf St., Victoria, BC V8V 4V6 Canada. (604)388-4324. FAX: (604)388-6166. Art Director: Leigh Lundgren. Estab. 1977. Tourist magazine featuring general information on shopping and attractions for the tourist market. Monthly. Circ. 30,000. Accepts previously published artwork. Original artwork returned to artist at the job's completion. Sample copies available. Art guidelines available.

Illustrations: Approached by 10 illustrators/year. Buys 20 illustrations/year from freelancers. Prefers lifestyle and scenic themes and realistic styles. Considers watercolor and acrylic. Send query letter with tearsheets, photographs, slides and transparencies. Samples are filed. Reports back to the artist only if interested. Call to schedule an appointment to show a portfolio. Portfolio should include tearsheets, photographs and slides. Buys first, one-time or reprint rights. Payment negotiable. Pays on publication.

WHISPERING WIND MAGAZINE, 8009 Wales St., New Orleans LA 70126. Editor: Jack B. Heriard. Magazine emphasizing American Indian crafts and culture. Features historical and how-to articles and ethnic and historical Native American (Indian) essays. "Readership is 52% Indian, 49% 15-35 years of age." Bimonthly. Circ. 8,000. Accepts previously published material. Original artwork returned after publication if requested. Sample copy $4.

Cartoons: Uses 3 cartoons/year from freelancers. "Must be Indian-oriented—no stereotypes." Prefers single panel with gagline, b&w line drawings. Send query letter with roughs. Samples are returned by SASE. Reports back within 5 days. Negotiates rights purchased. No payment.

Illustrations: Works on assignment only. Prefers traditional style. Looks for "attention to detail, accuracy of subjects and clothing from a historical perspective. Avoid, stereotyping Indian clothing (all Indians wear war bonnets, etc.)." Send query letter with photocopies. Samples are returned by SASE. Reports back within 5 days. Negotiates rights purchased. No payment.

WILDFIRE, Box 9167, Spokane WA 99209. (509)326-6561. Editor: Matthew Ryan. Magazine emphasizing nature, Native American values, spirituality and new art topics. "We promote Native American spirituality, earth awareness, ecology, natural child birth/raising, sexuality and relationships, alternative lifestyles, earth changes and prophecy." Quarterly. Circ. 41,000. Accepts previously published material. Original artwork is returned to the artist after publication. Sample copies $2.95.

Cartoons: Approached by 10-15 cartoonists/year. Buys 2 cartoons/issue from freelancers. "Am looking for more." Prefers themes featuring nature vs. technology or common sense vs. experts, "non-sarcastic." Prefers b&w line drawings or b&w washes. Send samples of style. Samples are filed or are returned by SASE if requested by artist. Reports back within 1 month. Buys first rights. Pays $20 (varies), b&w.

Illustrations: Approached by 10-15 illustrators/year. Send query letter with brochure. Samples are filed or are returned only if requested by artist. Reports back within months. Write to schedule an appointment to show a portfolio, which should include b&w tearsheets. Buys first rights. Pays $35 (varies), b&w.

Tips: "Read sample copy! Send samples of work (b&w only) and orientation (what can you create specifically for our view)."

*WILDLIFE ART NEWS, 3455 Dakota Ave. S., St. Louis Park MN 55416-0246. (612)927-9056. FAX: (612)927-9353. Publisher: Robert Koenke. Estab. 1982. Trade journal; magazine format; "the largest magazine in wildlife art originals, prints, duck stamps, artist interviews and industry information." Bimonthly. Circ. 45,000. Accepts previously published artwork. Original artwork returned to artist at job's completion. Sample copy $5. Art guidelines free for SASE with first class postage.

Cartoons: Buys 12 cartoons/year from freelancers. Prefers nature, wildlife and environmental themes; single panel. Send query letter with roughs. Sample are not filed and are returned by SASE. Reports back within 1 month. Buys first rights. Pays $50, b&w.

Illustrations: Approached by 50 illustrators/year. Works on assignment only. Prefers nature and animal themes. Considers pen & ink and charcoal. Send query letter with brochure, resume, SASE, photocopies and transparencies. Samples are not filed and are returned by SASE if requested by artist. Reports back within 3 weeks. Mail appropriate materials: color tearsheets, slides and photocopies. Buys first rights. "We do not pay for the artists for illustration in publication material."

Tips: "Interested wildlife artists should send SASE, 3-7 slides or transparencies, short biography and be patient!"

*WILSON LIBRARY BULLETIN, 950 University Ave., Bronx NY 10452. (212)588-8400. Editor: Mary Jo Godwin. Emphasizes the issues and the practice of library science. Published 10 times/year. Circ. 13,000. Free sample copy. Uses freelance artists mainly for cartoons and logos.

Cartoons: Approached by 25-30 cartoonists/year. Buys 2-3 cartoons/issue from freelancers on education, publishing, reading, technology and libraries; single panel with gagline. Mail finished art and SASE. Reports back only if interested. Buys first rights. Pays $100, b&w line drawings and washes; on acceptance.

Illustrations: Approached by 10-15 illustrators/year. Buys 1-2 illustrations/issue from freelancers. Works on assignment only. Send query letter, business card and samples to be kept on file. Do not send original work that must be returned. Reports back only if interested. Call for appointment to show portfolio. Buys first rights. Pays $400, color washes; $100-200, b&w line drawings and washes, inside; $25, spot drawings; on publication.

Tips: Artist should have "knowledge of our publication and its needs."

*WINES & VINES, 1800 Lincoln Ave., San Rafael CA 94901. (415)453-9700. Editor: Philip E. Hiaring. Emphasizes the grape and wine industry in North America for the trade—growers, winemakers, merchants. Monthly. Circ. 5,800. Accepts previously published material. Original artwork not returned after publication.

Cartoons: Buys approximately 3 cartoons/year. Prefers single panel with gagline; b&w line drawings. Send query letter with roughs to be kept on file. Material not kept on file is not returned. Reports within 1 month. Buys first rights. Pays $10.

Illustrations: Send query letter to be kept on file. Reports within 1 month. Buys first rights. Pays $50-100, color, cover; $15, b&w, inside; on acceptance.

*WINNING!, 15115 S. 76th E. Ave., Bixby OK 74008. (918)366-4441. FAX: (918)366-6250. Managing Editor: Simon P. McCaffery. Estab. 1976. Consumer magazine; emphasizing all aspects of legal gaming, especially state and foreign lotteries, sweepstakes and Las Vegas style casino gaming. We also include travel articles.

Monthly. Circ. 150,000. Accepts previously published artwork. Original artwork returned after publication. Sample copy $1. Art guidelines available.
Cartoons: Approached by 20-30 cartoonists/year. Buys 1-2 cartoons/issue, 12-15 cartoons/year from freelancers. Prefers "anything related directly to gaming"; with gagline, b&w line drawings. Send query letter with samples of published or unpublished work. Samples are filed or returned by SASE if requested by artist. Reports back within 2 weeks. Buys first North American rights or reprint rights. Pays $50, b&w, $75, color.
Illustrations: Approached by more than 50 illustrators/year. Buys 1-2 illustrations/issue, 10-12 illustrations/year from freelancers. Works on assignment only. Prefers themes and how-to illustrations. Prefers pen & ink. Send query letter with brochure, tearsheets, slides and SASE. Samples are filed or returned by SASE if requested by artist. Reports back within 10 days. Write to schedule an appointment to show a portfolio or mail appropriate materials: thumbnails and b&w tearsheets, slides and photocopies. Buys first North American rights or reprint rights. Pays $100, b&w, $200, color, inside. Pays within 30 days of acceptance.
Tips: "Be familiar with the current gaming industry and attitudes. Illustrations must be up-beat and people-oriented."

*WOMEN'S SPORTS & FITNESS, Suite 421, 1919 14th St., Boulder CO 80302. (303)440-5111. FAX: (303)440-3313. Art Director: Ian Paton. Estab. 1974. Consumer magazine. "Women's sports publication targeting women 20-40 years old." Monthly. Circ. 300,000. Accepts previously pubished artwork. Original artwork returned to artist at job's completion. Sample copies not available. Art guidelines not available.
Illustrations: Approached by 30-40 illustrators/year. Buys 3-4 illustrations/issue, 24-30 illustrations/year from freelancers. Works on assignment only. Prefers non-technical styles—lively, both real and slightly surreal, sometimes cartoonlike. Considers airbrush, colored pencil, watercolor and pastel. Send query letter with brochure and resume. Samples are filed. Reports back to the artist only if interested. Mail appropriate materials: thumbnails, tearsheets, and slides. "Various forms are acceptable." Rights purchsed vary according to project. Pays $50-300, color, inside; on acceptance.
Tips: "Send a brochure/promotional piece. We will certainly look at the work and keep it on file for upcoming projects/issues."

WONDER TIME, 6401 The Paseo, Kansas City MO 64131. (816)333-7000. Editor: Evelyn Beals. Estab. 1969. "Story paper" emphasizing inspiration and character-building material for first and second graders, 6-8 years old. Weekly. Circ. 40,000. Does not accept previously published material. Original artwork not returned to the artist after publication. Sample copies for SASE with 50¢ postage.
Illustrations: Approached by 6-10 illustrators/year. Buys 1 illustration/issue from freelancers. Works on assignment only. Send query letter with tear sheets or photocopies to be kept on file. Reports only if interested. Buys all rights. Pays $40, b&w; $75, color cover. Pays $40, b&w; $75, color inside; on acceptance.
Tips: "Include illustrations of children in your portfolio. I do not want to see fantasy art."

WOODENBOAT, Box 78, Brooklin ME 04616. (207)359-4651. Editor: Jonathan A. Wilson. Managing Editor: Jennifer Elliott. Concerns designing, building, repairing, using and maintaining wooden boats. Bimonthly. Circ. 103,000. Previously published work OK. Sample copy $4.
Illustrations: Buys 48 illustrations/year on wooden boats or related items. Send query letter with samples and SASE. Reports in 1-2 months. "We are always in need of high quality technical drawings. Rates vary, but usually $25-350. Buys first North American serial rights. Pays on publication.
Tips: "We work with several professionals on an assignment basis, but most of the illustrative material that we use in the magazine is submitted with a feature article. When we need additional material, however, we will try to contact a good freelancer in the appropriate geographic area."

WOODMEN OF THE WORLD, 1700 Farnam St., Omaha NE 68102. (402)342-1890. Editor: George M. Herriott. For members of the Woodmen of the World Life Insurance Society and their families. Emphasizes Society and member activities, insurance and health issues, American history, general interest topics and humor. Monthly. Circ. 475,000. Previously published material acceptable. Original artwork returned after publication, if arrangements are made. Free sample copy.
Cartoons: Approached by 50 cartoonists/year. Buys 15 cartoons/year from freelancers. Interested in general interest subjects; single panel. Send finished cartoons. SASE. Pays $15, b&w; $25, color. Reports in 2 weeks. Buys various rights. Pays $10, b&w line drawings, washes and halftones; on acceptance.
Illustrations: Approached by 10 illustrators/year. Works with 3-4 illustrators/year. Buys 5-10 illustrations/year; buys 3-4/year from freelancers. Interested in general topics, including seasonal, humorous, historical and human interest. Prefers mixed media. Works on assignment only. Send samples of art style, prices and references for files. Prefers to see finished art. SASE. Reports in two weeks. Buys one-time rights. Payment varies according to job.
Tips: Especially looks for creative material that takes a different approach to a story or cartoon. "Vary the media used and techniques."

*WORDPERFECT, THE MAGAZINE, 270 W. Center St., Orem UT 84057. (801)226-5555. FAX: (801)226-8804. Art Director: Nickie Egan. Consumer magazine "for WordPerfect users. It's an upbeat, colorful, conceptual magazine; hence, no computers are illustrated—since everyone knows what they look like." Monthly. Circ. 150,000. Accepts previously published artwork. Samples copies available. Art guidelines available.
Illustrations: Approached by 25 illustrators/year. Buys 10 illustrations/issue, 120 illustrations/year from freelancers. Works on assignment only. Prefers anything conceptual—no computers. Considers pen & ink, airbrush, colored pencil, mixed media, watercolor, acrylic, oil, pastel, collage, marker and charcoal. Send query letter with resume, tearsheets, photographs, photocopies and slides. Samples are filed or are returned upon request. Reports back to the artist only if interested. Call or write to schedule an appointment to show a portfolio or mail appropriate materials. Portfolio should include color tearsheets, slides and photocopies. Buys one-time rights. Pays $700, color, cover; $300, color, inside.
Tips: "I prefer abstract art and photos dealing with a computer environment—but avoid using any computers."

THE WORK BOAT, Box 1348, Mandeville LA 70470. (504)626-0298. Editor: R. Carpenter. Emphasizes news of the work boat industry for those involved with towboats, barges, oil rigs, dredges, crew boats and tugboats. Bi-monthly. Circ. 13,600.
Illustrations: Approached 2-3 illustrators per year. Works with 3-4 illustrators/year. Buys 8-9 illustrations/year from freelancers. Uses freelance artists mainly for covers and *occasionally* for story illustration. Suitable subjects are tow boats, pushboats, tug boats, offshore crew/supply boats, dredges; photos for cover. "Must evoke feeling of working in our industry. Action required. Allow 3 months lead for seasonal covers." Send query letter with color prints or slides. SASE. Reports in 4 weeks. Pays on acceptance.
Tips: "We prefer direct contact. We usually have a specific topic in mind. No cold submissions without reading the magazine."

WORKBENCH, Modern Handcraft, Inc., 4251 Pennsylvania, Kansas City MO 64111. Editor-in-Chief: Robert N. Hoffman. Estab. 1957. For woodworkers and do-it-yourself persons. Bimonthly. Circ. 870,000.
Cartoons: Buys 15 cartoons/year from freelancers. Interested in woodworking and do-it-yourself themes; single panel with gagline. Submit art. SASE. Reports in 1 month. Buys all rights, but may reassign rights to artist after publication. Pays $40 minimum, b&w line drawings; on acceptance.
Illustrations: Works with 10 illustrators/year. Buys 100 illustrations/year from freelancers. Artists with experience in the area of technical drawings, especially house plans, exploded views of furniture construction, power tool and appliance cutaways, should write for free sample copy with SASE and artists' guidelines. Pays $50-1,200, b&w; $100-1,500, color, inside.

*WORLD TRADE, 4940 Campus Dr., Newport Beach CA 92660. (714)757-1404. FAX: (714)757-1996. Photo Editor: Linda Lawler. Estab. 1988. Trade journal; magazine format; read by upper management, presidents and CEO's of companies with international sales." Bimonthly. Circ. 37,000. Accepts previously published artwork. Original artwork is returned to artist at job's completion. Sample copies not available. Art guidelines not available.
Cartoons: Approached by 2-3 cartoonists/year. Buys 3 cartoons/issue, 18-20 cartoons/year; single panel; with gagline, b&w line drawings. Send query letter with brochure and samples of work. Samples are filed. Reports back to the artist only if interested. Buys first rights or reprint rights. Pays $25-50, b&w.
Illustrations: Approached by 15-20 illustrators/year. Buys 2-3 illustrations/issue, 18-20 illustrations/year. Works on assignment only. "We are open to all kinds of themes and styles." Considers pen & ink, colored pencil, mixed media and watercolor. Send query letter with brochure and tearsheets. Samples are filed. Reports back to the artist only if interested. Call to schedule an appointment to show a portfolio or mail appropriate materials. Portfolio should include original/final art, tearsheets and slides. Buys first rights or reprint rights. Pays $50, b&w, $200-300, color, cover; $100-200, b&w, $100-200, color inside; on publication.
Tips: "Send an example of your work. We prefer previous work to be in business publications. Follow up with a telephone call."

WRITER'S DIGEST, 1507 Dana Avenue, Cincinnati OH 45207. Art Director: Carole Winters. Associate Editor: Bill Strickland (for cartoons). Emphasizes freelance writing for freelance writers. Monthly. Circ. 200,000. Original artwork returned after publication. Sample copy $2.
Cartoons: Buys 3 cartoons/issue from freelancers. Theme: the writing life—cartoons that deal with writers and the trials of writing and selling their work. Also, writing from a historical standpoint (past works), language use and other literary themes. Prefers single panel with or without gagline. Send finished cartoons. Material returned by SASE. Reports back within 1 month. Buys first rights or one-time rights. Pays $50-85, b&w; on acceptance.
Illustrations: Buys 4 illustrations/month from freelancers. Theme: the writing life (b&w line art primarily). Works on assignment only. Send nonreturnable samples to be kept on file. Accepts photocopies as samples. Write for appointment to show portfolio. Buys one-time rights. Pays $400, color, cover; $50-300, inside, b&w; on acceptance.

Tips: "We're also looking for black-and-white spots of writing-related subjects. We will buy all rights. $15-25 per spot."

WRITER'S YEARBOOK, 1507 Dana Ave., Cincinnati OH 45207. Submissions Editor: Bill Strickland. Emphasizes writing and marketing techniques, business topics for writers and writing opportunities for freelance writers and people trying to get started in writing. Annually. Original artwork returned with one copy of the issue in which it appears. Sample copy $3.95. Affiliated with *Writer's Digest.* Cartoons submitted to either publication are considered for both.
Cartoons: Uses 3-6 freelance cartoons/issue. "All cartoons must pertain to writing—its joys, agonies, quirks. All styles accepted, but high-quality art is a must." Prefers single panel, with or without gagline, b&w line drawings or washes. "Verticals are always considered, but horizontals—especially severe horizontals—are hard to come by." Send finished cartoons. Samples returned by SASE. Reports within 3 weeks. Buys first North American serial rights, one-time use. Pays $50 minimum, b&w; on acceptance.
Tips: "A cluttery style does not appeal to us. Send finished, not rough art, with clearly typed gaglines. Cartoons without gaglines must be particularly well executed."

YELLOW SILK: Journal of Erotic Arts, Box 6374, Albany CA 94706. (415)644-4188. Publisher: Lily Pond. Estab. 1981. Emphasizes erotic literature and arts for well educated, highly literate readership, generally personally involved in arts field. Quarterly. Circ. 15,000. Does not accept previously published material. Returns original artwork after publication. Sample copy $6.
Cartoons: Buys 12 cartoons/year. Acquires 0-3/issue from freelancers. Prefers themes involving human relationships and/or sexuality " 'All persuasions; no brutality' is editoral policy. Nothing tasteless." Accepts any cartoon format. Send query letter with finished cartoons or photocopies to be kept on file. Include phone number, name and address on each sample. Material not filed is returned by SASE with correct stamps, no meters. Reports only if SASE included. Buys first or reprint rights. Negotiates payments. Minimum payment plus 3 copies; on publication.
Illustrations: Acquires 10-20/issue by one artist if possible. Considers "anything in the widest definitions of eroticism except brutality, bondage or S&M. Nothing tasteless. We're looking for work that is beautiful, artistically. Considers this category somewhat misnamed. We publish fine arts as opposed to illustration. No pornography. All sexual persuasions represented." Prefers acrylic, then pen & ink, watercolor, oil, pastel, collage and mixed media. Send originals, photocopies, slides, photostats, good quality photographs. Color and b&w examples in each submission are preferred. Include name, address and telephone number on all samples. Samples not filed returned by SASE. Reports back within 8 weeks. To show portfolio, mail original/final art, b&w and color, photostats, photographs, photocopies and slides. Buys first rights or reprint rights. Negotiates payment plus copies; on publication.
Tips: "Artistic quality is of equal or higher importance than erotic content. There are too many people doing terrible work thinking it will sell if it's sexual. Don't send it to me! Also hard-edge S&M images seem disturbingly more frequent. Don't send us those, either !!"

*ZILLIONS, 256 Washington St., Mount Vernon NY 10553. Art Director: Robert Jenter. Magazine emphasizing stories, puzzles, how-to articles and product ratings for children age 8-14. Bimonthly. Circ. 140,000.
Illustrations: Approached by 50 illustrators/year. Works with 10-20 artists/year. Buys artwork for 3-4 stories/issue from freelancers. "We tend toward realism, but not necessarily—work can be primitive and fun, but must be sophisticated." Should be color work; not original art. Send query letter with photocopies and an SASE. Samples are filed. Reports back only if interested. Call to schedule an appointment to show a portfolio. Buys first rights. Pays $250-1,000; payment is on a per story basis; on acceptance.

Other magazines

Each year we contact all publishers currently listed in *Artist's Market* requesting they give us updated information for our next edition. We also mail listing questionnaires to new and established publishers who have not been included in past editions. The following magazines either did not respond to our request to update their listings for 1991 (if they indicated a reason, it is noted in parentheses after their name), or they are magazines which did not return our questionnaire for a new listing (designated by the words "declined listing" after their names).

Ad Astra
The Altadena Review (moved; no forwarding address)
American Bookseller
American Rodder
American Salon

Aqua-Field Publications
The Atlantic Monthly (declined listing)
Aura Literary/Arts Review
Australian Women's Weekly
Auto Racing Digest (out of

business)
The Autograph Collector's Magazine
Baker Street Publications
Banjo Newletter
Basketball Digest

Bay and Delta Yachtsman
Better Homes & Garden (declined listing)
Bon Appetit (declined listing)
Boundary Magazine
Bowling Digest
Bread
Business Today (declined listing)
California Garden
Calli's Tales
Campus USA Magazine
Canadian Research (no longer published)
Car and Driver (declined listing)
Carolina Quarterly
The Cattleman
Children's Album
China Painter
Cincom Solutions Magazine
Cinefantastique
Collegiate Microcomputer
Contemporary Christian Magazine
Cookbooks for Causes (asked to be deleted)
Country Journal
Crit, The Journal of the American Institute of Architecture Students
Cryptologia
Dakota Country
Decor
The Disciple
Diver Magazine
EAP Digest
Easyriders
The Economist (declined listing)
The Ecphorizer
Electronic Media
Equilibrium
Elle (declined listing)
Esquire (declined listing)
The Exceptional Parent
Family Motor Coaching
Fantasy Tales
The Fiddlehead
Fishing World (asked to be deleted)
Food and Wine (declined listing)
Football Digest
Forest Notes
Fortune (declined listing)
Frets Magazine
Gladstone Publishing

Glamour (declined listing)
Glass Digest
Good Health (moved; no forwarding address)
Guideposts
Harper's (declined listing)
Harper's Bazaar (declined listing)
Hockey Digest
Horse Illustrated
Hospitals Magazine
Independent Agent Magazine
Indianapolis 500 Yearbook
Industrial Machinery News
Inside Sports
Insurance Sales (needs have changed)
Journal of Reading
The Legal Reformer and Citizens Legal Manual Series
Ladies Home Journal (declined listing)
Life Magazine (declined listing)
McCall's (declined listing)
Mad Magazine (declined listing)
Marvel Comics
MB News
Medical Economics for Surgeons
Member Magazine
Men's Guide to Fashion
Metropolitan Home (declined listing)
Miller/Freeman Publications
The Mind's Eye
Modern Plastics
Money Magazine (declined listing)
Mother Jones (declined listing)
Motor Trend
Mountain Family Calendar
My Weekly
National Dragster
NCAA Sports Championship Programs
New Jersey Goodlife Magazine
New Realities
New York Magazine (declined listing)
The New York Times Magazine (declined listing)
Newsweek (declined listing)
Northeast Outdoors
Oceans (out of business)
Offshore
Ontario Out of Doors

Opportunity Magazine
Oregon River Watch
Pangloss Papers
Paraplegia News
Pediatric Annals
Pennsylvania Sportsman
Pet Business
PGA Magazine
Phoenix Home & Garden Magazine
Pig Iron
Plainswoman
Playboy (declined listing)
Primavera
Profit
Psychic Guide Magazine (asked to be deleted)
Rolling Stone (declined listing)
Room of One's Own
Rosicrucian Digest
Sacramento Magazine
Salt Water Sports (moved; no forwarding address)
Savings Institutions (no longer works with freelancers)
Scientific American (declined listing)
Scott Stamps Monthly Magazine (no longer works with freelancers)
Self (declined listing)
The Sensible Sound
Skiing
Soccer Digest
Spitball
Spy Magazine (declined listing)
Stork Magazine (no longer published)
Student Assistance Journal
TFR-The Freelancer's Report (out of business)
Time (declined listing)
Tole World
Tourist Attractions & Parks
Trains Illustrated
Treasure Chest
TV Guide
Utne Reader (declined listing)
US Magazine (declined listing)
Vanity Fair (declined listing)
Vogue (declined listing)
Video Choice Magazine
Virtue Magazine
Whole Life
Wisconsin Restaurateur
Women's Enterprise

Newspapers & Newsletters

USA Today, referred to by critics as "McPaper" because it provides quick information and little intellectual nourishment, is representative of the status of the newspaper industry today. Faced with a decrease in advertising and a decline in circulation, more and more newspapers are attempting to appeal to the TV generation by following *USA Today*'s lead—offering briefer bits of news, brighter colors and lots of graphics. Because of budget constraints and greater importance placed on the visual, there is more opportunity for the freelance artist. Newspaper graphics have joined the computer age, software replacing rapidographs and T-squares as essential tools of the trade. Large dailies were the forerunners in computerizing production, but now alternative papers and newsletters are using desktop publishing to illustrate and design their publications as well as produce them.

Fortunately, computers will never usurp the freelancer's place at newspapers. Illustrations are always needed as hooks to pull the potential reader into a story, especially when an emotionally laden topic involves interpretation. The traditional Sunday tabloids are now slick, news-weekly style magazines, requiring sophisticated graphics for the cover and the interior in order to compete with local magazines for advertising.

Alternative weeklies feel they lead the way in using graphic innovation by using dramatic covers and inside art. They have emerged from homespun publications to become slick, profitable businesses with upscale readers. With such staples as politics, social issues and investigative pieces, alternative weeklies require conceptual illustrations with an emotional kick. Alternatives are more likely to use innovative, cutting-edge work than dailies to accompany their provocative stories.

When sending samples to a newspaper's art director, include black-and-white work that shows your conceptual abilities. If you don't have any published work to show, illustrate a current news item, accompanying it with the headline and story. Because of tight deadlines, newspapers prefer to work with local artists, who also have a grasp of local events and personalities. Refer to this section's Close-up on Kerry Gavin to get a greater sense of what newspapers are looking for.

If you're interested in becoming an editorial cartoonist, try a weekly first, rather than a daily where an editorial cartoonist is probably already entrenched. Make an appointment with the editor to show samples, which should include caricatures, especially of local figures.

Most newsletters fall into two categories: informative and promotional. Targeted to business executives, informative newsletters convey specific information about a specialized topic to a select audience, such as stock investors or business executives. On the other hand, promotional newsletters not only present facts, but also opinions and miscellaneous items of interest to employees, club members, customers or dealers. They are usually distributed free of charge, instead of by subscription as informative newsletters are. Newsletters use mostly black-and-white line art to simplify production. If you are interested in submitting work to newsletters, send tearsheets, photostats or photocopies of black-and-white work that reflect the newsletter's focus. Before you submit work, however, request past copies in order to understand the publication's slant. In your cover letter, explain that in the package there are samples that can be kept on file; since space is limited, your work may not be needed at the time but might fit a future slot.

Getting published in newspapers and newsletters has its rewards. If your work appears on the editorial page or on the cover of Sunday supplements, your work will be seen in thousands of homes, bringing you increased recognition in your community. However, high visibility is offset by low payment; many newsletters pay in complimentary copies.

For further information and other names and addresses, consult *Writer's Market*, *The Newspaper and Allied Services Directory*, *Gale Directory of Publications*, *Editor & Publisher*, and *Newsletter Directory*.

*THE AGING CONNECTION, Suite 512, 833 Market St., San Francisco CA 94103. (415)442-0433. FAX: (415)882-4280. Editor: Paul Kleyman. Estab. 1979. Newspaper for professionals in aging. "The bimonthly paper is read by professionals in aging, from social workers to directors of senior centers. It covers public policy issues and innovations." Circ. 10,000. Accepts previously published artwork. Original artwork returned after publication. Sample copy available: 65¢. Art guidelines not available.
Cartoons: Approached by 1-2 freelance cartoonists/year. Buys 1 freelance cartoon/issue. Buys 6 freelance cartoons/year. Preferred themes are "aging from the point of view of people who serve older persons. No stereotypes about sexy or forgetful elders. We like toons that satirize the system." Prefers single, double and multiple panel, with gagline; b&w line drawings. Send query letter with sample of work, brief description or rough of idea. Samples are returned if requested by artist. Reports back within 30 days. Buys one-time rights. Pays $25, b&w.
Illustrations: Approached by 2 freelance illustrators/year. Buys 1-2 freelance illustrations/issue. Artists work on assignment only. Prefers pen & ink. Send query letter with SASE, tearsheets and photocopies. Samples are filed, if liked and returned by SASE if requested by artist. Reports back within 30 days. Call to schedule an appointment to show a portfolio which should include original/final art and b&w tearsheets. Buys one-time rights. Pays $25-50, b&w, inside; on acceptance.

AMERICAN LAWYER NEWSPAPERS GROUP, 2 Park Ave., New York NY 10016. (212)973-6789. Art Director: Julie Patrick. Estab. 1986. Weekly and daily newspapers and tabloids. Emphasizes law and business. 10 publications in Miami, Atlanta, Newark NJ, Stamford CT, San Francisco, Dallas, Manhattan, and Washington DC. Circ. 3,000-15,000. Accepts previously published material. Returns original artwork to the artist after publication. Sample copy available. Art guidelines available.
Cartoons: Buys 52+ freelance cartoons/year. Prefers editorial or political cartoons and caricatures. Prefers political and legal themes. Prefers single panel without gagline; b&w line drawings and b&w washes 30-45 picas wide. Send query letter with samples of style. Samples are filed. Reports back only if interested. Negotiates rights purchased. Pays $75-300, b&w. Pays on publication.
Illustration: Buys 52+ freelance illustrations/year. Prefers line art. Send query letter with brochure showing art style. Samples are filed. Reports back only if interested. Call to schedule an appointment to show a portfolio which should include roughs, original/final art, tearsheets, photostats and photographs. Negotiates rights purchased. Pays $75-300, color, inside. Pays on publication.

*AMERICAN MEDICAL NEWS, 535 N. Dearborn St., Chicago IL 60610. (312)645-4441. FAX: (312)645-4445. Editor: Dick Walt. Estab. 1958. Emphasizes news and opinions on developments, legislation and business in medicine. For physicians. Weekly newspaper. Circ. 315,000. Original artwork not returned after publication. Free sample copy.
Cartoons: Senior Editor: Sher Watts. Uses 1 freelance cartoon/issue. Buys 10 freelance cartoons/year. Receives "dozens" of submissions/week from freelancers. Interested in medical themes; single panel. Prefers to see finished cartoons. Send SASE. Reports in 4 weeks. Usually buys first North American rights. Pays up to $100, b&w; on acceptance.
Illustrations: Contact: Kevin O'Neil, graphics editor. Number of freelance illustrations used/issue varies; number bought/issue from freelancers varies. Prefers realistic style on a medical theme. Works on assignment only. Send query letter with brochure showing art style. Samples returned by SASE. "We don't look at many

The asterisk before a listing indicates that the listing is new in this edition. New markets are often the most receptive to freelance submissions.

portfolios, but portfolio should include original/final art, and color tearsheets." Usually buys first North American rights. Pays $250-350; "we have paid as much as $600 for single illustration." Pays on acceptance.
Tips: "I will look at any cartoons. I usually work with artists only from the Chicago area, because we need to see them in person. Portfolios should include tearsheets and brochures. We are using fewer cartoons overall."

APA MONITOR, American Psychological Association, 1200 17th St. NW, Washington DC 20036. (202)955-7690. Editor: Laurie Denton. Managing Editor: John Bales. Monthly tabloid newspaper for psychologists and other behavioral scientists. 72-80 pages. Circ. 75,000.
Cartoons: Buys 0-2 b&w freelance cartoons/month. Buys 10-20 freelance cartoons/year. Pays $50 on acceptance.
Illustrations: Buys 5-8 freelance illustrations/month. Uses 30 freelance illustrations/year on current events and feature articles in behavioral sciences/mental health area. Washington area artists preferred. Works on assignment only. Query with resume, tearsheets and photocopies. Sample copy $3. SASE. To show a portfolio, mail appropriate materials or call to schedule an appointment; portfolio should include original/final art and final reproduction/product. Original artwork returned after publication, if requested. Buys first North American serial rights. Pays $200, b&w cover and inside; on acceptance.
Tips: "Be creative, think about topics relevant to psychology. I look for ability to develop simple, clean graphics to complement abstract, complex ideas." Uses freelance talent mostly for "story illustrations; covers." Does not want to see "too much stuff; samples bigger than 8½×11."

BALLS AND STRIKES NEWSPAPER, 2801 N.E. 50th St., Oklahoma City OK 73111. (405)424-5266. Communications Director and Senior Editor: Bill Plummer III. Editor and Production and Design Director: Larry Floyd. Official publication of the Amateur Softball Association. Emphasizes amateur softball for "the more than 30 million people who play amateur softball; they come from all walks of life and hold varied jobs." Published 8 times/year. Circ. 300,000+. Previously published material OK. Original work returned after publication. Free sample copy available.
Illustrations: Uses 2-4 illustrations/issue. No drug or alcohol themes. Works on assignment only. Send query letter with resume and business card to be kept on file. Samples returned. Reports in 3 days. Buys all rights. Pays on publication.

BOOKPLATES IN THE NEWS, Apt. F, 605 N. Stoneman Ave., Alhambra CA 91801. (213)283-1936. Director: Audrey Spencer Arellanes. Emphasizes "bookplates for those who use bookplates, whether individuals or institutions, those who collect them, artists who design them, art historians, genealogists, historians, antiquarian booktrade and others for tracing provenance of a volume; also publishes yearbook annually." Quarterly. Circ. 250. Original work returned after publication. Previously published material OK "on occasion, usually from foreign publications." Sample copy $5; art guidelines for SASE with postage for 3 ounces.
Illustrations: Illustrations are bookplates. "Appearance of work in our publications should produce requests for bookplate commissions." Send query letter and finished art. Reports in 3 weeks. No payment.
Tips: "We only publish bookplates, those marks of ownership used by individuals and institutions. Some artists and owners furnish 250 original prints of their bookplate to be tipped-in quarterly. Membership is international; this is reflected in artwork from around the world."

THE BOSTON PHOENIX, 126 Brookline Ave., Boston MA 02215. (617)536-5390. Design Director: Cleo Leontis. Weekly. Circ. 150,000. Original work returned after publication by SASE. Sample copy $3.50; send requests for sample copy to circulation department.
Illustrations: Uses 2-8 b&w illustrations/issue, occasional color; buys all from freelancers. On assignment only. To show a portfolio, send samples of style (no originals) and resume to be kept on file for possible future assignments. Call for appointment. Buys one-time rights. Pays on publication.

BUILDING BRIEFS, Dan Burch Associates, 2338 Frankfort Ave., Louisville KY 40206. (502)895-4881. FAX: (502)893-1912. Program Manager: Sharon Hall. Estab. 1981. Newsletter. Emphasizes design/build and conventional methods of construction for commercial and industrial buildings, plus other topics such as landscaping, security and energy-saving ideas. Directed to potential clients of a building contractor in the nonresidential market, company presidents, board members and managerial personnel who will construct or renovate their buildings. Bimonthly. Circ. 25,000+. Original artwork returned after publication. Sample copy available.
Cartoons: Buys 1 freelance cartoon/issue. Buys 12 freelance cartoons/year. Prefers themes related to construction; light humor, simple line art. Prefers single panel with gagline; b&w line drawings. Send query letter with finished cartoons to be kept on file. Material not kept on file is returned. Reports only if interested. Buys one-time rights. Pays $50, b&w; on publication.
Tips: "Spend a little time researching the commercial building industry. Talk to a building contractor. One industry publication where more can be learned is *Metal Construction News*." Wants to see "cartoons; no negative humor."

*CARTOON WORLD, Box 30367, Lincoln NE 68503. (112)435-3191. Editor/Publisher: George Hartman. Estab. 1936. Newsletter "slanted to amateur and professional freelance cartoonists." Monthly. Circ. 300. Accepts previously published material. Returns original artwork after publication. Sample copy $5; art guidelines available.
Cartoons: Buys 1-2 freelance cartoons/issue. Buys 24 freelance cartoons/year. Does not want individual cartoons; seeks articles on cartooning, illustrated with cartoons, that will benefit other cartoonists. Topics as how to cartoon, how to create ideas, cartoon business plans, hints and markets. Send query letter with originals only. Reports within 10 days. Material will not be returned nor considered for publication without return postage. To show a portfolio, mail final reproduction/product. Buys reprint rights. Pays $5/8½x11 page; on acceptance.
Tips: "Anything sent to us must be by professionals who had lots of experience on cartooning or gagwriting."

*'"CHECK THE OIL!" Box 1000, Westerville OH 43081-7000. (614)891-0398. Editor: Jerry Keyser. Estab. 1982. Newsletter format. Bimonthly "addressing those interested in the history and collectible artifacts of the petroleum industry." Circ. 1,800 "and growing." Accepts previously published artwork. Original artwork returned at job's completion. Sample copy available. Art guidelines not available.
Cartoons: Buys 2-3 freelance cartoons/year "but we are looking for more." Theme must be related to the petroleum industry. Prefers b&w line drawings. Send query letter with roughs. Samples are filed or are returned by SASE if requested. Reports back only if interested. Negotiates rights purchased. Pays $10 and up, b&w; on acceptance.
Illustrations: Buys 3-4 freelance illustrations/year. Theme must be related to the petroleum industry. Send query letter with rough or thumbnail. Samples are filed or are returned by SASE if requested. Reports back to artist only if interested. To show a portfolio, mail appropriate materials. Negotiates rights purchased. Pays $50 for b&w; $100 for color, cover. Pays $25 and up, b&w, inside; on acceptance.
Tips: "To break into our publication, you should have focused, creative material."

CHICAGO READER, 11 E. Illinois, Chicago IL 60611. (312)828-0350. Editor-in-Chief: Robert A. Roth. Cartoon/Illustration Editor: David Jones. For young adults in lakefront neighborhoods interested in things to do in Chicago and feature stories on city life. Weekly. Circ. 131,000. Sample copy $2.
Cartoons: Buys 9 freelance cartoons/issue on any topic; single, double and multi-panel. Pays $10 and up. "At present, we carry eight regular cartoon features, plus one or more irregularly-appearing ones. While we are not actively looking for more, we will consider anything, and find the space if the material warrants it." Send photocopies (no originals). Buys one-time rights; pays by 15th of month following publication.
Illustrations: Buys 3 freelance illustrations/issue on assigned themes. Send photocopies or arrange interview to show portfolio. SASE. Buys one-time rights. Pays by 15th of month following publication. Cover and inside: Pays $120-220, b&w line drawings and washes.

THE CHRISTIAN SCIENCE MONITOR, 1 Norway St., Mail Stop P-214, Boston MA 02115. (617)450-2361. FAX: (617)450-2595. Design Director: John Van Pelt. Estab. 1908. Newspaper emphasizing analytical reporting of current events; diverse features and news features for well-educated, well-informed readers in all fields—especially politicians, educators and business people. Daily. Circ. 130,000. Original artwork returned after 3 months. Sample copy and art guidelines available.
Illustrations: Buys 100 freelance illustrations/year. Buys 1-2 freelance illustrations/week. Uses freelance artwork mainly for portraits and opinion illustration. Prefers editorial ("op-ed") conceptual themes; portraits. All color. Works on assignment only. Send samples to be filed. Samples should be 8½x11 photocopies; no originals. Samples not returned. Reports only if interested. Buys first rights. Pays $125-250, color, on publication.
Tips: "Show color samples. I do not want to see medical subjects. Be selective about the work you show."

THE CHRONICLE OF HIGHER EDUCATION, Suite 700, 1255 23rd St. NW, Washington DC 20037. (202)466-1035. FAX: (202)296-2691. Art Director: Peter Stafford. Estab. 1966. Emphasizes all aspects of higher education for college and university administrators, professors, students and staff. Weekly. Circ. 80,000. Sample copy available. Mainly uses freelance talent for illustration of Op/Ed articles and occasional spots and cartoons.
Cartoons: Uses approximately 75 cartoons/year. Prefers higher education related themes, i.e., sports, campus life, high cost of tuition, student loans and energy conservation on campus. Prefers single panel with gagline; b&w line drawings or b&w washes. Send query letter with samples of style to be kept on file. Material not kept on file is returned only if requested. Reports only if interested. Buys one-time rights. Pays on publication.
Illustrations: Buys 2 freelance illustrations/week. Uses 2 illustrations/issue; buys all from freelancers. Uses a variety of styles, depending on the tone of the story. Works on assignment only. Send query letter with photostats or good quality photocopy for line work; photographs or slides for halftone work, business card and tearsheets to be kept on file. Samples are returned only if requested. Reports only if interested. Buys one-time rights. Pays $200 and up depending on size, b&w, inside. Pays on publication.

Tips: "Always looking for artists that can take a fresh approach to subjects that have been illustrated many times in the past."

*THE CHRONICLE OF PHILANTHROPY, Suite 755, 1255 23rd St.NW, Washington DC 20037. (202)466-1205. FAX: (202)296-2691. Art Director: Jojo Gragasin, Jr.. Estab. 1988. Trade journal; newspaper format "covering the news of corporate and individual giving, foundations, fundraising, taxation, regulation, management and more." Biweekly. Circ. 20,000. Accepts previously published artwork. Original artwork returned at the job's completion by request. Sample copies and art guidelines available.

Cartoons: Approached by 3 freelance cartoonists/year. Buys 1-2 freelance cartoons issue. Buys 25-30 freelance cartoons/year. Prefers a philanthropic theme. Prefers single panel, with gagline and without gagline; b&w line drawings or b&w washes. Send query letter with finished cartoons. Samples are not filed and are returned. Reports back within 30 days. Buys first rights. Pays $100, b&w.

Illustrations: Approached by 5 freelance illustrators/year. Buys 2-4 freelance illustrations/year. Artists work on assignment only. Send query letter with brochure, tearsheets and photocopies. Samples are filed or are returned by SASE if requested by artist. Reports back within 30 days. To show a portfolio, mail roughs, original/final art and b&w and color tearsheets. Buys first rights. Pays $250-450, color, inside; on publication.

*THE CONSTANTIAN, 123 Orr Rd., Pittsburgh PA 15241. (412)831-8750. Editor: Randall J. Dicks. Estab. 1970. "We (Constantian Society) are monarchists and royalists, interested in monarchy as a political system and royalty as persons and personalities." Bimonthly newsletter. Circ. 500. Previously published work OK. Sample copy for SASE with postage for 3 ounces.

Cartoons: Buys 1-2 freelance cartoons/year. "We have not used many cartoons but we are certainly willing to consider them. We take our subject seriously, but there is room for humor. It is best to write us about the idea first and send samples." Send query letter with resume and samples. To show a portfolio, mail appropriate materials and SASE. Reports within 1 month. Buys various rights. Pays $10-20, b&w line drawings; on acceptance or publication.

Illustrations: "We use a lot of decorative drawings and work which relate to our subject matter (heraldic items of different nationalities, coats of arms, monograms, etc.)." We have a number of new projects and publications in mind, and may need cover art and other illustrations for booklets or brochures. Include SASE. Reports within 1 month. Rights purchased vary. Pays $10 and up, b&w line drawings; on acceptance or publication.

Tips: "Now we are using a Macintosh computer for our journal—it has new look, and there are changes in format. Artists should have some understanding of our subject—monarchy and royalty. Cartoons must relate to monarchy or royalty—but not ridicule or deride them!"

CONSTRUCTION SUPERVISION & SAFETY LETTER, 24 Rope Ferry Rd., Waterford CT 06386. (203)442-4365. Editor: DeLoris Lidestri. Emphasizes construction supervision for supervisors who work with their crews. Covers bricklayers, carpenters, electricians, painters, plasterers, plumbers and building laborers. Semimonthly. Circ. 3,700. Original artwork not returned after publication. Free sample copy.

Cartoons: Uses 1-3 freelance cartoons/issue. Receives 5-7 submissions/week from freelancers. Uses "situations that deal with supervision in construction. Cartoons that depict both men and women as workers and/ or supervisors needed. No sexist material, please." Format: single panel, b&w line drawings with gagline. Prefers to see finished cartoons. Include SASE. Reports in 2 weeks. Buys all rights. Pays $15 on acceptance.

Tips: "Send cartoons that deal with supervision to me. But any to do with construction safety send to Winifred Bonney, editor. CL has expanded from four pages to eight pages. We have a four-page safety section now. We want to see cartoons that do no harm to anyone. Gentle humor is fine. We do not want to see sexism or racism."

*CONTEST NEWS-LETTER, Box 589, La Grange KY 40031. (502)222-9051. Editor: Deni Hamilton. Estab. 1974. Monthly newsletter "for people who enter sweepstakes as a hobby. Lists new sweepstakes rules, tips on winning, etc." Circ.700,000. Accepts previously published artwork. Original artwork not returned after publication. Sample copy and art guidelines free for SASE with first-class postage.

Cartoons: Approached by 6-8 cartoonists/year. Buys 2 cartoons/issue, 12 cartoons/year. Prefers sweepstakes related themes and styles. Prefers single panel with gagline "at the bottom; we set it in type;" vertical b&w line drawings. Send query letter with roughs. Samples are not filed and are returned by SASE if requested by artist. Reports back only if interested. Buys all rights. Pays $25, b&w; on acceptance.

Tips: "Know the subject; reflect its quirks, joys, disappointments with humor."

COSMICIRCUS PRODUCTIONS/HUMANIST NEWSLETTER, 414 S. 41st St., Richmond CA 94804. (415)451-5818. Editor: Rey King. Estab. 1974. Newsletter. Also produces spoken work audio tapes/video tapes. Newsletter contains listings of new alternative media audio and video tapes, articles on political, occult and social issues (especially conspiracy theories). Monthly. Circ. 1,500. Accepts previously published artwork.

Cartoons: Buys 3-6 cartoons/year. Preferred themes include information on cults, sexuality, anarchy, occultism, humanism, activism, alternative energy etc. Considers single, double or multiple panel; b&w line drawings. Send query letter with samples of style. Samples are filed or are returned by SASE. Reports back within 2 months. Negotiates rights purchased. Pays $5-20, b&w; on publication.

Illustrations: Buys illustraitons mainly for spots and feature spreads. Buys 3-6 illustrations/year. Considers pen & ink, airbrush, mixed media, collage and marker. Send photocopies and photographs. Samples should show "shock value, educational, alternative to status quo." Samples not filed are returned by SASE. Reports back within 2 months. To show a portfolio, mail b&w photostats and photographs. Buys one-time rights. Pays $5-20, b&w; on publication.

*THE COUNTRY PRESS, Box 5024, Durango CO 81302. Contact: Editor. Estab. 1984. Newsletter. "A yearly directory dedicated to artists and craftspersons searching for outlets for their products." Circ. varies. Free information for SASE with first-class postage. Art guidelines not available.

Cartoons: Prefers country and Victorian themes and styles; b&w line drawings. Send query letter with brochure. Samples are filed or are returned by SASE if requested. Reports back within 2 weeks.

*DETROIT FREE PRESS, 321 W. Lafayette, Detroit MI 48226. (313)222-6516. Features Graphics Director: Deborah Withey. Daily newspaper and magazine for the Detroit Metropolitan area and Michigan. Circ. 750,000, newspaper; 1.5 million, magazine. Original artwork returned after publication. Sample copy and art guidelines not available.

Illustrations: Approached by 50 freelance illustrators/year. Buys 2 freelance magazine and 3 freelance newspaper illustrations/issue. Buys 250 freelance illustrations/year. Artists work on assignment only. Prefers contemporary illustration. Send query letter with brochure, business card and samples. Samples are filed. Reports back to the artist only if interested. Write to schedule an appointment to show a portfolio, which should include original/final art and b&w and color tearsheets. Buys first rights. Pays $150, b&w; $300, color, cover; $150, b&w; $300, color, inside; on acceptance.

THE EAST HARTFORD GAZETTE, 54 Connecticut Blvd., East Hartford CT 06108. Editor: Bill Doak. Estab. 1885. Weekly newspaper emphasizing local news, politics, development. "A community newspaper with a hometown feel." Circ. 21,000. Accepts previously published material. Returns original artwork after publication. Sample copy available.

Cartoons: Buys 6 freelance cartoons/year. Prefers editorial or political cartoons and humorous illustrations on local issues. Prefers single panel with gagline; b&w line drawings, 5x7, 8x10. Send query letter with finished cartoons. Samples not filed are returned only if requested. Pays $15, b&w.

Tips: "Know our type of publication."

*EASY READER, Box 726, 1233 Hermosa Ave., Hermosa Beach CA 90254. (213)372-4611. Editor: George Wiley. Estab. 1971. Weekly newspaper emphasizing local, regional and national news typical of the alternative press. "We concentrate largely on local issues of interest to readers in the South Bay area of Los Angeles. But we also use national material, particularly with an aggressive political slant. We want high-impact art. No happy faces." Circ. 60,000. Accepts previously published material sometimes. Returns original artwork to the artist after publication. Sample copy for SASE with first-class postage.

Cartoons: Buys 5 freelance cartoons/issue. Buys 260 freelance cartoons/year. Prefers editorial or political cartoons and caricatures. Style should be biting, no-holds-barred, "but no blue material." Prefers b&w line drawings and b&w washes, 8½x11. Send query letter with samples of style, roughs and finished cartoons. Samples are filed or are returned by SASE. Reports back within 3 weeks. Buys first rights or one-time rights. Pays $50, b&w; $150, color, cover; $25, b&w; $35, color, inside; on publication. Color seldom used.

Illustration: Buys 20 or more cover illustrations/year from freelancers. Works on assignment only. Send query letter with brochure, resume and samples. Samples are filed or are returned by SASE. Reports back within 3 weeks with SASE. Call to schedule an appointment to show a portfolio. Buys first rights or one-time rights. Pays $100, b&w; $150, color, cover; on publication.

Tips: "Nothing cute, nothing sentimental, nothing folksy—we want well-conceived artwork that concisely and simply makes its point. Irreverence is okay, even encouraged, as is caricature. A sense of humor helps."

THE ECO-HUMANE LETTER, The International Ecology Society, 1471 Barclay St., St. Paul MN 55106-1405. (612)774-4971. Editor: Stephanie J. O'Brien. Publisher: R.J.F. Kramer. Periodic newsletter. Emphasizes animals/environment. Features "select article reprints, action alerts, general data for those interested in the protection of animals and nature." Circ. 6,000. Accepts previously published material. Sample copy for SASE with first-class postage, no returns guaranteed.

Cartoons: Prefers gag cartoons, editorial or political cartoons. Prefers single panel, double panel, multi-panel with or without gagline; b&w line drawings and b&w washes. Prefers any size if readable. Send query letter with samples of style, roughs and finished cartoons. Samples are not filed and are not returned. Reports back only if interested. Buys all rights. Pays up to $50, b&w; on publication.

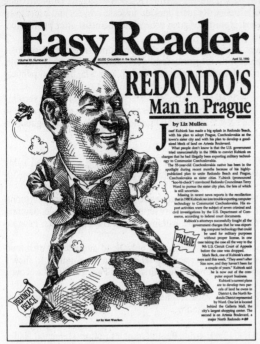

Los Angeles-based illustrator/cartoonist Matt Wuerker designed this playful caricature for a cover of Easy Reader. He received $100 for the dip-pen piece, which he completed in two days.

Illustrations: Prefers line art. Send query letter or resume. Samples are not filed and are not returned. Reports back only if interested. To show a portfolio, mail appropriate materials. Buys all rights. Pays up to $50, b&w, cover; up to $50, b&w, inside; on publication.
Tips: "Cover all bases. Volunteer for good causes."

FIGHTING WOMAN NEWS, 114382 Cronridge Dr., Owings Mills MD 21117 . Editor: Frances Steinberg. Estab. 1975. Emphasizes women's martial arts for adult women actively practicing some form of martial art; 90% college graduates. Quarterly. Circ. 5,000. Accepts previously published material, "but we must be told about the previous publication." Sample copy $3.50; art guidelines for SASE with postage for two ounces.
Cartoons: Buys 0-1 cartoon/issue from freelancers. Cartoon format open; no color. Send query letter with samples of style to be kept on file. Material not filed is returned by SASE. Reports as soon as possible. Buys one-time rights. Pays in copies.
Illustrations: Works with 1-5 freelance illustrators/year. Buys 4-10 freelance illustrations/year, 3-4 freelance illustrations/issue. "No woman black-belt beating up men or 'sexy' themes. We need ordinary women of varying ages, races, sizes, etc. wearing ordinary martial arts practice wear performing common, everyday martial arts activities. Any historical figures must be accurately garbed; fantasy or fictional characters obviously can't be accurate but must be workable."
Tips: "What works best for us is to have a few samples on file plus a rough idea of the artist's interest and availability. Then we can send out stuff that needs an illustration and ask if she can do it."

*THE FREEDONIA GAZETTE, Darien 28, New Hope PA 18938. (215)862-9734. Director: Paul Wesolowski. The purpose of this organization, the Marks Brothers Fan Club, is "to gather information on the lives and careers of the Marx Brothers and their impact on the world." It is a membership organization with approximately 400 members. Members consist of anyone interested in the Marx Brothers: students, professionals, fans.
Needs: Works with 2-3 freelance artists/year. Uses artists for illustration and layout of the *The Freedonia Gazette*. Prefers pen & ink and marker; illustrations which relate in some way to the Marx Brothers.
First Contact & Terms: Send query letter with tearsheets, photocopies and photographs. Samples are filed. Reports back within 3 weeks. To show a portfolio, mail b&w thumbnails, roughs, original/final art, tearsheets and photographs. "Portfolio should suggest the ability to draw or caricature one or more Marx Brothers."
Tips: "TFG is a not-for-profit organization. All writers, artists and editors volunteer their services. The only payment we offer is a complimentary copy of any issue your work appears in. We're oblivious to trends. We've filled a niche and are happy here."

FULTON COUNTY DAILY REPORT, 2 Park Ave., New York NY 10016. (212)973-6789. Art Director: Julie Patrick. Daily newspaper. Emphasizes law and business. Readers include upscale lawyers and executives. Circ. 4,000. Accepts previously published material. Returns original artwork to the artist after publication. Sample copy available. Art guidelines available.

Cartoons: Prefers editorial or political cartoons. Prefers current legal and national issues. Prefers single panel without gagline; b&w line drawings 30 picas wide for print. Send query letter with samples of style. Samples are filed. Reports back only if interested. Negotiates rights purchased. Pays $75, b&w; on publication.

Illustrations: Buys 52 + freelance illustrations/year. Prefers line art. Send query letter with brochure showing art style. Samples are filed. Reports back only if interested. Call to schedule an appointment to show portfolio which should include roughs, original/final art and b&w tearsheets and photographs. Negotiates rights purchased. Pays $75-150, color, inside. Pays on publication.

THE GRAPEVINE WEEKLY, 108 S. Albany St., Ithaca NY 14850. (607)272-3470. Managing Editor: Fred Yahn. "We are an alternative newsweekly that covers the news, issues, people, arts and entertainment of Tompkins County, N.Y." Weekly. Circ. 18,000. Original artwork is returned after publication. Sample copies $.50.

Cartoons: Cartoon editor: Linda McCandless. Buys 3 freelance cartoons/issue. Buys 150 freelance cartoons/year. Prefers single or multiple panel; b&w line drawings. Send query letter with samples of style. Samples are filed. Samples not filed are returned by SASE. Reports back within 4 weeks. Buys first rights. Pays $5-10, b&w.

Illustrations: Buys 3 freelance illustrations/issue. Works on assignment only. Send query letter with tearsheets. Samples are filed. Reports back within 4 weeks. Call or write to schedule an appointment to show a portfolio, which should include thumbnails, tearsheets and b&w. Buys first rights. Pays $10-50, b&w, cover; $10-15, b&w inside; on publication.

Tips: "The artist should be from Tompkins County. We look for simple line illustrations that reproduce cleanly without losing their intended shading. No intricate shading."

GUARDIAN, 33 W. 17th ST., New York NY 10011. (212)691-0404. Photo/Graphics Editor: Mahmood Nadia. Independent radical newspaper with national and international news and cultural reviews for nonsectarian leftists and activists. Weekly. Circ. 20,000. Accepts previously published material. Original artwork returned by SASE after publication. Sample copy available; art guidelines free for SASE.

Cartoons: Buys 7 freelance cartoons/issue. Prefers b&w, pen & ink, scratch board; progressive themes. Prefers single, double or multiple panel; b&w line drawings. "Third world, gay and lesbian artists especially encouraged to submit work." Send query letter with sample of style not larger than 8½x11" to be kept on file. Material not filed is returned by SASE. Reports only if interested. Write for appointment to show portfolio. Negotiates rights purchased. Pays $15, b&w; on publication.

Illustrations: Buys 3 freelance illustrations/issue. "We need left-wing political themes." Themes: progressive politics, issues. Send query letter and photocopies not larger than 8½x11" to be kept on file. Samples not filed are returned by SASE. Reports only if interested. To show a portfolio, mail original/final art, b&w tearsheets, photostats and photographs. Negotiates rights purchased. Pays $15, b&w, cover, inside; on publication.

HIGH COUNTRY NEWS, Box 1090, Paonia CO 81428. (303)527-4898. Editor: Betsy Marston. Emphasizes economic and environmental issues, Rocky Mountain regional pieces for national audience, all ages, occupations. Biweekly. Circ. 8,000. Accepts previously published material and simultaneous submissions. Original artwork returned after publication if accompanied by postage.

Illustrations: Uses 5 freelance illustrations/issue; buys 3 freelance illustrations/issue. Send query letter with samples and/or tearsheets to be kept on file. Prefers photocopies as samples. Samples not kept on file are returned by SASE. Reports within 1 month. Buys one-time rights. Pays after publication.

INTENSIVE CARING UNLIMITED, 910 Bent Lane, Philadelphia PA 19118. (215)233-4723. Editor-in-Chief: Lenette Moses. Estab. 1983. Bimonthly newsletter. "Our publication provides support and information for parents whose children are premature or high-risk, those with handicaps or medical problems, parents going through high-risk pregnancy and grieving parents." Circ. 3,000. Accepts previously published material. Returns original artwork after publication. Sample copy and art guidelines available.

Cartoons: Uses 1 freelance cartoon/issue. Buys 5-6 freelance cartoons/year. Prefers humorous illustrations. Interested in family issues. Prefers single panel with or without gagline; b&w line drawings, 4x2. Call editor to schedule an appointment to show a portfolio, or send query letter with samples of style. Samples are filed and are not returned. Reports back within 3 weeks.

Illustrations: Uses 12 freelance illustrations/issue. Prefers line art. Call editor to schedule an appointment to show a portfolio, or send query letter with samples. Samples are filed or are returned if requested. Reports back within 3 weeks.

Tips: "As a nonprofit organization, we are not able to pay for artwork. However, artists may retain all rights. We will use almost any quality line drawing of family topics, offering an artist exposure to our circulation of 3,000. Chance of acceptance is increased when artist contacts editor for list of upcoming article topics."

*ISTHMUS, 14 West Mifflin St., Madison WI 53703. (608)251-5627. Art Director: Christine Dehlinger. Estab. 1976. Weekly tabloid. "Weekly urban newspaper: hard news and analysis, lifestyle and arts/entertainment. Features, opinion and reviews. Readers are 25-49, educated, affluent. Citywide distribution." Circ. 55,000. Original artwork not returned after publication. Sample copy free for SASE with first-class postage and 9×12 SAE. Art guidelines not available.
Cartoons: Approached by 40 freelance cartoonists/year. Buys 3 freelance cartoons/issue. Buys 156 freelance cartoons/year. Prefers single, double or multiple panel and b&w line drawings. Send query letter with finished cartoons (photocopies). Samples are filed. Reports back to the artist only if interested. Rights purchased vary according to project. Pays $15, b&w; on publication.
Illustrations: Approached by 20 freelance illustrators/year. Buys 1-3 freelance illustrations/issue. Buys 20 freelance illustrations/year. Artists work on assignment only. Send query letter with samples. Samples are filed. Reports back to the artist only if interested. To show a portfolio, mail b&w tearsheets and photocopies. Rights purchased vary according to project. Pays $50, b&w, cover; $20, b&w, inside.
Tips: "Send samples every few months. Have distinctive style, but be versatile. Must be able to work on short notice."

THE JOURNAL, Addiction Research Foundation, 33 Russell St., Toronto, Ontario M5S 2S1 Canada. (416)964-9235. Editor: Anne MacLennan. Concerns drug and alcohol research, treatment, prevention and education. Monthly. Circ. 12,000. Free sample copy and guidelines.
Cartoons: Uses cartoons occasionally; buys 1/month from freelancers. Receives 1 submission/month from freelancers. Interested in "themes relating to alcohol and other drug use." Prefers finished cartoons. Pays from $30, 3x5 minimum cartoons; on publication.
Illustrations: Buys 1 freelance illustration/month. Send photocopies. Write to schedule an appointment to show a portfolio, which should include roughs and b&w samples. Pays $200 b&w, cover and inside; on publication.

KEEPERS VOICE, 2309 State St., Saginaw MI 48602. (517)799-8208. Editor: Bob Barrington. Professional association publication emphasizing law enforcement and corrections for correctional officers and police officers. Bimonthly. Circ. 9,000. Previously published material and simultaneous submissions OK. Original work returned after publication. Sample copy and art guidelines available.
Cartoons: Uses 2-4 freelance cartoons/issue. Prefers themes related to corrections (jails and prisons); single panel with gagline. Send roughs and resume. Samples returned by SASE. Reports in 1 week. Buys all rights. Pays $50-150/b&w or color; on publication.
Illustrations: Uses 1 freelance illustration/issue. Interested in anything related to corrections (jails and prisons). Provide resume and samples to be kept on file for possible future assignments. Send resume and samples of style. Samples returned. Reports in 1 week. Buys all rights. Pays $50-150 cover; $30-100 inside, b&w line drawings and b&w or color washes; on publication.

*LAWYERS MONTHLY, 30 Court Square, Boston MA 02108. (617)227-6034. FAX: (617)227-8824. Editor: Michelle E. Bates. Estab. 1987. Trade journal; newspaper format; "a feature supplement to six law newspapers; covers law, lawyers and legal issues." Monthly. Circ. 65,000. Original artwork returned after publication. Sample copy free for SASE with first-class postage. Art guidelines not available.
Cartoons: Prefers civil litigation and law practice themes. Prefers single panel; b&w line drawings. Send query letter with finished cartoons. Samples are filed or are returned by SASE. Reports back within 1 month. Buys first rights. Pays $50, b&w.
Illustrations: Prefers b&w line drawings which illustrate concrete concepts. Prefers pen & ink and charcoal. Send query letter with SASE, tearsheets and photocopies. Samples are filed. Reports back within 1 month. To show a portfolio, mail b&w tearsheets, slides and photocopies. Buys first rights. Pays $100, b&w, cover; $50, b&w, inside.
Tips: "Send informed illustrations depicting concrete concepts or issues."

THE MANITOBA TEACHER, 191 Harcourt St., Winnipeg, Manitoba R3J 3H2 Canada. (204)888-7961. FAX: (204)831-0877. Editor: Mrs. Miep van Raalte. Estab. 1919. Emphasizes education for teachers and others in Manitoba. 4 issues/year between July 1 and June 30. Circ. 16,900. Free sample copy and art guidelines.
Cartoons: Uses less than 2 freelance cartoons/year relating to education in Manitoba. Prefers single panel, b&w line drawings with gagline. Send roughs, samples of style and SAE (nonresidents include IRC). Reports in 1 month. Pays $10, b&w, cover; $5, b&w, inside.
Illustrations: Interested in b&w line drawings for inside. Send roughs, samples of style and SAE (nonresidents include IRC). Reports in 1 month.
Tips: Especially needs cartoons and illustrations related directly to the Manitoba scene. "Inquire before sending work."

Close-up

Kerry Gavin
Illustrator

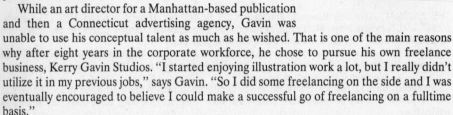

While an undergraduate at Pratt Institute, Kerry Gavin was encouraged to develop creative thinking and conceptualization. Now, as a freelance illustrator and designer, Gavin says this aspect of his artistic education has proven invaluable.

While an art director for a Manhattan-based publication and then a Connecticut advertising agency, Gavin was unable to use his conceptual talent as much as he wished. That is one of the main reasons why after eight years in the corporate workforce, he chose to pursue his own freelance business, Kerry Gavin Studios. "I started enjoying illustration work a lot, but I really didn't utilize it in my previous jobs," says Gavin. "So I did some freelancing on the side and I was eventually encouraged to believe I could make a successful go of freelancing on a fulltime basis."

Gavin discovered "I worked considerably harder and considerably longer . . . and was more satisfied with my results than in any other previous job circumstance" as a freelancer. "So I just decided to jump out and give it a shot."

To be sure, Gavin has been a smashing success on his own. From his studio in his Vernon, Connecticut home, he has worked in illustration for major magazines and newspapers. His impressive, diverse client list includes *The New York Times*, *The Washington Post*, *Family Circle*, *Industry Week*, *Glamour*, *The Boston Globe*, *Good Housekeeping*, *The Utne Reader*, *Prevention*, *Publishers Weekly*, The Oxford University Press, *Golf Illustrated*, *Playboy* and *The Cleveland Plain Dealer*. For his efforts Gavin has received recognition from several peer groups. The Society of Illustrators, United Press International, The Connecticut Art Directors Club, The Ad Club of New Jersey and many others have awarded Gavin for excellence in his field.

The switch from the corporate climate to self-employment was an "easy evolution," says Gavin, especially with budgeting his time and dealing with art directors and deadlines. "As an art director, I was the one buying services from illustrators. I became familiar with what the art director expects. So in that context it was easy for me to understand what to do when the time came to invert the positions."

Gavin feels that his home studio provides an excellent environment for his illustration. "I have few interruptions. My commute is minimal and I prefer it that way. I think I have the discipline it takes to get up and go to work every day. My average day is fairly long—usually 10-12 hours. I've been fortunate to get a good amount of work."

Gavin's first steady client was *The Hartford Courant* and he has since continued to work for major newspapers. But the market for magazines has grown substantially, prompting the illustrator to seek more clients in the magazine field. "Magazines have become a big part of what I'm doing—and a lot of it has to do with marketing. There are more magazines and thus more opportunities for assignments." He mentions that periodicals comprise 60-70 percent of his client workload.

Magazine work is also more appealing because of pay scale, he says. Magazines pay more because color is used more frequently, and color illustration generally leads to a bigger paycheck.

Many of Gavin's clients present him with a general, loose art direction. "The art directors I've worked with steadily over the last few years have not had firm ideas. That's why they call me, because they know they don't need firm ideas. Some people need to be channeled more ... to help them narrow down the way they execute a piece. I like the room I'm given because I work best with conceptual freedom—and this has resulted in a steadiness of clients. My work will be off the wall a bit, but they (art directors) seem to know which wall it will bounce off."

Although he does not recommend fulltime freelancing for every illustrator, Gavin believes that with a few smart marketing steps, a willing and talented artist can succeed. Gavin points out the basic rule of "knowing your style and your potential markets" as the most important. "It would be nice to just go in and say 'Oh, I think I'll do work for *Time*,' but if you don't do their style, you may be beating your head against the wall."

Second, generate a list of possible clients. Gavin's first resource for contacts was *Artist's Market*, but he also advises to "go to as many newsstands as possible" to scope out magazines and newspapers that would be interested in a particular style of work. When finding potential publications, copy the masthead in order to find the person to contact directly for submission information—usually the art director. College libraries are also a great resource because they carry trade publications and other publications that are not found on the newsstands.

After doing all the legwork and research, Gavin suggests a freelancer either do a mailing or walk his portfolio around to possible clients. In most cases though, unless one lives in a major publishing center, hoofing around town to find clients is too inefficient in the long run.

For an effective mailing, Gavin suggests narrowing all contacts to a feasible mailing list and sending work samples. Tearsheets of previously published work ("never send the original," warns Gavin) or reproductions of that work are the most acceptable. Reproductions, such as the color postcards Gavin has used for the last eight years, are surprisingly inexpensive and have a turnaround time of about six weeks.

After initial contacts are made, repeat mailings, more research, more legwork and, above all, outstanding and prompt illustration are a must to keep a steady list of active clients.

—Brian C. Rushing

Used to accompany an article in the Boston Globe, this black-and-white illustration conveys Gavin's ability to conceptualize and gives one a sense of the enjoyment he has doing it. It is not a repeat of what is said in the article, but rather a playful addition.

MILWAUKEE LABOR PRESS, 633 S. F Hawley Rd., Milwaukee WI 53214. (414)771-7070. Managing Editor: Carole Casamento. Estab. 1942. Tabloid. "Readership consists of members of AFL-CIO and Teamster Unions and their families. Advocacy journalism with views of organized labor." Monthly. Circ. 86,000. Accepts previously published artwork. Original artwork is returned after publication. Sample copy available.
Cartoons: Buys 1 freelance cartoon/issue. Buys 12 freelance cartoons/year. Prefers themes dealing with labor vs. big business, issues such as financial, world situation, unemployment, buy American. Prefers cartoons with gagline; b&w line drawings. Send query letter with finished cartoons. Samples not filed are returned by SASE. Reports back within 5 days. Buys first rights. Pays $25, b&w; on acceptance.
Illustrations: Buys 1 freelance illustration/issue. Buys 12 freelance illustrations/year. Considers pen & ink, collage, marker, charcoal pencil and calligraphy. Send query letter with photocopies. Reports back within 5 days. To show a portfolio, mail b&w original/final art. Buys first rights. Pays $25, b&w; on acceptance.
Tips: "The front page and/or editorial page" are most open to illustrators.

NATIONAL ENQUIRER, Lantana FL 33464. Cartoon Editor: Michele L. Cooke. Weekly tabloid. Circ. 6,000,000.
Cartoons: Buys 450 freelance cartoons/year on "all subjects the family reader can relate to, especially animal and husband-wife situations. Captionless cartoons have a better chance of selling here." Receives 2,000 freelance cartoons/week, buys 9 freelance cartoons/week. Especially needs Christmas cartoon spread (submit by July). Mail 8½ × 11" art. SASE or material is discarded. Reports in 3 weeks. "No portfolios, please." Buys first rights. Pays $300 maximum, b&w single panel; $40 every panel thereafter; on acceptance. "No critiques of artwork given."
Tips: "Study 5-6 issues before submitting. Check captions for spelling. New submitters should send introductory letter. All cartoonists should include phone and social security number on cartoon back. Know your market. We have no use for political or off-color gags. Neatness counts and sloppy, stained artwork registers a negative reaction. Besides neatness, we also look for correct spelling and punctuation on captions and in the body of the cartoon, accurate rendering of the subject (if the subject is a duck, make it look like a duck and not a goose, swan or chicken), and *most important* is visual impact! Prefers 8½ × 11 instead of halfs."

NETWORK WORLD, 161 Worcester Rd, The Meadows, Framingham MA 01701. (508)875-6400. Art Director: Dianne Barrett. Tabloid. Emphasizes news and features relating to the communications field. Weekly. Returns original artwork after publication.
Illustrations: Number purchased/issue varies. Themes depend on the storyline. Works on assignment only. Send query letter with brochure and photocopies to be kept on file. Write for appointment to show portfolio. Reports only if interested. Buys first rights. Pays $175 and up, b&w; $300 and up, color, inside; on acceptance.

NEW YORK ANTIQUE ALMANAC, Box 335, Lawrence NY 11559. (516)371-3300. Editor: Carol Nadel. Estab. 1975. For art, antiques and nostalgia collectors/investors. Monthly tabloid. Circ. 52,000. Reports within 4-6 weeks. Previously published work OK. Original artwork returned after publication if requested. Free sample copy.
Cartoons: Uses 1 freelance cartoon/issue; buys 1 freelance cartoon/issue. Receives 1 submission/week from freelancers. Interested in antique, nostalgia and money themes. Prefers finished cartoons. Include SASE. Reports in 4 weeks. Buys all rights, but may reassign rights to artist after publication. Pays $25, b&w; on publication.

NEWS & VIEWS, Suite 1122, 4450 General DeGaulle, New Orleans LA 70131. (504)367-0711. Contact: Huey Mayronne. Monthly newsletter. Emphasizes installment lending repossessions. Circ. 30,000. Accepts previously published material. Returns original artwork to the artist after publication. Sample copy available. Art guidelines not available.
Cartoons: Prefers gag cartoons, editorial or political cartoons, caricatures and humorous illustrations. Prefers single, double or multiple panel with or without gagline. Send query letter with finished cartoons. Samples are filed or are returned only if requested by artist. Reports back within 1 month. Negotiates rights purchased. Pays on acceptance.
Illustration: Buys various freelance illustrations/year. Works on assignment only. Send query letter with brochure showing art style, resume, business card and samples. Samples are filed or are returned if requested. Reports back within 1 month. To show a portfolio, mail original/final art. Buys all rights. Pays on acceptance.
Tips: "Send a brief resume, samples and approximate prices."

NEWSDAY, 235 Pinelawn Rd., Melville NY 11050. (516)454-3508. Art Director: Jack Sherman. Daily newspaper. Circ. 500,000. Original artwork returned after publication. Sample copy and art guidelines available.
Illustrations: Buys 4-5 freelance illustrations/week. Send query letter with brochure showing art style. Samples not filed are returned. Reports only if interested. Call to schedule an appointment to show a portfolio, which should include original/final art, final reproduction/product, b&w and color tearsheets, photostats and photos. Buys one-time rights. Pays $350 for b&w and $400 for color, cover; $100-250 for b&w; $150-300 for color, inside. Pays on publication.

Tips: "Let your portfolio talk for you."

NORTH MYRTLE BEACH TIMES, Box 725, North Myrtle Beach SC 29597. (803)249-1122 or 249-3525. FAX: (803)249-7012. Publisher: Pauline L. Lowman. Estab. 1971. Semiweekly. Circ. 9,500. Simultaneous submissions OK. Original work returned after publication if requested. Free sample copy and art guidelines.
Cartoons: Buys approximately 200 freelance cartoons/year. Uses 2 cartoons/issue. Interested in editorial themes; double panel b&w line drawings with gagline. Send query letter with resume and samples of style. Samples returned by SASE. Reports in 2 weeks. To show a portfolio, mail appropriate materials or call to schedule an appointment. Material not copyrighted. Pays $5-15, b&w; on acceptance.
Illustrations: Uses editorial themes. Send query letter with samples of style. Samples returned by SASE. Reports in 2 weeks. Material not copyrighted. Pays on publication.
Tips: "Be original and able to express ideas well. Be neat with work and have interesting samples to show. New trends include more graphics and color being used throughout."

NORTHEAST OUTDOORS, Box 2180, Waterbury CT 06722-2180. (203)755-0158. FAX: (203)755-3480. Editor: Jean Wertz. Estab. 1968. Emphasizes all facets of camping and hiking, with articles on camping areas, equipment and individual accounts of trips. For campers living in the Northeastern states. Monthly. Circ. 14,000. Free sample copy and guidelines for photos and art.
Cartoons: Uses 1 cartoon/issue. Interested in family camping and recreational vehicles, all in Northeastern states setting; single panel with gagline. Send finished cartoons and SASE. Reports in 2-4 weeks. Buys one-time rights. Pays $20, b&w line drawings; on acceptance.
Illustrations: "We rarely use illustrations unless accompanying a story; drawings to accompany a manuscript would be a welcome change (rarely do we find writer/artists submitting). In terms of marketing, an artist could send a few samples along with a query letter to find out if any upcoming stories need illustrations."
Tips: Wants to see "no hunting cartoons at all. I only buy 1 fishing cartoon per year."

***NOVASCOPE**, Box 283, Upperville VA 22176. (703)687-3314. FAX: (703)687-4113. Publisher: Mark E. Smith. Estab. 1985. General interest regional magazine, "specifically history and preservation, environment, current events, personalities and lifestyles." Monthly. Circ. 60,000. Accepts previously published artwork. Original artwork returned after publication. Sample copy free for SASE with first-class postage. Art guidelines not available.
Cartoons: Approached by 6 freelance cartoonists/year. Buys 1-2 freelance cartoons/issue. Buys 20 cartoons/year. Prefers styles which are reproduceable in b&w, like pen & ink. Prefer single panel; b&w line drawings. Send query letter with finished cartoons. Samples are filed. Reports back to the artist only if interested. Buys one-time rights or rights purchased vary according to project. Pays $15, b&w.
Illustrations: Approached by freelance 25 illustrators/year. Buys 1-2 freelance illustrations/issue. Buys 20 freelance illustrations/year. Prefers tasteful themes and styles, family acceptable. Prefers pen & ink, collage, airbrush, marker and charcoal. Send query letter with brochure, resume, SASE, tearsheets and photostats. Samples are filed. Reports back to the artist only if interested. To show a portfolio, mail thumbnails and b&w photostats. Pays $15, b&w; on publication.

***NUTRITION HEALTH REVIEW**, 171 Madison Ave., New York NY 10016. (212)679-3590. Features Editor: Frank Ray Rifkin. Tabloid. Emphasizes physical health, mental health, nutrition, food preparation and medicine. For a general audience. Quarterly. Circ. 165,000 paid. Accepts simultaneous submissions. Sample copy for SASE with first-class postage.
Cartoons: Uses 10 cartoons/issue. Interested in health, diet, illness, medications and psychology. Prefers single panel with gagline; b&w line drawings, 5x4. Send finished cartoons; samples returned by SASE if not purchased. Reports within 30 days. Buys first rights. Pays $15+, b&w; on acceptance.
Illustrations: Buys 10 freelance illustrations/issue. Send brochure showing art style to be kept on file; call or write for appointment to show portfolio, which should include roughs and original/final art. Samples returned by SASE. Buys first rights. Pays $50 and up; on acceptance.

***OFFSHORE, The Boating Magazine of New England, NY and NJ**, 220-9 Reservoir St., Needham MA 02194. (617)449-6204. Art Director: Dave Dauer. Monthly. Circ. 35,000. Accepts previously published material. Original artwork returned after publication. Sample copy for SASE with $2 postage.
Cartoons: Buys 2 cartoons/issue from freelancers. Prefers single panel; b&w line drawings. Send query letter with samples of style to be kept on file. Material not filed is returned by SASE. Reports within 1 week. Buys first rights. Pays $30-50, b&w; on acceptance.
Illustrations: Buys 2 illustrations/issue from freelancers. Prefers hard line. Works on assignment only. Send photostats or tearsheets to be kept on file. Samples not filed are returned by SASE. Reports within 1 week. Buys first rights. Pays $50-75, b&w; on acceptance.

***THE ORANGE COUNTY REGISTER**, 625 N. Grand, Santa Ana CA 92701. (714)953-7759. FAX: (714)542-5037. News Editor: Bill Dunn. Visuals Graphics Editor: Tia Lai. Estab. 1889. Newspaper. Daily with "full-color broadsheets; for a sophisticated upscale urban market, the most competitive market in the USA."

Circ. 350,000 daily; 400,000 Sunday. Accepts previously published artwork. Original artwork returned after publication. Sample copy available. Art guidelines not available.

Illustrations: Approached by 50-75 freelance illustrators/year. Buys 15 freelance illustrations/year. Works on assignment only. Preferred themes or styles depend on story assigned. Send query letter with brochure, resume, business card and samples. Samples are filed. Reports back only if interested. Call or write to schedule an appointment to show a portfolio, which should include b&w and color tearsheets, photographs and slides. Buys one-time rights. Pays $150, b&w; $300, color, cover; $75, b&w; $200, color, inside; on publication.

Tips: "Show solid work, the ability to be dependable and make deadlines. You need to be able to show strong conceptual work."

PARENTS & TEENAGERS MAGAZINE, Group Publishing, Box 481, 2890 N. Monroe, Loveland CO 80539. (303)669-3836. FAX: (303)669-3269. Art Director: Jean Bruns. Estab. 1988. An interdenominational newsletter providing encouragement and information on current issues affecting teenagers, for Christian families with teenagers. Bimonthly. Original artwork is returned after publication if requested. Sample copy $1. Art guidelines free for SASE with first-class postage.

Cartoons: Buys 1-3 freelance cartoons/issue. Prefers cartoons related to teenage or family themes. Prefers a "well-developed, contemporary, professional style. No sexual innuendo or ethnic or religious putdowns." Prefers single panel with gagline; b&w line drawings or washes. Send finished cartoons. Samples are photocopied for files. Samples not filed are returned by SASE. Reports back within 1 month. Buys one-time rights. Pays $40-60 negotiable, b&w; on publication.

Illustrations: Buys illustrations mainly for spots, b&w only. Buys up to 10 illustrations/issue. Works on assignment only. Prefers pen & ink; considers mixed media, pencil, wash and pastel. Send query leter with brochure, tearsheets, photostats, photocopies and slides. "Show a professional attitude, technique and style, good conceptual ability, and the ability to translate an idea into a unique, well-crafted illustration." Samples are filed. Reports back only if interested. Call or write to schedule an appointment to show a portfolio, which should include original/final art, tearsheets, slides and photostats. Buys first rights "usually. Occasionally negotiates additional rights." Pays $25 minimum, b&w, inside; on publication.

Tips: "Demonstrate an ability to depict different age groups well and a sense of contemporary style."

THE PEACE NEWSLETTER, 924 Burnet Ave., Syracuse NY 13203. (315)472-5478. Estab. 1936. Newsletter. "*The Peace Newsletter* is a Central New York voice for peace and justice. Reporting on local, national and international politics and human rights issues." Monthly. Circ. 5,000. Accepts previously published artwork. Original artwork is returned after publication if requested. Sample copy free for SASE with first-class postage. Art guidelines not available.

Cartoons: Acquires 5 cartoons/issue. "We cannot buy artwork or cartoons—people donate their art." Prefers cartoons with political slant. Send query letter with finished cartoons. Samples are filed. Reports back only if interested. "We do not pay for submissions."

Illustrations: Uses illustrations mainly for covers, spots and article highlights. Uses 60 illustrations/year. Prefers pen & ink and photography. Also uses marker and calligraphy. Send query letter with photographs. Reports back only if interested. To show a portfolio, mail original/final art and b&w photographs.

Tips: "Just send us materials we can use!"

*THE PIPE SMOKER'S EPHEMERIS, 20-37 120 St., College Point NY 11356. Editor/Publisher: Tom Dunn. Estab. 1964. Newsletter. "Irregular" quarterly. "For pipe smokers and anyone else who is interested in its varied contents." Accepts previously published artwork. Original artwork not returned after publication. Sample copies free for SASE with first-class postage. Art guidelines not available.

Cartoons: Send query letter with finished cartoons. Samples are filed or are returned. Reports back within 1 week.

Illustration: Send query letter with samples. Samples are filed or are returned. Reports back within 1 week. To show a portfolio, mail original/final art. "We do not pay for submissions but do provide free copies of issue wherein artwork appears."

Tips: Send "material suitable to journal; be willing to accept international exposure/fame."

*POSTCARD CLASSICS, Box 8, Norwood PA 19074. Editor: Dr. James Lewis Lowe. Estab. 1960. "A bimonthly journal for collectors, dealers and archivists of antique (pre-1920) picture postcards including views, greetings and picture postcards issued for special events, i.e., expositions, fairs, parades, elections, etc." Circ. 1,000. Returns original artwork after publication. Sample copy for large SASE with 3 oz. first-class postage.

Cartoons: Buys 1 freelance cartoon/issue. Buys 8-10 freelance cartoons/year. Seeks "dignified humor relating to postcards." Prefers single panel with gagline; b&w line drawings, 4x5. Send finished cartoons. Samples are filed. Does not report back. Pays in copies.

Tips: Does not want to see "slapstick or 'adult' " artwork.

PRESS-ENTERPRISE, Box 792, Riverside CA 92502. (714)684-1200. Assistant Managing Editor/Features & Art: Sally Ann Maas or Art Director: Carolita Feiring. Daily general circulation newspaper in Southern California. Circ. 155,000. Original artwork returned after publication.
Illustrations: Buys 1 freelance editorial illustration/week. Works on assignment only. Send query letter, resume and samples to be kept on file. Samples not filed are returned only if requested. Negotiates rights purchased. Write for appointment to show portfolio. Pays for illustration by the project, $35-150; on acceptance.
Tips: "Resume and samples absolute necessity." Looks for "ability to conceptualize editorially; the ability to draw well is not enough." A common mistake freelancers make is "not learning about the publication before selecting portfolio pieces."

PUBLICATIONS CO., 7015 Prospect Pl. NE, Albuquerque NM 87110 . (505)884-7636. Estab. 1956. Emphasizes general business for companies, service organizations, etc. and journalism in schools. Monthly. Accepts previously published material. Sample copy and art guidelines free for SASE.
Cartoons: Buys 100 freelance cartoons/year. Buys several cartoons/issue from freelancers. Prefers business, industry, factory, schools, and teen situations, plus seasonal material as themes. Prefers single panel with gagline; b&w line drawings. Send query letter with samples of style or finished cartoons. Material not filed is returned by SASE. Reports within 1 month. Buys reprint rights. Pays $5-10; on acceptance.
Illustrations: Works with 8 freelance illustrators/year. Buys 100 illustrations/year from freelancers. Prefers business, industry, factory, school and teen situations, plus seasonal material as themes. Send query letter with original art. Samples not filed are returned by SASE. Reports within 1 month. Buys reprint rights. Pays $25-40, b&w; on acceptance.

PURRRRR! The Newsletter for Cat Lovers, HCR 227, Islesboro ME 04848. (207)734-6745. Publisher/ Editor: Agatha Cabaniss. Estab. 1981. Bimonthly newsletter. "Want humorous, upbeat slant. Mixture of solid news and humor. Interested in people working with animal welfare. Includes cartoons and poems." Circ. over 400. Accepts previously published material. Returns original artwork after publication. Sample copy $2.
Cartoons: Buys 15-18 freelance cartoons/year. Buys 2-3 freelance cartoons/issue. Prefers gag cartoons or humorous illustrations featuring cats. Prefers single panel, double panel or multiple panel with or without gagline; b&w line drawings. Send query letter with samples of style, roughs or finished cartoons. Samples are filed "if we might want them in the future." Samples not filed are returned by SASE. Reports back within 7 days. Buys one-time rights. Pays $5-10, b&w; on acceptance.
Tips: The most common mistake freelancers make is "remaking a cartoon for a cat cartoon. We see a good market for beginning cartoonists developing."

*S.F. WEEKLY, 230 Ritch St., San Francisco CA 94107. (415)541-0700. Art Director: Rupert Kinnard. News and entertainment magazine; newspaper format; "arts and entertainment alternative, committed to representing the diversity of the Bay Area—to include men, women, people of color, lesbians, gays, etc." Weekly. Circ. 60,000. Accepts previously published artwork. Original artwork returned after publication. Sample copy available. Art guidelines not available.
Cartoons: Approached by 15 freelance cartoonists/year. Buys 2 freelance cartoons/issue. Buys 104 freelance cartoons/year. Prefers cartoons with a political slant; single panel, b&w line drawings. Send query letter with photocopies. Samples are filed. Reports back only if interested. Buys one-time rights. Pays $25, b&w; $50, color.
Illustrations: Approached by 100 freelance illustrators/year. Uses freelance artists mainly for cover illustrations and spot illustrations for articles. Buys very few illustrations/year. Works on assignment only. No particular themes preferred. Prefers pen & ink. Send query letter with brochure, SASE, tearsheets, photocopies and photostats. Samples are filed. Reports back only if interested. To show a portfolio, mail tearsheets and photocopies. Buys one-time rights. Pays $50, b&w; $90, color, cover; $30, b&w; $50, color, inside. Pays on publication.
Tips: "The only way to break into the *S.F. Weekly* is to be very unique and political, with an appreciation and respect for the diversity of our total community."

*SALESMANSHIP AND FOREMANSHIP AND EFFECTIVE EXECUTIVE, Dartnell Corporation, 4660 N. Ravenswood Ave., Chicago IL 60640. (312)561-4000. FAX: (312)561-3801. Art Director: G.C. Gormaly, Jr. Emphasizes salesmanship. Monthly. Previously published material OK.
Cartoons: Uses 1 freelance cartoon/issue. Buys approximately 150 freelance cartoons/year. Prefers single panel with or without gagline, b&w line drawings or b&w washes. Send query letter and samples of style. Samples returned. Reports in 1 month. Negotiates rights purchased. Pays $20-50, b&w; on acceptance.
Illustrations: Uses illustrations occasionally; seldom buys from freelancers. Send query letter and samples of style to be kept on file for possible future assignments. Samples not kept on file are returned. Reports in 2 months. Buys reprint rights. Pays $100-300 cover, $100-150 inside, b&w line or tone drawings; on acceptance.

San Francisco artist Roger Licot received $75 for this pen-and-ink illustration for the San Francisco Weekly. Art director Rupert Kinnard was looking for a "clean and simple design technique," and says the piece is successful because "it works well with the headline and is immediately intriguing."

© 1990 Roger Licot

SAN ANTONIO LIGHT, Box 161, San Antonio TX 78291. (512)271-2704. Assistant Managing Editor: Jeffrey Heinke. Daily newspaper. Circ. 160,000 daily, 240,000 Sunday.
Cartoons: Buys 5 freelance cartoons/week. Buys 200 freelance cartoons/year. Prefers editorial or political cartoons and humorous illustrations. Prefers b&w line drawings and b&w and color washes. Send query letter with samples of style. Samples are filed and are not returned. Reports back only if interested. Buys one-time rights. Pays $50, b&w; $75-85, color; on acceptance.
Illustration: Buys 30-50 freelance illustrations/year. Works on assignment only. Send query letter with brochure. Samples are filed and are not returned. Reports back only if interested. To show a portfolio, mail tearsheets or photostats. Buys one-time rights. Pays $75-150, b&w, $100-300, color, cover; on acceptance.
Tips: "I work with tight deadlines (3-7 days) very often. However, we use a lot of illustration."

SAN FRANCISCO BAY GUARDIAN, 520 Hampshire St., San Francisco CA 94110. (415)255-3100. Art Director: John Schmitz. For "a young, liberal, well-educated audience." Circ. 70,000. Weekly newspaper. Include SASE. Pays 60 days after publication.
Cartoons: Run weekly in "Local Color" column. Prefers local cartoonists. Pays $15.
Illustrations: Weekly assignments given to local artists. Pays $25-50.
Tips: "New artists must submit samples and letter/resume before calling. No portfolio reviews are given without previous written introduction. Turnaround time is generally short, so long-distance artists generally will not work out."

SKYDIVING, Box 1520, DeLand FL 32721. (904)736-9779. Editor: Michael Truffer. Emphasizes skydiving for sport parachutists, worldwide dealers and equipment manufacturers. Monthly. Circ. 8,600.
Cartoons: Uses 1-2 cartoons/issue; buys 0-1 freelance cartoons/issue. Receives 1-2 submissions/week from freelancers. Interested in themes relating to skydiving or aviation. Prefers single panel b&w line drawings with gagline. Send finished cartoons or samples of style and SASE. Reports in 1 week. Buys one-time rights. Pays $10 minimum for b&w; on publication.
Tips: Artists "must *know* parachuting; cartoons must be funny."

SOUTHERN ILLINOISAN, 710 N. Illinois, Carbondale IL 62901. (618)529-5454. FAX: (618)457-2935. Marketing Director: Sharon Walters. Estab. 1947. Daily newspaper emphasizing "regional and world news covering nine counties in southern Illinois." Circ. 38,500 (Sunday). Returns original artwork to the artist after publication. Sample copy avilable.

Cartoons: Prefers editorial or political cartoons and caricatures, national issues. Prefer single panel b&w line drawings. Send query letter with samples of style, roughs and finished cartoons. Samples returned by SASE. Reports back only if interested. Negotiates rights purchased. Pays on acceptance.

Illustration: Buys 10 freelance (local, by assignment) illustrations/year. Prefers line art. Works on assignment only. Send query letter with samples. Samples are not filed and are returned by SASE if requested. Reports back only if interested. Write to schedule an appointment to show a portfolio which should include thumbnails, roughs, b&w and color original/final art, tearsheets, final reproduction/product, photostats and photographs. Negotiates rights purchased. Pays on acceptance.

Tips: "Remember you are competing with syndicated work. Find a niche that you do extremely well and that also has interest for my readers, my market."

THE STATE JOURNAL-REGISTER, 1 Copley Plaza, Box 219, Springfield IL 62705. (217)788-1477. Graphics Editor: Barry Locher. Estab. 1831. Emphasizes news and features for the town and surrounding area. Daily. Circ. 70,000.

Illustrations: Buys 25-40 illustrations/year. Uses freelance artists mainly for covers and section fronts. "Uses approximately 6-7 photographs/issue and occasionally graphs, charts, maps, artwork. We buy only some illustrations from freelancers, not all. Staff does some work." Works on assignment only. Send query letter with samples to be kept on file. Samples are returned if not kept on file. Negotiates rights purchased. Pays $100, b&w; $175, color; on publication.

Tips: "We use cartoons and illustrations, either straightforward or abstract styles. I do not want to see any layout or advertising. If you send published illustrations, I like to have some indication of the content of the story the illustration accompanied. Also like to have some indication of how fast the artist can turn out work, as newspapers generally require a quicker turnaround time."

*STETHOSCOPE, DIGEST, Physicians Planning Service, 292 Madison Ave., New York NY 10017. (212)949-5900. Editor: James J. Arden, American Professional Practice Association and the National Association of Residents and Interns. Bimonthly economic newsletters geared toward in-practice physicians, residents and interns. Circ. 50,000. Returns original artwork after publication. Sample copy for SASE with first-class postage.

Cartoons: Buys 1 freelance cartoon/issue from freelancers. Prefers single panel with or without gagline; b&w line drawings and b&w washes. Send query letter with roughs. Samples are filed or are returned by SASE. Reports back within 4 weeks only if interested. Negotiates rights purchased. Pays $25-50, b&w; on publication.

*SUDS 'N' STUFF, Box 6402, Oceanside CA 92056. (619)724-4447/940-0605. Publisher: Michael J. Bosak, III. Estab. 1978. Monthly newletter emphasizing beer. "Interested in new beers on the market, interesting stories regarding old breweries, mini-breweries, national and international events concerning beer, interesting people in the beer industry, historical events concerning beer. Example: 'Why did the Pilgrims land at Plymouth Rock? They ran out of beer.' Readers are all ages, mostly college graduates." Circ. 8,000. Accepts previously published material. Original artwork is returned to artist after publication. Sample copy free for SASE with 50¢ postage.

Cartoons: Prefers mutiple panel without gagline; b&w line drawings. Send query letter. Samples not filed are not returned. Reports back within 1 month. Negotiates rights purchased. Pays $10 and up, b&w.

Illustrations: Send query letter with brochure. Does not want to see "crude work or ideas."

THE SUN, 15 Kearney Sq., Lowell MA 01852. (508)458-7100. FAX: (508)453-7177. Graphics Director: Mitchell Hayes. Estab. 1878. Daily newspaper emphasizing lifestyle, business, home, fashion, food and entertainment. "*The Sun* is a progressive mid-size daily newspaper." Circ. 58,000. Accepts previously published material. Returns original artwork to the artist after publication.

Illustration: Works with approximately 20 freelance illustrators/year. Buys approximately 125-200 freelance illustrations/year. Prefers bold woodcut style or scratch board for b&w, and all types of color work for color assignments. Majority of illustration is color. Works on assignment only. Send query letter with brochure or samples. Samples are filed and are not returned. Will call if interested. Pays $75-100, b&w; $150-300, color; on publication.

Tips: "Although we don't have a large budget, we do provide excellent tearsheets and little art direction. Through these practices we have been able to use established and talented illustrators who prefer the freedom from demanding art directors."

*THE SUN, 399 N. "D" St., San Bernardino CA 92401. (714)889-9666. Graphics Director: Betts Griffone. Newspaper. Daily, "owned by Gannett. The audience is the bedroom community of LA and Orange County." Circ. 100,000. Original artwork not returned after publication. Sample copy available; art guidelines not available.

Cartoons: Approached by 3 freelance cartoonists/year. Prefers single panel; b&w line drawings. Send query letter with examples. Samples are filed. Reports back only if interested. Buys all rights. Pays $3, b&w.

Illustrations: Approached by 3-4 freelance illustrators/year. Buys 15-20 freelance illustrations/year. Works on assignment only. Send query letter with sample. Samples are filed. Reports back only if interested. Write to schedule an appointment to show a portfolio, which should include thumbnails, roughs, original/final art and b&w and color tearsheets and slides. Buys all rights. Pays $25, b&w; $35, color, cover; $20, b&w, inside; on publication.

Tips: "Be persistent. Just keep sending samples."

*SYRACUSE NEW TIMES, 1415 W. Genesee St., Syracuse NY 13204-2156. (315)422-7011. FAX: (315)422-1721. Editor: Mike Greenstein. Estab. 1969. Tabloid. Weekly for young adults. Circ. 45,000. Accepts previously published artwork. Original artwork not returned after publication. Sample copy free for SASE with first-class postage. Art guidelines not available.

Cartoons: Approached by 100 freelance cartoonists/year. Buys 3-4 freelance cartoons/issue. Buys 150-200 freelance cartoons/year. Preferred themes are current issues. Prefers single panel. Send query letter with finished cartoons. Samples are sometimes filed or are returned by SASE. Reports back within 2 weeks only if interested. Buys one-time rights. Pays on publication.

Illustration: Approached by 12 freelance illustrators/year. Buys 1 freelance illustration/issue. Buys 20 freelance illustrations/year. Samples are not filed and are returned by SASE. Reports back in 2 weeks. To show a portfolio, mail original/final art. Buys one-time rights. Pays $50 for b&w, cover. Pays $30 for b&w, inside. Pays on publication.

Tips: "The best way to break in is to move here."

TOWERS CLUB, USA NEWSLETTER, Box 2038, Vancouver WA 98668. (206)574-3084. Chief Executive Officer: Jerry Buchanan. Emphasizes "anything that offers a new entrepreneurial opportunity, especially through mail order. The newsletter for 'Find a Need and Fill It' people." Readers are 80% male with average age of 48 and income of $35,000. Monthly except May and December. Circ. 4,000. Previously published material and simultaneous submissions OK. Original work returned after publication by SASE. Sample copy $3.

Cartoons: Uses 1 cartoon/issue; buys all from freelancers. Interested in themes of selling how-to-do-it information, showing it as a profitable and honorable profession; single panel with gagline, b&w line drawings. Send finished cartoons. Samples returned by SASE. Reports in 1 week. Buys one-time rights. Pays $15-25, b&w; on publication.

Illustrations: Uses 5-7 freelance illustrations/issue. Interested in realistic, illustrative art depicting typists, computers, small print shop operations, mail order, etc.; no comical themes. Especially needs line drawings of typists/writers/office workers, money, mail delivery, affluent people, intelligent and successful faces, etc. Send brochure showing art style. Provide samples to be kept on file for possible future assignments. Samples not kept on file are returned by SASE. Reports in 1 week. Buys one-time rights. Makes some permanent purchases. Pays $15, b&w; on acceptance.

Tips: "Newsletters are going more to using typesetting and artwork to brighten pages. Subscribe to our *TOWERS Club, USA* newsletter and study content and artwork used. Normally $60 per year, we will give 40% discount to artists who show us a portfolio of their work. Our theme will lead them to much other business, as we are about creative self-publishing/marketing exclusively. Many cartoonists have little or no genuine sense of humor. I suggest they tie in with someone who does and split the fee. Illustrators should see several copies of the publication they hope to draw for before submitting their samples. It could save a lot of postage. I do not want to see general, arty, avant-garde work."

TREASURE CHEST, (Venture Publishing Co.), #211A, 253 W. 72 St., New York NY 10023. (212)496-2234. Assistant Publisher: R. Hess. Estab. 1988. Newspaper emphasizing antiques,collectibles, collectors and collecting. Monthly.

Cartoons: Buys 1+ freelance cartoon/issue. Buys 12-15 freelance cartoons and caricatures/year. Send samples. Samples are filed or are returned by SASE. Reports back within 3 weeks. Negotiates rights purchased. Pays $20-25, b&w.

Illustrations: Prefers illustrations of antiques, collectibles, collectors and collections. Prefers line drawings. To show a portfolio, mail final reproduction/product photographs. Pays $20-30, b&w.

Tips: Uses freelance talent mainly for "covers, spots, etc." Looks for "relevant samples; rough ideas relevant to our publication."

WDS BOOK AUTHOR'S NEWSLETTER, Writers Digest School, 1507 Dana Ave., Cincinnati OH 45207. (513)531-2222. Editor: Ms. Kirk Polking. Semi-annual newsletter emphasizing writing and marketing information for Writer's Digest School students. Circ. 3,000.

Cartoons: Needs work related to the publishing of novels and nonfiction books. Buys 3-4/year. Send either finished art or roughs and SASE. Reports in 3 weeks. Pays $10, b&w.

*THE WINE SPECTATOR, Suite 2014, 601 Van Ness, San Francisco CA 94102. (415)673-2040. FAX: (415)673-0103. Production Manager: Donna Marianno Morris. Estab. 1978. Tabloid emphasizing wine for wine lovers—consumer and trade. Bimonthly. Circ. 100,000. Original artwork not returned after publication.
Illustrations: Works on assignment only. Send samples to be kept on file. Call for appointment to show portfolio. Prefers photostats or tearsheets as samples. Does not report back. Buys all rights. Pays $100-200, b&w; $200-250, color cover; $50-150, b&w; $150-200, color, inside; on publication.
Tips: "We are using more photography."

WOMEN ARTISTS NEWS, Box 3304, Grand Central Station, New York NY 10163. (212)666-6990. Editor: Rena Hansen. For women in all the arts with focus on the visual arts fields. Circ. 5,000. Photocopied submissions OK. Original artwork returned after publication. Pays on publication "when funds available." Sample copy for $3. Also uses artists for layout and brochures. Needs photographs.
Cartoons: Receives 1 submission/week from freelancers. Contact Feature Editor. Accepts cartoons on art and artists; double panel. Send finished art. Reports in 4 weeks. Pays $0-5, b&w washes.
Illustrations: Uses 20-30 illustrations (photographs)/issue; buys 4/issue from freelancers. Receives 10 submissions/week from freelancers. Provide samples (roughs) or published work to be kept on file for future assignments. Reports in 4 weeks. Pays for design by the hour, $10. Buys all rights on a work-for-hire basis.

WOMEN WISE, 38 S. Main St., Concord NH 03301. (603)225-2739. Contact: Editorial Committee. Estab. 1978. Quarterly tabloid. Emphasizes women's health and political issues. Features "updated health information with a feminist analysis. Audience is primarily women." Circ. 9,000. Accepts previously published material. Returns original artwork after publication. Sample copy and art guidelines available. Pays $15, cover; 1-year subscription, inside.
Cartoons: Buys 1 freelance cartoon/year. Prefers editorial or political cartoons. Send query letter. Reports back only if interested, but will send back originals.
Illustrations: Prefers line drawings—women and health related. Send query letter with brochure showing art style or resume, business card and samples. Samples are filed or are returned. Reports back only if interested. Call or write to schedule an appointment to show a portfolio. Pays $15, b&w, cover; on publication. Pays in subscriptions for inside.
Tips: "Seeking artists who can match art with stories, who can convey a clear feminist message through their work."

*THE WRITER'S NOOK NEWS, Suite 181, 38114 Third St., Willoughby OH 44094. (216)975-9865. Editor/Publisher: Eugene Ortiz. Estab. 1985. Newsletter. Quarterly "published for the enrichment of all writers, established or aspiring, regardless of field or genre. It covers markets, contests, events, how-to, poetry to playwriting, fiction, nonfiction, book reviews, Q&A for beginners, etc." Circ. 2,000. Returns originals after publication if requested. Sample copies for 9×12 SASE with 45¢ first-class postage. Art guidelines not available.
Cartoons: Approached by 2-3 freelance cartoonists/year. Buys 2-3 freelance cartoons/issue. Buys 6-12 freelance cartoons/year. Prefers themes related to writing. Prefers single panel, with gagline; b&w line drawings. Send query letter with finished cartoons. Samples are not filed and are returned by SASE if requested. Buys first rights. Pays $5, b&w; on acceptance.
Tips: "Get a sample copy or two, then submit a small batch of finished pieces (no more than twelve). I'll pick out what I like and return the rest with a check."

Newspapers/'90-'91 changes

The following newspapers appeared in the 1990 edition of *Artist's Market* but are not in the 1991 edition. Those which did not respond to our request for an update of their listings may have done so for a variety of reasons—they may be out of business for example, or they may be overstocked with submissions. If they indicated a reason, it is noted in parentheses after their name.

The American Newspaper Carrier
Arizona Republic
Banana Rag (asked to be deleted)
The Bridge Covered: Covered Bridge Post Cards
Cirtoen Car Club Newsletter
COA Review
The Comdex Show Daily
Crafter's Link (asked to be deleted)
The Crimson Fullmoon

The Episcopalian (out of business)
For Parents
The Foreman's Letter
The Legal Reformer and Citizens Legal Manual Series
Los Angeles Daily News
Medical Abstracts Newsletter (overstocked)
The Miami Herald (not accepting new artists)
National Librarian (not using freelance artwork)

Pennywhistle Press (asked to be deleted)
Personnel Advisory Bulletin
Psych Discourse
Southern Jewish Weekly
Telebriefs
Transport World
Union Electric News
Utility Supervision
Velonews (asked to be deleted)
The Vindicator
Westart

Music theater, dance, opera — each of these performing arts categories seeks originality, dynamic design and strong imagery, but always with the goal of passing along information. Not only do artists literally set the stage for these groups, but they also provide visual exposure through promotional materials such as programs, brochures, flyers and invitations.

The needs of these groups vary according to their particular medium. Musical groups such as symphonies require artwork mainly for posters, programs and brochures. Similarly, ballet, opera and theater companies require the talents of artists for promotional materials, but they also need scene designers and painters, costume designers and lighting specialists for their productions. Public relations director Michael Sande of A Contemporary Theatre in Seattle says he looks for freelance artists with "originality, creativity and the ability to grasp concepts from the written word — plays and discussions with theater artists (directors, playwrights and the marketing department)." Performing arts companies also look for affordability.

A recent survey done by the Theatre Communications Group found that, although attendance grew last year to an all-time high of 19 million, "many theaters across the country remain precariously poised on the brink of instability, and nearly one-half of the theaters in the study registered operating deficits for the year." Economic difficulties have also been experienced by symphonies and dance companies. The Denver Symphony declared bankrupcy last fall, and the Martha Graham Company and Dance Theatre of Harlem have been forced to lay off their dancers for two to five months this season.

It's best to work with a local performing arts group first to become acquainted with the demands of the field. If you find that you have an empathy for one category over another, perhaps a preference for dance rather than theater, then focus your efforts in your area of preference.

As with any market area, research performing arts groups as much as possible before approaching them with your work. Some groups have only seasonal needs, such as summer theaters, so check to see if this information is listed and when the group's needs are heaviest. Residencies are also available, perfect for the artist seeking summer employment and a weekly salary. For additional information, look to this section's Close-up of Randi Robin, a designer who works closely with Steppenwolf Theatre Company, 1990 Tony-award winner for its play "The Grapes of Wrath."

For further names and information regarding performing arts, consult the *American Dance Directory*, *Dance Magazine*, the *Summer Theatre Directory*, *American Theatre Association Directory*, *Theatre Profiles*, the *Music Industry Directory*, *Musical America* and the Central Theatre's *Opera/Musical Theatre Companies and Workshops in the United States and Canada*.

ALBERTA BALLET, 141 18th Ave. SW, Calgary, Alberta T25 0B8 Canada. (403)245-4222. FAX: (403)245-6573. Marketing Manager: Dorothy Evaskevich. Estab. 1966. 18 member dance ensemble.
Needs: Approached by 10 freelance artists/year. Works with 2-3 freelance artists/year. Freelance art needs are heaviest in spring. Artists work on assignment only. Uses freelance artists for advertising design, illustration and layout; brochure design and layout; poster design and illustration.
First Contact & Terms: Send query letter with photographs, photocopies and photostats. Samples are not filed and are returned. Reports back within 5 days. Call to schedule an appointment to show a portfolio, which should include slides and samples of previous work. Pays for design by the project, $600 minimum. Pays for illustration by the project, $600-1,500. Payment depends on budget and artist's experience. Buys one-time rights or all rights.
Tips: "Know something about the company before coming in."

AMERICAN BALLET, 86 Main St., Pascoag RI 02859. (401)568-0015 or 568-1680. Administrator: Paul Christiansen. Estab. 1983. "The American Ballet offers the best in ballet, from fairy tale classics to the contemporary."
Needs: Approached by 100 freelance artists/year. Works with 25 freelance artists/year. Needs "scenic artists and ballet guest artists." Prefers artists with experience in costuming, scenic design and ballet. Uses freelance artists for costume design, lighting, set design, scenery and guest ballet artists.
First Contact & Terms: Send query letter with resume. Samples are filed or are returned. Reports back within 30 days. Write to schedule an appointment to show a portfolio, which should include b&w photographs. Pays for design and illustration by the hour, $10. Rights purchased vary according to project.
Tips: "Be business-like in approach. Reliable and responsible artists are given first preference."

AMERICAN THEATRE DANCE CO., INC., Box 861, Coconut Grove FL 33233. (305)856-8825. Director: Diane Pariser. Promotion and management of dancers and musicians (bands, companies and other arts groups).
Needs: Works with 5 freelance artists/year. Freelance art needed through the year. Works on assignment only. Uses artists for advertising and brochure design, illustration and layout and poster design and illustration.
First Contact & Terms: Send query letter with brochure. Samples are filed. Reports back only if interested. Call to schedule an appointment to show a portfolio. Pays for design and illustration by the project, $100-350. Considers complexity of project and available budget when establishing payment. Buys one-time rights, reprint rights or all rights.
Tips: Artists should have "some experience doing artwork for performers."

ARDEN THEATRE COMPANY, 4940 Disston St., Philadelphia PA 19135 (street address). Box 508, Edgemont PA 19028 (mail address). (215)332-4930. General Manager: Amy L. Murphy. Estab. 1988. "Brings to life the greatest stories of all time by the greatest storytellers of all time; ultimate theatre, ranges from literary adaptation to drama to musicals."
Needs: Works with 10-20 freelance artists/year. Freelance art needs are heaviest in August-May. Artists work on assignment only. Prefers local artists only. Uses freelance artists for advertising design, illustration and layout; brochure design, illustration and layout; poster design and illustration; set design; costume design; lighting and scenery.
First Contact & Terms: Send query letter with brochure, resume, tearsheets, photographs, photocopies or "any representative work." Samples are filed. Reports back to the artist only if interested. "If artist would like information returned—please request." Call to schedule an appointment to show a portfolio or mail "any and all samples." Pays for design by the project, $100-1,000. Pays for illustration by the project, $100-300. Rights purchased vary according to project.
Tips: "Brochure/graphic design work needed now. Most hiring is done from April through October—but we are always interested in local artists' work."

THE ARKANSAS ARTS CENTER CHILDREN'S THEATRE, 10th & Commerce, Little Rock AR 72202. (501)372-4000. Artistic Director: Bradley D. Anderson. Estab. 1979. "A professional children's theater with 6 man staging and 3 tours per season (September-May). House seating is 389. We have over 2,000 subscribers and reach over 120,000 people statewide."
Needs: Number of freelance artists works with/year varies. Freelance art needs are seasonal. Needs heaviest September-May. Artists work on assignment only. Prefers artists with experience in children's theater and contemporary and classic children's literature. Uses freelance artists for brochure design and illustration, poster design and lighting.
First Contact & Terms: Send query letter with resume and SASE. Samples are not filed and are returned by SASE if requested by artist. Reports back to the artist only if interested. To show a portfolio, mail photographs and slides. Payment varies, dependent upon project and position. Rights purchased vary according to project.
Tips: "Always write first. Do not expect to be contacted unless we are interested."

ATLANTA SYMPHONY ORCHESTRA, 1293 Peachtree St. NE, Atlanta GA 30309. (404)898-1197. FAX: (404)898-9297. Director of Publications: Cynthia Bryson. Estab. 1950. Nonprofit. "Largest arts organization in the Southeast."
Needs: Approached by 15 freelance artists/year. Works with 6 freelance artists/year. Freelance art is needed throughout the year. Artists work on assignment only. Prefers local artists only. Uses freelance artists for advertising design, illustration and layout; brochure design, illustration and layout; and poster design and illustration. Various looks "but all must exemplify class and dignity."
First Contact & Terms: Send query letter. Samples are filed or are returned by SASE if requested by artist. Reports back to the artist only if interested. Write to schedule an appointment to show a portfolio or mail appropriate materials. Portfolio should include thumbnails, original/final art and b&w tearsheets and photographs. Payment to freelance artists for design and illustration depends on complexity of project, available budget and turnaround time. Rights purchased vary according to project.

Tips: "We have high-visibility work that is excellent for an artist portfolio."

BERKSHIRE PUBLIC THEATRE, INC., Box 860, 30 Union St., Pittsfield MA 01202. (413)445-4631. Director: Frank Bessell. Regional repertory theatre with an artistic and technical company of 100, an administrative staff of 15 and an audience of 30,000 yearly. "A year-round company performing classical and contemporary drama, musicals and cabarets, original works and children's theatre. Company of about 100 – is ever expanding."
Needs: Works with 10 freelance artists/year. Needs are heaviest with the beginning of each production, an average of 1/month. Uses artists for advertising and brochure design, illustration and layout; poster design and illustration; set and costume design; lighting and scenery. Prefers charcoal/pencil or silk screen photography.
First Contact & Terms: Send query letter with resume and samples to be kept on file. Call or write to schedule an appointment to show a portfolio, which should include thumbnails, roughs, original/final art, final reproduction/product and color and b&w tearsheets, photostats, photographs or "anything that best represents you." Pays by the project for design, $500 maximum; pays by the project for illustration; negotiates payment. "Sometimes barters exchanges in lieu of dollars."
Tips: Art must be "clean and sharp, meticulous detail, new and exciting, *not canned*." There is more use of warmer "Pantone colors, more creative use of layout – as a result, there is more direct collaboration to fill our needs."

BETHUNE BALLET THEATREDANSE, Suite 221, 8033 Sunset Blvd., Los Angeles CA 90046. (213)874-0481. Artistic Director: Zina Bethune. Ten member multimedia ballet company "incorporating visual technology (film, video, laser, animation and special effects) to enhance and expand the traditional theater of dance."
Needs: Works on assignment only. Uses artists for advertising, brochure, poster, program, set and costume design; lighting; scenery; film and video; special effects, i.e., lasers, image transference, etc.
First Contact & Terms: Send query letter with brochure, resume, business card and samples to be kept on file. Write for appointment to show portfolio. Prefers good representation of artist's work as samples. Samples not returned. Reports only if interested. Pays by the project, $50 minimum. Negotiates pay considering complexity of project, available budget and skill and experience of artist.
Tips: Artists should use "the movement and sweep of dance to express a variety of concepts and images. As a dance company, whose concept is a futuristic one, this helps us capture who and what we are. Research the company's needs before submitting to them and "do not send material that needs to be returned."

BOARSHEAD: MICHIGAN PUBLIC THEATER, 425 S. Grand Ave., Lansing MI 48933. (517)484-7800. Director of Marketing and Public Relations: Cheryl Dunn-Sermon. Nonprofit equity regional theater with a season running from September-May. Seating capacity 250.
Needs: Needs heaviest in late summer or early winter. Uses artists for brochure design, illustration and layout; and poster design.
First Contact & Terms: Send query letter with brochure showing art style or resume. Samples are filed or are returned by SASE if requested. Reports back within 1-2 weeks. Write to schedule an appointment to show a portfolio or mail roughs and final reproduction/product. Pays for design by the project, $50 minimum. Pays for illustration by the project. Considers how work will be used when establishing payment. Negotiates rights purchased.
Tips: "Prefer single designs to be utilized for theater productions – advertising, programs, posters and brochures."

CAPITAL REPERTORY COMPANY, Box 399, Albany NY 12201-0399. (518)462-4531. Marketing Director: Susan Phillips. Professional equity (Lort D) theatre.
Needs: Approached by 20-40 freelance artists/year. Works with 5-10 freelance illustrators and 3-6 freelance designers/year. Freelance needs are seasonal; needs heaviest from September-June. Works on assignment only. Uses freelance artists mainly for promotional pieces i.e. brochure, postcard and poster illustration. Also uses artists for advertising illustration, set and costume design, lighting and scenery. Prefers illustrations for individual plays to be used on self-mailers and in brochures.
First Contact & Terms: Send resume, tearsheets, photostats, photocopies and slides. Samples are filed or are returned if requested. Reports back only if interested. Call or write to show a portfolio, which should include b&w tearsheets and photostats. Pays for illustration by the project, $75 minimum. Considers complexity of project, skill and experience of artist and available budget when establishing payment. Buys all rights.

CENTER THEATER, 1346 West Devon Ave., Chicago IL 60660. (312)508-0200. Production Manager: R.J. Coleman. Estab. 1981. "We are a professional not-for-profit theater with a training program for actors."
Needs: Approached by 2 freelance artists/year. Works with 6 freelance artists/year. Freelance art needs are seasonal. Needs heaviest in the fall and spring. Artists work on assignment only. Uses freelance artists for advertising, brochure, poster and costume design; lighting; advertising layout; set design and scenery.

First Contact & Terms: Send query letter with brochure, resume, SASE, photographs and photocopies. Samples are filed or are returned by SASE if requested by artist. Reports back within 3 months. Write to schedule an appointment to show a portfolio, which should include photostats and slides. Pays for design by the project, $35-200. Pays for illustration by the project, $100-500. Rights purchased vary according to project.
Tips: "As a nonprofit, most of our design work is done gratis. After the initial gratis project, there is usually an opportunity for paying work if there is mutual satisfaction."

CHARLESTON BALLET, 822 Virginia St. E., Charleston WV 25301. (304)342-6541. Director/Choreographer: K. R. Pauley.
Needs: Works with 2-4 freelance artists/year. Works on assignment only. Uses artists for advertising, brochure, poster, set and costume design and scenery.
First Contact & Terms: Send a resume, tearsheets, photographs and slides. Samples are filed or are returned if requested. Reports back only if interested. Write to schedule an appointment to show a portfolio, which should include color and b&w final reproduction/product. Pays for design and illustration by the project, $100 maximum. Considers how work will be used when establishing payment. Buys reprint rights.

CHEYENNE SYMPHONY ORCHESTRA, Suite 203, Box 851, Cheyenne WY 82003. (307)778-8561. Executive Director: Betty Flood. Estab. 1954. Symphony association with 950 members; 5 subscription concerts.
Needs: Approached by 5 freelance artists/year. Works with 2 freelance artists/year. Freelance art needs are heaviest in the fall and spring. Artists work on assignment only. Prefers local artists only. Uses freelance artists for advertising design, illustration and layout and brochure design, illustration and layout.
First Contact & Terms: Send query letter with SASE and appropriate samples. Samples are filed or are returned by SASE if requested by artist. Reports back to the artist only if interested. To show a portfolio, write an appropriate letter. Pays for design or illustration by the project.

CIRCLE REPERTORY COMPANY, 161 Ave. of the Americas, New York NY 10013. (212)691-3210. FAX: (212)675-8098. Director of Communications: Gary W. Murphy.
Needs: Works with several freelance artists/year. Freelance art needs are seasonal. Needs heaviest in May and September. Works on assignment only. Uses artists for advertising and brochure design, illustration and layout; poster design and illustration.
First Contact & Terms: Send query letter with brochure showing art style or resume and samples. Samples are sometimes filed or are returned by SASE. Reports only if interested. Write to schedule an appointment to show a portfolio, which should include color and b&w thumbnails, original/final art and final reproduction/product. Negotiates payment for design and illustration. Considers complexity of project, skill and experience of artist, client's budget, how work will be used, turnaround time and rights purchased when establishing payment. Negotiates rights purchased.
Tips: "Every season brings a new look to Circle Rep. The 'look' lasts for the entire season. Artists applying to Circle Rep should take into account all elements of a theatre season including subscription brochures, newsletters, single ticket ads and benefit invitations."

CITIARTS/THEATRE CONCORD, 1950 Parkside Dr., Concord CA 94519. (415)671-3065. FAX: (415)671-3375. Contact: Richard Elliott. Produces musicals, comedy and drama year round. Assigns 30-50 freelance jobs/year.
Needs: Works with up to 10 freelance illustrators and 28 freelance designers/year. Works on assignment only. Uses artists for costume design; flyers; graphic/set design; posters; programs; theatrical lighting; advertising and brochure design, illustration and layout.
First Contact & Terms: Query, then mail slides or photos. Samples returned by SASE. Reports back on future assignment possibilities. Call or write to schedule an appointment to show a portfolio, which should include thumbnails, roughs, original/final art and b&w photographs. Pays for design by the project, $500-3,000. Pays for illustration by the project, $100-1,000.
Tips: In a portfolio, artists should "specifically include items relating to live theater productions in any way."

CIVIC BALLET CENTER AND DANCE ARTS, 25 S. Sierra Madre Blvd., Pasadena CA 91107. (818)792-0873. Director: Elly Van Dijk. Home of the Pasadena Civic Ballet, Inc., a pre-professional ballet company, a nonprofit organization. Offers classes in classical ballet, modern, jazz, creative dance for all ages and levels.
Needs: Works with about 15 freelance artists/year.
First Contact & Terms: Los Angeles-area artists preferred; performing experience a plus. Send query letter with resume to be kept on file. Reports only if interested and needed. Pays by the hour, $10-30. Considers skill and experience of artist when establishing payment.

COMMONWEALTH OPERA, INC., (formerly Project Opera), 160 Main St., Northampton MA 01060. (413)584-8811. Artistic Director: Richard R. Rescia. Productions of opera.
Needs: Needs heaviest in the fall and spring. Uses artists for set and costume design and scenery.
First Contact & Terms: "We use regional artists where possible." Send query letter with resume and photocopies to be kept on file. Samples not filed are returned by SASE. Pays for design by the hour, $6-12. Pays for illustration by the project, $250 maximum. Considers complexity of project and project's budget when establishing payment.
Tips: Looking for "abstractions that bring set design etc., down to its basic, simplest terms."

CONTEMPORARY DANCE THEATER, INC., Box 19220, Cincinnati OH 45219. (513)751-2800. Artistic Director: Jefferson James. Publicity Director: Kathy Valin. Dance company with a dance studio, also a national dance presenter.
Needs: Works with several freelance artists/year. Freelance art needed throughout the year. Uses artists for advertising, brochure, costume and poster design. Prefers contemporary but accessible look.
First Contact & Terms: Send query letter with brochure, resume and samples. Samples are not filed and are returned only if requested by artist. Reports back only if interested. Write to schedule an appointment to show a portfolio. Pays for design by the project, $50-200. Pays for illustration by the project, $25-200. Considers complexity of project, skill and experience of artist and available budget when establishing payment. Negotiates rights purchased.
Tips: The artist "needs experience presenting visual image of alternative art form. Be sensitive to its particular needs." In portfolio would like to see "work done for arts organizations or other non-mainstream organizations."

A CONTEMPORARY THEATRE (ACT), 100 W. Roy St., Seattle WA 98119. (206)285-3220. Public Relations Director: Michael Sande. Estab. 1965. "The mission of A Contemporary Theatre is to produce plays that challenge and test contemporary mores and societal perceptions and to be willing to set a theatrical tone which opens society to penetrating inquiries and examinations."
Needs: Approached by 10 freelance artists/year. Works with 2-3 freelance artists/year. Freelance art needs are seasonal. Needs heaviest from November-May. Works on assignment only. Prefers artists with experience in designing for performing arts organizations. Uses freelance artists for advertising, brochure and poster design; advertising, brochure and poster illustration; advertising and brochure layout. Prefers contemporary styles.
First Contact & Terms: Send query letter with brochure, resume and samples of promotional work. Samples are filed. Reports back to the artist only if interested. Write to schedule an appointment to show a portfolio which should include original/final art and b&w photostats and tearsheets. Pays for design by the project, $200-1,000. Pays for illustration by the project, $50-300. Rights purchased vary according to project.

THE CRICKET CONTEMPORARY THEATRE, 9 West 14th St., Minneapolis MN 55403. (612)871-3763 or 871-2244. Marketing Director: Glenn Morehouse. Production Manager: Richard Rauscher. Estab. 1971. "We are a contemporary theater producing 5 shows/season with additional special 'concerts.' We have a 213 seat house and 1,000 subscribers."
Needs: Approached by 20 freelance artists/year. Works with 25 freelance artists/year. Freelance art needs are seasonal. Needs heaviest from September-June. Artists work on assignment only. Prefers artists with experience in theater. Uses freelance artists for advertising, brochure and poster design; advertising, brochure and poster illustration; lighting and brochure layout. Style preferred depends on the play.
First Contact & Terms: Send query letter with resume. Samples are filed. Reports back to the artist only if interested. Write to schedule an appointment to show a portfolio, which should include original/final art and b&w slides. Pays for design by the project, $600 minimum. Pays for illustration by the project. "So far, all of our illustration has been donated."
Tips: "Our season runs September-June. I would suggest contacting the theater in July or August to find out what the next season's plays will be and if there are opportunities for design. We also display fine art in our lobby for each show. The Cricket's Commission on art sold is 21½%. So far, we have sold 2 pieces out of our lobby this season and around 10 pieces last season."

DANCE KALEIDOSCOPE, 429 E. Vermont, Indianapolis IN 46202. (317)634-8484. Contact: Tami Paauwe. Professional modern dance repertory company which tours the Midwest and beyond. The repertory comes largely from guest choreographers out of New York City.
Needs: Works with several freelance artists/year; needs heaviest in October, March and May. Uses artists for advertising, brochure, program, set and costume design; advertising, brochure and program layout; advertising illustration, posters, lighting and scenery. Prefers clean, bold style "that depicts movement inherent in the product." Prefers pen & ink, airbursh, charcoal/pencil, watercolor, acrylic and pastel.
First Contact & Terms: Local artists only with previous experience in the arts, "who enjoy the challenge of working within a limited budget. Artist must be willing to take direction from the board of directors." Send query letter with brochure, resume, business card, samples and tearsheets to be kept on file. Call for

appointment to show a portfolio. Samples not returned. Reports only if interested. Pays for design by the project, $0-200 average. Considers complexity of project, available budget, turnaround time and rights purchased when establishing payment.

Tips: "We want to see brochure designs, logos, letterhead designs and poster art – directly art-related, revealing fluid but bold lines/art. Artist must have an understanding of the arts (especially dance) and respect the company's need to use copy in some publications. DK is a not-for-profit organization."

DANCELLINGTON INC., Box 20346, ParkWest Finance Station NY 10025. (212)724-5565. FAX: (212)362-4183 % Mercedes. President/Artistic Director: M. Ellington. Estab. 1986. Tap dance company with 6-16 members. Performs at concerts, jazz festivals, theater works, live and taped performances.

Needs: Approached by 10 freelance artists/year. Works with 5 freelance artists/year. Freelance art is needed throughout the year. Artists work on assignment only. Prefers artists with experience in stage management and lighting design. Uses freelance artists for advertising design, illustration and layout; brochure design, illustration and layout; photography and videotape. Prefers theatrical look; variations of media and types of styles, music etc. "Entertainment is not necessarily reality."

First Contact & Terms: Send query letter with resume and photographs. Samples are filed. Reports back within 2 weeks. To show a portfolio, mail photographs. Pays for design and illustration by the project, $750-2,000. Buys first rights or negotiates rights purchased.

MARK DeGARMO AND DANCERS, Suite 24, 179 E. 3rd St., New York NY 10009. (212)353-1351. Artistic Director: Mark DeGarmo. "Mark DeGarmo and Dancers is an ensemble of six professional dancers dedicated to the development and performance of original modern dance. The variety of programs ranges from an informal lecture-demonstration to a full-evening concert with costumes, music, sets, and technical personnel. Also available are individual classes, teaching/choreographing residencies, solo or duet performances, and special children's performances." Works with 4 freelance artists/year. Freelance art needed throughout the year. Works on assignment only. Uses artists for advertising and brochure design, illustration and layout; poster design and illustration; set and costume design; lighting.

First Contact & Terms: Send query letter with cover letter, resume and xeroxes. Samples are filed or are returned by SASE. Reports back only if interested. Write to schedule an appointment to show a portfolio, which should include photostats and photographs. Pays for design and illustration by the job, $150-2,200. Considers complexity of project, skill and experience of artist, available budget, how work will be used, turnaround time and rights purchased when establishing payment. Negotiates rights purchased.

DIMENSIONS DANCE THEATER, 606 60th St., Oakland CA 94609. (415)428-2466. Contact: Booking Representative. "Dimensions Dance Theater is a modern dance company and school, which promotes the knowledge and appreciation of ethnic dance. The company presents African, jazz and modern dance idioms to create an innovative repertoire noted for its dynamism. The company consists of 15 dancers and 5 drummers."

Needs: Works with several freelance artists/year. Freelance art needed throughout the year. Works on assignment only. Uses artists for advertising, brochure and poster design; lighting and scenery.

First Contact & Terms: Send query letter with brochure. Samples are filed. Reports back only if interested. Call to schedule an appointment to show a portfolio, which should include color and b&w thumbnails, roughs, original/final art, final reproduction/product, tearsheets, photostats, photographs, slides and transparencies. Pays for design by the project, $50 minimum. "Depends on item being developed." Considers complexity of project, skill and experience of artist, available budget, how work will be used, turnaround time and rights purchased when establishing payment. Buys all rights.

Tips: Looking for "good work, creativity, affordability."

DULUTH BALLET, The Depot, 506 W. Michigan St., Duluth MN 55802. (218)722-2314. Office Staff: Willy McManus. Artistic Director: Nancy Gibson. Managing Director: Diane Jacobs. Ballet company of 8 dancers with a repertoire ranging from modern/contemporary to classical dance styles.

Needs: Works with 3-4 freelance artists/year; needs heaviest approximately one month before summer, fall and winter concerts. Uses artists for advertising design, illustration and layout.

First Contact & Terms: Send query letter with brochure, resume and samples to be kept on file. Prefers photostats and photography as samples. Samples returned by SASE if not kept on file. Call or write for appointment to show portfolio. Pays for design by the project, $50-100 average. Pays for illustration by the project, $50-200 average. Considers complexity of project, available budget, skill and experience of artist, how work will be used, turnaround time and rights purchased when establishing payment.

Tips: "Make sure work is appropriate to our situation. Sometimes we receive material that has no application to what we are doing."

SCOTT EVANS ORCHESTRAS & ENTERTAINMENT, 660 N.E. 139th St., N. Miami FL 33161. (305)891-4449 or 891-0158. Art Director: Scott Evans. Estab. 1978. "I produce, direct, orchestrate and create shows and productions of all types."

Needs: Works with freelance artists during the holidays. Artists work on assignment only. Uses freelance artists for advertising, brochure, catalog, poster, set and costume design; advertising, brochure, catalog and poster illustration; lighting; advertising, brochure and catalog layout and scenery.

First Contact & Terms: Send query letter with brochure showing art style or resume and tearsheets. Samples are filed or are returned. Reports back only if interested. Call or write to show a portfolio, which should include whatever the artists thinks appropriate. Pays for design and illustration by the project, $35-50 minimum to $150-300 maximum. Rights purchased vary according to project.

Tips: "Be precise, reasonably priced and prompt."

FLORIDA STUDIO THEATRE, 1241 North Palm Ave., Sarasota FL 34236. (813)366-9017. Artistic Director: Richard Hopkins. Estab. 1973. "We are an intimate theater seating 165-3,800 subscribers; the season runs from January-June."

Needs: Works with 4-10 freelance artists/year. Freelance art needs are seasonal. Needs heaviest in January-May. Artists work on assignment only. Uses freelance artists for costume design, advertising illustration and set design. The look preferred "depends on the assignment."

First Contact & Terms: Send query letter with resume, photographs and slides. Samples are filed. Reports back to the artist only if interested. Write to schedule an appointment to show a portfolio, which should include original/final art, slides and photographs. Payment for design is based on assignment and experience. Pays for design by the project, $50-1,200. Rights purchased vary according to project.

FMT, Box 92127, Milwaukee WI 53202. Co-Director: Mike Moynihan. Theatre company.

Needs: Works with 2-4 freelance artists/year. Uses artists for advertising and brochure design, illustration and layout; product, costume and textile design; calligraphy; paste-up; posters and direct mail.

First Contact & Terms: Send query letter with brochure showing art style or resume and tearsheets, photostats, photocopies, slides and photographs. Samples not filed are returned if accompanied by SASE. Reports only if interested. To show a portfolio, mail appropriate materials or write to schedule an appointment; portfolio should include original/final art, final reproduction/product and color tearsheets, photostats and photographs. Pays for design by the project, $25-500. Pays for illustrations by the project, $25-75. Considers complexity of project, available budget and turnaround time when establishing payment.

FOOTPATH DANCE COMPANY, 16704 Chagrin Blvd., Cleveland OH 44120. (216)491-8282. Managing Director: Brynna Fish. Estab. 1976. Modern dance company, national touring, local and school performances.

Needs: Works with 4-5 freelance artists/year. Freelance art is needed throughout the year. Artists work on assignment only. Prefers local artists only with experience in PR for the performing arts. Uses freelance artists for advertising, brochure, poster, costume and set design; lighting. Prefers modern styles.

First Contact & Terms: Send query letter with brochure and resume. Samples are filed. Reports back to the artist only if interested. Call to schedule an appointment to show a portfolio or mail appropriate materials. Portfolio should include roughs, tearsheets, original/final art and photographs. Pays for design by the project, $100-3,000. Pays for illustration by the project, $25-200. Rights purchased vary according to project.

GUS GIORDANO JAZZ DANCE CHICAGO, 614 Davis St., Evanston IL 60201. (312)866-6779. Executive Director: Betsy Whipple. Jazz dance company consisting of 8-10 members.

Needs: Works with 2-3 freelance artists/year. Prefers Chicago area artists. Works on assignment only. Uses artists for advertising, promotion (posters, etc.), costume design; lighting and scenery.

First Contact & Terms: Samples returned by SASE. Reports within weeks. Send resume to be kept on file for possible future assignments. Pays for design and illustration by the project, $100-500.

Tips: Looks for "someone with dedication to the performing arts who understands the needs of a nonprofit organization, including its limitations."

THE GROUP THEATRE COMPANY, 3940 Brooklyn Ave. NE, Seattle WA 98105. (206)685-4969. Marketing Director: Laura Newton. Professional theatre promoting a full theatrical season using flyers, brochures and posters. Other events generate invitations, etc.

Needs: Works with 6 freelance artists/year. Prefers local artists only. Uses artists for advertising illustration; brochure design, illustration and layout; posters and annual reports.

First Contact & Terms: Send query letter with brochure showing art style or resume, tearsheets and photocopies. Samples not filed are returned by SASE. Reports only if interested. Call or write to schedule an appointment to show a portfolio, which should include thumbnails, roughs, final reproduction/product and color tearsheets. Payment is negotiable.

Tips: "We really negotiate each project. We are a non-profit organization. If you rigidly demand a top-of-the market fee, we're probably not for you."

HARTFORD BALLET, 226 Farmington Ave., Hartford CT 06105. (203)525-9396. FAX: (203)249-8116. Executive Director: John Simone. Nationally recognized company under the artistic direction of Michael Uthoff, with a repertory in classical and contemporary ballet; mainstage performances include 15 local performances of the annual holiday "Nutcracker" and other productions featuring full-length and repertory world premieres and revivals.

Needs: Freelance artists needed for brochure and advertising design, particularly in the spring and fall. Designers also needed for costume, poster and scenic design; depending upon the needs of the current production.

First Contact & Terms: Send query letter and samples of work to be kept on file. Write for an appointment to show portfolio, which should include "good photos, designs of costumes (if applicable); good examples of previous b&w and four color graphic design work; examples of copywriting for advertising/graphic work." If return of samples is requested, send SASE. Terms discussed before any work is contracted. Fees based upon project needs.

Tips: "We need a contemporary style with strong sales emphasis." Looks for "consistency, reliability; good, accurate estimates of job costs."

MATTI LASCOE DANCE THEATRE CO., 1014-A Cabrillo Park Dr., Santa Ana CA 92701. (714)542-1463. Artistic Director: Matti Lascoe. Sixteen member Caribbean dance and music ensemble with drummers and the Trinidad Steel Drum Band. Concert is called "Caribbean Splash."

Needs: Works with 2 freelance artists/year; needs heaviest from September-November, January-May. Uses artists for advertising, brochure, set and costume design; lighting and scenery.

First Contact & Terms: Experienced artists only. Send resume, photographs and tearsheets to be kept on file. Write for artists' guidelines. Samples returned by SASE only if requested. Reports only if interested. Pays for design and illustration by the project. Considers available budget when establishing payment.

LINCOLN SYMPHONY ORCHESTRA ASSOCIATION, Suite 211, 1200 N. Lincoln NE 68508. (402)474-5610. Executive Director: Richard Frevert. Estab. 1926. Symphony orchestra presenting 20-25 concerts annually.

Needs: Approached by 4-5 freelance artists/year. Works with 1-2 freelance artists/year. Freelance art is needed throughout the year. Artists work on assignment only. Prefers artists with experience in performing arts promotion. Uses freelance artists for advertising design, illustration and layout; brochure design, illustration and layout; poster design and illustration.

First Contact & Terms: Send query letter with brochure, resume and tearsheets. Samples are filed. Reports back to the artist only if interested. Call to schedule an appointment to show a portfolio, which should include thumbnails, roughs, original/final art and b&w and color samples. Pays for design by the project, $200-1,000. Pays for illustration by the project, $100-500. Negotiates rights purchased.

LOS ANGELES CHAMBER ORCHESTRA, Suite 300, 315 W. 9th St., Los Angeles CA 90015. (213)622-7001. FAX: (213)955-2071. Director of Marketing: George Sebastian. Estab. 1968. Classical music company.

Needs: Approached by 25-50 freelance artists/year. Works with 4-6 freelance artists/year. Freelance art is needed throughout the year. Artists work on assignment only. Prefers local artists only with experience in brochure production and advertising. Uses freelance artists for advertising design, illustration and layout; brochure design, illustration and layout; poster design and illustration. Prefers "a young, fresh look."

First Contact & Terms: Send query letter with brochure. Samples are filed. Does not report back, in which case the artist should "contact this office." Call to schedule an appointment to show a portfolio, which should include original/final art. Pays for design and illustration by the project. "Each project differs significantly." Rights purchased vary according to project.

Tips: "Forget that we are a classical music organization."

MICHIGAN OPERA THEATRE, 6519 Second Ave., Detroit MI 48202. (313)874-7850. Marketing Director: Julia M. Saylor. "We are the ninth largest opera company in the United States (out of 100) based on operating budget. Our season repertory is a combination of musical theatre, classic operetta and grand opera. Our subscriber base is 9,500 patrons, plus over 100,000 single ticket buyers."

Needs: Works with 20 freelance artists/year. Freelance art needed throughout the year. Works on assignment only. Uses artists for advertising and brochure design, illustration and layout; catalog design; poster design and illustration.

First Contact & Terms: Send query letter with resume, tearsheets and photostats. Reports only if interested. Write to schedule an appointment to show a portfolio, which should include color and b&w original/final art and final reproduction/product. Pays for design by the project, $50 minimum. Pays for illustration by the hour, $25-50. "Since our needs vary greatly, from a small two-color postcard to a 100+ page perfectbound program book, our payments do also. We are a nonprofit agency; therefore, we do not pay sales tax and we generally look to save money, which is why we prefer to deal with freelancers." Considers complexity of project, skill and experience of artist, available budget, how work will be used and turnaround time when establishing payment.

Tips: "Innovation and a real understanding of opera really helps in marketing our product to the public. Often times, opera scares people, and we have found that the more knowledgeable our public is about our art form, the less scared they are."

MID-WILLAMETTE BALLET ENSEMBLE, Box 55, Salem OR 97308. (503)363-1403. Director, Salem Ballet School: Elfie Stevenin, DMA-DEA. Dance company of 15 ensemble students performing locally for community events and traditional concerts.
Needs: Works with 3 freelance artists for poster design, photography and brochure design; all fund-raising through parent organization only. Needs heaviest in fall and spring. Local artists only—"for the most part, they are artists who have children enrolled in classes."
First Contact & Terms: Send business card to be kept on file. Pays for design by the project. Considers available budget when establishing payment.

MILWAUKEE CHAMBER THEATRE, 152 W. Wisconsin Ave., Milwaukee WI 53203. (414)276-8842. General Manager: Lesley Smith. Estab. 1980. "We are a professional equity theater company that offers classical and contemporary productions in a 200-seat theater with 1,200 subscribers."
Needs: Approached by 25 freelance artists/year. Works with 6 freelance artists/year. Freelance art needs are seasonal. Needs heaviest September-June. Artists work on assignment only. Uses freelance artists for costume design, lighting, set design and scenery.
First Contact & Terms: Send query letter with brochure, resume and color photographs. Samples are filed. Reports back to the artist only if interested. Call or write to schedule an appointment to show a portfolio or mail appropriate materials. Pays for design by the project, $500-1,200.
Tips: "Call for appointment in the spring or summer for the following year. Then make a follow-up call to us."

THE MINNESOTA OPERA, Suite 20, 400 Sibley St., St. Paul MN 55101. (612)221-0122. FAX: (612)292-1854. Marketing Director: Kathy Davis. Opera/musical theater production company, presenting 4 operas (21 performances total) and a month-long run of an American musical.
Needs: Works with 2-4 freelance artists/year. Freelance art needed throughout the year. Works on assignment only. Uses artists for advertising and brochure design, illustration and layout; poster design and illustration.
First Contact & Terms: Send query letter with brochure, resume, tearsheets, photocopies and slides. Samples are filed or are are returned only if requested by artist. Reports back only if interested. Write to schedule an appointment to show a portfolio or mail roughs and final reproduction/product. Pays for design by the hour, $25-40 and by the project. Pays for illustration by the project, $100-750. Considers complexity of project, skill and experience of artist and available budget when establishing payment. Buys reprint rights.
Tips: Looking for freelance artists with the "ability to work with diverse needs, creativity with limited budgets."

MISSISSIPPI SYMPHONY ORCHESTRA, Box 2052, Jackson MS 39225. (601)960-1565. Assistant General Manager: Kate Treyens. Estab. 1944. "Largest performing arts organization in Mississippi. Over 1,000 subscribers."
Needs: Approached by 5 freelance artists/year. Works with 2 freelance artists/year. Needs are heaviest from September-April. Artists work on assignment only. Prefers local artists only. Uses freelance artists for advertising design, illustration and layout; brochure design, illustration and layout; and poster design and illustration.
First Contact & Terms: Send query letter with brochure and resume. Samples are filed. Reports back to the artist only if interested. Write to schedule an appointment to show a portfolio, which should include original/final art and b&w samples. Pays for design by the hour, $20, by the project, $1,000. Pays for illustration by the hour, by the project, $200. Rights purchased vary according to project.

ELISA MONTE DANCE CO., 39 Great Jones St., New York NY 10012. (212)533-2226. Manager: Bernard Schmidt. Modern dance company "with strong international flavor."
Needs: Works with 2-3 freelance artists/year. Prefers local artists. Works on assignment only. Uses artists for advertising, brochure and catalog design, illustration and layout; mechanicals; posters; and direct mail. Prefers collage.
First Contact & Terms: Send query letter with brochure showing art style or resume, photocopies or photographs. Samples not filed are returned by SASE only if requested by artist. Reports only if interested. Call or write to schedule an appointment to show a portfolio, which should include roughs, final reproduction/product and color photographs. Pays for design by the project, $400-1,000. Pays for illustration by the project, $100-400. Considers complexity of project, skill and experience of artist and how work will be used when establishing payment.

THE NEW CONSERVATORY CHILDREN'S THEATRE AND SCHOOL, 25 Van Ness, San Francisco CA 94102. (415)861-4914. Executive Director: Ed Decker. Estab. 1981. "We are a performing arts school for youth ages 4-19."

This promotional piece was designed by Ciri Johnson of Brooklyn, New York for the Elisa Monte Dance Company. Managing director Bernard Schmidt wanted a piece that would "capture the spirit of the dance company." He believes the piece is successful because "it is clean and interesting, prompting the curiosity of whoever looks at the design cover."

© 1990 Elisa Monte Dance Co.

Needs: Approached by 20 freelance artists/year. Work with 2-6 freelance artists/year. Freelance art needed throughout the year. Artists work on assignment only. Prefers local artists only. Uses freelance artists for brochure design, lighting, advertising layout, set design and scenery.
First Contact & Terms: Send query letter with brochure, resume, SASE and tearsheets. Samples are filed. Reports back to the artist only if interested. Write to schedule an appointment to show a portfolio or mail appropriate materials. Pays for design and illustration by the project. Payment depends on the job. Rights purchased vary according to project.

NEW JERSEY SHAKESPEARE FESTIVAL, Drew University, Madison NJ 07940. Artistic Director: Paul Barry. Contemporary and classical theatrical troupe.
Needs: Works with 1-2 freelance illustrators and 3 freelance designers/year. Assigns 3-6 freelance jobs/year. Design work for costumes, sets, props and lighting is seasonal, May-December. Uses artists for advertising, costumes, designer-in-residence, direct mail brochures, exhibits, flyers, graphics, posters, programs, sets and theatrical lighting.
First Contact & Terms: Query with resume or arrange interview to show portfolio. Include SASE. Reports within 1 week. Interviews for designers are held in March and April. Provide resume to be kept on file for future assignments. Pays $1,200-1,400/show for set and costume design (large shows).
Tips: "Our season has expanded to 27 playing weeks." An artist's work should display an "understanding of historical period, good use of color, practicality and fit of costumes. Sets should show an ease to build, and to change from one show to another."

NEW YORK CITY OPERA NATIONAL COMPANY, NY State Theater, Lincoln Center, New York NY 10023. (212)870-5635. Administrative Director: Nancy Kelly. "Opera company founded in 1979 by Beverly Sills as a national touring company with the purpose of bringing opera to areas of the country without resident opera associations. Its primary function is to provide young singers with an opportunity to gain performing experience; veteran singers use the tours to try new roles before singing them in New York."
Needs: Needs for freelance artists heaviest prior to tours in winter. Uses artists for set and costume design. Style should be "relatively simple and representational. It must capture the essential character of the opera." Prefers pen & ink, airbrush and collage. "Scenic and costume designers should be aware of the rigors of traveling productions and should think about portability and economics." Artists also used for graphics for marketing the current production.
First Contact & Terms: Previous experience is advisable; union memberships are required for set and costume design. Send query letter with resume to be kept on file. Reports only if interested. Pays for design and illustration by the project, $500-800; "varies according to design; follows union rates." Considers complexity of project and available budget when establishing payment.
Tips: "The use of artists is tied specifically to whatever opera we may be performing in a given year. We generally tour in the January-April time period and hire artists one year ahead of each tour. Send us examples of work of a similar nature to what we need, such as posters promoting plays, operas, etc. Elaborate colored

illustrations are useless to us, since our advertising is limited to two-color posters and flyers."

NEW YORK HARP ENSEMBLE, 140 W. End Ave., New York NY 10023. Director: Dr. Aristid von Wurtzler. Concert group which tours the U.S., Europe, Africa, South America, Australia and the Near and Far East.
Needs: Works with 1 freelance designer/year, summer only. Local artists only. Works on assignment only. Uses freelance artists for direct mail brochures, posters, programs and record cover layouts.
First Contact & Terms: Submit samples (brochures, posters and record covers). Samples returned by SASE. Reports back on future assignment possibilities. Provide flyer to be kept on file for future assignments. Pays by the project for design and illustration. Considers available budget and skill and experience of artist when establishing payment.

OAKLAND ENSEMBLE THEATRE, 1428 Alice St., Oakland CA 94612. (415)763-7774. Public Relations Director: Victoria Kirby. "Committed to producing insightful, engaging and substantive works of theatre particularly as they relate to pluralism in America's national life. Our frame of reference is Black."
Needs: Works with 2-3 freelance artists/year. Freelance art needs are seasonal. Needs heaviest from July-March. Works on assignment only. Uses artists for advertising and brochure design, illustration and layout; poster design and illustration; set design; costume design; lighting and scenery.
First Contact & Terms: Send query letter with brochure showing art style or resume and samples. Samples are filed or are returned by SASE only if requested. Reports back within 3 weeks. Write to schedule an appointment to show a portfolio. Pays for illustration/design by the hour, $35-50. Considers complexity of project, skill and experience of artist and available budget when establishing payment.

OLYMPIC BALLET THEATRE, Anderson Cultural Center, 700 Main St., Edmonds WA 98020. (206)774-7570. Artistic Directors: John and Helen Wilkins. Ballet company with 20 dancers, approximately 100 members and a Board of Trustees of 20, which does a full-length "Nutcracker" Spring Showcase and tour, lecture-demo's and mini-performances.
Needs: Works with 2 freelance artists/year. Needs heaviest in fall, winter and spring. Uses freelance artists for advertising, brochure, catalog, poster and program design and illustration; set and costume design.
First Contact & Terms: Works on assignment only. Call or write for appointment to show portfolio. Pays by the project, $25-1,000 for design; $25-400 for illustration. Considers complexity of project and project's budget when establishing payment.
Tips: Looks for "imagination, attention to detail; clear thinker about the project and related business matters."

OMAHA MAGIC THEATRE, 1417 Farnam St., Omaha NE 68102. (402)346-1227. Artistic Director: JoAnn Schmidman. Estab. 1968. "Our company and audience are a cross-cultural, inter-generational mix. Our audience is a true cross-section of the community."
Needs: Works with 3-8 freelance artists/year. Freelance art needed throughout the year. Uses freelance artists for set and costume design, lighting, scenery and " 'images' – visuals often projected on overheads throughout the play into performance space." Prefers non-naturalist, non-realistic styles.
First Contact & Terms: Send query letter with resume and slides. Samples are returned by SASE. Reports back within 3 months. Pays for design by the project, $1,000-2,500. Negotiates rights purchased.
Tips: "The plays we produce are the most avant of the avant-garde. The plays we produce must in some way push form and/or content to new directions."

PARADISE AREA ARTS COUNCIL, 6686 Brook Way, Paradise CA 95969. (916)877-8360. President: Thomas E. Wilson. June art festival by various mediums. Send SASE.
Needs: Prefers local artists. Needs heaviest in June and December. Works on assignment only. Uses artists for brochure, poster and costume design. Prefers "a smart, clean, exciting style."
First Contact & Terms: Send query letter with brochure showing art style. Reports within 1 month. To show a portfolio, mail appropriate materials, which should include final reproduction/product and photographs. Pays for illustration/design "by negotiation with artists."
Tips: "First-class promotional materials are necessary." There is a "great need for excellent projection of the arts."

PENNSYLVANIA STAGE COMPANY, 837 Linden St., Allentown PA 18101. (215)434-6110. Production Manager: Peter Wrenn-Meleck. "We are a LORT theatre, located 2 hours from New York City devoted to a diverse repertory of new and classic works presented on a proscenium stage. Our house seats 274 people, and we currently have 6,000 subscribers."
Needs: Works with 15 freelance artists/year; "We need freelance designers for our season which runs from October-July." "Artists must be able to come to Allentown for design consultation and construction." Works on assignment only. Uses artists for set, costume, and lighting design. "As a growing professional regional theatre, we have increased needs for graphic artists, photography and illustration for print materials (brochures, flyers) and particularly for our program magazine, *Callboard*, which is published seven times a year.

First Contact & Terms: Send query letter with resume. Prefers photostats, slides, b&w photos, color washes, roughs, as samples. Samples returned by SASE. Reports back whether to expect possible future assignments. Provide resume to be kept on file for possible future assignments. Pays by the project, $500-1,500 average, for design; $25-125 for print material. Considers complexity of project, available budget, and skill and experience of artist when establishing payment.
Tips: "We prefer that designers have extensive experience designing for professional theater."

RUDY PEREZ PERFORMANCE ENSEMBLE, Box 36614, Los Angeles CA 90036. (213)931-3604. Artistic Director: Rudy Perez. Performance art and experimental dance company, also known as the Rudy Perez Dance Theater, is a nonprofit organization dependent on funding from National Endowment for the Arts and the California Arts Council, corporate and private fundings; box office and bookings currently in the LA area.
Needs: "The work is mainly collaborations with visual artists and composers." Uses artists for publicity before performances and updating press kits, brochures, etc.
First Contact & Terms: Send query letter with brochure and resume to be kept on file. Reports within 1 week. "Since we are a nonprofit organization we depend on in-kind services and/or negotiable fees."
Tips: Artists should have "an interest in dance and theatre."

PHILADELPHIA DANCE CO. (Philadanco), 9 N. Preston St., Philadelphia PA 19104-2210. (215)387-8200. Executive Director: Joan Myers Brown. 14 member dance company performing contemporary, neoclassic, jazz and modern works.
Needs: Works with 2-3 freelance artists/year. Freelance art needed throughout the year. Works on assignment only. Uses artists for advertising design and layout; brochure, poster and costume design; lighting and scenery.
First Contact & Terms: Send query letter with brochure showing art style. Samples are filed or are returned only if requested. Reports back within 25 days. Write to schedule an appointment to show a portfolio, which should include previous work samples. Pays for design and illustration by the hour, $100-1,000. Considers complexity of project and client's budget when establishing payment. Negotiates rights purchased.
Tips: "Philadanco is becoming more sophisticated in its printed matter and requires designs to reflect the maturity of the company. We look at past work with dancers/dance companies and at contemporary styles in photography and pen and ink."

PHILHARMONIC ORCHESTRA OF FLORIDA, 1430 N. Federal Hwy., Ft. Lauderdale FL 33304. (305)561-2997. Director of Marketing: Michael D. Foden.
Needs: Works with 2 freelance artists/year; needs heaviest in October-May. Uses freelance artists for brochure design, illustration and layout; poster design and illustration.
First Contact & Terms: Send query letter with resume, tearsheets, photostats, photocopies or brochure showing art style. Samples are filed and are not returned. Reports back only if interested. Write to schedule an appointment to show a portfolio. Pays for design and illustration by the hour, $50 minimum. Considers complexity of project, available budget and rights purchased when establishing payment.

PICCOLO OPERA COMPANY, Lee Jon Associates, 18662 Fairfield Ave., Detroit MI 48221. (313)861-6930. Contact: Lee Jon Associates. Opera company, performs in English; productions staged and in costume. Travels around the country. Performs for adults and for youngsters, with piano or orchestra.
Needs: Works on assignment only. Prefers artists with layout experience. Uses artists for advertising design, brochure illustration and layout, poster design and set design. Pays by the project, $50-300; negotiable. Considers available budget, skill and experience of artist and creative talent of artist when establishing payment.
First Contact & Terms: Send query letter with resume, samples and SASE. Reports in 3-4 weeks.
Tips: When reviewing work, especially looks for "the impact of subject matter. Artists shouldn't overemphasize the design at the expense of the information; consider color in relation to legibility. We deal in emotions and the nostalgia aroused by music, so look for more 'romantic' design." Also interested in cartoon-style illustrations.

PIONEER PLAYHOUSE OF KENTUCKY, Danville KY 40422. (606)236-2747. Contact: Eben Henson. Regular summer stock theatre.
Needs: Works with 10 freelance artists/year; needs heaviest in summer. Uses artists for advertising, poster, set and costume design; lighting and scenery. Prefers artists willing to work in the nature of apprenticeship. Works on assignment only. Uses artists for the design, illustration and layout by advertising and brochures; the illustration and layout of catalogs; set design; costume design; lighting and scenery.
First Contact & Terms: Send query letter and material to be kept on file. Reports within 4 weeks. Call to schedule an appointment to show a portfolio. No payment of salary; apprenticeships provide room and board.
Tips: "For persons breaking into any form of the theatre, apprenticeship is necessary. First, one must establish himself with a reputable theater in order to advance in the theatrical profession."

POSEY SCHOOL OF DANCE, INC., Box 254, Northport NY 11768. (516)757-2700. President: Elsa Posey. Private school/professional training in performing arts.
Needs: Works with 4 or more freelance artists/year; needs heaviest in spring and fall. Prefers regional artists willing to work within nonprofit performing arts budget. Works on assignment only. Uses artists for advertising and brochure design, illustration and layout; poster and program design and illustration; set and costume design; lighting and scenery. Also uses artists for a newsletter and for advertising copy. Interested in *appropriate* cartoons.
First Contact & Terms: Send query letter with resume, tearsheets, photostats and photocopies. Samples returned by SASE. Reports within 4 weeks. To show a portfolio, mail tearsheets and photostats. Pays for design and illustration by the project, $25-250. Negotiates payment. Considers complexity of project, available budget, skill and experience of artist, how work will be used and rights purchased when establishing payment.
Tips: Artist must have "illustrative ability with understanding of dance, dancer's body and movement. Looking for honesty and a more personal approach."

PURDUE CONVOCATIONS AND LECTURES, CA-3, Rm. 9, Purdue University, West Lafayette IN 47907. (317)494-9412. FAX: (317)494-0540. Director of Publicity: Loretta Hiner. Estab. 1950s. "We present the performing arts. We have 1,200 friends and a mailing list of 15,000."
Needs: Approached by 2 freelance artists/year. Works with 1 freelance artist/year. Needs are heaviest in October-November. Artists work on assignment only. Prefers artists with experience in the performing arts. Uses freelance artists for brochure design and illustration. "Prefers cutting-edge styles, yet work should be welcoming, moving away from highbrow."
First Contact & Terms: Send query letter with brochure, resume, tearsheets and photostats. Samples are filed. Reports back to the artist only if interested. Call to schedule an appointment to show a portfolio. Portfolio should include thumbnails, photostats and slides. Pays for illustration/ design by the project, $75-2,000. Buys all rights.
Tips: "We like to have a lot of input and will often ask for changes."

RENAISSANCE DANCE COMPANY OF DETROIT: Dances of Court and Country in Elizabethan England, Apt. 903, 15 E. Kirby, Detroit MI 48202. (313)875-6354. Artistic Director: Harriet Berg. Main area of performance: *Mme. Cadillac Dance Theater: Dance and Drama of* the French Colonial period.
Needs: Assigns 4 jobs/year. Uses artists for flyers, programs, announcements and ads.
First Contact & Terms: Prefers pen & ink and calligraphy. Send query letter and SASE. Negotiates pay.
Tips: "We are a struggling dance company with a good deal of exposure. Is there an artist willing to do a public-service project for us in exchange for opportunity and broad distribution?"

THE REPERTORY DANCE THEATRE (RDT), Box 8088, Salt Lake City UT 84108. (801)581-6702. FAX: (801)581-7880. General Manager: Kathy Johnson. 10-member modern dance company with national touring, home seasons in Salt Lake City and summer workshops.
Needs: Works with 2-3 freelance artists/year; needs heaviest in summer and fall. Uses artists for advertising and brochure design, illustration and layout; poster design and illustration.
First Contact & Terms: Prefers local artists. Send query letter with resume, brochure, tearsheets and samples to be kept on file. Prefers "any samples which best represent work"; samples should be dance or movement related. Samples returned by SASE if not kept on file. Reports within 2 weeks. Works on assignment only. Pays for illustration/design by the project or "pro bono." Negotiates payment according to complexity of project and available budget.

RITES AND REASON, Brown University, Box 1148, Providence RI 02912. (401)863-4177. FAX: (401)863-3700. Contact: Managing Director. Black performing arts organization.
Needs: Uses freelance artists for all aspects of theater productions. Assigns 12 freelance jobs/season.
First Contact & Terms: Query with resume and SASE. Pays for design by the project, $300-3,000.
Tips: "We are the professional theatre component of the Afro-American studies program at Brown University. Our original productions of drama, music and dance primarily concern the interpretation of black people's experiences in the New World. A multidisciplinary approach to research and performance is used by artists and scholars who work together in creation of new productions. An effort is made, through the performing arts, to bring members of the community to a forum where they are given the opportunity to confront scholars and artists, and to critique their work. The dialogues with the community direct subsequent scholarly research that often becomes the basis for other new productions."

ROOSEVELT PARK AMPHITHEATRE, Middlesex County Department of Parks and Recreation, Box 661, New Brunswick NJ 08903. (201)548-2884. Producing Director: Phyllis Elfenbein. Musical theatre.
Needs: Works with 10 freelance artists/year; needs heaviest in spring through summer. Works on assignment only. Uses artists for set and costume design, lighting and scenery.
First Contact & Terms: Send query letter and resume. Prefers samples to be brought in person. Reports within 3 weeks. To show a portfolio, mail appropriate materials or write to schedule an appointment. Pays up to $1,500 for design; salary.

Tips: "We prefer slides of finished sets and costumes for productions."

SALT LAKE SYMPHONIC CHOIR, Box 45, Salt Lake City UT 84110. (801)466-8701. Contact: Manager.
Needs: Works with 5 illustrators and 2 designers/year; fall only. Works on assignment. Uses artists for advertising, billboards, costumes, direct mail brochures, flyers, posters, programs, theatrical lighting and record jackets.
First Contact & Terms: Mail resume, brochure and flyer to be kept on file. Include SASE. Negotiates pay by the project.

SAN DIEGO REPERTORY THEATRE, 79 Horton Plaza, San Diego CA 92101-6144. (619)231-3586. FAX: (619)235-0939. Marketing Director: Mark Mandel. Estab. 1976. "We are located downtown and are San Diego's largest professional theater with nearly 7,000 subscribers and more than 100,000 annually attend. We specialize in contemporary drama and musicals, new plays and the unique interpretation of classics."
Needs: Approached by 3-4 freelance artists/year. Works with 2-3 freelance artists/year. Freelance art needs are seasonal. Needs heaviest from November-March. Artists work on assignment only. Prefers local artists with experience in title illustration and non-traditional corporate marketing. Uses freelance artists for advertising design and layout; brochure design, illustration and layout; costume, lighting and set design. Prefers "a contemporary and bold look with a heavy use of photos and bold headlines."
First Contact & Terms: Send query letter with brochure and client listing. Samples are not filed and are returned by SASE if requested by artist. Reports back to the artist only if interested. To show a portfolio, mail thumbnails, roughs and original/final art. Pays for design by the project, $150-750. Pays for illustration by the project, $75-150. Rights purchased vary according to project.
Tips: "We are particularly interested in artists with expertise in combining illustration and design to completion. We prefer viewing 2-3 thumbnails to start. Some research is needed for illustration (reading plays first). Biggest annual project is the season brochure, usually 3-4 PMS or 4-color process."

San Francisco Artist Andrea Fong created this pen-and-ink promotional illustration for the San Francisco Opera Center's production of "Lucia di Lammermoor."

SAN FRANCISCO OPERA CENTER, War Memorial Opera House, San Francisco Opera, San Francisco CA 94102. (415)565-6435. FAX: (415)621-7508. Manager: Christine Bullin. Assistant to the Manager: Lucinda Toy. SFOC is the umbrella organization for the affiliate programs of the San Francisco Opera.
Needs: Works with 3-4 freelance artists/year; needs heaviest in summer preparing for fall and spring seasons. Uses artists for advertising, brochure and program design, illustration and layout; set and costume design; posters; lighting; scenery; PR and educational packets.

First Contact & Terms: Send query letter with brochure, resume, business card, photostats, slides and photographs to be kept on file. Write for appointment to show portfolio. Reports only if interested. Pays for design and illustration by the project, $50-300 average. Considers available budget, how work will be used and rights purchased when establishing payment.

SINGING BOYS OF PENNSYLVANIA, Box 110, State College, East Stroudsburg PA 18301, or Box 206, Wind Gap PA 18091. (717)421-6137 (business office) or (215)759-6002. Director: K. Bernard Schade. "Touring boy choir." Needs heaviest in fall and winter.
Needs: Local artists only. Works on assignment only. Uses artists for direct mail brochures, flyers, posters and record jackets; design, illustration and layout of advertising and brochures; poster, set and costume design; lighting and scenery.
First Contact & Terms: Query. Pays for design by the project, $100-250.

BETH SOLL & COMPANY/DANCE PROJECTS, INC., Box 825, Prudential Station, Boston MA 02199. (617)547-8771. Manager: Sally Fabens. Estab. 1977. Modern dance company with 6 dancers.
Needs: Works with 4-10 freelance artists/year. Freelance art is needed throughout the year. Artists work on assignment only. Prefers local artists only. Uses freelance artists for brochure design, illustration and layout; poster design and illustration; set and costume design; lighting and scenery.
First Contact & Terms: Contact through artist agent or send query letter with brochure, resume, photostats, photographs or photocopies. Samples are filed and arenot returned. Reports back to the artist only if interested. To show a portfolio, mail thumbnails, photostats, roughs, original/final art and photographs. Pays for illustration/design by the project, "payment dependent upon grants and funds available." Rights purchased vary according to project.
Tips: "Do not call. Do not rely on material being returned unless SASE is included in material sent."

SOUTHWEST JAZZ BALLET COMPANY, Box 38233, Houston TX 77238. (713)694-6114. Contact: President. Professional touring ballet company; producers of "America in Concert."
Needs: Works with 5 freelance artists/year. Works on assignment only. Uses artists for advertising illustration, brochure illustration and layout, poster illustration, costume design and scenery.
First Contact & Terms: Send query letter with resume and "end product" to be kept on file. Reports within 1 month. Call or write to schedule an appointment to show a portfolio, which should include final reproduction/product. Pays by the project. Considers complexity of project when establishing payment.
Tips: Looking for '40s Americana style.

STEPPENWOLF THEATRE COMPANY, 2851 N. Halsted St., Chicago IL 60657. (312)472-4515. FAX (312)472-4282. Marketing Manager: Jodi Royce. Estab. 1976. "We are a theatrical ensemble of 23 actors producing a 5 play subscription season."
Needs: Approached by 8-10 freelance artists/year. Works with 2-3 freelance artists/year. Freelance art is needed throughout the year. Artists work on assignment only. Prefers local artists only. Uses freelance artists for advertising, brochure, catalog and poster design; advertising and poster illustration; advertising, brochure and catalog layout. Prefers a bold and professional, but fun and unique look.
First Contact & Terms: Send query letter with brochure, resume, SASE, tearsheets or a sampling of work in any convenient format. Samples are filed or are returned by SASE if requested by artist. Reports back within 2 weeks. Call to schedule an appointment to show a portfolio, which should include original/final art, tearsheets and photographs. Pays for design by the project, $250 maximum. "Our usual designer receives a promotional listing for donating the majority of her work." Pays for illustration by the project, $200 maximum. "Sometimes we offer an in-kind payment; i.e. tickets to Steppenwolf." Rights purchased vary according to project.
Tips: "Our design needs are sporadic and always under impossible deadlines. A broad sample of work which shows capabilities is best for our impromptu design decisions. We choose by the style we need represented. Artists' ability to work with client's suggestions and ideas is of utmost concern."

MARK TAPER FORUM, 135 N. Grand Ave., Los Angeles CA 90012. (213)972-7259. FAX: (213)972-0746. Art Director: Chris Komuro. Inhouse agency for the Mark Taper Forum of the Los Angeles Music Center. Provides advertising and posters for live theatre.
Needs: Works with 10 freelance artists/year. Prefers local artists only. Uses artists for advertising design and illustration, brochure illustration, paste-up and mechanicals. Prefers painterly styles, graphic b&w styles.
First Contact & Terms: Send brochure showing art style or tearsheets, photostats and slides. Samples not filed are returned by SASE. Reports only if interested. Call or write to schedule an appointment to show a portfolio, which should include color and b&w original/final art, final reproduction/product and tearsheets. Pays for design by the hour, $15-20. Pays for illustration by the project, $300-1,000. Considers client's budget; "this is non-profit theatre."
Tips: "Strong illustrative skills should be demonstrated."

THE THEATRE BALLET OF SAN FRANCISCO, Suite 163, 2215 R Market S., San Francisco CA 94114. Director: Merriem Lanova. Estab. 1970. "Offers ballet productions with audiences averaging about 1,000."
Needs: Rarely works with freelance artists. Needs are heaviest in the fall. Artists work on assignment only. Uses freelance artists for advertising design, brochure design and layout, costume and set design and scenery.
First Contact & Terms: Send query letter with photocopies. Samples are filed. Call to schedule an appointment to show a portfolio.
Tips: "Keep trying as conditions change, sometimes even for the better."

THEATRE PROJECT COMPANY, Suite 10H, 634 N. Grand, St. Louis MO 63103. (314)531-1315. FAX: (314)533-3345. Artistic Director: William Freimuth. Estab. 1975. "We are a small professional theater offering new and progressive plays with 260 seats."
Needs: Works with 10 freelance artists/year. Freelance art is needed throughout the year. Artists work on assignment only. Uses freelance artists for advertising, brochure and poster design; costume design; advertising, brochure and poster illustration; lighting; advertising and brochure layout; set design; scenery and sound.
First Contact & Terms: Send query letter with resume. Samples are filed or are returned by SASE if requested by artist. Reports back to the artist only if interested. Call to schedule an appointment to show a portfolio, which should include "what's appropriate; varies according to the type of artist you are." Pays for design by the project, $200-750. Pays for illustration by the project, $50-200. "The fee for design and illustration depends on the type of artist." Rights purchased vary according to project.
Tips: "We are a growing company that is preparing to move into a new performing arts center in downtown St. Louis (mid-1991). Essentially, this will place our theater company 'on Broadway,' so to speak."

THEATRE-BY-THE-SEA, 364 Cards Pond Rd., Matunuck RI 02879. (401)782-3644. Producer: Richard Ericson, Fourquest Entertainment, Inc. Season: May-October. Proscenium stage with fly system. Send resume.
First Contact & Terms: Pays for design by the project (negotiable).

THEATRE-IN-THE-SCHOOLS, INC., Suite 3-2, 220 E. 4th St., New York NY 10009. (212)533-0416. Executive Director: Tim Jeffryes. Estab. 1983. "We are a touring theater to schools."
Needs: Approached by 1 freelance artist/year. Freelance art needs are seasonal. Needs heaviest in the spring. Artists work on assignment only. Uses freelance artists for advertising, brochure and poster design; advertising, brochure and poster illustration; advertising and brochure layout; set design and scenery.
First Contact & Terms: Send query letter with brochure, resume, SASE and photocopies. Samples are filed or are returned by SASE if requested by artist. Reports back to the artist only if interested. To show a portfolio, mail appropriate materials. Pays for design by the hour, $10-20; by the project, $100-250.
Tips: "Be prepared to deal with someone totally ignorant about freelance artists."

THREE RIVERS SHAKESPEARE FESTIVAL, B-39, Cathedral of Learning, University of Pittsburgh, Pittsburgh PA 15260. (412)624-6467. Producing Director: Attilio Favorini. "The Three Rivers Shakespeare is the classical professional theatre company in residence at the University of Pittsburgh. Three plays are performed through the months of May-August: two Shakespeare, and one classical."
Needs: Freelance art needs are seasonal. Needs heaviest from May-August. Uses artists for set design, costume design, lighting and scenery.
First Contact & Terms: Send query letter with brochure. Samples are filed or are returned by SASE only if requested by artist. Reports back only if interested. Call or write to schedule an appointment to show a portfolio, which should include original/final art, final reproduction/product, photographs and slides. Pays for design by the project, $1,750 minimum. Considers skill and experience of artist and available budget when establishing payment.

TOURING CONCERT OPERA COMPANY, INC., 228 E. 80th St., New York NY 10021. (212)988-2542. Artistic Director: Priscilla Gordon. Performs opera internationally.
Needs: Works with many freelance artists/year. Freelance art needed throughout the year. Uses artists for advertising and brochure design, illustration and layout; poster design and illustration; set and costume design; lighting and scenery.
First Contact & Terms: Send resume and samples. Samples are filed. Reports back only if interested. To show a portfolio, mail photostats. Payment is negotiated.

VALOIS COMPANY OF DANCERS, CPA 1028, University of Toledo, Toledo OH 43606. (419)537-4922. Art Director: Elaine Valois. Resident modern dance company active in public schools, workshops and mini-concerts and full performance. Consists of 5-9 upperclassmen/graduates in dance.
Needs: Works with 6 freelance artist/year. Needs heaviest in spring. Prefers local artists. Uses artists for advertising and brochure design, illustration and layout; poster design and illustration; costume design and lighting. "Student artists often help us, and we continue to support them and purchase from them when they go professional."

First Contact & Terms: Send query letter with brochure, business card and photostats to be kept on file. Samples not kept on file are returned only if requested. Reports within 2 weeks. To show a portfolio, mail appropriate materials or call to schedule an appointment; portfolio should include final reproduction, "any representation." Pays for design by the hour, $35-50; by the project, $500-1,000; by the day, $75-100. "Photos should be included. Financial history should not." Considers complexity of project, available budget and how work will be used when establishing payment.

Tips: "We have noticed more inventive use of photographic material blended in with graphics."

VICTORY GARDENS THEATER, 2257 N. Lincoln Ave., Chicago IL 60614. (312)549-5788. Managing Director: Marcelle McVay. "Subscriber-based not-for-profit professional theater, dedicated to the development of new works and using Chicago talent."

Needs: Works with 10-20 freelance artists/year. Works with developing or experienced, local artists on assignment only. Uses artists for advertising, brochure, catalog and poster design and illustration; set, lighting and costume design. Prefers marker and calligraphy, then collage and computer illustration.

First Contact & Terms: Send query letter with resume and tearsheets to be kept on file. Samples not filed are returned by SASE. Reports back only if interested. Pays for poster design by the project, $100-300 average; pays set, lighting and costume design according to U.S.A.A. Considers complexity of project, project's budget, skill and experience of the artist and turnaround time when establishing payment.

Tips: "Send examples of all types of brochures, posters, etc. I would like to see work done for other theatre arts organizations." Desiring non-corporate look, but slick. The ability to encapsulate dramatic themes in striking, retentive, attention-getting visual images working within constraints of time, budget, and copy."

VIRGINIA OPERA, 160 Virginia Beach Blvd., Norfolk VA 23510. (804)627-9545. FAX: (804)622-0058. Public Relations Director: Eilene Rosenblum.

Needs: Works with 1-2 freelance artists/year; needs heaviest in spring and summer. Works on assignment only. Uses freelance artists for advertising and brochure design, illustration and layout; poster design and illustration. Prefers collage, colored pencil, watercolor, acrylic, oil and pastel.

First Contact & Terms: Send resume and tearsheets, photostats, slides or portfolio of work. Samples are filed or are returned only if requested. Reports back only if interested. Call to schedule an appointment to show a portfolio, which should include original/final art, final reproduction/product, tearsheets, photostats and photographs. Pays for design and illustration by the project, $100 minimum. Considers complexity of project, skill and experience of artist, available budget and how work will be used when establishing payment. Negotiates rights purchased.

Tips: "Virginia Opera symbolizes excellence and always projects an image of quality. We are respected in our field as one of the leading regional opera companies in the country, and our image should reflect such. Opera is a very beautiful art form—lavish sets and costumes—and our artwork should convey that image."

WEST COAST ENSEMBLE, 6240 Hollywood Blvd., Hollywood CA 90028. (213)871-8673. Artistic Director: Les Hanson. Estab. 1982. "The West Coast Ensemble is a nonprofit theater company with two intimate theaters."

Needs: Approached by 25 freelance artists/year. Works with 15 freelance artists/year. Freelance art needed throughout the year. Artists work on assignment only. Prefers local artists with experience in set lighting and costume design.

First Contact & Terms: Send query letter with resume. Samples are filed. Reports back to the artist only if interested. To show a portfolio, mail original/final art and photographs. "Payment depends on the budget of the production." Pays for design by the project. Buys all rights.

WOLF TRAP FARM PARK FOR THE PERFORMING ARTS, The Wolf Trap Foundation, 1624 Trap Rd., Vienna VA 22182. The Foundation serves as the administrative arm of the Park with the National Park Service maintaining the Park grounds. "Wolf Trap is the only national park for the performing arts. As a national park, Wolf Trap serves the nation as well as international visitors." Publishes newsletter entitled *Wolf Trap Opera Company.*

Needs: Approached by 8 freelance artists/year. Works with 2 freelance illustrators and 4 freelance designers/year. Uses artists for advertising, brochure, and magazine design, illustration and layout and AV presentations, exhibits and displays.

First Contact & Terms: Send a query letter with resume and tearsheets, which will be kept on file. Samples not filed are returned only if requested. Reports back within 3-4 weeks. Call or write for an appointment to show a portfolio. Pays by the project. Considers available budget, skill and experience of the artist and turnaround time when establishing payment.

Tips: "We are a nonprofit organization and do not have a large budget for outside services."

Close-up

Randi Robin
Graphic Designer
Steppenwolf Theatre

Steppenwolf Theatre Company, according to principal graphic designer Randi Robin, "likes to see itself on the cutting edge, taking the extra step, sometimes risking safe productions for more innovative ones. This philosophy is [also] reflected in the theater's innovative graphic design and illustration." And this philosophy must work since Steppenwolf's production of "The Grapes of Wrath" won the 1990 Tony Award's Best Drama of the Year.

Robin, who has donated her services to Steppenwolf for the past six years, works independently as a graphic designer and works with the theater company on a freelance basis. She remains actively involved, overseeing 80-90 percent of the printing of production posters, stage bills and invitations.

Robin states that she primarily utilizes illustrations to convey a visual image of a play to an audience, even though this approach tends to be more time consuming than the use of photography. She keeps the work of freelance illustrators on file until she encounters a particular project the work is suitable for, and then calls the artist. If an agreement can be reached regarding fees and time constraints, the artist is assigned to the project. The process begins with preliminary pencil sketches, which must be approved by both Robin and the theater. When any necessary changes have been made, a medium is chosen. The average poster is completed within three weeks.

With Steppenwolf's promotions, Robin tries to convey a visual image of the play to the audience. Just as each play is different from the other, so too are the promotions. These two posters illustrate the variety of Steppenwolf's design and the way the typography ties in with the image.

Reprinted with permission of the artists

Robin is approached by 30-50 freelance artists per year and actually works with 10-15. She advises freelance artists to be adaptable and to show a broad range of styles and media, including one-color, four-color and black and white. "This is especially important with plays," she explains, "since they are all so different from one another. For example, the artist who designed the [promotion] for 'A Walk in the Woods' had a certain German Expressionist style that was appropriate for that play."

The title of a promotion is just as important as the illustration, stresses Robin. "To me, the most successful [promotions] have unique titles. It is very important that the type be merged with the image." She admits, however, that if a play is good and has favorable reviews, the promotion itself is not important.

Robin looks to the arts section of *The New York Times* for current trends in theater design and illustration, but is unable to see any clearly defined trends in the Chicago area, which is "very diversified." Specifically, says Robin, Steppenwolf tends to be "very esoteric in its thinking of what the image of a play should be, and I tend to be more broad. By working together, I think we reach a good middle ground."

Working with a theater company presents a unique challenge to the freelance designer and illustrator, according to Robin. "It can be difficult to work with theater people because they are artists in their own right. So, if an artist is working for them, he must have a certain love for the theater. Concessions must be made on the part of the artist." Through her own donation of time and effort at Steppenwolf, Robin exemplifies this dedication to the theater. "I enjoy my work at Steppenwolf immensely and will continue to do it for as long as they want me."

—Roseann Shaughnessy

ANNA WYMAN DANCE THEATRE, 927 Granville St., 3rd Floor, Vancouver, British Columbia V6Z 1L3 Canada. (604)662-8846. Artistic Director: Anna Wyman. 18-member modern dance company.
Needs: Works with several freelance artists/year. Uses artists for advertising, brochure and program design, illustration and layout; set and costume design; poster design and illustration; lighting and scenery.
First Contact & Terms: All commercial artists are subject to portfolio review and recommendation/approval by Artistic Director Anna Wyman. Send query letter with brochure, resume, business card, tearsheets, photostats, photocopies, slides and photographs to be kept on file. Samples not kept on file are returned only if requested. Reports within weeks. Portfolio should include thumbnails, roughs, original/final art, final reproduction/product and b&w tearsheets, photostats and photographs. Call or write for appointment to show portfolio. Pays by the project. Considers complexity of project and available budget when establishing payment.

Record Companies

Album and CD cover design and illustration are the big drawing cards for freelance artists in this section, but don't overlook promotional materials and collaterals for assignments. The recording industry offers an opportunity for creativity, since most companies have no set theme for the artwork they seek, but want the illustrator/designer to capture the mood evoked by the music in an attention-getting manner.

Artwork for album covers must be distinctive, provocative and appropriate to the performer and his music. Rock bands now have distinct visual styles, sharpened by their participation in videos. Gospel and country & western artists favor a more conservative image. Artwork for classical albums tends to be either representational or abstract, capturing the images of noted composers of the past or of historical genres. Because artwork must be appropriate for both long-play record albums and CD boxes, there is more vertical emphasis.

Creative directors at record companies are looking for a distinctive style that has a strong visual impact. If you wish to explore this market, study the current relationship of art and music on covers and promotional pieces by visiting record stores. Your sample package should include examples that reflect a strong graphic image that literally beckons a viewer. You don't have to live in one of the recording capitals to land the job, since most work is on assignment only. When negotiating a contract, remember to ask for a credit line on the album jacket and then later, a number of samples for your portfolio. Skills such as layout and paste-up are useful to fill many production jobs at record companies.

The names and addresses of hundreds of record companies and affiliated services, such as design, artwork and promotions, are listed in the *Songwriter's Market 1991*, *Billboard International Buyer's Guide*, the *California Music Directory* and the *Music Industry Directory*.

ALEAR RECORDS, Route 2, Box 114, Berkeley Springs WV 25411. (304)258-2175. Owner: Jim McCoy. Estab. 1973. Produces tapes and albums: country/western. Recent releases: "Mysteries of Life," Carroll County Ramblers; "The Real McCoy of Country Music" and "Jim McCoy Touches Your Heart," by Jim McCoy.
Needs: Produces 12 soloists and 6 groups/year. Works with 3 visual artists/year. Works on assignment only. Uses artists for CD cover design and album/tape cover illustration.
First Contact & Terms: Send query letter with resume and SASE. Samples are filed. Reports back within 30 days. To show a portfolio, mail roughs and b&w samples. Pays by the project, $50-250.

ALPHABEAT, Box 12 01, D-6980 Wertheim/Main West Germany 9342-841 55. Owner: Stephan Dehn or A&R Marga Zimmerman. Produces CDs, tapes and albums: rhythm and blues, soul, disco, rap, pop, new wave, electronic and house; solo and group artists.
Needs: Uses artists for CD cover design and illustration, album/tape cover design and illustration, brochure design and illustration, catalog design, illustration and layout, direct mail packages, advertising design and illustration.
First Contact & Terms: Send query letter with brochure, tearsheets, photostats, resume, photographs, slides, SASE, photocopies and IRC. Samples are returned by SASE with IRC. To show a portfolio, mail appropriate materials. Payment depends on product. Rights purchased vary according to project.

AMERICAN MUSIC CO./CUCA RECORD & CASSETTE MFG. CO., Box 8604, Madison WI 53708. Vice President, Marketing: Daniel W. Miller. Produces polka, rock and roll, soul, country/western and folk. Recent releases: "Mule Skinner Blues," by The Fendermen; and "Listen to Me," by Legend.
Needs: Produces 1-5 records/year. Uses artists for album cover design and illustration; primarily uses caricatures and line drawings.
First Contact & Terms: Send query letter with business card and samples; may be kept on file. Prefers color slides as samples. Samples not filed are returned by SASE. Reports to the artist only if interested. Pays by the project, $25-100 average. Considers available budget when establishing payment. Purchases all rights.

Tips: Uses mostly "artists who are beginners."

THE AMETHYST GROUP LTD., 96 McGregor Downs, W. Cola SC 29169-2850. Contact: Record co. and management. Produces rock and roll, disco, soul, rhythm and blues; solo artists. Recent releases: "Complicated Love," by True Identity; "Pace of a Pretty Face," by J. Blues.
Needs: Produces 3 soloists and 5 groups/year. Uses artists for album cover and brochure design, direct mail packages and promotional materials.
First Contact & Terms: Send query letter with resume and samples. Samples are returned by SASE. Reports back within 5 weeks. Write to show a portfolio, which should include b&w photographs. Pays by the project, $25 minimum. Considers available budget and rights purchased when establishing payment. Negotiates rights purchased.
Tips: "Be realistic and practical. Express talent not hype; be persistent."

APON RECORD COMPANY, INC., Steinway Station, Box 3082, Long Island City NY 11103. (212)721-8599. President: Andre M. Poncic. Produces classical, folk and pop.
Needs: Produces 20 records/year. Works with 10 visual artists/year. Uses artists for album cover design and illustration, catalog illustration and layout, posters.
First Contact & Terms: Works on assignment only. Send brochure and samples to be kept on file. Write for art guidelines. Samples not filed are returned by SASE. Reports to the artist within 60 days only if interested. Considers available budget when establishing payment. Purchases all rights.

ART ATTACK RECORDINGS, INC., Box 31475, Fort Lowell Station, Tucson AZ 85751. (602)881-1212. President: William Cashman. Produces rock and roll, country/western, jazz, pop, rhythm and blues; solo artists.
Needs: Produces 4 records/year; works with 4 recording artists/year. Works with 5 visual artists/year. Uses artists for album cover design and illustration; catalog design and layout; advertising design, illustration and layout, posters.
First Contact & Terms: Works on assignment only. Send query letter with brochure, business card, tearsheets or photographs to be kept on file. Samples not filed are returned by SASE only if requested. Reports only if interested. Write for appointment to show portfolio. Original artwork not returned to artist. Pays by the hour, $10-25 average. Considers complexity of project and available budget when establishing payment. Purchases all rights.

ARZEE RECORD COMPANY and ARCADE RECORD COMPANY, 3010 N. Front St., Philadelphia Pa 19133. (215)426-5682. President: Rex Zario. Produces rock and roll, country/western, rhythm and blues. Recent releases: "Rock Around the Clock," by James E. Myers; "Worlds Apart," by Ray Whitley; "Why Do I Cry Over You," by Bill Haley.
Needs: Produces 25 records/year. Works with 150 visual artists/year. Uses artists for brochure and catalog design, posters.
First Contact & Terms: Send query letter with brochure and tearsheets to be kept on file. Samples not filed are returned by SASE if requested. Reports within 6 weeks. Originals not returned after job's completion. Call for appointment to show portfolio. Buys all rights.

AVM CORPORATION, 8 August Bebel, Langen West Germany 6070. (6103)24017. FAX: (6103)26203. Estab. 1986. Produces CDs, tapes and albums: rock and roll, rhythm and blues, classical, soul, disco, rap, pop; solo and group artists. Recent releases: "One Day at the Time," by Bobby Kimbal (Ex-Toto); "Alive and Kicking in L.A.," by Hazel O'Connor; and "101 Greatest Classics," by London Symphony Orchestra.
Needs: Produces 6-8 soloists and 12-15 groups/year. Works with 5 visual artists/year. Uses artists for CD cover design and illustration, album/tape cover design and illustration, catalog design, direct mail packages, advertising design and illustration, posters.
First Contact & Terms: Send query letter with brochure. Samples are filed or returned by SASE if requested by artist. Reports back within 1 month. Write to schedule an appointment to show a portfolio, which should include roughs, photographs or copies. Payment negotiable. Buys all rights.

AZRA INTERNATIONAL, Box 459, Maywood CA 90270. (213)560-4223. Artist Development: D.T. Richards. Produces rock and roll and novelty records, by group and solo artists. Recent releases: "Salute the New Flag," by Mad Reign; "I Wanna Wrestle You," by Mad Matt; "And the Dead Shall Rise,", by Ripper.
Needs: Produces 6 soloists and 6 groups/year. Uses artists for album cover design and illustration.
First Contact & Terms: Send query letter. Samples are filed or are returned by SASE. Reports back within 1 week. Call to show a portfolio. Pays by the project, $100 minimum. Considers how work will be used when establishing payment. Negotiates rights purchased.
Tips: Looking for originality.

BILLY BAKER & ASSOCIATES, 3345 Hollins Ferry Rd., Baltimore MD 21227. (301)247-7447. FAX: (301)247-7445. Owner: William Baker. Estab. 1988. Produces tapes: country/western. Recent releases: "Carolina Blue," "Count the Times" and "Sad Eyes," by Johnny Ray Anthony.

Needs: Produces 10 soloists/year. Works with 50 visual artists/year. Uses artists for CD cover design, album/tape cover design and illustration, brochure illustration, catalog design, direct mail packages, advertising illustration, posters.
First Contact & Terms: Send query letter with brochure and photographs. Samples are filed. Reports back within 3 weeks only if interested. Call to schedule an appointment to show a portfolio or mail appropriate materials: b&w photographs. Rights purchased vary according to project.

BERANDOL MUSIC LIMITED, 110A Sackville St., Toronto, Ontario M5A 3E7 Canada. (416)869-1872. FAX: (416)869-1873. A&R Director: Tony T. Procewiat. Produces rock and roll, classical, disco and educational records. Recent releases: "Love Theme from Canada," by The Cosmic Orchestra; "The Magic Singing Animal Farm," by David Walden; "The Beastles Party Album," by the Beastles.
Needs: Produces 2 soloists and 2 groups/year. Works with 2 visual artists/year. Works on assignment only. Uses artists for album cover design and illustration, brochure design and illustration, direct mail packages and posters.
First Contact & Terms: Send query letter with brochure showing art style. Samples are filed. Reports back within 5 weeks. To show a portfolio, mail final reproduction/product. Pays by the project, $500-5,000. Considers skills and experience of artist and how work will be used when establishing payment. Buys all rights.

B.G.S. PRODUCTIONS LTD., Newtown St., Kilsyth, Glasgow G65 0JX Scotland. 0236-821081. Director: Dougie Stevenson. Produces rock and roll, country/western, jazz and folk; solo artists. Recent releases: "From Scotland With Love," by Sydney Devine; "The Pipes and Strings of Scotland," instrumental; and "Lena Martell Today."
Needs: Produces 20 records/year. Works with 2 visual artists/year. Uses artists for album cover design and illustration; brochure design, illustration and layout; catalog design, illustration and layout; advertising design, illustration and layout; posters.
First Contact & Terms: Send brochure, resume and samples to be kept on file. Call or write for appointment to show portfolio. Accepts photostats, photographs, photocopies or tearsheets as samples. Samples not filed are returned only if requested. Reports only if interested. Pays by the hour, $20 average. Considers available budget when establishing payment. Purchases all rights.

BIG BEAR RECORDS, P.O. Box, Birmingham B16 8UT England. (021)454-7020. Managing Director: Jim Simpson. Produces soul, jazz, rhythm and blues. Recent releases: "King Pleasure and the Biscuit Boys," "Bill Allred's Good Time Jazz Band," and "Lady Sings the Blues."
Needs: Produces 10 records/year. Works with 2 visual artists/year. Uses artists for album cover design and illustration.
First Contact & Terms: Works on assignment only. Send query letter with photographs or photocopies to be kept on file. Samples not filed are returned only by SAE (nonresidents include IRC). Negotiates payment. Considers complexity of project and how work will be used when establishing payment. Purchases all rights.

BOUQUET-ORCHID ENTERPRISES, Box 11686, Atlanta GA 30355. (404)355-7635. President: Bill Bohannon. Produces country, pop and contemporary gospel.
Needs: Produces 10 records/year; 5 of which have cover/jackets designed and illustrated by freelance artists. Uses artists for record album and brochure design.
First Contact & Terms: Send query letter with resume and samples. "I prefer a brief but concise overview of an artist's background and works showing the range of his talents." Include SASE. Reports within 2 weeks. Negotiates payment.

BOVINE RECORD COMPANY, 593 Kildare Rd., London Ontario N6H 3H8 Canada. (416)277-3908. President: Jack Moorhouse. Estab. 1977. Produces tapes: rock and roll, country/western; solo artists. Recent releases: "It's Time to Go," by John Moorhouse; "Reconsider Me," by Solid Ivory Brothers; and "Honky Tonk Angel," by Merle Morgan.
Needs: Produces 2 soloists and 2 groups/year. Works with 10 visual artists/year. Prefers local artists only. Works on assignment only. Uses artists for album/tape cover illustration and design, brochure illustration, direct mail packages, advertising design, posters.
First Contact & Terms: Send query letter with brochure, SASE and photographs. Samples are filed or are returned by SASE. Reports within 2 months. To show a portfolio, mail b&w and color photographs. Pays by the project.
Tips: "Circulate your best projects."

CDE, Box 310551, Atlanta GA 30331-0551. President: Charles Edwards. Produces disco, soul, jazz, rhythm and blues.
Needs: Produces 6-10 records/year; 100% of the album covers assigned to freelance designers, 100% to freelance illustrators. Assigns varying number of freelance jobs/year. Works on assignment only. Uses artists for album cover, poster, brochure and advertising design and illustration and direct mail packages. No set style, "we are open-minded to any style."

First Contact & Terms: Send query letter with brochure showing art style, photostats and original work. Samples not returned. Reports within 2 months. Original work returned after job's completion "by request." Negotiates payment. Buys first rights or negotiates rights purchased.
Tips: "The business needs new and creative people."

CHAPMAN RECORDING STUDIOS, 228 W. 5th St., Kansas City MO 64105. (816)842-6854. Contact: Chuck Chapman. Produces rock and roll, soul, country, jazz, folk, pop, rhythm and blues. Recent releases: "I Will Never Die" by Freddie Hart; "Phrogs, Pharaohs & Phorgiveness" by Paul Land & Ray Hildebrand.
Needs: Produces 25 records/year; 15 of which have cover/jackets designed and illustrated by freelance artists. Interested in record album design; no paintings.
First Contact & Terms: Send brochure or material that can be kept on file for future reference. Negotiates pay based on set fee/job.
Tips: "Original album jacket artwork has taken a jump within our operation."

COMMA RECORDS & TAPES, Box 2148, D-6078, Neu Isenburg West Germany. 06102-52696. FAX: 06102-52696. Contact: Marketing Department. Estab. 1972. Produces CDs, tapes and albums: rock and roll, rhythm and blues, classical, country/western, soul, folk, disco, pop; group and solo artists.
Needs: Produces 70 soloists and 40 groups/year. Works with 10 visual artists/year. Uses artists for CD cover and album/tape cover and brochure design and illustration, posters.
First Contact & Terms: Send query letter with brochure, tearsheets, photostats, photographs, SASE, photocopies and transparencies. Samples are not filed and are returned by SASE if requested by artist. Reports back to the artist only if interested and SASE enclosed. To show a portfolio, mail copies of final art and b&w photostats, tearsheets, photographs and transparencies. Payment negotiated. Buys first rights and all rights.

COSMOTONE RECORDS, Box 71988, Los Angeles CA 90071-0988. Record Producer: Rafael Brom. Produces rock, disco, country/western, folk, pop, educational; group and solo artits. Recent releases: "Padre Pio" by Lord Hamilton and "No. 1" by R.B.
Needs: Produces 3 soloists and 1 group/year. Works with 4 visual artists/year. Prefers artists with 10 years experience minimum. Works on assignment only. Uses artists for album brochure and advertising, catalog design and illustration, catalog layout, direct mail packages, posters and videos.
First Contact & Terms: Send query letter with resume, photocopies and slides. Samples not filed are not returned. Reports back only if interested. Pays by the project, $100 minimum. Considers complexity of project and skills and experience of artist when establishing payment. Buys all rights.

COWBOY JUNCTION FLEA MARKET & PUBLISHING CO., Highway 44 and Junction 490, Lecanto FL 32661. (904)746-4754. Secretary: Elizabeth Thompson. Estab. 1957. Produces tapes and albums: country/western and bluegrass. Recent releases: "Heart of Love," by Buddy Max; "Falina I Love You," by Wally Jones; and "Cedar Chips," by Leo Vargason.
Needs: Produces 3 soloists and 3 groups/year. Works with 12 visual artists/year. Uses artists for album/tape cover illustration and design and direct mail packages.
First Contact & Terms: Send query letter with SASE. Samples are not filed and are returned by SASE. To show a portfolio, mail "whatever one has."
Tips: "Display at Cowboy Junction Flea Market on Tuesday or Friday; come to our Country/Western–Bluegrass Music Show Saturday at 2 pm and show us and all involved your works. Closed July and August."

CREOLE RECORDS LTD., The Chilterns France Hill Drive, Camberley Surrey GU15 3QA England. 0276-686077. FAX: 0276-686055. Manager: Steve Tantum. Produces dance, disco, soul and pop; group and solo artists. Recent releases: "I Want to Wake Up with You" by Borns Gardiner.
Needs: Produces 45 records/year. Produces 5 soloists and 4 groups/year. Works with 6 visual artists/year. Uses artists for album cover design and illustration; advertising design, illustration and layout and posters.
First Contact & Terms: Send resume and samples to be kept on file. Accepts any samples. Samples not filed are returned by SAE (nonresidents include IRC). Reports within 3 weeks. Original art sometimes returned to artist if SAE. Payment varies. Considers complexity of project, available budget, skill and experience of commercial artist, how work will be used and rights purchased when establishing payment. Buys all rights.

CURRENT RECORDS/MANAGEMENT, 366 Adelaide St. E., Toronto, Ontario MSA 3X 9 Canada. (416)361-1101. FAX: (416)867-9501. Product Manager: Shelley-Lynn Pybus. Estab. 1983. Produces CDs, tapes and albums: rock and roll, rap, pop and dance music; solo and group artists. Recent releases: "Uptown," by Machinations (Australia); "Human Sexuality," by Mystery Romance (Canada); and "The Black Earth," by The Black Earth (England).
Needs: Produces 1-2 soloists and 5 groups/year. Works with several visual artists/year. Prefers artists with experience in album design. Works on assignment only. Uses artists for CD cover design, album/tape cover design and illustration, advertising illustration and posters.

First Contact & Terms: Send query letter with brochure, tearsheets, resume, photographs and SASE. Samples are filed if interested or are returned by SASE if requested by artist. Reports within 1 week. Call if in Toronto or mail your best work. "Payment depends on the budget. If it's a new act, we don't spend a big budget, if act is huge—there is a larger budget." Rights purchased vary according to project.

Tips: "As long as you believe in your work, you're creative, in the sense that you are original and can always expand on an idea. Don't give up! It only takes one and you're on your way!"

CURTISS RECORDS, Box 1622, Hendersonville TN 37077. President: W. Curtiss. Estab. 1970. Produces CDs, tapes and albums: rock and roll, rhythm and blues, country/western, jazz, soul, folk, disco, rap, pop and gospel; solo and group artists. Recent releases: "Big Heavy" and "Real Cool," by Rhythm Rockers.

Needs: Produces 8-10 soloists and 5-10 groups/year. Works with 3-12 visual artists/year. Works on assignment only. Uses artists for CD cover design and illustration, album/tape cover design and illustration, brochure design and illustration, catalog design, illustration and layout, direct mail packages, advertising design and illustration and posters.

First Contact & Terms: Send query letter with brochure, photographs and SASE. Samples are sometimes filed or are returned by SASE. Reports within 3-4 weeks. Write to schedule an appointment to show a portfolio, which should include original/final art and b&w and color photographs and SASE. Pay varies. Negotiates rights purchased.

CURTISS UNIVERSAL RECORD MASTERS, Box 4740, Nashville TN 37216. (615)865-4740. Manager: S.D. Neal. Produces soul, country, jazz, folk, pop, rock and roll, and rhythm and blues. Recent releases by Dixie Dee & The Rhythm Rockers, and Ben Williams.

Needs: Produces 6 records/year; some of which have cover/jackets designed and illustrated by freelance artists. Works on assignment only. Uses artists for album cover and poster design.

First Contact & Terms: Send business card and samples to be kept on file. Submit portfolio for review. Include SASE. Reports within 3 weeks. Originals returned to artist after job's completion. Negotiates pay based on artist involved. Negotiates rights purchased.

DEMI MONDE RECORDS AND PUBLISHING LTD., Foel, Llanfair Caereinion, Powys SY21 OR2 Wales. (0938)810758. Managing Director: D. Anderson. Estab. 1984. Produces CDs, tapes and albums: rock and roll, rhythm and blues and pop; group artists. Recent releases are by Hawkwind, Gong and Atomic Rooster.

Needs: Produces 10 groups/year. Works with 7 visual artists/year. Works on assignment only. Uses artists for CD cover design and illustration, album/tape cover design and illustration, brochure illustration, catalog design, illustration and layout, direct mail packages and advertising design.

First Contact & Terms: Send query letter with resume, photographs, SASE and photocopies. Samples are filed. Reports back to the artist only if interested. To show a portfolio, mail photostats and photographs. Pays by the project. Payment varies. Buys all rights.

DIGIMIX INTERNATIONAL RECORDS LTD., Sovereign House, 12 Trewartha Rd., Praa Sands Penzance, Cornwall TR20 9ST England. (0736)762826. FAX: (0736)763328. Music Director: Roderick Jones. Estab. 1989. Produces CDs, tapes and albums: rock and roll, rhythm and blues, classical, country/western, jazz, soul, folk, disco, rap, pop, gospel/Christian instrumental, educational; group and solo artists. Recent releases: "The Light and Shade of Eddie Blackstone," by Eddie Blackstone; "The Digimix House of Dance," a compilation of various artists; and "The Intimate Classical Guitar," a compilation of various artists.

Needs: Works on assignment only. Uses artists for CD cover design and illustration, album/tape cover design and illustration, brochure design and illustration, catalog design and illustration, direct mail packages, advertising design and posters.

First Contact & Terms: Send query letter with brochure, tearsheets, photostats, resume, photographs, SASE/IRC's and photocopies. Samples are filed. Reports to the artist only if interested. To show a portfolio, mail roughs and "definitely do not send" original/final art unless requested, b&w and color photographs, "anything which would benefit." Pays by the project. Payment negotiable. Rights purchased vary according to project.

Tips: "Identify the market—be commercial and appealing with each project. Categorize a portfolio into identifying musical categories."

DKP PRODUCTIONS, INC., 731 N. Harvard, Villa Park IL 60181. (708)941-0232. FAX: (708)941-0257. Director of Marketing: Mike Brandvold. Estab. 1986. Produces CDs, tapes and albums: rock and roll. Recent releases: "Renaissance Junkyard," by The Ultraviolet and "Phase II and Into The Night," by Defcon.

Needs: Produces 2 groups/year. Works with 2 visual artists/year. Prefers artists with experience in album design. Works on assignment only. Uses artists for CD cover design and illustration, album/tape cover design and illustration and posters.

First Contact & Terms: Send query letter with brochure, tearsheets, resume and photocopies. Samples are filed. Does not report back, in which case the artist should "contact us." Call to schedule an appointment to show a portfolio. Pays by the project. Buys all rights.

DYNACOM COMMUNICATIONS, INC., Box 702, Snowdon Station, Montreal, Quebec H3X 3X8 Canada. General Manager: D. Leonard. Produces rock and roll, disco, soul, country/western, jazz, folk, pop, educational, and rhythm and blues.

Needs: Produces 10 records/year. Uses artists for album cover design and illustration; brochure, catalog and advertising design, illustration and layout; direct mail packages and posters.

First Contact & Terms: Send query letter with brochure, resume, business card, photostats, slides or photographs and tearsheets. Samples not returned. Works on assignment only. Considers complexity of project, available budget, skill and experience of artist, how work will be used, turnaround time and rights purchased when establishing payment. Negotiates rights purchased.

EXECUTIVE RECORDS, 11 Shady Oak Trail, Charlotte NC 28210. (704)554-1162. Executive Director: Butch Kelly. Produces rock and roll, disco, soul, country/western, jazz, classical, gospel, pop and rhythm and blues; group and solo artists. Recent releases include "Super Star" and "I Just Want Somebody to Love" by L.A. Star and "Show Me Love" by Jay Wylie.

Needs: Produces 9 records/year by 4 groups and 5 soloists. Works with 3 groups and 3 solo recording artists/year. Works with 2 visual artists/year. Seeks artists with 3 years experience. Works on assignment only. Uses artists for album cover design, advertising design and layout and direct mail packages.

First Contact & Terms: Send query letter with brochure, resume and photographs to be kept on file. Samples not filed returned by SASE. Reports back only if interested. Original art sometimes are returned to the artist. To show a portfolio, mail original/final art and color photographs with SASE. Pays by the project, $25-100 average. Considers available budget and skill and experience of commercial artist when establishing payment. Buys all rights.

Tips: "Just be original. We like to see more color. It's affected my use in a more positive way."

FACTORY BEAT RECORDS, INC., 521 5th Ave., New York NY 10175. Produces disco, pop, contemporary and rhythm and blues. Recent releases: "Dance It Off" and "I Love Your Beat," by Rena; "Let's Slip Away" and "Everybody's Doin' It," by Charles T. Hudson.

Needs: Produces 2 albums/year.

First Contact & Terms: Send query letter with brochure and original work to be kept on file. Samples not filed are returned by SASE. Reports only if interested. Originals not returned to artist after job's completion. Considers available budget when establishing payment. Negotiates rights purchased.

FARR MUSIC AND RECORDS, Box 1098, Somerville NJ 08876. Contact: (201)722-2304. Candace Campbell. Produces rock and roll, disco, soul, country/western, folk and pop; group and solo artists.

Needs: Produces 12 records/year by 8 groups and 4 soloists. Works with 40 visual artists/year. Uses artists for album cover design and illustration, brochure and catalog design, advertising design and illustration and posters.

First Contact & Terms: Send query letter with resume, tearsheets, photostats, photocopies, slides and photographs to be kept on file. Samples not filed are returned by SASE. Reports within 3 weeks. To show a portfolio, mail roughs, final reproduction/product and color photographs. Original art returned to the artist. Buys first rights or all rights.

FINER ARTS RECORDS/TRANSWORLD RECORDS, Suite 115, 2170 S. Parker Rd., Denver CO 80231. (303)755-2546. FAX: (303)755-2617. President: R. Bernstein. Produces rock and roll, disco, soul, country/western, jazz, pop and rhythm and blues records by group and solo artists. Recent releases: "Israel Oh Israel" (a new Broadway musical), "Bonnie Delaney," "Kaylen Wells" and "Leeona Miracle." New recording artists ready for release.

Needs: Produces 2-3 soloists and 2-3 groups/year. Uses artists for album cover design and illustration and posters.

First Contact & Terms: Send query letter with brochure showing art style or resume and tearsheets, photostats and photocopies. Samples are filed or returned only if requested. Reports back only if interested. Write to schedule an appointment to show a portfolio. Pays by the project, $500 minimum. Considers complexity of project, available budget and turnaround time when establishing payment. Buys all rights and negotiates rights purchased.

FINKELSTEIN MANAGEMENT CO. LTD./TRUE NORTH RECORDS, Suite 301, 151 John St., Toronto Ontario M5V 2T2 Canada. (416)596-8696. FAX: (416)596-6861. Director: Jehanne Languedoc. Estab. 1969. Produces CDs, tapes and albums: rock and roll, folk and pop; solo and group artists. Recent releases: "Big Circumstance" and "Stealing Fire," by Bruce Cockburn, and "Barney Bentall & The Legendary Hearts," by Barney Bentall.

Needs: Produces 1 soloist and 2 groups/year. Works with 4 or 5 visual artists/year. Prefers artists with experience in album cover design. Uses artists for CD cover design and illustration, album/tape cover design and illustration, posters and photography.

First Contact & Terms: Send query letter with SASE. Samples are filed or are returned by SASE if requested by artist. Reports only if interested. Call to schedule an appointment to show a portfolio which should contain "whatever you feel is an accurate representation of your work." Pays by the project. Buys all rights.

FRECKLE RECORDS, Pioneer Square, Box 4005, Seattle WA 98104. (206)682-3200. General Manager: Jack Burg. Produces folk and pop; group and solo artists. Recent release: "A Collection" by Reilly & Maloney.
Needs: Produces 3 records/year. Uses artists for album cover design and illustration, brochure and advertising design and layout and posters.
First Contact & Terms: Prefers local experienced artists. Works on assignment only. Send query letter with brochure, resume, business card and samples to be kept on file. Call or write for appointment to show portfolio. Samples not filed are returned by SASE. Reports only if interested. Pays by the project. Considers complexity of project, available budget, skill and experience of commercial artist, how work will be used, turnaround time and rights purchased when establishing payment. Negotiates rights purchased.

FRONTLINE MUSIC GROUP, (formerly Frontline Records), Suite 200, 2955 E. Main St., Irvine CA 92714. (714)660-3888. FAX: (714)660-3899. Vice President Creative Services: Ed McTaggart. Estab. 1986. Produces rock and roll records by group and solo artists. Recent releases: "Out of the Darkness," by Bloodgood; "Wake Up," by Mark Farner; "In Your Face," by Shout and "Once Dead," by Vengeance Rising.
Needs: Produces 5 soloists and 10 groups/year. Works with 8 visual artists/year. Prefers local (Orange County/LA County) artists. Will accept photo transparencies from out of state. Works on assignment only. Uses artists for album cover design and illustration; brochure design and illustration; catalog design, illustration and layout; direct mail packages; advertising design and illustration and posters.
First Contact & Terms: Send query letter with resume and tearsheets, photostats, photocopies, slides and sample LP covers. Samples are filed. Reports back only if interested. Call to schedule an appointment to show a portfolio, which should include color and b&w roughs, original/final art, final reproduction/product and photographs. Pays for design by the hour, $10-20. Pays for illustration by the project, $300-1,500. Considers available budget, how work will be used and turnaround time when establishing payment. Buys one-time rights, all rights or negotiates rights purchased.
Tips: "I need artists that like creative challenges."

GALACTIC GRAPHICA, 44 Archdekin Dr., Brampton, Ontario L6V 1Y4 Canada. (416)572-7474. Controller: Randall. Estab. 1984. Produces CDs, tapes and albums: rock and roll, rhythm and blues, country, jazz; solo artists. Recent releases: "Rebel-U-Tion," by Lynne and the Rebels; "Audio Radiance for the Radio Audience," by Roto-noto; and "Big Problems in the Small Town," by Steve Middleton.
Needs: Produces 10 groups/year. Works with 2 visual artists/year. Works on assignment only. Uses artists for CD cover and album/tape cover design and illustration.
First Contact & Terms: Send query letter with tearsheets, resume and SASE. Samples are filed or returned by SASE if requested by artist. Reports back within 5 weeks only if interested. To show a portfolio, mail b&w photostats and photographs. Pays by the project. Rights purchased vary according to project.

GLOBAL RECORDS, Bakersfield Records, Chris Music Publishing, Sara Lee Music Publishing, 133 Arbutus Ave., Box 396, Mantistique MI 49854. Contact: Art Department. Produces soul, country/western, folk, rhythm and blues and contemporary gospel; group artists. Recent releases "Diamonds & Pearls," by Paradons; Milestone Records and Tapes, K-Tel Albums and cassettes.
Needs: Produces 11 records/year. Works with 2 visual artists/year. Uses artists for advertising design, illustration and layout; also advertising design for other businesses.
First Contact & Terms: Prefers amateur artists. Works on assignment only. Send query letter with brochure to be kept on file. Prefers photographs or tearsheets as samples. Samples returned by SASE. Reports within 3 months. Original artwork not returned to artist. Negotiates payment by the project. Considers available budget when establishing payment. Purchases all rights.
Tips: "We prefer a query first as to current needs. Don't send portfolio unless we ask." Looking for "one who can portray in a unique, interesting different way—not surrealism—but up to current music, CD ads in various music trades, etc."

GRASS ROOTS RECORDS, Box 532, Malibu CA 90265. (213)463-5998. President: Lee Magid. Estab. 1985. Produces CDs, tapes and albums: rock and roll, rhythm and blues, country/western, jazz, soul, rap, pop, black gospel, dance, salsa and Afro-Cuban; solo and group artists. Recent releases: "What Shall I Do?" by Tramaine Hawkins and "Welcome to the Blues," by Perry Walker.
Needs: Produces 8 soloists and 4 groups/year. Works with 4 visual artists/year. Works on assignment only. Uses artists for CD cover, album/tape cover and brochure design and illustration, catalog design, illustration and layout, direct mail packages, advertising illustration, posters and visuals for videos.
First Contact & Terms: Send query letter with photostats. Samples are filed and not returned. Reports only if interested. Portfolio should include color photostats. Pays by the project. Buys all rights. Negotiates rights purchased.

Tips: "Keep on submitting—someone will bite. Don't get too fancy if you're looking for a break."

HARD HAT RECORDS AND CASSETTE TAPES, 519 N. Halifax Ave., Daytona Beach FL 32018. (904)252-0381. FAX: (904)252-0381. Vice President, Sales/Promotion: Bobby Lee. Produces rock and roll, country/western, folk and educational; group and solo artists. Publishes high school/college marching band arrangements. Recent releases: "Sand in my Shoes & V-A-C-A-T-I-O-N" by the Hard Hatters; "Just a Piece of Paper," "Country Blues," "Can't Get Over Lovin' You," and "Only Lies" by the Blue Bandana Country Band.
Needs: Produces 12-30 records/year. Works with 2-3 visual artists/year. Works on assignment only. Uses artists for album cover design and illustration, advertising design and sheet music covers.
First Contact & Terms: Send query letter with brochure to be kept on file one year. Samples not filed are returned by SASE. Reports within 2 weeks. Write for appointment to show portfolio. Pays by the project. Considers complexity of project, available budget, skill and experience of artist, how work will be used, turnaround time and rights purchased when establishing payment. Purchases all rights.
Tips: "Video is playing a bigger part in the art market for record and tape companies. The market for this medium of musical entertainment has its own styles and needs."

HULA RECORDS, INC., Box 2135, Honolulu HI 96805. (808)847-4608. President: Donald P. McDiarmid III. Produces pop, educational and Hawaiian records; group and solo artists.
Needs: Produces 1-2 soloists and 3-4 groups/year. Works on assignment only. Uses artists for album cover design and illustration, brochure and catalog design, catalog layout, advertising design and posters.
First Contact & Terms: Send query letter with tearsheets and photocopies. Samples are filed or are returned only if requested. Reports back within 2 weeks. Write to schedule an appointment to show a portfolio. Pays by the project, $50-350. Considers available budget and rights purchased when establishing payment. Negotiates rights purchased.

JAY JAY, NE 35 62nd St., Miami FL 33138. (305)758-0000. President: Walter Jagiello. Produces country/western, jazz and polkas. Recent releases: "Polka Jazz," by The Raz Mataz Dixieland Jazz Band; "Polka Music Is My Life," and "Li'l Wally Sings," by Li'l Wally; "Polka Specials," by John Check and "Claude Musczynski Plays," by Claude Musczynski.
Needs: Produces 6 albums/year. Works on assignment only. Uses artists for album cover design and illustration, brochure design, catalog layout; advertising design, illustration and layout and posters.
First Contact & Terms: Send brochure and tearsheets to be kept on file. Call or write for appointment to show portfolio. Samples not filed are returned by SASE. Reports within 2 months. Pays by the project. Considers skill and experience of artist when establishing payment. Purchases all rights.

K.A.M. EXECUTIVE RECORDS, 11 Shady Oak Trail, Charlotte NC 28210. (704)554-1162. Creative Director: Butch Kelly. Produces disco, soul, country/western, jazz, pop, rhythm and blues; group and solo artists. Recent releases: "M.C. Perpetrators," by Lady Crush & DJ Jazz and "Street Dancin," by Fresh Air.
Needs: Produces 4 soloists and 3 groups/year. Works with 1 visual artist/year. Prefers artists with 3 years of experience. Works on assignment only. Uses artists for album cover, brochure and catalog design, advertising design and illustration and posters.
First Contact & Terms: Send brochure or resume, tearsheets, photostats, and photocopies. Samples are filed or are returned by SASE only if requested by artist. Reports back within 2 months or only if interested. Write to schedule an appointment to show a portfolio, which should include color final reproduction/product, photostats and photographs. Pays by the project, $50 minimum. Considers available budget, skills and experience of artist and rights purchased when establishing payment. Buys all rights; negotiates rights purchased.
Tips: "Be creative with new ideas."

KICKING MULE RECORDS, Box 158, Alderpoint CA 95411. Manager: Ed Denson. Produces guitar, banjo and dulcimer records. Catalog 100. Recent releases: "Elizabethians Dulcimer," by Randy Wilkinson; "Run-off," by Chris Proctor; and "Dialogs," by Beppe Gambetta.
Needs: Buys 10-20 designs/year. Especially needs book design and layout, cover art and book graphics.
First Contact & Terms: Query with full-size covers or layouts; local artists only. Does not wish to see illustrations. Include SASE. Reports in 4 weeks. Buys all rights. Pays $2.50/page, layout of tab books; $300, album cover design; $100, album liner design.
Tips: "Get to know the performers—they often pick their own designers."

KIMBO EDUCATIONAL, 10 N. 3rd Ave., Long Branch NJ 07740. Production Coordinators: Amy Laufer and James Kimble. Educational record/cassette company. Produces 8 records and cassettes/year for schools, teacher supply stores and parents. Contents primarily early childhood physical fitness, although other materials are produced for all ages.

Needs: Works with 3 freelance artists/year. Local artists only. Works on assignment only. Uses artists for ads, catalog design, album covers and flyer designs. Artist must have experience in the preparation of album jackets or cassette inserts.

First Contact & Terms: "It is very hard to do this type of material via mail." Write or call for appointment to show portfolio. Prefers photographs or actual samples of past work. Reports only if interested. Pays for design and illustration by the project, $200-500. Considers complexity of project and budget when establishing payment. Buys all rights.

Tips: "The jobs at Kimbo vary tremendously. We are an educational record company that produces material from infant level to senior citizen level. Sometimes we need cute 'kid-like' illustrations and sometimes graphic design will suffice. A person experienced in preparing an album cover would certainly have an edge. Prefer working with local talent. We are an educational firm so we cannot pay commercial record/cassette art prices."

KING KLASSIC RECORDS, Box 8532, Waukegan IL 60079. (708)336-5619. Manager: Dennis Bergeron. Estab. 1985. Produces CDs, tapes and albums: rock and roll and heavy metal. Recent releases: "Hellcats," by Hellcats; "Black Sanctuary," by Genocide; and "Monster of Steel," by Oxenkiller.

Needs: Produces 4 groups/year. Works with 6 visual artists/year. Prefers local artists with experience in photography. Uses artists for CD cover and album/tape cover design and illustration, advertising illustration and logo design.

First Contact & Terms: Send query letter with resume, tearsheets, photographs or photostats. Samples are filed. Reports within 2 weeks. Write to schedule an appointment to show (or mail) a portfolio which should include b&w and color photographs. Pays by the project, $25-600. Rights purchased vary according to project.

HOWARD KNIGHT ENTERTAINMENT GROUP, 1609 Congress Rd., Eastover SC 29044. (803)776-8397. President: Howard A. Knight, Jr.. Estab. 1969. Produces CDs, tapes and albums: rock and roll, rhythm and blues, country/western, folk, pop, educational; solo and group artists. "Our primary label is Pegasus Records." Recent releases: "Naughty and Nice," by Almost Nuts Band; "A Woman's Way," by Mundo Earwood; and "Our Latest," by The Bandit Band."

Needs: Produces 6 soloists and 4 groups/year. Prefers local artists only. Will work with new artists and help them, if they are reasonable (both to deal with and their fees). Works on assignment only. Uses artists for CD cover, album/tape cover, brochure advertising design and illustration, catalog design, illustration and layout, direct mail packages, posters, press kits and logos for artists.

First Contact & Terms: Send query letter with brochure, resume and SASE. Samples are filed. Reports within 2-6 weeks. "Whatever you wish to submit which shows off your artistic ability" should be submitted by mail. Pays by the project, $75-1,000. Rights purchased vary according to project.

Tips: "Work with small acts and labels at a reasonable fee in order to build a quality, professional portfolio and then approach larger acts, agents, labels etc."

KOTTAGE RECORDS, Box 121626, Nashville TN 37212. (615)726-3556. President: Neal James. Estab. 1972. Produces CDs and tapes: rock and roll, rhythm and blues, country/western, soul, pop; solo and group artists. Recent releases: "Tell Me," by Kenny Carr; "22," by Jeremiah Hedge; and "Love Don't Lie," by Ted Yost.

Needs: Produces 6 soloists and 2 groups/year. Works with 3 visual artists/year. Works on assignment only. Uses artists for CD cover and album/tape cover design and illustration, brochure and advertising design, posters and video covers.

First Contact & Terms: Send query letter with resume and SASE. Samples are not filed and are returned by SASE if requested by artist. Reports within 3 weeks. Write to schedule an appointment to show a portfolio, which should include b&w and color tearsheets and photographs. Pays by the project, $50 and up. Rights purchased vary according to project.

LAMON RECORDS INC., 6903 E. Harris Blvd., Charlotte NC 28215. (704)537-0133. FAX: (704)535-4515. Chairman of Board: Dwight L. Moody Jr. Produces rock and roll, country/western, folk, rhythm and blues and religious music; group artists. Recent releases: "Cotton Eyed Joe," by Carlton Moody and the Moody Brothers.

Needs: Works on assignment only. Uses artists for album cover design and illustration, brochure design, direct mail packages and advertising design.

First Contact & Terms: Send brochure and tearsheets. Samples are filed and are not returned. Reports back only if interested. Call to schedule an appointment to show a portfolio or mail appropriate materials. Considers skill and experience of artist and how work will be used when establishing payment. Buys all rights.

Tips: "Include work that has been used on album covers, CD covers or cassette covers."

LANA RECORDS/TOP SECRET RECORDS, Box 12444, Fresno CA 93777-2444. (209)266-8067. Director: Robby Roberson. Produces rock and roll, classical, disco, soul, country/western, jazz, folk, pop, educational, rhythm and blues; group and solo artists. Recent releases: "There," by Oh Lamour and "Has It All Ended," by Rick Holley.

Needs: Produces 5 soloists and 5 groups/year. Prefers at least 2 years of experience or past credits. Uses artists for album cover, brochure and catalog design and illustration; catalog layout; direct mail packages; advertising design and illustration; and posters.

First Contact & Terms: Send query letter with resume and photocopies. Samples are filed or are returned by SASE. Reports back within 2 weeks. Write to schedule an appointment to show a portfolio or mail photostats. Pays by the project, $50. Considers complexity of project and rights purchased when establishing payment. Buys all rights.

Tips: "Be honest about what you are capable of doing."

LANDMARK COMMUNICATIONS GROUP, Box 148296, Nashville TN 37214. President: Bill Anderson Jr. Estab. 1980. Produces CDs and tapes: country/western and gospel. Recent releases: "Jesus Is Lord," by Joanne Cash Yates and Johnny Cash and "Play It Again, Sam," by Michael Lee Pickern.

Needs: Produces 6 soloists and 2 groups/year. Works with 3 visual artists/year. Works on assignment only. Uses artists for CD cover design and album/tape cover illustration.

First Contact & Terms: Send query letter with brochure. Samples are filed. Reports back within 1 month. Portfolio should include tearsheets and photographs. Rights purchased vary according to project.

LARRCO INDUSTRIES OF TEXAS, INC. KLARRCO SATELLITE RADIO AND T.V. DIVISION, Box 3842, Houston TX 77253-3842. (713)691-0778. President: Dr. L. Herbst. Estab. 1987. Produces tapes, albums, videos and film: rock and roll, country/western, soul, folk, educational and gospel; solo and group artists.

Needs: Produces 1 soloist and 1 group/year. Works on assignment only. Uses artists for album/tape cover design and illustration; brochure design and illustration; catalog design, illustration and layout; direct mail packages; advertising design and illustration; posters; and commercials.

First Contact & Terms: Send query letter with brochure, tearsheets, photostats, resume, photographs, slides, SASE and transparencies. Samples are filed or are returned by SASE if requested by artist. Reports back within 1 month. To show a portfolio, mail b&w and color photostats, slides, roughs, tearsheets transparencies, original/final art and photographs. Pays by the project, $25-25,000. Rights purchased vary according to project.

These are two examples of freelance artwork commissioned by managing director Ron Lee of Lematt Music Ltd. in Buckinghamshire, England. He says, above all else, he looks for originality in artists. ©1989 Lematt Music Ltd.

LEMATT MUSIC LTD./Pogo Records Ltd./Swoop Records/Grenouille Records/Zarg/R.T.F.M. Records-Check Records/Lee Music Ltd., % Stewart House, Hill Bottom Rd., Sands, IND, EST, Highwycombe, Buckinghamshire England. 0494-436301/436401. Telex: 837173. Manager, Director: Ron Lee. Produces rock and roll, disco, country/western, pop, and rhythm and blues; group and solo artists. Recent releases "American Girl," by Hush; "Children Of The Night," by Nightmare; and "Phobias," by Orphan.

Needs: Produces 25 records/year; works with 12 groups and 6 soloists/year. Works with 1-2 visual artists/ year. Works on assignment only. Uses a few cartoons and humorous and cartoon-style illustrations where applicable. Uses artists for album cover design and illustration; advertising design, illustration and layout; and posters.

First Contact & Terms: Send query letter with brochure, resume, business card, slides, photographs and videos to be kept on file. Samples not filed are returned by SASE (nonresidents send IRCs). Reports within 3 weeks. To show a portfolio mail original/final art, final reproduction/product and photographs. Original artwork sometimes returned to artist. Considers complexity of project, available budget, skill and experience of artist, how work will be used and turnaround time when establishing payment. Payment negotiated.

JOHN LENNON RECORDING MUSIC LINE INTERNATIONAL (CEPAC), Suite 200/314, 131 Blour St. W., Toronto, Ontario M5S 1R8 Canada. (416)962-5000/966-0983. FAX: (416)961-0124. Producer/Arranger: John P. Eastman. Agent: Joseph Sudano. Estab. 1979. Produces CDs, tapes and albums: rhythm and blues, rap and pop; group and solo artists. Recent releases: "Fantasy Love," by Blysse; "You're Changing," and "Summer Nights," by Carl Ellison and the Mixx.
Needs: Produces 5 soloists and 2 groups/year. Works with 1-3 visual artists/year. Works on assignment only. Uses artists for brochure design and illustration.
First Contact & Terms: Send query letter with resume and SASE. Samples are not filed and are returned by SASE. Reports back within months. To show a portfolio, mail b&w samples. Pays by the hour, $25-35. Pays by the project or by the day, $200-280. Rights purchased vary according to project.

LINK RECORDS, 277 Church St., New York NY 10013. (212)334-9556. FAX: (212)219-8713. Label Director: John Hudson. Estab. 1985. Produces CDs, tapes and albums: rock and roll. Recent Releases: "Multinational Pop Conglomerate," by Full Fathom Five; "Hit by Hit," by Godfathers; "Learning Time," by Winter Hours; and "Multinational Pop Conglomerate," by Full Fathom Five.
Needs: Produces 2-3 groups/year. Works with 2-3 visual artists/year. Prefers artists with experience in LP, CD, cassette design and other label related work i.e. ads, catalogs, etc. Uses artists for CD cover design, album/tape cover design and illustration, advertising design and posters.
First Contact & Terms: Send query letter with resume, tearsheets, slides, transparencies and other samples. Samples are filed. Reports back to the artist only if interested. To show a portfolio, mail tearsheets, photographs, slides, transparencies and printed samples. Pays by the project. Buys all rights.

LITTLE RICHIE JOHNSON AGENCY, Box 3, Belen NM 87002. (505)864-7442. FAX: (505)864-7442. General Manager: Tony Palmer. Produces country/western records. Recent releases: "Step Aside," and "I Don't Want to See You Cry," by Jerry Jaramillo.
Needs: Produces 5 soloists and 2 groups/year. Works on assignment only. Prefers local artists only. Uses artists for album/tape cover design and advertising design.
First Contact & Terms: Send query letter with brochure showing art style or photographs. Samples are filed or are returned by SASE only if requested. Reports back only if interested. To show a portfolio, mail photographs. Pays by the project. Considers complexity of project and available budget when establishing payment. Rights purchased vary according to project.

LUCIFER RECORDS, INC., Box 263, Brigantine NJ 08203. (609)266-2623. President: Ron Luciano. Produces pop, disco and rock and roll.
Needs: Produces 2-12 records/year. Experienced artists only. Works on assignment only. Uses artists for album cover design; brochure design, illustration and layout; catalog design; direct mail packages; advertising layout, design and illustration; and posters.
First Contact & Terms: Send query letter with resume, business card, tearsheets, photostats or photocopies. Reports only if interested. Original art sometimes returned to artist. Write to show a portfolio, or mail tearsheets and photostats. Pays by the project. Considers budget, how work will be used, rights purchased and the assignment when establishing payment. Negotiates pay and rights purchased.

JACK LYNCH ENTERPRISES/NASHVILLE COUNTRY PRODUCTIONS, 351 Millwood Dr., Nashville TN 37217-1609. (615)366-9999. President: Col. Jack Lynch. Estab. 1963. Produces CDs, tapes and albums: country/western, MOR, bluegrass and gospel. Recent releases: "Bluegrass Holiday," by Ralph Stanley, The Country Gentlemen, Larry Sparks and Dave Evans.
Needs: Produces 1-12 soloists and 1-12 groups/year. Works with 1-12 visual artists/year. Prefers local artists only with experience in the music industry. Works on assignment only. Uses artists for CD cover design and album/tape cover design.
First Contact & Terms: Send query letter with brochure, resume and SASE. Samples are filed or are returned by SASE if requested by artist. Reports back to the artist only if interested. To show a portfolio, call or mail appropriate materials, which should include b&w and color samples. Pays by the hour, $10-25; by the project or by the day, $100-500. Buys all rights or rights purchased vary according to project.

MAJEGA RECORDS/PRODUCTIONS, 240 E. Radcliffe Dr., Claremont CA 91711. (714)624-0677. President: Gary K. Buckley. Produces country and pop records, audiovisual presentations; i.e., filmstrips, slide/sound sync and multimedia programs. Recent releases: "Steppin Out," by The Gospelmen; "Sending a Copy Home," by Jody Barry; and "Sky's the Limit," by Michael Noll.
Needs: Produces about 6 records/year; 4 of which have covers/jackets designed and illustrated by freelance artists. Works on assignment only. Uses artists for album covers, ad illustration, logo design, cartoons, charts/graphs and other promotional materials.
First Contact & Terms: Send query letter with resume, brochure, flyer and samples (2-3 tearsheets of varied styles if possible) to be kept on file for future assignments. "Samples provided should be relevant to type of work requested." Samples returned by SASE. Reports back on future assignment possibilities. Negotiates pay according to complexity of project and available budget.

Tips: "Look at existing covers and be conscious of the style of music inside. This will illustrate what the industry is accepting and give the artist a solid base to start creating from."

MEDA RECORDS INC., Box 21748, Detroit MI 48221. (313)862-5880. President: Mertis John. Produces soul, jazz, pop, gospel and rhythm and blues; group and solo artists. Recent releases: "Christmas Comes But Once A Year," by The Lamp Sisters; "Trafficmania," by Joe Hunter; and "Jesus Is Mine," by Lessie Williams.
Needs: Produces 8 soloists and 2-3 groups/year. Works with 4-5 visual artists/year. Works on assignment only. Uses artist for album cover design and illustration and advertising design.
First Contact & Terms: Send query letter with samples. Samples not filed are returned by SASE only if requested by artist. Reports back within 2 weeks only if interested. Write to schedule an appointment to show a portfolio, or mail final reproduction/product. Pays by the project, $75 minimum. Considers complexity of project, available budget and how work will be used when establishing payment. Buys all rights.

MIRROR RECORDS INC; HOUSE OF GUITARS BLVD., 645 Titus Ave., Rochester NY 14617. (716)544-3500. Art Director: Armand Schaubroeck. Produces rock and roll, heavy metal, middle of the road and new wave music. Recent releases: "Over the Rainbow," by Don Potter; "Here Are the Chesterfield Kings" and "I Shot My Guardian Angel," by Armand Schaubroeck Steals; "The Village Churchmice"; "The Chesterfield" and "Stop," by the Kings; and "Through the Eyes of Youth," by Immaculate Mary.
Needs: Produces 4 records/year; all of which have cover/jackets designed and illustrated by freelance artists. Uses artists for catalogs, album covers, inner sleeves and advertising design. "Always looking for new talent."
First Contact & Terms: Send query letter with brochure showing art style, samples and SASE. Reports within 1 month. Negotiates pay based on amount of creativity required, artist's previous experience, amount of time and artist expense.

MODERN MUSIC VENTURES, INC., 5626 Brock St., Houston TX 77023. (713)926-4431. FAX: (713)926-2253. Vice President Operations: Peter T. Freimanis. Estab. 1986. Produces CDs, tapes and albums: rock and roll, classical, country/western, jazz, disco, rap, latin (especially Tejano); solo artists and group artists. Recent releases: "La Primeva Vez," by Rick Gonzales and the Choice; "Fantasy," by Dizzy Gillespie and Arnett Cobb.
Needs: Produces 6 soloists and 6 groups/year. Works with 3 visual artists/year. Prefers artists with experience in cover art, artist photographs, etc. Works on assignment only. Uses artists for CD and album/tape cover design and illustration, posters, banners, logos, etc.
First Contact & Terms: Send query letter with samples. Samples are filed. Pays by the project, $100-2,500. Rights purchased vary according to project.
Tips: "Work 'on spec' with a small independent in order to obtain a final product as demo, in support of other materials."

MONTICANA RECORDS, Box 702, Snowdon Station, Montreal, Quebec H3X 3X8 Canada. General Manager: D. Leonard. Produces rock and roll, disco, soul, country/western, pop, educational and rhythm and blues.
Needs: Works with 4 freelance artists/year. Uses artists for album cover, brochure, catalog and advertising design; album cover, catalog and advertising illustration; brochure, catalog and advertising layout; and posters.
First Contact & Terms: Send query letter with brochure, resume, business card, photostats, slides, photographs and tearsheets. Samples not returned. Reports only if interested. Originals not returned to artist after job's completion. Pays by the hour, $5-20 average; by the project, $75-300 average. Considers complexity of project, available budget and skill and experience of artist when establishing payment. Buys all rights.

MUSICA SCHALLPLATTEN VERTRIEB GES.M.B.H., Webgasse 43, A-1060, Wien (Vienna) Austria Europe. (01)597-56-46. FAX: (01)597-56-46-36. A & R Manager: Manfred Blaschko. Estab. 1949. Produces CDs, tapes and albums: rock and roll, pop, disco; solo and group artists. Recent releases: "What's Wrong," by Andy Baum & The Trix; "Hansi Lang," by Hansi Lang; and "Special Night," by Hallucination Company.
Needs: Number of soloists produces each year varies. Number of visual artists works with each year varies.
First Contact & Terms: Send query letter with brochure, photographs and photocopies. Samples are filed and are not returned. Reports back to the artist only if interested. To show a portfolio, mail thumbnails and photographs. Pay varies. Buys reprint rights.
Tips: "We would like to see some photographs of work by the artist. Samples will be filed and the artist will be contacted from us if we have a job for him."

NERVOUS RECORDS, 4/36 Dabbs Hill Ln., Northolt, Middlesex England. (01)963-0352. FAX: (01)961-8110. Contact: R. Williams. Produces rock and roll and rockabilly. Recent releases: "Roll Over," by Ronnie & the Jitters; "At My Front Door," by Freddy Frogs; and "Do You Feel Restless," by Restless.

Needs: Produces 7 albums/year; works with 7 groups and soloists/year. Works with 3-4 visual artists/year. Uses artists for album cover, brochure, catalog and advertising design.

First Contact & Terms: Send query letter with samples; material may be kept on file. Write for appointment to show portfolio. Prefers tearsheets as samples. Samples not filed are returned by SAE (nonresidents include IRC). Reports only if interested. Original art returned to the artist. Pays for design and illustration by the project, $50-200 average. Considers available budget and how work will be used when establishing payment. Purchases first rights.

Tips: "We have noticed more use of imagery and caricatures in our field so fewer actual photographs are used." Wants to see "examples of previous album sleeves, in keeping with the style of our music."

NISE PRODUCTIONS INC., 413 Cooper St., Camden NJ 08102. (609)963-3190. General Manager: Sandy Perchetti. Head of A&R: Dan McKeown. Produces rock and roll, disco, soul, country/western, educational and rhythm and blues; group and solo artists. A&R; also Production Offices for Power Up Records, distributed nationally by Sutra, New York NY.

Needs: Produces 20 records/year; works with 4 recording artists/year. Works with 2 visual artists/year. Uses artists for album cover design and illustration; and brochure design, illustration and layout.

First Contact & Terms: Works on assignment only. Send query letter with samples to be kept on file. Write for appointment to show portfolio. Samples not filed are returned by SASE. Reports within 2 weeks. Pays by job. Considers available budget when establishing payment. Purchases all rights.

NORTHWEST INTERNATIONAL ENTERTAINMENT, (formerly Etiquette Productions), 5503 Roosevelt Way NE, Seattle WA 98105. (206)524-1020. FAX: (206)524-1102. Art Director: David Sterling. Produces rock and roll, soul, jazz, pop, rhythm and blues; group and solo artists. Recent releases: "Live Fanz Only," by The Sonics; and "Hey La La Lee," by Kinetics.

Needs: Produces 2-3 soloists and 2-3 groups/year. Works with 2-3 visual artists/year. Works on assignment only. Uses artists for album cover design and illustration and posters.

First Contact & Terms: Send query letter with brochure or resume and tearsheets, photostats and photocopies. Samples are filed or are returned by SASE. Reports back within 1 month. Write to schedule an appointment to show a portfolio. Pays by the project, $50 minimum. Considers complexity of project, available budget, skill and experience of artist, how work will be used, turnaround time and rights purchased when establishing payment. "We buy whatever rights are applicable to our needs."

Tips: "Send resume and samples—if we are interested, we will contact you." Looking for "creativity and orginality."

NUCLEUS RECORDS, Box 111, Sea Bright NJ 07760. President: Robert Bowden. Produces country/western, folk and pop. Recent release: "Always" and "Make Believe," by Marco-Sison.

Needs: Produces 2 records/year. Artists with 3 years' experience only. Currently works with no freelance artists. Works on assignment only. Uses artists for album cover design.

First Contact & Terms: Send query letter with resumes, original work and photographs. Write for appointment to show a portfolio, which should include photographs. Samples are returned. Pays for design by the project, $150-200. Pays for illustration by the project, $125-150. Reports within 1 month. Originals returned to artist after job's completion. Considers skill and experience of artist when establishing payment. Buys all rights.

OHIO RECORDS, Box 15208, Las Vegas NV 89114. A&R Director: Russ Delaney. Produces country/western; group and solo artists. Recent releases: "Sounds of Ethel Delaney and her Buckeye Strings," by Ethel Delaney.

Needs: Produces 1 album, 2 singles/year. Uses artists for album cover design, brochure design and posters. Works on assignment only. Uses artists for album cover design and illustration and posters.

First Contact & Terms: Send samples to be kept on file. Accepts any samples. Samples not filed are returned by SASE. Reports only if interested. Pay is negotiable. Considers available budget when establishing payment.

ORBIT RECORDS, Box 120675, Nashville TN 37212. (615)255-1068. Owner: Ray McGinnis. Produces rock and roll and country/western. Recent releases: "The Sound of the Sun Going Down," by Kim Tsoy; and "Blame It on the Moonlight," by Da-Kota.

Needs: Produces 8 soloists and 2 groups/year. Works on assignment only. Uses artists for album cover design and illustration.

First Contact & Terms: Send query letter with resume and samples. Samples are filed or are returned by SASE only if requested. Reports back within 1 month only if interested. Write to show a portfolio, or mail appropriate materials. Pays by the project. Considers complexity of project when establishing payment.

ORIGINAL CAST RECORDS; BROADWAY/HOLLYWOOD VIDEO PRODUCTIONS, Box 10051, Beverly Hills CA 90213. (213)761-2646. Executive Producer: Doris Chu. Produces educational and original cast musicals, children's shows, operettas, videotapes and movies. Recent releases: "Piano Bar," with Kelly Bishop, "Nefertiti," and "Christy," by various artists.

Needs: Produces 10 records/year; all of which have cover/jackets designed and illustrated by freelance artists. Interested in musical poster art style, realistic styles, graphic designs, etc. Looking for artists with costume and set design experience. Uses artists for record album design, insert designs, album illustration and graphics, brochure design, video production design, print ad design and illustration.
First Contact & Terms: Send brochure or materials that can be kept on file for future reference. Include SASE. Reports in 1 month or when assignment becomes available. Negotiates pay based on amount of creativity required and artist's previous experience/reputation "and also set fee/job of $1-75 for cover design and execution including paste-up; up to $150 for album cover front and back." Contact Doris Chu for information regarding internship of 6+ weeks.

ORINDA RECORDS, 111 Deerwood Pl., San Ramon CA 94583. (415)831-4890. President: C.J. Black. Art Director: Michael Robert Phillips. Produces classical, jazz and pop records; about 3-6 albums per month.
First Contact & Terms: Send samples and tearsheets. Samples not filed are returned only if requested. Reports only if interested. To show a portfolio, mail appropriate materials. Buys all rights.

OUR GANG ENTERTAINMENT, INC., 33227 Lake Shore Blvd., Eastlake OH 44095. (216)951-9787. FAX: (216)974-1004. Art Director: Linda L. Lindeman. Produces rock and roll, jazz, pop, educational, rhythm and blues, exercise albums and promotional advertising discs. Recent releases: "All For You," by Link; "Dancersize," by Carol Hensel and "Vintage Gold," collections of masters.
Needs: Produces 10 records/year. Assigns 50-75 freelance jobs/year. Uses artists for album cover, poster, brochure and advertising design and illustration; brochure and advertising layout; and direct mail packages. Theme depends on nature of the job; "we often use airbrush illustrations, line drawings of exercise positions and routines." Especially needs illustration of human features and positions.
First Contact & Terms: Artist must show ability to produce. Send query letter with resume and samples; call or write for appointment to submit portfolio for review. Prefers photostats, slides or originals as samples. Samples returned. Reports in 2 weeks. Works on assignment only. Original work not returned to artist after job's completion. Pays for design and illustration by the project, $150-500. Considers available budget and turnaround time when establishing payment. Buys all rights.
Tips: "We have a need for logo design; abstract and old fashioned designs are becoming a trend."

PARC RECORDS, INC., Box 547877, Orlando FL 32854-7877. (407)894-0021. FAX: (407)896-4597. Contact: Art Director. Produces rock and roll and pop records; group and solo artists. Recent releases: "Lightning Strikes Twice," by Molly Hatchet; and "Body Language," by Ana.
Needs: Produces 3 soloists and 3 groups/year. Uses artists for album cover design and illustration, brochure and direct mail package design and advertising design and illustration.
First Contact & Terms: Contact only through artist's agent. Reports back only if interested. Pays for design and illustration by the project, $150-10,000. Considers available budget when establishing payment.

PETER PAN INDUSTRIES, 88 St. Francis St., Newark NJ 07105. (201)344-4214. Creative director (A&R/Art): Dave Hummer. Produces rock and roll, disco, soul, pop, educational, rhythm and blues, aerobics and self-help; group and solo artists. Recent releases: "Total Shape Up," by Joanie Greggins; and "Dance to Fitness," by Jody Watley.
Needs: Produces 15 records/year. Works with many visual artists each year. Uses artists for album cover design and illustration; brochure, catalog and advertising design, illustration and layout; direct mail packages; posters; and packaging.
First Contact & Terms: Works on assignment only. Send query letter with samples to be kept on file; call or write for appointment to show portfolio. Prefers photocopies or tearsheets as samples. Samples not filed are returned only if requested. Reports only if interested. Original artwork returned to artist. Payment open. Considers complexity of project and turnaround time when establishing payment. Purchases all rights.

PINK STREET RECORDS, INC., Box 694, Highland Park IL 60035. (312)831-4162. Vice President: Charles Altholz. Estab. 1985. Produces rock and roll, disco and pop; group and solo artists. Recent releases: "Ten-28" and "E-Motion," by Ten-28; and "I Won't Sing in My Underwear," by Illicit.
Needs: Produces 3 soloists and 3 groups/year. Works with 2 visual artists/year. Works on assignment only. Uses artists for album cover design and illustration, direct mail packages, advertising design and illustration and posters.
First Contact & Terms: Send query letter with tearsheets. Samples are filed. Reports back within 3 weeks. Write to schedule an appointment to show a portfolio, which should include color roughs, final reproduction/product and photographs. Pays by the hour, $50 minimum. Considers complexity of project, available budget, skill and experience of artist, how work will be used, turnaround time and rights purchased when establishing payment. Negotiates rights purchased.
Tips: Looks for "an understanding of promotion and advertising principles applied to make a clear, simple impact visually. Include hot, exciting finished work in your portfolio."

PLANKTON RECORDS, 236 Sebert Rd., Forest Gate, London E7 ONP England. (081)534-8500. Senior Partner: Simon Law. Produces rock and roll, rhythm and blues, funk and gospel; solo and group artists. Recent releases: "Blue Blood," by the Medals; "Sold-Sight Unseen," by the Zipcodes; and "In Difference," by Marc Catley and Geoff Mann.
Needs: Produces 2 soloists and 2 groups/year. Works with inhouse artists and 1 freelance artist/year. "We usually work with a freelance visual artist if he or she is connected with and sympathetic to the recording artist." Works on assignment only. Uses artists for album cover design and illustration.
First Contact & Terms: Send query letter with brochure. Samples not filed are returned by SASE and IRC. Reports back within 2 months. Pays for design and illustration by the project, $100-200. Considers available budget when establishing payment. Buys reprint rights.
Tips: "All the products that we release have a Christian bias, regardless of musical style. This should be borne in mind before making an approach."

PLAY RECORDS, INC., Bos 6541, Cleveland OH 44101. (216)467-0300. President: John Latimer. Estab. 1985. Produces CDs, tapes and albums: rock and roll, pop, reggae; solo and group artists. Recent releases: "The Bellows," by the Bellows; "Glacial Groove," by Serious Nature; and "I-Tal U.S.A.," by I-Tal U.S.A.
Needs: Produces 3-4 soloists and 3-4 groups/year. Works with 2 visual artists/year. Works on assignment only. Uses freelance artists for CD cover design and illustration; album/tape cover design and illustration; brochure design and illustration; catalog design, illustration and layout; direct mail packages; advertising design and illustration; and posters.
First Contact & Terms: Send query letter with SASE and photocopies. Samples are filed or are returned by SASE. Reports back to the artist only if interested. To show a portfolio, mail photocopies. Pays by the project. Buys all rights.

PRAIRIE MUSIC LTD., Box 438, Walnut IA 51577. (712)784-3001. President: Bob Everhart. Estab. 1967. Produces tapes and albums: folk, traditional, country and bluegrass. Recent releases: "Time After Time," by Bob Everhart; "Smoky Mountain Heartbreak," by Bonnie Sanford; and "Fishpole John," by Bob Everhart.
Needs: Produces 2 soloists and 2 groups/year. Works with no visual artists at present. Prefers artists with experience in traditional rural values. Works on assignment only. Uses artists for album/tape cover design and illustration and posters.
First Contact & Terms: Send query letter with resume, photocopies and photostats. Samples are filed. Reports back within 4 months only if interested. To show a portfolio, mail b&w photostats. Pays by the project, $100-250. Buys one-time rights.

RAPP PRODUCTION INC./DO IT NOW PRODUCTIONS INC., Route 16, Box 560, Cain Circle, Gainesville GA 30506. (404)889-8624. Promotions: Marci Wheeler. Estab. 1964. Produces CDs, tapes and albums: rock and roll, rhythm and blues, classical, country/western, jazz, soul, folk, disco, rap, pop and Christian; solo and group artists. Recent releases: "Faith Of a Child," by Dan Carroll; "Songs For Human Beings," by Movin' Mountains; and "Eyes of His Father," by Ron Dennis Wheeler.
Needs: Produces 10-20 soloists and 10-20 groups/year. Works with 10-20 visual artists/year. Works with artist reps.; prefers experienced local artists only. Works on assignment only. Uses artists for cover design and illustration; album/tape cover design and illustration; brochure design and illustration; catalog design, illustration and layout; direct mail packages; advertising design and illustration;and posters.
First Contact & Terms: Send query letter with brochure, resume, SASE, tearsheets, photographs, photocopies, photostats and transparencies. Samples are filed or are returned by SASE if requested by artist. Reports back to the artist only if interested. To show a portfolio, mail "best introductions or lasting impressions." Payment depends on need at the time. Rights purchased vary according to project.

RECORD COMPANY OF THE SOUTH, 5220 Essen Ln., Baton Rouge LA 70808. (504)766-3233. Art Director: Ed Lakin. Produces rock and roll and rhythm and blues. Recent releases: "Don't Take It Out On The Dog," by Butch Hornsby; "World Class," by Luther Ken; and "Off My Leg," by Terry Burhans.
Needs: Produces 5 records/year; 20% of the album covers are assigned to freelance illustrators. Assigns 1 job/year. Uses artists for album cover and poster illustration and direct mail packages.
First Contact & Terms: Prefers artists from the South. Make contact through agent; send query letter with brochure/flyer and samples. Prefers photostats and slides as samples. Samples returned by SASE. Reports within 3 weeks. Works on assignment only; reports back on whether to expect possible future assignments. Provide brochure/flyer to be kept on file for possible future assignments. Original work returned to artist after job's completion. Pays by the project, $500-1,000 average; by the hour, $40-70 average; or a flat fee of $1,000 for covers. Considers complexity of project and available budget when establishing payment. "We generally buy first rights and reprint rights."
Tips: "Illustrators need to stay on the cutting edge of design." Make personal contact before sending samples. "Look at Dave Bathel's work out of St. Louis—hottest graphic designer in the country."

R.E.F. RECORDING CO./FRICK MUSIC PUBLISHING CO., 404 Bluegrass Ave., Madison TN 37115. (615)865-6380. Contact: Bob Frick. Produces country/western and gospel. Recent releases: "I Found Jesus in Nashville" and "Release Me," by Bob Scott Frick; "Unworthy," by Bob Myers; and "Scripture In Song," by Larry Ahlborn.
Needs: Produces 30 records/year; works with 10 groups artists/year. Works on assignment only.
First Contact & Terms: Send resume and photocopies to be kept on file. Write for appointment to show portfolio. Samples not filed are returned by SASE. Reports within 10 days only if interested.

RELATIVITY RECORDS, 187-07 Henderson Ave., Hollis NY 11423. (718)464-9510. Art Director: David Bett. Estab. 1979. Produces CDs, tapes and albums: rock and roll, jazz, rap, pop and heavy metal; solo artists. Recent releases: "Passion and Warfare," by Steve Val; "Harder Than You," by 24-7 Spy 2; and "Twisted Into Form," by Forbidden.
Needs: Produces 5 solo and 20 groups/year. Works with 10 freelance artists/year. Perfers artists with experience in "anything from underground comic-book art to mainstream commercial illustration." Works on assignment only. Uses artists for CD and album cover, brochure and catalog illustration; posters; logo art; and lettering.
First Contact & Terms: Send resume and color photostats. Samples are not filed and are not returned. Reports back only if interested. Call or write to show a portfolio, which should include color and b&w slides or transparencies. Pays by the project, $500-1,500. Considers complexity of project, available budget and rights purchased when establishing payment. Rights purchased vary according to project.
Tips: "We seek creative young people with imagination. Avoid the obvious"

RHYTHMS PRODUCTIONS, Whitney Bldg., Box 34485, Los Angeles CA 90034. President: R.S. White. Estab. 1955. Produces albums, tapes and books: educational children's. Recent titles include "Adventures of Professor Whatzit and Carmine Cat," by Dan Brown and Bruce Crook.
Needs: Works on assignment only. Prefers California artists. Produces 12 records and cassettes/year, all of which have covers/jackets designed and illustrated by freelance artists. Works with 1-2 visual artists/year. Prefers artists with experience in cartooning. Uses freelance artists for album/tape cover design and illstration and children's books..
First Contact & Terms: Send query letter photocopies and SASE. Samples are filed or are returned by SASE if requested by the artists. Reports within 1 month. "We do not review portfolios unless we have seen photocopies we like." Pays by the project. Buys all right.
Tips: "We like illustration that is suitable for children. We find that cartoonists have the look that we prefer. However, we also like art that is finer and that reflects a quality look for some of our more classical publications."

ROBBINS RECORDS, INC, HC80, Box 5B, Leesville LA 71446. National Representative: Sherree Stephens. Produces country/western and religious records. Recent releases: "Jesus Amazes Me," "Wait Till You See My Miracle Home," and "Since I've Had A Change Of Heart," by Sherrie Stephens and J.J. Stephens.
Needs: Produces various number of records/year. Works with various number of freelance artists/year. Works on assignment only. Uses artists for album cover design and posters.
First Contact & Terms: Send brochure to be kept on file. Reports only if interested. Originals not returned to artist after job's completion. Write for appointment to show portfolio. Pays by the project. Considers skill and experience of artist, how work will be used and rights purchased when establishing payment. Buys all rights.
Tips: Looking for "originality."

ROCKLAND MUSIC, INC., 117 W. Rockland, Box 615, Libertyville IL 60048. (708)362-4060. Contact: Perry Johnson. Estab. 1985. Produces rock and roll, country/western, pop, educational and rhythm and blues; group and solo artists. Recent releases: "This Feels Like Love to Me," by Sacha Distel; "Honeybear Rap," by Honeybears; and "Hooper's Active Music for Children," by Bill Hooper.
Needs: Produces 10 soloists and 5 groups/year. Works with 3 visual artists/year. Uses artists for album cover design and illustration, brochure design and posters.
First Contact & Terms: Send query letter with brochure showing art style or resume and samples. Samples are filed or are returned by SASE only if requested. Write to schedule an appointment to show a portfolio. Negotiates payment. Considers complexity of project, available budget and skills and experience of artist when establishing payment.
Tips: "Call or write first to see what our needs at the time are."

ROWENA RECORDS & TAPES, 195 S. 26th St., San Jose CA 95116. (408)286-9840. Owner: Jeannine O'Neal. Estab. 1967. Produces CDs, tapes and albums: rock and roll, rhythm and blues, country/western, soul, rap, pop and new age; group artists. Recent releases: "Before, After," by Sister Suffragette; "Heartbeat," by The Reed Sisters; and "New American Music," by Jeannine O'Neal.

Needs: Produces 20 soloists and 5 groups/year. Uses artists for CD cover design and illustration, album/tape cover design and illustration and posters.
First Contact & Terms: Send query letter with brochure, resume, SASE, tearsheets, photographs, photocopies and photostats. Samples are filed or are returned by SASE. Reports back within 1 month. To show a portfolio, mail original/final art. "Artist should submit prices."

SAN-SUE RECORDING STUDIO, Box 773, Mt. Juilet TN 37122. (615)758-5999. Owner: Buddy Powell. Estab. 1970. Produces tapes and albums: rock and roll, country/western and pop. Recent releases: "Little People," by Sue Powell; "My Way," by Jerry Baird; and "Which Way You Going Billy," by Sandi Powell.
Needs: Produces 20 soloists and 5 groups/year. Works with 3-4 visual artists/year. Works on assignment only. Uses artists for CD cover design, album/tape cover design and illustration, advertising design and posters.
First Contact & Terms: Send query letter with brochure, resume and SASE. Samples are filed or are returned by SASE. Reports back within 10 days. Write to schedule an appointment to show a portfolio, which should include photostats.

SEASIDE RECORDS, 100 Labon, Tabor City NC 28463. (919)653-2546. President: Elson H. Stevens. Produces rock and roll, country/western, pop, rhythm and blues, beach music and gospel. Recent releases: "Here I Go Again," by Angela; and "On the Down Side," by T.J. Gibson.
Needs: Work with various visual artists/year. Works on assignment only. Uses artists for album cover design and illustration, direct mail packages, posters and sleeves.
First Contact & Terms: Send query letter with brochure. Samples are filed. Reports back within 60 days. Call to schedule an appointment to show a portfolio, which should include color and b&w final reproduction/product. Pays by the project, $200 minimum. Considers complexity of project and available budget when establishing payment. Buys all rights.
Tips: "Be prepared." Wants to see "finished project. Do not send draft works."

SHAOLIN FILM & RECORDS, Box 387, Hollywood CA 90078. (818)506-8660. FAX: (818)761-5731. Vice President of A&R: Michelle McCarty. Estab. 1984. Produces CDs, tapes and albums: rock and roll, pop, folk and movie soundtracks; group and solo artists. Recent releases: "Temptation," by Richard O'Connor; and "Coyote in a Graveyard," by The Coyote.
Needs: Produces 1 soloist and 2 groups/year. Works with 1 visual artist/year. Works on assignment only. Uses freelance artists for CD cover design and illustration; album/tape cover design and illustration; brochure design and illustration; catalog design, illustration and layout; direct mail packages; advertising design and illustration and posters.
First Contact & Terms: Send query letter with brochure, resume, SASE, tearsheets, photographs and photocopies. Samples are filed "if we like them" or returned by SASE. Reports back within 1 month. To show a portfolio, mail original/final art and b&w and color photostats, slides, tearsheets and photographs. Pays by the project, $50-200. Buys all rights.
Tips: The best way for a freelance artist to break into CD/album/tape design and illustration is to "work for a loss, supplying art and ad work for new, unsigned bands. Develop a style, variety, experience and portfolio."

SIRR RODD RECORD & PUBLISHING COMPANY, Box 58116, Philadelphia PA 19102-8116. President: Rodney J. Keitt. Estab. 1985. Produces disco, soul, jazz, pop, rhythm and blues; group and solo artists. Recent releases: "Fashion & West Oak Lane Jam," by Klassy K; and "The Essence of Love/Ghetto Jazz," by Rodney Jerome Keitt.
Needs: Produces 2 soloists and 3 groups/year. Works with 1 visual artist/year. Works on assignment only. Uses artists for album cover design and illustration, direct mail packages, advertising design and illustration and posters.
First Contact & Terms: Send query letter with resume, photostats, photocopies and slides. Samples are filed and are not returned. Reports back within 2 months. Write to show a portfolio, which should include color thumbnails, roughs, final reproduction/product, photostats and photographs. Pays by the project, $100-3,500. Considers available budget, skills and experience of artist, how work will be used and rights purchased when establishing payment. Buys reprint rights or negotiates rights purchased.
Tips: "Treat every project as though it was a major project. Always request comments and criticism of your work."

SLAMDEK/SCRAMDOWN, Box 43551, Louisville KY 40253. (502)244-8694. Submissions Analyst: Kelly S. Kemper. Estab. 1986. Produces CDs, tapes and DATs: rock and roll, alternative rock, college, hardcore, etc. Recent releases: "Blurry," by Hopscotch Army; "If The Spirits are Willing," by Endpoint; and "Memphis Sessions," by Slambang Vanilla Featuring Jesus Rosebud.
Needs: Produces 5-10 groups/year. Prefers artists with experience in color and photograph integration. Works on assignment only. Uses artists for CD cover design and illustration; album/tape cover design and illustration; brochure design and illustration; catalog design, illustration and layout; advertising design and illustration;and posters.

First Contact & Terms: Send query letter with SASE, tearsheets and photographs. Samples are filed. Reports back within 90 days. To show a portfolio, mail color tearsheets and photographs. Payment varies. Rights purchased vary according to project.
Tips: "What is garbage to you may be a goldmine to someone else. Expect nothing and you won't be disappointed."

SPHEMUSATIONS, 12 Northfield Rd., One House, Stowmarket Suffolk IP14 3HE England. 0449-613388. General Manager: James Butt. Produces classical, country/western, jazz and educational records. Recent releases: "Little Boy Dances," by G. Sudbury; "The Magic of Voice & Harp," by P. Scholomowitz and Andre Back; and "P. Mendel: Route 56," by Paul Mendel.
Needs: Produces 6 soloists and 6 groups/year. Works with 1 visual artist/year. Works on assignment only. Uses artist for album cover design and illustration, brochure design and illustration, catalog design and layout, direct mail packages, advertising design and illustration and posters.
First Contact & Terms: Contact through artist's agent or send query letter with resume, tearsheets, photostats and photocopies. Samples are filed or are returned only if requested. Reports back within 6 weeks. Write to show a portfolio, which should include final reproduction/product and color and b&w photostats and photographs. Pays for illustration by the project, $500-2,000. Considers complexity of project, available budget, skills and experience of artist, how work will be used, turnaround time and rights purchased when establishing payment. Buys reprint rights, all rights or negotiates rights purchased.
Tips: Looks for "economy, simplicity and directness" in artwork for album covers.

SRSF RECORDINGS/ENTERTAINMENTS ENTERPRISES, Box 14131, Denver CO 80214. President: Sharon Smith-Fliesher. Estab. 1980. "Our company produces and distributes musical works in the form of cassettes, 45's, LP's and CD's;" members are musicians. Publishes periodical newsletter entitled *Lambda Performing Arts Guild Directory*.
Needs: Works with 6 freelance artists/year. Uses freelance artists mainly for album design/artwork. Also uses freelance artists for advertising layout, brochure design, illustration and layout. Prefers line art.
First Contact & Terms: Send query letter with brochure, resume, tearsheets, photostats and photocopies. Samples are filed or are returned by SASE only if requested. Reports back within 6 weeks. Mail appropriate materials: roughs, original/final art, b&w photostats, tearsheets, final reproduction/product. Pays for design/illustration by the hour, $10-15. Buys all rights. "Our company caters to the gay and lesbian community."

STARCREST PRODUCTIONS, 209 Circle Hills Dr., Grand Forks ND 58201. (701)772-6831. President: George Hastings. Produces country, pop and gospel music. Recent releases "North Dakota Country Centennial Album," by Mary Joyce.
Needs: Produces 5 records/year, all of which have cover/jackets designed and illustrated by freelance artists. Uses artists for jacket and brochure design and print ad illustration.
First Contact & Terms: Send query letter, samples and SASE. Reports in 2 months. Negotiates pay based on amount of creativity required.

SUSAN RECORDS, Box 4740, Nashville TN 37216. (615)865-4740. Manager: Susan Neal. Produces rock and roll, disco, soul, country/western, rock-a-billy, jazz, pop and rhythm and blues; group and solo artists. Recent release: "That's It Baby," by Dixie Dee.
Needs: Produces 15 records/year. Uses artists for album cover design and illustration; brochure design, illustration and layout; catalog design, illustration and layout; advertising design and layout.
First Contact & Terms: Send brochure, business card, SASE and photographs to be kept on file unless return requested. Samples not filed are returned by SASE. Reports within 15 days. Original art returned to the artist. Write for appointment to show a portfolio. Considers available budget and rights purchased when establishing payment. Negotiates rights purchased.

TEROCK RECORDS, Box 4740, Nashville TN 37216. Manager: S.D. Neal. Estab. 1959. Produces CDs, tapes and albums: rock and roll, jazz, rap, rhythm and blues, soul, pop, rock-a-billy, country/western, disco; solo and group artists. Recent releases: "Changes," by Ritchie Derwald; "Bright Lights," by Dixie Dee & the Rhythm Rockers; and "Wild Rock," by Mickey Finn.
Needs: Produces 6 soloists and 4-8 groups/year. Works with various visual artists/year. Works on assignment only. Uses artists for CD cover design and illustration, album/tape cover design and illustration, direct mail packages, posters, brochure design and illustration, advertising design and illustration, and catalog layout.
First Contact & Terms: Send query letter with bruchure, SASE, photographs and photocopies. Samples are filed or are returned by SASE if requested by artist. Reports back within 3 weeks. Write to schedule an appointment to show a portfolio or mail appropriate materials. Portfolio should include roughs, original/final art and b&w and color photostats and photographs. Payment varies. Negotiates rights purchased.

RIK TINORY PRODUCTIONS, 180 Pond St., Box 311, Cohasset MA 02025. (617)383-9494. Artist Relations: Claire Babcock. Produces rock and roll, classical, country/western, jazz, folk, pop, educational, rhythm and blues; group and solo artists. Recent releases: "Here's To You, L.A.," by Rik Tinory;and "Feeling Like I'm

Wanted," by Jimmy Parker. Also pre-production for Aerosmith album "Pump."
First Contact & Terms: Pays by the project. Considers how work will be used when establishing payment. Buys all rights.
Tips: "We do not accept unsolicited material. A phone call or letter describing what the artist's intentions are is necessary. Include SASE."

TOM THUMB MUSIC, (division of Rhythms Productions), Box 34485, Los Angeles CA 90034. President: Ruth White. Record and book publisher for children's market.
Needs: Works on assignment only. Prefers local artists with cartooning talents and animation background. Uses artists for catalog cover and book illustration, direct mail brochures, layout, magazine ads, multimedia kits, paste-up and album design. Artists must have a style that appeals to children.
First Contact & Terms: Buys 3-4 designs/year. Send query letter with brochure showing art style or resume, tearsheets and photocopies. Samples are filed or are returned by SASE. Reports within 3 weeks. Pays by the project. Considers complexity of project, available budget and rights purchased when establishing payment. Buys all rights on a work-for-hire basis.

TOP RECORDS, 4, Galleria del Corso, Milano Italia. (02)791141. FAX: 00392791141. Estab. 1975. Produces CDs, tapes, albums: rock and roll, rap, rhythm and blues, soul, pop, folk, country/western, disco; solo and group artists. Recent releases "You Set My Heart on Fire," by Tina Charles; "Contrabbandieri Di Musica," by Goran Kuzmicac; and "Space Vampires," by Henry Mancini.
Needs: Produces 5 soloists and 5 groups/year. Works with 2 visual artists/year. Works on assignment only.
First Contact & Terms: Send query letter with brochure. Samples are filed or are returned. Reports back within 2 weeks. Call to schedule an appointment to show a portfolio or mail appropriate materials. Portfolio should include original/final art and photographs. Buys all rights.

TREND® RECORDING AND DISTRIBUTING CO., Box 201, Smyrna GA 30081. (404)432-2454. President: Tom Hodges. Produces soul, country, pop, rhythm and blues, middle-of-the-road music and jazz. Recent releases include "Cadillac on My Mind/Let Me Know," by Marlon Frizzell.
Needs: Produces 3 records/year by 1 group and 2 soloists. Works with 3 visual artists/year. Freelance artists design and illustrate 1 cover/jacket per year.
First Contact & Terms: Send query letter with samples. Samples are not filed and are returned by SASE. Send brochure or samples that can be kept on file for future reference. Include SASE. Reports in 4 weeks. Write to schedule an appointment to show a portfolio or mail tearsheets. Pays $20-1,000. Negotiates pay based on amount of creativity required and how the work will be used. Buys reprint rights.
Tips: Looking for "originality."

TURF HANDLER RECORDS, INC., 807 NW 2nd Ave., Ft. Lauderdale FL 33311. (305)764-2310. A&R: Mr. Maniac. Estab. 1987. Produces tapes, albums, rap, rhythm and blues; solo and group artists. Recent Releases: "We Can Make You Dance," by MC Classy Rick; and "Do It to The Drummers Beat," by M.C. Kyle.
Needs: Produces 2 soloists and 1 group/year. Works with 3 visual artists/year. Works on assignment only. Uses artists for album/tape cover design and illustration, posters, and advertising design.
First Contact & Terms: Send query letter with brochure, resume, photographs and photocopies. Samples are filed. Reports back to the artists only if interested. To show a portfolio, mail roughs, original/final art and b&w and color photostats and photographs. Pays by the project. Buys all rights.
art is marketable."

UGLY DOG RECORDS, Box 1583, Brantford, Ontario N3T 5V6 Canada. (519)753-2081. President: John Mars. Estab. 1976. Produces tapes and albums: rock and roll, jazz and rhythm and blues. Recent releases: "Electric Playground," by The Children; "Annihilated Surprise," by Stuart Broomer and John Mars; and "Wild Thing," by the Popp Tarts.
Needs: Produces 1 group/year. "I do almost all the work myself." Uses artists for album/tape cover design and illustration, posters, brochure design and illustration, advertising design and illustration, concert and bar flyers and press releases.
First Contact & Terms: Send query letter with resume, SASE, tearsheets, photographs and photostats. Samples are filed or are returned by SASE if requested by artist. Reports back within 60 days. To show a portfolio, mail photostats and photographs. Pays by the project, $100-1,000. One-time rights.
Tips: "Know the basic rules that make a jacket work. Be meticulously neat. Be original to the point of going out on a limb."

VELVET PRODUCTION CO., 517 W. 57th St., Los Angeles CA 90037. (213)753-7893. Manager: Aaron Johnson. Produces soul and rhythm and blues. Recent releases: "There Are Two Sides to Every Coin," by Arlene Bell; and "I Ain't Jiving, Baby," by Chick Willis.

Needs: Produces 6 records/year. Works with 6 freelance artists/year. Experienced artists only. Works on assignment only. Uses artists for posters, album cover illustration, brochure design and catalog layout.

First Contact & Terms: Send query letter with brochure showing art style or resume, photostats and photocopies to be kept on file. Samples not kept on file are returned by SASE. Reports only if interested. Original artwork is returned after job's completion. Write for appointment to show a portfolio. Pays by the project, $50-200 average. Negotiates rights purchased.

WARNER BROS. RECORDS, 3300 Warner Blvd., Burbank CA 91505. (818)953-3361. FAX: (818)953-3232. Art Dept. Assistant: Michelle Barish. Produces CDs, tapes and sometimes albums: rock and roll, jazz, rap, rhythm and blues, soul, pop, folk, country/western; solo and group artists. Recent releases: "I'm Breathless," by Madonna; "Behind the Mask," by Fleetwood Mac; and "Back on the Block," by Quincy Jones. Releases approximately 150 total packages/year.

Needs: No restrictions regarding freelance artists. Works on assignment only. Uses freelance artists for CD cover design and illustration; album tape cover design and illustration; brochure design and illustration; catalog design, illustration and layout; advertising design and illustration; and posters.

First Contact & Terms: Send query letter with brochure, tearsheets, resume, slides and photographs. Samples are filed or are returned by SASE if requested by artist. Reports back to the artist only if interested. Call or write to schedule an appointment to show a portfolio or mail appropriate materias. Portfolio should include roughs, original/final art and b&w and color tearsheets, photographs, slides and transparencies. "Any of these are acceptable." Pays by the hour, $12-35; by the project. Buys all rights.

Tips: "Send a portfolio—we tend to use artists or illustrators with distinct/stylized work—rarely do we call on the illustrators to render likenesses; more often we are looking for someone with a conceptual or humorous approach."

ZANZIBAR RECORDS, 2019 Noble, Pittsburgh PA 15218. (412)351-6672. Label Manager: John C. Antimary. Estab. 1980. Produces CDs, tapes and albums: rock and roll, progressive rock; solo artists. Recent releases: "The Sounding," by The Affordable Floors; "Festival of Fun," by Post Mortem; and "Best of Graffiti," by Acoustic Solo Artists.

Needs: Produces 6-8 groups/year. Works with 2-3 visual artists/year. Works on assignment only. Uses artists for CD cover design and illustration, album tape cover design and illustration and advertising design.

First Contact & Terms: Send query letter with SASE. Samples are filed or are returned by SASE if requested by artist. Reports back to the artist only if interested. To show a portfolio, mail thumbnails and roughs. Pays by the project. Rights purchased vary according to project.

Z-ZONE RECORDS, Box 256577, Chicago IL 60625. President: George Peck. Estab. 1986. Produces rock and roll, classical, disco, soul, country/western, jazz, folk, pop, educational, rhythm and blues; group and solo artists. Recent releases: "Bambi," by Bambi & Z Zone; and "George Peck," by George Peck.

Needs: Produces 4-5 soloists and 5-8 groups/year. Works with 1-2 visual artists/year. Uses artists for album cover, brochure and catalog design, illustration and layout; direct mail packages; advertising design and illustration; and posters.

First Contact & Terms: Send query letter with photocopies and slides. Samples are filed or are returned by SASE only if requested by artists. Reports back only if interested. Write to schedule an appointment to show a portfolio or mail roughs and color and b&w photographs. Pays by the project, $400-650. Considers rights purchased when establishing payment. Buys all rights.

Syndicates & Clip Art Firms

Syndicates are basically agents for cartoonists, selling comic strips, panels and editorial cartoons to newspapers and magazines. They also handle merchandising of licensed products. Features can be daily, daily and Sunday, Sunday only, weekly (no day specified) or, in the case of magazines, monthly or bimonthly. Strips usually originate with the syndicate, while editorial cartoons usually appear first in the editorial cartoonist's base newspaper, then in other papers that subscribe through the syndicate.

Syndicates are facing a shrinking market. There are fewer daily newspapers today than there were ten years ago, with the survivors confronting shrinking newsholes and more coverage of local events. Therefore, syndicate salespeople have fewer and less eager markets for new material. Also, editors hesitate to drop a long-established strip for a newcomer, because such moves always result in a deluge of reader complaints.

There is good news, however. The slow but steady growth in the number of syndicated women cartoonists continues; there are now about 10 women among the 200 syndicated cartoonists. Also, the number of minority characters in strips has increased. Another trend reveals that more editorial cartoonists are creating strips for the comic pages, such as Bruce Beattie's "Snafu."

Selling to syndicates is not an easy task, but it is achievable. (Read this section's Close-up on Jim Davis to see how he did it.) Facing a shrinking market, syndicates are generally looking for a "sure thing," a feature they feel will be worth investing the $25,000 needed to promote and sell a new strip to newspapers. In general, syndicates look for originality, quality, salability and timeliness. Characters must have universal appeal in order to attract a diversity of readers.

The best approach to selling your work to syndicates is to submit work that has already been published regularly in a paper. This proves to the syndicate that you have established a loyal following and have produced a strip on a regular basis. Send a package to the syndicate's cartoon editor that contains a brief cover letter summarizing your idea, short biographical sketches of each character you show, and two dozen cartoon samples (never originals) on 8½ × 11 white paper. Unpublished cartoonists should build up their portfolios by cartooning for local papers before submitting work to a syndicate.

An alternative to syndication is self-syndication. Nicole Hollander proved it can be done with her strip "Sylvia." (Read the Close-up on her in the Greeting Card section to find out what her feelings are on self-syndication and doing a strip.) In this situation, cartoonists act as their own salespeople, sending packets to newspapers and other likely outlets. This requires developing a mailing list, promoting the strip periodically and developing a pricing, billing and collections structure. If you're a good businessperson, this might be the route for you.

Before signing a contract with a syndicate, consult an attorney to review its terms. A checklist of favorable terms includes: (1) creator ownership of the strip and its characters; (2) periodic evaluation of the syndicate's performance; (3) a five-year contract without automatic renewal; and (4) a percentage of gross, instead of net, receipts.

Clip art firms provide their clients—individuals, associations and businesses—with camera-ready illustrations, cartoons, spot drawings and decorative art for use in newsletters, brochures, advertisements and more. Generally clip art is rendered in black and white in a realistic manner to adapt to any use. Clip art falls into certain subject areas, such as animals, food, clothing or medicine. Though all rights are generally purchased, try to receive name credit alongside your work. Computer software now supplies clip art, so clip art firms must provide more unique material than in the past.

For regular updates on syndicates and clip art firms, read *Editor & Publisher*'s weekly column on the subject. Also, the weekly trade magazine publishes an annual directory, which includes syndicates. Writer's Digest Books has published a new market book just for cartoonists, *Humor and Cartoon Markets*.

ADVENTURE FEATURE SYNDICATE, Suite 400, 329 Harvey Dr., Glendale CA 91206. (818)247-1721. Executive Editor: R.E. Dairo. Syndicates to 200 newspapers and book publishers.
Needs: Buys from 20 freelance artists/year. Considers single, double and multi-panel cartoons. Prefers mystery, science fiction, adventure and drama as themes. Also needs comic strip, comic book, graphic novel and panel cartoonists.
First Contact & Terms: Send query letter with resume, photostats and tearsheets to be kept on file. Samples not kept on file are returned by SASE. Reports within 30 days. Write for appointment to show portfolio. Pays 50% of gross income; on publication. Considers salability of artwork when establishing payment. Buys reprint rights or negotiates rights purchased.
Tips: "Comic strips need a four-week presentation package reduced to newspaper size. Include an outline of artwork's storyline that could be used for a promotional kit. We also must have return envelope and postage to return submissions!"

*ALLIED FEATURE SYNDICATE, Drawer 48, Joplin MD 64802-0048. (417)673-4743. FAX: (417)673-2802. Editor: Robert Blanset. Estab. 1940. Syndicate serving 50 outlets: newspapers, magazines, etc.
Needs: Approached by 100 freelance artists/year. Buys from 10 or more freelance artists/year. Introduces 25-50 new strips/year. Considers comic strips, gag cartoons, caricatures, editorial/political cartoons, illustrations and spot drawings. Prefers single panel, double panel, multiple panel with or without gagline; b&w line drawings, b&w washes and color washes.
First Contact & Terms: Sample package should include cover letter, photocopies and finished cartoons. One sample of each should be included. Samples are filed or are returned by SASE if requested by artist. Does not report back. "On some occasions we do contact the artist." Call to schedule an appointment to show a portfolio. Portfolio should include b&w samples. Pays 50% of net proceeds; on publication. Buys first rights. Offers automatic renewal. Syndicate owns original art and the characters. "This is negotiable with artist. We always negotiate."

AMERICAN NEWSPAPER SYNDICATE, 9 Woodrush Dr., Irvine CA 92714. (714) 559-8047. Executive Editor: Susan Smith. Estab. 1987. Syndicates to U.S. and Canadian medium and large-sized general interest and special interest newspapers.
Needs: Wants to syndicate 5 new cartoonists this year. Looking for b&w and color comic strips, comic panels, editorial cartoons, illustrations and spot drawings. "We are particularly looking for humorous features that are fresh, contemporary and genuinely funny. We also will consider dramatic serial strip concepts that are unique and that have strong characters. We need features that can run daily and Sunday. Material should appeal to all ages and can be on any subject."
First Contact & Terms: Send query letter with copies of 6 weeks of dailies and character sketches. Samples not kept on file are returned by SASE. Please do *not* send original art. Reports within 3 weeks. Buys U.S. newspaper rights. Wants to sign contracts with cartoonists to produce material on a regular basis. Also looking for merchandising and licensing possibilities.
Tips: "We are willing to take on material that may be considered too unconventional by the other syndicates. Because of our understanding of the newspaper syndication market, we feel we can find a place for the previously unpublished cartoonists. We urge you to be fresh and original. Be yourself. Don't try to imitate

The asterisk before a listing indicates that the listing is new in this edition. New markets are often the most receptive to freelance submissions.

other, well-known cartoonists. Develop three-dimensional characters in open-ended situations that will provide ample opportunities for comic possibilities. Ask yourself: do I *really like* these characters? Is this feature *really* funny? Would I want to read it every day? When you can honestly answer yes to these questions, you may have a feature that is a potential hit."

ART PLUS REPRO RESOURCE, Box 1149, Orange Park FL 32067-1149. (904)269-5139. Publisher: Wayne Hepburn. Estab. 1983. Clip art firm serving about 12,000 outlets, including churches, schools, associations and ministries.
Needs: Buys 40-60 cartoons and 200-1,000 illustrations/year from freelance artists. Prefers illustrations and single panel cartoons with gagline and b&w line art. Maximum size is 7x10 and must be reducible to 20% of size without losing detail. "We need very graphic material." Prefers religious or educational themes.
First Contact & Terms: Send photocopies. Samples not filed are returned by SASE. Guidelines and catalog available for 9x12 SASE with 2 first-class stamps. Reports back within 2 months. To show a portfolio, mail roughs and photostats. Pays $5-50; on acceptance. Buys all rights.
Tips: "All our images are published as clip art to be reproduced by readers in their bulletins and newsletters for churches, schools, associations, etc. We need art for holidays, seasons and activities; new material every 3 months. We want singlepanel cartoons, not continuity strips."

B M ENTERPRISES, Box 421, Farrell PA 16121. (412)342-5300. President: William (Bill) Murray. Estab. 1980. Syndicates to 400 weekly newspapers, schools and national and regional magazines.
Needs: Buys from 12 freelance artists/year. Considers single, double and multiple panel cartoons; b&w line and spot drawings. Prefers humorous themes. Also uses artists for advertising.
First Contact & Terms: Prefers published artists only; however, others may submit. Works on assignment only. Send query letter with resume and tearsheets to be kept on file. Sample package should contain a minimum of 5 copies of work. Write for artists' guidelines. Samples not kept on file are returned by SASE. Reports within 30 days. Write for appointment to show a portfolio. Pays flat fee, $8-50; on acceptance. Considers skill and experience of artist when establishing payment. Buys all rights.
Tips: "Submit only best work. Send only humorous or family-oriented work; no profanity or rough sketches. If you are rejected, submit again." Sees trend toward "more advanced syndicated strips via the use of computers."

BLACK CONSCIENCE SYNDICATION, INC., 21 Bedford St., Wyandanch NY 11798. (516)491-7774. President: Clyde R. Davis. Estab. 1987. Syndicate serving regional magazines, schools, daily newspapers and television.
Needs: Considers comic strips, gag cartoons, caricatures, editorial or political cartoons, illustrations and spot drawings. Prefers single, double or multipanel cartoons. "All material must be of an importance to the Black community in America and the world." Especially needs material on gospel music and its history.
First Contact & Terms: Send query letter with resume, tearsheets and photocopies. Samples are filed or are returned by SASE only if requested by artist. Reports back within 2 months. Call to show a portfolio, which should include tearsheets. Pays 50% of gross income; on publication. Considers client's preferences when establishing payment. Buys first rights.
Tips: "All material must be inspiring as well as informative. Our main search is for the truth."

BRILLIANT ENTERPRISES, 117 W. Valerio St., Santa Barbara CA 93101. Art Director: Ashleigh Brilliant. Estab. 1967. Serves hundreds of daily newspapers.
Needs: Buys from various number of freelance artists/year. Considers illustrations with text. Prefers pen & ink.
First Contact & Terms: Samples are not filed and are returned by SASE. Reports back within 3 weeks. Pays flat fee of $50 minimum; on acceptance. Buys all rights.
Tips: "Our products and publications are so unusual that freelancers who do not first carefully study our line will only be wasting their time and ours. First contact should be made by sending for our catalog ($2 plus SASE)."

CAROL BRYAN IMAGINES, THE LIBRARY IMAGINATION PAPER, 1000 Byus Dr., Charleston WV 25311. Editor: Carol Bryan. Estab. 1978. Syndicates clip art for 3,000 public and school libraries. Sample issue $1.
Needs: Buys 6-15 freelance illustrations/issue. Considers gag cartoons, illustrations and spot drawings. Prefers single panel; b&w line drawings. Prefers library themes—"not negative towards library or stereotyped (example: showing a spinster librarian with glasses and bun)."
First Contact & Terms: Send query letter with tearsheets, photocopies and finished cartoons. Send no more than 6 samples. Samples are filed or are returned by SASE. Reports back within 3 weeks. Pays flat fee, $10-25; on publication. Buys one-time or reprint rights.
Tips: "Seeing a sample issue is mandatory—we have a specific style and have been very successful with it. Your style may blend with our philosophy. Need great cartoons that libraries can publish in their newsletters."

CARTOONEWS INTERNATIONAL, Trump Tower, 721 Fifth Ave., New York NY 10022. (212)980-0855. Contact: Manager. Syndicate servicing over 500 daily newspapers.
Needs: Considers editorial/political cartoons from "only interns in New York City area who wish to perfect their cartoon skills." Prefers pen & ink.
First Contact & Terms: To show a portfolio, send resume and finished cartoons. Include 10 samples. Samples are not filed and are not returned. Pays $5-10/hour.

CITY NEWS SERVICE, Box 39, Willow Springs MO 65793. (417)469-2423. President: Richard Weatherington. Estab. 1969. Editorial service providing editorial and graphic packages for magazines.
Needs: Buys from 12 or more freelance artists/year. Considers caricature, editorial cartoons and tax and business subjects as themes; considers b&w line drawings and shading film.
First Contact & Terms: Send query letter with resume, tearsheets or photocopies. Samples should contain business subjects. "Send five or more black and white line drawings, color drawings, shading film or good line drawing editorial cartoons." Does not want to see comic strips. Samples not filed are returned by SASE. Reports within 4-6 weeks. To show a portfolio, mail tearsheets or photostats. Pays 50% of net proceeds; pays flat fee, $25 minimum. "We may buy art outright or split percentage of sales." Considers complexity of project, skill and experience of artist and how work will be used and rights purchased when establishing payment.
Tips: "We have the markets for multiple sales of editorial support art. We need talented artists to supply specific projects. We will work with beginning artists. Be honest about talent and artistic ability. If it isn't there then don't beat your head against the wall."

*COMMUNITY FEATURES, Dept. C, Box 75, Berkeley CA 94701-0075. Art Editor: B. Miller. Syndicates to 270 daily and weekly newspapers and consumer magazines. Mails brochure of new syndicated offerings to over 700 newspapers. Guidelines $1 and #10 SASE. Specify "artists' guidelines."
Needs: Interested in professional quality b&w illustrations, spot drawings, line art, square single, double and multiple panel cartoons; illustrated educational panels, how-to, etc. Does not seek color. Looking for illustrators and editorial cartoonists for regular assignments.
First Contact & Terms: Send tearsheets, veloxes, PMTs or excellent photocopies (published and unpublished) that can be kept on file. Do not send artboards. Reports within 3-6 weeks. Buys various rights. Purchases some one-shot. Will consider line-art on all topics listed in guidelines. Pays $20-500 flat rate for one-shot and occasional work; 50% commission for regularly appearing features. Pays on publication.
Tips: "We look for a bold, modern look. Submit very clear copies. Include SASE if return is desired. Often, freelancers go to too much trouble and expense in sending elaborate packages with long cover letters. The work always speaks for itself! Best to leave samples of your work on file with us, and we will contact you as the need arises. (No artwork is distributed to our clients without artist's written approval.) Pet peeve: misspelled captions!"

*CONTINENTAL FEATURES/CONTINENTAL NEWS SERVICE, Suite 265, 341 W. Broadway, San Diego CA 92101. (619)492-8696. Director: Gary P. Salamone. Parent firm established August, 1981. Syndicate serving 3 outlets: house publication, publishing business and the general public through the *Continental Newstime* magazine. Guidelines available to the artist for SASE.
Needs: Approached by 10-12 freelance artists/year. Number of new strips introduced each year varies. Considers comic strips and gag cartoons. Prefers single panel with gagline. "In the next 12 months we foresee a need for cartoonists specializing in true-to-life figures to assist existing Continental cartoonist to meet demand of the general public." Maximum size of artwork 8×10, must be reducible to 65% of original size.
First Contact & Terms: Sample package should include cover letter and photocopies. 10-15 samples should be included. Samples are filed or are returned by SASE if requested by artist. Reports back within 1 month with receipt of SASE only if interested. To show a portfolio, mail photocopies and cover letter. Pays 70% of gross income; on publication. Rights purchased vary according to project. The minimum length of the contract is one year. The artist owns the original art and the characters.
Tips: "Continental Features/Continental News Service does not consider highly abstract or stick-figure art."

CREATORS SYNDICATE, INC., 5777 W. Century Blvd., Los Angeles CA 90045. (213)337-7003. President: Richard S. Newcombe. Vice President, General Manager: Anita Medeiros. Estab. 1987. Serves 1,700 daily newspapers, weekly and monthly magazines.
Needs: Buys from 100 freelance writers and artists/year. Considers comic strips, gag cartoons, caricatures, editorial or political cartoons and "all types of newspaper columns."
First Contact & Terms: Send query letter with brochure showing art style or resume and "anything but originals." Samples are not filed and are returned by SASE. Reports back within 2 months. Write to show a portfolio, which should include tearsheets and photostats. Pays 50% of net proceeds. Considers saleability of art work and client's preferences when establishing payment. Negotiates rights purchased.

DYNAMIC GRAPHICS INC., 6000 N. Forest Park Dr., Peoria IL 61614-3592. (309)688-8800. Art Director: Frank Antal. Distributes to thousands of magazines, newspapers, agencies, industries and educational institutions.

Needs: Works with 30-40 artists/year. Prefers illustration, graphic design and elements; primarily b&w, but will consider some 2- and full-color. "We are currently seeking to contact established illustrators capable of handling b&w and highly realistic illustrations of contemporary people and situations."

First Contact & Terms: Submit portfolio with SASE. Reports within 1 month. Buys all rights. Negotiates payment. Pays on acceptance.

Tips: "Concentrate on mastering the basics in anatomy and figure illustration before settling into a 'personal' or 'interpretive' style!"

EDITOR'S CHOICE CLIP ART, Box 715, Liverpool NY 13088. (919)453-1010. Editor: Peggy Ries. Clip art firm. Distributes bimonthly to major corporations who publish employee newsletters or magazines.

Needs: Serious and humorous editorial illustration, graphics, standing heads, etc. Works with many artists on a regular basis. Prefers line illustrations in pen & ink, scratchboard, etc., or pencil illustration on textured board. Also buys graphic symbols. Work is related to business and industry, employee relations, health and wellness, physical fitness, family life, recreation, etc.

First Contact & Terms: Experienced illustrators and graphic designers only. Works on assignment only. Send query letter, resume and samples to be kept on file. Reports within 60 days. Prefers photocopies as samples. "Include information on remuneration required." Samples returned by SASE if not kept on file. Original art not returned at job's completion. Buys all rights or negotiates limited use fee. Pays $20-200 for illustrations; negotiates payment amount, varies according to project. Pays on acceptance.

Tips: "Only accomplished illustrators will be considered. Amateurs need not apply. Send 10-12 samples that show an individual's diversity of styles and techniques. We need illustrations that are easily reproducible. Pen or pencil illustrations must be clear and of good quality. We have no use for color illustrations."

EDITORS PRESS SERVICE, INC., 330 W. 42nd st., 15th Floor, New York NY 10036. (212)563-2252. FAX: (212)563-2517. Vice President: John P. Klem. Estab. 1933. Syndicate servicing 1,700 publications: daily and weekly newspapers and magazines. International sales only.

Needs: Buys from 3-5 freelance artists/year. Introduces 1-2 new strips/year. Considers comic strips, gag cartoons, caricatures, editorial/political cartoons and illustrations. Considers single, double or multi panel. Prefers pen & ink. Prefers non-American themes. Maximum size of artwork: 11×17.

First Contact & Terms: Send cover letter, finished cartoons, tearsheets and photocopies. Include 24-48 strips/panels. Does not want to see original artwork. Samples not filed are returned. Reports back within 14 days. To show a portfolio, mail appropriate materials. Pays 50% of gross income. Buys all rights. Minimum length of contract: two years. Artist owns original art and characters.

Tips: Last year there were "fewer new strip launches. Look for niches. Do not copy existing successful features. Study the existing competition. Read newspaper!" Looking for "well written gags and strong character development."

RICHARD R. FALK ASSOCIATES, 1472 Broadway, New York NY 10036. (212)221-0043. President: R. Falk. Estab. 1940. Syndicates to regional magazines and daily newspapers.

Needs: Buys from 3-4 freelance artists/year. Works on assignment only. Considers caricatures, editorial or political cartoons and spot drawings. Prefers line drawings. Prefers theatrical and entertainment themes.

First Contact & Terms: "Only send simple flyers, throwaway illustrations, Xeroxes." Reports back only if interested. Pays flat fee or $100-500 on acceptance. Considers clients' preferences when establishing payment. Buys one-time rights.

Tips: "Do not send original work, only nonreturnable photocopies."

*FILLERS FOR PUBLICATIONS, 7015 Prospect Pl. NE, Albuquerque NM 87110. (505)884-7636. President: Lucie Dubovik. Distributes to magazines and newspapers.

Needs: Buys 72 pieces/year from freelancers. Considers single panel, 4×6 or 5×7 cartoons on current events, education, family life, retirement, factory and office themes; clip art and crossword puzzles. Inquire for subject matter and format.

First Contact & Terms: Send query letter with samples of style and SASE. Samples are returned. Reports in 3 weeks. Previously published and simultaneous submissions OK. Buys first rights. Pays $7, cartoons, line drawings; $25/page of clip art; on acceptance.

Tips: Does not want to see comic strips.

Close-up

Jim Davis
Cartoonist

For those serious about becoming syndicated, Jim Davis, creator of "Garfield," advises, "Don't give up. I received a thousand rejection notices before I finally got the nod from United Media. I know it's tough. There's a lot of talent out there and only so many spots on a comics page. I think I once heard that most syndicates receive 10,000 submissions a year, and only two or three actually ever become syndicated. It's probably a lot like trying to break into Hollywood, possibly harder."

So how did Davis get discovered and become a star? When Davis was starting out, he took samples of his work to admired cartoonist and fellow Indiana-resident Tom K. Ryan of "Tumbleweeds" to have his work critiqued. Ryan ended up offering him a job, which Davis stayed with for nine years. "I worked days, evenings and weekends for Tom. He didn't have a set schedule and since my job was to do balloons, borders and backgrounds on 'Tumbleweeds,' I did the work whenever Tom had it ready for me." From Ryan he learned what it takes to maintain a syndicated feature and was afforded the time, income and confidence to pursue syndication himself.

His first cartoon character was an insect. "I filled in the off hours working on 'Gnorm Gnat.' I can't say my time was organized then. I just worked whenever I needed to, which was all the time." He wasn't to find success with Gnorm. "I just kept getting rejections from syndicates without ever knowing exactly what was wrong. Finally a comics editor said to me, 'Bugs? Who wants to be eating breakfast and reading a comic strip about a bunch of bugs? Who can relate to bugs?' That's when I started looking for a more appealing character. Another cartoonist once said every cartoonist has 100,000 bad drawings and bad gags inside himself. Hopefully, I used up most of those bad gags and drawings before 'Garfield.' "

The forerunner to "Garfield" was a strip called "Jon," based on a cartoonist (himself) and his cat Garfield. It was run in the *Pendleton Times*, a weekly magazine in Indiana, whose editor happened to be a good friend of his. He says this was a good way for him to test out his idea and get more experience. "A lot of cartoonists start off in campus or other local newspapers. A hopeful cartoonist could also test the waters by becoming a 'ghost' gag writer."

"Garfield" now has a much larger audience than "Jon" did, appearing in over 2,300 papers a day, in such faraway places as Zimbabwe. What accounts for the cat's success? "His personality traits—overeating and oversleeping—are universal," says Davis. "Garfield says and does things that humans can't get away with, but probably think and feel. He's been called an anti-hero because he champions the causes of slothfulness and gluttony. Also, it doesn't hurt that there are millions of cat lovers out there."

It is "humor first and foremost, followed by interesting art" that he feels make for a successful strip. He adds, "I think great artwork can make a strip, although I'm not so sure bad artwork can break a strip." Examine Winsor McCay's "Little Nemo in Slumberland" and Hal Foster's "Prince Valiant," now successfully carried on by John Cullen Murphy, for examples of superior artwork. On the other hand, there are a few strips where the artwork is pretty amateurish, but the characters and humor are so great that the art doesn't really matter. The perfect mix, of course, is a nice blend of good writing and good art. Bill Watterson found that perfect mix in "Calvin and Hobbes." Other favorite cartoonists and strips include Mort Walker ("Beetle Bailey" and "Hi and Lois"); Mike Peters ("Mother Goose and Grimm"); Johnny Hart ("B.C."); Lynn Johnston ("For Better or Worse"); and Charles Schultz, who he says taught him "the power of the light-hearted treatment of the gentle things in life."

He shuns questions such as how many and what types of characters a strip should have, citing Berke Breathed's "Opus," (a penguin) and Gary Larson's amoeba and other off-the-wall characters as ones that no one could have guessed would be a hit. "As far as situations that work best in a comic strip," he says, "I always say cartoonists simply hold a mirror up to life and show it back with a humorous twist."

When submitting work Davis advises the cartoonist to know of each syndicates' requirements. "But," he says, "almost all of them want to see four to six weeks worth of material, both daily and Sunday strips. They prefer photocopies or stats, not originals. They're looking for innovative, interesting characters and themes and neat, consistent drawings. It doesn't hurt to have a 'back-story' about your strip, or a character sheet that shows your major characters. Include a resume or cover letter to tell the syndicate a bit about yourself. I don't think there is any gimmick to having your submission stand out. In fact, I believe most editors feel gimmicky packages, ones that are oversized or flashy are simply a pain in the neck."

When asked to explain the ubiquity of the "Garfield Stuck-On-You" doll on car windows, Davis says it was thought of by a designer on his staff and designed to stick on bedroom windows. "I think the fad of sticking it on car windows was born in Los Angeles where people 'live' in their cars, probably to make it seem homier and because their cars and all their accessories are extensions of their personalities. It was crazy and wonderful. I couldn't have planned this type of 'event' in a million years."

— Lauri Miller

Reprinted with permission of UFS, Inc.

Despite the well defined personalities of the insects in "Gnorm Gnat," people seemed unable to identify with them, and in Gnorm's last appearance, he was crushed by a giant foot. Davis came up with the idea of "Garfield" by doing market research and determining that many strips featured dogs, but none appealed to cat lovers.

FOTO EXPRESSION INTERNATIONAL, Box 1268, Station "Q"., Toronto Ontario M4T 2P4 Canada. (416)841-9788. FAX: (416)841-5593. Director: M.J. Kubik. Serving 35 outlets.
Needs: Buys from 80 freelance artists/year. Considers b&w and color single, double and multiple panel cartoons, illustrations and spot drawings.
First Contact & Terms: Send query letter with brochure showing art style or resume, tearsheets, slides and photographs. Samples not filed returned by SASE. Reports within one month. To show a portfolio, mail final reproduction/product and color and b&w photographs. Artist receives percentage; on publication. Considers skill and experience of artist and rights purchased when establishing payment. Negotiates rights purchased.
Tips: "Quality and content are essential. Resume and samples must be accompanied by a SASE or, out of Canada, International Reply Coupon is required."

*FUTURE FEATURES SYNDICATE, Suite 117, 1923 Wickham Rd., Melbourne FL 32935. Media Director: Jerry Forney. Estab. 1989. Syndicate serving hundreds of outlets: daily and weekly newspapers and magazines. Guidelines not available
Needs: Approached by over 400 freelance artists/year. Buys from "many new artists"/year. Introduces 8-10 new strips/year. Considers comic strips, gag cartoons and editorial/political cartoons. Prefers single, double and multiple panel with or without gagline; b&w line drawings. Prefers "unpublished creative art themed for general newspaper audiences; standard newspaper format." Also uses freelance artists for promotional commercial art; standard newspaper format. "However, the market for this type of art is limited." Maximum size of artwork is 8½×11 panel, 5×20 strip; must be reducible to 25% of original size.
First Contact & Terms: Sample package should include photocopies and "short paragraph stating why you want to be a syndicated cartoonist." 12 samples should be included. Samples are filed or are returned by SASE if requested by artist. Reports back within 1 month. "Will attempt to add personal note to each inquiry." Write to schedule an appointment to show a portfolio, which should include original/final art. Pays 50% of gross income; on publication. Buys reprint rights. Minimum length of contract is 2 years. Offers automatic renewal. Artist owns original art; syndicate owns characters.
Tips: "We want to see a level of work that can be maintained on a daily strip or feature. If you have ability, we work with you to promote it."

PAULA ROYCE GRAHAM, Suite 20 G, 2770 W. 5th St., Brooklyn NY 11224. (718)372-1920. Contact: Paula Royce Graham. Syndicates to newspapers and magazines.
Needs: Considers b&w illustrations. Uses artists for advertising and graphics.
First Contact & Terms: Send business card and tearsheets to be kept on file. Write for artists' guidelines. Samples returned by SASE only if requested. Reports within days. Write for appointment to show a portfolio. Pay is negotiable; on publication. Considers skill of artist, client's preferences and rights purchased when establishing payment. Buys all rights.
Tips: "Keep it simple."

GRAPHIC ARTS COMMUNICATIONS, Box 421, Farrell PA 16121. (412)342-5300. President: Bill Murray. Estab. 1980. Syndicates to 200 newspapers and magazines.
Needs: Buys 400 pieces/year from freelance artists. Humor through youth and family themes preferred for single panel and multipanel cartoons and strips. Needs ideas for anagrams, editorial cartoons and puzzles, and for new comic panel "Sugar & Spike."
First Contact & Terms: Query for guidelines. Sample package should contain 5 copies of work, resume, SASE and cover letter. Reports within 4-6 weeks. No originals returned. Buys all rights. Pays flat fee, $8-50.
Tips: "Trends seem to be heading in the area of real life problems and work with animals. Send copies of your best work. If rejected, submit again."

GRAPHIC NEWS BUREAU, gabriel graphics, Box 38, Madison Square Station, New York NY 10010. (212)254-8863. Cable: NOLNOEL. Director: J.G. Bumberg. Custom syndications and promotions to customized lists, small dailies, suburbans and selected weeklies.
Needs: Represents 4-6 freelance artists/year. Prefers artists within easy access. No dogmatic, regional or pornographic themes. Uses single panel cartoons, illustrations, halftones in line conversions and line drawings.
First Contact & Terms: Send query letter only. Reports within 4-6 weeks. Returns original art after reproduction on request with SASE. Provide 3x5 card to be kept on file for possible future assignments. Negotiates rights purchased; on publication.
Tips: "A new, added service provides for counseling and conceptualizing in graphics/management/communications when and where printing is an integral part of the promotion, product, service."

HISPANIC LINK NEWS SERVICE, 1420 N St. NW, Washington DC 20005. (202)234-0737. General Manager: Hector Ericksen-Mendoza. Syndicated column service to 200 newspapers and a newsletter serving 1,300 private subscribers, "movers and shakers in the Hispanic community in U.S., plus others interested in Hispanics."

Needs: Buys from 20 freelance artists/year. Considers single panel cartoons; b&w, pen & ink line drawings. Work should have a Hispanic angle; "most are editorial cartoons, some straight humor."

First Contact & Terms: Send query letter with resume and photocopies to be kept on file. Samples not filed returned by SASE. Reports within 3 weeks. Call for appointment to show portfolio or contact through artist's agent. Pays flat fee of $25 average; on acceptance. Considers clients' preferences when establishing payment. Buys reprint rights and negotiates rights purchased; "while we ask for reprint rights, we also allow the artist to sell later."

Tips: "While we accept work from all artists, we are particularly interested in helping Hispanic artists showcase their work. Cartoons should offer a Hispanic perspective on current events or a Hispanic view of life."

HOSPITAL PR GRAPHICS, Box 715, Liverpool NY 13088. (315)453-1010. FAX: (315)453-3950. Editor: Peggy Ries. Estab. 1981. Clip art firm. Distributes monthly to hospitals and other health care organizations.

Needs: Uses illustration, drawings, spot drawings and graphic symbols related to health care for use in brochures, folders, newsletters, etc. Prefers sensitive line illustrations, spot drawings and graphics related to hospitals, nurses, doctors, patients, technicians and medical apparatus. Also buys cartoons.

First Contact & Terms: Experienced illustrators only, preferably having hospital exposure or access to resource material. Works on assignment only. Send query letter, resume, photostats or photocopies to be kept on file. "Send 10 to 20 different drawings which are interesting and show sensitive, caring people." Does not want to see "color illustration or styles that cannot be reproduced easily." Samples returned by SASE if not kept on file. Reports within 1 month. Original art not returned at job's completion. Buys all rights. Pays flat rate of $20-over 200 for illustrations; negotiates payment, which varies according to project. Pays on acceptance.

Tips: "We are looking to establish a continuing relationship with freelance graphic designers and illustrators. Illustration style should be serious, sensitive and somewhat idealized. Send enough samples to show the variety (if any) of styles you're capable of handling. Indicate the length of time it took to complete each illustration or graphic, and/or remuneration required. Practice drawing people's faces. Many illustrators fall short when drawing people."

*INTERCONTINENTAL MEDIA SERVICES, Box 2801, Washington DC 20013. (202)775-1113. FAX: (202)457-8852. Executive Editor: E. Von Rothkirch. Estab. 1924. Syndicate serving up to 400 outlets: daily and weekly newspapers. Guidelines available for SASE.

Needs: Approached by 50 freelance artists/year. Buys from 5-10 freelance artists/year. Introduces 3-5 new strips/year. Considers comic strips, gag cartoons, caricatures, editorial/political cartoons and illustrations. Prefers single or multiple panel with gagline; b&w line drawings. Maximum size of artwork "standard"; must be reducible to 50% of original size.

First Contact & Terms: Sample package should include cover letter, resume and finished cartoons. 6 samples should be included. Samples are filed or are returned by SASE if requested by artist. Reports back within 1 month. Call or write to schedule an appointment to show a portfolio, which should include original/final art. Pays 50% of net proceeds; on publication. Buys all rights. Offers automatic renewal. The syndicate owns the original art and the characters.

JSA PUBLICATIONS, INC., Box 37175, Oak Park MI 48237. (313)546-9123. Director: Joe Ajlouny. Estab. 1982. Serves 12 outlets, mainly magazines and books.

Needs: Buys from 24 freelance artists/year. Considers greeting cards, comic strips, map art, caricatures, editorial or political cartoons. Prefers pen & ink and airbrush. Prefers panels to strips.

First Contact & Terms: Send query letter with resume and samples. Include enough to accurately express artist's talent and styles. Samples are filed or are returned by SASE only if requested. Reports back within 4 weeks only if interested. Call to schedule an appointment to show a portfolio. Pays flat fee of $50-900; on publication. Considers client's preferences and rights purchased when establishing payment. Negotiates rights purchased.

Tips: All submissions "must be of professional quality. Have a superior method of expression. By this we mean it must distinguish the artist from all others, especially true of comic strips or panels, except they must be funny or telling too!" Develop a theme and title concept and stick to it. We prefer educational, informational, contemporary submissions."

LEOLEEN-DURCK CREATIONS/LEONARD BRUCE DESIGNS, Suite 226, Box 2767, Jackson TN 38302. (901)668-1205. Director/Cartoonist: Leonard Bruce. Estab. 1985. Serves 5 outlets. Serves daily and weekly newspapers, charities, local papers, national magazines and other syndicates.

Needs: Buys from 10 freelance artists/year. Works on assignment only. Considers comic strips, gag cartoons, caricatures and editorial or political cartoons. Prefers single panel cartoons. Prefers pen & ink, very detailed with washes. Prefers off-the-wall, science fiction, animals and pets and children's themes.

First Contact & Terms: Send brochure showing art style, resume and photocopies. Sample package should include background information sheet of strip and artist, resume and photo of artist, 18 samples of previous published works and SASE. Samples are not filed and are returned by SASE. Reports back within 3 weeks only if interested. Write to schedule an appointment to show a portfolio or mail b&w photostats. Pays 10% of net proceeds; on publication. Considers skill and experience of artist and saleability of artwork when establishing payment. Buys first rights.

Tips: "Send your best work, blocked out panel cartoons and print neatly. Be able to accept rejections and work to refine your material. Always send in an SASE with samples. We are a small company and we will try to work with and for the artist so that everyone will benefit." Notices trend toward "different current themes, not family strips but divorced mom with kids, etc."

LOS ANGELES TIMES SYNDICATE, 218 S. Spring St., Los Angeles CA 90012. (213)237-7987. Executive Editor: Steven Christensen. (213)237-3213.

Needs: Comic strips, panel cartoons and editorial cartoons. "We prefer humor to dramatic continuity. We consider only cartoons that run 6 or 7 days/week. Cartoons may be of any size, as long as they're to scale with cartoons running in newspapers." (Strips usually run approximately $6^7/16 \times 2$, panel cartoons $3\frac{1}{8} \times 4$; editorial cartoons vary.)

First Contact & Terms: Submit photocopies or photostats of 24 dailies. Submitting Sunday cartoons is optional; if you choose to submit them, send at least four. Reports within 2 months. Include SASE. Syndicate buys all rights.

Tips: "Don't imitate cartoons that are already in the paper. Avoid linework or details that might bleed together, fade out or reproduce too small to see clearly. We hardly ever match artists with writers or vice versa. We prefer people or teams who can do the entire job of creating a feature."

MCLEAN PROVIDENCE JOURNAL AND ARLINGTON COURIER, Box 580, McLean VA 22101. (703)356-3320. Editor: David Dear. Estab. 1986. Syndicates to weekly newspapers and local guide books.

Needs: Buys from 2 freelance artists/year. Prefers local or Virginia artists. Considers comic strips, gag cartoons, caricatures, editorial or political cartoons, illustrations and spot drawings. Prefers pen & ink with washes.

First Contact & Terms: Send query letter with brochure or resume and tearsheets. Samples are filed and samples not filed are returned by SASE. Reports back only if interested. To show a portfolio, mail tearsheets. Pays flat fee, $5-90; on publication. Considers clients' preferences when establishing payment. Negotiates rights purchased.

Tips: "We prefer local artists from North Virginia who have local themes in their work."

METRO CREATIVE GRAPHICS, INC., 33 W. 34th St., New York NY 10011. (800)223-1600. Contact: Andrew Shapiro. Estab. 1910. Clip art firm. Distributes to 6,000 daily and weekly paid and free circulation newspapers, schools, graphics and ad agencies and retail chains.

Needs: Buys from 100 freelance artists/year. Considers single panel illustrations and line and spot drawings; b&w and color. Prefers all categories of themes associated with retail, classified, promotion and advertising. Also needs covers for special-interest tabloid section.

First Contact & Terms: Send query letter with brochure showing style or photostats, photocopies, slides, photographs and tearsheets to be kept on file. Samples not kept on file returned by SASE. Reports only if interested. To show a portfolio, mail appropriate materials or call to schedule an appointment. Works on assignment only. Pays flat fee of $25-800; on acceptance. Considers skill and experience of artist, saleability of artwork and clients' preferences when establishing payment.

Tips: "Metro provides steady work, lead time and prompt payment. All applicants are seriously considered. Don't rely on 1-2 samples to create interest. Show a variety of styles and special ability to draw people in realistic situations. If specialty is graphic design, think how you would use samples in advertising."

MINORITY FEATURES SYNDICATE, Box 421, Farrell PA 16121. (412)342-5300. Chairman of the Board: Bill Murray. Estab. 1980. Clip art firm serving approximately 500 outlets.

Needs: Buys from 600 freelance artists/year. Considers single, double and multi-panel cartoons; illustrations and spot drawings. Prefers b&w pen & ink line drawings with family themes. Also uses artists for advertising art. Also publishes comic books. Query first.

First Contact & Terms: Published artists only. Works on assignment only. Send query letter and resume to be kept on file; write for artists' guidelines. Prefers photocopies as samples, minimum of 5 copies. Samples returned by SASE. Reports only if interested. Pays flat fee, $8-50; on acceptance. Considers rights purchased when establishing payment. Buys all rights.

Tips: "Submit only your best efforts. If rejected, submit again. Trends seem to be heading in the area of real-life problems and work with animals."

NATIONAL NEWS BUREAU, 1318 Chancellor St., Philadelphia PA 19107. (215)546-8088. Editor: Harry Jay Katz. Syndicates to 1,000 outlets and publishes entertainment newspapers on a contract basis.
Needs: Buys from 500 freelance artists/year. Prefers entertainment themes. Uses single, double and multiple panel cartoons, illustrations; line and spot drawings.
First Contact & Terms: To show a portfolio, send samples and resume. Samples returned by SASE. Reports within 2 weeks. Returns original art after reproduction. Send resume and samples to be kept on file for future assignments. Negotiates rights purchased. Pays flat rate, $5-100 for each piece; on publication.

OCEANIC PRESS SERVICE, Box 6538, Buena Park CA 90622-6538. (714)527-5650. FAX: (714)527-0268. Manager: J. West. Estab. 1957. Syndicates to 300 magazines, newspapers and subscribers in 30 countries.
Needs: Buys several hundred pieces/year from freelancers. Considers cartoon strips (single, double and multiple panel) and illustrations. Prefers camera-ready material (tearsheets or clippings). Themes include published sex cartoons, family, inflation, juvenile activity cartoons, and covers for paperbacks (color transparencies). "No graphic sex or violence. Poke fun at established TV shows. Bad economy means people must do their own home, car and other repairs. How-to articles with b&w line drawings are needed. Magazines will buy less and have more features staff-written. Quality is needed. People like to read more about celebrities, but it has to have a special angle, not the usual biographic run-of-the-mill profile. Much will be TV related. I'd like to see a good cartoon book on Sherlock Holmes, on Hollywood, on leading TV shows."
First Contact & Terms: Send query letter with photostats and samples of previously published work. Accepts tearsheets and clippings. Send SASE. Reports within 1 month. Pays 50% of net proceeds. Originals returned to artist, or put on auction. Guidelines $1 with SASE.
Tips: "The trend is definitely toward the women's market: money saving topics, service features – how to do home repair – anything to fight inflation; also unusual cartoons about unusual happenings; unusual sports; and cartoons with sophisticated international settings, credit cards, air travel. We would like to receive more clippings for foreign reprints. Competition is keen – artists should strive for better quality submissions."

PROFESSIONAL ADVISORY COUNSEL, INC., Suite 106, 5815 Melton Dr., Oklahoma City OK 73132. (405)728-8000. President: Larry W. Beavers. Estab. 1952. Syndicate serving approximately 1,000 international outlets.
Needs: Buys from freelance artists/year. Introduces 40 new strips/year. Considers illustrations and spot drawings; b&w and color. Prefers camera-ready artwork. Also uses artists for advertising. Considers any media.
First Contact & Terms: Send query letter and roughs with 3-5 samples to file. Samples returned by SASE only if requested. Especially looks for "simplicity and fast-relating/assimilating potential." Reports only if interested. Write for appointment to show portfolio and for artists' guidelines. Pays flat fee, $150-400 average; on acceptance. Buys all rights.
Tips: "Make your contact quick, concise and to-the-point."

RELIGIOUS NEWS SERVICE, Box 1015, Radio City Station, New York NY 10101. (212)315-0870. Photo Editor: Judy Weidman. Estab. 1935. Syndicate serving 200 Catholic, Jewish and Protestant weekly newspapers.
Needs: Buys from 25+ freelance artists/year. "We buy a lot from a few freelancers." Considers comic strips, gag cartoons, caricatures, editorial/political cartoons, illustrations and spot drawings. Prefers clean, photoready work. Prefers religious, social themes. Maximum size 16×20; must be reducible to 25% of size.
First Contact & Terms: Send cover letter, finished cartoons and photocopies. Include 8-12 samples; "1-2 OK, too." Samples are filed or are returned by SASE only if requested. Reports back within 7-10 days. Call or write to schedule an appointment to show a portfolio, or mail b&w original/final art. Pays flat fee; $25-50; on publication. Negotiates rights purchased. Artist owns original art and characters.
Tips: "Include b&w art only; no fine art. Do not send preachy, overly subjective work."

*REPORTER, YOUR EDITORIAL ASSISTANT, 7015 Prospect Pl., NE, Albuquerque NM 87110. (505)884-7636. Editor: George Dubow. Syndicates to newspapers and magazines from secondary level schools and colleges.
Needs: Considers single panel cartoons on teenage themes.
First Contact & Terms: Mail art and SASE. Reports in 3 weeks. Buys first rights. Originals returned to artist only upon request. Pays $5-10.
Tips: Does not want to see comic strips.

SINGER MEDIA CORP., 3164 Tyler Ave., Anaheim CA 92801. (714)527-5650. Executive Vice President: Veena Uberoi. Syndicates to 300 worldwide magazines, newspapers, book publishers and poster firms; strips include *They Changed History*, and *How It Began*. Artists' guidelines $1.
Needs: Buys several thousand freelance pieces/year. Considers singe, double and multiple panel cartoon strips; family, children, sex, juvenile activities and games themes. Especially needs business, outer space and credit card cartoons of 3-4 panels. Prefers to buy reprints or clips of previously published material.

First Contact & Terms: To show a portfolio, send query letter with tearsheets. Show 10-12 samples. "Prefer to see tearsheets or camera ready copy or clippings." Include SASE. Reports within 2-3 weeks. Returns originals to artist at job's completion if requested at time of submission with SASE. Licenses reprint or all rights; prefers foreign reprint rights. Pays 50% commission.
Tips: "Send us cartoons on subjects like inflation, taxes, sports or Christmas; we get thousands on sex. Everyone wants new ideas—not the same old characters, same old humor at the doctor or psychiatrist or at the bar. More sophistication is needed. Background is also needed—not just 2 people talking."

SYNDICATED WRITERS & ARTISTS, INC., 2901 N. Tacoma Ave., Indianapolis IN 46218. (317)924-5143. Executive Editor: Eunice Trotter. Serves numerous newspapers.
Needs: Buys from 3-4 freelance artists/year. Considers editorial or political cartoons; pen & ink or line drawings. Prefers minority issues.
First Contact & Terms: To show a portfolio, send resume and samples. Samples are filed or are returned by SASE. Reports back only if interested. Pays 40% of gross income or flat fee of $15 minimum; on publication. Considers skill and experience of artist and client's preferences when establishing payment. Buys all rights.

TEENAGE CORNER INC., 70-540 Gardenia Ct., Rancho Mirage CA 92270. President: Mrs. David J. Lavin. Syndicates rights.
Needs: Prefers spot drawings and illustrations.
First Contact & Terms: Send query letter and SASE. Reports within 1 week. Buys one-time and reprint rights. Negotiates commission. Pays on publication.

TRIBUNE MEDIA SERVICES, INC., 64 E. Concord St., Orlando FL 32801. (305)839-5650. Editor: Mike Argirion. Syndicate serving daily and Sunday newspapers.
Needs: Seeks comic strips and newspaper panels.
First Contact & Terms: Send query letter with resume and photocopies. Sample package should include "2-3 weeks of daily and Sunday strips or panels." Samples not filed are returned. Reports within 4-6 weeks. Pays 50% of net proceeds.

UNITED MEDIA, 200 Park Ave., New York NY 10166. Director of Comic Art: Sarah Gillespie. Estab. 1978. Syndicate servicing U.S. and international newspapers. Guidelines available for SASE. "United Media consists of United Feature Syndicate and Newspaper Enterprise Association. Submissions are considered for both syndicates. Duplicate submissions are not needed."
Needs: Introduces 2-4 new strips/year. Considers comic strips and comic panels. Considers single, double and multiple panels. Prefers pen & ink. Maximum size of artwork: 8½×11.
First Contact & Terms: Send cover letter, finished cartoons and photocopies. Include 36 dailies, "Sundays not needed in first submissions." Do not send "oversize submissions, concepts but no strip." Samples are not filed and are returned by SASE. Reports back within 3 months. "Does not view portfolios." UFS pays 50% of net proceeds. NEA pays flat fee, $400 and up a week. Buys all rights. Minimum length of contract 5 years and 5 year renewal. Automatic renewal. 50/50 ownership of art; syndicate owns characters.
Tips: "Send copies, but not originals. Dailies only are needed on first submissions. Send a cover letter and resume. Do not send mocked-up licensing concepts." Looks for "originality, art and humor writing." Be aware of long odds; don't quit your day job; work on developing your own style and humor writing. Worry less about 'marketability'—that's our job."

UNIVERSAL PRESS SYNDICATE, 4900 Main St., Kansas City MO 64112. Editorial Director: Lee Salem. Syndicate serving 2750 daily and weekly newspapers.
Needs: Considers single, double or multiple panel cartoons and strips; b&w and color. Prefers photocopies of b&w, pen & ink, line drawings; "other techniques are reviewed, but remember that this material will be published in newspapers."
First Contact & Terms: Reports within 4 weeks. To show a portfolio, mail photostats. Buys syndication rights. Send query letter with resume and photocopies.
Tips: "A well-conceived comic strip with strong characters, good humor and a contemporary feel will almost always get a good response. Be original. Don't be afraid to try some new idea or technique. Don't be discouraged by rejection letters. Universal Press receives 100-150 comic submissions a week, and only takes on two or three a year, so keep plugging away. Talent has a way of rising to the top."

WHITEGATE FEATURES SYNDICATE, 71 Faunce Dr., Providence RI 02906. (401)274-2149. Talent Manager: Eve Green. Estab. 1988. Syndicate serving daily newspapers and magazines.
Needs: "We're new but we're planning on 6 or more strips next year. Do one now." Considers comic strips, gag cartoons, editorial/political cartoons, illustrations and spot drawings; single, double and multi panels. Also needs artists for advertising and publicity. Work must be reducible to strip size.

First Contact & Terms: Send cover letter, resume, tearsheets, photostats and photocopies. Include about 12 strips. Samples are filed or are returned by SASE. Reports back within 1½ months. Does not report back if no SASE included. To show a portfolio, mail tearsheets, photostats, photographs and slides; include b&w. Pays 50% of net proceeds upon syndication. Negotiates rights purchased. Minimum length of contract 5 years (flexible). Artists owns original art; syndicate own characters (negotiable).

Tips: Include in a sample package "info about youself, tearsheets of previous work, notes about the strip and enough samples to tell what it is. Please don't write asking if we want to see; just send samples." Looks for "good writing, strong characters, good taste in humor. We like people who have been cartooning for a while and have been printed. Try to get published in local newspapers."

Syndicates/'90-'91 changes

The following syndicates appeared in the 1990 edition of *Artist's Market* but are not in the 1991 edition. Those which did not respond to our request for an update of their listings may be out of business for example, or they may be overstocked with submissions. If they indicated a reason, it is noted in parentheses after their name.

American-International Syndicate (investigating complaint)
Fastbreak Syndicate Inc.

Interpress of London and New York (not accepting artwork)
News USA (asked to be deleted)

Reviews and Previews
United Cartoonists Syndicate (asked to be deleted)

Services & Opportunities

Organization of Interest

Membership in an organization can be helpful to you, the artist, for a variety of reasons. An organization can introduce you to other artists, which can be both a social and vocational benefit; it can offer support when the going gets tough; its activities—such as seminars, workshops, conferences and publications—can be educational in an art, business and/or legal sense; and sometimes it can be a financial aid, offering grants and access to such benefits as insurance and a credit union. Each of the following listings describes the purpose of the organization, what is required for membership, and what it offers its members. For further information, write or call the organizations that interest you.

AMERICAN CENTER FOR DESIGN, (formerly STA), Suite 500, 233 E. Ontario, Chicago IL 60611. (312)787-2018. FAX: (312)649-9518. Estab. 1927.
Purpose: "A national association of design professionals, educators and students. In addition to promoting excellence in design practice, it serves as a national center for the accumulation and dissemination of information regarding the role and value of design."
Membership: Membership is open to those individuals engaged in the practice, direction, or instruction of design, those engaged in an allied profession in the active support of the American Center for Design's objectives, businesses or institutions which support activities or education in design. Student, $50; Apprentice (any individual who has graduated from a design school within the last two years), $70; Regular or full, $100/80; Associate, $100/80. Membership is available. Write or call for membership information.
Offerings: 2-3 meetings/month and curated design exhibitions throughout year. Design student conference and regularly scheduled presentations by recognized designers. Publishes annual *Design Journal*; *Statements*: a publication of interviews, articles and book reviews published 3 times per year; *Bulletin*: a monthly newsletter providing information on current American Center for Design events and activities, including new member listing; *Creative Registry*: a monthly publication listing employment opportunities; and *100 Show Annual*: a catalog of winning entries from the 100 Show. Also publishes a directory listing member names, titles, work addresses and phone numbers.

AMERICAN INSTITUTE OF GRAPHIC ARTS, 1059 Third Ave., New York NY 10021. (212)752-0813. Estab. 1914.
Purpose: "National, nonprofit organization of graphic design and graphic arts professionals. AIGA sponsors competitions, exhibitions, publications, professional seminars and educational activities to promote excellence in the graphic design profession."
Membership: Student Member (full-time student), $35; Junior Member (practiced or taught graphic design less than 3 years), $140; Member Graphic Design (practiced or taught graphic design 3 years or more), $175; Member Allied Field (practiced or taught in allied field 3 years or more), $175; Institutional Member (library, educational institution, nonprofit organization, $175; Corporate Member (graphic design firm or corporation, entitled to 5 individual memberships), $875; Junior Member (practiced or taught graphic design less than 3

years), $140; "there is a one-time application fee of $20." Membership is available; write or call for membership information.
Offerings: Chapter meetings. Sponsors AIGA National Conference every 2 years (only national conference on graphic design) and also 4 competitions annually. Publishes *Graphic Design USA* and *AIGA Journal of Graphic Design*. Special programs include a library, gallery, travelling shows and slide archives. Membership directory lists members geographically and alphabetically.

AMERICAN SOCIETY OF ARCHITECTURAL PERSPECTIVISTS, BAC 320 Newbury St., Boston MA 02115. (617)846-4766. President Emeritus: Frank M. Costantino. Estab. 1986.
Purpose: Nonprofit business organization promoting the professional interest of architectural illustrators and establishing a communication network among members throughout the U.S., Canada, Japan, England and other countries. Approximate current membership: 350.
Membership: Open to architectural illustrators, architects, students and other related professionals. Must have professional practice of architectural delineation (formal guidelines still being determined). Regular or full membership, $75. Membership is available; write for membership information.
Offerings: Two meetings/year. Annual exhibition. Awards Hugh Ferriss Memorial Prize. Publishes exhibit booklet of winning entries and a newsletter. Membership directory lists membership, contract format, pricing guidelines, tax information and foreign renderers associations.

AMERICAN SOCIETY OF ARTISTS, INC., Box 1326, Palatine IL 60078. (312)751-2500 or (708)991-4748. Estab. 1972.
Purpose: National professional membership organization of fine artists (with American Artisans, its crafts division).
Membership: Juried membership, a limited number in each category and media; juried via slide/photo with application for membership. Regular or full, $50; Associateship, $30; Patronship, $30. "Note: Patronship and Associateship are not memberships." Membership is available; write or call for membership information.
Offerings: About 25 shows/year. Lecture and demonstration service – if a member qualifies for participation in this, they are "booked" for lectures, demos, workshops and seminars for various groups – they "present" them. Awards include honorary membership and certificates of appreciation. Publishes quarterly *A.S.A. Artisan*: includes show and exhibition listings and information for and about members. Other services include supplies, publicity and access to other benefits including insurance, credit union, etc. Publishes a directory available only to certain "working" members.

ART DIRECTORS CLUB OF CINCINNATI, Box 68062, Cincinnati OH 45206. Contact: Membership Chairman.
Purpose: To develop the standards of art education in the Cincinnati community, extend vocational guidance to young artists, elevate advertising and industrial art standards in Cincinnati, serve as a guide to its members in their dealings with artists and craftsmen and raise the standards of business procedure. Also to have its members contribute their time and talent in the development of creative ideas and designs for humanitarian, charitable and other worthwhile endeavors and encourage artistic and professional development among its members. Approximate current membership: 150.
Membership: Open to art directors, designers, illustrators, photographers, craftsmen, administrative heads of schools, museums, people over art directors. Regular or full, $50; $30 application fee. Membership is available; write or call for membership information.
Offerings: Meetings 2nd Tuesday of month September-May. Special speakers 6 times a year. Annual competition, show and banquet in March. Publishes monthly newsletter *The Director* outlining meetings, new members, upcoming events and news. Other services include: annual showing of clips, club Christmas party open to all. Publishes a directory for members.

ART DIRECTORS CLUB OF LOS ANGELES, Suite 410, 7080 Hollywood Blvd., Los Angeles CA 90028. (213)465-8707. Estab. 1948.
Purpose: To provide a forum for the exchange of ideas in the advertising/design community. Approximate current membership: 450.
Membership: Open to all graphic arts professionals and students. Regular or full, $100; Associate, $100; Affiliate, $100; Student, $25. Membership is available; write for membership information.
Offerings: Monthly meetings. Annual competition. Offers various workshops and seminars. Publishes the *Show Annual*, full-color and hard bound.

ART DIRECTORS CLUB OF PHILADELPHIA, 2017 Walnut St., Philadelphia PA 19103. (215)569-3650. FAX: (215)569-1410. Account Executive: Louise MacFarland. Estab. 1920.
Purpose: "To bring together creatives in the Delaware Valley." Approximate current membership: 550.
Membership: Open to everyone approved by Board of Directors. Regular or full, $130; student, $25; Group. Membership is available; write or call for membership information.
Offerings: 1 meeting/month, except summer. 1 exhibit of the Art Directors' Contest winners. Annual contest: Art Directors Call for Entries. Publishes bimonthly newsletter and annual book of entry winners. Publishes source book listing all creatives in Delaware Valley by category.

ART INFORMATION CENTER, Suite 412, 280 Broadway, New York NY 10007. (212)227-0282. Director: Dan Concholar. Estab. 1959.
Purpose: "A networking referral service for fine art, with a staff of 1, interns and volunteers."
Membership: Open to professional fine artists and dealers. $10 fee to place slides, data in information bank for artists; consultations by appointment. Write or call for membership information.

ARTS EXTENSION SERVICE, Division of Continuing Education, University of MA, Amherst MA 01003. (413)545-2360. FAX: (413)545-3405. Arts Resource Coordinator: Brenda D'addamio. Estab. 1973.
Purpose: "A service organization with a fulltime professional staff of 6, serving as a catalyst for better management of the arts for organizations and individual artists."
Membership: Not a membership organization. "We provide services for all who are interested in them."
Offerings: Arts Management workshops. "We present the New England Film and Video Festival every year." Publishes a number of softbound books such as *Fairs & Festivals of the Northeast and Southeast, The Artist in Business* and *Fundamentals of Arts Management.*

ASSOCIATION OF HISPANIC ART, (AHA), INC., 173 E. 116th St., New York NY 10029. (212)860-5445. Director of Technical Assistance: Daniela Montana. Estab. 1975.
Purpose: "AHA is an arts service organization dedicated to the advancement of Latino arts, artists and organizations as an integral part of the cultural life of the nation."
Membership: Open to the general public. Technical assistance is available to Hispanic artists and organizations. Individuals, $15; Organizations, $25. Membership is available; write for membership information.
Offerings: Visual Artists, Financial Management and Organizational Development workshops. Publishes *AHA Hispanic Arts News,* a monthly newsletter, technical assistance manuals, *Directory of Hispanic Arts Organizations* and the *Directory of Hispanic Visual Artists in the Northeast.*

ASSOCIATION OF MEDICAL ILLUSTRATORS, 2692 Huguenot Springs Rd., Midlothian VA 23113. (804)794-2908. Executive Director: Margaret H. Henry. Estab. 1946.
Purpose: "Devoted to: (1) advancement of medical illustration; (2) advancement of medical and health education; (3) education of its members; and (4) cooperation with related professions. Approximate current membership: 900.
Membership: Open to medical illustrators, graphic artists, designers, art directors, communication directors, etc. Active members must have a sponsor and undergo portfolio review. Associate members are elected as their dues are received. Active or full, $135; Associate, $115; Overseas, $70; Student, $40; Sustaining Corporate, $1,000. Membership is available; write or call for information.
Offerings: Annual meetings that include exhibitions. Two days of seminars preceding meetings. Publishes newsletters, *Journal of Biocommunication* and *Sourcebook of Medical Illustrators.* Special programs include insurance, legal advice, job placement, consulting network and contract forms. Membership directory lists members alphabetically and geographically, along with members of related groups, such as Health Science Communications Association, medical sculptors, biological photographers and biomedical communications directors.

BLACK CREATIVE PROFESSIONALS ASSOCIATION, Box 34272, Los Angeles CA 90034. (213)964-3550. President: David G. Brown. Estab. 1988. Approximate current membership: 150.
Purpose: Nonprofit association "to assist in professional advancement and education of members, provide referral resource for minority talent function as mentors and provide emotional support."
Membership: Open to anyone. Regular or full, $50. Membership is available; call for membership information.
Offerings: Meetings once a month. No exhibitions or trade shows, "but have plans for them in the future." Workshops once a month on a variety of art-related subjects. Future plans for contest. Publishes a monthly newsletter. Other services include a scholarship program with UCLA and discounts at art stores and on services. Publishes a directory listing all members and the services/skills they have to offer.

BRITISH AMERICAN ARTS ASSOCIATION, 116 Commercial Street, London E1 6NF United Kingdom. (071)247-5385. FAX: (071)247-5256. Executive Director: Jennifer Williams. Estab. 1978.
Purpose: "Arts service organization providing info and advice to artists and arts administrators working in transatlantic cultural exchange."
Membership: Membership is not currently available; write for membership information.
Offerings: Occasional workshops on varied subjects. Publishes newsletter.

CALIFORNIA LAWYERS FOR THE ARTS, Building C, Room 255, Fort Mason Center, San Francisco CA 94123. (415)775-7200; 315 W. Ninth St., Los Angeles CA 90015. (213)623-8311. Executive Director: Alma Robinson. Estab. 1974.

Purpose: "Nonprofit organization providing legal services and information for artists and art organizations of all disciplines, as well as resources on artists' housing. CLA has a membership of over 1,000 individuals and organizations which receive member discounts on lawyer referrals, workshops, seminars and the use of the research library."
Membership: Open to artists and organizations of all disciplines. Working Artist, $20; General Individual, $35; Panel Attorney, $50; Patron, $100-1,000; Student, $15; Small Organization, $40; Large Organization, $75. Membership is available; write or call for information.
Offerings: Weekly and monthly clinics; workshops and seminars. Publishes quarterly newsletter, *Artistic License* and books such as *Alternative Dispute Resolution, Legislative Masterpieces: A Guide to California Arts Legislation* and *The Visual Artist's Seminar Handbook*. Special programs include copyright clinics, tax workshops, nonprofit organization formation and management.

CHICAGO ARTISTS' COALITION, 5 W. Grand Ave., Chicago IL 60610. (312)670-2060. Executive Director: Arlene Rakoncay. Estab. 1975.
Purpose: An artist-run, nonprofit service organization for visual artists. "Our purpose is to create a positive environment in which artists can live and work. Our primary objectives are improved benefits, services and networking opportunities for artists; increased exhibitions and sales of local and regional artists' work; greater financial support of the arts from government sources, foundations and corporations; and protection of artists from unfair business practices and censorship." Approximate membership: 1,900.
Membership: Open to all visual artists. Regular, $30; Student, $18; Seniors, $20. Write or call for membership information.
Offerings: Bimonthly program meetings with slide presentations or panel discussions, an annual tax and recordkeeping workshop, an annual business of art conference. Publishes monthly *Artists' Gallery Guide* and *Bookkeeping for Artists, An Artist's Resource Book*. Other services include 2 health insurance plans, a fine art insurance plan for works of art, a job referral service, slide registry, discounts at art supply stores, a resource center and an emergency assistance program.

COALITION OF WOMEN'S ART ORGANIZATIONS, 123 East Beutel Rd., Port Washington WI 53074. (414)284-4458. Estab. 1977.
Purpose: "We are a national advocacy organization and have a 10,000 plus membership of individuals and organizations, such as National Artists Equity, National Women's Caucus for Art."
Membership: Open to anyone in the arts community who wishes to keep abreast of proposed national legislation and other issues that affect artists. Organizations, $25; Individuals, $10. Members must pay yearly dues. Write for membership information.
Offerings: 1 annual meeting/yearly at the College Art Association conference. Holds panels at Women's Caucus for Art and/or College Art Association conference held in February each year. Publishes *CWAO NEWS*, a monthly to keep members informed of salient information: proposed federal arts legislation, arts at issue, women's art issues etc.

COLORADO CALLIGRAPHERS' GUILD, Box 6746, Denver CO 80206. Contact: Secretary. Estab. 1978.
Purpose: Educational group. Approximate membership: 175.
Membership: Open to anyone. Regular or full, $20. Membership is available; write for membership information.
Offerings: Quarterly meetings. Sponsors open and juried shows of calligraphy. Has afternoon and 2 day workshops. Publishes *Inkcetera*, 3/year newsletter. Publishes a directory listing members.

COMMUNICATING ARTS GROUP OF SAN DIEGO, INC., Suite F, 3108 Fifth Ave., San Diego CA 92103. (619)295-5082. Administrator: Ms. Sydney Cleaver. Estab. 1950.
Purpose: A networking group for those in the graphic art field.
Membership: Open to professionals and students in graphic arts as well as related fields. Regular or full and Corporate memberships. Membership is available; write or call for membership information.
Offerings: Monthly meetings. Trade shows and exhibitions. Has "the best contest of advertising/editorial art done in San Diego County." Publishes "quarterly newsletter *Vision*, monthly newsletter *Glimpse* and an annual showbook of SanDi winners. Special programs include the SanDi Awards Show, a golf outing and a beach party." Publishes a directory of members for members only.

CONNECTICUT VOLUNTEER LAWYERS FOR THE ARTS (CTVLA), Connecticut Commission on the Arts, 227 Lawrence St., Hartford CT 06106. (203)566-4770. CTVLA Coordinator: Linda Dente. Estab. 1974.
Purpose: "This is a pro bono lawyer association made up of about 200 attorneys throughout Connecticut. The purpose of the CTVLA is to supply free legal help to Connecticut artists and arts organizations."
Membership: Eligibility requirements for artists to receive free legal help are 1) The artist must be a Connecticut resident. 2) The artist's legal problem must relate to his/her work as an artist; or in the case of arts organizations, the problem must relate directly to the organization. 3) The artist must qualify financially

by meeting standards set by the Connecticut Bar Association Committee on Arts and the Law. No fee or type of membership. Services are available; write or call about eligibility.

Offerings: "We provide benefits to artists, not to our members. We host conferences and workshops dealing with arts concerns and the law. These conferences are aimed at increasing artists' awareness of the laws pertaining to them."

DUTCHESS COUNTY ARTS COUNCIL, 39 Market St., Poughkeepsie NY 12601. (914)454-3222. Executive Director: Sherre Wesley. Estab. 1964.

Purpose: "An arts service organization with a membership of 40 cultural organizations and 470 individuals. DCAC seeks to establish the Mid-Hudson Valley Region as one of the premier locations for high quality cultural activities in New York State."

Membership: "Encouraged among artists and cultural organizations, educators and schools, professionals, nonprofit groups and all individuals interested in the arts." Benefactor, $250; Donor, $150; Patron, $100; Supporter, $50; Contributor, $35; Friend, $25. Membership is available; write or call for membership information.

Offerings: Annual membership meeting; others are on an as-needed basis. "DCAC's technical assistance workshops cover a broad range of topics, such as graphics techniques, advocacy, grant writing, marketing and financial management." County Executive Arts Awards are given to individuals and institutions who contribute significantly to the artistic vitality of Dutchess County. Publishes *ARTSCENE*, a quarterly newsletter providing news and information about DCAC and regional arts issues and activities, and The *Arts-In-Education Quarterly* provides news and information of interest to artists and art groups who are involved in educational programs. *The Artists Skills Bank* lists regional artists by specialities and skills and the *Arts-in-Education Registry* lists artists and cultural organizations which sponsor or participate in educational programs. Other services include raising and regranting funds to support the arts programming of artists and cultural groups and ARTSCAPE, an annual arts festival.

ETHNIC CULTURAL PRESERVATION COUNCIL, 6500 S. Pulaski, Chicago IL 60629. (312)582-5143. Executive Director: Carole Miller. Estab. 1977.

Purpose: Research and resource center for ethnic community and organization/artists.

Membership: Open to everyone. Individual, $15; Organization, $25. Membership is available; write for membership information.

Offerings: 4 programs/year plus special lectures, information on other people and events. Photograph and textile exhibitions. Workshops for young and old, of all ethnic groups.

GRAPHIC ARTISTS GUILD, 11 W. 20th St., New York NY 10011-3704. (212)463-7730. FAX: (212)463-8779. Executive Director: Paul Basista. Estab. 1967.

Purpose: "GAG is a national advocacy organization dedicated to uniting within its membership all persons engaged in the graphic arts professions, improving industry standards and improving the economic and social conditions of professional artists and designers."

Membership: Membership open to all professional graphic artists; at least 51% of income must be derived from artwork. Regular or full, $100, $135, $175; Associate, $95; Student, $55; One-time initiation, $25. Write or call for membership information.

Offerings: Monthly meetings at chapter levels. The 1st National Conference is planned for June 1991. Offering professional education geared toward business issues. Publishes *Graphic Artists Guild Handbook, Pricing & Ethical Guidelines* and *Graphic Artists Guild Directory of Illustration*. Other services include legal and accounting referrals, insurance plans, a placement center, job referral network, a professional education program and artist-to-artist hotline.

THE GUILD OF NATURAL SCIENCE ILLUSTRATORS, Box 652, Ben Franklin Station, Washington DC 20044. (301)762-0189. Administrative Assistant: Leslie Becker. Estab. 1968.

Purpose: A nonprofit organization for scientific illustrators, educational and professional.

Membership: Open to students, professional artists and individuals interested in the field of scientific illustration. "Potential members must have an interest in scientific illustration as a career and/or be employed in our field or an allied field, i.e.: curator, instructor, or exhibit (museum) worker." Regular or full, $30. Membership is available; write for membership information.

Offerings: Meetings every month, except June, July and August. Has 1 annual exhibit at the national meeting and a permanent traveling exhibit. Offers quarterly weekend workshops in Washington DC and a summer workshop for 2 weeks, out of town. Awards are given at the national meeting. Publishes 1 annual journal of scientific illustration and 10 newsletters/year. Publishes *Creative Source Directory* of members' work every 3 years.

INDEPENDENT FILMMAKER PROGRAM, 2021 N. Western Ave., Los Angeles CA 90027. (213)856-7787. Coordinator: Andrea Alsberg. Estab. 1968.
Purpose: Administered by the American Film Institute, the IFP is organized to support experienced film and video artists. Applicants must submit a completed work on film (16mm/35mm) or ¾″ video. Must be U.S. citizen or permanent resident (with green card). Cannot be enrolled as a student in an educational institution. Deadline for entries is September 14, 1990.
Membership: Offers grants for independent film/video makers.

INTERNATIONAL SCULPTURE CENTER (ISC), 1050 Potomac St., NW, Washington DC 20007. (202)965-6066. FAX: (202)965-7318. Executive Director: David Furchgott. Estab. 1979.
Purpose: "A nonprofit organization of 10,000 members; devoted to advancement of contemporary sculpture and the professional development of sculptors."
Membership: Membership open to anyone; all are eligible. Regular or full, $40; Associate, $100; Professional, $250. Membership is available; write or call for membership information.
Offerings: Offers exhibitions, conferences, lectures, panel discussions and workshops. Publishes *Sculpture* magazine, a 4-color bimonthly and *Insite*, a quarterly newsletter for upper-level members only. Holds the International Sculpture Conference every 2 years. Other services include the Sculpture Source, a computerized visual registry linking artists with potential exhibitors and purchasers of sculpture.

INTERNATIONAL SOCIETY OF COPIER ARTISTS, 800 West End Ave., New York NY 10025. (212)662-5533. Director: Louise Neaderland. Estab. 1981.
Purpose: "There are 110 contributing artist members and 40 institutional subscribers to the *I.S.C.A. Quarterly* of original xerographic art. The purpose is to promote the use of the copier as a creative tool and educate the public through exhibitions, lectures, slide shows and workshops.
Membership: Open to artists who use the copier as a creative tool to make prints and book works. Applicant must submit 3 slides or samples of their Xerographic work. If accepted annual membership fee is $30 in the Continental U.S. and $40 for foreign members. Each artist must contribute work to at least two of the four issues of the *I.S.C.A. Quarterly* in each year. Subscriptions are available for $90 per year (U.S.) or $110 outside the U.S. Membership is available; write or call for membership information.
Offerings: Board of directors meets once each year. Offers the traveling exhibition ISCAGRAPHICS of Xerographic prints and book works. Has workshops, lectures and slide shows on using the copier as a creative tool to produce prints and artists' books. Publishes *I.S.C.A. Directory of Xerographic Print and Bookmakers*.

KANSAS LAWYERS FOR THE ARTS, % Susan Whitfield-Lungren, Suite 212, 400 N. Woodlawn, Wichita KS 67208. (316)686-1133. Acting Director: Susan Whitfield-Lungren. Estab. 1987.
Purpose: Referral and information service for artists and arts organization; not a membership organization.
Offerings: Has workshops and seminars on subjects such as contracts and copyright. Publishes directory *Register of Lawyers*.

LAWYERS FOR THE CREATIVE ARTS, Suite 411, 213 W. Institute Pl., Chicago IL 60610. (312)944-2787. FAX: (312)944-2195. Executive Director: Daniel Mayer. Estab. 1972.
Purpose: Offers legal assistance and education to artists and arts organizations.
Membership: Assistance is available to all Illinois artists and arts organizations. Individual, $20; Group, $50.
Offerings: Offers workshops and seminars; topics include copyright for film/video and not-for-profit incorporation. Publishes *Copyright Basics for the Visual Artist* and many other publications. "Please contact for a publication list."

MICHIGAN ASSOCIATION OF CALLIGRAPHERS, Box 55, Royal Oak MI 48068-0055. (313)656-9790. President: Jacqueline Sullivan. Estab. 1978.
Purpose: "To promote the art of calligraphy in Michigan and surrounding states." Approximate current membership: 200.
Membership: Open to "anyone interested in calligraphy." $25 dues/year.

MICHIGAN GUILD OF ARTISTS AND ARTISANS, 118 N. Fourth Ave., Ann Arbor MI 48104. (313)662-3382. Director: Ralph Kohlhoff. Estab. 1971.
Purpose: "A nonprofit membership organization of artists, providing marketing and other services to individual artists and crafts persons."
Membership: Open to all American artists and artisans. "If the artist wishes to exhibit in the Guild Art Fairs, slides of work must be submitted for evaluation by juries of member peers." Exhibition, $50; Associate, $35; Student, $30; Supporting $30. Membership is available; write or call for membership information.
Offerings: 1 meeting/month for board and committees. Exhibitions in a member gallery in downtown Ann Arbor. Has workshops on "How to Market Your Art Work." Has Best of Guild art shows. Publishes the bimonthly *Unlimited Editions* newsletter and the *Guild Membership Directory*.

MIDWEST WATERCOLOR SOCIETY, 111 W. Washington Blvd., Lombard IL 60148. (No central office). (708)629-0443. Estab. 1976.
Purpose: "To preserve the integrity of transparent watercolor when national shows were accepting pastel, mixed media, collage, anything on paper."
Membership: "Open to any adult in the U.S. and Canada (patron members who do not paint themselves are also eligible for membership). Payment of dues brings newsletter and free entry in show (2 slides). When you have 3 acceptances hung in annual show, you're eligible for MWS letters. Then you must join." Regular, $20; Life, $300. Membership is available; write or call for membership information: Lu Penner, Box 230, Hudson WI 54016. (715)386-2560.
Offerings: Free Fashion entry. Annual meeting, exhibition awards dinner at opening of annual juried show at Neville Public Museum in Greenbay, Wisconsin. 5 day workshop in conjunction with show opening. 4-5 annual awards.

OCEAN STATE LAWYERS FOR THE ARTS (OSLA), Box 19, Saunderstown RI 02874-0019. (401)789-5686. Executive Director: David M. Spatt, Esq.. Estab. 1984.
Purpose: Nonprofit corporation providing free and reduced fee legal counsel to artists and arts organizations, as well as lectures, seminars and workshops.
Membership: "Counsel only offered on questions of law regarding arts and entertainment, i.e. copyright, contract, etc." Offers workshops on such topics as copyrights, contracts and collection of overdue accounts. Publishes *OSLA Arts & Laws*, quarterly newsletter providing legal information of interest to artists.

PANTONE COLOR INSTITUTE, Suite 319, 6324 Variel Ave., Woodland Hills CA 91367. (818)340-2370. Executive Director: Leatrice Eiseman. Estab. 1985.
Purpose: The institute researches the psychology of color, societal color trends, how individuals interact with color on a daily basis and its overall impact. Its studies and research are provided to industries and consumers worldwide through newsletter.
Membership: Open.
Offerings: Sponsors annual awards program. Publishes *Pantone Color News*, quarterly.

PEWABIC POTTERY, 10125 E. Jefferson, Detroit MI 48214. (313)822-0954. FAX: (313)822-0966. Executive Director: Mary Roehm. Estab. 1902.
Purpose: "A turn of the century art pottery nonprofit membership supported organization, whose focus lies in the design and fabrication of architectural tile and vessels, as well as advancement in the ceramic arts. Pewabic is a gallery, museum and educational facility."
Membership: Membership available to those interested and willing to pay annual membership dues. Individual, $35; Family, $50; Student, $25. Membership is available; write or call for membership information.
Offerings: One membership meeting/year. 9 exhibitions/year. Nationally recognized clay artists and art historians give workshops and seminars throughout the year. Publishes the *Pewabic Pottery* newsletter. Other services include the 2-year post graduate Craftsmen-in-Residence Program, adult and children classes, summer workshops, lectures, workshops and seminars.

PHILADELPHIA VOLUNTEER LAWYERS FOR THE ARTS, 251 S. 18th St., Philadelphia PA 19103. (215)545-3385. Director: Dorothy Manou. Estab. 1978.
Purpose: PVLA operates a free legal referral service for individual artists and nonprofit arts groups who have art-related legal problems or questions, but who cannot afford to retain their own attorneys. PVLA programs and publications are designed to educate artists, attorneys and other interested persons about the kinds of legal problems facing artists and art groups and to familiarize them with available solutions.
Membership: Membership is not available.
Offerings: Sponsors numerous workshops and programs on business, legal and tax issues for visual and performing artists. Publishes extensive mail-order book catalogs, including publications on business and legal issues i.e., *Legal Guide For Visual Artists, Guide to Artist-Gallery Agreements, Guide to Copyright, Trademark and Patent* and *Money for Artists*.

SACRAMENTO ILLUSTRATOR'S GUILD, 609 N. 10th St., Sacramento CA 95814. (916)454-3556. President: Buz Teach. Director Emeritus: William Boddy. Estab. 1984..
Purpose: "The Sacramento Illustrators Guild is a promotional, educational organization dedicated to the pursuits of illustrators in the commercial art field." Approximate current membership: 150-200.
Membership: Open to anyone. Acceptance as a professional member is based upon a portfolio review and the willingness of that person to perform one Guild-related task/year. Professional, $45; Supporting, $30. Membership is available; write or call for membership information.
Offerings: Monthly meetings. Offers workshops, meetings and seminars. "Illusions in Design" is an annual showcase of member's illustration. Also the annual Poster Competition. Publishes monthly newsletter *Second Monday* and *S.I.G. Members Directory*.

SAN DIEGO LAWYERS FOR THE ARTS, Suite 400, 1205 Prospect St., La Jolla CA 92037. (619)454-9696. Director: Peter Karlen. Estab. 1979.
Purpose: "Small organization designed to help fine artists and commercial artists with 'preventative' law and with their legal problems."
Offerings: Offers lectures, workshops and seminars. Also available are art law articles and bulletins.

SAN FRANCISCO SOCIETY OF ILLUSTRATORS, 633 Masonic, San Francisco CA 94117. (415)387-1992. President: Michele Manning. Estab. 1962.
Purpose: "To promote and stimulate interest in continued use of illustration; to help broaden the illustrator's horizon toward high ideals in pictorial art; to encourage members to maintain a constant quality and creative level in illustration; and to aid the illustrator in business matters, contracts, ethics, referrals and promotion."
Membership: "The Society encourages membership only to professionals who are devoted to quality in illustration and who adhere to the Society's standards of fair practice and ethics. Members sponsor various exhibits and an annual show, host evening functions with out-of-town illustrators, support and participate in the Air Force Documentary Art Program and contribute their art and time for numerous organizations." To qualify for membership, prospective members are required to participate in a portfolio review, which is held 3 times a year in January, May and September. Initiation fee, $50. Annual dues, $100. Publishes newsletter and directory available to members only.

SEATTLE DESIGN ASSOCIATION, Box 1097, Main Office Station, Seattle WA 98111. Membership Chairman: Jim Arrabito. Estab. 1977.
Purpose: "Committed to supporting the personal and professional growth of members of the graphic arts community through education, sharing of information and recognition of achievement." Approximate current membership: 188.
Membership: Regular or full, $50; Student, $25. Membership is available; write for membership information.
Offerings: 4-6 events/year. 2 biannual events: 12×12 auction and the SDA Award Show. Publishes a catalog of the SDA Award show winners and newsletter only available to members.

THE SOCIETY FOR CALLIGRAPHY & HANDWRITING, Box 31963, Seattle WA 98103. Secretary: Julie Kennedy. Estab. 1975.
Purpose: "To provide instruction in the form of workshops and seminars to members and the community." Approximate current membership: 150.
Membership: Open to anyone for yearly dues of $15. Membership is available; write for membership information.
Offerings: Monthly meetings. 1 exhibition/year. 3-4 workshops/year. Publishes bimonthly newsletter and membership directory, available only to members.

SOCIETY OF ILLUSTRATORS OF LOS ANGELES, Suite 400, 5000 Van Nuys Blvd., Sherman Oaks CA 91403. (818)784-0588. Executive Secretary: Alyce Heath. Estab. 1955.
Purpose: "To maintain and advance the highest standards of professionalism in illustration in the service of the communities of art and humanities."
Membership: Open to illustrators and persons allied to illustration. Regular members must undergo a portfolio review. Regular, $85; Associate, $85; Student, $25. Membership is available; write or call for information.
Offerings: Monthly meetings. Sponsors Illustration West exhibition. Presents awards at Illustration West. Sometimes organizes workshops or seminars. Publishes *Medium*. "We are able to supply a list of illustrators based on their specialties. There is a charge based on requirements."

SOCIETY OF NEWSPAPER DESIGN, The Newspaper Center, Box 17290, Dulles International Airport, Washington DC 20041. (703)620-1083. Executive Director: Ray Chattman. Estab. 1979.
Purpose: "Dedicated to the betterment of newspapers through design. Its more than 2,600 members worldwide represent the full spectrum of newspaper disciplines from the art department through the publisher's office."
Membership: Open to all with a working interest in newspapers and newspaper design. Regular, $55; Student, $35. Membership is available; write for more information.
Offerings: Annual meetings plus regional workshops. Sponsors annual Best of Newspaper Design competition. Publishes *Design* six times/year and *The Best of Newspaper Design* annually.

TEXAS ACCOUNTANTS & LAWYERS FOR THE ARTS, 1540 Sul Ross, Houston TX 77006. (713)526-4876. Contact: Program Director. Estab. 1979.
Purpose: "TALA provides free legal and accounting services to arts organizations and low-income artists in Texas."
Membership: Open to anyone. "Artists' income must not exceed $15,000; problem must be art-related; must be Texas resident. Organization, $25-50; Artist, $20. Membership is available; write or call for membership information.

Offerings: Art-related legal/accounting seminars (tax, copyright, etc.) are held on a regular basis. Publishes *Art Law and Accounting Reporter* (quarterly journal) and six booklets on art-related legal or accounting matters. Other services include SCRAP (arts materials recycling program).

TEXTILE ARTS CENTRE, 916 W. Diversey, Chicago IL 60614. (312)929-3655. Director: Julianne Mankowski. Estab. 1986.
Purpose: Nonprofit organization promoting the education and presentation of textile art.
Membership: Open to anyone. Student/Senior, $20; Individual, $30; Family, $40; Professional, $60; Friend, $100; Advocate, $250. Membership is available; write/call for membership information.
Offerings: Annual meetings; 7 gallery exhibits annually. Courses are offered quarterly in textiles, design, weaving, knitting, basketry etc. Has 2 competitions annually. Publishes *Members Only* newsletter, a technical journal on textile related information offered to members of TAC only. Also offers lectures.

TOLEDO VOLUNTEER LAWYERS FOR THE ARTS, 421-A N. Michigan St., Toledo OH 43624. (419)243-3125. Executive Director: Arnold N. Gottlieb. Estab. 1988.
Purpose: Offers legal services to individuals and organizations on art related issues.
Membership: Membership is not available.
Offerings: No meetings. Offers periodic seminars on legal rights and responsibilities, taxation, contracts, copyrights, etc. Other services include a lending library.

URBAN TRADITIONS, Suite 1880, 55 East Jackson, Chicago IL 60604. (312)663-5400. Director: Margy Mc-Clain. Estab. 1982.
Purpose: "Not-for-profit group that promotes, researches and presents ethnic and traditional arts of urban ethnic cultural communities."
Membership: Open to artists, cultural organizations and those with general interest in subject area. "Most members are actively involved in an art form reflecting their own cultural heritage, or present multiethnic arts programs. Members also include supporters of various ethnic/traditional arts." Individual, $20; Institutional, $35. Membership is available; write or call for membership information.
Offerings: Irregular meetings. Consults to exhibitions. Offers workshop "Presenting Ethnic Arts," for organizations or artists. Publishes *Expressions*, a newsletter of ethnicity, the arts and cultural affairs. Other services include concerts and school programs.

VISUAL ARTISTS & GALLERIES ASSOCIATION (V.A.G.A.), Suite 2626, 1 Rockefeller Plaza, New York NY 10021. (212)397-8353. Estab. 1978.
Purpose: "Formed in response to problems created by changes in the U.S. copyright law and changing state legislation on property rights, V.A.G.A. is the U.S. affiliate of an international consortium of artist copyright agencies."
Membership: Open to artists, galleries, art consultants. New, $60; Renewal, $45; Estate, $100; Gallery, $150. Membership is available: write or call for information.
Offerings: Worldwide copyright protection. Publishes *Art Law* newsletter. Promotion of artist's work. License negotiation (working as artist's agent, 30% fee). Personal copyright answers plus federal copyright forms. A review of documents pertaining to the sale, consignment or license of artist's work to museums, galleries, corporations, etc. Legal inquiry and referral. Insurance information we researched and recommend. Artfile, a visual resource for scholars, curators, art book publishers to locate art.

VISUAL ARTISTS ASSOCIATION, 2550 Beverly Blvd., Los Angeles CA 90057. (213)388-0477. Estab. 1981.
Purpose: To offer educational and business networking.
Membership: Open to students, provisional and general members. Must be in school or in business. Regular or full, $100; Student, $50; Provisional, $75. Membership is available; write or call for membership information.
Offerings: Monthly meetings. Offers workshops. Publishes newsletter entitled *LA Visual.* "Call to find out about other services."

VOLUNTEER LAWYERS FOR THE ARTS, 1285 Avenue of the Americas, New York NY 10019. (212)977-9270. Executive Director: Sharon G. Luckman. Estab. 1969.
Purpose: To provide the arts community with free legal assistance and comprehensive legal education. VLA's conferences and publications provide the arts community with easy-to-understand information on art law issues.
Membership: Open to everyone, legal community and general public. Regular, $50; Associate, $100. Write or call for information.
Offerings: Invitations to special events, conferences, workshops, access to VLA Arts Law Library. Discounts on publications. Subscriptions to *Journal for Associates* and discounts on seminars.

WASHINGTON LAWYERS FOR THE ARTS, Suite 512, Jones Bldg., 1331 Third Ave., Seattle WA 98101. (206)223-0502. Estab. 1976.
Purpose: "We provide low-cost or pro-bono legal services to artists/arts organizations on arts-related matters."
Membership: Open to "any artist or arts organization who wishes to support us." Associate, $25. Membership is available; write for membership information.
Offerings: Workshops on copyright, contracts, taxes and nonprofit status.

WOMEN IN DESIGN/CHICAGO, Suite 2400, 400 W. Madison, Chicago IL 60606. (312)648-1874. President: Lynn Holler Zurowski. Estab. 1977.
Purpose: A locally based, nonprofit organization of approximately 350 members. "We focus on the goals and interests of women designers and women in design related professions."
Membership: Open to anyone. Regular, $36; Corporate, $125; Patron, $300; Student, $25. Membership is available; write or call for information.
Offerings: Board meetings once a month. Workshops or seminars once or twice a month. Awards every other year. Publishes newsletter every other month. Special programs twice a year. Annual directory lists members. Woman of the Year Award.

WOMEN IN DESIGN / LOS ANGELES, 1875 Oak Tree Dr., Los Angeles CA 90041. (213)251-3737. Contact: Membership Chairperson. Estab. 1977.
Purpose: Professional organization of 250 designers, artists, illustrators, art directors and others.
Membership: Open to professionals and students, "those interested in our networking, educational programs and special events." Regular, $65; Student, $30/year. Membership is available; write or call for membership information.
Offerings: 2 meetings/month. Exhibitor at industry show Tools of the Trade (graphics), Show 'n Sell (annual show and sale of members' work) and West Week (exhibitor at annual trade show for interior/furniture/fabric designers). Holds hands-on studio visits to artists and biannual seminar on career-building techniques. Frequent design competitions for materials publicizing events and organization. Publishes *Women in Design Network*. Special programs include Portfolio Night, Resume Night. *Women in Design / LA Directory* includes members' names, addresses, phones, specialties. Special section includes self-promotional materials and samples sumitted by members.

WOMEN IN THE ARTS FOUNDATION, INC., % R. Crown, 1175 York Ave., New York NY 10021. (212)751-1915. Executive Coordinator: Roberta Crown. Estab. 1971.
Purpose: "WIA is working to overcome discrimination against women artists. Through meetings, newsletters, education programs, negotiations with museums, galleries and collectors, WIA works to change outdated concepts and attitudes regarding women as professional artists. WIA has provided opportunities for women to exhibit work and has addressed unfair jurying practices; we also provide information about networking to help women function effectively as professional artists.
Membership: Open to women in the arts, or those interested in the arts. Regular membership, $40. Write or call for membership information. Newsletter published quarterly-$9/yearly ($15 institutions).
Offerings: Monthly meetings. Approximately three or four exhibitions a year. Monthly workshops. Publishes catalogs of women's exhibits, prints of members' work and books with helpful information for artists.

WOMEN IN THE DIRECTOR'S CHAIR, 3435 N. Sheffield Ave., Chicago IL 60657. (312)281-4988. FAX: (708)475-1269. Artistic Director: Gretchen. Estab. 1980.
Purpose: "Not-for-profit media arts organization dedicated to exhibiting and promoting films and videos by women who reflect a diversity of cultures and experiences."
Membership: Open to anyone. Regular or full, $25; Student, $15; Two-year-full, $40. Membership is available; write or call for membership information.
Offerings: "There are regularly scheduled meetings which allow members to discuss their ideas, show works—in progress and obtain feedback and creative support from peers." Hosts the International Women Film and Video Festival. "A W.I.D.C. member is entitled to discounts on special screenings, seminars and workshops. We sponsor an essay contest for girls." Publishes newsletter providing members with information on upcoming events, news, etc.

Recommended Publications

Most of this additional reading material is available either in a library or bookstore, or from the publisher. To insure accurate names and addresses, use copies of these resources that are no older than a year.

ADVERTISING AGE, *740 Rush St., Chicago IL 60611. Weekly advertising and marketing tabloid.*
ADWEEK, *A/S/M Communications, Inc., 49 E. 21st St., New York NY 10010. Weekly advertising and marketing magazine. Also publishes annual* **ADWEEK AGENCY DIRECTORY** *in six regional editions.*
AIRBRUSH ACTION, *400 Madison Ave., Lakewood NJ 08701. Bimonthly magazine featuring product news and trends in airbrushing.*
AMERICAN ART DIRECTORY, *R.R. Bowker Company, 245 W. 17th St., New York NY 10011. Biennial directory listing art organizations, museums, newspapers which carry art notes and open art exhibitions.*
AMERICAN ARTIST, *1 Color Court, Marion OH 43305. Magazine featuring instructional articles on technique, profiles of successful artists, tips and reviews.*
AMERICAN CRAFT, *American Craft Council, 40 W. 53rd St., New York NY 10019. Available with membership to the American Craft Council. Monthly magazine which showcases the crafts.*
AMERICAN SHOWCASE, *American Showcase, Inc., 724 Fifth Ave., New York NY 10019. Annual talent sourcebook featuring illustrators and designers.*
ART BUSINESS NEWS, *Myers Publishing Co., 777 Summer St., Stamford CT 06901. Monthly tabloid covering art supplies and industry trends.*
ART CALENDAR, *Rt. 2, Box 273-C, Sterling VA 22170. Monthly magazine listing galleries reviewing portfolios, juried shows, percent-for-art programs, scholarships and art colonies, among other art-related topics.*
ART DIRECTION, *6th Fl., 10 E. 39th St., New York NY 10016-0199. Monthly magazine featuring art directors' views on advertising and photography.*
ART DIRECTORS ANNUAL, *Art Directors Club, 250 Park Ave. South, New York NY 10003. Annual showcase of work selected by the organization. Distributed by various bookstores in the area.*
ART IN AMERICA, *575 Broadway, New York NY 10012. Features in-depth articles on art issues, news and reviews. August edition of the monthly magazine is* **ART IN AMERICA'S ANNUAL GUIDE TO GALLERIES, MUSEUMS AND ARTISTS**, *which lists galleries and museums, a brief description of their focus and the contact person.*
ART NEW ENGLAND, *353 Washington St., Brighton MA 02135. Magazine with articles, regional reviews, gallery and exhibition listings.*
ART NOW GALLERY GUIDE, *320 Bonnie Burn Rd., Box 219, Scotch Plains NJ 07076. National and regional directories listing galleries and museums across the country.*
ART PRODUCT NEWS, *214 Second St. North, Post Office Drawer 117, St. Petersburg FL 33731. Bimonthly tabloid covering the latest developments and products in art supplies and equipment.*
THE ARTIST'S FRIENDLY LEGAL GUIDE, *North Light Publishing, 1507 Dana Ave., Cincinnati OH 45207. Comprehensive guide to copyright, contracts, moral rights and taxes. Includes contracts to be copied and used.*
THE ARTIST'S GUIDE TO PHILADELPHIA GALLERIES, *(by Amy Orr), Box 8755, Philadelphia PA 19101. Biennial guide to retail, cooperative and nonprofit galleries in Philadelphia.*
THE ARTIST'S MAGAZINE, *1507 Dana Ave., Cincinnati OH 45207. Monthly magazine featuring art instruction and marketing information.*
ARTnews, *Box 969, Farmingdale NY 11737. Monthly magazine featuring international news on gallery shows, plus interviews with painters and sculptors.*
ARTPAPER, *Visual Arts Information Service, Suite 303, 119 N. 4th St., Minneapolis MN 55401. Magazine with editorial on the arts; lists galleries, available grants, competitions and other opportunities for artists.*
ARTWEEK, *Suite 520, 12 S. 1st St., San Jose CA 95113. Weekly newspaper featuring articles on the West Coast art scene, news, reviews and a calendar of upcoming exhibitions and competitions.*
AUDIO VIDEO MARKET PLACE, *R.R. Bowker Company, Box 766, New York NY 10011. Directory listing audiovisual and film companies.*
BILLBOARD, *1515 Broadway, New York NY 10036. Tabloid covering trends in the music industry; published weekly. Also publishes annual* **BILLBOARD'S INTERNATIONAL BUYER'S GUIDE**, *a business-to-business directory which lists record companies.*
BUSINESS AND LEGAL FORMS FOR GRAPHIC DESIGNERS; BUSINESS AND LEGAL FORMS FOR

ILLUSTRATORS; BUSINESS AND LEGAL FORMS FOR FINE ARTISTS, *by Tad Crawford, North Light Publishing, 1507 Dana Ave., Cincinnati OH 45207. Each of these books provides different contracts and business forms with step-by-step instructions.*

CARTOON WORLD, *Box 30367, Lincoln NE 68503. Bimonthly newsletter listing cartoon markets.*

CHICAGO CREATIVE DIRECTORY, *Suite 810, 333 N. Michigan Ave., Chicago IL 60601. Annual talent sourcebook listing illustrators and designers in the Chicago area.*

CHICAGO MIDWEST FLASH, *Alexander Communications, 5th Fl., 215 W. Superior, Chicago IL 60610. Quarterly magazine, includes articles and news on graphic art and advertising in the Midwest.*

COLLECTOR'S MART, *WEB Publications, Inc., Suite 100, 650 Westdale Dr., Wichita KS 67209. Monthly magazine featuring collectibles.*

COMMUNICATION ARTS, *410 Sherman Ave., Box 10300, Palo Alto CA 94303. Magazine covering design, illustration and photography. Published 8 times a year.*

THE COMPLETE GUIDE TO GREETING-CARD DESIGN AND ILLUSTRATION, *by Eva Szela, North Light Publishing, 1507 Dana Ave., Cincinnati OH 45207. Book showing how to create, execute and sell designs for each greeting card style and subject.*

CREATIVE BLACK BOOK, *3rd Fl., 115 5th Ave., New York NY 10003. Annual talent sourcebook featuring illustrators and designers across the country.*

CREATIVE SOURCE, *Wilcord Publications Ltd., Suite 110, 511 King St. West, Toronto Ontario M5V 2Z4. Canada's annual talent sourcebook.*

DECOR, *Commerce Publishing Co., 408 Olive St., St. Louis MO 63102. Monthly magazine covering trends in art publishing, home accessories and framing.*

THE DESIGN FIRM DIRECTORY, *Wefler & Associates, Inc., Box 1591, Evanston IL 60204. Annual directory of design firms.*

dialogue: arts in the midwest, *Box 2572, Columbus OH 43216. Bimonthly magazine of arts in the region, featuring commentary, news, reviews and a calendar of events.*

DIRECTORIES IN PRINT, *Gale Research Co., Penobscot Building, Detroit MI 48226. Annual directory listing business and industrial directories, professional and scientific rosters and other lists and guides.*

EDITOR & PUBLISHER, *The Editor & Publisher Co., Inc., 11 W. 19th St., New York NY 10011. Weekly magazine covering latest developments in journalism and newspaper production. Publishes an annual directory issue listing syndicates and another directory listing newspapers.*

FINE ARTIST'S GUIDE TO SHOWING AND SELLING YOUR WORK, *by Sally Davis, North Light Publishing, 1507 Dana Ave., Cincinnati OH 45207. Complete guide to marketing your paintings and prints. Includes advice on how to evaluate a gallery, show or fair.*

FOLIO, *Box 4949, Stamford CT 06907-0949. Monthly magazine featuring trends in magazine circulation, production and editorial.*

GALE DIRECTORY OF PUBLICATIONS, *Gale Research Company, Penobscot Building, Detroit MI 48226. Annual guide to newspapers, magazines and journals.*

GETTING STARTED AS A FREELANCE ILLUSTRATOR OR DESIGNER, *by Michael Fleishman, North Light Publishing, 1507 Dana Ave., Cincinnati OH 45207. Book which presents information on self-promotion, portfolios and the markets open to freelancers.*

GETTING STARTED IN COMPUTER GRAPHICS, *by Gary Olsen, North Light Publishing, 1507 Dana Ave., Cincinnati OH 45207. Book about how to create contemporary computer graphics.*

GIFTS AND DECORATIVE ACCESSORIES, *Geyer-McAllister Publications, 51 Madison Ave., New York NY 10010. Monthly magazine covering trends and events in the fields of giftware, decorative accessories and collectibles.*

GIFTWARE NEWS, *Talcott Communications Inc., 1414 The Merchandise Mart, Chicago IL 60654. Monthly magazine featuring news in the fields of stationery, giftware and greeting cards.*

THE GRAPHIC ARTIST'S GUIDE TO MARKETING AND SELF-PROMOTION, *by Sally Davis, North Light Publishing, 1507 Dana Ave., Cincinnati OH 45207. Guide to creative marketing techniques for illustrators and designers.*

GRAPHIC ARTISTS GUILD'S DIRECTORY OF ILLUSTRATION, *Graphic Artists Guild, 8th Fl., 11 W. 20th St., New York NY 10011. Annual talent sourcebook featuring works of the guild's members.*

GRAPHIC ARTISTS GUILD HANDBOOK: PRICING & ETHICAL GUIDELINES, *F&W Publishing, 1507 Dana Ave., Cincinnati OH 45207. Pricing guide for major design and illustration markets.*

GRAPHIS, *Graphis U.S., Inc., 141 Lexington Ave., New York NY 10016. Bimonthly international journal of graphic design, including news, commentary, in-depth profiles and feature articles.*

GREETINGS MAGAZINE, *MacKay Publishing Corp., 309 Fifth Ave., New York NY 10016. Monthly magazine featuring updates on the greeting card and stationery industry.*

HOW MAGAZINE, *F&W Publishing, 1507 Dana Ave., Cincinnati OH 45207. Bimonthly magazine featuring trends in design and illustration.*

HOW TO MAKE MONEY IN NEWSPAPER SYNDICATION, *(by Susan Lane), Newspaper Syndication Specialists, Suite 326, Box 19654, Irvine CA 92720. Complete guide to marketing cartoons and features to syndicates and to syndicating your own work.*

HUMOR AND CARTOON MARKETS, *North Light Publishing, 1507 Dana Ave., Cincinnati OH 45207. Annual directory which lists names, addresses, contact people and marketing information for markets open to cartoonists.*

INTERIOR DESIGN, *249 W. 17th St., New York NY 10011. Monthly magazine featuring industry news and trends in furnishing and interior design.*

INTERNATIONAL DIRECTORY OF LITTLE MAGAZINES AND SMALL PRESSES, *Dustbooks, Box 100, Paradise CA 95969. Annual directory listing small, independent magazines, presses and papers.*

LEGAL GUIDE FOR THE VISUAL ARTIST, *by Tad Crawford, F&W Publishing, 1507 Dana Ave., Cincinnati OH 45207. Guide to art law covering copyright and contracts.*

LITERARY MARKET PLACE, *R.R. Bowker Company, 245 W. 17th St., New York NY 10011. Annual directory listing book publishers.*

MACWORLD, *501 Second St., San Francisco CA 94107. Magazine with feature articles and reviews centering around the Macintosh.*

MADISON AVENUE HANDBOOK, *Peter Glenn Publications, 17 E. 48th St., New York NY 10017. Annual directory listing advertising agencies, audiovisual firms and design studios in the New York area.*

MAGAZINE DESIGN AND PRODUCTION, *Suite 106, 8340 Mission Rd., Prairie Village KS 66206. Magazine with information on all aspects of magazine design and production; published monthly.*

MEDICAL MARKETING & MEDIA, *CPS Communications, Inc., Suite 215, 7200 W. Camino Real, Boca Raton FL 33431. Magazine covering medical and pharmaceutical marketing news. Published 15 times a year.*

MUSEUM & ARTS WASHINGTON, *Suite 222, 1707 L St., NW, Washington D.C. 20036. Bimonthly magazine of the fine arts in the Washington area.*

NEWSLETTERS IN PRINT, *Gale Research Co., Penobscot Building, Detroit MI 48226. Annual directory listing newsletters.*

O'DWYER DIRECTORY OF PUBLIC RELATIONS FIRMS, *J.R. O'Dwyer Company, Inc., 271 Madison Ave., New York NY 10016. Annual directory listing public relations firms, indexed by specialties.*

PARTY & PAPER RETAILER, *Suite 300, 500 Summer St., Stamford, CT 06901. Magazine for those interested in paper products. Also publishes annual* **SOURCE BOOK**, *which lists resources for party and paper related merchandise*

PLATE WORLD, *Plate World, Inc, 9200 N. Maryland Ave., Niles IL 60648. Monthly magazine focusing on news in the collectible plate industry.*

PRINT, *Ninth Fl., 104 Fifth Ave., New York NY 10011. Bimonthly magazine focusing on creative trends and technological advances in illustration, design, photography and printing.*

PROFILE, *Archimedia, Box 4403, Topeka KS 66604. Published annually in December; it is the official directory of the American Institute of Architects.*

PUBLISHERS DIRECTORY, *Gale Research Company, Penobscot Building, Detroit MI 48226. Annual directory offering detailed information on U.S. and Canadian publishers—major houses and small, independent presses.*

PUBLISHERS WEEKLY, *205 W. 42nd St., New York NY 10017. Weekly magazine covering industry trends and news in book publishing, book reviews and interviews.*

PUBLISHING NEWS, *Hanson Publishing Group, Box 4949, Stamford CT 06907-0949. Bimonthly newsmagazine of the publishing industry.*

REGIONAL THEATRE DIRECTORY, *Box 519, Dorset VT 05251. Annual directory of regional theaters.*

RSVP, *Box 314, Brooklyn NY 11205. Annual talent sourcebook listing illustrators and designers.*

SOUTHWEST ART, *Benjamin Franklin Tower, Suite 1440, 5444 Westheimer, Houston TX 77056. Monthly magazine which showcases the art and gallery scene of the Southwest. Also publishes an annual gallery guide.*

STANDARD DIRECTORY OF ADVERTISING AGENCIES, *National Register Publishing Co., Inc., 3004 Glenview Rd., Wilmette IL 60091. Annual directory listing advertising agencies.*

STANDARD PERIODICAL DIRECTORY, *Oxbridge Communications, Inc., Suite 636, 150 Fifth Ave., New York NY 10011. Biannual directory listing magazines, journals, newsletters, directories and association publications.*

STANDARD RATE AND DATA SERVICE, *3004 Glenview Rd., Wilmette IL 60091. Annual directory listing magazines, plus their advertising rates.*

STEP-BY-STEP GRAPHICS, *Dynamic Graphics, Inc., 6000 N. Forest Park Dr., Peoria IL 61614-3597. Bimonthly magazine featuring instruction for graphic design and illustration projects.*

THEATRE DIRECTORY, *Theatre Communications Group, Inc., 355 Lexington Ave., New York NY 10017. Directory listing theaters in the United States.*

THOMAS REGISTER OF MANUFACTURERS, *Thomas Publishing Co., 1 Penn Plaza, New York NY 10001. Multivolume directory listing manufacturers in all facets of business.*

U & lc, *Upper and Lower Case, 2 Hammarskjold Plaza, New York NY 10017. Newspaper format quarterly which includes feature articles, news and editorial for the graphic artist.*

ULRICH'S INTERNATIONAL PERIODICALS DIRECTORY, *R.R. Bowker Company, 245 W. 17th St., New York NY 10011. Annual directory listing international publications.*

VISUAL MERCHANDISING & STORE DESIGN, *Signs of the Times Publishing Company, 407 Gilbert Ave., Cincinnati OH 45202. Monthly magazine covering merchandise display and store interior design.*

WALLCOVERINGS MAGAZINE, *Suite 101, 15 Bank St., Stamford CT 06901. Offers up-to-date information on the wallcovering industry. Also publishes annual directory of national and international manufacturers, distributers and suppliers.*

WASHINGTON ART, *Art Calendar, Box 1040, Great Falls VA 22066. Directory of galleries, cooperatives and nonprofit spaces in the Washington, D.C. area.*

WITTY WORLD, *Box 1458, North Wales PA 19454. Quarterly magazine for professional and aspiring cartoonists covering international news about cartooning.*

WOMEN'S WEAR DAILY, *Fairchild Publications, 7 E. 12th St., New York NY 10003. Tabloid (Monday through Friday) focusing on women's and children's apparel.*

THE WORK BOOK, *Scott & Daughters Publishing, 940 N. Highland Ave., Los Angeles CA 90038. Annual talent sourcebook listing illustrators and designers in the Los Angeles area.*

WRITER'S MARKET, *Writer's Digest Books, 1507 Dana Ave., Cincinnati OH 45207. Annual directory listing markets for freelance writers. Lists names, addresses, contact people and marketing information for book publishers, magazines, greeting card companies and syndicates.*

Market conditions are constantly changing! If you're still using this book and it is 1992 or later, buy the newest edition of Artist's Market at your favorite bookstore or order directly from Writer's Digest Books.

Glossary

Acceptance (payment on). The artist is paid for his work as soon as the buyer decides to use it.

Adobe Illustrator® Macintosh drawing and painting software.

Airbrush. Small pencil-shaped pressure gun used to spray ink, paint or dyes to obtain graduated tonal effects.

Architectural delineator. An illustrator who sketches preliminary ideas for a presentation to a client.

ASAP. Abbreviation for "as soon as possible".

Ben-day. An artificial process of shading line illustrations, named after its inventor.

Biennially. Once every two years.

Bimonthly. Once every two months.

Biweekly. Once every two weeks.

Bleed. Area of a plate or print that extends (bleeds off) beyond the edge of a trimmed sheet.

Book. Another term for a portfolio.

Buy-out. The sale of all reproduction rights (and sometimes the original work) by the artist; also subcontracted portions of a job resold at a cost or profit to the end client by the artist.

Calligraphy. The art of fine handwriting.

Camera-ready. Art that is completely prepared for copy camera platemaking.

Cel art. Artwork applied to plastic film, especially used in animation; also an abbreviation for artwork on celluloid.

Cibachrome. Trademark for a full-color positive print made from a transparency.

Collaterals. Accompanying or auxiliary pieces, such as brochures, especially used in advertising.

Collotype. A screenless, flat printing process in which plates are coated with gelatin, exposed to continuous-tone negatives and printed on lithographic presses.

Color separation. Photographic process of separating any multi-color image into its primary component parts (cyan, magenta, yellow and black) for printing.

Commission. 1. Percentage of retail price taken by a sponsor/salesman on artwork sold. 2. Assignment given to an artist.

Comprehensive. Complete sketch of layout showing how a finished illustration will look when printed; also called a comp.

Consignment. Arrangement by which items are sent by an artist to a sales agent (gallery, shop, sales representative,etc.) for sale with the understanding the artist will not receive payment until work is sold. A commission is almost always charged for this service.

Direct-mail package. Sales or promotional material that is distributed by mail. Usually consists of an outer envelope, a cover letter, brochure or flyer, SASE, and postpaid reply card, or order form with business reply envelope.

Edition. The total number of prints published of one piece of art.

Etching. A print made by the intaglio process, creating a design in the surface of a metal or other plate with a needle and using a mordant to bite out the design.

Exclusive area representation. Requirement that an artist's work appear in only one outlet within a defined geographical area.

Gagline. The words printed, usually directly beneath a cartoon; also called a caption.

Gouache. Opaque watercolor with definite, appreciable film thickness and an actual paint layer.

Halftone. Reproduction of a continuous tone illustration with the image formed by dots produced by a camera lens screen.

IRC. International Reply Coupon; purchased at the post office to enclose with artwork sent to a foreign buyer to cover his postage cost when replying.

Keyline. Indentification, through signs and symbols, of the postions of illustrations and copy for the printer.

Kill fee. Portion of the agreed-upon price the artist receives for a job that was assigned, started, but then canceled.

Layout. Arrangement of photographs, illustrations, text and headlines for printed material.

Light table. Table with a light source beneath a glass top; especially useful in transferring art by tracing.

Lithography. Printing process based on a design made with a greasy substance on a limestone slab or metal plate and chemically treated so image areas take ink and non-image areas repel ink; during printing, non-image areas are kept wet with water.

Logotype. Name or design of a company or product used as a trademark on letterheads, direct mail packages, in advertising, etc., to establish visual identity; also called a logo.

Mechanicals. Paste-up or preparation of work for printing.

Ms, mss. Abbreviation for manuscript, manuscripts.

Niaf. Native art of such cultures as African, Eskimo, Native America, etc., usually associated with daily life.

Offset. Printing process in which a flat printing plate is treated to be ink-receptive in image areas and ink-repellant in non-image areas. Ink is transferred from the printing plate to a rubber plate, and then to the paper.

Overlay. Transparent cover over copy, where instruction, corrections or color location directions are given.

Panel. In cartooning, the boxed-in illustration; can be single panel, double panel or multiple panel.

Paste-up. Procedure involving coating the backside of art, type, Photostats, etc., with rubber cement or wax and adhering them in their proper positions to the mechanical board. The boards are then used as finished art by the printer.

Perspective. The ability to see objects in relation to their relative positions and distance, and depict the volume and spatial relationships on paper.

Photostat. Black-and-white copies produced by an inexpensive photographic process using paper negatives; only line values are held with accuracy. Also called stat.

Pin registration. The use of highly accurate holes and special pins on copy, film, plates and presses to insure proper positioning and alignment of colors.

PMT. Photomechanical transfer; Photostat produced without a negative, somewhat like the Polaroid process.

P-O-P. Point-of-purchase; a display device or structure located with the production or at the retail outlet to advertise or hold the product to increase sales.

Print. An impression pulled from an original plate, stone, block screen or negative; also a positive made from a photographic negative.

Publication (payment on). The artist is paid for his work when it is published.

Quark XPress® Computer page layout program—the electronic equivalent of both a phototypesetter and a drawing board, allowing the artist to design pages with all type and images in place and output them as single page mechanicals. Other such programs are PageMaker®, Ventura Publisher® and Ready Set Go®.

Query. Letter of inquiry to an editor or buyer eliciting his interest in a work you want to illustrate or sell.

Rendering. A drawn representation of a building, interior, etc., in perspective.

Retail. To sell directly to the consumer.

Roughs. Preliminary sketches or drawings.

Royalty. An agreed percentage paid by the publisher to the artist for each copy of his work sold.

SASE. Abbreviation for self-addressed, stamped envelope.

Semiannual. Once every six months.

Semimonthly. Once every two weeks.

Semiweekly. Twice a week.

Serigraph. Silkscreen; stencil method of printing involving a stencil adhered to a fine mesh cloth and stretched tightly over a wooden frame. Paint is forced through the holes of the screen not blocked by the stencil.

Simultaneous submissions. Submission of the same artwork to more than one potential buyer at the same time.

Speculation. Creating artwork with no assurance that the buyer will purchase it or reimburse expenses in any way, as opposed to creating artwork on assignment.

Spot drawing. Small illustration used to decorate or enhance a page of type, or to serve as a column ending.

Storyboard. Series of panels which illustrates a progressive sequence or graphics and story copy for a TV commercial, film or filmstrip. Serves as a guide for the eventual finished product.

Tabloid. Publication where an ordinary newspaper page is turned sideways.

Tearsheet. Published page containing an artist's illustration, cartoon, design or photograph.

Template. Plastic stencil containing various sizes of commonly used shapes, symbols or letters which can be traced one at a time.

Thumbnail. A rough layout in miniature.

Transparency. A photographic positive film such as a color slide.

Type spec. Type specification; determination of the size and style of type to be used in a layout.

UPS. Universal Postal Union; a coupon for return of first-class surface letters.

Velox. Photoprint of a continuous tone subject that has been transformed into line art by means of a halftone screen.

Video. General category comprised of videocassettes and videotapes.

Wash. Thin application of transparent color or watercolor black for a pastel or gray tonal effect.

Wholesale. To sell (usually in large quantities) to an outlet for resale rather than directly to the consumer.

Can't find a listing? Check the end of each market section for the '90-'91 Changes lists. These lists include any market listings from the 1990 edition which were either not verified or deleted in this edition.

Can't find a listing? Check the end of each market section for the '90-'91 Changes lists. These lists include any market listings from the 1990 edition which were either not verified or deleted in this edition.

Can't find a listing? Check the end of each market section for the '90-'91 Changes lists. These lists include any market listings from the 1990 edition which were either not verified or deleted in this edition.

Can't find a listing? Check the end of each market section for the '90-'91 Changes lists. These lists include any market listings from the 1990 edition which were either not verified or deleted in this edition.

Can't find a listing? Check the end of each market section for the '90-'91 Changes lists. These lists include any market listings from the 1990 edition which were either not verified or deleted in this edition.

Can't find a listing? Check the end of each market section for the '90-'91 Changes lists. These lists include any market listings from the 1990 edition which were either not verified or deleted in this edition.

Can't find a listing? Check the end of each market section for the '90-'91 Changes lists. These lists include any market listings from the 1990 edition which were either not verified or deleted in this edition.

Other Art Books from
Writer's Digest Books/North Light Books

Annual Directories

Children's Writer's & Illustrator's Market, edited by Lisa Carpenter $16.95 (paper)
Humor & Cartoon Markets, edited by Bob Staake $16.95 (paper)
Novel & Short Story Writer's Market, edited by Robin Gee $18.95 (paper)
Photographer's Market, edited by Sam Marshall $21.95 (cloth)
Poet's Market, edited by Judson Jerome $19.95 (cloth)
Songwriter's Market, edited by Mark Garvey $19.95 (cloth)
Writer's Market, edited by Glenda Tennant Neff $24.95 (cloth)

Graphics/Business of Art

Airbrush Artist's Library (6 in series) $12.95 (cloth)
Airbrush Techniques Workbooks (8 in series) $9.95 each
Airbrushing the Human Form, by Andy Charlesworth $19.95 (cloth)
The Art & Craft of Greeting Cards, by Susan Evarts $15.95 (paper)
Basic Graphic Design & Paste-Up, by Jack Warren $13.95 (paper)
Business & Legal Forms for Graphic Designers, by Tad Crawford $19.95 (paper)
Click: The Brightest in Computer-Generated Design, by Ellen Gerken $39.95 (cloth)
Color Harmony: A Guide to Creative Color Combinations, by Hideaki Chijiiwa $15.95 (paper)
Colorworks, (5 in series) $24.95 (cloth)
Complete Airbrush & Photoretouching Manual, by Peter Owen & John Sutcliffe $24.95 (cloth)
The Complete Guide to Greeting Card Design & Illustration, by Eva Szela $27.95 (cloth)
Creating Dynamic Roughs, by Alan Swann $27.95 (cloth)
Creative Ad Design & Illustration, by Dick Ward $32.95 (cloth)
Creative Director's Sourcebook, by Nick Souter and Stuart Neuman $89.00 (cloth)
Creative Typography, by Marion March $27.95 (cloth)
Design Rendering Techniques, by Dick Powell $29.95 (cloth)
Dynamic Airbrush, by David Miller & James Effler $29.95 (cloth)
Fashion Illustration Workbooks (4 in series) $8.95 each
Fantasy Art, by Bruce Robertson $24.95 (cloth)
Getting It Printed, by Beach, Shepro & Russon $29.50 (paper)
The Graphic Artist's Guide to Marketing & Self-Promotion, by Sally Prince Davis $15.95 (paper)
Graphics Handbook, by Howard Munce $14.95 (paper)
Handbook of Pricing & Ethical Guidelines, 7th edition, by The Graphic Artist's Guild $22.95 (paper)
HOT AIR: An Explosive Collection of Top Airbrush Illustration, by Werner Steuer $39.95 (cloth)
How to Design Trademarks & Logos, by Murphy & Row $24.95 (cloth)
How to Draw & Sell Cartoons, by Ross Thomson & Bill Hewison $18.95 (cloth)
How to Draw & Sell Comic Strips, by Alan McKenzie $18.95 (cloth)
How to Draw Charts & Diagrams, by Bruce Robertson $24.95 (cloth)
How to Understand & Use Design & Layout, by Alan Swann $24.95 (cloth)
How to Understand & Use Grids, by Alan Swann $27.95 (cloth)
How to Write and Illustrate Children's Books, edited by Treld Pelkey Bicknell and Felicity Trotman, $22.50 (cloth)
Living by Your Brush Alone, by Edna Wagner Piersol $16.95 (paper)
Make It Legal, by Lee Wilson $18.95 (paper)
Making Your Computer a Design & Business Partner, by Blount and Walker $27.95 (paper)
Marker Rendering Techniques, by Dick Powell & Patricia Monahan $32.95 (cloth)
Marker Techniques Workbooks (8 in series) $9.95 each
North Light Dictionary of Art Terms, by Margy Lee Elspass $12.95 (paper)
Papers for Printing, by Mark Beach & Ken Russon $34.50 (paper)
Preparing Your Design for Print, by Lynn John $27.95 (cloth)
Presentation Techniques for the Graphic Artist, by Jenny Mulherin $24.95 (cloth)
Print Production Handbook, by David Bann $16.95 (cloth)
PROMO: The Best in Self-Promotion Pieces, by Rose DeNeve $39.95 (cloth)
Ready to Use Layouts for Desktop Design, by Chris Prior $27.95 (cloth)
Studio Secrets for the Graphic Artist, by Jack Buchan $29.95 (cloth)

Type: Design, Color, Character & Use, by Michael Beaumont $24.95 (cloth)
Using Type Right, by Philip Brady $18.95 (paper)

Watercolor

Fill Your Watercolors with Light & Color, by Roland Roycraft $27.95 (cloth)
Flower Painting, by Paul Riley $27.95 (cloth)
Getting Started in Watercolor, by John Blockley $19.95 (paper)
The New Spirit of Watercolor, by Mike Ward $27.95 (cloth)
Painting Watercolor Portraits That Glow, by Jan Kunz $27.95 (cloth)
Sir William Russell Flint, edited by Ralph Lewis & Keith Gardner $55.00 (cloth)
Watercolor Painter's Solution Book, by Angela Gair $24.95 (cloth)
Watercolor — The Creative Experience, by Barbara Nechis $16.95 (paper)
Watercolor Tricks & Techniques, by Cathy Johnson $24.95 (cloth)
Watercolor Workbook, by Bud Biggs & Lois Marshall $19.95 (paper)
Watercolor: You Can Do It!, by Tony Couch $26.95 (cloth)
Webb on Watercolor, by Frank Webb $29.95 (cloth)

Mixed Media

The Art of Scratchboard, by Cecile Curtis $23.95 (cloth)
Catching Light in Your Paintings, by Charles Sovek $18.95 (paper)
Colored Pencil Drawing Techniques, by Iain Hutton-Jamieson $24.95 (cloth)
Complete Guide to Fashion Illustration, by Colin Barnes $32.95 (cloth)
The Complete Oil Painting Book, by Wendon Blake $29.95 (cloth)
The Figure, edited by Walt Reed $16.95 (paper)
Keys to Drawing, by Bert Dodson $19.95 (paper)
Make Your Own Picture Frames, by Jenny Rodwell $12.95 (paper)
Mixing Color, by Jeremy Galton $24.95 (cloth)
The North Light Illustrated Book of Painting Techniques, by Elizabeth Tate $27.95 (cloth)
Oil Painting: A Direct Approach, by Joyce Pike $26.95 (cloth)
Painting Murals, by Patricia Seligman $26.95 (cloth)
Painting with Acrylics, by Jenny Rodwell $19.95 (paper)
Pastel Painting Techniques, by Guy Roddon $24.95 (cloth)
The Pencil, by Paul Calle $17.95 (paper)
People Painting Scrapbook, by J. Everett Draper $26.95 (cloth)
Perspective Without Pain Workbooks (4 in series) $9.95 each
Photographing Your Artwork, by Russell Hart $16.95 (paper)
Putting People in Your Paintings, by J. Everett Draper $22.50 (cloth)
Tonal Values: How to See Them, How to Paint Them, by Angela Gair $24.95 (cloth)

To order directly from the publisher, include $3.00 postage and handling for one book,
$1.00 for each additional book. Allow 30 days for delivery.
North Light Books
1507 Dana Avenue, Cincinnati, Ohio 45207
Credit card orders
Call TOLL-FREE
1-800-289-0963
Prices subject to change without notice.

1991 Close-up Personalities

Artist: Lee Hammond

Luis Pérez
Associate Art Director
Page 268

Clare Wood
Illustrator
Page 80

Randi Robin
Graphic Designer
Page 597

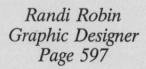